W9-BNV-300

FUNDAMENTALS OF SECURITIES REGULATION

FUNDAMENTALS OF SECURITIES REGULATION

SECOND EDITION

LOUIS LOSS

William Nelson Cromwell Professor of Law, Emeritus
Harvard University

LITTLE, BROWN AND COMPANY Boston and Toronto

Library of Congress Catalog Card No. 87-80721

ISBN NO. 0-316-53335-1

Third Printing

HAL

Published simultaneously in Canada
by Little, Brown & Company (Canada) Limited

Printed in the United States of America

SUMMARY OF CONTENTS

APPENDIXES

CONTENTS

CHAPTER 1

DEVELOPMENT OF THE SEC STATUTES

CHAPTER 2

DISTRIBUTION OF SECURITIES

CHAPTER 3

A WHAT! A "SECURITY" (HEREIN OF "ISSUER" AS WELL)

CHAPTER 4

"OFFER," "SALE," "UNDERWRITER," AND "DEALER"

CHAPTER 5

SECURITIES ACT EXEMPTIONS

CHAPTER 6

"CONTROL" CONCEPTS UNDER THE SEC STATUTES

CHAPTER 7

REGISTRATION AND POSTREGISTRATION PROVISIONS OF THE 1934 ACT

CHAPTER 8

MARKET REGULATION

CHAPTER 9

"FRAUD" AND MANIPULATION

CHAPTER 10

CIVIL LIABILITY

CHAPTER 11

THE SEC LAWYER

APPENDIXES

PREFACE

In the preface to the first edition, which spoke generally as of January 1, 1983, I said:

> From the practitioner's point of view, this is first cousin to a third edition of my treatise, following substantially the same arrangement of chapters. It is self-contained, not a supplement. But obviously it is not as comprehensive, whether for the pre-1969 period or since. So great has been the proliferation of cases and other literature in the almost fifteen years since the December 1, 1968, cut-off date of Volumes IV-VI that a new edition in the style of the treatise would probably extend to eight or ten volumes. As I said in the preface to the 1969 Supplement, "It may be that the one-man treatise, at least in a rapidly changing and expanding field like this, is a dying 'art form.' " This is not altogether bad: winnowing the leading cases and other materials out of the mass (or mess) should serve to improve readability.

The barely four-year life of the first edition, notwithstanding the publication of substantial annual supplements, attests to the phenomenon of ever increasing growth that characterizes this field. I have tried to reflect the major developments to an extent consistent with the "Fundamentals" in the title of this book and its limitation to a single volume.

This edition speaks generally as of May 15, 1987, and it will continue to be supplemented more or less annually.

Once more I express my warm thanks to Milton H. Cohen, Andrew L. Kaufman, and Margaret R. Loss for a critical reading of Chapter 3K, Chapter 11, and the variable contract discussion in Chapter 3E, respectively; to Nancy L. Campbell, Dana S. Wilson, and Lisa A. Wehrle at Little, Brown & Company for smoothing the editorial process; to Daniel G. Harmetz of the Harvard Law School Class of 1987 for his excellent research assistance; and to my long-time secretary, Julia Stephanian, who I hope knows how much I appreciate her.

L. L.

Cambridge, Massachusetts
October 1987

A NOTE ON FOOTNOTE NUMBERING

(1) The writer's footnotes are numbered consecutively in each subchapter (c. 1A, 1B, etc.).

(2) The writer's footnotes are interspersed with whatever footnotes are incorporated from cases or other materials that are set out substantially in full. Those footnotes are numbered as in their sources.

(3) The writer's own footnotes to such materials are identified by letters rather than numbers, together with the symbol, "Ed."

FUNDAMENTALS OF SECURITIES REGULATION

C H A P T E R 1

DEVELOPMENT OF THE SEC STATUTES

A. OF BUBBLES AND GIANTS

The Securities Act of 1933 did not spring full grown from the brow of any New Deal Zeus. It followed a generation of state regulation and several centuries of legislation in England. For the problems at which modern securities regulation is directed are as old as the cupidity of sellers and the gullibility of buyers.

A statute of Edward I, in 1285, authorized the Court of Aldermen to license brokers of some sort in the City of London, and there are said to be records of a number of prosecutions against unlicensed brokers before the year 1300.[1] Four centuries later, but still eighty years before the American Revolution, Parliament passed "An act to restrain the number and ill practice of brokers and stock jobbers."[2] And it was not long after that statute of 1697 that the "Bubble Mania" swept over France and England.

The story has often been told of the Mississippi Company, organized by the crafty John Law, and the South Sea Company, granted a monopoly by the British Government of the trading with South America and the Pacific Islands — and of how the two companies undertook to pay off the French and British public debts.[3] The bursting of the South Sea Bubble ruined thousands in all ranks of society. Reputations in the financial and political world were de-

C. 1A [1] S. Killik, The Work of the Stock Exchange (2d ed. 1934) 12.

[2] 8 & 9 Wm. 3 (1697) c. 32; see Lane, The Years Before the Stock Exchange, 7 History Today (1957) 760, 761.

[3] On the fascinating story of Law's Mississippi Company, see J. Francis, History of the Bank of England, Its Time and Traditions (1862) c. 7. See also P. Strong, Jessamy John (1947), a novel based on Law's life. The most scholarly treatment of the South Sea Bubble is in 1 W. Scott, The Constitution and Finance of English, Scottish and Irish Joint-Stock Companies to 1720 (1912) cc. 21-22. For popular accounts, see B. Melville, The South Sea Bubble (1921); G. Erleigh, The South Sea Bubble (1933).

stroyed wholesale. And the national disaster was aggravated by the numerous hoaxes that were developed by imitators. A thousand persons are said to have paid two guineas each in one morning as a first installment on a share in a company "for carrying on an undertaking of great importance, but nobody to know what it is."[4]

The result of all this was enforcement of the vague and prolix "Bubble Act" of 1720 — a piece of legislation that, ironically, had its origin in the political power of the South Sea Company itself and its desire to suppress less favored rivals without royal charters. In Maitland's words, "A panic-stricken Parliament issued a law, which, even when we now read it, seems to scream at us from the statute book."[5] The statute's recitals referred to "persons who contrive or attempt such dangerous and mischievous undertakings or projects, under false pretences of publick good, do presume * * * to open books for publick subscriptions, and draw in many unwary persons to subscribe therein towards raising great sums of money, whereupon the subscribers or claimants under them do pay small proportions thereof."[6] The act prohibited the use of false or irregular charters and the taking of subscriptions for such enterprises. It declared such matters to be a public nuisance subject to penalties and forfeitures. Brokers trading in such unlawful shares were rendered liable to lose their licenses. And (as if foreshadowing the American antitrust laws) merchants and traders whose business was injured by such unlawful organizations were given the right to sue for treble damages.

The Bubble Act was gradually whittled away and finally was repealed in 1825[7] — though as recently as 1906 counsel attempted, unsuccessfully, to have the statute applied as part of the received law of Idaho.[8] But with the growth of legitimate corporate enterprise, Parliament in the Companies Act of 1844 enacted the first modern prospectus requirement. This followed a landmark report (the first of a series of such reports about a generation apart) by a Select Committee on Joint Stock Companies under the chairmanship of Gladstone, who was then the young Tory President of the Board of Trade (now the Department of Trade and Commerce).[9] The 1844 act introduced the principle of compulsory disclosure

[4] Melville, op. cit. supra p. 1 n. 3, at 97.

[5] 3 Maitland, Collected Papers (1911) 390.

[6] 6 Geo. 1, c. 18, §18.

[7] 6 Geo. 4, c. 91. See A. DuBois, The English Business Company after the Bubble Act 1720-1800 (1938).

[8] Spotswood v. Morris, 12 Idaho 360, 85 Pac. 1094 (1906).

[9] 7 B. P. P. 1844.

through the registration of prospectuses inviting subscriptions to corporate shares.

In 1890 Parliament passed the Directors Liability Act (subsequently incorporated into the Companies Act), whose purpose it was to modify the common law of deceit, as it had been applied by the House of Lords the previous year in *Derry* v. *Peek,*[10] in order to subject corporate directors and promoters to civil liability for untrue statements in the prospectus without proof of scienter. And by the early 1900s, when the first American legislation made its appearance, the Companies Act of 1900 — which introduced an elaborate prescription of the contents of the prospectus — had pretty well fixed the British pattern as enforcement of a certain amount of affirmative disclosure going considerably beyond the negative injunction against fraud.

The financial life of the United States developed later, of course, than that of England. But John Law had his spiritual descendants in the Daniel Drews, Jim Fisks, and Jay Goulds.[11] And the growth of corporate enterprise produced much the same problems and abuses as had been met earlier in Great Britain.

The role of government in the protection of investors in the American economy of the closing decades of the twentieth century extends considerably beyond the proscription of fraud or even the policing of affirmative disclosure of corporate information. This is not to say that those two ends are not the basic foundation of any system of investor protection. Indeed, the disclosure problem is exacerbated by the very factors that have necessarily expanded government's role beyond those ends — the growth of the corporate giants and supergiants in modern society, with the concomitant dispersion of stock ownership and divorcement of ownership from control. Deft pens have written the story of "other people's money" and absentee ownership.[12] And by now a half-century of literature has built on the classic study in which Berle and Means traced the evolution of the corporate system as a "major social institution."[13]

[10] 14 A. C. 337 (1889).

[11] For some very readable accounts, see F. Davis, What Price Wall Street?, (1932); S. Holbrook, The Age of the Moguls (1953); M. Josephson, The Robber Barons (1934); H. Larson, Jay Cook (1936); R. O'Connor, Gould's Millions (1962); B. White, The Book of Daniel Drew (1911).

[12] See Brandeis, Other People's Money (1914); T. Veblen, Absentee Ownership and Business Enterprise in Recent Times (1923); W. Ripley, Main Street and Wall Street (1927).

[13] Berle and Means, The Modern Corporation and Private Property (1932) esp. bk. 1. See Corporations and Private Property, 26(2) J. L. & Econ. 235 (1983), a conference sponsored by The Hoover Institution on the fiftieth anniversary of the publication of Berle and Means. One study of data assembled in

Whether or not the economy is becoming increasingly concentrated, there is no doubt that it is now highly concentrated.[14] The "managerial revolution" that was in process when Berle and Means conducted their study in 1929 was said by 1966 to be "close to complete"; the portion of the 200 largest nonfinancial corporations that were under management control had increased from 44 percent in 1924 to 84.5 percent in 1963.[15] Indeed, Professor Berle in the late 1950s traced the progression from "ownership control" through "working control" and "management control" into a fourth stage: control by a relatively small group of institutions through their management of the spectacularly growing (and today far more huge) pension funds. The only right of the pensioner or policy holder is to receive money, a right depending "on a status position of some kind based on his having fulfilled a stated set of conditions." Thus it is, said Berle (with a touch of hyperbole), that "divorce between men and industrial things is becoming complete. A Communist revolution could not accomplish that more completely."[16]

---

the 1920s and 1930s revealed no significant relationship between a corporation's profitability and whether control was exercised by management or the owners. Stigler and Friedland, The Literature of Economics: The Case of Berle and Means, 26 J. L. & Econ. 237 (1983). Indeed, it has been asserted that the ownership-control divorcement, with all the problems it has created, "has been a major reason for the success of the modern corporate form as a business entity." Economic Report of the President (1985) 188.

[14]See S. Com. on Governmental Affairs, 96th Cong., 2d Sess., Structure of Corporate Concentration: Institutional Shareholders and Interlocking Directorates among Major U. S. Corporations (Com. Print 1980).

[15]See Larner, Ownership and Control in the 200 Largest Nonfinancial Corporations, 1929 and 1963, 56 Am. Econ. Rev. 777, 786-87 (1966).

[16]Berle, Power Without Property (1959) 75-76. The following make good reading: J. Livingston, The American Stockholder (1958) esp. c. 2; Manning, Book Review, 67 Yale L. J. 1477 (1958); E. Mason (ed.), The Corporation in Modern Society (1959); Manne, The "Higher Criticism" of the Modern Corporation, 62 Colum. L. Rev. 399 (1962), with a rebuttal in Berle, Modern Functions of the Corporate System, 62 Colum. L. Rev. 433 (1962).

Berle was prescient. Institutional ownership grew from 8.5 percent of the value of all outstanding securities listed on the New York Stock Exchange in 1933 [Securities Industry Study Report, S. Doc. No. 13, 93d Cong., 1st Sess. (1973) 113] to 35.4 percent by year-end 1980 [N. Y. Stock Exchange, Fact Book (1985) 55.] And institutional *trading* reached 64.9 percent of total dollar volume in the last quarter of 1980. N. Y. Stock Exchange, Public Transaction Study (1980) 56.

It has been reported that this tendency toward institutionalization of the stock market — which has created its own problems in securities regulation — "is likely to continue, though probably at a more moderate pace." M. Blume and I. Friend, The Changing Role of the Individual Investor (1978) 186; in general, see SEC, Institutional Investor Study Report, H. R. Doc. No. 92-64, 92d Cong., 1st Sess. (1971).

For a recent reappraisal of the "managerial revolution" postulate, with some

The other side of the dispersion-of-ownership coin is the New York Stock Exchange estimate that 47 million individuals owned shares of publicly traded corporations in mid-1985, up from 6.5 million in 1952, when the first such study was made by The Brookings Institution. This figure represents about one in every five Americans, and it is apart from the approximately 133 million persons with an indirect stake in the market through their pension plans, life insurance, and other intermediaries.[17]

These figures have inspired the discovery in some quarters that the United States has developed a new form of economy, "People's Capitalism" — a slogan that would seem to combine the best of both East and West.[18] It also has been suggested that the cloud has a silver lining after all. It may be that the very emancipation of the corporate manager from the concerns of ownership has been making him, as the editors of Fortune have put it, "a professional in the sense that like all professional men he has a responsibility to society as a whole."[19] Indeed, as far back as the middle 1920s Keynes referred to "the tendency of big enterprise to socialise itself" by management's considering the general stability and reputation of the institution more than maximum profit for the dissociated stockholders.[20] Even if the executives of large enterprises are no longer restrained by the owners, they cannot be impervious to "the subtle but all-pervasive influences exercised on them by the standards, values, and myths of the broader community in which they function."[21] It may even be, as Professor Berle himself ultimately discovered, that the modern enterprise is developing something surprisingly like a corporate soul.[22]

---

fresh data on control of the large corporation, see E. Herman, Corporate Control, Corporate Power (1981).

[17]Kimmel, Share Ownership in the United States (Brookings Institution 1952) 85, 89; N. Y. Stock Exchange, Shareownership 1985 (1986) 3; N. Y. Stock Exchange, Fact Book 1986 at 58.

[18]"The expression was developed by the Advertising Council, which prepared a 'People's Capitalism' exhibit, shown internationally under the auspices of the United States Information Agency." Perlo, "People's Capitalism" and Stock-Ownership, 48 Am. Econ. Rev. 333 (1958).

[19]Editors of Fortune (in collaboration with Davenport), U. S. A.: The Permanent Revolution (1951) 79.

[20]Keynes, The End of Laissez-Faire (1926) 42, republished in Keynes, Essays in Persuasion (1931) 314-15.

[21]Papandreou, Some Basic Problems in the Theory of the Firm, in 2 Am. Econ. Assn., A Survey of Contemporary Economics (Haley ed. 1952) 183, 198; cf. P. Drucker, The New Society (1949) 34-35, 339-43.

[22]Berle, The 20th Century Capitalist Revolution (1954) esp. cc. 3, 5. In the concluding lecture incorporated in that book, Professor Berle gracefully concedes that his well-known controversy with Professor E. Merrick Dodd in the early 1930s "has been settled (at least for the time being) squarely in favor of

As to all this the debate is far from over. Remarking that the "managerial" writers view business "as a kind of game in which profit has approximately the same significance as one's golf score," Professor Mason has contended that the managerial literature has not yet produced an ideology that justifies today's economic system — a system in which managers are supposed to manage for some diffuse, multivalued objective — as satisfactorily as classical economics performed the task for a nineteenth-century enterprise system committed solely to the profit objective.[23]

This much seems clear under any view: The important *law-shaping* factors in recent decades have in fact been the dispersion of ownership among great masses of stockholders — who clearly do *not* control regardless of who does — and the size of modern corporate entities.

At the same time, these are not the only antecedents of the SEC statutes: A collateral aspect of the separation of ownership and control was the development of the institution of "dummy directors" whose function it was to provide "snobbery appeal"[24] — "guinea-pig directors," as they have been called in England because of the once traditional fee of a guinea per meeting, accompanied by a free lunch.[25] And many other problems required legislative attention.

One of the foremost was the failure to furnish essential information to prospective investors when they were invited to buy securities. Others were the common law limitations on civil recovery by injured investors; the inadequacy of current information concerning companies with publicly held securities; the abuse of the proxy device by self-perpetuating managements; the abuse by corporate "insiders" of their favored position in order to trade in their corporations' securities for their own profit; the "private club" at-

---

Professor Dodd's contention." Id. at 169; see Berle and Means, The Modern Corporation and Private Property (1932) bk. II, c. 7, bk. IV, esp. cc. 1, 4; Dodd, For Whom Are Corporate Managers Trustees?, 45 Harv. L. Rev. 1145 (1932); Berle, For Whom Corporate Managers *Are* Trustees: A Note, 45 Harv. L. Rev. 1365 (1932); Dodd, Is Effective Enforcement of the Fiduciary Duties of Corporate Managers Practicable?, 2 U. Chi. L. Rev. 194 (1935). Dodd was already arguing that corporate powers were held in trust for the entire community, whereas Berle was reluctant to abandon the view that business corporations exist solely to make profit for their stockholders until there was offered "a clear and reasonably enforceable scheme of responsibilities to someone else." 45 Harv. L. Rev. at 1367.

[23] Mason, The Apologetics of "Managerialism," 31 J. Bus. U. Chi. 1, 7, 9 (1958); see also E. Mason (ed.), The Corporation in Modern Society (1959) c. 1.

[24] See Douglas, Directors Who Do Not Direct, 47 Harv. L. Rev. 1305 (1934).

[25] H. Samuel, Shareholders' Money (1933) 111 n. 1.

mosphere of the Nation's securities exchanges; the ease with which the securities markets could be manipulated; the lack of financial safeguards for brokers and dealers; the disproportionate amount of the Nation's available credit that at times was channeled into the securities markets at the expense, it was thought, of direct financing of commerce and industry; the practices of protective committees in corporate reorganizations; the abuses of the holding company and investment company devices; and the irresponsibility of trustees under corporate bond indentures.

The eight statutes under which the SEC operates — and it must be remembered that they are not an integrated code passed at a single legislative sitting — do not attack these problems with any single philosophy.

One recurrent group of themes centers around an assumption that various institutions operate according to certain "ideal" concepts: If directors are made civilly liable for misleading prospectuses unless they can affirmatively show that they exercised due care, they will really direct and not spread themselves too thin — so the theory goes. Trustees under corporate indentures should be made to act like real trustees. Other persons in a fiduciary position should be held to fiduciary standards — whether they are corporate "insiders" trading in their corporations' securities, or the managers or advisers of investment companies, or protective committee members in corporate reorganizations. There is also something of the idea that corporations ought to be run on the "town meeting" principle — a concept that, for all its naïveté, cannot be easily abandoned without an agonizing reappraisal of the major premise of Anglo-American corporation law to the effect that management is accountable to the owners of the enterprise.

A second (and somewhat overlapping) group of themes seems to be aimed at safeguarding the economy generally from the operation of the securities sector: Because of the "trigger" proclivities of the stock exchanges, they must be cleansed of manipulative influences and transformed into genuinely public institutions. Margin trading must be regulated as an integral part of supervising the Nation's banking and credit structure. And the crazy-quilt pattern of electric and gas holding companies built up in the 1920s, with their extreme separation of voting power from control, must undergo geographical integration and simplification of their capital structures with a view to protecting consumers as well as investors.

Then, too, there is the recurrent theme throughout these statutes of disclosure, again disclosure, and still more disclosure. Substantive regulation has its limits. But "The truth shall make you free."

B. STATE REGULATION OF SECURITIES: THE BLUE SKY LAWS

1. The Uniform Securities Act

Securities regulation in this country began around the turn of the century with public utility regulation, and most states still exempt public utility issues from the general securities statutes.[1] The first securities statute with teeth was enacted in Kansas in 1911. Kansas had been a stronghold of the Populist philosophy, and to this day the relative strictness of the Midwestern and Western securities statutes is probably a carryover from the era when an "Agrarian West" was bled by a "Moneyed East." Indeed, it was in Kansas, apparently, that the term "blue sky law" first came into general use to describe legislation aimed at promoters who "would sell building lots in the blue sky in fee simple."[2]

The fashion set by Kansas soon spread, so that today blue sky laws of one kind or another are found in every state, the District of Columbia, Puerto Rico, and all the Canadian provinces and territories.[3] In the *Blue Sky Cases* of 1917 the Supreme Court held that a number of these statutes neither violated the Fourteenth Amendment nor unduly burdened interstate commerce.[4] And, far from preempting the field, Congress in the SEC statutes specifically preserved the state legislation.[5]

In 1956 the National Conference of Commissioners on Uniform State Laws and the American Bar Association — after an unsuccessful experience with a 1929 Uniform Sale of Securities Act — promulgated a new Uniform Securities Act, which was drafted principally by the present writer after a two-year Study of State Securities Regulation conducted at the Harvard Law School under his

C. 1B [1]See Note, Public Utility Securities Regulation: A New Life for an Old Law, 7 Okla. City U. L. Rev. 271 (1982) (attempts to check imprudent plant expenditures before they occur through use of the authority over the issuance of long-term securities).

[2]Mulvey, Blue Sky Law, 36 Can. L. T. 37 (1916).

[3]For a bibliography by states, see Loss, Commentary on the Uniform Securities Act (1976) 181-203.

[4]Hall v. Geiger-Jones Co., 242 U. S. 539 (1917); Caldwell v. Sioux Falls Stock Yards Co., 242 U. S. 559 (1917); Merrick v. N. W. Halsey & Co., 242 U. S. 568 (1917).

[5]But see 11 U. S. C. §364(f), infra p. 286; Secondary Mortgage Market Enhancement Act of 1984, infra Supp. p. 664; cf. pp. 1533-39 infra. On federal-state cooperation, see pp. 307-08 infra.

direction.[6] That Act has been adopted, with the greater or lesser modifications that seem to be the curse of all "uniform" legislation, by thirty-six states in addition to the District of Columbia and Puerto Rico.[7] A number of additional states have adopted portions of the Act. This is particularly true of California, where the draftsman of the Corporate Securities Law of 1968 is understood to have borrowed as much of the Uniform Act as he thought would survive that state's relatively inhospitable climate for uniform legislation generally.

In August 1985 the National Conference of Commissioners on Uniform State Laws approved (subject to stylistic changes) a revised Uniform Securities Act.[8] But there were objections from both sides — the North American Securities Administrators Association, apparently because of the "deregulatory flavor of the act as a whole," and the American Bar Association representatives for opposite reasons.[9] Both sides are now advancing proposed amendments to the present Act, evidently agreeing on one proposition: that there is no need for an entirely new Act. Since the approval of the ABA (though not of the NASAA) is essential to the status of a "Uniform Act," the 1956 Act is still officially the Uniform Securities Act. Consequently, we shall simply note the major 1985 proposals at the places at which the Uniform Act is considered. Although the proposals reflect many changes,[10] there is also considerable evidence of paternity, so that frequently precedents under the 1956 Uniform Act will still be useful regardless of the present struggle's dénouement.

The Uniform Act is in four parts. The first three reflect the three traditional blue sky approaches: (I) antifraud provisions, (II) regulation of brokers and dealers (and more recently investment

[6] 7A U. L. A. 561 (master ed. 1978); see L. Loss and E. Cowett, Blue Sky Law (1958). Roughly the first half of that book treats the blue sky laws as they then were, and the second half is the text of the Uniform Act with the official comments as well as the more extensive comments of the draftsmen. The second part was republished, with an up-to-date bibliography by states, as Loss, Commentary on the Uniform Securities Act (1976).

[7] The fourteen states that have *not* adopted the Act are Arizona, California, Florida, Georgia, Illinois, Louisiana, Maine, New York, North Dakota, Ohio, Rhode Island, South Dakota, Texas, and Vermont.

[8] 1 CCH Blue Sky L. Rep. ¶¶5593 et seq. Maine and New Mexico have adopted versions of preliminary drafts.

[9] See 17 Sec. Reg. L. Rep. 1374, 1801-02 (1985); Hensley, The Development of a Revised Uniform Securities Act, 40 Bus. Law. 721 (1985).

[10] Among the more significant changes (apart from a few new definitions and a broadening of the exemptions) are the addition of administrative cease and desist orders (§602), declaratory orders (§706) subject to judicial review (§711(b)), and court-imposed civil penalties (§603(a)(1)(ii)). On the differences between the present and proposed Uniform Acts generally, see Sargent, Blue Sky Law, 14 Sec. Reg. L. J. 62 (1986).

advisers), and (III) registration of securities. Part IV contains the definitions, exemptions, and other provisions of general applicability, and tables indicate how much of Part IV is required depending on whether a state adopts only Part I or Parts I and II or all three parts. An additional table permits several different treatments of investment advisers.

Thus the Uniform Act is really several uniform acts in one. This reflects the great diversity that previously existed, to the point where it was not considered feasible to draft a single statute that would achieve general acceptance. In fact, however, except for the District of Columbia's omission of Part III, all the jurisdictions that have adopted the Uniform Act have taken all four parts *(mutatis mutandis),*[11] and most have adopted the broadest version with respect to investment advisers, treating them like brokers and dealers.[12]

To describe the first three parts of the Act in general terms:

Part I, Fraudulent and Other Prohibited Practices, contains only two sections: §101 outlaws fraudulent practices in connection with the *sale or purchase* of a security, and §102 has to do with fraudulent and other undesirable *investment advisory* activities. There are no exemptions from Part I. The sanctions are found in other parts of the Act. They include (1) criminal prosecution in the event of a willful violation,[13] (2) injunction, and (3) administrative proceedings to deny, suspend, or revoke registration when the violator is a broker-dealer, an agent of a broker-dealer or of an issuer, or an investment adviser. Moreover, although there is no civil liability for violation of Part I as such, provision is made in Part IV (§410(a)(2)) for civil liability in the case of *sales* made through fraud or misstatement.[14]

Part II, Registration of Broker-Dealers, Agents, and Investment Advisers, contains four sections. Section 201 requires the annual registration of broker-dealers, their agents, and investment advisers. Most of the exemptions from *securities* registration in Part IV do not apply. Any registered broker-dealer may act as an investment

[11] Nevada and New Jersey register only intrastate offerings, and the Colorado Uniform Act was amended in 1981 to register only those securities and broker-dealers not registered with the SEC.

[12] With forty jurisdictions requiring investment advisers to register, the SEC and the NASAA have developed a uniform form. SEC and NASAA Conference on Federal-State Securities Regulation, CCH Fed. Sec. L. Rep. ¶83,610 at 86,755 (1984); see p. 673 n. 9 infra.

[13] In State v. Ross, 104 N. M. App. 23, 715 P. 2d 471 (1986), the court held that convictions under the blue sky fraud provision and the general fraud provision did not amount to double jeopardy, since the elements of the two statutes were not the same.

[14] Civil liability is treated in Chapter 10.

adviser without registering separately in that capacity if his application so states and the administrator does not condition his registration. An issuer distributing its own securities does not have to register as a broker-dealer,[15] but the employees who represent the issuer in making the offering must register as "agents" as that term is defined in §401(b). The registration procedure is set out in §202, with provisions whereby the administrator by rule may require broker-dealers and investment advisers to maintain a minimum capital and may specify surety bonds for all registrants. Applications for registration automatically become effective on the thirtieth day after filing unless the administrator either accelerates the effective date or institutes a proceeding to deny registration. Section 203 contains a number of postregistration provisions having to do with books and accounts, financial reports, and the administrator's inspection or visitatorial power. Section 204 specifies eleven grounds on which the registration of a broker-dealer, agent, or investment adviser may be denied, suspended, or revoked, provided always that the administrator finds it in the public interest to take such action. One of these grounds is lack of qualification, and §204(b) provides, among other things, that in that connection the administrator may require applicants to take examinations.

Part III, Registration of Securities, contains six sections. Section 301 requires the registration of any security before it is offered or sold in the state unless the security or transaction is exempted under §402.[16] Sections 302-04 provide for three types of registration — by "notification," "coordination," and "qualification."[17] The first and third were quite common before the Uniform Act.

Under §302 the notification procedure is reserved for (1) issuers that have been in continuous operation for five years with no default or any senior security during the past three years and with a three-year average net earnings record of 5 percent on their common stock and (2) certain distributions of outstanding securities, whether or not they meet the first test. The registration statement in a notification case is substantially limited to the information that is essential to permit application of the statutory standards governing effectiveness under §306. In addition, the registration statement

[15] See p. 17 infra.

[16] For a detailed treatment of the Texas exemptions, which follow basically the pattern of the Uniform Act, see Lipsman, Exemptions under the Texas Securities Act: A Logical Framework for the Practicing Attorney, 22 Houston L. Rev. 725 (1985).

[17] In California the generic term has traditionally been "qualification" rather than "registration," and what is "registration by qualification" elsewhere is "qualification by permit" in California.

automatically becomes effective at a fixed hour on the second full business day after filing unless the administrator accelerates or institutes a stop-order proceeding to deny effectiveness. A number of Uniform Act jurisdictions have deleted the notification procedure in the light of the new coordination procedure.

The coordination procedure under §303 is limited to issues for which a registration statement has been filed with the SEC under the Securities Act of 1933. This reform, perhaps the most important in the entire statute, has been adopted by several nonuniform states (California, in substance Illinois, Maine, Ohio, South Dakota, and Texas).[18] A special procedure for such cases was relatively novel in the blue sky laws before the Uniform Act — although a measure of such coordination had been informally achieved in quite a few states, at least by those law firms with counsel who specialize in blue sky practice. The purpose of §303 was essentially to regularize this informal technique and to arrive at a coordination procedure that is definite and uniform. The section does this by streamlining the *content* of the registration statement and the *procedure* by which it becomes effective, but not the *substantive standards* governing its effectiveness.

The concept is essentially a simple one. If the SEC prospectus (together with such additional information filed with the SEC as the administrator may require) is filed in time, the registration statement becomes effective automatically at the state level the moment it becomes effective in Washington unless the administrator takes the affirmative step of instituting a stop-order proceeding under the substantive standards of the Uniform Act. There is also a special exemption designed to permit offers (but not sales) to be made during the waiting period between the filing and the effectiveness of the registration statement to the extent that such offers are permitted under the federal statute.[19] A coordination procedure was thus achieved without sacrificing the traditional regulatory philosophy of the states to the disclosure philosophy of the federal statute. And it has been suggested not only that the coordination system "had an enormously positive effect on the underwriter's ability to blue sky a national offering" but also that the widespread adoption

[18] Effective July 1, 1984, Illinois's "registration by notification" is substantially the Uniform Act's registration by coordination. And effective May 9, 1984, Hawaii's coordination provision was repealed in favor of an outright exemption for securities registered under the Securities Act of 1933. See also pp. 24-25 infra.

[19] §402(b)(12).

of this device enabled blue sky law to preserve its role in the regulation of national public offerings.[20]

The qualification procedure under §304 *must* be used when neither of the other procedures is available and *may* be used in any case. Here the administrator has plenary power to require information and to decide when the registration statement becomes effective, as well as to require the use of a prospectus.

Section 305 contains a number of provisions that are applicable to all or most registrations. For example, the administrator is authorized by rule or order to require escrow of securities, impounding of proceeds, and the use of a specified contract form as conditions upon registration by qualification or coordination.

Section 306 specifies nine grounds on which the administrator may issue a stop order denying, suspending, or revoking effectiveness of a registration statement if he finds it in the public interest to do so. These grounds apply equally to all three types of registration. The draftsmen's commentary has this to say about them:

> The *standards* in §306(a) are a cross-section of the existing standards somewhere between the two extremes: the simple "fraud" test exemplified by the Georgia statute and the "fair, just and equitable" or "sound business principles" language of states like California[21] and formerly Kansas. This is not a mere practical compromise. Administrative flexibility is important in this area, but it must always be balanced against the proper claim of legitimate business to as great a degree of specificity as the public interest will permit. Clause (F) of §306(a) refers to "unreasonable" *selling expense or promoters' participation or options*; this one clause should take care of many of the classic abuses which led to the development of such a thing as blue sky law. Among other grounds for action under §306(a), Clause (E) contains a *fraud* standard, Clause (A) contains a *full disclosure*

[20] Sargent, Blue Sky Law, 14 Sec. Reg. L. J. 62, 73 (1985).

[21] Today in California the Commissioner of Corporations may refuse to issue a permit unless he finds, among other things, that "the proposed plan of business of the applicant and the proposed issuance of securities are fair, just, and equitable, [and] that the applicant intends to transact its business fairly and honestly," except that (1) when he takes the initiative to suspend or revoke a permit that has already been issued, or in the first instance when the issuer has used the "notification" or "coordination" procedure, as well as in all nonissuer offerings, the *Commissioner* has the burden of showing that the proposed plan of business or issuance "is *not* fair, just, or equitable," and (2) neither standard applies in the case of a cash offering pursuant to a firm commitment underwriting in which the issue and all the underwriters are registered with the SEC. Cal. Corp. Code §25140.

standard, and Clause (B) refers to *violations* by the issuer and various other persons.[22]

2. New York and Other Atypical Jurisdictions

Because it would not be feasible to rely on local counsel in each state in which a multistate offering is to be made, a single lawyer or law firm will see to the registration of the offering wherever it is needed. This means that blue sky counsel must be familiar not only with the law of his own state but with all fifty-two statutes.[23] Students of the subject, therefore, will be relieved to know that, taken broadly, all fifty-two statutes are comparable — which is not surprising in view of the fact that the Uniform Act basically followed existing patterns — except for six jurisdictions that require separate mention:

Although the District of Columbia does not register securities, it does authorize the administrator to call for data by order in specific cases. This authority has been seldom if ever exercised.

New York's Martin Act,[24] passed in 1921, was supplemented in 1932 by very simple filing provisions with respect both to broker-dealers and to the securities they sell. But it is commonly referred to as a fraud act and falls primarily in that category. The basic provision, §352, is a grant of investigatory power to the Attorney

[22] Loss, Commentary on the Uniform Securities Act (1976) 83-84.

In 1984 the state regulators undertook to work toward developing procedures and guidelines with a view to providing greater consistency in the application of the various "merit" standards. SEC and NASAA Conference on Federal-State Securities Regulation, CCH Fed. Sec. L. Rep. ¶83,610 at 86,753, 86,756-58 (1984). For descriptions of some of the standards and conditions that are now commonly applied in the "merit" states, see id. at 86,757; Makens, Who Speaks for the Investor? An Evaluation of the Assault on Merit Regulation, 13 U. Balt. L. Rev. 435, 437-47 (1984). See also c. lC infra.

Other aspects of the Uniform Act, and of the blue sky laws generally, are considered in later portions of this book by way of comparison with the federal statutes.

There are two books on blue sky law that use the Uniform Act as a focal point. J. Long, Blue Sky Law (1985); H. Sowards and N. Hirsch, 11C Business Organizations: Blue Sky Regulation (1977); see also C. Moscow and H. Makens (eds.), Michigan Securities Regulation (1983). The Uniform Act aside, see Symposium on State Securities Regulation, 13 U. Balt. L. Rev. 435 (1984); P. Fass and D. Wittner, Blue Sky Practice for Public and Private Limited Offerings (1985 ed.) (securities of direct participation programs, i. e., real estate, oil and gas, equipment leasing, and cattle feeding).

[23] The North American Securities Administrators Association has achieved a considerable amount of uniformity of forms in cooperation with the SEC. See pp. 602-03 infra.

[24] Gen. Bus. Law, Art. 23-A.

General. The section has a majestic, one-sentence sweep: Whenever it appears to the Attorney General that, in connection with any security (or commodity) or investment advice, any person

> shall have employed, or employs, or is about to employ any device, scheme or artifice to defraud or for obtaining money or property by means of any false pretense, representation or promise, * * * shall have made, makes or attempts to make within or from this state fictitious or pretended purchases or sales of securities or commodities or * * * shall have employed, or employs, or is about to employ, any deception, misrepresentation, concealment, suppression, fraud, false pretense or false promise, or shall have engaged in or engages in or is about to engage in any practice or transaction or course of business relating to the purchase, exchange, investment advice or sale of securities or commodities which is fraudulent or in violation of law and which has operated or which would operate as a fraud upon the purchaser, * * * any one or all of which devices, schemes, artifices, fictitious or pretended purchases or sales of securities or commodities, deceptions, misrepresentations, concealments, suppressions, frauds, false pretenses, false promises, practices, transactions and courses of business are hereby declared to be and are hereinafter referred to as a fraudulent practice or fraudulent practices[,] or he believes it to be in the public interest that an investigation be made, he may in his discretion either require or permit such person * * * to file with him a statement in writing under oath or otherwise as to all the facts and circumstances concerning the subject matter which he believes it is to the public interest to investigate * * *.

The Attorney General or his representative may subpoena witnesses, examine them under oath before himself or a magistrate or court of record, and require the production of books and papers. When the Attorney General believes "from evidence satisfactory to him" that any person "has engaged in, is engaged in or is about to engage in any * * * fraudulent practices," or (under a 1958 amendment) whenever he shows a conviction anywhere of a crime involving securities or of any felony, he may bring an action in the name of the People against any person participating in any such practices to enjoin their continuation, and he may include an application to enjoin the defendant permanently from selling any securities in any capacity within the state. The court may grant as much of the relief sought as it "may deem proper." Refusal to testify or produce relevant papers in an investigation is *prima facie* proof of "fraudulent practices" so as to sustain a permanent injunction. Violation of an injunction, in addition to being contempt of court and a misdemeanor, may result in a civil penalty of $3000. And the court may appoint a receiver for "property derived * * * by means of * * * fraudulent practices," as well as any commingled property that cannot be identified, "for the benefit of all persons intervening * * * and establishing an interest in such property."

The New York courts have painted with a broad brush. As early as 1926 the Court of Appeals unanimously held that the term "fraud" includes "all deceitful practices contrary to the plain rules of common honesty." In the light of the legislative purpose, the words "fraud" and "fraudulent practice" are given "a wide meaning, so as to include all acts, although not originating in any actual evil design or contrivance to perpetrate fraud or injury upon others, which do by their tendency to deceive or mislead the purchasing public come within the purpose of the law." Hence a complaint for injunction is good if it alleges merely "a species of conduct commonly, although perhaps inaccurately, called equitable fraud, although the facts alleged do not connote what is commonly known as actual or intentional or legal fraud; i. e., false representations knowingly made and acted on, resulting in damage."[25]

On the broker-dealer front, the New York scheme is unquestionably the simplest. Every "dealer" or "broker" must file several documents, all of them quite simple: (1) A "state notice," containing merely the dealer's or broker's name and address, the state of incorporation, if any, and the names of the partners, if any, must be filed in the Department of State. (2) In addition, every dealer or broker must file a "broker-dealer statement" in the Department of Law, and (3) every salesman must file in the same place a "salesman's statement," containing "such information pertaining to the business history for the last preceding five years, criminal record and educational background of the applicant and [in the case of the broker-dealer statement] his or its partners, officers, directors or other principals thereof deemed pertinent by the attorney-general."[26] (4) The Attorney General may provide by rule or order for the filing of supplemental broker-dealer or salesman's statements to keep this information reasonably current. And (5) registration must be renewed every four years. (6) Finally, there must be filed in the Department of State a "further state notice" identifying each security offered "to the public" by the dealer and giving the name,

[25] People v. Federated Radio Corp., 244 N. Y. 33, 38-39, 41, 154 N. E. 655, 657, 658 (1926). This is one of the leading cases on the concept of fraud in securities legislation, state or federal.

[26] §359-e(3)(a), (b). Every salesman (with some exceptions) must also pass the NASAA's agents' examination. §359-e(3)(b). See p. 603 n. 9 infra.

address, and state of incorporation of the issuer. A number of categories of securities are exempted from this last requirement, and the manager of an underwriting or selling syndicate who maintains an office in the state normally files the "further state notice" on behalf of all members of the syndicate.

Violation of any of these filing requirements is defined as a "fraudulent practice" by §352. But, except for a 1963 amendment that requires every broker-dealer to maintain net capital of $5000,[27] there are no provisions concerning financial responsibility. There is no authority anywhere to deny or revoke or suspend registration on any standards. And the total information available from all the required filings does not amount to very much. In short, the registration requirements are merely an adjunct to the fraud provisions.

At the same time, New York defines "dealer" to include a "corporation selling or offering for sale * * * to the public within or from this state securities issued by it."[28] This kind of provision was quite common before the Uniform Act. One must not be surprised, however, when this Alice in Wonderland type of drafting — "When I use a word, it means just what I choose it to mean"[29] — produces strange results: It is understood to be the Attorney General's position that every corporation, domestic or foreign, that issues stock to employees in New York in connection with an employee stock option plan must register as a "dealer" unless an exemption is granted on application.[30]

The fraud and broker-dealer registration provisions aside, New York since late 1968 has required *securities* registration of intrastate offerings on a disclosure basis and with a notification procedure. In thus complementing the federal scheme, which exempts intrastate offerings, New York resembles Colorado, New Jersey, and Nevada. New York, however, goes further in requiring the registration of real estate syndication offerings generally.[31]

[27] §352-k1.

[28] §359-e1(a).

[29] Carroll, Through the Looking-Glass and What Alice Found There, c. 6.

[30] The exemption provision is §359-f2(e), and exemptions are granted very readily.

[31] N. Y. §352-e; see All Seasons Resorts, Inc. v. Abrams, 68 N. Y. 2d 81, 497 N. E. 2d 33 (1986); In the Matter of Council for Owner Occupied Housing, Inc. v. Abrams, 125 A. D. 2d 10, 511 N. Y. S. 2d 26, CCH Blue Sky L. Rep. ¶72,481 (3d Dept. 1987) (rulemaking does not extend to requiring correction of disclosed defects).

3. Insurance Securities

Regulation of insurance securities is frequently a world of its own. About a dozen jurisdictions have provisions in their *insurance* laws that regulate the issuance and sale of insurance securities quite comprehensively, generally with definitions, conditions for the issuance of permits and licenses, provisions for their revocation, filing fees, prohibitions of false advertising, penalties for issuance without a license or permit, limitations on organizational expenses, bond requirements, and provisions for subsequent financing.[32] About the same number of insurance laws have securities provisions of lesser scope.[33] Moreover, these provisions in the insurance statutes are apart from special provisions on insurance company securities that are occasionally found in the blue sky laws themselves.[34]

The net result is that regulation of insurance securities is sometimes within the exclusive jurisdiction of the insurance authorities, sometimes within the exclusive jurisdiction of the blue sky authorities (wherever there are no special provisions on insurance securities), and sometimes under the concurrent jurisdiction of both. Some of the statutes also distinguish between domestic and foreign or between authorized and unauthorized insurers.

Section 1204 of the New York Insurance Law (formerly §51) deserves special mention because it prohibits the unlicensed public sale of any security of an insurance company not authorized to do business in the state until one year from the first date upon which the security was "offered to the public" in New York. In the early 1960s it was held that that section's "endeavor to protect the public is * * * so emphatic that allowance of rescission in a proper case is in our opinion essential to carry out the Legislature's intent."[35] The court accordingly denied the defendant's motion for summary judgment. But the defendant won at trial on the ground that the exemption was satisfied by quotations in the "sheets"[36] indicating that the security had been traded over the counter for at least a

[32] E. g., Cal. Ins. Code §§820-60; Ill. Rev. Stat. c. 73, esp. §§627-44, 759.1, 759.2; Pa. Stat. Ann. (Purdon) Tit. 40, §§389-400.

[33] E. g., N. J. Rev. Stat. §17B:18-6; N. Y. Ins. Law §§1201, 1204. All these provisions are collected in CCH Blue Sky L. Rep.

[34] E. g., Ohio Rev. Code §1707-32. See Rosenblum, Potential Problems in the Blue Sky Area, [1982] Am. Council of Life Ins. Legal Section Proc. 39.

[35] Atkin v. Hill, Darlington & Grimm, 15 A. D. 2d 362, 366, 224 N. Y. S. 2d 553, 557 (1st Dept. 1962), *aff'd per curiam,* 12 N. Y. 2d 940, 188 N. E. 2d 790 (1963).

[36] This refers to the National Daily Quotation Service, published by the National Quotation Bureau, Inc., which is a subsidiary of Commerce Clearing House, Inc.

year, from which the defendant might justifiably have inferred, had he checked, that there had been a public offering at least a year previously. In other words, the court thought that it did not have to determine whether there had been a "public offering" during the one-year period in the sense in which newly issued securities are formally presented to the public; nor did it think it had to ascertain whether there had been actual sales in New York within that period.[37] This judgment was affirmed, the Appellate Division apparently concluding on the basis of the trial as distinct from what could be ascertained on motion for summary judgment:

> It is not every sale in derogation of the statute that can be rescinded. The purpose of the statute is, we believe, to prevent unlicensed foreign insurance companies from getting financing by offering their stock here by public sale. This court held that any buyer caught in such an operation could rescind the sale. The statute was not designed to allow a speculator to buy stock in such a company from a third person — neither the company nor one engaged in distributing its stock — and rest secure in the knowledge that if the stock turned out to be an advantageous investment he could keep it, and if not he could force the seller to take it back. In our opinion the record reveals just such a situation.[38]

Two members of the court dissented but wrote simply on the question of the exemption, disagreeing that it had been established by proof of only three sales and five over-the-counter quotations in New York during the year 1957.

4. Conflict of Laws

The increasingly interstate nature of the securities business has produced a complex congeries of problems in the conflict of laws: A broker-dealer in Boston sends sales literature to persons in California. Does the California statute apply? The Massachusetts statute? Both? A broker-dealer in New York calls a customer who lives in Connecticut or is vacationing in Florida. A contract between issuer and underwriter, or between dealer and customer, is signed in one state after preliminary negotiations in another. A corporation whose stockholders have preemptive rights and live in many states wants to raise additional capital through a public stock offer-

[37] 44 Misc. 2d 863, 254 N. Y. S. 2d 867 (Sup. Ct. 1964).

[38] 23 A. D. 2d 331, 332, 260 N. Y. S. 2d 482, 484 (1st Dept. 1965), *aff'd per curiam*, 18 N. Y. 2d 980, 224 N. E. 2d 723 (1966).

ing, and the blue sky administrators in one or more states refuse registration or insist on changes in the terms of the offering that are distasteful to the corporation and are not required in most states. A purchaser of an installment or periodic payment plan certificate issued by an investment company moves, before his payments are completed, to a state where the certificates cannot qualify for registration. A broker-dealer or investment adviser or issuer inserts an advertisement in the Wall Street Journal or Fortune, which circulate all over the country. In all these instances, and others, if a court should ultimately decide that there had been a violation of the law of one of the states that had a more or less peripheral relation to the transaction or the issue of securities, serious questions would arise of both civil and criminal liability and — perhaps most important of all as a practical matter — of enforceability of contract.

Because the thirty-five or forty reported blue sky decisions that predated the Uniform Securities Act defied generalization,[39] the proponents of the Uniform Act chose the codification route. And that Act reflects the fact that the problems are not of the classic conflict of laws type that requires the court to make a choice of law. Rather, two or more laws can apply at the same time:[40]

UNIFORM SECURITIES ACT, RELEVANT PROVISIONS OF PART IV

SECTION 401. [DEFINITIONS.]

When used in this act, unless the context otherwise requires:

["BROKER-DEALER."]

(c) * * * "Broker-dealer" does not include * * * (4) a person who has no place of business in this state if (A) he effects transactions in this state exclusively with or through (i) the issuers of the securities involved in the transactions, (ii) other broker-dealers, or (iii) banks, savings institutions, trust companies, insurance companies, investment companies as defined in the Investment Company Act of 1940, pension or profit-sharing trusts, or other financial institu-

[39]These cases are collected and analyzed in Loss, The Conflict of Laws and the Blue Sky Laws, 71 Harv. L. Rev. 209 (1957).

[40]Lintz v. Carey Manor, Ltd., 613 F. Supp. 543 (W. D. Va. 1985); see McClard, The Applicability of Local Securities Acts to Multi-State Securities Transactions, 20 U. Richmond L. Rev. 139 (1985).

tions or institutional buyers, whether acting for themselves or as trustees, or (B) during any period of twelve consecutive months he does not direct more than fifteen offers to sell or buy into this state in any manner to persons other than those specified in clause (A), whether or not the offeror or any of the offerees is then present in this state.

* * *

["INVESTMENT ADVISER."]

(f) * * * "Investment adviser" does not include * * * (6) a person who has no place of business in this state if (A) his only clients in this state are other investment advisers, broker-dealers, banks, savings institutions, trust companies, insurance companies, investment companies as defined in the Investment Company Act of 1940, pension or profit-sharing trusts, or other financial institutions or institutional buyers, whether acting for themselves or as trustees, or (B) during any period of twelve consecutive months he does not direct business communications into this state in any manner to more than five clients other than those specified in clause (A), whether or not he or any of the persons to whom the communications are directed is then present in this state * * *.

* * *

SECTION 414. [SCOPE OF THE ACT AND SERVICE OF PROCESS.]

[SELLERS.]

(a) Sections 101, 201(a), 301, 405, and 410 [which prohibit fraud, require the registration of broker-dealers, agents and securities, prohibit any representation of official approval, and create certain civil liabilities] apply to persons who sell or offer to sell when (1) an offer to sell is made in this state, or (2) an offer to buy is made and accepted in this state.

[BUYERS.]

(b) Sections 101, 201(a), and 405 apply to persons who buy or offer to buy when (1) an offer to buy is made in this state, or (2) an offer to sell is made and accepted in this state.

[OFFER IN THIS STATE.]

(c) For the purpose of this section, an offer to sell or to buy is made in this state, whether or not either party is then present in this state, when the offer (1) originates from this state or (2) is directed by the offeror to this state and received at the place to which it is directed (or at any post office in this state in the case of a mailed offer).[41]

[ACCEPTANCE IN THIS STATE.]

(d) For the purpose of this section, an offer to buy or to sell is accepted in this state when acceptance (1) is communicated to the offeror in this state and (2) has not previously been communicated to the offeror, orally or in writing, outside this state; and acceptance is communicated to the offeror in this state, whether or not either party is then present in this state, when the offeree directs it to the offeror in this state reasonably believing the offeror to be in this state and it is received at the place to which it is directed (or at any post office in this state in the case of a mailed acceptance).[42]

[PUBLICATIONS, RADIO, AND TELEVISION.]

(e) An offer to sell or to buy is not made in this state when (1) the publisher circulates or there is circulated on his behalf in this state any bona fide newspaper or other publication of general, regular, and paid circulation which is not published in this state, or which is published in this state but has had more than two-thirds of

[41] Application of the §414(c)(2) formula affords due process of law. Green v. Weis, Voison, Cannon, Inc., 479 F. 2d 462 (7th Cir. 1973). In Hayden v. McDonald, 742 F. 2d 423, 436 (8th Cir. 1984), involving the Minnesota Uniform Securities Act's equivalent of §12(1) of the Securities Act of 1933, infra p. 883, the court refused to apply the private offering "integration" doctrine (infra p. 326, par (3)) to establish Minnesota jurisdiction over those sales in the allegedly integrated offering that had resulted from out-of-state offers to sell.

[42] The court applied §414(a), (c), and (d) in Hall v. Johnston, 758 F. 2d 421 (9th Cir. 1985). In Newsome *ex rel.* Oklahoma Securities Commission v. Diamond Oil Producers, CCH Blue Sky L. Rep. ¶71,869 (Okla. Dist. Ct. 1983), the court applied §414(c)(1) even though the offer in the state to which it was directed had been made in accordance with the laws of that state. It would be incompatible with the purposes of the Act to exclude such sales from regulation, the court said, because that would create a "safe harbor" from which a promoter could operate with impunity so long as he never ventured into the states in which his purchasers resided. But cf. Kreis v. Mates Investment Fund, Inc., 473 F. 2d 1308 (8th Cir. 1973), a case under the Missouri Uniform Act that illustrates the mischief often created by adding provisos to this type of intricate statutory formulation.

its circulation outside this state during the past twelve months, or (2) a radio or television program originating outside this state is received in this state.

[INVESTMENT ADVICE.]

(f) Sections 102 and 201(c), as well as section 405 so far as investment advisers are concerned, apply when any act instrumental in effecting prohibited conduct is done in this state, whether or not either party is then present in this state.[43]

5. Partial Preemption Under the Federal Securities Code

The proponents of The American Law Institute's Federal Securities Code considered three possibilities with respect to federal-state relations:[44]

> (a) The first is complete preemption, as in §11361(a) (formerly §20a) of the Interstate Commerce Act (49 U. S. C. §11361(a); see 1 Loss 418-19) or, with modifications, the Commodity Futures Trading Act (7 U. S. C. §2).[45] If the period 1890-1914 had seen the enactment of federal securities laws along with the antitrust and ICC legislation, there might never have been any blue sky laws. Nevertheless, it is impossible to ignore the more than sixty years of blue sky history. Moreover, the blue sky authorities can continue to serve an important (if not indispensable) function with respect to essentially local offerings as well as local broker-dealers and investment advisers. And even with respect to nationwide offerings, there is no reason to assume that Congress would have been satisfied with a disclosure statute in 1933 if the blue sky laws had not already gone

[43] Section 414(g)-(h) provides for both consent to service of process and substituted service. For a thorough annotation of §414 of the Uniform Act, see J. Long, Blue Sky Law (1985) c. 3.

[44] 2 ALI, Federal Securities Code (1980) 966-67 (hereinafter cited as "Code"). Copyright 1980 by The American Law Institute and reprinted with its permission. On the Code, see p. 40 infra. The two volumes of the Code now contain a Second [pocket] Supplement (1981).

The Code's comments, in referring to today's section numbers as well as SEC releases, use the signals that the SEC uses: S for the Securities Act, X for the Securities Exchange Act, U for the Public Utility Holding Company Act, T for the Trust Indenture Act, N for the Investment Company Act, R for the Investment Advisers Act, and SIP for the Securities Investor Protection Act.

[45] For an argument in favor of preemption, whose theme is forcefully revealed in its title, see Campbell, An Open Attack on the Nonsense of Blue Sky Regulation, 10 J. Corp. L. 553 (1985).

further in most states: that is to say, their complete replacement now would require that serious consideration be given to the insertion of substantive standards, at least along the lines of the Uniform Securities Act's, in Part V of the Code. For all these reasons, the Code does not follow the route of complete preemption.

(b) The second possibility is a continuation of the *status quo:* duplicate regulation except in the rare instance of a conflict. [Citations omitted.] But, whatever the claims of history, they must be balanced against a decent regard for the principles of federalism in a country of fifty-odd jurisdictions with a view to both the legitimate needs of capital formation and the maximum effectiveness of the federal-state regulatory apparatus as a whole.

(c) What remains is the limited use of the Supremacy Clause to achieve what is not so much partial preemption (except in a constitutional sense) as federal-state integration or harmonization with reduction of unnecessary duplication of regulation. That is the philosophy of §1904, taken together with §514.

Whereas §1904 is designed to emphasize federal control of multistate distributions, §514 (which is a substantial expansion of the intrastate exemption in the Securities Act of 1933)[46] is an attempt to enhance the states' responsibility with respect to local distributions. The two sections evolved in the course of several years of collaboration with the North American Securities Administrators Association, which in 1977 endorsed the Code's federal-state scheme.[47]

The Code's first endeavor was to strengthen the Uniform Securities Act's scheme of registration by coordination[48] and make it nationwide. The commentary to the Code (brought current here to reflect subsequent legislation)[49] observes that the coordination technique has already been adopted, either verbatim or in substance, in Puerto Rico and thirty-nine states; that five more states accept the SEC registration statement or prospectus;[50] that the District of Columbia registers only broker-dealers, not securities; that

[46] See c. 5C infra.

[47] 2 Code 967-69.

[48] See p. 12 supra.

[49] Mississippi and New Hampshire have adopted the Uniform Act. There is a new statute in Maine. Florida's and Illinois's registration by "notification" is substantially the coordination scheme. Fla. Stat. §517.082; Ill. Rev. Stat. c. 121-1/2, §137.5A-B. Colorado now registers only intrastate offerings. Colo. Rev. Stat. (1973) §11-51-107(2). And Hawaii repealed the coordination section in favor of a provision that simply accepts the SEC prospectus. Hawaii Rev. Stat. (1968) §485-10(b)(4).

[50] Ariz. Rev. Stat. §44-1896; Ga. Code §10-5-9(5); Hawaii Rev. Stat. (1968) §485-10(b)(4); La. Rev. Stat. §51-708(10), 2d par.; N. D. Cent. Code §10-04-08, ¶4.

Colorado, Nevada, and New Jersey register only intrastate issues; that the only interstate offerings registrable in New York are those of real estate securities; and that this leaves only two states (Rhode Island and Vermont, plus New York with respect to real estate offerings) that would be substantially affected by a federally imposed coordination procedure. The Code would accordingly legislate complete preemption with respect to distribution of securities in the case of any state whose registration procedure was not substantially coordinated with the procedure under the Code by a date two years after the Code's enactment.[51]

There is also a preemption provision with respect to "blue chip" distributions as defined in the Code, "on the theory (a) that they almost universally get by the states' substantive requirements anyway, (b) that virtually all states already afford exemption to securities of a class listed on the New York Stock Exchange or frequently other specified exchanges * * * , and (c) that the present scheme makes for much unnecessary paper-shuffling that not only complicates the lives of blue sky lawyers but also (and this is more important) diverts the limited manpower of the blue sky administrators from those regulatory tasks for which they are perhaps better equipped than the SEC."[52]

C. THE BATTLE OF THE PHILOSOPHIES

When the Crash of 1929, followed by the Great Depression, finally led to the passage of the Securities Act of 1933 during the "hundred glorious days" of President Roosevelt's New Deal, the first problem was determining what the role of the federal government should be in the protection of investors. In addition to a couple of decades of experience with the blue sky laws — which varied, as we have seen, from New York's mild antifraud approach to California's "fair, just, and equitable" standard — Congress had available the English history of prospectus disclosure, the experience with capital control during World War I, the regulation of railroad securities by the Interstate Commerce Commission since 1920, and a long history of various federal incorporation and licensing proposals.

During its six-month life in 1918, the Capital Issues Committee (consisting of two members of the Federal Reserve Board, the

[51] §§1904(a), 2010(a); 2 Code 972-73.

[52] 2 Code 975. On existing preemption provisions, see pp. 242, 664, 871 n.3 infra. On judicial preemption, see pp. 533-39 infra.

Comptroller of the Currency, and four bankers) passed on more than 2000 applications to issue new securities, of which about 20 percent were disapproved.[1] But this was not investor protection. It was purely a rationing of capital to give effect to the Government's policy of "war business first."

Another result of the war was the Transportation Act of 1920, which was an incident of the return of the railroads to "private" ownership. That statute adopted a long-standing recommendation of the Interstate Commerce Commission by adding §20a to the Interstate Commerce Act in order to subject the purposes and uses of railroad issues to ICC authorization.[2] The same progression that had earlier marked the state legislation was thus repeated on the national scene. General securities registration was preceded by legislation of the public service variety dealing with the financing of railroads. Indeed, 1920 also saw the passage of the Federal Water Power Act, which authorized the Federal Power Commission (now the Federal Energy Regulatory Commission, in the Department of Energy) to regulate the amount and character of securities to be issued by public service licensees.[3]

The investor-protection aspects of the ICC securities provision — which was extended to motor carriers by the Motor Carrier Act of 1935 — are indirect. That provision is neither a blue sky law, in the sense that the ICC's primary interest is in giving investors a "fair shake" for their money, nor a disclosure statute. It takes its coloration from the Interstate Commerce Act and from its purpose of preventing a recurrence of the notorious financial scandals with their destruction of confidence in railroad investment. Accordingly, the statutory standards are phrased in terms of the contribution that the particular plan of financing would make to a healthy railroad system for the Nation. At the same time, the legislative history demonstrates that there was "universal recognition of the interrelation of sound railroad financing and the protection of investors, the latter being essential to maintaining confidence in railroad investment."[4] Without benefit of rule, moreover, it is the ICC's prac-

C. 1C [1] Report of Capital Issues Committee, H. R. Doc. No. 1485, 65th Cong., 3d Sess. (1918) 1, 5.

[2] Now 49 U. S. C. §11301.

[3] See 1 Loss 423-26.

[4] Breswick & Co. v. United States, 156 F. Supp. 227, 234 n. 15 (S. D. N. Y. 1957), *rev'd on other grounds* sub nom. Alleghany Corp. v. Breswick & Co., 355 U. S. 415 (1958). The classic treatise is I. Sharfman, The Interstate Commerce Commission (1931). For a summary discussion of the securities provision, see 1 Loss 412-23.

tice to require a prospectus comparable to that required by the SEC.[5]

Considerably deeper than any of these roots was the discussion, going back to 1885, of federal licensing or incorporation.[6] The Taft-Wickersham Permissive Federal Incorporation Bills were introduced in 1910[7] (Wickersham was Attorney General), and President Taft sent two messages to Congress on the subject that year and the next. It is an interesting footnote to history that in the 1912 campaign, when the Bull Moose platform declared for federal incorporation, Taft changed his attitude on the ground of undue concentration of power. Nevertheless, in his 1911 message he had recommended that corporations taking out federal charters should "be subject to rigid rules as to their organization and procedure, including effective publicity, and to the closest supervision as to the issue of stock and bonds by an executive bureau or commission in the Department of Commerce and Labor, to which in times of doubt they might well submit their proposed plans for future business."[8]

In recent years federal incorporation and licensing proposals of various sorts have received a boost from the current concern with respect to "corporate governance."[9] Today's proponents of federal incorporation of the largest corporations seem more interested in using that device not by way of corporate law reform or securities regulation but largely as a handle for such ends as more effective antitrust enforcement and protection of consumers and the envi-

[5] In contrast to the express preservation of state jurisdiction in the later SEC statutes, Congress made the ICC's jurisdiction "exclusive and plenary," to the point, apparently, where even the general corporation law of the state of incorporation may be ignored with respect to "anything relevant and material to the issuance of the securities and the corporate financial structure of the applicant." New York Central R. R., 295 ICC 19, 26 (1955). In Schwabacher v. United States, 334 U. S. 182 (1948), the Court held that an ICC order approving a merger overrode state statutes on dissenters' appraisal rights.

[6] 69-A FTC, Utility Corporations, S. Doc. No. 92, 70th Cong., 1st Sess. (1934) 137 et seq. The whole volume is devoted to this subject.

[7] S. 6186 and H. R. 20,142, 61st Cong., 2d Sess. (1910).

[8] See 16 Messages and Papers of the Presidents 7455, 7457, 7522 (1910), 17 id. 7652, 7654 (1911); 69-A FTC, Utility Corporations, S. Doc. No. 92, 70th Cong., 1st Sess. (1934) 8 et seq.; H. Cherrington, The Investor and the Securities Act (1942) 40.

[9] The American Law Institute is now studying the law relating to the fiduciary obligations of corporate officers, directors, and controlling stockholders. See D. Schwartz (ed.), Commentaries on Corporate Structure and Governance: The ALI-ABA Symposiums 1977-1978 (1979); ALI, Principles of Corporate Governance: Analysis and Recommendations, Tent. Drafts 2-6 (1985-87). See also pp. 430-32, 465-6 infra.

ronment.[10] Be that as it may, Congress in the SEC statutes opted for what is essentially a scheme of federal licensing: Corporations may keep their state charters, but various SEC provisions (not all of them limited to disclosure, as we shall see) apply *on top of* the state corporation law if corporations want to distribute securities to the public or engage in the brokerage or investment company business or various other activities. This is not federal licensing in the broad sense in which that technique is currently being advanced as an answer to the states' charter-mongering.[11] But it is certainly licensing in the generic sense.

The basic question that Congress faced in 1933 when at long last it got to the point of legislating was what the *standards* of the limited federal licensing should be. The diehards, who opposed *any* licensing or registration requirement, wanted to settle for a fraud act of the New York type — or, preferably, stern enforcement of the penal laws without even the power somewhere to enjoin frauds. Any preventive law, even of the purely injunctive type, would not work, it was said, and would only hinder honest business. Indeed, it has since been charged that if the SEC "had had jurisdiction during the early days of the development of the west we would have had no mining industry in the United States today"[12] — a statement that may well be true in its implication that securities regulation as we know it is a luxury that an earlier stage of "acquisitive" capitalism could not have afforded.

At the other extreme, not unnaturally, the merit philosophy of the blue sky laws had its proponents — and still does.[13] Professor

[10] See R. Nader, M. Green, and J. Seligman, Taming the Giant Corporation (1976); Schwartz, Federal Chartering of Corporations: An Introduction, 61 Geo. L. J. 71 (1972).

[11] Cary, Federalism and Corporate Law: Reflections upon Delaware, 83 Yale L. J. 663 (1974).

[12] Telegram from Secretary of Arizona Small Mine Operators Association in opposition to American-Canadian extradition treaty covering securities violations, Canada, Minutes of Proceedings and Evidence before H. C. Standing Comm. on External Affairs, No. 6 (Nov. 23, 1945) 147.

[13] See Hueni, Application of Merit Requirements in State Securities Regulation, 15 Wayne L. Rev. 1417, esp. at 1417-21, 1444-45 (1969); Goodkind, Blue Sky Law: Is There Merit in the Merit Requirements?, [1976] Wis. L. Rev. 79; Tyler, More about Blue Sky, 39 Wash. & Lee L. Rev. 899 (1982).

For a study that is said to affirm the efficacy of Texas's merit standards, see Walker and Hadaway, Merit Standards Revisited: An Empirical Analysis of the Efficacy of Texas Merit Standards, 7 J. Corp. L. 651 (1982), with Texas guidelines at 682-88. One of the standards in the "Revised Maine Securities Act," effective September 19, 1985, is that "The offering is being made on terms which are unfair, unjust, or inequitable."

For some difficulties in the administration of the disclosure philosophy, see

William O. Douglas, as he then was, published a pungent critique of the Securities Act of 1933 a few years before he was to be charged with its administration as Chairman of the SEC.[14] Although he considered it "sheer nonsense to talk of repealing the Securities Act or even of making substantial amendments," he also thought three propositions were "tolerably clear":

> First, that the Securities Act falls far short of accomplishing its purposes. Second, that in any programme for the protection of investors and in any genuine and permanent correction of the evils of high finance an Act like the Securities Act is of a decidedly secondary character. And, third, that a vigorous enforcement of the Act promises to spell its own defeat because it is so wholly antithetical to the programme of control envisaged in the New Deal and to the whole economy under which we are living.

As to the first two points, the "glaring light of publicity" on which the Act is based is not enough, Douglas wrote, because

> those needing investment guidance will receive small comfort from the balance sheets, contracts, or compilation of other data revealed in the registration statement. They either lack the training or intelligence to assimilate them and find them useful, or are so concerned with a speculative profit as to consider them irrelevant.

This means that the results of the act for the investor are primarily twofold: The disclosure requirement will in itself prevent some

---

pp. 150-57, 1071-72 infra.

For a comprehensive study of merit regulation, see Ad Hoc Subcommittee on Merit Regulation of the State Regulation of Securities Committee [ABA], Report on State Merit Regulation of Securities Offerings, 41 Bus. Law. 785 (1986). "No systematic evidence" was found that "merit regulation accomplishes its goals." Id. at 844. Nevertheless, "merit can play a useful, although limited, role in regulating a finite class of transactions in which market forces, private incentives, and federal and state disclosure requirements do not suffice to protect certain investors. Since merit regulation is not without cost, however, and because its benefits are limited, modesty of purpose and flexibility of means should be built into it. The merit states simply cannot — indeed should not — control the structure of governance and the quantum of risk associated with most registered securities offerings. Once that is accepted, merit regulation can begin to function as a less controversial aspect of the state-federal regulatory scheme." Id. at 852.

When a registrant has difficulty in a particular state, there are several possibilities: working out an extradisclosure solution to the particular merit problem; offering the securities only under specific "suitability" criteria (see p. 831 infra); submission of certain "undertakings" restricting the registrant's actions as a condition of effectiveness; or in the last analysis some restructuring or withdrawal, though the latter may prove fatal in "copy cat" states. Id. at 802.

[14] Douglas, Protecting the Investor, 23 Yale Rev. (N. S.) 521 (1934).

fraudulent transactions that cannot stand the light of publicity, and the judgment of those who do understand will be reflected in the market price and will seep down to the investor through his advisers. In addition, the stringent civil liability provisions of the act are a great advance over the hypertechnical common law. But this chief virtue of the statute is also one of its greatest weaknesses; for history teaches that "terroristic methods are notoriously feeble instruments for continuous control." Witness the Eighteenth Amendment.

The Act is also "superficial," Douglas went on to say. Registration will be hardest for well-established going concerns — "businesses with far flung units, with complicated details, with kaleidoscopic activities" — and easiest for "the oil well scheme, the gold mine venture, the holding company set-up, or the investment trust, in fact, any enterprise which is just beginning or whose activities, assets, and relations are simple." And at best the registration statement will be discounted shortly after its effectiveness "by a host of other bearish or bullish factors." There is no machinery for periodic reports,[15] nothing to control the power of self-perpetuating management or to protect the rights of minorities, nothing on the soundness or unsoundness of capital structure or on "the problem of mobilizing the flow of capital to various productive channels."

To be sure, the Act is but a first step. This, said Douglas, is where the third point comes in. The whole business is essentially a "nineteenth-century piece of legislation" that unrealistically envisages a return to "Main Street business." This explains, among other things, "the great reliance placed on truth about securities, as if the truth could be told to people who could understand it — a supposition which might be justified if little units of business were seeking funds and people were buying shares with the modicum of intelligence with which they are supposed to buy wearing apparel or horses." We cannot "turn back the clock" to simpler days. We must perfect a plan for control of our present forms of organization so as to harness the "instruments of production not only for the ancient purpose of profit but also for the more slowly evolving purpose of service in the sense of the public good." At the same time, although the type of control embodied in the state blue sky laws should not be condemned, it would if transplanted to the federal scene engage a government agency in "activity a thousand fold more complex than the analogous activity of the Interstate Commerce Commission in the railroad field." "The control needed is one which would combine regulation by industry with supervision

[15] Reporting came with the Securities Exchange Act of 1934.

by government." For example, a company that had cleared its security through the Code Authority and the supervisory governmental agency (these were the days of the NRA) would gain the benefits of a moderated Securities Act.[16] And ultimately there must be some form of control over access to the capital market. Thus spake Douglas.

Those who today discount the efficacy of the prospectus similarly stress its complexity, and refer to the proverbial horse who is led to the water's edge. Moreover there is always the question of disclosure to whom. To Aunt Minnie or Uncle Gus in Oshkosh (whose English cousin, the author recently learned, is Aunt Jane at Land's End)? Or to the financial analyst on the "creep down" theory? The difference is the gulf between arithmetic and atomic physics.

Despite these limitations, Congress opted for the British disclosure philosophy over the native merit philosophy of the blue sky laws.[17] "Show up the roguery," as The Times had put it in connection with the debate on the 1844 Companies Act, "and it is harmless."[18] Congress was conscious also of Louis D. Brandeis's statement seventy years later, in Other People's Money,[19] strongly urging publicity as a remedy for social and industrial diseases gen-

[16]Something of this idea was later to be incorporated in the 1938 Maloney Act amendment of the 1934 Act, which provided a measure of self-regulation of the business practices of the over-the-counter securities industry under the general aegis of the SEC. See pp. 617-24 infra.

[17]With p. 28 n. 13 supra, contrast Mofsky and Tollison, Demerit in Merit Regulation, 60 Marq. L. Rev. 367 (1977); Seligman, The Historical Need for a Mandatory Corporate Disclosure System, 9 J. Corp. L. 1 (1983).

The 1984 Bush report, by way of reduction of unnecessary regulatory costs, stated that state blue sky laws of the "merit" type "have often resulted in unnecessary economic barriers to the capital formation process." Blueprint for Reform: The Report of the Task Group on Regulation of Financial Services (1984) 42.

Illinois, traditionally one of the "tough" blue sky states, went over to a purely disclosure basis effective July 1, 1984. See Sosin and Fein, The Landmark 1983 Amendment to the Illinois Securities Law, 72 Ill. B. J. 206 (1983). So did the new Louisiana statute effective September 6, 1985. There are rumblings in Wisconsin. See 18 Sec. Reg. L. Rep. 1218 (1986). And Iowa, while retaining the Uniform Act's standards, has repealed the "unfair or inequitable" language that had been added to those standards. Moreover, other states have attempted to mitigate the impact of merit regulation in other ways. See Sargent, Blue Sky Law: The Challenge to Merit Regulation — Part I, 12 Sec. Reg. L. J. 276 (1984); id. — Part II, 12 Sec. Reg. L. J. 367 (1985).

In support of the conclusion that both the advocates and the opponents of merit regulation have failed to provide the analysis and data needed for a policy decision, see Makens, Who Speaks for the Investor? An Evaluation of the Assault on Merit Regulation, 13 U. Balt. L. Rev. 435 (1984).

[18]The Times, July 4, 1844, quoted in B. Hunt, The Development of the Business Corporation in England 1800-1867 (1936) 95 n. 12.

[19]C. 5, esp. 1st par.

erally and for excessive underwriters' charges specifically. "Sunlight is said to be the best of disinfectants; electric light the most efficient policeman." At the same time, the law should not try to keep investors from making bad bargains; it should not even undertake (except incidentally in connection with railroads and public service corporations) to fix bankers' profits. He cited the Pure Food Law as an example: It does not guarantee quality or prices, but it does help the consumer to judge quality by requiring the disclosure of ingredients. The length and complexity of some SEC prospectuses make one wish that Brandeis had recognized that *excessive* sunlight can cause skin cancer. Nevertheless, if any single person was the spiritual father of the Securities Act, it was he.

Two quotations a scant thirty-three years apart demonstrate the revolution in thinking. In hearings held in 1900 by the so-called Industrial Commission that had been created two years earlier, this exchange occurred between a member of the Commission and the president of American Sugar Refining Company:

> Q: You think, then, that when a corporation is chartered by the State, offers stock to the public, and is one in which the public is interested, that the public has no right to know what its earning power is or to subject them to any inspection whatever, that the people may not buy this stock blindly?
>
> A: Yes; that is my theory. Let the buyer beware; that covers the whole business. You can not wet nurse people from the time they are born until the time they die. They have got to wade in and get stuck, and that is the way men are educated and cultivated.[20]

In the debate on the bill that became the Securities Act of 1933, Representative (later Speaker) Rayburn stated simply:

> The purpose of this bill is to place the owners of securities on a parity, so far as is possible, with the management of the corporations, and to place the buyer on the same plane so far as available information is concerned, with the seller.[21]

As the Supreme Court has since put it, the SEC statutes embrace a "fundamental purpose * * * to substitute a philosophy of full disclosure for the philosophy of *caveat emptor* and thus to achieve a high standard of business ethics in the securities industry."[22] In short, Congress did not take away from the citizen "his inalienable

[20] 1 Industrial Commission, Preliminary Report on Trusts and Industrial Combinations, H. R. Doc. No. 476, 56th Cong., 1st Sess. (1900) 123.

[21] 77 Cong. Rec. 2918 (1933).

[22] SEC v. Capital Gains Research Bureau, Inc., 375 U. S. 180, 186 (1963); Affiliated Ute Citizens of Utah v. United States, 406 U. S. 128, 151 (1972).

right to make a fool of himself." It simply attempted to prevent others from making a fool of him.[23]

It must not be thought, however, that Disclosure and Merit are two gods that sit on separate but equal thrones. On the one hand, the Uniform Securities Act has a disclosure component, and most states today require the delivery of prospectuses. On the other hand, the indirect regulatory effect of a policed system of full and fair disclosure should not be underestimated: People who are forced to undress in public will presumably pay some attention to their figures.

Nevertheless, there *is* a difference, which is illustrated by the federal and state approaches to stock options. A registration guide published by the SEC in 1968 stated:

> If a material amount of options or warrants has been or is to be issued to promoters, underwriters, finders, principal stockholders, officers or directors, certain disclosure in regard thereto should be made in the prospectus, in addition to that required by Item 18 of Form S-1. Such additional disclosure should ordinarily include the following: that for the life of the options or warrants the holders thereof are given at nominal cost, the opportunity to profit from a rise in the market for securities of the class subject thereto, with a resulting dilution in the interest of security holders; that the terms on which the issuer could obtain additional capital during that period may be adversely affected; and that the holders of such options or warrants might be expected to exercise them at a time when the issuer would, in all likelihood, be able to obtain any needed capital by a new offering of securities on terms more favorable than those provided for by the options or warrants. Similar disclosure should also be made where securities with conversion privileges are issued to the above persons.[24] By contrast, the North American Securities Administrators Association has a statement of policy that begins, "Options or warrants to purchase securities issued or sold to persons other than all of the purchasers of the securities must be justified by the applicant," and goes on to recite the conditions under which various kinds of options or warrants are justified.[25]

All this is not to say that the only critics of the disclosure philosophy today would go further. There is an economic school that argues powerfully that "the costs to society of government-required

[23] The language is from the 1935 Report of the [Canadian] Royal Commission on Price Spreads (p. 38), although the recommendations of that commission came closer to the merit than the disclosure philosophy.

[24] Sec. Act Rel. 4936, ¶36 (1968). This is now reflected in Reg. S-K, Item 201(a)(2), and Sec. Act Rel. 6383, 24 SEC Dock. 1278-79 (1982).

[25] CCH NASAA Rep. ¶2801.

disclosure exceed the benefits."[26] Moreover, the "Efficient Capital Market Hypothesis," which has occupied a prominent place in the economics and finance literature of the last decade and more, implies not only that the SEC's mandated disclosure and its insider trading restrictions are ineffective but also that the very goal of egalitarian disclosure may be inappropriate.[27]

[26] Benston, An Appraisal of the Costs and Benefits of Government-Required Disclosure: SEC and FTC Requirements, 41 Law & Contemp. Prob. 30, 60 (1977); see also Bentson, Required Disclosure and the Stock Market: An Evaluation of the Securities Exchange Act of 1934, 63 Am. Econ. Rev. (No. 1) 132 (1973); S. Phillips and J. Zecher, The SEC and the Public Interest (1981); Jarrell, The Economic Effects of Federal Regulation of the Market for New Security Issues, 24 J. L. & Econ. 613 (1982); compare Stigler, Public Regulation of the Securities Markets, 19 Bus. Law. 721, 37 J. Bus. U. Chi. 117 (1964), with a reply in Friend and Herman, The S. E. C. Through a Glass Darkly, 37 J. Bus. U. Chi. 382 (1964); and for a general critique of the SEC's approach to life, particularly in the accounting field, see H. Kripke, The SEC and Corporate Disclosure: Regulation in Search of a Purpose (1979).

For a critique of the second Benston study's methodology and conclusions, see Friend and Westerfield, Required Disclosure and the Stock Market: Comment, 65 Am. Econ. Rev. (No. 3) 467 (1975); see also Benston, Required Disclosure and the Stock Market: Rejoinder, 65 Am. Econ. Rev. (No. 3) 473 (1975). In M. Blume and I. Friend, The Changing Role of the Individual Investor (1978) 208, the authors conclude that "economic as well as equity considerations seem to support the general value to investors of the greater financial disclosure that has taken place under the stimulus of Federal securities regulations." For a recent reexamination of the earlier studies, together with an analysis of some of the later ones, see Friend, Economic and Equity Aspects of Securities Regulation (Rodney L. White Center for Financial Research, Wharton School, U. Pa., Working Paper No. 7-82, 1982). See also Seligman, The Historical Need for a Mandatory Corporate Disclosure System, 9 J. Corp. L. 1 (1983).

It has been suggested, apropos of the critical school, that we "may be approaching a new stage, which can be called 'post-revisionism.'" Coffee, Market Failure and the Economic Case for a Mandatory Disclosure System, 70 Va. L. Rev. 717, 719 (1984).

[27] For a basic treatment, see T. Dyckman, D. Downes, and R. Magee, Efficient Capital Markets and Accounting: A Critical Analysis (1975). For a more technical treatment, widely regarded as the landmark essay, see Fama, Efficient Capital Markets: A Review of Theory and Empirical Work, 25 J. Fin. 383 (1970). For a brief in support of the hypothesis, see Note, The Efficient Capital Market Hypothesis, Economic Theory and the Regulation of the Securities Industry, 29 Stan. L. Rev. 1031 (1977). For a bibliography, see Fischel, Finance Theory in Securities Fraud Cases Involving Actively Traded Securities, 38 Bus. Law. 1, 4 n. 9 (1982).

In Fisher v. Plessey Co., Ltd., 559 F. Supp. 442, 448 (S. D. N. Y. 1983), the court rejected an argument that under the efficient market theory the plaintiff could not complain that the market price for the subsidiary's debentures for which the parent was making a tender offer was understated because of certain nondisclosures in the tender offer materials. "It would turn the securities law upside down to hold that individual investors are not entitled to disclosure of material information on the assumption that the market has set a 'fair' price for the securities at issue." See also Wang, Some Arguments That the Stock Market Is Not Efficient, 19 U. C. Davis L. Rev. 41 (1986). More generally, see Gilson

Be all this as it may — and the SEC's disclosure policy continues to evolve — there is little likelihood as this is written that any legislative change will be in the direction of *more* basic regulation.[28]

D. THE SEC STATUTES IN A NUTSHELL AND THE FEDERAL SECURITIES CODE[1]

The federal securities legislation is administered by the Securities and Exchange Commission. The SEC, as an "independent" agency of five members appointed by the President and confirmed by the Senate for staggered five-year terms, exercises not only executive but also quasi-legislative (rulemaking) and quasi-judicial powers. There are seven related but separate statutes.[2] The first six were

---

and Kraakman, The Mechanisms of Market Efficiency, 70 Va. L. Rev. 549 (1984).

[28] The Advisory Committee on Corporate Disclosure — a group of thirteen lawyers, accountants, academics, financial executives, analysts, and other users of information, under the chairmanship of former Commissioner Sommer — concluded in 1976 (although not all its members agreed unreservedly) that the disclosure system of the 1933 and 1934 Acts as developed by the SEC "is sound and does not need radical reform or renovation," although the Commission should not be "indifferent to research which some would suggest has already or may in the future suggest a radical modification of this disclosure system," and that "Market forces and self-interest cannot be relied upon to assure a sufficient flow of timely and reliable information." 1 Report of the Advisory Committee on Corporate Disclosure to the Securities and Exchange Commission (1977) 2, I-II.

C. 1D [1] Chapter 1D is a condensation of Loss, Codification of the Federal Securities Law in the United States: A Case Study in Legislative Reform, in K. Ludwig and A. Soellner (eds.), Europäisches Rechtsdenken in Geschichte und Gegenwart (*Festschrift* in honor of Professor Helmut Coing of the University of Frankfurt, 1982).

[2] There has recently been a spate of much needed publications on the legislative history of some or all of the SEC statutes. See J. Ellenberger and E. Mahar, Legislative History of the Securities Act of 1933 and Securities Exchange Act of 1934 (11 vols. 1973); Fed. B. Assn., Securities Law Committee, Federal Securities Laws Legislative History 1933-1982 (4 vols., all 7 statutes, 1983); see also, for an exhaustive reference to the research tools, Sargent and Greenberg, Research in Securities Regulation: Access to the Sources of the Law, 75 L. Library J. 98 (1982).

There is an eighth statute under which the Commission functions. Under Chapter 11 of the new bankruptcy statute effective October 1, 1979 (11 U. S. C.) — as under the predecessor statute's Chapter X, dating from 1938 — the Commission serves as adviser to the court in corporate reorganization proceedings in which there is a substantial public interest. See 2 Loss c. 4B. As Judge Jerome Frank (who was Chairman of the SEC before he went to the Second Circuit) put it, Congress recognized that "reorganization is only in its superficial aspects litigation *inter partes* and that fundamentally it is an administrative problem of business and finance." Frank, Epithetical Jurisprudence and

enacted between 1933 and 1940; the seventh came in 1970; and most of them have been repeatedly amended.

The Securities Act of 1933 adapted the disclosure philosophy of the British prospectus provisions of 1929 by requiring the registration with the SEC of *distributions* of securities.

The Securities Exchange Act of 1934 was addressed to postdistribution *trading*. The static disclosure of the 1933 Act was thus transposed into a philosophy of continuous disclosure through the registration of all securities traded on exchanges, with rulemaking authority in the Commission to require the filing of periodic reports by both issuers and certain insiders (directors, officers, and 10 percent holders) as well as to regulate the solicitation of proxies. In 1964 and later these provisions were extended to certain securities traded in the over-the-counter market: any class of equity security held by at least 500 persons and issued by a company with at least $1,000,000 of gross assets, since increased by rule to $5 million. Then in 1968 Congress added regulation of "tender offers" ("takeover bids" as they are known in England and Canada and increasingly in the United States) to the statutory scheme.

In addition, the 1934 Act from the beginning has had three other themes: regulation of the exchange and over-the-counter markets; prevention of fraud and market manipulation; and control of securities credit by the Board of Governors of the Federal Reserve System as part of its authority over the Nation's credit generally.

Finally, the 1934 Act was virtually doubled in size in 1975 (and greatly complicated as a result of the patchwork process) by broadening the market regulation provisions, with a direction to the Commission to develop a national market system, and inserting the Commission for the first time into the clearance and settlement processes as well as regulation of the markets in municipal securities.

A major theme of the 1934 Act is self-regulation under the gen-

---

the Work of the Securities and Exchange Commission in the Administration of Chapter X of the Bankruptcy Act, 18 N. Y. U. L. Q. Rev. 317 (1941).

"In December 1983 the Commission reoriented its bankruptcy program shifting its emphasis from an active day-to-day participation in a limited number of cases to a more issue-oriented participation in a greater number of cases." Corp. Reorg. Rel. 338, 31 SEC Dock. 1097 (1984), citing Corp. Reorg. Rel. 331, 29 SEC Dock. 949 (1984). See The Securities and Exchange Commission's Role in Bankruptcy Reorganization Proceedings, Report by Commissioner Longstreth, CCH Fed. Sec. L. Rep. ¶83,463 (1983).

It is the Commission's position that its advisory role under §1109(a), under which it has no right of appeal, does not eliminate its right to participate in a reorganization like any other "party in interest" under §1109(b), with appeal rights, when necessary or appropriate to carry out its law enforcement responsibilities under the securities laws (as, typically, when funds frozen in an earlier Commission enforcement action have been transferred to the trustee).

eral aegis of the SEC. There are now four types of "self-regulatory organizations": the national securities exchanges; the National Association of Securities Dealers, Inc., which is registered with the Commission as a "national securities association" to regulate participants in the over-the-counter market; since 1975, registered clearing agencies; and also since 1975, the Municipal Securities Rulemaking Board.

The next of the seven statutes in chronological order, the Public Utility Holding Company Act of 1935, pervasively regulates electric and gas holding companies and their subsidiaries in order to assure their compliance with the statutory standards of geographical integration and corporate simplification.[3]

The Trust Indenture Act of 1939 supplements the 1933 Act when a distribution consists of debt securities. A trust indenture must be filed and qualified with the Commission, with a mass of specified provisions that are designed to impose appropriate obligations on the trustee, particularly in the event of default. And there must be a corporate trustee that satisfies a batch of stringent tests to assure its independence from both the obligor and every underwriter.[4]

[3] On the Holding Company Act generally, see D. Hawes, Utility Holding Companies (1984). In December 1981 the Commission, pointing out that its "task of reorganizing the Nation's gas and electric companies was completed twenty years ago," unanimously recommended repeal of this Act as having "served its basic purpose." Letter of Dec. 21, 1981, from Chairman Shad to Senator D'Amato, 14 Sec. Reg. L. Rep. 56 (1982). This recommendation was endorsed by the 1984 Bush report. Blueprint for Reform: The Report of the Task Force on Regulation of Financial Services (1984) 95. But it seems to have met unexpected opposition in the Congress — presumably because it contains no safeguards against recreation of the pre-1935 conditions — and the Commission apparently is not pressing it.

[4] The Trust Indenture Act is peculiar in its enforcement technique. Once an indenture that purports to meet the statutory standards is qualified, the Commission is *functus officio*. Congress presumably thought that, particularly with an independent trustee as potential plaintiff, it could rely on the ordinary functioning of the law of contracts and trusts to assure that the indenture would be enforced. And for thirty-six years it was generally supposed that the applicable law would be state law, to be applied in state courts unless the usual requirements of federal diversity jurisdiction were satisfied, though the legislative history would be relevant as one of the sources of interpretation of the contract and presumably error in that respect could ultimately be reviewed by the Supreme Court. See Note, Hybrid State Law in the Federal Courts, 83 Harv. L. Rev. 280, 310-19 (1969).

Beginning in 1975, however, a series of District Court cases concluded that "this legislation must be viewed as an indirect method of imposing nationally uniform and clearly defined obligations upon those associated with the issuance of corporate debt"; that the very exclusion of the Commission from an enforcement role made it easier to imply a private right of action as a matter of federal law; and that the courts would apply federal law to "those questions of inter-

The Investment Company Act of 1940 is a complex piece of legislation for the still expanding and evolving investment company industry. Because that statute is not thoroughly considered throughout this book, its salient aspects are summarized in Chapter 1E.

Concurrently with the enactment of the Investment Company Act of 1940, Congress passed the Investment Advisers Act of 1940. This is the shortest and simplest statute in the series. It requires the registration of investment advisers of all types — ranging from the "investment counselors" at one extreme, whose individualized advisory clients are substantial institutional and individual investors, to the publishers of various sorts of market letters — and regulates a few of their practices.

The last of the seven statutes, the Securities Investor Protection Act of 1970, insures customers against their brokers' insolvency up to $500,000 for each account, except that the maximum is $100,000 to the extent that a claim is for cash rather than securities. This is made possible by a requirement that every broker or dealer registered with the SEC be a member of the Securities Investor Protection Corporation, which, though not a Government agency, was created by Congress and operates under some supervision by the SEC; an annual assessment of the members; and backing from the United States Treasury (which thus far has not had to be used) to the extent of $1 billion.[5]

The inevitable result of this episodic kind of legislation, enacted

---

pretation and enforcement of the indenture agreement to which the statute is specifically addressed, leaving the purely business aspects to state regulation, or to the pendent jurisdiction of the district courts." Morris v. Cantor, 390 F. Supp. 817, 822 (S. D. N. Y. 1975); see also In re Equity Funding Corp. of America Securities Litigation, 416 F. Supp. 161, 203 (C. D. Cal. 1976); Zeffiro v. First Pa. Banking & Trust Co., 623 F. 2d 290 (3d Cir. 1980), *cert. denied,* 456 U. S. 1005; cf. Caplin v. Marine Midland Grace Trust Co., 439 F. 2d 118, 123 n. 5 (2d Cir. *en banc* 1971), *aff'd,* 406 U. S. 416, 426-27 n. 17 (1971).

Speaking *obiter* in the *Caplin* case, the Second Circuit said "we would not regard it as unlikely that a class action could be maintained in federal court for violation of §315 of the Trust Indenture Act"; and the Supreme Court was able to *assume* that §315 would give rise to an action by the *indenture* trustee against a debenture holder, since it held that the *reorganization* trustee lacked standing in any event.

Whether or not these cases correctly construe the present law, their result is reflected in a more straightforward way in the Federal Securities Code that is about to be examined. See §§1305(c), 1719(a), 1822(a); 1 Code xxxvii-xl.

In general, see Friedman, Updating the Trust Indenture Act, 7 U. Mich. J. L. Reform 329 (1974).

[5] See Bloomenthal and Salcito, Customer Protection from Brokerage Failures: The Securities Investor Protection Corporation and the SEC, 54 U. Colo. L. Rev. 161 (1983).

often in response to crises, is a great many inconsistencies, a considerable number of both gaps and overlaps, and in general needless complexity in a field of the law that would not make light bedtime reading at best. In many areas, moreover, such as proxy solicitation and market stabilization, the statutory provisions are essentially a skeletal framework for elaborate SEC rules, which have all the force of law. And there have been some thousands of judicial decisions, not to mention cases decided by the Commission itself.

This state of affairs has made it apparent for some time that ultimately there would have to be a reexamination of the field of securities regulation as a whole, resulting ideally in the preparation of a code that would replace all the existing statutes, with incidental substantive changes, and that would also put appropriate portions of both the administrative rulemaking structure and the jurisprudence into legislative form. The author confronted the problem in a personal way as early as 1947, when he started to work on the first edition of his treatise on Securities Regulation. In the interest of an orderly presentation he treated the then six statutes as a single piece of legislation, which, as he stated in the preface, "is ideally what they should be."[6] Indeed, as early as 1939, when William O. Douglas left the Chairmanship of the Commission to become an Associate Justice of the Supreme Court of the United States, he stated in a letter to President Roosevelt that "eventually it should be possible to merge or consolidate the various registration or reporting requirements of the [then] three Acts to the end that information filed by a corporation under one statute would serve the purposes of all three statutes."[7]

In 1966 Mr. Milton H. Cohen of the Chicago Bar, who had directed the "Special Study of Securities Markets,"[8] published an article called " 'Truth in Securities' Revisited," which was a brilliant plea for integration of the two basic statutes of 1933 and 1934.[9] "Though the mills of God grind slowly,"[10] this article set in train a

[6] Loss, Securities Regulation (1951) vi.

[7] The author first learned of this letter, dated April 12, 1939, about five years ago from Professor Joel J. Seligman of the University of Michigan, who discovered it in the Douglas files at the SEC in connection with his writing a history of the Commission. J. Seligman, The Transformation of Wall Street (1982).

[8] See Report of Special Study of Securities Markets, H. R. Doc. No. 95, 88th Cong., 1st Sess. (5 vols. 1963). This most comprehensive study since the enactment of the 1933 and 1934 Acts was ordered by §19(d) of the 1934 Act, enacted in 1961. And it led, among other things, to the Securities Acts Amendments of 1964. See 4 Loss 2306-13.

[9] 79 Harv. L. Rev. 1340 (1966).

[10] Friedrich von Logau, Sinngedichte, III.ii.24, translated into English by H. W. Longfellow.

series of events that culminated in the drafting of the proposed Federal Securities Code. Shortly after the article's publication, the Committee on Federal Regulation of Securities of the American Bar Association's Section of Corporation, Banking and Business Law, in a conference held in Chicago in late 1966, reached a consensus in favor of a broad codification study.[11] And in late 1968 the Council of The American Law Institute, with informal promises of cooperation from both the SEC and the Council of the ABA section, undertook to produce a Federal Securities Code.

Following its usual practice, the Institute's Council appointed a "Reporter" (the present author),[12] several "Consultants," and a larger group of "Advisers." These groups counted among their number two United States Court of Appeals judges, the present Chief Justice of the Supreme Judicial Court of Maine, four former Chairmen and three former members of the SEC, a sitting member of the SEC (happily, the only one of 1968 vintage, when he was the General Counsel, to stay on the Commission throughout the work), a state securities commissioner who acted as liaison with the North American Securities Administrators Association, several law professors well known for their work in the securities field (including Professor L. C. B. Gower from London, who provided comparative insights into the British thinking, particularly with regard to "insider trading"), and a number of highly knowledgeable practitioners from various parts of the country.[13]

It is a firm tradition of the Institute that advisers serve in their individual capacities, not as representatives of various constituencies. However, members of the staffs of the SEC and of the appropriate subcommittees of both Houses of Congress were invited to meet with the advisory group on occasion. And the Reporter frequently went outside the advisory group either for assistance on specialized subjects or in order to ascertain the views of the self-regulatory organizations, various trade associations, and the federal bank regulatory agencies.

After almost eight years of sustained effort — during which the advisory groups met for two-day or three-day sessions several times a year and the much larger ABA committee held similar meetings

[11] Proceedings, Conference on Codification of Federal Securities Laws, 22 Bus. Law. 793 (1967).

[12] The author's colleague, Professor Victor Brudney, was later appointed Assistant Reporter for Part XIV (Investment Companies).

[13] The entire group is listed in 1 Code v-vi.

annually — a twenty-part Federal Securities Code[14] was approved by the Institute's Council and in May 1978 by the ALI membership.[15]

The Code's mass is reflected in the fact that, in bill form as it was printed by the subcommittee of the House of Representatives, it comes to 756 pages. Altogether there are upwards of 1000 subsections. There are considerable efficiencies of space when certain provisions that are reflected in several or all of the seven existing statutes are unified in the Code structure. But that shortening is counterbalanced by the fact that the Code for the first time puts a great deal of the case law and the Commission's regulations into statutory form.

This involved procedure of multiple reviews and repeated redrafting — sometimes *ad nauseam,* as it seemed to the Reporter — is nevertheless indispensable to a job of the Code's magnitude and complexity. In the words of a well-known and sympathetic commentator from Paris, the Institute's procedure is "*assez lourde, mais très sûre.*"[16] Even so, much remained to be done.

First of all, there was the matter of who would undertake the considerable task of attempting to get the Code enacted. It is the Institute's practice not to engage in legislative activities. Who, then, were to be the spokesmen for the Code in approaching members

[14]An enumeration of the twenty parts will convey some idea of the Code's scope:

I. Legislative Findings and Declarations.
II. Definitions.
III. Exemptions.
IV. Issuer Registration.
V. Distributions.
VI. Postregistration Provisions.
VII. Broker, Dealer, and Investment Adviser Registration and Qualifications.
VIII. Self-Regulatory Organizations.
IX. Market Regulation.
X. National Market and Clearance-Settlement Systems.
XI. Municipal Securities.
XII. Broker-Dealer Insolvency.
XIII. Trust Indentures.
XIV. Investment Companies.
XV. Utility Holding Companies.
XVI. Fraud, Misrepresentation, and Manipulation.
XVII. Civil Liability.
XVIII. Administration and Enforcement.
XIX. Scope of the Code.
XX. General.

[15]The Institute's discussion of the seven Tentative Drafts and the Proposed Final Draft may be found in the Institute's Proceedings for 1972-79.

[16]Tunc La révision du droit fédéral des sociétés aux États-Unis, 25 Rev. int. dr. comp. 693 (1973).

of Congress, in soliciting support from interested organizations, and in responding to whatever opposition might develop during the legislative process? *Faute de mieux,* several members of the advisory group together with the Reporter — making it very plain that they were acting only for themselves and without authority to speak for the Institute or the ABA or anybody else — formed themselves into a self-anointed working group dedicated to the adoption of the Code. And that group was generally accepted as if it had the sort of official standing that it lacked.

At the ABA level the Code was endorsed by a postal ballot majority of some 93 percent of the committee and in early 1979 was unanimously recommended to the Congress by both the Council of the Section of Corporation, Banking and Business Law and the House of Delegates.

With the Institute and the ABA thus in agreement, the task force faced the more formidable task of seeking the official endorsement of the SEC. In September 1980 — after almost two years of detailed discussion, first with an initially hostile staff and then with Chairman Williams and a few of his key people, as well as three public meetings of the Commission — the Commission announced its unanimous support for the Code with some sixty changes, of which the Reporter considered only six to be *relatively* major.[17] And in January 1982 the "Reagan Commission," after a review of the Code with the agreed changes that the Commissioners had undertaken because three of them had been appointed since the release of September 1980, "strongly" reaffirmed its support, stating that it "encourages others, including affected industry and professional groups, to join in this effort to improve the securities laws," and calling the Code "an enormous simplification."[18]

The Official Draft — which is to say, the *Institute's* final product — is the "Proposed Official Draft" as changed to reflect (1) comments received before and at the May 1978 meeting, (2) action taken at the meeting, (3) adjustments required by the subsequently

[17] Sec. Act Rel. 6242, 20 SEC Dock. 1483 (1980), reprinted in 1 Code (2d Supp. 1981) 13, with appendixes at 1 and 17. This *entente cordiale* was made possible not only by a series of compromises in which both sides yielded ground but also by the Commission's reservation of the right to bring six "separable issues" to the attention of Congress at any time *apart from* the Code. These are issues of high political and emotional content, such as whether the Commission should be given explicit authority (which it has always considered to be implicit in the present statutes) to discipline lawyers and accountants practicing before it. Since the Commission recognized, realistically, that any one of those issues would be likely to derail the entire codification effort, it did not insist on their resolution in connection with Congress's consideration of the Code.

[18] Sec. Act Rel. 6377, 24 SEC Dock. 670, 671 (1982).

enacted bankruptcy statute, which the Reporter was authorized to make with the Council's concurrence by the vote approving the Code, and (4) postmeeting changes of an editorial or technical nature that the Reporter was likewise authorized by that vote to make in accordance with the Institute's practice. The Official Draft, together with a detailed commentary and cross-references to existing law, was published in 1980 in two volumes.

A second pocket supplement, published in 1981, contains the SEC's first release (with the Reporter's analysis of the changes attached) together with the text of all the amendments of the Official Draft that were required to reflect that release, as well as the legislative amendments of late 1980 and a few miscellaneous amendments of a minor nature. In short, the two volumes as amended by the Second Supplement reflect the text of the Code as it was expected to be introduced in Congress.

In that form — which reflects a further painstaking review by the Office of Legislative Counsel of the House of Representatives — the Code was printed in bill style by the appropriate subcommittee of the House.[19] And shortly before the 1980 election that subcommittee publicly scheduled hearings on the Code for January 1981. That represented the Code's legislative high water mark. Apart from the 1980 election, with the consequent committee changes in the Congress, opposition was heard from certain industry quarters, and there was a small but vocal minority in the ABA committee. Nevertheless, the Code had had and continues to have a considerable impact on the development of the law in a number of respects:

(1) As additional legislation or rulemaking is considered in the future, the draftsmen are apt to look to the Code as a model. Thus, the judicial review provision of the 1934 Act, §25(a), was modified in the 1970 amendments on the model of an early draft of Code §1818. And Rule 176 under the 1933 Act, with respect to the circumstances affecting the determination of what constitutes reasonable investigation under §11, comes from Code §1704(g).

(2) The Code has encouraged administrative reform. One example is the Commission's program of integrating the disclosure requirements of the 1933 and 1934 Acts,[20] which found its inspiration largely in the Code's scheme of company registration.[21] Another is the nonpublic offering concept of thirty-five buyers (not

[19]Com. Print, 97th Cong., 1st Sess. (Mar. 16, 1981). It is this version of the Code that is occasionally described in this book.

[20]See p. 146 infra.

[21]See 1 Code xxvii-xxviii.

offerees) together with "accredited investors" (the Code's "limited offering" and "institutional investors" concepts)[22] in Rule 506.

(3) What is perhaps most significant is that portions of the Code — particularly Parts XVI and XVII, on fraud and civil liability — have been cited in several dozen cases (several in the Supreme Court) as if they were a restatement of existing law.[23]

This is not the place for a description of the Code's major reforms. Suffice it merely to list a few: (1) a functional arrangement in twenty parts, written in straightforward English, with section and subsection headings and numerous cross-references that facilitate comprehension; (2) *company* registration, with continuous disclosure, as a substitute for multiple registration of *securities;* (3) a considerable degree of deregulation through the inclusion of provisions that would replace several of the Commission's most abstruse rules; (4) codification of the complex area of extraterritoriality;[24] (5) a significant degree of "preemption" of the state securities laws, achieved with the endorsement of the North American Securities Administrators Association;[25] and (6) a logical restructuring of the entire field of civil liability. This last category does not completely codify the law of "insider trading" — some of which must be allowed to continue to evolve *ad hoc* in the common law tradition — but nevertheless gives fairly precise answers to some twenty-five questions[26] raised by the ubiquitous Rule 10b-5.[27]

E. SALIENT FEATURES OF THE INVESTMENT COMPANY ACT OF 1940

The Investment Company Act (often called "the 1940 Act" despite the Investment Advisers Act of the same year) cannot be treated here as extensively as the 1933 and 1934 Acts. But it *is* referred

[22] See 1 Code xxix-xxx.

[23] E. g., Blue Chip Stamps v. Manor Drug Stores, 421 U. S. 723, 730, 767 (1975); Foremost-McKesson, Inc. v. Provident Securities Co., 423 U. S. 232, 240 n. 11 (1976); TSC Industries, Inc. v. Northway, Inc., 426 U. S. 438, 445 (1976); Chiarella v. United States, 445 U. S. 222, 228 n. 9 (1980); Dirks v. SEC, 463 U. S. 646, 650 n. 3 (1983). In Stern v. Merrill Lynch, Pierce, Fenner & Smith, Inc., 603 F. 2d 1073, 1100 (4th Cir. 1979), Butzner, J., dissenting, said that the circumstances of the Code's development "assure [its] acceptance as informed commentary, although it has not yet been enacted into law."

[24] See c. 1F infra.

[25] The text of the Association's resolution appears in 2 Code 967-69.

[26] See 2 id. 656-67.

[27] See c. 9B infra.

to from time to time in the exposition of those two statutes. Hence this summary, which does not purport to be complete.[1]

1. The "Investment Company" Concept

The Investment Company Act is definitely a regulatory statute for an industry that was thought to require something more than the disclosure treatment of the 1933 and 1934 Acts. Investment companies engage primarily in the business of investing and reinvesting in securities of other companies. They are basically institutions that provide a medium for public investment in pools of corporate securities. Their *raison d'être* is diversification of risk with professional management. In theory they are the "poor man's" investment counselors. In origin largely Scottish via Boston, they have emerged as an important element in the financial world only within the last fifty or sixty years.

The several types of investment companies are classified by the statute into three basic groups. Some of the Act's provisions apply to all investment companies, others only to one or two classes or subclasses:

a. Face-Amount Certificate Companies

These companies issue face-amount installment certificates, which, in essence, are unsecured obligations to pay either (1) a specified amount to the holder at a fixed future date if all the required payments are made or (2) a cash surrender value on surrender of the certificate prior to maturity.[2]

b. Unit Investment Trusts

In the "unit" or "fixed" investment trusts there is no obligation to pay any specified amount. Typically the holder of a share in such a trust has merely an undivided interest in a package of specified securities that is held by a trustee or custodian. There is no board of directors, and management discretion in the handling of the

C. 1E [1] For an exhaustive study, see T. Frankel, The Regulation of Money Managers: The Investment Company Act and the Investment Advisers Act (4 vols. 1979-80).

[2] §§2(a)(15), 4(1).

portfolio is entirely eliminated or reduced to a minimum.[3] Indeed, the trust's sole asset is almost always the shares of a single open-end investment company (a type to be described in a moment), and the unit investment trust issues "periodic payment plan certificates" that represent the indirect interest of the trust's investors in the shares of the underlying investment company.[4] There is thus a "trust on a trust," the certificates of the unit investment trust forming the underlying security for the periodic payment plan certificates.

c. Management Companies

The residual and largest group of investment companies — all those that are not face-amount certificate companies or unit investment trusts — consists of the "management companies."[5] They are organized as corporations, or occasionally business trusts, and they normally have a board of directors or trustees with considerable freedom in selecting the types and amounts of investment. They issue certificates or shares that are equity securities representing a fluctuating interest in a fund (as in the case of unit investment trusts) rather than a fixed obligation to pay a specified amount (as in the case of face-amount certificate companies).

Management investment companies are subdivided into "open-end" companies (popularly called "mutual funds") and "closed-end" companies, and each of these is in turn subdivided into "diversified" and "nondiversified" companies.[6] An open-end company is one that is offering or has outstanding any "redeemable security" — defined as a security that entitles the holder on demand to receive approximately his proportionate share of the issuer's net assets or its cash equivalent.[7] Almost all open-end companies continuously offer new shares to the public in order to cover redemptions and to increase their funds available for investment. Closed-end companies do not have redeemable securities; they may occasionally offer new securities to the public as any industrial company does, but the usual way to acquire their shares is on the open market. The definition of a "diversified" management company is based on a mathematical test of the degree of diversification of the portfolio. Most open-end companies are in fact diversified.

[3] §4(2).
[4] §2(a)(26).
[5] §4(3).
[6] §5.
[7] §2(a)(31).

As of September 30, 1985, 2458 registered investment companies were active, of which 1735 were open-end, 177 were closed-end, 541 were unit trusts, and 5 were face-amount certificate companies, and the approximate market value of the assets of all these companies aggregated $525 billion.[8]

2. History of the Act

The problems of the industry flow from the very nature of the assets of investment companies. Because those assets are usually liquid and readily negotiable, control of the companies' large funds of cash and securities offered many opportunities for exploitation by unscrupulous management. The industry's problems and abuses were thoroughly explored by the SEC in a four-year study that had been ordered by Congress in §30 of the Public Utility Holding Company Act.[9] The Investment Company Act evolved from a bill that was based on the conclusion and recommendations in the Commission's report. After hearings had been held on a bill drafted by the Commission, the industry and the Commission worked out a compromise bill that passed without a dissenting vote — and that statute stood substantially without amendment for thirty years.

In 1962 the Wharton School of Finance and Commerce in the University of Pennsylvania completed a study that the SEC had commissioned in 1958,[10] and in December 1966 the Commission sent its own report to Congress.[11] All this eventuated in the Investment Company Amendments Act of 1970, which introduced considerable change. And in late 1980 the Small Business Investment Incentive Act amended the 1940 Act in order to relieve from a number of the statutory restrictions in the interest of financing relatively small business ventures.[12]

[8] 51 SEC Ann. Rep. 109 (1985).

[9] SEC Report on the Study of Investment Trusts and Investment Companies, in 5 parts with 6 supplemental reports, all cited in 1 Loss 147 n. 52; see the findings in Inv. Co. Act §1.

[10] A Study of Mutual Funds Prepared for the Securities and Exchange Commission by the Wharton School of Finance and Commerce, H. R. Rep. No. 2274, 87th Cong., 2d Sess. (1962). The study was later updated and expanded. I. Friend, M. Blume, and J. Crockett, Mutual Funds and Other Institutional Investors: A New Perspective (1970).

[11] SEC, Public Policy Implications of Investment Company Growth, H. R. Rep. No. 2337, 89th Cong., 2d Sess. (1966).

[12] See Thomas and Roye, Regulation of Business Development Companies under the Investment Company Act, 55 So. Cal. L. Rev. 895 (1982). See also p. 306 infra.

3. The Registration and Regulatory Provisions

As under the other SEC statutes, the technique of the Investment Company Act is first of all to require registration — in this case, registration of all investment companies that make use of the mails or interstate facilities — so as to have a handle for the regulatory scheme. Most of the required information is similar to that contained in registration statements filed under the 1933 and 1934 Acts, from which investment companies are not exempted. But the 1940 Act registration statement must also recite the registrant's policy with respect to specified subjects — such as diversification, issuance of senior securities, borrowing and lending money, engaging in underwriting, and investing in real estate or commodities — that may not be changed without the vote of a majority of the outstanding voting securities.[13]

The very first task of the draftsmen of the statute was to create a definition of "investment company" precise enough to distinguish those companies subject to the registration requirement from holding companies on the one hand and operating companies on the other. Their solution was a quantitative definition in terms of the portion of a company's assets that are "investment securities." Thus, one of the several definitions is a company that "is engaged or proposes to engage in the business of investing, reinvesting, owning, holding, or trading in securities" and owns "investment securities" exceeding 40 percent of its total assets (exclusive of Government securities and cash); and the term "investment securities" is in turn defined to exclude securities of majority owned subsidiaries that are not themselves investment companies.[14] There is a declaratory order procedure whereby a company that comes within this definition is given an opportunity to establish that it is engaged in some other business, either directly or through majority owned subsidiaries or controlled companies.[15] Several categories are automatically ex-

[13] §§8(b), 13; cf. §21.

[14] This rule of thumb has given rise to the phenomenon of the inadvertent investment company, which falls within the 40 percent test either (1) during its start-up period, when it may temporarily invest the proceeds of its initial distribution in securities until it can begin its non-investment company operations, or (2) as a result of the sale of an operating division for securities (or cash that is temporarily invested in securities) or an unsuccessful tender offer. See Rosenblat and Lybecker, Some Thoughts on the Federal Securities Laws Regulating External Investment Management Arrangements and the ALI Federal Securities Code Project, 124 U. Pa. L. Rev. 587, 601-03 (1976). The problem is solved in the Code by means of a temporary exclusion from the definition. §202(80)(C); cf. Rules 3a-1, 3a-2.

[15] §§3(a), (b).

cluded from the definition, notably any issuer whose outstanding securities (other than short-term paper) are beneficially owned by not more than 100 persons and that "is not making and does not presently propose to make a public offering of its securities."[16] The Act also contains a number of exemptions in addition to giving the Commission the broadest authority to exempt any person, security, or transaction or any class of persons, securities, or transactions — by rule or order, conditionally or unconditionally — from any or all the provisions of the Act.[17]

The regulatory provisions that attach to all registered companies (absent some exemption) are designed to accomplish five main objectives: (1) honest and unbiased management, (2) greater participation in management by security holders, (3) adequate and feasible capital structures, (4) sound financial statements and accounting practices, and (5) correction of abuses in selling practices.[18]

The amendments of 1970 gave the Commission a good deal, but not all, of what it wanted:

SEC, 37th ANNUAL REPORT
1971

In proposing mutual fund legislation in 1967, the Commission recognized that most of the specific abuses aimed at in the Investment Company Act had been substantially eliminated. However, the dramatic growth of the industry and accompanying changes created new situations which were not anticipated in 1940. While the industry accepted or even welcomed many of the changes proposed by the Commission, it took exception to the principal recommendations of the Commission, and as a result these were modified in the legislation passed by Congress. The most significant aspects of that legislation, which also included certain amendments of the Investment Advisers Act of 1940, are described below.

Investment Advisory Fees

The 1970 Act amends the Investment Company Act by adding a new Section 36(b) (effective June 14, 1972) which specifies that the investment adviser of a registered investment company has a fiduciary duty with respect to the receipt of compensation for ser-

[16] §3(c)(1).
[17] §6, esp. §6(c).
[18] 10 SEC Ann. Rep. 162-63 (1944).

vices or payments of a material nature paid by such company or its shareholders to the adviser or an affiliate of the adviser. An action for breach of this duty may be brought in a Federal court by the Commission or by a shareholder on behalf of the company. * * * Section 36(b) further provides that the court is to give such consideration as it deems appropriate to approval of the compensation or payments in question by the board of directors and to approval or ratification by the shareholders.[a]

* * *

While the Commission had originally recommended adoption of a standard of "reasonable" management compensation, it considered the fiduciary standard finally agreed upon and adopted as equivalent in substance. Clearly, the new provision represents a significant improvement over the prior standards of "corporate waste" and "gross abuse of trust" applicable under state and federal law, respectively.

Sales Charges

In the area of sales charges imposed on investors in mutual fund shares, the 1970 Act amended Section 22(b) of the Investment Company Act to provide that the National Association of Securities Dealers, Inc. (NASD) may by rule prohibit its members from offering such shares at a price which includes an "excessive sales load but shall allow for reasonable compensation for sales personnel, broker-dealers, and underwriters, and for reasonable sales loads to investors." Previously, the NASD was authorized only to prohibit an "unconscionable or grossly excessive sales load." The 1970 Act also provides that at any time after 18 months from the date of its enactment, or after the NASD has adopted rules under amended Section 22(b), the Commission may alter or supplement the rules of the NASD. * * *[b]

[a]Ed.: This section will be considered in the Civil Liability chapter. See p. 985 infra.

[b]Ed.: See NASD Rules of Fair Practice, Art. III, §26, CCH NASD Manual ¶2176; SEC Rule 22c-1.

The typical open-end investment company is virtually unique on the American scene in that it is externally managed pursuant to a management contract made with a close corporation that is organized by the investment company's promoters to function as investment adviser and is affiliated with the principal underwriter of the investment company's shares.

Section 15 of the Act requires that any contract with an investment adviser

THE FRONT-END LOAD ON CONTRACTUAL PLANS

Other significant amendments of the 1940 Act relate to the so-called "front-end load" on periodic payment plan certificates (i. e., certificates issued in connection with contractual plans for the accumulation of fund shares on an installment basis). Formerly, there was no right to a refund for an investor who did not want or was unable to continue payments to the end of the plan under which as much as 50 percent of the payment made during the first year could be deducted for sales charges. Thus, planholders who did not complete their payments were disadvantaged in terms of the portion of their payments actually invested in shares.

The 1970 Act, through amendment of Section 27 of the 1940 Act, provides a desirable improvement in investor protection in this area. Under the new provisions, sales charges on contractual plans may be imposed under either of two alternative methods. Under the so-called "spread load" alternative (which must be elected by written notice to the Commission), the sales load is restricted to not more than 20 percent of any payment and not more than an average of 16 percent over the first 4 years of the plan. Under the other alternative, periodic payment plan certificates may still be sold with a 50 percent front-end load, but plan sponsors must refund, to any investor surrendering his certificate within the first 18 months of the plan, that portion of the sales charges which exceeds 15 percent of the gross payments made, as well as paying him the value of his account. The 1970 Act further provides that, regardless of the alternative followed, an investor is entitled to a full refund of the value of his account plus all sales charges if he cancels his plan within 45 days from the mailing by the custodian bank of notice of the charges to be deducted and of his cancellation right. Such a notice must be mailed within 60 days after issuance of his certificate. The Commission is authorized to make rules requiring contractual plan sponsors to maintain specified reserves to meet refund obligations

---

be approved initially by a majority of the outstanding voting securities, and that any contract with either an adviser or a principal underwriter be approved annually by such a vote or by the board of directors if the contract is to continue for more than two years. Moreover, an advisory contract may be terminated at any time on sixty days' notice, without penalty, by either the investment company's board or a vote of stockholders.

So far as the investment company's board itself is concerned, §10 limits "interested persons" (as broadly defined in §2(a)(19)) to 60 percent of all the directors. And, in effect, a *majority* of the board must be independent if certain inside persons are principal underwriters or regular brokers for the investment company. On top of this, §17 prohibits certain transactions in which there is a conflict of interest.

and specifying the notice to be given to investors regarding their refund rights.

Fund Holding Companies

Provisions of the Investment Company Act relating to fund holding companies (i. e., investment companies whose portfolios consist either entirely or largely of the securities of other investment companies) were also amended, so as to limit the creation of new fund holding companies and the further enlargement of existing companies. Concern with such companies has centered on the fact that they result in "layering" of sales charges and administrative and other expenses to investors and may have a disruptive effect on the funds whose securities are held in their portfolios. Section 12(d)(1) of the 1940 Act formerly prohibited a registered investment company, subject to certain exceptions, from purchasing more than 3 percent of the outstanding voting stock of another investment company unless it already owned at least 25 percent. This limitation was inadequate, since it applied only to purchases by *registered* investment companies. Hence, a foreign-based fund holding company not subject to registration under the Act could make unlimited investments in registered investment companies.

Under the 1970 amendments, no investment company may have more than 10 percent of the value of its assets invested in securities of other investment companies. However, that limitation is made inapplicable to a *registered* investment company if certain conditions are met, principally that: (1) not more than 3 percent of the outstanding stock of any one investment company is owned by the holding company and (2) the sales load of the holding company cannot exceed 1½ percent. In addition, the portfolio fund is not obligated to redeem its securities held by the holding company in an amount exceeding 1 percent of its outstanding securities in any period of less than 30 days.

Performance Fee Advisory Contracts

The 1970 Act, in accordance with the Commission's recommendation, amended the Investment Advisers Act by deleting the exemption from the coverage of its provisions formerly provided for an investment adviser whose only clients are registered investment companies. The Advisers Act was further amended so as to prohibit an investment adviser from performing or entering into an advisory contract with a registered investment company providing for certain types of "performance fees," i. e., compensation based on the realized or unrealized appreciation of the investment company's portfolio.

The Commission had originally recommended a flat prohibition of performance fee arrangements between investment advisers and registered investment companies. It considered that such arrangements give advisers incentives to take undue risks and noted that many fee arrangements were unfair or so complex that it was virtually impossible to understand them. However, after discussion with industry representatives, the Commission agreed to an exception for certain limited types of performance fees. The amendments as adopted exempt from the prohibition against performance fee compensation an arrangement based on a percentage of a registered investment company's net asset value averaged over a specified period, which provides for proportionate increases and decreases in compensation on the basis of investment performance of the company as measured against an appropriate index of securities prices or such other measure of investment performance as the Commission may specify.

Expanded Commission Enforcement Authority

The 1970 Act added a new subsection (b) to Section 9 of the Investment Company Act to provide additional grounds for disqualification of persons from affiliation with an investment company. Formerly only persons subject to certain convictions or injunctions were so disqualified. The new provision parallels comparable provisions in the Securities Exchange and Investment Advisers Acts providing for remedial action through administrative proceedings. It empowers the Commission, after notice and opportunity for hearing, to prohibit any person, either permanently or for such time as may be appropriate, from serving a registered investment company in the capacities of employee, officer, director, member of an advisory board, investment adviser, depositor or principal underwriter or as an affiliated person of its investment adviser, depositor, or principal underwriter. The Commission may take such action if it finds (1) that such person has willfully violated, or willfully aided and abetted violations by another, of any provision of the Securities Act, Securities Exchange Act, Investment Company Act, or Investment Advisers Act, or any rule or regulation thereunder, or has willfully made or caused to be made a materially false or misleading statement in any registration statement, application or report filed under the Investment Company Act, and (2) that such action is in the public interest.

F. TRANSNATIONAL TRANSACTIONS

1. General

The extraterritorial reach of various provisions of the SEC statutes has engaged the courts (and occasionally the Commission) in upwards of fifty reported cases, most of them decided in the last decade or so. And in an electronic age in which "world class" securities are listed on exchanges around the globe, so that they are traded twenty-four hours a day, the volume of transnational securities business is bound to increase in the 1980s and beyond.

The Board of Governors of the Federal Reserve System referred to the emergence of New York, London, and Tokyo as "a single round-the-clock global market" when in December 1986 it admitted two Japanese investment houses to the small group of "primary dealers" in United States Government securities.[1] And the SEC has approved various linkages with foreign exchanges: Boston-Montreal,[2] American-Toronto,[3] Midwest-Toronto,[4] NASD-London.[5] And in early 1985 the SEC solicited public comment on internationalization both of public offerings and of the markets generally.[6]

C. 1F [1] N.Y. Times, Dec. 12, 1986, p. D1, col. 4. See p. 611 infra.

[2] Boston Stock Exchange, Inc., Sec. Ex. Act Rel. 21,449, 31 SEC Dock. 758 (1984); Sec. Ex. Act Rel. 21,925, 32 SEC Dock. 1152 (1985).

[3] Sec. Ex. Act Rel. 22,442, 34 SEC Dock. 105 (1985).

[4] Sec. Ex. Act Rel. 23,075, 35 SEC Dock. 481 (1986). The Midwest and London Exchanges have also instituted a joint clearance and settlement link. Wall St. J., Aug. 11, 1986, p. 16, col. 4.

[5] Sec. Ex. Act Rel. 23,158, 35 SEC Dock. 684 (1986); Sec. Ex. Act Rel. 23,729, 36 SEC Dock. 1024 (1986). The former Stock Exchange, London, is now the International Stock Exchange of the United Kingdom and the Republic of Ireland, Ltd. For proposed modifications in this pilot program, see Sec. Ex. Act Rel. 24,364, 38 SEC Dock. 148 (1987). Entirely abroad it has been reported that Montreal has reached agreements with London and Paris that will let British and French companies list their shares in Montreal on the basis solely of British or French disclosure and regulatory requirements. Wall St. J., May 22, 1986, p. 34, col. 1.

[6] In order to provide a context for the former solicitation, the Commission suggested two conceptual approaches designed to facilitate multinational offerings in the United States, the United Kingdom, and Canada. Under the "reciprocal" approach (which commentators are apparently favoring) the three countries would agree that a prospectus accepted in an issuer's domicile would be accepted in the other countries if it met certain standards. Under the "common prospectus" approach a single prospectus would be filed simultaneously in each of the three countries. Sec. Act Rel. 6568, 32 SEC Dock. 707 (1985); Sec. Ex. Act

There are eight leading cases in the Second Circuit, Judge Friendly writing in five of them.[7] And all fifty-odd cases have been litigated with little guidance from either the statutes themselves or the Commission's rules. The Commission has never used its rulemaking authority under §30(b) of the 1934 Act, the only extraterritorial provision of anything like general applicability, which makes that statute inapplicable "to any person insofar as he transacts a business in securities without the jurisdiction of the United States, unless he transacts such business in contravention of such rules and regulations as the Commission may prescribe as necessary or appropriate to prevent the evasion of this title."[8]

The unsure and at times contorted growth of judicial doctrine in this area pointed to a provision on extraterritoriality in the Code that would, it was hoped, combine and distill the best of the judicial and rulemaking processes. Except for its rulemaking aspect, §1905 of the Code was drafted as if it were a restatement of existing law.

Rel. 21,958, 32 SEC Dock. 1241 (1985); see generally id. at 1244-45.

In July 1986 the International Association of Securities Commissions — representing the governments and securities markets of fifty-eight countries, all of the major free market economies except for some reason Japan — took tentative steps toward international regulation. 18 Sec. Reg. L. Rep. 1049 (1986); see also 19 id. 24 (1987). In September 1986 the SEC, the CFTC, and the United Kingdom Department of Trade and Industry entered into an agreement to facilitate the exchange of information on enforcement of their respective securities and commodities laws. CCH Fed. Sec. L. Rep. ¶84,017. See generally Frankel *et al.*, Symposium: The Internationalization of the Securities Markets, 4 B. U. Int'l L. J. 1 (1986); Report of the SEC to the House Committee on Energy and Commerce on the Internationalization of the Securities Markets: Interim Progress Report (Oct. 9, 1986).

On the securities regulatory structures in various countries, see R. Rosen, International Securities Regulation (looseleaf); see also Bloomenthal, International Capital Markets and Securities Regulation, Clark Boardman Securities Law Series, Vols. 10, 10-A *passim* (1982); J. Robinson (ed.), International Securities Law and Practice (1985).

[7] Schoenbaum v. Firstbrook, 405 F. 2d 200 (2d Cir. 1968), *modified on other grounds*, 405 F. 2d 215 (2d Cir. *en banc* 1968), *cert. denied* sub nom. Manley v. Schoenbaum, 395 U. S. 906; Leasco Data Processing Equipment Corp. v. Maxwell, 468 F. 2d 1326 (2d Cir. 1972); Bersch v. Drexel Firestone, Inc., 519 F. 2d 974 (2d Cir. 1975), *cert. denied* sub nom. Bersch v. Arthur Andersen & Co., 423 U. S. 1018; IIT v. Vencap, Ltd., 519 F. 2d 1001 (2d Cir. 1975); IIT v. Cornfeld, 619 F. 2d 909 (2d Cir. 1980); Fidenas AG v. Compagnie Internationale pour l'Informatique CII Honeywell Bull, S. A., 606 F. 2d 5 (2d Cir. 1979); Psimenos v. E. F. Hutton & Co., 722 F. 2d 1041, 1044-45 (2d Cir. 1983) (commodity trading); AVC Nederland B. V. v. Atrium Investment Partnership, 740 F. 2d 148 (2d Cir. 1984). The three in which Judge Friendly did *not* write are *Schoenbaum, Fidenas,* and *Psimenos.*

[8] See also Sec. Ex. Act §§7(f) (infra p. 660), 12(g)(3) (infra p. 68), 30(a); Holding Co. Act §10(c)(2); Inv. Co. Act §7(d); Sec. Inv. Prot. Act §3(a)(2).

Then, in May 1986, The American Law Institute approved the Restatement of Foreign Relations Law of the United States (Revised), which contains a special section, §416, on "Jurisdiction to Regulate Activities Related to Securities: Law of the United States." We here set out the Code provisions with the commentary, and then consider the relationship between these two products of the Institute.[9]

FEDERAL SECURITIES CODE §1905 WITH COMMENTS[a]

SEC. 1905.

(a) APPLICATION EXTRATERRITORIALLY

(1) Within the limits of international law, this Code * * * applies

(A) with respect to

(i) a sale or purchase of a security, an offer to sell or buy a security, or an inducement not to buy or sell a security;

(ii) a proxy solicitation or other circularization of security holders;

(iii) a tender offer or a recommendation to security holders in favor of or opposition to a tender offer; or

(iv) any activity as an investment adviser

[9] See Loss, Extraterritoriality in the Federal Securities Code, 20 Harv. Int'l L. J. 305 (1979), which is based on the commentary to §1905; Lowenfeld, Public Law in the International Arena: Conflict of Laws, International Law, and Some Suggestions for Their Interaction, c. 3, The Approach in Action — United States Regulation of Securities Transactions, in 2 Collected Courses of the Hague Academy of International Law (1980) (an unfavorable critique of §1905 by one of the Restatement's Associate Reporters); Bloomenthal, International Capital Markets and Securities Regulation, 10-A Clark Boardman Securities Law Series (1982), Part III, Extraterritorial Application of U. S. Securities Laws; Larose, Conflicts, Contacts, and Cooperation: Extraterritorial Application of the United States Securities Laws, 12 Sec. Reg. L. J. 99 (1984) (comparative analysis of existing law, the Code, and the Restatement); Goelzer *et al.*, The Draft Restatement: A Critique from a Securities Regulation Perspective, 19 Int'l Law. 431 (1985) (same, constituting a favorable critique of §1905, by members of the SEC's staff, in contrast to the Draft Restatement).

[a] ED.: Copyright 1980 by The American Law Institute and reprinted with its permission. The comments collect all the relevant cases, but most citations are here omitted without further indication.

that occurs within the United States although it is initiated outside the United States;

(B) with respect to a nonresident of the United States that has a status described in section 1902(b),[b] to the extent that the Code attaches consequences to such a status;

(C) for purposes of section 1821,[c] with respect to an attempt, solicitation, or conspiracy outside the United States to commit a violation of this Code within the United States; and

(D) with respect to any other prohibited, required, or actionable conduct (i) whose constituent elements occur to a significant (but not necessarily predominant) extent within the United States, or (ii) some or all of whose constituent elements occur outside the United States but cause a substantial effect within it (of a type that this Code is designed to prevent) as a direct and reasonably foreseeable result of the conduct.

(2) Within the limits of international law, part XVI[d] applies with respect to an act specified in section 1905(a)(1)(A) that is initiated within the United States although it occurs outside the United States.

(b) NONAPPLICATION EXTRATERRITORIALLY

(1) Except as provided in section 1905(a)(2), this Code * * * does not apply with respect to an act specified in section 1905(a)(1)(A) that occurs outside the United States although it is initiated within the United States.

(2) Section 702[e] does not apply with respect to a broker, dealer, municipal broker, municipal dealer, or investment adviser, not a resident of the United States, to the extent that he does business with (A) a person outside the United States, or (B) a non-national of the United States who is present as a nonresident within the United States and was previously a customer or client.

(3) Section 702 does not apply with respect to a broker or dealer, not a resident of the United States, to the extent that he participates in a distribution or a limited offering if his only connection with the United States as a broker or dealer, so far as the distribution or limited offering is concerned, consists of (A) taking down securities for sale outside the United States, and (B) participating solely through

[b]ED.: This section refers to a person registered under the Code in any capacity, a person who has to file ownership or tender offer reports under §605 or 606 (so far as those sections are concerned), a participant in a registered clearing agency, or an associate or person acting on behalf of any such person.

[c]ED.: This is the penal section.

[d]ED.: Part XVI is entitled "Fraud, Misrepresentation, and Manipulation."

[e]ED.: This section requires the designated persons to register.

his group membership in group activities of a principal underwriter who is a registered broker or dealer.

(c) RULEMAKING AUTHORITY

Within the limits of international law and section 1905(a)(1)(D), and in the light of the significance of effects within the United States of particular acts or conduct, the Commission, by rule —

(1) may provide (A) that this Code does not apply with respect to the subject matter of section 1905(a), (B) that it does apply with respect to the subject matter of section 1905(b), and (C) that it does or does not apply with respect to any other subject matter; and

(2) shall prescribe the extent to which section 402[f] applies with respect to an issuer that is not a resident of the United States.

* * *

COMMENT

(1) There are several possible solutions to the variegated problems of extraterritoriality that have produced a substantial amount of litigation in recent years:

(a) The Code could simply perpetuate X30 * * * and for the rest leave the matter to the courts. But, aside from the fact that X30 covers only a relatively narrow band of the SEC spectrum, that section is both equivocal and illogical.

It is equivocal in referring to a person insofar as he transacts a business in securities "without the jurisdiction of the United States"; for it is not stated whether this refers to the territorial jurisdiction of the United States or its extraterritorial jurisdiction in the international law or the American constitutional law sense. Presumably it means the former in view of the authority of the Commission to adopt rules, which could hardly go beyond the several jurisdictional bases of the statute such as use of the mails or registration as a broker-dealer. But in *SEC* v. *United Financial Group, Inc.*, 474 F. 2d 354, 357-58 (9th Cir. 1973), the court without discussion read it the other way.

X30(b) is, in any event, illogical in the sense that it has been interpreted to exclude the transacting of "a business in securities" but not an isolated act outside the territorial limits of the United

[f]ED.: This section is the successor to §12(g) of the 1934 Act (infra p. 411), which requires the registration of any company with $1 million of assets (raised to $5 million by Commission rule) and 500 security holders.

States. *Schoenbaum* v. *Firstbrook,* 405 F. 2d 200, 207 (2d Cir. 1968), *modified on other grounds,* 405 F. 2d 215 (2d Cir. *en banc* 1968), *cert. denied* sub nom. *Manley* v. *Schoenbaum,* 395 U. S. 906.

* * *[g]

(b) An early draft of §1905(a), along the lines of §§17 and 18 of the [original] Restatement of Foreign Relations Law of the United States, consisted simply, in substance, of §§1905(a)(1)(D) and 1905(c), without the introductory reference to the limits of international law (which is borrowed from §3(3) of the Restatement):

(i) The situation in §1905(a)(1)(D)(ii) — and the more extreme of the two — was litigated in the *Schoenbaum* case (supra Comment (1)(a)). That was a stockholder's derivative action under Rule 10b-5 in which the plaintiff alleged that the directors of a Canadian corporation *with its stock listed on the American Stock Exchange* had authorized the sale of treasury shares *in Canada* at a price that was inadequate in the light of certain oil discoveries not yet disclosed to the public. The court stated:

> We believe that Congress intended the Exchange Act to have extraterritorial application in order to protect domestic investors who have purchased foreign securities on American exchanges and to protect the domestic securities market from the effects of improper foreign transactions in American securities. In our view, neither the usual presumption against extraterritorial application of legislation nor the specific language of Section 30(b) show Congressional intent to preclude application of the Exchange Act to transactions regarding stocks traded in the United States which are effected outside the United States, when extraterritorial application of the Act is necessary to protect American investors.

405 F. 2d at 206.

[g]ED.: The remainder of §1905 codifies the Foreign Corrupt Practices Act (§1905(d), now in part Sec. Ex. Act §30A), and provides for *in personam* jurisdiction with notice abroad (§1905(e)-(f)). See the text and commentary in 2 Code 996-1006. It should be noted in this connection that all of the first six Acts provide a broad choice of venue — in the case of the 1934 Act, the district where "any act or transaction constituting the violation occurred," or the district where the defendant "is found or is an inhabitant or transacts business" — and that process may be served "in any other district of which the defendant is an inhabitant or wherever the defendant may be found." Sec. Ex. Act §27. This literally permits worldwide service so far as American law is concerned. And the courts have given the venue provisions a broad reading. See 3 Loss 2007-12; 6 id. 4143-56; Smith, No Forum at All or Any Forum You Choose: Personal Jurisdiction over Aliens under the Antitrust and Securities Laws, 39 Bus. Law. 1685 (1984).

In Sec. Act Rel. 5068 (1970), the Commission justified guidelines with respect to the applicability of the statutes to the sale of mutual fund shares abroad by referring, *inter alia,* to the possibility that "Loss of confidence in the integrity of American registered investment companies could trigger widespread redemptions resulting in losses to foreign and domestic investors and damage to the United States securities market." * * *

The leading case here, of course, is *United States* v. *Aluminum Co. of America,* 148 F. 2d 416, 444 (2d Cir. 1945), which held that certain agreements made by foreign companies outside the United States were illegal under §1 of the Sherman Act. But cf. *Bersch* v. *Drexel Firestone, Inc.,* 519 F. 2d 974, 989 (2d Cir. 1975), *cert. denied* sub nom. *Bersch* v. *Arthur Andersen & Co.,* 423 U. S. 1018, where Judge Friendly said that "there is subject matter jurisdiction of fraudulent acts relating to securities which are committed abroad only when these result in injury to purchasers or sellers of those securities in whom the United States has an interest, not where acts simply have an adverse effect on the American economy or American investors generally."[h]

(ii) The situation in §1905(a)(1)(D)(i) — where *some* of the constituent elements occur in the United States — is illustrated by *Leasco Data Processing Equipment Corp.* v. *Maxwell,* 468 F. 2d 1326 (2d Cir. 1972), *on remand,* 68 F. R. D. 178 (S. D. N. Y. 1974), also a Rule 10b-5 action, this one for damage allegedly resulting from the purchase of shares of a British company on the London Stock Exchange. If all the alleged misrepresentations had occurred in England, Judge Friendly stated, "we would entertain most serious doubt whether, despite [the *Aluminum* and *Schoenbaum* cases], §10(b) would be applicable simply because of the adverse effect of the fraudulently induced purchases in England of securities of an English corporation, *not traded in an organized American securities market,* upon an American corporation whose stock is listed on the New York Stock Exchange and its shareholders." 468 F. 2d at 1334 (italics supplied). But "it tips the scales in favor of applicability when substantial misrepresentations were made in the United States (id. at 1337), as they allegedly were not only by agents physically within the United States but also by telephone and mail. The court saw no reason why, "for purposes of jurisdiction to impose a rule, making tele-

[h]ED.: See also IIT v. Cornfeld, 619 F. 2d 909, 916-17 (2d Cir. 1980), decided after publication of the Code.

phone calls and sending mail to the United States should not be deemed to constitute conduct within it." Id. at 1335.[i]

* * *

But cf. *Bersch* v. *Drexel Firestone, Inc.*, supra Comment (1)(b)(i), 519 F. 2d at 987 (United States activities that "are merely preparatory or take the form of culpable nonfeasance and are relatively small in comparison to those abroad" do not suffice);[j] *Ogdeninvest, A. G.* v. *Hessische Landesbank-Girozentrale,* CCH Fed. Sec. L. Rep. ¶96,555 at 94,321 (S. D. N. Y. 1978) (when both parties are foreign corporations, fraudulent acts themselves must be performed in United States "in the absence of a more than negligent effect upon the United States or its citizens").[k]

* * *

(c) Section 1905(a)-(c), accordingly, proceeds on a four-way basis: (i) §1905(a)(1)(A)-(C) attempts a statutory formulation of the rules of international law with respect to the extraterritorial application of the most significant areas of the Code; (ii) §1905(a)(1)(D) subjects the residue to the undefined limits of international law; (iii) §1905(b)

[i]ED.: In Grunenthal GmbH v. Hotz, 712 F. 2d 421 (9th Cir. 1983), where the only misrepresentation in the United States was a repetition of a representation first made abroad, the court stated, in reversing a dismissal for lack of subject matter jurisdiction, that the fact that the conduct in this country had been "based on convenience" was of little significance. See also Psimenos v. E. F. Hutton & Co., Inc., 722 F. 2d 1041 (2d Cir. 1983) (complaint under Commodity Exchange Act by Greek citizen who bought American futures contracts on American commodity exchanges through Athens and Paris offices of defendant American broker on basis of false pamphlet emanating from defendant's New York office); Tamari v. Bache & Co. (Lebanon), S. A. L., 730 F. 2d 1103 (7th Cir. 1984), *cert. denied,* 469 U. S. 871 (complaint under Commodity Exchange Act by Lebanese citizens against Lebanese subsidiary of Delaware corporation where trading on American commodity exchanges followed contacts between the parties in Lebanon was sustained under both the "conduct" and the "effects" theory).

[j]ED.: But such activities assume a different aspect when they involve United States securities. IIT v. Cornfeld, 619 F. 2d 909, 918 (2d Cir. 1980).

[k]ED.: See also Plessey Co., PLC v. General Electric Co., PLC, 628 F. Supp. 477, 500-02 (D. Del. 1986). The *Bersch* holding was with respect to foreign plaintiffs. And some citations are omitted, including Fidenas A. G. v. Compagnie Internationale pour l'Informatique CII Honeywell Bull, S. A., 606 F. 2d 5 (2d Cir. 1979) (all parties were foreign, the essential core of the alleged fraud was in Switzerland, and any activities in the United States were "clearly secondary and ancillary"). See also Fidenas AG v. Honeywell, Inc., 501 F. Supp. 1029 (S. D. N. Y. 1980) (same result in action against American parent corporation of previous defendants); Doll v. James Martin Associates (Holdings), Ltd., 600 F. Supp. 510 (E. D. Mich. 1984).

specifies certain areas in which the Code does *not* apply extraterritorially; and (iv) §1905(c)(1) gives the Commission rulemaking authority that permits it not only to reverse the rebuttable "in" and "out" presumptions (as it were) of §1905(a)-(b) but also to fill the gap covered by neither (a) nor (b). All this is subject to the introductory limitation to "international law," however ascertained, as well as §1905(a)(1)(D). See Comment (11)(a) and (e).

This pattern not only blends the judicial expertise in international law (public and private) with the administrative expertise in the securities aspects of international commerce, but also recognizes that it is essential to distinguish between *power* in the international law sense and *policy.* See *Bersch,* supra Comment (1)(b)(i), 519 F. 2d at 985. This §1905 does by making the coverage of the Code quite broad (at least *prima facie*) and relying largely on Commission rules to tailor that expression of power to the appropriate policy considerations in the myriad contexts that could result in litigation (as many already have) under the Code. At the same time, the draft neither exhausts the limits of international law nor attempts to anticipate more than the more common and repetitive factual configurations.

(2) §§1905(a)(1)(A), 1905(a)(2), 1905(b): The pattern here is — in terms, for example, of a simple offer into or out of the United States — to cover both cases so far as "fraud" is concerned (§1905(a)(2)), but, so far as Part V[l] is concerned, to reach only the offer *into* the United States (§1905(a)(1)(A)), not the offer *out* of the United States (§1905(b)). But all this is true only *prima facie,* in the absence of contrary rules (within the limits of international law) under §1905(c).[m]

(3) §1905(a)(1)(A): (a) * * *

(b) Presumably everybody would agree that the making of an offer from another country into the United States by mail or telephone is subject to S5 and 17(a) [the registration and fraud provisions] even though neither the seller nor an agent of the seller sets foot in the United States. * * * This is the classic case of the shot across a boundary — the so-called "subjective territorial principle." See [original] Restatement §18, Comment c, Illus. 2.

(c) Presumably the same would be true of proxy solicitations or tender requests made in the United States from a point outside solely by use of the mails or telephone, whether or not the statutory

[l]ED.: Part V, entitled "Distributions," is basically today's 1933 Act registration and prospectus scheme.

[m]ED.: With respect to §1905(a)(1)(A)(i), see AVC Nederland B. V. v. Atrium Investment Partnership, 740 F. 2d 148, 154 n. 9 (2d Cir. 1984).

provisions were limited to registered securities (as, for example, X14(e) is not).

(4) §§1905(a)(2), 1905(b): The converse situation — the offer *from* the United States — is just as clearly covered by the "*objective* territorial principle" of international law. That is to say, there is no question of the propriety of a state's applying its laws so as to avoid its territory's being used as a base to injure persons in other states. [Original] Restatement §17(a), esp. Comment a, Illus. 2; *IIT* v. *Vencap, Ltd.*, 519 F. 2d 1001, 1017 (2d Cir. 1975); *United States* v. *Cook*, 873 F. 2d 281 (5th Cir. 1978); *Continental Grain (Australia), Pty. Ltd.* v. *Pacific Oilseeds, Inc.*, 592 F. 2d 409 (8th Cir. 1979).

See also *SEC* v. *Kasser*, 548 F. 2d 109 (3d Cir. 1977), *cert. denied* sub nom. *Churchill Forest Industries (Manitoba), Ltd.* v. *SEC*, 431 U. S. 938. "We are reluctant to conclude," Judge Adams [there] stated, "that Congress intended to allow the United States to become a 'Barbary Coast,' as it were, harboring international securities 'pirates.' "

This accounts for §1905(a)(2), which so applies the "fraud" provisions. But *policy* does not require that Part V (successor to the registration and prospectus provisions of the 1933 act) extend as far as it might under international law. In the past the Commission has attacked this problem by construing S4(2) as exempting from registration transactions not involving any public offering *within the United States.* 1 Loss 368-70; 4 id. 2407-11. More recently its counsel have disclaimed that position, relying instead, apparently, on the Commission's withholding action in these cases as a matter of prosecutor's discretion. See Answering Brief of SEC, p. 47, n. 47 (1972), in *SEC* v. *United Financial Group, Inc.*, 474 F. 2d 354 (9th Cir. 1973).[n]

[n]ED.: On the same condition securities may be sold abroad concurrently with an offering in the United States under Regulation D (infra p. 313) as long as the issuer does not elect to rely *solely* on Regulation D for sales to foreign persons. Reg. D, Prel. Note 7. The Commission's staff has even permitted a domestic intrastate offering under §3(a)(11) (see c. 5C infra) in tandem with an offering abroad. Scientific Mfg., Inc., CCH Fed. Sec. L. Rep. ¶77,505 (letter 1983). See generally Clark, Debt Securities, in Practising Law Institute, Sixteenth Annual Institute on Securities Regulation (1984) c. 4 at 37-43. But the securities sold abroad must not seep back into the United States; they must "come to rest" abroad. Sec. Act Rel. 4708 (1964). For the precautions usually taken to assure that result — which is no small matter in an age of computerized trading, linkages, and depositories — see Morgenstern, Real Estate Securities and the Foreign Investor — Some Problems and a Proposal, 11 Sec. Reg. L. J. 332, 343-46 (1984); Evans, Offerings of Securities Solely to Foreign Investors, 40 Bus. Law. 69 (1984) (with description of "no action" letters); Singer Co. (letter, Aug. 7, 1974) (debt securities); Procter & Gamble Co. (letter, Feb. 21,

Section 1905(b) is an elaboration of this policy, subject to rules that might provide otherwise under §1905(c)(1).

(5) §1905(a)(1)(B): (a) This section rests on a person's *status* rather than his acts. See *Fontaine* v. *SEC,* 259 F. Supp. 880 (D. P. R. 1966), *stay denied,* CCH Fed. Sec. L. Rep. ¶91,892 (1st Cir. 1967), described in 5 Loss 3410-11. With respect to the reference to §1902(b)(3) * * * in *Roth* v. *Fund of Funds, Ltd.,* 405 F. 2d 421 (2d Cir. 1968), *cert. denied,* 394 U. S. 975, a Canadian corporation with its offices in Switzerland was held liable under X16(b) [which provides for the recapture of certain insiders' short-term trading profits] when as a more-than-10 percent holder it had bought and sold on an American exchange, using New York brokers and paying for the purchases through a New York bank. But (subject to the introductory limitation to international law and the Commission's rulemaking authority to provide otherwise) §1905(a)(1)(B) would produce the same result even with respect to purchases and sales abroad.

(b) However, the "to the extent" clause contemplates only provisions that attach to status — for example, §1714 (successor to X16(b)) and the broker-dealer hypothecation and recordkeeping rules. International *offers* and other *transactions* that are effected by brokers or dealers, whether they are American or foreign and whether the offers are into or out of the United States, are governed by §1905(a)(1)(A), (a)(2) and (b) rather than (a)(1)(B).

* * *

(7) §1905(a)(1)(D): See Comment (1)(b)(i)-(ii). The "conduct" may consist of culpable nonfeasance. And the "constituent elements" phrase is not limited to acts essential to the establishment of the "prohibited, required, or actionable conduct." Thus, Clause (i) is broad enough, in the context of §1602(a)(1), to cover a sale consummated in England pursuant to negotiations in both England and the United States even though the only misrepresentations occurred in the negotiations abroad. But in such a case the emphasis is on "significant * * * extent." Cf. *Bersch,* supra Comment (1)(b)(i), 519 F. 2d at 987; *IIT,* supra Comment (4), 519 F. 2d at 1018. As here used, that phrase contemplates a qualitative rather than a merely quantitative analysis — just as the "constituent elements" phrase refers generally to the various acts that make up the conduct in

---

1985) (same). Infra Red Associates, Inc. (letter, Sept. 11, 1985) (somewhat less developed guidelines for equity securities).

question instead of being limited to such discrete steps in the conduct as offer, acceptance, and so on.[o]

(8) §1905(b)(2)(A): This reflects *Schoenbaum* (supra Comment (1)(a)). And the negative implication reflects the holding in *SEC* v. *Myers,* 285 F. Supp. 743, 746 (D. Md. 1968), that a Canadian investment adviser could be enjoined from violating the registration provision of the Advisers Act if he were conducting a "business" *in the United States.* See also 2 Loss 1291, n. 15, 4th par.

* * *

(9) §1905(b)(2)(B): This contemplates, for example, the Canadian broker who uses the telephone to service a customer who is vacationing in Florida. If only Canadian brokers were involved, this clause might be limited to customers who were themselves Canadian nationals; but the clause is phrased in terms of any nonnational of the United States in deference particularly to European or Japanese brokers, who are perhaps increasingly likely to have a multinational clientele. The further limitation to persons who were *previously* customers or clients is designed to preclude a nonresident broker's building up a business with aliens more or less permanently in the United States unless he registers, and it does so more simply than would be the case with a fixed time limitation on the customer's presence in the United States.

(10) §1905(b)(3): This reflects the administrative construction, but without limitation to buyers who are nonnationals of the United States. Sec. Act Rel. 4708 (1964) 2, following Report to the President of the United States from the Task Force on Promoting Increased Foreign Investment in United States Corporate Securities and Increased Foreign Financing for United States Corporations Operating Abroad (1964) 7; see also 5 Loss 3353-54.

(11) §1905(c)(1): (a) The introductory language of §1905(a)(1)(2) and (c) reflects Chief Justice Marshall's admonition that "an act of Congress ought never to be construed to violate the law of nations if any other possible construction remains." *The Charming Betsy,* 2

[o]ED.: In O'Driscoll v. Merrill Lynch, Pierce, Fenner & Smith, Inc., CCH Fed. Sec. L. Rep. ¶99,486 (S. D. N. Y. 1983), the court entertained Rule 10b-5 jurisdiction over an Irish national with respect to claims pertaining to the period after his arrival in the country even though the alleged churning had been devised abroad, because his residency gave him the right to the same protection as United States citizens; but a foreign company that he had organized to buy and hold his stock could not present 10b-5 claims because it could not allege direct causation of its losses by acts within the United States.

Cranch 64, 118 (1804), quoted in *McCulloch* v. *Sociedad Nacional de Marineros de Honduras,* 372 U. S. 10, 21 (1963).

That concept, of course, leaves the not insignificant question of determining what the international law is in a given context. See, e. g., in connection with the originally proposed rules for foreign issuers under X12(g), 21 Record of N. Y. C. B. A. 240, 252 (1966). Moreover, there is the risk — which the Commission presumably will consider under the "public interest" and other standards of §1804(b) [the rulemaking provision] — that excessive extraterritoriality might damage the country's trade position. But it is precisely in the grey area that Commission rules under §1905(c)(1) may be expected to be particularly helpful.

(b) Today some situations are clearly covered without benefit of express statutory provisions or rules. * * *

(c) Other cases are in a grey area under present law — for example, the Canadian newspaper that sells a relatively small number of copies in Miami hotels to Canadians vacationing in Florida. Literally a security advertised for sale in the newspaper is the subject of an "offer" in Florida. But does S12(1) apply if only one or two copies are mailed to Canadian subscribers while temporarily in Florida? The solution in §414(e)(1) of the Uniform Securities Act is a provision to the effect that there is no "offer" in the state when "the publisher circulates * * * in this state any bona fide newspaper or other publication of general, regular, and paid circulation which is not published in this state or which is published in this state but has had more than two-thirds of its circulation outside this state during the past twelve months." Without suggesting that this approach would be appropriate in the context of Part V, it is an indication of one sort of rule that the Commission might adopt under §1905(c)(1).

(d) So far there have been a number of negative cases to counterbalance the affirmative cases that have been cited * * *.

* * *

(e) In short, §1905(c)(1) does not give the Commission a completely free hand. * * *

(f) Rules could also consider the *nationality* basis of jurisdiction under international law. [Original] Restatement §30; X7(f). That is to say, an act not otherwise within the Code might be brought within it if the actor were an American national. But normally nationality alone is not considered sufficient to establish that a particular statute extends that far. And the nationality principle does not necessarily apply, for example, to transactions abroad merely because they are with American servicemen or other nationals. For "A state does not have jurisdiction to prescribe a rule of law attaching legal consequences to conduct of an alien outside its territory merely on the ground that the conduct affects one of its nationals." Restatement §30(2).[p]

* * *

(12) §1905(c)(2): This is X12(g)(3). * * *[q]

The later Restatement is not basically inconsistent with the Code. In the words of the Reporters' notes:

> A somewhat different approach to securities regulation based on minimum contacts with the United States is taken in §1905 of the proposed Federal Securities Code (1980) of the American Law Institute. As stated in the introduction to that work, §1905 was designed to make substantive coverage of the Code quite broad, but always "within the limits of international law." This Restatement seeks to define those limits, including the principle of reasonableness for the exercise of jurisdiction to prescribe and apply a state's law, and the method for applying it. Since the proposed Federal Securities Code calls for vesting maximum power in the Securities and Exchange Commission subject to narrowing the exercise of that power by regulation, this Chapter would also guide the Commission in its rulemaking.[10]

Two important differences are the flexibility of this rulemaking authority and, in contrast with the antitrust field, the absence from all of the SEC litigation so far of conflict with foreign states' interests.[11]

On the latter point, that is to say, "no instance is known in which a transaction challenged under U. S. law — such as misrepresenta-

[p]ED.: In Grunenthal GmbH v. Hotz, 712 F. 2d 421, 426 n. 9 (9th Cir. 1983), the court noted *obiter* that "the Second Circuit's apparent application of different tests depending on the nationality of the plaintiff may raise constitutional questions."

[q]ED.: The Commission's rules under §12(g)(3) are considered infra pp. 70-72. Section 7(f) of the 1934 Act, with respect to margin trading, is reflected in the margin section of the Code. §918(d). For cases under the Commodity Exchange Act, see Note, Extraterritorial Application of Fraud Provisions of the Commodity Exchange Act, 41 Wash. & Lee L. Rev. 1215 (1984).

[10]Tent. Draft No. 7 (1986) 25.

[11]Id. at 23.

tion or insider trading — was asserted to be mandated by the law of a foreign state."[12] Nevertheless, on the enforcement level, the SEC has had to develop a number of mechanisms.[13] In 1984 the Commission, pointing to the dramatic increase in foreign participation in the United States securities markets, invited comment on a "waiver by conduct" approach that would be enacted into federal legislation. The concept is that a purchase or sale of a security in the United States market from a foreign country would constitute (1) an implied consent to disclosure of information and evidence relevant to the transaction for purposes of any Commission investigation, administrative proceeding, or action for injunctive relief that might arise out of the transaction, and (2) appointment of the American executing broker as agent for service of process or subpoenas, as well as a consent to the exercise of *in personam* jurisdiction by United States courts and the Commission.[14]

A waiver law might well make it easier to get American courts to subpoena information or evidence located abroad. But the Commission's very reference to a "waiver by conduct" law as representing, "in large measure, an appeal for nations with secrecy laws to apply principles of comity"[15] indicates that a foreign court that would not recognize the "effects" doctrine[16] would not be apt to feel differently about a constructive waiver.

2. Registration of Foreign Securities [§12(g)(3) and Rule 12g3-2]

Foreign securities, whether governmental or corporate, are exempted neither from the 1933 Act nor from §12(a) of the 1934 Act, which requires the registration of securities listed on ex-

[12] Ibid.

[13] See Fedders, Policing Internationalized U. S. Capital Markets: Methods to Obtain Evidence Abroad, 18 Int'l Law. 89 (1984).

[14] Sec. Ex. Act Rel. 21,186, 31 SEC Dock. 14 (1984). See Symposium, Policing Trans-Border Fraud in the United States Securities Markets, 11 Brooklyn J. Int'l L. 475 (1985); Liftin, Our Playing Field, Our Rules: An Analysis of the SEC's Waiver by Conduct Approach, 11 Brooklyn J. Int'l L. 525 (1985). The Commission stated that there were about 15 countries with secrecy laws and 16 with blocking laws. The latter, of course, cannot be waived by private parties, because they are considered to protect national rather than private interests when they prohibit the disclosure, copying, inspection, or removal of documents located in the enacting state by way of compliance with orders of foreign authorities. Sec. Ex. Act Rel. 21,186, 31 SEC Dock. 14, 18 (1984). See, e. g., U. K. Limitation Amendment Act 1980, Acts 1980, c. 24.

[15] Sec. Ex. Act Rel. 21,186, 31 SEC Dock. 14, 21 (1984).

[16] See p. 60 supra.

changes.[17] Quite the contrary, the Commission sometimes uses Rule 408 under the 1933 Act — which requires a registration statement to include, in addition to the specified information, whatever "further material information * * * may be necessary to make the required statements * * * not misleading" — in order to call for disclosure with respect to various economic, political, and legal considerations pertaining to such matters as taxation, risks of expropriation and currency devaluation, and stockholders' rights. The Commission nevertheless has made some practical concessions with respect to disclosure of management remuneration: it accepts aggregate figures when disclosure of individual remuneration is not made under the customs and practices of the particular country.[18] It also has allowed some deviation in financial reporting. In adopting a new Form 20-F in 1979 by way of consolidating the 1934 Act registration and annual report forms for certain foreign private issuers at a level somewhere between the prior forms and the general Forms 10 and 10-K, the Commission stated that its staff stood ready to discuss modifications in particular cases.[19]

So far as §12(g) is concerned, the problem is much more difficult. For the foreign issuer is not seeking access to the American capital market by way of either a distribution or a listing on a stock exchange. It is *prima facie* subject to the registration requirement if it has $5 million of assets and a class of equity security held of record by 500 persons. The Commission, out of considerations of enforcement difficulties, protection of existing markets in foreign securities, and greater flexibility,[20] would have preferred the Senate's formula, which would have exempted all foreign securities unless the Com-

[17] Foreign *governmental* securities are exempted from §15(d) of the 1934 Act, infra p. 436.

[18] Form 20-F, Item 11; see Garrett, Is the SEC a Barrier to New York's Role in International Finance?, Sec. Reg. L. Rep. No. 257, p. D-2 (1974).

[19] Sec. Ex. Act Rel. 16,371, 18 SEC Dock. 1118, 1119 (1979). Form 20-F facilitated the later extension of the integrated disclosure system under the 1933 and 1934 Acts to foreign private issuers eligible for that form. Sec. Act Rel. 6360, 24 SEC Dock. 3, 5 (1981); Sec. Act Rel. 6437, 26 SEC Dock. 964 (1982), infra p. 148 n. 6. The Commission thus "sought to balance the policies of protecting investors by requiring substantially the same disclosure from domestic and foreign issuers and of promoting the public interest by encouraging foreign issuers to register their securities with the Commission." Id. at 965. For a fuller account of this evolution, together with an enumeration of some of the basic differences between United States and foreign accounting practices and an account of the activities of regional and international bodies with respect to the harmonization of accounting requirements, see Thomas, International Accounting and Reporting, 15 N. Y. U. J. Int'l L. & Pol. 517 (1983).

[20] 1 Investor Protection, Hearings on H. R. 6789 before Subcom. of House Com. on Int. & For. Commerce, H. R. 6793, S. 1642, 88th Cong., 1st Sess. (1963) 179.

mission, by either rule or order, should find "that a substantial public market for the equity securities of such issuer or of a class of issuers which includes such issuer exists in the United States and that continued exemption * * * is not in the public interest or consistent with the protection of investors."[21] The House turned the formula around, however, so that §12(g)(3) as enacted makes no distinction *prima facie* between domestic and foreign securities. Instead it authorized the Commission, either by rule or on its own motion (after notice and opportunity for hearing) by order, to exempt any foreign security, including a certificate of deposit for a foreign security, "if the Commission finds that such exemption is in the public interest and is consistent with the protection of investors."

After inviting comment on a set of proposed rules that produced protests by the British and Canadian Governments, as well as an opinion by the Committee on International Law of The Association of the Bar of the City of New York that the proposed rules would violate international law as they applied to foreign corporations without securities either listed or publicly offered in the United States,[22] the Commission in 1967 adopted a considerably revised set of rules and forms that reflected its view with respect to "the continuing improvement in the quality of the information now being made public by foreign issuers."[23]

Under this scheme of things, pursuant primarily to Rule 12g3-2 as last amended in 1984:[24]

(1) American depositary receipts for foreign securities are exempted from §12(g) outright.

(2) Any class of securities of a foreign issuer (which is defined by Rule 3b-4 to mean a foreign government, a foreign national, or a corporation or other organization incorporated or organized under the laws of a foreign country) is likewise exempted if it has fewer than 300 holders resident in the United States.[25]

(3) Securities of all foreign *private* issues except those that are essentially United States companies are automatically exempted if

[21] §12(g)(2)(E) as contained in S. 1642, 88th Cong. (1963); see S. Rep. No. 379, 88th Cong., 1st Sess. (1963) 29-31.

[22] 21 Record A. B. C. N. Y. 240, 252 (1966).

[23] Sec. Ex. Act Rel. 8066 (1967). A temporary exemptive rule had been in effect meanwhile.

[24] Sec. Ex. Act Rel. 20,264, 28 SEC Dock. 1263 (1984).

[25] But the exemption in Rule 12g-1 with respect to issuers with *less than $5 million of assets* (see p. 411 infra) is inapplicable with respect to a security of a foreign *private* issuer that is quoted in an interdealer quotation system (which is to say, NASDAQ, infra p. 600).

information of specified categories is furnished to the Commission. A foreign issuer is considered to be essentially a United States company if "(1) more than 50 percent of the outstanding voting securities of such issuer are held of record either directly or through voting trust certificates or depositary receipts by residents of the United States; and (2) the business of such issuer is administered principally in the United States or 50 percent or more of the members of its Board of Directors are residents of the United States." When this definition is not satisfied, the required information is limited to whatever "the issuer since the beginning of its last fiscal years (A) has made or is required to make public pursuant to the law of the country of its domicile or in which it is incorporated or organized, (B) has filed or is required to file with a stock exchange on which its securities are traded and which was made public by such exchange, or (C) has distributed or is required to distribute to its security holders."[26] Moreover, this exemption has not been available since October 1983 to any company with a security listed on an American exchange or reporting under §15(d)[27] or with a security quoted in an "automated interdealer quotation system"; for those companies have sought a public market for their securities in the United States. But the Commission, when it amended Rule 12g3-2 in October 1983, indefinitely "grandfathered" all issuers that were then in NASDAQ and in compliance with the reporting obligations (except that Canadian issuers were "grandfathered" for only two years).[28]

(4) Insofar as a "foreign private issuer" has registered under §12 — even §12(b) (for exchange listing) rather than §12(g) — Rule 3a12-3(b), by reference to Form 20-F, affords an exemption from the proxy and insider trading provisions of §§14 and 16. Non-Canadian companies enjoy this exemption even when they have a security listed on an exchange or they report under §15(d). But the exemption applies to Canadian companies only to the extent that they register under §12(g) and do not have a listed security or a reporting obligation under §15(d).

(5) In order to inform brokers, dealers, and investors of the unavailability of information in the United States with respect to certain foreign issuers, the Commission undertook from time to time to issue lists of issuers from which it had received information. It added that, although no sanction would attach to any broker or dealer by reason of transactions in securities listed as neither regis-

[26] There is only a partial English translation requirement. Rule 12g3-2(b)(4).
[27] See p. 436 infra.
[28] Rule 12g3-2(d); see Sec. Ex. Act Rel. 20,264, 28 SEC Dock. 1263 (1983).

tered nor exempt, "the Commission expects that brokers and dealers will consider this fact in deciding whether they have a reasonable basis for recommending these securities to customers."[29] The latest published list includes 559 issuers.[30]

The saving grace in this maze — and the description here is not complete — is that it is inevitably more difficult to attempt to present a composite picture than it is for one to pick his way through the various registration, reporting, proxy, tender offer, and insider trading provisions and the relevant exemptions once he has a particular kind of foreign issuer in mind (with regard, for example, to whether or not it is Canadian, whether or not it has a security listed or that it wants to list on an American exchange, and whether or not it has registered under the 1933 Act so as to be subject to the reporting requirement under §15(d) of the 1934 Act). At best, however, this complex of rules and forms is not calculated to reassure foreign businessmen and lawyers who already have a mental image of a multi-tentacled monster with its head in Washington and the oddly vinous name, SEC.

G. ADMINISTRATIVE LAW ASPECTS

When writing in a field like securities regulation, which is an amalgam of everything from contracts and torts to corporations and international law, it is difficult to draw precise boundary lines around the subject matter. Administrative law — judicial review, rulemaking, investigation, subpoena enforcement, and the governmental injunction (not to mention the criminal sanction) — is a case in point. Some of this matter is more or less peculiar to the SEC. Thus we cover (or at least touch) at appropriate places the administrative enforcement procedures of the SEC and the self-regulatory organizations,[1] judicial review of the Commission's final orders in the Courts of Appeals,[2] and the availability of various kinds of ancillary relief in SEC injunctive proceedings.[3] So far as the bulk of admin-

[29] Sec. Ex. Act Rel. 8066 (1967).
[30] Sec. Ex. Act Rel. 22, 355, 33 SEC Dock. 1242 (1985).

C. 1G [1] See pp. 630-36 infra.
[2] See p. 635 infra; 3 and 6 Loss, c. 12C.
[3] See pp. 751 n. 80, 1004-11 infra. On "equity" for an injunction, see Rondeau v. Mosinee Paper Corp., 422 U. S. 49 (1975), infra p. 531. On the prerequisites for an injunction generally, see SEC v. National Student Marketing Corp., 457 F. Supp. 682, 715-16 (D. D. C. 1978), infra p. 1051. "It is fair to say that the current judicial attitude toward the issuance of injunctions on the

istrative law is concerned, however, the SEC is simply another administrative agency — and so we leave that matter to the writers in that field.[4]

basis of past violations at the SEC's request has become more circumspect than in earlier days." SEC v. American Board of Trade, Inc., 751 F. 2d 529, 536 (2d Cir. 1984).

The overwhelming proportion of SEC-initiated injunctions are entered by consent with a statement that the defendant "neither admits nor denies" the Commission's allegations. In March 1986 the Department of Justice issued guidelines with respect to negotiating consent judgments and settlements. See 54 U. S. L. Wk. 2492. Although they are specifically directed to lawyers in the Executive establishment, they might well be useful in the SEC context.

In SEC v. Randolph, 564 F. Supp. 137 (N. D. Cal. 1983), *rev'd,* 736 F. 2d 525 (9th Cir. 1984), the lower court's refusal to approve a consent injunction was reversed, the appellate court holding (1) that there was a constitutional case or controversy notwithstanding the parties' having "arrived in court with the proposed judgment in hand"; (2) that enforcement of the settlement agreement on normal contract principles did not offer the security of a judgment; and (3) that, so far as public interest was concerned, the court should have deferred to the judgment of the Commission, particularly since its resources were limited.

This pressure to settle can only be aggravated by Parklane Hosiery Co., Inc. v. Shore, 439 U. S. 322 (1979), where the Court held that a defendant found to have violated in a *litigated* SEC injunctive action was collaterally estopped from relitigating the same factual issue in a class action brought against him by a private plaintiff with respect to the same transaction. Other questions, like reliance and causation, may still be open, but the plaintiff will obtain a partial summary judgment to the effect that the defendant committed the violation alleged by the Commission. On the exceptions to the *Parklane* case, see Chemetron Corp. v. Business Funds, Inc., 682 F. 2d 1149, 1188-92 (5th Cir. 1982), *vacated and remanded on other grounds,* 460 U. S. 1007 (1983). On the impact of adjudications by the Commission itself, see Stillman, Collateral Estoppel Implications of SEC Adjudications, 42 Bus. Law. 441 (1987).

[4]See 3 and 6 Loss, c. 12; Code, Part XVIII.

CHAPTER 2

DISTRIBUTION OF SECURITIES

A. DISTRIBUTION TECHNIQUES

The registration and prospectus provisions of the Securities Act of 1933 can be understood — and their effectiveness evaluated — only on the background of the techniques by which securities are distributed in the United States. With a healthy obeisance in honor of the still new "shelf registration" technique, there are three basic types of so-called underwriting that are in common use, sometimes with variations.[1]

C. 2A [1]*Caveat:* Chapter 2A describes the traditional distribution techniques as they existed before the Commission adopted Rule 415 on an experimental basis in the spring of 1982. Since that rule and its potentially vast implications for capital formation and investment banking practices could not readily be understood without an analysis of the 1933 Act and the administrative practices that led to the rule's adoption, its consideration must be postponed until later in Chapter 2. See p. 136 infra. At any rate, the traditional distribution techniques are not dead; and, however much they may change under the impact of Rule 415, they are at the very least essential background.

For the rest, Chapter 2A is limited to distributions — which is to say, *public* offerings — of corporate securities. Many of the techniques and procedures used in the distribution of municipal and industrial revenue bonds differ substantially from those followed in the corporate area. On private placements, see c. 5E infra. On offerings of outstanding shares by means of "block distributions," see 1 Code 273-77. Other techniques that in recent years have accounted for a substantial volume have been dividend reinvestment plans, "TRASOPs," and employee thrift plans. In fact, dividend reinvestment plans have enabled companies, particularly utilities, to raise such large amounts of equity capital that utility common stock issues in the traditional manner have decreased in number. TRASOPs are a special form of employee stock ownership plan created by the Tax Reduction Act of 1975. §301(d), Int. Rev. Code §409, 26 U. S. C. §409. "From the employee's standpoint, they are a combined stock bonus and stock purchase plan. That is, employees can receive shares of the employer at no cost to them under such a plan, and they also may be given the opportunity to purchase additional shares of the employer at half the prevailing market price." Sec. Act Rel. 6188, 19 SEC Dock. 465, 484 (1980).

In general, see K. Bialkin and W. Grant (eds.), Securities Underwriting: A Practitioner's Guide (1985).

1. Strict or "Old-Fashioned" Underwriting

Under the traditional English system of distribution — which is no longer common in that country — the issuer did not sell to an investment banking house for resale to the public, either directly or through a group of dealers. Instead a designated "issuing house" advertised the issue and received applications and subscriptions from the public on the issuer's behalf after an announced date. When sufficient applications had been received, an announcement was made that "the lists are closed," and the issuer proceeded to allot the securities directly to the applicants or subscribers, using various methods of proration in the event of an oversubscription. Securities firms normally subscribed to new issues not for their own accounts with a view to resale at a profit, but only as brokers for the accounts of their customers. Before the public offering was thus made, the issue was "underwritten" in order to ensure that the company would obtain the amount of funds it required.

This was underwriting in the strict insurance sense. For a fee or premium, the underwriter agreed to take up whatever portion of the issue was not purchased by the public within a specified time. And, just as insurance companies frequently reinsure large underwritings with other companies in order to distribute the risk, so the initial underwriter often protected himself by agreements with sub-underwriters, to which the issuer was not a party. The typical underwriting syndicate was not limited to investment bankers or so-called issuing houses. It included or might consist entirely of insurance companies or investment trusts or other institutions, or even large individual investors, who thus obtained large blocks of securities at less than the issue price. Accordingly, the underwriters planned to hold for investment any securities they might be required to take. Even the issuing houses that found themselves required to take up unsubscribed portions of issues were inclined to hold them temporarily until they found a buyer on favorable terms, instead of trying to resell them immediately, at a loss if necessary, as underwriters generally do in this country when issues get "sticky."

This method of distribution is called in the United States "strict" or "old-fashioned" or "standby" underwriting. It is seldom if ever used here except in connection with offerings to existing stockholders by means of warrants or rights. But in that field its use, though with important modifications, is common. Usually stockholders are thus given a prior opportunity to purchase at a price below the market. If the discount is sufficiently large, and especially if the issuer is well established, the services of investment bankers may be dispensed with entirely. But it is common practice for the issuer to enter into a "standby agreement" with an investment banker.

Almost invariably the agreement is made with a syndicate of such bankers formed by the firm that is first approached, in which event that firm generally acts as syndicate manager. The trend has been toward larger and larger syndicates; they sometimes number well over a hundred members. The underwriters may receive by way of compensation a fixed percentage of the entire issue for assuming the risk of standing by during the week or so of the rights offering, or a smaller percentage so computed plus an additional concession (sometimes called the "work-out" cost) on any portion of the issue unsubscribed by security holders and hence required to be taken up by themselves. The method of compensation has been subject to a good deal of variation.

In the last few decades this standby technique for the handling of rights offerings has been developed to a fine point. In order to reduce the market risk of standing by during the rights period, the underwriters often purchase rights that are offered in the market by security holders who do not wish to acquire the new securities, exercise the rights themselves, and offer the stock for sale without waiting for the expiration of the rights offering. This also avoids an unfavorable reception of the public offering by reason of the market impact of a large block of unsubscribed stock.

Another — and less common — method of rights offerings is the so-called dealer-manager plan. The issuer merely arranges with one or more investment banking firms to pay a per-share commission to any dealers who promote the exercise of rights during the subscription period and whose names appear on the exercised warrants. This is a form of best-efforts arrangement, but sometimes it is combined with an ordinary standby agreement.

Rights offerings generally have undergone a good deal of experimentation, and the procedures are far from uniform. Their popularity is largely accounted for, presumably, by the substantial saving in costs as compared with other methods of distribution through investment bankers.

2. Firm-Commitment Underwriting

"Firm-commitment" underwriting is not technically underwriting in the classic insurance sense. But its purpose and effect are much the same in that it assures the issuer of a specified amount of money at a certain time (subject frequently to specified conditions precedent in the underwriting contract) and shifts the risk of the market (at least in part) to the investment bankers. Traditionally the issuer would simply sell the entire issue outright to a group of securities firms, represented by one or several "managers" or "principal underwriters" or "representatives"; they in turn would sell at a price differential to a larger "selling group" of dealers; and they would sell at another differential to the public. In a very limited sense the process is comparable to the merchandising of beans or automobiles. The issuer is the manufacturer of the securities; the members of the underwriting group are the wholesalers; and the members of the selling group are the retailers. But it is not quite so simple. Except in the case of open-end investment companies, securities of particular issuers are distributed not continually but once in a long time, and then in a large batch. And the securities market is quite a different animal from the market for canned beans.

Before the Securities Act of 1933 — particularly during the period of tremendous industrial and business expansion that began roughly in 1900 — the procedure underwent an elaborate development. The risk of handling the increasingly large securities offerings of the Nation's industrial units had to be spread, and methods had to be developed to merchandise the securities among the ever-growing numbers of investors spread across the continent.

Jay Cooke is credited with having introduced the "underwriting syndicate" into this country in the sale of a $2 million bond issue by the Pennsylvania Railroad in 1870.[2] By the turn of the century it was common in the case of large offerings for a single investment banker to do the "origination" — that is, carry on the preliminary negotiations with the issuer, make the investigations deemed necessary, and then purchase the issue from the issuer. The banker was chosen (and still is to a large extent except when the law requires competitive bidding) on the basis of his past relationships with the issuer and his past performance. The "origination" stage was followed by the process of "syndication": In order to spread the commitment, the originating banker would immediately sell the issue to a small "original purchase group." And that group would in turn sell to a larger "banking group"; or the members of the latter group might occupy the status of "old-fashioned underwriters." The originating banker would become a member of the purchase group; the members of that group would likewise become members of the banking group; and the originating banker would manage both groups. When the issue was not too large, the inter-

[2]See H. Larson, Jay Cooke (1936) 314 et seq.

mediate group might be omitted. In either event, the two or three steps followed each other very closely. The function of both groups was to spread the risk — although the process also permitted the originating banker to make participations available on favorable terms to large distributors, to those firms that had reciprocated in the past or might do so in the future, to those he might count on in less favorable times, and to those suggested by the issuer. In any event, these groups were not designed primarily to do the actual distributing; often the members of the groups were not organized for retailing purposes. The public sale would be effected, for the account of whichever group last bought the issue, by the manager (the originating banker) through an organization of employees and agents, which would sometimes include those members of the purchase and banking groups who were geared for retail distribution.

With the increase in the number and size of securities issues during World War I, as well as the development of coast-to-coast telephone and wire systems, both groups tended to grow in membership and, in order to facilitate the actual mechanics of distribution, it became customary to add still another step to the elaborate process: Instead of the originating banker's selling through agents and employees, a much larger and more dispersed "selling group" or "selling syndicate" would take the issue from the banking group; those members of the earlier group or groups with distributive facilities would join this new group; and it, too, would be managed by the originating banker. These developments also tended to speed up the distribution process and shorten the lives of the several groups.

The passage of the Securities Act of 1933, as well as the new federal securities transfer taxes that were imposed in 1932, made for a simplification of this system.[3] Under the statute only negotiations between the issuer and "underwriters" are permitted before the filing of the registration statement. Until then the securities may not be offered to the public or even to dealers who are not "underwriters" within the statutory definition. And until the actual effective date of the registration statement, no sales or contracts may be made except with underwriters. This, in practice, means that today the interval between the signing of the underwriting contract and the effectiveness of the registration statement, during which whoever is committed to purchase at a fixed price cannot

[3] There has been no federal stock transfer tax since year-end 1965. 79 Stat. 136 (1965).

legally shift his liability against a decline in a frequently volatile market, has been reduced to an hour or two.

One result of this has been the development of the "market out" clause in the underwriting contract. Although the use of this clause is by no means universal and in practice it is not considered "cricket" to take advantage of it, it typically provides that the manager of the underwriting group (or the representatives of the group) may terminate the agreement if before the date of public offering (or before the date of the closing or settlement between underwriters and issuer) the issuer or any subsidiary sustains a material adverse change, or trading in the securities is suspended, or minimum or maximum prices or government restrictions on securities trading are put into effect, or a general banking moratorium is declared, or in the judgment of the managing underwriter (or, alternatively, the representatives of the underwriters or a majority in interests of the several underwriters) material changes in "general economic, political, or financial conditions" or the effect of international conditions on financial markets in the United States make it impracticable or inadvisable to market the securities at specified public offering price. This clause is much broader than the traditional *force majeure* provision.[4]

Another result of the Securities Act and the former transfer taxes has been a tendency to reduce the number of transfers between groups and to enlarge the number of "underwriters" who bear the initial risk. In effect, the originating banker and the purchase and banking groups have all been combined into a single "underwriting syndicate or group."

It is difficult to generalize about the practice today, because it may vary substantially from issue to issue. Each of the prominent banking houses tends to develop variations of its own. Nevertheless, certain patterns are familiar. Quite early the underwriter, specifically negativing any obligation, gives the issuer sufficient assurance, either orally or by a "letter of intent," to warrant the issuer's going ahead with the extensive work and expenses that are necessary. The single underwriting group is then created by a contract among its members (usually called the "agreement among purchasers" or the "agreement among underwriters") whereby they agree to be rep-

[4] The Delaware Supreme Court has held that the typical "market out" clause does not render the underwriting agreement void for lack of mutuality, because the underwriters' "absolute judgment" means "a judgment based upon sincerity, honesty, fair dealing and good faith, not one evidencing caprice or bad faith." Blish v. Thompson Automatic Arms Corp., 30 Del. Ch. 538, 569, 64 A. 2d 581, 597 (1948).

resented in their negotiations with the issuer by one or two or three of their number, whom it is currently the style to call merely the "representatives of the underwriters." It is the latter who, as successors to the old originating bankers, take the initiative and run the show. Through them all the underwriters enter into a "purchase contract" directly with the issuer. In order to limit exposure under §11 of the 1933 Act,[5] the liability of each underwriter to the issuer is several rather than joint. The trend has been toward larger underwriting groups, whose members are more and more able to do their own distributing. For that reason, and because of the tremendous expansion of the retail capability of many of the underwriting houses, there has also been a tendency to deemphasize formal "selling groups."

Typically the underwriters authorize their representatives to reserve out of the syndicate account (the "pot") whatever amount of the issue the latter choose for sale to selling-group dealers — sometimes termed simply "selected dealers" — as well as institutional investors.[6] The dealers are usually selected by the representatives, or in any event approved by them if suggested by other members of the underwriting group. The degree of formality that surrounds the organization of the selling group (if there is one) or the selection of the "selected dealers" depends largely on the predilections of the representatives. Usually the dealers sign some sort of uniform "dealer offering letter" that is sent to them by the representatives.

The method of determining the participants of the several underwriters is by no means fixed. How much a particular house gets is apt to depend on its prestige, its capital, its distributing capacity, its geographical location, whether it has any special outlets (perhaps connections with large pension funds or the like), and frequently the issuer's wishes. The participation of a given house is not necessarily related to the amount it can distribute. Some houses join the group primarily as underwriters, with a view to making a profit out of assuming their shares of the risk, and they may give up most or all of their participations for sale by the representatives, for their account, to institutions and dealers. In other words, the amount reserved for such sale is not always prorated among the accounts of all the underwriters. Sometimes it is, but sometimes each member

[5] See p. 896 infra.

[6] Also in many debt issues underwriters arrange for "delayed delivery contracts" between institutional buyers and the issuer. These contracts relieve the underwriters from the obligation to buy the amount of securities that the contracts cover. The issuer assumes the credit risk of the institutions, and the underwriters are paid a commission in lieu of a spread with respect to those securities.

of the group indicates to the representatives what proportion of its share it would like to have for its own retail distribution. The portion that particular houses thus distribute at retail usually varies between 25 and 75 percent. Those underwriters who want more for their own retail distribution become "selected dealers." Not infrequently, too, the representatives reserve the right, in checking on the progress of the distribution, to take securities away from those underwriters that are slow and allocate them to members of the selling group whose distribution has been more successful. In any event, the representatives are obligated under the "agreement among purchasers" to notify each underwriter, on or before the public offering date, of the amount of its securities that has not been reserved for offering to institutions and dealers, so that the several underwriters will know how much they have to distribute.

As often as not the representatives are authorized, as the syndicate managers were before 1933, to "stabilize" the market on behalf of the underwriting group, although in practice the authority frequently remains unused especially in debt issues; this is a complex process (strictly regulated under the 1934 Act) whose purpose is to "peg" or put a floor under the market so as to prevent the overhanging supply of securities that are being distributed from depressing the market before and during the distribution.[7] There has also been a continuation of the practice whereby during the life of the underwriting syndicate all the underwriters and participating dealers make a concurrent public offering at a uniform price and at uniform concessions allowed by them to other dealers, although the representatives usually reserve the right to terminate price restrictions even during the life of the syndicate. The public offering price (within the limits negotiated with the issuer) and all dealers' concessions and discounts are determined by the representatives — usually with the concurrence of a specified proportion of the underwriters, and sometimes with discretion in the former (which is not customarily used) to change the price. Although the liability of each underwriter to the issuer is several, the members of the group

[7] On stabilization see p. 859 infra. Still another device for reducing the underwriters' risk is the practice of overalloting — that is to say, selling more shares than the underwriters are obligated to purchase. This creates a short position, which may help to establish a better after-market; for any shares resold by original buyers will in effect have been placed in advance through the overallotment sales. In addition, the underwriters are often given a "Green Shoe option," which has nothing to do with footwear but is named after a company: an option to buy additional shares from the issuer, or sometimes from selling shareholders, for the sole purpose of covering overallotments. There are usually maximum limitations with respect to the percentage of the offering that is subject to the option and the option's life.

are responsible for their proportionate shares of the underwriting expenses, including carrying costs, and they participate *pro rata* in the stabilizing account.

In recognition of the representatives' directing the whole process (like the old originating banker), they are usually paid, out of the gross spread on the entire issue, a management fee of perhaps one-quarter of a point on a bond or some fixed percentage of the spread. This fee, which is split if there is more than one representative, is beyond the regular concession on whatever securities they underwrite or retail for their own account. For example, the underwriters may buy a million shares of stock from the issuer at 23 and sell part of them to selected dealers at, say, 23.8 with a view to a public offering price of 25. The nonmanaging underwriters may allow the representatives 5 percent of their spread of .8. And the selected dealers may sell at a discount of one-quarter of a point (in other words, at 24 3/4) to any other dealer who is a member of the National Association of Securities Dealers (NASD) or frequently foreign dealers on certain conditions. To the extent that any underwriter sells at retail, it gets the entire spread of 2 points, less the management fee, the discount, if any, that it allows to dealers generally, and, of course, its share of the expenses of the syndicate. The spreads in this illustration are arbitrary. Depending on all the circumstances, particularly how much selling effort the issue is expected to require, the retailers may get either more or less than half of the entire spread. In general, their portion of the entire spread seems to have increased in recent years.

Two recent trends will bear watching:

(1) Although traditionally investment bankers that are required to take down unsold portions of "sour" offerings do not hold the securities long, some have recently been acting like their "merchant banking" counterparts abroad by investing their capital in leveraged buy-outs of established companies as well as funneling seed money into new venture capital companies. This development has not been without controversy in terms of the impact of such investments on the independence of the investment bankers' future financing advice to clients, as well as the impairment of their liquidity. (A buy-out of a company is "leveraged" when most of the purchase price is provided by newly arranged debt that the company itself will pay back and the remainder comes from equity investors who end up with all of the stock.)[8]

[8] See Bleakley, Wall St.'s Merchant Bankers, N. Y. Times, Nov. 19, 1984, p. D1; Sterngold, Wall St. Buys into the Action, N. Y. Times, June 19, 1986, p. 29. See also p. 500 infra ("junk bonds").

(2) The entire syndication procedure may be going the way of the elaborate pre-1933 system. Although 98 percent of common stock issues (measured in dollars) were syndicated as recently as 1981, by 1985 more than 30 percent were sold entirely by the managing underwriters. With 50-85 percent of even a syndicated deal going to institutional investors in the light of the increasing institutionalization of the market, syndication does not buy much extra distribution.[9]

So far we have been considering *negotiated* offerings, whether or not syndicated. In 1941 the SEC adopted Rule 50, a competitive bidding rule for underwritings (with some exceptions) under the Public Utility Holding Company Act. The ICC and a dozen states, including New York, have similar requirements for utility issues in at least some cases. And in one form or another competitive bidding has been the accepted method of financing for municipal and public instrumentality bonds since the beginning of the century, Massachusetts having led the way by statute in 1870. This method of underwriting is rarely used, at least for industrial common stock issues, when it is not required. But in total dollar amount it looms large.[10]

[9] Wall St. J., Feb. 24, 1986, p. 15. This is apart from the impact of Rule 415, the "shelf registration" rule. See p. 136 infra.

[10] Some years ago this method was followed by many utilities even though they no longer were subjected to Rule 50 or to a state regulatory requirement. With the phenomenon of highly volatile debt markets, however, the technique has proven in many instances to be very costly. As a result it is seldom used unless required by law, and even in those cases regulatory authorities have often granted exemptions.

In recent years a novel form of competitive bidding has made its appearance, the so-called Dutch auction:

> The Dutch auction differs in certain material respects from the practice of competitive bidding. Principally, the bids which are submitted need not cover the entire amount of the offering in order to be accepted. Each bidder, including institutions and individuals as well as registered broker-dealers, indicates the amount of the offering which is wanted, and the yield [which is a function of price and interest rate]. Each bid received will, on the final date designated for entry of bids, become an irrevocable offer to purchase the amount of bonds indicated unless the bid is withdrawn.
>
> In addition, the closing price is based upon the yields specified in the bids. After closing the invitation period, the bids are listed in ascending order of yields. The bid with the lowest yield is accepted first, and then other bids at successively higher yields are accepted up to those bids with the highest yield required to reach the total amount of the offering. The highest accepted yield is the yield at which all of the bonds are awarded. Upon determination of the yield, the interest rate and price are fixed by the issuer. The securities will be awarded to the successful bidders at a

Suffice it to say that competitive bidding works in much the same way as firm-commitment underwriting of the negotiated variety, except for the initial stage. The houses interested in a particular issue that is to be offered at competitive bidding organize their respective underwriting syndicates for the purpose of submitting bids. The manager of each bidding syndicate holds a meeting of the members to determine the price they will bid. Then the syndicate with the successful bid distributes in the usual manner.[11]

3. Best-Efforts Underwriting

Companies that are not well established are not apt to find an underwriter that will give a firm commitment and assume the risk of distribution. Of necessity, therefore, they customarily distribute their securities through firms that merely undertake to use their best efforts.[12] Paradoxically, this type of distribution is also preferred on occasion by companies that are so well established that they can do without any underwriting commitment, thus saving on cost of distribution. The securities house, instead of *buying* the issue *from* the company and reselling it as principal, *sells* it *for* the company as agent; and its compensation takes the form of an agent's com-

---

uniform price based upon the accepted yield.

Finally, there is no managing underwriter creating an underwriting syndicate, and no underwriting discount or commissions. There are no agreements entered into covering resale prices. As a result, prices can vary among resellers.

Exxon Corp., CCH Fed. Sec. L. Rep. ¶81,198 at 88,159 (letter 1977).

See generally Note, Auctioning New Issues of Corporate Securities, 71 Va. L. Rev. 1381 (1985).

[11] From the point of view of the structuring of the legal profession, it is interesting that issuers that are subject to Rule 50 follow the practice of designating independent counsel to act for the bidders with the understanding that they will be compensated by the successful bidders. After a special study the Commission early concluded that "the existing practice of designation by the issuer of independent counsel to represent the bidders will be permitted to continue, but that adequate disclosure of such matters as the identity of the independent counsel and the proposed fees of such counsel to be paid by the successful bidders will be required and close scrutiny will be given to the reasonableness of such fees and to the relationship of the independent counsel to the issuer." Holding Co. Act Rel. 3118 (1941).

[12] It must not be assumed that every promotional company can find even a best-efforts underwriter. The problems of financing "small business" are profound. See p. 305 infra. In the Small Business Investment Incentive Act of 1980 Congress amended the Investment Company Act to encourage the formation of "business development companies" ("venture capital companies," as they are known in the street) that would invest in new ventures, and also added an exemption in §4(6) of the 1933 Act (infra pp. 306-08).

mission rather than a merchant's or dealer's profit. There may still be a selling group to help in the merchandising. But its members likewise do not buy from the issuer; they are subagents. This, of course, is not really underwriting; it is simply merchandising.[13]

The term "best efforts" is used also in a broader sense to include all offerings through investment bankers, whether or not on an agency basis, otherwise than by "firm" agreements to purchase for resale. In this sense the term includes (1) offerings on an agency basis (through rights or otherwise) of high-grade securities not requiring underwriting, (2) offerings through purchases and resales by a dealer firm acting as principal but without any commitment to buy more than it can resell, or more than a specified portion of the offering, and (3) open-end investment company shares that are sold on a continuous dealer basis. Moreover, there are variations on the theme: In "all-or-none" underwriting, closing is conditioned on sale of all the securities; if they are not sold, the offering terminates and no subscriptions are accepted. In "minimum-maximum" underwriting, unless a specified minimum number of securities have been sold, the offering terminates; once the minimum is reached, the deal closes and the underwriters may nevertheless continue to sell any amount up to the maximum.

4. American Investment Banking in General

It should be apparent from what has been said that there is nothing immutable about the three general methods of distribution. The investment banking industry, being very much alive, is continually studying and developing new techniques. One generalization, however, is safe. The formal underwriters in this country are invariably investment bankers. Commercial banks and trust companies and their affiliated securities companies used to underwrite in large volume. But all companies engaged "in the business of receiving deposits" had to stop with the (somewhat less than complete) divorcement of commercial and investment banking in the Banking Act of 1933 (the Glass-Steagall Act).[14] Insurance companies, com-

[13] See Dale v. Rosenfeld, 229 F. 2d 855 (2d Cir. 1956).

[14] See 1 Loss 1189-90. On the Glass-Steagall philosophy generally, which is much debated currently, see Kurucza, Brokerage Activities and Investment Banking, in Practising Law Institute, Fifteenth Annual Institute on Securities Regulation (1984) c. 20; Comment, Securities Activities under the Glass-Steagall Act, 35 Emory L. J. 463 (1986); Investment Company Institute v. Federal Deposit Ins. Corp., 815 F. 2d 1540 (D. C. Cir. 1982). See also p. 219 n. 51 infra.

mercial banks, and, to a lesser extent, investment companies and other institutional investors do play a prominent part in the financing of many companies, particularly in the case of high-grade bonds. But they are not syndicate members as they once were in both England and America. They are commonly consulted by the investment bankers and have portions of certain issues reserved for them by the syndicate manager, as we have seen, so that they are in a sense silent partners in the syndicate. Or in many cases the issuer, instead of making a public offering, merely effects a "private placement" of its bonds (sometimes through an investment banker that obtains a commission of perhaps one point) with a number of institutional investors for their own portfolios.

With rare exceptions, the insurance companies, the largest investors of all, do not even bid for bonds that are offered competitively. This was one of the Government's complaints in its antitrust action against seventeen prominent investment banking firms — although Judge Medina ultimately found in 1953 that the Government had not proved its allegation that a number of large insurance companies had entered into a noncompeting agreement with most of the defendant firms at a series of meetings held in the office of the New York Superintendent of Insurance in December 1941, after three large life insurance companies had won a $90 million issue of American Telephone & Telegraph debentures.[15]

B. REGISTRATION AND PROSPECTUS PROVISIONS OF THE 1933 ACT

1. The Statutory Pattern

The 1933 Act is concerned primarily with *distributions.* Post distribution *trading* was to be the subject of further legislation, which turned out to be the 1934 Act.

The registration and prospectus provisions aside, there are only four sections in the 1933 Act that make conduct unlawful or actionable, and three of them may be disposed of summarily at this point: Section 17, which will be considered in a later chapter, is a general antifraud provision — applicable to the sale of all securities, whether registered or exempt from registration — that was a harbinger of what was to come the next year; and that section has a

[15] United States v. Morgan, 118 F. Supp. 621, 823-26, esp. 826 (S. D. N. Y. 1953).

civil liability analogue in §12(2). Section 23 prohibits misrepresentation with respect to the effect of registration. And §24 makes it a crime not only willfully to violate any other provision (§17 or 23 or 5, the registration section) but also willfully to include a misstatement or half-truth in a registration statement.

The entire balance of the statute serves merely to implement the central registration provision, §5. That scheme of involuted drafting does not facilitate comprehensibility. One begins, naturally enough, with §5 itself. But that section covers the universe: read alone, it makes it unlawful for a humble investor named John Doe ("any person") to use the mails or any means of interstate commerce to sell 100 shares of General Motors (or, for that matter, part or all the outstanding stock of Doe Corp., Doe's family business) to his friend, Richard Roe, unless a registration statement is in effect and he delivers a specified prospectus. But that can't be right: Doe was presumably one of the class to be *protected* by the statute, not *regulated.*

The answer lies in §4(1), which exempts "transactions by any person other than an issuer, underwriter, or dealer."[1] Doe seems to be in the clear, because the "issuer" is Doe *Corp.* and certainly Doe, one supposes, is neither a "dealer" nor an "underwriter." But slow down. These are all defined terms, and §2(11) makes an "underwriter" out of anyone (whether or not he owns a pair of striped trousers) who has purchased a security, "with a view to [its] distribution," either from the "issuer" or from anybody who is in a "control" relationship with the issuer; and, whatever "control" and "distribution" (which are *not* defined terms) may mean, (1) Doe may well be a controlling person of his family corporation, so that (2) Roe, if he contemplates a reoffering of the stock to the highest bidder he can find, may well be engaged in a "distribution" so as to become an "underwriter," with the result that (3) the §4(1) exemption is lost after all.

If this is not bad enough, Doe's lawyer will find that §5(c) prohibits any "offer" of a security unless a registration statement has been *filed*, and that §2(3) defines "offer" to include "every attempt or offer to dispose of * * * a security" — which is a far cry from

C. 2B [1]The 1954 and 1964 amendments require caution in considering pre-1954 literature. The principal purpose in 1954 was to permit offers, as distinct from sales, during the waiting period between the filing and the effectiveness of a registration statement, and this entailed adding a §5(c); the original Act made no distinction between the prefiling and waiting periods. Also, until 1964 what is now §§4(1), 4(2), and 4(3) was all §4(1) with three unnumbered clauses, and the present §4(4) was §4(2). Section 4(5) was added in 1975 and §4(6) in 1980.

what he learned as a first-year law student. And among other artificialities, he will discover that, when §5 refers to a "prospectus," that term, as defined in §2(10), includes any written communication that either offers or "confirms" the sale of a security.

The artichoke will have to be addressed layer by layer:

Section 5 was designed to place the facts before the investing public in two ways: First, adequate and accurate information in the form of a "registration statement" was to be made a matter of public record for a period of twenty days; this waiting or "cooling" period was to be used only to inform prospective investors about the issue and not to attempt to sell it. Secondly, underwriters and dealers were to furnish prospective investors with a prospectus based on the information in the registration statement. This is still the basic pattern of the statute, except that it was amended in 1954 to permit certain types of *offers* (but not *sales*) during the waiting period.

As amended in 1954, §5 is in three parts, which do not altogether coincide with the three stages in the registration process: the prefiling stage, the waiting period, and the posteffective stage.

Before a registration statement has been filed, §5(c), which was added in 1954, prohibits any use of interstate facilities or the mails to "offer to sell." Since that term is defined in §2(3) to include "every attempt or offer to dispose of, or solicitation of an offer to buy, a security or interest in a security, for value," it goes well beyond the common law concept of an offer. *A fortiori* it would be unlawful to *sell* or *deliver* a security in the prefiling stage even if the statute said nothing more. But §5(a) expressly prohibits sales or deliveries at any time before the *effective* date of the registration statement, which of course includes the prefiling stage. And the term "sale" is defined by §2(3) to include "every contract of sale or disposition of a security or interest in a security, for value."

During the waiting period between filing and effectiveness, §5(b)(1) prohibits the use of interstate facilities or the mails to transmit any "prospectus" unless it meets the requirements of §10, which prescribes the contents of the statutory prospectus. Since the term "prospectus" is defined by §2(10) to mean a *written* offer (with certain exceptions), there is no prohibition against *oral* offers (even by *inter*state telephone) during the waiting period as there is before filing. And, as we shall see, §§10 and 2(10) contemplate rules permitting the use of certain types of documents that are considerably less extensive than the full statutory prospectus. But §5(b)(1) prohibits the use of interstate facilities or the mails to transmit any other *written* offers during the waiting period; §5(a) prohibits the use of interstate facilities or the mails to *sell* or *deliver,* as in the prefiling stage; and §5(c) prohibits the use of interstate facilities or the mails even to make *offers* while any public examination or proceeding looking toward a "stop order" or "refusal order" under §8 is pending during the waiting period or, of course, while such an order is operative.

After the effective date sales may be freely made. But *offers* are limited by §5(b) as in the waiting period, except that the term "prospectus" is defined in §2(10) with a view to permitting supplementary selling literature (that is, literature accompanied or preceded by a full §10 prospectus) only *after* the effective date. In any event, the full prospectus must accompany any interstate or mailed *delivery* of the security under §5(b)(2) if it has not *preceded* delivery. And the actual *entry* of a stop order or refusal order bars the use of interstate facilities or the mails even to make *offers,* although the mere *pendency* of a proceeding or examination under §8 does not have this effect except during the waiting period.

Section 5 must be read in the light of the definitions contained in §2 and the exemptions contained in §§3 and 4. We have already noticed §4(1) and its interreaction with the definition of "underwriter" in §2(11) to bring *underwritten* secondary distributions in *control* situations within §5.[2] Now suppose Doe is a dealer in securities by profession, but it has been years since General Motors has issued any new securities. He must then look to §4(3), which exempts all "transactions by a dealer" (and the term "dealer" is defined in §2(12) to include a broker) *except* that (1) dealers that are participants in the distribution are subject to §5 for as long as it may take them to get rid of their unsold allotments or subscriptions and (2) *all* dealers (even those that have played no role whatever in the distribution proper) are subject to §5 for a minimum of forty days after the effective date (ninety days if securities of the issuer have not previously been sold pursuant to an earlier effective registration statement) unless the Commission shortens either period by rule or order.

This is the provision that indicates "that the act is, in the main, concerned with the problem of distribution as distinguished from trading."[3] Congress felt that there had to be some minimum post-effective period during which all dealers, whether members of one of the distributing groups or not, should be required to use a stat-

[2] See p. 88 supra. A primary distribution is a distribution of securities (including treasury shares) by the issuer, and a secondary distribution is a distribution of outstanding securities by their owner.

[3] H. R. Rep. No. 85, 73d Cong., 1st Sess. (1933) 15.

utory prospectus in order to avoid a particular dealer's claiming "that the securities he was offering for sale were not acquired by him in the process of distribution but were acquired after such process had ended"; and in 1933 Congress arbitrarily picked a period of one year "because, generally speaking, the average public offering has been distributed within a year, and the imposition of requirements upon the dealer so far as that year is concerned is not burdensome."[4] The period was reduced to a minimum of forty days in the 1954 amendments, and the 1964 amendments not only extended the period to ninety days for first registrations but also authorized the Commission by rule or order to shorten the forty-day period as well as the ninety-day period.

Then there is §4(2), which exempts "transactions by an issuer not involving any public offering."[5]

In other words, §5 (quite apart from the other definitions and exemptions) must be read as if it applied to *any transaction by an issuer or underwriter in connection with a "primary" distribution* (that is, a *public* offering) *by the issuer, or a "secondary" distribution by a person in a control relationship with the issuer, or any transaction by a dealer within forty* (sometimes ninety) *days after the beginning of such a distribution* (unless the period is shortened by the Commission) *or during such longer period as he personally may be engaged in distributing.* And even this statement must be limited by a clause in §2(3) that excepts from the definitions of the terms "offer" and "sale" any "preliminary negotiations or agreements" with underwriters. This has the effect of permitting the formation of the underwriting group before the effectiveness or even the filing of the registration statement, although there is no exemption for "offers" or "sales" by underwriters to selling group dealers.

The method and procedure of registration are specified in §§6 and 8, and the contents of the registration statement and prospectus are prescribed, subject to the Commission's rulemaking power, in §§7 and 10 and Schedule A of the Act (Schedule B in the case of securities issued by foreign governments). Under §8 the registration statement automatically becomes effective on the twentieth day after filing unless the Commission fixes an earlier date; the filing of an amendment before the effective date of the registration statement starts the twenty-day period running again unless the amendment is filed with the consent of the Commission (a process popularly called "acceleration"); and, if the registration statement is materially

[4] Id. at 16.
[5] See c. 5E infra.

deficient, the Commission, after notice and hearing, may at any time enter a stop order suspending its effectiveness, subject to judicial review in the appropriate Court of Appeals under §9.

Section 11 of the Act imposes civil liability on the issuer, its officers and directors, the underwriters, accountants, engineers, and other experts in the event the registration statement contains material misstatements or omits to state material facts; §12(1) imposes civil liability upon any person who offers or sells a security in violation of §5; and §12(2) imposes civil liability upon any person who offers or sells any security (whether or not registered) by means of material misstatements or omissions to state material facts. The rest of the statute contains investigation, injunction, criminal penalty, rulemaking, and a few miscellaneous provisions.

2. The Jurisdictional Base of §5

For constitutional reasons §5, as well as the antifraud provisions of §§12(2) and 17 and of the 1934 Act, refers (not always in the same connective language) to use of the mails or interstate commerce.

Although Congress, in the judicial atmosphere of the day, may have "meant to exert its power to the full constitutional extent permitted by the commerce clause and the postal clause,"[6] it now seems fairly clear that the jurisdictional base of the section could be constitutionally expanded so that it would apply to all steps in the process of selling — from offer to delivery and payment — if the mails or interstate facilities were used in any one step. And that is what the Code would do.[7] As it is, each of the five prohibitions in §5 stands alone so far as the jurisdictional base is concerned — and in this respect no change was effected by the 1954 amendments. Literally, that is to say, a dealer may offer or sell in any manner he likes, whether before filing or without a prospectus after filing, as long as he does not use the mails or interstate facilities to do so — even though they may later be used in sending a confirmation of the transaction or delivering the security. This is apart, of course, from the fact that *oral* offers are now permitted during the waiting period even by *inter*state telephone, as they always were after the effective date.

On the face of the statute it is thus possible to offer and sell

[6] Schillner v. H. Vaughan Clark & Co., 134 F. 2d 875, 878 (2d Cir. 1943).
[7] §1902(d).

without even a technical violation, either before or after effective registration, and deliver a statutory prospectus for the first time with the confirmation or the security — if, indeed, the mails or interstate facilities are used at that stage. This is hardly the kind of informed investing that was contemplated when the Securities Act was passed. A prospectus that comes with the security does not tell the investor whether or not he should buy. It tells him whether he has acquired a security or a lawsuit. As an English investment banker is said to have remarked, "What you chaps have is not a prospectus but a retrospectus."[8] Indeed, one may question whether the ordinary investor will examine the prospectus at all after skillful sales talk has already convinced him to part with his money. It is therefore irrelevant that the oral contract of sale may not be legally enforceable against the buyer, either because of the statute of frauds or because of difficulties of proof. The fact is that an investor who is psychologically committed is much less apt to study the prospectus than one who is trying to make up his mind.

For these reasons the Code would rationalize the prospectus delivery requirement by moving in two directions. When the issuer is a "one-year registrant" — which is to say, a company (under the Code's scheme of registering companies rather than securities) that has been registered, and hence is subject to the Code's continual reporting provisions, for at least a year — there would be no prospectus requirement at all except for sales out of underwriters' or selling group dealers' allotments or subscriptions.[9] On the other hand, with respect to securities of *non*-one-year registrants — which is to say, those new or relatively new to the marketplace — the buyer would have a privilege of disaffirmance for two business days after he had received a prospectus (or, during the waiting period a so-called "preliminary prospectus").[10]

All this is not to imply a grudging construction of §5 as it stands. It is now fairly well established in the lower courts (1) that the use of a common carrier or even a private car or one's own two feet to cross a state line suffices, since a highway or a bridge that joins two

[8] SEC, Disclosure to Investors (The Wheat Report) (1969) 106.

[9] §512(3). A company would register (1) on acquiring $1 million of assets and 500 security holders, (2) on the first "distribution" of its securities, (3) on becoming an investment company, or (4) on becoming a utility holding company (see Part IV); all four categories would then be equally subject to the continuous disclosure requirements of Part VI, except that investment and utility holding companies would be subject to substantive regulation under Parts XIV and XV; and today's 1933 Act registration statement would become a much simpler "offering statement" (see Part V).

[10] §504(b).

states (if not the vehicle or the pedestrian's feet) is a means of interstate commerce;[11] (2) that, on the rationale of the mail fraud cases, use of the mails or interstate commerce in *making payment* is their use "to offer" and "to sell" within the meaning of §§5(c) and 5(a)(1) on the theory that payment is an essential element of a sale and that the seller should reasonably have foreseen that payment might be made by one of the jurisdictional means;[12] and (3) that even the *intra*state telephone is a means or instrument of communication "in interstate commerce" notwithstanding the arguably broader reference in §10(b) of the 1934 Act, that statute's general fraud provision, to a means or instrumentality "of" interstate commerce.[13]

3. The Prefiling Period

Before we proceed further, a word of caution: Everything said in the remainder of this Chapter 2B, as well as Chapter 2C on the registration *procedure,* is subject to the still relatively recent adoption of Rule 415, which in certain circumstances permits registration "for the shelf" instead of the traditional registration for specified offerings to be made essentially forthwith.[14] However the practice

[11] E. g., MacClain v. Bules, 275 F. 2d 431, 433 (8th Cir. 1960); Hill York Corp. v. American Int'l Franchises, Inc., 448 F. 2d 680, 693 (5th Cir. 1971). The term "interstate commerce" is defined in §2(7) of the 1933 Act.

[12] E. g., Lennerth v. Mendenhall, 234 F. Supp. 59, 63 (N. D. Ohio 1964) (mailing a check was "indispensable to the whole transaction"); cf. United States v. Wolfson, 405 F. 2d 779, 783-84 (2d Cir. 1968) (selling broker's mailing of confirmation to *seller*). Under the mail fraud statute, see, e. g., United States v. Roylance, 690 F. 2d 164 (10th Cir. 1982).

[13] E. g., Lennerth v. Mendenhall, 234 F. Supp. 59, 63 (N. D. Ohio 1964); Clarence E. Thornton, 42 SEC 751, 753 n. 4 (1965); Ingraffia v. Belle Meade Hospital, Inc., 319 F. Supp. 537 (E. D. La. 1970); Loveridge v. Dreaugoux, 678 F. 2d 870 (10th Cir. 1982). *Contra*: e. g., Franklin Savings Bank v. Levy, 406 F. Supp. 40, 42 (S. D. N. Y. 1975), *rev'd on other grounds,* 551 F. 2d 521 (2d Cir. 1977). The fraud provisions of the 1933 Act, §§12(2) and 17, likewise say "in."

The affirmative cases are perhaps weakened by the 1975 amendment of the definition of "interstate commerce" in §3(a)(17) of the 1934 Act, but not §2(7) of the 1933 Act, to include "intrastate use of (A) any facility of a national securities exchange or of a telephone or other interstate means of communication, or (B) any other interstate instrumentality." Quite clearly that amendment merely codified existing law so far as Rule 10b-5 is concerned. Myzel v. Fields, 386 F. 2d 718, 727 n. 2 (8th Cir. 1967), *cert. denied,* 390 U. S. 951; Lawrence v. SEC, 398 F. 2d 276, 279 n. 2 (1st Cir. 1968); Kerbs v. Fall River Industries, Inc., 502 F. 2d 731, 737-38 (10th Cir. 1974); Aquionics Acceptance Corp. v. Kollar, 503 F. 2d 1225 (6th Cir. 1974); Gower v. Cohn, 643 F. 2d 1146, 1151 (5th Cir. 1981). Section 3(a)(17) was not mentioned in *Loveridge,* supra.

[14] See pp. 135–43 infra.

under that rule may develop, an exegesis of the historical norm is essential to an understanding of the "shelf" phenomenon.

a. Preliminary Negotiations with Underwriters

Before a registration statement has been filed, §§5(a)(1) and 5(c) prohibit the use of the mails or interstate facilities not only to sell the security but also "to offer to sell or offer to buy through the use or medium of any prospectus or otherwise." But §2(3) excepts from the definitions of the terms "sell" and "offer to sell," as well as the term "offer to buy" as used in §5(c), "preliminary negotiations or agreements between an issuer (or any person directly or indirectly controlling or controlled by an issuer, or under direct or indirect common control with an issuer) and any underwriter or among underwriters who are or are to be in privity of contract with an issuer (or any person indirectly or directly controlling or controlled by an issuer, or under direct or indirect common control with an issuer)." Before the 1954 amendments, when the prohibition against the use of the mails or interstate facilities to offer to sell or buy extended until the effectiveness rather than the filing of the registration statement, this exception was even more essential as a means of getting the distribution under way.

Just as the express exception for preliminary negotiations between issuer and underwriter was a clear indication that Congress intended in the original act to "delay the actual organization of the selling group and the disposition of the security to the dealers until the registration statement shall have become effective"[15] it should be equally clear now that the organization of the selling group must be delayed until the registration statement has been *filed.* In fact, it is clear from the legislative history that the "offer to buy" prohibition was originally inserted solely for the purpose of preventing *dealers* from making offers to buy from underwriters during the waiting period — or, as §5 has now been amended, before the filing of the registration statement. "Otherwise," the House committee observed, "the underwriter, although only entitled to accept such offers to buy, after the effective date of the registration statement, could accept them in the order of their priority and thus bring pressure upon dealers, who wish to avail themselves of a particular security offering, to rush their orders to buy without adequate con-

[15] H. R. Rep. No. 85, 73d Cong., 1st Sess. (1933) 12.

siderations of the nature of the security being offered."[16] In other words, an ordinary investor is not prohibited from making an offer to buy a security from the issuer or an underwriter or dealer before the filing date, although no person in these three categories may solicit or accept his offer or make any attempt to sell to him.[17]

Quite apart from the legislative history, any such offer to buy is exempted by §4(1) as a transaction "by any person other than an issuer, underwriter, or dealer"; for, even though the offeree is the issuer or an underwriter or dealer, the word "transactions" in the several exemptions under §4 is simply a shorthand term for offers (including offers to buy) and sales, which are all that §5 prohibits and consequently all that §4 needs to exempt from. Again, since §2(3) permits an issuer to make an offer to sell to a prospective underwriter before the filing date, there should certainly be no objection in principle to a prospective underwriter's approaching an issuer in the first instance with an offer to buy. When the issuer itself is making an offer to buy its own securities — at least when the offer goes to a substantial number of security holders — §5(c) would seem literally to apply in the sense that there is no specific exemption or exclusion; for that *is* an offer (and hence a transaction) "by an issuer." On the other hand, however tempting it might have been before the special legislation of 1968 to reinforce Rule 10b-5 under the 1934 Act by using §5(c) to attack the problems of inadequate disclosure by issuers in public tender offers, not merely the legislative history of §5(c) but the whole registration structure of the 1933 Act is utterly inconsistent with any concept of issuers' registering public offerings to buy.

Now that it is clear that the exception in §2(3) does *not* extend to negotiations or agreements *beyond* the underwriting level, there remains the question of what it does encompass. The juxtaposition of the word "preliminary" is somewhat ambiguous. Apparently it does not modify the word "agreements" — or perhaps it means merely that the agreements must be preliminary to the effectiveness of the registration statement — because the House committee report states that "Underwriting agreements can thus be entered into prior to the time of the filing of the registration statement."[18] In practice the SEC has not interfered with the making of firm contracts to sell between issuer and underwriter at any time. Indeed, it has always insisted on having the registration statement disclose

[16] Id. at 11.

[17] But see Morgan, Offers to Buy Under the Securities Act of 1933, [1983] Ariz. St. L. J. 809.

[18] Id. at 12.

the underwriting data before it becomes effective. But it is not common for the securities actually to be transferred to the underwriters until after effectiveness.

Since §2 introduces all the definitions by the phrase "unless the context otherwise requires,"[19] it is arguable that the "preliminary negotiations" clause, though it literally excludes from the definitions of "sell" and "offer to sell," should be treated like a §4 exemption so as not to extend to the fraud provisions.[20] At any rate, the Code cuts through the entire morass by simply exempting from the Code's successor to §5 "an offer or sale to an underwriter."[21]

b. "Beating the Gun"

The 1954 legitimation of "offers" during the waiting period substantially solved one important aspect of the old problem of "beating the gun." For there is no longer much pressure in the prefiling days personally to solicit and accept "indications of interest" — a euphemism for the making of "offers" in the statutory sense — in view of the few weeks that will be available for the making of "offers" while the registration statement is being processed. The aspect of the problem that survived the 1954 amendments was the practice that some issuers, underwriters, and dealers followed of "conditioning the market" before the filing of a registration statement through such devices as press interviews, speeches, special reports to stockholders, market letters, and so on. This is a problem that arises not only in the prefiling stage but also during the waiting period and even after effectiveness, because the *method* of offering is restricted at least as long as the distribution continues.

In 1969 the Commission had this to say:

> * * * the increasing obligations and incentives of corporations to make timely disclosures concerning their offerings raise a question as to a possible conflict between the obligation to make timely disclosure and the restriction on publication of information concerning an issuer which may have securities "in registration." The Commission believes that such a conflict may be more apparent than real. Events resulting in a duty to make prompt disclosure under the anti-fraud provisions of the securities laws or timely disclosure policies of self-regulatory organizations at a time when a registered

[19] See p. 245 infra.

[20] In any event, there is no reference at all to agreements with underwriters in the 1934 Act.

[21] §512(1).

offering of securities is contemplated are relatively infrequent and normally may be effected in a manner which will not unduly influence the proposed offering. Disclosure of a material event would ordinarily not be subject to restrictions under Section 5 of the Securities Act if it is purely factual and does not include predictions or opinions.[22]

And in 1971:

It has been suggested that the Commission promulgate an all inclusive list of permissible and prohibited activities in this area. This is not feasible for the reason that determinations are based upon the particular facts of each case. However, the Commission as a matter of policy encourages the flow of factual information to shareholders and the investing public. Issuers in this regard should:

1. Continue to advertise products and services.

2. Continue to send out customary quarterly, annual and other periodic reports to stockholders.

3. Continue to publish proxy statements and send out dividend notices.

4. Continue to make announcements to the press with respect to factual business and financial developments; i. e., receipt of a contract, the settlement of a strike, the opening of a plant, or similar events of interest to the community in which the business operates.

5. Answer unsolicited telephone inquiries from stockholders, financial analysts, the press and others concerning factual information.

6. Observe an "open door" policy in responding to unsolicited inquiries concerning factual matters from securities analysts, financial analysts, security holders, and participants in the communications field who have a legitimate interest in the corporation's affairs.

7. Continue to hold stockholder meetings as scheduled and to answer shareholders' inquiries at stockholder meetings relating to factual matters.

In order to curtail problems in this area, issuers in this regard should avoid:

1. Issuance of forecasts, projections, or predictions relating but not limited to revenues, income, or earnings per share.

2. Publishing opinions concerning values.

In the event a company publicly releases material information concerning new corporate developments during the period that a registration statement is pending, the registration statement should

[22] Sec. Act Rel. 5009 (1969). The exclusion here of "predictions" and "opinions" — as well as "forecasts" and "projections" in the later release of 1971 (infra) — is not affected by the Commission's later relaxation of its traditional hostility to profit forecasts in prospectuses and proxy statements. See pp. 162–64 infra. Paragraph 2 of the 1971 release (infra) excludes even "opinions concerning [present] values."

be amended at or prior to the time the information is released. If this is not done and such information is publicly released through inadvertence, the pending registration statement should be promptly amended to reflect such information.[23]

The issuer confronts still other §5 problems in the course of its corporate life:

(1) A corporation in need of additional capital requires a vote of shareholders to authorize additional shares, and those shareholders have preemptive rights.

(2) The same corporation is informed by a prospective underwriter that its interest is conditioned on a *waiver* of preemptive rights.

(3) A corporation would like to inform its shareholders of a contemplated rights offering — which, absent §5, would be the decent thing to do in order to avoid the possibility of some shareholders' selling their shares and missing out on the value of the rights.

(4) A prospective underwriter that wants to get rid of an outstanding issue of callable preferred that is overhanging the market insists that the stock be called, and the issuer, again out of a sense of sound shareholder relations, would like to inform its preferred shareholders when making the call that they will be given an opportunity to subscribe to a new issue for a limited time after the effective date of the registration statement.

The Commission interposed no objection to any of these practices. And today the answer is found in Rule 135, adopted in 1955 with respect to rights offerings and ultimately extended in 1970 to *all* offerings. That rule provides that a person proposing to make a public offering is not considered to make an "offer," so far as §5 is concerned, if the notice states that the offering will be made only by means of a prospectus and contains no more than six categories of information. But six does not mean seven: There is no reference to price, and a divided Second Circuit held that the announcement of a target company (Piper Aircraft) in a hostile takeover attempt by Chris-Craft Industries that a package exchange offer by a friendly third company (Bangor Punta) would be valued at "$80 or more" overstepped Rule 135 and violated §5.[24]

[23] Sec. Act Rel. 5180 (1971). See p. 98 n. 22 supra.

[24] Chris-Craft Industries, Inc. v. Bangor Punta Corp., 426 F. 2d 569, 574-75 (2d Cir. *en banc* 1970). A 1982 amendment permits information with respect to interest rate, conversion ratio, and subscription price, in the case of a rights offering of a security listed on an exchange or quoted in NASDAQ (see p. 600 infra), to be disseminated through the facilities of the consolidated transaction reporting system (see p. 692 infra) or NASDAQ or the Dow Jones broad tape if

On the other hand, Rule 135 does not exhaust the Commission's discretion. This is evident from a development under the 1968 addition of §14(d) to the 1934 Act in order to give the Commission jurisdiction over tender offers.[25] Sometimes two companies agree in principle to a merger, after which one of them (the "acquiring company") makes a cash tender offer for less than all the equity securities of the other (the "acquired company"), with the idea that, if the acquiring company does not obtain as many shares as it wants in the tender offer, stockholders of the acquired company may elect, before the vote on the merger, to receive cash in lieu of securities of the acquiring company. This presents something of a dilemma, in that the very disclosure of these merger negotiations that is required with respect to the tender offer pursuant to §14(d)(1) of the 1934 Act might be said to be a form of "gun-jumping" with respect to the securities of the acquiring company emanating from the subsequent statutory merger. But the Commission has released a staff letter reversing its affirmative position on that question.[26]

Dealers face similar line-drawing problems with respect to recommending, or including in their market letters, securities that are in registration. For them the Commission adopted a *series* of rules in 1970:[27]

> *Rule 137.* This new rule is designed to clarify the status of dealers not participating in a distribution. It permits publication and distribution by a dealer in the regular course of business of information, opinions, or recommendations regarding securities of a reporting company [under the 1934 Act] which has filed or proposes to file a registration statement under the [1933] Act.
>
> *Rule 138.* New Rule 138 permits a broker-dealer participating in an offering of non-convertible senior securities [that meet specified conditions, primarily a three-year reporting history under the 1934 Act] to publish opinions or recommendations concerning the issuer's common stock, and vice versa. [The rationale of this rule lies in the fact that the market for senior securities is largely institutional.]
>
> *Rule 139.* New Rule 139 permits a broker-dealer participating in an offering to publish at regular intervals, as part of a comprehensive list of securities, opinions or recommendations concerning the

---

the information is already disclosed in a registration statement on file. Rule 135(c).

[25] See c. 7E infra.

[26] United Technologies Corp., CCH Fed. Sec. L. Rep. ¶81,679 (letter 1978); Sec. Act Rel. 5927, 14 SEC Dock. 894 (1978). The acquiring company may not go beyond the disclosure required by §14(d)(1) by, for example, issuing press releases or granting interviews. Id. at 898; cf. Sheinberg v. Fluor Corp., 514 F. Supp. 134 (S. D. N. Y. 1981).

[27] Sec. Act Rel. 5101 (1970).

issuer provided it is a reporting company [under the 1934 Act or, as the rule was extended in 1984,[28] it meets the qualifications for one of the "blue chip" forms, S-3 or F-3,[29] and distributes the publication "with reasonable regularity in the normal course of business]." The opinion or recommendation, however, must not be given special prominence, and must not be more favorable than the last previous opinion distributed before the broker-dealer became a participant.

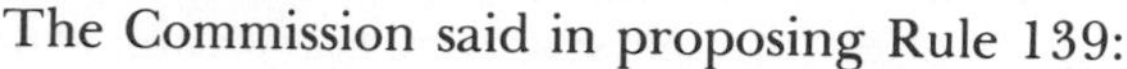

The Commission said in proposing Rule 139:

> Some relaxation of restrictions in this area appears necessary, particularly with respect to issuers which are continuously "in registration." Otherwise investors may be deprived of the broker-dealer's opinion when buying or selling securities in the trading markets.[30]

All this, however, is in a particular state of flux because of the "shelf registration" rule. For the time being, at least, the Commission is permitting research reports beyond Rule 139 until three business days before the commencement of sales.[31]

4. The Waiting Period

a. The Offer-Sale Distinction

Actual contracts of sale are still illegal under §5(a)(1) and not merely unenforceable if entered into before the effective date. But issuers, underwriters, and dealers should find no difficulty in so regulating their conduct during the waiting period as to avoid making "sales." Obviously no such person should make an offer in the common law sense that, if accepted by the buyer before the effective date, would create an illegal contract. And the acceptance of funds, or the segregation of funds held previously for a customer, would presumably be evidence of an illegal contract.

Perhaps the safest technique is to solicit offers to buy, which the seller can then accept after the effective date. But this is not the only possible technique. The 1954 legislative reports refer also to

[28] Sec. Act Rel. 6550, 31 SEC Dock. 454 (1984). This was incidental to the integrated disclosure system.

[29] See p. 147 infra. The Commission stated that the amended Rule 139 would apply to S-3 or F-3 registrants using the "shelf registration" rule. Sec. Act Rel. 6550, 31 SEC Dock. 454, 455 n. 10 (1984).

[30] Sec. Act Rel. 5010 (1969).

[31] Sec. Act Rel. 6383, 24 SEC Dock. 1262, 1294 n. 94 (1982).

the possibility of "conditioning offers."[32] An offer to sell that is conditioned merely on the effectiveness of the registration statement, and that is accepted on the same condition, might well be held to result in a contract to sell — a contract that is conditioned on effective registration, but still a contract and hence a violation of §5(a)(1). Nevertheless, since the offeror is the lord of his offer, he can presumably make a conditional and revocable offer to sell if it is made clear that the offer cannot be accepted until the effective date. Or he can simply "offer" in the statutory sense by soliciting "indications of interest" and state that no offer for a contract (in the common law sense) will be made until the effective date. The advantage of the latter procedure, which is the most common, is that there is no common law offer outstanding that the statutory offeror will have to revoke if he changes his mind before the effective date.

We turn now to a consideration of the several ways in which offers (in the statutory sense) may legally be made during the waiting period.

b. Types of Statutory Offers: Introduction

DISKIN v. LOMASNEY & COMPANY

United States Court of Appeals, Second Circuit, 1971
452 F. 2d 871

Before FRIENDLY, Chief Judge, FEINBERG, Circuit Judge, and DAVIS, Associate Judge.

FRIENDLY, Chief Judge. During the summer of 1968 plaintiff Diskin had conversations with defendant Lomasney, general partner of defendant Lomasney & Co., a broker-dealer, with respect to securities of two companies, Ski Park City West, S. I. and Continental Travel, Ltd. Lomasney & Co. had agreed to sell up to 60,000 common shares of the former on a "best efforts" basis and was the principal underwriter for the sale of 350,000 common shares of the latter. A preliminary registration statement with respect to the shares of Continental Travel had been filed with the Securities and Exchange Commission on August 28, 1968, but did not become effective until February 11, 1969. On September 17, 1968, Lomasney sent Diskin a final prospectus for the Ski Park City West, S. I., stock, along with a letter, the body of which read as follows:

[32] S. Rep. No. 1036 at 15 and H. R. Rep. No. 1542 at 23, 83d Cong., 2d Sess. (1954).

> I am enclosing herewith, a copy of the Prospectus on SKI PARK CITY WEST. This letter will also assure you that if you take 1,000 shares of SKI PARK CITY WEST at the issue price, we will commit to you the sale at the public offering price when, as and if issued, 5,000 shares of CONTINENTAL TRAVEL, LTD.

On the same day Diskin placed an order for the 1,000 shares of Ski Park City West and received a written confirmation. He later paid for these, and the validity of their offer and sale is unquestioned.

On February 12, 1969, Lomasney sent Diskin a confirmation of the sale of 5,000 shares of Continental Travel at $12 per share, apparently without any further communication. Diskin received from Lomasney a final prospectus and registration statement for these shares prior to February 28, 1969, when he paid the bill of $60,000, and received delivery. On November 19, 1969, Diskin demanded rescission. Having received no answer, he brought this action [under §12(1)] in the District Court for the Southern District of New York on January 6, 1970, claiming that the letter of September 17, 1968, insofar as it related to shares of Continental Travel, was a violation of §5(b)(1) of the Securities Act of 1933. * * *

[The District Court dismissed on the ground that the Continental portion of the letter came within the exclusion in the last sentence of §2(3).]

* * *

We have considered whether, despite the error in dismissing the complaint on this ground, the judgment could be affirmed on the basis that a registration statement concerning the Continental Travel shares had been filed prior to September 17, 1968, although it had not yet become effective. See §5(c). However, the mere filing of a registration statement does not ensure the legality of *any* written offer made during the post-filing, pre-effective period; to be lawful, such written offers must be made by way of a "prospectus" which meets the requirements of §10. See §5(b)(1). See also H. R. Rep. No. 1542, reprinted in U. S. Code Cong. & Admin. News, 83d Cong., 2d Sess. 2973, 2983, 2996-2997 (1954). We perceive no basis for disagreeing with Professor Loss' summary of the law in this respect:

> In sum, there are five legal ways in which offers may be made during the waiting period even if the mails or interstate facilities are used: by means of (1) oral communication, (2) the "tombstone ad," whether the old-fashioned variety under §2(10)(b) or the ex-

> panded type under Rule 134 (successor to the old "identifying statement"), (3) the preliminary prospectus under Rule 433 [issued pursuant to §10(b)][a] (successor to the "red herring prospectus"), (4) the "buff card" type of summary prospectus independently prepared under §10(b) and Rule 434, and (5) the summary prospectus filed as part of the registration statement under §10(b) and Rule 434a (successor to the old "newspaper prospectus" but not limited to newspapers).[b]

I Loss, Securities Regulation 243 (2d ed. 1961). See also Jennings & Marsh, Securities Regulation 89-92 (2d ed. 1968). The letter of September 17, 1968, was none of these. Indeed, the confirmation of February 12, 1969, was a further violation unless a prospectus had been furnished, see §§2(10) and 5(b)(1), which the agreed statement does not say.

We pass therefore to the arguments which defendants made in their memorandum, which the district court did not reach. These were (1) that the letter was not an "offer" but was a mere expression of willingness to sell; (2) that the violation was cured by Diskin's receipt of a prospectus prior to the actual purchase; and (3) that the action was brought more than one year after the violation and was thus untimely under §13 of the Securities Act.

Although there is a paucity of authority on these issues, we think none constituted a valid defense. The statutory language defining "offer" in §2(3) "goes well beyond the common law concept of an offer." I Loss, supra, at 181; cf. Carl M. Loeb, Rhoades & Co., Securities Exch. Act Release No. 5870, at 7-8 (1959); People v. Jacques, 137 Cal. App. 2d 823, 832, 291 P. 2d 124, 129-130 (1955). Consequently, we entertain no doubt that the portion of the letter of September 17 dealing with the Continental Travel shares constituted an "offer" within §2(3). Moreover, whether or not a dealer can lawfully "make a conditional and revocable offer to sell [without employing any of the five established procedures] if it is made clear that the offer cannot be accepted until the effective date," see I Loss, supra, at 224, the offer of September 17 did not measure up to that standard since it was not revocable. This case, where Lo-

[a]Ed.: Brackets are the court's. This rule was renumbered 430 in 1982.

[b]Ed.: In 1982 former Rules 434 and 434a were consolidated into Rule 431. See p. 110 infra. For an argument that the prohibition of other forms of advertising securities (without regard to fraud) violates the First Amendment in its application to commercial speech, see Schoeman, The First Amendment and Securities Advertising, 41 Bus. Law. 377 (1986); cf. Lowe v. SEC, 472 U. S. 181 (1985), infra p. 678.

masney apparently confirmed the sale without any further word from Diskin, would be a peculiarly unattractive one for endeavoring to carve out an exception to the statutory words. Indeed, as previously indicated, the confirmation, if unaccompanied by a prospectus, was itself a violation of §5(b)(1).

On the second point, we again agree with Professor Loss that "[w]hatever doubt there may once have been as to the applicability of §12(1) to illegal offers [followed by legal sales] was resolved when the original definition of sale was split into separate definitions of 'sale' and 'offer' in 1954, with the incidental amendment of §12(1) to refer to any person 'who offers or sells a security in violation of section 5' so as 'to preserve the effect of the present law' by not excluding the newly permissible pre-effective offers from liabilities under §12." III Loss, supra, at 1695-96. With respect to the one-year period of limitation, although §13 dates this from the "violation" in cases of claims under §12(1), it would be unreasonable to read §13 as starting the short period for an action at a date before the action could have been brought — a construction which might lead in some extreme cases to a running of the statute of limitations before the claim had even arisen. Furthermore, the limitation argument would be wholly drained of force if, as seems likely, the confirmation of February 12, 1968, was itself a violation.

The result here reached may appear to be harsh, since Diskin had an opportunity to read the final prospectus before he paid for the shares. But the 1954 Congress quite obviously meant to allow rescission or damages in the case of illegal offers as well as of illegal sales. Very likely Congress thought that, when it had done so much to broaden the methods for making legal offers during the "waiting period" between the filing and the taking effect of a registration statement, it should make sure that still other methods were not attempted. Here all Lomasney needed to have done was to accompany the September 17, 1968 letter with any one of the three types of prospectus for the Continental shares mentioned in the extract we have quoted from Professor Loss' treatise. Very likely Congress thought a better time for meaningful prospectus reading was at the time of the offer rather than in the context of confirmation and demand for payment. In any event, it made altogether clear that an offeror of a security who had failed to follow one of the allowed paths could not achieve absolution simply by returning to the road of virtue before receiving payment.

The judgment dismissing the complaint is reversed, with instructions to enter judgment for the plaintiff that, upon delivery of 5,000 shares of Continental Travel, Ltd., he shall receive $60,000 with interest from February 28, 1969, and costs.

c. Oral Offers

The only prohibition in §5(b)(1) runs to the use of a "prospectus" relating to a security with respect to which a registration statement has been filed unless the prospectus meets the requirements of §10. This makes it important to determine precisely what is meant by the term "prospectus" as used in §5(b)(1). The draftsmen of the statute employed two terms that must not be confused. Section 5(b)(1) refers to a "prospectus that meets the requirements of section 10" — the section that specifies (or permits the Commission by rule to specify) the contents of several types of prospectuses required or permitted to be used in connection with the registration process. They include the full, final prospectus (sometimes referred to as a complete or formal or statutory prospectus) as well as (for some purposes) the so-called "preliminary prospectus" and two types of summary prospectuses (all of which will be discussed later). On the other hand, §5(b)(1) also uses the one word "prospectus," and that term is defined in §2(10) to mean, with certain exceptions, "any prospectus, notice, circular, advertisement, letter, or communication, written or by radio or television, which offers any security for sale or confirms the sale of any security." Any writing that in fact offers a security for sale (in the statutory sense) comes within this definition, notwithstanding an attempted disclaimer to the effect that it is not to be construed as an offer to sell or that the securities are being offered only by a prospectus that will be furnished on request.

But there is another side to this coin. Since §5(b)(1) speaks in terms of a "prospectus," and that term is defined in §2(10) as an offer made in writing (or by radio or television), it is perfectly lawful to make *oral* offers at any time after the filing date even though they are not accompanied or preceded by a §10 prospectus. This has nothing to do with the jurisdictional base. A pre*filing* offer made by personal contact is legal only because it involves no use of the mails or of any interstate facilities. But after the filing date an oral offer may be made even by *inter*state telephone because an oral offer is in no case a "prospectus." It is in such a case — when there is an oral offer during the waiting period followed by a contract entered into orally either after the effective date or without use of the interstate telephone during the waiting period — that §5(b)(2), with its requirement that the *delivery of the security* be accompanied or preceded by a complete prospectus, becomes significant.[33]

[33] It does not follow that one may say anything he wants. For example, it is

d. The "Tombstone Ad" [§2(10)(b), Rule 134]

In any event, if any person subject to §5 does make use of the mails or interstate facilities to send a "prospectus" after the filing date, §5(b)(1) demands that the "prospectus" meet the requirements of §10. But there is an important exception to the definition. Section 2(10)(b) provides that "a notice, circular, advertisement, letter, or communication in respect of a security shall not be deemed to be a prospectus if it states from whom a written prospectus meeting the requirements of section 10 may be obtained and, in addition, does no more than identify the security, state the price thereof, state by whom orders will be executed, and contain such other information as the Commission, by rules or regulations deemed necessary or appropriate in the public interest and for the protection of investors, and subject to such terms and conditions as may be prescribed therein, may permit." The last clause, giving the Commission authority to expand the contents of the document by rule, was added in the 1954 amendments. Because of the format that advertisements took under the pre-1954 language — and still do for the most part —they are universally if somewhat mournfully known as "tombstone ads."[34]

The reason for the extreme strictness as to the content of the "tombstone ad" in 1933 was that it was not designed as selling literature. That was to be the function of the §10 prospectus. Section 2(10)(b) was designed to afford merely a device for screening out those prospective customers who might be sufficiently interested in the particular security to ask for a statutory prospectus. The rulemaking power was inserted in 1954 in view of "the wide variations in the types of issuers, securities, and offerings subject to the Securities Act" and was designed "to permit appropriate variation in the contents of such advertisements under such safeguards as

---

prudent not to admit the press to preeffective meetings but to limit attendance to representatives of sophisticated institutions and securities firms. Moreover, the information discussed should be consistent with what is contained in the prospectus. For one thing, not infrequently the SEC comment letter asks for the dates, times, places, and lists of all people attending all due diligence or information meetings, with a statement that what was discussed was within the confines of the information set forth in the prospectus. See Lovejoy, Initial Public Offerings: Prefiling and Pre effective Publicity, in Practising Law Institute, Thirteenth Annual Institute on Securities Regulation (1982) c. 21.

[34] Not infrequently the "tombstone ad" announces that the issue has already been sold. In that event its function is merely to advertise the underwriters rather than the security.

may be necessary in the circumstances."[35] But the Commission emphasized, in proposing the adoption of its Rule 134 in 1955, "that such communications are intended to be limited to announcements identifying the existence of a public offering and the availability of a prospectus and they are not to be selling literature of any kind."[36]

Rule 134 permits a document, without constituting a "prospectus," to include fourteen categories of information. But it does not permit the sender of the communication to solicit an indication of interest unless (1) the communication is accompanied or preceded by a §10 prospectus and (2) it contains a statement to the effect that until the effective date no offer can be accepted, no part of the purchase price can be received, any offer to buy may be withdrawn or revoked, and any indication of interest will involve no obligation or commitment of any kind. Nevertheless, it can only further the purpose of the statute and rule to include a detachable form, as is sometimes done, on which the recipient may simply request a copy of the prospectus (or before the effective date, the "preliminary prospectus," which will be examined next).[37]

e. The Preliminary Prospectus [§10(a), Rule 430]

The "tombstone ad" aside, the only offer in writing (or by radio or television) that §5(b)(1) permits in the waiting period is a prospectus meeting the requirements of §10. Section 10(a) governs the contents of the full statutory prospectus, and §10(b), which will be examined next, directs the Commission to adopt rules permitting the use of an abbreviated or summary prospectus for certain purposes. But the Commission has always had ample power elsewhere in §10 to add to or subtract from the contents of the full prospectus.[38] And, of course, §5(b)(1) as amended in 1954 permits the use of a §10 prospectus at any time after the filing date, not merely after the effective date as it had previously read. Consequently, without finding it necessary to advert to its new §10(b) power, the Commission in 1954 adopted Rule 433, renumbered 430 in 1982, to the effect that "A form of prospectus filed as a part of the

[35] S. Rep. No. 1036 at 13 and H. R. Rep. No. 1542 at 22, 83d Cong., 2d Sess. (1954).

[36] Sec. Act Rel. 3535 (1955).

[37] There is also a special Rule 134a for options material. See p. 235 n. 12 infra.

[38] §§10(a)(4), 10(c), 10(d).

registration statement shall be deemed to meet the requirements of section 10 of the Act for the purpose of section 5(b)(1) thereof prior to the effective date of the registration statement" if it contains substantially the information required to be included in the full prospectus under §10(a) "except for the omission of information with respect to the offering price, underwriting discounts or commissions, discounts or commissions to dealers, amount of proceeds, conversion rates, call prices, or other matters dependent upon the offering price." The caption "Preliminary Prospectus" and the following legend must appear in red ink on the outside front cover:

> A registration statement relating to these securities has been filed with the Securities and Exchange Commission but has not yet become effective. Information contained herein is subject to completion or amendment. These securities may not be sold nor may offers to buy be accepted prior to the time the registration statement becomes effective. This prospectus shall not constitute an offer to sell or the solicitation of an offer to buy nor shall there be any sale of these securities in any State in which such offer, solicitation or sale would be unlawful prior to registration or qualification under the securities laws of any such State.[39]

f. Summary Prospectuses [§10(b), Rule 431]

The new §10(b) that was inserted in 1954 provides:

> In addition to the prospectus permitted or required in subsection (a), the Commission shall by rules or regulations * * * permit the use of a prospectus for the purposes of subsection (b)(1) of section 5 which omits in part or summarizes information in the prospectus specified in subsection (a). A prospectus permitted under this subsection shall, except to the extent the Commission by rules or regulations * * * otherwise provides, be filed as part of the registration statement but shall not be deemed a part of such registration statement for the purposes of section 11. * * *

The exception from §11 liability was designed to encourage the use of summary prospectuses. Of course, any deficiency that carried through to the full §10(a) prospectus despite the Commission's processing would create liability under §11. Section 11(a) in any event extends liability only to any part of the registration statement that was deficient "when such part became effective." Consequently,

[39]This requirement now appears in Regulation S-K, infra p. 149, Item 501(c)(8).

§10(b) was not necessary in order to immunize from §11 liability in the case of summary prospectuses used before the effective date. Moreover, apart from the new suspension power in §10(b) itself, 10(b) prospectuses remain subject not only to the Commission's stop-order and other administrative powers under §8, but also to the general provisions of §§12(2) and 17(a), which impose civil and criminal sanctions upon a person who sells any security by means of fraud or half-truths. It seems odd, nevertheless, to exempt from civil liability under §11 the issuer and underwriters, who are responsible for what goes into a summary prospectus, but to impose civil liability under §12(2) upon the dealer, who will have to use a summary prospectus (if at all) as he finds it.

In 1982 a single Rule 431 replaced two old ones, Rule 434 for summaries prepared by independent statistical organizations and Rule 434a for summaries prepared as part of the registration statement if the particular form so provided. The present Rule 431, which likewise applies only if the particular form so provides, requires that summary prospectuses of both kinds be filed as a part of the registration statement. In any event, the rule is available only if the registrant has reported for the past three years under the 1934 Act and has had a default-free record since the end of the last fiscal year. A summary prospectus *must* contain whatever information is specified in the instructions to the particular form; *may* reflect other information contained in the registration statement or specified in Rule 134(a), the "tombstone ad" rule; may employ "such condensed or summarized form as may be appropriate in the light of the circumstances under which the [summary] prospectus is to be used"; and must be captioned a "Preliminary Summary Prospectus" when used before the effective date. There is a filing requirement as part of the registration statement in terms of five business days before use, subject to acceleration.

It must not be overlooked that summary prospectuses are considered to meet the requirements of §10 only for the purpose of §5(b)(1). That is to say, a summary prospectus meeting the requirements of the rule may be sent through the mails or interstate channels even before either a preliminary or a final statutory prospectus, but the rule does not affect the requirement of §5(b)(2) that the complete §10(a) prospectus precede or accompany any *delivery* of the security that is effected by use of the mails or interstate means.

In any event, summary prospectuses have not been widely used at least in recent years. Standard & Poor's Corporation, which used to be the prime user of the old Rule 434, in 1968 gave up its practice of summarizing filed prospectuses on folded-over cards and selling them in bulk to dealers for distribution to their customers during the waiting period. And — whether because of the cost of even a column or less in a national newspaper or because institutional investors, at least, want to see the entire preliminary prospectus — other summaries are rarely used except perhaps for some local offerings. Even so, the Commission included instructions with respect to summary prospectuses in the new forms it adopted in 1982.[40]

g. State Blue Sky Laws

Opening up the SEC waiting period in 1954 to offers aggravated a problem that had always existed under the blue sky laws, because most of the state statutes (including the Uniform Securities Act)[41] incorporate the pre-1954 federal formula of prohibiting offers and sales alike before effective registration. The Uniform Securities Act has a special exemption for "any offer (but not a sale) of a security for which registration statements have been filed under both this act and the Securities Act of 1933 if no stop order or refusal order is in effect and no public proceeding or examination looking toward such an order is pending under either act"[42] — leaving it to the federal statute and rules to regulate the types of offers. And there is a variety of "outs" in states that have not adopted that exemption, including (so far as offers to *dealers* are concerned) the quite common exemption (found in the Uniform Act)[43] for offers and sales to dealers.

5. The Posteffective Period

a. In General

Since §5(b)(1) as amended in 1954 applies to all transactions after the filing date, the waiting-period and posteffective problems substantially overlap. The permissible methods of offering are the same,

[40] See p. 146 infra. There is also a special rule for investment company advertisements in a newspaper or magazine or on radio or television. Rule 482. Use of the summary prospectus by itself is apart from the Commission's encouraging the inclusion of summaries as part of lengthy or complex prospectuses. See p. 127 n. 17 infra.
[41] §301.
[42] §402(b)(2).
[43] §402(b)(8).

except that (1) the "preliminary prospectus" under Rule 430 and the preliminary summary prospectus under Rule 431 are limited by their nature to the waiting period, (2) the full §10(a) prospectus is, of course, available, and (3) there is (as we shall see) one device, supplemental selling literature, that is peculiar to the posteffective period. But the big difference is that the effectiveness of the registration statement terminates the prohibition in §5(a) against using the mails or interstate facilities to *sell* or *deliver* the security.

b. Prospectus with Delivery or Confirmation

It is here that §5(b)(2) enters the picture for the first time: Unless the buyer has already received a complete §10(a) prospectus, it is unlawful to *deliver* the security through the mails or in interstate commerce without sending such a prospectus along with it. There is no requirement that the buyer must have received the full prospectus *from the seller himself.* But the seller would be wise to obtain a receipt for the earlier prospectus.

Moreover, the buyer's prior receipt of a *summary* §10(b) prospectus will not satisfy §5(b)(2), because the reference there is to "a prospectus that meets the requirements of subsection (a) of section 10" and Rule 431 applies expressly "for the purpose of section 5(b)(1)," not §5(b)(2). Nor will it suffice that the buyer received during the waiting period a *preliminary* 10(a) prospectus without price and related data; for Rule 430 similarly permits such a prospectus only "for the purpose of section 5(b)(1)." And a "tombstone ad" under Rule 134, expanded or otherwise, obviously is not "a prospectus that meets the requirements of subsection (a) of section 10"; it is not a "prospectus" at all. Indeed, even if the buyer has previously received a *complete* 10(a) prospectus, he must presumably be given another one with delivery of the security if in the interim the earlier prospectus has been changed so that it is no longer current.

Now suppose the seller mails a *confirmation* of the transaction before he mails the security. In 1941 the Commission's General Counsel expressed the opinion that the term "prospectus" as used in §5(b)(1) was defined in §2(10) broadly enough to include an ordinary confirmation.[44] Under this view, the net result of §§5(b)(2) and 5(b)(1) combined is that a full prospectus must precede or accompany delivery or confirmation, whichever *first* occurs by

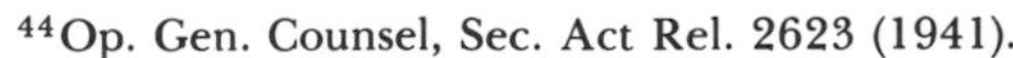

[44]Op. Gen. Counsel, Sec. Act Rel. 2623 (1941).

use of the mails or interstate facilities.[45] Whether or not this was an unduly broad reading of §2(10) as it then stood — and the interpretation was never formally challenged — it has now been codified by the 1954 expansion of the definition of "prospectus" in §2(10) to include any written communication that "confirms the sale of any security."

c. The Statutory Prospectus

The Second Circuit has held that "implicit in the statutory provision that the prospectus contain certain information is the requirement that such information be true or correct," so that a prospectus "does not meet the requirements of §10(a) * * * if information required to be disclosed is materially false or misleading."[46] At first blush this seems logical enough. Certainly one is not entitled to file an utterly inadequate document and have it considered a §10(a) prospectus. But *query:* There is no apparent need to find a violation of §5(b) when by hypothesis there is a more serious violation of §17(a), the fraud provision. And to consider *every* material defect to destroy the document's status as a §10(a) prospectus ignores an important distinction between the civil liability provisions of §§12(1) and 12(2). A violation of §5 creates strict liability under §12(1), whereas proof of a material misstatement does not entitle the §12(2)

[45] Since §5(b)(1) refers to a prospectus that meets the requirements of §10 — not, as does §5(b)(2), to a prospectus that meets the requirements of §10(a) — it may seem at first blush that a confirmation may properly be sent along with or after a *summary* prospectus. It is perfectly true that, since §5(b)(1) does refer broadly to a §10 prospectus and since a summary prospectus under Rule 431 does meet the requirements of subsection (b) of §10, mailing the summary prospectus as such would not violate §5(b)(1). But a confirmation is itself a "prospectus" as defined in §2(10) unless, under §2(10)(a), "a written prospectus meeting the requirements of *subsection (a)* of section 10" accompanies or has preceded it. (Italics supplied.) Hence the mailing of the *confirmation* would violate §5(b)(1) although the mailing of the Rule 431 prospectus would not. (This is perhaps as good an example as any of the need for some statutory simplification in this area.)

[46] SEC v. Manor Nursing Centers, Inc., 458 F. 2d 1082, 1098 (2d Cir. 1972); cf. Great Sweet Grass Oils, Ltd., 37 SEC 683, 694 n. 1 (1957), *aff'd per curiam* sub nom. Great Sweet Grass Oils, Ltd. v. SEC, 256 F. 2d 893 (D. C. Cir. 1958) (reporting requirement under Sec. Ex. Act §13(a) "necessarily embodies the requirement that such reports be true and correct"); GAF Corp. v. Milstein, 453 F. 2d 709, 720 (2d Cir. 1971) (ownership reports under Sec. Ex. Act §13(d)).

plaintiff to a judgment if the defendant sustains his reasonable care defense.[47]

d. Supplementary Selling Literature

We have seen that §5(b)(1) prohibits the use of the mails or interstate facilities to send any non-§10 "prospectus" after the *filing* date, and that the term "prospectus" is defined in §2(10) to mean, in substance, any written offer. There are two exceptions to this definition. One is the provision in §2(10)(b) for the "tombstone ad," which may be used at any time after the *filing* of the registration statement. The other appears in §2(10)(a), which provides that "a communication sent or given *after* the effective date of the registration statement (other than a prospectus permitted under subsection (b) of section 10)[48] shall not be deemed a prospectus if it is proved that prior to or at the same time with such communication a written prospectus meeting the requirements of subsection (a) of section 10 at the time of such communication was sent or given to the person to whom the communication was made." The purpose of this clause is to permit the use of supplementary selling literature *after* the effective date if it goes along with or follows the full §10(a) prospectus but does not precede it. It need not be filed so far as the 1933 Act is concerned.[49] But §24(b) of the Investment Company Act requires the filing of selling literature of investment companies

[47] Similarly, so far as the 1934 Act is concerned, an action (including a private action if implied) for *failure* to file might avoid the scienter element in an action for a *false* filing under §18(a) or Rule 10b-5. And both §24 of the 1933 Act and §32(a) of the 1934 Act make it a crime willfully (and knowingly in the case of the 1934 Act) to make any materially false statement in a filing under those statutes.

The view expressed in the text was followed in SEC v. Southwest Coal & Energy Co., 624 F. 2d 1312, 1317-19 (5th Cir. 1980); see also SEC v. Blazon Corp., 609 F. 2d 960, 968-69 (9th Cir. 1979); Jefferies & Co. v. United Mo. Bank of Kansas City, CCH Fed. Sec. L. Rep. ¶99,257 at 96,145 (W. D. Mo. 1983).

[48] The parenthetical clause was presumably inserted in the 1954 amendments because of the peculiar language of §12(2), which imposes civil liability for misstatements in "a prospectus or oral communication."

[49] The NASD spot checks. In addition, it requires its members to file their sales literature with the Association within ten days *after* use. Advance filing is optional, except that a member that has not previously filed with the Association (or an exchange that has comparable standards) *must* file within ten days *before* use (1) until he has done so for a year or (2) on a determination by a District Business Conduct Committee that there is a reasonable likelihood that the member has departed and is reasonably likely to depart again from the "fair dealing" standards of the NASD's rule. NASD Rules of Fair Practice, Art. III, §35(a)-(c), CCH NASD Manual ¶2195.

(other than those of the closed-end type) within ten days *after* its use.[50]

e. Delivery to Buyer's Broker

Is delivery of a prospectus to the buyer's *broker* sufficient compliance with §5(b) by the seller and his broker even though the buyer's broker never delivers the prospectus to his principal? Presumably it is if the buyer's broker is authorized or otherwise empowered under general principles of agency law to receive delivery.

In the case of transactions effected on a stock exchange a Commission rule excuses the selling member (that is, the seller's broker) from delivering a prospectus in the usual way to the buying member (that is, the buyer's broker) if during the forty-day period the issuer or an underwriter has complied with requests made by the exchange from time to time to deliver to the exchange as many copies of the full prospectus as appear reasonably necessary to comply with the requests of its members and if the exchange delivers a copy to any member on his written request.[51] However, since Rule 174[52] excuses the prospectus delivery requirement altogether during the forty-day period with respect to issuers that are reporting companies under the 1934 Act (as all companies with securities listed on an exchange are), Rule 153 is significant only so long as there are unsold allotments.[53]

Whether the buyer's broker (in a transaction on or off an exchange) is himself under a statutory duty to deliver the prospectus to his principal will depend, within the forty-day period, on whether or not he has done any soliciting. A buyer's broker who has not solicited the buy order does not "*sell*" to the buyer even within the broad definition in §2(3); he *buys for* him. Hence he is not covered by §5.

[50]The statutory fraud provisions apply, of course, and in 1979 the SEC adopted an interpretative rule for investment company sales literature (Rule 156) that replaced a considerably more detailed "Statement of Policy." The reason for the shift was to emphasize the industry's principal responsibility in the area. See Sec. Act Rel. 6140, 18 SEC Dock. 801 (1979). Then in late 1986 the Commission solicited comment with respect to new rules, as well as amendments to several rules and forms under both Acts, affecting the advertising of mutual funds and insurance company separate accounts offering variable annuities. Sec. Act Rel. 6660, 36 SEC Dock. 659 (1986).

[51]Rule 153. This has been called a "formal genuflection." Cohen, "Truth in Securities" Revisited, 79 Harv. L. Rev. 1340, 1351 (1966).

[52]See p. 117 infra.

[53]See pp. 90-91 supra.

f. The Dealers' Exemption

(*i*) *In general:* Transactions by the issuer or an underwriter are always subject to §5(b) whenever they occur. But what dealers are subject to the prospectus requirement and for how long? We have already noticed the requirement in the original Act (now Clause (B) of §4(3)) that all dealers, whether or not engaged in the distribution in the usual sense, comply with the prospectus provisions with respect to all transactions for one year after the first public offering of a registered security — a period arbitrarily selected as marking the line between distribution and post-distribution trading — as well as the further requirement (now in Clause (C)) that dealers participating in the distribution comply with the prospectus provision for as long as it might take them to get rid of their unsold allotments or subscriptions. We have noticed also the reduction of the arbitrary period to forty days in 1954 and its 1964 extension to ninety days for first offerings, with authority in the Commission to shorten either period by rule or order.[54]

Although it was assumed that most offerings would begin during the waiting period, it was contemplated that an occasional offering might be postponed on account of market conditions or otherwise for some time after the effective date. For this reason what is now Clause (B) was reworded in the 1954 amendments so as to subject *all* dealers to the prospectus provision for forty days after the effective date or forty days after the posteffective offering to the public by the issuer or by or through an underwriter, whichever occurs later.

If the draftsmen had stopped here, however, dealers generally might never have been able to begin lawful trading in securities that had been illegally offered to the public without registration; or perhaps, anomalously, the statute would have been read literally to exempt dealers' transactions *immediately* after an illegal public offering. This made it necessary to insert another clause (now (A)) in order to make the dealers' exemption applicable forty days after "the first date upon which the security was bona fide offered to the public by the issuer or by or through an underwriter" without the filing of a registration statement. Clause (A) is not limited in so many words to transactions after illegal public offerings. But the language in question, apart from barring dealers' transactions immediately after an *exempt* public offering, could serve no other pur-

[54] Ibid.

pose, and the legislative history makes it clear that the purpose was as here described.[55]

The forty-day and ninety-day periods do not apply to a dealer still acting as an underwriter, since §4(3) exempts only transactions by dealers *qua* dealers and not transactions by dealers *qua* underwriters. At the same time, the exemption applies by its terms to a transaction by "an underwriter no longer acting as an underwriter in respect of the security involved in such transaction."

In 1964 the Commission exercised its new rulemaking authority in §4(3) by adopting Rule 174. Subject to the dealer's overriding obligation to deliver a prospectus while acting as an underwriter or disposing of an allotment or subscription, as well as the statutory exclusion of any stop-order interval in computing the prospectus-delivery period, the rule affords a number of dispensations:

(1) The statutory periods are waived altogether if the issuer was a reporting company under the 1934 Act immediately prior to the filing of the registration statement[56] or the registration statement covers American depositary receipts or voting trust certificates without registration of the underlying securities. (2) When a registration statement relates to offerings to be made from time to time — in the case of so-called shelf registrations — no new period applies for dealers trading after the period of forty or ninety days following the *first* offering for the account of any person under the registration statement. (3) The rule also preserves the Commission's authority under §4(3) to vary the statutory periods on application or on its own motion; and the Commission has delegated this authority to the Director of the Division of Corporation Finance, along with authority to reduce either the ninety-day or the forty-day period.

Finally, in order to inform dealers more readily of their obligation to deliver a prospectus, there must be a statement in bold face

[55] S. Rep. No. 1036 at 14 and H. R. Rep. No. 1542 at 22, 83d Cong., 2d Sess. (1954); see Sec. Act Rel. 4726 (1964) 2 n. 3; Atkin v. Hill, Darlington & Grimm, 15 A. D. 2d 362, 370 n., 224 N. Y. S. 2d 553, 561 n. 1 (1st Dept. 1962), *aff'd per curiam* 12 N. Y. 2d 940, 188 N. E. 2d 790 (1963).

[56] In December 1986 the Commission solicited comment on alternative proposal to extend the exemption. The first would (1) eliminate the delivery period for transactions in "reported securities" meeting specified size, public float, and operating history criteria, and (2) reduce the period to twenty-five days for transaction in "reported securities" not meeting one or more of those criteria. The second proposal, advanced by the Securities Industry Association, would apply the twenty-five-day period to cases where the issuer, as of the *effective* date of the registration statement, was listed on an exchange or authorized for quotation in something like NASDAQ. "Reported securities" are those included in the Consolidated Tape Association transaction reporting system or NASDAQ securities designated for trading in the National Market System (see c. 8F infra). Sec. Act Rel. 6682, 37 SEC Dock. 260 (1986).

or italic type on the inside front or outside back cover page of the prospectus stating the date on which the relevant statutory period will expire.[57]

(ii) Investment company securities: As part of the 1954 legislative program, §24(d) of the Investment Company Act was amended to require, in effect, that all dealers in investment company securities of the types that are continually being offered (namely, securities issued by face-amount certificate companies or redeemable securities issued by open-end management companies or unit investment trusts) be subject to the prospectus provisions as long as any security of the same class as the registered security is being offered. Because such companies normally registered once a year under the original Act, the one-year period during which all dealers had to use prospectuses was continually being renewed. If the reduction to forty days had applied in this context, independent dealers engaged in making a market for such shares would have been subject to the prospectus requirements for only forty days in each year, whereas dealers engaged in the distribution would always have had to use prospectuses.

This possibility was neither desirable in the public interest nor relished by the investment companies, which had to think of the competitive disadvantage it would entail for their regular distributors. Consequently, §24(d) was amended to provide that the dealers' exemption in the Securities Act does not apply to any transaction in an investment company security of any of the types here referred to "if any other security of the same class is currently being offered or sold by the issuer or by or through an underwriter in a distribution which is not exempted from section 5." At the same time, in order to mitigate any discrimination that might be suffered by independent dealers who should be unable to obtain prospectuses from the issuer or an underwriter, §24(d) was drafted to give the Commission power by rule to extend the dealers' exemption "with respect to any class of persons, securities, or transactions."

There is also a Rule 135a, which is directed to the problem of generic advertising. An advertisement or communication (normally by a booker or dealer looking for business) that does not refer specifically by name to a particular investment company or its securities (or to any nonexempted securities) is not considered to offer any security for sale if it is limited to specified categories of information with respect to investment companies generally.

[57] Reg. S-K, Item 502(e).

g. Offering of Additional Securities of an Outstanding Class

Not infrequently an issuer registers and distributes additional securities of a class already outstanding. A corporation, for example, has a million shares of common stock that have been outstanding and traded on a stock exchange or over the counter for years, and it issues an additional 300,000 shares. Or perhaps one of its controlling persons dies and his executor has to sell a large block of stock to meet estate taxes, so that a registration statement is filed for that purpose. Common sense tells us that a certificate for 100 shares of the old stock and a certificate for 100 shares of the new (or of the control block) are as fungible as two bushels of September wheat or two one-dollar bills. And so the law treats securities of the same class for most purposes. But not the Securities Act. Any dealer who sells one of the *new* shares within the statutory periods must use a prospectus. There is no warrant in the Act for excepting such a transaction merely because like securities are already outstanding. If the dealer is sure he is selling one of the *old* shares, on the other hand, there is likewise no warrant in the Act for subjecting him to the prospectus requirement just because additional shares of the same class have recently been distributed. But as a practical matter how is he to tell? Even if the old and new certificates are distinguished by serial numbers, ready differentiation is incompatible with the realities of securities trading. Over-the-counter dealers, for example, customarily solicit and obtain buy orders for securities that they do not carry in inventory, and then go out and acquire them in the market. How can a dealer tell when he solicits his customer's buy order whether he will be delivering a new or an old security? In the one case his solicitation must comply with §5(b)(1); in the other case it need not.[58]

The short answer is that the only thing the dealer can do is play safe and comply with §5(b) in all his trading for the applicable period. This is not an altogether satisfactory solution. When the new issue is a fraction of the size of the old — perhaps a relatively small secondary distribution — to subject all trading to the prospectus requirement for the statutory period is definitely a case of tail wagging dog. But the problem is not nearly so serious as it was when dealers had to use prospectuses for an entire year, particularly in the light of Rule 174.[59] Under the present statutory framework, moreover, there seems to be no complete solution short of elimi-

[58] Cf. Barnes v. Osofsky, 373 F. 2d 269 (2d Cir. 1967), infra p. 904 n. 69.
[59] See pp. 116–18 supra.

nating any arbitrary period altogether, which would be a case of avoiding tail-wag-dog at the price of having baby-thrown-out-with-the-bath.

C. THE REGISTRATION PROCEDURE

1. A Study in Administrative Technique

a. The Statutory Pattern

If an experienced English company law solicitor were asked for the first time to examine the 1933 Act and describe how the registration machinery worked, this is what he would say: "Under §§6 and 7 one files with the SEC something called a 'registration statement,' which contains information specified by Commission rule, is accompanied by a filing fee, and is signed by specified persons. Under §8(a) there is a twenty-day waiting period between filing and effectiveness, and the filing of a preeffective amendment starts the twenty-day period running again, unless in either case the Commission declares otherwise.[1] Apparently the Commission examines the registration statement, because §8(d) provides for something you chaps call a 'stop order' to prevent effectiveness if the Commission concludes after some sort of hearing that the registration statement is materially deficient. And under §9 a stop order may be reviewed, on a substantial evidence basis, in one of your Courts of Appeals, subject to further review on certiorari in the Supreme Court."

This is a perfectly accurate description. But, if the Commission had followed this procedure literally, the Act would have been a disaster, especially during the period from 1933 to 1954 when §5 prohibited "offers" as well as sales during the waiting period. It required four great administrative inventions — monuments to the vaunted flexibility of the administrative process — to make the Act work.

C. 2C [1]The Commission's giving its "consent" under §8(a) to the filing of an amendment (it never exercises its "order" power under that section) is popularly called "acceleration."

b. The "Red Herring" Fiction

Section 5 was based on a conceptual dilemma that plagued both Commission and industry for twenty-one years. Although any form of preeffective solicitation by use of the mails or interstate facilities was categorically forbidden, the whole theory of the waiting period was that the information contained in the registration statement would be disseminated so that the investing public would be able to make an intelligent determination whether to buy when the statement became effective. This "cooling" period as it was known — something not found in the English model — reflected Congress's view that the process of distribution must be slowed down:

> The compulsory 30-day inspection period before securities can be sold is deliberately intended to interfere with the reckless traditions of the last few years of the securities business. It contemplates a change from methods of distribution lately in vogue which attempted complete sale of an issue sometimes within 1 day or at most a few days. Such methods practically compelled minor distributors, dealers, and even salesmen, as the price of participation in future issues of the underwriting house involved, to make commitments blindly. This has resulted in the demoralization of ethical standards as between these ultimate sales outlets and the securities-buying public to whom they had to look to take such commitments off their hands. This high-pressure technique has assumed an undue importance in the eyes of the present generation of securities distributors, with its reliance upon delicate calculations of day-to-day fluctuations in market opportunities and its implicit temptations to market manipulation, and must be discarded because the resulting injury to an underinformed public demonstrably hurts the Nation. It is furthermore the considered judgment of this committee that any issue which cannot stand the test of a waiting inspection over a month's average of economic conditions, but must be floated within a few days upon the crest of a possibly manipulated market fluctuation, is not a security which deserves protection at the cost of the public as compared with other issues which can meet this test.[2]

But how was dissemination to be distinguished from solicitation? An underwriter with a firm commitment — or a dealer who hoped to have a firm commitment immediately upon effectiveness — was apparently expected to disseminate information without in any way puffing his wares. Salesmen, however, are not educators, and the

[2] H. R. Rep. No. 85, 73d Cong., 1st Sess. (1933) 7-8. The thirty-day period was reduced to twenty before passage.

concept of a reluctant salesman soon proved to be as chimerical as the dream of a nation without a thirst.

Nevertheless, the administrators of the statute had a job to do. Consequently, before the Act was many months old, the Federal Trade Commission (which administered the 1933 Act until the SEC was created by the 1934 Act) took a hint from the report of the House committee and issued a release to the effect that, although the making and acceptance of offers conditioned upon the effectiveness of the registration statement "would obviously fly in the face of the general purposes of the Act," it would be permissible during the waiting period, and indeed would carry out the general purposes of the statute, for an issuer or underwriter to distribute circulars that described the security as in a §10 prospectus but were "clearly and unmistakably marked to indicate that they are informative only, negativing without equivocation either impliedly or expressly an intent to solicit offers to buy or to make an offer to sell."[3]

This release was the origin of the so-called "red herring prospectus" — a document that got its name from a legend superimposed on each page to the effect that a registration statement had been filed with the SEC but had not yet become effective, that the information in the circular was subject to correction and change without notice, that under no circumstances was the circular to be considered an offer to sell or a solicitation of an offer to buy, and that no offer to buy or sell should be made and no order would be accepted until the effective date of the registration statement. This is now history, except that the "red herring prospectus" was the seed of today's "preliminary prospectus" under Rule 430 and, although one no longer has to indulge in the "red herring" fiction since the 1954 legalization of waiting period offers, these documents are still referred to quite commonly as "red herring prospectuses."[4]

c. The Letter of Comment

In practice the heavy artillery of §8(d) is reserved for flagrant cases.[5] Instead, without benefit of specific statutory authority, the

[3] Sec. Act Rel. 70 (1933); see H. R. Rep. No. 85, 73d Cong., 1st Sess. (1933) 12-13.

[4] See p. 108 supra. Of the many treatments of the "red herring prospectus," one deserves mention if only because of its title. Kennedy, Labor Pains in the Birth of a Red Herring, 34 U. K. C. L. Rev. 198 (1966).

[5] A stop order proceeding may be initiated "at any time," either before or after the effective date. The Commission has never used the alternative preef-

Commission early developed a very workable examination procedure. For many years every registration statement was examined by the security analysts, lawyers, and accountants in one of the branches of what is now called the Division of Corporation Finance. Except for some companies that have repeatedly registered earlier offerings, relatively few registration statements are found to be in entirely acceptable shape when they are filed.

In the overwhelming majority of cases, however, no thought is given to the institution of a formal proceeding. Instead, the examining branch drafts a letter of comment (originally, and more candidly, called a "deficiency letter") specifying the respects in which it appears that the registration statement is deficient. Non-routine letters are reviewed by an Assistant Director of the Division in order to coordinate the work of the several branches, and novel questions of policy may be considered by the Director or Associate Director or the entire Commission. The staff is available for personal or telephonic conferences after receipt of the letter of comment.[6] Almost invariably an amendment is filed, and it is unnecessary to resort to formal proceedings against the registration statement. Amendments are examined in the same manner as the registration statement, and sometimes a further letter of comment and one or more additional amendments are required.

If the statement could not be appropriately amended within the statutory twenty-day period, the issuer used to be asked to file a simple "delaying amendment" by telegram or letter, which served under §8(a) to start the twenty-day period running again. But Rule 473, which prescribed that procedure, was amended in 1961 to make available an optional procedure, usually followed, whereby a single filing serves in effect as a series of constructive delaying amendments until the Division is satisfied with the registration statement.

In 1968, because of the logjam caused by increased volume of filings, the Commission announced an "emergency" procedure

---

fective procedure under §8(b).

With the recent increase in filings (40 percent to a record of 6100 in fiscal 1983) the number of stop order proceedings has also gone up. See McLucas, Stop Order Proceedings under the Securities Act of 1933: A Current Assessment, 40 Bus. Law. 515 (1985). That writer (id. at 518 n. 20) corrects the present author's "never" by citing two early "refusal order" proceedings. Gold Producers, Inc., 1 SEC 1, 18 FTC 619 (1933); cf. International Investors Fund System, Inc., 1 SEC 461 (1936).

[6] *Prefiling* conferences, which have grown rare with an overburdened staff, come at a price: once a question has been asked in advance of a filing, there may be no practical alternative to waiting for the answer, which can delay a filing considerably.

whereby, after a cursory review by a staff officer, counsel would be advised in one of three ways (later increased to four): (1) that the registration statement was so poorly drafted or otherwise presented problems so serious that no further review would be made (a hint that the registration statement should be withdrawn); (2) that the staff had made only a cursory review and would provide no written or oral comments; (3) that limited comments would be given; or (4) that the filing would be subject to the regular review process.[7] The time saving was dramatic. In June and July 1969 about 40 percent of the registration statements received expedited or summary treatment, and for them the median time between filing and notification of either minor comment or none was 8 days, in contrast to 49 days between filing and comment letter with respect to those registration statements that got regular treatment.[8] Then in late 1980 the Commission went over to a concept of what it calls "selective review": All first-time registrants, but only about 5 percent of repeat registrants, receive a thorough review. Certain others are not reviewed at all. The registrant is notified within two or three days after the filing whether its registration statement will be reviewed. If not, it will become effective at any time more than forty-eight hours after filing that the registrant requests.[9]

To be sure, there is another angle to all this informality from the point of view of the science of government. Although in theory the Commission's staff merely "suggests" amendments, the practicalities of financing do not allow any real alternative to complying. The privilege of testing the staff's views by defending a stop-order proceeding is an expensive one in terms of the success of the financing. And, although the Commission's final order is subject to judicial review, a court proceeding that may take a year or more is hardly a realistic way to determine whether a company in need of financing is right in insisting that a particular item of information may properly go in the footnotes rather than the text of the financial statements.[10] Besides, the registrant that receives less than a full review must pay a dual price: (1) The comment letter process is something of an insurance policy against potentially ruinous liability under §11.

[7] Sec. Act Rel. 4934 (1968), 5231 (1972).

[8] Smith (SEC Commissioner), An Overview of the Registration Statement Process (address before Practising Law Institute, New York, Sept. 18, 1969) 7.

[9] See SEC News Digest, Nov. 17, 1980, p. 1. On the procedures with respect to registration statements of investment companies, see Sec. Act Rel. 6510, 29 SEC Dock. 1005 (1984).

[10] In the entire history of the Commission only one stop order has been judicially reviewed on its merits, and it was affirmed. Oklahoma-Texas Trust v. SEC, 100 F. 2d 888 (10th Cir. 1939).

(2) Counsel for, say, a cement company cannot be sure, when he follows the time-honored technique of using the last effective registrant statement for a cement company as a model, that it passed through the staff's fire![11]

d. The Price Amendment

In practice, particularly in the case of large issues, the required information concerning the offering price and related matters (the specific terms of the securities, redemption and sinking fund provisions, call and conversion prices), as well as the underwriting arrangements, is normally filed by amendment after the rest of the statement has been reviewed and informally cleared by the staff, or after notification that the registration statement will not be reviewed, and only a short time before the anticipated offering date. In order to avoid the necessity of fixing the price and terms of the security several days or perhaps several months before the anticipated offering, and because underwriters simply would not accept a firm commitment and run the risk of market changes during all that time, or would demand exorbitant compensation for doing so,[12] it is customary for the underwriters to sign their purchase contract with the issuer only after they receive notice of staff clearance (or non-review notification), to file the so-called price amendment immediately, and to request that it be accelerated so that the statement will become effective within, typically, an hour or two.[13] The contract is conditioned on a specified effective date and hour. And it is the Commission's policy to grant such acceleration requests ordinarily, whether or not the registration statement has been re-

[11] Ironically, moreover, the SEC's streamlined review has led some blue sky officials to conclude that they should bear an increasing review responsibility in connection with initial public offerings. Lovejoy, Initial Public Offerings: The Due Diligence Process and Blue Sky Problems, in Practising Law Institute, Thirteenth Annual Institute on Securities Regulation (1982) c. 22 at 382.

[12] Another reason for minimizing the interval between the signing of the underwriting contract and the effectiveness of the registration statement, so far as the underwriters are concerned, is that immediately upon the signing the Commission's capital rule for broker-dealers under the 1934 Act deducts from the underwriter's net capital as a liquidity factor (depending on the type of securities) specified percentages of the value of the securities representing the underwriter's open contractual commitment. Rule 15c3-1, infra p. 638.

[13] If it is requested that the registration statement become effective at a particular hour, Rule 461(a) requires that the Commission be advised to that effect not later than the second business day before the desired effective date.

viewed.[14] This practice also permits the issuer and underwriters to "hit the market" — that is, select an effective date in the light of what they regard to be favorable market conditions.

e. Acceleration

Finally, there is the acceleration power itself. But, apart from its implementing the price amendment technique, the Commission has used it to develop a fine-honed tool for accomplishing more effective disclosure — and, some have said on occasion, has abused it for other ends.[15] That is to say, there is decidedly another side to the acceleration coin. To the extent that acceleration of the price amendment is a valuable privilege — one indispensable to the issuer's ability to obtain a firm underwriting commitment — the Commission's authority to deny acceleration in specific cases gives it an effective sanction.[16] How has that authority been used in practice?

(i) One cannot cavil, under the disclosure philosophy, with the Commission's statement of policy in Rules 460 and 461:

> Rule 460(a) Pursuant to the statutory requirement that the Commission in ruling upon requests for acceleration of the effective date

[14] See Rule 461(b). The procedure would be further streamlined by a proposed Rule 430A that would permit the registration statement to become effective on certain conditions without price and related data, which would either (1) be included in the final prospectus and incorporated by reference into the registration statement or (2) be the subject of a posteffective amendment. Sec. Act Rel. 6672, 36 SEC Dock. 1064 (1986).

[15] Oddly, the §8(a) standards are found only in the sentence that permits the Commission to reduce the twenty-day period between filing and effectiveness, a grant of authority that until recently has rarely been used. Nevertheless, the Commission has always assumed that those standards must be read into the second sentence, on acceleration of preeffective amendments. Presumably the courts would so read the second sentence in order to avoid a constitutional question of delegation of legislative power.

[16] The Commission has authorized the Director of the Division of Corporation Finance to grant but not to deny acceleration.

The best-efforts underwriter, of course, can more readily wait out the twenty days. Indeed, even the firm-commitment underwriter is not vitally dependent on acceleration of the price amendment when there is no preexisting market for the securities to be offered. In that situation the negotiated price can be inserted in the original filing, with an "out" clause in the underwriting agreement to take care of an abrupt change in market conditions generally during the waiting period.

Registration statements on Form S-8, which applies to certain employee offerings, become effective on the twentieth day after filing regardless of any preeffective amendments, and delaying amendments are not permitted. Rules 473(d), 475(a). This is also the practice with respect to dividend reinvestment plans.

of a registration statement shall have due regard to the adequacy of the information respecting the issuer theretofore available to the public, the Commission may consider whether the persons making the offering have taken reasonable steps to make the information contained in the registration statement conveniently available to underwriters and dealers who it is reasonably anticipated will be invited to participate in the distribution of the security to be offered or sold.

(b) As a minimum, reasonable steps to make the information conveniently available would involve the distribution, to each underwriter and dealer who it is reasonably anticipated will be invited to participate in the distribution of the security, a reasonable time in advance of the anticipated effective date of the registration statement, of as many copies of the proposed form of preliminary prospectus permitted by Rule 430 as appears to be reasonable to secure adequate distribution of the preliminary prospectus.

(c) The granting of acceleration will not be conditioned upon

(1) The distribution of a preliminary prospectus in any state where such distribution would be illegal * * *

Rule 461 * * *

(b) * * * the following are included in the situations in which the Commission considers that the statutory standards of section 8(a) may not be met and may refuse to accelerate the effective date:

(1) Where there has not been a bona fide effort to make the prospectus reasonably concise and readable, so as to facilitate an understanding of the information required or permitted to be contained in the prospectus.[17]

(2) Where the form of preliminary prospectus, which has been distributed by the issuer or underwriter, is found to be inaccurate or inadequate in any material respect, until the Commission has received satisfactory assurance that appropriate correcting material has been sent to all underwriters and dealers who received

[17] Without specific reference to its acceleration power, the Commission requires a summary "where the length or complexity of the prospectus makes such a summary appropriate," as well as the inclusion, when "appropriate," of an introductory "discussion of the specific factors that make the offering speculative or one of high risk," with a cross-reference on the outside front cover. Reg. S-K, Items 501(c)(4), 503(a) and (c). This so-called "poison pen summary" with respect to high risk issues is a bit debatable if it is to lay the ground for a stop order as distinguished from nonacceleration. Arguably, as long as all the required information is set out in a logical order that stresses neither the favorable nor the unfavorable data, the Commission is no more justified in insisting on concentrating all the poison at the beginning than the registrant would be in concentrating the honey there and relegating the poison to the back pages.

In adopting Form N-1A for certain open-end investment companies, the Commission stated that prospectuses longer than twelve printed pages should include a synopsis "where the length or complexity of the prospectus makes a synopsis appropriate." Sec. Act Rel. 6479, 28 SEC Dock. 682, 686 (1983).

such preliminary prospectus or prospectuses in quantity sufficient for their information and the information of others to whom the inaccurate or inadequate material was sent.[18]

(ii) The Commission has sometimes required a broader distribution. In the case of most speculative new issues, for example, it has conditioned acceleration on the distribution of a properly amended preliminary prospectus not only among selling-group dealers but also to each customer to whom the underwriters and selling-group dealers expect to confirm. And, when the issuer is not a reporting company under the 1934 Act, Rule 15c2-8, one of the over-the-counter antifraud rules under §15(c)(2) of that Act, requires the dealer to deliver a preliminary prospectus at least *forty-eight hours before* the anticipated mailing of confirmations.[19]

(iii) Rule 461 warns further that the Commission "may refuse" to accelerate when (A) the issuer, a controlling person, or an underwriter is under investigation; (B) a firm-commitment underwriter fails to meet the financial responsibility requirements of Rule 15c3-1 under the 1934 Act; (C) persons connected with the offering may have manipulated the market; or (D) the NASD has not issued a "no objection" statement when it is required by its rules to review the underwriters' compensation or any other arrangements among the registrant and securities firms participating in the distribution. All this seems logical enough, at least if the NASD clause is not read as a basis for denial of acceleration when the NASD considers the disclosed compensation or other arrangements to be improper.[20]

(iv) Somewhat more controversial has been the Commission's use of its acceleration power to enforce its view that indemnification of an officer or director (or a person in control of the issuer) against statutory liabilities is unenforceable, however valid the indemnification may be as a matter of state law, because it tends to frustrate

[18] As with the former "red herring prospectus," the risk of being required to circulate corrected material can be substantially reduced or eliminated by merely holding up any circulation of preliminary prospectuses until receipt of the staff's first letter of comment.

[19] See also Sec. Act Rel. 4968 (1969). Rule 15c2-8 provides further that "a broker-dealer participating in a distribution must take reasonable steps to see to it that any person desiring a copy of a preliminary or final prospectus receives a copy. Each salesman who is expected to offer the securities must receive a copy of the preliminary prospectus and, if he is expected to offer the securities after the effective date of the registration statement, he must receive a copy of the final prospectus. The managing underwriter must take reasonable steps to see that broker-dealers participating in the distribution receive a sufficient number of copies of the prospectus to comply with the rule and with" §5(b). Sec. Act Rel. 5101 (1970).

[20] Rule 461(b)(3)-(7).

the *in terrorem* purpose of individual liability under §11 for negligent deficiencies in the registration statement. When there is provision for such indemnification and it has not been waived, the Commission will not accelerate unless the registration statement includes a statement of the Commission's view and an undertaking to the effect that any claim for indemnification (other than payment of the expenses of a successful defense) will not be honored without a judicial test.[21] This policy will be considered in the chapter on Civil Liability as part of the indemnification-contribution-insurance complex under the SEC statutes generally.[22]

(v) As early as 1945 the Commission announced that it considered that the statutory standard for acceleration was "not met in cases where the selling stockholder does not bear his equitable proportion of the expense of registration."[23] And occasionally the Commission experimented with other types of cases. For example, the Commission for some years denied acceleration when the registration statement related to a preferred stock with a par or stated value substantially less than its liquidation preference (or any equity security junior thereto) unless an agreement was made to restrict surplus (so as to prevent dividends on any junior security) until the total capital and surplus at least equalled the amount of the liquidation preference.[24] The Commission justified that policy on the grounds that the description of the terms of the several classes of securities in such cases was apt to give a misleading impression of the registrant's capitalization notwithstanding disclosure of the disparity between liquidation preference and par or stated value, and that the "public interest" standard of §8(a) was not satisfied when the capital structure was such that the contributions of one class of stockholders might be distributed to another class in the form of dividends.

Although these two practices were included when the Commission first proposed to formalize its policy,[25] they were abandoned without explanation when it took final action in the form of a note to Rule 460 (replaced in 1982 by Rule 461).[26] Particularly since those policies were the hardest to defend, there was an inference that the note was meant to be exclusive. But that was not done

[21] This is sometimes called the Johnson & Johnson formula after an early registration statement in which it was developed.

[22] See p. 1037 infra.

[23] Sec. Act Rel. 3055 (1945).

[24] Sec. Act Rel. 3672 (1956).

[25] Proposed note to Rule 460, ibid.

[26] Sec. Act Rel. 3791 (1957).

expressly.[27] And the suspicion grew that the Commission intended to leave the door open at least a crack when the Chairman publicly stated in 1958 that there was a clear inference, from the Commission's action in abandoning some of the proposals that "really had little to do with disclosure problems," that acceleration would be granted if the papers were otherwise in order and the note were satisfied — "unless legal ingenuity has thought up some new gadget."[28]

In 1949 a Hoover Commission "task force" cited the indemnification policy, as well as the Commission's policy on "bail-outs" by controlling stockholders, in support of its conclusion that the Commission had exceeded its statutory authority by thus attempting through its acceleration power to achieve objectives unrelated to the principle of disclosure.[29] And in 1958 the American Bar Association's criticism went to the point of suggested legislation to except the price amendment altogether from the power to deny acceleration.[30]

This criticism, of course, assumes the major premise that the Commission's authority under §8(a) is strictly limited to considerations of disclosure. Quite apart from acceleration, the registration statement is supposed to be accurate and adequate if a stop order is to be avoided under §8(d). Consequently, it seems reasonable to suppose that §8(a) requires something more than ordinary disclosure when it imposes on the Commission the duty to consider how readily the facts in the registration statement can be understood by the investing public in less time than the full statutory period.

It may be assumed that in statutory context these general standards alone do not suffice to turn what is basically a disclosure statute into a piece of legislation that gives the Commission authority to approve or disapprove securities on their merits.[31] But the Commission has never claimed this power. And it has now abandoned

[27] Any doubt was dispelled when the Commission stated in 1968, after referring to the note to Rule 460: "Other instances occur from time to time which cause the Commission to deny acceleration requests." Sec. Act Rel. 4910 (1968).

[28] Gadsby, Proposed Legislation Regarding Acceleration Policies, 187 Com. & Fin. Chron. 2171, 2190 (1958).

[29] Task Force Report on Regulatory Commissions [Appendix N] Prepared for the Commission on Organization of the Executive Branch of the Government (1949) 148-49.

[30] See 83 A. B. A. Rep. 839-42 (1958).

[31] Standards like "the public interest and the protection of investors" must be read in statutory context. New York Central Securities Corp. v. United States, 287 U. S. 12, 24-25 (1932) ("public interest" in Interstate Commerce Act); Pan American World Airways, Inc. v. United States, 371 U. S. 296, 308-09 (1963) (Civil Aeronautics Act).

the two policies — in the "bail-out" and restricted surplus cases — that, however sound they were as a matter of corporation law, were the hardest to justify under disclosure-oriented standards. Insofar as the policies on indemnification, investigations, market manipulation and underwriters' financial responsibility go beyond the disclosure philosophy, there is probably enough flexibility in the standards of §8(a) to justify them.

2. Posteffective Problems

a. Date As of Which Registration Statement Speaks

As of what date does the registration statement speak? On this fundamental question the statute is not too clear on its face. Section 8(d) authorizes a stop order "If it appears to the Commission at any time that the registration statement includes any untrue statement * * *." It does not use the past tense, "included." This would seem consistent with the statement of the House committee that, "In determining whether a stop order should issue, the Commission will naturally have regard to the facts as they then exist and will stop the further sale of securities even though the registration statement was true when made, [and] it has become untrue or misleading by reason of subsequent developments."[32] On the other hand, §11 imposes civil liability on the issuer and other persons "In case any part of the registration statement, when such part became effective, contained an untrue statement * * *. The two sections can be reconciled with each other — although §11 cannot be reconciled with the statement of the House committee — by reading the phrase "at any time" in §8(d), in accordance with its position as a matter of syntax, to modify the verb "appears" rather than "includes." At any rate, the second reported opinion of the Federal Trade Commission decided that the registration statement was required to be true and adequate only as of its effective date.[33]

Under this approach the primary purpose, at least, of the posteffective amendment procedure in §8(c) is to permit posteffective correction of belatedly discovered deficiencies that existed as of the effective date. As we shall see, however, the practice has come a long way from this static concept.

[32] H. R. Rep. No. 85, 73d Cong., 1st Sess. (1933) 20.

[33] Charles A. Howard, 1 SEC 6, 9-10, 18 FTC 626, 630-31 (1934). If the state of the registrant's knowledge or the facts change between the filing and effective dates, the registration statement must be corrected by amendment.

First it is necessary to look at the mechanics of §8(c) itself.[34] The filing of a posteffective amendment does not suspend the effectiveness of the registration statement. It may indicate that the statement as unamended is deficient. But in the absence of a stop order the statement remains in effect and sales may legally be made so far as §5 is concerned. The question of the effective date of the amendment is important chiefly from the point of view of civil liability under §11. Until the amendment is declared effective by the Commission, it cannot be the basis of liability under the language of that section. By the same token a person who buys between the filing and the effectiveness of the amendment can recover on the basis of the unamended registration statement if it is deficient (unless, knowledge always being a defense under §11, the defendant is able to prove that the filing of the amendment itself brought knowledge of the deficiencies in the registration statement to the buyer); on the other hand, whether a person who buys after the effectiveness of the amendment can similarly recover is at least open to question.

All this is not to say that the issuer, underwriters, and dealers can ignore all posteffective developments that materially alter the picture presented in the registration statement. Posteffective amendment is not the only means of achieving currency. The Federal Trade Commission put it this way:

> Let us suppose that the registration statement contained a statement to the effect that the registrant owned 500 acres of timbered land, and that after the registration statement became effective a forest fire destroyed the timber on 250 of these acres. The statement made by the registrant would still reflect the truth as of the time that the registration statement became effective and thus would give no ground for the issuance of a stop order. Vendors, who knew or should have known of this fact, would, however, thereafter be under a duty to disclose that fact to their customers in order to avoid the

[34] A posteffective amendment becomes effective "on such date as the Commission may determine." Posteffective amendments to registration statements for employee offerings on Form S-8 become effective on filing. Rule 464. And this is also the practice with respect to dividend reinvestment plans. Cf. p. 126 n. 16 supra. In May 1984 the SEC amended Rules 485(b) and 486(b), which had previously permitted certain posteffective amendments filed by open-end investment companies and unit investment trusts to become effective automatically on filing. The rule amendments extend the automatic procedure to posteffective amendments filed solely for the purpose of complying with an undertaking to file an amendment containing financial statements within four to six months after the effective date of the registration statement (with the privilege of delaying the effective date, presumably at the registrant's request, until any subsequent day through the twentieth day after the date of the filing). Sec. Act Rel. 6533, 30 SEC Dock. 553 (1984).

> liabilities of Section 12(2); and the Commission could proceed by injunction against such nondisclosing vendors under Section 17(a).
> On the other hand, let us suppose that the statement that the registrant owned 500 acres was based upon a mistaken survey, and that after the registration statement became effective a second and correct survey disclosed that the registrant only owned 250 acres. In such a case, the statement would be untrue as of the time that the registration statement became effective, and the Commission could proceed by stop order unless appropriate amendments were made to the registration statement.[35]

The Commission might have referred to the possibility of still further sanctions attendant on use of a prospectus that did not disclose the fire: a common law deceit action, various blue sky liabilities, and criminal prosecution under §17(a), the mail fraud statute, and state statutes on obtaining money or property by false pretenses (not to mention Rule 10b-5 if the Commission had been prescient).

The traditional procedure was to disclose the posteffective change (the fire in the FTC's example) by putting a sticker on the prospectus and filing copies as required by SEC rule,[36] not by way of an amendment that might be subject to a stop order or §11 liability. On the other hand, because §10(a) of the Act requires the prospectus to "contain the information contained in the registration statement," the registrant must file the later prospectus as a posteffective amendment to the registration statement if the new information is *substituted* for the old and not merely *added* to it. And, when numerous and significant changes since the original effective date have made the original prospectus obsolete, the Commission has said, " 'supplementation' of the outmoded prospectus necessarily results in an obscure and uncoordinated presentation."[37] Beyond that, it has been true for some time that "the staff generally requires that posteffective amendments be filed to reflect material changes."[38] Indeed, Commission counsel in 1972 characterized the line of cases going back to the FTC as not dictated by statutory interpretation at all but as based on a series of discretionary refusals to exert statutory authority for reasons of policy and convenience. The Commission, its counsel contended, had never followed the old FTC approach when posteffective developments involved "a major and substantial change in the basic nature and terms of the public of-

[35] Charles A. Howard, 1 SEC 6, 10, 18 FTC 626, 631 (1934).

[36] Rule 424(c).

[37] Franchard Corp., 42 SEC 163, 184-85 (1964). In that case a supplemented prospectus was in fact filed as an amendment and the Commission found that its form was misleading.

[38] Sec. Act Rel. 6276, 21 SEC Dock. 1052, 1075 (1980).

fering which was deliberately, willfully and voluntarily effected by the issuer and selling shareholders."[39]

Whatever the merit of this argument, there is nevertheless one statutory exception to the rule that the registration statement must be amended whenever the prospectus is changed rather than supplemented. Section 10(a)(3) provides that, "when a prospectus is used more than nine months after the effective date of the registration statement, the information contained therein shall be as of a date not more than sixteen months prior to such use, so far as such information is known to the user of such prospectus or can be furnished by such user without unreasonable effort or expense." There is no requirement that this so-called "nine-month prospectus" be filed as an amendment to the registration statement, even though a Commission rule permits (but does not require) the omission from such a prospectus of any information previously required to be contained in the prospectus insofar as the prospectus contains later information on the same subjects (including the latest available certified financial statements) as of a date not more than sixteen months prior to its use; for §10(a)(3) obviously cuts across the clause in the first part of §10(a) to the effect that the prospectus shall "contain the information contained in the registration statement." It is necessary merely to file ten copies of the prospectus with the Commission.[40] In other words, whereas the substitution of information in a prospectus used *less* than nine months after the effective date requires a posteffective amendment, the same substitution *after* nine months does not. This means, of course, that nine-month prospectuses are not subject to stop order or to civil liability under §11.

Gradually, however, a series of exceptions has been eating up the rule that the nine-month prospectus need not be filed as an amendment. Under §24(e)(3) of the Investment Company Act, nine-month prospectuses of investment companies that make continuous offerings do have to be filed as posteffective amendments. That special class of issuer aside, the Commission developed the practice over the years, in the case of various kinds of deferred or continuous offerings, of requiring an undertaking to file any nine-month prospectuses as posteffective amendments.[41] And it normally follows the practice whenever there is only a best-efforts underwriter or none at all.

[39] Brief for Appellees, pp. 47-48, SEC v. Manor Nursing Centers, Inc., 458 F. 2d 1082 (2d Cir. 1972).

[40] Rules 427, 424(c).

[41] See Form S-4, Item 22(a); Reg. S-K, Item 512(h)(2).

One can readily understand the Commission's exacting the post-effective amendment procedure as a condition of recognizing the exigencies of certain types of deferred or continuous offerings. It is considerably more difficult to understand, in the light of the juxtaposition of §§7, 8(c), and 10(a)(3), a general requirement that would in effect transpose §10(a)(3) to §7. That end *would* be achieved by the Code, which would also require a posteffective amendment *whenever* the prospectus was "supplemented or changed" or whenever an amendment was necessary "to correct (A) a material deficiency in the offering statement [today's registration statement] as of its effective date, or (B) a statement of a material fact in the offering statement that becomes a misrepresentation by reason of a subsequent event."[42]

b. Registration for the "Shelf" (Rule 415)

In any event, §10(a)(3) is not designed to permit issuers to register unlimited amounts of securities with the thought of presently distributing some and having the rest conveniently registered in the event that a need for further capital should arise in the indefinite future. Section 6(a) of the act concludes by stating that "A registration statement shall be deemed effective only as to the securities specified therein as proposed to be offered." In order to avoid the registration of securities "for the shelf," the Commission has traditionally construed this provision, in the context of the statute as a whole, as if the word "presently" (in the sense of "soon") preceded the phrase "proposed to be offered." The Commission, accordingly, has made it clear by rule that the registration of additional securities, even though they are of the same class as other securities that are already effectively registered, must be effected through a separate statement rather than by way of amendment of the earlier statement. The same policy explains the Commission's practice of requiring a registrant to include in the registration statement an undertaking to file a posteffective amendment reducing the amount of securities registered in certain contingencies. This practice is followed, for example, in conversion situations with respect to securities not taken down at the expiration of the conversion period.

It used to be followed also in the case of open-end investment companies, which continuously stand ready to redeem their outstanding shares and, usually, to sell new shares to the public. So

[42] §508.

that they would never run out of registered shares, they used to follow the practice of filing approximately once a year a registration statement that covered as many shares as they expected to be able to sell during the following twelve months. Since they naturally tended to err on the side of plenty, the Commission customarily required an undertaking that any shares remaining unsold after eighteen months would be "deregistered" by a posteffective amendment. In the 1954 amendment program, however, a new §24(e) was added to the Investment Company Act so as to permit those investment companies engaged in continuous offerings (most open-end management companies, face-amount certificate companies, and unit investment trusts) to register additional securities under the 1933 Act either by filing a new registration statement as they formerly did or by filing an appropriate amendment, approximately once a year, to the latest effective registration statement for securities of the same class.[43]

The open-end investment company is the classic case of the continuous offering. But the practical exigencies presented by a number of other types of either continuous or deferred offerings — the latter are more properly "shelf registrations" though the two categories blur into each other — have persuaded the Commission to bend the last sentence of §6(a) so as to ameliorate the burden of filing successive registration statements. In 1982 the Commission, after stating that its substantial experience with various types of shelf registrations had not made it aware of major abuses and that a restrictive policy was not necessary or appropriate, formalized and radically liberalized the administrative practice in a new Rule 415, which has three conditions designed to assure "[1] a bona fide intention to offer and sell, [2] accurate current information and [3] liability protection under the Securities Act."[44]

The first condition of the rule, as originally adopted, limited the amount of registerable securities to what "is reasonably expected to

[43] The filing of current information as a part of the registration statement at approximately yearly intervals is assured by providing, as we have seen (supra p. 134), that no nine-month prospectus relating to a security issued by any such company, within the meaning of §10(a)(3) of the Securities Act, is considered to meet the requirements of §10 unless it has been filed as part of a posteffective amendment that has become effective. In 1970 the Investment Company Act was further amended by the addition of §24(f), which, in effect, permits *nunc pro tunc* registration of oversales in addition to authorizing the Commission by rule to permit the registration of an indefinite number of securities in the first instance. See Rules 24e-1, 24e-2, 24f-1, 24f-2.

[44] Sec. Act Rel. 6276, 21 SEC Dock. 1052, 1073 (1980); Sec. Act Rel. 6334, 23 SEC Dock. 387 (1981). The rule was adopted in Sec. Act Rel. 6383, 24 SEC Dock. 1262, 1288-94 (1982).

be offered and sold within two years," with exceptions that codified past practice.[45] The radical innovation, however, was the rule's permitting offerings to be made from time to time during the two-year period "at the market," through the facilities of an exchange or an over-the-counter marketmaker,[46] if in the case of a primary offering of equity securities, (1) the securities were sold through one or more underwriters named in the statutory prospectus,[47] (2) the registrant met the applicable requirements of the contemporaneously adopted Form S-3 (which is to say, the securities were widely followed by financial analysts),[48] and (3) the amount of securities registered, when voting stock, did not exceed 10 percent of the nonaffiliate "float."[49]

A number of prominent underwriting houses strenuously objected that the two-year innovation might have serious impacts on the capital raising process. The new Form S-3 is so skeletal, as we shall see in a moment, that any of some 2000 companies eligible for that form may file a single registration statement designating the amount of bonds and stocks it wants to put on its "shelf" for issuance during the next two years and, when it considers interest rates and other factors to be propitious, may quite readily enter the market with relatively small chunks of securities. The result, in the words of a financial journalist, could be not only to "alter the style

[45] Although Rule 415(b) makes the rule inapplicable to foreign governments, "seasoned foreign governments are permitted to use shelf registration in a manner substantially similar." Sec. Act Rel. 6499, 29 SEC Dock. 138, 148 (1983).

The Commission, in its various attempts over the years to adjust the last sentence of §6(a) to the exigencies of warrants and convertible securities, has had to ignore the two anomalies in that sentence: (1) The clear negative implication is that the issue of a right that *is* immediately exercisable does involve a present offer of the security it calls for; this would seem to be so even though the right, though immediately exercisable as a legal matter, will not be exercised for some time as a practical matter, if ever, because the exercise price is substantially higher than the current market price of the stock called for. (2) The delayed "offer" concept applies only when the right is "originally issued or transferred with a security"; thus, when warrants are issued independently of any other security, there is again by negative implication an immediate "offer" of the security they call for although they may not be immediately exercisable even as a legal matter.

[46] Present Rule 415(a)(4).

[47] "The SEC has required underwriter participation because it asserts that the direct involvement of an underwriter provides discipline upon [at-the-market] offerings of equity securities and helps to ensure that accurate and current disclosure is made to investors in the prospectus and that the prospectus delivery requirements of the Securities Act are met." Ferrara and Sweeney, Shelf Registration under SEC Temporary Rule 415, 5 Corp. L. Rev. 308, 313 n. 22 (1982).

[48] See p. 148 infra.

[49] The "float" refers to the amount of stock outstanding and available for trading after deduction of large blocks (whether or not held by affiliates) that are not likely to enter the market.

and role of investment bankers" but also to "tear asunder some of the traditional relationships and pecking orders that have governed the nation's capital markets since the early 20th century." Without time, necessarily, for lead underwriters to form syndicates, and with smaller amounts involved, the "blue chip" issuers would have "much greater flexibility and incentive to shop around for investment banks" — indeed, the syndicate might be eliminated — and investment bankers might be eschewed entirely in favor of selling the entire issue to one or a few institutional buyers (a so-called "bought deal").[50]

The Commission's language in response was more bland. "Recognizing the importance of the views and concerns of the commentators,"[51] it inserted the S-3 and 10 percent float conditions with respect to primary offerings of equities; adopted the rule for only a nine-month period, to expire December 10, 1982; and promised public hearings and a further opportunity to comment during that period.[52]

In the light of these hearings and a great many diverse comments, the Commission extended the rule to year-end 1983 with only one modification: removal of the posteffective amendment requirement to reflect the addition or deletion of a "managing underwriter," because of "the lack of clarity in this area and the difficulty of interpretation and operation of the managing underwriter concept."[53]

Then in November 1983 the Commission, finding that the rule "has operated efficiently and has provided registrants with important benefits in their financings, most notably cost savings," extended the rule indefinitely.[54] But the concerns that had been expressed about disclosure and "due diligence"[55] persuaded the Commission to limit the rule to "those offerings where the benefits of shelf registration are most significant and where the disclosure

[50] See Friedman, Investment Banks' New Day, N. Y. Times, Mar. 11, 1982, p. D1, col. 3; Ehrbar, Upheaval in Investment Banking, 106 Fortune 90 (Aug. 23, 1982). For a wryly incisive comparison of primary stock distributions twenty-five years ago and today, thanks largely to Rule 415, see Pryor and Smith, Significant Changes in Primary Stock Distributions over the Last 25 Years, Nat'l L. J., Aug. 9, 1982, p. 21; Pryor and Smith, Disclosure and Capital Formation Policies, Nat'l L. J., Aug. 16, 1982, p. 15.

[51] Sec. Act Rel. 6383, 24 SEC Dock. 1262, 1288 (1982).

[52] Id. at 1288-89. In Sec. Act Rel. 6391, 24 SEC Dock. 1502 (1982), the Commission set forth a substantial number of issues on which it invited comment at hearings to begin on June 28, 1982.

[53] Sec. Act Rel. 6423, 26 SEC Dock. 3, 8 (1982).

[54] Sec. Act Rel. 6499, 29 SEC Dock. 138, 139 (1983).

[55] See Supp. p. 149 n. 8 infra.

and due diligence concerns are mitigated by other factors":[56] only primary offerings (including offerings by a parent or subsidiary of the issuer) on Form S-3 or F-3[57] (the "dark blue chips" in the sense of "a continuous stream of high quality corporate information about registrants widely followed in the marketplace") apart from shelf offerings of the traditional varieties, all of which were codified.[58]

This codification was accomplished mechanically by listing ten types of offerings to which Rule 415 is limited, the first nine being in substance exceptions to the tenth, which covers the S-3 (or F-3) case.[59]

> (i) Securities which are to be offered or sold solely by or on behalf of a person or persons other than the registrant, a subsidiary of the registrant or a person of which the registrant is a subsidiary;
>
> (ii) Securities which are to be offered and sold pursuant to a dividend or interest reinvestment plan or an employee benefit plan of the registrant;
>
> (iii) Securities which are to be issued upon the exercise of outstanding options, warrants or rights;
>
> (iv) Securities which are to be issued upon conversion of other outstanding securities;
>
> (v) Securities which are pledged as collateral;
>
> (vi) Securities which are registered on Form F-6 [American depository receipts];
>
> (vii) Mortgage related securities, including such securities as mortgage backed debt and mortgage participation or pass through certificates;
>
> (viii) Securities which are to be issued in connection with business combination transactions;
>
> (ix) Securities the offering of which will be commenced promptly, will be made on a continuous basis and may continue for a period in excess of 30 days from the date of initial effectiveness;[60] or
>
> (x) Securities registered (or qualified to be registered) on Form S-3 or Form F-3 which are to be offered and sold on a continuous

[56] 26 SEC Dock. at 139.

[57] The rule as originally adopted contained the S-3 restriction only for equity offerings "at the market."

[58] 29 SEC Dock. at 144.

[59] Rule 415(a)(1).

[60] Examples of the Clause (ix) category are "customer purchase plans; exchange, rights, subscription and rescission offers; offers to employees, consultants or independent agents; offerings on a best efforts basis; tax shelter and other limited partnership interests; commodity funds; condominium rental pools; time sharing agreements; real estate investment trusts; farmers' cooperative organizations or others making distributions on a membership basis; and continuous debt sales by finance companies to their customers." 29 SEC Dock. at 146 (1983).

> or delayed basis by or on behalf of the registrant, a subsidiary of the registrant or a person of which the registrant is a subsidiary.

The two-year formula limits only Clauses (viii)-(x).[61]

So much for the first of the three conditions of the rule: a *bona fide* intention to offer and sell. So far as the other two conditions are concerned:

The second (accurate current information) requires undertakings to file posteffective amendments reflecting material postregistration events (any "fundamental change" so far as the prospectus is concerned) as well as the nine-month prospectus provision in §10(a)(3).[62] The term "fundamental," the Commission said, "is intended to reflect current staff practice under which posteffective amendments are filed when major and substantial changes are made to information contained in the registration statement." Numerous small changes can become cumulatively "fundamental." But a short sticker will continue to be permitted for material changes that are not "fundamental" and can be stated accurately and succinctly in that form.[63]

The third condition (liability protection) requires a further undertaking

> That, for the purpose of determining any liability under the Securities Act of 1933, each such post-effective amendment shall be deemed to be a new registration statement relating to the securities offered therein, and the offering of such securities at that time shall be deemed to be the initial bona fide offering thereof.
>
> To remove from registration by means of a post-effective amend-

[61] "According to SEC staff, the offering may extend beyond the two-year period so long as it was reasonably expected, upon initial registration, to culminate within two years." Ferrara and Sweeney, Shelf Registration under SEC Temporary Rule 415, 5 Corp. L. Rev. 308, 310 (1982). Moreover, the rule "contemplates an issuer's selling the securities registered on the shelf in a succession of different kinds of offerings." Sec. Act Rel. 6383, 24 SEC Dock. 1252, 1288 (1982). But "The use of a single shelf registration statement for widely diverse plans of financing may be inappropriate in cases where a complete description of each plan of distribution to which the filing relates, together with a discussion of the impact on the issuer of such plan alone and in combination with the other contemplated financings, becomes so complex as to reduce substantially the effectiveness of the disclosures. In such cases, more than one registration statement may be necessary." Id. at 1291.

[62] Rule 415(a)(3); Reg. S-K, Item 512(a)(1). It is the administrative practice to require a two-day wait before *any* posteffective amendment becomes effective.

[63] Sec. Act Rel. 6383, 24 SEC Dock. 1262, 1290 (1982). "* * * there is no need to maintain an accurate and current, or 'evergreen,' prospectus when no offers or sales are being made pursuant to the shelf registration." Id. at 1289. An example is a rights offering when the market price of the stock is substantially below the exercise price. Sec. Act Rel. 6334, 23 SEC Dock. 387, 394 (1981).

ment any of the securities being registered which remain unsold at the termination of the offering.[64]

It is difficult still to assess fully the impact of Rule 415 on capital formation and investment banking practices. The deregulation aspects are clear: gun-jumping questions with respect to securities taken off the shelf are eliminated; and, except for the relatively rare case where a posteffective amendment is required, underwriters and dealers may confirm sales orally immediately after the terms of the particular offering are agreed to without waiting for the filing of a price amendment or SEC processing or declaration of effectiveness. But there are also a number of legal considerations: the issuer that wants to offer debt securities must qualify an indenture that is "open-ended";[65] regulated companies, such as public utilities, must work out procedures for authorization in advance;[66] and issuers must also make their peace with the state blue sky administrators. Moreover, the potential changes in techniques of capital formation loom large: the more frequent offering of securities in smaller batches may lead to semiprivate placements effected through single underwriters without syndication, as we have already noticed;[67] we may even see the development of some form of competitive bidding; and institutional investors may come to play a more direct role in capital formation.

These and other considerations — including the impact on regional broker-dealers, the risk of aggravating the trend toward institutionalization of the markets, and the risk to underwriters' due

[64] Rule 415(a)(3); Reg. S-K, Item 512(a)(2)-(3).

[65] With respect to the accommodation of the Trust Indenture Act to shelf registrations, see letter, Div. of Corp. Fin., CCH Fed. Sec. L. Rep. ¶77,345 (1982).

[66] In 1982 the Commission issued a statement of policy with respect to the application of the competitive bidding rule under the Holding Company Act (Rule 50, supra p. 84) in the context of Rule 415 offerings. Holding Co. Act Rel. 22,623, 26 SEC Dock. 39 (1982). "Determining that the formal competitive bidding procedures specified in paragraph (b) of Rule 50 were inconsistent with those possible under the shelf registration rule, the Commission stated that registered holding companies and their subsidiaries could adopt alternative procedures to those described in paragraph (b) of Rule 50 to develop and procure two or more competitive offers for securities which have been authorized for sale by the Commission." Sec. Act Rel. 6499, 29 SEC Dock. 138, 148 (1983).

[67] See pp. 137-38 supra. *Query* which is the more prudent course when the issuer effects a classic private placement during the two-year period: (1) to avoid any "integration" problem (see p. 326, par. (3), infra), or (2) to take the securities off the shelf and run the risk of making a statutory "underwriter" out of an institution that buys in the private placement and later resells (see pp. 255, 385-86 infra)? See Williams, Problems in the Application of the 1933 Act and Rules Thereunder to Shelf Offerings, in Practising Law Institute, Fourteenth Annual Institute on Securities Regulation (1983) c. 9 at 115-16.

diligence and the disclosure system generally — led Commissioner Thomas to write an extensive opinion dissenting from the initial extension of the rule without substantial change.[68] And her dissent from the final extension would have limited the application of the rule in the S-3 (or F-3) situation to debt securities.[69] On the other hand, Chairman Shad estimated that under the rule as revised shelf offerings of equity securities would amount to less than 5 percent of the total volume of equity offerings.[70]

Even apart from Rule 415, the propriety and enforceability of the Commission-exacted extrastatutory undertakings are moot questions, since the Commission's authority seems never to have been challenged. In principle, it is not easy to answer the trenchant criticism of the entire practice made by a former General Counsel of the SEC: "But it would seem that, to the extent that an undertaking (other than one specifically prescribed by statute) does no more than obligate an issuer to do what is required by law, it is unnecessary; and that, to the extent that an undertaking imposes an obligation to do something not required by law, it is unwarranted."[71] The pragmatic answer is that it may be too much to expect complete logic and philosophic consistency in a field as complex as this. Perhaps the important thing is that all this seems to work. Indeed, to the extent that the undertaking technique represents an attempt to accommodate the policy and requirements of the statute to the exigencies of certain types of offerings that raise questions under the last sentence of §6(a) — to say nothing of the attempt to facilitate capital formation by the new Rule 415 — the Commission has managed to soften the impact of that statutory provision and still to achieve substantially the statutory purpose of providing investors with current information, subject to the sanctions of the Act, at a time close to the actual sales activity or investment decision.[72]

[68] 26 SEC Dock. at 9. See also Committee of Publicly Owned Companies, Shelf Registration: Strategies, Techniques, Pitfalls, Case Studies (1983).

[69] 29 SEC Dock. at 150.

[70] 15 Sec. Reg. L. Rep. 2171 (1983). For statistics on the types of shelf registrations from March 1982 through September 1983, see 29 SEC Dock. at 140-41 (1983). In general, see Practising Law Institute, Fourteenth Annual Institute on Securities Regulation (1983) cc. 4, 5, 7, 9. On volume and cost savings, together with a critique leading to proposed statutory amendments, see J. Auerbach and S. Hayes, Investment Banking and Diligence: What Price Deregulation? (1986) cc. 7-9.

[71] Throop, Recent Developments with Respect to Rule 133, 15 Bus. Law. 119, 127 (1959).

[72] In Item 512 of Regulation S-K the Commission has enumerated the undertakings that are applicable to various kinds of offerings: (a) Rule 415 offer-

Nevertheless, altogether apart from logical symmetry, all this creates practical problems:

(1) Since the undertakings are given by the issuer but many of the acts bringing them into play are acts by the underwriter that may occur in the future, the issuer should protect itself by appropriate agreement with the underwriter. And conversely, the underwriter will want an appropriate registration covenant from the issuer.[73]

(2) A posteffective amendment designed to make only minor changes may nevertheless have the effect of reaffirming other facts that were true when the registration statement originally became effective but have since become untrue. Therefore, care must be taken that the contents of the entire registration statement are accurate and complete as of the effective date of the posteffective amendment.

(3) As long as the Commission uses its §4(3) authority to waive delivery of prospectuses after expiration of the forty-day or ninety-day period following the *first* of several "shelf" offerings[74] it is an academic question whether the Commission through this undertaking technique could extend the statutory periods during which all dealers must deliver prospectuses under §4(3). But the problem remains whether the statute of limitations imposed upon §11 actions by §13 can be extended by any such process of levitation. When Congress wanted to accomplish a similar result in connection with the 1954 amendment of §24(e) of the Investment Company Act to permit the registration of additional securities of open-end companies to be effected under the Securities Act by amending an earlier registration statement instead of filing a new one, it expressly extended the statute of limitations.[75]

---

ings; (b) filings incorporating subsequent Exchange Act documents by reference; (c) warrants and rights offerings; (d) competitive bids; (e) incorporated annual and quarterly reports; (f) employee plans on Form S-8; (g) equity offerings of non-reporting registrants; (h) registration on Form S-14, S-4, or F-4 of securities offered for sale; and (i) acceleration of effectiveness.

[73] See p. 365 infra.

[74] Rule 174(c); see p. 117 supra.

[75] Section 507 of the Code cuts through the present statutory morass with a series of short and simple provisions:

> (a) *Continuous Distributions.* — Except as the Commission provides otherwise by rule, (1) an issuer may include as many continuously offered securities in an offering statement as it specifies, either initially or by amendment, and (2) a registered investment company may include retroactively in an offering statement, by amendment, continuously offered securities already issued.
>
> (b) *Deferred Distributions.* — The Commission, by rule or order, may

D. CONTENTS OF THE REGISTRATION STATEMENT AND PROSPECTUS (HEREIN OF THE SEC'S ACCOUNTING ROLE)

1. Integration of the Disclosure Provisions of the 1933 and 1934 Acts

This is not the place for a detailed treatment of how to prepare a registration statement. That is more art than science in any event, and it is learned in the doing. All we can profitably do here is tune the fiddle before placing it in the learner's hands.[1]

Section 7 provides, in substance, that the registration statement shall contain the information, and be accompanied by the documents, specified in Schedule A (or Schedule B in the case of securities issued by a foreign government or one of its political subdivisions), except that the Commission may by rule add to or subtract from the specified information and documents with respect to any class of issuers or securities. Similar flexibility marks §10, which provides that the statutory prospectus shall contain "the information contained in the registration statement" except for certain documents referred to in the schedules and subject to the Commission's power to adopt rules adding, subtracting, and classifying. Additional authority is given the Commission by §19(a), the general provision on rulemaking, to define "accounting, technical, and trade terms" used in the Act and to prescribe the form in which required information shall be set forth and the methods to be followed in the preparation of accounts and financial statements. The Commission has used this authority from the beginning not only to adopt a number of general rules but also to adapt the specifications

---

permit the filing of an offering statement by any issuer, or its preeffective or posteffective amendment to increase the amount of securities offered, in connection with a deferred distribution.

(c) *Ninety-day Rule.* — Except as provided in section 507(a) or (b) or by rule or order, an offering statement may be filed only if it is proposed to begin the offering of the securities by the ninetieth day after its effective date and the offering statement so states.

C. 2D [1] Limitation of space prevents setting out the excellent description of the entire process of "going public" in Wheat and Blackstone, Guideposts for a First Public Offering, 15 Bus. Law. 539 (1960). On the advantages and disadvantages of going public in the first place, see Schneider, Manko, and Kant, Going Public: Practice, Procedure and Consequences (Packard Press 1986).

of Schedule A to the circumstances of particular types of issuers by promulgating a substantial number of separate forms.[2]

Much as new law school professors are reputed to prepare very strict examinations and to become less exacting as they mellow, the Commission has found it possible, as it has accumulated experience, to relax the requirements substantially without impairing the interests of investors — though this is not to say, of course, that experience has not also dictated a tightening of requirements here and there. There has always been a substantial variety of forms for different types of issues and, in recent years, issuers of different qualities. But it is possible to discern four stages in the maturation process:

(1) Until the early 1940s all the forms consisted of the registration statement proper, in question-and-answer form, and the prospectus, which had to repeat much the same information in narrative form.

(2) In 1942 the Commission adopted Form S-1, which, after many modifications, is still the residual form. That form and others in the "S" series made the prospectus the basic part of the registration statement and simply required additional information to be included as Part II. Part II, which has remained in question-and-answer form, is a public document that is used by analysts and financial services, but it does not have to be delivered to anyone. A "hooker" in Part II is a requirement for disclosure of recent sales of unregistered securities and a statement of the exemption relied on. The result is sometimes the inclusion in the financial statements of a substantial contingent liability under §12(1), or even deferral of the offering.[3]

(3) In 1970 the Commission adopted Form S-16, and later ex-

[2] So far as Schedule B is concerned, the Commission has never adopted a form for foreign government issues. Each registration is handled *ad hoc.* But the Commission does have a few rules that expatiate on the schedule. Rules 490-94. And by now the "follow the leader" practice has resulted in a considerable amount of uniformity. When foreign governments guarantee the principal and interest of securities issued by state-owned utilities or other entities, Schedule B is applied to the guaranteed securities as well as the guarantees. Sec. Act Rel. 6424, 26 SEC Dock. 20 (1982); see Greene and Adee, The Securities of Foreign Governments, Political Subdivisions, and Multinational Organizations, 10 N. C. J. Int'l L. & Com. Reg. 1 (1985).

[3] In Sec. Act Rel. 6479, 28 SEC Dock. 682 (1983), the Commission adopted Form N-1A under the Securities and Investment Company Acts by way of establishing a *three*-part registration statement. The first part is a "simplified prospectus," which is all that has to be delivered. The second is a "statement of additional information" available to prospective investors without charge and on request. The third is the old Part II. This form is for all open-end investment companies other than "small business investment companies" and insurance company "separate accounts."

tended its scope on an optional basis to cover issuers that (among other conditions) had a three-year reporting history under the 1934 Act and a specified income record. The prime characteristic of Form S-16 was a highly condensed prospectus, with incorporation by reference of all reports and proxy statements filed under the 1934 Act (including such material filed in the future) together with a statement of any material changes of an adverse nature in the registrant's affairs since the date of the latest certified financials.[4] This was an important step in integration of the filing requirements of the 1933 and 1934 Acts.[5] Some registration statements on Form S-16 became effective in as little as forty-eight hours.

(4) Form S-16 disappeared and the integration program was carried a great step further in 1982 — about as far as possible short of the Code's registration of companies rather than securities.

SECURITIES ACT RELEASE NO. 6383: ADOPTION OF INTEGRATED DISCLOSURE SYSTEM

24 SEC Dock. 1262

Securities and Exchange Commission, 1982

* * *

* * * It was long clear that the transaction-oriented framework of the Securities Act and the disclosure system which developed thereunder often overlap with, and produce disclosure duplicative of, that prepared independently in response to the status-oriented framework of the Exchange Act and the continuous disclosure system operating thereunder. * * *

* * *

New Forms S-1, S-2 and S-3 provide the basic framework for the registration of securities under the Securities Act. These Forms establish three categories for registration statements. The same information will be required to be part of Securities Act registration statements in all categories, either presented in, or delivered with, the prospectus or incorporated by reference from another docu-

[4] Sec. Act Rel. 5117 (1970). Form S-16 followed a recommendation of the "Wheat Report" prepared by an SEC staff group under the direction of then Commissioner Wheat. Disclosure to Investors: A Reappraisal of Federal Administrative Policies under the '33 and '34 Acts (1969).

[5] See Cohen, "Truth in Securities" Revisited, 79 Harv. L. Rev. 1340 (1966), supra p. 39; Sec. Act Rel. 6235, 20 SEC Dock. 1175 (1980).

ment. Differences among the three Forms reflect the Commission's determination as to (1) when this required information must be presented in full in the prospectus delivered to investors, (2) when certain of the delivered information may be presented on a streamlined basis and supplemented by documents incorporated by reference, and (3) when certain information may be incorporated by reference from documents in the Exchange Act continuous reporting system without delivery to investors.

Generally, it is the registrant-oriented portion of the information relating to a public offering, as opposed to the transaction-specific information, which sometimes may be satisfied otherwise than through full prospectus presentation. Much of this registrant-oriented information is the same as that which is required to be presented in annual reports to the Commission on Form 10-K and in annual reports to security holders, as well as in quarterly and current reports on Forms 10-Q (17 CFR 249.308a) and 8-K (17 CFR 249.308), respectively. Information about the offering, however, will not have been reported on in any other disclosure document or otherwise have been publicly disseminated and thus will be required to be presented in the prospectus in all cases.

The registration statement for the first category is Form S-1. It requires complete disclosure to be set forth in the prospectus and permits no incorporation by reference. Form S-1 is to be used by registrants in the Exchange Act reporting system for less than three years and also may be used by any registrants who choose to do so or for whom no other form is available.

The second category of registration statement is Form S-2, which combines reliance on incorporating Exchange Act reports by reference with delivery to investors of streamlined information. Registrants in the Exchange Act reporting system for three years may use this Form, which allows them to choose to either: (1) deliver a copy of their annual report to security holders along with the prospectus describing the offering or (2) present registrant-oriented information comparable to that of the annual report in the prospectus along with the description of the offering. In either case, the more complete information in the Form 10-K is incorporated by reference into the prospectus.

Form S-3, in reliance on the efficient market theory, allows maximum use of incorporation by reference of Exchange Act reports and requires the least disclosure to be presented in the prospectus and delivered to investors. Generally, the Form S-3 prospectus will present the same transaction-specific information as will be presented in a Form S-1 or S-2 prospectus. Information concerning the registrant will be incorporated by reference from Exchange Act reports. The prospectus will not be required to present any information concerning the registrant unless there has been a material change in the registrant's affairs which has not been reported in an Exchange Act filing or the Exchange Act reports incorporated by reference do not reflect certain restated financial statements or other financial information.

* * *

Form S-3 is available, in substance, for American companies (and under certain circumstances foreign private issuers) that have reported under the 1934 Act for the past three years and have had a default-free record since the end of the last fiscal year, but only if (1) the nonaffiliate float is at least $150 million or (2) the voting stock held by nonaffiliates has an aggregate value of at least $100 million and an annual trading volume of at least 3 million shares. In addition, because investment grade debt securities are generally bought on the basis of interest rates and security ratings, they (as well as investment grade preferred stocks) are eligible for Form S-3 regardless of the float.[6]

Underwriters were said to be reluctant to have Form S-16 used out of fear of §11 liability for incorporated documents with whose preparation they had not been involved.[7] And, if they insisted on beefing up the prospectus with additional information such as a description of the issuer's business and summary financial information, they increased the risk of liability, arguably, by picking and choosing without benefit of SEC guidelines. Here the Commission took a leaf out of the Code by adopting a rule to the effect that one of the circumstances to be considered in determining whether a defendant acted reasonably is "Whether, with respect to a fact or document incorporated by reference, the particular person had any

[6]There are also special provisions for (1) secondary offerings, (2) rights offerings, dividend or interest reinvestment plans, and conversions, (3) majority-owned subsidiaries, and (4) rights offerings by foreign private issuers. And in late 1982 the Commission extended the integrated disclosure system to most foreign private issuers through the adoption (*inter alia*) of Forms F-1, F-2, and F-3. Sec. Act Rel. 6437, 26 SEC Dock. 964 (1982).

[7]See Sec. Act Rel. 5879, 13 SEC Dock. 509, 511 (1977).

responsibility for the fact or document at the time of the filing from which it was incorporated."[8]

With respect to the forms generally:

(1) There are a number of specialized forms: for example, S-4 for business combination transactions, S-8 for certain employee offerings, S-18 for offerings up to $7.5 million, and N-1A for investment companies.[9]

(2) In the 1982 integration amendments the Commission expanded Regulation S-K, which it had adopted in 1977,[10] to provide a reservoir of all substantive data (other than financial statements, which are the subject of Regulation S-X, the general accounting regulation) from which registration statements under both Acts, together with reports and proxy statements under the 1934 Act, draw.[11] Accordingly, counsel will first select the proper registration (or report) form, which will direct him to the appropriate sections of Regulation S-K for that form's (or report's) specific disclosure requirements, and he will then look to Regulation C (or Regulation 12B under the 1934 Act) for the preparation and filing *procedures.*

(3) Traditionally the Commission's staff discouraged disclosure of security ratings except in limited circumstances. But in the 1982 integration program the Commission *permitted* registration statements and reports (as well as "tombstone ads") to disclose ratings assigned by nationally recognized rating organizations to classes of debt securities (whether or not convertible) and preferred stock.[12]

(4) Rule 408 requires, in addition to the specific items in a reg-

[8] Rule 176(h); Code §1704(g)(6); see also Rule 412; Sec. Act Rel. 6383, 24 SEC Dock. 1262, 1296 (1982). An underwriter that has an ongoing relationship with a particular company may also perform its §11 "due diligence" by having its counsel participate in the preparation of the annual and quarterly reports under the 1934 Act and obtaining an accountant's "comfort letter" when the reports are filed. Moreover, the Commission found in adopting Rule 415 that registrants and their lawyers, accountants, and underwriters were developing new "due diligence" procedures. It thought the trend toward an issuer's retaining independent counsel to perform on an ongoing basis the historical "due diligence" function on behalf of potential underwriters — along the lines of the historical procedure with respect to competitive bidding under the Holding Company Act (see p. 85 n. 11 supra) — was a particularly significant development. Sec. Act Rel. 6499, 29 SEC Dock. 138, 143 (1983). See generally Practising Law Institute, Fourteenth Annual Institute on Securities Regulation (1983) cc. 6, 8; Nicholas, The Integrated Disclosure System and Its Impact upon Underwriters' Due Diligence: Will Investors Be Protected?, 11 Sec. Reg. L. J. 3 (1983).

[9] On Forms S-14 and S-18, see pp. 293, 308 infra.

[10] Sec. Act Rel. 5893, 13 SEC Dock. 1217 (1977).

[11] A number of industry guides are attached at the end of Regulation S-K. Items 801-02. See also SEC, The Disclosure Practices Manual (1982).

[12] Rules 134(a)(14), 436(g); Reg. S-K, Item 10(c) (Commission policy); Sec.

istration statement, the inclusion of such further material information, if any, as may be necessary to make the required statements, in the light of the circumstances under which they are made, not misleading.

(5) After its first public offering a company must file reports on Form S-R, semiannually until termination of the offering, to cover (a) the status of the offering when there is a best-efforts underwriter and (b) application of the proceeds.[13]

The next step in this historical development is likely to be the most radical of all. At 11:13 in the morning of September 24, 1984, the Chairman of the SEC inserted an eight-inch "floppy" disc into a computer terminal that sped 85 pages of corporate data into the agency's public files — an event that he called "a step through the looking glass into a future wonderland."[14] We shall have to get used to another acronym: "EDGAR," for Electronic Data Gathering, Analysis, and Retrieval.[15] After a period of testing with some hundreds of pilot companies that voluntarily filed on floppy discs as well as over telephone lines, the Commission in June 1986 requested comment on rulemaking changes necessary to require a wide range of electronic filings under all the statutes except the Advisers Act.[16] Ultimately, it is contemplated, persons will have instant access to the Commission's electronic files while sitting at business or home computers.[17]

2. Disclosure Standards

It remains to consider briefly a few troublesome matters of philosophical approach to type of disclosure.

A chronic problem, perhaps endemic to any disclosure system, is a tendency toward prolixity in prospectuses. This has been due

---

Act Rel. 6383, 24 SEC Dock. 1262, 1282-85 (1982). Indeed, the availability of Form S-3 is conditioned on such ratings.

[13] Rule 463. For a detailed discussion of registration expenses — legal, accounting, and printing — see Schneider, Manko, and Kant, Going Public: Practice, Procedure, and Consequences (Packard Press 1983) 27-31.

[14] N. Y. Times, Sept. 25, 1984, p. D1, col. 1.

[15] Sec. Act Rel. 6519, 30 SEC Dock. 54 (1984) (soliciting comment from potential users); Sec. Act Rel. 6539, 30 SEC Dock. 1048 (1984) (adoption of temporary rules and forms to facilitate EDGAR's operation).

[16] Sec. Act Rel. 6651, 35 SEC Dock. 1215 (1986).

[17] See generally 51 SEC Ann. Rep. 20-22 (1985); Langevoort, Information Technology and the Structure of Securities Regulation, 98 Harv. L. Rev. 747 (1985). Mechanically, politically, and financially, however, all is not yet clear sailing. See Ingersoll, EDGAR, The SEC's Planned Data System Remains in High-Tech Limbo As New Bid Deadline Nears, Wall St. J., Nov. 28, 1986, p. 36, col. 1.

partly to the conservatism of lawyers who worry about the broad liabilities under §11 and partly to the Commission staff's insistence on "hard information." A former Chairman of the Commission had a little fun with what he called the "lugubrious approach to life and company affairs" that has marked prospectuses from the beginning:

> Or suppose General Eisenhower's D-Day order had to be filed with the SEC. "The officers who planned this assault, including myself, have never before planned anything like this. In fact, I have never commanded any troops in combat. The airborne and other methods being employed have never before been tried by our Army. The weather forecast is only slightly favorable and such forecasts have a high degree of unreliability. Therefore, there is no assurance that any of you will reach Normandy alive, or, if you do, that you can secure the beach."[18]

Things have improved somewhat in this respect since the Commission in the early 1970s lifted its previous ban against established corporate symbols or trademarks, as well as photographs of management, principal properties, and important products.[19] A Boston Gas Company prospectus of September 1, 1971 — which was innovative also in its relatively bold use of color in a map and picture — abbreviated 35 pages of text and financial information into an opening summary of 4 pages. Not surprisingly, that was promptly dubbed the "Mother Goose summary." Nevertheless, the problem, as two lawyers highly experienced in this area have observed, is perhaps intractable:

> The prospectus is a somewhat schizophrenic document, having two purposes which often present conflicting pulls. On the one hand, it is a selling document. It is used by the principal underwriters to form the underwriting syndicate and a dealer group, and by the underwriters and dealers to sell the securities to the public. From this point of view, it is desirable to present the best possible image. On the other hand, the prospectus is a disclosure document, an insurance policy against liability. With the view toward protection against liability, there is a tendency to resolve all doubts against the company and to make things look as bleak as possible. In balancing the purposes, established underwriters and experienced counsel, guided at least in part by their knowledge of the SEC staff attitudes, traditionally lean to a very conservative presentation. They avoid glowing adjectives, subjective evaluations and predictions about

[18]Garrett, Public Relations and Corporate Disclosures (address to Public Relations Society of America, Los Angeles, Sept. 25, 1975).
[19]Sec. Act Rel. 5171 (1971).

the future. The prospectus is limited to provable statements of historic fact. The layman frequently complains that all the glamor and romance has been lost. "Why can't you tell them," he says, "that we have the most aggressive and imaginative management in the industry?" It takes considerable client education before an attorney can answer this question to his client's satisfaction.[20]

Another philosophical problem that defies neat solution in a disclosure system is the extent to which there should be a disclosure of the integrity, ability, and diligence of management. This problem transcends the prospectus to implicate all disclosure documents, particularly proxy literature.

In *Franchard Corp.*, a leading case decided in 1964, the Commission started with the premise, "Of cardinal importance in any business is the quality of its management."[21] And it thought that the very difficulty of disclosing management's integrity or ability in any meaningful way, which made generalization misleading, made specific disclosures all the more important. Therefore, it found that a registration statement was misleading because of its failure to disclose (1) the issuer's transfers to its controlling stockholder and chief executive officer of large sums that he used in his own ventures and (2) pledges of his stock by that stockholder, a man whose reputation as a real estate syndicator was an important investor attraction, as security for high-interest loans that placed him in a strained financial condition, created a likelihood of a shift in control, and gave rise to potential conflicts of interest with shareholders in fixing the issuer's financial policy. The Commission considered it irrelevant that the omitted facts were unknown to the other officers and directors.

Self-dealing, in other words, is material even if it does not affect the company's financial condition, because it has a direct hearing on management *integrity* and *competence*. This is especially true when stockholders are asked to vote for directors.[22] But *diligence* is another matter. In the *Franchard* case the Commission went on to say that the required identification of the members of the board was not an implied representation that they would exercise the degree of diligence that might be required by the varying standards of state

[20] Schneider, Manko, and Kant, Going Public — Practices, Procedures and Consequences (Packard Press 1986) 12.

[21] 42 SEC 163, 169 (1964).

[22] In Treadway Companies v. Cave Corp., 638 F. 2d 357 (2d Cir. 1980), the court ordered a new election in a proxy context, because the stockholders had voted at a time when a court order had prevented their obtaining material information with respect to the integrity and competence of candidates for the board.

corporation law. Despite the standard of care specified in §11, the Act does not purport "to define federal standards of directors' responsibility in the orderly operations of business enterprises and nowhere empowers us to formulate administratively such regulatory standards."[23] Particularly because the state courts for various reasons, including the complexity and diversity of business activities, have shown "a marked reluctance to interfere with good faith business judgments," a general requirement of "information in Securities Act prospectuses as to whether directors have performed their duties in accordance with the standards of responsibility required of them under state law would stretch disclosure beyond the limitations contemplated by the statutory scheme and necessitated by considerations of administrative practicality."[24]

The Commission observed that it had required disclosure concerning directors' performance in situations involving a virtual abdication of responsibility or when the prospectus had made affirmative representations by which their performance could be tested. "But the disclosures sought here by the staff would require evaluation of the entire conduct of a board of directors in the context of the whole business operations of a company in the light of diverse and uncertain standards. In our view, this is a function which the disclosure requirements of the Securities Act cannot effectively discharge. It would either result in self-serving generalities of little value to investors or grave uncertainties both on the part of those who must enforce and those who must comply with that Act."[25]

Judge Frankel put it more dramatically a few years later:

> * * * it is bemusing, and ultimately pointless, to charge that directors perpetrated a "material omission" when they failed to (a) discover and adjudge faithless motives for their actions and (b) announce such a discovery in reporting the products of their managerial efforts and judgment. The securities laws, while their central insistence is indeed upon disclosure, were never intended to attempt any such measures of psychoanalysis or reported self-analysis. The unclean heart of a director is not actionable, whether or not it is "disclosed," unless the impurities are translated into actionable deeds or omissions both objective and external.[26]

It has been held, similarly, that *motive* (for example, entrench-

[23] Franchard Corp., 42 SEC 163, 176 (1964).
[24] Id. at 178.
[25] Ibid.
[26] Stedman v. Storer, 308 F. Supp. 881, 887 (S. D. N. Y. 1969); cf. Kademian v. Ladish Co., 792 F. 2d 614, 627 (9th Cir. 1986).

ment of control) need not be disclosed[27] so long as the facts are adequately stated and the motive is not "manipulative or deceptive."[28]

But the Commission itself soon distinguished *Franchard* in a disciplinary proceeding against a broker-dealer firm that acted as investment adviser and underwriter for two investment companies. In view of the failure to provide unaffiliated directors of each investment company with relevant information on important investments and other transactions, the Commission found that the implication inherent in each prospectus that those directors were discharging their responsibilities to the other members of the board and to shareholders, and that investors were being accorded the benefits of responsible and objective observation and consideration of the investment company's activities by unaffiliated directors, was materially misleading. In *Franchard*, by contrast, not only was the board regularly informed as to the company's affairs; it was also obvious that a single individual would exercise the dominant role in managing the operations.[29]

There are no neat answers here. In 1980 the Commission's General Counsel expressed the view that "*Franchard* is best captured as a philosophical rumination of the Commission on the corporate governance process at an early point in time."[30] And the Commission's concern became painfully apparent to many companies in connection with the post-Watergate disclosures of what were euphemistically called "questionable payments" abroad — a development that resulted in the outlawry of such practices by the Foreign

[27] Golub v. PPD Corp., 576 F. 2d 759, 765 (8th Cir. 1978); Biesenbach v. Guenther, 588 F. 2d 400, 402 (3d Cir. 1978); Rodman v. Grant Foundation, 608 F. 2d 64, 71 (2d Cir. 1979); District 65, UAW v. Harper & Row, Publishers, Inc., 576 F. Supp. 1468, 1486 (S. D. N. Y. 1983) (no duty to disclose motive, breach of fiduciary duty, or possible alternatives to management's proposals); Steinberg v. Pargas, Inc., CCH Fed. Sec. L. Rep. ¶91,979 at 90,878-79 (S. D. N. Y. 1985).

[28] Vaughn v. Teledyne, Inc., 628 F. 2d 1214, 1221 (9th Cir. 1980).

[29] Imperial Financial Services, Inc., 42 SEC 717 (1965).

[30] Ferrara, Current Issues Between Corporations and Shareholders: Federal Intervention into Corporate Governance, 36 Bus. Law. 759, 769 (1980); see also Ferrara, Disclosure of Management Integrity and Competency — Sliding Down the "Slippery Slope" of Materiality, in L. Gower, L. Loss, and A. Sommer (cochairmen), New Trends in Company Law Disclosure (London conference under auspices of Law & Business, Inc., New York, and Institute of Advanced Legal Studies, U. of London, 1980) 148; Schneider, Soft Information Disclosure: A Semi-revolution, in Practising Law Institute, Fifteenth Annual Institute on Securities Regulation (1984) c. 2 at 44-53.

Corrupt Practices Act of 1977.[31] In its 1976 "Report to Congress on Questionable and Illegal Payments," the Commission, stating that "investors should be vitally interested in the quality and integrity of management," emphasized that disclosure of conflicts of interest and special perquisites to management

> reflects the deeply held belief that the managements of corporations are stewards acting on behalf of the shareholders, who are entitled to honest use of, and accounting for, the funds entrusted to the corporation and to procedures necessary to assure accountability and disclosure of the manner in which management performs its stewardship.[32]

As the court stated in holding that a corporation's failure to disclose an insider's kickbacks from one of its suppliers violated both the reporting and proxy rules under the 1934 Act, "One does not elect as a director an individual who is using the corporation he represents for personal gain."[33] On the other hand, the Ninth Circuit in 1981, speaking to the proxy rules under §14 of the 1934 Act, drew

> a sharp distinction * * * between allegations of director misconduct involving breach of trust or self-dealing — the nondisclosure of which is presumptively material — and allegations of simple breach of fiduciary duty/waste of corporate assets — the nondisclosure of which is never material for §14(a) purposes. * * *
>
> * * * The distinction between "mere" bribes and bribes coupled with kickbacks to the directors makes a great deal of sense, indeed, is fundamental to a meaningful concept of materiality under §14(a) and the preservation of state corporate law.

[31] 91 Stat. 1494 (1977). That Act amended §13(b) of the 1934 Act with respect to accounting standards (see p. 161 infra), added §30A to the 1934 Act in order to forbid foreign bribes with respect to companies reporting under that Act, and, altogether apart from the SEC, authorized the Attorney General to institute injunctive (as well as criminal) proceedings in the event of foreign bribes by "domestic concerns" that were not reporting companies under the 1934 Act. See Symposium, The Foreign Corrupt Practices Act: Domestic and International Implications, 9 Syracuse J. Int'l L. & Commerce 235 (1982); United States v. McLean, 738 F. 2d 655 (5th Cir. 1984), *cert. denied,* 470 U. S. 1050 (employee cannot be convicted without prior conviction of employer).

[32] S. Com. on Banking, Housing & Urban Affairs, 94th Cong., 2d Sess. (Com. Print 1976).

[33] SEC v. Kalvex, Inc., 425 F. Supp. 310, 315 (S. D. N. Y. 1975); see also Roeder v. Alpha Industries, Inc., 814 F. 2d 22, 25-26 (1st Cir. 1987). Nor does one "elect as a trustee or director an individual *who knows, or should know,* that other directors or trustees are using the corporation for a personal gain and vote in favor of such transactions, or raise no objection to such transactions." Perelman v. Pennsylvania Real Estate Investment Trust, 432 F. Supp. 1298, 1303-04 (E. D. Pa. 1977).

* * *

> Absent credible allegations of self-dealing by the directors or dishonesty or deceit which inures to the direct, personal benefit of the directors — a fact that demonstrates a betrayal of trust to the corporation and shareholders and the director's essential unfitness for corporate stewardship — we hold that director misconduct of the type traditionally regulated by state corporate law need not be disclosed in proxy solicitations for director elections. This type of mismanagement, unadorned by self-dealing, is simply not material or otherwise within the ambit of the federal securities laws. * * *[34]

The ultimate question of materiality is a bit easier to determine when there is or has been a proceeding of some sort. With respect to events that occurred during the past five years and that are "material to an evaluation of the ability or integrity of any director," or nominee for a directorship or executive officer, there must be disclosure (*inter alia*) whether the person (1) was convicted or is a defendant in a criminal proceeding, or (2) was the subject of any

[34]Gaines v. Haughton, 645 F. 2d 761, 776-79 (9th Cir. 1981), *cert. denied,* 454 U. S. 1145; but cf. Decker v. Massey-Ferguson, Ltd., 681 F. 2d 111, 115-19 (2d Cir. 1982). The impact of Santa Fe Industries, Inc. v. Green, 430 U. S. 462 (1977) infra p. 803, is apparent.

This and other cases have led two commentators to conclude:

> Despite litigation during the past ten years regarding the independent standing of integrity of management disclosures under the federal securities laws, the primary issues remain unresolved. The case law has failed to develop uniform standards of analysis and in some instances appears to be inconsistent with the general standards of materiality articulated by the Supreme Court. Thus, the case law is instructive only in those isolated instances of corporate misconduct that conform to familiar factual patterns viewed as material in prior decisions by both the courts and the commission; namely, misconduct that (1) involves self-dealing or concurrent financial materiality, or (2) is the subject of pending proceedings or has already resulted in convictions, fines, or administrative sanctions against the corporation or individual members of senior management. In such instances, the weight of authority requires disclosure. The statutes, case law, and commission's regulations, however, provide no definitive guidance relating to disclosure of illegal conduct by members of senior management that falls outside those boundaries.

Branch and Rubright, Integrity of Management Disclosures under the Federal Securities Laws, 37 Bus. Law. 1447, 1478-79 (1982); see also Longstreth, SEC Disclosure Policy Regarding Management Integrity, 38 Bus. Law. 1413 (1983); Block, Barton, and Olah, Judicial Limitations on Federal Disclosure Requirements Regarding Management Integrity, 14 Sec. Reg. L. J. 354 (1987). For a discussion of the evolution toward a more active SEC role in "corporate governance," see Steinberg, The Securities and Exchange Commission's Administrative, Enforcement, and Legislative Programs and Policies — Their Influence on Corporate Internal Affairs, 58 Notre Dame Law. 173, 216-18 (1982); see also p. 465 infra.

judicial limitation with respect to a security or commodity transaction or "any type of business practice."[35]

In a criminal case the Second Circuit has refused to stretch the required disclosure to include *uncharged* criminal conduct.[36] And on the civil side the same court has reacted similarly to unadjudicated allegations of "breach of trust," at least when not involving the company in question.[37] But, notwithstanding the inapplicability of the Commission's rule to unadjudicated civil allegations, most courts require disclosure of lawsuits pending against director-nominees when the allegations are material.[38]

3. THE SEC AND ACCOUNTING

If this is not the place for a "how to do it" discussion of how to register, *a fortiori* there is room for only a minimal treatment of the SEC's role in the world of accounting. That role goes far beyond the matter of financial data required to be included in the 1933 Act registration statement. For comprehensive financial statements are required also by the 1934 Act and the Holding Company and Investment Company Acts. Moreover, both the 1933 and 1934 Acts authorize the Commission to define accounting terms and to prescribe "the items or details to be shown in the balance sheet and earning statement, and the methods to be followed in the preparation of accounts, in the appraisal or valuation of assets and liabilities, in the determination of depreciation and depletion, in the differentiation of recurring and nonrecurring income, in the differentiation of investment and operating income, and in the preparation, where the Commission deems it necessary or desirable, of consolidated balance sheets or income accounts of any person" in a control relationship with the issuer.[39]

[35] Reg. S-K, Item 401(f).

[36] United States v. Matthews, 787 F. 2d 38, 46-50 (2d Cir. 1986).

[37] GAF Corp. v. Heyman, 724 F. 2d 727 (2d Cir. 1983).

[38] See Michaelson, "Breach of Trust": The Duty to Disclose Pending Litigation in a Contest for Corporate Control, 37 Rutgers L. Rev. 1 (1984); Beatty v. Bright, 318 F. Supp. 169 (S. D. Iowa 1970); Robinson v. Penn Central Co., 336 F. Supp. 655 (E. D. Pa. 1971); Rafal v. Geneen, 368 F. Supp. 255, 261 (E. D. Pa. 1972); cf. Zell v. InterCapital Income Securities, Inc., 675 F. 2d 1041, 1044 (9th Cir. 1982) (proxy statement seeking shareholder approval to retain investment management firm failed to disclose that the firm and its principals had been named as defendants in many lawsuits alleging fraud and other misconduct).

[39] Sec. Act §19(a); Sec. Ex. Act §13(b); cf. Inv. Co. Act §38(a); see also id., §§30(e), 31(c), 32. The "bible" here for many years was L. Rappaport, SEC Accounting Practice and Procedure (3d ed. 1972). For a current treatment, see J. Burton, R. Palmer, and R. Kay, Handbook of Accounting and Auditing (1981

To the extent of its jurisdiction as so prescribed, one would expect the Commission's impact on accounting principles and practices to be substantial. For what is the purpose of accounting if not full and fair disclosure? Indeed, if it is true (as the saying went) that the SEC "made a lady out of Wall Street," it is equally true that it had a great deal to do with raising public accountancy to the status of a genuine profession.

Actually the Commission's impact has been considerably broader than a literal reading of the statutes would indicate. In the first place, accountants that develop certain habits in preparing financial statements for filing with the SEC are apt to carry those habits over to non-SEC work. The Commission's stringent view on auditors' independence has also influenced the profession generally. And, although the SEC cannot directly regulate the reports sent to stockholders as distinct from those filed under the several statutes, we shall see later that the Commission (perhaps dubiously) has used its proxy rules under §14 of the 1934 Act to assert a significant measure of *indirect* control over the financial statements contained in stockholders' reports.[40]

For some years — partly but not entirely because of the pressure of an inflationary economy on historical cost concepts — the accounting world has been in ferment. There has been an explosion of litigation — SEC disciplinary proceedings, civil actions, both SEC-initiated[41] and private,[42] and even criminal prosecutions of partners

---

with 1987 update). The Code in §1805 gathers the accounting and records provisions of all the SEC statutes with some changes.

In United States v. Arthur Young & Co., 465 U. S. 805, 810-11 (1984), where the Court held that there was no work-product privilege for tax accrual work papers prepared by an independent auditor during a routine review of a company's financial statements for compliance with the securities laws, Chief Justice Burger stated for a unanimous Court: "Corporate financial statements are one of the primary sources of information available to guide the decisions of the investing public. In an effort to control the accuracy of the financial data available to investors in the securities markets, various provisions of the federal securities laws require publicly held corporations to file their financial statements with the Securities and Exchange Commission." Also: "By certifying the public reports that collectively depict a corporation's financial status, the independent auditor assumes a *public* responsibility transcending any employment relationship with the client. The independent public accountant performing this special function owes ultimate allegiance to the corporation's creditors and stockholders, as well as to investing public. This 'public watchdog' function demands that the accountant maintain total independence from the client at all times and requires complete fidelity to the public trust." Id. at 817-18.

[40] See p. 434 infra.

[41] In Peat, Marwick, Mitchell & Co., Acctg. Ser. Rel. 173, 7 SEC Dock. 301 (1975), *modified,* Acctg. Ser. Rel. 173A, 12 SEC Dock. 361 (1977), the Commission announced a settlement of four injunctive actions with respect to four separate audits. The settlement contemplated, among other things, a compre-

in leading firms of accountants. Most disciplinary proceedings, brought under Rule 2(e) of the Commission's Rules of Practice,[43] have resulted, like the typical injunctive action, in settlements calling for such steps as review of the firm's auditing procedures by persons satisfactory to the Commission's Chief Accountant, completion of continuing professional education programs, and "peer review."[44] And the Second Circuit has permitted a criminal jury to find that financial statements did not fairly present the facts even though they followed "generally accepted accounting principles" (GAAP).[45] The Commission is fond of quoting Judge Friendly's statement: "In our complex society the accountant's certificate and the lawyer's opinion can be instruments for inflicting pecuniary loss more potent than the chisel or the crow-bar."[46]

Another cause of the ferment has gone to the essence of the Commission's role in the establishment of accounting principles. Apart from its general accounting regulation, Regulation S-X — which specifies the financial statements to be included in the registration and reporting forms and, insofar as it requires a particular method of accounting, is not believed to conflict "with the basic policy of relying on the FASB [the Financial Accounting Standards Board] for leadership in establishing financial accounting and reporting standards"[47] — the Commission has chosen to rely for the most part on the profession to establish generally accepted account-

---

hensive investigation of the firm's audit practices by a committee selected by the firm and the Commission's staff.

[42] E. g., Herzfeld v. Laventhol, Krekstein, Horwath & Horwath, 540 F. 2d 27 (2d Cir. 1976).

[43] The validity of this rule as applied to accountants was sustained in Touche, Ross & Co. v. SEC, 609 F. 2d 570 (2d Cir. 1979); Davy v. SEC, 792 F. 2d 1418 (9th Cir. 1986). See c. 11B infra.

[44] E. g., Benjamin Botwinick & Co., Acctg. Ser. Rel. 168 (1975); John E. Harrington, AAE Rel. 81, 34 SEC Dock. 859, 870-71 (1985). On April 1, 1987, the Commission published for comment proposed rule amendments that would require that filed financial statements be certified by an independent accountant that has undergone a peer review of its accounting and auditing practice within the last three years. "Available information," the Commission stated, "supports the position that peer review contributes to the improvement of the quality of audits, which in turn improves the reliability of financial statements." Sec. Act Rel. 6695, 37 SEC Dock. 1364 (1987). "Accountants would have the option of satisfying the requirement by undergoing a peer review under the auspices of an acceptable peer review organization ('PRO') or, alternatively, by having their peer review supervised directly by the Commission." Id. at 1366.

[45] United States v. Simon, 425 F. 2d 796 (2d Cir. 1969), *cert. denied*, 397 U. S. 1006; see also United States v. Natelli, 527 F. 2d 311 (2d Cir. 1975), *cert. denied*, 425 U. S. 934.

[46] United States v. Benjamin, 328 F. 2d 854, 863 (2d Cir. 1964), *cert denied sub nom.* Howard v. United States, 377 U. S. 953.

[47] Sec. Act Rel. 6233, 20 SEC Dock. 1115, 1118 (1980).

ing principles. This approach goes back to the famous Accounting Series Release 4 of 1938 — the "great treaty" as Chairman Garrett called it.[48]

In 1972 a study committee appointed under the chairmanship of former Commissioner Wheat by the American Institute of Certified Public Accountants rejected the idea of a new government rule-making authority in favor of a Financial Accounting Standards Board of seven full-time members selected by a Financial Accounting Foundation that would also see to the Board's financing and review its operations.[49] With this apparatus in place, the Commission announced that it would regard only those principles, standards, and practices promulgated in the FASB's "statements and interpretation" as having substantial authoritative support for purposes of Release 4.[50]

This self-abnegation has been attacked from various quarters, both legislative[51] and private.[52] But in a series of reports the SEC

[48]SEC Codification of Financial Reporting Policies §101; Garrett, The Accounting Profession and Accounting Principles (address before Second Annual Robert M. Trueblood Memorial Conference, Ill. C. P. A. Foundation, Chicago, Oct. 3, 1975) 5. The Commission, however, has been historically in advance of the profession so far as standards of accountants' independence are concerned. See, e. g., Acctg. Ser. Rel. 296, 23 SEC Dock. 566 (1981), SEC Codification, supra, §§601.01, 604.01.

In Financial Reporting Release 1, 25 SEC Dock. 2 (1982), the Commission announced the publication of a codification of the relevant portions of the 100 Accounting Series Releases. SEC Codification of Financial Reporting Policies (1982). The Accounting Series Releases were then replaced by two new series: Financial Reporting Releases for accounting and auditing matters of general interest, and Accounting and Auditing Enforcement Releases for enforcement matters. See AAE Rel. 1, 25 SEC Dock. 4 (1982).

[49]AICPA, Establishing Financial Accounting Standards (1972).

[50]Acctg. Ser. Rel. 150, 3 SEC Dock. 275 (1973), SEC Codification of Financial Reporting Policies §101; see also Acctg. Ser. Rel. 280, 20 SEC Dock. 1115 (1980), SEC Codification, loc. cit. supra. For a case reflecting disparate views among the members of the Commission with respect to whether a particular subject comes within the category of professional judgment, see American Express Co., AAE Rel. 101, 35 SEC Dock. 1163, 1171-72 (1986).

[51]See Federal Regulation and Regulatory Reform, Report by Subcom. on Oversight & Investigations, House Com. on Int. & For. Commerce, 94th Cong., 2d Sess. (the "Moss Report") (1976) 18, 32-39, 51-52; Subcom. on Reports, Acctg. & Mgmt. of S. Com. on Gov't Operations, The Accounting Establishment: A Staff Study, 95th Cong., 1st Sess. (1977), leading to the report of the subcommittee itself, Improving the Accountability of Publicly Owned Corporations and Their Auditors (the "Metcalf Report") (1977); see also Oversight of the Accounting Profession: Hearings before Subcom. on Governmental Efficiency & the District of Columbia, S. Com. on Governmental Affairs, 96th Cong., 1st Sess. (1979) (successor to Metcalf subcommittee); SEC and Corporate Audits, Hearings before Subcom. on Oversight and Investigations, House Com. on Energy & Commerce, 99th Cong., 1st Sess. (1985).

[52]Some have complained that the Commission has not gone far enough. See

has stuck to its guns, relying primarily on the establishment in 1977 of a new SEC Practice Section within the AICPA Division of CPA Firms, whose work is overseen by a Public Oversight Board of nonaccountants.[53]

Still another bone of contention — this time between the Commission and the profession — grew out of §13(b)(2) of the 1934 Act, which found its way into the law as part of the Foreign Corrupt Practices Act of 1977. That section broadly requires every reporting company to "(A) make and keep books, records, and accounts, which, in reasonable detail, accurately and fairly reflect the transactions and dispositions of the assets of the issuer," and (B) maintain a system of internal accounting controls sufficient to provide those "reasonable assurances" that the section specifies.[54] Proposed SEC rules that would have required all annual reports filed with the Commission or mailed under the proxy rules to include a management statement on internal accounting control, reported on by an independent accountant, encountered substantial opposition and were withdrawn, the Commission later noting the significant private sector initiatives in the area.[55]

Arthur Andersen & Co., Establishing Accounting Principles — A Crisis in Decision Making (1965) 3, 9 and *passim;* Kripke, The SEC, the Accountants, Some Myths and Some Realities, 45 N. Y. U. L. Rev. 1151, 1175-1204 (1970). At the other extreme, it has been asserted that "the SEC's accounting disclosure requirements are of small, if any, relevance to investors * * *." Benston, The Effectiveness and Effects of the SEC's Accounting Disclosure Requirements, in H. Manne (ed.), Economic Policy and the Regulation of Corporate Securities (1968) 23, 50.

[53] SEC, Report to Congress on the Accounting Profession and the Commission's Oversight Role, 95th Cong., 2d Sess. (Com. Print 1978), reprinted without appendixes and the much longer SEC *staff* report, CCH Fed. Sec. L. Rep. ¶81,634. Two more reports under the same title were submitted in 1979 and 1980. See also 50 SEC Ann. Rep. 17-19 (1984). For a short fifty-year summary of the relationship between the SEC and the accounting profession, see Moran and Previts, The SEC and the Profession, 1934-84: The Realities of Self-Regulation, 158 J. Accountancy 68 (1984). For a general discussion of the interaction of the SEC and the accounting profession, see 7 J. Comp. Bus. & Capital Market L. 233, esp. Seligman, The SEC and Accounting: A Historical Perspective, id. at 241 (1985).

[54] See [ABA] Committee on Corporate Law and Accounting, A Guide to the New Section 13(b)(2) Accounting Requirements of the Securities Exchange Act of 1934, 34 Bus. Law. 307 (1978); same committee, Practical Implications of the Accounting Provisions of the Foreign Corrupt Practices Act of 1977, and Recent Developments (transcript of a program), 35 Bus. Law. 713 (1980). For the legislative history, see Lewis v. Sporck, 612 F. Supp. 1316 (N. D. Cal. 1985).

[55] Sec. Ex. Act Rel. 15,772, 17 SEC Dock. 421 (1979); Sec. Ex. Act Rel. 16,877, 20 SEC Dock. 310 (1980); Sec. Ex. Act Rel. 18,451, 24 SEC Dock. 746 (1982). The Commission, however, did use its new authority to adopt Rules 13b-1 and 13b-2, which prohibit the falsification of corporate records or accounts as well as a director's or officer's making materially false, misleading, or

There has also been a radical change in the SEC's views with respect to "soft information," notably profit forecasts. Traditionally the Commission disallowed forecasts in prospectuses and proxy statements as distinct from shareholders' reports or discussions with financial analysts. Then a number of cases gave pause. In one, brought under §11, the court held that a registration statement filed in connection with a takeover bid should have disclosed the target insurance company's "surplus surplus" (that is to say, the surplus in excess of the amount required by the state insurance authorities) despite counsel's advice that the estimates were too unreliable; for the surplus surplus was one of the principal reasons for the takeover attempt.[56] In another case the court rejected a complaint against a chemical company because the shortfall had been due to a recession that had hit synthetic fiber producers with particular impact, and the company over a period of years had carefully developed internal forecast figures that were consistent with the published figures, and the published forecast had fit into a continuing framework of regular dissemination of company news, good or bad.[57]

Partly at least under the impact of these cases, it must be presumed, the Commission announced in 1973, after a public rulemaking proceeding, that it would permit but not require reasonably based projections, under rules to be issued for comment, in the case of companies with a history of reported earnings and internal budgeting.[58] But then the Commission began to back and fill a bit. In 1976, because of the questioning comments[59] it had received on a

incomplete statements to an accountant in connection with an audit or examination or the preparation or filing of required reports. Sec. Ex. Act Rel. 15,570, 16 SEC Dock. 1143, 1147-48 (1979). See Michael R. Murray, Sec. Ex. Act Rel. 23,067, 35 SEC Dock. 435 (1986) (company controller who was highest ranking accounting employee, though not a decision maker, had a duty to the company and its stockholders not to assist, or even acquiesce, in false financial statements).

[56] Feit v. Leasco Data Processing Equipment Corp., 332 F. Supp. 544 (E. D. N. Y. 1971).

[57] Dolgow v. Anderson, 53 F. R. D. 64 (E. D. N. Y. 1971), *aff'd per curiam,* 464 F. 2d 437 (2d Cir. 1972); see also Polin v. Conductron Corp., 552 F. 2d 797, 806 n. 28 (8th Cir. 1977), *cert. denied,* 434 U. S. 857. Contrast this "rule of reason" approach with the "highly probable" realization test of Beecher v. Able, 374 F. Supp. 341 (S. D. N. Y. 1974) —which supported the worst expectations of those who opposed forecasts as too dangerous legally — although the court after trial found that there was no recklessness as required by Rule 10b-5 as long as there was *some* basis for the prediction. Id., CCH Fed. Sec. L. Rep. ¶95,303 (S. D. N. Y. 1975).

[58] Sec. Act Rel. 5362, 1 SEC Dock. No. 1, p. 4 (1973).

[59] See Financial Executives Research Foundation, Public Disclosure of Business Forecasts (1972), a two-part study by a management consulting firm and a law firm, which reported that more than 97 percent of the responding companies

set of proposed "safe harbor" rules[60] and the diversity of views expressed, the Commission withdrew its proposal and said it would neither encourage nor discourage forecasts. The Commission added, nevertheless, that it would not object to good faith projections that had a reasonable basis and an appropriate format and were accompanied by information adequate to enable investors to make their own judgments. The Commission also went out of its way to express its belief that appropriate projections should not create civil liability simply because they turned out to be erroneous.[61]

By late 1978 the Commission had apparently developed enough confidence to publish a comprehensive release together with staff guides[62] and alternative versions of a proposed "safe harbor rule."[63] Among other things, the release discussed the duty to correct projections known to have become misleading. But the Commission imposed no reporting or operating history or other status criteria, and it stated that, although disclosure of assumptions underlying projections was desirable, it was not essential.[64]

Finally, in order to encourage projections both in filings and generally, the Commission in mid-1979 adopted "safe harbor" rules under the 1933 and 1934 Acts, to the effect that a "forward looking statement" is not a "fraudulent statement" unless the plaintiff shows a lack of reasonable basis or good faith.[65] Although the rules as proposed for comment would have put the burden of proof with respect to reasonableness and good faith on the defendant, the

---

prepared sales, expense, and earnings forecasts, but that all companies expressed concern over the consequences of releasing their internal figures.

[60] Sec. Act Rel. 5581, 6 SEC Dock. 746 (1975).

[61] Sec. Act Rel. 5699, 9 SEC Dock. 472 (1976).

[62] Sec. Act Rel. 5992, 16 SEC Dock. 81 (1978).

[63] Sec. Act Rel. 5993, 16 SEC Dock. 90 (1978).

[64] In 1982 the Commission promulgated a detailed statement of its policy with respect to projections in all disclosure documents. Reg. S-K, Item 10(b). See Bradshaw v. Jenkins, CCH Fed. Sec. L. Rep. ¶99,719 at 97,909 (W. D. Wash. 1984) (defendants had no duty to disclose their estimates of future loan write-offs and litigation liabilities in proxy solicitation material); Howing Co. v. Nationwide Corp., 625 F. Supp. 146, 153-54 (S. D. Ohio 1985) (proxy and tender offer rules require disclosure of soft information only if the underlying predictions "are substantially certain to hold"); Kademian v. Ladish Co., 792 F. 2d 614, 625 (7th Cir. 1986) (court referred to "the general proposition that there is no duty to disclose internal valuations under the federal securities laws").

[65] Rules 175 and 3b-6, adopted by Sec. Act Rel. 6084, 17 SEC Dock. 1048 (1979). See Rubin v. Long Island Lighting Co., 576 F. Supp. 608, 613 n. 8 (E. D. N. Y. 1984). In Jackson v. Daniels, CCH Fed. Sec. L. Rep. ¶92,045 (D. N. M. 1985), Rule 175 was held inapplicable for a number of reasons.

Commission deferred to the recommendation of its Advisory Committee on Corporate Disclosure.[66]

The Code's solution is a definition of "fact" to include "a promise, prediction, estimate, projection, or forecast," with a provision that such a fact "is not a misrepresentation if it (i) is made in good faith, (ii) has a reasonable basis when it is made, and (iii) complies with any applicable rule so far as underlying assumptions or other conditions are concerned."[67]

[66]See p. 35 n. 28 supra. In Flynn v. Bass Brothers Enterprises, Inc., 744 F. 2d 978 (3d Cir. 1984), the court, taking note of the administrative evolution, said that appraisals must be disclosed "in appropriate cases," but the court declined to apply that view retroactively to a tender offer that had preceded the Commission's about-face. Cf. Weinberger v. Rio Grande Industries, Inc., 519 A. 2d 116, 126-29 (Del. Ch. 1986) (Delaware law). In contrast to this case-by-case approach, the rule in the Sixth Circuit is that "soft information such as asset appraisals and projections must [as distinct from may] be disclosed only if the reported values are virtually as certain as hard facts." Starkman v. Marathon Oil Co., 772 F. 2d 231, 241 (6th Cir. 1985), *cert. denied,* 106 S. Ct. 1195. See also Walker v. Action Industries, Inc., 802 F. 2d 703 (4th Cir. 1986), *cert. denied,* 107 S. Ct. 952 (court summarized cases and held that there was no duty under the circumstances to disclose financial projections).

[67]§§202(55)(B), 202(96)(B). On burden of proof, see 1 Code 158, Comment (e); on duty to correct, see §1602(b)(2). On contingent liabilities, see c. 11D infra. See generally Schneider, Soft Information Disclosures: A Semi-revolution in Practising Law Institute, Fifteenth Annual Institute on Securities Regulation (1984) c. 2. It is there suggested (1) that, "even before the recent change of orientation, the SEC had developed a double standard, depending on whether soft information was favorable or adverse" (id. at 21), and (2) that the evolving requirement for "management discussion and analysis" (see pp. 161-62 infra) is another indication of the Commission's change of view (id. at 24-25). See also Schneider, Mandatory Disclosure of Appraisals and other Soft Information: A Comment on *Flynn* v. *Bass Brothers,* in Practising Law Institute, Sixteenth Annual Institute on Securities Regulation (1984) c. 16.

CHAPTER 3

A WHAT! A "SECURITY" (HEREIN OF "ISSUER" AS WELL)

A. A PRELIMINARY THOUGHT

The definition in §2(1) of the 1933 Act borrowed from the earlier blue sky definitions, which had already developed something of a judicial gloss. And §401(l) of the Uniform Securities Act is identical with §2(1) except for the oil and gas language and the exclusion of orthodox insurance and annuities from §401(l).[1] But there are enough variations, with additional phrases in some of the state statutes, to indicate caution with respect to interchangeability of federal and state precedents. Indeed, the 1933 and 1934 federal definitions themselves are not identical, as we shall see.

Even so, such is the complexity of the financial world that after seven decades and more of securities regulation there is still a constant stream of cases that seek to draw the line between "securities" and real property or tangible or intangible personal property or various hybrids emanating from the banking and insurance industries. The definition has been before the Supreme Court no fewer than nine times.

B. DEBT SECURITIES

1. Notes

The definitions of "security" in both §2(1) of the 1933 Act and §3(a)(10) of the 1934 Act begin by including "any note."[1] At the

C. 3A [1] See pp. 205-06 infra.

C. 3B [1] There *is* a difference: §3(a)(3) of the 1933 Act merely *exempts from registration* (as distinct from the fraud provisions) "Any note, draft, bill of exchange, or bankers' acceptance which arises out of a current transaction or the

same time, all the definitions are introduced by the phrase, "unless the context otherwise requires."[2] Even apart from this legislative rubber, two propositions are clear:

(1) A public offering of instruments that are denominated "notes" but might just as well be called "debentures" or "bonds" is clearly an offer of a "security." Else we might expect to see all debt instruments termed "notes."[3]

(2) Just as clearly, the personal "note" given as a down payment on a television set is *not* a "security." Else every unsatisfactory picture tube might end up in federal court, without regard to diversity of citizenship or jurisdictional amount, as a fraudulent "purchase" of a "security" in violation of Rule 10b-5.

The difficulty, as usual, comes somewhere between these two extreme propositions. Three overlapping approaches have developed:[4]

---

proceeds of which have been or are to be used for current transactions, and which has a maturity at the time of issuance of not exceeding nine months, exclusive of days of grace, or any renewal thereof the maturity of which is likewise limited," whereas §3(a)(10) of the 1934 Act (without reference to the "current transaction" test) *excludes* such short-term paper *from the definition,* so that one would expect even the fraud provisions of the 1934 Act to be inapplicable. But on the premise that the two definitions are *in pari materia* (see Tcherepnin v. Knight, 389 U. S. 332, 335-36 (1967)), the courts in Rule 10b-5 cases have ignored the maturity factor. See McClure v. First National Bank of Lubbock, Tex., 497 F. 2d 490, 495 (5th Cir. 1974), *cert. denied,* 420 U. S. 930, where the court conceded that "The original scrivener of the definitional section [3(a)(10)] may well wonder what happened to his carefully drawn exemption on the way to the courthouse * * *."

On the preliminary question whether a note's maturity does exceed nine months, the court in Chemical Bank v. Arthur Andersen & Co., 726 F. 2d 930, 937 (2d Cir. 1984), *cert. denied,* 469 U. S. 884, held that the date of issuance was critical with respect to an original issuance, but that the answer was not so clear with respect to a renewal:

> It can be argued that the word "likewise" in the final clause of §3(a)(3) picks up the entire phrase "a maturity at the time of issuance of not exceeding nine months." On the other hand, it can be contended that the term "likewise" embraces only the words "a maturity of not exceeding nine months" since * * * it makes little business sense to exclude a period when renewed notes were still outstanding but overdue.

[2] See p. 245-46 infra.

[3] See, e. g., Llanos v. United States, 206 F. 2d 852 (9th Cir. 1953), *cert. denied* 346 U. S. 923; People v. Milne, 690 P. 2d 829 (Colo. 1984) (Colorado Unif Sec. Act); Robertson v. White, 635 F. Supp. 851 (W. D. Ark. 1986) (state statute offering of demand notes to 1600 members of farmers' cooperative).

[4] SEC v. Diversified Industries, Inc., 465 F. Supp. 104, 108-11 (D. D. C. 1979). The court held that a ten-year purchase money mortgage note given as par payment for real estate was a "security" under all three approaches.

A. THE COMMERCIAL/INVESTMENT DICHOTOMY TEST OF THE [FIRST,] THIRD, FIFTH, SEVENTH, AND TENTH CIRCUITS

The "investment/commercial dichotomy test," which has been followed in the [First,] Third, Fifth, Seventh, and Tenth Circuits, is premised on the view that Congress's concern in enacting the securities laws was with practices associated with investment transactions and that the securities laws were not designed to regulate commercial transactions. See *C. N. S. Enterprises, Inc.* v. *G. & G. Enterprises, Inc.*, 508 F. 2d 1354, 1359 (7th Cir.) *cert. denied,* 423 U. S. 825 (1975). The decision of the U. S. Court of Appeals for the Seventh Circuit in *C. N. S. Enterprises, Inc.* contains a helpful description of the investment/commercial test.

* * *

Although a case-by-case approach has been adopted under the commercial/investment dichotomy approach, courts have focused on certain factors to guide the application of the test. Despite the defendants' contentions to the contrary, one of the factors the courts have focused on in applying the test is the nature of the assets acquired in exchange for the notes. The defendants are correct in pointing out that every time an investment asset is acquired, the notes have not been determined to be securities under this test. See *Lino* v. *City Investing Co.*, 487 F. 2d 689 (3d Cir. 1973) (franchise); *C. N. S. Enterprises, Inc.* v. *G. & G. Enterprises, Inc.*, 508 F. 2d 1354 (7th Cir.), *cert. denied,* 423 U. S. 825 (1975) (dry cleaning business); *Bellah* v. *First National Bank,* 495 F. 2d 1109 (5th Cir. 1974) (cattle business).[5] Nevertheless, the asset acquired has been recognized to be an important, and often determinative, factor in the court's determination. In *McClure* v. *First National Bank,* 497 F. 2d 490 (5th Cir. 1974), *cert. denied,* 420 U. S. 930 (1975), Judge Roney analyzed prior federal decisions and concluded:

> [W]here notes have been deemed securities within the meaning of the securities laws, either of two factors * * * usually indicated the investment overtones of the underlying transaction. * * * [The] notes were [either] offered to some class of investors, [or] were * * * acquired * * * for speculation or investment. * * * Second, * * * the borrower [obtained] investment assets, directly or indirectly, in exchange for its notes.

Id. at 493-94. [Citations omitted.] * * *

[5]See also Futura Development Corp. v. Centex Corp., 761 F. 2d 33, 40-41 (1st Cir. 1985), *cert. denied,* 106 S. Ct. 147; cf. Union National Bank of Little Rock v. Farmers Bank, Hamburg, Ark., 786 F. 2d 881, 884-85 (8th Cir. 1986); but cf. Zabriskie v. Lewis, 507 F. 2d 546 (10th Cir. 1974).

The Court finds that the note issued by Penn-Dixie in part payment for the real estate would qualify as a security under the investment/commercial test. First the land was not acquired to provide housing for a family or to build a new corporate headquarters, but was acquired for purely investment purposes. Second, the note was issued by a publicly held corporation, Penn-Dixie, to a trust not normally in the business of making loans, the JDL Trust. See *Lino* v. *City Investing Co.*, 487 F. 2d 689, 696 (3d Cir. 1973). Third, the duration of the note, ten years, signifies a long-term stake in the progress of the investment, since the collateral for the loan, the land itself, would fluctuate in value with the success of the venture. Therefore, the Court finds that in the "complete context of [this] transaction," id. at 696 n. 15, the note was a security under the investment/commercial dichotomy test of the [First,] Third, Fifth, Seventh, and Tenth Circuits.[6]

B. The Risk Capital Test of the Ninth Circuit

The U. S. Court of Appeals for the Ninth Circuit applies a risk capital test in determining whether a note is a security.[7] See *Amfac Mortgage Corp.* v. *Arizona Mall, Inc.*, 583 F. 2d 426 (9th Cir. 1978). Under this test, the ultimate inquiry is whether the lender has contributed risk capital subject to the entrepreneurial or managerial efforts of others. *United California Bank* v. *THC Financial Corp.*, 557 F. 2d 1351, 1358 (9th Cir. 1977); *Great Western Bank & Trust* v. *Kotz*, 532 F. 2d 1252, 1257 (9th Cir. 1976).[8] Six factors have been considered in *Amfac Mortgage, Great Western,* and *United California Bank* to determine if the lender has contributed risk capital. The factors focused on are: (1) time, (2) collateralization, (3) form of the obligation, (4) circumstances of issue, (5) relationship between the amount borrowed and the size of the borrower's business, and (6) the contemplated use of the funds. * * *

[6] The commercial-investment dichotomy was chosen for the Code, which excludes from the "security" definition "a note or evidence of indebtedness issued in a primarily mercantile or consumer, rather than investment, transaction not involving a distribution." §202(150)(B)(iii).

[7] On the origin of this test, see p. 203 infra. But, since it is merely an elaboration of *Howey* (infra p. 184) for certain types of transactions, it has been held not to preclude finding a security in the context of an offering of notes secured by deeds of trust on real property through following the usual *Howey* rationale. Wright v. Schock, 571 F. Supp. 642 (N. D. Cal. 1983), *aff'd on other grounds,* 742 F. 2d 541 (9th Cir. 1984).

[8] See also Underhill v. Royal, 769 F. 2d 1426, 1430-31 (9th Cir. 1985) (public offering of notes underlying a "collateral loan agreement/promissory note"); Ahern v. Gaussoin, 611 F. Supp. 1465, 1474-77 (D. Ore. 1985); cf. People v. Schock, 152 Cal. App. 3d 379, 199 Cal. Rptr. 327 (1984) (state statute).

C. The Literal Approach of the Second Circuit

The broadest approach to determining whether a note constitutes a security under the federal securities laws has been taken by the U. S. Court of Appeals for the Second Circuit. In *Exchange National Bank* v. *Touche Ross & Co.*, 544 F. 2d 1126 (2d Cir. 1976), Judge Friendly, writing for the court, held that a party asserting that a note with a maturity longer than nine months is not a security within the 1934 Act [or that a note with a shorter maturity is within it], has the burden of proving that the "context" requires that result. In the course of his opinion, Judge Friendly offered some guidance for future cases:

> One can readily think of many cases where [the context otherwise requires] — the note delivered in consumer financing, the note secured by a mortgage on a home, the short-term note secured by a lien on a small business or some of its assets, the note evidencing a "character" loan to a bank customer, short-term notes secured by an assignment of accounts receivable, or a note which simply formalizes an open-account debt incurred in the ordinary course of business (particularly if, as in the case of the customer of a broker, it is collateralized). When a note does not bear a strong family resemblance to these examples and has a maturity date exceeding nine months, §10(b) of the 1934 Act should generally apply.[9]

[9]544 F. 2d at 1137-38. In Chemical Bank v. Arthur Andersen & Co., 726 F. 2d 930, 938 (2d Cir. 1984), *cert. denied*, 469 U. S. 884, Judge Friendly, understandably, took umbrage at the "literal" characterization: "* * * despite the pejorative label attached by some courts [citations omitted], we do not regard *Exchange National Bank* as a 'literalist' or even a 'neo-literalist' approach. Its position was and is that the words of the statute are not to be disregarded, as some other approaches have done, * * * but are to be given significance 'unless the context otherwise required.' "

It has been held that neither a fixed rate of interest nor a short term (one year) precludes a note from being a security. Hunssinger v. Rockford Business Credits, Inc., 745 F. 2d 484 (7th Cir. 1984). Conversely, in Chemical Bank v. Arthur Andersen & Co., supra, at 938-39, Judge Friendly stated for the court that the context required that certain "Replacement Notes" with a maturity exceeding nine months *not* be considered securities within §10(b) or §17(a); that this result was supported both by dictum in Marine Bank v. Weaver, 455 U. S. 551 (1982) (infra p. 173), and by the plaintiff banks' failure to cite any appellate decision "in which a note evidencing a loan made by a commercial bank to finance current operations of a borrower has been held to constitute a security within the federal securities laws"; that the examples in *Exchange National Bank* "were not graven in stone"; and that the court was simply adding "notes evidencing loans by commercial banks for current operations to the categories previously listed."

See also Davis v. Avco Financial Services, Inc., 739 F. 2d 1057, 1063 (6th Cir. 1984), *rehearing, and rehearing en banc, denied*, CCH Fed. Sec. L. Rep. ¶91,668 (7th Cir. 1984), *cert. denied*, 470 U. S. 1005 (notes executed to a finance company in the ordinary course of its business were not securities even though the com-

2. Note Participations and Syndications

Suppose now that the circumstances preclude a note's being a security. Might there still be a security, in the nature of an "investment contract" or "certificate of interest or participation in a profit-sharing agreement," when two or more lenders take "participations" in the loan or the loan is "syndicated"?

In a loan "participation" the loan is made by a single bank, which in turn assigns participations to other banks, insurance companies, and perhaps pension funds, without any direct relation between the assignees and the borrower. In a loan "syndication" the first bank offers other banks the opportunities to be *pro rata* direct lenders.[10]

The recent cases hold that participations are not "securities."[11] And those holdings should apply *a fortiori* to syndications.

3. "Repos"

The "retail repo" (for "retail repurchase agreement") had a life of only a decade or so. By mid-1986 it had been supplanted by bank certificates of deposit and "money market" accounts. But against the possibility of its return — together with whatever historical value it may have — a brief treatment here is indicated. The Commission in a 1981 release had this to say:[12]

---

pany knew that the loan proceeds would be used for a securities investment encouraged by the company's manager). Cf. South Carolina National Bank v. Darmstadter, 622 F. Supp. 226 (D. S. C. 1985), *aff'd without published opinion* (4th Cir. 1986), *cert. denied,* 107 S. Ct. 951. For a general statement, see SEC v. American Board of Trade, Inc., 751 F. 2d 529, 538-39 (2d Cir. 1984).

[10] See generally Frankel, Loan Participations and the *Becker* Case, in Practising Law Institute, Sixteenth Annual Institute on Securities Regulation (1984) c. 22; Note, International Loan Syndications, the Securities Acts, and the Duties of a Lead Bank, 64 Va. L. Rev. 897 (1978).

[11] United American Bank of Nashville v. Gunter, 620 F. 2d 1108, 1115-19 (5th Cir. 1980); American Fletcher Mortgage Co. v. United States Steel Credit Corp., 635 F. 2d 1247, 1253-55 (7th Cir. 1980), *cert. denied,* 451 U. S. 911; Union Planters National Bank of Memphis v. Commercial Credit Business Loans, Inc., 651 F. 2d 1174, 1179-85 (6th Cir. 1981), *cert. denied,* 454 U. S. 1124; Union National Bank of Little Rock v. Farmers Bank, Hamburg, Ark., 786 F. 2d 881 (8th Cir. 1986); Citizens State Bank v. Federal Deposit Ins. Corp., 639 F. Supp. 758 (W. D. Okla. 1986); cf. Vorrius v. Harvey, 570 F. Supp. 537 (S. D. N. Y. 1983) (salesman's participation in a loan offered by his commodity trading firm employer); J. Henry Schroder Bank & Trust Co. v. Metropolitan Savings Bank, 117 A. D. 2d 515, 497 N. Y. S. 2d 931 (1st Dept. 1986) (New York Martin Act). *Contra:* Commercial Discount Corp. v. Lincoln First Commercial Corp., 445 F. Supp. 1263, 1267 (S. D. N. Y. 1978). For a tabular analysis of a dozen cases, see Scholl and Weaver, Loan Participations: Are They "Securities"?, 10 Fla. St. U. L. Rev. 215, 224-25 (1982).

[12] Sec. Act Rel. 6351, 23 SEC Dock. 1000 (1981).

The use of so-called "retail repurchase agreements" ("retail repos") as a means for banks and savings and loan associations to raise short-term capital is becoming increasingly widespread in the U. S. financial markets. These retail repos typically are, in economic reality, debt obligations of banks and savings and loan associations that are collateralized by an interest either in a security that is a direct obligation of, or is guaranteed as to principal and interest by, the United States or any agency thereof ("government security"), or a pool of such securities. Retail repos are issued to the general public in denominations of less than $100,000 and with maturities of less than 90 days.

* * *

The following statement by the Comptroller of the Currency would appear to have particular relevance to the adoption of sound disclosure practices in connection with retail repo programs:

> * * * The customer should be advised (1) that the Retail Repo is an obligation of the issuing bank and that the underlying security serves as collateral; (2) that the bank will pay a fixed amount, including interest on the purchase price, regardless of any fluctuation in the market price of the underlying security; (3) that the interest rate paid is not that of the underlying security; and (4) that general banking assets will most likely be used to satisfy the bank's obligation under the Retail Repo rather than proceeds from the sale of the underlying security. In addition, the customer should be advised at the time of purchase of the actual or approximate market value of the underlying security interest and he should be clearly warned that the Retail Repo is not a deposit, is not FDIC insured, and is not guaranteed in any way by the U. S. Government or any agency thereof. Language generally associated with deposits must be avoided to prevent creating the impression that insured deposits are being offered. The customer must be informed that he may become an unsecured creditor of the bank to the extent the market value of his security interest falls below the amount of the funds invested.

* * * In addition, the no-action positions contained in the [attached] letters do not apply to transactions in which the issuer of the retail repos holds itself out as offering an investment, as opposed to a collateral, interest in a government security or pool of such securities. Characterizing an arrangement as involving a bank's or savings and loan association's "money market fund" or otherwise implying that retail repos are investment interests in a government security or pool of such securities may therefore raise disclosure and other questions under the securities laws.

The no-action letters set forth herein deal solely with retail repos, which are a relatively recent phenomenon. The letters do not discuss more traditional repurchase agreements that have been in use for a number of years. These traditional repurchase agreements essentially are short-term contracts to sell and repurchase entire government securities in large denominations. While the primary purpose of this release is to address the application of the federal securities laws to retail repos, the Commission believes it also would be useful to indicate briefly its views on these other types of repos.

Traditional repurchase agreements differ from retail repos in several significant respects. For example, traditional repos usually have a shorter duration (one day is not untypical), involve larger amounts (one million dollars is not uncommon), are privately negotiated rather than mass marketed, and involve entire government securities which often are delivered directly to the purchaser, an event which rarely, if ever, occurs in a retail repo transaction.

The economic realities of traditional repurchase agreements suggest that such agreements are not themselves separate securities.[13] For purposes of the federal securities laws, however, they are deemed to involve the purchase and sale of the U. S. government securities to which they relate. As a result, the antifraud provisions of such laws would apply to the offer, sale and purchase of U. S. government securities occurring in connection with traditional repurchase agreements.[14]

The new retail repos, by contrast, *were* considered by the Commission to be securities themselves, for the "no action" letters emphasized the application of the fraud provisions and excused registration under the exemptions in §§3(a)(2) and 3(a)(5) for securities of banks and savings and loan associations.[15]

[13] American Bank & Trust Co. v. Wallace, 702 F. 2d 93 (6th Cir. 1983); but cf. First National Bank of Las Vegas, N. M. v. Estate of Russell, 657 F. 2d 668 (5th Cir. 1981).

[14] Manufacturers Hanover Trust Co. v. Drysdale Securities Corp., 801 F. 2d 13, 19 (2d Cir. 1986), *cert. denied* sub. nom. Arthur Andersen & Co. v. Manufacturers Hanover Trust Co., 107 S. Ct. 952.

[15] See Note, Lifting the Cloud of Uncertainty over the Repo Market: Characterization of Repos As Separate Purchases and Sales of Securities, 37 Vand. L. Rev. 401, 424 (1984); City of Harrisburg v. Bradford Trust Co., 621 F. Supp. 463, 469-70 (M. D. Pa. 1985); In the Matter of Bevill, Bresler & Schulman Asset Management Corp., 67B. R. 557, CCH Fed. Sec. L. Rep. ¶92,966 (D. N. J. 1986) (participants in repo and reverse repo transactions were "customers" within Sec. Inv. Prot. Act).

In late 1985 the Board of Governors of the Federal Reserve System announced a supervisory policy on repo transactions of depository institutions with securities dealers and others. Fed. Res. Rel., Nov. 1, 1985. And in January 1986 the Commission amended Regulation S-X, the accounting regulation, to require disclosure by registrants of the nature and extent of their repos (and "reverse repos"), as well as the degree of risk involved, if their commitments

4. Bank Certificates of Deposit

There are two Supreme Court cases in this area:

In *Tcherepnin* v. *Knight* depositors in a savings and loan association that was in voluntary liquidation were able to void their purchases for violation of Rule 10b-5 (the general antifraud rule under the 1934 Act), and thus to get themselves in a creditor position, on the ground that withdrawable and transferable (but nonnegotiable) capital shares issued to evidence savings accounts were securities.[16]

In *Marine Bank* v. *Weaver,* which involved a fixed-interest certificate of deposit issued by a bank, the Court distinguished *Tcherepnin* on the grounds (1) that buyers there not only had voting rights but also received dividends based on profits, not a fixed rate of interest, and (2) that a bank certificate of deposit differed from other long-term debt obligations because of federal bank regulation and insurance, so that there was no need for SEC-type protection against fraud.[17]

---

exceed 10 percent of total assets. Reg. S-X, §501.07; Sec. Act Rel. 6621, 34 SEC Dock. 1295 (1986). (A "reverse repo" is a *purchase* with an agreement to *resell.*)

For a report of investigation, see Fidelity Financial Corp., Sec. Ex. Act Rel. 18,927, 25 SEC Dock. 1056 (1982). For an in-depth explanation, see SEC v. Miller, 495 F. Supp. 465 (S. D. N. Y. 1980). For an analysis from the point of view of banking and other bodies of law as well as securities regulation, see Porter, Eighty-Nine-Day Agreements for the Sale and Repurchase of Fractional Interests in Governmental Securities, 98 Banking L. J. 343 (1981); Porter, Retail Repurchase Agreements Revisited, 99 Banking L. J. 676 (1982).

[16] 389 U. S. 332 (1967).

[17] 455 U. S. 551 (1982); see also Brockton Savings Bank v. Peat, Marwick, Mitchell & Co., 577 F. Supp. 1281 (D. Mass. 1983); Wolf v. Banco Nacional de México, 739 F. 2d 1458, 1460-62 (9th Cir. 1984), *cert. denied,* 469 U. S. 1108; Callejo v. Bancomer, S. A., 764 F. 2d 1101, 1125 n. 33 (5th Cir. 1985); West v. Multibanco Comermex, S. A., 807 F. 2d 820, 826-27 (9th Cir. 1986).

In *Wolf* the court read *Marine Bank's* regulatory references as applicable to a Mexican bank, since "Mexico thoroughly regulates its banks and * * * no Mexican bank has become insolvent in fifty years." But the court placed the burden of proving adequate regulation against insolvency on the bank.

For an analysis of the foreign bank point as well as a half-dozen other questions with respect to certificates of deposit — in the light of the Court's cautioning that "Each transaction must be analyzed and evaluated on the basis of the content of the instruments in question, the purposes intended to be served, and the factual setting as a whole" (455 U. S. at 560 n. 11) — see Greene and Norman, CDs As Securities, 17 Rev. Sec. Reg. 793 (1984).

But cf. Gary Plastic Packaging Corp. v. Merrill Lynch, Pierce, Fenner & Smith, Inc., 756 F. 2d 230 (2d Cir. 1985), where the court held that Merrill Lynch's "CD Program" involving certificates of deposit specially created by a number of banks gave rise to investment contracts, because "a significant portion of the customer's investment depends on Merrill Lynch's managerial and financial expertise."

5. "Evidence of Indebtedness"

In holding that a letter of commitment that guaranteed forthcoming loans was an "evidence of indebtedness," the Tenth Circuit said that that term "is not limited to a promissory note or other simple acknowledgement of a debt owing and is held to include all contractual obligations to pay in the future for consideration presently received."[18] But "evidence of indebtedness," like "note," is so broad as to preclude a literal reading. Surely, just as my promissory note given in connection with my installment purchase of a television set is not a "note," the credit card sales slip that I sign for a restaurant meal is not an "evidence of indebtedness."[19] And the same criteria developed in the "note" cases should be helpful here.

A further complication is presented here by the presence of the phrase only in the 1933 Act, not the 1934 Act. The Supreme Court did not rely on the omission when it reversed the Seventh Circuit's decision that a bank certificate of deposit was a security under the 1934 Act. As Judge Cummings stated in his dissenting opinion below, "The author of the 1934 Act may have decided that inclusion of 'evidence of indebtedness' would be poor draftsmanship, that term being inconsistent with the exclusion of 'any note, draft, bill of exchange, or banker's acceptance.' "[20] On the other hand, the absence of the phrase was held by the Second Circuit to preclude an open-account loan from being a security.[21]

C. OIL AND GAS

Oil and gas financing is a strange world with a vocabulary all its own. Established companies normally issue the usual types of se-

[18] United States v. Austin, 462 F. 2d 724, 736 (10th Cir. 1972), *cert. denied,* 409 U. S. 1048.

[19] Cf. McGovern Plaza Joint Venture v. First of Denver Mortgage Investors, 562 F. 2d 645 (10th Cir. 1977) (neither a construction loan commitment nor a permanent loan commitment purchasd by a real estate developer in the normal course of business from a *bona fide* lender was a "security," court distinguishing *Austin,* supra n. 18); United States v. Namer, 680 F. 2d 1088, 1096-97 (5th Cir. 1982) (similar); People v. Dempster, CCH Blue Sky L. Rep. ¶72,034 at 70,582 (Mich. App. 1983) (*held,* without reference to the "evidence of indebtedness" phrase in the Michigan Uniform Securities Act, receipts for money to be invested in precious metals were not "securities" because no money was actually being invested).

[20] Marine Bank v. Weaver, 371 F. 2d 374, 380 n. 3 (1967), *rev'd,* 455 U. S. 551 (1982).

[21] Zeller v. Bogue Electric Mfg. Corp., 476 F. 2d 795, 800-01 (2d Cir. 1973), *cert. denied,* 414 U. S. 908.

curities. But in the century and more since the beginnings of the commercial petroleum industry certain peculiar forms of financing have evolved. In the typical case the development of an area with an oil potential is dependent on a favorable geologist's report, although the established companies are apt to get large amounts of acreage under option even before doing any geological or geophysical work. If the report is favorable, the process of leasing or "blocking" the tract begins. Representatives of one or more producers or speculators obtain leases to the oil and gas rights on as many of the individual tracts as they can. The tracts are typically "granted, demised, leased and let" to the lessee "for the sole and only purpose of mining and operating oil and gas and laying pipelines" during a stated term of years. The lessor receives, in addition to an immediate "cash bonus" in some cases, a promise on the part of the lessee to pay a stated rental per acre for every year in which a well is not drilled, and a further promise of a stated percentage, usually one-eighth, of the oil and gas actually produced and sold or its value at the prevailing market price.

This one-eighth interest is the "landowner's royalty interest," and it commonly finds its way into the securities markets in lots of fractional undivided portions after having been transferred to banks as collateral for loans or having been sold to an oil royalty dealer. Thus the sale of these interests is not a device for financing the drilling of a well. It is merely a method of sharing the risk involved, or receiving the immediate enjoyment of an income that would otherwise be spread over a number of years, or both.

The *lessee's* interest is termed the "working interest." If the lessee is an established producing company, it may retain all of the working interest. On the other hand, if it does not have independent resources, it may sell fractional undivided shares of the lease to raise working capital, or it may give a part interest in the lease to a drilling contractor, who in turn may sell all or part of his share to finance the drilling. As in the case of the "landowners' royalty interests," which are fractions of the one-eighth portion, these "working interests," which are fractions of the seven-eighths portion, may nominally give rights of participation either in the oil or gas or in the proceeds from its sale. If the fractional undivided interests in the seven-eighths portion are not subject to any of the expense of development, operation, or maintenance, they are commonly known as "overriding royalty interests." If they *are* subject to any part of that expense, they are known simply as "working interests" — or, in certain circumstances that are not typical, "participating interests." Occasionally, too, interests called "oil or gas payments" may be created out of the seven-eighths interest; these resemble "overriding royalty interests" in that they are not subject to any portion of the expense, but they are limited to a maximum amount fixed either in barrels of oil or in cubic feet of gas or in dollars. This precise terminology is not too fixed, but it has been adopted by the Commission.[1]

Both the landowner's royalty interest and the working interest are *sui generis.* Their precise nature, and particularly the problem whether they are realty or personalty, have much occupied the courts in connection with taxation, inheritance, dower and curtesy, and the formal prerequisites of legal instruments. The answers have varied from state to state and within particular states, depending upon the legal ends sought to be subserved.

For purposes of the Securities Act, however, it is irrelevant whether these interests are real or personal property, and it is equally irrelevant whether they are transferred by deed or by contract. Section 2(1) was amended in 1934 to make clear that it covers any "fractional undivided interest in oil, gas, or other mineral rights." The Federal Trade Commission thereupon took the position that "The word 'rights' is broad enough to make the definition applicable to interests which are regarded as giving ownership of the oil or gas in place as well as to interests which merely afford the owner the right to produce oil or gas."[2] However, there is no "fractional undivided interest" if the *whole* landowner's royalty interest is transferred, even though under the terms of the lease the holder may be entitled to only one-eighth or some other portion of the production.[3]

The 1934 amendments also supplied a special definition of the term "issuer" with respect to these fractional undivided interests to mean "the owner of any such right or of any interest in such right (whether whole or fractional) who creates fractional interests therein for the purpose of public offering."[4] If there is no "public offering" by an issuer, an exemption is available in any event under §4(2). But the exemptions generally do not apply to the antifraud provisions in §§12(2) and 17. So it is necessary to decide whether a "security" is involved when an owner of an entire leasehold creates fractional interests (or an owner of fractional interests creates smaller fractional interests) for the purpose of a private offering that he

C. 3C [1] Reg. B, Rule 300. See Penturelli v. Spector, Cohen, Gaden & Rosen, P. C., 779 F. 2d 160, 165-67 (3d Cir. 1985), citing the text.

[2] Sec. Act Rel. 185 (1934).

[3] See Fearneyhough v. McElvain, 598 F. Supp. 905 (C. D. Ill. 1984).

[4] Woodward v. Wright, 266 F. 2d 108 (10th Cir. 1959).

makes *fraudulently.* This question was answered affirmatively in a case in which the court permitted recovery under §12(2) but not under §12(1).[5] In other words, there can be a "security" without an "issuer," the definition of the latter term being important only because the "issuer" must sign the registration statement under §6(a) and is absolutely liable for material defects in it under §11. By contrast, §§12 and 17(a) refer to any "person" who sells.

At the state level, the draftsmen of the Uniform Securities Act substituted the phrase, "any certificate of interest or participation in an oil, gas, or mining title or lease or in payments out of production under such a title or lease," because some such phraseology was common in the state statutes.[6] The "certificate of interest or participation" locution was also substituted for the "fractional undivided interest" phrase in §3(a)(10) of the 1934 Act.[7]

The "fractional undivided interest" phrase in §2(1) has been applied in a number of cases.[8] But the financing techniques in this area are so variegated that it is not always clear whether a particular transaction involves a "security" by virtue of either that phrase or some other portion of the definition. Can it be assumed on the one hand, for example, that every transfer of a fractional undivided working interest in an oil or gas leasehold results in a "security" if what is involved essentially is a development contract among only a few persons, especially if they are equally sophisticated in oil and gas matters? Can it be assumed, on the other hand, that a public offering of small portions of a leasehold does not involve a "security" under some other portion of the definition merely because they are divided by metes and bounds instead of being "fractional undivided interests"? The first question was answered in the neg-

[5] Ibid.

[6] §401(*l*); see Loss, Commentary on the Uniform Securities Act (1979) 106.

[7] It is nevertheless the administrative view that the ordinary oil royalty is a security under the 1934 Act — if not under this portion of the definition, then under the catchall phrases. Indeed, the 1934 Act definition may well go further than its 1933 Act counterpart in the sense that a "certificate of interest * * * in any * * * lease" is perhaps broad enough to include any portion of an entire leasehold interest, whether or not an undivided portion.

[8] See, e. g., Penturelli v. Spector, Cohen, Gaden & Rosen, P. C., 779 F. 2d 160 (3d Cir. 1985), citing the text (coal leases). For a description of the so-called "industry deal," see Pezold and Richey, The "Industry Deal" among Oil and Gas Companies and the Federal Securities Acts, 16 Tex. Tech. L. Rev. 827, 831 (1985): an "undivided fractional interest in an oil and gas lease, coupled with an 'operating agreement' whereby the party proposing the 'prospect' [which is to say, a defined geographical area as distinct from an undefined geologic idea] oversees, or 'operates,' the drilling of a test well on the lease." Although these interests seem quite clearly to fall within the "fractional undivided interest" language, it is said that the oil and gas industry has not viewed them as "securities." Id. at 834.

ative by a sharply divided Illinois Supreme Court, whose dissenters accused the majority of having "left the world of realism."[9] And the second question produced the first case on the definition of "security" in the Supreme Court of the United States — a case whose relevance transcends the oil and gas sphere:

SECURITIES AND EXCHANGE COMMISSION v. C. M. JOINER LEASING CORPORATION

Supreme Court of the United States, 1943
320 U. S. 344

MR. JUSTICE JACKSON delivered the opinion of the Court.

The Securities and Exchange Commission brought this action in District Court to restrain respondents from further violations of §§5(a) and 17(a)(2) and (3) of the Securities Act of 1933. The District Court denied relief and the Circuit Court of Appeals affirmed upon a construction of the statute which excludes from its operation all trading in oil and gas leases. 133 F. 2d 241. As this presents a question important to the administration of the Act we granted certiorari.

Respondents and one Johnson, a defendant against whom a decree was taken by consent, engaged in a campaign to sell assignments of oil leases. The underlying leases, acreage from which was being sold, are not in the record. They required, as appears from the assignments, annual rental in case of delayed drilling of §1 per year. It also seems that these leases were granted by the landowners on an agreement that a test well would be drilled by the lessees. One Anthony blocked up leases on about 4,700 acres of land in McCulloch County, Texas, in consideration of drilling a test well. Defendant Joiner testified that he acquired 3,002 of these acres for "practically nothing except to drill a well." Anthony was a driller and agreed to do the drilling which the Joiner Company undertook to finance, expecting to raise most of the funds for this purpose from the resale of small parcels of acreage. The sales campaign was by mail addressed to upwards of 1,000 prospects in widely scattered parts of the country and actual purchasers, about fifty in number, were located in at least eighteen states and the District of Columbia. Leasehold subdivisions offered never exceeded twenty acres and

[9] Hammer v. Sanders, 8 Ill. 2d 414, 429, 134 N. E. 2d 509, 517 (1956), *cert. denied*, 352 U. S. 878. It has been said that this "has been honored more in its avoidance than in its acceptance." Witter v. Buchanan, 132 Ill. App. 3d 273, 282, 476 N. E. 2d 1123, 1130 (1985).

usually covered two and a half to five acres. The prices ranged from $5 to $15 per acre. The largest single purchase shown by the record was $100, and the great majority of purchases amounted to $25 or less. All buyers were given the opportunity to pay these sums in installments, and some did so.

The sales literature nowhere mentioned drilling conditions which the purchaser would meet or costs which he would incur if he attempted to develop his own acreage. On the other hand, it assured the prospect that the Joiner Company was engaged in and would complete the drilling of a test well so located as to test the oil-producing possibilities of the offered leaseholds. The leases were offered on these terms: "You may have ten acres around one or both wells at $5 per acre cash payable by August 1st, 1941 and $5 per acre additional payable November 1st, 1941 or thirty days after both wells are completed." Other language in the advertising literature emphasized the character of the purchase as an investment and as a participation in an enterprise.

The trial court made findings of what amounted to fraud, and the Circuit Court of Appeals approved, saying, "the evidence would justify stronger findings of fraud." However, both courts refused injunction because, as the Court of Appeals stated, it could "find simply sales and assignments of legal and legitimate oil and gas leases, i. e., sales of interests in land." It was thought that these assignments could not be proved to be "securities" or "investment contracts" under §2(1) of the Act.

Undisputed facts seem to us, however, to establish the conclusion that defendants were not, as a practical matter, offering naked leasehold rights. Had the offer mailed by defendants omitted the economic inducements of the proposed and promised exploration well, it would have been a quite different proposition. Purchasers then would have been left to their own devices for realizing upon their rights. They would have anticipated waiting an indefinite time, paying delayed drilling rental meanwhile until some chance exploration proved or disproved the productivity of their acres. Their alternative would have been to test their own leases at a cost of $5,000 or more per well.

But defendants offered no such dismal prospect. Their proposition was to sell documents which offered the purchaser a chance, without undue delay or additional cost, of sharing in discovery values which might follow a current exploration enterprise. The drilling of this well was not an unconnected or uncontrolled phenomenon to which salesmen pointed merely to show the possibilities of the offered leases. The exploration enterprise was woven into these leaseholds, in both an economic and a legal sense; the undertaking to drill a well runs through the whole transaction as the thread on which everybody's beads were strung. * * *

* * *

It is clear that an economic interest in this well-drilling undertaking was what brought into being the instruments that defendants were selling and gave to the instruments most of their value and all of their lure. The trading in these documents had all the evils inherent in the securities transactions which it was the aim of the Securities Act to end.

It is urged that the definition of "security" which controls the scope of this Act falls short of including these transactions. Respondents invoke the "*ejusdem generis* rule" to constrict the more general terms substantially to the specific terms which they follow. And they invoke the ancient maxim "*expressio unius est exclusio alterius*" to exclude sales of leasehold subdivisions by the acre because the statute expressly includes sales of leasehold subdivisions by undivided shares.

Some rules of statutory construction come down to us from sources that were hostile toward the legislative process itself and thought it generally wise to restrict the operation of an act to its narrowest permissible compass. However well these rules may serve at times to aid in deciphering legislative intent, they long have been subordinated to the doctrine that courts will construe the details of an act in conformity with its dominating general purpose, will read text in the light of context and will interpret the text so far as the meaning of the words fairly permits so as to carry out in particular cases the generally expressed legislative policy.[8]

In the Securities Act the term "security" was defined to include by name or description many documents in which there is common trading for speculation or investment. Some, such as notes, bonds, and stocks, are pretty much standardized and the name alone carries well-settled meaning. Others are of more variable character and were necessarily designated by more descriptive terms, such as "transferable share," "investment contract," and "in general any

[8] This Court has refused to follow the "*ejusdem generis*" rule, even in criminal cases, where its application seemed to conflict with the general purpose of an act. [Citations omitted.]

It has also treated the maxim "*expressio unius est exclusio alterius*" as but an aid to construction. [Citations omitted. See c. 3M infra.]

interest or instrument commonly known as a security." We cannot read out of the statute these general descriptive designations merely because more specific ones have been used to reach some kinds of documents. Instruments may be included within any of these definitions, as matter of law, if on their face they answer to the name or description. However, the reach of the Act does not stop with the obvious and commonplace. Novel, uncommon, or irregular devices, whatever they appear to be, are also reached if it be proved as matter of fact that they were widely offered or dealt in under terms or courses of dealing which established their character in commerce as "investment contracts," or as "any interest or instrument commonly known as a 'security.'" The proof here seems clear that these defendants' offers brought their instruments within these terms.

It is urged that because the definition mentions "fractional undivided interest in oil, gas or other mineral rights," it excludes sales of leasehold subdivisions by parcels. Oil and gas rights posed a difficult problem to the legislative draftsman. Such rights were notorious subjects of speculation and fraud, but leases and assignments were also indispensable instruments of legitimate oil exploration and production. To include leases and assignments by name might easily burden the oil industry by controls that were designed only for the traffic in securities. This was avoided by including specifically only that form of splitting up of mineral interests which had been most utilized for speculative purposes. We do not think the draftsmen thereby immunized other forms of contracts and offerings which are proved as matter of fact to answer to such descriptive terms as "investment contracts" and "securities."

Nor can we agree with the court below that defendants' offerings were beyond the scope of the Act because they offered leases and assignments which under Texas law conveyed interests in real estate. In applying acts of this general purpose, the courts have not been guided by the nature of the assets back of a particular document or offering. The test rather is what character the instrument is given in commerce by the terms of the offer, the plan of distribution, and the economic inducements held out to the prospect. In the enforcement of an act such as this it is not inappropriate that promoters' offerings be judged as being what they were represented to be.

Finally it is urged that we must interpret with strictness the scope of this Act because violations of it are crimes. Some authority is cited and a great array could be assembled to support the general proposition that penal statutes must be strictly construed. An almost equally impressive collection can be made of decisions holding that remedial statutes should be liberally construed. What, then, shall we say of the construction of a section like this which may be the basis of either civil proceedings of a preventive or remedial nature or of punitive proceedings, or perhaps both?

Different courts have given different answers to the general question. * * * The weight of authority is committed to a liberal construction, although some courts tend toward strict construction, and some have seemed to differentiate according to the use being made of the statute, inclining to a strict construction when a criminal penalty is being imposed and a more liberal one when civil remedies are being applied.

* * *

In the present case we do nothing to the words of the Act; we merely accept them. It would be necessary in any case for any kind of relief to prove that documents being sold were securities under the Act. In some cases it might be done by proving the document itself, which on its face would be a note, a bond, or a share of stock. In others proof must go outside the instrument itself as we do here. Where this proof is offered in a civil action, as here, a preponderance of the evidence will establish the case; if it were offered in a criminal case, it would have to meet the stricter requirement of satisfying the jury beyond reasonable doubt.

We hold that the court below erred in denying an injunction under the undisputed facts of this case and its findings. The judgment is *reversed*.

MR. JUSTICE ROBERTS is of the opinion that the judgment should be affirmed.

MR. JUSTICE DOUGLAS took no part in the consideration or decision of this case.

The Fifth Circuit later said:

> In [*SEC* v. *W. J. Howey Co.*, 328 U. S. 293 (1946), infra p. 184] the element of expectation of "profits solely from the efforts of the promoter or a third party," which are "to come solely from the efforts of others" [citations omitted], as well as that case's restatement of the Joiner holding in the broadest of terms, certainly overcomes any imputation that language in Joiner that the "drilling of

> this well was not an unconnected or uncontrolled phenomenon" etc. meant to require that the collateral activity be that of the seller or one under his control. Loss, Securities Regulation, 1955 Supp. p. 149, as much as says so: "Mr. Justice Jackson's statement that 'The exploration enterprise was woven into these leaseholds, in both an economic and a legal sense,' would seem to apply equally in principle whether the exploration is being done under the seller's control or by a third person." * * *[10]

The last few decades have seen the development of a new method of financing, the "oil program," in which the security is not an undivided interest in *one* well but an interest, under a variety of contractual arrangements, in a joint venture or limited partnership whose function is to develop a *number* of profitable drilling prospects. These programs are sold for the purpose of raising funds to acquire leases on prospect acreage and to drill wells, although producing properties are sometimes acquired as well. Ultimately fractional undivided interests in the completed wells may be distributed to the participants. And additional payments may be required for completion and exploration costs, at the risk of forfeiture for nonpayment. Customarily the programs are created at annual or more frequent intervals, with emphasis on the tax advantages flowing from "pass-through" treatment of drilling costs and certain other deductions.

As these programs increased in number and dollar amount, they began to take on the characteristic of investment companies whose portfolio "securities" were various kinds of oil and gas interests rather than stocks. But §3(c)(9) of the Investment Company Act excludes "Any person substantially all of whose business consists of owning or holding oil, gas, or other mineral royalties or leases, or fractional interests therein, or certificates of interest or participation in or investment contracts relative to such royalties, leases, or fractional interests." And there are so many differences from the typical mutual fund that application of many of the provisions of the Investment Company Act would raise serious problems. For one thing, the conflict between that Act's philosophy of an investor-controlled management and the philosophy of the passive investor implicit in the limited partnership arrangement presents difficulties.

The upshot was that the Commission in 1972 transmitted to Congress a proposed Oil and Gas Investment Act, which was intended to deal only with "blind pool" oil programs that provide pass-through tax treatment and generally offer their securities or

[10]Roe v. United States, 287 F. 2d 435, 439 n. 5 (5th Cir. 1961).

participations to the public.[11] But legislation of that kind does not seem likely in the foreseeable future.[12]

D. THE "INVESTMENT CONTRACT" CONCEPT

1. General

For some reason Justice Jackson seemed reluctant in *Joiner* to adopt in so many words the interpretation of "investment contract" that had been widely followed by the state courts. That was left for the next Supreme Court case — still the seminal case — three years later:

SEC v. W. J. HOWEY COMPANY

Supreme Court of the United States, 1946
328 U. S. 293

Mr. Justice Murphy delivered the opinion of the Court.

This case involves the application of §2(1) of the Securities Act of 1933 to an offering of units of a citrus grove development coupled with a contract for cultivating, marketing and remitting the net proceeds to the investor.

* * *

Most of the facts are stipulated. The respondents, W. J. Howey Company and Howey-in-the-Hills Service, Inc., are Florida corporations under direct common control and management. The Howey Company owns large tracts of citrus acreage in Lake County, Florida. During the past several years it has planted about 500 acres annually, keeping half of the groves itself and offering the other half to the public "to help us finance additional development." Howey-in-the-Hills Service, Inc., is a service company engaged in cultivating and developing many of these groves, including the harvesting and marketing of the crops.

Each prospective customer is offered both a land sales contract and a service contract, after having been told that it is not feasible to invest in a grove unless service arrangements are made. While the purchaser is free to make arrangements with other service com-

[11] S. 3884, 92d Cong., 2d Sess., 118 Cong. Rec. 26,967 (1972).
[12] §202(80)(B)(x); 1 Code 125.

panies, the superiority of Howey-in-the-Hills Service, Inc., is stressed. Indeed 85% of the acreage sold during the 3-year period ending May 31, 1943, was covered by service contracts with Howey-in-the-Hills Service, Inc.

The land sales contract with the Howey Company provides for a uniform purchase price per acre or fraction thereof, varying in amount only in accordance with the number of years the particular plot has been planted with citrus trees. Upon full payment of the purchase price the land is conveyed to the purchaser by warranty deed. Purchases are usually made in narrow strips of land arranged so that an acre consists of a row of 48 trees. During the period between February 1, 1941, and May 31, 1943, 31 of the 42 persons making purchases bought less than 5 acres each. The average holding of these 31 persons was 1.33 acres and sales of as little as 0.65, 0.7 and 0.73 of an acre were made. These tracts are not separately fenced and the sole indication of several ownership is found in small land marks intelligible only through a plat book record.

The service contract, generally of a 10-year duration without option of cancellation, gives Howey-in-the-Hills Service, Inc., a leasehold interest and "full and complete" possession of the acreage. For a specified fee plus the cost of labor and materials, the company is given full discretion and authority over the cultivation of the groves and the harvest and marketing of the crops. The company is well established in the citrus business and maintains a large force of skilled personnel and a great deal of equipment, including 75 tractors, sprayer wagons, fertilizer trucks and the like. Without the consent of the company, the land owner or purchaser has no right of entry to market the crop;[2] thus there is ordinarily no right to specific fruit. The company is accountable only for an allocation of the net profits based upon a check made at the time of picking. All the produce is pooled by the respondent companies, which do business under their own names.

The purchasers for the most part are non-residents of Florida. They are predominantly business and professional people who lack the knowledge, skill and equipment necessary for the care and cultivation of citrus trees. They are attracted by the expectation of substantial profits. It was represented, for example, that profits during the 1943-1944 season amounted to 20% and that even greater profits might be expected during the 1944-1945 season, although only a 10% annual return was to be expected over a 10-

C. 3D [2] Some investors visited their particular plots annually, making suggestions as to care and cultivation, but without any legal rights in the matters.

year period. Many of these purchasers are patrons of a resort hotel owned and operated by the Howey Company in a scenic section adjacent to the groves. The hotel's advertising mentions the fine groves in the vicinity and the attention of the patrons is drawn to the groves as they are being escorted about the surrounding countryside. They are told that the groves are for sale; if they indicate an interest in the matter they are then given a sales talk.

* * *

Section 2(1) of the Act defines the term "security" to include the commonly known documents traded for speculation or investment. This definition also includes "securities" of a more variable character, designated by such descriptive terms as "certificate of interest or participation in any profit-sharing agreement," "investment contract" and "in general, any interest or instrument commonly known as a 'security.' " The legal issue in this case turns upon a determination of whether, under the circumstances, the land sales contract, the warranty deed and the service contract together constitute an "investment contract" within the meaning of §2(1). An affirmative answer brings into operation the registration requirements of §5(a), unless the security is granted an exemption under §3(b). The lower courts, in reaching a negative answer to this problem, treated the contracts and deeds as separate transactions involving no more than an ordinary real estate sale and an agreement by the seller to manage the property for the buyer.

The term "investment contract" is undefined by the Securities Act or by relevant legislative reports. But the term was common in many state "blue sky" laws in existence prior to the adoption of the federal statute and, although the term was also undefined by the state laws, it had been broadly construed by state courts so as to afford the investing public a full measure of protection. Form was disregarded for substance and emphasis was placed upon economic reality. An investment contract thus came to mean a contract or scheme for "the placing of capital or laying out of money in a way intended to secure income or profit from its employment." *State* v. *Gopher Tire & Rubber Co.*, 146 Minn. 52, 56, 177 N. W. 937, 938. This definition was uniformly applied by state courts to a variety of situations where individuals were led to invest money in a common enterprise with the expectation that they would earn a profit solely through the efforts of the promoter or of some one other than themselves.

By including an investment contract within the scope of §2(1) of the Securities Act, Congress was using a term the meaning of which had been crystallized by this prior judicial interpretation. It is therefore reasonable to attach that meaning to the term as used by Congress, especially since such a definition is consistent with the statutory aims. In other words, an investment contract for purposes of the Securities Act means a contract, transaction or scheme whereby a person invests his money in a common enterprise and is led to expect profits solely from the efforts of the promoter or a third party, it being immaterial whether the shares in the enterprise are evidenced by formal certificates or by nominal interests in the physical assets employed in the enterprise. Such a definition necessarily underlies this Court's decision in *S. E. C.* v. *Joiner Corp.,* 320 U. S. 344, and has been enunciated and applied many times by lower federal courts. It permits the fulfillment of the statutory purpose of compelling full and fair disclosure relative to the issuance of "the many types of instruments that in our commercial world fall within the ordinary concept of a security." H. Rep. No. 85, 73rd Cong., 1st Sess., p. 11. It embodies a flexible rather than a static principle, one that is capable of adaptation to meet the countless and variable schemes devised by those who seek the use of the money of others on the promise of profits.

The transactions in this case clearly involve investment contracts as so defined. The respondent companies are offering something more than fee simple interests in land, something different from a farm or orchard coupled with management services. They are offering an opportunity to contribute money and to share in the profits of a large citrus fruit enterprise managed and partly owned by respondents. They are offering this opportunity to persons who reside in distant localities and who lack the equipment and experience requisite to the cultivation, harvesting and marketing of the citrus products. Such persons have no desire to occupy the land or to develop it themselves; they are attracted solely by the prospects of a return on their investment. Indeed, individual development of the plots of land that are offered and sold would seldom be economically feasible due to their small size. Such tracts gain utility as citrus groves only when cultivated and developed as component parts of a larger area. A common enterprise managed by respondents or third parties with adequate personnel and equipment is therefore essential if the investors are to achieve their paramount aim of a return on their investments. Their respective shares in this enterprise are evidenced by land sales contracts and warranty deeds, which serve as a convenient method of determining the investors' allocable shares of the profits. The resulting transfer of rights in land is purely incidental.

Thus all the elements of a profit-seeking business venture are present here. The investors provide the capital and share in the earnings and profits; the promoters manage, control and operate the enterprise. It follows that the arrangements whereby the investors' interests are made manifest involve investment contracts, regardless of the legal terminology in which such contracts are clothed. The investment contracts in this instance take the form of land sales contracts, warranty deeds and service contracts which respondents offer to prospective investors. And respondents' failure to abide by the statutory and administrative rules in making such offerings, even though the failure result from a *bona fide* mistake as to the law, cannot be sanctioned under the Act.

This conclusion is unaffected by the fact that some purchasers choose not to accept the full offer of an investment contract by declining to enter into a service contract with the respondents. The Securities Act prohibits the offer as well as the sale of unregistered, non-exempt securities. Hence it is enough that the respondents merely offer the essential ingredients of an investment contract.

We reject the suggestion of the Circuit Court of Appeals, 151 F. 2d at 717, that an investment contract is necessarily missing where the enterprise is not speculative or promotional in character and where the tangible interest which is sold has intrinsic value independent of the success of the enterprise as a whole. The test is whether the scheme involves an investment of money in a common enterprise with profits to come solely from the efforts of others. If that test be satisfied, it is immaterial whether the enterprise is speculative or non-speculative or whether there is a sale of property with or without intrinsic value. See *S. E. C.* v. *Joiner Corp.*, supra, 352. The statutory policy of affording broad protection to investors is not to be thwarted by unrealistic and irrelevant formulae.[a]

The *Howey* formula has not been limited by any means to the production of vitamin C. Many schemes have been held with almost monotonous consistency to involve "investment contracts" on the

[a]ED.: Justice Frankfurter dissented on the ground that the Supreme Court should not disturb the findings in which both lower courts had concurred.

See also Marine Bank v. Weaver, 455 U. S. 551, 556 (1982), supra p. 173, where the Court held that an agreement under which two investors pledged a bank certificate of deposit to enable a company to obtain working capital in return for a 50 percent interest in the company's anticipated profits was not a "security," because it was a "unique agreement, negotiated one-on-one by the parties," that was neither designed for public trading nor meant for a number of potential investors.

basis of a purported sale or lease of some form of tangible property subject to an arrangement whereby the seller retains possession and control of the property with a view to earning a profit for the nominal owners or lessees. Proof of some sort of pooling arrangement among investors (as in the *Howey* case) helps, but it is not essential.[1] And the catalogue is as variegated as the imaginations of promoters.

Many of them involve animals, preferably of either a fecund or a fur-bearing variety. A person "sells" pairs of silver foxes, for example, with the idea that he will supply the expert care (for a charge, of course) and in due time nature will supply lots of pups — one is tempted to say "a true stock dividend."[2] But the technique has been applied even to the considerably less glamorous, but more reliable, barnyard cow, which offers not only earnings from her milk but also capital gains on her calves and — when her milking days are but a nostalgic memory and she makes the supreme sacrifice — on her own poor carcass as well.[3] Indeed, the latest zoological medium seems to be earthworms, which rate high on the fecundity scale because their bisexuality makes it possible for any two worms to reproduce.[4]

The courts attempt to draw the line, however, where neither the element of a common enterprise nor the element of reliance on the

[1] E. g., El Khadem v. Equity Security Corp., 494 F. 2d 1224, 1229 (9th Cir. 1974); Pacific Coast Coin Exchange of Canada, Ltd. v. Ontario Securities Commission, [1978] 2 S. C. R. 112, 80 D. L. R. 3d 529 (Can. Sup. Ct.); Union Home Loans, Sec. Ex. Act Rel. 19,346, 26 SEC Dock. 1346, 1348 (1982); see also United States v. Jones, 712 F. 2d 1316, 1321 (9th Cir. 1983), *cert. denied* sub nom. Webber v. United States, 464 U. S. 986 (sale and leaseback of truck trailers). On the question whether an interest in a discretionary commodities account with a broker is a security only if there is "horizontal commonality" (some sort of "common enterprise" among customers similarly situated) as distinct from "vertical commonality" (a "common enterprise" between broker and customer), see p. 238 infra.

[2] SEC v. Payne, 35 F. Supp. 873 (S. D. N. Y. 1940).

[3] E. g., McLish v. Harris Farms, Inc., 507 F. Supp. 1075 (E. D. Cal. 1980); see also GRM v. Equine Investment & Management Group, 596 F. Supp. 307 (S. D. Tex. 1984); Ronnett v. American Breeding Herds, Inc., 124 Ill. App. 3d 842, 464 N. E. 2d 1201 (1984) (Illinois act); Kefalos v. Bonnie Brae Farms, Inc., 630 F. Supp. 6 (E. D. Ky. 1985); Comment, Equine Syndications: Are They Securities?, 6 N. Ky. L. Rev. 361 (1979) (thoroughbred stallions). But "the Commission has uniformly taken the position that a share in a stallion syndicate is not a security, provided the syndicate manager does no more than care for the horse and perform certain ministerial functions for the syndicate." Campbell, Stallion Syndicates As Securities, 70 Ky. L. J. 1131, 1147 (1988). Questions arise when the syndicate manager goes further. But "purchasers of interests in stallion syndicates invariably are in the horse business and are purchasing breeding rights to use in their particular programs." Id. at 1152.

[4] Smith v. Gross, 604 F. 2d 639 (9th Cir. 1979); Sec. Ex. Act Rel. 15,345, 16 SEC Dock. 221 (1978).

efforts of another is present. For example, no "investment contract" is involved when a person invests in real estate, with the hope perhaps of earning a profit as the result of a general increase in values concurrent with the development of the neighborhood, as long as he does not do so as part of an enterprise whereby it is expressly or impliedly understood that the property will be developed or operated by others.[5]

We cannot consider here all the permutations of the "investment contract" phenomenon. But we shall examine developments in the most significant areas.

2. Partnerships

It seems clear, from the reference to partnerships in §2(2) as well as the specification in Schedule A of the partners' names and addresses "if the issuer be a partnership," that interests in partnerships *may* be securities. Here, too, some sort of line must be drawn. The easy case is the public offering of freely transferable limited partnership interests, which is functionally equivalent to a public offer-

[5]Gordon v. Terry, 684 F. 2d 736, 740 n. 4, *cert. denied,* 459 U. S. 1203 (11th Cir. 1982). The holding in that case was that an investor might show sufficient dependence on the promoter's expertise to establish an investment contract despite the written agreement's giving the investor substantial control, but that the investor had the burden of proving such dependency, with respect to each defendant separately, as to render him incapable of exercising the power that the agreement vested in him.

See also Perry v. Gammon, 583 F. Supp. 1230 (N. D. Ga. 1984) (sale of apartment complexes to a limited partnership that retained ultimate control over its investment, as evidenced by its decision to retain the managing agent as well as a provision in the sales contract authorizing the partnership to disaffirm the management agreement on short notice); Lopez v. Richards, 594 F. Supp. 488 (S. D. Miss. 1984); McConnell v. Frank Howard Allen & Co., 574 F. Supp. 781 (N. D. Cal. 1983); Adams v. State, 443 So. 2d 1003 (Fla. App. 1983) (agreements to buy rabbit breeding kits with membership in association that pelted rabbits and negotiated with furriers); Stenger v. R. H. Love Galleries, Inc., 741 F. 2d 144 (7th Cir. 1984) (paintings); cf. Villeneuve v. Advance Business Concepts Corp., 730 F. 2d 1403 (11th Cir. *en banc* 1984) (distributorship for the sale of self-watering planters); Behar v. Professional Network Systems, Inc., — F. Supp. — , CCH Fed. Sec. L. Rep. ¶93,155 (S. D. N. Y. 1987) (although plaintiff was to receive a specified percentage of the revenues generated by a seminar scheme, he was not a passive investor in a public offering but rather exercised considerable bargaining power).

But cf. McEldowney v. Allied Commercial Realty Co., CCH Blue Sky L. Rep. ¶71,864 (D. Ore. 1982) (*held,* under state law, sale of a fractional undivided interest in land pursuant to a leaseback agreement under which buyer was entitled to rental receipts but not a share of the profits of development was an investment contract in view of buyer's expectation of profit from increased appreciation of the property after development).

ng of preferred stock.[6] Not surprisingly, limited partnership nterests are traded on the stock exchanges. But such interests have been treated like securities for purposes of the fraud provisions even without the public element.[7] Indeed, even interests in something called a *general* partnership may be securities when the venture, though a general partnership *de jure,* functions *de facto* like a limited partnership.[8] And, conversely, *limited* partnership interests are *not* securities if their owners do participate actively in running the business.[9]

[6] E. g., SEC v. Murphy, 626 F. 2d 633, 640-41 (9th Cir. 1980); Siebel v. Scott, 725 F. 2d 995, 998 (5th Cir. 1984), *cert. denied,* 467 U. S. 1242 (it suffices that limited partnership interests were securities in the seller's hands though not in the buyer's); cf. Mayer v. Oil Field Systems Corp., 721 F. 2d 59, 65 (2d Cir. 1983), citing the text (limited partnership interests are securities, at least when there is a considerable number of limited partners); Less v. Lurie, 789 F. 2d 624 (8th Cir. 1986) (because investors alleged that a partnership was a shadow formed as part of a general scheme to defraud that also included misrepresentations and was operated in connection with the purchase of securities, a claim was stated regardless of whether the partnership interests were themselves securities).

[7] McGreghar Land Co. v. Meguiar, 521 F. 2d 822 (9th Cir. 1975); Goodman v. Epstein, 582 F. 2d 388, 408-09 (7th Cir. 1978). When a corporation is organized to be the general partner of a series of limited partnerships — a common phenomenon in recent years in the perpetual search for "tax shelters" — the corporation might be the "issuer" (or at least a co-issuer) of the limited partnership interests as the entity responsible for the success or failure of the enterprise. Cf. SEC v. Murphy, 626 F. 2d 633, 642-44 (9th Cir. 1980); SEC v. Holschuh, 694 F. 2d 130, 139 (7th Cir. 1982).

[8] Williamson v. Tucker, 645 F. 2d 404, 422-24 (5th Cir. 1981), *cert. denied,* 454 U. S. 897; Morrison v. Pelican Landing Development, CCH Fed. Sec. L. Rep. ¶98,863 (N. D. Ill. 1982); McConnell v. Frank Howard Allen & Co., 574 F. Supp. 781 (N. D. Cal. 1983); SEC v. Professional Associates, 731 F. 2d 349, 357 (6th Cir. 1984); but cf. Odom v. Slavik, 703 F. 2d 212, 215 (6th Cir. 1983); Stewart v. Germany, 631 F. Supp. 236, 238-40 (S. D. Miss. 1986); Roark v. Belvedere, Ltd., 633 F. Supp. 765, 767-68 (S. D. Ohio 1986); Rivanna Travelers Unlimited v. Thompson Travelers, Inc., 650 F. Supp. 1378 (W. D. Va. 1986); Deutsch Energy Co. v. Mazur, 813 F. 2d 1567 (9th Cir. 1987).

In Cohen v. Goodfriend, 642 F. Supp. 95, 98-100 (E. D. N. Y. 1986), where the plaintiff alleged that he did not know he was a general partner because what he had been sold had been represented to be a limited partnership interest, there was held to be a security.

[9] Rodeo v. Gillman, 787 F. 2d 1175 (7th Cir. 1986); see also Darrah v. Garrett, CCH Fed. Sec. L. Rep. ¶91,472 (W. D. Ohio 1984); Bank of America National Trust & Savings Assn. v. Hotel Rittenhouse Assn., Inc., 595 F. Supp. 800, 806 (E. D. Pa. 1984), citing the text; Federal Deposit Ins. Corp. v. Eagle Properties, Ltd., CCH Fed. Sec. L. Rep. ¶92,304 at 92,082-83 (W. D. Tex. 1985). It is relevant here that the New Uniform Limited Partnership Act that was approved in 1985 significantly expands a limited partner's right to control the enterprise. See Comment, Are Limited Partnership Interests Securities? A Different Conclusion Under the California Limited Partnership Act, 18 Pac. L. J. 125 (1986).

A limited partnership interest does not stop being a security when accom-

In short, it is substance, not form, that controls here, too.[10] The problem, as Judge Frank put it when he was Chairman of the SEC is to distinguish between the public offering of securities parading as "limited partnership interests" and "an offering of a half interest in a hamburger stand."[11]

3. Real Estate and "Stock"

Analysis of this branch of the "security" definition begins with *United Housing Foundation, Inc. v. Forman*,[12] where the Supreme Court held that shares in a nonprofit, cooperative housing corporation (Co-op City) were neither "stock" nor "investment contracts." So far as the "stock" component of the definition is concerned, the shares had none of the traditional characteristics: dividends conditioned on an apportionment of profits, subjection to pledge, voting rights proportional to number of shares owned, and possibility of appreciation in value. And an "investment contract" was precluded by the "non-profit" nature of the project and the focus on the acquisition of a place to live.

As Justice Powell wrote for a six-to-three majority:[13]

> A
>
> We reject at the outset any suggestion that the present transaction, evidenced by the sale of shares called "stock," must be considered a security transaction simply because the statutory definition of a security includes the words "any * * * stock." Rather we adhere to the basic principle that has guided all of the Court's decisions in this area:
>
> > [I]n searching for the meaning and scope of the word "security" in the Act[s], form should be disregarded for substance

---

panied by an option to buy out the general partners. Rodeo v. Gillman, supra at 1180.

In Goodwin v. Elkins & Co., 730 F. 2d 99 (3d Cir. 1984), *cert. denied*, 469 U. S. 831, the three judges relied on three separate grounds in holding that a general partner's interest in a limited brokerage partnership was not a security (1) because a general partner's role under the Uniform Partnership Act extended by law well beyond the permitted role of a passive investor; (2) because state partnership law aside, a general partner with the degree of participation in partnership affairs in the case at bar could not have entered into an investment contract; and (3) solely because the terms of the partnership agreement detailed numerous duties for a general partner.

[10] In general, see Yeomans v. Simon, 791 F. 2d 341, 344-47 (5th Cir. 1986)

[11] 212 Sat. Eve. Post 28 (Apr. 27, 1940), 26 (June 1, 1940), 26 (June 15 1940).

[12] 421 U. S. 837 (1975).

[13] Id. at 848-53.

> and the emphasis should be on economic reality. *Tcherepnin* v. *Knight,* 389 U. S. 332, 336 (1967).

See also *Howey,* supra, at 298 [p. 184 supra].

* * * Because securities transactions are economic in character Congress intended the application of these statutes to turn on the economic realities underlying a transaction, and not on the name appended thereto. Thus, in construing these Acts against the background of their purpose, we are guided by a traditional canon of statutory construction:

> [A] thing may be within the letter of the statute and yet not within the statute, because not within its spirit, nor within the intention of its makers. *Church of the Holy Trinity* v. *United States,* 143 U. S. 457, 459 (1892).

See also *United States* v. *American Trucking Assns.,* 310 U. S. 534, 543 (1940).[14]

* * *

In holding that the name given to an instrument is not dispositive, we do not suggest that the name is wholly irrelevant to the decision whether it is a security. There may be occasions when the use of a traditional name such as "stocks" or "bonds" will lead a purchaser justifiably to assume that the federal securities laws apply. This would clearly be the case when the underlying transaction embodies some of the significant characteristics typically associated with the named instrument.

* * *

B

The Court of Appeals, as an alternative ground for its decision, concluded that a share in Riverbay was also an "investment contract" as defined by the Securities Acts. Respondents further argue that in any event what they agreed to purchase is "commonly known as a 'security' " within the meaning of these laws. In considering these claims we again must examine the substance — the economic realities of the transaction — rather than the names that may have been employed by the parties. We perceive no distinction, for present purposes, between an "investment contract" and an "instrument commonly known as a 'security.' " In either case, the basic test for distinguishing the transaction from other commercial dealings is

> whether the scheme involves an investment of money in a

[14] * * * See * * * 1 L. Loss, Securities Regulation 493 (2d ed. 1961) ("substance governs rather than form: * * * just as some things which look like real estate are securities, some things which look like securities are real estate").

common enterprise with profits to come solely from the efforts of others. *Howey*, 328 U. S. at 301.[16]

This test, in shorthand form, embodies the essential attributes that run through all of the Court's decisions defining a security. The touchstone is the presence of an investment in a common venture premised on a reasonable expectation of profits to be derived from the entrepreneurial or managerial efforts of others. By profits, the Court has meant either capital appreciation resulting from the development of the initial investment, as in *Joiner,* supra (sale of oil leases conditioned on promoters' agreement to drill exploratory well), or a participation in earnings resulting from the use of investors' funds, as in *Tcherepnin* v. *Knight,* supra (dividends on the investment based on savings and loan association's profits). In such cases the investor is "attracted solely by the prospects of a return" on his investment. *Howey*, supra at 300. By contrast, when a purchaser is motivated by a desire to use or consume the item purchased — "to occupy the land or to develop it themselves," as the *Howey* Court put it, ibid. — the securities laws do not apply. See also *Joiner*, supra.

In the present case there can be no doubt that investors were attracted solely by the prospect of acquiring a place to live, and not by financial returns on their investments. * * * [a]

[16] This test speaks in terms of "profits to come *solely* from the efforts of others." (Emphasis supplied.) Although the issue is not presented in this case, we note that the Court of Appeals for the Ninth Circuit has held that the "word 'solely' should not be read as a strict or literal limitation on the definition of an investment contract, but rather must be construed realistically, so as to include within the definition those schemes which involve in substance, if not form, securities." SEC v. Glenn W. Turner Enterprises, Inc., 474 F. 2d 476, 482, *cert. denied,* 414 U. S. 821 (1973). We express no view, however, as to the holding of this case.

[a] ED.: The Court rejected the lower court's view that a form of profit was inherent in the possibility of net income derived from the leasing of commercial facilities, professional offices, and parking spaces, as well as the operation of community washing machines, and the use of any income from these conveniences to reduce tenant rental costs. "Conceptually, one might readily agree that net income from the leasing of commercial and professional facilities is the kind of profit traditionally associated with a security investment. See *Tcherepnin* v. *Knight* supra. But in the present case this income — if indeed there is any — is far too speculative and insubstantial to bring the entire transaction within the Securities Acts." 421 U. S. at 856.

Still another "profit" theory that the Court rejected was based on the tax deductibility of the portion of the monthly rental charge applied to interest on the mortgage. Id. at 855. This language was distinguished in Kolibash v. Sagittarius Recording Co., 626 F. Supp. 1173, 1178-79 (S. D. Ohio 1986), where the *primary* benefit that the investors expected to receive was the tax benefit to be derived from participating in a master recording tax shelter scheme.

Cf. All Seasons Resorts, Inc. v. Abrams, 68 N. Y. 2d 81, 497 N. E. 2d 33 (1986) (memberships constituting only a license for use of a system of outdoor resort campgrounds); Dumbarton Condominiums Assn. v. 3120 R St. Associates

More recently claims have been made that the condominium is uperior to the stock cooperative.[14] A condominium is a multi-unit building in which each occupant owns his apartment in fee simple ogether with a proportionate undivided interest in the common reas.[15] In any event, at the other extreme from either device is he syndication of an office building or of a residential development n which the investor's interest is not equated with residence; the Empire State Building, in effect, "went public" in 1961 by means of the registration of $39 million of participations in the partnership nterests of several general partners in Empire State Building Associates, which was to acquire a net 114-year lease on the building nd land.[16]

In between is the Florida vacation home that *is* lived in during he winter months but rented out during most of the year. In 1973 he Commission published guidelines:[17]

> * * * Resort condominiums are one of the more common interests in real estate the offer of which may involve an offering of securities. However, other types of units that are part of a development or project present analogous questions under the federal securities laws. Although this release speaks in terms of condominiums, it applies to offerings of all types of units in real estate developments which have characteristics similar to those described herein.

---

td. Partnership, 657 F. Supp. 226, CCH Fed. Sec. L. Rep. ¶93,221 (D. D. C. 987) (some condominium units were bought as investments and some as resiences).

[14] See Comment, Community Apartments: Condominium or Stock Cooperave?, 50 Calif. L. Rev. 299 (1962).

[15] On condominiums generally, see Berger, Condominium: Shelter on a Statory Foundation, 63 Colum. L. Rev. 987 (1963).

[16] SEC File No. 2-18,741 (1961). See generally Kroll, The Why and the How Real Estate Syndications, 14 Record A. B. C. N. Y. 71 (1959), 5 Prac. Law.) (Mar. 1959); Berger, Real Estate Syndication: Property, Promotion, and the eed for Protection, 60 Yale L. J. 725 (1960); cf. Gallagher v. Balkind, CCH ed. Sec. L. Rep. ¶92,373 (S. D. N. Y. 1985).

Whether or not the SEC statutes apply in the real estate context, the Interate Land Sales Full Disclosure Act, enacted as Title XIV of the Housing and rban Development Act of 1968, as amended, 15 U. S. C. §§1701 et seq., ovides, on the model of §5 of the 1933 Act, that developers selling or leasing hundred or more unimproved lots pursuant to a common promotional plan ust file a "statement of record" with the Department of Housing and Urban evelopment and give each buyer or lessee a "property report" before he signs y agreement, with a right in the buyer or lessee to revoke within seven days. here is also a fraud provision, modeled on §17(a) of the 1933 Act, that applies ien the number of unimproved lots is 25 or more. And at the state level there a Uniform Land Sales Practice Act. 7A U. L. A. 371 (1966).

[17] Sec. Act Rel. 5347 (1973); see Mosher v. Southbridge Associates, Inc., 552 Supp. 1231 (W. D. Pa. 1982).

* * *

* * * The "profits" that the purchaser is led to expect may consist of revenues received from rental of the unit; these revenues and any tax benefits resulting from rental of the unit are the economic inducements held out to the purchaser.

* * *

In summary, the offering of condominium units in conjunction with any one of the following will cause the offering to be viewed as an offering of securities in the form of investment contracts:

1. The condominiums, with any rental arrangement or other similar service, are offered and sold with emphasis on the economic benefits to the purchaser to be derived from the managerial efforts of the promoter, or a third party designated or arranged for by the promoter, from rental of the units.
2. The offering of participation in a rental pool arrangement; and
3. The offering of a rental or similar arrangement whereby the purchaser must hold his unit available for rental for any part of the year, must use an exclusive rental agent or is otherwise materially restricted in his occupancy or rental of his unit.

In all of the above situations, investor protection requires the application of the federal securities laws.

If the condominiums are not offered and sold with emphasis on the economic benefits to the purchaser to be derived from the managerial efforts of others, and assuming that no plan to avoid the registration requirements of the Securities Act is involved, an owner of a condominium unit may, after purchasing his unit, enter into a non-pooled rental arrangement with an agent not designated or required to be used as a condition to the purchase, whether or not such agent is affiliated with the offeror, without causing a sale of a security to be involved in the sale of the unit. Further a continuing affiliation between the developers or promoters of a project and the project by reason of maintenance arrangements does not make the unit a security.

In situations where commercial facilities are a part of the common elements of a residential project, no registration would be required under the investment contract theory where (a) the income from such facilities is used only to offset common area expenses and (b) the operation of such facilities is incidental to the project as a whole and are [*sic*] not established as a primary income source for the individual owners of a condominium or cooperative unit.

* * *

Another in-between case is stock in a *private* cooperative that is the holder's residence — the classic cooperative apartment that has been described as a "child of a marriage of a long-term lease with a stock certificate,"[18] — and that, unlike Co-op City, presents the same possibility of capital appreciation as any real estate investment. There, nevertheless, the Second Circuit has said there is no security.[19]

Housing cooperatives and condominiums aside, the Supreme Court's perfectly sound conclusion has considerably broader implications: If not all stock is "stock," what about the sale of a *business* (or part of a business) that simply takes the form of a stock transfer? After a four-to-four split among the Circuits, the Supreme Court neatly pulled together its previous decisions in *Landreth Timber Co. v. Landreth,* Justice Powell writing for all but Justice Stevens:[20]

II

It is axiomatic that "[t]he starting point in every case involving construction of a statute is the language itself." [Citations omitted.] As we have observed in the past, this definition is quite broad, *Marine Bank* v. *Weaver,* 455 U. S. 551, 556 (1982), and includes both instruments whose names alone carry well-settled meaning, as well as instruments of "more variable character [that] were necessarily designated by more descriptive terms," such as "investment contract" and "instrument commonly known as a 'security.'" *SEC* v.

[18] Isaacs, "To Buy or Not to Buy: That Is the Question" * * * What Is a Cooperative Apartment?, 13 Record A. B. C. N. Y. 203, 210 (1958).

[19] Grenader v. Spitz, 537 F. 2d 612 (2d Cir. 1976); cf. Bender v. Continental Towers Ltd. Partnership, 632 F. Supp. 497 (S. D. N. Y. 1986) (condominium conversion plan); but cf. N. Y. Gen. Bus. Law, Art. 23-A, §§352-ee, 353, applied in State v. Rachmani Corp., CCH Blue Sky L. Rep. ¶72,146 (Sup. Ct. 1984) (cooperative apartment conversion).

The real estate industry has recently developed various kinds of "shared-equity programs," which are designed to provide first-time purchasers with a realistic opportunity of finding an affordable house, as well as to prevent the displacement of tenants through condominium conversion. These goals are achieved by using the funds of an investor who acquires an equity interest in the property and a share of appreciation on sale or refinancing, as well as a tax shelter by way of deductions for interest expense and sometimes depreciation. See Fields, Real Estate Interests As Investment Contracts: An Update and a New Application — The Shared-Equity Program, 12 Real Est. L. J. 307 (1984), discussing Electronic Realty Associates, Inc., CCH Fed. Sec. L. Rep. ¶77,050 (letter 1981).

With respect to the acquisition, sale, or servicing of mortgages or deeds of trust generally, see Sec. Act Rel. 3892 (1958). With respect to mortgage-backed securities ("securitization" of mortgages), see p. 232 n. 2 infra.

[20] 471 U. S. 681, 685-94 (1985).

C. M. Joiner Leasing Corp., 320 U. S. 344, 351 (1943). The face of the definition shows that "stock" is considered to be a "security" within the meaning of the Acts. As we observed in *United Housing Foundation, Inc.* v. *Forman,* 421 U. S. 837 (1975), most instruments bearing such a traditional title are likely to be covered by the definition. Id., at 850.

As we also recognized in *Forman,* the fact that instruments bear the label "stock" is not of itself sufficient to invoke the coverage of the Acts. Rather, we concluded that we must also determine whether those instruments possess "some of the significant characteristics typically associated with" stock, id., at 851, recognizing that when an instrument is both called "stock" and bears stock's usual characteristics, "a purchaser justifiably [may] assume that the federal securities laws apply," id., at 850. * * *

Under the facts of *Forman,* we concluded that the instruments at issue there were not "securities" within the meaning of the Acts. * * *

In contrast, it is undisputed that the stock involved here possesses all of the characteristics we identified in *Forman* as traditionally associated with common stock. Indeed, the District Court so found. Moreover, unlike the situation in *Forman,* the context of the transaction involved here — the sale of stock in a corporation — is typical of the kind of context to which the Acts normally apply. It is thus much more likely here than in *Forman* that an investor would believe he was covered by the federal securities laws. Under the circumstances of this case, the plain meaning of the statutory definition mandates that the stock be treated as "securities" subject to the coverage of the Acts. * * *

III

Under other circumstances, we might consider the statutory analysis outlined above to be a sufficient answer compelling judgment for petitioner.[3] Respondents urge, however, that language in our previous opinions, including *Forman,* requires that we look beyond the label "stock" and the characteristics of the instruments involved to determine whether application of the Acts is mandated by the economic substance of the transaction. Moreover, the Court of Appeals rejected the view that the plain meaning of the definition would be sufficient to hold this stock covered, because it saw "no principled way," 731 F. 2d at 1353, to justify treating notes, bonds, and other of the definitional categories differently. We address these concerns in turn.

[3] Professor Loss suggests that the statutory analysis is sufficient. L. Loss Fundamentals of Securities Regulation 212 (1983). * * *

A

It is fair to say that our cases have not been entirely clear on the proper method of analysis for determining when an instrument is a "security." This Court has decided a number of cases in which it looked to the economic substance of the transaction, rather than just to its form, to determine whether the Acts applied. * * * [Justice Powell here discusses the *Joiner* and *Howey* cases.]

* * *

Respondents contend that *Forman* and the case on which it was based required us to reject the view that the shares of stock at issue here may be considered "securities" because of their name and characteristics. Instead, they argue that our cases require us in every instance to look to the economic substance of the transaction to determine whether the *Howey* test has been met. According to respondents, it is clear that petitioner sought not to earn profits from the efforts of others, but to buy a company that it could manage and control. Petitioner was not a passive investor of the kind Congress intended the Acts to protect, but an active entrepreneur, who sought to "use or consume" the business purchased just as the purchasers in *Forman* sought to use the apartments they acquired after purchasing shares of stock. Thus, respondents urge that the Acts do not apply.

We disagree with respondents' interpretation of our cases. First, it is important to understand the contexts within which these cases were decided. All of the cases on which respondents rely involved unusual instruments not easily characterized as "securities." See n. 3, supra. Thus, if the Acts were to apply in those cases at all, it would have to have been because the economic reality underlying the transactions indicated that the instruments were actually of a type that falls within the usual concept of a security. In the case at bar, in contrast, the instrument involved is traditional stock, plainly within the statutory definition. There is no need here, as there was in the prior cases, to look beyond the characteristics of the instrument to determine whether the Acts apply.

* * *

Second, we would note that the *Howey* economic reality test was designed to determine whether a particular instrument is an "investment contract," not whether it fits within *any* of the examples listed in the statutory definition of "security." Our cases are consistent with this view. * * * Moreover, applying the *Howey* test to traditional stock and all other types of instruments listed in the

statutory definition would make the Act's enumeration of many types of instruments superfluous. *Golden* v. *Garafalo,* 678 F. 2d 1139, 1144 (C.A. 2 1982). See *Tcherepnin* v. *Knight,* 389 U. S. 332, 343 (1967).

Finally, we cannot agree with respondents that the Acts were intended to cover only "passive investors" and not privately negotiated transactions involving the transfer of control to "entrepreneurs." * * * [6]

B

We now turn to the Court of Appeals' concern that treating stock as a specific category of "security" provable by its characteristics means that other categories listed in the statutory definition, such as notes, must be treated the same way. Although we do not decide whether coverage of notes or other instruments may be provable by their name and characteristics, we do point out several reasons why we think stock may be distinguishable from most if not all of the other categories listed in the Act's definition.

Instruments that bear both the name and all of the usual characteristics of stock seem to us to be the clearest case for coverage by the plain language of the definition. * * * Unlike some instruments, therefore, traditional stock is more susceptible of a plain meaning approach.

Professor Loss has agreed that stock is different from the other categories of instruments. He observes that it "goes against the grain" to apply the *Howey* test for determining whether an instrument is an "investment contract" to traditional stock. L. Loss, Fundamentals of Securities Regulation 211-212 (1983). As Professor Loss explains,

> It is one thing to say that the typical cooperative apartment dweller has bought a home, not a security; or that not every installment purchase "note" is a security; or that a person who charges a restaurant meal by signing his credit card slip is not selling a security even though his signature is an "evidence of indebtedness." But *stock* (except for the residential wrinkle) is so quintessentially a security as to foreclose further analysis. Id., at 212 (emphasis in original).

(1) The Court concurrently came out the same way in affirming

[6] In criticizing the sale of business doctrine, Professor Loss agrees. He considers that the doctrine "comes dangerously close to the heresy of saying that the fraud provisions do not apply to private transactions; for nobody, apparently, has had the temerity to argue that the sale of a *publicly* owned business for stock of the acquiring corporation that is distributed to the shareholders of the selling corporation as a liquidating dividend does not involve a security." L. Loss, Fundamentals of Securities Regulation 212 (1983) (emphasis in original) (footnote omitted).

Gould v. *Ruefenacht,*[21] where the plaintiff had bought half of a sole shareholder's stock, promising to participate in the management. Observing that "In 'economic reality,' considerably less than 100%, and often less than 50%, of outstanding shares may be a controlling block,"[22] the Court stated:[23]

> Application of the sale of business doctrine also would lead to arbitrary distinctions between transactions covered by the Acts and those that are not. Because applicability of the Acts would depend on factors other than the type of characteristics of the instrument involved, a corporation's stock could be determined to be a security as to the seller, but not as to the purchaser, or as to some purchasers but not others. Likewise, if the same purchaser bought small amounts of stock through several different transactions, it is possible that the Acts would apply as to some of the transactions, but not as to the one that gave him "control." See *Ruefenacht* v. *O'Halloran,* [737 F. 2d 320, 335 (9th Cir. 1984)]. Such distinctions make little sense in view of the Act's purpose to protect investors. Moreover, the parties' inability to determine at the time of the transaction whether the Acts apply neither serves the Acts' protective purpose nor permits the purchaser to compensate for the added risk of no protection when negotiating the transaction.

(2) Presumably there must still be a determination whether a particular instrument had the attributes of "stock." In a 1982 case in the Second Circuit,[24] the transaction involved was held to be not a purchase of the publicly traded shares of a company but rather a buy-out of its assets, including instruments labeled "stock" of closely held subsidiaries.

(3) The "essential characteristics" approach rather than *Howey* certainly lends itself better to an analysis of such phrases as "voting trust certificate" and "certificate of deposit for a security."[25]

(4) It cannot be assumed that *United Housing* is altogether a sport.

[21] 471 U. S. 701 (1985).

[22] Id. at 705, quoting from King v. Winkler, 673 F. 2d 342, 346 (11th Cir. 1982).

[23] 471 U. S. at 705-06.

[24] Seagrave Corp. v. Vista Resources, Inc., 696 F. 2d 227 (2d Cir. 1982), *clarified,* 710 F. 2d 95 (2d Cir. 1983), *cert. dismissed by consent,* 468 U. S. 1226.

[25] See c. 3H infra. In Meason v. Bank of Miami, 652 F. 2d 542, 549 (5th Cir. 1981), *cert. denied,* 455 U. S. 939, the court declined to apply the *Howey* test to a certificate of deposit issued by an offshore bank. And in Penturelli v. Spector, Cohen, Gaden & Rosen, P. C., 779 F. 2d 160 (3d Cir. 1985), the court applied the *Landreth-Ruefenacht* rather than the *Howey* analysis to the mineral phrases in the 1933 and 1934 Act definitions of "security" (see pp. 176–77 supra). But cf. Parvin v. Davis Oil Co., 524 F. 2d 112 (9th Cir. 1975); Simon v. Fribourg, 650 F. Supp. 321 (D. Minn. 1986), citing the text.

There are negative "stock" holdings with respect to "stock" in a nonprofit corporation entitling its Ute Indian holders to graze livestock on rangeland maintained by the issuer [26] and stock of a Federal Land Bank Association.[27] And there is an SEC "no action" letter with respect to stock in a title insurance company whose membership was limited to practicing lawyers in three states, the entire benefit of ownership of shares being the ability to write title insurance.[28]

(5) It remains to be seen whether the split of authority at the level of the state blue sky laws will survive the *Landreth* case.[29]

4. FRANCHISES

Many of *Howey*'s progeny have involved various franchise arrangements. Indeed, one case grew out of a franchise operation on how to run franchise operations.[30] Although *Howey* without more would have sufficed in those cases in which the franchisee virtually sat on his hands and relied "solely" on the franchisor to earn him a return on his investment, the courts have developed two theories for covering even those cases in which the franchisee "makes the hamburgers."

One, which arose under the Hawaii Uniform Securities Act, read the "solely" of *Howey* as referring to the *managerial* efforts of the franchisor. That is to say, since in fact *Howey* involved *no* investment participation, the "solely" was dictum.[31] That holding was soon adopted by the SEC,[32] and at least *obiter* by the Supreme Court when it referred in the cooperative housing case to the "entrepreneurial or managerial efforts of others."[33]

[26] Hackford v. First Security Bank of Utah, CCH Fed. Sec. L. Rep. ¶99,402 (10th Cir. 1983), *cert. denied,* 464 U. S. 827.

[27] Dau v. Federal Land Bank of Omaha, 627 F. Supp. 346, 350 (N. D. Iowa 1985).

[28] Attorney's Title Guaranty Fund, Inc., CCH Fed. Sec. L. Rep. ¶77,402 (letter 1983).

[29] In favor of the doctrine, see C & C Electric Construction Co., Inc. v. Rogers, 281 Ark. 178, 182, 663 S. W. 2d 707, 709 (1984); Carver v. Blanford, 288 S. C. 309, 342 S. E. 2d 406 (1986); Star Supply Co. v. Jones, 665 S. W. 2d 194 (Tex. App. 1984). *Contra:* Fox v. Ehrmantraut, 28 Cal. 3d 127, 615 P. 2d 1383 (1980); Tech Resources, Inc. v. Estate of Hubbard, 246 Ga. 583, 272 S. E. 2d 314 (1980); Condux v. Neldon, 83 Ill. App. 3d 575, 404 N. E. 2d 523 (1980); Specialized Tours, Inc. v. Hagen, 392 N. W. 2d 520 (Minn. 1986).

[30] Lino v. City Investing Co., 487 F. 2d 689 (3d Cir. 1973).

[31] State v. Hawaii Market Center, Inc., 52 Hawaii 642, 485 P. 2d 108 (1971).

[32] Sec. Act Rel. 5211 (1971).

[33] United Housing Foundation, Inc. v. Forman, 421 U. S. 837, 852 (1975); see also id. at 852 n. 16. For square holdings under the federal legislation, see

The other technique for extending *Howey* — which the Hawaii court used in tandem with the first[34] — is the so-called "risk capital" theory. That theory, which originated in a 1961 opinion of Justice Traynor of the California Supreme Court, has it that a security is involved regardless of the franchisee's activities when the franchisees provide the "risk capital" for the business."[35]

California and a number of other states now have special franchise investment statutes that interrelate in various ways with their blue sky laws.[36]

E. INSURANCE AND BANK HYBRIDS

1. Insurance Hybrids

The current trend toward "one-stop financial marketing," together with the increasing competition of the securities, insurance, and banking industries for the business of managing the billions of private pension funds, has resulted in the development of interesting — and to no little extent perplexing — hybrids.

Our story starts with §3(a)(8) of the 1933 Act, which exempts "any insurance or endowment policy or annuity contract or optional

---

SEC v. Glenn W. Turner Enterprises, Inc., 474 F. 2d 476 (9th Cir. 1973), *cert. denied,* 414 U. S. 821; SEC v. Koscot Interplanetary, Inc., 497 F. 2d 473 (5th Cir. 1974); Davis v. Avco Financial Services, Inc., 739 F. 2d 1057, 1063 (6th Cir. 1984), *rehearing, and rehearing en banc, denied,* CCH Fed. Sec. L. Rep. ¶91,668 (6th Cir. 1984), *cert. denied,* 470 U. S. 1005, 1135. There are also blue sky cases. E. g., American Gold & Diamond Corp. v. Kirkpatrick, 678 P. 2d 1343 (Alaska 1984); cf. Activator Supply Co., Inc. v. Wurth, 239 Kan. 610, 722 P. 2d 1081 (1986).

[34] See also Pacific Coast Coin Exchange of Canada v. Ontario Securities Commission, [1978] 2 S. C. R. 112, 80 D. L. R. 2d 529, a case involving the sale of bags of silver coins.

[35] Silver Hills Country Club v. Sobieski, 55 Cal. 2d 811, 814-16, 361 P. 2d 906, 908-09 (1961), followed in 49 Ops. Cal. Att. Gen. 124, CCH Blue Sky L. Rep. ¶70,747 (1967). At the time of these opinions the California definition included any "beneficial interest or title to property, profits, or earnings." In its original form §2(1) included the comparable phrase, "certificate of interest in property, tangible or intangible," which was removed in the 1934 amendments as perhaps involving "too broad and uncertain application." H. R. Rep. No. 1838, 73d Cong., 2d Sess. (1934) 39. Moreover, Justice Traynor's opinion involved memberships in a new country club. But the Attorney General's opinion was directed to franchise operations. See also, e. g., Mitzner v. Cardet Int'l, Inc., 358 F. Supp. 1262 (N. D. Ill. 1973); but cf. Bitter v. Hobey Int'l, Inc., 498 F. 2d 183 (9th Cir. 1974). See generally Stevenson and O'Leary, Definition of a Security: Risk Capital and Investment Contracts in Washington, 3 U. Puget Sound L. Rev. 83 (1980); Annot., "Risk Capital" Test for Determination of Whether Transaction Involves Security * * *, 68 A. L. R. Fed. 89 (1984).

[36] See Cal. Franchise Investment Law, Cal. Corp. Code §§31,000-19.

annuity contract, issued by a corporation subject to the supervision of the insurance commissioner, bank commissioner, or any agency or officer performing like functions, of any State or Territory of the United States or the District of Columbia."[1]

This is a perfect example of how it sometimes does not pay to be too cautious. True, all forms of insurance except pure term have some investment element, and insurance companies are among the largest institutional investors. But without this exemption, and without any specific reference to insurance policies in the definition of "security," and at a time when *Paul* v. *Virginia* was still the law of the land,[2] it is hardly conceivable that Congress would have subjected insurance policies to federal control *sub silentio,* even control of the disclosure variety. As it is, §3(a)(8) seems on its face to create a negative implication that insurance policies *are* securities, which are exempt from the registration requirements but are subject to the antifraud provisions. Nevertheless, the Commission early took the position that insurance or endowment policies or annuity contracts issued by regularly constituted insurance companies were not intended to be securities, and that in effect §3(a)(8) is supererogation.[3] This undoubtedly carries out the legislative intention; for the House report states that the purpose of the exemption "makes clear what is already implied in the act, namely, that insurance policies are not to be regarded as securities subject to the provisions of the act."[4] And it has been held under a number of the blue sky

C. 3E [1]In addition, §3(c)(3) of the Investment Company Act excludes any "insurance company" from the definition of "investment company."

[2]8 Wall. 168 (U. S. 1869), overruled by United States v. South-Eastern Underwriters Assn., 322 U. S. 533 (1944).

[3]See the writer's testimony on behalf of the Commission in Securities Exchange Acts Amendments, Hearings before Subcom. of S. Com. on Banking & Currency on S. 2408, 81st Cong., 2d Sess. (1950) 33. The Supreme Court has referred *obiter* to the exemption as "clearly supererogation." Tcherepnin v. Knight, 389 U. S. 332, 342 n. 30 (1967); see also Grainger v. State Security Life Ins. Co., 547 F. 2d 303, 305 (5th Cir. 1977), *rehearing denied,* 563 F. 2d 215 (5th Cir. 1977), *cert. denied,* 436 U. S. 932. In Sec. Act Rel. 658, 31 SEC Dock. 908, 912 n. 25 (1984), the Commission at long last formally acknowledged that §3(a)(8) was an "exclusion."

[4]H. R. Rep. No. 85, 73d Cong., 1st Sess. (1933) 15, cited in SEC v. Variable Annuity Life Ins. Co. of America, 359 U. S. 65, 74 n. 4 (1959) (Brennan, J., concurring). On this approach, "an insurance company's financial guarantee bond insuring the timely payment of amounts due under debentures to be offered publicly by a non-insurance subsidiary of an insurance company" has been treated as within §3(a)(8). Sec. Act Rel. 6688, 37 SEC Dock. 774, 777 (1987), infra p. 614 n. 58.

laws that orthodox annuity contracts issued by life insurance companies are not securities.[5]

The question of categorization as between the two major fields of insurance (in the generic sense of the term as including annuities) and securities arose most acutely with the development of the so-called "variable annuity" in the mid-1950s. The variable annuity was the answer of an important segment of the insurance industry to the problem of tailoring the traditional annuity to an inflationary economy. The distinguishing feature of the variable annuity is that the annuitant's payments purchase units in a fund of securities, much as in the case of an open-end investment company. The accumulation in the annuitant's account is valued at maturity, and the insurance company promises to pay him thereafter not a fixed number of dollars monthly (though some contracts offer fixed payment options) but the dollar value, fluctuating with each monthly payment as the value of the portfolio fluctuates, of the annuity units to which it is determined at maturity that the annuitant is entitled on the basis of capital contribution, age, and (at one time at least) sex. That is to say, the first payment after maturity is determined by reference to standard annuity tables, on the basis of an assumed net investment rate of a certain percentage per annum, but the figure thus obtained is converted to annuity units by dividing it by the then value of an annuity unit. Thereafter the dollar value of a unit and hence the amount of subsequent monthly payments fluctuate as the value of the portfolio goes up or down.[6]

Of course, this marriage of the insurance and mutual fund concepts would not work unless the buyers' funds were invested, typically, in common stocks (though today there are balanced and bond and even money market plans). But all the states, as well as Puerto Rico and Congress for the District of Columbia, have now adjusted their insurance statutes or regulations in one way or another to make possible the issuance of variable contracts.[7]

At the state level the Uniform Securities Act made explicit what

[5] E. g., Haberman v. Equitable Life Assurance Society, 224 F. 2d 401, *corrected on rehearing*, 225 F. 2d 837 (5th Cir. 1955), *cert. denied*, 350 U. S. 948 (phrase "or other evidence of indebtedness" must be construed *ejusdem generis* in Texas act; nor is annuity "any other instrument commonly known as a security").

[6] See generally G. Johnson and D. Grubbs, The Variable Annuity (2d ed. 1970); Frankel, Variable Annuities, Variable Insurance and Separate Accounts, 51 B. U. L. Rev. 173 (1971); T. Frankel, The Regulation of Money Managers: The Investment Company Act and the Investment Advisers Act (1978) *passim*; Proceedings of Conference on Variable Annuities and Variable Life Insurance, 32 Bus. Law. 675 (1977).

[7] Notwithstanding D. C. Code §35-639, the District of Columbia, alone, does not permit variable contracts.

seemed to be the view of the great majority of blue sky administrators in the mid-1950s to the effect that variable annuities were securities, which should not be exempted from registration. But the appropriate clauses were inserted in brackets in 1958, so that they could be deleted by any state that might conclude that variable annuities were sufficiently regulated by the insurance authorities to warrant excluding them from the blue sky law along with orthodox annuities.[8] And all but a handful of states exclude variable annuities in one form of language or another.

The problem at the federal level was more difficult, not only because §3(a)(8) of the Securities Act exempts any "annuity contract" issued by a corporation subject to the supervision of some insurance authority, without further qualification, but also because Congress, promptly after the Supreme Court had overruled *Paul* v. *Virginia* in 1944, had declared in the McCarran-Ferguson Insurance Regulation Act that "No Act of Congress shall be construed to invalidate, impair or supersede any law enacted by any State for the purpose of regulating the business of insurance."[9] Nevertheless, the SEC in 1956 sued in the District of Columbia to enjoin a local life insurance company, Variable Annuity Life Insurance Company (known as VALIC), from selling variable annuities without registration under both the Securities Act and the Investment Company Act. The District Court, finding that the contracts had characteristics of both securities and insurance, concluded that both statutes would apply "if it were not for the clear and explicit language of the McCarran Act and the fact that the defendants [a second similar company had intervened] are licensed and regulated by the insurance departments of this District and the States where they operate." The Court of Appeals affirmed on the ground that "The definitions in the Securities Act and the Investment Company Act indicate that if the insurance commissioner of a state subjects the business to his supervision, it is the business of insurance." The Supreme Court reversed by a vote of five to four. The majority, though bowing to the long tradition of regulating "insurance" at the state level, emphasized that the words "insurance" and "annuity" had to be construed as federal terms in a federal statute. And they concluded that, although those concepts should not be frozen into the mold they fitted when the federal statutes were passed, "the concept of 'insurance' involves some investment risk-taking on the part of the company" — "a guarantee that at least some fraction

[8] §§401(*l*), 402(a)(5).
[9] §2, 15 U. S. C. §1012.

of the benefits will be payable in fixed amounts." The dissenters, emphasizing that these were not cases where the label "annuity" had simply been attached to a securities scheme in an effort to avoid federal regulation, were unable to join in what was termed the majority's "preoccupation with a constricted 'color matching' approach to the construction of the relevant federal statutes which fails to take adequate account of the historic congressional policy of leaving regulation of the business of insurance entirely to the States."[10]

The *VALIC* case inevitably left a number of both conceptual and practical problems in its wake, particularly with respect to the application of the Investment Company Act, which our "story line" cannot ignore despite our primary concern with the Securities Act. At times during and after the litigation, as it later appeared, the Commission was perhaps overinclined to analyze the variable annuity in terms of whether its investment or insurance characteristics predominated. But it soon recognized that a variable annuity was neither solely an investment contract nor solely an insurance contract, and that the insurance and investment elements could be segregated with sufficient precision so that the former might be regulated by the state insurance authorities and the latter by the Commission.

VALIC was organized to be purely a variable annuity company. The typical structure that the Commission contemplated in the case of an established insurance company that sought to sell variable annuities (backed by the assets in a legally separate account for the benefit of variable annuity contract holders) was the incorporation by the insurance company of an investment fund as an open-end

[10]SEC v. Variable Annuity Life Ins. Co. of America, 155 F. Supp. 521, 526 (D. D. C. 1957), *aff'd*, 257 F. 2d 201, 205 (D. C. Cir. 1958), *rev'd*, 359 U. S. 65, 71, 96 (1959). The concurring opinion of Justice Brennan contains a more reasoned exposition of the insurance-security dichotomy than Justice Douglas's opinion for the Court. Dean Landis, one of the principal draftsmen of the 1933 Act, wrote after this case that no member of the conference committee, where the exemption originated, "could possibly have envisaged that some two decades later the traditional annuity contract would be turned into this type of a pro rata interest in a group of securities," and that Justice Harlan's dissenting opinion misread the history of the Act in several respects. Landis, The Legislative History of the Securities Act of 1933, 28 Geo. Wash. L. Rev. 29, 47 n. 24 (1959).

Of course, the Supreme Court's ruling that variable annuities were "securities" within the 1933 Act is necessarily a holding that the McCarran-Ferguson Act does not bar the application of the 1933 Act to the issuance of securities by insurance companies. For a later interpretation of the McCarran-Ferguson Act, in the context of the SEC's proxy rules, see SEC v. National Securities, Inc., 393 U. S. 453 (1969).

management investment company that would be registered under the 1940 Act, with the insurance company holding the shares of the "investment company," and as a practical matter controlling it, but with a "pass-through" of voting power from the insurance company to the contract holders; and the insurance company might enter into an advisory contract with the "investment company." Under the practice that has evolved, however, there have been certain modifications of this pattern, as we shall see.

Prudential, the early champion of the variable annuity among the traditional insurance companies, ultimately conceded that it was governed by the Supreme Court decision as far as registration under the Securities Act was concerned notwithstanding the fact that its long-established business in standard insurance would dwarf its proposed business in variable annuities. But it insisted that, even though a company that sold variable annuities exclusively might not come within the categorical exclusion of any "insurance company" from the definition of an "investment company" by §3(c)(3) of the 1940 Act, Prudential certainly was an "insurance company." It accordingly sought a declaratory order from the Commission to that effect, or in the alternative a number of exemptions. The Commission denied the application, and its order was affirmed on judicial review.

Prudential, the Commission said, "is not itself an investment company, but it is the creator of one — and proposes to be its 'investment adviser' and 'principal underwriter.' "[11] Insurance companies, in its view, were excluded from the definition of "investment company" only because they would otherwise fall within the statute by reason of the investment activities that were a necessary ingredient of their insurance business. In short, the fact that a pure variable annuity life insurance company might itself register as an "investment company" did not mean that the same means of compliance with the statute should apply to a company like Prudential. In its case the "investment company" that would register would be not a subsidiary corporation but the separate fund created by Prudential to make possible the sale of variable annuities; for §3(a) of the Investment Company Act defines "investment company" to mean any "issuer" that does certain things and §2(a)(21) defines "issuer" in terms of a "person" and §2(a)(27) defines "person" to include a "company" and §2(a)(8) defines "company" to include a "fund."[12]

[11] Prudential Ins. Co. of America, 41 SEC 335, 340-41 (1963), *aff'd* sub nom. Prudential Ins. Co. of America v. SEC, 326 F. 2d 383 (3d Cir. 1964), *cert. denied*, 377 U. S. 953.

[12] Cf. SEC v. American Board of Trade, Inc., 751 F. 2d 529, 536 (2d Cir. 1984).

Thus was born what has become irreverently known as the Commission's "ectoplasmic theory." The fund may or may not have a legal identity for ordinary purposes. For example, the enabling provision in the New York Insurance Law, on the one hand, insulates the separate account from the other business of the company and, on the other hand, specifies that the assets in all separate accounts "shall be the property of the insurer."[13] But, be that as it may, for purposes of the Investment Company Act the separate account is an "investment company" distinct from the insurance company. And it seems to be the Commission's view that the "security" is not the variable contract but the "accumulation unit," which "must be located, despite any difficulty in the wording of a particular form of contract."[14] If all this startles at first blush, it must be remembered that a corporation, too, is a *persona ficta;* one gets used to the idea.

By now a considerable number of these "ectoplasms" have been registered, although sometimes, for a variety of reasons, the insurance company creates a wholly owned subsidiary that in turn creates a separate account to be the registrant under both Acts,[15] with the subsidiary or sister subsidiaries acting as its investment adviser and underwriter. Some sort of committee is created to act as the fund's "board of directors," and it is the members of that pseudo-board rather than the directors of the insurance company itself that (1) are elected by the contract holders so as to meet the requirement in §16(a) of the Act and (2) have to comply with §10, on affiliations of directors.

It is not easy to reconcile the "ectoplasmic" concept of an autonomous management for the separate account with (1) the common requirement of the insurance laws (like the corporation laws generally) that the corporation's board of directors is responsible for the conduct of its affairs and (2) the difficulties with respect to any blanket delegation of that responsibility. But the variable annuity laws and regulations of many states now provide for control of the separate account's assets by its board of managers. And, for the rest, the difficulty of fitting an "ectoplasm" on the 1940 Act's Procrustean bed — an image that is a pretty good test of a legal mind —

[13] §4240(a)(5), (12).

[14] Prudential Ins. Co. of America, supra p. 208 n. 11, 41 SEC at 347.

[15] The administrative view is that the insurance company (or the subsidiary) is a co-issuer. See p. 608 n. 18 infra; 4 Loss 2522.

has been ameliorated by the Commission's use of its plenary power under §6(c) of that Act to exempt by either rule or order.[16]

Meanwhile the question remains, even under the 1933 Act, of determining *how much* risk an insurance company must assume in order to avoid SEC jurisdiction. A so-called Flexible Fund Annuity that was obviously designed, by an old-line insurance company (as distinct from a company like VALIC), to impose just enough investment risk-taking on the company to satisfy the VALIC formula resulted in a second Supreme Court decision ten years later, this time by a bench that followed *VALIC* unanimously.[17] So far as the Investment Company Act is concerned, the Court adopted the Commission's suggestion that it remand the case for further consideration of the question — which the courts below had not reached because of their view that the contract itself was exempt — whether the "Flexible Fund" was an "investment company." In observing that this question was a "difficult one"[18] and that United Benefit, unlike VALIC, was in the main an insurance company exempted from the Investment Company Act, without citing the Third Circuit's opinion in the *Prudential* case, the Court seems to have invited the Court of Appeals to consider as a fresh issue the status under the Investment Company Act of a conventional insurance company that issues a security in the nature of a variable annuity. At that point, however, United Benefit Life apparently lost its stomach for litigation, so that this particular symphony remains unfinished.

Still another congeries of "security" and related problems is presented by the diversity of *group* annuity contracts with a variable element that have been developed in recent years, to some extent in response to the Self-Employed Individuals Tax Retirement Act of 1962, popularly known as the Keogh Act or "H. R. 10," which permits self-employed persons to enjoy in some measure the tax

[16] In 1969 the Commission adopted a series of rules to codify some of its *ad hoc* exemptions. See Inv. Co. Act Rel. 5738 (1969); see also Inv. Co. Act Rel. 13,687, 29 SEC Dock. 718 (1983); Inv. Co. Act Rel. 13,688, 29 SEC Dock. 722 (1983).

[17] SEC v. United Benefit Life Ins. Co., 387 U. S. 202 (1967), *rev'g* 359 F. 2d 619 (D. C. Cir. 1966); see also Peoria Union Stock Yards Co. Retirement Plan v. Penn Mutual Life Ins. Co., 698 F. 2d 320 (7th Cir. 1983), *rehearing denied,* CCH Fed. Sec. L. Rep. ¶99,162 (7th Cir. 1983); cf. Grainger v. State Security Life Ins. Co., 547 F. 2d 303 (5th Cir. 1977), *rehearing denied,* 563 F. 2d 215 (5th Cir. 1977); but cf. Olpin v. Ideal National Ins. Co., 419 F. 2d 1250 (10th Cir. 1969), *cert. denied,* 397 U. S. 1074; Otto v. Variable Annuity Life Ins. Co., 808 F. 2d 512 (7th Cir. 1986) 814 F. 2d 1127 (7th Cir. 1987).

[18] 387 U.S. at 212.

deferral privileges available to corporate employees in connection with qualified pension plans.[19]

The *Prudential* case provides no direct teaching with respect to group contracts. For, although Prudential intended to offer group as well as individual variable contracts, the Third Circuit followed the Commission in excluding group plans from the scope of its opinion in the light of the fact that the Commission was dealing with the problems of group plans in its administrative capacity.[20] In this state of affairs all that can be said is that these contracts seem sufficiently different from *variable* annuities sold *individually* — in their historical development from the group annuity contracts that have been written for over forty years (with participation by the employer one way or another in the insurer's experience with respect to investment earnings, mortality and expenses), in the material risks assumed by the insurer, in the motivation and character of the persons (usually substantial employers) to whom the contracts are sold, and in the general manner of their negotiation and sale — so that it cannot be assumed that the Supreme Court would follow *VALIC* and its sequel. After all, the SEC won *VALIC* by one vote, and there have been changes in the Court.

At any rate, after the Commission had experimented with exemptive rules, Congress in 1970 amended §3(a)(2) of the 1933 Act and §3(a)(12) of the 1934 Act so that (as further amended in essentially technical respects in 1980) they exempt "any security arising out of a contract issued by an insurance company" in connection with employee plans that come within specified sections of the Internal Revenue Code. Congress likewise amended §3(c)(11) of the Investment Company Act (as it is now numbered) to exclude substantially the same plans from the definition of "investment company." But the 1933 Act exemption does not apply (1) if any part of the corpus or income in excess of the employer's contribution is allocated to the purchase of securities of the employer or an affiliate or (2) with respect to "Keogh plans." The former exception precludes use of exempt employee plans as an indirect method of financing the employer, and the second reflects the thought that self-employed persons unsophisticated in the securities field should have at least the disclosure protections of the 1933 Act in view of the fairly complex nature of "Keogh plans" as an equity investment.

[19] 76 Stat. 809 (1962), now Int. Rev. Code §401, 26 U. S. C. §401; for a succinct description of that act, see Mundheim and Henderson, Applicability of the Federal Securities Laws to Pension and Profit-Sharing Plans, 29 Law & Contemp. Prob. 795, 797-800 (1964).

[20] 326 F. 2d at 384 n. 1.

Section 3(a)(2) does provide that the Commission in its discretion "shall" exempt interests in "Keogh plans" by rule or order. And the Commission, after repeatedly exercising its order authority in the case typically of law or brokerage or accounting partnerships that did not fall within the statutory exemption for corporate plans,[21] adopted Rule 180 in late 1981 in order essentially to codify these *ad hoc* exemptions.[22] It also took the occasion to endorse its staff's view that there are two securities in these cases, both of which fall within the exemption: the interest of the plan in the trust or insurance company separate account in which plan assets are invested, and, when employees voluntarily contribute, their interests in the plan.[23]

So far we have been speaking of variable annuities. Now what about variable life insurance?[24] Equity-linked insurance policies have been available in different forms in the Netherlands since about 1960, in Great Britain since about 1970, and more recently in Canada.

The Commission and the industry disagree on the applicability of the *VALIC* case. The industry contends that, "as long as insurance protection and mortality considerations are dominant, principal and central, and investment aspects are subordinate, secondary, and auxiliary," there is no security.[25] At the same time, the industry is trying to live with the Commission's view: that, apart from limited exemptions from the Investment Company Act,[26] variable life in-

[21] E. g., Salomon Brothers Profit Sharing Plan, Sec. Act Rel. 5852, 12 SEC Dock. 1462 (1977). Quite a few "Keogh plans" also function under either the intrastate exemption in §3(a)(11) (infra c. 5C) or the private offering exemption (infra c. 5E).

[22] Sec. Act Rel. 6363, 24 SEC Dock. 68 (1981).

[23] Sec. Act Rel. 6188, 19 SEC Dock. 465, 467 (1980); see also Sec. Act Rel. 6281, 21 SEC Dock. 1372, 1378-79 (1981); but see International Brotherhood of Teamsters v. Daniel, 439 U. S. 551, 564-65 (1979), infra p. 221. The word "trust" looks forward to the bank plans, infra p. 220.

[24] In addition to the citations at p. 205 n. 6 supra, see D. Olson and H. Winkleboss (eds.), Variable Life Insurance: Current Issues and Developments (1971).

[25] The quotation is from Kroll and Cohen, The Insurance-Security Identity Crisis, 46 Geo. Wash. L. Rev. 790 (1978), a perceptive essay on the drawing of the line.

[26] See Rules 6c-3, 6e-2, adopted by Inv. Co. Act Rel. 9482, 10 SEC Dock. 751 (1976). Rule 6e-2 defines "variable life insurance contract." These exemptions are based in part on the exemptions granted by order in Equitable Variable Life Ins. Co., Inv. Co. Act Rel. 8888, 7 SEC Dock. 588 (1975), the first company to offer variable life insurance. See also Rule 6e-3(T), adopted on a temporary basis by Inv. Co. Act Rel. 14,234, 31 SEC Dock. 859 (1984), for a new type of whole life insurance product to be funded by separate accounts with provision for flexible payments and death benefits.

Today there are several dozen companies in the variable life field. Traditionally the policy owner is given no ownership interest in the separate account.

surance is subject to regulation under all the SEC statutes (including the 1934 Act's broker-dealer registration provisions and the Investment Advisers Act) in conjunction with state insurance laws and regulations.[27]

More recently the life insurance industry has been developing other novel products. In 1977 the Commission invited comment with respect to the offer and sale of certain contractual arrangements issued by life insurance companies and generally known as "guaranteed investment, interest or income contracts, tax deferred annuity contracts and similar products":

> The contracts which are the subject of study by the staff take a variety of forms but, in general, they provide for the payment of money to a life insurance company (in a single sum or in installments); include promises by the insurer to pay interest at a guaranteed rate with or without the possibility of excess interest; and permit the purchase of an annuity at a future date at an annuity purchase rate which may or may not be guaranteed in the contracts. They appear to be of two basic types: contracts which guarantee a low rate of interest and provide for the possibility that excess interest will be credited by the insurance company ("excess interest contracts") and contracts which guarantee a relatively high rate of interest and generally are written for a short period of time (5 to 12 years) ("high interest contracts").
>
> * * *
>
> * * * the emphasis in the advertising and marketing of these contracts is clearly on their use as investment vehicles for the accumulation of capital. * * * In addition, an insurance company may have its own agents distributing all its other products but choose to have these new contracts distributed through broker-dealers.[28]

Rather, the separate account is used as an index in the sense that the policy owner's benefits may go up (or down) in accordance with the results of the separate account. Consequently, unlike the situation with respect to variable annuities, where the "security" is considered to be the "accumulation unit" rather than the variable contract (see p. 209 supra), the "security" under this scheme is necessarily the life insurance policy itself. However, there is a trend, at least in the case of universal life (see p. 215 infra), toward registering *units* as with respect to variable annuities.

[27] Inv. Co. Act Rel. 7644, 1 SEC Dock. No. 1, p. 1 (1973). The Code excludes from the definition of "security" — so that even the fraud provisions do not apply — any "insurance policy" issued by an "insurance company" as defined, as well as any "annuity contract" under which an "insurance company" "promises to pay one or more sums of money that are fixed or vary in accordance with a cost-of-living index or on any other basis specified by rule." §202(150)(B)(vi)-(vii).

[28] Sec. Act Rel. 5838, 12 SEC Dock. 915, 916-17 (1977).

After experimenting with a published statement of policy,[29] the Commission in 1986 adopted Rule 151,[30] a "safe harbor" rule to the effect that an "annuity contract or optional annuity contract" — language broad enough to cover "what are generally known as guaranteed investment contracts"[31] — comes within the §3(a)(8) exclusion if (1) the insurer is subject to state insurance regulation, (2) the insurer assumes the "investment risk as prescribed in the rule," and (3) the contract "is not marketed primarily as an investment."[32]

Since there were traditional annuity contracts before 1933 that involved no assumption of mortality or longevity risks by the insurer, the Commission did not include such a requirement as a separate element of the rule. But it cautioned that the presence or absence of a mortality risk assumption might be relevant with respect to contracts *outside* the safe harbor.[33]

The Commission addressed also the so-called "deposit fund rider," which "typically is associated with an insurance contract and permits moneys in excess of the minimum purchase payments for the principal contract to be deposited with the insurer and credited with interest at a discretionary rate":[34]

[29] Sec. Act Rel. 6050, 17 SEC Dock. 182 (1979).

[30] Sec. Act Rel. 6645, 35 SEC Dock. 952 (1986). The Commission concurrently withdrew its 1979 guidelines. Sec. Act Rel. 6051, 17 SEC Dock. 190 (1979).

[31] Sec. Act Rel. 6645, 35 SEC Dock. 952 at 952 (1986). At the same time, the rule applies to all insurance companies, not merely to separate accounts. Guaranteed investment contracts are not funded through separate accounts. Mason and Roth, SEC Regulation of Life Insurance Products — On the Brink of the Universal, 15 Conn. L. Rev. 505 (1983). Moreover, the §3(a)(2) exemption is broad enough since the 1980 amendments to include guaranteed investment contracts and other arrangements sold to tax-qualified plans that are funded by an insurance company's *general* account (as distinct from a separate account).

[32] With respect to the marketing condition, the Commission emphasized that it had never said "that an insurer in marketing its product cannot describe the investment nature of the contract, including its interest rate sensitivity and tax-favored status. * * * [A] marketing approach that fairly and accurately describes both the insurance and investment features of a particular contract, and that emphasizes the product's usefulness as a long-term insurance device for retirement or income security purposes, would undoubtedly 'pass' the rule's marketing test." Id. at 962.

[33] Id. at 954.

[34] Id. at 963 n. 51. More specifically,

> Certain deposit fund riders, which may be marketed in conjunction with either a life insurance policy or an annuity contract, appear to be designed to function as an alternative to a bank savings account. Such arrangements ordinarily provide that: (1) a basic premium must be paid for the annuity or life insurance; (2) additional sums contributed by the investor are held on deposit by the insurance company; and (3) interest is credited on such deposits at a rate which might change from time to time. The contract may provide that sums accumulated during the accumulation

> For purposes of rule 151, the Commission is of the view that it is appropriate to determine the status of all deposit fund riders separately from the contracts to which they relate. Such an approach * * * focuses primarily on the fundamental question of whether the insurer is assuming a significant degree of investment risk * * *. If a deposit fund rider is structured as a security it should be treated as such, regardless of the status of the contract to which it is attached or the nature of its relationship to that contract.[35]

Meanwhile the evolution continues apace. The year 1978 saw the introduction of "universal life insurance" in the United States.[36] This is a product that provides for guaranteed policy values, as well as the pooling of risks and losses characteristic of conventional whole life policies; but, typically, it also permits the policy owner to change the amount and timing of the premiums and (as long as underwriting requirements are met) the size of the death benefit as his needs change.[37] Universal life as such is funded through the company's general account, not a special account as with variable life of the traditional kind (if one may use that adjective with so relatively new a product). But it was perhaps inevitable that universal life would be crossed with traditional variable life to produce: "flexible premium variable life insurance."[38]

The difficulty with all these insurance hybrids — and there will be more — is that, in the last analysis, there is no escaping the fact that there is a continuous spectrum from a one-year term life insurance policy, which is pure insurance, through the various forms of straight life and endowment policies, to annuities and life insurance, both fixed and (in varying degrees) variable, to mutual fund shares and ultimately common stock, which represent pure investment.

> period may be used, at a later date, to purchase an annuity at guaranteed purchase rates or to purchase other forms of insurance protection. Often, the investor is permitted to withdraw money from the deposit fund at will.

Sec. Act Rel. 6051, 17 SEC Dock. 190, 194 (1979). Cf. Olpin v. Ideal National Ins. Co., 419 F. 2d 1250 (10th Cir. 1969), *cert. denied,* 397 U. S. 1074.

[35] Sec. Act Rel. 6645, 35 SEC Dock. 952, 963 (1986).

[36] Mason and Roth, SEC Regulation of Life Insurance Products — On the Brink of the Universal, 15 Conn. L. Rev. 505, 551 n. 186 (1983).

[37] See Fleming, Universal Life: Finding a Safe Harbor Under the Securities Act of 1933, 34 Fed'n Ins. Counsel Q. 421 (1984).

[38] On this evolution, see Inv. Co. Act Rel. 13,632, 29 SEC Dock. 294 (1983), where the Commission at the industry's suggestion solicited comments on various issues with respect to flexible premium variable life insurance under the Investment Company Act.

2. Bank Hybrids

The variable annuity experience, together with the 1962 statute that transferred authority over the trust powers of national banks from the Board of Governors of the Federal Reserve System to the Comptroller of the Currency,[39] forced the SEC to take a position with respect to the activities of banks when they commingle customers' investments in one form or another.

The Board's Regulation F did not prohibit national banks from operating *individual* "managing agency accounts" (that is to say, accounts in which banks act not as trustees but simply as investment advisers on an agency basis) for a fee. It simply limited *commingling* of those accounts to "common trust funds" (that is to say, as the term was defined in Regulation F[40] and still is in §584(a) of the Internal Revenue Code, funds maintained by a bank "exclusively for the collective investment and reinvestment of monies contributed thereto by the bank in its capacity as a trustee, executor, administrator, or guardian") or, when authorized by the trust instrument or court order, employee plans.[41] But banks could not accept small managing agency accounts as a practical matter because they were too expensive to administer. And the operation of common trust funds "as investment trusts for other than strictly fiduciary purposes" was prohibited, as was any publicizing of the earnings of the funds or the value of their assets.

Even then the Commission had an uneasy feeling about interests in these commingled funds. For, quite apart from the fraud provisions, the §3(a)(2) exemption for "any security issued or guaranteed by any bank," as well as the exclusion of any "bank" from the definition of "investment company" in §3(c)(3) of the 1940 Act, has always been understood as applying to the bank itself and securities with a claim against the bank's assets (a construction substantially confirmed in the 1970 amendment of §3(a)(2) to the effect that "a security issued or guaranteed by a bank shall not include any interest or participation in any collective trust fund maintained by a bank"). Rightly or wrongly, the Commission's rationale for staying its hand in those days was the exemption in §4(2) of the Securities Act for transactions "not involving any public offering." This rationale also served to reenforce the position of nonaction under the Investment Company Act insofar as §3(c)(1) of that stat-

[39] 76 Stat. 668, 12 U. S. C. §92a.
[40] §10(c), 2 Fed. Reg. 2976 (1937), as amended, 20 Fed. Reg. 3305 (1955).
[41] Id., §17(a).

ute excludes from the definition of "investment company" any issuer whose outstanding securities are beneficially owned by not more than one hundred persons and "which is not making and does not presently propose to make a public offering of its securities."

The Commission's hand was forced when the Comptroller of the Currency in 1963 revised his Regulation 9 (as the Board's Regulation F had been redesignated) by not only abandoning the Board's "*bona fide* fiduciary purpose" concept but also permitting collective investment (when not in contravention of local law) in (1) a fund consisting of assets of tax-exempt trusts or (2) a so-called "common trust fund, maintained by the bank exclusively for the collective investment and reinvestment of monies contributed thereto by the bank in its capacity as managing agent under a managing agency agreement expressly providing that such monies are received by the bank in trust."[42]

It is still provided that no bank administering a collective investment fund may "issue any certificate or other document evidencing a direct or indirect interest in such fund in any form."[43] But the passage of the Keogh Act very substantially expanded the tax-exempt category, and the other was specifically intended to permit the commingling of managing agency accounts.[44]

All this led to a clash between the Comptroller and the Commission in both the courts and Congress. The *banks'* objections to SEC encroachment were probably based not only on a natural enough disinclination to become subject to the jurisdiction of yet another federal regulatory agency, but also on the fear that their submission might be construed as an admission that they were violating the Glass-Steagall Banking Act of 1933, which divorced commercial from investment banking. That fear proved to be well founded, as we shall see in a moment.

[42] Reg. 9, §9.18(a), 12 C. F. R. §9.18(a).

[43] Id., §9.18(b)(13).

[44] The Comptroller redefined "managing agent" in a 1964 amendment of Regulation 9 as a relationship that imposes upon the bank "the fiduciary responsibilities imposed upon trustees under will or deed"; and that is when the description of the managing agency common trust fund was changed to require that the managing agency agreement provide expressly that the bank shall hold the monies received "in trust." §9.1(h). These amendments were intended to facilitate the ruling that the Internal Revenue Service had issued in early 1964 to the effect that a collective managing agency fund maintained pursuant to Regulation 9 would qualify as a "common trust fund" under §584 of the Code. Rev. Rul. 64-59, [1964]-1 Cum. Bul. 193. Since a common trust fund would be financially improbable without this tax exemption and §584 extends only to funds that comply with the regulations governing common trust funds of national banks, Regulation 9 actually affects all banks, state as well as national, that establish common trust funds.

The logjam began to break in late 1963. Prudential filed a registration statement under the Securities Act for interests in a "Keogh fund." A few weeks later, the National Bank of Detroit ruptured the banking industry's solid front by filing a similar registration statement. Soon a number of registrations became effective for commingled bank funds used as the investment media for "Keogh plans" sponsored by associations like the American Bar Association and the American Medical Association. And finally, in August 1965, the First National City Bank of New York (now Citibank), having obtained the Comptroller's approval of a collective investment fund for managing agency accounts with a minimum value of $10,000, applied for a number of exemptions from the Investment Company Act, with a view to registering under the Securities Act if its application should be granted, as it was.[45]

The Commission's order followed by a day the opening of hearings on the most recent of a series of exemptive bills, and the Comptroller inexplicably canceled his appearance. This combination of the First National City Bank exemptive order and the Comptroller's *volte face* seemed to put the quietus on the pending bill.

A few weeks later, however, the NASD sought judicial review of the Commission's order in the Court of Appeals for the District of Columbia Circuit, and the Investment Company Institute (together with a few of its members) sued the Comptroller of the Currency in the District Court for the District of Columbia for a declaratory judgment to the effect that his permitting national banks to sponsor their own mutual funds violated the provisions of the Banking Act on divorcement of investment and commercial banking. The ICI won below. The Court of Appeals, deciding both cases together, sustained both the SEC and the Comptroller. On the banking laws, the court held that the words "security" and "underwriter" in the Securities Act were "terms of art with a high gloss" whose "expansive definitions under the Securities Act cannot be imported wholesale into the Glass-Steagall Act when the two statutes serve different purposes." The Supreme Court took the opposite view and reversed the *ICI* case, thus vacating the *NASD* case as moot.[46]

[45] First National City Bank, 42 SEC 924 (1966), *rehearing denied,* Inv. Co. Act Rel. 4563 (1966).

[46] Investment Company Institute v. Camp, 274 F. Supp. 624 (D. D. C. 1967), *rev'd* sub nom. NASD v. SEC, 420 F. 2d 83, 89 (D. C. Cir. 1969), *rev'd* sub nom. Investment Company Institute v. Camp, 401 U. S. 617 (1971). Three Circuits have distinguished this case, holding that units of beneficial interest in a bank's *trust* fund containing individual retirement account assets were not Glass-Steagall securities even though there was registration under both 1933 and 1940 Acts. Investment Company Institute v. Clark, 789 F. 2d 175 (2d Cir.

It seems quite clear from Justice Stewart's opinion that, if the banking laws were to be amended to allow pooled managing agency accounts, the SEC statutes would apply. Meanwhile, just as United Benefit Life tested the boundaries of *VALIC*,[47] First National City Bank tested the *ICI* case by introducing a Special Investment Advisory Service whereby the Bank gave Merrill Lynch investment direction over a group of accounts, each at least $25,000 in size, to be managed on a uniform basis. Merrill Lynch charged nothing for custody and bookkeeping, since its compensation came from commissions. The SEC alleged in a complaint for injunction that the Service was an unregistered "investment company" with a present value of some $35 million and more than 1000 security holders. And the case was settled on terms that left the bank free to offer a service, on a nondiscretionary basis only, pursuant to which it would make investment recommendations for a fee and any person deciding to act on the recommendations would transfer an order to a broker-dealer selected from a list of at least three provided by the bank.[48]

The Comptroller has also permitted various kinds of automatic investment services, which permit customers to buy any of a preselected list of common stocks by means of a predetermined monthly charge to their checking accounts, as well as dividend reinvestment plans by arrangement with issuers.[49] The SEC status of these mutations is not yet clear. There have been some "no action" letters, although the question seems a bit closer with respect to dividend reinvestment plans because of the issuer's involvement.[50]

Not surprisingly, "With banks and securities firms trying to move into each others' turf and with conglomerates attempting to muscle into the financial arena," new problems under both the banking and the securities laws are continually arising.[51]

1986), *cert. denied,* 107 S. Ct. 421; Investment Company Institute v. Conover, 790 F. 2d 925 (D. C. Cir. 1986), *cert. denied,* 107 S. Ct. 421; Investment Company Institute v. Clark, 793 F. 2d 220 (9th Cir. 1986), *cert. denied,* 107 S. Ct. 421.

[47] See p. 210 supra.

[48] SEC v. First National City Bank, Litig. Rel. 4534 (S. D. N. Y. 1970).

[49] Comptroller of Currency letter, June 10, 1974, CCH Fed. Sec. L. Rep. ¶79,817.

[50] See Sec. Act Rel. 5515, 4 SEC Dock. 623 (1974).

[51] In recent years there has been considerable controversy, engendering a good deal of litigation, with respect to the Glass-Steagall Act's separation of commercial and investment banking. For a comprehensive discussion, see Fischer, Gram, Kaufman, and More, The Securities Activities of Commercial Banks: A Legal and Economic Analysis, 51 Tenn. L. Rev. 467 (1984); Pitt and Williams, The Glass-Steagall Act: Key Issues for the Financial Services Industry, 11 Sec. Reg. L. J. 234 (1983) c. 27; Mulhern, Bank-Brokerage Activities, in Practising Law Institute, Fourteenth Annual Institute on Securities Regulation (1983) c.

So far as tax-exempt plans are concerned, Congress treated banks as it did insurance companies in 1970.[52] And the Code proposes a novel treatment of the "mini-account" problem — how to provide a needed service to the investor who cannot quite afford custom-tailored investment advice — by defining "mini-account client" and relying on regulation of the investment advisory rather than the Securities Act and Investment Company Act types.[53]

F. EMPLOYEE BENEFIT PLANS

With respect to those benefit plans of various kinds that are *not* administered or funded through an insurance company or a bank or an investment company, there may be two separate securities, as we have seen,[1] and the §3(a)(2) exemption may apply to both: the participation interests of the *plans* in the collective investment vehicles in which they invest their assets, and the *employees'* interests in their respective plans. The former are always securities; they have been considered in the last section of this chapter, in the discussion of the insurance and banking hybrids. The latter (whether in combination with the former or whether the particular employer administers its own plan) may or may not be securities; it is this question that we now explore.[2]

In 1979 the Supreme Court, in *International Brotherhood of Teamsters* v. *Daniel,*[3] held, in a class action under the fraud provisions of the 1933 and 1934 Acts, that a noncontributory, compulsory pension plan met none of the *Howey* elements for an investment contract: "Looking at the economic realities, it seems clear that an

---

27; Lybecker, Bank Collective Investment Management Activities, in Practising Law Institute, Fifteenth Annual Institute on Securities Regulation (1984) c. 21. See also p. 86 n. 14 supra.

[52] See p. 211 supra. Congress concurrently amended §3(a)(2) of the 1933 Act and §3(a)(12) of the 1934 Act to exempt "any interest or participation in any common trust fund or similar fund maintained by a bank exclusively for the collective investment and reinvestment of assets contributed thereto by such bank in its capacity as trustee, executor, administrator, or guardian." See the definition of "common trust fund" in Securities Act Rule 132 and Exchange Act Rule 3a12-6.

[53] §§202(80)(B)(xiv), 202(95), 202(150)(B)(ix), 914(c); see 1 Code 396-407. See generally Wade, Bank-Sponsored Collective Investment Funds: An Analysis of Applicable Federal Banking and Securities Laws, 35 Bus. Law. 361 (1980).

C. 3F [1] See p. 212 supra.

[2] The Commission has published two exhaustive releases of its staff's views on all aspects of employee benefit plans. Sec. Act Rel. 6188, 19 SEC Dock. 465 (1980); Sec. Act Rel. 6281, 21 SEC Dock. 1372 (1981).

[3] 439 U. S. 551 (1979).

employee is selling his labor primarily to obtain a livelihood, not making an investment";[4] nor could the employer's contributions be equated with an investment by the employee in a "defined benefit" plan in which payments are not tied to the time worked. And the Court rejected the theory below that pension benefits contained a profit element to the extent they exceeded employer contributions so as to depend on earnings from the assets.

The Court then rejected an argument from the 1970 amendment that extended the §3(a)(2) exemption to participations in certain tax-exempt plans,[5] reading that amendment as recognizing "only that a pension plan had 'an interest or participation' in the fund in which its assets were held, not that prospective beneficiaries of a plan had any interest in either the plan's bank-maintained assets or the plan itself."[6] And the Court likewise rejected an argument from longstanding administrative construction, finding that[7]

> the SEC's present position is flatly contradicted by its past actions. Until the instant litigation arose, the public record reveals no evidence that the SEC had ever considered the Securities Acts to be applicable to noncontributory pension plans. In 1941, the SEC first articulated the position that voluntary, contributory plans had investment characteristics that rendered them "securities" under the Acts. At the same time, however, the SEC recognized that noncontributory plans were not covered by the Securities Acts because such plans did not involve a "sale" within the meaning of the statutes. [Citations omitted.][21]
>
> In an attempt to reconcile these interpretations of the Securities Acts with its present stand, the SEC now augments its past position with two additional propositions. First, it is argued, noncontributory plans are "securities" even where a "sale" is not involved. Second, the previous concession that noncontributory plans do not involve a "sale" was meant to apply only to the registration and reporting requirements of the Securities Acts; for purposes of the antifraud

[4] Id. at 560.
[5] See p. 211 supra.
[6] 439 U. S. at 565.
[7] Id. at 566-67.
[21] Subsequent to 1941 the SEC made no further efforts to regulate even contributory, voluntary pension plans except where the employees' contributions were invested in the employer's securities. * * * It also continued to disavow any authority to regulate noncontributory, compulsory plans. See letter from Assistant Director, Division of Corporate Finance, May 12, 1953, [1978] CCH Fed. Sec. L. Rep. ¶2105.51; letter from Chief Counsel, Division of Corporate Finance, Aug. 1, 1962, [1978] CCH Fed. Sec. L. Rep. ¶2105.52; Hearings Before the Senate Committee on Banking and Currency [on Mutual Fund Legislation of 1967, 90th Cong., 1st Sess., pt. 3 (1967)] * * *; 1 L. Loss, Securities Regulation 510-511 (2d ed. 1961); 4 id., at 2553-2554 (2d ed. 1969). * * *

> provisions, a "sale" is involved. As for the first proposition, we observe that none of the SEC opinions, reports, or testimony cited to us address the question. As for the second, the record is unambiguously to the contrary.[22] Both in its 1941 statements and repeatedly since then, the SEC has declared that its "no sale" position applied to the Securities Act as a whole. [Citations omitted.] Congress acted on this understanding when it proceeded to develop the legislation that became ERISA. * * * As far as we are aware, at no time before this case arose did the SEC intimate that the antifraud provisions of the Securities Acts nevertheless applied to noncontributory pension plans.

Finally, "Whatever benefits employees might derive from the effect of the Securities Acts are now provided in more definite form through ERISA"[8] (the Employee Retirement Income Security Act).[9]

Query how much of the Commission's traditional view survives Mr. Daniel's misfortune:

(1) Although the Court expressed no opinion on the Commission's "bifurcated sale" arguments,[10] the Commission has abandoned that concept. It now construes the term "sale" no more broadly for the fraud provisions than for registration purposes.[11]

(2) Otherwise the face of *Daniel,* where the plan was both compulsory and noncontributory,[12] requires no change in the Commis-

[22] On occasion the SEC has contended that because §2 of the Securities Act and §3 of the Securities Exchange Act apply the qualifying phrase "unless the context otherwise requires" to the Acts' general definitions, it is permissible to regard a particular transaction as involving a sale or not depending on the form of regulation involved. See 1 L. Loss, Securities Regulation 524-528 (2d ed. 1961); 4 id., at 2562-2565 (2d ed. 1969). The Court noted the contention in SEC v. National Securities, Inc., 393 U. S. 453, 465-466 (1969). On previous occasions the SEC appears to have taken a different position: In 1943 it submitted an *amicus* brief in the Ninth Circuit arguing that a transaction must be a sale for all purposes of the Securities Act or for none, and it did not begin to rely on its "regulatory context" theory until 1951. See Brief for the SEC in National Supply Co. v. Leland Stanford Junior University, [134 F. 2d 689 (9th Cir. 1943)]; 1 L. Loss, supra, at 524 n. 211; Cohen, Rule 133 of the Securities and Exchange Commission, 14 Record of N. Y. C. B. A. 162, 164-165 (1959). We also note that, with respect to statutory mergers, the area in which the SEC originally developed its theory as to the bifurcated definition of a sale, the SEC since has abandoned its position and finds the presence of a "sale" for all purposes in the case of such mergers. See 17 C. F. R. §5230.145 (1978). In view of our disposition of this case, we express no opinion as to the correct resolution of the divergent views on this issue.

[8] 439 U. S. at 570.

[9] 88 Stat. 829, 29 U. S. C. §§1021-30 (1974).

[10] 439 U. S. at 567-68 n. 22, supra p. 222.

[11] Sec. Act Rel. 6188, 19 SEC Dock. 465, 483 (1980).

[12] See also Bauman v. Bish, 571 F. Supp. 1054, 1062-65 (N. D. W. Va. 1983), where *Daniel* was followed with respect to a compulsory and noncontributory

sion's traditional position — which it tried to enlarge in its *amicus curiae* capacity — to the effect that there is no "sale" unless a plan is both voluntary and contributory. Lower courts have applied *Daniel* in the compulsory-contributory case[13] and even in the voluntary-contributory case that the Commission would cover.[14] But much may still depend on the circumstances.[15] Notwithstanding the Commission's view that it is irrelevant to the "security" question whether the plan is a "defined benefit plan" (one that pays fixed or determinable benefits without regard to the plan's earnings) rather than a "defined contribution plan" (one in which benefits vary with the investment success of the plan and perhaps other factors),[16] even a voluntary-contributory plan does not look like a "security" when one's pension is not based on the plan's income; consequently, cases of that type[17] may be distinguished from even voluntary-contributory cases that are not defined benefit plans.

(3) So far as indirect distribution of the employer's own securities is concerned,[18] very few *pension* plans are funded by investment in company stock with employee money. All of such plans that have been registered (and quite a few have been) are so-called thrift plans, which are almost always optional rather than compulsory, although they are structured as "profit-sharing plans" to qualify them under §401 of the Internal Revenue Code. They often provide from two to four investment media, including a portfolio of common stocks, Government bonds, and securities of the employer, whichever the employee chooses. Many plans are expressly designed to limit the amount that can be used to purchase the employer's securities to the amount of the employer's contribution for the express purpose of avoiding registration.

(4) What is the significance to all this of the exclusion in §3(c)(11) of the 1940 Act of any "employee's stock bonus, pension, or profit-

---

"employee stock ownership plan" (ESOP). But cf. Foltz v. U. S. News & World Report, Inc., 627 F. Supp. 1143, 1159 (D. D. C. 1986).

[13] Black v. Payne, 591 F. 2d 83, 87-88 (9th Cir. 1979), *cert. denied*, 444 U. S. 867.

[14] Tanuggi v. Grolier, Inc., 471 F. Supp. 1209 (S. D. N. Y. 1979); Newkirk v. General Electric Co., CCH Fed. Sec. L. Rep. ¶97,216 (N. D. Cal. 1979); Coward v. Colgate-Palmolive Co., 686 F. 2d 1230 (7th Cir. 1982), *cert. denied*, 460 U. S. 1070; O'Neil v. Marriott Corp., 538 F. Supp. 1026 (D. Md. 1982); Cunha v. Ward Foods, Inc., 545 F. Supp. 94 (D. Hawaii 1982).

[15] See Faulk v. Bagley, 88 F. R. D. 153, 164 (M. D. N. C. 1980).

[16] Sec. Act Rel. 6188, 19 SEC Dock. 465, 471-72 (1980).

[17] See the *Black*, *Tanuggi*, *Coward*, and *Cunha* cases, supra p. 223 nn. 13, 14.

[18] See p. 211 supra; and see generally H. Weyher and H. Knott, The Employee Stock Ownership Plan (1982). With respect to the factors determining when the employer's participation in *market* purchases of its stock requires registration, see Sec. Act Rel. 6188, 19 SEC Dock. 465, 483 (1980).

sharing trust" that meets certain requirements, as well as the direction to the Commission in §6(b) of the 1940 Act to exempt any "employees' security company" on application to whatever extent it considers appropriate under specified standards? If these things are not *prima facie* "investment companies," why exclude or exempt them? And can it be that interests in an investment company are not "securities"?[19]

The Code's Reporter breathed a sigh of relief when *Daniel* was decided and promptly recommended that the Code say nothing on the question, thus leaving it to the courts to prick out *Daniel*'s boundaries. But the Code's comments evidence a clear preference for amending ERISA to the extent that the protection it affords is not as adequate as the SEC's — on the theory that "the SEC should no more be in the business of regulating *bona fide* pension (or pension-related) plans (even on a 'fraud' basis) than orthodox insurance policies or annuities."[20]

G. PREORGANIZATION CERTIFICATES OR SUBSCRIPTIONS (HEREIN OF JOINT VENTURES)

"There is more reason for the application of this [blue sky] law to unorganized business concerns," the Oregon Supreme Court has said, "than to those having a recognized legal entity."[1] This was said without benefit of any statutory reference to preorganization subscriptions. The promoters were simply held to be selling stock in a corporation as yet unborn. The specific reference to any "preorganization certificate or subscription" in §2(1) represents a concession on the part of Congress as much as it does assurance of complete coverage. Without it there would be no way legally to solicit the public in advance of incorporation, since there would be no "issuer" to sign the registration statement. As the statute stands, the preorganization certificates or subscriptions are securities distinct from the ultimate stock, and their issuers are the promoters,

[19] The same questions may be asked, of course, with respect to the exemption in §3(a)(2) of the 1933 Act on the Commission's view that the exemption extends to the employee's interest in the plan as well as the plan's interest in its investment medium. See p. 212 supra. But we have seen that the exemption for insurance policies and annuities in §3(a)(8) has not been taken to establish that these insurance products are securities. See p. 204 supra.

[20] See 1 Code 225-27.

C. 3G [1] State v Whiteaker, 118 Ore. 656, 661, 247 Pac. 1077, 1079 (1926).

who may thus effect registration before the corporation is organized. However, since this does not preclude the necessity of filing a separate registration statement for the stock after the corporation is formed, promoters normally incorporate first in order to avoid double registration. Few preorganization subscriptions have ever been registered.

It seems clear that, although a "preorganization certificate" requires a writing, a "preorganization subscription" does not. It is specifically recognized in the legislative history that there may be a "security" under some parts of the definition even though all the negotiations are oral.[2]

There is a nice question of determining the extent to which the preorganization subscription rationale should be applied to the formation of a close corporation. And the question is complicated by the theory developed by some of the state courts — and implicit, as we have seen, in the delineation of the "investment contract" phrase in §2(1) of the 1933 Act — that no "security" is involved in a joint venture, at least if nothing has yet been incorporated when the joint venture is put together.[3] The federal exemption for private offerings would normally preclude the necessity of registration in this kind of case. But the identical question could arise in an action under §12(2) or Rule 10b-5 — or conceivably in an enforcement proceeding under §17(a) — for misstatements in the alleged sale of subscriptions.

A 1952 decision of the California Supreme Court (*Holmberg* v. *Marsden*) is typical of one point of view as applied to one type of

[2]This was said with reference to the 1934 amendment that added the words "interest or" in the present clause, "any interest or instrument commonly known as a 'security.' " "It is also intended to apply the Act to interests commonly known as 'securities,' " the conference report said, "whether or not such interests are represented by any document or not [*sic*]. Thus the statute will apply to inscribed shares, and its provisions cannot be evaded by simply refraining from issuing to the subscriber any documentary evidence of his interest." H. R. Rep. No. 1838, 73d Cong., 2d Sess. (1934) 39. In SEC v. W. J. Howey Co., 328 U. S. 293, 299 (1946), the Court said it was "immaterial whether the shares in the enterprise are evidenced by formal certificates or by nominal interests in the physical assets employed by the enterprise." See also Sulkow v. Crosstown Apparel, Inc., 807 F. 2d 33, 36 (2d Cir. 1986). But "The absence of a physical document presents difficulties for the plaintiff because it must nonetheless prove the existence of subject matter jurisdiction based on the existence of a written or oral security not available for examination by the court." Canadian Imperial Bank of Commerce Trust Co. v. Fingland, 615 F. 2d 465, 467 (9th Cir. 1980).

[3]E. g., Nicholl v. Ipsen, 130 Cal. App. 2d 452, 458-59, 278 P. 2d 927, 930 (1955), and cases cited; but cf., e. g., Brown v. Cole, 155 Tex. 624, 291 S. W. 2d 704 (1956). Under the express statutory exemptions for joint adventures that exist in a few states, see, e. g., Grabendike v. Adix, 335 Mich. 128, 55 N. W. 2d 761 (1952).

case. The plaintiff and the two defendants had agreed to organize a corporation, each taking a one-third interest. When this company went the way of many other new businesses, the plaintiff tried to get his money back on the ground that no permit had been secured for the issuance of the stock at the time of his payment. He prevailed in the appellate court, but the California Supreme Court reversed, holding that there was evidence to support the factual findings of the trial court to the effect that the defendants had not offered or sold preorganization subscriptions to the plaintiff but had merely participated with him in organizing the enterprise. The fact that the proposal had originated with the defendants was not considered conclusive when weighed against the circumstances that the plaintiff had participated actively in the business. "Whether the three men, as among themselves, be termed partners, joint venturers, or copromotors [*sic*] of a corporation * * * it is obvious that the trial court was justified in concluding that they stood on an equal footing as entrepreneurs."[4] Consequently there appeared to the court to be no more reason for the defendants to reimburse the plaintiff than the other way around.

In most of the state cases thus far cited the statutory definition did not explicitly include preorganization subscriptions. But the blue sky laws have sometimes been applied to preorganization solicitations nevertheless. Might it not follow, conversely, that the explicit inclusion of preorganization subscriptions is no assurance that the statute *will* apply to every promotion of a close corporation? Certainly a respectable argument could be made for reaching the same result arrived at by the California court in the *Holmberg* case if in similar circumstances one of the organizers of the corporation were to sue the others under §12(2) of the federal statute. We have noticed and shall notice other instances when a cautious use of the introductory phrase in §2 — to the effect that the several definitions apply "unless the context otherwise requires" — had led to a result different from that produced by a literal reading of the statutory words but more consistent with the statutory purpose.[5]

[4] Holmberg v. Marsden, 39 Cal. 2d 592, 597, 248 P. 2d 417, 419-20 (1952); cf. Goodman v. DeAzoulay, 539 F. Supp. 10 (E. D. Pa. 1981), *defendant's motion for summary judgment granted in part and denied in part,* 554 F. Supp. 1029 (E. D. Pa. 1983); but cf., e. g., Trump v. Badet, 84 Ariz. 319, 327 P. 2d 1001 (1958). For additional blue sky cases both ways, see 4 Loss 2490-91.

[5] See c. 3B supra; pp. 227-28 infra.

H. VOTING TRUST CERTIFICATES, CERTIFICATES OF DEPOSIT, AND RECEIPTS

The ordinary voting trust certificate or certificate of deposit — the latter is usually but not always issued by a protective committee in the course of a corporate reorganization — is recognizable enough.[1] But certain types of solicitation may well result in the offer of such certificates — or at least securities in the nature of such certificates — even though the particular words are not used. Thus, although the ordinary solicitation of a corporate proxy or of a power of attorney by a protective committee raises no question under the 1933 Act, there may be circumstances in which it amounts to an offer of a "security." For example, proxies might be solicited under an arrangement amounting to a voting trust. Or a committee might seek authority not merely to represent bondholders or stockholders in a pending reorganization proceeding, but also to bind them to a particular plan of reorganization or to accept new securities without any further assent on their part. If there is difficulty in saying this amounts to an offering of "certificates of deposit" when there are no certificates, there are other toeholds: The committee would seem to be offering "preorganization subscriptions" to the securities of the reorganized corporation. Or, if the outstanding securities are stamped to indicate that they are subject to a lien for their *pro rata* share of the committee's expenses, the stamp would seem to be a "receipt" for a security. Or, as a last resort, there is the clause, "any interest * * * commonly known as a 'security,' " which was presumably intended as a catchall for this sort of contingency.

Conversely, not all instruments that are in form "receipts" for securities are themselves "securities." Congress could not have intended to require registration when the issuer of the receipt acts in a purely ministerial capacity and has only the obligations of an ordinary bailee. For example, a bank or trust company, retained to act as depositary by a corporation or a committee of security holders, may issue receipts as part of the mechanics of a voluntary reorganization, the receipts merely evidencing the depositors' right either to receive certain new securities or to have their old securities returned depending on specified contingencies (such as the number

C. 3H [1] A bank "certificate of deposit" that is a debt of the bank itself is a very different animal. See Marine Bank v. Weaver, 455 U. S. 551, 557 n. 5 (1982); SEC v. American Board of Trade, Inc., 751 F. 2d 529, 536 (2d Cir. 1984).

of securities deposited by a given date). The new securities called for by the plan will be registered (unless an exemption is available), but the receipts themselves are hardly "securities." In other words, the phrase "receipt for" a security is more or less *ejusdem generis* with "certificate of deposit," and is essentially another statutory handle to cover instruments that are certificates of deposit in substance without being so termed. In close cases this may draw a fine line. But the touchstone should always be substance rather than form — whether it operates to include or to exclude.

So far as identifying the "issuer" of these types of securities is concerned — a matter that is important not only in determining who must sign the registration statement but also in assessing the issuer's virtually absolute liability under §11 — there is a specific provision in §2(4):

> * * * with respect to certificates of deposit, voting-trust certificates, or collateral-trust certificates, or with respect to certificates of interest or shares in an unincorporated investment trust not having a board of directors (or persons performing similar functions) or of the fixed, restricted management, or unit type,[2] the term "issuer" means the person or persons performing the acts and assuming the duties of depositor or manager pursuant to the provisions of the trust or other agreement or instrument under which such securities are issued * * *.

This makes it clear that the physical issuer of these types of securities — the depositary — is not the "issuer." It is not clear whether that is all that this clause means — in which event the "issuer" is the voting trust or the committee as an entity — or whether the voting trustees or the committee members were intended to be the "issuer" in either their official or their personal capacities. It is probably the former, but this question is not too important, since §2(4) goes on to say that

> in the case of an unincorporated association which provides by its articles for limited liability of any or all of its members, or in the case of a trust, committee, or other legal entity, the trustees or members thereof shall not be individually liable as issuers of any security issued by the association, trust, committee, or other legal entity.

In any event, in determining who is "performing the acts and assuming the duties of depositor or manager," it is necessary once

[2] See pp. 45-46 supra.

again to look to the substance of the arrangements in each case, however desirable it would be to have a more definite criterion.

Take the so-called American depositary receipt, which goes back to the "substitute certificates" developed by the financial community in the 1920s as a device to facilitate American trading in foreign securities.[3]

In the 1920s the depositor was generally an American investment house that was anxious to facilitate the sale of a block of shares it held in a foreign company. It would enter into an agreement with a domestic bank as depositary. The foreign company would not be a party to the agreement, but the American investors would automatically become parties by purchasing the receipts. The depositor normally reserved the right to exercise managerial control over the deposit, and the depositary bank undertook merely to hold the foreign shares and to issue receipts against them.

For some time, however, it has been common for the depositary bank to assume the initiative by announcing that it stands ready to issue receipts against the deposit of designated foreign securities. The depositors, who are generally domestic dealers or private shareholders, then undertake to have their foreign securities lodged with the depositary's foreign agent in return for American depositary receipts to be issued by the depositary bank. There is no longer a formal deposit agreement, except as it may be evidenced in the receipts themselves. And the foreign company is still not involved, except that the depositary bank normally receives its permission in advance to issue the receipts.

In 1955, in response to the pressure to facilitate the banks' of-

[3] See Williams, Trading in the United States in Foreign Securities and Securities Distributed Outside the United States Without Registration Under the Securities Act of 1933, in 6 Practising Law Institute, Sixth Annual Institute on Securities Regulation (1975) 327, 333; Royston, The Regulation of American Depositary Receipts: Americanization of the International Capital Markets, 10 N. C. J. Int'l L. & Com. Reg. 83 (1985).

"ADRs" are convenient not only when the shares are in bearer form but also when the normal unit of trading in the foreign market is not suited to the American market, or when there are inconvenient requirements of foreign law. J. Stephenson and W. Williams, A Lawyer's Guide to International Business Transactions (2d ed. 1980) 70.

Actually foreign equity securities are traded in three forms in the United States: (1) as issued in the country of incorporation ("ordinary shares"); (2) as issued specifically for use in the United States and frequently with different procedural rights ("American shares"); and (3) most commonly in the form of ADRs.

There have also been quite a few converse instances where banks have issued bearer depositary receipts in foreign countries ("Continental Depositary Receipts") against securities of American corporations in order to accommodate them to the European custom of trading in bearer instruments.

fering of American depositary receipts, the Commission adopted Form S-12,[4] replaced in 1983 by Form F-6, which applies if (1) the ADR holder may withdraw the deposited securities at any time (subject to a few mechanical exceptions), (2) the deposited securities are offered pursuant to a 1933 Act registration or in transactions that would be exempt if effected in the United States, and (3) the issuer of the deposited securities reports under the 1934 Act (or the securities qualify for the insurance company exemption in §12(g)(2)(G)). Rule 174(a)[5] applies to all F-6 registrations. Under Form F-6, as was the case under Form S-12, the entire prospectus, which today consists of only two items of information specified in the form, may be embodied in the receipts themselves.[6] By way of further streamlining, the signature instructions state simply that "The legal entity created by the agreement for the issuance of ADRs shall sign the registration statement as registrant." And the form provides specifically that the depositary is not to be deemed an issuer or a person controlling the issuer notwithstanding its signing the registration statement in the name of the altogether fictitious "entity." This awe-inspiring (and altogether laudable) demonstration of administrative flexibility means that nobody has the liability of an "issuer" under §11 so far as Form F-6 is concerned.[7]

I. EQUIPMENT TRUST CERTIFICATES

There is still another special provision in §2(4) for "equipment-trust certificates or like securities," with respect to which "the term 'issuer' means the person by whom the equipment or property is or is to be used." This is to make it clear that the issuer is the carrier that thus finances its rolling stock, whoever may be the physical issuer of the certificates. The manufacturer of the equipment transfers title to a trustee, who is the nominal issuer of equipment trust certificates. The certificates are secured by a lease or conditional sale agreement under which the railroad obtains possession of the equipment. The purpose of this financing device is, by placing title in the trustee, to avoid subjecting the equipment to the lien of the after-acquired property clauses that are typical in railroad mort-

[4]Sec Act Rel. 3593 (1955).

[5]See p. 148 n. 6 supra.

[6]The form requires undertakings to file and transmit certain information from time to time.

[7]If the issuer of the deposited securities sponsors the ADR arrangement, the registration statement must be signed also by the issuer and certain others.

gages.[1] Although equipment trust certificates are not included *eo nomine* in §2(1), any doubt that they are "securities" is set at rest by the special provision defining their "issuer" in §2(4) as well as their exemption by §3(a)(6).

A financial writer claimed in 1955 that equipment trust certificates as a vehicle of financing have been applied to only one type of commercial property aside from railroad and trolley cars, buses, and airplanes — namely, "jukeboxes."[2] The exaggeration in that statement is only slight.[3] At any rate, an example of the "like securities" referred to in the equipment trust clause of §2(4) would presumably be a lease-back arrangement where for tax purposes a corporation conveys certain land and buildings in fee to a trustee and takes back a perpetual or long-term lease. If the trustee issues certificates of beneficial interest in the property, the "issuer" would seem to be the lessee.

Since all the purposes of equipment trust certificates can be equally served without the formality of a trust by conditional sales contracts[4] — which was not true in all states before the Uniform Commercial Code — equipment trust certificates may well be on their way to extinction. Whether or not conditional sales contracts are "like securities" today — as they probably are — the Code's definitions of both "security" and "issuer" refer specifically to an "equipment trust certificate (including a conditional sale contract or similar interest or instrument serving the same purpose)."[5]

J. GUARANTEES

The reference to a "guarantee" of a security in the 1934 amendment of §2(1) makes it clear that the guarantor is the issuer only of the guarantee and not of the security guaranteed.[1] The House committee report on the amendment also emphasizes that "the omission of specific mention of guarantors [in the definition of the term 'issuer'] * * * will make it clear that guarantors are to be

C. 3I [1] In general, see Hawks and Wood, Marketing Railroad Equipment Trust Certificates, 45 ICC Prac. J. 466 (1978).

[2] M. Mayer, Wall Street: Men and Money (1955) 38.

[3] For scattered instances outside the transportation industries, see 1 Dewing, The Financial Policy of Corporations (5th ed. 1953) 207-08. This means that most equipment trust certificates are exempted anyway under §3(a)(6).

[4] See Sec. Act §3(a)(6) as amended in 1976.

[5] §§202(85)(D), 202(150)(A). The definition of "issuer" refers to a "similar security" rather than a "similar interest or instrument."

C. 3J [1] H. R. Rep. No. 1838, 73d Cong., 2d Sess. (1934) 39. See Hugo Stinnes Corp., 7 SEC 622, 635 (1940).

treated as issuers of securities only if the guarantees are incorporated in securities distributed to investors."[2] Presumably the guarantee may be of either principal or interest or both.

The statute does not refer specifically to the "assumption" by *B* of securities issued by *A*. But obviously, if the holders of *A*'s securities have anything to say about the assumption, *B* is in substance offering its securities in exchange for *A*'s, and registration of *B*'s securities is required unless some exemption is available.

K. WARRANTS, OPTIONS, AND COMMODITY FUTURES

Until October 1982 the relevant part of the definition in both the 1933 and 1934 Acts referred only to any "warrant or right to subscribe to or purchase" any of the previously mentioned securities. In 1982 those Acts were amended to insert before this language

> any put, call, straddle, option, or privilege on any security, certificate of deposit, or group or index of securities (including any interest therein or based on the value thereof), or any put, call, straddle, option, or privilege entered into on a national securities exchange relating to foreign currency.[1]

The story of how this came about, as well as how the question of option securities came to be affected by the world of commodity futures, is best told historically.

The original definition clearly covered the ordinary warrants or rights to purchase shares of the same corporation — or occasionally

[2] H. R. Rep. No. 1838, 73d Cong., 2d Sess. (1934) 39. Cf. James v. Meinke, 778 F. 2d 200, 204-05 (5th Cir. 1984), where a guarantee agreement executed by an investor in consideration of a promise that he would receive additional stock was held not to be an "investment contract" for purposes of Rule 10b-5. The court did not mention the fact that the definition of "security" in §3(a)(10) of the 1934 Act did not include a "guarantee."

Banks' standby letters of credit by way of back-up for securities issues have been treated administratively as "tantamount to guarantees" so as to exempt the securities to which they pertain. Sec. Act Rel. 6688, 37 SEC Dock. 774, 776 (1987), infra p. 614 n. 58.

On GNMA-guaranteed securities, see p. 237 n. 16 infra.

C. 3K [1] 96 Stat. 1409. In contrast to this language, which covers an *option* on a certificate of deposit, the definitions in the two 1940 Acts were concurrently amended to include a certificate of deposit itself. This variation is designed to make an "investment company," under the 40 percent test of §3(a)(3) of the Investment Company Act (see p. 48 n. 14 supra), out of any "money fund" that invests heavily in certificates of deposit.

a related corporation — that are customarily traded both on the exchanges and in the over-the-counter market.[2] Moreover, although "warrant" may be a term of art that assumes some sort of certificate, undoubtedly rights to purchase securities are themselves "securities" even when they are not evidenced by any writing but are announced in a letter to security holders. However announced or evidenced, warrants and rights have a dual personality. They are themselves "securities" at the same time that they represent offers to sell other securities.

In a 1961 decision, the first case in which the Commission allowed restricted stock options under the Holding Company Act, it held that the options were nonetheless "securities" under that Act by virtue of their being nontransferable.[3] Nevertheless, it is still arguable, as in the case of the ordinary promissory note given to a bank or another private lender, that a literal reading is not always indicated and that a nontransferable option that is incident to a contract for personal services is not a "security" even for purposes of the fraud provisions of the 1933 Act. This leaves another unavoidable shadow area.

In financial jargon "puts" and "calls" are in a different category from "warrants" and "rights," although all are forms of options. A put is an option to sell at a certain price within a certain period, and a call is a similar option to buy. The economic *raison d'être* of these options is to serve as a hedge (a form of insurance) against future market movements. For example, a person who is long may buy a put as insurance that he will be able to sell if the market falls to a certain level, and a person who is short may buy a call to ensure that he will be able to cover (buy) if the market rises to a certain figure. At the same time, these instruments provide a cheap form of speculation.[4] Since they had served as manipulative devices, the

[2] See Entel v. Guilden, 223 F. Supp. 129, 130 n. 4 (S. D. N. Y. 1963): "The Atlas Corporation has for many years used perpetual warrants as a major means of acquiring equity capital." In permitting a warrant holder to bring a derivative action under §17(e) of the Investment Company Act, the court there pointed out that the definition of "security" in §2(a)(35) included any "warrant or right to subscribe to or purchase" any stock. "An Atlas warrant, thus, can be fairly described as a 'distilled' share of Atlas common — the sweet liquor of speculation concentrated with some of the dregs of investment 'responsibility' left behind." Id. at 130.

[3] Middle South Utilities, Inc., 40 SEC 509, 511-12 (1961).

[4] A 1961 SEC staff report stated: "From the data collected and from interviews it appears that only a small number of options are bought for insurance. * * * The brokers interviewed were unanimous in the opinion that the reason most persons bought options was the opportunity it afforded them for speculation on a small amount of capital." SEC, Div. of Trading & Exchanges, Report on Put and Call Options (1961) 76-77.

Commission was given authority in §9(b)-(d) of the 1934 Act to regulate puts and calls by rule.[5]

Until 1973 these instruments were generally written in bearer form by more or less professional investors, endorsed by stock exchange houses, and then bought and sold in the over-the-counter market. This procedure continues to some extent. But the main ballgame has undergone a radical change since the creation of the Chicago Board Options Exchange in 1973, followed soon by options trading on the American, Philadelphia, and Pacific Stock Exchanges, with the New York Stock Exchange joining the fray in 1982.[6] The CBOE pioneered two concepts: (1) contract standardization so that options were made fungible by fixing the exercise months and exercise ("striking") prices, and (2) establishment (and now joint ownership by all the options exchanges) of The Options Clearing Corporation, which is the issuer, as well as the guarantor, of the traded options.[7]

How, then, do these instruments stand under §5 of the 1933 Act? A call is a "right to * * * purchase" a security within the literal language of the original definition; but a put is a right to *sell.* The Sixth Circuit held without elucidation that this language "clearly includes options to purchase or sell stock."[8] Alternatively, both types of option are such an integral part of securities trading that it seemed entirely reasonable to subsume them under the phrases, "investment contract" and "interest or instrument commonly known as a 'security.' "

At any rate, the definition was evidently thought sufficient to include options for purposes of broker-dealer registration, and might have been thought sufficient all along for registration purposes under the 1933 Act. Presumably one reason for the Commission's

[5] See p. 851 infra.

[6] See p. 241 n. 35 infra.

[7] See Report of the Special Study of the Options Markets to the Securities and Exchange Commission, House Com. Print 96-IFC3, 96th Cong., 1st Sess. (1978), discussed in Lipton, The Special Study of the Options Market: Its Findings and Recommendations, 7 Sec. Reg. L. J. 299 (1980); Poser and Brodsky, Amex Options Regulation, 8 Rev. Sec. Reg. 959 (1975); Markham and Gilberg, Stock and Commodity Options — Two Regulatory Approaches and Their Conflicts, 47 Albany L. Rev. 741 (1983). For the basics see Johnson, Is It Better to Go Naked on the Street? A Primer on the Options Market, 55 Notre Dame Law. 7 (1979); Poser, Options Account Fraud: Securities Churning in a New Context, 39 Bus. Law. 571, 586-92 (1984). On the role of organized options markets in capital formation, see Mendelson, Exchange Traded Options and the Supply of Capital, 2 J. Comp. L. & Sec. Reg. 65 (1979); Rubinstein, An Economic Evaluation of Organized Options Markets, 2 J. Comp. L. & Sec. Reg. 49 (1979).

[8] Mansbach v. Prescott, Ball & Turbin, 598 F. 2d 1017, 1026 n. 40 (6th Cir. 1979).

not requiring 1933 Act registration, or perhaps never squarely facing the question, was that pre-1973 options were not issued as classes of fungible securities and were not subjects of public offerings in any significant sense.

When the mechanisms for offering and trading of fungible options were inaugurated in 1973, after close Commission scrutiny under both Acts, it was thought essential to have a disclosure document covering rights to sell as well as rights to buy (and, interestingly, containing disclosures for the benefit of writers of options, which is to say, sellers, not merely purchasers). At this point the SEC staff insisted, and apparently no one questioned, that options had to be registered under the 1933 Act, as they have been by The Options Clearing Corporation in the capacity of issuer.

Then in 1982 the Commission adopted an elective Form S-20 for the registration of standardized options, together with Rule 9b-1 under the 1934 Act by way of providing an *Exchange* Act "disclosure document" for use along with the new form.[9] That document, which contains general information concerning standardized options and option trading, is prepared by *the options markets,* is filed with the Commission in preliminary form sixty days before its use,[10] and is "intended to enhance investor understanding of standardized options by presenting all essential information about such options in a more readable Exchange Act disclosure document."[11] At the same time, a prospectus is available for investors who are interested in more detailed information about the *issuer* of the options; but another new rule, 153b under the 1933 Act, provides that the prospectus delivery requirement is satisfied by depositing copies of the prospectus with each options market on which the options are traded.[12]

Enter the Commodity Futures Trading Commission Act of 1974,[13] which amended the Commodity Exchange Act by expanding its

[9] Sec. Act Rel. 6426, 26 SEC Dock. 136 (1982).

[10] The document must be kept current by the filing of amendments thirty days before use; and both the original document and any amended document must be filed in definitive form not later than their use. The Commission may accelerate either period.

[11] Sec. Act Rel. 6426, 26 SEC Dock. 136 at 136 (1982).

[12] Cf. Rule 153, supra p. 115. The Commission concurrently adopted Rule 135b in order to exclude the disclosure document from §12(1) liability by providing that it "shall not be deemed to constitute an offer to sell or offer to buy any security" for purposes of §5, and adopted Rule 134a in order similarly to exclude from a "prospectus" status, under certain conditions, any materials "limited to explanatory information, describing the general nature of the standardized options markets or one or more strategies."

[13] 88 Stat. 1389 (1974), scattered in 7 U. S. C.

coverage beyond edible commodities and transferring its administration from the Department of Agriculture to the newly created Commodity Futures Trading Commission. In the process Congress defined "commodity" to mean a couple of dozen edible items, "and all other goods and articles" (except onions for some reason)[14]

> and all services, rights, and interests in which contracts for future delivery are presently or in the future dealt in: *Provided*, That the [Commodity Futures Trading] Commission shall have exclusive jurisdiction[15] with respect to accounts, agreements (including any transaction which is of the character of, or is commonly known to the trade as, an "option," "privilege," "indemnity," "bid," "offer," "put," "call," "advance guaranty," or "decline guaranty"), and transactions involving contracts of sale of a commodity for future delivery, traded or executed on a contract market designated pursuant to section 5 of this title or any other board of trade, exchange, or market * * * : *And provided further*, That, except as hereinabove provided, nothing contained in this section shall (i) supersede or limit the jurisdiction at any time conferred on the Securities and Exchange Commission or other regulatory authorities under the laws of the United States or of any State, or (ii) restrict the Securities and Exchange Commission and such other authorities from carrying out their duties and responsibilities in accordance with such laws. Nothing in this section shall supersede or limit the jurisdiction conferred on courts of the United States or any State. Nothing in this chapter shall be deemed to govern or in any way be applicable to transactions in foreign currency, security warrants, security rights, resales of installment loan contracts, repurchase options, government securities, or mortgages and mortgage purchase commitments, unless such transactions involve the sale thereof for future delivery conducted on a board of trade. * * *

We shall first explore the security-commodity line apart from the ambit of the CFTC's exclusive jurisdiction and then consider the impact of the commodity legislation on that question:

(1) Clearly the term "security" does not comprehend a commodity futures contract *per se*[16] any more than it does an orthodox life

[14] In Board of Trade of the City of Chicago v. SEC, 677 F. 2d 1137, 1142 n. 9 (7th Cir. 1982), *vacated as moot*, 559 U. S. 1026 (1982), the court could not resist suggesting "a physiological basis for the onion producers' crying."

[15] Com. Ex. Act §2(a)(1)(A); 7 U. S. C. §2. The Futures Trading Act of 1982 (see p. 241 infra), which added (B), 96 Stat. 2294; 7 U. S. C. §2a, inserted at this point: "except to the extent otherwise provided in subparagraph (B) of this part."

[16] Sinva, Inc. v. Merrill Lynch, Pierce, Fenner & Smith, Inc., 253 F. Supp. 359, 366-67 (S. D. N. Y. 1966); Berman v. Dean Witter & Co., Inc., 353 F. Supp. 669 (C. D. Cal. 1973) (Japanese yen futures); Rasmussen v. Thomson &

insurance policy.[17] The security and commodity worlds, like the world of insurance, were so distinct in 1933 that Congress would expressly have included commodity futures in the definition, as a few states have,[18] if it had so intended.

(2) *Discretionary* commodity accounts, however, may involve the kind of reliance on the broker's efforts that will result in "investment contracts."[19] For that matter, so may discretionary *securities* accounts.[20] And the discretionary authority need not be embodied

---

McKinnon Auchincloss Kohlmeyer, Inc., 608 F. 2d 175, 177 (5th Cir. 1979) (commodities adviser does not have to register under Investment Advisers Act). So, too, with respect to a *forward* contract, although in the particular case the so-called "stand-by with pair-off" involving GNMA certificates was held to be both an investment contract and an "evidence of indebtedness" because the defendant had offered a guaranteed return. SEC v. G. Weeks Securities, 678 F. 2d 649 (6th Cir. 1982); see also John Kilpatrick, Sec. Ex. Act Rel. 23,251, 35 SEC Dock. 914, 915-17 (1986).

A "forward contract" is "an off-exchange, usually privately negotiated agreement, generally among commercial or institutional parties for a specified amount and quality of a commodity for deferred delivery at a specified date, in which actual delivery generally is contemplated, physically possible, and often occurs." Committee on Commodities Regulation of the Association of the Bar of the City of New York, The Forward Contract Exclusion: An Analysis of Off-Exchange Commodity-Based Instruments, 41 Bus. Law. 853 (1986).

A GNMA ("Ginnie Mae") certificate represents an interest in a pool of government-underwritten residential mortgages. The GNMA (Government National Mortgage Association), an agency of the federal government, guarantees timely payment of the mortgage principal and interest. GNMAs have fairly standardized terms and therefore may be pooled and marketed for investment. The issuers are usually mortgage bankers who earn their compensation by organizing pools of GNMAs. Abeles v. Oppenheimer & Co., 597 F. Supp. 532 (N. D. Ill. 1983) *summary judgment for defendants,* 662 F. Supp. 290 (N. D. Ill. 1986); see also Board of Trade of City of Chicago v. SEC, 677 F. 2d 1137, 1138-39 (7th Cir. 1982), *vacated as moot,* 459 U.S. 1026 (1982).

On mortgage-related securities ("securitization" of mortgages) more generally, see Dayan and Pratt, Mortgage-Related Securities, in Practising Law Institute, Sixteenth Annual Institute on Securities Regulation (1984) c. 6; K. Lore, Mortgage-Backed Securities: Developments and Trends in the Secondary Mortgage Market (1985); Murray and Hadaway, Mortgage-Backed Securities: An Investigation of Legal and Financial Issues, 11 J. Corp. L. 203 (1986). On guarantees as securities, see p. c. 3J.

On precious metal contracts, see Noa v. Kay Futures, Inc., 638 F. 2d 77 (9th Cir. 1980); SEC v. Belmont Reid & Co., Inc., 794 F. 2d 1388 (9th Cir. 1986); Sec. Act Rel. 5552, 6 SEC Dock. 2 (1974); Committee on Commodities Regulation, supra, at 891-95.

[17] See p. 204 supra.

[18] E. g., N. Y. Gen. Bus. Law, Art. 23-A, §352.1; Wis. Stat., c. 189, §551.02(13)(a). *Contra:* Cal. Ad. Code, Tit. 10, c. 3, Rule 260.019, CCH Blue Sky L. Rep. ¶11,750 ("security" does not include "any discretionary account maintained by a customer with a commodity broker").

[19] Commercial Iron & Metal Co. v. Bache & Co., Inc., 478 F. 2d 39 (10th Cir. 1973); Moody v. Bache & Co., Inc., 570 F. 2d 523, 526 (5th Cir. 1978).

[20] Alvord v. Shearson Hayden Stone, Inc., 485 F. Supp. 848, 851-53 (D. Conn. 1980); Savino v. E. F. Hutton & Co., 507 F. Supp. 1225, 1235-39 (S. D.

in a formal contract as long as the broker in fact controls the account.[21]

(3) The cases are in disarray with respect to the kind of "common enterprise" required to make an "investment contract" out of a discretionary account. The broadest view is satisfied with "vertical commonality"; that approach recognizes a "common enterprise" between broker and customer, without insisting on any sort of pooling among customers' accounts.[22] A stricter view does insist on such pooling: "horizontal commonality."[23] The strictest view is not satisfied, at least with merely vertical commonality, unless the broker himself shares in the enterprise apart from his commissions.[24]

N. Y. 1981); Levine v. Merrill Lynch, Pierce, Fenner & Smith, Inc., 639 F. Supp. 1391, 1395 (S. D. N. Y. 1986).

[21] Scheer v. Merrill Lynch, Pierce, Fenner & Smith, Inc., CCH Fed. Sec. L. Rep. ¶95,086 (S. D. N. Y. 1975).

[22] SEC v. Continental Commodities Corp., 497 F. 2d 516, 520-23 (5th Cir. 1974) (options on commodity futures); Troyer v. Karcagi, 476 F. Supp. 1142, 1147-48 (S. D. N. Y. 1979), and cases cited at 1147 n. 7; Alvord v. Shearson Hayden Stone, Inc., 485 F. Supp. 848, 853 (D. Conn. 1980); McGill v. American Land & Exploration Co., 776 F. 2d 923 (10th Cir. 1985); but cf. In re Federal Bank & Trust Co., Ltd. Securities Litigation, CCH Fed. Sec. L. Rep. ¶91,565 (D. Ore. 1984) (no vertical commonality in fact); Silverstein v. Merrill Lynch, Pierce, Fenner & Smith, Inc., 618 F. Supp. 436 (S. D. N. Y. 1985); Nakagawa v. Ellis & Ellis Associates, Inc., — F. Supp. —, CCH Fed. Sec. L. Rep. ¶93,028 (D. Hawaii 1986) (no vertical commonality in fact). This view is supported by the holdings that pooling of accounts is not a prerequisite to other kinds of investment contracts. See p. 189 supra.

[23] Milnarik v. M-S Commodities, Inc., 457 F. 2d 274 (7th Cir. 1972), *cert. denied*, 409 U. S. 887; Curran v. Merrill Lynch, Pierce, Fenner & Smith, Inc., 622 F. 2d 216, esp. at 224-25 (6th Cir. 1980), *aff'd on other grounds* sub nom. Merrill Lynch, Pierce, Fenner & Smith, Inc. v. Curran, 456 U. S. 353 (1982) (even though the account was misrepresented as including the essential elements of horizontal commonality); Salcer v. Merrill Lynch, Pierce, Fenner & Smith, Inc., 682 F. 2d 459 (3d Cir. 1982); cf. Marine Bank v. Weaver, 455 U. S. 551, 559-60 (1982), supra p. 173.

The horizontal view, too, has not been limited to discretionary accounts. See Dahl v. English, 578 F. Supp. 17 (N. D. Ill. 1983) (sale of unique works of art in lithographic plate form at different prices through different contracts executed at different times); Hart v. Public Homes of Mich. Corp., 735 F. 2d 1001 (6th Cir. 1984) (sale and leaseback of model homes). And it is proper to look beyond the instruments in question to find that the required horizontal commonality existed. SEC v. Professional Associates, 731 F. 2d 349, 354-55 (6th Cir. 1984). But it does not suffice to show horizontal commonality that the defendant brokers traded in the same commodity future on behalf of several customers at the same time. Silverstein v. Merrill Lynch, Pierce, Fenner & Smith, Inc., 618 F. Supp. 436, 439 n. 2 (S. D. N. Y. 1985).

[24] Lopez v. Dean Witter Reynolds, Inc., 805 F. 2d 880 (9th Cir. 1986), and earlier 9th Cir. cases cited; Savino v. E. F. Hutton & Co., 507 F. Supp. 1225, 1237-38 (S. D. N. Y. 1981); Kaufman v. Magid, 539 F. Supp. 1088, 1097 (D. Mass. 1982); Xaphes v. Merrill Lynch, Pierce, Fenner & Smith, Inc., 597 F. Supp. 213, 216 (D. Me. 1984); Mechigian v. Art Capital Corp., 612 F. Supp. 1421 (S. D. N. Y. 1985); Shotto v. Laub, 635 F. Supp. 835 (D. Md. 1986). The cases cited supra p. 238 n. 23 do not consider this question.

(4) There is authority for the proposition that a commodity futures contract for a Government security involves a "contract to buy" the underlying security and hence constitutes, within §3(a)(13) of the 1934 Act, a "purchase" of a security for purposes of Rule 10b-5.[25]

(5) Commodity *options* are no more securities *per se* than are commodity futures contracts.[26] But "naked" options — calls not backed by ownership of the commodity futures called for — have been held to be investment contracts, apparently because of the introduction of a substantial, investor "enterprise risk," as well as

[25]Paine, Webber, Jackson & Curtis, Inc. v. Conaway, 515 F. Supp. 202, 210 (N. D. Ala. 1981); Fisher v. Dean Witter Reynolds, Inc., 526 F. Supp. 558 (E. D. Pa., Giles, J., 1981). *Contra:* P & C Investment Club v. Becker, 520 F. Supp. 120 (E. D. Pa., Ditter, J., 1981). The SEC staff has taken a "no action" position under the several statutes to the extent that investment in futures contracts on financial instruments, as well as any advice with respect to such contracts, is limited to futures contracts on Treasury instruments, GNMA certificates (see p. 237 n. 16 supra), and commercial paper, all of which are exempted from registration under the 1933 Act. Boston Futures Fund 1, CCH Com. Fut. L. Rep. ¶20,915 (1979) (letter).

So, too, with respect to "forward" contracts to buy GNMA certificates (see p. 237 n. 16 supra). Berk v. Oppenheimer & Co., CCH Fed. Sec. L. Rep. ¶99,436 (N. D. Ill. 1983); Abrams v. Oppenheimer Government Securities, Inc., 737 F. 2d 582 (7th Cir. 1984) (*a fortiori* in view of absence of CFTC authority). The same result has been reached on a slightly different theory that the purchase or sale of a GNMA certificate forward contract is inextricably tied to the sale of the underlying security. Plymouth-Home National Bank v. Oppenheimer & Co., CCH Fed. Sec. L. Rep. ¶99,265 (N. D. Ill. 1983). But "It does not logically follow that a futures contract based on a security is itself a security." Conroy v. Andeck Resources '81 Year-End, Ltd., 137 Ill. App. 3d 375, 383, 484 N. E. 2d 525, 532 (1985). For an exhaustive treatment, see Miller, Regulation of Trading in Ginnie Maes, 21 Duquesne L. Rev. 39 (1982).

In February 1984 the SEC adopted Rule 3a12-7 to designate as exempted securities under the 1934 Act over-the-counter options on Government securities when (1) the options are traded otherwise than on an exchange or NASDAQ and (2) they relate to securities representing obligations of at least $250,000:

> While the Commission staff has generally taken the position that OTC government options are securities separate from the exempt securities underlying them, the Commission has not, as a general administrative matter, required registration of firms that limit their activities to government securities and OTC government options. * * * The rule's principal purpose is to accommodate market professionals and institutions that trade OTC government options incidentally to their primary business and who, but for their dealings in those options, would not be subject to registration and other requirements of the Exchange Act.

Sec. Ex. Act Rel. 10,625, 29 SEC Dock. 963, 964 (1984).

[26]Glazer v. National Commodity Research & Statistical Service, 547 F. 2d 392 (7th Cir. 1977); but cf. SEC v. American Commodity Exchange, Inc., 546 F. 2d 1361, 1366 (10th Cir. 1976) (purported commodity options sold as part of a scheme to generate fees).

the seller's undertaking to advise customers with respect to the most opportune moment to sell or exercise their options or to sell specific futures contracts.[27]

The impact on all this of the "exclusive jurisdiction" language in the CFTC Act's definition of "commodity" was unclear.[28] But the two Commissions jointly announced in December 1981 that, pending the enactment of clarifying amendments to the securities and commodities laws, they had "resolved a range of issues regarding their respective jurisdictions * * * over a host of instruments generally described as 'financial futures' or 'financial options' ":[29]

(1) The agreement left untouched the CFTC's exclusive jurisdiction over commodity futures trading on boards of trade in *futures contracts* (or options on futures contracts) on securities issued or guaranteed by the United States Government or other SEC-exempted securities (except municipals).

(2) On the other hand, the agreement recognized the SEC as the sole federal regulator of the securities *options* markets. And, in recognition of the SEC's unique responsibilities over the markets for corporate and municipal securities, the two agencies specified certain criteria to govern approval by the CFTC of futures trading in a *group* or *index* of such securities, in addition to affording the SEC an opportunity for an oral hearing before the CFTC (together with judicial review) in order to present the bases for any objection.

This estimable example of administrative harmony hit a snag, however, in the Seventh Circuit. In early 1981 the SEC had ap-

[27] SEC v. Continental Commodities Corp., 497 F. 2d 516 (5th Cir. 1974); SEC v. Commodities Options Int'l, Inc., 553 F. 2d 628 (9th Cir. 1977); Searsy v. Commercial Trading Corp., 560 S. W. 2d 637 (Tex. 1977) (state act). See generally Long, The Naked Commodity Option Contract As a Security, 15 Wm. & Mary L. Rev. 211 (1973); Long, Commodity Options — Revisited, 25 Drake L. Rev. 75 (1976).

[28] See p. 236 supra. In general, see Bromberg, Commodities Law and Securities Law — Overlaps and Preemptions, 1 J. Corp. L. 217 (1976); Guttman, The Futures Trading Act of 1978: The Reaffirmation of CFTC-SEC Coordinated Jurisdiction over Security/Commodities, 28 Am. U. L. Rev. 1 (1978); Raisler, Adams, and Donley-Hoopes, Discretionary Commodity Accounts: Why They Are Not Governed by the Federal Securities Laws, 42 Wash. & Lee L. Rev. 743 (1985). *Query:* It is still not clear whether the "exclusive jurisdiction" language forecloses the question whether a discretionary commodity account is an investment contract for purposes of civil actions. See id. at 766-67; George v. Omni Capital Int'l, Ltd., 795 F. 2d 415, 419-22 (5th Cir. 1986), and cases cited; Cady v. A. G. Edwards & Sons, Inc., 648 F. Supp. 621, 624-26 (D. Utah 1986).

[29] SEC and CFTC press release (CFTC Rel. 853-81), Dec. 7, 1981, CCH Fed. Sec. L. Rep. ¶83,062; see Longstreth (SEC Commissioner), The SEC-CFTC Accord: Accommodation in the Public Interest (remarks to Securities and Commodities Law Committees of Chicago Bar Assn., Chicago, Apr. 16, 1982).

proved proposed rule changes by the Chicago Board Options Exchange, a securities exchange,[30] designed to accommodate trading in options on GNMA securities.[31] On petition of the Chicago Board of Trade, which had traded GNMA *futures* since 1975, the Seventh Circuit in a split decision reversed. The majority not only held that the SEC was without jurisdiction because of the CFTC statute — the two Commissions could not by agreement "reapportion their jurisdiction in the face of a clear, contrary statutory mandate"[32] — but also went on, gratuitously, to say that GNMA options were not even "securities" despite the "right to * * * purchase" language of the definition.[33]

This case was promptly overruled by the enactment of the October 1982 amendments to the 1933 Act.[34] The Commission thereupon approved a number of changes in the rules of the Chicago Board Options Exchange and the American and Philadelphia Stock Exchanges to allow them to begin trading in various financial instruments,[35] and the Supreme Court vacated the Seventh Circuit decision as moot.[36] Then, as part of the Futures Trading Act of 1982, Congress enacted the SEC-CFTC "treaty" into law.[37]

[30] See p. 234 supra.

[31] Chicago Board Options Exchange, Inc., Sec. Ex. Act Rel. 17,577, 22 SEC Dock. 186 (1981). See p. 239 n. 25 supra.

[32] Board of Trade of the City of Chicago v. SEC, 677 F. 2d 1137, 1142 n. 8 (7th Cir. 1982), *vacated as moot,* 459 U. S. 1026 (1982).

[33] 677 F. 2d at 1155-61.

[34] See p. 232 supra.

[35] Sec. Ex. Act Rels. 19,125-34, 26 SEC Dock. 464-92 (1982); see also American Stock Exchange, Inc., Sec. Ex. Act Rel. 19,263, 26 SEC Dock. 1027 (1982) (options on certificates of deposit); American Stock Exchange, Inc., Sec. Ex. Act Rel. 19,264, 26 SEC Dock. 1033 (1982) (options on various stock indexes on Amex, CBOE, and NYSE, marking the NYSE's first entry into the listed options market); Options Clearing Corp., Sec. Ex. Act Rel. 19,274, 26 SEC Dock. 1051 (1982) (foreign currency options); New York Stock Exchange, Inc., Sec. Ex. Act Rel. 20,669, 29 SEC Dock. 1092 (1984) (issues raised by NYSE's entry into the industry index options market). Releases 19,263-64 discuss the economic functions of these various interests, the Commission expressing its belief that, unless serious regulatory concerns were identified, "the marketplace generally should be permitted to determine whether a particular contract meets the needs of market participants." Sec. Ex. Act Rel. 19,263, 26 SEC Dock. at 1029.

[36] Board of Trade of the City of Chicago v. SEC, 459 U. S. 1026 (1982).

[37] 96 Stat. 2294 (1983); see H. R. Rep. No. 97-964 (1982); Rosen, The Impact of the Futures Trading Act of 1982 on Commodity Regulation, 15 Sec. Reg. L. Rep. 142 (1983). The statute departs from the "treaty" in giving the SEC an effective veto over any application submitted to the CFTC on or after December 9, 1982, for designation of a stock index future or an option on such a future.

The statute prohibits future contracts (as well as options on such contracts) based on individual securities except exempted securities (other than municipals) under §3 of the 1933 Act or §3(a)(12) of the 1934 Act. Com. Ex. Act §2(a)(1)(B)(v), 7 U. S. C. §2a(v). Since the legislative history of the 1982 amend-

For good measure the 1982 legislation amended §28(a) of the 1934 Act to provide that no state law with respect to gaming contracts or the like invalidates any put, call, or other security, or applies to any related activity, if the instrument is traded pursuant to rules of a self-regulatory organization (which is to say, an exchange or the NASD) that are filed with the SEC. This provision reflects the introduction of cash settlements for index trading, without the at least theoretical anticipation of ultimate delivery that characterizes trading in commodity futures (as well as trading in individual securities insofar as such trading is permitted).[38]

In late 1983 the SEC took the position with the CFTC that four stock index futures contracts proposed by the Chicago Mercantile Exchange did not satisfy the statutory criteria of the Commodity Exchange Act. Particularly, the SEC felt that the contracts were susceptible to manipulation and did not represent a "substantial segment" of the market.[39] This and other incidents led to a second accord between the two Commissions, with the publication of guidelines for designation as a contract market for futures contracts (or options on such contracts) involving a nondiversified industry index of domestic equity securities.[40]

In late 1984 a joint study by the Board of Governors of the Federal Reserve System, the CFTC, and the SEC concluded (*inter alia*) (1) that the futures and options markets served a useful purpose by providing a means for shifting economic risks, (2) that those markets appeared to have no measurable negative influence on capital formation, and (3) that, with the SEC and CFTC committed to

---

ments indicates that Congress did not intent to forbid the marketing of futures on British Government bonds (so-called "gilts") in the United States so long as neither the settlement of the futures contracts nor trading in the bonds themselves occurred in the United States, the Commission adopted Rule 3a12-8 to designate those bonds (together with Canadian Government securities) as "exempted securities" under §3(a)(12) for the purpose of permitting futures trading in the United States under the terms of the Commodity Exchange Act. The exemption now covers (1) futures trading (2) with respect to securities that are issued by the Government of the United Kingdom, Canada, or Japan and not registered under the 1933 Act (or the subject of an American depositary receipt so registered) if (3) the contracts are not deliverable in the United States. Sec. Ex. Act Rel. 20,708, 29 SEC Dock. 1188 (1984); Sec. Ex. Act Rel. 23,423, 36 SEC Dock. 117 (1986); Sec. Ex. Act Rel. 24,209, 37 SEC Dock. 1161 (1987).

[38] See p. 241 n. 37 supra.

[39] Letter, Nov. 29, 1983, CCH Fed. Sec. L. Rep. ¶83,460.

[40] Sec. Ex. Act Rel. 20,578, 29 SEC Dock. 817 (1984); see N. Y. Times, Jan. 30, 1984, p. D6, col. 2. These guidelines were promptly challenged by the Chicago Board of Trade in an injunctive action against both Commissions, which the court dismissed for failure to exhaust the administrative remedies. Board of Trade of the City of Chicago v. CFTC, CCH Fed. Sec. L. Rep. ¶91,437 (N. D. Ill. 1984).

cooperating toward achieving greater harmonization of existing federal regulation over those markets, additional legislation establishing an appropriate regulatory framework would not be warranted.[41]

L. JUDGE OR JURY?

In principle, the line between the functions of judge and jury on the "security" question would seem to be drawn as follows:

(1) If the underlying facts are in dispute in a criminal case, they must go to the jury, and it is reversible error for the judge to instruct flatly that there is an "investment contract" instead of instructing that the jury should find an "investment contract" if it credits certain facts essential to constitute such a "security." "The plea of not guilty puts all in issue, even the most patent truths. In our federal system, the Trial Court may never instruct a verdict either in whole or in part "[1]

(2) This is equally true with respect to a civil action at law, except that the burden of proof is in terms of a preponderance of the evidence rather than the reasonable doubt rule.

(3) When the underlying facts on the "security" question are sufficiently one-sided in a civil action at law so that a verdict for the other side would have to be set aside, the judge (if the other elements of the action are established) may direct a verdict for the first side.[2]

[41] Board of Governors of the Federal Reserve System, CFTC, and SEC, A Study of the Effects on the Economy of Trading in Futures and Options (1984), of which c. 1 is reprinted in CCH Fed. Sec. L. Rep. ¶83,723.

It seems that both securities and futures markets "may be viewed as social rather than exclusively economic structures." Baker, The Social Structure of a National Securities Market, 89 Am. J. Sociology 775, 776 (1984) (sociological analysis of the stock options market).

See generally J. Seligman, The SEC and the Future of Finance (1985) c. 2, The Structure of the Options Markets; Mallen v. Merrill Lynch, Pierce, Fenner & Smith, Inc. 605 F. Supp. 1105 (N. D. Ga. 1985), citing the text.

C. 3L [1] Roe v. United States, 287 F. 2d 435, 440-41 (5th Cir. 1961), *cert. denied,* 368 U. S. 824; see also Farrell v. United States, 321 F. 2d 409, 414-16 (9th Cir. 1963), *cert. denied,* 375 U. S. 992 (court approved jury instruction on question whether certain trust deed notes were "notes" or "evidences of indebtedness" or "investment contracts"); Gibbs v. United States, 559 F. 2d 28 (10th Cir. 1976), *cert. denied,* 434 U. S. 1015; United States v. Johnson, 718 F. 2d 1317 (5th Cir. *en banc* 1983) (National Stolen Property Act). See also, under the California statute, People v. Figueroa, 41 Cal. 3d 714, 715 P. 2d 680 (1986).

[2] Ahrens v. American-Canadian Beaver Co., Inc., 428 F. 2d 926, 928 (10th Cir. 1970); Great Western Bank & Trust Co. v. Kotz, 532 F. 2d 1252, 1255 (9th Cir. 1976). Cf. also SEC v. W. J. Howey Co., 328 U. S. 293 (1946), supra p.

(4) So far as the esoteric types of "security" are concerned, the question is far less likely to be determinable as a practical matter from the face of a written instrument alone.[3] But, when that is so under the conceded facts, it is not error, even in a criminal case, to refuse an instruction giving an abstract definition of "security" in the language of the statute.[4]

(5) In any case, the "security" question under the federal statute is to be determined as a matter of federal law, regardless of the impact of state law.[5]

M. A FEW FINAL WORDS ABOUT STATUTORY CONSTRUCTION

Justice Jackson's language in the *Joiner* case rejecting the liberal-strict construction approach[1] in favor of reading "text in the light of context" was a breath of fresh air that one hoped might counter the pressure, as Justice Schaefer of the Illinois Supreme Court put it, toward "a jurisprudence of words or phrases divorced from facts and capable of generating new words and phrases with independent

184, an action for injunction that the Commission lost on the "investment contract" point in both lower courts but won in the Supreme Court. Justice Frankfurter dissented on the ground that the majority had ignored the federal two-court rule with respect to findings of fact. But the majority obviously thought that it was free to decide the question as one of law, since it said that "Most of the facts are stipulated." Id. at 294.

[3]Aldrich v. McCulloch Properties, Inc., 627 F. 2d 1036, 1039 (10th Cir. 1980). In SEC v. Professional Associates, 731 F. 2d 349 (6th Cir. 1984), the court held that it was proper to consider evidence extrinsic to the terms of the document involved, and that the classification of an investment as a "trust" did not *ipso facto* prevent it from being a security if it amounted to an investment contract.

[4]Tarvestad v. United States, 418 F. 2d 1043, 1048 (8th Cir. 1969) (no more specific instruction was requested); United States v. Austin, 462 F. 2d 724, 735-36 (10th Cir. 1972), *cert. denied,* 409 U. S. 1048 (court conceded that *Roe,* supra p. 243 n. 1, was substantially indistinguishable, but "in this six-week trial * * * establishing guilt beyond all reasonable doubt, we do not believe that reversal would be justifiable"); United States v. Carman, 577 F. 2d 556, 562-63 (9th Cir. 1978). See also, under the California statute, People v. Skelton, 109 Cal. App. 3d 691, 712-14, 167 Cal. Rptr. 636, 646-48 (1980), and cases cited.

[5]SEC v. C. M. Joiner Leasing Co., 320 U. S. 344, 352 (1943) (reversing holding below that "defendants' offerings were beyond the scope of the Act because they offered [oil] leases and assignments that under Texas law conveyed interests in real estate"); SEC v. Variable Annuity Life Ins. Co. of America, 359 U. S. 65, 69 (1959); Farrell v. United States, 321 F. 2d 409, 416 (9th Cir. 1963), *cert. denied,* 375 U. S. 992 (California law limiting personal liability of makers of trust deed notes *held* not determinative).

C. 3M [1]320 U. S. at 350-51, supra pp. 181-82.

lives."[2] And one does occasionally find echoes of this suspicion of maxims.[3]

But not all judges seem eager to be liberated from the ratrace that caused a Texas court to say that the blue sky law "should be considered as a penal statute when it is sought to enforce the penalty, and as a remedial statute when it is sought to enforce the [civil] remedy."[4] In short, the old maxims have a good deal of staying power, and advocates may be pardoned for following the judges' rhetoric when it suits their purpose.[5] Indeed, an appellate court has quoted from Justice Jackson's opinion to support the proposition that the Securities Act "should be liberally construed"![6]

The further Jackson adjuration to read "text in the light of context"[7] is reflected in the statutes themselves insofar as their definitional sections apply "unless the context requires otherwise."[8] The Supreme Court has referred to this phrase in stating that "Congress itself has cautioned that the same words may take on a different coloration in different sections of the securities laws."[9] In that case the Court did not have to decide whether the Commission's former Rule 133, its so-called "no sale rule" with respect to mergers and

[2] Schaefer, Book Review, 84 Harv. L. Rev. 1558, 1559-60 (1971); cf. Pound, Common Law and Legislation, 21 Harv. L. Rev. 383, 386-87, 401-02 (1908).

[3] See Herman & MacLean v. Huddleston, 459 U. S. 375, 387 n. 23 (1983), infra p. 976; United States v. Charnay, 537 F. 2d 341, 348 (9th Cir. 1976), *cert. denied*, 429 U. S. 1000; United States v. Chiarella, 588 F. 2d 1358, 1368 n. 16 (2d Cir. 1978), *rev'd on other grounds* sub nom. Chiarella v. United States, 445 U. S. 222 (1980). As Justice White has said (in a non-SEC case) of the maxim that penal statutes should be strictly construed:

> But that canon "is not an inexorable command to override common sense and evident statutory purpose," United States v. Brown, 333 U. S. 18, 25 [1948], and does not "require that the act be given the 'narrowest meaning.' It is sufficient if the words are given their fair meaning in accord with the evident intent of Congress." United States v. Raynor, 302 U. S. 540, 552 [1938]. * * *

United States v. Cook, 384 U. S. 257, 262-63 (1966).

[4] Dempsey-Tegeler, Inc. v. Flowers, 465 S. W. 2d 208, 211 (Tex. Civ. App. 1971).

[5] See pp. 939-40 infra. Contrast Murphy, J., in M. Kraus & Bros., Inc. v. United States, 327 U. S. 614, 626 (1946) ("certainly a criminal conviction [under the Emergency Price Control Act of 1942] ought not to rest upon an interpretation reached by the use of policy judgments rather than by the inexorable command of relevant language"), with Warren, C. J., in Tcherepnin v. Knight, 389 U. S. 332, 336 (1967) ("we are guided by the familiar canon of statutory construction that remedial legislation should be construed broadly to effectuate its purposes").

[6] Creswell-Keith, Inc. v. Willingham, 264 F. 2d 76, 80 (8th Cir. 1959).

[7] 320 U. S. at 351, supra p. 180.

[8] Sec. Act §2; Sec. Ex. Act §3(a); Holding Co. Act §2(a); Trust Ind. Act §303; Inv. Co. Act §2(a); Inv. Adv. Act §202(a).

[9] SEC v. National Securities, Inc., 393 U. S. 453, 465-66 (1969).

the like,[10] precluded a sale for purposes of Rule 10b-5, because the rule itself was limited to §5. And it later left open the question whether the "context" language permitted different interpretations of "sale" for purposes of applying the registration and fraud provisions to interests in employee pension plans.[11] Nevertheless, although there is a split of authority, a number of lower courts have applied the word "context" as referring not only to the context of the statute itself but also to "the surrounding factual circumstances."[12] And there is support for that view in the legislative history.[13]

[10] See p. 292 infra.

[11] International Brotherhood of Teamsters v. Daniel, 439 U. S. 551, 567 n. 22 (1979), supra p. 222 n. 22.

[12] E. g., Emisco Industries, Inc. v. Pro's, Inc., 543 F. 2d 38, 39 (7th Cir. 1976); Exchange National Bank v. Touche Ross & Co., 544 F. 2d 1126, 1137-38 (2d Cir. 1976), supra p. 169, *semble*. *Contra:* American Bankers Assn. v. SEC, 804 F. 2d 739, 753-54 (D. C. Cir. 1986).

[13] Early versions of the 1933 bills said: "unless the *text* requires otherwise." S. 875 and H. R. 4314, §2, 73d Cong. (1933). The "context" language was substituted in H. R. 5480.

CHAPTER 4

"OFFER," "SALE," "UNDERWRITER," AND "DEALER"

A. "SALE" AND "OFFER" [§2(3)]

1. Exchanges of Securities and Alterations of Their Terms

The Commission has not attempted any metaphysical distinction between "value" and "consideration." By now, however, it is pretty well understood that certain types of disposition are regarded as made for "value" and others not. Thus, it is clear on the face of the statute that an exchange of one security for another is a sale: witness the exemptions provided by §§3(a)(9) and 3(a)(10) for certain types of exchange offerings,[1] as well as the reference in the definition of "security" to certificates of deposit, voting trust certificates, and receipts, which are normally issued only in exchange for outstanding securities. The Commission has likewise held that securities issued in settlement of open-book or contract obligations are issued for value.[2] The stamping of outstanding bonds to evidence their holders' consent to an extension of maturity has been treated by the courts as if it were an exchange of new bonds for old and hence a sale; the absence of a new certificate is regarded as irrelevant.[3] On the same rationale it is equally unimportant that

C. 4A [1]See pp. 276, 283 infra.

[2]Resources Corp. Int'l, 7 SEC 689, 730 (1940).

[3]SEC v. Associated Gas & Electric Co., 99 F. 2d 795 (2d Cir. 1938). This case was decided under the Holding Company Act, which defines the term "sale" even more broadly to include "any sale, disposition by lease, exchange or pledge, or other disposition," with no mention of "value." §2(a)(23). Moreover, that Act requires an effective declaration not only in order to "sell" any security but also in order to "issue" any security or "to exercise any privilege or right to alter the * * * rights of the holders of an outstanding security." §6(a). But the

the extension may not even be evidenced by any stamping; dissenters' bonds, for example, may be bought in and the maturity of the others extended by means of an amendment of the underlying indenture.

There is always the question, however, whether the rights of security holders have been so substantially affected by the particular change in the terms of the outstanding security that it becomes a new security. For example, a change in interest or dividend rate or liquidation preference or underlying security, or a change in the identity of the issuer, would seem quite clearly to result in a new security. On the other hand, there is likely to be agreement that a mere change in the name of the security (perhaps from common to Class B stock), or a change in the name of the issuer without a change of identity, or certain types of charter amendment affecting the powers of the directors, do not make a new security. In between come a great variety of other changes — for example, from par to no par or vice versa, changes in par or stated value, changes in redemption or cumulative or conversion features, various changes in voting rights. There the answer must depend on the context, and in fact it varies in different contexts under the SEC statutes themselves.[4]

2. GIFTS

It would be hard to make a "sale" out of a *bona fide* gift.[5] Thus, just as the Commission regarded noncontributory employee plans as not involving a "sale" of an investment contract,[6] so, too, with respect to *stock* issued to employees as a bonus (that is to say, without any contractual commitment). But the situation is otherwise when stock is offered as a reward for meeting certain sales quotas or other

---

court spoke only in terms of a "sale" within the meaning of the Holding Company Act, and it is impossible to read the opinion without concluding that its rationale applies equally to the Securities Act. See, e. g., Keys v. Wolfe, 709 F. 2d 413 (5th Cir. 1983) (certain changes in investment contracts with respect to a pecan growing scheme might be sufficient to create a sale of a security). "Thus, before changes in the rights of a security holder can qualify as the 'purchase' of a new security under Section 10(b) and Rule 10b-5, there must be such a significant change in the nature of the investment or in the investment risks as to amount to a new investment." Id. at 417; see also Bull v. American Bank & Trust Co., 641 F. Supp. 62, 68-69 (E. D. Pa. 1986), and cases cited; cf. Ahern v. Gaussoin, 611 F. Supp. 1465.

[4] Cf. p. 576 n. 94 infra.

[5] Cf. Shaw v. Dreyfus, 172 F. 2d 140 (2d Cir. 1949), *cert. denied,* 337 U. S. 907 (Sec. Ex. Act §16(b)).

[6] See p. 221 supra.

measures of performance. And it must be remembered that even a *gift* of a *warrant* involves an "offer" of the security it calls for, so that the registration and prospectus provisions must be satisfied for the latter security before the gift is made of the warrant. Since it is no extra trouble, it is customary (though not necessary) to register the gift warrants along with the ultimate securities.

3. Pledges

In *Rubin* v. *United States*,[7] a criminal case, the Supreme Court held that a pledge of stock to a bank as collateral for a loan was an "offer" and "sale" within §2(3) of the 1933 Act for purposes of §17(a), the general fraud provision of the 1933 Act:

> Obtaining a loan secured by a pledge of shares of stock unmistakably involves a "disposition of * * * [an] interest in a security, for value." Although pledges transfer less than absolute title, the interest thus transferred nonetheless is an "interest in a security." The pledges contemplated a self-executing procedure under a power that could, at the option of the pledgee (the bank) in the event of a default, vest absolute title and ownership. Bankers Trust parted with substantial consideration — specifically, a total of $475,000 — and obtained the inchoate but valuable interest under the pledges and concomitant powers. It is not essential under the terms of the Act that full title pass to a transferee for the transaction to be an "offer" or a "sale."[8]

We consider later, in connection with the definition of "underwriter," whether the *Rubin* case extends to making the lender an "underwriter" for purposes of determining the applicability of §5, the registration provision.[9]

4. Stock and Liquidating Dividends

A stock dividend "does not distribute property but simply dilutes the shares as they existed before."[10] That is to say, it just cuts the

[7] 449 U. S. 424 (1981).

[8] Id. at 429-30. Justice Blackmun concurred on the theory that the pledge was simply a type of disposition. Id. at 432.

[9] See p. 259 infra.

[10] Hafner v. Forest Laboratories, Inc., CCH Fed. Sec. L. Rep. ¶91,443 at 94,741 (S. D. N. Y. 1964), *aff'd*, 345 F. 2d 167 (2d Cir. 1965). So, too, with respect to a stock split (or, presumably, a reverse stock split). Gurvitz v. Breyman

same pie into smaller slices. At the same time — perhaps because enough people think that enough other people will be deluded by stock dividends — "the market may in some instances place value on them."[11]

Presumably the 1933 conference committee was aware of this Janus-faced phenomenon when it omitted a House provision exempting stock dividends because "they do not constitute a sale, not being given for value."[12] And the General Counsel of the Commission early expressed the opinion that, although "the waiver or surrender of a right or claim" ordinarily constitutes "value," there is no sale when a dividend is declared in cash or stock in the alternative and a stockholder's election of the stock waives his right to the cash.[13] He distinguished the case, however, where the board gives stockholders an opportunity to waive a cash dividend that has already been declared and to receive it in the form of securities, since stockholders ordinarily acquire the vested rights of creditors on the public declaration of a cash dividend out of surplus. The same rationale would seem to apply to securities offered in exchange for accrued dividends on preferred stock.

A like analysis should apply in principle to dividends payable in *portfolio* securities, which are really partial liquidations, as long as it is not a case where certain classes of existing security holders are "bought out" by the distribution of portfolio securities in exchange, each holder being permitted to decide for himself whether or not to accept the offer.[14] But in the late 1960s the Commission became aware that some people had developed corporate shell games out of this spin-off technique in order to obtain the advantages of a public market by the back door rather than through registration. The Commission addressed perhaps the simplest model in a 1969 release:[15]

> Frequently, the pattern involves the issuance by a company, with little, if any, business activity, of its shares to a publicly-owned com-

---

& Co., 379 F. Supp. 1283 (S. D. N. Y. 1974). The title of one article adhering to this view is exceptionally expressive: Sosnick, Stock Dividends Are Lemons, Not Melons, 3 Calif. Mgmt. Rev. 61 (Winter 1961).

[11] Hafner v. Forest Laboratories, Inc., supra p. 249 n. 10, 345 F. 2d at 168.

[12] H. R. Rep. No. 152, 73d Cong., 1st Sess. (1933) 25; Sec. Act Rel. 3728 (1956) 3.

[13] Sec. Act Rel. 929 (1936). It is on this theory that open-end investment companies do not deliver prospectuses in distributions pursuant to dividend investment programs when each stockholder has the option of taking the dividends in cash or shares. SEC, Public Policy Implications of Investment Company Growth, H. R. Rep. No. 2337, 89th Cong., 2d Sess. (1966) 216.

[14] Cf. p. 798 infra.

[15] Sec. Act Rel. 4982 (1969).

pany in exchange for what may or may not be nominal consideration. The publicly-owned company subsequently spins off the shares to its shareholders with the result that active trading in the shares begins with no information on the issuer being available to the investing public. Despite this lack of information, moreover, the shares frequently trade in an active market at increasingly higher prices. Under such a pattern, when the shares are issued to the publicly-owned or acquiring company, a sale takes place within the meaning of the Securities Act and if the shares are then distributed to the shareholders of the acquiring company, that company may be an underwriter within the meaning of Section 2(11) of the Act as a person "who purchased from an issuer with a view to * * * the distribution of any security" or as a person who "has a direct or indirect participation in any such undertaking."

While the distribution of the shares to the acquiring company's shareholders may not, in itself, constitute a distribution for the purposes of the Act, the entire process, including the redistribution in the trading market which can be anticipated and which may indeed be a principal purpose of the spin off, can have that consequence. * * *

The theory has been advanced that since a sale is not involved in the distribution of the shares in a spin off that registration is not required and that even if it is required, no purpose would be served by filing a registration statement and requiring the delivery of a prospectus since the persons receiving the shares are not called upon to make an investment judgment.

This reasoning fails, however, to take into account that there is a sale by the issuer and the distribution thereafter does not cease at the point of receipt by the initial distributees of the shares but continues into the trading market involving sales to the investing public at large. Moreover, it ignores what appears to be primarily the purpose of the spin off in numerous circumstances which is to create quickly, and without the disclosure required by registration, a trading market in the shares of the issuer. * * * In the circumstances of a spin off, when the shares are thereafter traded in the absence of information about the issuer, the potential for fraud and deceit is manifest.[16]

Variations on the theme tend toward the Byzantine.[17] And the

[16] See also Sec. Ex. Act Rel. 19,284, 26 SEC Dock. 1145 (1982).

[17] See SEC v. Harwyn Industries Corp., 326 F. Supp. 943 (S. D. N. Y. 1971); SEC v. Datronics Engineers, Inc., 490 F. 2d 250 (4th Cir. 1973), *cert. denied,* 416 U. S. 937; United States v. Rubinson, 543 F. 2d 951, 958 n. 18 (2d Cir. 1976), *cert. denied sub nom.* Chester v. United States, 429 U. S. 850. In the first of these cases the court held that §§2(3) and 5 did not require that the "value" flow from the immediate parties who got the stock, but denied a preliminary injunction because, among other reasons, the defendants had relied on advice of counsel in the light of prevailing business practices and of the Commission's past acquiescence in unregistered spin-offs. See Schneider, Shell Cor-

Commission has used both barrels in return. In 1971 the Commission, resorting to its antifraud rulemaking authority under §15(c)(2) of the 1934 Act[18] to reinforce the disclosure scheme of the 1933 Act, adopted Rule 15c2-11, which prohibits broker-dealers from publishing over-the-counter quotations unless specified information is available with respect to the security and its issuer. The Commission referred to shell distributions through the spin-off device as one of the occasions for the rule.[19]

The 1969 release specifically did not "attempt to deal with any problems attributable to more conventional spin offs."[20] And for some time Commission counsel have been understood to take the position that *any* spin-off requires registration unless the issuer of the dividend security is (1) a reporting company under the 1934 Act or (2) undertakes to register under the 1934 Act promptly and some sort of statement as to the effect of the transaction accompanies the dividend. This position is perhaps more straightforward than defensible under the present statutory structure. A simple, bright line test requires legislation, and the Code supplies it in defining "offer" and "sale" to *include* "a dividend consisting of a security of another company that is not a one-year registrant" and to *exclude* any other "security dividend."[21]

B. "UNDERWRITER" [§2(11)]

1. General

The determination whether a particular person is an "underwriter" is important for a number of reasons. Underwriters are subject to civil liability under §11 for deficiencies in the registration statement. Various items of the registration forms call for information concerning each underwriter. And, as we have already seen, whether a person is an "underwriter" sometimes determines the availability of both the "preliminary negotiations" clause in §2(3) and the §4(1)

porations and Spin-Offs, in Practising Law Institute, First Annual Institute on Securities Regulation (1969) c. 15.

[18] See p. 707 infra.

[19] Sec. Ex. Act Rel. 9310 (1971).

[20] Sec. Act Rel. 4982 (1969).

[21] §202(143)(F)(iv) and (G)(iv). The definition excludes also "a split or reverse split." §202(14)(G)(v). A two-for-one split is of course, the equivalent of a 100 percent stock dividend.

exemption for "transactions by any person other than an issuer, underwriter, or dealer."[1]

The term "underwriter" is defined not with reference to the particular person's general business but on the basis of his relationship to the particular offering. No distinction is made between professional investment bankers and rank amateurs. Any person who performs one of the specified functions in relation to the offering is a statutory underwriter even though he is not a broker or dealer. Conversely, even a professional investment banker is *not* a statutory underwriter in effecting a distribution on behalf of a person not in a control relationship with the issuer, or in arranging a private placement on behalf of the issuer or a person in a control relationship with the issuer.[2]

The language of the definition is broad enough to cover at least the three basic types of underwriting that have been described in the preceding chapter: firm-commitment, best-efforts, and "old-fashioned." Section 2(11) reads as follows (the letters are added to indicate the six elements of the definition):

> The term "underwriter" means any person who [a] has purchased from an issuer with a view to, or [b] offers or sells for an issuer in connection with, [c] the distribution of any security, or [d] participates or has a direct or indirect participation in any such undertaking, or participates or has a participation in the direct or indirect underwriting of any such undertaking; but [e] such term shall not include a person whose interest is limited to a commission from an underwriter or dealer not in excess of the usual and customary distributors' or sellers' commission. [f] As used in this paragraph the term "issuer" shall include, in addition to an issuer, any person directly or indirectly controlling or controlled by the issuer, or any person under direct or indirect common control with the issuer.

2. The Control Clause

The second sentence of §2(11) tends to confuse because the introductory clause, "As used in this paragraph," is overlooked. A person in a control relationship with the issuer is *not* an "issuer" *except* for purposes of reading the control language into the *first*

C. **4B** [1]See pp. 88, 95, supra.

[2]On the private placement point, see Bd. of Gov. of Fed. Res. System, Statement Concerning Applicability of the Glass-Steagall Act to the Commercial Paper Placement Activities of Bankers Trust Co., CCH Fed. Sec. L. Rep. ¶83,780 at 87,474 n. 29 (1985), citing the text in the form of 1 Loss 547.

sentence. The draftsmen were simply trying to avoid a single, long sentence. In other words, it is as if §2(11) defined the term "underwriter" to mean any person who bought from or sold for either the issuer or a person in a control relationship with the issuer, and so on.

The second sentence nevertheless has two functions:

> The first function is to require the disclosure of any underwriting commission which, instead of being paid directly to the underwriter by the issuer, may be paid in an indirect fashion by a subsidiary or affiliate of the issuer to the underwriter. Its second function is to bring within the provisions of the bill redistribution whether of outstanding issues or issues sold subsequently to the enactment of the bill. All the outstanding stock of a particular corporation may be owned by one individual or a select group of individuals. At some future date they may wish to dispose of their holdings and to make an offer of this stock to the public. Such a public offering may possess all the dangers attendant upon a new offering of securities. Wherever such a redistribution reaches significant proportions, the distributor would be in the position of controlling the issuer and thus able to furnish the information demanded by the bill. This being so, the distributor is treated as equivalent to the original issuer and, if he seeks to dispose of the issue through a public offering, he becomes subject to the act.[3]

It is the second of these two functions that is the more significant, and that has created the problems under the "control" clause. Since the same or similar questions of control pervade all the SEC statutes, the discussion of what constitutes control within the meaning of §2(11) will be reserved for a later chapter.[4] In general, the Commission has applied the pragmatic test: Is the particular person in a position to obtain the required signatures of the issuer and its officers and directors on a registration statement? No other criterion would do, since the controlling person himself is not an "issuer" except for purposes of §2(11).

3. Purchasing from an Issuer

The term "purchased," which is not separately defined in the Act, presumably is complementary to the word "sold" or "sell."[5]

[3] H. R. Rep. No. 85, 73d Cong., 1st Sess. (1933) 13-14.

[4] See c. 6 infra.

[5] SEC v. Guild Films Co., Inc., 279 F. 2d 485, 489 (2d Cir. 1960), *cert. denied* sub nom. Santa Monica Bank v. SEC, 364 U. S. 819.

Clearly it includes an exchange.[6] The substance of the transaction controls. The Commission held that a firm was an underwriter under this language because it had loaned money to an individual to enable him to exercise an option to buy a controlling block of stock and the firm was to share in the profits and risks of the undertaking.[7] In another case the issuer's president was held to be an underwriter because his activities in connection with two previous registrations justified the inference that he would exercise purchase warrants and resell the registered stock in substantial volume, as he did, even though he received no price differential and was treated no differently from other stockholders.[8]

The status of a large warrant holder who wishes to exercise his warrants and distribute the underlying securities, but who is not connected with the issuer in any way, is unclear. He does fall literally within the definition of "underwriter," even though he may be the last person in the world the issuer would choose to act in that capacity in the usual sense. Indeed, the humble investor who buys 100 shares of a registered issue with the hope of a quick turnaround profit by reselling on the stock exchange likewise falls literally within the definition, because she has purchased "with a view to * * * distribution"; the term "distribution" is more or less synonymous with "public offering,"[9] and a sell order given to a stock exchange broker results in an offer to the highest bidder anywhere in the world, which is certainly a "public offering." But surely that result would be even more inane than to say that a tremendous shareholder who exercises stock purchase rights can *never* be an underwriter.

How, then, to separate the big from the small potatoes? Commission counsel have tried a number of pragmatic solutions. For a while they applied a rule of thumb in terms of 10 percent of the issue.[10] Gradually they began to consider that percentage as simply

[6] Hayes Mfg. Corp., 23 SEC 574, 576-77 (1946).

[7] Sweet's Steel Co., 4 SEC 589 (1939).

[8] Kinner Airplane & Motor Corp., Ltd., 2 SEC 943, 946-48 (1937).

[9] See H. R. Rep. No. 1838, 73d Cong., 2d Sess. (1934) 41; Gilligan, Will & Co. v. SEC, 267 F. 2d 461, 466-68 (2d Cir. 1959), *cert. denied*, 361 U. S. 896; cf. Securities Industry Assn. v. Board of Governors of Federal Reserve System, 807 F. 2d 1052, 1064 (2d Cir. 1986). On "public offering," see c. 5E infra.

[10] The then Director of the SEC's Division of Corporation Finance stated: "The presumption came up in the context of one filing and perhaps a lecture or two. It was never the Commission's position, and [a predecessor] tells me it was not even a division position, but these things tend to take on a life of their own." Williams, Problems in the Application of the 1933 Act and the Rules Thereunder to Shelf Offerings, in Practising Law Institute, Fourteenth Annual Institute on Securities Regulation (1983) c. 9 at 117.

one factor together with other circumstances such as the total amount of the issuer's securities outstanding, the size of the "float," and whether the issuer was a reporting company under the 1934 Act. And in recent years "no action" letters have tended simply to apply the volume figures in Rule 144, which is considered in a later chapter: the greater of (1) 1 percent of the amount outstanding or (2) the average weekly reported volume of trading during the last four weeks.[11] But, as we shall see there, this area is something of a morass.

The SEC staff *has* agreed that

> Insurance companies and similar institutional investors generally should not be deemed underwriters under Section 2(11) with regard to the purchase of large amounts of registered securities provided such securities are acquired in the ordinary course of their business from the issuer or underwriter of those securities and such purchasers have no arrangement with any person to participate in the distribution of such securities.[12]

4. Selling for an Issuer

This part of the definition, too, is broad enough to cover a person who solicits exchanges of securities on behalf of the issuer.[13] However, the ordinary protective committee in reorganization is not considered to be an "underwriter"; when it delivers the new securities to its depositors, it is acting for them and not for the issuer.[14] Whether directors or officers or employees of the issuer who sell on its behalf are underwriters or are merely performing their official corporate functions is a question of fact in each case. If their selling activity is only an incidental function of their regular duties and they receive no additional compensation, they are not regarded as underwriters, since a corporation can act only through individuals.[15] But a different conclusion is required when they spend a major part of their time and effort in selling activities and receive special compensation.[16] It should be highly relevant also whether they are

[11] Rule 144(e), infra pp. 373-74.

[12] American Council of Life Ins., CCH Fed. Sec. L. Rep. ¶77,526 (letter 1983).

[13] Chain Stores Depot Corp., 7 SEC 1015, 1024 (1940).

[14] Commonwealth Bond Corp., 1 SEC 13, 17, 18, FTC 635, 641 (1934).

[15] Free Traders, Inc., 7 SEC 913, 921-22 (1940).

[16] Beta Frozen Food Storage, Inc., 37 SEC 387, 392 (1956). It would also be evidentiary of an "underwriter" status, presumably, if they rather than the issuer were to hire or pay salesmen, or pay any part of the selling expenses, or maintain separate offices for handling sales.

specially hired in connection with the company's selling activities, particularly if they have a background in the securities business either as professional promoters or otherwise.[17]

The Second Circuit has made it clear that a person may be an underwriter under this part of the definition even though it has no contractual relationship or understanding with the issuer. The first holding to this effect was made in the course of reversing a District Court judgment that had dismissed the Commission's complaint for an injunction to restrain future violations of §5 by a Chinese benevolent association. The association had received some $600,000 from members of various Chinese communities in the Eastern states for the purpose of acquiring Chinese "Liberty Bonds." The association would deliver the money to the New York agency of the Bank of China, together with written applications for bonds by the respective purchasers, and the New York agency would transmit the funds to its branch in Hong Kong, which would return the bonds to the New York branch. Neither the association nor any of its members had ever received any compensation from any source. The motive was purely patriotic. A majority of the court nevertheless concluded:

> Whether the Chinese government as issuer authorized the solicitation, or merely availed itself of gratuitous and even unknown acts on the part of the defendant whereby written offers to buy, and the funds collected for payment, were transmitted to the Chinese banks does not affect the meaning of the statutory provisions which are quite explicit. In either case the solicitation was equally for the benefit of the Chinese government and broadly speaking was for the issuer in connection with the distribution of the bonds.[18]

5. Donees and Pledgees

The question whether a donee or pledgee may be an "underwriter" implicates both the "purchasing from" and the "selling for" parts of the definition. There have been registrations for secondary distributions effected by charitable donees of controlling persons. The theory, presumably, was that registration would have been required if the controlling person had himself distributed the shares

[17] Cf. American Gyro Co., 1 SEC 83, 93 (1935) (several stock salesmen engaged at 25 percent commission). A related question is whether an officer, director, or employee of the issuer selling its securities must be registered as a broker under the 1934 Act. See p. 606 infra.

[18] SEC v Chinese Consolidated Benevolent Assn., Inc., 120 F. 2d 738, 740 (2d Cir. 1941), *cert. denied,* 314 U. S. 618.

through an underwriter for cash and contributed the cash to a charitable institution — a procedure that would not have been nearly so favorable for him from the tax point of view. Even so, secondary distributions by controlling persons are exempted under §4(1) unless there is an "underwriter" in the picture. And one may question whether a court would agree that a charitable donee was a person that had "purchased from" or was "selling for" the controlling person within the meaning of §2(11).[19]

The case for finding an "underwriter" is stronger, for example, when securities are given to a university on condition that a building be named after the donor, or when the donee is a charitable foundation identified in name and purpose with the donor. The case for making a "sale" out of a charitable gift may also be a bit stronger when there was a prior pledge to make the gift, though there is undeniably a bootstrap quality about this approach. But apparently the Commission does not stop with either of these situations. It has referred publicly to a letter of Commission counsel stating that the answer "may be given only after consideration of all the relevant facts including the intents and purposes of the donor, any understandings or agreements between the donor and donee, and the needs and policies of the donee," and that, "As a general rule, registration may be required when a gift of securities is made by a control person under circumstances in which a redistribution to the public by the donee may reasonably be anticipated."[20]

The fact is that the charitable gift cases that have been registered so far have involved gifts requiring the immediate use of cash, for example, to build a library. But this test exalts account-juggling, in that the donee can simply use unrestricted funds or sell other securities out of its portfolio in order to finance the donor's project and hold the donor's securities for investment.

The donor, of course, may always condition his gift on the donee's holding for investment — though that may reduce its value for income tax purposes. Or the donee may avoid an "underwriter" status by reselling privately for investment — though, here again, unless the donor were to restrict his gift accordingly, he might be involved in a distribution by the donee as "underwriter" in accordance with the Commission's view, and any such restriction, again, would presumably diminish the value of the gift for tax purposes.

The case of a noncharitable donee — for example, a daughter of the controlling person who, in order to diversify her portfolio,

[19] See pp. 254-57 supra.

[20] Letter of Chief Counsel, Div. of Corp. Fin., Aug. 8, 1962, CCH Fed. Sec. L. Rep. ¶1551.60, cited in Sec. Act Rel. 4669 (1964) n. 5.

sells a substantial block of securities that she has received from her father as a wedding gift — is different still. On the one hand, the lack of any tax advantage to the donor weakens the Commission's case. But on the other hand, the family relationship makes it easier to say that the daughter is an "underwriter" in the sense that she is "selling for" her father.[21]

In the pledge context the question typically arises when a controlling person secures his own or the issuer's note by pledging stock that he holds. But the question may arise also when a lender takes a stock pledge from a noncontrolling person who is himself an underwriter. That, in fact is how the question arose in the leading case.[22] Unable to pay a past due stock-secured note, the borrower arranged with the bank to deposit as additional collateral a different stock that a subsidiary of his had just obtained. Within a few days the banks began a public sale of the most recently pledged stock. And the Commission got a §5 injunction on its traditional view that a pledgee could avoid underwriter status only if it was a *bona fide* pledgee now seeking to sell collateral it acquired in good faith to secure the debt.[23]

The Second Circuit affirmed on an altogether different basis:[24]

> The banks cannot be exempted on the ground that they did not "purchase" within the meaning of §2(11). The term, although not defined in the Act, should be interpreted in a manner complementary to "sale" which is defined in §2(3) as including "every * * * disposition of * * * a security or interest in a security for value * * * ." In fact, a proposed provision of the Act which expressly exempted sales "by or for the account of a pledge holder or mortgagee selling or offering for sale or delivery in the ordinary course of business and not for the purpose of avoiding the provisions of the Act, to liquidate a *bona fide* debt, a security pledged in good faith as collateral for such debt," was not accepted by Congress. S. 875, 73rd Cong., 1st Sess. (1933) §126. [Citation omitted.]
>
> * * *
>
> The banks have contended that they were "*bona fide* pledgees" and therefore "entitled upon default to sell the stock free of restrictions." They assume that "good faith" in accepting the stock is a

[21] Compare the charitable and noncharitable gift cases under §16(b) of the 1934 Act. See 2 Loss 1082-84.

[22] SEC v. Guild Films Co., Inc., 279 F. 2d 485 (2d Cir. 1960), *cert. denied* sub nom. Santa Monica Bank v. SEC, 364 U. S. 819.

[23] SEC v. Guild Films Co., Inc., 178 F. Supp. 418 (S. D. N. Y. 1959).

[24] 279 F. 2d at 489.

sufficient defense. See Loss, Securities Regulation, 346 (1951). But the statute does not impose such a "good faith" criterion. The exemption in §4(1) was intended to permit private sales of unregistered securities to investors who are likely to have, or who are likely to obtain, such information as is ordinarily disclosed in registration statements. See *S. E. C.* v. *Ralston Purina Co.*, 1953, 346 U. S. 119. The "good faith" of the banks is irrelevant to this purpose. It would be of little solace to purchasers of worthless stock to learn that the sellers had acted "in good faith." Regardless of good faith, the banks engaged in steps necessary to this public sale, and cannot be exempted.

Without imputing to the banks any participation in a preconceived scheme to use the pledge of these securities as a device for unlawful distribution, it may be noted that when the 50,000 shares of Guild Films stock were received on February 12, 1959, the banks knew that they had been given unregistered stock and that the issuer had specifically forbidden that the stock "be sold, transferred, pledged or hypothecated in the absence of an effective registration statement for the shares under the Securities Act of 1933 or an opinion of counsel to the company that registration is not required under said Act." Furthermore, from [pledgor's] prior unfulfilled promises, the banks should have known that immediate sale was almost inevitable if they were to recoup their loans from the security received.

(1) The first question in analyzing this case is whether *Rubin*[25] controls. That is to say, does *Rubin* decide either the question whether a pledge is a "sale" or the question whether a pledgee is an "underwriter" for purposes of §5? The §5 question may arise in a number of ways even though banks do not ordinarily make loans to companies that are collateralized by their own shares. For quite commonly the borrower does pledge the stock of a subsidiary in order to obtain funds for the operations of that subsidiary, or of the parent borrower itself or of some other subsidiary. Indeed, the borrower may borrow in order to *acquire* control of a company whose shares he pledges to secure the loan. Or the pledged shares may be controlled by a *guarantor* of the loan, as in the case where a bank makes a loan to a closely held corporation but asks for the personal guarantees of the owners and takes a pledge of the stock of the borrowing company in order to protect itself against a change in ownership.

(2) On the assumption that *Rubin* does not *govern* in these §5 contexts, it is still easier probably, under the language of §2(3), to say that a pledge involves a "sale" to the pledgee than that it does

[25] See p. 249 supra.

not.[26] Even so, is it not a *non sequitur* to say that the pledgee is an "underwriter" as having purchased "with a view to * * * distribution"? For it requires a forced reading of that phrase to say that a *bona fide* lender is calculating more on foreclosure than on repayment. So, if the pledgee is a purchaser but is *not* an underwriter, is not the §4(2) exemption available? And, if the pledgee *is* an "underwriter" *arguendo,* is not the pledge itself excluded from the definition of "sale" by the "preliminary negotiations" clause of §2(3)?

(3) On the other hand, even if the pledge itself is not a "sale" and the pledgee is not *ab initio* an "underwriter" for purposes of §5, is it not persuasive to argue that the pledgee does purchase *on foreclosure* and, if it forecloses "with a view to * * * distribution," becomes an "underwriter" at that time? Alternatively, can the foreclosing pledgee be brought under the "sells for" phrase in §2(11) because of its obligation to account to the pledgor for any amount by which the proceeds of the foreclosure sale exceed the debt; or does the "sells for" phrase contemplate more than that?

(4) What if the pledgor loses control of the issuer between date of pledge and date of foreclosure?

(5) Until *Guild Films* it had been generally considered that a *bona fide* pledge did not involve an "offer" or "sale" and that, in any event, a foreclosure sale by a *bona fide* pledgee of securities deposited as collateral by the issuer or a control affiliate was exempt under §4(1) unless the pledgee was himself in a control relationship with the issuer and also used an underwriter.[27] The Commission argued as appellee in that case that every pledgee did engage in a "pur-

[26] There is a series of 10b-5 cases so holding. See Kerbs v. Fall River Industries, Inc., 502 F. 2d 731, 739 (10th Cir. 1974); Mallis v. Federal Deposit Ins. Corp., 568 F. 2d 824, 828-30 (2d Cir. 1977), *cert. dismissed* sub nom. Bankers Trust Co. v. Mallis, 435 U. S. 381; Mansbach v. Prescott, Ball & Turben, 598 F. 2d 1017, 1029 (6th Cir. 1979); Chemical Bank v. Arthur Andersen & Co., 726 F. 2d 930, 939-45 (2d Cir. 1984), *cert. denied,* 469 U. S. 884 (notwithstanding the absence from §3(a)(14) of the phrase, "or interest in a security"). *Contra* (i. e., no sale): First National Bank of Commerce of Dallas v. All American Assurance Co., 583 F. 2d 1295 (5th Cir. 1978); Lincoln National Bank v. Herber, 604 F. 2d 1038 (7th Cir. 1979); cf. McClure v. First National Bank of Lubbock, Tex., 497 F. 2d 490 (5th Cir. 1974), *cert. denied,* 420 U. S. 930; Shelter Mutual Ins. Co. v. Public Water Supply District No. 7 of Jefferson County, Mo., 569 F. Supp. 310, 322-24 (E. D. Mo. 1983), *aff'd on other grounds,* 747 F. 2d 1195 (8th Cir. 1984). The first two *contra* cases preceded *Rubin.*

[27] See Throop and Lane, Some Problems of Exemption Under the Securities Act of 1933, 4 Law & Contemp. Prob. 89, 124 (1937). In A. D. M. Corp. v. Thomson, 707 F. 2d 25, 26-27 (1st Cir. 1983), *cert. denied,* 464 U. S. 938, the court referred to *Guild Films* as dictum, citing authorities both ways and letters not insisting on registration for resale. But it did not have to decide the question; for, even on the assumption that §5 applied, the court concluded that the Act did not automatically invalidate sales in violation of §5.

chase" within the meaning of §2(11), but that whether registration would be required for a *bona fide* foreclosure sale "is not the issue here, because clearly these are not the facts in the instant case."[28] If, therefore, the appellate court had affirmed on the lower court's reasoning to that effect, the case would have been of little consequence. Since the last paragraph of the appellate opinion did, in effect, agree that this was not a case of a *bona fide* pledge, can the rest of the opinion be regarded as dictum?[29]

(6) Why was the Second Circuit so eager to address itself to a question of great importance that was not at all necessary to the decision — a question that could not have been fully argued, with all its implications for the world of commercial banking, and that one cannot assume would have been decided the same way after a proper argument directed to the facts of an altogether different case? With great respect to those who joined in the opinion, would it not have been better if they had heeded the Supreme Court's admonition:

> Courts should avoid passing on questions of public law even short of constitutionality that are not immediately pressing. Many of the same reasons are present which impel them to abstain from adjudicating constitutional claims against a statute before it effectively and presently impinges on such claims.[30]

(7) The SEC for its part, although it had not requested the appellate court to go so far, eagerly clasped the entire opinion to its corporate bosom. "Although we believe, as the court below held, that registration would be required even if this had been an ordinary collateral situation," the Commission stated in its brief in opposition to the banks' unsuccessful petition for certiorari, "there can be no doubt that registration is required where the securities to be sold were actually transferred and taken with the specific intention that they be distributed in order to obtain repayment of the loan."[31] Was this statement fair to the Supreme Court, or was it an example of overzealous advocacy that came dangerously close

[28] Brief for SEC, pp. 16, 23. That is to say, a *bona fide* pledgee is a bank that "takes unregistered securities as collateral for a loan which the debtor plans to pay at maturity, and which the bank can reasonably expect will be so retired, but because of unforeseen and untoward circumstances the debtor is unable to pay, compelling the bank to resort to the collateral." Id. at 23.

[29] See Lincoln National Bank v. Herber, 604 F. 2d 1038 (7th Cir. 1979).

[30] Eccles v. Peoples Bank of Lakewood Village, Cal., 333 U. S. 426, 432 (1948).

[31] Brief for SEC in Opposition, pp. 7-8, Santa Monica Bank v. SEC, 364 U. S. 819 (1960).

to a half-truth in not indicating how recently the Commission had decided so to "believe"?

(8) What should a bank (or other lender) do to protect itself in view of both *Rubin* and *Guild Films?* The first answer that generally comes to mind, when the borrower is an issuer or control affiliate, is to obtain an immediate "shelf" registration, or the borrower's promise to use his best efforts to obtain registration if required, or both.[32] Even the former, however, requires an undertaking with the Commission to file a posteffective amendment to reflect any "fundamental change"; and a registration covenant is cold comfort at best when by hypothesis the lender will be dealing with a registrant that in the event of foreclosure will be probably hostile and possibly insolvent. Therein, indeed, lies the greatest danger of the *Guild Films* case — that borrowers may find it more difficult to finance by pledging the shares of controlled companies, registration covenants notwithstanding. But the person who does decide to lend should consider these protective measures for what they are worth. Moreover, although it might be argued that the pledgor's good faith is not so essential to the exemption as the pledgee's, it is understood to have been the administrative view for some period even before *Guild Films* that both parties must contemplate in good faith, when the loan is made, that it will be repaid. Consequently, the careful lender will also see to it (as he normally will quite apart from the Securities Act) that there is objective evidence of the borrower's probable ability to make repayment.

There are other devices that may be used either as alternatives or in addition to a registration covenant:

(a) The Uniform Commercial Code authorizes the disposition of collateral after default "by public or private proceedings" as long as "every aspect of the disposition including the method, manner, time, place and terms" are "commercially reasonable" and (unless the collateral is perishable "or threatens to decline speedily in value or is of a type customarily sold on a recognized market") the debtor is given "reasonable notification of the time * * * after which any

[32] See p. 136 supra. Rule 415(a)(1)(v) permits "shelf" registration for securities "pledged as collateral." Under either alternative, in order for the bank to protect itself against the possibility that the borrower may lose control otherwise than through a disposition of the pledged securities, an act that, of course, is under the bank's control, the borrower might be asked to get the appropriate promises from the issuer itself. Or, at the very least, the pledgor should agree, by way of minimizing the possibility of his loss of control, that he will not sell or pledge any of his unpledged holdings before discharging the loan; and any such agreement, in order to bind innocent buyers or pledgees of those holdings, should be accompanied by a legend on the shares restricting transferability.

private sale * * * is to be made."[33] Moreover, "The fact that a better price could have been obtained by a sale at a different time or in a different method from that selected by the secured party is not of itself sufficient to establish that the sale was not made in a commercially reasonable manner."[34] Indeed, the lender may ask the borrower to secure a "take out" or "pick up" letter from a satisfactory third party who will agree with the lender that upon the lender's demand or the pledgor's default he will either buy, or seek or secure somebody who will buy, the pledged securities for investment.[35]

(b) Since a private sale for investment is apt to entail a substantial discount below the market price, banks normally buttress the right of private sale by a specific provision in the loan agreement. Although §9-501(3) of the Uniform Commercial Code generally precludes waiver or variation of the Code's safeguards of the debtor's rights, it does permit the parties by agreement to "determine the standards by which the fulfillment of these rights and [the secured party's] duties is to be measured if such standards are not manifestly unreasonable."

(c) When the loan is collateralized by securities in addition to the "control" stock, the lender can simply liquidate the other collateral first and realize on the "control" stock only as a last resort. Here again, in order to avoid any question of the lender's right to determine which collateral to dispose of first, a suitable provision might be written into the loan agreement. The agreement might also reserve the lender's right to require the borrower to substitute collateral.

(d) The Commission permits a pledgee to sell "control" stock through a broker under the brokerage exemption in §4(4) as elucidated by Rule 144.[36] Once more, an agreement permitting the use of that procedure may prevent a later complaint by the debtor that a less restricted method of sale might have brought a higher price. Moreover, it may be well to obtain agreements by the controlling stockholders to file the reports necessary to activate Rule 144.

(e) Subject to a similar agreement, the pledgee might try to use

[33] §9-504(3).

[34] §9-507(2).

[35] See, e. g., Meadow Brook National Bank v. Levine, CCH Fed. Sec. L. Rep. ¶91,496 (N. Y. Sup. Ct. 1965). It has been said that "This is not a practical solution." Lehr, Some Securities Law Issues in Lending on Pledged Stock, 38 Bus. Law. 91, 119 n. 139 (1982).

[36] See pp. 352, 374 infra; Hueter, The Plight of the Pledgee Under Rule 144, 3 Sec. Reg. L. J. 111 (1975).

the intrastate exemption[37] rather than the private offering exemption in selling the security on foreclosure. But, insofar as the application of that exemption to secondary distributions by controlling persons is treated differently from its application to primary distributions,[38] a sale on foreclosure of a loan made to the *issuer* would probably be considered in the primary category on the theory that the lender (i) is an "underwriter" rather than a controlling person and (ii) is, under the law of pledge, selling for the issuer.

6. Participation in an Underwriting

The House report, after referring to the other portions of the "underwriter" definition, went on to say:

> The definition of underwriter is also broad enough to include two other groups of persons who perform functions, similar in character, in the distribution of a large issue. The first of these groups may be designated as the underwriters of the underwriter, a group who, for a commission, agree to take over pro rata the underwriting risk assumed by the first underwriter. The second group may be termed participants in the underwriting or outright purchase, who may or may not be formal parties to the underwriting contract, but who are given a certain share or interest therein.[39]

It seems quite clear, therefore, that the language of §2(11) is intended to cover the "old-fashioned underwriter."[40] Whether he is an underwriter only with respect to the amount sold, or also with respect to the unsold portion he takes down, is not clear; the former is understood to be the administrative construction if the portion taken down by the underwriter is held for investment. In any event, the Commission's Rule 142 has the effect of excluding an "old-fashioned underwriter" from the definition if his sole function in the distribution is confined to an undertaking entered into with one of the principal underwriters (*not with the issuer itself*) to purchase all or some specified proportion of the securities remaining unsold after the lapse of some specified period of time, and if he purchases those securities for investment. It is required also that he have no affiliation of any kind with any of the principal underwriters. The Commission's General Counsel has observed that this rule was "adopted in recognition of the value of secondary capital in facili-

[37] See c. 5C infra.
[38] See p. 300 infra.
[39] H. R. Rep. No. 85, 73d Cong., 1st Sess. (1933) 13.
[40] For a description of this type of underwriting, see p. 76 supra.

tating the flow of investment funds into industry, and of the fact that the owners of such secondary capital cannot practicably perform the duty of thorough investigation and analysis imposed by the Act on the underwriter proper." In emphasizing that the rule "in no way limits the responsibility of the underwriter who actually serves as a conduit for the distribution of securities to the public," this opinion points out that "Disproportionate commissions or service fees would raise a serious doubt whether the functions of the persons concerned were in fact confined as prescribed in the rule."[41]

Section 2(11), particularly the clause here marked [d], also extends beyond the "old-fashioned underwriter." The section was amended in conference "to make clear that a person merely furnishing an underwriter money to enable him to enter into an underwriting agreement is not an underwriter."[42] The report went on to say: "The test is one of participating in the underwriting undertaking rather than that of a mere interest in it." The Commission has accordingly applied the definition to a person appointed by the principal underwriter as "exclusive selling agent," as well as a person who by arrangement with the principal underwriters undertook to see that a daily print would be made on the stock exchange tape.[43] Presumably the definition applies likewise to a "sub-underwriter" whom the principal underwriters put in charge of the distribution in a particular area of the country. Certainly there is no requirement of privity of contract with the issuer (or a person in a control relationship with the issuer).[44] The "participation" test was not met, however, with respect to warrant holders who simply delivered their warrants to the underwriters, who exercised them and distributed the shares,[45] or with respect to stockholders (of four years' standing) whose shares were included in the underwriting agreement for shares to be issued by the company.[46]

The ordinary "finder" who receives a cash fee from either the issuer or the underwriter or both for bringing them together is not himself an underwriter if he does not otherwise participate in the

[41] Sec. Act Rel. 1862 (1938).

[42] H. R. Rep. No. 152, 73d Cong., 1st Sess. (1933) 24. But cf. Sweet's Steel Co., 4 SEC 589 (1939), supra p. 255 n. 7.

[43] Reiter-Foster Oil Corp., 6 SEC 1028, 1036-41 (1940).

[44] The Commission has found it convenient to refer in its registration forms to the "principal underwriter." That term is defined in Rule 405 to mean "an underwriter in privity of contract with the issuer * * * ."

[45] McFarland v. Memorex Corp., 493 F. Supp. 631, 644-47 (N. D. Cal. 1980).

[46] In re Activision Securities Litigation, 621 F. Supp. 415, 423 (N. D. Cal. 1985).

distribution.[47] On the other hand, "Whenever the finder is deemed to be an underwriter by reason of the receipt of securities for services, or otherwise, he should be identified as such in the prospectus."[48] But it does not follow that the receipt of securities for a finder's services will automatically make the finder an underwriter. He will not be an underwriter if he takes the securities for investment, although (1) the securities he receives should be included in the registration statement and (2) it will be more difficult for a finder *who is engaged in the securities business* to persuade the Commission on the eventual resale of his securities that he is not an underwriter despite his investment undertaking.[49]

7. The Usual and Customary Commission

The "usual and customary * * * commission" clause of §2(11) seeks to draw the line between "sub-underwriters" and ordinary selling group dealers. And Rule 141 settles most of the questions by providing that the term "commission" includes the remuneration, commonly known as a "spread," that is received by a dealer who buys and sells as *principal;* that the term "commission from an underwriter or dealer" includes any commission paid by an underwriter or dealer who is in a control relationship with the issuer;[50] that the "usual and customary" commission may not exceed the amount allowed to other persons for comparable services; and that a person *is* an underwriter, regardless of the amount of his com-

[47] South Umpqua Mining Co., 3 SEC 233, 241 (1938); Sec. Act Rel. 4936 (1968) par. 11.

[48] Ibid. In Republic Bank of Oklahoma City, 18 Sec. Reg. L. Rep. 1828 (1986), the "commercially reasonable" test persuaded the staff to grant a "no action" letter to permit a public sale of pledged shares on foreclosure under specified procedures designed to provide some assurance that a distribution would not occur: (1) the public notice of sale would state that the bank reserved the right to bid for and buy the shares; (2) they would be sold only as a block to a single buyer; (3) the buyer would represent that he was acquiring the shares for his own account and not with a view to resale; (4) the certificates would be legended to show that the stock was restricted; and (5) prospective purchasers would be provided access to certain financial information.

[49] It has been said under the California statute that, when a finder goes beyond bringing a buyer and seller together so that they may make their own contract without aid from him, any participation by him in the negotiations, however slight, will make him a "broker," who cannot recover a fee without registration as such. Evans v. Riverside Int'l Raceway, 237 Cal. App. 2d 666, 675-76, 47 Cal. Rptr. 187, 192 (1965).

[50] This makes it clear that the fact that the underwriter is an "issuer" within the meaning of the second sentence of §2(11) does not *per se* place any dealer receiving a commission from him in the "underwriter" category.

mission, if his function "is the management of the distribution of all or a substantial part of the particular issue" or if he "performs the functions normally performed by an underwriter or underwriting syndicate." Section 2(11) itself is specific that the commission may not be received from the issuer.

C. "DEALER" [§2(12)]

Two propositions are apparent on the face of the definition of "dealer" as "any person who engages either for all or part of his time, directly or indirectly, as agent, broker, or principal, in the business of offering, buying, selling, or otherwise dealing or trading in securities issued by another person":

(1) In contrast to the definition of "underwriter," this definition does depend on the person's general activities rather than his conduct in the particular offering. And it is settled in a variety of contexts, as has been said of §2(12), that the concept of "doing business" requires a degree of continuity — certainly more than an isolated transaction.[1]

(2) Although in common parlance a dealer is a principal and a broker is an agent, and although §4(4) exempts certain "brokers' transactions" without defining "broker," §2(12) defines "dealer" to include a "broker." This overeconomy of language was corrected for purposes of the 1934 Act, which separately defines the two terms in accordance with the English language.[2] "The sole object of this definition," the 1933 House report states, "is thus to subject brokers to the same advertising restrictions [and, it might have added, to the same prospectus delivery requirement pursuant to the dealers' exemption in the present §4(3)] that are imposed upon dealers, so as to prevent the broker from being used as a cloak for the sale of securities."[3]

The brokerage portion of the definition is broad enough to include an auctioneer who is regularly (although not necessarily exclusively) engaged in the business of auctioning securities. Moreover, although banks are specifically excluded from the 1934 Act definitions of "broker" and "dealer," they are not excluded from the definition in §2(12) of the 1933 Act. Presumably, therefore, the

C. 4C [1]deBrun v. Andromeda Broadcasting Systems, Inc., 465 F. Supp. 1276, 1279 (D. Nev. 1979).

[2]§§3(a)(4), 3(a)(5), discussed infra p. 604.

[3]H. R. Rep. No. 85, 73d Cong., 1st Sess. (1933) 14.

ordinary commercial bank, which under the federal banking laws can legally act as broker though not (except, basically, in governments and municipals) as dealer, is a "dealer" under the §2(12) definition,[4] and hence must deliver a prospectus in executing a customer's buy order that it has solicited (so that the exemption for unsolicited brokerage transactions in §4(4) is not available).[5] In a case in which the Commission censured a bank for aiding and abetting an illegal distribution by selling 20,000 shares of common stock for a customer through an account that it maintained with a New York Stock Exchange member firm, the Commission stated:

> In our opinion, if banks wish to maintain brokerage accounts for the convenience of their customers or others, it is incumbent upon them to take precautions to avoid the use of such accounts in connection with unlawful distributions of unregistered securities. * * * Generally speaking, it would seem that the bank would be expected to follow procedures substantially equivalent to those which we have required brokers-dealers to establish and maintain * * * . We would consider that, alternatively, a bank could meet its responsibilities by requesting the broker-dealer with which it maintains its account to conduct the necessary investigation of the circumstances surrounding a proposed securities transaction, of course with the full cooperation of the bank.[6]

[4] On the Glass-Steagall Act's separation of commercial and investment banking, see p. 219 n. 51 supra.

[5] Cf. Hyman v. Gregory & Sons, 44 Misc. 2d 102, 252 N. Y. S. 2d 919 (Sup. Ct. 1964), where the court applied the brokerage exemption to a bank executing an unsolicited buy order for a customer without considering whether the bank was a "dealer" in the first place.

[6] Southern Cal. First National Bank of San Diego, 44 SEC 652, 653-54 (1971).

CHAPTER 5

SECURITIES ACT EXEMPTIONS

A. GENERAL

The exemption in §3(a)(1) for offerings pending in 1933 has long since spent its force. The exemptions in §§3(a)(2), (3), (6), and (8), as well as §§4(1) and 4(3), have already been referred to.[1] And the exemptions in §§3(a)(4) and (5) for securities issued by certain eleemosynary institutions, savings and loan associations, and farmers' cooperatives, as well as the §4(5) exemption for certain first-lien notes, require no discussion here.[2] That leaves for consideration (the letters indicating subchapters) (B) the exchange and reorgani-

C. 5A [1]On §3(a)(2), see pp. 211-12, 214 n. 31, 216, 220 supra; p. 612 n. 43 infra; on §3(a)(3), see p. 165 n. 1 supra; on §3(a)(6), see c. 3I supra; on §3(a)(8), see pp. 203-04 supra; on §4(1), see p. 88 supra, p. 351 infra; on §4(3), see p. 116 supra.

[2]Section 3(a)(2) exempts securities issued or guaranteed by banks, and §3(a)(5) exempts securities issued by certain savings and loan associations. The 1984 Bush report recommended that all public issues of securities by banks and savings and loans should be subject to the registration requirements of the 1933 Act. Blueprint for Reform: The Report of the Task Force on Regulation of Financial Services (1984) 92-93.

In Rembold v. Pacific First Federal Savings Bank, 798 F. 2d 1307 (9th Cir. 1986), the court held that enactment of the judicial review provisions of the National Housing Act with respect to orders of the Federal Home Loan Bank Board did not affect a private securities fraud action by stockholders complaining of misrepresentations in a savings institution's required stock offering circular that followed FHLBB approval of a conversion plan.

"Bank" is defined in §3(a)(2) to mean "any national bank, or any banking institution organized under the laws of any State, territory, or the District of Columbia, the business of which is substantially confined to banking and is supervised by the State or territorial banking commission or similar official." The Commission has nevertheless taken the position that American branches and agencies of foreign banks are "functionally indistinguishable from their domestic counterparts" when they are "subject to domestic regulation by federal or state banking authorities that is substantially equivalent to that applied to domestic banks." Sec. Act Rel. 6661, 36 SEC Dock. 746, 747 (1986).

With respect to farmers' cooperatives, see Centner, Retained Equities of Agricultural Cooperatives and the Federal Securities Acts, 31 U. Kan. L. Rev. 245 (1983). With respect to §4(5), see p. 664 infra.

zation exemptions in §§3(a)(7), (9), and (10) and the bankruptcy statute, (C) the intrastate exemption in §3(a)(11), (D) the exemptions for "small" issues in §4(6) and the rules under §§3(b) and 3(c), (E) the nonpublic offering exemption in §4(2), and (F) the brokers' exemption in §4(4). But first a number of general observations:

1. Exempted Securities Versus Exempted Transactions

A moment's glance at §§3 and 4 will reveal that the dichotomy between the "exempted securities" and the "exempted transactions" was not carefully considered. The exemptions in §§3(a)(2) to 3(a)(8) are genuine security exemptions. But there is nothing peculiar about the securities, or the issuers of the securities, that are exempted under §§3(a)(1), 3(a)(9)-(11), 3(b), and to some extent 3(c). All those exemptions were created because (or in the case of §3(c) partly because) of the circumstances surrounding the particular offering.

The fact is that the present 3(a)(9) and 3(a)(10) exemptions were originally §4(3) and that the present 3(a)(11) exemption was originally §5(c). It was essentially a legislative accident that placed these exemptions among the "exempted securities" in the 1934 amendments. The express purpose of the shift was merely to codify the Federal Trade Commission's previous interpretation[3] that, when the issuer was excused from registration under §4(3) or §5(c), dealers could trade immediately notwithstanding the nonapplicability of the dealers' exemption in the then §4(1) (now §4(3) as renumbered in 1964, which is not to be confused with the original §4(3) of 1933-34 vintage) to transactions within "one year [now forty days] after the first date upon which the security was *bona fide* offered to the public."[4] As sometimes happens when statutes are amended, the attempt to solve one problem created another that was even more serious — namely, the anomaly of having several transaction exemptions included among the security exemptions. What should have been done, of course, was to amend the *dealers'* exemption to make it clear that the nonexempt period applies only when the particular issue is subject to the registration requirement.[5]

It is not simply a matter of statutory neatness. If these few sec-

[3] Sec. Act Rel. 97, part 7 (1933).
[4] H. R. Rep. No. 1838, 73d Cong., 2d Sess. (1934) 40.
[5] See Code §512(2).

tions are to be read literally as exempting the securities themselves, presumably a control affiliate's distribution of securities previously issued under one of these exemptions (or a redistribution after a reacquisition by the issuer) would itself be exempt. On the basis of the legislative history the Commission's General Counsel early took the position that a secondary distribution would not be exempt, because §§3(a)(9), 3(a)(10), and 3(a)(11) were in substance transaction exemptions.[6] Later this view was formally adopted by the Commission itself.[7]

2. Fraud Provisions

None of the exemptions in either §3 or §4 extends to the fraud provisions of §17 or the provision in §12(2) creating civil liability for the sale of securities by misleading statements or omissions.[8] There is one exception to this statement: §12(2) is by its terms inapplicable to the governmental, bank, and other securities exempted under §3(a)(2), not to mention the fraud provisions of the 1934 Act.[9] But even those securities are subject to §17. In other words, it is unlawful for any person to employ a fraudulent scheme in the sale of even a United States Government bond by use of the mails or any facilities of interstate commerce. This conclusion, of course, is subject to whatever may be the general law with respect to (1) presumption of substantive inapplicability of statutes to the Government itself and (2) sovereign immunity of the Government and its agents.[10]

[6] Op. Gen. Counsel, Sec. Act Rel. 646 (1936).

[7] Thompson Ross Securities Co., 6 SEC 1111, 1117-18 (1940); Sec. Act Rel. 4434 (1961) (§3(a)(11)); Gearhart & Otis, Inc., 42 SEC 1, 27 (1964), *aff'd* sub nom. Gearhart & Otis, Inc. v. SEC, 348 F. 2d 798 (D. C. Cir. 1965) (§§3(a)(1), 3(b)).

[8] §17(c) and introductory clauses of §§3(a) and 4. In United States v. Naftalin, 441 U. S. 768, 777-78 (1979), the Court held that §17(a) "was intended to cover any fraudulent scheme in an offer or sale of securities, whether in the course of an initial distribution or in the course of ordinary market trading."

[9] Harmsen v. Smith, 693 F. 2d 932, 939-40 (9th Cir. 1982), *cert. denied,* 464 U. S. 822.

[10] All the statutes *except* the 1933 Act and its first cousin, the 1939 Act, codify the first proposition. Sec. Ex. Act §3(c); Holding Co. Act §2(c); Inv. Co. Act §2(b); Inv. Adv. Act §202(b). On both propositions, see Code §304 and cases cited in the comment. On the question whether municipalities (or states) and their agents can be reached under the fraud provisions — from the point of view of the Tenth and Eleventh Amendments as well as statutory construction and both legislative and official immunity — see the discussion in In re Washington Public Power System Securities Litigation, 623 F. Supp. 1466, 1476-83 (W. D. Wash. 1985). The definition of "person" in §3(a)(9) of the 1934 Act

3. Burden of Proof

In 1938 the Ninth Circuit said of the private offering exemption that "the terms of such an exception to the 'general policy' of the act must be 'strictly construed' against the claimant of its benefit."[11] This was before the *Joiner* case.[12] Whether or not the injunction of the Supreme Court to look to statutory context rather than maxims of construction applies to this statement of the Ninth Circuit, the more important holding of the Court of Appeals — since repeated by the Supreme Court itself in the context of the same exemption — was that the burden of proving an exemption is on the person who claims it.[13] That is the generally accepted view under the blue sky laws as well.[14] By the same token, the burden of pleading the exemption is also upon the defendant; it is not necessary to negative all the statutory exemptions in an indictment or any other initial pleading.[15]

All this seems reasonable and fair enough as applied to genuine exemptions like those for bank securities, short-term commercial paper, and so on. The defendant has the burden simply of going forward with evidence of his pleaded exemption. The plaintiff retains the ultimate burden of proof by a preponderance of the evidence or, in a criminal case, beyond a reasonable doubt.[16] But

---

was extended in 1975 to include governments. This was held to create a right of action against the municipal defendants so far as the statute is concerned.

[11] SEC v. Sunbeam Gold Mines Co., 95 F. 2d 699, 701 (9th Cir. 1938); see also, e. g., Hill York Corp. v. American Int'l Franchises, Inc., 448 F. 2d 680, 691-92 (5th Cir. 1971); Quinn & Co. v. SEC, 452 F. 2d 943, 945-46 (10th Cir. 1971), *cert. denied*, 406 U. S. 957.

[12] SEC v. C. M. Joiner Leasing Corp., 320 U. S. 344, 350-51 (1943), supra p. 178.

[13] SEC v. Ralston Purina Co., 346 U. S. 119, 126 (1953); see also FTC v. Morton Salt Co., 334 U. S. 37, 44-45 (1948) (a "general rule of statutory construction"). In Whitehall Corp., 38 SEC 259, 268-70 (1958), the Commission carried this rule to the point of finding a violation *without any evidence of offers to nonresidents* simply because the respondent had not sustained the burden of proving that the offers represented by certain interim certificates had been restricted to residents.

[14] E. g., Commonwealth v. David, 365 Mass. 47, 53-54, 309 N. E. 2d 484, 488 (1974); Brown v. Cole, 155 Tex. 624, 634, 291 S. W. 2d 704, 711 (1956). The Uniform Securities Act codifies the rule. §402(d); see People v. Dempster, 396 Mich. 700, 242 N. W. 2d 381 (1976), infra n. 16 (not an unconstitutional burden); cf. State v. Fairchild, 298 S. E. 2d 110 (W. Va. 1982).

[15] Edwards v. United States, 312 U. S. 473 (1941).

[16] In People v. Dempster, 396 Mich. 700, 242 N. W. 2d 381 (1976), the court so construed §402(d) of the Uniform Securities Act: "* * * once the state establishes a prima facie case of statutory violation, the burden of going forward, i. e., of injecting some competent evidence of the exempt status of the securities, shifts to the defendant. However, once the defendant properly injects the issue,

suppose, for example, that the question is whether the defendant was a controlling person of the issuer within the meaning of §2(11). Even in a civil action under §12(1), and *a fortiori* in a criminal prosecution, it might still be argued that, when a statute is drafted with a universal prohibition like §5 and a §4(1) type of "exemption" that looks in turn to the last sentence of §2(11), to permit the plaintiff to prove merely a sale of an unregistered security to him by use of the mails and to shift to the defendant the burden of proving lack of control are so far at odds with the usual burden of proof that Congress would have been more specific if it had intended such a departure. So, too, with respect to the nonpublic offering exemption in §4(2). The exemptions altogether, including §§4(1)-(4), probably cover more than 99 percent of all transactions in securities. In short, they are not really exemptions at all but simply "a drafting technique used to extract, from the overall universe of sales, that small segment which is in fact subject to registration."[17]

Admittedly the line between genuine and formal exemptions for purposes of assigning the burden of going forward (and presumably of pleading) would not be easy to draw. In the criminal law generally the Supreme Court held in 1975 that the Maine rule that required a homicide defendant to prove that he had acted in the heat of passion or with sudden provocation in order to avoid a mandatory life sentence for murder violated the due process requirement that the prosecution prove beyond a reasonable doubt every fact necessary to constitute the crime charged.[18] Then two years later the Court distinguished the 1975 case, stating: "To recognize at all a mitigating circumstance does not require the State to prove its nonexistence in each case in which the fact is put in issue, if in its judgment this would be too cumbersome, too expensive, and too inaccurate."[19] The securities cases, state and federal, reflect this perplexity.[20]

---

the State is obliged to establish the contrary beyond a reasonable doubt." 396 Mich. at 714, 242 N. W. 2d at 388. The *David* case, supra p. 274 n. 14, is to the same effect apart from the Uniform Act. See also People v. Figueroa, 41 Cal. 3d 714, 720-21, 715 P. 2d 680, 684-85 (1986).

[17] Section 4(2) and Statutory Law: A Position Paper of the Federal Regulation of Securities Committee, Section of Corporation, Banking and Business Law of the American Bar Association, 31 Bus. Law. 485, 503 (1975). Substantially this entire paper is set out infra p. 328; see esp. pp. 346-47 infra.

[18] Mullaney v. Wilbur, 421 U. S. 684 (1975).

[19] Patterson v. New York, 432 U. S. 197, 209 (1977).

[20] In United States *ex rel.* Shott v. Tehan, 365 F. 2d 191, 194 (6th Cir. 1966), *cert. denied,* 385 U. S. 1012, a *habeas corpus* proceeding by a lawyer who had been convicted in Ohio of failing to register a single promissory note as well as

B. EXCHANGES AND REORGANIZATIONS

1. Voluntary Exchanges [§3(a)(9)]

Section 3(a)(9) exempts "Any security exchanged by the issuer with its existing security holders exclusively where no commission or other remuneration is paid or given directly or indirectly for soliciting such exchange." The philosophy of this exemption is not altogether easy to understand in view of the skepticism that the legislative history reflects concerning voluntary reorganizations. The following rather weak explanation in the conference report indicates that the exemption may represent little more than a horse-trade compromise between the two houses:

> The House provision * * * exempting * * * the sale of stock to stockholders is omitted from the substitute * * * . Sales of stock to stockholders become subject to the act unless the stockholders are so small in number that the sale to them does not constitute a public offering. The Senate agreed that the mere exchange with its security holders of one form of security for another by an issuer where no commission or other remuneration is paid, shall be exempt. This exemption is considered necessary to permit certain voluntary readjustment of obligations. Inasmuch as any exchange that involves the payment of a commission of any sort is not exempt, there is no danger of the provision being used for purposes of evasion.[1]

In any event, the exemption is quite narrow: (a) The issuer of both securities must be the same. (b) Under the administrative construction no part of the offering may be made to persons other

---

failing to register as a dealer in that connection, the court held that shifting the burden of proving an exemption for notes "not offered * * * for sale to the public" was "not unreasonable, nor does it offend any principle of justice, nor does it constitute a denial of due process of law." See also United States v. Abrams, 29 F. R. D. 178, 181 (S. D. N. Y. 1961), *convictions aff'd*, 357 F. 2d 539 (2d Cir. 1966), *cert. denied*, 384 U. S. 1001; Pennaluna & Co., Inc. v. SEC, 410 F. 2d 861, 865 (9th Cir. 1968), *cert. denied*, 396 U. S. 1007. *Contrast* United States v. Re, 336 F. 2d 306, 317 (2d Cir. 1964), *cert. denied*, 379 U. S. 904 (conviction on §5 count *rev'd* for failure to prove that controlling person was source of shares sold); United States v. Prince, 496 F. 2d 1289, 1291 (5th Cir. 1974), *cert. denied*, 419 U. S. 1107 (court stated without comment that lower court had granted one defendant's post-conviction motion for a judgment of acquittal because prosecution had failed to prove that the stock was not exempt); Gaskin v. State, 248 Ark. 168, 179, 450 S. W. 2d 557, 563 (1970); State v. Goetz, 312 N. W. 2d 1 (N. D. 1981), *cert. denied* sub nom. Goetz v. North Dakota, 455 U. S. 924 (eight personal notes); State v. Frost, 57 Ohio St. 2d 121, 387 N. E. 2d 235 (1979).

C. 5B [1]H. R. Rep. No. 152, 73d Cong., 1st Sess. (1933) 25.

than existing security holders or even to existing security holders other than by way of exchange. (c) There may be no paid solicitation.

a. Identity of the Issuer

The reference to exchanges "by the issuer with its existing security holders" precludes application of the exemption in such instances as when a parent offers its securities in exchange for those of a subsidiary or vice versa, or when a successor corporation offers its securities in exchange for those of a predecessor, or when certificates of deposits are issued by a committee in exchange for the securities deposited, or when the securities of a successor corporation are issued in exchange for certificates of deposit representing securities of a predecessor corporation, or when voting-trust certificates are issued in exchange for the securities that are placed in trust. In all these cases the issuer of the security being "sold" is different from the issuer of the security being received in exchange.

Changes in the composition of a committee that has issued certificates of deposit or in the trustees under a voting trust would not seem to result in a change of identity of the "issuer" if effected in accordance with the provisions of the deposit agreement or the trust instrument. This would seem to be equally true with respect to the renewal of a voting trust pursuant to a provision in the original trust instrument.[2] On the other hand, when the original trust instrument contains no renewal provision or when none is permitted by the local law, solicitation of the holders of the expiring voting-trust certificates to deposit their underlying securities in a new trust requires registration because the new trust is a different "issuer" from the old.[3]

b. Exclusively in Exchange

It is not clear from the position of the word "exclusively" whether it modifies "exchanged" or the phrase "with its existing security holders." The Commission has made the word do double duty.

[2] Some corporation statutes expressly provide for a renewal of the term. E. g., Del. Gen. Corp. Law, Del. Code, Tit. 8, §218(b); N. Y. Bus. Corp. L. §621(d).

[3] Reserve Life Ins. Co. v. Provident Life Ins. Co., 499 F. 2d 715, 722 (8th Cir. 1974), *cert. denied*, 419 U. S. 1107.

Under its construction — which seems as logical as any, and as much as an exemption of such parenthood deserves — the exemption is lost if existing security holders of the issuer are asked to give up anything in addition to their old securities *or* if any part of the new offering is made (whatever the consideration) to persons other than the issuer's security holders.

So far as the first of these conditions is concerned, the Commission has two interpretative rules. One defines the term "exchanged" so that the issuer may require the surrender of the outstanding securities "to be accompanied by such payment in cash by the security holder as may be necessary to effect an equitable adjustment, in respect of dividends or interest paid or payable on the securities involved in the exchange, as between such security holder and other security holders of the same class accepting the offer or exchange."[4] The other, in substance, permits the *issuer* to make payments to its security holders in connection with an exchange; in other words, although anything of value (other than the old securities) coming from the *security holders* will destroy the exemption, except as permitted by the first of these two rules, the payment of cash by the *issuer* will not.[5]

Query: Are the securities issued in "exchange" when the consideration is the waiver of unpaid interest coupons? Should a distinction be drawn between unpaid interest coupons — which, if severed from the bonds and assigned by the bondholders, would presumably be considered "evidences of indebtedness" and hence securities in their own right for purposes of applying the fraud provisions — and unpaid interest not evidenced by coupons? Are accrued but unpaid dividends on preferred stock, or cash dividends declared on preferred or common, different? Undeclared dividends, even though accrued and cumulative, are not a debt.

So far as the second condition is concerned — that the offering be made exclusively to existing security holders — there is no requirement that it be made to all members of a given class of holders. On the other hand, when part of an issue is offered in exchange with existing security holders and the rest, say, is offered for cash to a sufficiently small number of nonholders and in such a way that that part considered alone would not involve a public offering, the 3(a)(9) exemption is considered to be destroyed. Inherent in this proposition are two questions:

First, what is an "issue" of securities? The term "issue," which is

[4] Rule 149.
[5] Rule 150.

read into §3(a)(9) by interpretation of the word "exclusively," is explicit in two other exemptions that will be examined shortly.[6] It is a word that is widely used in the financial world without much attention to its precise meaning. It used to be the Commission's general approach that a difference *either* between classes[7] *or* between plans of financing in time and circumstances[8] resulted in a separate "issue" so long as in either event the difference was substantial.[9] For example, if new Series B bonds were offered in exchange for outstanding Series A bonds, and new Series C bonds differing substantially from the Series B were sold to a few insurance companies in order to raise the funds necessary to redeem those Series A bonds whose holders did not accept the exchange offer, the Series B would be exempted under §3(a)(9) and the Series C as a private offering under §4(2). Again, so far as different segments of the *same* class are concerned, the Commission put it this way in discussing one of the other exemptions that expressly involves the "issue" concept:

> The determination whether securities are being offered as part of a single "issue" will depend upon a consideration of various factors concerning the methods of sale and distribution employed to effect the offerings and the disposition of the proceeds. If the offerings may be segregated into separate blocks, as evidenced by material differences in the use of the proceeds, in the manner and terms of distribution, and in similar related details, each offering will be a separate "issue." In the main, of course, each case must be determined upon the basis of its own facts.[10]

More recently the Commission has taken the position that a genuine difference in *class* is not conclusive but merely one factor to be considered.[11] In any event, two batches of securities without substantial differences are considered a single "issue": to use SEC jargon, they are "integrated."[12]

[6] §§3(a)(11), 3(b), infra cc. 5C, 5D.

[7] Op. General Counsel, Sec. Act Rel. 2029 (1939). Cf. the definition of "class" in Sec. Ex. Act §§12(g)(5) and 15(d) as including "all securities of an issuer which are of substantially similar character and the holders of which enjoy substantially similar rights and privileges."

[8] Unity Gold Corp., 3 SEC 618 (1938); see also Sec. Act Rel. 4434 (1961) (§3(a)(11)).

[9] Hillsborough Investment Corp. v. SEC, 276 F. 2d 665 (1st Cir. 1960); SEC v. Murphy, 626 F. 2d 633, 645 (9th Cir. 1980).

[10] Unity Gold Corp., 3 SEC 618, 625 (1938); see also Currie v. Cayman Resources Corp., 595 F. Supp. 1364, 1376-77 (N. D. Ga. 1984).

[11] The Commission has so read Sec. Act Rel. 4552 (1962). See Sec. Act Rel. 6274, 21 SEC Dock. 1013, 1020 (1980); Prelim. Note 3 to Rule 146.

[12] E. g., Doran v. Petroleum Management Corp., 545 F. 2d 893, 901 n. 9 (5th Cir. 1977) ("participants" and "special participants" in limited partnership);

Secondly, on the assumption that there is a single issue (that is, a single *class* of securities being offered in a single *plan of financing*), under what circumstances may different exemptions be combined? The answer to this question depends on which exemptions are being considered. Naturally both of the exemptions that are sought to be combined must be capable of combination if registration is to be avoided. So far as §3(a)(9) is concerned, it is not capable of combination with any other exemption, as we have seen.

Another problem under this branch of the 3(a)(9) exemption is created by the provision in §2(3) to the effect that the issuance of a security pursuant to a delayed conversion privilege is not a "sale" until the privilege is exercised. In such a case, clearly, the 3(a)(9) exemption is available for the future conversions. On the other hand, when a company issues preferred stock *immediately* convertible into common (regardless of the practicability of immediate conversion from the point of view of market prices), there is a present "offer" of the common. What, then, is the status of the common under §3(a)(9)? In a sense, the consideration given for the common is simply the preferred stock. On the other hand, when a purchaser pays $100 for a share of convertible preferred that he immediately converts into common, it does not seem altogether realistic to consider that he did not have his eye in part on the common when he parted with his money. The administrative construction has gone from one extreme to the other and has now come pretty solidly to rest in the middle. The Federal Trade Commission required immediate registration of both securities, even to insisting on a double registration fee. Then for a while SEC counsel followed the view that the exemption was available notwithstanding immediate convertibility. But for many years the Commission has required registration of the common along with the preferred on the ground that the *initial offer* (in the common law sense) is not an exchange transaction, while regarding the actual *sale* (in that sense) as exempt. In other words, although §3(a)(9) is not considered to exempt the initial offer of the common stock from the *registration* provisions of

---

see Morrissey, Integration of Securities Offerings — the ABA's "Indiscreet" Proposal, 26 Ariz. L. Rev. 41 (1984). In the context of the increased use of limited partnerships as financing vehicles, see Integration of Partnership Offerings: A Proposal for Identifying a Discrete Offering, 37 Bus. Law. 1591 (1982) (position paper of an ABA committee). For a proposal that the Commission recognize by rule that "the time clearly has come for a complete reformulation of the integration doctrine," see Am. B. Assn. Committee on Federal Regulation of Securities, Integration of Securities Offerings: Report of the Task Force on Integration, 41 Bus. Law. 595 (1986).

The staff is understood to consider the integration formula that governs the intrastate, small issue, and private offering exemptions (see Rule 147(b)(2), infra pp. 296-98, and Rule 502(a), infra pp. 313-14) in other contexts as well.

§§5(a) and 5(c), it is considered to exempt its actual issuance from the *prospectus* provisions of §5(b). More than that, the exemption extends also to the *continuing* offer of the common inherent in the convertible securities once they have all been issued, so that it is not necessary for the issuer to use a series of nine-month prospectuses under §10(a)(3) as long as the convertible security is outstanding.

Query: Suppose the issuer offers common stock to the public for cash at the same time that it is offering preferred immediately convertible into common. Or suppose an offering of common by way of conversion is outstanding when additional common is offered for cash. Does the cash offering of the common automatically destroy the §3(a)(9) exemption for the issuance of the common upon conversion?

c. Nonpayment of Remuneration for Soliciting Exchanges

The problems that arise with respect to this final condition of the §3(a)(9) exemption are somewhat simpler. The predecessor exemption in the original Act had prohibited the payment of remuneration "in connection with such exchange" rather than "for soliciting such exchange." The latter language was substituted in the 1934 amendments in order to codify the Federal Trade Commission's interpretation that fees paid, for example, to lawyers or accountants or printers did not destroy the exemption.

The exemption will still be destroyed, however, when any remuneration is paid "directly or indirectly" for soliciting exchanges. This presumably covers remuneration received by the solicitors from sources other than the issuer, whether directors, officers, employees, or outsiders. The question whether the issuer's employees or officers or directors may solicit is much the same as whether they are "underwriters."[13]

Query:

(1) Does the condition with respect to the absence of remuneration preclude the issuer's using paid solicitors to obtain the security holders' *authorization* of the new issue that is then offered to them by way of exchange?[14]

(2) Not infrequently an issuer forces conversions by calling the convertible security for redemption and seeks to protect its cash

[13] See pp. 256-57 supra.
[14] Cf. p. 99 supra.

position, in the event of an unfavorable market break that could cause many shareholders to let their shares be redeemed, by retaining one or more investment bankers to buy the convertible security at a fraction over the call price, convert, and distribute the underlying security. Is this activity precluded by §3(a)(9)?

d. The Exemption in General

(i) *When-issued trading:* So far as when-issued trading in the contemplated securities is concerned, the Commission has interposed no objection, presumably on the theory that the dealers' exemption under §4(3) is available when the ultimate issuance will be exempt under §3(a)(9).[15] On the other hand, it is clear that the dealers' exemption is not available for when-issued trading in advance of an offering that is subject to the registration requirement, since it would be a form of "beating the gun." Consequently, the dealer who offers or sells a security on a when-issued basis in contemplation of an offering under §3(a)(9) is at the mercy of the issuer's failing to comply with all the conditions of the exemption, as well as the issuer's changing its plans and registering the securities after all. Either of these eventualities would put the dealer in the position of having retroactively violated §5, with a consequent contingent liability to his buyers under §12(1) even if the Commission should take no action against him.[16]

[15] See Loss and Vernon, When-Issued Securities Trading in Law and Practice, 54 Yale L. J. 741, 782-86 (1945).

[16] Certain dealers actually found themselves in this predicament in connection with a Brazilian debt refunding in 1944. The Brazilian Government had five series of bond issues outstanding and various political subdivisions had twenty-five series. According to a plan of readjustment that was originally proposed, the federal government was to issue five series of new bonds in exchange for the five old series of its own bonds, and the bonds of the political subdivisions were to be refunded by new bonds that were to be issued by those subdivisions and guaranteed by the federal government. The refunding of the federal bonds was entitled to an exemption under §3(a)(9), but a registration statement was filed to cover the federal guarantee of the subdivisions' twenty-five series. After a substantial amount of when-issued trading had occurred in the new federal bonds that it was thought would be exempted under §3(a)(9), the registration statement was amended to reflect a radical change in the plan of readjustment: the federal government offered thirty new series of its own bonds in exchange for all the outstanding series. Since there was to be a single new federal issue, part of which was to be exchanged with persons other than existing security holders of the federal government, there could be no 3(a)(9) exemption for any part of the new bonds, and a serious question arose as to the status of outstanding when-issued contracts. In view of the fact that the trading had occurred in good faith in reliance on the original plan, the Commission did not interfere with the

(ii) *The requirement of good faith:* It goes without saying that "Section 3(a)(9) is applicable only to exchanges which are *bona fide,* in the sense that they are not effected merely as a step in a plan to evade the registration requirements of the Act." This view was early expressed by the Commission's General Counsel in an opinion in which he stated that the determination of the *bona fides* of the exchange would depend on

> factors such as the length of time during which the securities received by the issuer were outstanding prior to their surrender in exchange, the number of holders of the securities originally outstanding, the marketability of such securities, and also the question whether the exchange is one which was dictated by financial considerations of the issuer and not primarily in order to enable one or a few security holders to distribute their holdings to the public.[17]

(iii) *Code treatment:* The Code rationalizes the 3(a)(9) exemption in both directions by (A) limiting it to securities of "one-year registrants" and (B) in that area deleting the exclusivity requirement with respect to nonconversion exchanges and opening the exemption to securities issued on the exercise of warrants as well as conversions so long as there is no paid solicitation.[18] As a substitute for the delivery of a prospectus on exercise, holders of warrants and convertible securities will receive whatever reports the Commission requires to be sent.[19]

2. Judicially or Administratively Approved Exchanges [§§3(a)(7), 3(a)(10), and 11 U. S. C. §§364(f), 1125(e), 1145]

Until October 1, 1979, §3(a)(10) and the exemptions in §§264, 393, and 518 of Chapters X-XII of the old Bankruptcy Act substantially overlapped, as §77(f) of that Act, the exemption for "reorganization rails," substantially overlapped §3(a)(6) of the 1933 Act. But the Bankruptcy Reform Act as it is popularly called — it is officially Title 11 of the United States Code — repealed §77 and Chapters X-XII in favor of a single new chapter on reorganization,

---

consummation of the contracts. N. Y. Herald Tribune, May 27, 1944, p. 17, col. 6; N. Y. Times, July 3, 1944, p. 18, col. 6. No opinion was expressed, however, on the legality of these contracts; the buyers were left to whatever civil remedies they might have.

[17] Op. Gen. Counsel, Sec. Act Rel. 646 (1936).

[18] §512(7)-(8).

[19] §§602(a)(2), 602(e).

Chapter 11. And in the process Congress amended §3(a)(10) (and also §3(a)(9)) to exclude from the exemption "a security exchanged in a case under Title 11." This codified the Commission's lately developed view (of dubious merit) under the pre-1979 version of §§3(a)(9) and 3(a)(10).

Otherwise §3(a)(10) embodies none of the restrictions that surround the 3(a)(9) exemption. There is no requirement of identity of the issuers. The new securities may be issued in exchange for claims or property interests as well as outstanding securities; indeed, the consideration may *in part* be cash.[20] Although the exemption does not apply to the issuance of securities *entirely* for cash, there is nothing in its language to prevent combining it with another exemption (if one can be found that does not itself suffer from a marital disability). Finally, the 3(a)(10) exemption is not destroyed by the payment of remuneration for soliciting exchanges.

Section 3(a)(10), on the other hand, does have peculiar conditions and raises peculiar problems of its own:

(a) The syntax requires the construction that a *state* governmental authority must be *expressly* authorized by law to approve not only the terms and conditions of the exchange but also their *fairness.*[21] This is not so with respect to a court or a *federal* official or agency. But the court or the federal official or agency must still hold the requisite hearing on the fairness of the terms and conditions and presumably have jurisdiction to do so.[22] And there is implicit in the language of §3(a)(10) a requirement of adequate notice to all persons to whom it is proposed to issue securities.[23]

(b) The exemption does not apply to the issuance of certificates of deposit unless the court or agency expressly approves the terms and conditions of their issuance after the same type of hearing that is specified for any other securities that are to be exempted. The

[20] *Query:* Does a judicial or quasi-judicial determination of the issuer's insolvency render its stock valueless so as to destroy the exemption for new securities issued in consideration of the shares and cash?

[21] Op. Gen. Counsel, Sec. Act Rel. 312 (1935). Although it is a corollary of this position that the approving authority must be expressly authorized to hold the hearing, it is unnecessary that the hearing be mandatory under the applicable state law. Ibid. All this applies equally to state bank and insurance authorities. Institutional Corp. of America, CCH Fed. Sec. L. Rep. ¶78,133 (letter 1971).

[22] Op. Gen. Counsel, Sec. Act Rel. 312 (1935).

[23] Ibid.

courts on occasion have held such hearings so that deposits might be solicited by committees under the exemption.[24]

(c) Just as it is unlawful to offer securities on condition of their future registration, it is the Commission's position that there may be no solicitation of exchanges in advance of the approval that is expected under §3(a)(10).[25] This statement must be qualified, however, to the extent that the particular statute or procedure governing the hearing requires tentative indications of approval of a plan by security holders before the court or authority will give its approval. Otherwise the operation of §3(a)(10) would be stymied. In such cases even formal receipts or certificates of deposit are unobjectionable if their legal effect is equivalent solely to the requisite indication of approval.[26]

The new bankruptcy statute, effective October 1, 1979, contains three relevant sections. Since they are fairly complex and are yet to be widely construed, they will be set out in full text with the technical amendments enacted in 1984[27] and explanatory comments in the footnotes:[28]

[24] In re Saenger Theatres, Inc., CCH Bktcy. L. Rep. ¶308 (E. D. La. 1934). Any "court" will do; it may even be foreign. And the matter *sub judice* need not be a reorganization. It may be a judicially approved settlement of a class or derivative action. See Ash, Reorganizations and Other Exchanges Under Section 3(a)(10) of the Securities Act of 1933, 75 Nw. U. L. Rev. 1, 37-40 (1980). For the first use of §3(a)(10) in settling an action brought by the SEC itself, see SEC v. Blinder, Robinson & Co., Inc., 511 F. Supp. 799 (D. Colo. 1981); for a discussion of the "fairness" criteria there applied, see Glanzer, Schiffman, and Packman, Settlement of Securities Litigation Through the Issuance of Securities Without Registration: The Use of Section 3(a)(10) in SEC Enforcement Proceedings, 50 Ford. L. Rev. 533 (1982).

SEC administrative action under the Holding Company Act may also do the trick. Utah Power & Light Co., Holding Co. Act Rel. 13,748 (1958) 10 n. 7; Holding Co. Act Rel. 16,081 (1968).

A few states have specifically adjusted their blue sky laws to conform to the language of §3(a)(10). Cal. Corp. Code §25142; N. C. Gen. Stat. §78A-30; Ohio Rev. Code §1707.04; Ore. Rev. Stat. §59.095. And since the late 1960s a substantial number of states have enacted insurance legislation directed to the acquisition of control of an insurance company through an exchange offer by a holding company created by it for that purpose. See Ash, supra, at 51-59. On the preclusive effect of a California administrative finding of fairness, see Plaine v. McCabe, 797 F. 2d 713, 718-21 (9th Cir. 1986).

[25] This is considered by the Commission to rule out when-issued trading under the §4(3) dealers' exemption in advance of the §3(a)(10) approval.

[26] Op. Gen. Counsel, Sec. Act Rel. 296 (1935).

[27] 98 Stat. 333 (1984).

[28] See Morgan, Application of the Securities Laws in Chapter 11 Reorganizations Under the Bankruptcy Reform Act of 1978, [1983] U. Ill. L. Rev. 861; In re Stanley Hotel, Inc., 13 B. R. 926 (D. Colo. Bkrtcy. Ct. 1981).

RELEVANT PROVISIONS OF TITLE II, UNITED STATES CODE

§364. Obtaining Credit

(a) If the trustee is authorized to operate the business of the debtor under section 721, 1108, or 1304 of this title, unless the court orders otherwise, the trustee may obtain unsecured credit and incur unsecured debt in the ordinary course of business allowable under section 503(b)(1) of this title as an administrative expense.[29]

* * *

(f) Except with respect to an entity that is an underwriter as defined in section 1145(b) of this title, section 5 of the Securities Act of 1933 (15 U. S. C. 77e), the Trust Indenture Act of 1939 (15 U. S. C. 77aaa et seq.), and any State or local law requiring registration for offer or sale of a security or registration or licensing of an issuer of, underwriter of, or broker or dealer in, a security does not apply to the offer or sale under this section of a security that is not an equity security.

* * *

§1125. Postpetition Disclosure and Solicitation

(a) In this section —

(1) "adequate information" means information of a kind, and in sufficient detail, as far as is reasonably practicable in light of the nature and history of the debtor and the condition of the debtor's books and records, that would enable a hypothetical reasonable investor typical of holders of claims or interests of the relevant class to make an informed judgment about the plan, but adequate information need not include such information about any other possible or proposed plan; and

[29]The purpose of this exemption is to finance the reorganization. Section 3(a)(7) of the 1933 Act remains, presumably because it covers certificates issued by a receiver as well as by a trustee in bankruptcy. And that section is not limited, as §364(f) is, to non-equity securities and non-underwriter transactions. But the first limitation is superfluous in view of the practice of financing reorganizations only with debt securities. And, even if the non-underwriter limitation is not read into §3(a)(7), the receiver or trustee relying on that section would not have the advantage of the preemption clause in §364(f), which is new.

(2) "investor typical of holders of claims or interests of the relevant class" means investor having —

(A) a claim or interest of the relevant class;

(B) such a relationship with the debtor as the holders of other claims of interests of such class generally have; and

(C) such ability to obtain such information from sources other than the disclosure required by this section as holders of claims or interest in such class generally have.

(b) An acceptance or rejection of a plan may not be solicited after the commencement of the case under this title from a holder of a claim or interest with respect to such claim or interest, unless, at the time of or before such solicitation, there is transmitted to such holder the plan or a summary of the plan, and a written disclosure statement approved, after notice and a hearing, by the court as containing adequate information.[30] The court may approve a disclosure statement without a valuation of the debtor or an appraisal of the debtor's assets.

(c) The same disclosure statement shall be transmitted to each holder of a claim or interest of a particular class, but there may be transmitted different disclosure statements, differing in amount, detail, or kind of information, as between classes.

(d) Whether a disclosure statement required under subsection (b) of this section contains adequate information is not governed by any otherwise applicable nonbankruptcy law, rule, or regulation, but an agency or official whose duty is to administer or enforce such a law, rule, or regulation may be heard on the issue of whether a disclosure statement contains adequate information. Such an agency or official may not appeal from, or otherwise seek review of, an order approving a disclosure statement.[31]

(e) A person that solicits acceptance or rejection of a plan, in good faith and in compliance with the applicable provisions of this

[30] The application of this section to a rejection as well as an acceptance of a plan produces the anomaly that the required "disclosure statement" may be prepared by a person other than the debtor. Moreover, apart from the possibility of a creditor's soliciting rejections of a proposed plan that he thinks is unfair, he may also desire to solicit acceptances of his own plan.

[31] See pp. 457-58, 1st par., infra.

title, or that participates, in good faith and in compliance with the applicable provisions of this title, in the offer, issuance, sale, or purchase of a security, offered or sold under the plan, of the debtor, of an affiliate participating in a joint plan with the debtor, or of a newly organized successor to the debtor under the plan, is not liable, on account of such solicitation or participation, for violation of any applicable law, rule, or regulation governing solicitation of acceptance or rejection of a plan or the offer, issuance, sale, or purchase of securities.[32]

* * *

§1145. Exemption from Securities Laws

(a) Except with respect to an entity that is an underwriter as defined in subsection (b) of this section, section 5 of the Securities Act of 1933 (15 U. S. C. 77e) and any State or local law[33] requiring registration for offer or sale of a security or registration or licensing of an issuer of, underwriter of, or broker or dealer in, a security[34] does not apply to —

[32]Section 1125(e) is not an exemption for the securities coming out of a reorganization — that is the function of §1145 — but a limitation on civil liability. This section is not only directed to the proxy rules but also designed to preclude civil liability for good faith solicitations of sales and purchases of securities in connection with a plan, on the theory that the policing of the solicitations would be by the court.

The Commission's staff takes a "no action" position with respect to failure to comply with the reporting and proxy solicitation requirements of §§13 and 14. But it is the administrative construction, which seems sound, that failure to take advantage of the "safe harbor" afforded by the "good faith" provision of §1125(e) activates all the SEC fraud provisions, including Rule 13e-3(b)(1), the "going private" antifraud rule (see pp. 522-23 infra). Bennett Petroleum Corp., 16 Sec. Reg. L. Rep. 23 (letter 1983).

"Good faith" has the flavor of the scienter standard enunciated in the *Hochfelder* case under Rule 10b-5 (infra p. 774). See H. R. Rep. No. 95-595, 95th Cong., 2d Sess., 5 U. S. Code Cong. & Ad. News 5963 (1978). That is to say, presumably only a knowing or intentional omission or misrepresentation of material fact will result in a finding of lack of good faith.

See generally Epling and Thompson, Securities Disclosure in Bankruptcy, 39 Bus. Law. 855 (1984), whose authors note the switch from the old reorganization exemptions' basis in the court's passing on the substantive merits of the plan to the disclosure philosophy of the securities laws.

See also Bankruptcy Rules 3016 (due date of disclosure statement), 3017 (procedure).

[33]This preemption clause, like that in §364(f), is new.

[34]Title 11 has its own definition of "security" in §101(35), which includes an "investment contract or certificate of interest or participation in a profit-sharing agreement or in an oil, gas, or mineral royalty or lease" only if the contract or interest is registered under the 1933 Act or exempted pursuant to §3(b).

(1) the offer or sale under a plan of a security of the debtor, of an affiliate participating in a joint plan with the debtor, or of a successor to the debtor under the plan —

(A) in exchange for a claim against, an interest in, or a claim for an administrative expense in the case concerning, the debtor or such affiliate; or

(B) principally[35] in such exchange and partly for cash or property;

(2) the offer of a security through any warrant, option, right to subscribe, or conversion privilege that was sold in the manner specified in paragraph (1) of this subsection, or the sale of a security upon the exercise of such a warrant, option, right, or privilege;

(3) the offer or sale, other than under a plan, of a security of an issuer other than the debtor or an affiliate,[36] if —

(A) such security was owned by the debtor on the date of the filing of the petition;

(B) the issuer of such security is —

(i) required to file reports under section 13 or 15(d) of the Securities Exchange Act of 1934 (15 U. S. C. 78m or 78o(d)); and

(ii) in compliance with the disclosure and reporting provision of such applicable section; and

(C) such offer or sale is of securities that do not exceed —

(i) during the two-year period immediately following the date of the filing of the petition, four percent of the securities of such class outstanding on such date; and

(ii) during any 180-day period following such two-year period, one percent of the securities outstanding at the beginning of such 180-day period; or

[35] Note that §3(a)(10) says "partly" in exchange.

[36] This limited exemption for the sale of a *portfolio* security of the debtor is new.

(4) a transaction by a stockbroker[37] in a security that is executed after a transaction of a kind specified in paragraph (1) or (2) of this subsection in such security and before the expiration of 40 days after the first date on which such security was *bona fide* offered to the public by the issuer or by or through an underwriter, if such stockbroker provides, at the time of or before such transaction by such stockbroker, a disclosure statement approved under section 1125 of this title, and, if the court orders, information supplementing such disclosure statement.

(b)(1) Except as provided in paragraph (2) of this subsection and except with respect to ordinary trading transactions of an entity that is not an issuer, an entity is an underwriter under section 2(11) of the Securities Act of 1933 (15 U. S. C. 77b(11)), if such entity —

(A) purchases a claim against, interest in, or claim for an administrative expense in the case concerning, the debtor, if such purchase is with a view to distribution of any security received or to be received in exchange for such a claim or interest;

(B) offers to sell securities offered or sold under the plan for the holders of such securities;

(C) offers to buy securities offered or sold under the plan for the holders of such securities, if such offer to buy is —

(i) with a view to distribution of such securities; and

(ii) under an agreement made in connection with the plan, with the consummation of the plan, or with the offer or sale of securities under the plan; or

(D) is an issuer, as used in such section 2(11), with respect to such securities.

(2) An entity is not an underwriter under section 2(11) of the Securities Act of 1933 or under paragraph (1) of this subsection with respect to an agreement that provides only for —

[37] Perhaps to keep lawyers on the *qui vive,* §101(39) of Title 11, in contrast to the definition of "dealer" in §2(12) of the 1933 Act to include a broker, defines "stockbroker" to include a dealer. At any rate, this new exemption supplements the dealers' exemption in §4(3) of the 1933 Act, which does not apply, under its Clause (A), to transactions during the forty-day period covered by §1145(a)(4) (although §1145(a)(4) seems to overlook the fact that §4(3) is inapplicable for *ninety* days in the case of a first registrant).

(A)(i) the matching or combining of fractional interests in securities offered or sold under the plan into whole interests; or

(ii) the purchase or sale of such fractional interests from or to entities receiving such fractional interests under the plan; or

(B) the purchase or sale for such entities of such fractional or whole interests as are necessary to adjust for any remaining fractional interests after such matching.

(3) An entity other than an entity of the kind specified in paragraph (1) of this subsection is not an underwriter under section 2(11) of the Securities Act of 1933 with respect to any securities offered or sold to such entity in the manner specified in subsection (a)(1) of this section.[38]

(c) An offer or sale of securities of the kind and in the manner specified under subsection (a)(1) of this section is deemed to be a public offering.[39]

(d) The Trust Indenture Act of 1939 (15 U. S. C. 77aaa et seq.) does not apply to a commercial note issued under the plan that matures not later than one year after the effective date of the plan.[40]

[38] Section 1145(a) exempts only the issuance of the securities in the reorganization, or the debtor's sale of a portfolio security; it is a transaction exemption, not a securities exemption. In our discussion of the 1933 Act's definition of "underwriter" we have noticed the problem whether a person who takes a large part of a registered issue with a view to distribution is an "underwriter" so as to preclude the §4(1) exemption. See p. 255 supra. And we shall later notice the same problem with respect to a person who takes a large block in an exempted exchange under §3(a)(9) or 3(a)(10) or in a private offering exempted under §4(2). See pp. 357-78, 387 infra. Section 1145(b)(3) solves the problem, to the extent of a non-"underwriter" within §1145(b)(1), in the context of securities coming out of a Chapter 11 reorganization.

[39] The purpose of this provision is understood to be to prevent a construction of Rule 144, along the lines of former Rule 155 as interpreted in Sec. Act Rel. 4248 (1960) (see 1 Loss pp. 673-86; 4 id. 2659), so as to impose restrictions on the resale of convertible securities received in a reorganization.

By way of complementing the §5 exemption in §1145, §1129(d) provides that, "on request of a party in interest that is a governmental unit, the court may not confirm a plan if the principal purpose of the plan is the avoidance of * * * section 5 of the Securities Act of 1933 * * *."

[40] Section 1145 rendered largely obsolete the roughly comparable "safe harbor" Rule 148 that had been adopted a year earlier. Sec. Act Rel. 5918, 14 SEC Dock. 587 (1978). The SEC staff has taken the position that the rule is no longer applicable to bankruptcy reorganizations. Calstar, Inc., 17 Sec. Reg. L.

3. MERGERS AND SIMILAR EVENTS [RULE 145]

Despite the perceived presence of a "sale" in exchanges of securities and significant alterations of their terms,[41] and despite the definitional implication from the registration exemptions in §§3(a)(9) and 3(a)(10) for various exchange offerings by way of reorganization or otherwise, the SEC, almost from its first day, took the view that the ordinary merger or consolidation or sale of assets for securities (as well as the ordinary reclassification of a single company's capital structure) did not involve an "offer" or "sale" if under the applicable law or charter provision a vote of a specified majority bound the entire class (subject only to any dissenters' statutory appraisal rights). This so-called "no sale theory" was premised on the concept that stockholders participating in a class vote were simply acting as one of the corporate organs, without the element of *individual* volition that is essential to a "sale."

Both on that account and because the theory did not apply to reorganizations that took the form of share-for-share exchanges, the theory was unforgivably formalistic. And the hole it created was a wide one. Consequently, although the Ninth Circuit early sustained the theory with only a reference to the Commission's brief as *amicus curiae,*[42] the short (really the long) of it is that, after gradually whittling away at the rule that embodied the theory (former Rule 133), the Commission in 1972 finally screwed up the courage to repeal that rule in favor of a new Rule 145 that says there *is* a "sale."[43]

The Committee on Administrative Law of the Association of the Bar of the City of New York — happily — could not resist a reminder, when the Commission had earlier proposed to repeal Rule 133, that what it called "a serious legal problem" had been similarly solved in Sir William S. Gilbert's Iolanthe:

Rep. 1820 (letter 1985). But it remains on the books, presumably because it extends also to "securities which were in the debtor's portfolio either at the time proceedings were commenced under * * * the Securities Investor Protection Act, or at the time the Federal Deposit Insurance Corporation was appointed as a receiver for the debtor's assets."

The draftsman of Title 11 necessarily worked on the basis of today's Securities Act. On the substantially different — and, one hopes, simpler — treatment of secondary (that is to say, nonissuer) transactions in the Code, see p. 376 infra.

[41] See p. 247 supra.

[42] National Supply Co. v. Leland Stanford Jr. University, 134 F. 2d 689, 694 (9th Cir. 1943), *cert. denied,* 320 U. S. 773.

[43] Sec. Act Rel. 5316 (1972). For the history, see 1 Loss 518-39.

QUEEN: * * * And yet (*unfolding a scroll*) the law is clear — every fairy must die who marries a mortal!

LORD CHANCELLOR: Allow me, as an Old Equity draftsman, to make a suggestion. The subtleties of the legal mind are equal to the emergency. The thing is really quite simple — the insertion of a single word will do it. Let it stand that every fairy shall die who doesn't marry a mortal, and there you are, out of your difficulty at once![44]

In 1959, when the Commission had amended Rule 133 to limit its application, it had adopted Form S-14 as an optional form for use when registration was required in a merger-type transaction. That form required the same information as a "proxy statement" or "information statement" under §14 of the 1934 Act.[45] And, when such a statement was sent to the security holders who were to vote, as it had to be if their security was registered under the 1934 Act, there could be a "wrap-around" prospectus consisting of the proxy or information statement inside an S-14 cover.[46]

In 1985 the Commission applied the principles of the integrated disclosure system[47] to business combination transactions by adopting Form S-4.[48] The new Form S-4 not only (1) replaced Form S-14 with its application to transactions of the Rule 145 type, but also (2) was clarified and to some extent expanded to cover short-form mergers, exchange offers for securities of the issuer or another person, and reoffers of securities registered on the new form. Concurrently, moreover, just as Forms F-1 to F-3 complement Forms S-1 to S-3 with respect to most foreign private issuers,[49] the Commission adopted Form F-4 to complement the new S-4 in that area.[50] And somewhat later the Commission adopted an S-4-type Form N-14 for management investment companies and business development companies[51] in business combination transactions.[52]

The "wrap-around" idea survives to permit the S-4 (or F-4) prospectus to serve as the proxy statement. And compliance with Form

[44] Act II, quoted in Purcell, A Consideration of the No-Sale Theory Under the Securities Act of 1933, 24 Brooklyn L. Rev. 254, 279 n. 78 (1958).

[45] See p. 459 infra.

[46] Rule 153a defines "preceded by a prospectus" in §5(b)(2) to take into account changes in the body of stockholders between the date of voting and the date of delivery of a prospectus. And there is a "tombstone ad" provision in Rule 145(b)(1).

[47] See p. 146 supra.

[48] Sec. Act Rel. 6578, 32 SEC Dock. 1280 (1985).

[49] See p. 148 n. 6 supra.

[50] Sec. Act Rel. 6579, 32 SEC Dock. 1312 (1985).

[51] See p. 338 infra.

[52] Sec. Act Rel. 6611, 34 SEC Dock. 645 (1985).

N-14 satisfies the proxy rules under both the Exchange and Investment Company Acts (unless a separate proxy submission, as for an election of directors, accompanies the merger proxy). But Form S-1 (or F-1) remains available for mergers or exchange offers, enabling registrants to "choose to use Form S-1 [or F-1] and to have the company being acquired prepare its own proxy statement so that the company being acquired will assume liability for the information in its own proxy statement."[53]

Rule 145 does not apply to a reclassification consisting simply of a "stock split, reverse stock split, or change in par value" or to a merger or consolidation whose sole purpose is to change an issuer's domicile.[54] But the release adopting the rule[55] states that a "short-form merger"[56] involves a "sale" despite the absence of *any* vote of the subsidiary's stockholders and despite the silence of the rule itself. This view is reflected in the Code because it is sound in policy:

> Even a short-form merger comes within the definition. This is consistent with the disclosure philosophy; for the minority holders should be able to make up their minds intelligently whether to demand their statutory appraisal rights or seek injunctive relief. That is to say, the mere fact that they have no vote on the merger is no more significant than it is in an ordinary merger in which the surviving company already owns more than the percentage of shares required for approval.[57]

Whether a short-form merger involves a "sale" today is another question. The Second Circuit in a case under Rule 10b-5 has held that it does.[58]

As that case demonstrates, bringing mergers and the like within the definition of "sale" has an important impact on state corporation law with respect to mergers. Even before the adoption of Rule 145, the "no sale theory," as the Commission took pains to point out when it codified the theory as Rule 133, was limited to §5 as distinct from the fraud provisions of the 1933 and 1934 Acts.[59]

[53] Sec. Act Rel. 6578, 32 SEC Dock. 1280, 1284 n. 24 (1985).

[54] On the scope of the rule's application to transfers of assets for securities, see Rule 145(a)(3).

[55] Sec. Act Rel. 5316 (1972).

[56] See, e. g., Del. Gen. Corp. L., Tit. 8, §253, which permits the merger of a 90 percent subsidiary into its parent without a stockholder vote, subject to dissenters' appraisal rights.

[57] 1 Code 188.

[58] Vine v Beneficial Finance Co., Inc., 374 F. 2d 627 (2d Cir. 1967), *cert. denied*, 389 U. S. 970.

[59] Sec. Act Rel. 3420 (1951).

This makes Rule 10b-5 and the other fraud provisions available as a basis for attacking mergers and the like and, since state law cannot foreclose federal remedies, to do so even when the merger statute declares that the appraisal remedy is exclusive (usually in the absence of fraud).[60]

If an exemption is available under §3(a)(9)-(11) or 4(2), nothing in Rule 145 affects that result.[61]

An early draft of the Uniform Securities Act attempted to codify the SEC's then "no sale theory" by *exempting* mergers and the like only from the *registration* requirement.[62] But the final draft excludes mergers and the like from the *definitions* of "offer" and "sale," even for fraud purposes — this on the dual theory that merger provisions at the state level should be relegated to the corporation statutes, and that fraud may be attacked at the state level by means of all the usual remedies at common law and in equity.[63]

C. INTRASTATE ISSUES [§3(a)(11)]

In 1961 the Commission published a general release on §3(a)(11),[1] and this was followed in 1974 by a second release that discussed the newly adopted Rule 147, a "safe harbor" rule that creates certainty at the price of strictness.[2] This means that, on the one hand, the rule assures safety if all its sometimes stringent conditions are satisfied and that, on the other hand, an issuer that fails to satisfy one

[60] Swanson v. American Consumer Industries, Inc., 415 F. 2d 1326, 1332-33 (7th Cir. 1969).

[61] Sec. Act Rel. 5463, 3 SEC Dock. 600, 601-02 (1974).

[62] Harvard Law School Study of State Securities Regulation — A Proposed Uniform Securities Act — Second Draft (Loss and Cowett 1955) §§401(j)(7), 402(b)(8).

[63] §401(j)(6)(C); see Loss, Commentary on the Uniform Securities Act (1976) 102-04.

C. 5C [1] Sec. Act Rel. 4434 (1961).

[2] Sec. Act Rel. 5450, 3 SEC Dock. 349 (1974). The rule is not available, however,

> to any person with respect to any offering which, although in technical compliance with the provisions of the rule, is part of a plan or scheme by such person to make interstate offers or sales of securities. In such cases, registration would be required. In addition, any plan or scheme that involves a series of offerings by affiliated organizations in various states, even if in technical compliance with the rule, may be outside the parameters of the rule and of Section 3(a)(11) if what is being financed is in effect a single business enterprise.

Id. at 354.

or more conditions may still fall back on the statutory language itself.

The scheme here will be to set out the text of the 1961 release and to include in the footnotes, in addition to the usual commentary, an indication of the differences between §3(a)(11) unadorned and Rule 174.

SECURITIES ACT RELEASE NO. 4434: SECTION 3(a)(11) EXEMPTION FOR LOCAL OFFERINGS

Securities and Exchange Commission, 1961[1]

* * *

"Issue Concept"[a]

A basic condition of the exemption is that the entire issue of securities be offered[b] and sold exclusively to residents of the state in question. Consequently, an offer to a non-resident which is considered part of the intrastate issue will render the exemption unavailable to the entire offering.

Whether an offering is "a part of an issue," that is, whether it is an integrated part of an offering previously made or proposed to be made, is a question of fact and depends essentially upon whether the offerings are a related part of a plan or program. *Unity Gold Corporation,* 3 S. E. C. 618, 625 (1938); *Peoples Securities Company,* SEA Release No. 6176, Feb. 10, 1960. Thus, the exemption should not be relied upon in combination with another exemption for the different parts of a single issue where a part is offered or sold to non-residents.[c]

[1][Under §24(d) of the Investment Company Act] the Section 3(a)(11) exemption for an intrastate offering is not availabe for an investment company registered or required to be registered under the Investment Company Act. But the Commission may exempt specific issues from §24(d) as it may from any other provision of the 1940 Act.]

[a]Ed.: See pp. 278-79 supra.

[b]Ed.: An offer to a nonresident destroys the exemption for the entire issue even if no sales are made to nonresidents. SEC v. Hillsborough Investment Corp., 173 F. Supp. 86, 87-88 (D. N. H. 1958), *permanent injunction,* 176 F. Supp. 789 (D. N. H. 1959), *aff'd on other grounds* sub nom. Hillsborough Investment Corp. v. SEC, 276 F. 2d 665 (1st Cir. 1960). On the other hand, mere delivery to a nonresident who had been a resident at the time of the sale, or acceptance of payment from such a person, should not be fatal.

[c]Ed.: In recent years, however, the staff has not objected to a concurrent offering to persons in a foreign country who are neither citizens nor residents of the United States. Scientific Mfg., Inc., CCH Fed. Sec. L. Rep. ¶77,505 (letter 1983).

* * *

Moreover, since the exemption is designed to cover only those security distributions, which, as a whole, are essentially local in character, it is clear that the phrase "sold only to persons resident" as used in Section 3(a)(11) cannot refer merely to the initial sales by the issuing corporation to its underwriters, or even the subsequent resales by the underwriters to distributing dealers. To give effect to the fundamental purpose of the exemption, it is necessary that the entire issue of securities shall be offered and sold to, and come to rest only in the hands of residents within the state. If any part of the issue is offered or sold to a non-resident, the exemption is unavailable not only for the securities so sold, but for all securities forming a part of the issue, including those sold to residents. Securities Act Release No. 201 (1934); *Brooklyn Manhattan Transit Corporation,* 1 S. E. C. 147 (1935); *S. E. C.* v. *Hillsborough Investment Corp.,* 173 F. Supp. 86 (D. N. H. 1958); *Hillsborough Investment Corp.* v. *S. E. C.,* 276 F. 2d 665 (C. A. 1 1960); *S. E. C.* v. *Los Angeles Trust Deed & Mortgage Exchange, et al.,* 186 F. Supp. 830, 871 (S. D. Cal. 1960), *aff'd* 285 F. 2d 162 (C. A. 9 1960) [*cert. denied,* 366 U. S. 919].[d] It is incumbent upon the issuer, underwriter, dealers

[d]ED.: The Commission has repeatedly held that a single sale (or presumably, under its view, a single offer) to a nonresident destroys the exemption for the entire issue. E. g., Armstrong, Jones & Co., 43 SEC 888, 890-94 (1968), *rehearing denied,* 43 SEC 993 (1968), *aff'd* sub nom. Armstrong, Jones & Co. v. SEC, 421 F. 2d 359 (6th Cir. 1970), *cert. denied,* 398 U. S. 958 (underwriter had reason to believe that two residents who signed subscription agreement were nominees for nonresidents). Part of a single issue may not be sold under the 3(a)(11) exemption even if the balance is registered. Sec. Act Rel. 97, part 10 (1933); see Texas Glass Mfg. Corp., 38 SEC 630, 634 (1938); cf. Unity Gold Corp., 3 SEC 618, 625-26 (1938). In such a case, however, the Commission would be unlikely to take any action except to require the registration statement to disclose a contingent liability under §12(1) for selling in violation of §5 — though there would seem to be no defense to such liability.

Presumably a *gift* could be made to a nonresident. SEC v. Hillsborough Investment Corp., supra, 173 F. Supp. at 90 n. 2. And nonresidents could be bought out for cash. West Side National Bank of San Angelo, 563 Sec. Reg. L. Rep. No. 563, p. C-3 (letter 1980). A *bona fide* attempt to obtain a waiver of preemptive rights from a nonresident stockholder should not be regarded as an "offer." Cf. p. 99 supra. Otherwise, even if it were feasible to reserve the nonresident's shares until he found himself in the state, and to effect purchase, payment, and delivery without use (direct or indirect) of the mails or interstate commerce, the offer and sale to the nonresident would still destroy the exemption for the entire offering. But see p. 299 n. h infra.

Rule 147(b)(2) provides that all securities of the issuer offered or sold pursuant to a registration statement or a §3 or §4(2) exemption *before* the six-month period immediately preceding or *after* the six-month period immediately following any offer or sale pursuant to Rule 147 will be deemed not to be part of the

and other persons connected with the offering to make sure that it does not become an interstate distribution through resales. It is understood to be customary for such persons to obtain assurances that purchases are not made with a view to resale to non-residents.[e]

Doing Business Within the State

In view of the local character of the Section 3(a)(11) exemption, the requirement that the issuer be doing business in the state can only be satisfied by the performance of substantial operational activities in the state of incorporation. The doing business requirement is not met by functions in the particular state such as bookkeeping, stock record and similar activities or by offering securities in the state.[f] Thus, the exemption would be unavailable to an offering by a company made in the state of its incorporation of undivided fractional oil and gas interests located in other states even though the company conducted other business in the state of its incorporation. While the person creating the fractional interests is technically the "issuer" as defined in Section 2(4) of the Act, the purchaser of such security obtains no interest in the issuer's separate business within the state. Similarly, an intrastate exemption would not be available to a "local" mortgage company offering interests in out-of-state mortgages which are sold under circumstances to constitute them investment contracts. Also, the same position has been taken of a sale of an interest, by a real estate syndicate organized in one state to the residents of that state, in property acquired under a sale and leaseback arrangement with another corporation organized and engaged in business in another state.

If the proceeds of the offering are to be used primarily for the purpose of a new business conducted outside of the state of incorporation and unrelated to some incidental business locally conducted, the exemption should not be relied upon. *S. E. C. v. Truckee Showboat, Inc.*, 157 F. Supp. 824 (S. D. Cal. 1957). So also, a Section 3(a)(11) exemption should not be relied upon for each of a series

---

issue if there are no offers or sales of the same or a similar class by or for the issuer *during* either six-month period.

[e]Ed.: Rule 147(f) requires the issuer to take specified precautions to preserve the exemption: (1) placing a legend on the certificate to indicate that the securities have not been registered and to call attention to the nine-month holding provision (see p. 302 n. m l infra); (2) issuing stop transfer instructions to the transfer agent (or making a notation in the appropriate records of the issuer itself if it has no transfer agent; (3) obtaining a written representation of his residence from each buyer; and (4) making written disclosure of the limitations on resale.

[f]Ed.: Mark E. O'Leary, 43 SEC 842, 847 (1968), *aff'd* sub nom. O'Leary v. SEC, 424 F. 2d 908 (D. C. Cir. 1970).

of corporations organized in different states where there is in fact and purpose a single business enterprise or financial venture whether or not it is planned to merge or consolidate the various corporations at a later date. *S. E. C.* v. *Los Angeles Trust Deed & Mortgage Exchange, et al.,* 186 F. Supp. 830, 871 (S. D. Cal. 1960), *aff'd* 285 F. 2d 162 (C. A. 9 1960).[g]

Residence Within the State

Section 3(a)(11) requires that the entire issue be confined to a single state in which the issuer, the offerees and the purchasers are residents. Mere presence in the state is not sufficient to constitute residence as in the case of military personnel at a military post. *S. E. C.* v. *Capital Funds, Inc.,* No. A46-60 [Litig. Rel. 1805], D. Alaska, 1960.[h] The mere obtaining of formal representations of

[g]Ed.: See also SEC v. Freeman, CCH Fed. Sec. L. Rep. ¶96,361 at 93,243 (N. D. Ill. 1978).

Rule 147(c)(2) applies three cumulative standards to the "doing business" concept, in terms of 80 percent of (1) gross revenues for specified periods, (2) assets, and (3) local use of net proceeds from the sale, in addition to requiring that the issuer's "principal office" be located in the state. For a number of illustrations, see Sec. Act Rel. 5450, 3 SEC Dock. 349, 352-53 (1974).

[h]Ed.: This reflects a construction of "resident" to mean "domiciled" in the conflict-of-laws sense. The legislative committees, in connection with the 1954 amendments that added the words "offered and," stated that "the exemption * * * has not been considered available unless the entire issue of securities was offered and sold exclusively to persons domiciled in the one State." For this statement the reports cited a 1937 opinion of the General Counsel (Sec. Act Rel. 1459), which did go into the "offer" point but was silent on the meaning of "resident." S. Rep. No. 1036 at 13 and H. R. Rep. No. 1542 at 22, 83d Cong., 2d Sess. (1954). What obviously happened is that the SEC lawyers who drafted the legislative reports employed one of the recognized bootstrap techniques of making "legislative history" by having the committees "approve" an administrative construction. To be sure, the interpretation of "resident" as a statutory term depends on the statutory context. 1 Beale, The Conflict of Laws (1935) §10.3. But one is intrigued by the picture of a securities salesman's examining a prospective buyer on his *animus manendi* before making him an "offer." And Rule 147(d)(2) defines "residence" in terms of "principal residence" while abandoning the *animus manendi* element. See Sec. Act Rel. 5450, 3 SEC Dock. 349, 353 (1974). But the Commission still cautions, at least so far as the rule is concerned, that "Temporary residence, such as that of many persons in the military service, would not satisfy the provisions of paragraph (d)." Ibid.

At least so far as the rule is concerned, the residence of a "business organization" is "the state or territory in which it has its principal office, unless it is an entity organized for the specific purpose of acquiring securities in the offering, in which case it will be deemed to be a resident of a state only if all of the beneficial owners of interests in such entity are residents of the state." Ibid.

In the case of buyers who take the security in two or more names, whether the tenure is joint, common, or by the entirety, presumably both or all must be residents. But, if the one who is a resident supplies the entire purchase price, he might be considered to be making a gift of a part interest to the other without

residence and agreements not to resell to non-residents or agreements that sales are void if the purchaser is a non-resident should not be relied upon without more as establishing the availability of the exemption.

An offering may be so large that its success as a local offering appears doubtful from the outset. Also, reliance should not be placed on the exemption for an issue which includes warrants for the purchase of another security unless there can be assurance that the warrants will be exercised only by residents. With respect to convertible securities, a Section 3(a)(9) exemption may be available for the conversion.[i]

A secondary offering by a controlling person in the issuer's state of incorporation may be made in reliance on a Section 3(a)(11) exemption provided the exemption would be available to the issuer for a primary offering in that state. It is not essential that the

---

destruction of the exemption. Needless to say, the exemption does not permit offers or sales to resident agents of nonresident principals. Sec. Act Rel. 97, part 9 (1933). In the case of buyers on an installment basis who become nonresidents before all the installments are paid, the legality of accepting further installment payments and making delivery to the former residents should depend on whether there was a mutually enforceable sale in the first instance with a mere postponement of delivery until completion of payment, in which event payment and delivery could be completed, or whether there was in substance a series of separate sales, in which event obviously none could be effected after termination of residence. SEC v. American Founders Life Ins. Co. of Denver, Colo., CCH Fed. Sec. L. Rep. ¶90,861 (D. Colo. 1958); cf. Hill v. Equitable Bank, N. A., 599 F. Supp. 1062, 1072-77 (D. Del. 1984) (statute of limitations); cf. also pp. 579-81 infra (Sec. Ex. Act §16(b)).

Rule 147(c)(1) addresses the term "resident" for purposes of the *issuer's* being "resident within" the state:

> A corporation, limited partnership or business trust must be incorporated or organized pursuant to the laws of [the particular] state or territory. Section 3(a)(11) provides specifically that a corporate issuer must be incorporated in the state. A general partnership or other form of business entity that is not formed under a specific state or territorial law must have its principal office within the state or territory. [See Grenader v. Spitz, 390 F. Supp. 1112, 1117 (S. D. N. Y. 1975), *reaff'd*, CCH Fed. Sec. L. Rep. ¶95,300 (S. D. N. Y. 1975), *rev'd on other grounds*, 537 F. 2d 612 (2d Cir. 1976), *cert. denied*, 429 U. S. 1009.] The rule also provides that an individual who is deemed an issuer, e. g., a promoter issuing preincorporation certificates, will be deemed a resident if his principal residence is in the state or territory. As initially proposed, the rule provided that in a partnership, *all* the general partners must be resident within such state or territory. The Commission has reconsidered this provision in light of the provisions applicable to corporations and determined to treat all business entities in a similar manner.

Sec. Act Rel. 5450, 3 SEC Dock. 349, 352 (1974).

[i]ED.: With respect to convertibles, see p. 302 n. n infra.

controlling person be a resident of the issuer's state of incorporation.[j]

RESALES

From these general principles it follows that if during the course of distribution any underwriter, any distributing dealer (whether or not a member of the formal selling or distributing group),[k] or any dealer or other person purchasing securities from a distributing dealer for resale were to offer or sell such securities to a non-resident, the exemption would be defeated. In other words, Section 3(a)(11) contemplates that the exemption is applicable only if the entire issue is distributed pursuant to the statutory conditions. Consequently, any offers or sales to a non-resident in connection with the distribution of the issue would destroy the exemption as to all securities which are a part of that issue, including those sold to residents regardless of whether such sales are made directly to non-residents or indirectly through residents who as part of the distribution thereafter sell to non-residents. It would furthermore be immaterial that sales to non-residents are made without use of the mails or instruments of interstate commerce. Any such sales of part of the issue to non-residents, however few, would not be in compliance with the conditions of Section 3(a)(11), and would render the exemption unavailable for the entire offering including the sales to residents. *Petersen Engine Co., Inc.,* 2 S. E. C. 892, 903 (1937); *Professional Investors,* 37 S. E. C. 173, 175 (1956); *Universal Service,* 37 S. E. C. 559, 563-564 (1957); *S. E. C.* v. *Hillsborough Investment Corp.,* 173 F. Supp. 86 (D. N. H. 1958); *Hillsborough Investment Corp.* v. *S. E. C.,* 276 F. 2d 665 (C. A. 1 1960).[l]

This is not to suggest, however, that securities which have actually come to rest in the hands of resident investors, such as persons purchasing without a view to further distribution or resale to non-residents, may not in due course be resold by such persons, whether directly or through dealers or brokers, to non-residents without in-

[j] ED.: The exemption for secondaries is not reflected in the rule, although the release preserved the "long standing administrative interpretations of Section 3(a)(11)." Id. at 351; Rule 147, Prel. Note 4.

[k] ED.: J. A. Hogle & Co., 36 SEC 460, 463-64 (1955).

[l] ED.: Clearly, however, only those buyers (resident or nonresident) to whom sales *are* made by use of the mails can recover under §12(1). That is to say, a sale (whether to a resident or to a nonresident) cannot itself violate §5 if no use is made of the jurisdictional means in any step of the transaction; but even a face-to-face sale to a nonresident makes illegal those sales (whether to residents or to nonresidents) that do involve some use of the mails or interstate facilities.

any way affecting the exemption.[m] The relevance of any such resales consists only of the evidentiary light which they might cast upon the factual question whether the securities had in fact come to rest in the hands of resident investors. If the securities are resold but a short time after their acquisition to a non-resident this fact, although not conclusive, might support an inference that the original offering had not come to rest in the state, and that the resale therefore constituted a part of the process of primary distribution; a stronger inference would arise if the purchaser involved were a security dealer.[n] It may be noted that the non-residence of the underwriter or dealer is not pertinent so long as the ultimate distribution is solely to residents of the state.[o]

USE OF THE MAILS AND FACILITIES OF INTERSTATE COMMERCE

The intrastate exemption is not dependent upon non-use of the mails or instrument of interstate commerce in the distribution. Securities issued in a transaction properly exempt under this provision may be offered and sold without registration through the mails or by use of any instruments of transportation or communication in interstate commerce, may be made the subject of general newspaper advertisement (provided the advertisement is appropriately limited to indicate that offers to purchase are solicited only from, and sales will be made only to, residents of the particular state involved), and

[m] ED.: By way of providing objective standards for determining when the securities have in fact "come to rest," Rule 147(e) permits resales only to residents for nine months from the last sale by the issuer. Compare the similar problem under the private offering exemption in §4(2), infra p. 357. In this respect the rule is more lenient than the 1961 release: whereas that release limits reoffers as well as resales, the rule release referred to the reoffer restriction as impractical. Sec. Act Rel. 5450, 3 SEC Dock. 349, 353 (1974). *Query* whether the stricter unwritten rule really survives. In Busch v. Carpenter, 598 F. Supp. 519 (D. Utah 1984), the court held that, since the nine-month period was a safe harbor provision, seven months could suffice under the exemption.

[n] ED.: When a convertible security is sold pursuant to the rule, resales of either the convertible security or the underlying security may be made during the nine-month period only to residents. But a conversion itself, if exempted pursuant to §3(a)(9) of the Act, does not begin a new period. In the case of warrants and options, sales upon exercise, if done in reliance on the rule, begin a new period. Rule 174, Note 1; Sec. Act Rel. 5450, 3 SEC Dock. 349, 353 (1974).

[o] ED.: Whitehall Corp., 38 SEC 259, 268-71 (1958), *semble* (Commission did not question the use of a Texas underwriter for a purportedly Arkansas issue). So, too, with respect to the transfer agent. Letter from Acting Chief Counsel, Div. of Corp. Fin., SEC, Sept. 28, 1956, CCH Fed. Sec. L. Rep. ¶76,411. Presumably, however, there would be some question in the case of a nonresident underwriter not selling as agent but buying for resale, at least if the underwriter retained any part of the issue after completing the distribution.

may even be delivered by means of transportation and communication used in interstate commerce, to the purchasers.[p] * * *

CONCLUSION

In conclusion, the fact should be stressed that Section 3(a)(11) is designed to apply only to distributions genuinely local in character. From a practical point of view, the provisions of that section can exempt only issues which in reality represent local financing by local industries, carried out through local investments. Any distribution not of this type raises a serious question as to the availability of Section 3(a)(11). Consequently, any dealer proposing to participate in the distribution of an issue claimed to be exempt under Section 3(a)(11) should examine the character of the transaction and the proposed or actual manner of its execution by all persons concerned with it with the greatest care to satisfy himself that the distribution will not, or did not, exceed the limitations of the exemption. Otherwise the dealer, even though his own sales may be carefully confined to resident purchasers, may subject himself to serious risk of civil liability under Section 12(1) of the Act for selling without prior registration a security not in fact entitled to exemption from registration. * * *

* * *

Rule 147 makes for considerable certainty.[3] But the exemption is still no bargain: witness, for example, the transformation of "doing business" — which to the man in the street would mean *some* business, possibly a *substantial* portion of the total business, and *conceivably* the *primary* portion[4] — into a triple 80 percent test. As it is, the several conditions and their strict reading by the Commission quite justify the Chairman's statement in 1958 that "as a practical matter the intrastate exemption is loaded with dynamite and must

[p]ED.: Coastal Finance Corp. v. Coastal Finance Corp. of North Providence, 387 A. 2d 1373, 1376 (R. I. 1978).

[3]See Commentary, Securities Regulation: SEC Rule 147: Ten Years of SEC Interpretation, 38 Okla. L. Rev. 507 (1985).

[4]In Chapman v. Dunn, 414 F. 2d 153 (6th Cir. 1969), the court concluded that the issuer "must conduct a predominant amount of his business" within the state. But, since all the land covered by the oil and gas leases managed by a Michigan office was in Ohio, the Michigan activities in fact were apparently insubstantial.

be handled with very great care."[5] Its limited usefulness is all the more apparent in the light of other exemptions. If the offering is not over $5 million, an exemption may well be available in many cases pursuant to §4(6) or 3(b),[6] with none of the risk inherent in §3(a)(11). And, if the offering is larger, it is difficult to see how the very restrictive conditions of §3(a)(11) can be satisfied unless the entire issue is placed with a relatively few persons for investment, in which event the exemption for private offerings under §4(2) may be available without regard to the residence of the issuer or the buyers.

Nevertheless, the exemption is there. It was presumably intended to be used. And it is in fact used. This inevitably raises the question: If a single sale or perhaps a single offer (or, indeed a single resale or reoffer by a resident buyer before the securities have "come to rest") to a nonresident destroys the exemption forevermore for the entire issue, what are the practical consequences of a mistake made in good faith, or of a properly supervised salesman's disregard of his instructions to confine his activities to residents? There can be no criminal liability without proof of willfulness, and there have been relatively few criminal prosecutions of any kind under §5 alone. But in a proceeding to revoke a broker-dealer's registration under the 1934 Act, which requires a finding both of willfulness and of public interest, the Commission held that evidence of the broker-dealer's reliance on advice of counsel and of his effort in good faith to restrict the offering to residents was relevant only to the question whether the public interest required the imposition of a sanction and did not negative a finding of a willful violation.[7] By the same token, it is the Commission's policy, once the exemption has been lost under its view, however innocently, to threaten injunctive proceedings if the offering is continued without registration, to require that the registration statement disclose a contingent liability under §12(1) with respect to the shares already sold in violation of §5, and to insist that the issuer offer rescission to those persons on the basis of a statutory prospectus.

One can understand the enforcement agency's attitude that it should construe all exemptions strictly until the courts hold otherwise. And it is true, almost by hypothesis, that the Commission, when it examines the prospectuses that are used in purportedly exempt offerings (if, indeed, any prospectuses are used at all), will find material misstatements or omissions as compared with the pro-

[5] Gadsby, The SEC and the Financing of Small Business, 14 Bus. Law. 144, 148 (1958).

[6] See p. 348 and c. 5D infra.

[7] Whitehall Corp., 38 SEC 259, 273-74 (1958).

spectuses that buyers would have received in the event of registration. Yet it is difficult to believe that Congress intended to make the issuer an absolute insurer of every offeree's residence and of every salesman's integrity. Unless the standard is one of due care — which includes reasonable supervision of all selling agents and may well require something more than an automatic acceptance of the buyer's representation — the exemption is virtually read out of the statute. Perhaps it should be. But that presumably is why Congress sits. Meanwhile, although it is usually impracticable to litigate with the Commission when an issuer is primarily interested in completing its financing — and although prudent counsel, with the potentialities of strict liability under §12(1) and of class actions in mind, will think twice before counseling reliance on §3(a)(11) (with or without Rule 147), particularly in the case of a substantial public offering — a seller against whom a claim is made for rescission or damages under §12(1) would be well advised to defend if he thinks he used reasonable care.

In the preparation of the Code it was early decided to develop a successor exemption "that would serve the need without undue risk to either the user or the investor"[8] or, if that turned out to be impracticable, to delete the exemption altogether as little more than a trap for the unwary. As matters turned out after several false starts, a considerable expansion of the exemption was the other side of the partial preemption coin.[9] This effort to enhance the states' responsibility with respect to "local distributions"(the Code's term) produced an endorsement of the Code's federal-state balance by the North American Securities Administrators Association.[10]

D. "SMALL" ISSUES [§§3(b), 4(6)]

1. THE "SMALL BUSINESS" DILEMMA

"Small business" is the darling of Congress and the essence of the American dream. But "small business" is also the source of many of the frauds and other problems at which securities regulation is directed. In a 1941 report to Congress the Commission stated that its "experience demonstrates that the evils of high pressure salesmanship and of selling on the basis of inadequate infor-

[8] 2 Code 970.
[9] See §§514, 1904.
[10] See 2 Code 966-81.

mation are particularly prevalent in small issues."[1] It is not that "captains of industry" are inherently more saintly than struggling entrepreneurs or promoters. It is simply that successful business people, like successful politicians, sometimes become statesmen, whereas new business enterprises invitably have a high mortality rate. Partly on that account, new businesses — and to a lesser extent old businesses that are relatively small — find it hard to obtain financing, and more expensive when they do.

Still, a healthy capitalistic system dare not allow small enterprise to dry up. And so over the years both Congress and the SEC have addressed the problem of financing small business in various (not always consistent) ways. For example:

Under the Small Business Investment Act of 1958, "small business investment companies," themselves financed in part by the Small Business Administration, were designed to provide a source of both equity capital and loan funds to eligible small business;[2] and Congress concurrently added §3(c) to the 1933 Act, under which the SEC adopted Regulation E in order conditionally to exempt offerings by SBA-licensed small business investment companies up to $500,000, now $5 million, each year (except that no single non-issuer offering may exceed $100,000).[3] Again, the Regulatory Flexibility Act of 1980 requires each agency, among other things, to publish a plan for periodic review of all rules with a significant impact on a substantial number of small entities.[4] And the Small Business Investment Incentive Act of 1980 amended the Investment Company Act by establishing a new regulatory system for certain investment companies called "business development companies."[5]

C. 5D [1]SEC, Report on Proposals for Amendments to the Securities Act of 1933 and the Securities Exchange Act of 1934, H. R. Com. Print, Com. on Int'l & For. Commerce, 77th Cong., 1st Sess. (1941) 17.

[2]15 U.S.C. §§661-96.

[3]On the increase, see Sec. Act Rel. 6546, 31 SEC Dock. 292 (1984). The $5 million figure is the maximum permitted by §3(b) (infra p. 309). Section 3(c) has no maximum.

[4]5 U. S. C. §§601-12; see Sec. Act Rel. 6323, 22 SEC Dock. 1319 (1981).

[5]94 Stat. 2275 (1980). Section 2(a)(48) of the 1940 Act defines a "business development company," in effect, as a domestic, closed-end company that (1) is operated for the purpose of making investments in small and developing as well as financially troubled businesses, (2) makes available significant managerial assistance to its portfolio companies, and (3) has notified the Commission of its election to be subject to the system of regulation established by §§55-65 of the 1940 Act. The 1984 amendment of Regulation E (supra) also extended the exemption to business development companies. See generally Thomas and Roye, Regulation of Business Development Companies Under the Investment Company Act, 55 So. Cal. L. Rev. 895 (1982); Bergman, Business Development Companies, 17 Rev. Sec. Reg. 877 (1984).

As part of the same piece of legislation Congress enacted also the Omnibus Small Business Capital Formation Act of 1980[6] and the Small Business Issuers' Simplification Act of 1980.[7]

The former Act added §19(c) to the 1933 Act in order to encourage cooperation between the SEC and state securities authorities by way of achieving "maximum uniformity in Federal and State standards" (including uniform forms and a uniform registration exemption for "small issuers") and "minimum interference with the business of capital formation." Toward these ends the Commission is directed to conduct, at least annually, a conference with representatives of associations of state securities officials, self-regulatory organizations, and private organizations involved in capital formation. And other provisions (which are not mechanically incorporated into any of the existing SEC statutes) direct the Commission to "gather, analyze, and make available to the public, information with respect to the capital formation needs, and the problems and costs involved with new, small, medium-sized, and independent businesses,"[8] and to make the results available to the Small Business Administration; to "conduct an annual Government-business forum to review the current status of problems and programs relating to small business capital formation"; and to "use its best efforts to identify and reduce the costs of raising capital in connection with the issuance of securities by firms whose aggregate outstanding securities and other indebtedness have a market value of $25,000,000 or less."[9]

The Small Business Issuers' Simplification Act of 1980 added §4(6) to the 1933 Act in order to exempt

> transactions involving offers or sales by an issuer solely to one or more accredited investors, if the aggregate offering price of an issue of securities offered in reliance on this paragraph does not exceed the amount allowed under section 3(b) of this title, if there is no

[6] 95 Stat. 2291 (1980), scattered in U. S. C.

[7] 15 U. S. C. §§77b, 77d(6).

[8] Code §1903(g)(1) substitutes "independent businesses that are (A) new, or (B) small or medium-sized" — wording that better expresses what is understood to have been intended.

[9] See SEC Government-Business Forum on Small Business Capital Formation, Final Report (Nov. 1982), which made a number of recommendations, by no means limited to securities regulation. Five such reports have thus far been published, the last in February 1987. See Sec. Act Rel. 6689, 37 SEC Dock. 782 (1987). And in Sec. Act Rel. 6474, 28 SEC Dock. 474 (1983), the SEC and the NASAA announced public hearings pursuant to §19(c) and requested comments on increased uniformity in state and federal regulation. See SEC and NASAA Conference on Federal-State Securities Regulation, CCH Fed. Sec. L. Rep. ¶83,610 (1984).

advertising or public solicitation in connection with the transaction by the issuer or anyone acting on the issuer's behalf, and if the issuer files such notice with the Commission as the Commission shall prescribe.[10]

The term "accredited investor" is defined in a new §2(15) of the 1933 Act to mean, in substance, a bank, registered investment company, or licensed small business investment company, or any other person specified by Commission rule "on the basis of such factors as financial sophistication, net worth, knowledge, and experience in financial matters, or amount of assets under management."[11] This is substantially the Code's definition of "institutional investor" for purposes of its "limited offering" concept.

Even before this legislation, the SEC, for its part, held a series of hearings throughout the country in 1978-79 with respect to the effects of its rules and the disclosure requirements of the statutes on the ability of small businesses to raise capital.[12] And in 1979 it adopted a simplified Form S-18 for cash offerings up to $5 million (now $7.5 million)[13] by certain domestic or Canadian corporate issuers that are not already reporting companies under the Exchange Act. The narrative disclosure called for is somewhat less extensive than it is in Form S-1. And audited financial statements, which are required for only two rather than the three fiscal years of Form S-1, must comply only with generally accepted accounting principles, not with Regulation S-X.[14]

Much earlier than all this the joint effort of Congress *and* Commission produced a series of "small issue" exemptions from §5 of the 1933 Act. Section 3(b) gives the Commission rulemaking authority to exempt any "issue" up to a maximum amount that has grown in stages from $100,000 in 1933-45 to $5 million since late 1980. And the Commission has adopted a series of exemptions

[10]The §3(b) amount (see p. 309 infra) is now $5 million, and the notice requirement is reflected in Form D.

[11]The Commission has further defined the term in Rule 215. See p. 314 n. 59 infra.

[12]Sec. Act Rel. 5914, 14 SEC Dock. 314 (1978).

[13]See Sec. Act Rel. 6489, 28 SEC Dock. 1171 (1983).

[14]Sec. Act Rel. 6049, 17 SEC Dock. 153 (1979). The S-18 form (which may not be used by companies reporting under the 1934 Act) may be filed in the SEC Regional Office where the company conducts or intends to conduct its principal business operations. See generally Arnold and Hopkins, Small Firm Securities Registration in S-18 Era: Perceptions of Professionals, 8 Corp. L. Rev. 135 (1985). The difficulty is that those who use Form S-18 tend to take refuge by including the fuller disclosure of Form S-1 for fear of liability under §11.

under that section that provide a panoply from which to choose in accordance with the facts of the particular case.

2. Regulation A

a. Maximum Offering Price

The principal exemption under §3(b) (at least until recent years) has always been Regulation A, which now consists of Rules 251-64.[15] It is often referred to as "short-form registration." But, of course, it is not registration at all. It is a conditional exemption. Among other differences, §11 liability for false registration statements does not attach to selling literature used in Regulation A offerings; there only §12(2), Rule 10b-5,[16] and perhaps §17(a) apply by way of civil liability.

Although the §3(b) authority now goes to $5 million, the Regulation A limit is $1.5 million in aggregate offering price (inclusive of any securities offered or sold pursuant to any other exemption under §3(b) or in violation of §5(a) within a year before the commencement of the proposed offering). But that figure applies only when the offering is for the account of (1) the issuer, (2) the estate of a decedent who owned the securities at his death if they are offered within two years after that date, or (3) a control affiliate of the issuer (except that the maximum is $100,000 for the account of any single affiliate other than an estate). Otherwise the maximum is $300,000 rather than $1.5 million (with the same limitation per affiliate).[17] In any event, when portions of a "hot issue" are withheld or taken by insiders and then sold at a higher price in the market shortly after the initial offering, one must guard against the limitation's being exceeded; for the distribution is not completed until the stock "ultimately comes to rest in the hands of the investing public."[18]

[15] For what is substantially a treatise on Regulation A as it then stood, written by a lawyer who was in charge of Regulation A interpretations in the SEC's New York Regional Office, see Weiss, Regulation A Under the Securities Act of 1933 — Highways and Byways, 8 N. Y. L. F. 3 (1962); Weiss, Highways and Byways Revisited, 15 N. Y. L. F. 218 (1969).

[16] See p. 726 infra.

[17] Rule 254.

[18] R. A. Holman & Co. v. SEC, 366 F. 2d 446, 449, 450 (2d Cir. 1966), *amended on rehearing*, 377 F. 2d 665 (2d Cir. 1967), *aff'g* R. A. Holman & Co., 42 SEC 866, 869 (1965), *cert. denied*, 389 U. S. 991. Par value is irrelevant.

b. The "Issue" Concept

The §3(b) limitation is imposed on any "issue" — the same term used in §3(a)(11)[19]. The Commission early refused to construe that term "to permit the exemption of small portions of large financing operations," either by claiming exemption for a small portion and registering the remainder or by the formality of successive yearly filings under the regulation if the shares otherwise constituted a single "issue." This view, expounded in the leading *Unity Gold* case,[20] has not been changed so far as the "issue" concept in the intrastate exemption or the similar concept read into the 3(a)(9) exemption is concerned.[21] But it was expressly abandoned, presumably under the Commission's statutory power to define "technical" terms,[22] in the 1941 revision of Regulation A.[23] The 1941-53 regulation specifically permitted the full amount to be offered in any twelve-month period, year after year; or that amount might be offered under the exemption and the balance immediately registered, without regard to whether the successive offerings constituted an integrated plan of financing.[24] And this is still the Commission's view, although the specific provision was omitted, presumably as surplusage, in the revised regulation.

Nevertheless, in 1948, when the limit was $100,000, the Commission repeated its *Unity Gold* language almost word for word in order to hold that there had been a single "issue," all of which had been sold in violation of §5, when 74,000 shares of stock had been offered under Regulation A at $1 and five months later 50,000 additional shares had been offered without benefit of registration or any other exemption.[25] Of course, the 50,000 shares were sold illegally under any view. But the Commission's going out of its way to hold that the first 74,000 shares had also been sold in violation can mean only that the relaxation of the "issue" concept incorporated in the 1941 revision of Regulation A is not to be extended by interpretation.[26] Moreover, under a special rule that the Commission adopted in the 1956 revision for promotional companies

Mines & Metals Corp. v. SEC, 200 F. 2d 317, 319-20 (9th Cir. 1952), *cert. denied*, 345 U. S. 941.

[19] See p. 296 supra.

[20] Unity Gold Corp., 3 SEC 618, 625 (1938).

[21] See pp. 278-79, 296 supra.

[22] §19(a).

[23] Sec. Act Rel. 2410 (1940).

[24] Former Rule 220(e), Sec. Act Rel. 2410 (1940).

[25] Herbert R. May, 27 SEC 814, 817-20 (1948).

[26] Cf. Batkin & Co., 38 SEC 436, 448 (1958).

and those without a specified earnings record, the "issue" includes, unless a specified escrow or similar arrangement is made,

> (1) all securities issued prior to the filing of the offering statement,[27] or proposed to be issued, for a consideration consisting in whole or part of assets or services and held by the person to whom issued; and
> (2) all securities issued to and held by or proposed to be issued, pursuant to options or otherwise, to any director, officer or promoter of the issuer, or to any underwriter, dealer or security salesman.[28]

There are, however, limited exclusions in computing the aggregate offering price.[29]

c. Offering Statement

Unless the Commission accelerates the period on a written request, no securities may be offered under Regulation A until ten business days after the filing with the appropriate Regional Office of an offering statement on Form 1-A in three parts: (I) Notification; (II) Offering Circular; and (III) Exhibits.[30] As with a registration statement, the filing of an amendment starts the period running anew unless the Commission accelerates.

There are also provisions modeled on the "tombstone ad," preliminary prospectus, and post-offering report rules, as well as the nine-month prospectus provision.[31] But Regulation A goes even further in requiring (1) that the offering circular be furnished, in the case of a company that does not report under the 1934 Act, forty-eight hours before the confirmation is mailed,[32] and (2) that copies of all sales literature be filed five days before use.[33]

On the other hand, no offering circular is required at all with respect to an offering of not more than $100,000 by a nonpromo-

[27] See pp. 311-12 infra.
[28] Rule 253(c).
[29] Rule 254(d).
[30] Rule 255. Regulation A does not require an audit. But state authorities and underwriters frequently do, and the SEC *encourages* audits. In any event, the issuer, if not already a registrant under §12(g) of the 1934 Act (see p. 411 infra), is apt to become one, and thus to have to have an audit after completion of the offering. And the cost of an audit to a start-up company is not great.
[31] See pp. 107, 108, 134, 150 supra.
[32] Rule 256(a).
[33] Rule 258.

tional company, except for the filing (not the use) of the nonfinancial information normally required in an offering circular.[34]

d. Exclusions and Suspensions

In substance, Regulation A is available only to issuers that are incorporated and also have their principal business operations in the United States or Canada.[35] Investment company securities and fractional undivided interests in oil, gas, or mineral rights are excluded.[36] Certain criminal, injunctive, or disciplinary records (sometimes called the "bad boy" provisions) bar access to the exemption.[37] So does noncompliance with the reporting requirements of the 1934 Act when they apply.[38] And the Commission has reserved the authority temporarily or permanently to suspend the exemption on certain findings.[39]

e. Code

Regulation A has suffered from a mild odor in the olfactory glands of some investment bankers and lawyers:[40] Frauds there have been here. But, quite apart from the fact that Regulation A has been used by some relatively small but established companies, its reputation reflects to a large extent the inevitable risk of investing in new and unproved enterprises.

Although the importance of Regulation A offerings when measured by the universe of capital formation is small, a 1982 staff study by SEC economists[41] concluded that, "in comparison with the other vehicles available for the raising of funds, in particular by smaller or new enterprises, the Regulation A exemption may possess char-

[34] Rule 257.

[35] Rule 252(a).

[36] Rule 252(b).

[37] Rule 252(c)-(e).

[38] Rule 252(f).

[39] Rule 261.

[40] 1 SEC, Report of Special Study of Securities Markets, H. R. Doc. No. 95, 88th Cong., 1st Sess. (1963) 496-97. These offerings have suffered also from the "hot issue" sobriquet. See CCH NASD Manual ¶2151.06; Grienenberger, The "Hot Issue" Amendments and New Disclosure Guides, in Practising Law Institute, Fifth Annual Institute on Securities Regulation (1974) c. 4.

[41] SEC, Directorate of Economic and Policy Analysis, An Analysis of the Use of Regulation A for Small Offerings (1982) esp. c. 1, History and Background of Regulation A.

acteristics which are attractive to prospective issuers and not possessed by alternative capital raising vehicles."[42]

3. Regulation D

In 1975 the Commission adopted a Rule 240 in order conditionally to exempt certain offerings up to $100,000 annually by closely held issuers.[43] And effective in February 1980 it adopted a much broader Rule 242, which on certain conditions exempted issues up to $2 million in a six-month period if the number of buyers (not offerees) was limited to thirty-five apart from "accredited persons" as defined.[44] In 1982, the Commission adopted Regulation D as an amalgam of those two rules (with changes) and the former Rule 146 with respect to the statutory exemption for nonpublic offerings.[45] Regulation D consists of six rules. Rules 504-06 replace Rules 240, 242, and 146. And Rules 501-03 contain definitions and conditions that apply to the regulation generally (that is to say, to all three exemptions). Consequently, Rules 504 and 505 will be discussed here, and Rule 506 will be discussed in the next subchapter in connection with the private offering exemption in §4(2).

Rule 504, since it is "an effort by the Commission to set aside a clear and workable exemption for small offerings by small issuers to be regulated by state 'Blue Sky' requirements" and to be subject only to antifraud provisions at the federal level,[46] is limited to primary offerings of securities whose issuers are neither reporting companies under the 1934 Act nor investment companies.[47] The limit is $500,000 in twelve months, inclusive of all offerings made under any §3(b) exemptive rule or in violation of §5.[48] There is the same type of "integration" provision, in terms of six months on either side of the offering, that appears in Rule 147, the intrastate exemp-

[42] Id. at 6.

[43] Sec. Act Rel. 5560, 6 SEC Dock. 132 (1975).

[44] Sec. Act Rel. 6180, 19 SEC Dock. 295 (1980).

[45] Sec. Act Rel. 6389, 24 SEC Dock. 1166 (1982). On the former Rule 146, see p. 324 infra. For a considerable number of staff interpretations of Regulation D, see Sec. Act Rel. 6455, 27 SEC Dock. 347 (1983); see also Warren, A Review of Regulation D: The Present Exemption Regimen for Limited Offerings Under the Securities Act of 1933, 33 Am. U. L. Rev. 355 (1984); J. Long, 1985 Blue Sky Law Handbook: Developments in State Securities Regulation (1984) 5-62 to 5-117; Wertheimer, Problems of Small Issues, in Practising Law Institute, Fifteenth Annual Institute on Securities Regulation (1984) c. 7.

[46] Sec. Act Rel. 6389, 24 SEC Dock. 1166, 1168 (1982).

[47] Rule 504(a).

[48] Rule 504(b)(2).

tion "safe harbor" rule.[49] Although there is no preoffer filing requirement, notices of sales must be filed on Form D at specified times.[50] There may be no "general solicitation or general advertising."[51] And, so far as resales are concerned, the securities have the status of those acquired in a private offering.[52] But these last two conditions do not apply to offers and sales made exclusively in one or more states in accordance with their requirements of registration and pre-sale delivery of a disclosure document[53] — a conditional bow to state regulation that is a bit inconsistent philosophically with the express negation in Rule 504 of any requirement that specific information be furnished to buyers.[54]

The Rule 505 exemption applies to primary offerings by any issuer other than an investment company or an issuer disqualified under Rule 252(c)-(f) of Regulation A,[55] and it extends to the full $5 million permitted by §3(b) (with the same "integration" treatment as in Rule 504).[56] Moreover, the treatment with respect to general solicitation or advertising, resales, and filings is the same in both rules (without the bow to state law that is in Rule 504). But the greater liberality of Rule 505 is balanced by additional conditions: The issuer must "reasonably believe" that there are not more than thirty-five buyers,[57] with an elaborate prescription of how to calculate the number,[58] a prescription that excludes an "accredited investor" from the count.[59] And, except for sales only to "ac-

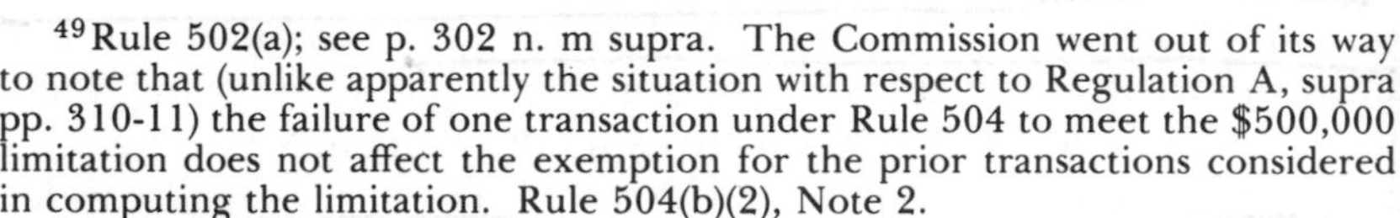

[49] Rule 502(a); see p. 302 n. m supra. The Commission went out of its way to note that (unlike apparently the situation with respect to Regulation A, supra pp. 310-11) the failure of one transaction under Rule 504 to meet the $500,000 limitation does not affect the exemption for the prior transactions considered in computing the limitation. Rule 504(b)(2), Note 2.

[50] Rule 503.

[51] Rule 502(c).

[52] Rule 502(d). See p. 357 infra.

[53] Rule 504(b)(1).

[54] Rule 502(b)(1)(i).

[55] Rules 505(a), 505(b)(2)(iii).

[56] Rule 505(b)(2)(i).

[57] Rule 505(b)(2)(ii). This formula was borrowed from the Code's concept of a "limited offering." See p. 348 infra.

[58] Rule 501(e). See Morgenstern, Corporations, Partnerships and Trusts As Purchasers Under Regulation D, 7 Real Est. Sec. J. 46, 46-49 (1986).

[59] The statutory definition of this term in §2(15) (see p. 308 supra) is enlarged in Rule 215 to include (among others) any director, executive officer, or general partner of the issuer, any buyer of at least $150,000 of securities if that amount does not exceed 20 percent of his net worth, and any natural person whose net worth exceeds $1 million or who had more than $200,000 of income in each of the two past years and reasonably expects to do as well in the current year; and the entire definition from §2(15) and Rule 215 is repeated in Rule 501(a) for ease of reference. The rich, apparently, are honorary financial sophisticates. See Morganstern, supra n. 58, at 49-65.

credited investors," the issuer must furnish each buyer, before the sale, with prescribed information centered basically around (1) the last annual report to stockholders and various filings under the 1934 Act when the issuer is a reporting company under that Act and (2) Part I of Form S-18[60] in other cases.[61]

Regulation D was expressly designed, in part, to achieve uniformity between state and federal exemptions in order to facilitate capital formation consistent with the protection of investors. And in 1983 the North American Securities Administrators Association approved a "Uniform Limited Offering Exemption" statute that incorporates Rule 505,[62] with additional conditions.[63] A footnote contemplates the possibility of a state's accepting Rule 506 offerings "within the ambit of this exemption." But it cautions that the absence of a dollar limit there creates regulatory concerns, in recognition of which it states that "Rule 506 is not adopted as part of the basic ULOE."[64]

4. LIMITED SALES TO "ACCREDITED INVESTORS" [§4(6)]

Cutting across all this, as we have already noticed,[65] is Congress's 1980 gift of §4(6). That exemption, which is, of course, self-operative except for the Commission's authority (reflected in Form D) to require the filing of notice, extends to offerings up to the §3(b) limit (now $5 million) to "accredited investors." Section 4(6) is thus a hybrid that combines elements of §3(b) (small size) and §4(2)

[60] See p. 308 supra.
[61] Rule 502(b).
[62] See p. 314 supra.
[63] CCH NASAA Rep. ¶6201.
[64] Id., n. 1. See generally SEC and NASAA Conference on Federal-State Securities Regulation, CCH Fed. Sec. L. Rep. ¶83,610 at 86,753-54, 86,761-62 (1984); SEC, Directorate of Economic and Policy Analysis, An Analysis of Regulation D (1984) esp. at 1 and Ex. A; J. Long, 1985 Blue Sky Law Handbook: Developments in State Securities Regulation (1984) 5-118 to 5-135. Some form of ULOE has been adopted in a majority of states, and both the SEC and the NASAA are encouraging its universal adoption. Sec. Act Rel. 6561, 31 SEC Dock. 1044, 1046 (1984). For a detailed state-to-state analysis, including a tabular summary, see Hainsfurther, Summary of Blue Sky Exemptions Corresponding to Regulation D, 38 Sw. L. J. 989 (1984).

In late 1986 the SEC with the cooperation of the NASAA proposed revisions to Form D designed to make it a uniform notification form that could be filed with the Commission and the states. Sec. Act Rel. 6650, 35 SEC Dock. 1090 (1986). And in January 1987 the Commission proposed a number of general amendments to Regulation D. Sec. Act Rel. 6683, 37 SEC Dock. 588 (1987).
[65] See pp. 307-08 supra.

(private offerings). But, as the following colloquy demonstrates, the gift was not too generous:

MR. FLEISCHER [OF THE NEW YORK BAR]: If Section 4(2) is presently available for sales to institutions, why would one bother using the 4(6) exemption?

MS. WERTHEIMER [OF THE DALLAS BAR]: One would not, and the exemption has limited utility.

Remember that much of the impetus for Section 4(6) came from the White House Small-Business Conference. Partnerships had been complaining about not being able to use Rule 242, which was already in existence, and this exemption may have been a bone that was thrown them, although in its present form it is limited to institutional sales. Mickey, do you know any more about the background than that?

MS. BEACH [ASSOCIATE DIRECTOR, DIVISION OF CORPORATION FINANCE, SEC]: Not really. I think you are right, that it may very well be that this is not a significant extension of the existing Rule 242 exemption. In many ways it is more restrictive than Rule 242, since no securities may be sold to individuals and no big-ticket purchasers are included as accredited investors. As Art said, if you sell only to institutions, Section 4(2) probably presents no problem.[66]

5. SPECIALIZED EXEMPTIVE RULES

There are three exemptions under §3(b) that are specialized in one way or another:

(1) Regulation B (Rules 300-46) conditionally exempts offerings of various species of fractional undivided interests in oil or gas rights up to $250,000 per year. Among other conditions, there may be no sales or payment until forty-eight hours after delivery of a specified "offering sheet," which must also be filed, and the Commission requires satisfactory assurance that notification of the offering has been furnished to the authorities in each state in which it is to be made.[67]

(2) In 1959, concurrently with the adoption of an interpretative rule to the effect that the levying of an assessment on assessable

[66] Wertheimer, Small Offerings: Recent SEC and Legislative Initiatives, in Practising Law Institute, Twelfth Annual Institute on Securities Regulation (1981) c. 17 at 293. In addition, §4(6) (like Rules 505 and 506 but unlike Regulation A) is limited to primary offerings by issuers.

[67] Rule 310(e). This requirement applies even though a particular state itself requires no filing. Sec. Act Rel. 5662, 8 SEC Dock. 807 (1975). On Regulation B generally, see SEC v. Hansen, CCH Fed. Sec. L. Rep. ¶91,426 at 98,115-17 (S. D. N. Y. 1984).

stock involves an "offer" and "sale," the Commission adopted Regulation F (Rules 651-56) in order to exempt (1) "Assessments on assessable stock of any corporation incorporated and having its "principal business operations" in the United States and (2) "Assessable stock of any such corporation offered or sold at public auction or otherwise for the purpose of realizing the amount of an assessment levied thereon." In computing the $300,000 maximum permitted in any twelve-month period by the regulation, there must be included "all assessments levied on assessable stock of the issuer" and all securities offered under any §3(b) exemptive rule or sold in violation of §5(a). There are filing and suspension procedures.

(3) Rule 236 conditionally exempts a reporting company's share offerings up to $300,000 to provide funds to be distributed to the issuer's shareholders in lieu of issuing fractional shares or scrip certificates in connection with a stock dividend or merger or the like.

E. PRIVATE OFFERINGS [§4(2)]

1. The Statutory Exemption Historically

Section 4(2) exempts "transactions by an issuer not involving any public offering." These nine words support a substantial gloss.

The legislative history is of little help except insofar as the general tone may be set by the House committee's reference to this exemption as permitting "an issuer to make a specific or an isolated sale of its securities to a particular person," and to the exemption generally as directed to transactions "where there is no practical need for [the bill's] application or where the public benefits are too remote."[1]

The administrative construction was early set in an opinion of the SEC's General Counsel to the effect that the determination whether a particlar transaction involves a public offering depends on all the surrounding circumstances. Apart from the number of offerees, he said, important factors are their relationship to each other and to the issuer, the number of units offered, and the manner of offering.[2]

In that opinion, which was written in the context of a proposed offering of $1,766,000 of preferred stock to twenty-five persons, the General Counsel had thought it "a much wiser policy for me

C. 5E [1]H. R. Rep. No. 85, 73d Cong., 1st Sess. (1933) 5, 7, 15-16.
[2]Sec. Act Rel. 285 (1935).

not to express an opinion * * * as to whether a public offering is involved." Nevertheless, while emphasizing the necessity of considering all surrounding circumstances, he did not withdraw the opinion referred to by him as having been expressed by his office that "under ordinary circumstances an offering to not more than approximately 25 persons is not an offering to a substantial number and presumably does not involve a public offering." And in the case of an offering to institutional investors the Commission was known not to object to a hundred or more offerees.

That was the rubric until the Supreme Court decided *SEC v. Ralston Purina Co.* in 1953,[3] to the effect that long-time offerings of treasury stock to "key employees" were "public" offerings. During the preceding five years the company had thus sold nearly $2 million of stock. In Justice Clark's words:

> In each of these years, a corporate resolution authorized the sale of common stock "to employees * * * who shall, without any solicitation by the Company or its officers or employees, inquire of any of them as to how to purchase common stock of Ralston Purina Company." A memorandum sent to branch and store managers after the resolution was adopted advised that "The only employees to whom this stock will be available will be those who take the initiative and are interested in buying stock at present market prices." Among those responding to these offers were employees with the duties of artist, bakeshop foreman, chow loading foreman, clerical assistant, copywriter, electrician, stock clerk, mill office clerk, order credit trainee, production trainee, stenographer, and veterinarian. The lowest salary bracket of those purchasing was $2,700 in 1949, $2,435 in 1950 and $3,107 in 1951. The record shows that in 1947, 243 employees bought stock, 20 in 1948, 414 in 1949, 411 in 1950, and the 1951 offer, interrupted by this litigation, produced 165 applications to purchase. No records were kept of those to whom the offers were made; the estimated number in 1951 was 500.
>
> The company bottoms its exemption claim on the classification of all offerees as "key employees" in its organization. Its position on trial was that "A key employee * * * is not confined to an organization chart. It would include an individual who is eligible for promotion, an individual who especially influences others or who advises others, a person whom the employees look to in some special way, an individual, of course, who carries some special responsibility, who is sympathetic to management and who is ambitious and who the management feels is likely to be promoted to a greater responsibility." That an offering to all of its employees would be public is conceded.

[3] 346 U. S. 119 (1953).

The Securities Act nowhere defines the scope of §4(1)'s private offering exemption. Nor is the legislative history of much help in staking out its boundaries. * * *

Decisions under comparable exemptions in the English Companies Acts and state "blue sky" laws, the statutory antecedents of federal securities legislation, have made one thing clear — to be public an offer need not be open to the whole world.[7] In *Securities and Exchange Comm'n* v. *Sunbeam Gold Mines Co.*, 95 F. 2d 699 (C. A. 9th Cir. 1938), this point was made in dealing with an offering to the stockholders of two corporations about to be merged. Judge Denman observed that:

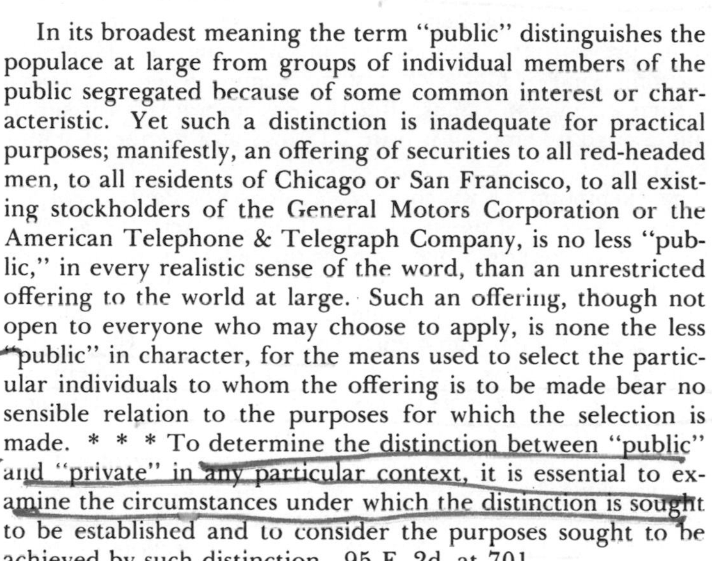

> In its broadest meaning the term "public" distinguishes the populace at large from groups of individual members of the public segregated because of some common interest or characteristic. Yet such a distinction is inadequate for practical purposes; manifestly, an offering of securities to all red-headed men, to all residents of Chicago or San Francisco, to all existing stockholders of the General Motors Corporation or the American Telephone & Telegraph Company, is no less "public," in every realistic sense of the word, than an unrestricted offering to the world at large. Such an offering, though not open to everyone who may choose to apply, is none the less "public" in character, for the means used to select the particular individuals to whom the offering is to be made bear no sensible relation to the purposes for which the selection is made. * * * To determine the distinction between "public" and "private" in any particular context, it is essential to examine the circumstances under which the distinction is sought to be established and to consider the purposes sought to be achieved by such distinction. 95 F. 2d, at 701.

* * *

Exemption from the registration requirements of the Securities Act is the question. The design of the statute is to protect investors by promoting full disclosure of information thought necessary to informed investment decisions. The natural way to interpret the private offering exemption is in light of the statutory purpose. Since exempt transactions are those as to which "there is no practical need for [the bill's] application," the applicability of §§4(1) [now §4(2)]

[7] Nash v. Lynde, [1929] A. C. 158; In re South of England Natural Gas and Petroleum Co. Ltd., [1911] 1 Ch. 573; cf. Sherwell v. Combined Incandescent Mantles Syndicate, Ltd., 23 T. L. R. 482 (1907). See 80 Sol. J. 785 (1936).

People v. Montague, 280 Mich. 610, 274 N. W. 347 (1937); In re Leach, 215 Cal. 536, 12 P. 2d 3 (1932); Mary Pickford Co. v. Bayly Bros., 68 P. 2d 239 (1937), *modified,* 12 Cal. 2d 501, 86 P. 2d 102 (1939).

should turn on whether the particular class of persons affected needs the protection of the Act. An offering to those who are shown to be able to fend for themselves is a transaction "not involving any public offering."

The Commission would have us go one step further and hold that "an offering to a substantial number of the public" is not exempt under §4(1). We are advised that "whatever the special circumstances, the Commission has consistently interpreted the exemption as being inapplicable when a large number of offerees is involved." But the statute would seem to apply to a "public offering" whether to few or many.[11] It may well be that offerings to a substantial number of persons would rarely be exempt. Indeed nothing prevents the commission, in enforcing the statute, from using some kind of numerical test in deciding when to investigate particular exemption claims. But there is no warrant for superimposing a quantity limit on private offerings as a matter of statutory interpretation.

The exemption, as we construe it, does not deprive corporate employees, as a class, of the safeguards of the Act. We agree that some employee offerings may come within §4(1), e. g., one made to executive personnel who because of their position have access to the same kind of information that the Act would make available in the form of a registration statement. Absent such a showing of special circumstances, employees are just as much members of the investing "public" as any of their neighbors in the community. Although we do not rely on it, the rejection in 1934 of an amendment which would have specifically exempted employee stock offerings supports this conclusion. The House Managers, commenting on the Conference Report, said that "the participants in employees' stock-investment plans may be in as great need of the protection afforded by availability of information concerning the issuer for which they work as are most other members of the public." H. R. Rep. No. 1838, 73d Cong., 2d Sess. 41.

* * * the court below thought the burden [of proof] met primarily because of the respondent's purpose in singling out its key employees for stock offerings. But once it is seen that the exemption question turns on the knowledge of the offerees, the issuer's motives, laudable though they may be, fade into irrelevance. The focus of inquiry should be on the need of the offerees for the protections afforded by registration. The employees here were not shown to have access to the kind of information which registration would

focus: need of offerees for information

[11] See Viscount Sumner's frequently quoted dictum in Nash v. Lynde: " 'The Public' * * * is of course a general word. No particular numbers are prescribed. Anything from two to infinity may serve: perhaps even one, if he is intended to be the first of a series of subscribers, but makes further proceedings needless by himself subscribing the whole." [1929] A. C. 158, 169.

disclose. The obvious opportunities for pressure and imposition make it advisable that they be entitled to compliance with §5.

Ralston Purina has produced no end of mischief:

(1) True, the language of §4(2) came out of the British Companies Act 1929.[4] But, both §4(2) and the legislative history being as sparse as they are, was there any policy reason to follow the House of Lords in worrying about number and type of offerees rather than buyers? How is an offeree hurt if he does not buy?

(2) Suppose an offering is made to ten "self-fending" types, all of whom buy, and one "*non*-self-fender" who does *not* buy. Should the first ten be able to recover under §12(1)?

(3) When the *Ralston* approach is carried to the point where an offer to a single person becomes a "public" offering,[5] have we not left the world of reason — or, at least, abandoned the English language?

(4) In considering whether an offering to not more than a relatively small number of persons (perhaps twenty-five) may safely be assumed to be private notwithstanding any other factors, arguably the Court's rejection of a quantity limit was not directed to a number *below* which an offering might be deemed *private* but was by way of reply to the Commission's argument that the substantial number of offerees in the *Ralston* case conclusively established without more that the offering was *public*. In other words, the Court, still arguably, rejected a rule of thumb on the top side, not the bottom side.

At least as late as 1961, the present writer thought it "apparent from an examination of the subsequent cases and other expressions

[4]This language was retained as late as the Companies Act 1985. 1985 Acts c. 6, §56(3)(b), with an elaborate set of provisions defining the term, §§58(3), 59, 60. But the Financial Services Act 1986, which repealed the entire part of the 1985 Act dealing with "Capital Issues," abandoned the "public offering" phrase in favor of a provision that authorizes the Secretary of State — in practice, presumably the Securities and Investments Board (see p. 618 n. 10 infra) — to exempt by order "advertisements appearing to him to have a private character, whether by reason of a connection between the person issuing them and those to whom they are addressed or otherwise." 1986 Acts c. 60, §160(6)(a).

[5]G. Eugene England Foundation v. First Federal Corp., 663 F. 2d 988, 990 (10th Cir. 1973); see also Klapmeier v. Telecheck Int'l, Inc., 482 F. 2d 247, 254 (8th Cir. 1973) (stock-for-stock exchange with seven persons, all represented by one of them in negotiating a merger); Meadow Brook National Bank v. Levine, CCH Fed. Sec. L. Rep. ¶91,496 at 94,870 (N. Y. Sup. Ct. 1965) (dictum that, taken out of context, indicates the possibility that an offering to a single person in need of protection might not be exempted); but see Milnarik v. M-S Commodities, Inc., 320 F. Supp. 1149, 1153 (N. D. Ill. 1970), *aff'd on other grounds*, 457 F. 2d 274 (7th Cir. 1972), *cert. denied*, 409 U. S. 887 (despite *Ralston*, "an offering has never been held to be a public offering when it has been extended to only one person").

of the Commission's views" that "On the pragmatic rather than the semantic level, * * * the Supreme Court's opinion seems to have had little effect on the traditional position taken by the Commission except perhaps to strengthen it."[6] By 1969, however, he had to say: "Since 1958 or so, * * * the number of Commission disavowals of any safe numerical test, though mostly dicta, has grown to the point that one can no longer assume as a practical matter that an offering to not more than some twenty-five persons (or any lesser number) will be considered exempt even so far as Commission intervention as distinct from civil liability under §12(1) is concerned."[7]

What happened in the interim was a series of cases — most of them, as chance had it, in the Fifth Circuit[8] — that gradually narrowed the exemption to the point where the court in *Doran* v. *Petroleum Management Corp.*, the latest of these cases, went out of its way to emphasize that its earlier decisions had not meant to lay down any categorical requirement that every offeree be an "insider"[9] (presumably in the sense of the law that has developed under Rule 10b-5).[10] The "insider" approach is precisely what SEC counsel had argued in one of the earlier Fifth Circuit cases,[11] although a member of the Commission was quick to make a public disavowal.[12]

In *Doran* — which involved an offering of oil well limited partnership interests to eight sophisticated oil and gas investors, of whom the plaintiff was one of the five who accepted — the court held that sophistication itself was not enough. Sophistication is not a substi-

[6] 1 Loss 661-62 (1961).

[7] 4 Loss 2644 (1969). The Commission's General Counsel did say in December 1970: "As a rule, the Commission does not take after small transactions in the situation where the Supreme Court said we might. Unless we feel that there is more to it than a registration problem, we do not normally object, at least in court, to situations where the securities are offered to some fifteen or twenty people." Loomis, The Federal Securities Laws, 7 Ga. S. B. J. 353, 361 (1971). But see Thomas D. Conrad, Jr., 44 SEC 725 (1971), where the Commission held that, when the offerees were unsophisticated and "clearly did not have access to the same kind of information that registration would have supplied," the fact that there were only nine offerees and that the bonds were by their terms nontransferable did not suffice to make the offering private. See pp. 343-44 infra.

[8] 545 F. 2d 893 (5th Cir. 1977), and cases cited; see also Lawler v. Gilliam, 569 F. 2d 1283, 1289-91 (4th Cir. 1978).

[9] 545 F. 2d at 906-08.

[10] See c. 9B infra.

[11] Brief of SEC at 28, SEC v. Continental Tobacco Co. of S. C., 463 F. 2d 137 (5th Cir. 1972).

[12] Owens, A Look at the Private Offering Exemption As It Approaches Its Fortieth Birthday, Sec. Reg. L. Rep. No. 152, p. G-1 at G-2 (1972).

tute for availability of the information that registration would provide. Unless each offeree has been furnished that information directly, the defendant must show that each offeree had "access" — which is to say, "a relationship based on factors such as employment, family, or economic bargaining power that enables the offeree effectively to obtain such information."[13]

(5) It has been the accredited doctrine for some time that statutes should not be read literally, or even construed in accordance with a "legislative intention" that is often (as in this case) mythical or at best unclear, but that the correct approach is that enjoined on us by Justice Jackson in *Joiner*: to fathom the "dominating general purpose" and to go ahead with the business of interpretation "so far as the meaning of the words fairly permits so as to carry out in particular cases the generally expressed legislative policy."[14] Even so, do the two simple English words, "public offering," fairly permit the supersophisticated gloss that has surrounded them? At least from hindsight, would it not have been better if the Justices in *Ralston* had acted a bit less "professorial," simply agreeing with the Commission's position that at some point the number of offerees is so large (or presumably so small) as not to permit of debate, and had left the in-between cases to be decided on the basis of all the relevant circumstances as the Commission's General Counsel had viewed the matter in 1935?[15]

(6) If a person keeps lions in his backyard and one of them chews up a neighbor, it is altogether reasonable to hold him liable without proof of negligence; for the man-eating propensities of wild beasts are well known. But, when a §12(1) imposes liability on one who violates §5 — a question that raises all sorts of difficult subsidiary questions under §§2-4 — isn't the combination of strict liability and a fuzzy substructure an abominable kind of jurisprudence?

The fact is — a point made with his usual felicity by the late Ray Garrett, Jr., a few years before he was to become Chairman of the SEC — that the Fifth Circuit series involved promotional offerings, which are but one of four discernible *loci classici* under the §4(2) rubric. The other three are offerings to employees, the issuance of

[13] 545 F. 2d at 903. Even a showing of "availability" (in the sense of actual information or access) "is not independently sufficient to establish that the offering qualified for the private placement exemption, but it is necessary to gain the exemption and is to be weighed along with the sophistication and number of the offerees, the number of units offered, and the size and manner of the offering." Id. at 904.

[14] SEC v. C. M. Joiner Leasing Corp., 320 U. S. 344, 350-51 (1943), supra p. 178.

[15] See p. 317 supra.

securities in payment of acquisitions of other companies, and (foremost of all) institutional placements. *Ralston* furnishes adequate guide for the employee category. But acquisition offerings are vastly different, in that the offerees are usually identified and finite in number and negotiations are usually extensive. And institutional investors are well able to care for themselves without all the "sophistication" and "access" paraphernalia erected on the foundation of Ralston's annual offerings to "chow loading foremen" and other management-anointed "key employees."[16]

2. The "Safe Harbor" of Rule 506

The situation cried out for rulemaking. The Bar uttered appropriate cries. And in 1974 the Commission responded, perhaps not altogether in a way that the Bar wished, with Rule 146, which was replaced by a somewhat simpler Rule 506 as part of the Regulation D that was adopted in 1982.

Rule 506, with its condition of reasonable belief that there are not more than thirty-five buyers apart from an unlimited number of "accredited investors,"[17] is not too different from Rule 505[18] — which presumably accounts for their integration into the same Regulation D, to the point where most of the conditions of Rule 506 are found in Rules 501-03. This includes the treatment with respect to "integration," general solicitation or advertising, resales, filings, and disclosure to buyers.[19] The basic differences are two:

(1) Since Rule 506 is based on §4(2), not §3(b), there is no limitation with respect to aggregate offering price.

(2) The issuer must "reasonably believe immediately prior to making any sale that each purchaser who is not an accredited investor * * * has such knowledge and experience in financial and business matters that he is capable of evaluating the merits and risks of

[16] Garrett, Private Offerings Under the Securities Act of 1933 (unpublished address before 11th Annual Corporate Counsel Institute, Chicago, Oct. 5, 1972), condensed in Garrett, The Private Offering Exemption Today, in Practising Law Institute, Fourth Annual Institute on Securities Regulation (1973) c. 2.

[17] See pp. 314-15 supra.

[18] See p. 314 supra.

[19] See pp. 313-14 supra. If the offering exceeds $7.5 million, so that Form S-18 cannot be used as a point of reference (see p. 308 supra), and the issuer is not a reporting company under the 1934 Act, the reference is to Part I of whatever form the issuer would be entitled to use. Rule 502(b)(2)(i)(B).

his prospective investment."[20] The rule, however, perpetuates the former Rule 146's invention of a "purchaser representative" whose knowledge and experience (and there may be more than one) may supplement or be substituted for the purchaser's. That term is elaborately defined to insure independence from the issuer (except when the purchaser is a relative of his representative or a trust, estate, or corporation related in a specific manner to its representative) as well as knowledge and experience.[21]

The language of the rule itself must be carefully studied, of course, since each of the highly structured conditions must be satisfied by one who wants to enter its "safe harbor." A number of those conditions deserve special mention:

(1) Significantly, the Commission in Rule 146 shifted for the first time to maximum number of *buyers* rather than offerees. An early version of the Code referred to thirty-five buyers plus an unlimited number of "institutional investors."[22] This was designed basically as a return to the very early administrative view except for the change from offerees to buyers and the increase from twenty-five to thirty-five. Rule 506(b)(2)(i) follows this approach.

(2) The "offeree representative" concept that found its way into securities regulation with Rule 146 led the staff to say that a lawyer who is included in a list of such representatives and receives compensation for his advisory services is not excluded from the definition of "investment adviser" as a "lawyer * * * whose performance of such [legal] services is solely incidental to the practice of his profession,"[23] and hence he must register under the Investment Advisers Act.[24]

[20] Rule 506(b)(2)(11). Cf. Anastasi v. American Petroleum, Inc., 579 F. Supp. 273 (D. Colo. 1984), decided under the former Rule 146, which specifically required "reasonable inquiry." The court held that an issuer that had relied on the alleged misrepresentations of investors regarding their financial suitability had no cause of action for contribution against the investors for damages it had sustained by loss of the exemption, because those alleged misrepresentations could not have caused the loss of the exemption if the issuer had conducted an adequate investigation into the offerees' background.

[21] Rule 501(h). See People v. Morrow, 682 P. 2d 1201 (Colo. App. 1983) (state law).

[22] Code §§202(41)(B), 202(74).

[23] Inv. Adv. Act §202(a)(11)(B).

[24] Winstead, McGuire, Sechrest & Trimble, CCH Fed. Sec. L. Rep. ¶80,131 (letter 1975). The letter contrasted the case of the lawyer who served "in an isolated instance." The two types of persons most likely to serve are (1) the selling broker-dealer and (2) a lawyer, accountant, or financial planner. For an analysis of their potential liability to the buyers they represent, other buyers of the Rule 506 offering, the SEC, and the issuer, see Stern, Potential Liability of Purchaser Representatives, 39 Bus. Law. 1801 (1984). The selling broker-dealer is not disqualified under the definition in Rule 501(h), but the conflict of interest

(3) Although §4(2) does not contain the word "issue" that is found in §§3(a)(11) and 3(b),[25] the "issue" or "integration" concept is read into the word "involving" just as it is read into the word "exclusively" in §3(a)(9). The Commission has stated that "it is clear that the private offering exemption [§4(2)] cannot be available for a *portion* of a 'single' offering."[26] But Regulation D contains a six-month "safe harbor," like that in Rule 147(b) with respect to intrastate offerings, on either side of the D offering.[27]

(4) In 1978 the Commission, stating that its experience with Rule 146 had demonstrated "the need to be able to perceive misuses of the rule and, thus, to become aware of, and prevent, frauds in their incipient stages," added a requirement, now reflected in Rule 503, that certain reports of sales be filed.[28] The filing burden is not great. But there is no indication that the Commission took into account the *dis*advantages of a reporting requirement in an exemptive rule: Congress intended all the statutory exemptions to work automatically. And, once more, there is the spectre of strict liability under §12(1) if a report is filed a day late. Indeed, in the ordinary case, as Professor Kripke pungently put it, of "one pizza twirler who sells to another pizza twirler for $75,000 the capital stock of a

gives enough pause to have caused some broker-dealer firms to prohibit the practice as a matter of policy.

[25] See pp. 296, 310 supra.

[26] Herbert R. May, 27 SEC 814, 819-20 (1948); Crowell-Collier Publishing Co., Sec. Act Rel. 3825 (1957) 5. The Commission has made two exceptions to the integration doctrine by rule so far as the private offering exemption is concerned. One of them is Rule 254(d)(2) of Regulation A, to the effect that securities offered to a single majority-control parent of the issuer in connection with a *pro rata* offering to stockholders may be segregated from the other securities involved in the offering. The other is a special rule that affords a *locus poenitentiae* to an issuer that starts with a private offering and *subsequentily* decides to make a public offering or file a registration statement: in such a case the exemption is considered to apply to the transactions not involving any public offering at the time that they were effected. Rule 152. The staff, moreover, is understood to apply Rule 152 when the private offering is for "seed money," that is to say, funds required to get a business under way. Cf. Verticom, Inc., 18 Sec. Reg. L. Rep. 302 (letter 1986). But there is no similar dispensation for an issuer that thinks it can get by under §3(a)(9) or §3(a)(11) but finds it necessary to register in order to complete the financing. In such a case, at least in principle and presumably so far as civil liability under §12(1) is concerned, there is a single issue no part of which qualifies for exemption.

[27] See p. 297 n. d supra.

[28] Sec. Act Rel. 5912, 14 SEC Dock. 306, 307 (1978). This requirement followed a strong recommendation in a General Accounting Office report that had described a rash of private placement frauds. General Accounting Office, Action Needed to Better Protect Investors from Fraud in Purchasing Privately Placed Securities (1980).

corporation which owns a pizza parlor," counsel, at least if not expert in the law and lore of securities regulation, normally will not even think of a federal registration requirement, let alone the conditions his client must meet if he wants to be sure to gain an exemption.[29]

(5) To get back to Genesis, where does the Commission get the authority to adopt a rule like 506 (as implemented by Rules 501-03)? In theory the rule is interpretative, not substantive. But is a detailed rule that runs for several columns in the SEC Docket, complete with filing requirements, a definition of a "technical" or "trade" term, or does it otherwise fall within the scope of §19(a) of the Act — a provision that authorizes "such rules and regulations as may be necessary to carry out the provisions of this title, including rules and regulations governing registration statements and prospectuses * * * , and defining accounting, technical, and trade terms used in this title"?[30]

(6) The Commission has emphasized that the rule is a "safe harbor."[31] Compliance with every condition assures the §4(2) exemption. But the Commission did not (and, aside from what a court might consider to be a proper use of its rulemaking authority, could not) take away anything that Congress gave in §4(2).[32] One who relies on §4(2) *apart* from the rule is simply on his own, as if there had never been a rule. Since it is unnecessary to choose between §4(2) *per se* and Rule 506, prudent counsel who uses the rule will so structure the offering as to be able to establish a §4(2) defense if it turns out that one or more conditions of the rule have not been satisfied.[33]

[29] Kripke, SEC Rule 146: A "Major Blunder," N. Y. L. J., July 5, 1974, p. 1, col. 3.

[30] The 1975 legislation amended §3(b) of the 1934 Act by adding "other" in the present "technical, trade, accounting, and other terms." But the comparable §19(a) of the 1933 Act remains in its original form.

[31] Sec. Act Rel. 6389, 24 SEC Dock. 1166, 1178 n. 33 (1982).

[32] Mary S. Krech Trust v. Lake Apartments, 642 F. 2d 98, 102 (5th Cir. 1981).

[33] In 1976 the Commission invited comment on the operation of then Rule 146 and whether it should be rescinded or revised. Sec. Act Rel. 5779, 11 SEC Dock. 1116 (1976). Fifteen months later the Commission stated that the majority of comments favored retention of the rule and "did not indicate that the rule impedes the flow of venture capital or facilitate the fraudulent offering of securities." Sec. Act Rel. 5913, 14 SEC Dock. 310, 311 (1978).

3. The Statutory Exemption Today

As evidence that §4(2) lives, consider:

SECTION 4(2) AND STATUTORY LAW: A POSITION PAPER OF THE FEDERAL REGULATION OF SECURITIES COMMITTEE, SECTION OF CORPORATION, BANKING AND BUSINESS LAW OF THE AMERICAN BAR ASSOCIATION

31 Business Lawyer 485 (1975)[a]

* * *

Introduction

* * *

In the Release announcing adoption of the Rule, the Commission emphasizes that Rule 146 is not the exclusive basis for determining whether the Section 4(2) exemption is available. Additionally, issuers may continue to rely on the exemption "by complying with the relevant administrative and judicial interpretations in effect at the time of the transaction." For a number of reasons discussed below, the body of law relevant to the availability of the Section 4(2) exemption otherwise than in reliance upon Rule 146, referred to in this position paper as "Statutory Law," is and will continue to be important notwithstanding the adoption of Rule 146. For example, institutional private placements of straight debt issues routinely continue to rely on Statutory Law. We anticipate that issuers and their attorneys in noninstitutional private placements as well will continue to rely on Statutory Law in many situations, sometimes by choice, sometimes by necessity and finally sometimes through accident or inadvertence.

Unfortunately, there have been differing views expressed, even among experienced securities lawyers, as to the state of the Statutory Law on certain points. There is considerable uncertainty as to

[a]Ed.: Copyright 1975, American Bar Association. Reprinted with the permission of the Association and its Section of Corporation, Banking, and Business Law. Some citations are omitted and citation style is here adjusted. Attached to this paper are two appendices. Appendix A contains a survey of the literature with respect to §4(2). Appendix B lists a number of cases dealing with the section. For an updated version of the substance of this paper written by its principal draftsman, see Schneider, The Statutory Law of Private Placements, 14 Rev. Sec. Reg. 869 (1981). The references to Rule 146 should now read 506.

the effect and force of the existing judicial interpretations, many of which have been influenced by extreme positions taken by the Commission in litigation. In large part as a result of those litigation positions, there is also considerable uncertainty as to the administrative interpretations. The legislative history of Section 4(2) is scanty, as is apparent from the present confused state of the law, and is susceptible of widely differing interpretations. There have been relatively few published administrative interpretations of Section 4(2) by the Commission. In any event, the authority of the Commission in this area is somewhat circumscribed by relevant judicial decisions. Furthermore, the judicial precedents are not particularly helpful because many involve fact situations where the result — usually the denial of the exemption and therefore a victory for the purchaser of the unregistered securities — could well be justified on other grounds, such as fraud or a material misrepresentation or omission in connection with the sale, in addition to a relatively broad distribution of securities. Additionally, many of the cases have been decided more on procedural than on substantive grounds, and, some of the most troublesome judicial pronouncements in the decisions constitute dicta rather than clear holdings.

We recognize, therefore, that it is difficult, if not impossible, to state accurately what the Statutory Law is. Nevertheless, we have set forth in this position paper practical guidelines which represent what we believe is an interpretation of Statutory Law which is consistent with the language of the Securities Act of 1933, the legislative history of Section 4(2), the purposes and policies of the Act and the principal judicial decisions on the subject. We believe that the interpretations discussed herein should be followed by the courts.

SOURCES OF STATUTORY LAW

LEGISLATIVE HISTORY[b]

* * *

ADMINISTRATIVE[c]

* * *

An administrative interpretation in 1962[8] stressed another aspect found in earlier interpretations, namely, that the offerees must have

[b]ED.: See p. 317 supra.

[c]ED.: The report here describes the early General Counsel opinion in Sec. Act Rel. 285 (1935). See p. 317 supra.

access to information about the issuer. We believe that the requirement of access to information might be satisfied independent of the transaction by virtue of a preexisting relationship — for example, where the purchaser is an executive officer of the issuer. Or, access to information can arise through the economic bargaining power of an offeree who did not have prior first hand knowledge of the issuer. Thus, in the traditional institutional private placement, purchasers who had no prior information about the issuer could obtain the information they desired as a result of their economic bargaining power.

Access through economic bargaining power seemed to be a generally accepted approach until doubt was cast upon the doctrine, at least as far as the Commission's position was concerned, by the Commission's appellate brief in *SEC* v. *Continental Tobacco Co., Inc.* That brief reiterated every restriction that any of the authorities had mentioned over the years, including the suggestion that a qualified offeree was required to have "a relationship to the company tantamount to that of an 'insider.' "[10] The Commission's reply brief raised further doubts regarding certain generally accepted notions (discussed below) with respect to offeree qualification. The reply brief suggested that a desire to consult counsel tends to disqualify an offeree by asserting: "Indeed, the very fact that investors consider it is necessary to rely upon an attorney in their purchase of stock demonstrates that the investors are unfamiliar with the company, cannot 'fend for themselves' and therefore need the 'protections afforded by registration.' "[11] Contrary to the Commission's contention, it is the highly sophisticated investors, those least needing the benefits of a registration statement, who are most likely to rely on counsel.

JUDICIAL PRECEDENTS

Turning to the judicial precedents, *SEC* v. *Ralston Purina Co.*, focused on the offerees' lack of need for the Act's protection. It articulated the test in terms of the offerees' ability to "fend for

[8]Sec. Act Rel. 4552 (1972).

[10]Brief for Appellant at 28. This interpretation was expressly rejected in Woolf v. S. D. Cohn & Co., 515 F. 2d 591 (5th Cir. 1975), *vacated on other grounds* sub nom. S. D. Cohn & Co. v. Woolf, 426 U. S. 944 (1976). [See also Doran v. Petroleum Management Corp., 545 F. 2d 893, 900 (5th Cir. 1977, supra p. 322.]

[11]Reply Brief for Appellant at 2.

themselves," and "access" to the "kind of information which registration would disclose." The court did not elaborate upon the meaning of the term "access." The case, however, involved an offering to hundreds of employees. It was clear that many of them had neither economic bargaining power nor a relationship to the company which would give them an independent means of obtaining necessary information.

The subsequent judicial precedents have not been particularly helpful. In most of the reported cases decided since *Ralston Purina,* the issuers and their control persons lost. Many of these cases involved egregious fact situations, typically tainted with a clearly public distribution and misrepresentation, in which the issuers should have lost. The courts, however, have used extremely broad dicta which, if taken literally, would leave little viability in the exemption under the statute. The narrow holdings of many of these cases turn on a simple procedural aspect of the cases — the failure of the issuer to offer evidence necessary to carry the burden of proving that the exemption was available. In many of the cases, the issuer offered no evidence regarding crucial factors necessary to establish the exemption, such as the method by which the offering was made, the number of offerees or their qualifications.

In those cases where the issuer prevailed on the merits, it is clear that the courts did not require full compliance with the dicta enunciated in those cases where the issuers lost.

We add a caveat. Certain of the early cases which were decided favorably to the issuers might not be decided the same way today, in the light of later circuit court precedents. Also, it is noteworthy that some of these cases involve interests in oil and gas ventures where a purchaser, asserting a Section 5 violation, was refusing to honor his purchase commitment when the holes were dry. The courts might have found the equities in that factual setting to be somewhat different from the equities in the normal rescission suit. Nonetheless, we believe it is fair to conclude that a distinctly different attitude toward the exemption emerges from a reading of the cases in which the issuers prevailed, as contrasted with the more numerous cases where the exemption was held to be unavailable. When the facts were more favorable to the issuer, the courts seemed to interpret the requirements for exemption in a less demanding manner.

SEC Chairman Garrett, at the PLI Fourth Annual Securities Institute (when he was still a private practitioner) characterized the result of the various authorities, legislative, judicial, and administrative, as:

> [A] kind of mishmash. The issuer is now told that all of these factors have something to do with whether he has an exemption under Section 4(2), but he is never given a hint as to the proper proportions in the brew. The saving recipe is kept secret, a moving target which he can never be sure he has hit.[15]

GUIDELINES

Where does this leave us? We believe that there are only four attributes of any real significance in determining whether the exemption is available under Statutory Law. This combination of factors provides a reasonable test to identify those transactions where the registration provisions of the Act are not needed to implement its statutory purpose. The other factors frequently mentioned in the precedents are of very minor significance, or none at all. We believe the four essential attributes relate to the following — (1) offeree qualification; (2) availability of information; (3) manner of offering; and (4) absence of redistribution. Each of these will be discussed separately. We further believe, as more fully noted below, that all of the four foregoing attributes must be approached flexibly and in recognition of the fact that they do not constitute abstract concepts whose parameters are fixed. Furthermore, these four attributes are intimately related; indeed, the question of qualification of offerees and the manner in which information is imparted to such offerees may justifiably be regarded as correlatives from the standpoint of determining the applicability of the exemption to a specific private placement under Statutory Law.

While we suggest some practical guidelines below, we are not attempting to lay down precise tests on any of the four relevant factors. This position paper is not intended to be an exact definition of Statutory Law, in the sense that compliance with all of the suggestions herein would necessarily assure the availability of the exemption or, conversely, that failure to comply in some detail would necessarily result in the unavailability of the exemption. As it has evolved, the exemption has become far too complex and the transactions in which it may be relied upon far too varied to permit any precise and all-encompassing definition of its exact limits in anything but the most abstract terms. This no doubt explains why Rule 146 was cast in terms of a non-exclusive safe harbor.

[15] Garrett, The Private Offering Exemption Today, in Practising Law Institute, Fourth Annual Institute on Securities Regulation (1973) c. 2 at 10-11.

The analysis below is designed to be consistent with the basic public policy objective, which is to provide registration for investors who need the Act's protections through the rather burdensome registration process. The conclusions reached below attempt to balance the practical needs of various classes of investors for the benefits of registration (over and above the protections arising under the federal securities anti-fraud provisions), and the burdens on issuers of compliance with the registration process. Hopefully, the guidelines set forth should provide a basis of exemption for various broad categories of transactions for which the registration process seems inappropriate or unnecessary — among them, the institutional private placement, and the financing of a small business among individuals closely associated with the venture.

To a large extent, our discussion focuses on the type of equity private placements which are typically sold to individuals or others who are not professional investors or venture capitalists, and which often involve a relatively high degree of risk. So-called institutional private placements have been undertaken for many years in a fairly standardized pattern. Such transactions involve sophisticated institutional investors making relatively large purchases of debt or, less often, equity securities. No significant interpretive problems have been experienced in applying the provisions of Section 4(2) to such institutional transactions, and nothing in this position paper is intended to cast doubt on the propriety of prevailing practices in the institutional private placement field.

* * *

We also note in passing that issuers effecting private placements may have additional requirements to satisfy under state blue sky laws, which are beyond the scope of the present discussion. Parenthetically, we note that several state blue sky authorities recently have published rules or statements of policy, in proposed or final form, which appear to condition their exemptions for private placements upon compliance by issuers with all of the provisions of Rule 146. We believe that these actions by state blue sky administrators are inappropriate, and overlook the sound policy reasons which prompted the SEC to make Rule 146 nonexclusive. We believe that there are many transactions which, as a policy matter, should be exempt from both federal and state registration requirements, even though they do not meet the many technical requirements of Rule 146.

OFFEREE QUALIFICATION

From the standpoint of framing precise or objective standards, qualification of offerees is probably the most troublesome of all the attributes of the exemption. We believe that offerees in a private placement should be deemed qualified on any one of several bases. They may be qualified on the basis of their ability to understand the risk. This attribute is sometimes called "sophistication." They may be qualified on the basis of their ability to assume the investment risk, so called "wealth." Or, they may be qualified on the basis of a personal relationship to the issuer or a promoter. The qualifying relationships include, but are not necessarily limited to, family ties, friendship, an employment relationship or a pre-existing business relationship. In our view, *Ralston Purina* does not exclude these alternative approaches. Because of the personal relationship factor, Promoter *X* might be justified in allowing a close family member, his best friend and his right-hand man in the business to participate in a private placement, while Promoter *Y*, who is a stranger to these people, would not be justified in including them in an otherwise identical offering which relied upon the Section 4(2) exemption. We believe that the public benefits are too remote and there is no practical need for the burdens of applying the registration provisions (as contrasted with anti-fraud provisions) when the offerees have such close relationships to the offeror. We note that when such close personal ties exist, a decision to make an investment may be motivated, wholly or in part, by non-economic factors unrelated to financial risks and benefits of the investment.

We suggested above that an offeree might qualify solely on the basis of his ability to assume the risk. We add a caveat. We might have serious reservations about including a very wealthy person as an offeree in a highly risky private placement, based solely upon his ability to assume the risk, if he had no understanding of financial matters, and no competent advisor. On the other hand, if an equally wealthy offeree was an experienced business man with some general understanding of financial matters, we would consider him qualified as an offeree based upon his ability to assume the risk, even though he lacked a high degree of sophistication.

Several other observations concerning offeree qualification are relevant.

(1) *Risk-Bearing Ability:* First, with respect to the offeree's ability to assume the risk, we believe it is relevant to consider, in very broad and general terms, the extent of the risk of loss in judging whether the offeree can assume it. There have been expressions

from the Commission that the appropriate inquiry is whether the offeree can afford to lose all of the money to be invested. Notwithstanding such suggestions, under Statutory Law as well as Rule 146, we believe that both the total amount of money invested, and also the likelihood that all or part of it will be lost, must be considered.[d]

Specifically, other things being equal, it may well be that Offeree *X* is qualified to participate in a private placement of a high-grade mortgage bond, where the likelihood of substantial loss is minimal, but not in a highly speculative common stock offering involving a significant probability of total loss. In short, risk-bearing ability may require a judgment regarding the general level of the risks inherent in the particular investment, not merely a reference to the total amount invested.

(2) *The Offeree Representative Principle:* We believe that Statutory Law gives some recognition to the offeree representative principle which is formalized in Rule 146 — that is, a person other than an offeree may be able to advise an offeree or otherwise protect the offeree's interests so as to qualify the offeree. Two cases seem to recognize this principle in the acquisition setting.[18] The point is also recognized tangentially in at least one non-acquisition case.[19] In *Klinkel* v. *Krekow*,[20] an unreported U. S. District Court memorandum decision, the court accepted the parties' agreement in a rescission suit that information disclosed to the son of the plaintiff-purchaser was deemed known by plaintiff and "to the extent sophistication and investment philosophy of an offeree are relevant, those of [the son] should control."

(3) *Manner of Disclosure:* We suggest that a determination of the offeree's ability to understand the risk may well vary with the manner and scope of the disclosure made to him. The more careful, painstaking and detailed the disclosure is, the more readily one may find that a particular offeree is able to understand the risk. Consider any business which is not particularly well known to the investing public generally. Without the availability of appropriate information to the offeree, by way of access or as a result of being furnished by the issuer, most persons would not be able to qualify as offerees on the basis of ability to understand the risk. On the

[d]ED.: Rule 506 eliminated the risk test in former Rule 146(d) as an alternative to knowledge and experience.

[18]Klapmeier v. Telecheck Int'l, Inc., 482 F. 2d 247 (8th Cir. 1973); Bowers v. Columbia General Corp., 336 F. Supp. 609 (D. Del. 1971).

[19]See Woodward v. Wright, 266 F. 2d 108, 115 (10th Cir. 1959). [ED.: For a later square holding, see Barry v. Ceres Land Co., CCH Fed. Sec. L. Rep. ¶99,008 (D. Minn. 1978).]

[20]W. D. Wash., No. 317-71C2, Aug. 16, 1974.

other hand, if a carefully prepared disclosure document is submitted to them, the same group of investors might well qualify as persons who can understand the risk.

This point may have an important bearing in preparing disclosure materials. If the offerees are all thoroughly familiar with the particular business, it may be sufficient to disclose only distinctive aspects of the particular issuer. On the other hand, if the offerees are not familiar with the issuer's business, the disclosure should also give them more general information about the industry and type of business.

(4) *Degrees of Sophistication:* We consider it important to recognize that there are degrees of sophistication. The inquiry as to whether an offeree is adequately sophisticated should not be approached in a categorical or absolute fashion, since the concept entails weighing of relative factors. All those who are not sufficiently sophisticated to qualify as offerees of every type of security for every type of offering should not be lumped together. The unsophisticated range from the total incompetent in financial matters, and possibly other matters as well, to the worldly man of business who knows a good deal about money matters but who has had limited experience in corporate finance and private placements. A good many presidents of companies going public are not "sophisticated" in matters of corporate finance, in the normal sense of the term "sophisticated."

Indeed, we suggest that the term "sophistication" is somewhat misused in this context. It is a shorthand way of expressing a rather complex thought, and quite possibly the use of the term is not entirely accurate. The relevant inquiry should be whether the investor can understand and evaluate the nature of the risk based upon the information supplied to him. The relevant inquiry should not be whether the investor is *au courant* in all of the latest nuances and techniques of corporate finance. To the extent that the term "sophistication" raises inquiries of the latter type, the use of the term may tend to becloud the inquiry.

(5) *Non-Qualifed Offerees:* Is the exemption lost for the entire transaction where one or more of the offerees (or purchasers) fails to meet the appropriate tests? The question may arise in a variety of factual settings, as illustrated by the following extreme hypotheticals. Assume that the issue concerning the availability of the exemption is raised in each case in a Section 12(1) rescission suit brought by a qualified purchaser, who is seeking a return of his purchase price after the investment turns out to be unprofitable. The plaintiff charges that the offering as a whole did not qualify for the exemption.

Case No. 1: The offeror makes the offers with total disregard as to the qualifications of the offerees. In fact, most of the offerees and purchasers are not qualified.

Case No. 2: The offeror uses a high degree of care in preclearing offerees. In hindsight, it appears that only one offeree was not appropriately qualified. When the offer was made to him, the offeror had reasonable grounds to believe that the offeree was qualified, relying in part on information supplied by the offeree which was subsequently discovered to be untrue. Prior to the sale, when the true facts were discovered, the nonqualified offeree was eliminated from the private placement and the securities were sold only to qualified offerees, but no effort was made to terminate the pending offering as to the qualified offerees.

The language in the cases discussing the point indicates that the exemption is unavailable unless every offeree (even those who did not become purchasers) meets the qualification test.[21] However, virtually all such cases more closely resemble Case No. 1 above, rather than Case No. 2. If the issue were to arise in a circumstance similar to Case No. 2, we believe that a court should, and probably would, either find the exemption available vis-à-vis the plaintiff, or find some other basis for denying the plaintiff the right to rescind his transaction.[22]

There is not enough precedent to make specific predictions concerning the broad range of circumstances which might be presented. We think, however, it would be appropriate for courts to consider, in passing on the availability of the exemption, such factors as the status of the plaintiff (e. g., whether he is qualified as an offeree), whether the defendant acted reasonably in making offers to offerees who were not in fact qualified, the extent of the offers which were made to non-qualified offerees, what remedial action, if any, was taken by the defendant upon learning of the non-qualification, and the procedural setting in which the issue arises.

Note that the exemption remains available under Rule 146 even if a sale was made to a non-qualified person, as long as the issuer had reasonable grounds to believe and, after making reasonable inquiry, did believe that each offeree-purchaser was qualified. The general philosophy of protecting an issuer, and ultimately its existing investors, when the issuer acts reasonably was further empha-

[21] E. g., Lively v. Hirschfeld, 440 F. 2d 631, 633 (10th Cir. 1971); Repass v. Rees, 174 F. Supp. 898 (D. Colo. 1959).

[22] See A. C. Frost & Co. v. Coeur D'Alene Mines Corp., 312 U. S. 38 (1941); Value Line Fund, Inc. v. Marcus, CCH Fed. Sec. L. Rep. ¶91,523 (S. D. N. Y. 1965); Schneider and Zall, Section 12(1) and the Imperfect Exempt Transaction: The Proposed I & I Defense, 28 Bus. Law. 1011 (1973).

sized by the SEC in its recent amendment of Rule 146(g).[23] Prior to the amendment, the 35 purchaser ceiling was absolute, and the benefits of the Rule were lost if there were more, despite the issuer's reasonable and good faith belief to the contrary. As amended, the Rule remains available where there are more than 35 purchasers, so long as the issuer has reasonable grounds to believe, after making reasonable inquiry, that there are no more than 35 purchasers.

(6) Economic Bargaining Power: The concept of economic bargaining power has become a widely accepted concept under Statutory Law, and is used in a somewhat imprecise way to describe an attribute of offerees who have "access" to information.[24]

If the plain meaning of the expression "economic bargaining power" is considered, the term would seem to have no necessary connection with the sophistication of the offeree or his background in financial matters, as illustrated by the following two examples:

(a) A small privately held company desperately needs funds, and the only potential investor identified by the sole stockholder is his neighbor. The neighbor has $20,000 to invest but little experience in finance. The stockholder offers a 20 percent interest in the company for $20,000, and the neighbor wants 30 percent. Given the relative position of the company and the neighbor, arguably the neighbor has great leverage, or economic bargaining power, to impose his terms and conditions and satisfy his other requirements, before he parts with his money.

(b) A small insurance company is invited by a lead institution to purchase a $1,000,000 unit in a $50,000,000 placement of high grade debt securities. As a practical matter, the insurance company may have very little ability to negotiate any terms in the transaction with the issuer or make any independent investigation. Its alternatives are to accept or reject the deal as packaged by the lead institutional investor based upon the offering memorandum supplied, and it knows that any efforts to act too independently might well decrease the likelihood of its being invited into future trans-

[23] Sec. Act Rel. 5585, 6 SEC Dock. 829 (1975).

[24] See, e. g., Note to Rule 146(e), which states: "Access can only exist by reason of the offeree's position with respect to the issuer. Position means an employment or family relationship or economic bargaining power that enables the offeree to obtain information from the issuer in order to evaluate the merits and risks of the prospective investment." [Rule 146(e) referred to each officer's access to "the same kind of information that is specified in Schedule A of the Act" as an alternative to his being furnished with that kind of information prior to sale. Rule 506 does not refer to "access," although it does not require any information to be furnished to an "accredited investor" (Rule 502(b)(1)(i)), which includes any director, executive officer, or general partner of the issuer (Rule 501(a)(4)).]

actions. Arguably, the insurance company has very little economic bargaining power in this transaction.

Notwithstanding the foregoing analysis, however, we think the term economic bargaining power, as used in the private placement context, should be understood as a term of art. It is, to a large extent, an attribute which an offeree may be presumed to have based upon several factors including, but not necessarily limited to, available resources, financial experience and history as an investor. It is not to be determined primarily from a factual analysis of the relative bargaining strengths of a particular issuer vis-à-vis a particular offeree in a given factual setting.

INFORMATION

A second general attribute relates to the scope and manner of disclosure of information. It is generally considered necessary that each offeree have some information about the issuer, or at least access to that information, prior to the sale. It is not necessary in all cases for the offeree to have had the information prior to, and independent of, the transaction. In some situations, the information may be supplied to the offeree in connection with the transaction at the time the offering is made.

It is difficult to set forth a precise standard to determine when the information requirement can be satisfied by having the information supplied, in connection with the transaction, to offerees who did not previously have such information. Clearly supplying the information is a generally accepted practice where institutional type offerees are involved. Institutions normally are presumed to have "access" to the information by virtue of their economic bargaining power. In addition, the practice of supplying information is acceptable in certain instances where qualified individual offerees are involved; otherwise, individuals could never participate in a private placement of an issuer which has not made extensive prior public disclosures, unless the individuals had preexisting relationships which made them privy to information about the issuer. In practice, the law has not been interpreted so restrictively. To the contrary, the participation of individuals in the private placement of a private company has been widely accepted for a long time, even if the offerees had no knowledge about the issuer prior to their receipt of information in connection with the transaction.

The information required to be supplied need not be nearly as extensive as the information called for by Schedule A of the 1933 Act, or by Form S-1, although the Form S-1 requirements provide a useful guideline. The statutory exemption does reflect a legislative policy decision that occasions exist where there is no need for the expense and delay of providing a registration statement, or its non-filed equivalent. It is probably adequate to give basis information concerning the issuer's financial condition, results of operations, business, property and management.

Indeed, it is doubtful whether all of the foregoing categories of information are required in every case. Many private placements by a small closely-held company are completed with little or no formal disclosure documentation. If the buyer shows no interest in information regarding executive compensation, for example, the exemption should not be lost by the failure of the issuer to supply such information, especially if the remuneration is reasonable and just about what the buyer would have expected had he considered the matter.

In some private placements, especially those involving closely held companies, even more basic information in reliable form may be unavailable. *Livens* v. *William D. Wilter, Inc.*,[25] held that a private placement was proper despite the absence of reliable financial statements, since the buyer was advised that reliable financial statements were unavailable and he was willing, in effect, to take the risk. Significantly, in *Livens* the exemption applied although the court found that at the time of the purchase no one, neither the sellers nor the purchaser, appreciated the full extent of the deficiency in the issuer's financial records, and in a sense the purchaser was misled, albeit unintentionally, by the seller.

Statutory Law does not require that disclosures be made, or that information be conveyed, in writing, if the result can be accomplished in another manner such as an oral presentation, a tour of physical facilities, inspection of products, or allowing the offeree to communicate directly with others such as customers, suppliers and bankers. In fact, most private companies which accept an occasional new investor do not prepare a narrative prospectus-type disclosure document. Many supply no written material at all to the investor, subject to the possible exception of financial statements which have been prepared for other purposes.

Of course, written disclosures are very helpful as a matter of proof, to establish what information was conveyed. In some cases,

[25] 374 F. Supp. 1104 (D. Mass. 1974); see also Cowles v. Dow Keith Oil & Gas, Inc., 752 F. 2d 508, 513 (10th Cir. 1985), *cert. denied*, 107 S. Ct. 74 ("because [the defendant] conducted 'a minor operation' drilling only 'shallow wells,' [the plaintiffs] had about as much means of acquiring information and knowledge as did the defendant").

it may well be helpful to concentrate the written disclosures on what is, essentially, a list of risk factors such as one might find in a so-called "introductory statement" to a statutory prospectus. The purchaser may be asked for written acknowledgment that he is aware of these risk factors. He might also be requested to acknowledge that he is familiar with the business, has had an opportunity to ask questions and has received the information requested. (We do not suggest, however, that inviting the offeree to ask for any information he wishes adequately substitutes in all cases for supplying him with information in written or other readily usable form.) In some cases, as a mechanical matter, these suggested acknowledgments can be incorporated into a simple subscription agreement which the investor signs at the time of the purchase.

MANNER OF THE OFFERING

The third general attribute of a proper private placement under Statutory Law relates to the manner of offering. In general, the offering should be made through direct communication with qualified offerees or their representatives, whether by the issuer itself or through an agent of the issuer. All forms of general advertising and mass media circulation should be avoided. The number of offers made may have evidentiary significance, as discussed below, in determining whether the manner of an offering was proper.

A related question is the determination of when an offer is made. At one extreme, we find nothing objectionable if a full service brokerage firm advertises generally for customers, even though some of them may eventually become offerees in a specific private placement. A detailed discussion of this subject is beyond the scope of this paper except for the following generalizations. On the one hand, "offer" for purposes of Statutory Law is defined broadly and might include attempts to sell specific investments which fall far short of an offer capable of acceptance under traditional contract law principles. On the other hand, inquiries to screen preliminary indications of general interest in a broad category of investments do not amount to offers. In *SEC* v. *Universal Major Industries Corp.*,[26] the Court indicated that it was not the manner of the offering, but rather the class of offerees which determines whether the exemption is available. Read in context, we do not interpret this case as holding that the manner of offering is irrelevant, but merely that an

[26] CCH Fed. Sec. L. Rep. ¶95,229 at 98,210 (S. D. N. Y. 1975), *aff'd on other grounds*, 546 F. 2d 1044 (2d Cir. 1976).

offering made in a proper manner will nonetheless fail to qualify if the class of offerees is inappropriate.

ABSENCE OF REDISTRIBUTION[e]

* * *

SIGNIFICANCE OF THE FACTORS

If all the foregoing attributes are met — qualification of the offerees, availability of information, manner of the offering and absence of a redistribution — the exemption should apply to the transaction notwithstanding the failure of that transaction to meet some of the other tests sometimes articulated in the traditional sources.

The Release promulgating Rule 146 noted that none of the foregoing factors, standing alone, would assure the availability of the exemption. We agree with the Release in this respect. However, the Release does not comment on the proposition which we have just made — that the presence of all of the factors together would normally satisfy the terms of the exemption.

For purposes of discussion and analysis, we have separated four attributes of a private placement, but we do not consider them to be totally self-contained and unrelated criteria. Rather, we view them as interrelated factors, the composite effect of which should result in an exempt transaction complying with the underlying statutory objective. To illustrate this interrelationship, we have noted the correlation between the scope and care of the information disclosures, on the one hand, and the qualification of an offeree based upon his ability to understand the risk, on the other hand.

To a large extent, this position paper reviews minimum requirements necessary to establish the Section 4(2) exemption. Assuming that the events have already occurred, we believe that the principles set forth should be of assistance in predicting how a court may decide if a transaction is challenged. We do not necessarily imply, however, that sound counseling or good business judgment dictates the planning of transactions to meet only the minimal standards. To the contrary, we have suggested that good practice might, in certain circumstances, suggest additional steps in order to assure the availability of the exemption — for example, see the discussion above

[e]ED.: See pp. 357-66 infra.

regarding the desirability of legends.[f] Additionally, we note that the cases which have been presented to the courts have typically involved complex fact situations and numerous interrelated issues. It may be difficult as a practical matter to defend the availability of the exemption if a transaction is planned to meet only the barest minimum standards. As an illustration, while Statutory Law does not require that written evidence be maintained concerning the identity and qualification of each offeree, the absence of such documentation may be very damaging to an issuer whose reliance upon the exemption is later challenged.

* * *

NUMBER OF OFFEREES

* * *

A much discussed subject regarding private placements is the significance of the number of offerees. It is the official dogma that the number of offerees (or purchasers) is not conclusive as to the availability or unavailability of the exemption. For many years, however, experienced counsel attached great significance to the number of offerees. Assuming an otherwise proper transaction, traditionally 25 qualified offerees was a widely accepted rule of thumb as an appropriate ceiling, at least when the noninstitutional type of offeree was involved. However, in *Ralston Purina,* the Supreme Court pointedly rejected the SEC contention that there could be a *maximum* number which could never be *exceeded* for the exemption to remain available. Indeed, if the 1933 Act itself imposes a maximum limit on the number of offerees, Rule 146 would be invalid under the Act, since it has no such limitation, although the Act appears to impose (and the Rule clearly does impose) a limit on the manner of the offering.

We believe that the adoption of Rule 146 will inevitably affect interpretations under Statutory Law. In the future, we expect that there will be much less concern among experienced counsel regarding the number of offerees as such. Rather, the focus of attention will be directed more to the manner of the offering. The total

[f]ED.: See p. 360 infra.

number of offerees may be considered relevant, if at all, primarily as evidence of the matter in which the offering was made.[g]

As a practical matter, we believe there has always been some relationship between the number of offerees considered acceptable and the level of the offerees' sophistication. Other things being equal, most counsel would feel comfortable with a larger number of offerees and purchasers, where the offerees are all sophisticated institutions rather than individuals. It is widely known that institutional private placements have occurred involving well over 100 purchasers.[h] We doubt that many experienced counsel would have felt comfortable with a private placement involving the same number of individual purchasers under similar circumstances.

The discussion throughout this position paper relates to a single offering. Consideration should also be given to the integration doctrine, which deals generally with the question of whether two or more transactions should be viewed as parts of the same offering.

SUBSTANTIAL COMPLIANCE WITH RULE 146

This analysis leads us to the question of whether substantial, but not total, compliance with Rule 146 will qualify a transaction for exemption under Statutory Law. We believe, as a policy matter, that this question should be answered in the affirmative in most cases, since the Rule is essentially, in its broad concepts (subject to exceptions — especially, but not exclusively, those dealing with documentation), an articulation of our understanding of Statutory Law. Of course, it becomes essential in any given case to consider the particular defect in the transaction under the Rule, in order to determine whether the statutory exemption applies.

If the Rule has made any significant departure from the Statutory Law, as it had been understood previously, it probably related to the number of offerees permitted. However, as previously indicated, this factor is likely to be one of declining significance under Statutory Law, as long as the matter of offering is appropriate and the number of offerees does not become excessive.

Rule 146 gave express recognition to the offeree representative concept, in order to qualify an offeree who was not independently

[g]ED.: In Western Federal Corp. v. Erickson, 739 F. 2d 1439, 1442-43 (9th Cir. 1984), the court still considered that one of the tests was the number of offerees.

[h]ED.: See Institutional Private Placements Under the Securities Act of 1933, A Paper of the Committee on Developments in Business Financing, Section of Corporation, Banking and Business Law of the American Bar Association, 31 Bus. Law. 515 (1975).

sophisticated. As previously indicated, however, we believe that this principle had some support in Statutory Law.

Under Rule 146, there are many mechanical requirements. Various items of documentation and record keeping are essential under the Rule. While these procedures are, by and large, desirable practices to follow, we do not consider them to be essential in order to establish the exemption under Statutory Law.

Turning to another point, the Rule has several requirements that the issuer have certain beliefs and/or reasonable grounds for certain beliefs — for example, that the offerees are qualified. We do not believe that Statutory Law has similar requirements. Specifically, we suggest that if the offerees are in fact qualified, the exemption would not be lost under Statutory Law because the issuer lacked a reasonable ground for so believing in advance.

Let us hasten to add that we would not advise clients to go into private placements without considerable care. Every effort should be made to make sure that the issuer has the beliefs required by the Rule, and that such beliefs are reasonably based. We are suggesting, however, that if counsel is consulted after the fact and is asked to render an opinion, the absence of a reasonable belief in advance by the issuer should not be a fatal defect if the circumstances were, in fact, as they should have been for the exemption to apply. We stress again, however, that it would be foolhardy to plan a transaction without forming appropriate beliefs in advance.

RELATIONSHIP BETWEEN SECTION 4(2) AND THE ANTI-FRAUD RULES

The issue of whether the disclosure is fraudulent is a different issue from whether a transaction violates the registration requirements. We do not believe that any fraud in connection with a private placement should automatically render Section 4(2) inapplicable — thereby converting every Section 12(2) case in a private placement into a Section 12(1) case as well — despite certain judicial intimations to the contrary.[31] But, as a practical matter, there is likely to be a close connection between the factors which determine whether Section 5 was violated and whether disclosure was adequate. That is, the more adequate, careful and painstaking the disclosure, the more likely it is that a court will find that the Section 4(2) exemption applied, including the fact that there were proper

[31] See Hill York Corp. v. American Int'l Franchises, Inc., 448 F. 2d 680 (5th Cir. 1971). [See also p. 888 n. 6 infra.]

and qualified offerees who could understand the risks based upon the disclosures made to them. On the other hand, the more defective the disclosure, the more likely it is, we believe, that a court will find the transaction to be non-exempt under Section 4(2).

* * *

BURDEN OF PROOF[i]

We would like to add a brief comment on the burden of proof. Following *Ralston Purina,* many cases have held that the burden of proof to establish the availability of the exemption is on the party relying upon it. It is reasoned that the Act is "remedial" and that "exemptions" are to be viewed narrowly. This analysis tends to ignore the fact that every sale of a security, public or private, is prima facie subject to registration if the jurisdictional means are used. This includes all of the millions of shares traded every day on the stock exchanges. The exemptions cover 99+% of all of the transactions. Viewed in this light, they are not really "exemptions" in the normal sense of exceptions to the general principle. Rather, they are a drafting technique used to extract, from the overall universe of sales, that small segment which is in fact subject to registration.

In any event, traditional statements about burden of proof make sense where the defendant makes no effort to demonstrate general compliance with the exemption. These statements are questionable, once the defendant has shown that the offering was conducted generally in a proper manner and that the plaintiff himself was a proper purchaser. If the law were otherwise, the defendant could never win a Section 12(1) case in a private placement context until he had presented affirmative evidence regarding such matters as the qualifications of each and every person to whom an offer was made. Once the defendant demonstrates that the overall procedures of the offering were properly conducted, is it likely that a court would impose such a burdensome requirement, or permit such a waste of judicial time? At some point, the burden should shift back to the plaintiff for him to show some defects in the transaction. In *Grenader* v. *Spitz,*[35] the court held that the defendant was entitled to rely on the intrastate offering exemption. The court apparently placed the burden on the plaintiff to show that the offerees were *not* residents of the State in question. Query whether a minor defect in a

[i]ED.: See also p. 274 supra.
[35]390 F. Supp. 1112 (S. D. N. Y. 1975).

transaction, which does not involve the plaintiff, should ever permit the plaintiff to rescind, if the transaction was generally conducted in a proper manner.

The way to test our hypothesis with respect to the burden of proof would be to consider the following hypothetical case: Assume that the defendant issuer is attempting to establish the availability of the exemption. The issuer proves affirmatively that the offering was conducted in a proper manner, with one minor exception with respect to one offeree. It also offers into evidence written questionnaires signed by each purchaser and offeree which, in every case but one, establish that the person was fully qualified. However, one purchaser, who was not the one seeking rescission of the transaction, simply completed the questions regarding current annual income and net worth by stating "more than $10,000." Let us further assume that such purchaser would not have qualified if his current annual income and net worth actually had been barely $10,000, although there is no reason from the record to suspect that the relevant amounts for him were in fact that low. After the record is closed, is it likely that any court would grant the plaintiff a directed verdict on the grounds that the defendant failed to carry the burden of proof regarding the qualifications of the particular offeree — not the plaintiff — who was reluctant to give specific information? We very much doubt it.

We believe that at some point practical realities and equitable considerations will prevail. Regardless of the language employed by the courts, once the party relying on the exemption has shown that the transaction was generally conducted in a proper manner, the burden of going forward should and probably will shift to the adverse party to demonstrate some material defect in the transaction.

* * *

---

4. The Code

This is one of the areas in which those who worked on the Code saw the greatest need for simplification and objectization. The Code's approach — aside from the treatment of the second (resale) stage, which we shall consider later[34] — has five elements:

[34] See p. 376 infra.

(1) The Code's successors to §5 apply only "in connection with a distribution."[35] That term is defined to mean "an offering other than (i) a limited offering or (ii) an offering by means of one or more trading transactions."[36] Clause (ii) need not detain use here.[37] The term "limited offering" is in turn defined as one in which "the initial buyers of the securities are institutional investors or not more than thirty-five other persons or both, or the seller reasonably so believes."[38]

(2) We have already noticed the Code's definition of "institutional investor," which is in part statutory and in part left to Commission rule.[39]

(3) We have noticed also the Code's scheme of *company* registration and the "one-year registrant."[40] When the issuer is *not* a one-year registrant, the Commission, by rule, may modify the definition of "limited offering" and "impose additional conditions, considering (I) the type of issuer and security, (II) the kind of market if any, and (III) similar criteria."[41]

(4) When the issuer *is* a one-year registrant, the Code's working group agreed with the Commission to amend the ALI-ABA-approved draft as the Code would go to Congress by giving the Commission the limited authority to require by rule that the most recent annual report (and all subsequent reports) be given to each non-institutional buyer unless (i) the security is traded in specified markets or (ii) the issuer has been a registrant for *three* years.[42] This reflects the view that there should be added to the one-year registrant's continuous disclosure rationale "some assurance that the market adequately reflects that disclosure."[43]

(5) The Code preserves the strict liability of §12(1)[44] as tempered by reducing the absolutism of today's substantive provisions. On this approach the presence of a "limited offering" is not conditioned on the absence of "general advertising," a fairly slippery term. Instead it is simply made "unlawful," subject to the usual sanctions, "for any person in connection with a limited offering * * * to

[35] §§502(a), 503(a), 504(a).

[36] §202(41)(A).

[37] See p. 377, par. (5) infra.

[38] §202(41)(B)(i)(I). There are two more conditions, which will be considered below because they are directed to the "second stage." See p. 377, par. (4) infra.

[39] §202(74); see p. 308 supra.

[40] See p. 93 n. 9 supra.

[41] §202(41)(B)(iii).

[42] §202(41)(B)(iv).

[43] 1 Code (2d Supp.) 23.

[44] Code §1702.

engage in general advertising in contravention of the rules of the Commission."[45]

5. STATE BLUE SKY LAWS

Counsel is not able to rest when he finds an exemption under §4(2), with or without Rule 506. If he is to avoid registration altogether, he must find some exemption also in every state (a term that as here used includes the District of Columbia and Puerto Rico) in which the offering is to be made. Each of the 52 states has one or more comparable exemptions except the District of Columbia, which does not register securities. We shall simply paint the general picture.

The statutes follow several themes (sometimes more than one in the same state), though with considerable variations even among the 38 states[46] that have adopted basically the Uniform Securities Act:

(1) The Uniform Act — partly because of the difficulties inherent in the undefined federal criterion of a "public offering" and partly because those states that previously had any sort of general exemption in this area usually phrased it in terms of a maximum number of buyers or offers or security holders — exempts offers to ten persons (other than institutional investors and broker-dealers) in the state during any twelve-month period, but only if the seller "reasonably believes that all the buyers in this state are purchasing for investment" and no remuneration is paid for soliciting, with authority in the administrator by rule or order to withdraw or further condition the exemption, or change the number of offerees permitted, or waive any of the conditions.[47] This is the basic theme in 40-odd states, although only a dozen or so keep the figure at 10. Elsewhere the number is raised most often to 15, 25, or 35.

(2) A handful of states have exemptions that limit the total number of security holders at the end of the offering rather than the number of offerees.

(3) Only some 10 states make general use of the undefined federal criterion of a "public offering." Some of these incorporate most of the federal exemptions by reference. In the latter group

[45] §503(b). On the term "general advertising," see J & C Investments v. Mid-South Drilling, Inc., 286 Ark. 320, 691 S. W. 2d 853 (1985) (state law).

[46] See p. 9 n. 7 supra.

[47] §402(b)(9). See, Loss Commentary on the Uniform Securities Act (1976) 124-30; Federman, Potential Liability from Indirect Remuneration in Private Oil and Gas Offerings, 11 Sec. Reg. L. J. 135 (1983).

presumably the federal precedents are binding, not merely persuasive, as a matter of state (not federal) law. And a substantial number of states have incorporated part or all of former Rule 146, or its successor, Rule 506, either by statute or administratively.[48]

(4) A few states with the almost universal exemption for an "isolated transaction" do not limit that exemption to nonissuer transactions.

(5) A great majority of the states, as well as §402(b)(8) of the Uniform Act, exempt sales to institutional investors.

(6) It is also relevant here that most of the statutes contain some sort of exemption for offerings to existing security holders — usually offers of additional *stock* to existing *stockholders* and only on condition that no commissions be paid. The comparable exemption in the Uniform Act is broader in that (a) it covers any offer to existing security holders, (b) it permits payment of "a standby commission," and (c) it waives the condition with respect to the payment of other remuneration if the issuer first files a notice specifying the terms of the offer and the administrator does not by order disallow the exemption within the next five full business days.[49]

F. TRADING TRANSACTIONS AND SECONDARY DISTRIBUTIONS

In this subchapter we examine various kinds of transactions whose common denominator is that the issuer is not a party. This includes "secondary distributions" of outstanding securities by their owner. It includes also the matter of resales after either a primary or a secondary offering, whether the offering is public or private — what we referred to in the §4(2) discussion as the "second stage" in the consideration of the private offering exemption,[1] although the resale problem extends well beyond the §4(2) context.

[48] See Regulation of Real Estate Securities, Including the Applicability of Federal Rule 146 and Its Use in State Blue Sky Laws, Report of Subcommittee on Syndications and Joint Ventures of the Committee on Real Estate Financing, American Bar Association, 13 Real Est., Probate & Trust J. 841, 846-52 (1978); see also p. 315 supra.

[49] §402(b)(11).

C. 5F [1] See p. 347 supra.

1. Private Nonissuer Transactions [§4(1)]

Section 4(1) exempts "Transactions by any person other than an issuer, underwriter, or deaer."[2] We have already noticed the definitions of these three terms and the interrelation between this exemption and the definition of "underwriter" so as to bring within §5 any secondary distribution of outstanding securities when the security holder is in a control relationship with the issuer and the distribution involves an underwriter.[3] Since §5 covers the universe — all persons and all transactions — this exemption is essential to permit Jones to sell his 100 shares of General Motors stock to Smith. Even if Jones's sale is of 1,000,000 shares to thousands of Smiths, there is still an exemption under §4(1) unless (1) Jones is an affiliate of General Motors (that is to say, there is a control relationship between them within the meaning of the second sentence of §2(11)), in which event anyone acting for him in making the distribution becomes an "underwriter," or (2) Jones is himself an "underwriter" because he purchased the security from General Motors with a view to distribution or because the circumstances warrant the conclusion that he is making the distribution for the benefit of General Motors. If Jones is neither an affiliate nor an underwriter, there is no limit on the size of a distribution he may make under the §4(1) exemption, even through an investment banking syndicate, because the investment bankers will not be "underwriters."

If Jones *is* an affiliate, arguably he may make a direct distribution — which is to say, a *public* offering — so long as he does not use an underwriter. But suppose that we metamorphose Jones into Jones *Corp.*, which wants to offer the stock of its subsidiary to its own thousands of shareholders. Would not a person who took even a few of the subsidiary's shares for resale on a market rise become literally an "underwriter"? And, since §4(1) exempts *transactions*, not *persons*,[4] would not such an "underwriter's" participation in the

[2] In Kohl v. Arlen Realty, Inc., 120 Misc. 2d 414, 465 N. Y. S. 2d 681 (Sup. Ct. 1983), the court held that a sheriff, as an arm of the court, was not an "issuer, underwriter, or dealer." "While there are no cases in New York directly in point, statutes have long recognized that the duties of the sheriff to sell securities to satisfy judgments must be unencumbered by any registration requirements." 120 Misc. 2d at 416, 465 N. Y. S. 2d at 683.

[3] See p. 88 supra.

[4] SEC v. Chinese Consolidated Benevolent Assn., Inc., 120 F. 2d 738, 741 (2d Cir. 1941), *cert. denied*, 314 U.S. 618 (1941), supra p. 257; see also SEC v. Culpepper, 270 F. 2d 241, 247 (2d Cir. 1959); SEC v. Holschuh, 694 F. 2d

transaction destroy the exemption so as to involve Jones Corp. in an illegal transaction?[5] This raises the same question of drawing the line between big and little buyers from the issuer itself that we have met in discussing the definition of "underwriter."[6] Significantly, the public utility holding companies that made secondary offerings of their subsidiaries' securities to their own security holders pursuant to §11(e) plans under the Holding Company Act took the prudent course of causing the securities to be registered.

2. Brokers' Transactions [§4(4)]

What, then, is the impact on all this of §4(4), which exempts "brokers' transactions" effected without the solicitation of customers' orders? As we have seen, the term "broker" is not separately defined.[7] All brokers are included within the definition of "dealer" in §2(12). It follows that the §4(4) exemption depends not upon a firm's generally acting as a broker but upon the capacity in which it executes the particular transaction. It follows also that the exemption is of no consequence at such times as the dealers' exemption in §4(3) is available. Its significance is that it permits an investor to cut his losses at any time, even while a stop order is in effect, by calling his broker.[8]

The brokers' exemption does not extend to the selling customer. It was established by the Federal Trade Commission that the exemption is limited to the broker's part of the transaction.[9] Thus, an *issuer* cannot avoid registration simply by having its securities sold through a broker, even though the issuer merely wishes to sell 100 shares of treasury stock on a stock exchange. Nor is the exemption available when the broker's principal is an *underwriter* or *dealer*. Whether or not the broker is liable in such cases as a participant in, or aider and abettor of, his *principal's* nonexempt transaction — as he is if he knows or has reasonable ground to believe that his principal is an issuer, underwriter, or dealer — the *principal* clearly violates §5. Conversely, when the principal is *not* an issuer, underwriter, or dealer, a §4(1) exemption for the principal's part

130, 137 (7th Cir. 1982); In re National Mortgage Equity Corp. Mortgage Pool Certificates Securities Litigation, 636 F. Supp. 1138, 1172-73 (C. D. Cal. 1986).

[5] The word "transaction" has always been read in the global sense of the entire offering rather than the sale from issuer to *A* and from *A* to *B*.

[6] See p. 255 supra.

[7] See p. 268 supra.

[8] H. R. Rep. No. 85, 73d Cong., 1st Sess. (1933) 16.

[9] Sec. Act Rel. 131 (1934).

of the transaction goes hand in hand with a §4(4) exemption for the broker's part.

Does this mean that an affiliate (who is not himself an underwriter or dealer) may sell his securities without limit as long as he does so through unsolicited brokers' transactions? Until 1946 the Commission followed this line: The fact that a broker effects an isolated transaction for an affiliate of the issuer does not make the broker an underwriter, even though he is selling for an "issuer" within the meaning of §2(11).[10] This assumes, however, that the broker does not exceed ordinary brokerage functions. If he does, he becomes an underwriter, with the result that his part of the transaction loses the 4(4) exemption and the affiliate's part loses the 4(1) exemption. What constitutes ordinary brokerage functions is a question of fact. Presumably the delegation of unusual discretion as to the time and manner of executing the affiliate's order, or the payment of more than a customary brokerage commission, would be fatal. And, although solicitation would normally seem to be part of the ordinary brokerage function, any solicitation that destroys the 4(4) exemption for the broker's part of the transaction destroys also the 4(1) exemption for the affiliate's part.[11] The caveat was always added, however, that a broker engaged in distributing any substantial block of securities would probably be compelled to perform functions beyond those normally exercised by brokers.

This caveat seemed adequate to draw the line between sporadic trading and secondary distributions until the "bull" market of 1945 and 1946. It became apparent, however, that large blocks of securities could be sold in that market without solicitation or any particular sales effort. For example, in a series of three orders entered between late December 1945 and May 1946, the Commission granted exemptions under the Holding Company Act for the sale by The United Corporation on the New York Stock Exchange

[10] True, an affiliate's broker who sells even 100 shares on a stock exchange is engaged in a "distribution" if that term is synonymous with "public offering." An implied exception is simply read into §2(11) for brokers when they execute transactions exempted under §4(4).

[11] It is a nice question whether the affiliate would be held to have engaged in an illegal transaction if he had had no knowledge or reasonable ground to believe that the broker had done any soliciting or in any way exceeded normal brokerage functions. This is in a sense the correlative of the question whether a particular broker participates in an illegal transaction when he does solicit or exceed normal brokerage functions but he has no knowledge or reasonable ground to believe that his selling customer is the issuer or in any way related to the issuer. Obviously there would be no criminal liability or basis for administrative disciplinary proceedings or injunctive action in either case. Whether there would be civil liability under §12(1) would make a nice examination question.

of a total of almost 600,000 shares of the common stock of its subsidiary, Columbia Gas & Electric Corporation. Since there was clear control and no registration statement had been filed under the Securities Act, it was obvious from the Commission's silence that exemption was assumed under §§4(1) and 4(4).[12]

A few months later, in the *Haupt* case, the Commission repudiated the implications of these orders and restated its position under §4(4). From December 15, 1943, to June 1, 1944, Ira Haupt & Company, a New York Stock Exchange member firm, had sold approximately 93,000 shares of the common stock of Park & Tilford, Inc., on behalf of the Schulte interests, who together owned some 91 percent of the outstanding stock. On December 15, 1943, Schulte had publicly announced that Park & Tilford was contemplating a distribution of whiskey to its shareholders at cost. (One must remember the date; whiskey was so scarce during the war that some thought Prohibition would come back *de facto.*) The stock advanced from 57⅝ on that day to a high of 98¼ on May 26. On that day Park & Tilford offered to sell to its stockholders at a reduced price six cases of whiskey for each share of stock. On May 31 the Office of Price Administration limited the negotiability of the purchase rights and the maximum profits on the resale of the liquor. The price of the stock dropped 10⅛ points that day and reached a low of 30⅝ in June. All the Schulte sales during this period were effected on the New York Stock Exchange through the Haupt firm. At first the firm received a series of orders to sell 200 or 300 shares at a time at a limited price. On March 7, however, the firm was authorized to sell up to 50,000 shares at 80 or better, and this number was later increased to 73,000 shares. It was stipulated that, during the period of 5½ months when the 93,000 shares were sold, 10 customers' men or representatives of the Haupt firm had solicited 21 customers, who had purchased approximately 4000 shares, and that the firm's chief statistician had prepared a written analysis of the stock for a customer, who had thereupon purchased 100 shares. This was the only evidence in the record with respect to solicitation.

In an administrative proceeding against the Haupt firm under the 1934 Act, the Commission stated:

> We conclude that Section [4(4)] cannot exempt transactions by an underwriter executed over the Exchange in connection with a

[12] United Corp., Holding Co. Act Rels. 6337 (1945), 6409 (1946), 6649 (1946). The first 200,000 shares were sold in only twenty-six days. Holding Co. Act Rel. 6409, supra.

> distribution for a controlling stockholder. Respondent has suggested that this conclusion is contrary to administrative interpretations issued by our staff and to the implications in recent orders issued in connection with applications of *The United Corporation* under the Public Utility Holding Company Act with respect to United's sale of common stock of a subsidiary through brokers on the New York Stock Exchange. The administrative interpretations referred to were to the general effect that an underwriter selling for a controlling stockholder over the exchange might conceivably be entitled to the exemption under Section [4(4)] if his activities were confined strictly to the usual brokerage functions, but that, as a practical matter, his activities could not be so confined in connection with a distribution of any substantial block of securities. These interpretations arrived at the same ultimate result as that which we have reached here. But the theory and the qualification of the interpretations — which we agree are inconsistent with our conclusion herein — were developed against the background of a very different market than is now prevalent. It has been only comparatively recently that the problem has been presented in the context of a market in which large blocks can frequently be sold without solicitations or other sales activity. In that context, the invalidity of the theory on which the interpretations were based has become apparent. We have reached our present conclusion on this phase of the case after careful consideration of the entire problem and, to the extent that the administrative interpretations referred to and the principle involved in the *United* case may be inconsistent with that conclusion, they must be overruled.[13]

The Commission had little trouble tying the Haupt firm into the violation. It found "no validity in the argument that a predetermination of the precise number of shares which are to be publicly dispersed is an essential element of a distribution." "Nor do we think," the Commission said, "that a 'distribution' loses its character as such merely because the extent of the offering may depend on certain conditions such as the market price." The Commission also rejected the firm's claim that it was not aware of the distribution intended by the Schulte interests. The Commission pointed out that only 7000 shares of the stock had been traded on the Exchange in the entire month of November; that 24,500 shares had been traded in the first two days following the announcement of the impending whiskey dividend; and that an additional 115,000 shares had been traded during the rest of that month. Under all the circumstances, the Commission found that "'The only reasonable

[13] Ira Haupt & Co., 23 SEC 589, 604-06 (1946).

conclusion that could have been reached by respondent was that it was intended that a large block would be sold."[14]

Although it could not be convincingly argued for a moment that Congress did not intend this kind of distribution to be subject to the registration requirement, the absence of any precise line between a nonexempt secondary distribution and the kind of brokerage transaction on behalf of an affiliate of an issuer that might still come within the brokerage exemption caused a good deal of concern among the brokerage fraternity. The argument was occasionally heard that, since "distribution" was supposed to be synonymous with "public offering," no broker could feel safe any longer in executing an order to sell 100 shares of stock on behalf of some officer or director of a corporation who might conceivably be deemed to be a member of a controlling group.

The upshot was the Commission's adoption eight years later, in 1954, of a Rule 154 (since replaced, as we shall see), which defined the term "broker's transactions" in §4(4) to include transactions by a broker acting as agent for a person in a control relationship with the issuer if, in addition to otherwise meeting the conditions of that section, he was "not aware of circumstances indicating that his principal is an underwriter in respect of the securities or that the transactions are part of a distribution of securities on behalf of his principal." And by way of "a ready guide for routine cases involving trading as distinguished from distributing transactions," the rule provided that there was not deemed to be a "distribution" if the transaction in question and all other sales of the same class of securities by or on behalf of the same person within the preceding six months did not exceed approximately 1 percent of the shares or units of an over-the-counter security and, in the case of a security traded on an exchange, the lesser of that amount or the aggregate reported volume of exchange trading during any week within the preceding four weeks. Whether transactions exceeding this formula constituted a "distribution" would depend on whether they involved an amount that was "substantial in relation to the number of shares or units of the security outstanding and the aggregate volume of trading in such security."[15]

[14] Id. at 598.

[15] Although the rule was expressly directed at §4(4), it was obviously contemplated that the seller's part of the transaction would be considered to be exempt under §4(1) whenever the broker's part came within the rule.

3. Resales After Private Offerings

Roughly the same period saw the playing out of another drama: what has here been referred to as the "second stage" of the private offering exemption in §4(2). That is to say, on the assumption that the number of initial offerees and all the other relevant factors are such as to justify the conclusion that the first stage of the transaction does not involve a public offering, it is still necessary to consider whether the purchasers' intent is to take for resale. If so, obviously, it is the number and type of *ultimate* offerees that are significant; otherwise a distribution by means of a sale to two or three firm-commitment underwriters for distribution would be a private offering.

The purchaser's intent is a question of fact, on which his own statement is evidentiary (not, of course, conclusive). The fact that a buyer does resell is not conclusive that he so intended when he bought. The private offering exemption does not impose an indefinite restraint on alienation — though naturally, the shorter the period before resale, the stronger would be the inference that there had been an intention to resell from the beginning unless the original purchaser could show some plausible reason why he had changed his mind. This came to be known as the "change of circumstances doctrine." Time, in other words, is relevant on the question of intent, but not conclusive.[16] Other factors, too, are very relevant: Whereas "insurance and investment companies * * * could quite readily sustain the burden of proof that they had purchased for investment," the nature of the business ordinarily carried on by a dealer or an investment banking house "would create an extremely strong presumption of purchase for resale."[17] If the buyer is neither an institutional investor on the one hand nor a securities firm on the other, the question must be asked whether his purchase of a block of securities of the particular size for investment is consistent with his general operations. Indeed, most of the factors enumerated in the 1935 opinion of the General Counsel[18] other than the number of offerees are hardly relevant except "where there are indications that the securities have been purchased for redistribution

[16] In Vohs v. Dickson, 495 F. 2d 607, 620-21 (5th Cir. 1974), where the court (*obiter*) found support for the finding below that the defendant had taken with investment intent, the court talked about the relevance of length of time, an investment letter, an unforeseen change of circumstances, the nature of the defendant's past investment and trading processes, and the character and scope of his business.

[17] Op. Gen. Counsel, Sec. Act Rel. 1862 (1938).

[18] Op. Gen. Counsel, Sec. Act Rel. 285 (1935).

and hence a public offering may be involved even though the initial offering is to an insubstantial number of offerees."[19]

In a 1938 opinion the General Counsel had expressed the view that retention of the securities for as long as a year "would create a strong inference that they had been purchased for investment." But he had added that even such an inference would fall, for example, "in the face of evidence of a pre-arranged scheme to effect a distribution at the end of the year."[20] The Commission later elaborated on this caveat:

> Holding for the six months' capital gains period of the tax statutes, holding in an "investment account" rather than a "trading account," holding for a deferred sale, holding for a market rise, holding for sale if the market does not rise, or holding for a year, does not afford a statutory basis for an exemption and therefore does not provide an adequate basis on which counsel may give opinions or businessmen rely in selling securities without registration.
>
> Purchasing for the purpose of future sale is nonetheless purchasing for sale and, if the transactions involve any public offering even at some future date, the registration provisions apply unless at the time of the public offering an exemption is available.[21]

It would seem to follow that the length of the holding that is required to negative an inference of an intent to distribute is affected by the relatively speculative or stable nature of the issuer. But, in the case of an established issuer with relatively stable earnings, it seems considerably less clear that (as asserted by a member of the Commission) "the happening or non-occurrence of an event in the affairs of the company or within the industry of which the company is a part, or that affects the general economy, is generally, in the absence of other persuasive factors, not the type of emergency or hardship situation that justifies reliance upon the change of circumstance doctrine."[22] One can understand the Commission's not being persuaded "that a person who had acquired a large block of securities in an airplane manufacturer but desired to sell his holdings upon learning of the launching of the first sputnik, because he suddenly believed that the age of missiles would supplant the use

[19] Brief of SEC, p. 38 n. 28, SEC v. Ralston Purina Co., 346 U. S. 119 (1953).

[20] Op. Gen. Counsel, Sec. Act Rel. 1862 (1938).

[21] Crowell-Collier Publishing Co., Sec. Act Rel. 3825 (1957) 6-7; see also Gilligan, Will & Co. v. SEC, 267 F. 2d 461, 468 (2d Cir. 1959), *cert. denied,* 361 U. S. 896, where the court affirmed disciplinary action taken by the Commission against one of the broker-dealers in the *Crowell-Collier* case.

[22] Orrick, Non-public Offerings of Corporate Securities — Limitations on the Exemption Under the Federal Securities Act, 21 U. Pitt. L. Rev. 1, 16 (1959).

of aircraft, had originally taken the securities for investment."[23] But the mere fact that an unanticipated technological advance affects an entire industry hardly precludes an inference that there has been a change of circumstances. Indeed, if it is to be taken as literally true that the exemption is destroyed by a vague intention to sell upon a substantial market movement in either direction, it is difficult to see how a resale could ever be made with safety except in the event of death, bankruptcy, or other personal disaster.

In their search for a crutch to lean on, some lawyers talked for a time of a "Cohen two-year rule," in reliance on remarks made by then Commissioner Manuel F. Cohen (later Chairman)[24] as well as a case in which a District Court concluded that a two-year holding was "an insuperable obstacle" to a finding that the defendant had taken the shares with a view to distribution "in the absence of any relevant evidence from which I could conclude he did not take the shares for investment."[25] But Commissioner Cohen indicated that certain factual situations would negative any two-year presumption, and the court might have been influenced by the necessity in a criminal contempt proceeding of proving "beyond a reasonable doubt" that the defendant's transactions had violated the court's injunction. Some lawyers then followed their own house rules in terms of three years or even five. But the Commission insisted that no specific period was conclusive or even presumptive of a "change of circumstances."

All this left a conscientious lawyer in a difficult position if he examined the issuer or the prospective buyers too closely on the question of investment intent; for few investors could honestly survive the examination, and a prospective buyer's very act of inquiring of counsel how long he must hold before reselling might require the answer that he has already entertained the fatal thought. For that matter, the prudent buyer's exaction of a registration covenant from the issuer in the event of a resale might itself damn the transaction. And it is difficult to see how a buyer acting in a *fiduciary* capacity could ever make the necessary representation consistently with his duty regularly to examine his investments with a view to making whatever changes are indicated. The late Ray Garrett put it very well some years before he became Chairman of the SEC:

> For reasons which will appear, one of the financial lawyer's most

[23] Id. at 17.

[24] See C. Israels (ed.), S. E. C. Problems of Controlling Stockholders and in Underwritings (1962) 30-31.

[25] United States v. Sherwood, 175 F. Supp. 480, 483 (S. D. N. Y. 1959).

...triguing tasks is that of explaining, for example, to a man who has just sold his business for stock, the precise state of mind which is appropriate for a good investment letter. The lawyer begins by saying that he must take for investment purposes, not for resale. And the dialogue runs: "Does that mean I can't ever sell it?" "No." "When, then?" "Only later when your reselling is consistent with your present investment intent." "In 6 months?" "No." "How long?" "Theoretically tomorrow if there is some change in circumstances — but don't you dare try it!" "What is a change of circumstances?" "Something basic and unforeseen." "Like needing the cash for a trip around the world?" "Do you expect to take a trip around the world?" And so on, ad infinitum.[26]

In this difficult state of affairs the Bar developed a number of safeguards:

(1) Every first-tier buyer is asked to sign an investment letter, which should be carefully drafted to explain what the buyer is being asked to sign. Some lawyers advise that a written explanation be given and that each buyer acknowledge in writing that it has been read. More properly, these letters should state negatively, more or less in the language of §2(11), that the buyers are *not* taking with a view to *distribution;* for a promise to hold for investment, or not to *resell,* would be inconsistent with a *private* resale for *investment,* which would not necessarily destroy the exemption (although even such resales are apt to increase the number of offerees dangerously by reason of the factor of geometric progression). And one should by all means avoid phrasing the letter in terms of holding for a fixed period. In principle even a long period would be worse than none; for it might be taken to indicate a present intention to resell at the end of the period.

(2) Transfer of the securities is restricted, with a notation on each certificate in order to meet the requirement of the Uniform Commercial Code for binding third persons.[27] A legend along these lines should be adequate when the seller has sufficient bargaining power to get it:

> These shares have been purchased for investment within the meaning of the Securities Act of 1933 and they may not be sold, transferred, pledged, or hypothecated without an effective registration statement under that Act or an opinion of counsel satisfactory to the company to the effect that the proposed transaction will be exempt from registration.

[26] Garrett, Federal Securities Act — An Introduction to Jurisdiction, [1961] U. Ill. L. F. 267, 293 n. 85.

[27] §8-204.

Depending on the relative bargaining power of the parties, the buyer, on the one hand, may have to agree to be bound by the opinion of the seller's counsel, and the seller, on the other hand, may have to agree to accept an opinion of the buyer's counsel or, conceivably, any counsel without further designation. Indeed, the buyer may be unwilling to accept legended certificates at all.[28]

(3) Sometimes a restriction on transfer is impracticable, or at least awkward, as, for example, when the seller is a controlling person who wants to rely on §4(1) for the sale of outstanding securities. In that event, an alternative to a restriction on transfer — or in any event a device to supplement the stamped certificate technique — is to deliver a "stop transfer notice" to the company or its transfer agent, with instructions to hold up transfer when a certificate affected by the notice is presented for registration of transfer until counsel for the company can pass on the matter.[29]

(4) It may be advisable, depending on the reliability of the buyers

[28] Alternatively, since it is not so much a pledge itself as a possible resale by the pledgee that must be guarded against (see p. 261 supra), it should be sufficient, if the buyer objects to the broader language, to substitute: "* * * they may not be sold or transferred by any person, including a pledgee, without * * *." In that event it may also be advisable, depending on the circumstances, to insert "or a donee" after "a pledgee," since the Commission has sometimes made "underwriters" out of donees, as we have seen (supra pp. 258-59), and the specific inclusion of a pledgee in the legend may create an undesirable negative implication.

Regulation D recites that the reasonable care that the issuer must exercise to assure that its buyers are not underwriters includes reasonable inquiry as to investment purpose, written disclosure of resale limitations, and an appropriate legend on the certificate. Rule 502(d).

An issuer may not delay registration of a transfer by unreasonably refusing to honor an opinion of counsel (or a "no action" letter from the SEC staff if that was bargained for). Kanton v. U. S. Plastics, Inc., 248 F. Supp. 353 (D. N. J. 1965). And an opinion of counsel may not be unreasonably withheld, at least when his refusal is "part of a deliberate and unwarranted attempt to forestall plaintiff's transfer of his stock while permitting favored shareholders to transfer their shares." Singer v. Whitman & Ransom, 83 A. D. 2d 862, 863, 442 N. Y. S. 2d 26, 27 (2d Dept. 1981). But, if the parties bargained for an opinion of counsel, a "no action" letter does not afford the same protection. Kenler v. Canal National Bank, 489 F. 2d 482 (1st Cir. 1973). In any event, a Securities Act barrier to a transfer does not necessarily defeat a claim for damages under UCC §8-204. Edina State Bank v. Mr. Steak, Inc., 487 F. 2d 640 (10th Cir. 1973), *cert. denied,* 419 U. S. 883.

"* * * defendants' allegedly wrongful refusal to remove the legend, without more, does not create a cause of action under Rule 10b-5." Madison Consultants v. Federal Deposit Ins. Corp., 710 F. 2d 57, 61 (2d Cir. 1983).

[29] For a discussion of the complexities raised by the Uniform Commercial Code, see Israels, in Current Problems of Securities Underwriters and Dealers, 18 Bus. Law. 27, 85-89 (1962). On the interrelation of the transfer agent's duties to (1) its issuer principal, (2) the UCC, and (3) the 1933 Act, see Morgan, Reconciling the "Conflicting" Duties to Transfer Agents and Issuers Under the Securities Act and the Uniform Commercial Code, 42 Ohio St. L. J. 879 (1981).

and the relative bargaining power of the parties, to require a statement of each buyer's financial condition by way of showing, for example, whether the amount of securities purchased is unduly large in relation to his financial means, or whether he borrowed to finance the purchase so that he might intend or be forced to resell in the near future in order to repay his loan. Prudence would seem also to dictate some inquiry, before making a sale, into the prospective buyer's record with respect to holding securities for long-term investment in the past.

In the last analysis, of course, the value of all such safeguards rests on the ability to persuade a court or the SEC that they are not empty rituals. But they may be particularly important with respect to civil or other liabilities:

(a) If first-tier buyers resell pursuant to a registration statement, there is no retroactive violation in the issuer's (or affiliate's) sale to them, because they turn out to have been "underwriters" within the expansive reading of the "preliminary negotiations" clause of §2(3).[30] Indeed, if the initial offering would be exempted under §4(2) (or §4(1) in the case of an affiliate) except for the fact that at least some of the buyers contemplate the possibility of a delayed distribution, it is questionable whether registration would be *proper* before the distribution (Rule 415 aside); for the last sentence of §6(a) indicates that the registration process was intended to have its impact at the point of *public offering*. By the same token, an investment representation hardly seems appropriate in such a case; instead the opinion of counsel for the issuer (or the affiliate) should more properly be couched in terms of the preliminary negotiations clause of §2(3) rather than §4(2) (or §4(1)). When the buyers are such that a §4(2) (or §4(1)) exemption would clearly be available if they were in fact taking for investment, but they want to be free to resell at any time subject to registration, there is no reason why the opinion of counsel cannot be phrased under both sections in the alternative; for the mere fact that only time will tell whether these candid persons did in fact buy "for investment" or were "underwriters" is no reason why the initial transaction should fall between two stools. Of course, if even one of the initial buyers takes for immediate distribution, there is no choice but to register; in that event, the technique of an undertaking to file a posteffective amendment before any delayed distribution by the others affords a practical solution to the dilemma.

(b) On the other hand, an *illegal* resale by first-tier buyers who

[30] See pp. 95-97 supra.

purported to take for investment raises different questions as far as the issuer's (or affiliate's) involvement in the violation is concerned, depending presumably on whether the issuer (or affiliate) had reasonable ground to question the initial investment representation. If so, the issuer (or affiliate) violates §5 along with the person reselling, either directly by virtue of participating in a nonexempt sale or as an aider and abettor. For these reasons, an issuer (or its transfer agent) should be particularly careful before registering a transfer of shares out of the names of persons who purported to buy from the issuer (or from an affiliate, though the *issuer's* involvement is somewhat less in that event) for investment. It may, of course, hold up a request to transfer for a reasonable time in order to investigate its legality. But it is not a proposition unique to §5 of the Securities Act that the issuer (or its transfer agent) may in either event guess wrong at the issuer's peril (if not the agent's as well) — whether it improperly registers a transfer or improperly declines to do so.

(c) The Commission staff has spoken forcefully about the *broker-dealer's* duty of investigation before he participates in an unregistered distribution:

> * * * [a] dealer who offers to sell, or is asked to sell a substantial amount of securities must take whatever steps are necessary to be sure that this is a transaction not involving an issuer, person in a control relationship with an issuer or an underwriter. For this purpose, it is not sufficient for him merely to accept "self-serving statements of his sellers and their counsel without reasonably exploring the possibility of contrary facts."
>
> The amount of inquiry called for necessarily varies with the circumstances of particular cases. A dealer who is offered a modest amount of a widely traded security by a responsible customer, whose lack of relationship to the issuer is well known to him, may ordinarily proceed with considerable confidence. On the other hand, when the dealer is offered a substantial block of a little-known security, either by persons who appear reluctant to disclose exactly where the securities came from, or where the surrounding circumstances raise a question as to whether or not the ostensible sellers may be merely intermediaries for controlling persons or statutory underwriters, then searching inquiry is called for.[31]

To this the staff has added:

> A firm's participation in an unregistered public distribution has fre-

[31] Sec. Act Rels. 4445 (1962), 5168 (1971). See also SEC v. Culpepper, 270 F. 2d 241 (2d Cir. 1959); SEC v. Mono-Kearsarge Consolidated Mining Co., 167 F. Supp. 248 (D. Utah 1958); Fitzgerald, De Arman & Roberts, Inc., Sec. Ex. Act Rel. 21,137, 30 SEC Dock. 1108 (1984).

quently been a major factor in the success of this unlawful activity since the firm affords sellers access to the market place and may create an appearance of propriety and substance otherwise lacking. * * *

* * *

While "the amount of injury called for necessarily varies with the circumstances of particular cases," all registered broker-dealers should establish minimum standard procedures to prevent and detect violations of the federal securities laws and to ensure that the firm meet its continuing responsibility *to know* both its customers and the securities being sold. * * *

Registered broker-dealers should also establish standard procedures as an initial step in their general investigation into the background of prospective customers and the source of the securities to be traded. * * *

* * *

The customer's responses or other particular circumstances may reasonably indicate that there is a duty to make further inquiries and verify the information received. * * *

Where it appears that securities to be sold were not acquired by open-market purchases, it must be determined whether their sale is exempted from registration under the Securities Act of 1933. Any determination that such an exemption exists should only be made after the broker-dealer has reviewed the facts surrounding the acquisition of the shares and competent outside counsel having no proprietary interest in the offering has furnished a supporting opinion describing the relevant facts in sufficient detail to provide an explicit basis for the legal conclusions stated. Of course, any firm receiving a sell order where the circumstances raise questions as to the propriety of the transactions should, in the exercise of its responsibilities, immediately alert the nearest Commission office.[32]

[32] Sec. Act Rel. 5168 (1971). See also Rule 144(g)(3), infra p. 374, which deems the term "brokers' transactions" in §4(4) to include a transaction in which (among other conditions) the broker "after reasonable inquiry is not aware of circumstances indicating that the person for whose account the securities are sold is an underwriter with respect to the securities or that the transaction is a part of a distribution of securities of the issuer." And the Commission has spoken on the meaning of "reasonable inquiry" in this context. Sec. Act Rel. 5223 (1972) 11. A broker or dealer is not entitled to rely on the absence of a restrictive legend. Butcher & Singer, Inc., Sec. Ex. Act Rel. 23,990, 37 SEC Dock. 544, 546 (1987), and cases cited. The Commission's further animadversions with respect to the role of counsel are considered infra c. 11A.

Violations are one thing and sanctions are another. A violation is not a crime, nor may it be the basis for administrative disciplinary proceedings against a broker-dealer, unless it was committed "willfully."[33] And an injunction requires "equity" — "some cognizable danger of recurrent violation."[34] *Civil* liability under §12(1) runs only to the seller's immediate buyer. When a lying first-tier buyer sues an innocent issuer (or affiliate), the doctrine of *in pari delicto* should apply, though this is less certain when *both* parties are playing games.[35] But an issuer (or affiliate) that in good faith had accepted investment representations from both *X* and *Y* might well be held liable to an innocent *Y* if *X* alone had misrepresented his intention and distributed the security. Whether a *dealer* who acted reasonably but got caught up in an illegal distribution would be liable to *his* buyers is a nice question — literally yes, with a right over presumably against the violators in common law tort.

Thus far we have been examining the resale problem from the issuer's (or affiliate's) point of view. The first-tier buyer, from his point of view, will want a registration covenant from the issuer (not just from the affiliate that is making a private offering under §4(1), since that very offering may weaken or destroy his control) in case the buyer will want to resell at a time or under circumstances when everybody agrees that registration is required (or, at any rate, when the issuer's counsel is of that opinion). A well drafted registration covenant will consider many variables and, again, will reflect the relative bargaining powers of the parties.[36] Sometimes, for example, the initial buyers from the issuer will have to be satisfied with a "piggyback" arrangement, whereby the issuer, instead of agreeing to register on a specified demand, agrees merely to give the initial buyers an opportunity to participate in any registration statement that the issuer may file in the future, with appropriate provisions with respect to payment of the expenses of registration and so on. These covenants are subject to specific performance whenever that

[33] Sec. Act §24; Sec. Ex. Act §15(b)(4)(D).
[34] United States v. W. T. Grant Co., 345 U. S. 629, 633 (1953).
[35] See p. 1034 infra.
[36] See Schneider and Manko, Rule 145, 5 Rev. Sec. Reg. 811, 821 n. 59 (1972).

relief is appropriate under the law of contracts.[37] But it is not always easy to get these agreements, because they may interfere with the issuer's future financing.

4. Rule 144

In 1972 the two tracks we have traveled in the last two sections of this subchapter — transactions by affiliates' brokers and resales after issuers' private offerings — converged in Rule 144. In the former aspect the rule replaced Rule 154. In the latter aspect Rule 144 is new. Both aspects are reflected in the rule's definition of "restricted securities" to mean securities "acquired directly or indirectly from the issuer, or from an affiliate of the issuer, in a transaction or chain of transactions not involving any public offering, or securities acquired from the issuer that are subject to the resale limitations of Regulation D under the Act, or securities that are subject to the resale limitations of Regulation D and are acquired in a transaction or chain of transactions not involving any public offering."[38]

The Commission's release on the adoption of the rule is as interesting for its tone as for its substance:[39]

> In brief, the rule provides that any affiliate or other person who sells restricted securities of an issuer for his own account, or any person who sells restricted or any other securities for the account of an affiliate of the issuer, is not deemed to be engaged in a distribution of the securities, and therefore is not an underwriter as defined in Section 2(11) of the Act, if the securities are sold in accordance with all the terms and conditions of the rule. * * *
>
> A number of persons have commented that it is not clear whether the rule, as proposed, was intended to be the exclusive means for selling restricted securities without registration under the Securities Act. In this connection, certain commentators asserted that the

[37] E. g., Kupferman v. Consolidated Research & Mfg. Corp., CCH Fed. Sec. L. Rep. ¶91,197 (S. D. N. Y. 1962); Siegler v. Living Aluminum, Inc., CCH Fed. Sec. L. Rep. ¶91,266 (N. Y. Sup. Ct. 1963); Waste Management, Inc. v. Deffenbaugh, 534 F. 2d 126 (8th Cir. 1976); Madison Fund, Inc. v. Charter Co., 427 F. Supp. 597 (S. D. N. Y. 1977) (breach of "piggyback" agreement); Canfield v. Reynolds, 631 F. 2d 169, 178 (2d Cir. 1980). But cf. Lipsky v. Commonwealth United Corp., 551 F. 2d 887 (2d Cir. 1976); Yoffee v. Keller Industries, Inc., 297 Pa. Super. 178, 443 A. 2d 358 (1982).

[38] Rule 144(a)(3). Rule 506 of Regulation D is, of course, a private offering rule; and Rules 504 and 505, though adopted under §3(b), have something of the private offering flavor.

[39] Sec. Act Rel. 5223 (1972).

Commission does not have the statutory authority to adopt such an exclusive rule while others stated that the Commission had such power and urged it to adopt an exclusive rule. The Commission does not believe it is necessary to reach these questions relating to its statutory authority at this time, since the rule as adopted is not exclusive. However, persons who offer or sell restricted securities without complying with Rule 144 are hereby put on notice by the Commission that in view of the broad remedial purposes of the Act and of public policy which strongly supports registration, they will have a substantial burden of proof in establishing that an exemption from registration is available for such offers or sales and that such persons and the brokers and other persons who participate in the transactions do so at their risk.

Moreover, with respect to restricted securities acquired after the effective date of the rule, the staff will not issue "no-action" letters relating to resales of such securities. Further, in connection with such resales, the Commission hereby puts all persons including brokers and attorneys on notice that the "change in circumstances" concept should no longer be considered as one of the factors in determining whether a person is an underwriter. The Commission recognizes that this concept has been in existence in one form or another for a long period of time. However, administrative agencies as well as courts from time to time change their interpretation of statutory provisions in the light of new considerations and changing conditions which indicate that earlier interpretations of such provisions are no longer in keeping with the statutory objectives. Thus, the "change in circumstances" concept in the Commission's opinion fails to meet the objectives of the Act, since the circumstances of the seller are unrelated to the need of investors for the protections afforded by the registration and other provisions of the Act.

Further, with respect to restricted securities acquired after the effective date of the rule but not sold pursuant to the provisions of the rule, the Commission hereby gives notice that in deciding whether a person is an underwriter, the length of time the securities have been held will be considered but the fact that securities have been held for a particular period of time does not by itself establish the availability of an exemption from registration.

* * *

Background and Purpose

* * *

Rule 144 is designed to implement the fundamental purposes of the Act as expressed in its preamble:

> To provide full and fair disclosure of the character of the securities sold in interstate commerce and through the mails, and to prevent fraud in the sale thereof * * *

The rule would also operate to inhibit the creation of public markets in securities of issuers concerning which adequate current information is not available to the public. At the same time, where adequate current information concerning an issuer is available to the public, the rule would permit the public sale in ordinary trading transactions of limited quantities of securities owned by persons controlling, controlled by or under common control with the issuer (hereinafter "affiliate") and by persons who have acquired restricted securities of the issuer.

This approach is consistent with the philosophy underlying the Act, that a disclosure law would provide the best protection for investors. * * *

* * *

Resales of securities acquired in private placements are frequently made under claims of an exemption pursuant to Section 4(1) of the Act, that is, a transaction by a person other than an issuer, underwriter, or dealer. This Section was intended to exempt only trading transactions between individual investors with respect to securities already issued and not to exempt distributions by issuers or acts of other individuals who engage in steps necessary to such distributions.

Generally the majority of questions arising under this Section have dealt with whether the seller is an "underwriter." The term underwriter is broadly defined in Section 2(11) of the Act to mean any person who has purchased from an issuer with a view to, or offers or sells for an issuer in connection with, the distribution of any security, or participates or has a direct or indirect participation in any such undertaking, or participates or has a participation in the direct or indirect underwriting of any such undertaking. The interpretation of this definition has traditionally focused on the words "with a view to" in the phrase "purchased from an issuer with a view to * * * distribution." Thus, an investment banking firm which arranges with an issuer for the public sale of its securities is clearly an "underwriter" under that Section. Not so well understood is the fact that individual investors who are not professionals in the securities business may be "underwriters" within the meaning of that term as used in the Act if they act as links in a chain of transactions through which securities move from an issuer to the public. It is difficult to ascertain the mental state of the purchaser at the time of his acquisition, and the staff has looked to subsequent acts and circumstances to determine whether such person took with a view to distribution at the time of his acquisition. Emphasis has been placed on factors such as the length of time the person has held the securities ("holding period") and whether there has been an unforeseeable change in circumstances of the holder. Experience has shown, however, that reliance upon such factors as the above has not assured adequate protection of investors through the maintenance of informed trading markets and has led to uncertainty in the application of the registration provisions of the Act.

Moreover, the Commission hereby emphasizes and draws attention to the fact that the statutory language of Section 2(11) is in the disjunctive. Thus, it is insufficient to conclude that a person is not an underwriter solely because he did not purchase securities from an issuer with a view to their distribution. It must also be established that the person is not offering or selling for an issuer in connection with the distribution of the securities and that the person does not participate or have a participation in any such undertaking, and does not participate or have a participation in any such underwriting of such an undertaking.

Rule 144, together with the other related rules and amendments, is designed to provide full and fair disclosure of the character of securities sold in trading transactions and to create greater certainty and predictability in the application of the registration provisions of the Act by replacing subjective standards with more objective ones.

Explanation and Analysis of the Rule

* * *

* * * In determining when a person is deemed not to be engaged in a distribution several factors must be considered.

First, the purpose and underlying policy of the Act to protect investors requires, in the Commission's opinion, that there be adequate current information concerning the issuer, whether the resales of securities by persons result in a distribution or are effected in trading transactions. Accordingly, the availability of the rule is conditioned on the existence of adequate current public information.

Secondly, a holding period prior to resale is essential, among other reasons, to assure that those persons who buy under a claim of a Section 4(2) exemption have assumed the economic risks of investment, and therefore, are not acting as conduits for sale to the public of unregistered securities, directly or indirectly, on behalf of an issuer. It should be noted that there is nothing in Section 2(11) which places a time limit on a person's status as an underwriter. The public has the same need for protection afforded by registration whether the securities are distributed shortly after their purchase or after a considerable length of time.

A third factor, which must be considered in determining what is deemed not to constitute a "distribution," is the impact of the particular transaction or transactions on the trading markets. It is consistent with the rationale of the Act that Section 4(1) be interpreted to permit only routine trading transactions as distinguished from distributions. Therefore, a person reselling securities under Section 4(1) of the Act must sell the securities in such limited quantities and in such a manner so as not to disrupt the trading markets. The larger the amount of securities involved, the more likely it is that such resales may involve methods of offering and amounts of compensation usually associated with a distribution rather than routine trading transactions. Thus, solicitation of buy orders or the payment of extra compensation are not permitted by the rule.

In summary, if the sale in question is made in accordance with all the provisions of the rule, as outlined below, any person who sells restricted securities shall be deemed not to be engaged in a distribution of such securities and therefore not an underwriter thereof. The rule also provides that any person who sells restricted or other securities on behalf of a person in a control relationship with the issuer shall be deemed not to be engaged in a distribution of such securities and therefore not to be an underwriter thereof, if the sale is made in accordance with all the conditions of the rule.

* * *

USE OF LEGENDS AND STOP-TRANSFER INSTRUCTIONS

Precautions by issuers are essential to assure that a public offering does not result from resale of securities initially purchased in transactions claimed to be exempt under Section 4(2) of the Act. (Attention is directed to Securities Act Release No. 5121 [1970] which discusses the use of legends and stop-transfer instructions as evidence of a non-public offering.) Although such assurance cannot be obtained merely by the use of an appropriate legend on stock certificates or other evidences of ownership, or by appropriate instructions to transfer agents, these devices serve a useful policing function, and the use of such devices is strongly suggested by the Commission and will be considered a factor in determining whether in fact there has been a private placement.

CONTRACTUAL REGISTRATION OR OTHER RIGHTS FOR RESALE OF RESTRICTED SECURITIES

Issuers, brokers, dealers, private placees and other holders of restricted securities are hereby put on notice that the Commission deems it appropriate that such persons when acquiring such securities, should consider contracting for registration or other rights, so that, if they desire to distribute their securities rather than resell in trading transactions pursuant to the rule, they can do so in a manner consistent with the provisions of the Act, i. e., by filing a registration statement or a notification under Regulation A. If the issuer does not file reports pursuant to Sections 13 or 15(d) of the Exchange Act, such persons should consider obtaining an agreement by the issuer to register voluntarily under that Act so that Rule 144 may be available.

* * *

Rule 144 is detailed and complex.[40] As Chairman Casey, under whose chairmanship the rule was adopted, later stated, "the price of clarity and predictability has been great."[41] A Lexis search in 1978 already revealed more than 4000 interpretations.[42] And two highly qualified commentators, concluding in 1977 that the rule "has proven a success," stated:

> In the last five years, the securities bar has been inundated with a veritable flood of interpretive letters which have penetrated virtually every crevice and cavity in the rule in which a latent ambiguity might be lurking. As of this late date, one might say that the unresolved interpretive questions which remain under the rule are generally of mind-boggling insignificance.[43]

So the partial summary here of the rule's six conditions must be taken with more than a grain of salt:[44]

(1) *Current public information:* There must be "adequate public information." This condition is satisfied if the issuer has been a reporting company under the 1934 Act for at least ninety days and has filed all required reports for twelve months (or for whatever shorter period it was required to file reports). If the issuer is not a reporting company, specified portions of the information required by Rule 15c2-11[45] must be publicly available. The rule provides

[40] See D. Goldwasser, A Guide to Rule 144 (2d ed. 1977); Sec. Act Rel. 6099, 17 SEC Dock. 1422 (1979) (summary of principal interpretations); Dept. of Commerce and SEC, Rule 144 Sales in the OTC Market: A Preliminary Analysis of the Impact of Rule 144 Sales in the OTC Market (1980); Fogelson, Rule 144 — A Summary Review, 37 Bus. Law. 1519 (1982).

[41] Casey, SEC Rules 144 and 146 Revisited, 43 Brooklyn L. Rev. 571, 587 (1977).

[42] H. Kripke, The SEC and Corporate Disclosure: Regulation in Search of a Purpose (1979) 42-43.

[43] Borden and Fleischman, The Continuing Development of Rule 144: Significant SEC Staff Interpretations, in Practising Law Institute, Eighth Annual Institute on Securities Regulation (1977) c. 4 at 91.

[44] All quotations are from Sec. Act Rel. 5223 (1972).

[45] See infra.

that "the person proposing to sell securities or the broker through whom they are to be sold shall be entitled to rely upon the issuer's statement in the latest * * * report that all required reports have been filed or upon a written statement from the issuer that all such reports have been filed, unless he knows or has reason to believe that the issuer has not complied with such requirements."

(2) *Holding period:* As stated in the Commission's release:[46]

> Securities sold in reliance upon the rule must have been beneficially owned and fully paid for by the seller for a holding period of at least two years prior to his sale as specified below. This condition is designed to assure that the registration provisions of the Act are not circumvented by persons acting, directly or indirectly, as conduits for an issuer in connection with resales of restricted securities. In order to accomplish this, the rule provides that such persons be subject to the full economic risks of investment during the holding period. Accordingly, the rule provides that giving the person from whom the securities were purchased promissory notes or other obligations to pay the purchase price, or entering into an installment purchase contract with such person, will not constitute payment of the purchase price unless certain conditions are met. These conditions are that the promissory note, obligation or contract must provide for full recourse against the purchaser of the securities, must be adequately secured by collateral other than the securities purchased and must have been discharged by payment in full prior to the sale of the securities.
>
> * * *
>
> There have been various holding periods provided for in proposed rules and applied over the years by administrative interpretations. After reexamination and reconsideration, the Commission believes, in keeping with the purposes of the Act in preventing the distribution of unregistered securities to the public, that the holding period should be two years in the context of the other provisions of the rule. The definitive holding period provided in the rule may be relied on only in connection with sales made pursuant to the rule.
>
> For the purpose of the rule, the doctrine of "fungibility" will not apply. That is, the acquisition during the two-year period of other securities of the same issuer, whether restricted or nonrestricted, will not start the holding period running anew.[47] However, a new

46 Sec. Act Rel. 5223 (1972).

47 Before Rule 144, and perhaps still when one is not relying on the theoretically nonexclusive rule, one who bought a block of securities from the issuer could not avoid the status of an "underwriter" by retaining that block for investment and simultaneously distributing another block of securities acquired from the issuer some time previously. See, e. g., Thomas C. Bennett, Jr., 43

provision has been added to the rule dealing with short sales, puts or other options to sell securities. The provision requires that if the securities sold are equity securities there shall be excluded in determining the holding period any period during which the seller had a short position in, or any put or other option to dispose of, any securities of the same class or any securities convertible into securities of such class. If the securities sold are nonconvertible debt securities, there must be excluded any period during which the seller had a short position in, or any put or other option to dispose of, any nonconvertible debt securities of the same issuer.

Certain securities acquired in connection with, or as a result of, ownership or acquisition of other securities, are deemed to have been acquired when such other securities were acquired. These include stock dividends (including stock dividends on securities initially acquired as stock dividends), stock splits, stock acquired in recapitalizations, conversions or contingent issuances of securities. The rule, as adopted, includes provision for contingent issuance of securities in a stock for stock transaction as well as in the stock for assets transaction provided for in the rule as proposed.

The holding periods of pledgor-pledgee-purchaser on default, donor-donee, settlor-trustee-beneficiary, and decedent-estate-legatee may be tacked.[48] But, as stated in the release, "A purchaser in a private placement or series of private placements would not be permitted to tack the holding period of the prior owner."

(3) *Amount of securities sold:* The amount of securities that normally may be sold in reliance on the rule during any three-month period is the greater of 1 percent of the outstanding class or average weekly reported volume during the past four calendar weeks. Here the pledge, gift, trust, and estate situations that enjoy tacking for purposes of computing the holding period are *aggregated* for purposes of applying the amount limitations. Moreover, as stated in the release, "The rule permits sales within successive 6-month [now

SEC 75, 81-82 (1966). For this purpose — and the same result might follow in principle if the one block was sold shortly *before* the other block was purchased — the two blocks were considered fungible despite the statutory nonfungibility that we have noticed is unavoidable for other purposes (see p. 116 supra). But there was considerable grey in this area. See 4 Loss 2578. There is an old rule, for example, to the effect that a person whose business consists chiefly of buying the securities of any one issuer with the proceeds of the sales of its own securities is to be regarded as engaged in the distribution of the securities of that issuer so as to become an underwriter of those securities. Rule 140.

[48]There is no holding period at all if the estate or selling legatee is not an affiliate of the issuer.

3-month] periods, but no accumulation [is] permitted." That is to say, year I's unused quota may not be carried over to year II.[49]

(4) *Manner of sale:* Sales must be made in "brokers' transactions" within §4(4) (as elaborated in the rule) or in transactions directly with a "marketmaker" as defined in §3(a)(38) of the 1934 Act (in substance, a dealer who holds himself out as being willing to buy and sell a particular security for his own account on a regular basis).[50] As stated in the release:

> * * * The broker may not solicit buy orders, but he may inquire of other brokers or dealers who have indicated an interest in the securities within the preceding 60 days.
>
> In addition, the rule provides that the broker shall make a reasonable inquiry to ascertain whether the seller is engaged in a distribution. Reasonable inquiry should include, among other matters, inquiry as to the length of time the seller has held the securities; the amount of securities the seller and "chargeable" persons have sold in the past six months; whether he intends to sell securities of the same class through any other means; the number of shares of the class outstanding or the relevant trading volume; and whether the seller has solicited or made any arrangement for the solicitation of buy orders, or has made any payment to any other person in connection with the proposed transaction.

(5) *Notice of offering:* The seller must file a prescribed notice with the Commission and the principal exchange (if any) on which the securities are traded. But there is a *de minimis* exception in terms of 500 shares or $10,000 of aggregate sale price.

(6) *Bona fide intention to sell:* Along the lines of the last sentence of §6(a), the "anti-shelf" provision, the person filing the notice must "have a *bona fide* intention to sell * * * within a reasonable time * * *."

In the case of sales by a nonaffiliate who has been a beneficial owner for *three* years, Rule 144(k) waives all six conditions except with respect to manner of sale and intention.[51]

As with respect to the impact of Rule 506 on the statutory exemption in §4(2), the question arises here of how much of the pre-144 gloss on §4(1) together with §2(11) survives Rule 144. The

[49] In re Bankers Trust Co. of Western N. Y., 93 A. D. 2d 583, 462 N. Y. S. 2d 924 (4th Dept. 1983), the court concluded that a trustee's decision to postpone a sale, so that he missed an opportunity to sell $500,000 worth of stock because of fluctuations in the volume of trading, was based on a judgment that the price would go up, which was not an imprudent decision. The lower court had found negligence.

[50] This condition does not apply to securities sold for an estate or its beneficiary that is not an affiliate.

[51] See Sec. Act Rel. 6488, 28 SEC Dock. 1170 (1983).

Commission in 1979 added Rule 144(j) to codify its repeated statements that the rule is not exclusive.[52] But, as we have seen, the release adopting Rule 144 (1) emphasized the "substantial burden of proof" in establishing exemption apart from the rule, (2) withheld the comfort of "no action" letters, (3) rejected *any* time period as itself establishing an exemption, and (4) announced that "the 'change in circumstances' concept should no longer be considered as one of the factors in determining whether a person is an underwriter."[53] One's heart grows cold!

The rule *has* elevated a good deal of prior lore into written form and thus has made things more predictable. But aside from the price in complexity, as well as the question we noticed with respect to Rule 506 whether the definitional and implemental rulemaking authority in §19(a) justifies so substantive a rule, it is not easy to comprehend how the Commission can abandon the "change of circumstances" concept that is so clearly implicit in 2(11)'s "with a view to * * * distribution." It is never possible to decide questions that lurk in a person's mind, like intention or motive, except by circumstantial evidence. It is not a matter of the Commission's not being absolutely bound by *stare decisis* or of the abandoned concept's being inconsistent with the need for investor protection — the two rationales mentioned in the adopting release. It is a matter simply of how far statutory language may be stretched.

It follows that, if the person who bought from an issuer (or affiliate) has held the securities long enough to make credible his assertion that he did not take them with a view to distribution — so that, as it used to be said, the securities have "come to rest" in his hands — he should not be brought within the "has purchased from" portion of the "underwriter" definition in §2(11), and his later distribution should be exempted under §4(1).

The securities Bar, understandably, seems loathe to do battle on this front. But *private* sales of restricted securities outside Rule 144 are fairly common, and neither the Commission nor the Bar seems to be much troubled by them. Because the SEC staff often has required such resales to meet some of the *Ralston*-type criteria for §4(2) offerings by an issuer, this variety of sale has been dubbed a "Section 4(1½)" transaction. But the answer, of course, is simply §4(1). Section 4(2) with its reference to "transactions by an issuer" can have no application to a resale unless the securities have not yet "come to rest" in the reseller's hands. In that event, it is appropriate for the sophistication and access criteria to be applied, but

[52] Sec. Act Rel. 6032, 16 SEC Dock. 1261, 1264 (1979).
[53] See p. 367 supra.

only for the purpose of assuring that the issuer's original §4(2) exemption has not been lost.[54]

There is a more fundamental objection to the entire "140 series" of rules: They represent an administrative philosophy that will not suffer the smallest mouse to escape the trap. In terms of cost-benefit analysis they ignore the inordinate price in complexity of catching the few smallest mice. Certainly this whole area, with or without the "140 series" of rules (now including Rule 506), is one of the best arguments for a code that would cut through the half-century accumulation of underbrush and emancipate both Government and the citizen from an archaic and tyrannic statutory structure.

5. Nonissuer Transactions Under the Code

The Code's treatment of resales and secondary distributions — which marks a substantial departure from existing law — follows this scheme:

(1) The "control" test is abandoned altogether except for purposes of civil liability and disclosure (as well as block trades to a limited extent).

(2) All distributions (primary as well as secondary) up to $200,000 are categorically *exempted* from the offering statement requirement as *de minimis* (subject to SEC rulemaking authority only in the $100,000-$200,000 range).[55] And the Commission's general authority to exempt any person, security, or transaction by rule or order from any or all provisions of the Code[56] will enable it to exempt even larger distributions with or without conditions.

(3) We have already noticed the "one-year registrant" concept;[57] the definition of "distribution" as "an offering other than (i) a limited offering or (ii) an offering by means of one or more trading transactions"; and the definition of "limited offering" in terms of thirty-five buyers and an unlimited number of "institutional investors."[58] This applies equally to *secondary* offerings.

[54]See The Section "4(1½)" Phenomenon: Private Resales of "Restricted" Securities, A Report to the [ABA] Committee on Federal Regulation of Securities from the Study Group on Section "4(1½)" of the Subcommittee on 1933 Act — General, 34 Bus. Law. 1961 (1979). This report does not consider the "change of circumstances" doctrine. But with respect to private resales it is consistent with the views here expressed. It also thought that a three-year holding period should be "well-nigh conclusive." Id. at 1975 n. 69.

[55]§512(5).

[56]§303.

[57]See p. 93 supra.

[58]§202(41), supra p. 348.

(4) The difficult problem with respect to holding period is simplified by a provision to the effect that there may be free and unlimited transfers within or outside the initial group of buyers as long as there are no more than thirty-five buyer-owners (apart from institutional investors) at any time for a year in the case of a one-year registrant or three years in other cases.[59] This is a much easier restriction on transferability both to interpret and to police, and after the one-year or three-year period there is no restriction at all. Moreover, the restriction itself, like the initial test of thirty-five, is expressed not in absolute terms but in terms of reasonable belief.[60]

(5) Whereas §4(4) today exempts only unsolicited *brokers'* transactions, and Rule 144 as amended a few years ago extends to transactions directly with marketmakers, the new "trading transaction" includes all routine dealer transactions as a matter of statute.[61]

(6) All secondary *distributions* not exempted by reason of small amount are treated alike. But in the case of a one-year registrant all that is required is the filing by the secondary distributor (not the issuer) of a very short "distribution statement" that contains simply the facts with respect to the secondary distributor and the terms of the distribution, together with a certification that the secondary distributor does not know any additional information that he would have to disclose under the antifraud provisions; and the distribution statement becomes effective on the third day after filing.[62]

(7) With respect to *non*-one-year registrants, the issuer must file a regular offering statement (today's registration statement), together with a company registration statement if it is not already a registrant, on demand. But this requirement is subjected to a number of qualifications designed, on the one hand, to avoid locking in market buyers and, on the other hand, to protect the issuer's legitimate interest:[63]

(a) The issuer has sixteen months to comply with the demand.

(b) The secondary distributor must pay the costs.

(c) The issuer has a right of indemnification against any underwriters with respect to material supplied by them.[64]

(d) The demand provision carries no "piggy-back" rights.

(e) The demand provision does not apply if the secondary dis-

[59] §202(41)(B)(i)-(ii). Moreover, the Commission is given rulemaking authority, which is considerably narrower with respect to one-year registrants. §202(4)(B)(iv)-(v). See p. 348, pars. (3)-(4) supra.

[60] §202(41)(B)(i)(I) and (viii).

[61] §202(41)(C).

[62] §510.

[63] §502(b).

[64] §1724(e)(1).

tributor executes an express waiver of his rights, is contractually or legally bound by a restriction on transfer that would be violated by the proposed distribution, or acquired the securities with knowledge that his seller executed such a waiver.

(f) The secondary distributor must present a reasonably supported opinion of counsel to the effect that the distribution could not otherwise be legally made.

(g) The issuer has the alternative of offering (or arranging for someone else to offer) to buy out the secondary distributor at a price to be determined by arbitration.

(8) There is a special exemption for block trades in securities of one-year registrants if, among other conditions, (a) the secondary distributor owns or reasonably believes that he owns not more than 15 percent of the voting securities and (b) in the event of 5-15 percent ownership he is not in a control relationship with the issuer and forwards a brief report of beneficial ownership to the SEC by the next business day after the contract to sell.[65]

6. Nonissuer Transactions Under the State Blue Sky Laws

Once more the lawyer's task is not finished until he examines the law with respect to nonissuer transactions in every state in which an offer is to be made.

Section 305 of the Uniform Securities Act provides:

[Effective Period, Withdrawal, and Non-Issuer Distributions.]

(i) Every registration statement is effective for one year from its effective date, or any longer period during which the security is being offered or distributed in a non-exempted transaction by or for the account of the issuer or other person on whose behalf the offering is being made or by any underwriter or broker-dealer who is still offering part of an unsold allotment or subscription taken by him as a participant in the distribution, except during the time a stop order is in effect under section 306. All outstanding securities of the same class as a registered security are considered to be registered for the purpose of any non-issuer transaction (1) so long as the registration statement is effective and (2) between the thirtieth day after the entry of any stop order suspending or revoking the effectiveness of the registration statement under section 306 (if the registration statement did not relate in whole or in part to a non-

[65] §512(4).

issuer distribution) and one year from the effective date of the registration statement. A registration statement may not be withdrawn for one year from its effective date if any securities of the same class are outstanding. A registration statement may be withdrawn otherwise only in the discretion of the [Administrator].

[REPORTS.]

(j) So long as a registration statement is effective, the [Administrator] may by rule or order require the person who filed the registration statement to file reports, not more often than quarterly, to keep reasonably current the information contained in the registration statement and to disclose the progress of the offering.

LOSS, COMMENTARY ON THE UNIFORM SECURITIES ACT (1976) 72-79

DRAFTSMEN'S COMMENTARY TO §305(i), §305(j) AND RELATED SECTIONS REFERRING TO NON-ISSUER DISTRIBUTIONS

Perhaps the most difficult aspect of the area of securities registration, and often the most ambiguous under the present statutes, is the application of the registration provisions to secondary distributions or other transactions not involving the issuer of the security. In many statutes it is difficult or impossible to say with any certainty when registration is required in such a case; who must or may register; how many units of the security should be registered; who may sell once a registration becomes effective; and, as a result, who is civilly liable. A related question is how long a registration statement remains in effect. These questions are dealt with in §305(i), §305(j) and a number of other provisions throughout the statute.

This is one of the few areas in which this Act breaks new ground, although part of the statutory scheme can be traced to existing patterns. Thus, most of the present statutes provide that a registration remains effective for one year. But the statutes are silent for the most part as to the effect of registration upon trading in outstanding securities of the class. A registration statement usually relates to a fixed number of shares sold at a specified price, or an indeterminate number of shares aggregating no more than a specified dollar amount. The status of resales of the registered securities by their initial purchasers is ambiguous. Quite a few statutes contain exemptions for resales when the security is listed in a recognized manual * * * , when an exemption is specially applied for * * * , or when the outstanding security meets some other test

* * *. When registration is clearly required before outstanding securities may be resold, the statutes not infrequently specify a special method of registration * * *. * * *

One solution for many of these problems would be to restrict the registration provisions to primary offerings * * *. * * * The Securities Act of 1933 is similarly restricted to primary offerings, except that registration is required when a person in a control relationship with the issuer makes a secondary distribution through an underwriter. * * * But, aside from the great difficulty in determining when "control" exists * * * , the tradition of registering outstanding securities is too strong in most states to be easily disturbed. The statutory scheme of this Act is essentially in that tradition, but it incorporates a number of devices which are designed to make for less unnecessary red tape and more certainty:

1. Section 301(a) applies broadly to any offer or sale by any person. Thus, it is literally unlawful for Jones to sell five shares of *X* Corp. to Smith unless there is registration or an exemption.

2. The term "non-issuer" is defined in §401(h) to mean simply "not directly or indirectly for the benefit of the issuer." * * *

3. Section 402(b)(1) exempts from registration "any isolated non-issuer transaction, whether effected through a broker-dealer or not." Some sort of "isolated transaction" exemption is universal or virtually so today, and a considerable body of case law has been developed.[a] This exemption takes care of Jones's sale of *X* Corp. to Smith, but obviously does not cover something like the offering of Ford stock by the Ford Foundation. Whether it covers something in between — say, Jones's sale of 500 or 1000 shares of *X* Corp. to several people more or less concurrently — depends on the construction of the word "isolated." In Massachusetts, where the exemption in §3(a) for "any isolated sale" is qualified, as this type of exemption usually is, by a provision that "this exemption shall not include a sale made in the course of repeated and successive transactions of a like character," the Supreme Judicial Court has stated that "two sales of securities, made one after the other within a period of such reasonable time as to indicate that one general purpose actuates the vendor and that the sales promote the same aim and are not so detached and separated as to form no part of a single plan, would be 'repeated and successive transactions.' " *Kneeland* v. *Emerton,* 280 Mass. 371, 389, 183 N. E. 155, 163 (1932); followed

[a]ED.: In Blinder, Robinson & Co., Inc. v. Goettsch, 403 N. W. 2d 772 (Iowa 1987), the court, citing the Code, sustained this sanction against a constitutional attack of vagueness.

in *Gales* v. *Weldon*, 282 S. W. 2d 522, 526 (Mo. 1955) (five sales in two months) * * *. * * *

4. On the other hand, there are in this statute, as there often are in the existing acts, other exemptions which frequently make resort to this exemption unnecessary. When the non-issuer distribution is something more than an "isolated transaction," however that phrase is construed, it may still be exempted under §402(a)(8) if the security is listed on a stock exchange, under §402(b)(3) if the distribution is effected through a registered broker-dealer who does not solicit orders or offers to buy, under §402(b)(6) if the transaction is by an executor or one of the other persons there enumerated, under §402(b)(7) if it is a transaction by a *bona fide* pledgee, under §402(b)(8) if the offer is made solely to institutional buyers and broker-dealers, or under §402(b)(9) if it is made to a limited number of persons. * * *

5. These exemptions of general applicability aside, §402(b)(2) affords an exemption which is specifically designed for certain non-issuer distributions. That exemption applies to

> any non-issuer distribution of an outstanding security if (A) a recognized securities manual contains the names of the issuer's officers and directors, a balance sheet of the issuer as of a date within eighteen months, and a profit and loss statement for either the fiscal year preceding that date or the most recent year of operations, or (B) the security has a fixed maturity or a fixed interest or dividend provision and there has been no default during the current fiscal year or within the three preceding fiscal years, or during the existence of the issuer and any predecessors if less than three years, in the payment of principal, interest, or dividends on the security.[b]

* * *

Apart from these existing types of exemption, the "manual" exemption for secondary distributions which is incorporated in Clause (A) of §402(b)(2) is of ancient vintage in some states, and it has been spreading in recent years. * * * The exemption in §402(b)(2)(A) is not so restricted as most of the existing manual exemptions. Not infrequently they apply only to sales by registered dealers, or require that the sale be at a price "reasonably related to the current market price," or contain other restrictions. On the other hand, not all of them provide, as this Act does, that the exemption may be denied or revoked by the Administrator. Under

[b]ED.: On the manual exemption, see Christensen v. Dean Witter Reynolds, Inc., CCH Blue Sky L. Rep. ¶72,045 at 70,612-13 (D. Minn. 1984).

§402(c) the Administrator may deny or revoke the exemption for a particular non-issuer distribution if he finds, in the language of §412(b), that denial or revocation "is necessary or appropriate in the public interest or for the protection of investors and consistent with the purposes fairly intended by the policy and provisions of this act." This same authority applies to all of the other exemptions enumerated in paragraph 4 of this commentary except the exemption for listed securities. * * * Moreover, there are other safeguards: The Administrator may define the term "recognized securities manual" by rule under §412(a). The fraud provisions of §§101 and 410(a)(2) apply. Broker-dealers and their agents who effect transactions exempted under §402(b)(2) are subject to the registration provisions of Part II and the Administrator's policing thereunder. And an Administrator who chooses to do so may keep track of the securities sold under this exemption by requiring under §203(a) that registered broker-dealers prepare and keep lists of those securities.

6. If no exemption is available for the non-issuer distribution, the security must be registered. This is when §305(1) becomes significant. Under the first sentence of that section every registration statement is effective for at least one year and for any longer period during which the security is being distributed, except while a stop order is in effect. To this extent, §305(i) is in the existing pattern, except that it is more specific. What is new is the second sentence. Under Clause (1) of that sentence all outstanding securities "of the same class" as the registered security are considered to be registered for the purpose of any non-issuer transaction so long as the registration statement remains effective. When the Administrator has permitted a registration statement to become effective, it seems perfectly safe to permit secondary trading in the same class of security without further ado for a period of at least one year. Compare the present exemptions described in paragraph 5 of this commentary. * * *

Moreover, since §305(j) gives the Administrator power by rule or order to require the registrant to file reports as long as the registration remains effective, current information will always be obtainable in respect of offerings which take more than one year to complete, and hence it seems proper to permit secondary trading for however long a registration remains in effect. Section 305(j) is actually somewhat broader than the average reporting provision in the statutes today, but it is basically consistent with the prevailing pattern. There are also other statutory protections: injunction under §408 against continued or threatened sales which would violate the antifraud provisions of §101; entry of a stop order under §306(a); criminal prosecution under §409 for fraudulent sales; and revocation of the registration of any broker-dealer who engages in such transactions under §304(a)(2)(B).

The net effect of this class registration technique is that whenever a registration statement has become effective, no matter who has filed it or how many units of the class have been registered, all securities *of the same class* can be legally traded by anybody *as if they were registered.* Whether the security being traded is "of the same class" as the registered security notwithstanding changes in its terms during the year presents a question of construction. * * *

7. It remains to explain Clause (2) of the second sentence of §305(i). This is designed to take care of the situation where the Administrator finds it necessary to enter a stop order during the year after the effective date. Obviously, when the registration which thus becomes the subject of a stop order was itself filed in connection with a non-issuer distribution, it would substantially nullify the effect of the stop order to continue to permit a secondary market on the class registration theory of the first sentence of §305(i). But, when the registration statement related entirely to a primary distribution by the issuer, and a substantial part of the offering was made in the state before the stop order was entered, there should be some way to avoid indefinitely locking in those people who were unfortunate enough to be buyers. On the one hand, it would not be in the public interest freely to permit this one set of unfortunates to dump their securities into the hands of another set of unfortunates. But, on the other hand, forever to stop all secondary trading after the entry of a stop order except for "isolated transactions" under §402(b)(1) would come very close to establishing a restraint on alienation, perhaps even with constitutional overtones under the due process clauses. Cf. *People* v. *Pace,* 73 Cal. App. 548, 238 Pac. 1089 (1925) * * *. The proposed solution is Clause (2).

8. The next problem under the class registration theory of the first sentence of §305(i) is raised by the possibility of withdrawal. For the reason stated in paragraph 8 of the official comment, §305(i) provides that a registration statement may not be withdrawn for one year from its effective date if any securities of the same class are outstanding. Under any other circumstances withdrawal is discretionary with the Administrator.

9. If no exemption is available for a non-issuer distribution and *a registration statement for securities of the same class is not effective,* there arises for the first time the necessity of filing a *special* registration statement to permit a non-issuer distribution. As in the case of a

distribution for the account of the issuer, registration may be effected here by coordination, or by notification under *either* §302(a)(2) or §302(a)(1),[c] or as a last resort by qualification. In any event, a registration for a non-issuer distribution, like any other registration, is deemed to register all outstanding securities of the same class, and thus to permit *anybody* to trade for a minimum of one year or however much longer it may take to complete the registered non-issuer distribution. It is thus immaterial, as stated in paragraph 9 of the official comment, whether the registration statement specifically covers 100 shares or 100,000 shares, because the Administrator may not permit the registration statement to become effective unless the statutory standards are satisfied.

* * *

10. There is one final problem with respect to non-issuer distributions, which is dealt with in §305(f). That section provides:

> In the case of a non-issuer distribution, information may not be required under section 304 or 305(j) unless it is known to the person filing the registration statement or to the persons on whose behalf the distribution is to be made, or can be furnished by them without unreasonable effort or expense.

This provision is designed only to take care of the case where the seller simply cannot obtain certified financial statements and other data normally required. It is a problem which is apparently worked out today at a pragmatic level. But it is a problem which cannot be ignored. Cf. *People* v. *Pace,* 73 Cal. App. 548, 238 Pac. 1089 (1925). If a person owns 5 percent of the stock of a company and decides to sell out precisely because he cannot get along with the management, there must be some way out of the impasse which results when the Administrator insists on information that the stockholder simply cannot obtain. The phrase "without unreasonable effort or expense" is borrowed from §10(a)(3) of the Securities Act of 1933, 15 U. S. C. §77j(a)(3), which is derived from a provision that was inserted by amendment in 1934 in order to prevent the blocking in of dealers who might still be subject to the statutory requirement that an up-to-date prospectus be used without being able to supply

[c]ED.: Section 302(a)(2) makes the notification procedure available for a non-issuer distribution, apart from the quality standards of §302(a)(1), "if (A) any security of the same class has ever been registered under this act or a predecessor act, or (B) the security being registered was originally issued pursuant to an exemption under this act or a predecessor act."

the required up-to-date information. The SEC has taken the position that, when the issuer itself or an underwriter or dealer who does have access to current information is still selling after the time when the prospectus must be brought up to date, the "unreasonable effort or expense" clause was not intended to apply to that expense which is merely incident to the correlation of the new information and the reprinting of the prospectus. * * * Similarly here, in the case of a non-issuer distribution by a person who is in a control relationship with the issuer or otherwise has access to required information, the "unreasonable effort or expense" clause is not meant to apply to that expense which is merely incident to supplying the information required to register. * * *[d]

7. The Resale Problem in Other Contexts Under the 1933 Act

a. Registered Securities and "Small Issues"

We have yet to consider the matter of resales by buyers of *registered* securities or of securities received in an intrastate offering, a merger or the like, or an exchange or reorganization.

Why worry about the buyer of a *registered* security who wants to resell? The answer, conceptually, is that, though in form an issuer registers its *securities,* in substance it registers *offerings* — or, more precisely perhaps, securities *with respect* to specified offerings. Surely an issuer that registered its stock and went public ten years ago and then five years ago "went private" by rebuying the public's stock, which thus became treasury shares, could not now go public once more without a fresh registration statement by arguing "once registered always registered." The same result would follow if one bought enough of the registered shares to become a controlling shareholder and now wanted to make a secondary distribution through an underwriter. These would be altogether different offerings from the original distribution, and a fresh registration would be required. By the same token, an institution, let us say, that bought a large (though noncontrolling) block of a registered issue

[d] Ed.: The scheme is substantially unchanged in the 1985 proposed Uniform Act except that (1) §402(2) broadens the exemption for non-issuer transactions in exchange-listed securities to cover all companies subject to the 1934 Act's reporting requirement for at least ninety days, and (2) the manual exemption in §402(3) is limited by the same ninety-day condition. See esp. §§3(f), 3(l), 3(m).

and later wanted to reoffer it publicly, even while the registration statement was fresh so far as its description of the *issuer* was concerned, would be an "underwriter" making a very different *offering* from the *issuer's*.[66]

This is so *conceptually*. And, as we noticed in considering whether a large warrant holder who exercises his warrants and acquires registered shares with a view to their public resale is an "underwriter," the Commission has experimented with various pragmatic solutions.[67] No definitive answer is possible at the moment beyond saying that staying within the recently expanded Rule 144 formula should afford a safe harbor by analogy.

Presumably all this is equally true of resales after public offerings pursuant to Regulation A or one of the other "small issue" exemptions except Rules 504 and 505. Since those two rules are based in part on the private offering rationale, the securities acquired are "deemed to have the same status as if they had been acquired in a transaction pursuant to Section 4(2)," and Rule 144 is expressly made applicable to their resale.[68]

b. Mergers and Similar Events [Rule 145]

Rule 145 defines "underwriter" for purposes of that rule to include any company (other than the issuer) whose assets or capital structure is affected by a merger or the like, as well as any control affiliate of any such company.[69] But there is an exception if (1) the securities are resold pursuant to all the conditions of Rule 144 except the two-year holding period and the notice requirement or (2) the reseller is not an affiliate of the *issuer* and satisfies the two-year requirement and the issuer has been a reporting company for at least twelve months and has filed all required reports during that period, or (3) the reseller has not been an affiliate of the issuer for three months and is a *three*-year beneficial owner.[70] With this much explicitness, it is not likely that any *non*affiliate of a constituent

[66] But see p. 255 supra. [S280]
[67] See pp. 255-56 supra.
[68] Rules 144(a)(3), 502(d), 504(b)(1); see p. 366 supra.
[69] Rule 145(c).
[70] Rule 145(d). In 1984 the Commission amended Rule 145(d) to apply the same resale provisions to securities acquired in business combinations pursuant to registration under Rule 145 as had previously applied to combinations pursuant to an exemption under Rule 144. Sec. Act Rel. 6508, 29 SEC Dock. 1000 (1984); see Barron, Control and Restricted Securities, 12 Sec. Reg. L. J. 286 (1984).

company would be considered an "underwriter" regardless of how large a block of the issuer's securities he acquired.

c. Voluntary Exchanges [§3(a)(9)]

If the §3(a)(9) offering, though an exempted exchange, was not a public offering — that is to say, if the §4(2) exemption also fit — the securities are "restricted securities" within Rule 144(a)(3). But the holding period dates back to the date of acquisition of the security surrendered for conversion.[71]

If the §3(a)(9) offering was a *public* offering, presumably the answer — or lack of answer — should be the same in principle as it is with respect to the resale of large blocks of *registered* securities.

d. Judicially or Administratively Approved Exchanges [§3(a)(10); 11 U. S. C. §1145]

Here again, the Commission applies the volume formula of Rule 144 by analogy with respect to resales of securities acquired pursuant to the §3(a)(10) exemption, as it used to with respect to the exemptions in Chapters X and XI of the old Bankruptcy Act.[72] The fact is that most *trade* creditors, at least, do take, in all probability, for distribution.

So far as Chapter 11 of the new bankruptcy statute is concerned, the text of an elaborate exemptive provision, with a special definition of "underwriter," has already been set out.[73] Under §1145(b)(3), in substance, one who does not fall within the *special* definition of "underwriter" in §1145(b)(1) is not a §2(11) underwriter, so that the §4(1) exemption is available with respect to resales of securities of the debtor (or an affiliate participating with it in a joint plan, or a successor to the debtor) received in the reorganization at least principally in exchange for claims against the debtor (or affiliate). In addition, §1145(a)(3) exempts, on conditions

[71] Rule 144(d)(4)(B).

[72] So, too, with respect to §1145(a) of the new bankruptcy statute. Although the reference in §1145(b)(1)(D) (supra p. 290) to "an issuer, as used in section 2(11)," literally forecloses the exemption to a control affiliate of the debtor, the SEC staff, relying in large part on congressional intent, has ruled that an affiliate may use Rule 144 (with no holding period) just as if the affiliate had received securities in any public offering. Calstar, Inc., 17 Sec. Reg. L. Rep. 1820 (letter 1985).

[73] See pp. 288-91 supra.

that are self-explanatory, an offer or sale of the debtor's (or an affiliate's) portfolio securities apart from a plan.

e. Intrastate Issues [§3(a)(11)]

The answer with respect to the resale of securities received in an intrastate offering is mercifully simple. Rule 147(e), as we have seen, provides a nine-month gestation period before the securities can be said to "come to rest" so that they may be sold to nonresidents.[74]

f. The Code

With the Code's treatment of resales without regard to the presence of either an "underwriter" or "control," all these pieces fall readily into place. Each proposed resale is judged separately to see whether a "distribution" is involved.[75]

[74] Sec. Act Rel. 5450, 3 SEC Dock 349, 353 (1974), supra p. 302 n. m.
[75] See pp. 376-78 supra.

CHAPTER 6

"CONTROL" CONCEPTS UNDER THE SEC STATUTES

A. THE STATUTORY CONTEXTS

The concept of "control" of a corporation or other entity pervades the statutes administered by the SEC. The context — perhaps also the meaning of the concept — varies from statute to statute and sometimes within a particular statute.

In the Securities Act the concept figures most prominently in determining which secondary distributions must be registered. For purposes of the definition of "underwriter" only, as we have seen, the term "issuer" includes "any person directly or indirectly controlling or controlled by the issuer, or any person under direct or indirect common control with the issuer."[1] There is also a provision — to be examined in the chapter on civil liabilities — to the effect that, when any person is civilly liable under the statute, the same liability extends in general to "Every person who, by or through stock ownership, agency, or otherwise, or who, pursuant to or in connection with an agreement or understanding with one or more other persons by or through stock ownership, agency, or otherwise, controls" the first person.[2] Finally, the registration forms require information with respect to the issuer's "parents," "subsidiaries," "affiliates," and "associates";[3] for this purpose the Commission's rules define an "affiliate" as "a person that directly, or indirectly through one or more intermediaries, controls or is controlled by, or is under common control with, the person specified," and define

C. 6A [1]See pp. 253-54 supra.

[2]§15, infra p. 1011. There is a similar provision in the Exchange Act except that the reference is merely to "Every person who, directly or indirectly, controls any person liable * * *." §20(a).

[3]See Sec. Act Sch. A(25); §19(a) (consolidated financial statements for issuer and any person in a control relationship).

"parent" and "subsidiary" as controlling and controlled affiliates respectively.[4]

The Trust Indenture Act, in disqualifying a proposed trustee who has any control relationship with an obligor or underwriter, borrows the language used to define "underwriter" in the Securities Act.[5]

The same language appears also in the sections of the Exchange Act that require registration statements for securities to contain specified categories of information with respect to the registrant and any person in a control relationship.[6] The provision in the Advisers Act on disclosure of education refers to "any controlling person."[7] The provisions of the Exchange and Advisers Acts on discipline and qualifications refer repeatedly to any "person associated" with a broker-dealer, exchange member or adviser,[8] a term defined in both Acts to include "any person directly or indirectly controlling or controlled by" the broker-dealer, member, or adviser.[9] And the Exchange Act provisions on registered securities associations as well as municipal and government securities are replete with the "person associated" phrase.[10] In addition, the tender offer provision of the Exchange Act directs the Commission to exempt offers that do not have the purpose or effect of "changing or influencing the control of the issuer";[11] the provision on issuers' purchases of their own shares apply equally to purchases by a person with the kind of control relationship described in the Securities Act (or "a person subject to the control of the issuer or any such person");[12] and the Commission has a rule under one of the fraud provisions of the Exchange Act that, in substance, requires any broker or dealer in a control relationship with the issuer of any security purchased or sold to disclose to the customer "the existence of such control."[13]

In neither the Securities Act (as supplemented by the Trust Indenture Act) nor the Exchange Act is "control" defined. In the two essentially regulatory statutes, the Holding Company and Investment Company Acts, the scheme is different. Both statutes re-

[4] Rule 405; see also Sec. Ex. Act Rule 12b-2.
[5] §310(b)(3); see also §310(b)(7).
[6] §§12(b), 12(g)(1).
[7] §203(c)(1).
[8] Sec. Ex. Act §§15(b)(1), 15(b)(2)(A), 15(b)(4), 15(b)(6), 15(b)(7)(A), 19(d)(1), 19(e)(1), 19(f)-(h); Inv. Adv. Act §§203(e), 203(f). See p. 392 n. 16 infra.
[9] Sec. Ex. Act §§3(a)(18), 3(a)(21); Inv. Adv. Act §202(a)(17).
[10] §§15A, 15B, 15C.
[11] §14(d)(8)(C).
[12] §13(e)(2); see also Sec. Ex. Act Rule 10b-18(a)(1), infra p. 867.
[13] Rule 15c1-5.

fer repeatedly to the control concept, and they contain elaborate definitions, with provision for declaratory orders by the Commission. In both cases the purpose is to establish relationships in which the absence of arm's-length dealing may exist, with opportunity for unfair treatment of investors.

The Holding Company Act does not define "control" as such, but it contains definitions of "holding company," "subsidiary company," and "affiliate" that determine the status of persons under the Act generally.[14] For purposes of the first two definitions, which are correlatives, Congress adopted as a point of departure a rule of thumb based upon 10 percent ownership. In substance, a 10 percent stockholder is presumed to be a holding company unless it proves that it is not, whereas any other company is presumed not to be a holding company unless the Commission establishes that it is. More particularly, any "company which directly or indirectly owns, controls, or holds with power to vote," 10 percent of the outstanding voting securities of a public utility company (that is, an electric or gas company) or of another holding company is itself a holding company unless the Commission, upon application, finds that it

> (i) does not, either alone or pursuant to an arrangement or understanding with one or more other persons, directly or indirectly control a public-utility or holding company either through one or more intermediary persons or by any means or device whatsoever, (ii) is not an intermediary company through which such control is exercised, and (iii) does not, directly or indirectly, exercise (either alone or pursuant to an arrangement or understanding with one or more other persons) such a controlling influence over the management or policies of any public-utility or holding company as to make it necessary or appropriate in the public interest or for the protection of investors or consumers that the applicant be subject to the obligations, duties, and liabilities imposed in this title upon holding companies.

On the other hand, regardless of the 10 percent figure, the Commission may declare "any person" to be a holding company upon a determination, after notice and opportunity for hearing, that it exercises such a controlling influence, either alone or with other persons.

The term "affiliate" is defined to include any person that "directly or indirectly owns, controls, or holds with power to vote, 5 per centum or more of the outstanding voting securities" of a spec-

[14] §§2(a)(7), 2(a)(8), 2(a)(11); see also §2(b).

ified company; or any company of whose outstanding voting securities that percentage is so owned, controlled, or held by a specified company; or any person or class of persons that the Commission determines, after notice and opportunity for hearing, to stand in such relation to a specified company "that there is liable to be such an absence of arm's-length bargaining in transactions between them as to make it necessary or appropriate in the public interest or for the protection of investors or consumers that such person be subject to the obligations, duties, and liabilities imposed in this title upon affiliates of a company."[15]

The Investment Company Act does define "control" as such. The scheme is roughly similar to that of the Holding Company Act except that Congress chose the figure 25 percent rather than 10 percent:

> "Control" means the power to exercise a controlling influence over the management or policies of a company, unless such power is solely the result of an official position with such company.
>
> Any person who owns beneficially, either directly or through one or more controlled companies, more than 25 per centum of the voting securities of a company shall be presumed to control such company. Any person who does not so own more than 25 per centum of the voting securities of any company shall be presumed not to control such company. A natural person shall be presumed not to be a controlled person within the meaning of this title. Any such presumption may be rebutted by evidence, but except as hereinafter provided, shall continue until a determination to the contrary made by the Commission by order either on its own motion or on application by an interested person. If an application filed hereunder is not granted or denied by the Commission within sixty days after filing thereof, the determination sought by the application shall be deemed to have been temporarily granted pending final determination of the Commission thereon. The Commission, upon its own motion or upon application, may by order revoke or modify any order issued under this paragraph whenever it shall find that the determination embraced in such original order is no longer consistent with the facts.[16]

[15] §2(a)(11). A number of other sections of the Holding Company Act refer to "control" without elaboration or definition, as in the 1933, 1934, and 1939 Acts. For example, §11(b)(1), on geographical integration, requires the Commission to permit a registered holding company to "continue to control" more than one integrated utility system if it makes certain findings. See also §§1(a)(4), 1(b)(3); cf. §§4(a)(6), 10(a)(1)(C), (F).

[16] §2(a)(9). The Commission borrowed the 25 percent test in Rule 19g2-1(b)(2), which has to do with enforcement by exchanges and the NASD of compliance with the statute by members and "persons associated," and borrowed

One impact of these determinations of a person's status comes under the provision of the Act that (with certain exceptions) prohibits "any registered investment company and any company or companies controlled by such registered investment company" from acquiring more than specified percentages of the voting stock of any other investment company or any insurance company unless the first company and any companies it controls already own in the aggregate at least 25 percent of the total outstanding voting stock of the company in question.[17] Other impacts come under the sections of the statute concerned with affiliations of directors and transactions of affiliated persons of registered investment companies.[18]

Oddly enough, the Investment Company Act sometimes puts the shoe on the other foot so far as control is concerned. Thus, a person is defined not to be an "investment company" if the Commission upon application declares that it is primarily engaged in a business other than that of investing, owning, or trading in securities "either directly or (A) through majority-owned subsidiaries or (B) through controlled companies conducting similar types of businesses." There it is to the applicant's advantage to prove control in order to escape registration under the statute.[19]

The Investment Advisers Act — which, in addition to the provisions already mentioned,[20] prohibits any transfer of "a controlling block" of a corporate investment adviser's voting securities without the consent of each client[21] — repeats the first sentence of the Investment Company Act's definition of "control," omitting the balance of that definition with its rebuttable presumption.[22]

B. DETERMINANTS OF "CONTROL"

It has been generally recognized, back far further than 1933, that practical control of a corporation does not require ownership of 51 percent of its voting securities — or anything like that amount. We have already noticed in the opening chapter the rarity of con-

---

the 10 percent test in Rule 19h-1(f)(2), which has to do with notice by a self-regulatory organization of membership or participation or association notwithstanding a statutory disqualification, finding "important distinctions between the policies underlying the two rules." Sec. Ex. Act Rel. 18,278, 24 SEC Dock. 76, 85 (1981).

[17] §12(d).

[18] §§10, 17(a), 17(d), 17(e).

[19] §3(b)(2).

[20] See p. 390 nn. 7-9 supra.

[21] §§202(a)(1), 205(2).

[22] §202(a)(12).

trol by majority ownership so far as the country's largest corporations are concerned, and the frequency of control by management with little or no voting power.[1] In 1912 the Supreme Court said in the Government's suit against the Union Pacific Railroad under the Sherman Act: "It may be true that in small corporations the holding of less than a majority of the stock would not amount to control, but the testimony in this case is ample to show that, distributed as the stock is among many stockholders, a compact, united ownership of 46% is ample to control the operations of the [Southern Pacific Railroad Company]."[2] As Judge Cardozo (as he then was) put it for the New York Court of Appeals in 1918, "A dominating influence may be exerted in other ways than by a vote."[3]

The legislative history demonstrates, consistently with this approach, that Congress took a broad view of control, even in the basic statutes in which it did not define the term. The House committee report stated with reference to the definition of "underwriter" in the Securities Act:

C. 6B [1]See pp. 3-4 supra.

[2]United States v. Union Pacific R. R. Co., 226 U. S. 61, 95-96 (1912). In Natural Gas Pipeline Co. v. Slattery, 302 U. S. 300, 307-08 (1937), the Court said, apropos of the control relationship between a gas company and its source of supply as bearing on the fixing of its rates: "We have not said, nor do we perceive any ground for saying, that the Constitution requires such an inquiry to be limited to those cases where common control of the two corporations is secured through ownership of a majority of their voting stock. We are not unaware that, as the statute recognizes, there are other methods of control of a corporation than through such ownership. Common management of corporations through officers or directors, or common ownership of a substantial amount, though less than a majority of their stock, gives such indication of unified control as to call for close scrutiny of a contract between them whenever the reasonableness of its terms is the subject of inquiry." In Denver & Rio Grande Western R. R. Co. v. United States, 387 U. S. 485, 499 (1967), the Court held that acquisition of 20 percent of the stock of Railway Express Agency by The Greyhound Corporation might constitute control.

[3]Globe Woolen Co. v. Utica Gas & Electric Co., 224 N. Y. 483, 489, 121 N. E. 378, 379-80 (1918). In Essex Universal Corp. v. Yates, 305 F. 2d 572, 580 (2d Cir. 1962), which was not an SEC case, Judge Clark (concurring) stated: "Surely in the normal course of events a management which has behind it 28.3 per cent of the stock has working control, absent perhaps a pitched proxy battle which might unseat it." And Judge Lumbard added, speaking only for himself, that in such a case, with a listed company, the person attempting to overcome the presumption of control would have to do more than "raise merely hypothetical possibilities of opposition by the other Republic shareholders to Essex' assumption of management control." Id. at 579. There would have to be a showing that there was "some other organized block of stock of sufficient size to out-vote the block Essex was buying, or else some circumstance making it likely that enough of the holders of the remaining Republic stock would band together to keep Essex from control." Ibid.; see also Gould v. Ruefenacht, 471 U. S. 701, 705 (1985), supra p. 201.

> The concept of control herein involved is not a narrow one, depending upon a mathematical formula of 51 percent of voting power, but is broadly defined to permit the provisions of the act to become effective wherever the fact of control actually exist.[4]

The same committee stated, in speaking of the concept of control as used in the registration and civil liability provisions of the Exchange Act:

> * * * when reference is made to "control," the term is intended to include actual control as well as what has been called legally enforceable control. * * * [5] It was thought undesirable to attempt to define the term. It would be difficult if not impossible to enumerate or to anticipate the many ways in which actual control may be exerted. A few examples of the methods used are stock ownership, lease, contract, and agency. It is well known that actual control sometimes may be exerted through ownership of much less than a majority of the stock of a corporation either by the ownership of such stock alone or through such ownership in combination with other factors.[6]

In the absence of a statutory definition of control in these two Acts, as well as the Trust Indenture Act,[7] the Commission has supplied its own definition by rule. There are rules under the three Acts, as well as the accounting regulation, that define "control" to mean "the possession, direct or indirect, of the power to direct or cause the direction of the management and policies of a person, whether through the ownership of voting securities, by contract, or otherwise."[8] There are also rules under these three Acts, as well as the Investment Company Act, that permit the registrant to disclaim the existence and any admission of control if its existence "is open to reasonable doubt," but in any event the registrant must state "the material facts pertinent to the possible existence of control."[9]

The Communications Act of 1934 uses the identical control lan-

[4] H. R. Rep. No. 85, 73d Cong., 1st Sess. (1933) 14.

[5] Citing Handy & Harmon v. Burnet, 284 U. S. 136 (1931).

[6] H. R. Rep. No. 1383, 73d Cong., 2d Sess. (1934) 26.

[7] This does not make the concept of "control" stock unconstitutionally vague for criminal purposes. "The meaning of 'control' under the [1933] act is no different than it is in normal everyday usage." United States v. Re, 336 F. 2d 306, 316 (2d Cir. 1964), *cert. denied*, 379 U. S. 904.

[8] Sec. Act Rule 405; Sec. Ex. Act Rule 12b-2; Trust Ind. Act Rule 0-2; Reg. S-X, Rule 1-02. Although these definitions were adopted for purposes of registration or qualification, they presumably apply by analogy in so far as the term "control" is used in other contexts.

[9] Sec. Act Rule 410; Sec. Ex. Act Rule 12b-22; Trust Ind. Act Rule 7a-26; Inv. Co. Act Rule 8b-22.

guage that is found in the Securities Act definition of the term "underwriter." The Federal Communications Commission is denied jurisdiction over any carrier "engaged in interstate or foreign communication solely through physical connection with the facilities of another carrier not directly or indirectly controlling or controlled by, or under direct or indirect common control with such carrier."[10] There is likewise no statutory definition of "control." In sustaining an order that found that one company controlled another, the Supreme Court set the tone for subsequent discussion of "control" in administrative contexts when it said in the *Rochester Telephone* case:

> The record amply justified the Communications Commission in making such findings. Investing the Commission with the duty of ascertaining "control" of one company by another, Congress did not imply artificial tests of control. This is an issue of fact to be determined by the special circumstances of each case. So long as there is warrant in the record for the judgment of the expert body it must stand. The suggestion that the refusal to regard the New York ownership of only one third of the common stock of the Rochester as conclusive of the former's lack of control of the latter should invalidate the Commission's finding, disregards actualities in such intercorporate relations. Having found that the record permitted the Commission to draw the conclusion that it did, a court travels beyond its province to express concurrence therewith as an original question. "The judicial function is exhausted when there is found to be a rational basis for the conclusions approved by the administrative body." [Citations omitted.][11]

The precedent is a particularly close one so far as the SEC acts are concerned, even to the point that the FCC spoke of "power to control the functions of Rochester,"[12] just as the SEC rule speaks of "power to direct * * * management and policies."

There has been relatively little litigation with respect to control, however, under the 1933, 1934, and 1939 Acts themselves. Most of the SEC control cases that have gone to court have arisen under the Holding Company Act. The Commission has won all of them, although the margin in one case was too close for comfort: The Ninth Circuit first affirmed, by a vote of two to one, the Commission's order denying an application by Pacific Gas & Electric Company to be declared not to be a subsidiary of The North American Company; it then reheard the case *en banc* and affirmed by an evenly

[10] §2(b), 47 U. S. C. §152(b)(2).
[11] Rochester Telephone Corp. v. United States, 307 U. S. 125, 145-46 (1939).
[12] See 307 U. S. at 145.

divided court; and the Supreme Court divided evenly in turn.[13] In these cases, however, the accent is on "controlling influence," which the Commission and the courts have said means "something less in the form of influence over the management or policies of a company than 'control' of a company." Whereas the existence of "control" constitutes an absolute bar under §2(a)(7) to the entry of an order declaring a company not to be a holding company, the existence of a "controlling influence" precludes such an order only under specified "public interest" standards.

The courts have held under the Holding Company Act that "latent power" is sufficient to constitute a "controlling influence";[14] that a "controlling influence may be effective without accomplishing its purpose fully";[15] and that the concept means essentially "susceptibility to domination."[16] As Justice Murphy stated for the Supreme Court in sustaining the constitutionality of the geographical integration requirement in §11(b)(1): "Historical ties and associations, combined with strategic holdings of stock, can on occasion serve as a potent substitute for the more obvious modes of control. [Citations omitted.] Domination may spring as readily from subtle or unexercised power as from arbitrary imposition of command."[17] It has also been held by the Commission that the presumption of control cannot be rebutted merely by asserting the existence of

[13] Pacific Gas & Electric Co., 10 SEC 39 (1941), *aff'd sub nom.* Pacific Gas & Electric Co. v. SEC, 127 F. 2d 378 (9th Cir. 1942), *aff'd per curiam on rehearing, with a dissenting opinion,* 139 F. 2d 298 (9th Cir. 1943), *aff'd per curiam,* 324 U. S. 826 (1945).

[14] Koppers United Co. v. SEC, 138 F. 2d 577, 580-81 (D. C. Cir. 1943), and cases cited.

[15] Detroit Edison Co. v. SEC, 119 F. 2d 730, 738-39 (6th Cir. 1941), *cert. denied,* 314 U. S. 618. "This phrase should be construed in the light of the purpose of the Act of which it is a part, and when understood in this setting and in the light of its ordinary signification, it means the act or process, or power of producing an effect which may be without apparent force or direct authority and is effective in checking or preventing action, or exercising restraint or preventing free action. The phrase as here used, does not necessarily mean that those exercising controlling influence must be able to carry their point." Ibid.

[16] See cases cited in American Gas & Electric Co. v. SEC, 134 F. 2d 633, 643 n. 22 (D. C. Cir. 1943), *cert. denied,* 319 U. S. 763. "Under some circumstances 'controlling influence may spring as readily from advice constantly sought as from command arbitrarily imposed.' " Id. at 642, citing Manchester Gas Co., 7 SEC 57, 62 (1940). Judge Stephens insisted in his dissenting opinion, on the other hand, that "control" and "controlling influence" are "two different types of presently effective control" — the first referring to control through "structural means" such as stock ownership, voting trusts, or interlocking officers or directors or the like, and the second referring to "such control as might result from the command of one mind over another, or from station or prestige, or from habituation to the policies of another." 134 F. 2d at 648-49.

[17] North American Co. v. SEC, 327 U. S. 686, 693 (1946).

control in others, since the "potentiality of exercising a controlling influence in the determination of the course of action of a company may exist in more than one person at the same time or from time to time.[18]

Yet, once it is admitted that control does not require ownership of a majority of the voting stock — and that, like "controlling influence," it may take many different forms[19] — many of the factors that determine the existence of a "controlling influence" apply equally to the determination whether there is "control." Just as the cases under the Holding Company Act emphasize "latent power," the Commission's rules under the 1933, 1934, and 1939 Acts speak (as we have seen) of the "power to direct * * * management." Control, the Commission has held under the Securities Act, "is not synonymous with direct operation of an enterprise"; it "may be inferred from the conduct of the parties."[20] As the Commission put it in its Report on Investment Trusts, "the word 'control' does not mean day-to-day management of the portfolio company, but means rather that major decisions are probably seldom taken without consulting the investment company or its sponsors, or that the control is at least potential and equivalent at all times to unusual

[18] M. A. Hanna Co., 10 SEC 581, 589 (1941) (Inv. Co. Act); see also Investors Mutual, Inc., 42 SEC 1071, 1086 (1966), *aff'd* sub nom. Phillips v. SEC, 388 F. 2d 964 (2d Cir. 1968) (control by each of two hostile groups); DeMarco v. Edens, CCH Fed. Sec. L. Rep. ¶91,856 at 95,935 (S. D. N. Y. 1966), *aff'd,* 390 F. 2d 836 (2d Cir. 1968) (vice-president of broker-dealer corporation, who *inter alia* had loaned large sums to president, was himself a controlling person despite president's being sole stockholder); United States v. Corr, 543 F. 2d 1042, 1050 (2d Cir. 1976).

[19] American Gas & Electric Co. v. SEC, 134 F. 2d 633, 641 n. 14 (D. C. Cir. 1943), *cert. denied,* 319 U. S. 763, and cases cited. A brokerage firm has been held civilly liable for a wire correspondent's violations of various provisions of the Exchange Act on the theory that it controlled the correspondent, even though the court expressly found no agency relationship. Hawkins v. Merrill Lynch, Pierce, Fenner & Beane, 85 F. Supp. 104, 123 (W. D. Ark. 1949); see also DeMarco v. Edens, CCH Fed. Sec. L. Rep. ¶91,856 at 95,934 (S. D. N. Y. 1966), *aff'd,* 390 F. 2d 836 (2d Cir. 1968) (court held that issuer controlled best efforts underwriter because it had selected the underwriter, fixed the offering price, and drafted the offering circular).

[20] Reiter-Foster Oil Corp., 6 SEC 1028, 1044 (1940). It does not follow, regardless of the literal definition of "parent" and its cross-reference to controlling persons, that the officers and directors as a group must always be listed as a "parent" in the registration statements and annual reports. For otherwise *every* corporation would have a "parent" in the form of its board and management. When a group of individuals or a family or several families control, the question becomes closer. An individual can also be a *controlled* person. SEC v. North American Research & Development Corp., 424 F. 2d 63, 67, 72 (2d Cir. 1970), where an individual was held to be an "issuer" under §2(11) because of his control of a woman who in turn controlled the company.

influence."[21] Again, "past history" has been emphasized not only as evidence of "controlling influence,"[22] but also as evidence of "control" itself. One of the leading Commission decisions on "control" is the *Morgan* case under the Trust Indenture Act, where the then J. P. Morgan & Co. Incorporated and Morgan Stanley & Co. Incorporated were held to be under common control so as to prevent the former, under §310(b)(3), from acting as indenture trustee when the latter acted as underwriter.[23] The Commission empha-

[21]SEC, Report on the Study of Investment Trusts and Investment Companies, Part 4, Control and Influence over Industry and Economic Significance of Investment Companies, H. R. Doc. No. 246, 77th Cong., 1st Sess. (1941) 2, quoted in Chicago Corp., 28 SEC 463, 468 (1948). In a very different context, cf. Communist Party of the U. S. A. v. Subversive Activities Control Board, 367 U. S. 1, 36-38 (1961):

> * * * Under §3(3) of the Act an organization cannot be found to be a Communist organization unless it is "substantially directed, dominated, or controlled by the foreign government or foreign organization controlling the world Communist movement." * * *
>
> We agree that substantial direction, domination, or control of one entity by another may exist without the latter's having power, in the event of noncompliance, effectively to enforce obedience to its will. * * *
>
> * * * A foreign government "dominates" or "controls" the "direction" of the world Communist movement through very different means and in very different ways than one organization "dominates" or "controls" another, or than an individual "dominates" or "controls" an organization. These differences do not deprive the concepts "domination" and "control" of ample meaning. Throughout various manifestations these concepts denote a relationship in which one entity so much holds ascendancy over another that it is predictably certain that the latter will comply with the directions expressed by the former solely by virtue of that relationship, and without reference to the nature and content of the directions. * * *

[22]American Gas & Electric Co. v. SEC, 134 F. 2d 633, 636 n. 8 (D. C. Cir. 1943), *cert. denied,* 319 U. S. 763, and cases cited; Chicago Corp., 28 SEC 463 (1948).

[23]J. P. Morgan & Co., 10 SEC 119 (1941). This case followed the Commission's order under the Holding Company Act, Dayton Power & Light Co., 8 SEC 950 (1941), which was affirmed in Morgan Stanley & Co. v. SEC, 126 F. 2d 325 (2d Cir. 1942). The *Dayton* case involved the Commission's former Rule U-12F-2, which, in general, prohibited the payment of any underwriters' fees to any affiliate of the issuer, or to any person found to stand in such relation to the issuer "that there is liable to be or to have been an absence of arm's-length bargaining with respect to the transaction," unless the underwriter had been awarded the securities as the most favorable bidder in open competition. The Commission had applied this rule in denying an underwriting fee to Morgan Stanley in connection with an offering of securities by Dayton Power & Light Company. The Commission's order, affirmed by the court, was based on the following four steps: (1) Dayton was wholly owned by Columbia Gas & Electric Corporation. (2) Columbia was controlled by United Corporation, which owned 19.6 percent of its stock. (3) United had been organized in 1929 by J. P. Morgan & Co. and another house, which had chosen the man who was still president; the court said that this was the most tenuous step but held that there was substantial evidence to support the Commission's conclusion. (4) Morgan Stan-

sized such factors as the origin and sponsorship of Morgan Stanley by J. P. Morgan & Co., the common Morgan name, the business relationships between the two firms,[24] their retaining of the same counsel,[25] and the family relations such as husband-wife and father-son among the several family groups that in the aggregate controlled both firms.

Certainly the additional factors that the Commission considered in its 1948 decision in the *Chicago Corporation* case under the Investment Company Act[26] are equally relevant in determining the existence of *A*'s "control" over *B* under those acts that do not define the term. There the Commission emphasized the amount of stock held;[27]

---

ley had been created by J. P. Morgan & Co., whose partners still held 45 percent of its preferred stock. This stock was disposed of to members of their families between the date of the Commission's opinion in the *Dayton* case and the date of its opinion in the proceeding under the Trust Indenture Act.

[24]See also United States v. E. I. du Pont de Nemours & Co., 366 U. S. 316, 332 (1961).

[25]This factor did not impress Judge Stephens, who said in his dissenting opinion in American Gas & Electric Co. v. SEC, 134 F. 2d 633, 654 (D. C. Cir. 1943), *cert. denied*, 319 U. S. 763: "The existence of a common law firm * * * of itself proves nothing." On the question whether counsel can himself be a controlling person, the court held in Westlake v. Abrams, 565 F. Supp. 1330 (N. D. Ga. 1983), that, absent counsel's participation in securities fraud or a blatant violation of ethical precepts, their vigorous performance of legitimate litigation activities for their client broker could not make them controlling persons, and their description as "general counsel" served only with respect to litigation matters, so that they could be distinguished from lawyers who acted only as advisers on the impact of the securities laws. See also Barker v. Henderson, Franklin, Starnes & Holt, 797 F. 2d 490, 494 (7th Cir. 1986) (ability of law and accounting firms "to persuade and give counsel is not the same thing as 'control' "). But see Seidel v. Public Service Co. of N. H., 616 F. Supp. 1342, 1362 (D. N. H. 1985).

[26]28 SEC 463 (1948).

[27]The Commission has elsewhere expressed doubt that "a voting trust (except possibly a voting trust established solely for the purpose of liquidation) can ever operate effectively to insulate the control which ownership of a block of stock carries." H. M. Byllesby & Co., 6 SEC 639, 654 (1940) (Holding Co. Act). Certainly control is not affected when the voting trustees are not completely independent of the depositors. Ibid. When they *are* independent of or perhaps even hostile to the beneficial owners and the termination of the trust is not imminent, the beneficial owners may indeed be insulated from control. And stock in a voting trust, or securities held otherwise in a representative capacity, might be considered along with other factors in determining whether the voting trustees or other representatives are themselves in control. The question is inevitably one of fact in each case. For example, the SEC has recognized that a stockholder that has given a proxy that is irrevocable until a specified event not within the stockholder's control (for example, the exhaustion of coal mines) is no longer in control. Clearfield Bituminous Coal Corp., 1 SEC 374 (1936); cf. Boise Gas Light & Coke Co., 2 SEC 269 (1937) (when preferred stock has elected a majority of the board for ten years because of failure of earnings, and imminent reorganization will leave 100 percent common stockholder with only 5 percent of the common, that stockholder no longer controls).

the number of *A*'s representatives on *B*'s board of directors; *A*'s strategic position through the number of representatives on the executive committee;[28] *A*'s demonstrated influence;[29] *A*'s position as *B*'s banker company when that is the case; the relative size and prestige of *A* and *B; A*'s veto power over mergers or consolidations through ownership of preferred stock; and *A*'s power to "break quorum" by abstaining from attending the stockholder's meeting or giving a proxy. Still another factor that may evidence control is a strong position as creditor.[30]

A person's clear ability to control the proxy machinery of a corporation when the stockholders are widely scattered is strong evidence of control.[31] At the same time, a determination of control by no means requires a showing that the person in question could win a proxy fight against the management. Both court and Commission have rejected any such "blood and thunder" concept of control. As long as the putatively controlling person and the man-

[28] Appointment or domination of the officers or members of the executive committee of the board is strong evidence of control, especially when the board seldom meets. Resources Corp. Int'l, 7 SEC 689, 716-18 (1940).

[29] Cf. SEC v. Franklin Atlas Corp., 154 F. Supp. 395 (S. D. N. Y. 1957) (manager of real estate venture who was not director, officer, or stockholder was found to be in "actual control" for purposes of Sec. Act §2(11)). Absence of a stock interest does not preclude a control finding. M. J. Merritt & Co., 42 SEC 1021, 1030-31 (1966), *aff'd per curiam* sub nom. Vickers v. SEC, 383 F. 2d 343 (2d Cir. 1967), and sub nom. Walker v. SEC, 383 F. 2d 344 (2d Cir. 1967) (partner of firm whose broker-dealer registration had been revoked had in effect continued its business through a corporate successor with a brother in the management).

[30] In re Falstaff Brewing Corp. Antitrust Litigation, 441 F. Supp. 62, 68 (E. D. Mo. 1977) (Sec. Ex. Act §20(a)); Touche, Niven, Bailey & Smart, 37 SEC 629, 662-67 (1957) (Reg. S-X, control flowing from *former* creditor position). In Metge v. Baehler, 577 F. Supp. 810, 818 (S. D. Iowa 1984), *aff'd*, 762 F. 2d 621, 630-32 (8th Cir. 1985), — *cert. denied* sub nom. Metge v. Bankers Trust Co., 106 S. Ct. 798 and 832, the court applied to a lending bank the same test of control that it held to be applicable generally — actual exercise of control over the corporation in question generally plus the power to control the specific transaction or activity in question — at least in the absence of the bank's obtaining the right to vote a controlling block of stock pledged as collateral. A right to enforce negative covenants does not necessarily establish control. Woodward & Lothrop, Inc. v. Schnabel, 593 F. Supp. 1385, 1400 (D. D. C. 1984). See generally Enstam and Kamen, Control and the Institutional Investor, 23 Bus. Law. 289, 319-25 (1968); Bartlett and Lapatin, The Status of a Creditor As a "Controlling Person," 28 Merc. L. Rev. 639 (1977).

[31] Chicago Corp., 28 SEC 463, 476 (1948); Thompson Ross Securities Co., 6 SEC 1111, 1120-21 (1940) (Sec. Act); Moulton v. Field, 179 Fed. 673, 675 (7th Cir. 1910), *cert. denied* sub nom. Gray v. Field, 219 U. S. 586, Berle, "Control" in Corporate Law, 58 Colum. L. Rev. 1212, 1213 (1958). Everything else being equal, the amount of stock required to give a particular person control decreases as the number of other holders increases and as the amount of stock usually represented at the annual meetings decreases.

agement of the putatively controlled company are friendly and cooperative, there is no point in speculating on the results of a proxy fight.[32]

It follows that control may rest with a *group* of persons, such as the members of the corporation's management (both directors and officers) and their families, or the members of one or more families not directly in the management, or a number of business associates. As we have noticed with reference to the Securities Act, the House report itself, by way of explaining the "control" clause in the definition of "underwriter," observed that "All the outstanding stock of a particular corporation may be owned by one individual or a select group of individuals."[33] This approach has been taken in a number of cases.[34] And it was the Commission's theme, of course, in the *Morgan* case under the Trust Indenture Act — the theme of common control by a number of family groups united by social and business connections.[35] It does not follow, however, that one member of such a group controls in all contexts. For example, whether a secondary distribution by one member requires registration under the Securities Act raises essentially a question of fact in each case whether that person has enough influence with the group to be able to obtain the issuer's signature on a registration statement. Hence it is for the jury when a jury sits.

The question has been much mooted whether a person's status as an officer or director in itself makes him a controlling person for purposes, for example, of registration under the Securities Act or disclosure by a broker-dealer of a control relationship with the issuer under the Commission's Exchange Act fraud rules. The Investment Company Act, as we have seen, specifically negatives control

[32] American Gas & Electric Co. v. SEC, 134 F. 2d 633, 639 (D. C. Cir. 1943), *cert. denied,* 319 U. S. 763; Chicago Corp., 28 SEC 463, 474-75 (1948).

[33] H. R. Rep. No. 85, 73d Cong., 1st Sess. (1933) 13-14, supra p. 279; see also Temporary National Economic Committee, Investigation of Concentration of Economic Power, Monog. No. 29, Distribution of Ownership in the 200 Largest Nonfinancial Corporations (1940) 101.

[34] Landay v. United States, 108 F. 2d 698, 704 (6th Cir. 1939), *cert. denied,* 309 U. S. 681 ("appellants by voting their shares of stock in a block completely dominated the corporation" and hence were properly convicted under Sec. Act §5); SEC v. Micro-Moisture Controls, Inc., 148 F. Supp. 558 (S. D. N. Y. 1957) (preliminary injunction), *reargument denied,* CCH Fed. Sec. L. Rep. ¶90,805 (S. D. N. Y. 1957), *final injunction,* 167 F. Supp. 716 (S. D. N. Y. 1958), *aff'd* sub nom. SEC v. Culpepper, 270 F. 2d 241 (2d Cir. 1959) (a broker-dealer who had bought shares with a view to distribution from two persons owning only 1½ percent of the stock was an "underwriter" because those two were part of a larger controlling group); Barnes v. Resources Royalties, Inc., 795 F. 2d 1359, 1364-66 (8th Cir. 1986).

[35] J. P. Morgan & Co., 10 SEC 119 (1941).

when the "power to exercise a controlling influence * * * is solely the result of an official position."[36] But even there the Commission held that an individual was a controlling person when his being president was the *result* rather than the *source* of his power; in that case the president owned less than 3 percent of the company's voting stock, but he had the confidence of four family groups that together accounted for over 31 percent.[37] Accordingly, although a person's being an officer or director does not create any *presumption* of control,[38] it is a sort of red light. It may take only one or two questions to bring out that a particular officer has no substantial influence, or that a particular director represents a minority interest (perhaps as the result of cumulative voting) that is out of sympathy with the controlling block. On the other hand, the answer to the first few questions may demonstrate the need for a fairly extensive inquiry into the entire relationship of the particular officer or director to the rest of the managing group.[39]

There is also food for thought here so far as estate planners are concerned: Does control cease with death? If control resulted solely from stock ownership, presumably it passes to the estate. Otherwise, presumably it does not. On the other hand, when an executor or administrator is an officer or director or otherwise a controlling person, the estate may well be under *common* control. Or a bank might be an executor of several estates or a trustee under a number of testamentary (or, for that matter, *inter vivos*) trusts that in the aggregate carry enough voting power to constitute control. As a writer with a literary bent put it in another connection, "some holders, it seems, are born to control, some achieve control, and some have control thrust upon them."[40]

In sum, the available authority seems to impel the conclusion that

[36] §2(a)(9), supra p. 392.

[37] Transit Investment Corp., 23 SEC 415 (1946).

[38] Burgess v. Premier Corp., 727 F. 2d 826, 832 (9th Cir. 1984).

[39] Obviously the *resignation* of a substantial stockholder as an officer or director cannot be conclusive that he no longer controls, since it may have had nothing to do with a disagreement on managerial policy.

[40] Note, Rule 134: SEC Regulation of Dispositions of Securities by Controlling Persons and Private Placees, 25 Vand. L. Rev. 845, 857 (1972). On these estate complications, see Rifkind, Securities Problems of the "Locked-in" Estate, 25 Bus. Law. 169 (1969). Cf. Barclays Bank, Ltd. v. Inland Revenue Commissioners, [1960] 3 W. L. R. 280 (H. L.), noted in Pennington, Control of a Company, 104 Sol. J. 1088 (1960) (testator who died owning beneficially 1100 shares out of a total of 8350, and holding 3650 other shares with three other persons as trustees under a trust created by him nineteen years earlier for his wife and children, *held* to have "the control of the company" for estate tax purposes, so that the 1100 shares should be valued by apportioning the value of the company's assets rather than on the basis of market).

the difference between "control" and "controlling influence" is one of degree. This is so much so that it is the Commission's policy not to permit its lawyers to express any views as to the existence or nonexistence of control except in the clearest cases. Once the meaning of "control" in a particular statutory context is understood, the parties themselves and their attorneys are in a much better position to determine whether or not control exists than any outside counsel.[41]

[41] For a thorough analysis and collection of authorities, see 1 T. Frankel, The Regulation of Money Managers: The Investment Company Act and The Investment Advisers Act (1978) 489-529.

The Code sweeps this Augean stable reasonably clean: (1) It abandons "control" as a criterion for determining which distributions must be the subject of an offering statement (the Code's successor to today's 1933 Act registration statement). (2) It contains a single Code-wide definition of "control" for disclosure and civil liability purposes, in terms of "controlling influence." (3) That definition adapts the 25 percent formula of the Investment Company Act as a rebuttable presumption one way or the other. (4) In addition to retaining the declaratory order procedure now in the Investment Company Act, which is obligatory on the Commission, the Code gives the Commission discretion to entertain applications for declaratory orders generally.

CHAPTER 7

REGISTRATION AND POSTREGISTRATION PROVISIONS OF THE 1934 ACT

This chapter considers those provisions of the 1934 Act — relating essentially to continuing disclosure by the issuer — that supplement the 1933 Act.[1] Under §12 the issuer must register every nonexempt security that (1) is listed on an exchange or (2) is (since a 1964 amendment) an equity security held of record by at least 500 persons if the issuer has total assets exceeding $5 million[2] (and is engaged in interstate commerce or in a business affecting interstate commerce, or any of its securities are traded by use of the mails or any means of interstate commerce).

Unlike the 1933 Act, whose disclosure scheme is transaction oriented and hence episodic, registration under the 1934 Act is designed to afford more or less continuous disclosure. This it does in four ways (which in some respects go beyond disclosure into substantive regulation): (1) Periodic reports must be filed under §13 (and in some cases under §15(d)). (2) Under §14(a) the solicitation of proxies with respect to registered securities must comply with the Commission's rules. (3) The Williams Act provisions, §§13(d)-(e) and 14(d)-(f), which were added in 1968 and amended in 1970, regulate tender offers and require certain beneficial ownership reports. (4) Section 16 imposes certain controls over insider-trading practices. These will be considered in the order indicated.

C. 7 [1]On the Commission's granting of confidential treatment pursuant to the 1933 and 1934 Acts, see Comizio, Keeping Corporate Information Secret: Confidential Treatment Under the Securities Act of 1933 and the Securities Exchange Act of 1934, 18 N. Eng. L. Rev. 787 (1982-83).

[2]The statutory figure in §12(g)(1) is $1 million, but it has been increased by rule to $5 million. See p. 411 infra.

A. REGISTRATION

1. Exchange-Listed Securities

Section 12(a) makes it unlawful for an exchange member or a broker or dealer to effect a transaction in any nonexempt security on a national securities exchange "unless a registration is effective as to such security for such exchange." The Exchange Act is not tied in with the Securities Act as is the Trust Indenture Act. Although the Commission has taken heroic steps in recent years to integrate the disclosure requirement of the 1933 and 1934 Acts,[1] registration under the one statute does not excuse registration under the other when it is otherwise required. If a particular security is offered to the public and forthwith listed on an exchange, it must be registered under both Acts. Indeed, a debt security offered to the public by a public utility holding company or a subsidiary and listed on an exchange must comply with four separate SEC statutes — the Securities Act, the Exchange Act, the Trust Indenture Act, and the Holding Company Act — except insofar as an exemption may be available under one or more of the statutes. By the same token, Exchange Act registration is required when the issuer desires to list on an exchange, even though the security has never been registered under the Securities Act because the security was publicly held before 1933 or was issued under a Securities Act exemption. Registration is effected by the issuer's filing an application *with the exchange,* duplicate originals being filed with the Commission.[2] The Exchange Act, unlike the Securities Act, contains no signature requirement, but in 1980 the Commission required the basic *annual report* form, Form 10-K, to include the signatures not only of the issuer's principal executive, financial, and accounting officers but also of a majority of the directors. This requirement, taken over from §6(a) of the Securities Act, was incidental to the Commission's integration movement: "The Commission believes that just as its rules and the administrative focus of the Division of Corporation Finance are being realigned to reflect the shift in emphasis toward relying on periodic disclosure under the Exchange Act, so too the attention of the private sector, including management, directors, accountants, and attorneys, must also be refocused towards Exchange Act filings if a sufficient degree of discipline is to be instilled in the system to make it work."[3]

Amendments may be filed either before or after registration be-

C. 7A [1]See p. 146 supra.
[2]§12(b).
[3]Sec. Act Rel. 6231, 20 SEC Dock. 1059, 1067 (1980).

comes effective,[4] which is thirty days after the Commission's receipt of certification by the exchange authorities that the security has been approved for listing and registration "or within such shorter period of time as the Commission may determine."[5] There is no statutory standard governing acceleration, and in practice most applications are accelerated under the following statement of policy:

> The Commission will consider requests for acceleration of the effective date of registration of securities in cases where, in its opinion, adequate and reasonably current information concerning the issuer has previously been filed and made available to the general public under any Act administered by the Commission. However, in passing upon requests for acceleration the Commission will also consider the following additional factors:
>
> (a) The adequacy of disclosure in the application for registration and its general compliance with the requirements of the Act and the rules and regulations thereunder;
>
> (b) The distribution of the securities being registered or the distribution of other securities related thereto;
>
> (c) The operation of the exchange's trading mechanism in relation to the date on which effective registration is requested;
>
> (d) Compliance with the registration requirements of the Securities Act of 1933;
>
> (e) Any other factors pertinent to the particular case, such as required stockholder approval; qualification under applicable State "Blue-sky" laws; authorization by appropriate State and Federal Agencies having jurisdiction; Court proceedings; and similar matters connected with the securities being registered or with other securities related thereto.
>
> Requests for acceleration of the effective date of registration of securities may be made either by the registrant or its authorized representatives or by the exchange on which registration is sought. Every request should be in writing and should state the grounds upon which it is based and the approximate date on which effective registration is desired.
>
> While the Commission will cooperate with registrants and with exchanges by acting upon requests for acceleration as promptly as possible, consistent with the public interest and the protection of investors, applications for registration should be filed early enough to allow at least ten days for examination of the application and consideration of the request for acceleration by the Commission.[6]

Until 1954 the procedure was to register, as under the 1933 Act,

[4] Rule 12b-15.

[5] §12(d) 1st sentence, as implemented by Reg. 12D1.

[6] Sec. Ex. Act Rel. 3985 (1941). The penultimate paragraph of this quotation is codified in Rule 12d1-2.

only as many units of a class of securities as had been issued (including treasury shares) rather than the entire class. In that year the Commission adopted a system of registration of entire *classes* of securities.[7] All applications for registration, past and future, are now "deemed to apply for registration of the entire class," and registration once effective automatically extends, without further application or exchange certification or Commission order, to additional securities *of the same class* "upon issuance." This is so even when the additional securities have not been authorized until after the effective registration of the class pursuant to the original application.[8] In view of the annual and current reporting requirements of §13, the Commission concluded that the filing of a new application was not necessary in the interest of investors except in the case of a new class (or a new series with different terms). But, since the Commission's new procedure affects only the *statutory* requirement of *registration,* the exchanges as part of their own *listing* procedures still require issuers to notify them how many securities of the class or series have actually been issued.

As in the case of the Securities Act, the Commission has adopted a number of specialized forms and a residual form, Form 10, which corresponds to the Securities Act's Form S-1. And we have already noticed the adoption of Regulation S-K in 1977, together with its expansion in 1982, as a repository for the types of information required in filings under both statutes.[9]

2. Over-the-Counter Securities

a. The Statutory Scheme

For thirty years after enactment of the Exchange Act there was a double standard of investor protection — a standard that resulted, more by accident than by design, from the piecemeal adoption of the SEC statutes but that nevertheless glowed with an incandescent illogic. If an investor happened to be a stockholder of a listed company, or a public utility holding company or a subsidiary of such a company, or an investment company, he had the protections afforded by the reporting requirements as well as (with some exceptions) the proxy rules and the insider-trading provisions. If, on the other hand, he happened to hold a security that did not fall within

[7] Sec. Ex. Act Rel. 4990 (1954).
[8] Rule 12d1-1.
[9] See p. 149 supra.

any of these categories but that had been offered to the public and registered under the 1933 Act since 1936, he was likely to have current information by virtue of §15(d) of the Exchange Act, but that was all; §15(d), enacted that year, subjected certain *Securities Act* registrants to the reporting requirement of the Exchange Act but not to the proxy or insider-trading provisions.[10] The third investor, who held an unlisted security in an industrial corporation that had not done any public financing since 1936, was still further from the fire; so far as he was concerned, the whole series of SEC statutes might just as well not have existed except for a few fraud provisions, no matter how large the corporation or how widely distributed its securities.

The limitation of §§12, 13, 14, and 16 of the original Exchange Act to listed securities was not due to any conviction on the part of Congress that similar safeguards were not equally essential with respect to securities traded in the over-the-counter market. The several exchanges were concrete organized institutions that one could see and touch, and it was a relatively simple matter to condition the use of those markets upon compliance with the registration and other provisions. By contrast, the over-the-counter market was an amorphous thing that did not present a ready platform on which to base similar provisions. As the Commission had occasion to observe in 1936: "Prior to the enactment of the statute, the over-the-counter market was one of the enigmas of our financial system. Authentic data were lacking with respect to its nature, its function, its size, and the technique of its operation."[11] It was not surprising, therefore, that, after setting up a fairly detailed system of regulation of the organized exchanges, Congress threw the entire problem of the over-the-counter market into the lap of the newly created Commission. Section 15 of the original Exchange Act simply made it unlawful, in contravention of whatever rules the Commission might prescribe as necessary or appropriate in the public interest and "to insure to investors protection comparable to that provided by and under authority of this title in the case of national securities exchanges," for any broker or dealer to use the mails or interstate facilities for the purpose of making a market otherwise than on an exchange. The Commission was authorized under the original §15 to provide, among other things, for registration of brokers or deal-

[10] See p. 410 infra.
[11] SEC, Report on the Feasibility and Advisability of the Complete Segregation of the Functions of Dealer and Broker (1936) 78.

ers making such a market, as well as registration of the *securities* there traded.[12]

Under this section the Commission adopted rules requiring the registration of over-the-counter brokers and dealers, as well as a few rudimentary antifraud rules. But in 1936 the Commission in a report to Congress referred to the impracticability of enforcing a registration requirement against the *issuers* of securities by prohibiting *brokers and dealers* from trading in securities not registered.[13] One of the solutions it suggested was requiring future registrants of substantial size under the Securities Act to undertake to make periodic reports thereafter. Accordingly, Congress added §15(d) (since amended), on reports by certain Securities Act registrants, and further amended §15 by codifying the Commission's rules on *broker-dealer* registration. But — solely for want of a practicable sanction — Congress omitted any reference to the registration of *securities* traded in the over-the-counter market.

It was a strange sort of regulatory scheme that gave individual members of the class to be regulated the power to decide whether the regulation should apply to them. This is apart from the dislocation of the traditional relationship between the exchanges and the over-the-counter market that was an inevitable result of regulating the one market and not the other. For, just as surely as water flows downhill, business will move from a regulated to an unregulated market.[14] The Wall Street Journal, resorting to another metaphor, saw "no reason why the laws for the protection of investors * * * should make fish of one group of corporations and fowl of another."[15]

[12] 48 Stat. 895-96 (1934). "This power is vitally necessary to forestall widespread evasion of stock exchange regulation by the withdrawal of securities from listing on exchanges, and by transferring trading therein to 'over-the-counter' markets where manipulative evils could continue to flourish, unchecked by any regulatory authority. Since the necessity for regulation of 'over-the-counter' markets will depend largely on the extent to which activities prohibited on exchanges are transferred to such markets, provision for their regulation has been made as flexible as possible." S. Rep. No. 792, 73d Cong., 2d Sess. (1934) 6. See also the legislative findings in §2, which do not discriminate between the two markets.

[13] SEC, Report on Trading in Unlisted Securities upon Exchanges (1936) 17-21, infra p. 593 n. d.

[14] An early comparative study referred to the experience under the German Stock Exchange Law of 1896, which, on the theory that the original incorporators would normally list on the Exchange in order to redistribute, safeguarded that channel very strongly, thus increasing the temptation of many incorporators to use other channels for distribution. See Kessler, The American Securities Act and Its Foreign Counterparts: A Comparative Study, 44 Yale L. J. 1133, 1140-41 (1935).

[15] Wall St. J., Feb. 8, 1950, p. 8, col. 1.

Legislative hearings were held on a number of occasions between 1941 and 1957, and a series of SEC reports documented the inadequate reporting and proxy-soliciting practices of many large, publicly held over-the-counter companies.[16] Finally — as if to prove once more that reform legislation, at least of the SEC variety, is hostage to some crisis — a delinquent child of the American Stock Exchange set the stage for a legislative solution. The Commission's expulsion of two partners of a member firm for fraud and market manipulation[17] resulted in an SEC investigation of the exchange, which was merged into a broader study that Congress ordered in late 1961. That was the famous "Special Study of Securities Markets" that we have already noticed.[18] And its recommendations ultimately produced the Securities Acts Amendments of 1964, which added §12(g)-(i) to the 1934 Act.

The technique seems simple on the background of the Commission's 1936 confession that no statutory mechanism could be found. It reflects, of course, a later constitutional milieu. Section 12(g)(1) provides simply that "every issuer which is engaged in interstate commerce, or in a business affecting interstate commerce, or whose securities are traded by use of the mails or any means or instrumentality of interstate commerce[19] shall," within 120 days after the last day of its fiscal year on which it has "total assets exceeding $1,000,000 and a class of equity security (other than an exempted security) held of record by" 500 or more persons, register that security; and in 1982 and 1986 the Commission used its §12(h) exemptive authority to recognize eighteen years of inflation by raising the $1 million figure first to $3 million and then to $5 million.[20] The registration statement becomes effective sixty days after filing, with authority in the Commission to accelerate.

The interrelation of §§12(b) and 12(g) is such that a particular company may be subject to both registration requirements. Section 12(g)(2)(A) exempts any security listed and registered on an exchange under §12(b). But a company of the requisite size with its common stock listed and an unlisted class of preferred held by at

[16] See 2 Loss 1152-64.

[17] Re, Re & Sagarese, 41 SEC 230 (1962).

[18] See p. 39 supra.

[19] See Bastian v. Lakefront Realty Corp., 581 F. 2d 685, 688 (7th Cir. 1978).

[20] Sec. Ex. Act Rel. 18,647, 25 SEC Dock. 49 (1982); Sec. Ex. Act Rel. 23,406, 36 SEC Dock. 56 (1986). The 500 figure was 750 for the first two years in order to ease the Commission's burden. With the increase to $5 million, it is expected that some companies with securities registered while the asset test was lower will have them remain registered so that they will qualify for trading in NASDAQ.

least 500 persons must register the preferred under §12(g). Moreover, §12(g)(1) specifically *permits* an issuer to register any class of equity security even though it is not required to be registered. The ordinary human does not willingly put his head in the lion's mouth. But even before the 1964 amendments, companies were occasionally known to list on an exchange in anticipation of a proxy contest so as to subject the opposition's material to the proxy rules, and today the tender offer provisions give some protection to a company that is an unwilling target. Again, it is conceivable that an underwriter will require registration before undertaking a distribution. And the privilege of voluntary registration will also take care of the company with almost 500 stockholders that prefers the lion's mouth to the cliff's edge.

It is from the point of view of the regulatory philosophy that §12(g) is particularly significant. For it is the first instance of compulsory registration in the 1933 and 1934 Acts. Companies could previously avoid registration — at a price, of course — by not going to the public or listing on an exchange. But a company that meets the size and ownership standards of §12(g) has no choice.

Apart from the reflection of a later constitutional atmosphere, one implication of the compulsory factor is that, whereas there are ready devices for the issuer's delaying the effectiveness of a registration statement under the 1933 Act or §12(b) of the 1934 Act until it is reasonably sure from the staff's comments (if any) that the registration statement is not materially deficient, an issuer cannot postpone the operative effect of §12(g) by merely deferring its public offering or its listing until the deficiencies are cured. The fact that a §12(g) registration statement may become effective after sixty days in deficient form presents no particular problem for the *Commission*. It has ample sanctions for obtaining amendments from a recalcitrant issuer with an effective registration statement. It is the issuer itself that may be in an uncomfortable position. Although the possibility of criminal prosecution under §32 for filing false or misleading statements may be discounted unless the issuer is utterly indifferent to its responsibilities, the issuer risks civil liability under §18 — not to mention Rule 10b-5.

b. Due Date of Registration Statement

The critical date under §12(g)(1) for application of the size and ownership criteria is the last day of the fiscal year.[21] Two proposi-

[21] McAlinden v. Wiggins, 543 F. Supp. 1004, 1005 (S. D. N. Y. 1982).

tions follow from this arbitrary choice: (1) Exceeding either or both figures *during* a fiscal year is irrelevant unless *both* criteria are satisfied on the last day. (2) If both criteria are met on the last day of the fiscal year, a registration statement must be filed within 120 days even though by then the company has less than $5 million of assets and fewer than 500 record holders of any class of equity security; the company (unless it obtains an exemptive order under §12(h)) must then look to the quite different standards governing *termination* of registration.

At first blush it would seem to be equally clear that there is nothing illegal or otherwise improper about having either the issuer or one or more stockholders buy out enough record holders to keep the total safely below 500 on the last day of the fiscal year. But this device presents a number of problems. First, any repurchases by the issuer itself would have to comply, of course, with the appropriate provisions of the state of incorporation governing repurchases with respect to capital and various kinds of surplus. Secondly, a question might be raised, normally in a stockholder's derivative action, whether a repurchase by the company, particularly when the company had never repurchased before, had been for a proper corporate purpose as a matter of state law. Thirdly, §20(c) of the 1934 Act, which was appropriately amended in 1964 in the light of the adoption of §12(g), makes it "unlawful for any director or officer of, or any owner of any securities issued by, any issuer required to file any document, report, or information under this title or any rule or regulation thereunder without just cause to hinder, delay, or obstruct the making or filing of any such document, report, or information." And, in any event, careful attention would have to be paid to Rule 12g5-1(b)(3):

> If the issuer knows or has reason to know that the form of holding securities of record is used primarily to circumvent the provisions of section 12(g) or 15(d) of the Act, the beneficial owners of such securities shall be deemed to be the record owners thereof.[22]

This is obviously a catch-all provision that is aimed at deterring the organization of holding companies, subsidiaries, or trusts for the primary purpose of avoiding registration. Finally, since an issuer or stockholder buying on the market would have no way of knowing whether the seller was selling out completely, any purchases for the purpose of reducing the number of shareholders would have to be negotiated transactions, and this would increase the likelihood of a court's finding a violation of Rule 10b-5, perhaps on the basis of a

[22] See Tankersley v. Albright, 374 F. Supp. 551, 557 (N. D. Ill. 1974).

failure to disclose that the purpose of the purchases was to avoid the rights of investors flowing from registration.

Even so, it is by no means clear that reducing the number of stockholders below the statutory figure would not be considered a proper avoidance of an arbitrary statutory test, comparable to avoiding §16(b) by holding a security for six months before selling it. It is not unknown for public companies to "go private" quite apart from §12(g).[23] Nevertheless, any management that ventured on this virgin territory should tread warily. And certainly an issuer that had to do so repeatedly would be well advised to give up and register.[24]

There are similar questions of avoidance and evasion with reference to the assets test. For example, a company with a seasonable business might legitimately avoid registration by adopting a natural fiscal year, ending on a date when reduced inventories have not been replenished and both receivables and bank loans are usually at their low points for the year. On the other hand, paying off a substantial bank debt just before the close of the fiscal year and then reborrowing the money early in the next fiscal year would be an obvious evasion. In between there is inevitably another gray area.

Do §§13, 14, and 16 apply when a class of security should be registered under §12(g) but has not been? The Code adopts the administrative construction[25] as sound in policy by making it generally "unlawful for a person who is required to be registered under any provision of this Code but is not so registered to do any act that it would be unlawful for him to do if he were registered."[26] And that view has some judicial support under existing law.[27] On the other hand, a negative answer today is suggested not only by a literal reading of §§13, 14, and 16, which apply only to "registered" securities, but also by the language of prior bills,[28] which would

[23] On the "going private" phenomenon, see pp. 522-23 infra.

[24] The converse question — whether dissident stockholders may force management to register by selling portions of their holdings to persons who are not already record holders — has been litigated, with an affirmative answer, at state law. Loretto Literary & Benevolent Institution v. Blue Diamond Coal Co., 444 A. 2d 256 (Del. Ch. 1982).

[25] See Townsend Corp. of America, 42 SEC 282, 316-17 (1964) (Inv. Co. Act).

[26] §2006(b); see 2 Code 1022.

[27] Reserve Life Ins. Co. v. Provident Life Ins. Co., 499 F. 2d 715, 724 (8th Cir. 1974), *cert. denied*, 419 U. S. 1107; but cf. Upson v. Otis, 155 F. 2d 606, 610 (2d Cir. 1946); Bastian v. Lakefront Realty Corp., 581 F. 2d 685, 689-91 (7th Cir. 1978).

[28] See 2 Loss 1153-62; 4 Loss 2310.

have applied the three sections to securities "registered or required to be registered." And there is presumably some limit to the administrative or judicial rewriting of statutes in order to repair drafting oversights. In any event, injunctive and criminal proceedings would still lie, of course, for violation of §12(g)(1) itself.

The question assumes practical importance, therefore, only in the context of civil liability. So far as §16(b) is concerned, the statute of limitations would be tolled pending the required registration.[29] And the plaintiff that would otherwise seek private relief for violation of the proxy rules might be well advised to argue, at least in the alternative, not (1) that §14 could be or had been violated by an unregistered company but (2) that a company that was about to solicit or had solicited proxies when it was in violation of the registration requirement of §12(g)(1) should no more be permitted to enjoy the fruits of its violation than a company whose proxy solicitation had violated §14. Moreover, this latter argument should be equally available to the Commission itself in an injunctive action directed to the proxy solicitation of a company that was in violation of the registration requirement.

c. Banks

Banks and insurance companies[30] were the areas that created the greatest difficulty in connection with the 1964 legislation.

On the one hand, bank securities had always been exempted from registration under the 1933 Act. This in turn had precluded operation of the reporting requirement in §15(d) of the 1934 Act.[31] And, although bank stocks had never been exempted from the registration requirement in §12(a) of the 1934 Act, the Commission had early created a "temporary" exemption from §12(a) for bank securities listed on June 30, 1935 (or securities of the same issuer

[29] See p. 543 infra; Whittaker v. Whittaker Corp., 639 F. 2d 516, 527-30 (9th Cir. 1981), *cert. denied,* 454 U. S. 1031. In Kay v. ScienTex Corp., 719 F. 2d 1009, 1015 (9th Cir. 1983), the court rejected the plaintiff's argument, based by analogy on the tolling cases, that the defendant should not be permitted to use the courts to his advantage by summary judgment until he filed the required reports, since failure to file would deprive the plaintiff of information necessary to present evidence of his trading. This estoppel argument, the court stated, would be stronger if the proponent were an individual shareholder; the issuer that was making the argument had its own records that reflected stock transfers by the defendant.

[30] With respect to insurance companies, see p. 424 infra.

[31] See p. 410 supra.

exchanged for them) until the adoption of a special form[32] and had never adopted a form. In any event, a tendency to withdraw bank stocks from listing had set in well before 1934. And, although several bank *holding companies* have stocks listed on the New York Stock Exchange, by 1963 there were only five listed bank stocks (all on the then Philadelphia-Baltimore-Washington Stock Exchange) in addition to fifteen that were traded on the Honolulu, Richmond, and Wheeling Stock Exchanges, all exempted exchanges.[33] Furthermore, all banks are regulated by federal or state banking authorities or both.[34] And the country's banks could not be expected to relish another layer of regulation, which might interfere with customary accounting methods and other operating practices.

On the other hand, existing regulation was oriented toward the protection of depositors rather than investors and the integrity of the market.[35] And the Special Study had marshalled impressive evidence that the financial reporting and proxy solicitation practices of banks fell far short of the standards imposed by §§13 and 14 of the Exchange Act.[36]

At some point the Commission apparently concluded that the most statesmanlike policy consistent with principle would be to recommend that the registration and other provisions of the bill should extend to bank securities but should be administered by the respective federal bank agencies. The result was §12(i), which — as amended in 1968 to add references to the new tender offer provisions in the Williams Act, and as extended to insured savings and loan institutions by the Depository Institutions Act of 1974[37] — vests the SEC's "powers, functions, and duties * * * to administer and enforce" §§12, 13, 14(a), (c), (d), and (f), and 16 in (1) the Comptroller of the Currency with respect to national and District of Columbia banks, (2) the Board of Governors of the Federal Re-

[32] Former Rule 12a-1, adopted by Sec. Ex. Act Rel. 291 (1935), and repealed as obsolete by Sec. Ex. Act Rel. 18,853, 25 SEC Dock. 794 (1982).

[33] 3 SEC, Report of Special Study of Securities Markets, H. R. Doc. No. 95, 88th Cong., 1st Sess. (1963) 36.

[34] SEC Legislation, Hearings Before Subcom. of S. Com. on Banking & Currency on S. 1642, 88th Cong., 1st Sess. (1963) 172-75 (description by Comptroller of the Currency of disclosure requirements applicable to national banks in 1963).

[35] See Murane, SEC, FTC, and the Federal Bank Regulators: Emerging Problems of Administrative Jurisdictional Overlap, 61 Geo. L. J. 37 (1972). On the difference between the disclosure requirements of the SEC and the bank regulatory agencies with respect to loans, credit quality, and foreign exposure, see Coombe and Lapic, Problem Loans, Foreign Outstandings, and Other Developments in Bank Disclosure, 40 Bus. Law. 485 (1985).

[36] 3 Special Study, op. cit. supra n. 33, at 35-39.

[37] §105, 88 Stat. 1500, 1503-04 (1974).

serve System with respect to all other member banks of the Federal Reserve System, (3) the Federal Deposit Insurance Corporation with respect to all other insured banks, and (4) the Federal Home Loan Bank Board with respect to institutions insured by the Federal Savings and Loan Insurance Corporation. The 1974 statute also amended §12(i) to require these agencies to adopt rules "substantially similar" to the SEC's unless they publish detailed reasons for their findings to the contrary.

The "powers, functions, and duties" referred to in §12(i) include authority to adopt definitional and other rules under §§3(b) and 23(a) and to act just as the Commission would with respect to the investigatory, injunctive, and criminal provisions as well as the several administrative sanctions.[38] Moreover, the Senate made it clear that the bill in no way limited other provisions of law giving authority to the federal and state banking agencies.[39] The SEC, however, retains a considerable amount of jurisdiction in this area.

First of all, most of the larger banks are now subsidiaries of bank holding companies, which (together with their affiliates) come within the SEC's jurisdiction if they fall within the standards of §12(g), since they are not "banks" as defined in §3(a)(6). This inevitably gives the Commission an indirect say on the financial and other disclosures acquired with respect to the subsidiary banks.[40]

Secondly, the enumeration of only a few sections in §12(i) leaves jurisdiction in the SEC to apply the various investigatory provisions and sanctions as far as any other sections, including the fraud and manipulation provisions, are concerned.[41] Moreover, since the bank agencies are given no authority to register over-the-counter broker-dealers under §15(b), it is clear that only the SEC may discipline registered broker-dealers for violation of *any* provision of the Exchange Act — including even those specified in §12(i) — in connection with bank securities. And it is the Commission's view that, although the bank agencies have the authority normally vested in

[38] S. Rep. No. 379, 88th Cong., 1st Sess. (1963) 63-64.

[39] Id. at 35-36.

[40] See Third National Corp., Sec. Ex. Act Rel. 11,396, 6 SEC Dock. 852 (1975).

[41] See Local 734 Bakery Drivers Pension Fund Trust v. Continental Ill. National Bank of Chicago, CCH Fed. Sec. L. Rep. ¶94,565 at 95,960 (N. D. Ill. 1973) (Rule 10b-5); SEC v. Warner, 652 F. Supp. 647, 649-50 (S. D. Fla. 1987). On the symbiosis of the SEC and banking provisions with respect to insiders, see Buchalter and Allen, Bank Insider Abuses: When Does the Ax Fall?, 96 Banking L. J. 804 (1979). In SEC and Comptroller of the Currency v. National Bank of Ga., Litig. Rel. 8395, 14 SEC Dock. 1029 (N. D. Ga. 1978), both agencies sued jointly, alleging violations of the fraud, reporting, and proxy provisions of the SEC statutes.

the Commission under §§12(j) and 12(k) to delist or summarily suspend trading in securities within their jurisdiction for violation of the provisions specified in §12(l), they have no authority under those provisions that affect exchange trading in securities generally as well as the organization and administration of the exchanges.[42]

d. Definitions[43]

(i) *"Class":* Section 12(g)(5) borrowed a special definition from §15(d):

> For the purposes of this subsection, the term "class" shall include all securities of an issuer which are of substantially similar character and the holders of which enjoy substantially similar rights and privileges.

This general problem keeps cropping up in a number of contexts. We have met it in connection with the "new security" question[44] and the voluntary exchange exemption;[45] and we shall meet it again in connection with §15(d)[46] and especially §16, on insider trading, which refers to beneficial holders of more than 10 percent of "any class of any equity security."[47] In terms of maximizing the statutory coverage, there are a built-in stress and strain. For purposes of §§12(g) and 15(d) — as well as the intrastate and private offering exemptions in §§3(a)(11) and 4(2) of the 1933 Act to the extent that different classes constitute separate "issues" or "offerings"[48] — it is in the Commission's interest to play down relatively minor differences between "Class A Common" and "Class B Common," or between two formally separate "classes" of convertible debentures, so as to produce one big, widely held "class." So, too, when it is a matter of matching a purchase of Class A against a sale of Class B for purposes of §16(b). But that approach cuts in the op-

[42] 2 Investor Protection, Hearings Before Subcom. of House Com. on Int'l & For. Commerce on H. R. 6789, H. R. 6793, S. 1642, 88th Cong., 1st Sess. (1963) 1365-66. See generally Mathewson, From Confidential Supervision to Market Discipline: The Role of Disclosure in the Regulation of Commercial Banks, 11 J. Corp. L. 139, 151-60.

The 1984 Bush report would centralize enforcement responsibility with respect to banks and savings and loans in the SEC. Blueprint for Reform: The Report of the Task Force on Regulation of Financial Services (1984) 64.

[43] The definition of "equity security" is considered infra p. 574.

[44] See p. 248 supra.

[45] See pp. 278-79 supra.

[46] See p. 436 infra.

[47] See p. 575 infra.

[48] See pp. 296-98, 326 supra.

posite direction as far as the 10 percent test in §16 is concerned. Presumably there is some limit to the freedom to give the same term different constructions in different sections of the same statute, particularly since the existence of a single "class" for purposes of §12(g) may be the sole basis for applying §16. And maximization of coverage itself may not be a strong enough solvent. Yet §3(a) of the 1934 Act, like §2(a) of the 1933 Act, introduces all the general definitions with the words, "unless the context otherwise requires." And — more to the point here — the definition of "class" in §§12(g)(5) and 15(d) is specifically limited to "the purposes of this subsection."

There is not much that has so far emerged in the way of guidelines. As always, of course, "form" must yield to "substance." This means that securities denominated "preferred" and "common" *may* constitute a single class. The mere fact that one security is convertible into another does not make them one class.[49] On the other hand, the result is apt to be different when both securities are of the same basic type, which is to say, common stock, preferred stock, unsecured debt, or secured debt. Convertibility aside, when, for example, two preferred issues differ with respect to one or more of their basic characteristics — voting rights, dividend preference, and preference on liquidation — an approach in terms of the purpose of the differences in the particular case, which would be roughly analogous to the "business purpose" test in tax law, would seem to be superior to the sort of "color matching" approach that Justice Harlan disparaged in his dissenting opinion in the variable annuity case,[50] even though the latter approach seems to be invited by the "substantially similar character" language of §12(g)(5).

(ii) *"Held of record" [Rule 12g5-1]:* Consistently with the reference in §12(g)(1) to holders "of record," this definitional rule simply supplies a series of explanations and qualifications, only a few of which require comment:

Securities held by two or more persons as co-owners, or as co-fiduciaries with respect to a single trust, estate, or account, are considered to have a single record holder. It follows, for example, that, when John Doe holds some securities in his own name and others as trustee, there are two record holders; that, when John and

[49] In Plessey Co., PLC v. General Electric Co., PLC, 628 F. Supp. 477 (D. Del. 1986), the court held, for purposes of determining whether a tender offer had been made by one British company to another, that the target's American depository receipts (convertible to Dollar Ordinary Shares) and those Dollar Shares (convertible to Sterling Ordinary Shares) were all separate classes.

[50] SEC v. Variable Annuity Life Ins. Co. of America, 359 U. S. 65, 96 (1959), supra p. 206.

Mary Doe hold securities as co-owners (whether the type of tenancy is joint or common or by the entirety or unknown) and each of them holds other securities in his or her own name, there is a total of three record holders; and that, when securities are held by John Doe, by Mary Doe, by John and Mary Doe as co-owners, by John Doe as custodian for a minor child, and by John and Mary Doe as trustees, there is a total of five record holders.

"Each outstanding unregistered or bearer certificate shall be included as held of record by a separate person, except to the extent that the issuer can establish that, if such securities were registered, they would be held of record, under the provisions of this rule, by a lesser number of persons." Since a convertible bond is defined as an "equity security" by §3(a)(11), this clause applies equally to convertible bonds in bearer form. That is to say, it is simply a matter of counting the number of bonds outstanding, regardless of denomination.

"Securities held, to the knowledge of the issuer, subject to a voting trust, deposit agreement or similar arrangement shall be included as held of record by the record holders of the voting trust certificates, certificates of deposit, receipts or similar evidences of interest in such securities: *Provided however*, That the issuer may rely in good faith on such information as is received in response to its request from a nonaffiliated issuer of the certificates or evidences of interest." Note the limiting words, "to the knowledge of the issuer." When that limitation is satisfied, the record holders of the voting-trust certificates or similar securities are counted twice, once to determine the number of holders of the underlying shares and again to determine the number of holders of the voting-trust certificates, which are themselves included within the definition of "equity security" under §3(a)(11). On the other hand, the rule as adopted does not, as the Commission originally proposed, look through brokers, dealers, banks, or their nominees to include the number of separate customers' accounts. That is to say, the brokerage firm that holds stock in "street name" for fifty customers is counted as a single holder. The Commission, apparently assuming that its authority in §12(g)(5) to define "held of record" *could* be stretched to include beneficial holders in this sense, stated that it had abandoned its original proposal in the interest of simplification but would "determine in the light of experience whether inclusion of these accounts at a future date is necessary or appropriate to prevent circumvention of the Act and to achieve the intended coverage on a uniform and acceptable basis."[51] Similar considerations

[51] Sec. Ex. Act Rel. 7492 (1965).

underlay the Commission's decision not to include employees with a direct beneficial interest in securities held by an employee plan.[52]

(iii) *"Total assets" [Rule 12g5-2]:* The assets test in §12(g)(1), too, presents a bit of a dilemma for both the Commission and corporate management. The Commission for its part must balance the conflicting policies of furthering the statutory coverage, which in an inflationary economy would tend to support asset revaluations, and encouraging conservative accounting, which would tend in the opposite direction. Conversely, management now has an incentive to make accounting adjustments downward in order to reduce total assets below the $5 million figure and thus avoid registration.

As long as the accounting principles followed by the company are supported by substantial authority, are adequately disclosed, do not unfairly portray the company's financial condition, and do not contravene a position expressed in a Commission rule or release, it is difficult to see how the Commission could object to this kind of avoidance. For, consistently with its general approach to accounting principles, the Commission has not prescribed detailed rules under §12(g) for valuing assets or computing reserves. Although this may result in some lack of uniformity in the application of the section, that consideration alone has not persuaded the Commission to undertake the formidable task of choosing between alternative methods of valuation when there is a substantial difference of opinion within the profession. Its definitional rule makes only two points:

(1) The term "total assets" refers to either the corporate or the consolidated balance sheet, whichever shows the larger figure, as required to be filed on the proper registration form and as prepared in accordance with Regulation S-X. This formula, of course, makes more acute the question whether consolidated statements should be prepared in the first place. Clearly the fact that a company may not have prepared consolidated financial statements in the past cannot be determinative for purposes of the $5 million test when generally accepted accounting principles would have dictated consolidated statements.

(2) "Where the security is a certificate of deposit, voting trust certificate, or certificate or other evidence of interest in a similar trust or agreement, the 'total assets' of the issuer of the security held under the trust or agreement shall be deemed to be the 'total assets' of the issuer of such certificate or evidence of interest." This means that the assets test is met by a voting trust that has half the stock of a company with $5 million of assets.

One thing that is perfectly clear is that the existence of a capital

[52] Ibid.

deficit is irrelevant as long as "total assets" exceed $5 million. On this basis registration might be required even on the part of a company that was insolvent in the bankruptcy sense.

3. Exemptions

a. General

The treatment of exemptions in the 1934 Act is quite different from that in the 1933 and 1939 Acts, essentially because the 1934 Act contains so many different kinds of substantive provisions:

(1) Section 3(a)(12) *defines* the term "exempted security" to include, in effect, only "direct obligations of or obligations guaranteed as to principal or interest" by an American governmental authority,[53] certain industrial development bonds by reference to the Internal Revenue Code,[54] and whatever other securities the Commission may exempt, conditionally or unconditionally, by rule. The Commission has broadly construed the term "direct obligations" as standing in contradistinction to the phrase "obligations guaranteed as to principal or interest," and hence has regarded state and municipal revenue bonds and special assessment bonds as exempt. Rules adopted under a section that excludes "exempted securities" obviously cannot be made applicable to the securities that are so defined by §3(a)(12). But the converse does not necessarily follow. The Commission apparently considers that its power to classify securities in the general rulemaking provisions is sufficiently

[53]Only the Secretary of the Treasury may designate for exemption securities issued or guaranteed by "corporations in which the United States has a direct or indirect interest," and that authority has been used sparingly.

[54]The Internal Revenue Code references comprehend industrial revenue bonds issued (1) for certain specific purposes or (2) in the face amount of not more than $1 million (or in certain cases $5 million). See Sec. Act Rel. 5103 (1970). On the various kinds of industrial development bonds, see Note, The Liability of Municipalities for State and Federal Securities Fraud in the Issuance of Industrial Development Bonds, 30 Okla. L. Rev. 704, 705-11 (1977).

The original 1934 Act did not include a government or political subdivision in the §3(a)(9) definition of "person." Accordingly, the courts held that, although industrial development bonds were not exempted, the municipality could not be sued under Rule 10b-5. Woods v. Homes & Structures of Pittsburgh, Kan., Inc., 489 F. Supp. 1270, 1280-82 (D. Kan. 1980), and cases cited; Brown v. City of Covington, 805 F. 2d 1266 (6th Cir. 1986). This was changed by amendment in 1975. See p. 627 infra.

broad to permit it to exclude "exempted securities" from rules adopted under provisions that do *not* exclude them.[55]

(2) Apart from those few securities that come within the definition of "exempted securities" in §3(a)(12), there is a considerable panoply of exemptions peculiar to §12(g). These include securities of investment companies, savings and loan associations, nonprofit issuers, cooperatives, insurance companies, and foreign issuers. In some respects these exemptions differ from their analogues in the 1933 Act.

(3) All these exemptions flow automatically from statute or rule. In addition, although §3(a)(12) limits the Commission to acting by rule rather than by order, the Commission has given itself an *ad hoc* exemptive authority in certain rules, for example, those on trading during distributions, market stabilization, and distributions through rights.[56] And §12(h), added in the 1964 amendments, authorizes exemption, by rule *or order,* from not only §12(g) but also §§13, 14, 15(d), and 16.

As a result of this statutory scheme, one who wishes to determine whether a particular kind of security or transaction is or may be exempted from a particular substantive provision of the statute must see first whether that provision by its terms excludes "exempted securities" or contains any special exemptions or exemptive authority. Then, in either event, he must determine whether the Commission has adopted an exemptive rule under that section. And, finally, either the particular section or a rule thereunder or §12(h) may afford him an opportunity to seek an exemptive *order.*

b. Insurance Companies [§12(g)(2)(G)]

Most of the §12(g) exemptions do not require discussion here. But one that does, because of both its intrinsic importance and its implications for federalism, is the exemption in §12(g)(2)(G) for securities of insurance companies.

We have already noted that, along with banks,[57] insurance companies were the area of greatest difficulty for Congress in connection with the 1964 legislation. The ultimate solutions, though philosophically similar in that jurisdiction over both categories was shifted

[55] See Rules 10b-6(d), 10b-7(n), which exclude "exempted securities" from the regulations on trading during distributions and on market stabilization although they are not excluded by §10(b).

[56] Rules 10b-6(h), 10b-7(o), 10b-8(f).

[57] See p. 415 supra.

for the most part from the SEC to the bank and insurance regulatory authorities, took quite different forms. Because there was no federal insurance agency on the scene to which jurisdiction could be transferred as it was to the federal bank agencies by §12(i), the device used was an exemption from §12(g)(1) that was made conditional on the existence of substantially similar regulation in the domiciliary state.

The SEC has never had jurisdiction over *mutual* insurance companies except on their occasional issuance of debt securities, because they do not issue stock and §3(a)(8) of the 1933 Act exempts insurance policies and annuities, which (as we have seen) are normally not "securities" in any event.[58] However, before 1964 there was no exemption from either the 1933 Act or the 1934 Act for insurance company *securities.* That was the entire point of the variable annuity controversy. Consequently a considerable number of insurance companies had registered issues under the 1933 Act. And, as a result, 169 insurance companies were reporting to the Commission under §15(d) of the 1934 Act as of June 30, 1963, though only 2 additional companies were listed on an exchange (and thus reporting under §13) on that date.[59] (In 1965 The Insurance Company of North America became the first new insurance company to be listed on the New York Stock Exchange since 1916; today there are some 30.)

So far as the merits are concerned, the Commission's "Special Study" of 1963, finding that "Insurance companies as a group * * * exhibit all of the inadequacies in reporting and proxy solicitations characteristic of the total group studied," concluded that they did not present a case for special treatment with respect to §§13, 14, and 16.[60] And in 1960 a group within the National Federation of Financial Analysts Societies concluded that annual stockholders' reports of the life insurance industry "are the poorest of any major industry in the United States."[61]

Nevertheless, the National Association of Insurance Commissioners (NAIC), representing the insurance regulatory authorities of all the states, the District of Columbia, and Puerto Rico, took a firm position that insurance companies should be exempted in accordance with the tradition of state regulation. The commissioners

[58] See p. 204 supra.

[59] 1 Investor Protection, supra p. 418 n. 42, at 176 n. 5.

[60] 3 SEC, Report of Special Study of Securities Markets, H. R. Doc. No. 95, 88th Cong., 1st Sess. (1963) 42.

[61] SEC Legislation, 1963, Hearings Before Subcom. of S. Com. on Banking & Currency on S. 1642, 88th Cong., 1st Sess. (1963) 25.

recognized that there was some validity to the contention that their procedures were directed primarily to the protection of policy holders rather than investors. But they sought an opportunity to demonstrate their ability effectively to protect investors as well.[62] And the Commission, as it did with the banks, went along presumably to avoid the danger of a serious floor fight on the entire bill. But, again as with banks, jurisdiction over insurance *holding* companies remains with the SEC.

Unhappily, perhaps because it was a relatively late insertion in the bill, §12(g)(2)(G) is not as precisely drafted as one might wish when it exempts

> any security issued by an insurance company if all of the following conditions are met:
>
> (i) Such insurance company is required to and does file an annual statement with the Commissioner of Insurance (or other officer or agency performing a similar function) of its domiciliary State, and such annual statement conforms to that prescribed by the National Association of Insurance Commissioners or in the determination of such State commissioner, officer or agency substantially conforms to that so prescribed.
>
> (ii) Such insurance company is subject to regulation by its domiciliary State of proxies, consents, or authorizations in respect of securities issued by such company and such regulation conforms to that prescribed by the National Association of Insurance Commissioners.
>
> (iii) After July 1, 1966, the purchase and sales of securities issued by such insurance company by beneficial owners, directors, or officers of such company are subject to regulation (including reporting) by its domiciliary State substantially in the manner provided in section 16 of this title.[63]

Citations to the relevant laws of all three categories in the 52 jurisdictions are readily available.[64] Suffice it here to note the pitfalls in all three clauses:

Two points are worth noting with respect to the first clause:

(1) Unlike the second and third clauses, the first clause requires not merely that the insurance company be "subject to" specified regulation but also that it comply by actually filing. This raises the question whether a late filing would destroy the exemption. Presumably every commissioner's control over the required filings is

[62] H. R. Rep. No. 1418, 88th Cong., 2d Sess. (1964) 10.

[63] In addition, Congress in §3(a)(19) incorporated the definition of "insurance company" from §2(a)(17) of the Investment Company Act.

[64] For the text of the provisions, see CCH Blue Sky L. Rep., where they are collected along with the "insurance securities laws."

great enough to authorize him to grant reasonable extensions, which would prevent non-compliance as a matter of state law and hence avoid any question under Clause (i). In any event, it is difficult to conceive of a company's failing to file its report for a given year until the last day of its next fiscal year, which is presumably the date for determining the availability of the exemption.[65] But the short answer would seem to be that any failure to file that was not excused as a matter of state law *would* hazard the exemption, at least if the failure extended beyond the end of the next fiscal year.

(2) Timing aside, the insurance commissioner's determination (at least in the absence of a genuine abuse of discretion on his part) is made conclusive on the question of substantial compliance. That is to say, Congress has not only delegated a legislative function, as it were, to an organization of state administrative officials; it has also precluded the SEC and the federal courts from examining (except perhaps in extreme cases) the question of compliance in an individual case.

In contrast with Clause (i), which quite clearly did not require additional state legislation, Clause (iii) just as clearly did. Accordingly, the NAIC adopted a model insider trading act. That model or similar legislation based on §16 of the Exchange Act has been adopted in all 52 jurisdictions. And the NAIC also adopted and recommended a set of rules and forms closely modeled on the SEC's. But problems remain aside from the variations that seem to plague all "uniform" state legislation. For example, since Clause (iii) refers to local regulation "substantially in the manner provided in" §16, there is a question how much weight the word "substantially" will bear. The SEC, for example, has adopted a pretty rigid rule defining beneficial ownership in various trust situations.[66] Although Clause (iii) does not require compliance with any regulations prescribed by the NAIC as Clause (i) does, any insurance commissioner who did not adopt the NAIC's model forms and rules — which for this reason were copied as closely as possible from the SEC's forms and rules — would be hazarding the exemption for companies incorporated in his jurisdiction. Even so, the NAIC and all the commissioners must watch carefully for future SEC rule or form amendments that tighten §16 and, therefore, automatically affect Clause (iii) of the exemption. And, forms and rules aside, what about judicial construction? The federal courts have developed an extremely strict test for computing the recoverable profits under

[65] Cf. §12(g)(1)(B) (due date of registration statement).
[66] Rule 16a-8.

§16(b) in cases of multiple transactions, refusing to permit either the tracing of certificates or a first-in-first-out presumption as under the tax laws.[67] The state courts are not bound to follow these federal precedents in interpreting state statutes as such, but they may well risk destruction of the entire exemption if they do not.

It is Clause (ii) that presents perhaps the toughest problems. To be sure, it is the only one of the three clauses that does not require that the state regulation conform "substantially" to either the NAIC or the SEC pattern. In the event, virtually all 52 jurisdictions have enacted enabling legislation to authorize their insurance commissioners to adopt the proxy rules, basically but not altogether like the SEC's, that the NAIC "strongly recommended" (it did not use the statutory word "prescribed") and that all 52 jurisdictions have adopted. But, unfortunately, the NAIC did not recommend a model proxy act as it did a model insider trading act; and the inevitable result is a hodgepodge.[68]

It must not be overlooked, moreover, that the exemptive scheme in §12(g)(2)(G) is on an all-or-none basis. That is to say, failure to comply with Clause (ii), for example, destroys the exemption not only with respect to §14 but also with respect to the reporting and insider trading provisions of §§13 and 16. Therefore, the absence or insufficiency of the proxy regulation required by Clause (ii) in a particular state may mean, for example, that a director that has diligently filed the required insider trading reports with the insurance commissioner will find himself sued several years later under §16(b) on the theory that no exemption was available and that the two-year statute of limitations in §16(b) was tolled during the period that he did not file reports with the SEC. Conversely, suppose that a state court — perhaps relishing its independence of the Supreme Court of the United States and the lower federal courts — reads the state statute's insider trading provisions less stringently than the federal precedents go. Having in mind the Supreme Court's holding that in a proper case a trial court, as a matter of federal law, may set aside any action taken by means of illegally solicited proxies,[69] a company that is soliciting proxies for some extraordinary event like a merger might well give serious consideration to the advisability of registering under §12(g) and complying with the SEC

[67] See pp. 558-61 infra.

[68] In 1980 the NAIC adopted a revised Regulation Regarding Proxies, Consents and Authorizations of Domestic Stock Insurers, which is modeled closely on the SEC's rules. [1980]-2 Proc. NAIC 309. But that revision is effective in only a few states.

[69] See pp. 491-95 infra.

proxy rules. Whatever the reason, a number of insurance companies have done so.

All in all, counsel for one of the large insurance companies concluded after a detailed survey of the action taken by the NAIC and the insurance commissioners in the light of §12(g)(2)(G):

> It seems doubtful that any of the industry or NAIC representatives who worked so diligently and effectively to secure the provisional insurance company exemption foresaw the multiplicity of problems posed by incorporation of the federal regulatory pattern in all the states. * * * If Congress should amend Section 16, presumably all the states will have to do likewise. If the SEC revises its rules under that section, at least if such revision should have the effect of narrowing exemptions, insurance commissioners will almost certainly have to follow suit. Eternal, unflagging vigilance will be the price of continued liberty, and to the extent that state regulation is as effective as it must be to maintain the exemption the liberty purchased may be largely illusory.[70]

The only observation one can add is that this proliferation of jurisdiction among 52 insurance commissioners and judicial systems, not to mention four federal bank and savings and loan agencies, does little to improve the disposition of a writer on the subject.

c. Exemptive Orders [§12(h)]

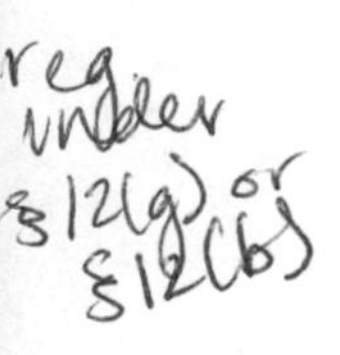

The authority under §12(h) to exempt by order is not limited to §12(g). It may be applied separately to §13, 14, or 15(d), whether the security is registered under §12(g) or under §12(b). And the Commission has used the authority in a great variety of cases, often granting exemption partially and conditionally.

In one case, for example, the Commission rejected contentions that an exemption was warranted by (1) the fact that only 456 of the 599 shareholders of record were residents of the United States, (2) the fact that 466 shareholders owned five shares or less, and (3) the very limited trading interest. But the Commission recognized that, in view of the absence of a continuing or professional market interest, the financial community that seeks out and disseminates information on file would not be served by compliance with the

[70] Kenney, Securities Regulation in the Insurance Business or S-X and the Single Standard, 19 Assn. Life Ins. Counsel Proc. 1, 52 (1965). For a discussion of the additional complexities in the event that an insurance commissioner should seek to enforce his state's proxy or insider trading legislation in the courts of another state, see 5 Loss 2758-59.

reporting requirements of §13(a) in the particular case. It accordingly exempted from that section, and waived certain of the financial requirements in connection with the filing of a registration statement, but also imposed a number of conditions: (a) that the financial statements included in the annual reports to shareholders and certified in accordance with generally accepted accounting principles be deemed incorporated by reference in the company's proxy or information statements so that §18 would be made applicable; (b) that the company, when acting as middleman between seller and buyer, furnish every offeree a copy of the most recent proxy or information statement and annual report; and (c) that the company inform the Commission annually of all sales and advise it promptly of any material change in the factual situation.[71]

4. NONSTATUTORY LISTING REQUIREMENTS OF THE EXCHANGES

Long before the Exchange Act the several exchanges had their own varying requirements for listing. These are unaffected by the Exchange Act, except for a residual power in the Commission (which was enlarged in the 1975 amendments) to disapprove new rules or rule changes generally before they become effective and to make changes in exchange rules.[72]

The development of the exchanges' listing rules was gradual. For many years all that the New York Stock Exchange demanded to know was that a company really existed and that its securities were authentic. The old viewpoint was that the function of an exchange was not to reform corporate practices but to maintain a "free and open" market for securities. The trend toward the modern disclosure requirements — like so many developments in this field — followed the increasing divorcement of management and ownership. Although the New York Stock Exchange was trying as early as the 1860s to get financial reports from companies whose securities were dealt in, and by 1909 was obtaining agreements to distribute annual financial statements to stockholders as a condition of listing, the development did not proceed in earnest until the boom that ended with the 1929 crash had got well under way, and it was then accentuated by the depression. Thus the Exchange has required since 1933 that the financial statements accompanying listing

[71] National Dollar Stores, Ltd., 43 SEC 881 (1968).
[72] §§19(b)(1)-(3), 19(c).

applications and those subsequently published or sent to stockholders be audited under specified standards by public accountants. And its requirements with respect to the publication of quarterly earnings and the sending of annual reports to stockholders antedate the SEC.

The disclosure requirements of the New York Stock Exchange largely, but not entirely, parallel those under the Exchange Act.[73] But the conditions of listing go beyond disclosure. The Exchange itself has described its requirements this way:

> The company must be a going concern or be the successor to a going concern. While the amount of assets and earnings and the aggregate market value are considerations, greater emphasis is placed on such questions as the degree of national interest in the company, the character of the market for its products, its relative stability and position in its industry, and whether or not it is engaged in an expanding industry with prospects for maintaining its position.[74]

The Exchange has repeatedly raised its *minimum* numerical standards so that it now looks in general for 1,100,000 publicly held shares; 2000 holders (including beneficial holders of stock held in "street name") of 100 shares or more; demonstrated earning power under competitive conditions of $2.5 million before taxes during the latest year and $2 million during the preceding two years; and an aggregate market value of $18 million for the publicly held shares.[75]

There are also a number of other conditions,[76] which are reflected in the Commission's 1977 release approving an Exchange rule designed to "require each domestic company with common stock listed on the NYSE, as a condition of initial and continued listing of its securities on the NYSE, to establish not later than June 30, 1978, and maintain thereafter, an audit committee comprised solely of directors independent of management and free from any relationship that, in the opinion of the board of directors, would interfere with the exercise of independent judgment as a committee member":[77]

[73] The listing application obligates the issuer to "furnish to the Exchange on demand such information concerning the Corporation as the Exchange may reasonably require." N. Y. Stock Ex. Listed Company Manual 901.01.13.

[74] Id. at 102.01.

[75] Ibid.

[76] For the current form of listing agreement, see id. 901.00. See generally Comment, Stock Exchange Listing Agreements As a Vehicle for Corporate Governance, 129 U. Pa. L. Rev. 1427 (1981).

[77] Sec. Ex. Act Rel. 13,346, 11 SEC Dock. 1945 (1977). See generally D. McCauley and J. Burton, Audit Committees (BNA Corp. Practice Series 1986);

The NYSE listing agreement, which has traditionally been a principal means by which the NYSE enforces its listing standards, was first adopted by the NYSE in 1899. That agreement, and the policies set forth in the NYSE Company Manual, have developed gradually over the years and impose a wide variety of requirements for initial and continued listing. Those policies frequently require a listed company to take action which it would not otherwise be required to take and prevent a listed company from taking action which would otherwise be permitted.[6] Furthermore, the NYSE has a general policy calling for timely and adequate disclosure of corporate affairs and has in past urged listed companies to consider the desirability of having at least two outside directors whose functions on the board would include giving particular attention to full disclosure of corporate affairs.

Consistent with its overall approach to listing policies, the NYSE, and the accounting profession, major corporations and others, including the Commission, have for many years recognized the advantages of corporate audit committees. Stronger support for audit committees independent of management developed in the wake of recent revelations of questionable and illegal corporate payments. In particular, the Commission has urged strengthening the indepen-

---

Comment, Corporate Financial Records and Internal Accounting Controls: What Does the SEC Expect of Audit Committee Members?, 9 N. C. J. Int'l L. & Com. Reg. 291 (1984).

[6] For example, since 1926, the NYSE has refused to list non-voting common stock, and currently it will delist the voting common stock of a company which creates a class of non-voting common stock or fails to solicit proxies for meetings of its stockholders. [N. Y. Stock Ex. Listed Co. Manual 313.00(A), 402.04, 802.00.] As a matter of policy, the NYSE refuses to list a class of stock whose voting rights are subject to unusual restrictions. Id., at [313.00(C)] et seq. Certain redemption schemes are prohibited. Id., at [311.01]. In authorizing additional shares distributed by a stock dividend, a company can be required to transfer from earned surplus to permanent capitalization an amount equal to the fair value of such shares. Id., at [703.02(A)]. A company whose board of directors is divided into more than three classes may not list its shares; if the board is divided into classes, they should be of approximately equal size and tenure, and the directors' terms of office should not exceed three years. Id., at [304.00]. Since 1940, listed preferred stock must have certain minimum provisions enabling holders to obtain board representation in the event of dividend default, and must be protected against compulsory change in rights and preferences. Id., at [703.05(A), (D)]. Shareholder approval is a prerequisite to listing securities to be used in connection with options or other remuneration plans for directors, officers, or employees; actions resulting in a change in the control of a company; and certain acquisitions. Id., at [312.00]. Where stockholder approval is needed for listing any additional securities, over 50 percent of all securities entitled to vote must be represented in the vote, and approval must be by a majority of votes cast. Id., at [312.00(B)]. Before a class of securities eligible for continued listing may be delisted, the proposed withdrawal must have been approved by a substantial percentage of the outstanding shares (generally 66⅔ percent) and not opposed by a substantial number of individual holders (generally 10 percent of the individual holders). Id., at [806.00]. * * *

> dence and vitality of corporate boards of directors and has suggested that, at least initially, those principles could be implemented by amending the listing requirements of the NYSE and other self-regulatory organizations, rather than by direct Commission action. * * *
>
> The NYSE's revision of its listing policies appears to be an appropriate way to implement, at this time, an independent audit committee requirement. * * * While independent audit committees will not eliminate all instances of abuse, their establishment can be an important step in a broader effort to remedy the problems of corporate accountability and disclosure that have been uncovered.
>
> * * * While the current proposal applies only to domestic companies, their compliance should not be deemed to place them at any inappropriate competitive disadvantage.

As early as 1968 the Exchange solicited comment on whether it should modify its traditional "one share, one vote" policy to permit supermajority voting requirements designed to ward off tender offers.[78] The subject is a controversial one, ringing the bell of "corporate democracy" as it does.[79] In the face of competitive pressure from the American Stock Exchange and the NASD, the New York Stock Exchange in late 1986 reluctantly proposed a rule change to permit stock with disparate voting rights on a number of conditions. These would include approval by two-thirds of all shares entitled to vote on the question as well as approval by independent directors (or a majority of independent directors when a majority of the board was independent).[80] In December 1986 the Commission held a two-day public hearing on the general subject, including the question whether its §19(c)(3) authority over self-regulatory organization rules[81] would enable it to impose the same rule on other self-regulatory organizations.[82]

In 1956 the Exchange announced a formal statement of policy covering so-called *backdoor* listings to codify its objection to indirect listings of companies that cannot meet the original listing standards: When an unlisted company proposes to combine with and into a listed company under circumstances that in the opinion of the Ex-

[78] See Mullaney, Guarding Against Takeovers—Defensive Charter Provisions, 25 Bus. Law. 1441 (1970).

[79] In favor of the traditional policy, see Seligman, Equal Protection in Shareholder Voting Rights: The One Common Share, One Vote Controversy, 54 Geo. Wash. L. Rev. 687 (1986). *Opposed:* D. Fischel, Organized Exchanges and the Regulation of Dual Class Common Stock (1986).

[80] Sec. Ex. Act Rel. 23,724, 36 SEC Dock. 1016 (1986).

[81] See p. 636 infra.

[82] Sec. Ex. Act Rel. 23,803, 36 SEC Dock. 1260. *An appendix to this volume brings this matter current to the date of the return of final proofs.*

change constitute an acquisition of a listed company by an unlisted company, the resulting company must meet the standards for original listing or the Exchange will refuse to list additional shares of the listed company for the purpose.[83]

The American Stock Exchange has a similar policy.[84] But its requirements generally are somewhat less strict, in line with its tradition as a "seasoner" for the "Big Board." Each case is considered on its merits. Some issues of corporations still in the development stage, and without demonstrated earning power, have been listed. Important factors in such cases are the company's management, the adequacy of its financing, and its prospects. The other exchanges run the gamut.

Whatever may be the rights of *stockholders* as third-party beneficiaries of a corporation's listing agreement, it has been held that a *prospective purchaser* has no such right that is enforceable in an action against the corporation for damages resulting from breach of its agreement with the Exchange to publish promptly its decision to pass a dividend. The market price had dropped after the delayed publication of the passed dividend, and the plaintiff claimed that she would have canceled an order to buy additional shares "good till canceled" if the decision to pass the dividend had been promptly published.[85]

B. REPORTS

1. IN CONNECTION WITH EXCHANGE ACT REGISTRATION

Section 13(a) of the Exchange Act requires every issuer of a security registered on an exchange to file with the Commission and the exchange (1) such information as the Commission may by rule require "to keep reasonably current" the information filed in registering and (2) such annual and quarterly reports as the Commission may by rule prescribe. The Commission has held that §13(a)

[83] N. Y. Stock Ex. Listed Company Manual 703.08(G), 801.00.

[84] CCH Am. Stock Ex. Guide ¶10,111 (back door listing).

[85] Mackubin v. Curtiss-Wright Corp., 190 Md. 52, 57 A. 2d 318 (1948). Corbin says: "It would have been helpful if the court had analyzed the purposes for which the exchange exacted the promise as a condition of listing." 4 Corbin, Contracts (1951) 49.

"necessarily embodies the requirement that such reports be true and correct."[1]

a. Annual Reports

A Commission rule requires the filing of an annual report, normally within ninety days after the close of the fiscal year, for each year after the last full fiscal year for which financial statements were filed in the application for registration.[2] The basic annual report form, corresponding to Form 10 for registration, is Form 10-K, and there are other forms in the "K" series corresponding to each of the specialized registration forms.

Information may be incorporated by reference from a proxy statement or from a report to security holders or from a prospectus into a 1934 Act registration statement or report.[3] And issuers are encouraged to integrate their annual reports to shareholders and those filed with the Commission. We have already noticed in the subchapter on accounting[4] that the Commission, without any direct authority over reports to security holders, has managed to assert a significant measure of indirect control by resort to its rulemaking authority with respect to proxy solicitations — this on the theory that the annual report to security holders, more than the occasional prospectus or even the proxy statement, should be recognized as "the most effective means of communication between management and security holders."[5]

The proxy rules have gradually been tightened so that today a proxy solicitation on behalf of the issuer with respect to an annual meeting for the election of directors must be accompanied or preceded by an annual report to security holders that includes, *inter alia*, (1) balance sheets for two years and income statements for three, all audited and prepared on a consolidated basis in substantial compliance with Regulation S-X, (2) selected financial data, and (3) management's analysis of financial condition and results of opera-

C. 7B [1]Great Sweet Grass Oils, Ltd., 37 SEC 683, 684 n. 1 (1957), *aff'd per curiam* sub nom. Great Sweet Grass Oils, Ltd. v. SEC, 256 F. 2d 893 (D. C. Cir. 1958); see p. 441 supra, where this approach is *queried.*

[2]Rule 13a-1; Form 10-K, Gen. Inst. A.

[3]Rule 12b-23. Financial statements incorporated by reference must satisfy the requirements of the form or report in which they are incorporated. Rule 12b-23(a)(1).

[4]See p. 158 supra.

[5]Sec. Ex. Act Rel. 11,079, 5 SEC Dock. 356, 357 (1974).

tions.[6] Unless the report itself satisfies Form 10-K, either the report or the proxy statement must contain an undertaking to supply a copy of the 10-K report on request without charge.[7] Copies of the report to security holders must also be mailed to the Commission "solely for its information," which is to say, the report is not considered to be filed for purposes of civil liability under §18.[8] And a company that has no securities registered under the 1934 Act but that is subject to §15(d), so that the proxy rules do not apply, must likewise furnish to the Commission (but not "file") any annual report or proxy material that *is* distributed, or must state that that is not the case.[9]

The Code recognizes the security holders' report as "the central device for continuous disclosure" by giving the Commission direct authority over its content.[10]

b. Quarterly and Current Reports

Every issuer that is required to file an annual report on Form 10-K (with a few exceptions) must file a quarterly report on Form 10-Q within forty-five days after the end of its first three fiscal quarters,[11] and a "current report" on Form 8-K within fifteen days after the occurrence of specified events of an extraordinary character that have not been reported previously.[12]

The *quarterly* report must include condensed financial data, which need not be audited but must follow generally accepted accounting

[6] Rule 14a-3(b)(1)-(9). Since the rule requires that the annual report "accompany or precede" the proxy materials, management must mail the annual report in a way that will "reasonably guarantee its timely arrival." Consequently an issuer's third-class mailing of its annual report four to five days in advance of the first-class mailing of its proxy materials violated the rule. Ash v. GAF Corp., 723 F. 2d 1090 (3d Cir. 1983).

[7] Rule 14a-3(b)(10).

[8] Rule 14a-3(c). This is without prejudice to the question whether Rule 10b-5 might apply.

[9] This requirement appears at the end of Form 10-K itself.

[10] §602(a)(2); see 1 Code 293-95.

[11] Rule 13a-13; Form 10-Q, Gen. Instr. A2. Separate publication of the results of operations for the fourth quarter is not required but is encouraged. Sec. Ex. Act Rel. 9559 (1972).

[12] Rule 13a-11; Form 8-K, Gen. Instr. B2. Registrants are "encouraged" to make voluntary reports of further events "promptly." Id., Gen. Instr. B2. And the Commission's staff also encourages the practice, voluntarily adopted by some companies, of announcing the availability of their current reports on request and in some cases distributing copies to their stockholders and other interested persons. Sec. Ex. Act Rel. 10,547, 3 SEC Dock. 210 (1973).

principles,[13] together with a management analysis of financial condition and results of operations.[14] That much of the report is not considered to be "filed" for purposes of civil liability under §18.[15] But, in addition, the report must include specified information with respect to legal proceedings, material changes in registered securities, defaults on senior securities, and matters submitted to a vote of security holders.

The extraordinary events that call for the filing of a *current* report are a change in control, the acquisition or disposition of a significant amount of assets, bankruptcy or receivership proceedings, a change of auditors, and a director's resignation because of a policy dispute.

When §13, together with the annual and current reporting rules and forms, was attacked in a criminal case as casting the defendants "into a hopelessly tangled rat maze," Judge Edelstein concluded: "The statutory and regulatory scheme is certainly more involved than the injunction, 'Thou shalt not steal.' But the conditions of society giving rise to the necessity for regulation are more involved than in the days of the patriarchs."[16]

2. IN CONNECTION WITH SECURITIES ACT REGISTRATION

Section 13 applied only to listed companies until the 1964 adoption of §12(g), although there are comparable reporting provisions with respect to registered holding companies and mutual service companies in the Holding Company Act[17] and the Investment Company Act specifically incorporates §13(a) of the Exchange Act among other reporting requirements.[18] We have already noticed the 1936 adoption of §15(d) of the Exchange Act.[19] That section survived in amended form the 1964 adoption of §12(g), because §15(d) is not limited, as §12(g) is, to classes of securities with 500 holders or

to equity securities. Since the original version continues to apply to

[13] Reg. S-X, §10-01.

[14] Reg. S-K, Item 11(b).

[15] Rule 13a-13(d).

[16] United States v. Guterma, 189 F. Supp. 265, 274 (S. D. N. Y. 1960). In the same case Judge Edelstein held (id. at 273) that a series of counts charging violations in connection with the filing of annual reports and current reports was not duplicitous under the "course of conduct" theory that the Supreme Court had expounded in United States v. Universal C. I. T. Credit Corp., 344 U. S. 218 (1952).

[17] §14; Rule 1(c); Form U5S.

[18] §30(a)-(e).

[19] See p. 410 supra.

pre-1964 registrants under the 1933 Act, our description of the section must start there.

In salient portion §15(d) as adopted in 1936 provided:

> Each registration statement hereafter filed pursuant to the Securities Act of 1933, as amended, shall contain an undertaking by the issuer[20] of the issue of securities to which the registration statement relates to file with the Commission, in accordance with such rules and regulations as the Commission may prescribe as necessary or appropriate in the public interest or for the protection of investors, such supplementary and periodic information, documents, and reports as may be required pursuant to section 13 of this title in respect of a security listed and registered on a national securities exchange, but such undertaking shall become operative only if the aggregate offering price of such issue of securities, plus the aggregate value of all other securities of such issuer of the same class (as hereinafter defined) outstanding, computed upon the basis of such offering price, amounts to $2,000,000 or more. The issuer shall file such supplementary and periodic information, documents, and reports pursuant to such undertaking, except that the duty to file shall be automatically suspended if and so long as * * * the aggregate value of all outstanding securities of the class to which such issue belongs is reduced to less than $1,000,000 computed upon the basis of the offering price of the last issue of securities of said class offered to the public. * * *

Section 15(d) was considerably simplified in the 1964 amendments so far as its prospective operation is concerned. Although the original version remains in force for purposes of determining the operative effect, under the old $2 million and $1 million tests, of undertakings contained in registration statements filed before August 20, 1964 (the "date of enactment" of the 1964 amendments), the reporting duty with respect to registration statements filed since that date flows directly from the section. Except for the old cases, the "awkward" undertakings under §15(d) are thus a thing of the past.[21]

[20] This is the only "undertaking" provision that has ever appeared in any of the SEC statutes, as distinct from the extrastatutory undertakings that are sometimes required under the 1933 Act. See pp. 140-42 supra. The sanction for enforcement of §15(d) undertakings is also unique. Congress concurrently amended the penal section of the statute to provide that, in lieu of any criminal penalty for failure to comply with an undertaking under §15(d), the issuer "shall forfeit to the United States the sum of $100" for every day the failure to comply continues. The forfeiture is "recoverable in a civil suit in the name of the United States." §32(b). The section has been a dead letter.

[21] S. Rep. No. 379, 88th Cong., 1st Sess. (1963) 69. A company with two or more registration statements effective under the 1933 Act, one or more filed

Regulation 15D generally parallels Regulation 13A. The §12(h) exemptive authority[22] has occasionally been used to exempt from §15(d) *ad hoc*. And the Commission's authority to enforce the statute by "mandamus"[23] (mandatory injunction under the Federal Rules of Civil Procedure) extends to §15(d).[24]

C. GETTING OUT ONCE YOU'RE IN

1. Voluntary Delisting

Although listing and registration are entirely discretionary with the issuer in the first instance, the issuer has no unqualified right to delist. Section 12(d) provides that "A security registered with a national securities exchange may be withdrawn or stricken from listing and registration in accordance with the rules of the exchange and, upon such terms as the Commission may deem necessary to impose for the protection of investors, upon application by the issuer or the exchange to the Commission."

All that the Commission's rules require is the filing of an application or notice in the event of something like a redemption or retirement.[1] And in other cases deregistration on application of an exchange (as distinct from the issuer) is granted automatically after a short time interval unless the Commission orders a hearing with respect to the possible imposition of terms.[2] Although the exchanges' status as self-regulatory organizations requires that an issuer that opposes delisting be given a hearing that satisfies the Fifth Amendment,[3] they also have "broad latitude * * * in making the critical judgment of when a company has failed to fulfill its responsibilities to such an extent that dealing on the Exchange in the

on or before August 20, 1964, and one or more since that date, must report under §15(d) if (and as long as) required *either* by any of the undertakings in the older registration statements *or* by the amended §15(d). Id. at 67-69.

[22] See p. 423 supra.

[23] §21(e); see SEC v. Union Corp. of America, 205 F. Supp. 518 (E. D. Mo. 1962), *aff'd per curiam* sub nom. Union Corp. of America v. SEC, 309 F. 2d 93 (8th Cir. 1962).

[24] The compliance order procedure in §15(c)(4) (infra p. 441) likewise extends to §15(d). For a discussion of some nice questions of interpretation of the scope of §15(d), see 5 Loss 2784-87.

C. 7C [1] Rule 12d2-2(a)-(b).

[2] Rule 12d2-2(c).

[3] Intercontinental Industries, Inc. v. American Stock Exchange, 452 F. 2d 935, 940-41 (5th Cir. 1971).

security is unwarranted."[4] Listing "is not a vested right which may not be terminated by changes in the importance of the company and its stock in the investment community."[5]

The New York Stock Exchange's delisting guidelines (which do not operate automatically) contain both numerical criteria and others: for example, a common stock might be delisted if the company issues a debt security with inadequate interest coverage and common stock equity of less than 25 percent.[6]

Application by exchanges normally raise no particular problem, because they have a selfish interest in retaining appropriate listings. Nor do issuers' applications when the securities have little value, or when they are to remain listed on another exchange. And initially, except for a few cases where the Commission dismissed factually misleading applications (without prejudice to their renewal) on the ground that security holders might have been misled into not appearing and objecting,[7] the only term the Commission imposed in granting the application was a brief delay. But, in order to counter what seemed to be a wave of delisting applications from regional exchanges that were motivated by a desire to avoid the disclosure impact of the statute, the Commission in 1944 imposed for the first time, as a "term" in granting the application under §12(d), the requirement of a shareholder vote; and, in view of the "grave questions" whether deregistration "would deprive the shareholders of substantial advantages without giving them or the [issuer] itself compensatory benefits,"[8] the Commission required a vote not only by a majority of shares but also by a majority of shareholders *per capita*. The fact that the issuer was a Massachusetts trust, whose shareholders had no vote at all under state law, emphasizes the supremacy of federal law here.[9]

[4] Id. at 940.

[5] Atlas Tack Corp. and Exchange Buffet Corp., 37 SEC 362, 365 (1956), *aff'd* sub nom. Exchange Buffet Corp. v. New York Stock Exchange, 244 F. 2d 507 (2d Cir. 1957), and Atlas Tack Corp. v. SEC, 246 F. 2d 311 (1st Cir. 1957).

[6] N. Y. Stock Ex. Listed Company Manual 801.00 to 809.00, esp. at 802.00.

[7] E. g., Automobile Finance Co., 9 SEC 571 (1941).

[8] Shawmut Assn., 15 SEC 1028, 1035, 1038 (1944), *aff'd* sub nom. Shawmut Assn. v. SEC, 146 F. 2d 791 (1st Cir. 1945), *motion to modify terms of vote denied*, 19 SEC 719 (1945). Most of the exchanges have their own voting requirements, which must be complied with under §12(d) before the issuer can apply for deregistration. But Boston, where Shawmut was listed, did not.

[9] 146 F. 2d at 795; cf. Phillips v. SEC, 153 F. 2d 27 (2d Cir. 1946), *cert. denied*, 328 U. S. 860 (plan under Holding Co. Act §11(e) need *not* provide for a stockholders' vote although it normally would be *required* by state law).

Cf. also United Funds, Inc. v. Carter Products, Inc., CCH Fed. Sec. L. Rep. ¶91,288 (Md. Cir. Ct. 1963), a non-SEC case of considerable significance as far as delisting is concerned. Carter had only one class of stock, with 3 million

This and two similar cases that followed — in all three of which management ultimately decided not to go to the shareholders — effectively checkmated the delisting trend.[10] And since the 1964

shares authorized and 2.6 million outstanding, of which Hoyt owned slightly more than 50 percent. In 1957 Hoyt and members of his family had made a public distribution of 500,000 shares, the prospectus stating that the company intended to apply for listing on the New York Stock Exchange. The plaintiffs, three investment companies, bought their shares in the public offering or afterwards. In 1962 the board recommended, and the shareholders after a solicitation under the SEC proxy rules approved, an amendment of the articles to create a new class of nonvoting common, of which 4 million shares were authorized, with an announcement that the board would declare a stock dividend share for share. Before that board meeting, the Exchange had advised that it would delist the common stock if the amendment became effective.

The court enjoined consummation of the proposed plan, holding (1) that the statement about listing, which had been made for the company's benefit as well as that of the seller's, had been meant to make the stock more attractive to investors and, under the usage and custom of the market, had been accepted as a promise that the listing would be continued in the absence of a proper corporate reason for discontinuance, and that the plaintiffs had relied upon that statement in buying, so that the promissory estoppel doctrine of §90 of the Restatement of Contracts applied without regard to absence of privity (an underwriter having intervened between the defendants and the plaintiffs); (2) that this contractual obligation of Carter applied equally to Hoyt in view of his implied representation and promise that through his control he would see that Carter complied with his stated intention; (3) that Hoyt had an additional obligation, apart from the law of contracts, based on the fiduciary duty of a majority holder toward the minority not to use his voting power for some ulterior purpose adverse to the interests of the company and its stockholders; (4) that the only real purpose was to enable the Hoyt family to diversify or reduce its large investment in Carter without reduction of its majority control; (5) that perpetuation of majority voting control in a single stockholder was not a proper corporate purpose; (6) that Exchange listing was a valuable corporate asset, so that delisting would cause special damage to minority stockholders, as contrasted with Hoyt and his family, by depriving them of the benefit of §§14 and 16, and hence injustice could be avoided only by the enforcement of the promise pursuant to §90; (7) that these conclusions with respect to the company's and Hoyt's contractual obligations applied also to the determination whether Hoyt had committed a breach of his fiduciary obligation; and (8) that, in conclusion, the proposed issuance of nonvoting common would violate the company's and Hoyt's contractual obligations, as well as Hoyt's duty as a fiduciary, and would substantially damage the plaintiffs, who had no adequate legal remedy.

On the significance of delisting, see also Gearhart Industries, Inc. v. Smith Int'l, Inc., 741 F. 2d 707, 725-26 (5th Cir. 1984); Norlin Corp. v. Rooney, Pace, Inc., 744 F. 2d 255, 268-69 (2d Cir. 1984).

[10] Torrington Co., 19 SEC 39 (1945); Suburban Electric Securities Co., 23 SEC 5, 11 (1946) (*two-thirds* majorities by shares and *per capita*). A few companies that did submit delisting proposals to their shareholders — either because of exchange rules or because they realized the Commission would insist on a vote — managed to obtain substantial majorities, in terms of shareholders as well as shares, notwithstanding their inclusion of a statement of the disadvantages of delisting in the proxy statements required to be sent to shareholders under the Commission's proxy rules. Apparently shareholders follow management here as in most matters. But one can only speculate on how a full and fair disclosure would have worked in the three cases in which the Commission wrote opin-

adoption of §12(g), of course, few companies would escape regulation by delisting.

2. Involuntary Delisting and Compliance Orders

The same statute that denies management the unqualified right to withdraw voluntarily from exchange listing and registration authorizes the Commission to impose involuntary delisting as one of the sanctions. Section 12(j) (successor to the pre-1975 §19(a)(2)) authorizes the Commission to suspend for not more than twelve months, or to revoke, registration on a finding (after notice and opportunity for hearing) that the issuer "has failed to comply with any provision of this" Act.

The remedy is draconian. When management fails to comply with some provision of the statute or the Commission's rules, it makes little sense to visit the sin on the innocent security holders by depriving them of an exchange market, not to mention the statutory advantages of registration. More than that, the remedy is unnecessary in view of the availability of a judicial action for mandatory injunction to require the filing of adequate reports.[11]

Indeed, the 1964 amendments added a new *administrative* remedy in §15(c)(4), which authorizes the Commission, if it finds (after notice and opportunity for hearing) that any person subject to §12, 13, 14, or 15(d) "has failed to comply with" any such provision "in any material respect," to publish its findings and order compliance, on whatever terms it specifies, by not only that person but also (as the section was amended by the Insider Trading Sanctions Act of 1984)[12] "any person who was a cause of the failure to comply due to an act or omission the person knew or should have known would contribute to the failure to comply."[13]

At first blush it seems odd to provide for an order that is not

---

ions — whether, to take one of them as an example, any substantial number of shareholders would have been sufficiently ill-advised, or sufficiently magnanimous, to vote for delisting in the face of disclosure that management thought the price of the shares on the exchange was too high and expected that the price would go down in the event of delisting! Id. at 5.

[11] SEC v. Atlas Tack Corp., 93 F. Supp. 111 (D. Mass. 1950).

[12] See p. 1008 infra.

[13] *Query* whether this language is broad enough to cover an accountant or lawyer or, in a proxy or tender offer context, a public relations firm or a proxy or tender offer soliciting firm.

The 1984 legislation also added §14. This includes not only the proxy provisions of §14(a)-(c) but also the tender offer provisions of §14(d)-(f), which were not enacted until 1968.

self-enforcing in the sense that failure to comply would subject any person either to contempt proceedings of any kind or to criminal prosecution. But §21(e) gives the District Courts jurisdiction to command compliance not only with the statute and rules but also with "orders thereunder." And §15(c)(4) serves the important function of permitting the Commission to resolve complex factual, accounting, and other technical questions in its own forum, just as it may use §12(j) with respect to listed securities.[14] That is to say, §15(c)(4) makes it possible for the Commission to appear in court as a lower tribunal whose quasi-judicial orders are being reviewed instead of as an ordinary plaintiff in an injunctive action. This, of course, is not unimportant. At the same time, there is no need to prove equity as there is when the Commission seeks injunctive relief.[15]

Most of the §15(c)(4) orders have been entered by consent,[16] just as §12(j) orders have normally resulted in compliance rather than delisting, presumably because most managements are not eager to lose their exchange market or, in any event, dislike the aroma of being *thrown* off.[17] In other words, the deregistration procedure, as applied to companies with securities actively traded, seemed to be developing into an administrative "means of correcting faulty statements."[18]

This makes it harder to understand a number of proceedings beginning in the late 1950s — proceedings not explicable in terms of getting rid of the "deadwood" in some exchanges' lists — that the Commission pursued to the bitter end of deregistration, emphasizing that use of the facilities of a national securities exchange was a "privilege involving important responsibilities," whose abuse violated "the integrity of the exchange market," and observing that regard must be had to the interests of potential investors as well as

[14]See S. Rep. No. 379, 88th Cong., 1st Sess. (1963) 66. Actually, although §15(c)(4) came into the law in 1964 in connection with §12(g), it is not limited to §12(g) registration and in fact it has been used against exchange-registered securities. Crescent Corp., 43 SEC 551 (1967).

[15]See generally McLucas and Romanowich, SEC Enforcement Proceedings Under Section 15(c)(4) of the Securities Exchange Act of 1934, 41 Bus. Law. 145 (1985). Of the 60 proceedings brought between 1975 and June 1985, some 46 are said to have concerned accounting and financial disclosures. Id. at 152. On the types of orders entered, see id. at 167-73.

[16]E. g., Hycel, Inc., Sec. Ex. Act Rel. 14,981, 15 SEC Dock. 315 (1978).

[17]See, e. g., Adolf Gobel, Inc., 35 SEC 535, 539 (1954). In the early years most orders under the former §19(a)(2), now §12(j), involved small companies with negligible assets and little or no investor interest, which had no business being on an exchange. 10 SEC Ann. Rep. 47 (1944).

[18]Associated Gas & Electric Co., 11 SEC 975, 1062 (1942).

existing stockholders.[19] Whatever their explanation, presumably those cases may be consigned to history in view of the Commission's statement in the hearings that led to the enactment of §15(c)(4):

> The sanction of delisting for failure to comply with the provisions of the act has been imposed only infrequently by the Commission because delisting would have the effect of relieving the issuer of the duty of complying with the disclosure provisions of the act and would deprive investors of an exchange market for the trading of their securities.[20]

3. TERMINATION OF §12(g) REGISTRATION

Under §12(g)(4) registration of any class of security is terminated ninety days after the issuer files a certification that the number of holders of record of that class of security is reduced below 300. But in 1982 the Commission by rule (concurrently with its increase of the statutory assets figure to $3 million) added an *alternative* deregistration standard in terms of falling below 500 holders if the issuer's total assets have not exceeded $3 million on the last day of each of the three most recent fiscal years.[21] The Commission may accelerate the ninety-day period. And, if it finds that the statutory certification is untrue, it is required (after notice and opportunity for hearing) to deny termination of registration, in which event termination is deferred pending final decision on the question of denial. Once a company becomes registered under §12(g), the mere fact that its assets fall below $3 million is irrelevant.

The first characteristic of this section that strikes the eye, in comparison with both §12(g)(1), under which the 500 test for initial registration is determined as of the last day of each fiscal year, and §15(d), under which the reporting requirement is suspended if there are fewer than 300 record holders of the particular class of securi-

[19] Great Sweet Grass Oils, Ltd., 37 SEC 683, 697-98 (1957), *aff'd per curiam* sub nom. Great Sweet Grass Oils, Ltd. v. SEC, 256 F. 2d 893 (D. C. Cir. 1958); see also Kroy Oils, Ltd., 37 SEC 683, 697-98 (1957).

[20] SEC Legislation, 1963, Hearings Before Subcom. of S. Com. on Banking & Currency on S. 1642, 88th Cong., 1st Sess. (1963) 402-03; 1 Investor Protection, Hearings Before Subcom. of House Com. on Intl. & For. Commerce on H. R. 6789, H. R. 6793, S. 1642, 88th Cong., 1st Sess. (1963) 183. *Query* SEC v. American Realty Trust, 429 F. Supp. 1148, 1178 (E. D. Va. 1977), *rev'd on other grounds*, 586 F. 2d 1001 (4th Cir. 1978), where the court (without discussion) cited §15(c)(4) as one reason for declining to order the filing of corrected annual reports.

[21] Rule 12g-4(a); Sec. Ex. Act Rel. 18,647, 25 SEC Dock. 49 (1982). This figure has not been increased to the current entry figure of $5 million.

ties at the *beginning* of a particular fiscal year, is that the statutory certification under §12(g)(4) may be filed at any time during the fiscal year. Furthermore, unless termination is denied on a finding that the certification with respect to the number of holders is untrue, the registration is *terminated*, not merely suspended like the reporting duty under §15(d).

Literally this would seem to be so even if the number of holders rises above 300 (or 500 under the rule's alternative) once more during the period between the filing of the certification and the effectiveness of the termination. But, of course, the security will have to be registered anew if there are as many as 500 holders (as well as $5 million of assets) by the end of the fiscal year during which registration was terminated or the end of any succeeding fiscal year. Moreover, the legislative history emphasizes that after termination of registration the Commission may still require the filing of reports with respect to periods while the security was registered.[22] Finally, because of the differences in the critical date for applying the statutory test of 300 stockholders under §15(d), it is quite possible that a reporting duty under §15(d) may for a short time survive the termination of §12(g) registration under the statutory test.

4. Suspension of §15(d) Reporting

Suspension of the reporting duty under §15(d) is now governed by a test in terms of 300 record holders of any class of securities to which the registration statement relates rather than the old $1 million test.[23] This is so with respect to all registration statements filed before or after August 20, 1964, except that (1) the old $1 million test continues to apply to those registration statements filed before that date as an *additional* "out" in accordance with the provisions of the undertaking,[24] and (2) in 1982 the Commission by rule added an *alternative* suspension standard comparable to the new alternative deregistration standard with respect to §12(g).[25]

[22] S. Rep. No. 379, 88th Cong., 1st Sess. (1963) 62; 1 Investor Protection, Hearings Before Subcom. of House Com. on Intl. & For. Commerce on H. R. 6789, H. R. 6793, S. 1642, 88th Cong., 1st Sess. (1963) 215.

[23] The duty to file is automatically suspended for any fiscal year (after the year in which the registration statement becomes effective) at whose beginning there are fewer than 300 record holders of each registered class.

[24] S. Rep. No. 479, 88th Cong., 1st Sess. (1963) 67.

[25] Rule 15d-6(a)(2); see p. 443 supra.

5. Suspension of Trading

Apart from the fact that the Commission's authority under §12(j) extends to the temporary suspension as well as the withdrawal of the *registration* of a security, there are certain circumstances under which either the exchange or the Commission may suspend *trading*. The difference between the two types of suspension is that a security that is suspended from trading retains its registered status.

a. Suspension of Trading by Exchange

The Act is silent on the point. But a rule of the Commission permits the exchanges to suspend trading in accordance with their own rules. It is required merely that the exchange promptly notify the Commission of the effective date of the suspension and of the restoration to trading, as well as the reasons for ordering or continuing the suspension. It goes without saying that any such suspension may not be continued to the point where it appears to the Commission that it is designed to evade the delisting provisions of §12(d).[26]

Brief exchange suspensions are frequent — several per trading day on the average — and typically they occur either when there is a substantial influx or imbalance of buy or sell orders or in the event of a news announcement considered to have significant implications for price.[27] Sometimes a suspension is initiated by a request from the issuer itself.[28]

Resumption of trading after a "news pending" interruption used to be delayed sometimes for several hours or more while awaiting a corporate announcement. But in January 1986 the New York Stock Exchange announced that, in the interest of providing a liquid market, it would normally reopen trading within approximately thirty

[26] Rule 12d2-1.

[27] See Hopewell and Schwartz, Temporary Trading Suspensions in Individual NYSE Securities, 33 J. Fin. 1355, 1372 (1978). See also, e. g., Wall St. J., May 3, 1966, p. 7, col. 2: Apparently because of an error by one or more specialists in establishing a post-merger opening price at about one-third what it should have been, the Exchange not only halted trading at 11:23 A.M. but also ordered all previous transactions cancelled, and trading did not reopen until the next day, after appointment of "a new temporary specialist."

[28] Cf. State Teachers Retirement Board v. Fluor Corp., 654 F. 2d 843 (2d Cir. 1981).

minutes, stating that no material news announcement had been released when that was the case.[29]

b. Suspension of Trading by SEC

In addition, an emergency suspension power is given the Commission directly by §12(k) (successor to the pre-1975 §19(a)(4)). That section authorizes the Commission, if in its opinion the public interest and the protection of investors so require,

> to suspend trading in any security (other than an exempted security) for a period not exceeding ten days, or with the approval of the President, summarily to suspend all trading on any national securities exchange or otherwise, in securities other than exempted securities, for a period not exceeding ninety days.

Although the New York Stock Exchange had to close for some four months in 1914 and again on fourteen scattered days in 1928 and November 1929 because of volume activity, as well as eleven days during the bank moratorium of March 1933,[30] it has not yet been necessary to invoke the emergency power to suspend all trading.

The story with respect to individual suspensions is very different. The Commission never used its summary power until 1944. The first order was entered on the day the company's president committed suicide, and it was followed by an investigation and public hearing with respect to the adequacy of the company's recent filings under both the 1933 and 1934 Acts.[31]

For a while the Commission regarded summary suspension as a highly extraordinary remedy, designed essentially for crisis situations. But over the years this authority developed into another disclosure device. After a warning by the Commission that it would consider temporary suspension of trading in securities of issuers that were delinquent in filing reports,[32] nearly 200 of the 279 suspension

[29] N. Y. Stock Ex. Special Membership Bul., Jan. 13, 1986; N. Y. Stock Ex. Listed Company Manual 202.07. On trading halts in connection with market rumors, see SEC, SEC Roundtable: Market Rumors and Trading Halts (1986) 7-10.

[30] N. Y. Stock Ex., Fact Book (1966) 37, 44-45. The Exchange closed without any action by the Commission twenty-eight minutes after President Kennedy's assassination on Friday, November 22, 1963, and most of the other exchanges followed. The weekend and a national day of mourning intervened before the resumption of trading the following Tuesday.

[31] Elastic Stop Nut Corp. of America, Sec. Ex. Act Rel. 3635 (1944).

[32] Sec. Ex. Act Rel. 10,214 (1973).

orders in fiscal 1974 fell in that category.[33] Between 1964 and November 1976 alone, the Commission suspended trading in 941 securities.[34] More than that:

(1) By 1959 the Chairman found it possible to say, by way of explaining a legislative proposal to insert a *pendente lite* suspension power in the then §19(a)(2), predecessor of today's §12(j), that "Lately, this grant of power [then §19(a)(4), now §12(k)] has been used to keep in effect a suspension of trading pending final disposition of delisting proceedings," although "No express authority for such action is contained in Section 19(a)(4).[35]

(2) The original §19(a)(4) covered only exchange trading. But from the beginning the Commission managed to extend its authority to the over-the-counter market by adopting an appropriate fraud-prevention rule under §15(c)(2)[36] and simply finding, whenever it suspended exchange trading, that the purpose of the suspension was "to prevent fraudulent, deceptive, or manipulative acts or practices." That practice was regularized by the 1964 amendments' adoption of an over-the-counter suspension authority in a §15(c)(5), which in the 1975 amendments was combined with the original §19(a)(4) into the present §12(k). The Senate committee said of the new §15(c)(5) in 1964:

> As under section 19(a)(4), the Commission could invoke this suspension power in those cases in which fraudulent or manipulative practices of the issuer or other persons have deprived the security of a fair and orderly market, or where some corporate event makes informed trading impossible and provides opportunities for the deception of investors. Trading would be resumed as soon as adequate disclosure and dissemination of the facts material to informed investment decision were achieved.[37]

In recent years the Commission has exercised its suspension authority primarily in the over-the-counter market, relying on the exchanges to act in their own markets.

(3) Another construction of the Commission ultimately led to a sharp defeat in the Supreme Court. Although the suspension power

[33] 40 SEC Ann. Rep. 77-78 (1974).

[34] Petition for cert., SEC v. Sloan, 436 U. S. 103 (1978).

[35] Gadsby, Current S. E. C. Legislative and Related Problems, 189 Com. & Fin. Chron. 1863, 1903 (1959). Sometimes the Commission also acted to prevent trading until it might obtain appropriate injunctive relief, usually against fraud or manipulation or an unregistered distribution in violation of §5 of the 1933 Act.

[36] Former Rule 15c2-2 as adopted in Sec. Ex. Act Rel. 3587 (1944). On §15(c)(2), see p. 707 infra.

[37] S. Rep. No. 379, 88th Cong., 1st Sess. (1963) 66.

has always been limited to ten days, the Commission from the beginning followed the policy of entering a series of orders until it considered that adequate information was available. Then, except when the suspension culminated in a delisting order or a final suspension order under former §19(a)(2) (now §12(j)), it timed the lifting of its suspension so that the public would have some opportunity to be informed of the facts before the resumption of exchange trading. It was perhaps not unreasonable for the Commission to conclude that a single ten-day suspension order did not exhaust its summary power with respect to the particular security if it made a new determination every ten days of the necessity of continuing the suspension under the statutory standards.[38] But the practice got out of hand. Consecutive orders were entered in 235 of the 941 suspensions between 1964 and November 1976.[39] And many lasted the better part of a year. The result was predictable: a sharp Supreme Court decision that "the Commission is not empowered to issue, based upon a single set of circumstances, a series of summary orders which would suspend trading beyond the initial 10-day period":[40]

> Even assuming that it is proper to suspend trading simply in order to enhance the information in the marketplace, there is nothing to indicate that the Commission cannot simply reveal to the investing public at the end of 10 days the reasons which it thought justified the initial summary suspension and then let the investors make their own judgments.
>
> * * * the Commission's argument amounts to little more than the notion that §12(k) *ought* to be a panacea for every type of problem which may beset the marketplace. This does not appear to be the first time the Commission has adopted this construction of the statute. As early as 1961 a recognized authority in this area of the law called attention to the fact that the Commission was gradually carrying over the summary suspension power granted in the predecessors of §12(k) into other areas of its statutory authority and using it as a *pendente lite* power to keep in effect a suspension of

[38] The Senate committee accepted this construction in connection with the 1964 amendments, while counseling "restraint" and action "with all diligence to develop the necessary facts in order that any suspension can be terminated as soon as possible." S. Rep. No. 379, 88th Cong., 1st Sess. (1963) 66-67.

[39] Petition for cert., SEC v. Sloan, 436 U. S. 103 (1978).

[40] Id. at 108. Presumably because there was no effective order to set aside, the Second Circuit's opinion concluded with a direction to the Commission — something extraordinary if not unique in its experience — "to discontinue forthwith its adoption and use of successive ten-day suspension orders * * *." Sloan v. SEC, 547 F. 2d 152, 158 (2d Cir. 1976), *cert. denied*, 434 U. S. 821.

trading pending final disposition of delisting proceedings. 2 L. Loss, Securities Regulation 854-855 (2d ed. 1961).

The author then questioned the propriety of extending the summary suspension power in that manner, id., at 854, and we think those same questions arise when the Commission argues that the summary suspension power should be available not only for the purposes clearly contemplated by §12(k), but also as a solution to virtually any other problem which might occur in the marketplace. We do not think §12(k) was meant to be such a cure-all. It provides the Commission with a powerful weapon for dealing with certain problems. But its time limit is clearly and precisely defined.[41]

The Commission is now very careful to find a different ground for a second order.[42] And it has continued the practice of cautioning broker-dealers who trade after termination of the suspension to consider all available information, including any subsequently issued by the company, and not to enter quotations in violation of the minimum information requirements of Rule 15c2-11.[43]

D. PROXIES

1. The Problem (Herein of Costs of Solicitation)

Corporate practice has come a long way from the common law's nonrecognition of the proxy device.[1] The widespread distribution of corporate securities, with the concomitant separation of ownership and management, puts the entire concept of the stockholders' meeting at the mercy of the proxy instrument. This makes the corporate proxy a tremendous force for good or evil in our eco-

[41] Id. at 157.

[42] See McDowell Enterprises, Inc., Sec. Ex. Act Rel. 16,682, 19 SEC Dock. 938 (1980) (no interval between the two suspension periods); Olympic Gas & Oil, Inc., Sec. Ex. Act Rel. 16,738, 19 SEC Dock. 1213 (1980) (three-week interval).

[43] Ibid.; on Rule 15c2-11, see p. 707 infra; on the Code's novel solution, see §§903(d), 1817(d)(1)(B).

C. 7D [1] Except for the universal statutory reversal of this common law rule, state proxy regulation is still a virtual void. On the historical development of proxy law generally, see Axe, Corporate Proxies, 41 Mich. L. Rev. 225 (1942). In NUI Corp. v. Kimmelman, 765 F. 2d 399 (3d Cir. 1985), the court reversed a holding that a statute that prohibited acquisition of control of a public utility through obtaining proxies without the approval of the Board of Public Utilities (a statute lobbied by the defendant in a proxy contest) was subject to the Supremacy Clause as interfering with the neutrality of the federal scheme; for there was no causal connection between the plaintiff's loss of the election and the statute. Cf. pp. 533-38 infra (state tender offer legislation).

nomic scheme. Unregulated, it is an open invitation to self-perpetuation and irresponsibility of management. Properly circumscribed, it may well turn out to be the salvation of the modern corporate system.

In the old days the stockholder typically received once a year a finely printed proxy card that he was urged to sign and return. Ordinarily the proxy authorized one or more persons to vote the stockholder's shares to elect directors and take any other action that was considered desirable. This was the sum and substance of the corporate owner's solemn right of suffrage. It was an accepted practice before the SEC proxy rules, as an eminent member of the corporate Bar has pointed out,

> to give the proxies power to approve, adopt, ratify and confirm all of the minutes of the board of directors since the date of the last annual meeting and all acts and transactions of the directors or officers taken pursuant thereto, although a detailed description of such minutes or action was customarily not included in the notice. Corporate practice varied as to whether at the meeting the presiding officer would merely state that the minute books were at hand and available for inspection by the stockholders prior to action upon the customary motion for approval and ratification, or whether a clerk would read the minutes aloud for several hours while the proxies designated by the stockholders sat around in bored silence. Some lawyers and managements regarded this so-called ratification by the stockholders of the acts of the management even though not set forth in detail in the notice of the meeting as being of great efficacy.[2]

Management had every advantage, moreover, if insurgent groups should have the temerity to wage a "proxy fight." It had the stockholders' lists. It stood to gain from stockholder inertia. And it had the overwhelming strategic advantage of access to the corporate treasury for the sometimes substantial costs of solicitation. As a British writer has put it, "it is easier to upset a Ministry than a Board of Directors, so long as a company remains a going concern."[3]

So far as the matter of costs is concerned, the relatively few cases in both the United States and England follow the general approach — an approach that had its inception before the day of campaign expenses running sometimes into seven figures — that reasonable expenditures in the interest of an intelligent exercise of the stockholders' judgment on the corporate policies to be followed

[2] Dean, Non-compliance with Proxy Regulations — Effect on Ability of Corporation to Hold Valid Meeting, 24 Corn. L. Q. 483, 490 (1939).

[3] H. Parkinson, Scientific Investment (1932) 134.

may properly be charged to the corporation, whereas expenditures that are solely in the interest of the directors' maintaining themselves in office may not. But, the courts say, even though the formal issue may be an election of directors, it does not necessarily follow that no question of corporate policy is involved.[4]

A 1955 New York case that might have clarified the general problem of solicitation costs produced an anticlimactic three-way split in the Court of Appeals without a majority opinion. The difficulty was that the plaintiff, in a derivative action to require reimbursement of the corporation, challenged various expenses — including professional proxy solicitation,[5] public relations counsel, entertainment, and chartered airplanes and limousines — as improper *per se,* conceding that they were "fair and reasonable" in amount.[6] Judge Froessel for himself, Chief Judge Conway, and Judge Burke followed the policy test and saw no need for the trial court to examine each of the challenged items in view of the concession as to their reasonableness. Judge Desmond concurred in the result only because the plaintiff, in failing to introduce any "evidentiary bases for a determination as to either lawfulness or reasonableness," had not made out a *prima facie* case; the record, as he saw it, did not present the "highly important" question whether it is lawful for a corporation to pay the expenses of a proxy contest, although he did go on to say that a heavy vote of stockholder ratification would not immunize "intrinsically unlawful" expenditures from attack.[7] Judges Van Voorhis, Dye, and Fuld dissented.

[4] E. g., Hall v. Trans-Lux Daylight Picture Screen Corp., 20 Del. Ch. 78, 171 Atl. 226 (Ch. 1934); Campbell v. Australian Mutual Provident Society, 99 L. T. 3 (P. C. 1908).

[5] For a description of one of the leading firms of proxy solicitors, Georgeson & Co., see The Old Touch, 30 New Yorker 24 (Mar. 27, 1954).

[6] Rosenfeld v. Fairchild Engine & Airplane Corp., 309 N. Y. 168, 172, 128 N. E. 2d 291, 292 (1955). Professor Eisenberg takes the view that, if the statutory principal of a limited term of office is to be respected, the directors must be regarded "as acting not as officeholders but as officeseekers"; that, in terms of fiduciary duties as distinct from authority, the rationale of the traditional test "loses sight of the crucial fact that toward the expiration of his term an incumbent director assumes the capacity of officeseeker as well as officeholder, thereby creating an irreconcilable conflict of interest"; that consequently the presence of a policy issue should not in itself justify board access to the corporate proxy machinery; and that a preferable approach would be a matching test under which management would not be allowed to use the corporate proxy machinery to wage a campaign that substantially exceeds that of the insurgents (so that, for example, management should be allowed to employ public relations counsel or proxy solicitors only if the insurgents do so or it is reasonably foreseeable that they will). Eisenberg, Access to the Corporate Proxy Machinery, 83 Harv. L. Rev. 1489, 1494-1502 (1970).

[7] 309 N. Y. at 174, 175, 176, 128 N. E. 2d at 293, 294, 295.

They thought it quite possible that the existence of a contest warranted the management "in circularizing the stockholders with more than ordinarily detailed information."[8] But they rejected the policy test as impracticable. In their view the plaintiff's concession of reasonableness did not relieve the defendants of the burden of going forward with evidence justifying their expenditures "once plaintiff had proved facts from which an inference of impropriety might be drawn."[9]

At any rate, even if the sauce goes to the ganders and *successful* insurgents may reimburse themselves from the treasury once the "outs" have become "ins" — a point on which the law is far from clear — there is still a great difference between the management's dipping into the corporate till at the outset and the insurgents' raising the funds themselves with a view to reimbursement *if* they win.

Altogether, a writer in the London Economist put it well when he said on Christmas Day in 1937:

> Company meeting procedure is a fitting topic for the festival of Christmas. Outwardly, it is a conglomeration of paradoxes whose superb unreason best suits the moment when paper hats are put on and logic leaves by the chimney. Approximately five thousand British public companies invite their shareholders, once every year, to a folk *moot.* If half the proprietors of even a moderate sized company attended, the chairman would have a larger audience than Signor Mussolini ever addressed from the Palazzo Venezia. No hall in England could possibly contain the 150,000 ordinary shareholders of Imperial Chemical Industries. But no secretary ever lost sleep on that account; for shareholders simply do not come trooping by battalions. Contrary to all theatrical canons, the best shows draw the thinnest houses. Only a passed dividend, a heavy loss or a reconstruction scheme can really pack the hall; a crowded meeting is usually an angry meeting. Shareholders who cannot attend, however, are given special facilities for voting in favour of the chairman's policy before they have heard his speech.[10]

2. The Regulatory Scheme

In §14(a) of the Exchange Act, Congress, abandoning the more specific standards of the original bills,[11] left the solicitation of prox-

[8] 309 N. Y. at 179, 128 N. E. 2d at 296.
[9] 309 N. Y. at 178, 128 N. E. 2d at 296.
[10] "The Chairman Said * * * ," 129 Economist 646 (1937).
[11] §13(a), S. 2693, H. R. 7852, 7855, 73d Cong., 2d Sess. (1934). See also

ies to SEC rulemaking under broad "public interest" standards. Neither the statute nor the rules are limited to ensuring full disclosure. The statutory language is considerably more general than it is under the specific disclosure philosophy of the 1933 Act. But the Commission's basic philosophy here has been one of disclosure. At any rate, it has analogized its rules to the disclosure requirements of the Securities Act — the rules *are* in a sense a little Securities Act — and has emphasized that its power under §14(a), unlike its authority under the Holding Company Act, does not extend to passing on the fairness or merits of any plan presented to security holders.[12] Within its authority, however, the Commission has recognized that the stockholder today can only address the assembled proxies which are lying at the head of the table."[13] Notwithstanding Professor Berle's characterization of the shareholders' meeting as "a kind of ancient, meaningless ritual like some of the ceremonies that go on with the mace in the House of Lords,"[14] the Commission has designed its rules so as to make the proxy device the closest practicable substitute for attendance at the meeting.

The Commission's approach to its quasi-legislative function under §14(a) has been an empirical one, but its philosophy has been consistent. The first rudimentary rules of 1935 set the basic three-way approach that has survived several general revisions and many amendments: (1) There must be a "brief description" of the matters to be considered, together with the action proposed to be taken by the holder of the proxy. (2) Nonmanagement solicitation must be facilitated. (3) A general fraud rule prohibits the making of any materially false or misleading statements.

As Regulation 14A stands, it consists of thirteen fairly detailed rules, together with a Schedule 14A that specifies in twenty-two items the information required in the proxy statement and a Schedule 14B that specifies the information to be included in the statement required to be filed for each "participant" in a *contested* election.[15]

Holding Co. Act §§12(e), 12(g)(3); Inv. Co. Act §§14(a), 20(a). With respect to §15(d) companies, see pp. 408-09 supra.

[12] Sec. Ex. Act Rel. 1350 (1937).

[13] Testimony of SEC Chairman Purcell in Securities and Exchange Commission Proxy Rules, Hearings Before House Com. on Intl. & For. Commerce on H. R. 1493, H. R. 1821, and H. R. 2019, 78th Cong., 1st Sess. (1943) 174.

[14] A. Berle, Economic Power and the Free Society (Fund for the Republic 1957) 7.

[15] In late 1986 the Commission updated and simplified the rules. One of the most significant changes applied the principles of the integrated disclosure system to proxy statements pursuant to a program undertaken in 1982. Sec. Ex.

In 1956 the Second Circuit upheld both the constitutionality of §14(a) and the validity of the rules "as applied either to management or to insurgent stockholder groups." The court rejected a defense that the section and rules were "unconstitutional as unauthorized delegations of legislative power and otherwise," the "otherwise" evidently referring to the argument of prior restraint under the First Amendment.[16]

3. Coverage, Definitions, and Exemptions

The rules use the term "proxy" as a generic reference to the statutory trilogy, "proxy or consent or authorization."[17] And, al-

---

Act Rel. 18,878, 25 SEC Dock. 924 (1982); Sec. Ex. Act Rel. 23,789, 36 SEC Dock. 1203 (1986).

See also Sec. Ex. Act Rel. 23,788, 36 SEC Dock. 1196 (1986), proposing a Rule 14a-14 with respect to notified or superseded documents.

For a comparative study of proxy regulation in the United States and Canada, see R. Crête, The Proxy System in Canadian Corporations (1986).

[16] SEC v. May, 229 F. 2d 123, 124 (2d Cir. 1956). In Curtis Publishing Co. v. Butts, 388 U. S. 130, 150 (1967), the Court stated: "Federal securities regulation, mail fraud statutes, and common-law actions for deceit and misrepresentation are only some examples of our understanding that the right to communicate information of public interest is not unconditional." Cf. also Donaldson v. Read Magazine, 333 U. S. 178, 191 (1948) (Court, in sustaining the postal fraud order statute, stated that the First Amendment did not inhibit legislation like the 1934 Act that is designed to prevent fraud or deception of the public with respect to such areas as securities). But cf. Lowe v. SEC, 472 U. S. 181 (1985), infra p. 678.

[17] Rule 14a-1. For a solicitation of consents pursuant to §228 of the Delaware General Corporation law — an almost universal type of provision under which stockholders' written consents may be substituted for a meeting — see Pabst Brewing Co. v. Jacobs, 549 F. Supp. 1068 (D. Del. 1982), *aff'd without published opinion,* 707 F. 2d 1392 (2d Cir. 1982), discussed in Quinn and Rudoff, Takeover on Consent: A View from the Inside, 12 Sec. Reg. L. J. 3 (1984). The consent device was not widely used until relatively recently, and it raises unique tactical considerations. See Finkelstein and Varallo, Action by Written Consent in Control Contests — Strategic and Legal Considerations, 14 Sec. Reg. L. J. 3 (1986).

In Greater Iowa Corp. v. McLendon, 378 F. 2d 783, 796-98 (8th Cir. 1967), the court, characterizing "consent" and "authorization" as "extremely broad words" that were "not limited by the word proxy" (id. at 796), held that a solicitation to enter into a voting trust was so analogous to a proxy solicitation as to be covered by the rules. Cf. also Reserve Life Ins. Co. v. Provident Life Ins. Co., 499 F. 2d 715, 725 (8th Cir. 1974). But voting trust certificates are "securities," and Rule 14a-2(a)(3) exempts any solicitation involved in the offer and sale of securities registered under the 1933 Act (except in connection with a merger-type transaction within Rule 145).

It does not follow that a plaintiff's demand on stockholders in a derivative action, whether made pursuant to Rule 23.1 of the Federal Rules of Civil Procedure or pursuant to a similar requirement of state law, is subject to §14(a). On the other hand, certain types of notices to stockholders in class actions may present a closer question, particularly if the stockholders are asked to contribute toward expenses.

though most proxy solicitations are directed to holders of *stock,* §14(a) applies to any kind of security as long as it is registered. Holders of debt securities are not uncommonly solicited to give consents or authorizations in connection with reorganizations or modifications of one kind or another.

The term "solicitation" is defined to include "(i) Any request for a proxy whether or not accompanied by or included in a form of proxy; (ii) Any request to execute or not to execute, or to revoke, a proxy; or (iii) The furnishing of a form of proxy or other communication to security holders under circumstances reasonably calculated to result in the procurement, withholding or revocation of a proxy."[18] Clause (2) makes it clear that the consent or authorization whose solicitation is subject to the rules "may take the form of failure to object or to dissent."[19] And Clause (3) makes it equally clear that the Commission's authority extends to any writings, whether or not they strictly solicit a proxy, that (in the words of Judge Learned Hand) "are part of a continuous plan ending in solicitation and which prepare the way for its success."[20] Analogy

[18] Rule 14a-1(j)(1).

[19] Ibid. See, e. g., Gaudiosi v. Mellon, 269 F. 2d 873 (3d Cir. 1959), *cert. denied,* 361 U. S. 902 (insurgent's wires to Swiss banks that were nominees for large blocks warning them not to vote for management without informing owners of contest and giving them an opportunity to determine how their stock should be voted were solicitations); Sargent v. Genesco, Inc., 492 F. 2d 750, 767-68 (5th Cir. 1974) (an "informational" letter sent to shareholders, whose vote was not required, to describe a proposed refinancing plan was a proxy solicitation on the theory that it encouraged shareholder inaction with respect to the plan).

[20] SEC v. Okin, 132 F. 2d 784, 786 (2d Cir. 1943); see also Studebaker Corp. v. Gittlin, 360 F. 2d 692, 696 (2d Cir. 1966); Suburban Electric Securities Co., 23 SEC 5, 11 n. 11 (1946) (attachment of blank proxy form to notice of meeting with statement that proxies were not being solicited); Data Probe Acquisition Corp. v. Datatab, Inc., 568 F. Supp. 1538, 1556 n. 7 (S. D. N. Y. 1983), *rev'd on other grounds,* 722 F. 2d 1 (2d Cir. 1983), *cert. denied,* 465 U. S. 1052 (letter allegedly intended as a statement of position under Rule 14e-2, infra p. 525, may serve as a proxy solicitation with respect to a competing merger agreement); Long Island Lighting Co. v. Barbash, 779 F. 2d 793 (2d Cir. 1985) (an advertisement urging that plaintiff utility company be converted to public ownership, and appearing while the company was engaged in a proxy fight with some of the proponents of conversion, *could* be a proxy solicitation, and the proxy rules *could* cover communications indirectly addressed to stockholders by appearing in publications of general circulation); but cf. Smallwood v. Pearl Brewing Co., 489 F. 2d 579, 600-01 (5th Cir. 1974), *cert. denied,* 419 U. S. 873.

Query whether the definition extends to a request for tenders when the tender offer is conditioned on the certificate's being deposited along with the proxy and there is no solicitation otherwise. See Rule 14a-2(a)(2). Suppose *X* makes a tender offer for the stock of *Y,* which resorts to the not uncommon stratagem of proposing a merger with *Z.* If *X* continues to press its bid after *Y* or *Z* begins to solicit proxies for the merger, will *X*'s literature amount to a request not to execute, or to revoke, proxies for the merger? Conversely, will *Y*'s literature

to the problem of "beating the gun" by issuing press releases and making speeches before the filing of a registration statement under the 1933 Act is not inapt.

At the same time, there are a number of activities that quite clearly do *not* amount to solicitation. One is the routine distribution of semiannual and quarterly reports, as well as "other communications containing information and comment concerning the business of the character normally sent to security holders by corporate management during the course of a fiscal year."[21] Again, the term "solicitation" as defined in the rules does not apply to the furnishing of a form of proxy to a security holder upon his unsolicited request, or to the performance of ministerial acts on behalf of a solicitor (such as the physical distribution of the proxy literature or management's required mailing of a security holder's communications).[22] And as a matter of administrative policy the Commission has never questioned the propriety of answering inquiries from the press as long as they have not been "planted" by the persons interested in obtaining proxies.[23]

Indeed, presumably because the cry of "free press" had been raised in connection with the Commission's consideration of the 1956 rule amendments, the Director of the Division of Corporation Finance took pains to emphasize in a letter to the General Manager of the American Newspaper Publishers Association that "The proxy rules do not control or regulate what a newspaper publishes."[24] Out of context this says too much. It seems quite clear, as the letter

---

directed nominally *against* X's offer be considered a solicitation of proxies *for* the merger? In Radol v. Thomas, 772 F. 2d 244, 253-55 (6th Cir. 1985), the court held that a two-step acquisition involving a tender offer and a subsequent merger did not require compliance with the proxy rules at the tender offer stage.

Query further the position of one who permits the use of his name in another's solicitation — as where a person is the proposed buyer of the company soliciting proxies for approval of the sale. Compare Yamamoto v. Omiya, 564 F. 2d 1319, 1323 (9th Cir. 1977), with SEC v. Falstaff Brewing Corp., 629 F. 2d 62, 68-69 (D. C. Cir. 1980). Moreover, there is always the aider and abettor doctrine, both criminal and civil. Cf. pp. 1016-23 infra.

[21] Sec. Ex. Act Rel. 5276 (1956).

[22] Rule 14a-1(j)(2). A party has not "solicited" proxies "absent some showing of active involvement by that person in the preparation or dissemination of the allegedly misleading materials." Caspary v. Louisiana Land & Exploration Co., 579 F. Supp. 1105 (S. D. N. Y. 1983), *aff'd per curiam*, 725 F. 2d 189 (2d Cir. 1984) (incumbent director fighting a proxy battle for reelection could not be held liable for a possibly misleading advertisement written and paid for by his father).

[23] For a collection of cases, see Cherno and Zelenty, Solicitations in Proxy Contests, 17 Rev. Sec. Reg. 965 (1984).

[24] See p. 454 n. 16 supra.

recognizes, that a publisher would be criminally liable (and probably subject to injunction as well) as an aider and abettor if he were willfully to publish, by way of advertisement, any soliciting material that was misleading or that had not been filed when it should have been. The same conclusion would follow in principle if it could be shown that a publisher, through a financial interest in the company being fought over or a business or personal relationship with persons in one camp or the other, had willfully lent himself to unlawful solicitation in the guise of news stories or editorial comment. And it almost goes without saying that the distribution of reprints or reproductions of news stories or editorial comment may subject their distributor to the proxy rules under certain circumstances.[25] But the specific message of the Director's letter is perfectly plain: The proxy rules do not apply to a newspaper's publication of news stories quoting the contending parties, or of editorial comments, or to a publisher's merely permitting reprints of either news or editorial matter from his newspaper.

The means by which the solicitation is made is of no consequence. Section 14(a) applies to any solicitation "by use of the mails or by any means or instrumentality of interstate commerce or of any facility of any national securities exchange or otherwise." This technique was obviously used in order to preserve the rest of the section if the words "or otherwise" should be stricken on constitutional grounds. The question, of course, is whether the dependence of the rules upon registration, which is based on use of the mails or interstate facilities, furnishes a sufficient constitutional foundation for regulating the ordinary word-of-mouth solicitation. Until the 1942 revision of the proxy rules the Commission played it safe and exempted solicitations not effected by use of the mails or interstate or exchange facilities. Since then, however, there has been no such exemption.[26] The constitutional question has not been raised, and it seems fair to conclude that there is no longer any substantial question (if there ever was).

There are nine exemptions apart from the exemptive authority in §12(h).[27] We have already noticed the treatment of certain foreign securities.[28] Three of the exemptions are designed to avoid duplication of regulation; they cover solicitations incident to a bankruptcy reorganization (the rule still refers to Chapter X of the old

[25] Sec. Ex. Act Rel. 5276 (1956).
[26] Sec. Ex. Act Rel. 3347 (1942).
[27] See p. 428 supra.
[28] Rule 3a12-3, supra p. 71. The other eight exemptions appear in Rule 14a-2.

Bankruptcy Act),[29] or an application or declaration under the Holding Company Act, or the registration of a security under the 1933 Act. There is also an exemption modeled on the "tombstone ad" provision of the Securities Act: This exemption permits any solicitation through the medium of a newspaper advertisement that informs security holders where they may obtain copies of a proxy statement, form of proxy, and any other soliciting material, and that does no more than name the issuer, state the reason for the advertisement, and identify the proposals to be acted upon by security holders.

Another exemption applies unconditionally to "Any solicitation by a person in respect of securities of which he is the beneficial owner." This permits the buyer to solicit and obtain the seller's proxy when the sale has occurred after the record date for determining the security holders who may vote at the meeting. It also reflects the practice whereby brokers or dealers carry securities in their own names as record owners for the accounts of their customers, usually for the reason that the securities are held in a margin account or that the "street name" facilitates transferability. In these cases the corporation, of course, recognizes only the record owner, and the exemption permits the beneficial owner to solicit a proxy from the broker if he wants to attend the meeting and vote himself or appoint his own substitute proxy.

Still another exemption contemplates the converse situation, where the broker or other record owner transmits the proxy literature to the customer (the beneficial owner) with a request for instructions. This exemption, which is subject to a number of conditions, complements the rules of the several exchanges with respect to their members' transmittal of proxy literature to their customers, the beneficial owners of the securities.[30]

The final two exemptions do not extend to Rule 14a-9, the general antifraud rule. One permits one person, under certain conditions, to furnish proxy voting advice to another with whom he has a business relationship. The other of these two exemptions covers *nonmanagement* solicitations of not more than ten persons. As in the case of the private offering exemption under the 1933 Act, the significant factor is the number of persons solicited rather than the number who actually give their proxies. And the maximum of

[29] See 11 U. S. C. §1125(d), supra p. 287, which in the bankruptcy context replaces §14(a) (together with §14(c), infra p. 490) as well as the old Chapter X exemption in Rule 14a-2(a)(4). See Poloron Products, Inc., 15 Sec. Reg. L. Rep. 796 (letter 1983).

[30] See pp. 486-90 infra.

ten solicitations is applicable not to each member of a given non-management group but to the group as a whole. Nor may one piece of soliciting material be sent to one group of ten persons and another piece to ten different persons. By the same token, the exemption does not permit the sending of follow-up material even to fewer than ten persons if more than ten were initially approached as part of the same solicitation campaign. On the other hand, the exemption applies to each of several opposition groups, not just the first. By way of rough analogy, the exception in the 1933 Act for preliminary negotiations with underwriters comes to mind. A beginning must be made somehow.

4. The Proxy Statement and Form of Proxy

a. The Filing Requirements

Like the Securities Act, the proxy rules contain, in effect, their "prospectus" requirement and their "registration" requirement, complete with waiting period. No solicitation subject to the rules may be made "unless each person solicited is concurrently furnished or has previously been furnished with a written proxy statement containing the information specified in Schedule 14A."[31] Preliminary copies of the proxy statement and form of proxy, as well as any other soliciting material to be distributed at the same time, must be filed with the Commission at least ten days before the final material is used.[32] In addition, copies of all the literature in definitive form must be mailed, concurrently with its distribution, to the Commission and each exchange on which *any* security of the issuer is listed.[33]

The filing of revised material does not start the ten-day period running again unless the material reflects "a fundamental change."[34] But, particularly when the staff asks for revised preliminary material, it may be prudent to wait for "clearance" of the revised material; for there is always the "fraud" rule to consider. The practice in such cases is to wait. But in late 1980 the staff stopped routinely examining all preliminary material, so that there is no point in waiting beyond the ten days unless the staff indicates during that period that there will be comments.

[31] Rule 14a-3(a).
[32] Rule 14a-6(a). The Commission may accelerate the period *ad hoc.*
[33] Rule 14a-6(c).
[34] Rule 14a-6, n. 1.

If the proxy statement is analogized to the Securities Act prospectus, the filing requirements so far mentioned already go further than they do under that Act in that supplemental soliciting material that is to accompany the proxy statement must be filed along with it, instead of being left merely to the fraud rule as supplementary selling literature is left to §17(a) of the Securities Act, the model for the proxy fraud rule. But the rules require also that preliminary copies of any "follow-up" material be filed at least two business days before its use and, if there is to be any personal solicitation, that copies of all written instructions or other materials furnished to the solicitors themselves be filed at least five days before they are so furnished.[35] *Advance* filing of "soliciting material in the form of speeches, press releases, and radio or television scripts" is optional.[36] It thus becomes once more a question of prudence whether to take advantage of the privilege not to file in advance and thus to assume the risk that the Commission will insist on the distribution of what it considers to be corrective material.

In the exceptional cases where a contest develops, the Commission's role is in part that of a mediator attempting to obtain the clarification or deletion of questionable statements. Partly to avoid wrangling by the opposing camps when there is a contest, partly because the preliminary material was often filed in incomplete form with a view to amendment during the ten-day waiting period, and partly because disclosure before examination would tend to defeat the very purpose of the rules and also make it harder to secure correction of misleading material, the preliminary material was not made public, whether in contested or uncontested cases, until some time after the passage of the Freedom of Information Act. But in 1976 the Commission amended the pertinent rule to make the preliminary material public (except as confidential treatment might be granted pursuant to that Act and the Commission's rule on confidential treatment)[37] when the definitive material is filed.[38]

b. The Form of Proxy

The form of proxy itself must indicate in bold-face type whether or not the proxy is solicited on behalf of the board.[39] The rules

[35] Rule 14a-6(b), (d). Again the Commission may accelerate.
[36] Rule 14a-6(h).
[37] Rule 24b-2. See p. 405 n. 1.
[38] Rule 14a-6(e), as amended in Sec. Ex. Act Rel. 13,030, 11 SEC Dock. 1075 (1976), renumbered 14a-6(f) by Sec. Ex. Act Rel. 23,789, 36 SEC Dock. 1203 (1986).
[39] Rule 14a-4(a)(1).

exclude proxies that confer authority to vote at more than one annual meeting.[40] And, because of the common law rule of agency whereby the latest proxy is the one that counts, the form of proxy must provide a specifically designated blank space for dating the proxy,[41] and there may be no solicitation of "(a) any undated or post-dated proxy; or (b) any proxy which provides that it shall be deemed to be dated as of any date subsequent to the date on which it is signed by the security holder."[42]

In addition, the form of proxy must "identify clearly and impartially each matter or group of related matters intended to be acted upon, whether proposed by the registrant or by security holders."[43] And it is required, in substance, that there be a box-type ballot: the form of proxy must permit the security holder to choose "between approval or disapproval of, or abstention with respect to, each matter or group of related matters referred to therein as intended to be acted upon, other than elections to office."[44] So far as elections are concerned, there is usually no point in merely voting *against* a slate; if a security holder does not like the nominees, he can either give his proxy to the opposition, if any, or simply not vote.

As amended in 1979, the rules require the proxy form to provide one of several designated methods for security holders to withhold authority to vote for each nominee.[45] In any event, authority may not be conferred to vote for any person to any office for which a *bona fide* nominee is not named in the proxy statement.

A proxy may confer discretionary authority only within specified limitations:[46] with respect to matters incident to the conduct of the meeting or unanticipated matters that may come before the meeting

[40] Rule 14a-4(d)(2).
[41] Rule 14a-4(a)(2).
[42] Rule 14a-10.
[43] Rule 14a-4(a)(3).
[44] Rule 14a-4(b)(1). Professor Gower, the preeminent British authority on company law, has made the intriguing suggestion that certain types of resolutions ought to be susceptible of being passed only on a postal ballot, with a prohibition against the dispatch of any voting papers until after a meeting had been held and the proposals discussed. "If this were done, meetings would produce a genuine debate instead of the present farce in which a handful of opposing orators harangue a complacent management secure in the knowledge that nothing that is said or left unsaid can affect the result." Gower, Investor Protection in the U. S. A., 15 Mod. L. Rev. 446, 452 (1952).
[45] Rule 14a-4(b)(2), as amended in Sec. Ex. Act Rel. 16,356, 18 SEC Dock. 997 (1979). A few states do count votes cast *against* a nominee in determining whether he has received the requisite number of votes. See Strong v. Fromm Laboratories, Inc., 273 Wis. 159, 77 N. W. 2d 389 (1956). In such cases issuers are instructed to provide a means for voting *against* a nominee in lieu of or in addition to providing a means for withholding authority to vote. Instr. 2 to Rule 14a-4(b).
[46] Rule 14a-4(c).

(including the election of a person to an office for which a *bona fide* nominee named in the proxy statement is unable to serve or "for good cause will not serve"); approval of the minutes of a prior meeting when approval does not amount to ratification of action taken at the meeting; any proposal properly omitted from the proxy statement under the "stockholder proposal" rule that will be examined later or the fraud rule;[47] or any matter as to which the security holder does not specify a choice, if the form of proxy states in bold type how it is intended to vote the shares in each such case.

This last privilege has been attacked on the ground that management is thus enabled to gain an unfair advantage from stockholder inertia, with the result that it is almost impossible for minority proposals to carry if all unmarked ballots are to be counted for the management. The rule has been defended, on the other hand, on the ground (1) that otherwise it would be impossible to obtain the favorable vote of a specified percentage of the outstanding shares as is required by state law for certain types of action, and (2) that it is necessary in order to avoid disfranchising stockholders who inadvertently fail to mark their ballots but who evidence a pro-management position by the very fact that they return proxies to the management.[48]

Along somewhat similar lines, the Commission thus far has also resisted a proposal that rings the bell of "corporate democracy" but would create difficult practical problems in the context of existing corporate laws and procedures — the proposal of a secret ballot. And in the 1948 amendments the Commission failed to adopt still another proposal — this time one that it had itself circulated for comment — to the effect that the form of proxy should contain no recommendation with respect to any matter to be acted upon.[49] At the same time, the Commission warned against "the use of the proxy form to electioneer for or against propositions to be voted upon." It stated that it would permit the form of proxy to include nothing beyond a simple statement of the management's favoring or opposing any of the propositions. Among the forbidden devices are arguments or recommendations, as well as "the use of arrows or any other visual device designed to direct the stockholder's attention to the place on the proxy for voting one way and away from the place for voting the contrary, and the switching of boxes in

[47] See pp. 468, 477 infra.
[48] See Dyer v. SEC, 266 F. 2d 33, 39 (8th Cir. 1959), *cert. denied*, 361 U. S. 835.
[49] Sec. Ex. Act Rel. 4114 (1948).

order to procure the result desired by the management."[50] There is no objection to the use of a distinctive color for either the form of proxy or the proxy statement. Indeed, this serves to reinforce the rule that requires the form of proxy to indicate in bold type whether or not it is solicited on behalf of the board.[51] But it does seem to be carrying a good thing a bit far for one side to print all of its materials on white paper with diagonal stripes of red and blue on the side, as a stockholders' committee did in a 1951 contest, and then to urge stockholders to vote "the red, white and blue proxy"![52]

Finally, either the proxy form or the proxy statement must provide "subject to reasonable specified conditions" that the shares will be voted and, when a choice is specified by means of a box-type ballot, that the specification will be honored.[53]

c. Content of the Proxy Statement

The first five items of Schedule 14A apply to proxy statements generally, regardless of the type of action proposed to be taken. They call for information with respect to (1) the revocability of the proxy, (2) dissenters' appraisal rights, (3) the identity of the persons on whose behalf the solicitation is being made and who are bearing its cost, (4) any "substantial interest" of the solicitors and other specified persons in the matters to be acted upon, and (5) the issuer's voting securities and their principal holders. Item 6 specifies in considerable detail the information required in connection with an election of directors; this is at least one of the matters involved in about 90 percent of all the proxy statements filed. And Items 8 through 22 relate to proposals of various other types: the selection of auditors; bonus, profit-sharing, and other remuneration plans; pension and retirement plans; options, warrants, or rights; the authorization or issuance of securities otherwise than for exchange; the modification or exchange of securities; mergers, consolidations, acquisitions of another issuer's securities, and similar matters; the acquisition or disposition of property; the restatement of accounts; reports of the management or of committees, as well as minutes of stockholders' meetings; matters submitted to a vote of security hold-

[50] Sec. Ex. Act Rel. 4185 (1948).

[51] Rule 14a-4(a)(1).

[52] E. Aranow and H. Einhorn, Proxy Contests for Corporate Control (2d ed. 1980) 175-76.

[53] Rule 14a-4(e); cf. Textron, Inc. v. American Woolen Co., 122 F. Supp. 305 (D. Mass. 1954).

ers without any requirement that they be so submitted; and charter and by-law amendments.

Financial statements are required by Item 15 only if action is to be taken with respect to the authorization, issuance, modification, or exchange of securities, or a merger, consolidation, acquisition, or similar matter. And we have already noticed the tie-in that the Commission has developed between proxy statements and reports to security holders.[54]

One item of Schedule 14A remains, and it clutches at the heartstrings. Item 7 (by reference to Regulation S-K) requires the proxy statement to include substantially the same information with respect to management remuneration as in Form 10-K, the basic annual report form: (1) the "cash compensation" (including bonuses and deferred compensation) paid by the registrant and its subsidiaries to each of the five highest paid "executive officers" receiving more than $60,000 as well as all executive officers as a group, (2) their pension, stock option, and other plans, and (3) their interest in "other compensation."[55]

It is the Commission's view that, on the one hand, information specifically required by Schedule 14A must be disclosed regardless of materiality, and that, on the other hand, when omitted information *is* material, the mere fact that it is not specifically called for by the schedule does not foreclose the possibility of a violation of Rule 14a-9, the "fraud" rule.[56]

In view of all this, it is not surprising to find a commentator concluding more than thirty years ago:

> In addition to requiring an adequate disclosure of pertinent information, the proxy rules are inevitably effecting, albeit in a negative way, the establishment of minimal standards of conduct for

[54] See pp. 434-35 supra.

[55] See Sec. Ex. Act Rel. 19,431, 27 SEC Dock. 1151 (1983). For a history of the remuneration disclosure requirement and the latest revision, see Sec. Ex. Act Rel. 19,431, 27 SEC Dock. 2 (1983).

[56] The lower courts are divided on the first proposition. The Commission's view is supported by Lewis v. Dansker, 357 F. Supp. 636 (S. D. N. Y. 1973), *modified on other grounds,* 68 F. R. D. 184 (S. D. N. Y. 1975); cf. Smillie v. Park Chemical Co., 466 F. Supp. 572, 577 (E. D. Mich. 1979) (such omissions "are material as a matter of law"). *Contra:* Kass v. Arden-Mayfair, Inc., 431 F. Supp. 1037, 1046 (C. D. Cal. 1977). On the second proposition, see Zell v. InterCapital Income Securities, Inc., 675 F. 2d 1041, 1044 (9th Cir. 1982). A proxy statement need not characterize disclosed information, nor should it set forth subjective motivations that underlie the votes of directors or controlling stockholders as long as all the material facts regarding their personal interests are disclosed. Mendell v. Greenberg, 612 F. Supp. 1543, 1550-51, 1553 (S. D. N. Y. 1985), *on later motion,* 113 F.R.D. 680 (S. D. N. Y. 1987).

> management; for there is little doubt that many transactions entered into by a company during the year preceding its annual meeting are undertaken by its management with one eye on the company's forthcoming proxy statement.[57]

Much more recently the Commission, under Chairman Williams, relied primarily on its proxy authority to explore the area of what has come to be called "corporate governance."[58] After soliciting written comments and then posing a series of questions,[59] the Commission in 1978 proposed a number of rules designed, among other things, to increase the information available to investors with respect to the structure, composition, and functioning of boards of directors.[60] And, after extensive public hearings, the Commission in stages adopted a number of these proposals,[61] including the present rule, which we have already noticed, that permits the withholding of authority to vote for individual candidates for the board.[62]

In publishing its 1978 proposals the Commission seemed to go beyond disclosure in expressing its belief that "it is desirable that [the audit, nominating, and compensation committees of the board], which have responsibilities in areas where disinterested oversight is most needed, normally be composed entirely of persons independent of management.[63] But in adopting certain of the 1978 proposals the Commission eschewed any purpose to prescribe the composition of the board or the mechanisms of corporate governance, adding: "While the federal securities laws generally embody a disclosure approach, it has long been recognized that disclosure may have beneficial effects on corporate behavior."[64] And the Commission backed off from the most controversial of its proposals, which would have required an identification of directors as "management director," "affiliated nonmanagement director," and "independent director." Instead it amended Regulation 14A to require a brief

[57] Caplin, Proxies, Annual Meetings and Corporate Democracy: The Lawyer's Role, 37 Va. L. Rev. 653, 667 (1951).

[58] See SEC, Div. of Corporate Finance, Staff Report on Corporate Accountability, S. Com. on Banking, Housing & Urban Affairs, 96th Cong., 2d Sess. (Com. Print 1980); Sec. Ex. Act Rel. 17,518, 21 SEC Dock. 1551 (1981) (statistical profile of boards of registered issuers).

[59] Sec. Ex. Act Rel. 13,482, 12 SEC Dock. 239 (1977); Sec. Ex. Act Rel. 13,901 (1977), 12 SEC Dock. 1630, with a staff-prepared summary of the comments in CCH Fed. Sec. L. Rep. ¶81,653 (1978).

[60] Sec. Ex. Act Rel. 14,970, 15 SEC Dock. 291 (1978).

[61] Sec. Ex. Act Rel. 15,384, 16 SEC Dock. 348 (1978); Sec. Ex. Act Rel. 16,356, 18 SEC Dock. 997 (1979).

[62] Rule 14a-4(b)(2), supra p. 461.

[63] Sec. Ex. Act Rel. 14,970, 15 SEC Dock. 291, 296-97 (1978).

[64] Sec. Ex. Act Rel. 15,384, 16 SEC Dock. 348, 350 (1978).

description of certain economic and personal relationships between each director and the issuer.[65] Indeed, it urged issuers *not* to "label" their directors until an adequate system of categorization might be developed.[66]

5. Contested Solicitations and Security Holder Proposals

A major problem in any system of proxy regulation is the equalization, so far as practicable, of the rights of management and of opposition security holders. The SEC rules attack this problem in three ways: (a) by assuring access to fellow security holders, (b) by imposing special requirements on all participants in *contested* elections, and (c) by opening the management's own proxy statement to legitimate proposals of security holders.[67]

a. Lists of Security Holders [Rule 14a-7]

The Commission's rules do not require the disclosure of security holders' lists. Rule 14a-7 neatly sidesteps all the state law problems of proper motive by giving management a choice. If it intends to make any solicitation subject to the proxy rules, it must either (1) furnish a list of the names and addresses of the holders of the particular security promptly on the written request of any security holder entitled to vote on the matter or (2) mail his proxy material for him, in either event at his expense.

At the same time, this rule is not preemptive: nothing in it derogates from whatever right the shareholder may have under state law to obtain a list.[68] In most cases, not surprisingly, the manage-

[65] See Sch. 14A, Item 6(b)(1); more generally, see Reg. S-K, Item 404.

[66] Sec. Ex. Act Rel. 15,384, 16 SEC Dock. 348, 355 (1978).

[67] See NUI Corp. v. Kimmelman, 593 F. Supp. 1457, 1469 (D. N. J. 1984), quoting the text, *rev'd on other grounds,* 765 F. 2d 399 (3d Cir. 1985). In Haas v. Wieboldt Stores, 725 F. 2d 71 (7th Cir. 1984), the court held that the plaintiff stated a claim for which relief could be granted when he alleged that the defendant corporation had changed the meeting date in order to make his proxy materials inaccurate.

[68] Alabama Gas Corp. v. Morrow, 265 Ala. 604, 93 So. 2d 515 (1957); Western Air Lines, Inc. v. Kerkorian, 254 A. 2d 240, 242 (Del. 1969); Smith v. Republic Pictures Corp., 144 N. Y. S. 2d 142 (Sup. Ct. 1955), *aff'd per curiam,* 286 App. Div. 1000, 145 N. Y. S. 2d 311 (1st Dept. 1955), *leave to appeal denied,* 286 App. Div. 1089, 147 N. Y. S. 2d 674 (1st Dept. 1955). Conceivably, however, the availability of the right to have management send out the dissident's

ment prefers the mailing alternative. And, by the same token the security holder would prefer a list, not only because he would just as soon not have the management see his material in advance so that it can get a reply into the hands of the security holders simultaneously, but also because he may want to do some personal solicitation, particularly of the larger holders.

b. Contested Elections [Rule 14a-11 and Sch. 14B]

Aside from the exemption for non-board solicitations of not more than ten persons and the fact that some of the items of information in Schedule 14A (such as management compensation) are by their nature inapplicable to opposition solicitations, the requirement of delivery of a proxy statement applies to all proxy solicitors equally, whether they are for or against the board. Indeed, although hotly contested proxy fights probably give the Commission as much cause as any of its variegated functions do to conclude that "A policeman's lot is not a happy one," it is perhaps a tribute to the Commission's impartial role of umpire that a few companies are said actually to have listed their securities on an exchange in anticipation of a proxy contest with the primary purpose of ensuring that the opposition's proxy material would be filed with the Commission and reviewed by its staff. Nevertheless, nonmanagement proxy statements are a rarity — though the period before the popularity of the tender offer as a form of corporate warfare saw a number of proxy battles that achieved epic proportions.

The result was the adoption in the mid-1950s of Rule 14a-11 and Schedule 14B. Rule 14a-11 applies only to contests for the election or removal of directors, not to contested solicitations on other matters. It requires every "participant" in such a solicitation (a term that is broadly defined except that it does not include the issuer itself) to file with the Commission, as well as each exchange on which *any* security of the issuer is listed, a statement containing the information specified by the schedule. And a summary of the greater part of the schedule must be incorporated in the proxy

literature will affect his right to a list as a matter of *state* law. See Sawers v. American Phenolic Corp., 404 Ill. 440, 452, 89 N. E. 2d 374, 381 (1949). *Contra:* Wood, Walker & Co. v. Evans, 300 F. Supp. 171 (D. Colo. 1969), *aff'd on other grounds,* 461 F. 2d 852 (10th Cir. 1972); Kerkorian v. Western Air Lines, Inc., 253 A. 2d 221, 225 (Del. Ch. 1969), *aff'd on other grounds* sub nom. Western Air Lines, Inc. v. Kerkorian, supra.

statement. Rule 14a-11 permits either side to solicit before furnishing a proxy statement, but only under specified conditions.

c. Security Holder Proposals [Rule 14a-8]

Security holders who are not willing or able to bear the expense of solicitation have another procedure available to them on voting matters not involving elections. Rule 14a-8 formalized the Commission's previous practice of occasionally suggesting that a management on notice of certain stockholder proposals set forth the proposals in its own proxy material, with provision for a yes-no vote, and state that the management intended to vote its stock and the proxies it received against the proposals unless otherwise directed. In salient part the rule provides:[69]

> (a) If any security holder of a registrant notifies the registrant of his intention to present a proposal for action at a forthcoming meeting of the registrant's security holders, the registrant shall set forth the proposal in its proxy statement and identify it in its form of proxy and provide means by which security holders can make the specification required by Rule 14a-4(b).[70] Notwithstanding the foregoing, the registrant shall not be required to include the proposal in its proxy statement or form of proxy unless the security holder (hereinafter, the "proponent") has complied with the requirements of this paragraph and paragraphs (b) and (c) of this Section:
>
> * * *
>
> (4) *Number of Proposals.* The proponent may submit no more than one proposal and an accompanying supporting statement for inclusion in the registrant's proxy materials for a meeting of security holders. * * *
>
> (b)(1) *Supporting Statement.* The registrant, at the request of the proponent, shall include in its proxy statement a statement of the proponent in support of the proposal, which statement shall not include the name and address of the proponent. A proposal and its supporting statement in the aggregate shall not exceed 500 words. * * *

[69] For a detailed treatment of the rule, with emphasis on its social responsibility implications, see H. Booth, The Shareholder Proposal Rule: SEC Interpretations and Lawsuits (Investor Responsibility Research Center 1987); see also Liebeler, A Proposal to Rescind the Shareholder Proposal Rule, 18 Ga. L. Rev. 425, 427-37 (1984).

[70] See p. 461, text at n. 42 supra.

(2) *Identification of Proponent.* The proxy statement shall also include either the name and address of the proponent and the number of shares of the voting security held by the proponent or a statement that such information will be furnished by the registrant to any person, orally or in writing as requested, promptly upon the receipt of any oral or written request therefor.

(c) The registrant may omit a proposal and any statement in support thereof from its proxy statement and form of proxy under any of the following circumstances:

(1) If the proposal is, under the laws of the registrant's domicile, not a proper subject for action by security holders;

(2) If the proposal, if implemented, would require the issuer to violate any state law or federal law of the United States, or any law of any foreign jurisdiction to which the issuer is subject, except that this provision shall not apply with respect to any foreign law compliance with which would be violative of any state law or federal law of the United States;

(3) If the proposal or the supporting statement is contrary to any of the Commission's proxy rules and regulations, including Rule 14a-9, which prohibits false or misleading statements in proxy soliciting materials;

(4) If the proposal relates to the redress of a personal claim grievance against the registrant or any other person, or if it is designed to result in a benefit to the proponent or to further a personal interest, which benefit or interest is not shared with the other security holders at large;

(5) If the proposal relates to operations which account for less than 5 percent of the registrant's total assets at the end of its most recent fiscal year, and for less than 5 percent of its net earnings and gross sales for its most recent fiscal year, and is not otherwise significantly related to the registrant's business;

(6) If the proposal deals with a matter that is beyond the registrant's power to effectuate;

(7) If the proposal deals with a matter relating to the conduct of the ordinary business operations of the registrant;

(8) If the proposal relates to an election to office;[71]

[71] See Dyer v. SEC, 289 F. 2d 242, 247 (8th Cir. 1961) (resolution to censure incumbent directors and declare them disqualified for reelection "was not one of attempt by by-law provision or otherwise to lay down general qualification standards for the office of director"); Rauchman v. Mobil Corp., 739 F. 2d 205 (8th Cir. 1984) (proposed by-law amendment that would prevent a citizen of an OPEC country from sitting on an oil company's board). For a history of the recurrent proposals over the years to permit stockholders to nominate directors in the issuer's proxy statement, see Hinsey, Nomination and Election of Corporate Directors, in Ray Garrett, Jr., Corporate and Securities Law Institute, Northwestern University School of Law, Standards for Regulating Corporate Internal Affairs (1981) 54.

(9) If the proposal is counter to a proposal to be submitted by the registrant at the meeting;

(10) If the proposal has been rendered moot;

(11) If the proposal is substantially duplicative of a proposal previously submitted to the issuer by another proponent, which proposal will be included in the registrant's proxy material for the meeting;

(12) If the proposal deals with substantially the same subject matter as a prior proposal submitted to security holders in the registrant's proxy statement and form of proxy relating to any annual or special meeting of security holders held within the preceding five calendar years, it may be omitted from the registrant's proxy materials relating to any meeting of security holders held within three calendar years after the latest such previous submission:

Provided, That —

> (i) If the proposal was submitted at only one meeting during such preceding period, it received less than five percent of the total number of votes cast in regard thereto; or
>
> (ii) If the proposal was submitted at only two meetings during such preceding period, it received at the time of its second submission less than 8 percent of the total number of votes cast in regard thereto; or
>
> (iii) If the proposal was submitted at three or more meetings during such preceding period, it received at the time of its latest submission less than 10 percent of the total number of votes cast in regard thereto; or

(13) If the proposal relates to specific amounts of cash or stock dividends.

(d) Whenever the registrant asserts, for any reason, that a proposal and any statement in support thereof received from a proponent may properly be omitted from its proxy statement and form of proxy, it shall file with the Commission, not later than 60 days prior to the date the preliminary copies of the proxy statement and form of proxy are filed pursuant to Rule 14a-6(a) or such shorter period prior to such date as the Commission or its staff may permit, six copies of the following items: (1) The proposal; (2) any statement in support thereof as received from the proponent; (3) a statement of the reasons why the registrant deems such omission to be proper in the particular case; and (4) where such reasons are based on matters of law, a supporting opinion of counsel. The registrant shall at the same time, if it has not already done so, notify the proponent of its intention to omit the proposal from its proxy statement and form of proxy and shall forward to him a copy of the statement of reasons why the registrant deems the omission of the proposal to be proper and a copy of such supporting opinion of counsel.

(e) If the registrant intends to include in the proxy statement a statement in opposition to a proposal received from a proponent, it shall, not later than ten calendar days prior to the date the preliminary copies of the proxy statement and form of proxy are filed pursuant to Rule 14a-6(a), or, in the event that the proposal must be revised to be includable, not later than five calendar days after receipt by the registrant of the revised proposal, promptly forward to the proponent a copy of the statement in opposition to the proposal.

In the event the proponent believes that the statement in opposition contains materially false or misleading statements within the meaning of Rule 14a-9 and the proponent wishes to bring this matter to the attention of the Commission, the proponent should promptly provide the staff with a letter setting forth the reasons for this view and at the same time promptly provide the registrant with a copy of such letter.

The rule does not permit the security holder himself to do any soliciting on the basis of his 500 words; if he wants to solicit, he must comply with the rules and furnish his own proxy statement. And the management is not limited to any maximum number of words in reply.

A recurrent question is what constitutes "a proper subject for action by security holders" within Rule 14a-8(c)(1). That rule was amended in 1954 to refer expressly to "the laws of the [registrant's] domicile." As to this the Commission probably has little choice under the statute. When the state law is clear that a particular matter is for the directors alone, that would seem to be decisive. If Congress had intended to give the Commission power to reallocate functions between the two corporate organs, so radical a federal intervention would presumably have been more clearly expressed. It would approach federal incorporation in all but name.

Even so, state law must not be allowed to frustrate federal regulation. In *SEC* v. *Transamerica Corp.*,[72] which arose at a time when the rule was silent with respect to the governing law, the registrant unsuccessfully opposed a proposal[73] to amend a by-law in order to eliminate the requirement that notice of any by-law amendment be contained in the notice of meeting. Management insisted, in the

[72] 163 F. 2d 511 (3d Cir. 1947), *cert. denied*, 332 U. S. 847.

[73] The proponent was one of the Gilbert brothers, Lewis and John, who have long played a unique role on the American corporate scene as full-time attenders at stockholder meetings. Lewis Gilbert has been called "the country's most celebrated minority stockholder." For a description of his corporate activities, see Bainbridge, The Talking Stockholder, 24 New Yorker 40 (Dec. 11, 1948), 33 (Dec. 18, 1948). See also p. 477 n. 93 infra.

words of the Third Circuit, that it was "entitled to use the notice requirement * * * as a biock or strainer to prevent any proposal to amend the by-laws, which it may deem unsuitable, from reaching a vote at an annual meeting of stockholders."[74] Applying Delaware law — but ignoring the possibility under that law of reserving authority over by-law amendments to the board under the statute or articles — the court considered that management's position "is overnice and is untenable,"[75] and therefore the proposal was a proper subject for stockholder action within the purview of the SEC rule.

That seems to be the holding, *as a matter of Delaware law.* But then, perhaps because the court realized that it did not have the last word in interpreting the state law, it added — whether by way of an alternative holding or *obiter* — a paragraph whose implications are not altogether clear:

> But assuming *arguendo* that this was not so, we think that we have demonstrated that Gilbert's proposals are within the reach of security-holder action were it not for the insulation afforded management by the notice provision of By-Law 47. If this minor provision may be employed as Transamerica seeks to employ it, it will serve to circumvent the intent of Congress in enacting the Securities Exchange Act of 1934. It was the intent of Congress to require fair opportunity for the operation of corporate suffrage. The control of great corporations by a very few persons was the abuse at which Congress struck in enacting Section 14(a). We entertain no doubt that Proxy Rule X-14A-7 [now 14a-8] represents a proper exercise of the authority conferred by Congress on the Commission under Section 14(a). This seems to us to end the matter. The power conferred upon the Commission by Congress cannot be frustrated by a corporate by-law.[76]

It does seem plain that, at the very least, the Commission's requirement cannot be evaded by means of procedural obstacles that are claimed to be lawful in the state of incorporation. On the other hand, given the *arguendo* assumption that By-Law 47 *would* be enforced "in all its strictness" by the Delaware courts, does not the court's "But" paragraph put the federal camel's nose in the Delaware tent? Or will the camel be allowed to proceed only to the extent that state law might otherwise be regarded as frustrating full implementation of the federal policy — which is to say, only as far as the Supremacy Clause requires? Presumably yes, especially in

[74] 163 F. 2d at 516.
[75] Id. at 518.
[76] Ibid.

view of the Commission's subsequent amendment of Rule 14a-8 to refer expressly to "the laws of the [registrant's] domicile."

This leaves the major question of determining the precise division of authority between stockholders and directors under the applicable state law. But the difficulty is that there is simply not very much state law to use as a guide in these matters. The typical corporation law provides, more or less as in the words of the Delaware statute, that "The business and affairs of every corporation organized under this chapter shall be managed by or under the direction of a board of directors, except as may be otherwise provided in this chapter or in its certificate of incorporation."[77] There may be an occasional provision that specifically requires board action on a given matter — for example, a provision giving the directors authority to amend or repeal by-laws when the certificate of incorporation so provides, as in Delaware, or giving them that authority unless the articles of incorporation provide otherwise, as in Illinois.[78] But, apart from these special provisions, a judicial decision barring shareholder action on a particular item of business as being contrary to the state's statutory scheme for the conduct of corporate affairs would be highly unusual. Consequently, with the Commission in the position in which the federal courts frequently find themselves under the *Erie* doctrine of guessing what the state courts would say, there is inevitably much room for the exercise of administrative discretion — and for resorting to the "burden of proof" (which the Commission puts on the company) and "benefit of the doubt" techniques in deciding individual cases.

Inevitably the Commission (normally its staff), while purporting to find and apply a generally nonexistent state law, has been building a "common law" of its own as to what constitutes a "proper subject" for shareholder action. It is a "common law" that undoubtedly would yield to a contrary decision of the particular state court. But it is perhaps equally likely that this body of "common law" will influence the state courts themselves when the rare cases come to them.[79] As for the handful of judicial opinions construing the rule, they must be read with care because of the rule's repeated amendment.

[77] Del. Gen. Corp. Law §141(a).

[78] Id., §109(a); Ill. Bus. Corp. Act of 1983, §2.25, 32 Smith-Hurd Ill. Ann. Stat. §2.25.

[79] See Medical Committee for Human Rights v. SEC, 432 F. 2d 659, 680 n. 29 (D. C. Cir. 1970), *vacated as moot*, 404 U. S. 403 (1972).

It is not easy to generalize in describing the rule's operation.[80] But a number of propositions seem reasonably clear apart from the relatively specific provisions like the exclusion by Rule 14a-8(c)(13) of proposals with respect to "specific amounts of cash or stock dividends":

(1) There is little question about proposals of the traditional type, such as independent auditors and stockholders' ratification of their selection, change of the place of stockholders' meeting, post-meeting reports, and cumulative voting.

(2) As the Commission went out of its way to observe in the note to Rule 14a-8(c)(1):

> Under certain states' laws, a proposal that mandates certain action by the issuer's board of directors may not be a proper subject matter for shareholder action, while a proposal recommending or requesting such action of the board may be proper under such state law.

(3) Form is important in the sense that an otherwise ineligible proposal may pass muster if cast in the form of an amendment of the articles or by-laws.

(4) In the 1970s — partly under the impact of the "ethical investor" movement centering around a number of churches and universities, joined more recently by a number of institutional investors and labor unions[81] — the traditional-type proposals gave way largely to the "social" or "ethical" type, such as disinvestment in tobacco stocks, withdrawal from South Africa, female and minority directors, consumer issues, and industrial safety.[82] In 1952 the rule was amended to exclude a proposal submitted "primarily for the purpose of promoting general economic, political, racial, religious, social or similar causes";[83] in 1972, in order to make the exclusion as objective as possible, that clause was amended to refer to any such matter "that is not significantly related to the business of the issuer

[80] For reviews of positions taken by the Commission's staff, see Warwick, Shareholder Proposals, in Practising Law Institute, Twelfth Annual Institute on Securities Regulation (1981) c. 5; Eisenberg, Current Applications of the Shareholder Proposal Rule, 15 Rev. Sec. Reg. 903 (1982); Cane, The Revered SEC Shareholder Proposal System: Attitudes, Results and Perspectives, 11 J. Corp. L. 57 (1985).

[81] See J. Simon, C. Powers, and J. Gunnemann, The Ethical Investor: Universities and Corporate Responsibility (1972); Blumberg, The Public's "Right to Know": Disclosure in the Major American Corporation, 28 Bus. Law. 1025, 1026-32 (1973); Feder, More Actions by Shareholders, N. Y. Times, Apr. 20, 1987, p. D1.

[82] See Schwartz The Public-Interest Proxy Contest: Reflections on Campaign GM, 69 Mich. L. Rev. 421 (1971).

[83] Sec. Ex. Act Rel. 4775 (1952).

or is not within the control of the issuer";[84] in 1976 the Commission substituted a Rule 14a-8(c)(5), which spoke simply of "a matter that is not significantly related to the issuer's business";[85] and the revision of 1983 introduced the present numerical test.[86]

In 1970, during the war in Vietnam and while this exclusion was still in its original form, the District of Columbia Circuit remanded to the Commission for more thorough consideration its exclusion of a proposal advanced by a committee of physicians that Dow Chemical Company stop making napalm. "We think," the court said, "that there is a clear and compelling distinction between management's legitimate need for freedom to apply its expertise in matters of day-to-day business judgment, and management's patently illegitimate claim of power to treat modern corporations with their vast resources as personal satrapies implementing personal political or moral predilections. It could scarcely be argued that management is more qualified or more entitled to make these kinds of decisions than the shareholders who are the true beneficial owners of the corporation; and it seems equally implausible that an application of the proxy rules which permitted such a result could be harmonized with the philosophy of corporate democracy which Congress embodied in section 14(a) of the Securities Exchange Act of 1934."[87]

(5) Because the National Environmental Policy Act of 1969 requires all federal agencies to consider that Act and administer their own statutes in accordance with that Act "to the fullest extent possible,"[88] environmental proposals must be considered as a distinct species of the "ethical" genus. But it is difficult to say how high a boost this legislation will give to environmental and ecological proposals that might otherwise be dubious under Rule 14a-8. It has been suggested that the Commission has not been as vigorous with

[84] Sec. Ex. Act Rel. 9784 (1972).

[85] Sec. Ex. Act Rel. 12,999, 10 SEC Dock. 1006 (1976). The previous reference to lack of control became the 14a-8(c)(6) exclusion of a matter "beyond the [registrant's] power to effectuate."

[86] Rule 15a-8(c)(5), supra p. 469. In Lovenheim v. Iroquois Brands, Ltd., 618 F. Supp. 554 (D. D. C. 1985), the court, construing the "significantly related" language as including ethical or social significance, required the inclusion of a proposal to study whether the forced feeding of geese by the defendant's French supplier of *paté de foie gras* (which constituted a minute part of its business) was inhumane.

[87] Medical Committee for Human Rights v. SEC, 432 F. 2d 659, 681 (D. C. Cir. 1970), *vacated as moot,* 404 U. S. 403. But cf. State *ex rel.* Pillsbury v. Honeywell, Inc., 291 Minn. 322, 191 N. W. 2d 406 (1971).

[88] 42 U. S. C. §4332; see Natural Resources Defense Council, Inc. v. SEC, 606 F. 2d 1031 (D. C. Cir. 1979).

respect to *disclosure* in the environmental area as it has been with respect to "questionable payments" abroad.[89]

Speaking of the stockholder proposal rule generally, and stating that "There is no way for us to write our rules with the surgical precision that preserves solely the values we desire, while foreclosing all possible abuse or inefficiency," and that "the Rule has effectively invested our staff with the power to decide complex issues of law, fact and policy without any real possibility of outside, objective appellate review," Commissioner Longstreth would have permitted the inclusion of *any* shareholder proposal except "those which state law would exclude (even after they have been expressed in the most acceptable language) and those which relate to the nomination of directors."[90] This later turned up as the last of three proposals on which the Commission sought comment in 1982 (on the assumption, on which it also invited the public's views, that shareholder access to the issuer's proxy statement should continue to be provided under the 1934 Act rather than being left to regulation under state law).[91] In the event, the Commission opted for the least radical of the three proposals, which simply revised the existing rule in a number of respects, the most significant being these:[92]

(1) The proponent must "be a record or beneficial owner of at least 1 percent or $1000 in market value of securities entitled to be voted at the meeting and have held such securities for at least one year."

(2) In order to avoid unnecessarily burdening the issuer with the cost of compliance with Rule 14a-8,

> Proponents who deliver written proxy materials to holders of more than 25 percent of a class of the registrant's outstanding securities entitled to vote with respect to the same meeting of security holders will be ineligible to use the provisions of Rule 14a-8 for the inclusion of a proposal in the registrant's proxy materials.

(3) The number of proposals that a proponent may submit in any one year was reduced from two to one.

(4) The proponent is entitled to a statement that, together with

[89] See Stevenson, The SEC and the New Disclosure, 62 Corn. L. Rev. 50 (1976); Sec. Act Rel. 5569, 6 SEC Dock. 257 (1975); Sec. Act Rel. 5627, 8 SEC Dock. 41 (1975); Sec. Act Rel. 5704, 9 SEC Dock. 540 (1976).

[90] Longstreth, The S. E. C. and Shareholder Proposals: Simplification in Regulation, CCH Fed. Sec. L. Rep. ¶83,067 at 84,707 (1981).

[91] Sec. Ex. Act Rel. 19,135, 26 SEC Dock. 494, 495 (1982).

[92] Sec. Ex. Act Rel. 20,091, 28 SEC Dock. 798 (1983). The third proposal would have permitted the issuer, with the approval of its security holders, to vary the procedures and to formulate eligibility criteria and bases for exclusion of proposals more or less restrictive than those set forth in the rule. Sec. Ex. Act Rel. 19,135, 26 SEC Dock. 494, 495 (1982).

the proposal itself, does not exceed 500 words. And the supporting statement must be included in the management's material at the proponent's request even though the management does not oppose the proposal.

(5) The registrant may, but need not, include the proponent's name and address in its proxy materials. If it chooses not to do so, it must indicate that it will provide that information on request.

Stockholder proposals generally are an area in which policy should negate a higgling approach. It is not too important that these proposals are not carried, or that disproportionate use is made of the rule by a few perennial proponents. The very opportunity to submit proposals, even of an advisory nature, affords a safety valve for stockholder expression at a price to management that would seem to be relatively slight. There is said to be "little doubt that the public interest shareholder proposal movement has affected corporate management, raised its consciousness about a number of ethical issues, and caused it to do some things it would not otherwise have done."[93] Moreover, if the rule is anachronistic in a day in which meetings are attended by "a few corporate officials and a heap of proxies,"[94] one should not underestimate its symbolic significance in an area in which no alternative philosophy has yet been developed for the classic theory of managerial responsibility to the owners of the business.[95]

6. FALSE OR MISLEADING STATEMENTS [RULE 14a-9]

a. General

Much as the registration and prospectus requirement of the Securities Act is complemented by a general fraud provision, the regulatory pattern built on the proxy statement is filled out by a rule

[93] Purcell, Management and the "Ethical" Investor, 57 Harv. Bus. Rev. 24, 30 (Sept.-Oct. 1979); see also Stevenson, The Corporation As a Political Institution, 8 Hofstra L. Rev. 39, 46-47 (1979). It is noteworthy that Transamerica Corporation, after strenuously contesting the Commission's ruling, adopted Gilbert's further proposals with respect to independent auditors and reports of meetings without submitting them to a stockholder vote. 14 SEC Ann. Rep. 54 (1948). Finally, at age 79, Gilbert won his first victory on January 30, 1987, when the shareholders of Chock-Full-O-Nuts Corporation backed his resolution to adopt the common practice of allowing stockholders to ratify management's choice of auditors. See Feder, More Actions by Shareholders, N. Y. Times, Apr. 20, 1987, p. D1, at D5. See also p. 471 n. 78 supra.

[94] Freeman, An Estimate of the Practical Consequences of the Stockholder's Proposal Rule, 34 U. Detroit L. J. 549, 554 (1957).

[95] But see Liebeler, A Proposal to Rescind the Shareholder Proposal Rule, 18 Ga. L. Rev. 425 (1984); Dent, SEC Rule 14a-8: A Study in Regulating Failure, 30 N. Y. L. S. L. Rev. 1 (1985).

now numbered 14a-9. This proxy "fraud" rule is the most elaborate formulation of any of the fraud provisions in that it not only combines the 1934 Act's prohibition of "false or misleading" statements (instead of the 1933 Act's narrower "untrue" statements) with the 1933 Act's express concern about omissions, but also introduces the concept of an omission to state any material fact "necessary to correct any statement in any earlier communication * * * which has become false or misleading."[96] And Rule 14a-9 is the portion of the proxy regulation that has most often been to court.

First of all, a note to Rule 14a-9 gives "some examples of what, depending upon particular facts and circumstances, may be misleading within the meaning of this rule":

> (a) Predictions as to specific future market values.[97]
>
> (b) Material which directly or indirectly impugns character, integrity or personal reputation, or directly or indirectly makes charges concerning improper, illegal or immoral conduct or associations, without factual foundation.[98]
>
> (c) Failure to so identify a proxy statement, form of proxy and other soliciting material as to clearly distinguish it from the soliciting material of any other person or persons soliciting for the same meeting or subject matter.
>
> (d) Claims made prior to a meeting regarding the results of a solicitation.

One side's omissions are not cured by the other side's disclosures.[99] Similarly, one's omissions are not automatically excused by his own disclosure in an earlier communication. "Perception of future events may take on a different cast as the future approaches,

[96]See Lebhor Friedman, Inc. v. Movielab, Inc., — F. Supp. — ,CCH Fed. Sec. L. Rep. ¶93,162 (S. D. N. Y. 1987). See also Rule 14a-11(c)(5); and see p. 464 n. 56 supra. This may require the postponement of a merger or the like if updating the proxy literature is impractical. See Gerstle v. Gamble-Skogmo, Inc., 478 F. 2d 1281, 1297 n. 15 (2d Cir. 1973). But in General Time Corp. v. Talley Industries, Inc., 403 F. 2d 159, 163 (2d Cir. 1968), *cert. denied,* 393 U. S. 1026, the court, assuming that Rule 14a-9 might be read as authorizing that type of relief, called it "strong medicine, especially when administered the very day of the stockholders' meeting," so that a correspondingly strong showing of materiality was required. Cf. p. 736 infra.

[97]Until the 1979 adoption of Rule 3b-6, the "safe harbor" rule for forward projections (see pp. 163-64 supra), Note (a) referred to "market value, earnings, or dividends."

[98]On the question, common to Rules 14a-7 and 14a-8, of liability for defamatory matter contained in security holders' material distributed by the company, see 2 Loss 913-15; 5 id. 2862-63.

[99]Kohn v. American Metal Climax, Inc., 458 F. 2d 255, 265 (3d Cir. 1972), *cert. denied,* 409 U. S. 874; Gladwin v. Medfield Corp., 540 F. 2d 1266, 1270 (5th Cir. 1976).

and, what is more important, later correspondence may act to bury facts previously disclosed."[100] This is not to say that previously disclosed facts may not be considered in the balance; "the adequacy of disclosure can be measured only by considering the total mix."[101]

In considering what is false or misleading there is some indication that a degree of freedom is permitted in proxy fights along the lines of the traditional concept of "puffing." In the analogous context of a contested tender offer Judge Friendly has cautioned that "Courts should tread lightly in imposing a duty of self-flagellation on officers with respect to matters that are known as well, or almost as well, to the target company; some issues concerning a contested tender offer can safely be left for the latter's riposte."[102] And he has also suggested that "the hurly-burly" of election contests might justify a less strict approach than something like a merger.[103] But the Second Circuit said earlier that it was not "the policy of Congress" to view stockholder's disputes "in the eyes of the law just as are political contests, with each side free to hurl charges with comparative unrestraint, the assumption being that the opposing side is then at liberty to refute and thus effectively deflate the 'campaign oratory' of its adversary."[104] To sum up in Judge Friendly's trenchant prose once more:

> While "corporations are not required to address their stockholders as if they were children in kindergarten," *Richland* v. *Crandall*, 262 F. Supp. 538, 554 (S. D. N. Y. 1967), it is not sufficient that overtones might have been picked up by the sensitive antennae of investment analysts.[105]

Counsel will know what rhetoric to employ on either side.

[100] Smallwood v. Pearl Brewing Co., 489 F. 2d 579, 605 (5th Cir. 1974), *cert. denied*, 419 U. S. 873.

[101] Id., 489 F. 2d at 606. But apparently no case has considered news accounts to be an adequate substitute for disclosure by the proxy solicitor. Bertoglio v. Texas Int'l Co., 488 F. Supp. 630, 643-44 (D. Del. 1980), *reargument or modification denied*, CCH Fed. Sec. L. Rep. ¶97,373 (D. Del. 1980).

[102] Missouri Portland Cement Co. v. Cargill, Inc., 498 F. 2d 851, 873 (2d Cir. 1974), *cert. denied*, 419 U. S. 883. On "puffing" in the sale of securities, see pp. 717-18 infra.

[103] Gerstle v. Gamble-Skogmo, Inc., 478 F. 2d 1281, 1300 n. 19 (2d Cir. 1973); see also Kennecott Copper Corp. v. Curtiss-Wright Corp., 584 F. 2d 1195, 1200 (2d Cir. 1978).

[104] SEC v. May, 229 F. 2d 123, 124 (2d Cir. 1956).

[105] Gerstle v. Gamble-Skogmo, Inc., 478 F. 2d 1281, 1297 (2d Cir. 1973); see also Gould v. American-Hawaiian Steamship Co., 535 F. 2d 761, 770-71 (3d Cir. 1976); Pavlidis v. New England Patriots Football Club, Inc., CCH Fed. Sec. L. Rep. ¶99,431 (D. Mass. 1983), *aff'd in part and vacated in part on other grounds*, 737 F. 2d 1227 (1st Cir. 1984); Goldman v. Belden, 754 F. 2d 1059, 1067 (2d Cir. 1985). In the tender offer context, see p. 528 infra.

It must also be borne in mind, apart from the jurisprudence on Rule 14a-9, that much of what is said in the later chapter on SEC fraud concepts generally is equally applicable here.[106] For example, the classic fact-opinion question that is commonly met in the field of fraud has arisen under the proxy rules — to result in a holding by the Second Circuit that the expression of a statement as an opinion does not preclude a violation when the opinion is groundless.[107]

For the rest, the great questions are (1) what is a "material" fact and (2) whether the rule requires proof of negligence or "scienter" or neither.

b. Materiality

The great case here is the Supreme Court's 1976 decision in *TSC Industries, Inc.* v. *Northway, Inc.*:[108]

> [In *Mills* v. *Electric Auto-Lite Co.*, 396 U. S. 375 (1970)] we attempted to clarify to some extent the elements of a private cause of action for violation of §14(a). In a suit challenging the sufficiency under §14(a) and Rule 14a-9 of a proxy statement soliciting votes in favor of a merger, we held that there was no need to demonstrate that the alleged defect in the proxy statement actually had a decisive effect on the voting. So long as the misstatement or omission was material, the causal relation between violation and injury is sufficiently established, we concluded, if "the proxy solicitation itself * * * was an essential link in the accomplishment of the transaction." 396 U. S., at 385. After *Mills*, then, the content given to the notion of materiality assumes heightened significance.
>
> The question of materiality, it is universally agreed, is an objective one, involving the significance of an omitted or misrepresented fact to a reasonable investor. Variations in the formulation of a general test of materiality occur in the articulation of just how significant a fact must be or, put another way, how certain it must be that the fact would affect a reasonable investor's judgment.
>
> The Court of Appeals in this case concluded that material facts include "all facts which a reasonable shareholder *might* consider important." 512 F. 2d, at 330 (emphasis added). This formulation of the test of materiality has been explicitly rejected by at least two courts as setting too low a threshold for the imposition of liability under Rule 14a-9. *Gerstle* v. *Gamble-Skogmo, Inc.*, 478 F. 2d 1281, 1301-1302 (C. A. 2 1973); *Smallwood* v. *Pearl Brewing Co.*, 489 F. 2d

[106] See c. 9A infra.
[107] SEC v. Okin, 137 F. 2d 862, 864 (2d Cir. 1943).
[108] 426 U. S. 438.

579, 603-604 (C. A. 5 1974). In these cases, panels of the Second and Fifth Circuits opted for the conventional tort test of materiality — whether a reasonable man *would* attach importance to the fact misrepresented or omitted in determining his course of action. See Restatement (Second) of Torts §538(2)(a) (Tent. Draft No. 10, Apr. 20, 1964). See also American Law Institute, Federal Securities Code §256(a) (Tent. Draft No. 2, 1973). * * *

In arriving at its broad definition of a material fact as one that a reasonable shareholder *might* consider important, the Court of Appeals in this case relied heavily upon language of this Court in *Mills* v. *Electric Auto-Lite Co.*, supra. That reliance was misplaced. The *Mills* Court did characterize a determination of materiality as at least "embod[ying] a conclusion that the defect was of such a character that it might have been considered important by a reasonable shareholder who was in the process of deciding how to vote." 396 U. S., at 384. But * * * [the] references to materiality were simply preliminary to our consideration of the sole question in the case — whether proof of the materiality of an omission from a proxy statement must be supplemented by a showing that the defect actually caused the outcome of the vote. It is clear, then, that *Mills* did not intend to foreclose further inquiry into the meaning of materiality under Rule 14a-9.

In formulating a standard of materiality under Rule 14a-9, we are guided, of course, by the recognition in *Borak* and *Mills* of the Rule's broad remedial purpose. * * *

We are aware, however, that the disclosure policy embodied in the proxy regulations is not without limit. See id., at 384. Some information is of such dubious significance that insistence on its disclosure may accomplish more harm than good. The potential liability for a Rule 14a-9 violation can be great indeed, and if the standard of materiality is unnecessarily low, not only may the corporation and its management be subjected to liability for insignificant omissions or misstatements, but also management's fear of exposing itself to substantial liability may cause it simply to bury the shareholders in an avalanche of trivial information — a result that is hardly conducive to informed decisionmaking. Precisely these dangers are presented, we think, by the definition of a material fact adopted by the Court of Appeals in this case — a fact which a reasonable shareholder *might* consider important. We agree with Judge Friendly, speaking for the Court of Appeals in *Gerstle*, that the "might" formulation is "too suggestive of mere possibility, however unlikely." 478 F. 2d, at 1302.

The general standard of materiality that we think best comports with the policies of Rule 14a-9 is as follows: An omitted fact is material if there is a substantial likelihood that a reasonable shareholder would consider it important in deciding how to vote. This standard is fully consistent with *Mills'* general description of materiality as a requirement that "the defect have a significant *propensity* to affect the voting process." It does not require proof of a substantial likelihood that disclosure of the omitted fact would have caused the reasonable investor to change his vote. What the standard does contemplate is a showing of a substantial likelihood that, under all the circumstances, the omitted fact would have assumed actual significance in the deliberations of the reasonable shareholder. Put another way, there must be a substantial likelihood that the disclosure of the omitted fact would have been viewed by the reasonable investor as having significantly altered the "total mix" of information made available.

The issue of materiality may be characterized as a mixed question of law and fact, involving as it does the application of a legal standard to a particular set of facts. * * * Only if the established omissions are "so obviously important to an investor, that reasonable minds cannot differ on the question of materiality" is the ultimate issue of materiality appropriately resolved "as a matter of law" by summary judgment. * * * In considering whether summary judgment on the issue is appropriate, we must bear in mind that the underlying objective facts, which will often be free from dispute, are merely the starting point for the ultimate determination of materiality. The determination requires delicate assessments of the inferences a "reasonable shareholder" would draw from a given set of facts and the significance of those inferences to him, and these assessments are peculiarly ones for the trier of fact. * * *

This definition of "material" has been followed (*mutatis mutandis*) in other SEC contexts.[109] This makes frequently for an interchangeability of precedent among Rule 14a-9, Rule 10b-5, and other SEC contexts in which materiality is at issue. And, of course, the factual variations are infinite. To take just a few recent holdings of a general nature:

(1) "The concept of full and fair disclosure under Rule 14a-9 cannot exclude an element of timeliness: not only the substance of the information but the timing of dissemination, its availability, must be considered."[110]

[109] Alton Box Board Co. v. Goldman, Sachs & Co., 560 F. 2d 916 (8th Cir. 1977) (Sec. Act §12(2)); Healey v. Catalyst Recovery of Pa., Inc., 616 F. 2d 641, 647 (3d Cir. 1980) (Rule 10b-5); SEC v. MacDonald, 699 F. 2d 47 (1st Cir. 1982) (same); Simpson v. Southeastern Investment Trust, 697 F. 2d 1257, 1259 (5th Cir. 1983) (court saw no appreciable distinction between Sec. Act §12(2) and Rule 10b-5); Flynn v. Bass Brothers Enterprises, Inc., 744 F. 2d 978, 985 (3d Cir. 1984) (Sec. Ex. Act §14(e)); SEC v. American Board of Trade, Inc., 751 F. 2d 529, 534 n. 4 (2d Cir. 1984), citing the text; Starkman v. Marathon Oil Co., 772 F. 2d 231 (6th Cir. 1985) (Rule 10b-5); Goss v. Clutch Exchange, Inc., 701 P. 2d 33, 35 n. 3 (Colo. 1985), citing the text (state equivalent of Sec. Act §12(2)).

[110] Woodward & Lothrop, Inc. v. Schnabel, 593 F. Supp. 1385, 1393 (D. D. C. 1984).

(2) "The fact that a proxy statement is drafted by insiders acting in their own interest does not change the standard of materiality. A fact does not become more material to the shareholder's decision because it is withheld by an insider, or because the insider might profit by withholding it."[111]

(3) However, "a self-dealing insider may have a 'heavier burden of disclosure' in the sense that he will find it more difficult to convince the court that he has met the requirements of §14(a)."[112]

(4) "Although it is clear that a court may base §14(a) liability on the fact that material information is disclosed piecemeal or buried in the footnotes to financial statements [citations omitted], it does not follow that such disclosures must be regarded as inadequate *per se.*"[113]

Finally, we have earlier considered the extent to which the 1933 Act requires disclosure of the integrity and ability of management.[114] That conundrum is further reflected here in the holdings that motive (for example, entrenchment of control) need not be disclosed[115] so long as the facts are adequately stated and the motive is not "manipulative or deceptive."[116]

[111] Pavlidis v. New England Patriots Football Club, 737 F. 2d 1227, 1231 (1st Cir. 1984).

[112] Ibid.

[113] Id. at 1232.

[114] See pp. 152-57 supra.

[115] Golub v. PPD Corp., 576 F. 2d 759, 765 (8th Cir. 1978); Biesenbach v. Guenther, 588 F. 2d 400, 402 (3d Cir. 1978); Rodman v. Grant Foundation, 608 F. 2d 64, 71 (2d Cir. 1979); District 65, UAW v. Harper & Row, Publishers, Inc., 576 F. Supp. 1468, 1486 (S. D. N. Y. 1983) (no duty to disclose motive, breach of fiduciary duty, or possible alternatives to management's proposals); Steinberg v. Pargas, Inc., CCH Fed. Sec. L. Rep. ¶91,979 at 90,878-79 (S. D. N. Y. 1985).

[116] Vaughn v. Teledyne, Inc., 628 F. 2d 1214, 1221 (9th Cir. 1980). In GAF Corp. v. Heyman, 724 F. 2d 727 (2d Cir. 1983), the court held that unadjudicated allegations of "breach of trust" made in a pending unrelated civil action against a director nominee by his sister were not material omissions from the nominee's proxy solicitations seeking election, since a reasonable shareholder would not "place much stock" in untested civil allegations not involving the company in question:

> Vast numbers of allegations arguably implicate a prospective director's "integrity and fitness." The ruling below, if left intact, would lead to a situation where proxy contestants, in order to minimize the risk of having an election set aside, would have to include in their solicitation materials descriptions, explanations, and denials regarding allegations in derivative actions, class actions, matrimonial disputes, and a host of other legal matters, all unrelated to the business of the subject corporation.

Id. at 743.

c. Scienter

none required

In *Gerstle* v. *Gamble-Skogmo, Inc.*,[117] where the plaintiffs in a class action claimed that the merger of their company into the defendant company had been procured by a false and misleading proxy statement, Judge Friendly wrote on the standard of culpability in damage actions for violation of Rule 14a-9:

> Judge Bartels held, 298 F. Supp. at 97, that "the basis for incorporating scienter into a Rule 10b-5 action does not exist in a Rule 14a-9 suit," and that "Negligence alone either in making a misrepresentation or in failing to disclose a material fact in connection with proxy solicitation is sufficient to warrant recovery." The Judge * * * [considered] that one strong ground for holding that Rule 10b-5 requires a showing of something more than negligence in an action for damages is that the statutory authority for the Rule, section 10(b) of the Securities Exchange Act, 15 U. S. C. §78j, is addressed to "any manipulative or deceptive device or contrivance," * * * whereas section 14(a) contains no such evil-sounding language.[118]
>
> We think there is much force in this. See *Gould* v. *American Hawaiian S. S. Co.,* 351 F. Supp. 853, 861-863 (D. Del. 1972); 5 Loss, Securities Regulation 2864-65 (2d ed. Supp. 1969). Although the language of Rule 14a-9(a) closely parallels that of Rule 10b-5, and neither says in so many words that scienter should be a requirement, one of the primary reasons that this court has held that this is required in a private action under Rule 10b-5 [citations omitted] is a concern that without some such requirement the Rule might be invalid as exceeding the Commission's authority under section 10(b) to regulate "manipulative or deceptive devices." See *SEC* v. *Texas Gulf Sulphur Co.*, 401 F. 2d [833] at 868 (Friendly, J., concurring); *Lanza* v. *Drexel & Co.*, 479 F. 2d [1277] at 1305; 3 Loss, supra, at 1766 (2d ed. 1962), 6 id. at 3883-85 (Supp. 1969). * * * We note also that while an open-ended reading of Rule 10b-5 would render the express civil liability provisions of the securities acts largely superfluous, and be inconsistent with the limitations Congress built into these sections, see *SEC* v. *Texas Gulf Sulphur Co.,* supra, 401 F. 2d [833] at 867-868; 3 Loss, supra, at 1785, a reading of Rule 14a-9 as imposing liability without scienter in a case like the present is completely compatible with the statutory scheme.
>
> Although this does not mean that scienter should never be required in an action under Rule 14a-9, a number of considerations

[117] 478 F. 2d 1281 (2d Cir. 1973).
[118] See p. 774 infra.

persuade us that it would be inappropriate to require plaintiffs to prove it in the circumstances of this case. First, many 10b-5 cases relate to statements issued by corporations, without legal obligation to do so, as a result of what the SEC has properly called "a commendable and growing recognition on the part of industry and the investment community of the importance of informing security holders and the public generally with respect to important business and financial developments." Securities Act Release No. 3844 (Oct. 8, 1957). Imposition of too liberal a standard with respect to culpability would deter this, particularly in light of the almost unlimited liability that may result. See *SEC* v. *Texas Gulf Sulphur Co.*, supra, 401 F. 2d at 867. Such considerations do not apply to a proxy statement required by the Proxy Rules, especially to one, like that in the present case, which serves many of the same functions as a registration statement, compare *Gould* v. *American Hawaiian S. S. Co.*, supra, 351 F. Supp. at 863 n. 12. Rather, a broad standard of culpability here will serve to reinforce the high duty of care owned by a controlling corporation to minority shareholders in the preparation of a proxy statement seeking their acquiescence in this sort of transaction, a consideration which is particularly relevant since liability in this case is limited to the stockholders whose proxies were solicited. * * *

Furthermore, the common law itself finds negligence sufficient for tort liability where a person supplies false information to another with the intent to influence a transaction in which he has a pecuniary interest. Restatement (Second) of Torts §552 (Tent. Draft No. 12, 1966); Prosser, Torts §107, at 706-09 (4th ed. 1971); *Gediman* v. *Anheuser Busch, Inc.*, 299 F. 2d 537, 543-546 (2 Cir. 1962). This is particularly so when the transaction redounded directly to the benefit of the defendant, in which case the common law would provide the remedies of rescission and restitution without proof of scienter. See Prosser, supra, §105, at 687-89; 3 Loss, supra, at 1626-27. It is unlikely that section 14(a) and Rule 14a-9 contemplated less.

We thus hold that in a case like this, where the plaintiffs represent the very class who were asked to approve a merger on the basis of a misleading proxy statement and are seeking compensation from the beneficiary who is responsible for the preparation of the statement, they are not required to establish any evil motive or even reckless disregard of the facts. Whether in situations other than that here presented "the liability of the corporation issuing a materially false or misleading proxy statement is virtually absolute, as under Section 11 of the 1933 Act with respect to a registration statement," Jennings & Marsh, Securities Regulation: Cases and Materials 1358 (3d ed. 1972), we leave to another day.

Later the Third Circuit applied the same negligence standard to outside directors that *Gerstle* had applied to the registrant.[119] But Judge Friendly had been careful to leave open the possibility of applying a scienter test in some circumstances. And the Sixth Circuit did so with respect to outside accountants.[120]

7. Securities Held in "Street" or "Nominee" Name [§14(b)]

A 1975 New York Stock Exchange survey reported that some 5 or 6 percent of all equity securities were held in "street" name (a phrase that refers to the form of nominee name that brokers use to register securities they hold for customers or for their own account) and something over 22 percent were held in "nominee" name (a phrase that refers to a partnership formed to act as record holder of securities held by institutional investors and financial intermediaries, mostly banks, for *their* customers or for their own account).[121] Whatever the reasons for this phenomenon — normally, so far as brokers are concerned, because the stock is held in margin accounts or because it is just more convenient for the customers — any split of the legal and beneficial ownership of shares creates a substantial problem when proxies are solicited, because management knows only the stockholders of record. And the problem has been exacerbated by the steps taken by the securities industry in the last decade and more to immobilize stock certificates in depositories in an attempt to cope with the burgeoning paperwork problem — a development that has greatly increased the proportion of shares held in the names of nominees in order to facilitate transfers among participants in a depository.[122]

[119] Gould v. American-Hawaiian Steamship Co., 535 F. 2d 761, 777-78 (3d Cir. 1976).

[120] Adams v. Standard Knitting Mills, Inc., 623 F. 2d 422 (6th Cir. 1980), *cert. denied*, 449 U. S. 1067. But in Fradkin v. Ernst, 571 F. Supp. 829, 843 (N. D. Ohio 1983), the court applied the negligence standard to the registrant and the corporate officials responsible for preparing the proxy statement.

Between the dates of *Gerstle* and *Adams*, the Third Circuit, in a case that involved only injunctive relief, said that, whatever might be the rule with respect to damages or rescission, "we have no hesitancy in recognizing that for prospective relief looking to the protection of the franchise the test for the purposes of Rule 14a-9 is the objective sufficiency of the disclosure." Ash v. LFE Corp., 525 F. 2d 215, 220 (3d Cir. 1975). But cf., under Rule 10b-5, Aaron v. SEC, 446 U. S. 680 (1980), infra p. 783.

[121] SEC, Div. of Corporate Finance, Staff Report on Corporate Accountability, S. Com. on Banking, Housing & Urban Affairs, 96th Cong., 2d Sess. (Com. Print 1980) 327-28.

[122] H. R. Rep. No. 92-1537 (1972) 5.

Congress specifically legislated for this problem in §14(b) to the extent of making it unlawful (as that section was amended in 1964) for an exchange member or a registered broker-dealer to give or withhold a proxy with respect to a registered security in contravention of the Commission's rules. But we have just noticed that banks' record ownership for the account of others exceeds that of brokers several times over. And, even within the scope of §14(b), the Commission, as of the time of the legislative studies leading to the 1975 amendments of the 1934 Act, had left the problem to the exchanges to handle.

The rules of the New York Stock Exchange[123] (and the rules of the other exchanges are more or less similar) require its member firms, upon the proxy solicitor's reimbursing them for out-of-pocket expenses, to transmit copies of all proxy material they receive to beneficial owners within the United States. Along with the proxy material, the member firm must transmit either (1) a request for voting instructions, together with a statement that it may give a proxy in its own discretion if no instructions are received within time periods specified by the rules, or (2) a signed proxy together with a letter informing the beneficial owner of the necessity for completing the proxy form and forwarding it to the proxy solicitor in order that the shares may be represented at the meeting. Except in compliance with these rules or at the direction of the beneficial owner, a member firm may not give a proxy. And in no event may it give a proxy without instructions if the signer of the proxy has knowledge of any contest or if the question is the authorization of a merger or consolidation "or any other matter which may affect substantially the rights or privileges of the stock." When a countersolicitation develops after a member firm has given a discretionary proxy in good faith, the question whether the proxy should be canceled is a matter that the Exchange leaves to each firm to decide for itself.

In general, these rules apply without regard to whether the particular security is subject to the SEC's proxy rules. But, if it is not, there are a number of other requirements: (1) If member firms or their employees solicit proxies (otherwise than by merely forwarding the solicitor's proxy material) or engage in specified other activities, a copy of Schedule B, which is equivalent to the SEC's Schedule 14B, must be filed with the Exchange. (2) Before a member or member firm or one of its employees solicits more

[123] N. Y. Stock Ex. Rules 450-60, CCH N. Y. Stock Ex. Guide ¶¶2450-60; see also CCH NASD Manual §4.

than ten security holders to sign a proxy or to vote or abstain from voting on any proposal in connection with a proxy contest, he must also file the information specified in Schedule A, which is equivalent to the SEC's Schedule 14A. (3) He may not even join with any other person in requesting more than ten security holders to sign a proxy, or to vote or abstain from voting on any proposal in connection with a proxy contest, unless the *other* person agrees to file Schedules A and B with the Exchange and to furnish a copy of the information contained in Schedule A (in substance, an SEC-type proxy statement) to each person solicited.

As part of the 1975 amendments Congress in §12(m) directed the Commission to study the problem and to determine (1) whether the practice of non-beneficial record ownership was consistent with the purposes of the 1934 Act and (2) "whether steps can be taken to facilitate communications between issuers and the beneficial owners of their securities while at the same time retaining the benefits of such practice." The Commission sent two reports to Congress.[124] And in 1977 it finally exercised its §14(b) authority to the extent of adopting Rule 14b-1 concurrently with its revision of Rule 14a-3(d).[125]

Under Rule 14a-3 as it now stands, a registrant that intends to solicit proxies may choose between alternate procedures for communicating with its beneficial holders, depending on whether it wants to communicate directly or is satisfied to communicate through the brokers or other record holders. Rule 14b-1 simply complements the registrant's obligation by requiring registered brokers and dealers to act accordingly.

The Commission expressed the view that the employment of an intermediary to compile and supply a list of beneficial owners would assure registrants that the lists would be compiled in a standardized manner and that their source would be kept confidential, in addition to making available economies of scale. The Ad Hoc Committee on Identification of Beneficial Owners that

[124] SEC, Preliminary Report on the Practice of Recording the Ownership of Securities in the Records of the Issuer in Other Than the Name of the Beneficial Owner of Such Securities (1975); SEC, Final Report on the Practice of Recording the Ownership of Securities in the Records of the Issuer in Other Than the Name of the Beneficial Owner of Such Securities (1976).

[125] Sec. Ex. Act Rel. 13,719, 12 SEC Dock. 1111 (1977); see also Advisory Committee on Shareholder Communications, Improving Communications Between Issuers and Beneficial Owners of Nominee Held Securities (1982); Sec. Ex. Act Rel. 19,291, 26 SEC Dock. 1150 (1982). Following these 1982 proposals, both rules were fine-tuned in 1983 and again in 1985. Sec. Ex. Act Rel. 20,021, 28 SEC Dock. 513 (1983); Sec. Ex. Act Rel. 22,533, 34 SEC Dock. 384 (1985).

had been appointed by the New York Stock Exchange selected for this purpose Election Corporation of America, which is governed in this function by a user board consisting of registrants, brokers, and other industry representatives. But there is no requirement that brokers employ that organization or any agent at all.[126]

The 1975 amendments also added §17A, which for the first time injected the Commission into the clearance and settlement process. Among other things, that section directs the Commission to "facilitate the establishment" of a national clearance and settlement system; requires the registration of clearing agencies and transfer agents[127] as self-regulatory organizations under specified standards and with certain obligations, including the disciplining of participants;[128] gives the Commission broad rulemaking authority with respect to the activities of registered clearing agencies and transfer agents; and goes so far as to direct the Commission to use its authority "to end the physical movement of securities certificates in connection with the settlement among brokers and dealers of transactions in securities." In 1979 the Commission used this rulemaking authority to adopt Rule 17Ad-8, which requires a registered clearing agency on request to provide to each issuer whose securities are held in the name of the clearing agency or its nominee a "securities position listing" of those participants in the clearing agency on whose behalf the agency holds the issuer's securities and the participants' respective positions in those securities as of a specified date.[129]

After nine more years Congress passed the Shareholder Communications Act of 1985, which amended §14(b), effective one year after its enactment in January 1986, to authorize the SEC to require bank and savings and loan nominees, as well as other nominees exercising fiduciary powers, to perform tasks with respect to the voting and distributions of proxies. The Commission may not require disclosure of the name of a beneficial owner in an

[126] Id. at 385-86, 388. In fact, virtually all brokers have contracted with an intermediary for this purpose. Sec. Ex. Act Rel. 23,847, 37 SEC Dock. 89, 96 (1986).

[127] The terms are defined in §§3(a)(23) and 3(a)(25).

[128] The term is defined in §3(a)(24).

[129] Sec. Ex. Act Rel. 16,443, 19 SEC Dock. 3 (1979). For a general description of the nominee practice, with recommendations, see Advisory Committee on Shareholder Communications, Improving Communications Between Issuers and Beneficial Owners of Nominee-Held Securities (1982). Apart from all this, certain 5 percent and 10 percent beneficial owners are required to file reports with the Commission under §§13(d), 13(g), and 16(a). See pp. 514-16, 542 infra.

account held by one of these nominees on the date of enactment unless the owner consents; but with respect to accounts opened *after* the date of enactment the Commission may require disclosure unless the customer objects. Rule 14b-2, which implements this legislation, parallels Rule 14b-1 to the extent possible.[130]

8. "Information Statements" When Proxies Are Not Solicited [§14(c)]

One of the defects of §14(a) was the ready means of avoidance by the simple device of not soliciting proxies — a particularly unfortunate practice because it may prevent the presence of a quorum and thus result in self-perpetuation of management. A number of exchanges began to require all listed companies to solicit proxies, to the point where the New York Stock Exchange in 1962 suspended trading in the one company that had defied all its efforts. But in the 1964 amendments, presumably because the new §12(g) would require the registration of a great many over-the-counter securities, Congress inserted §14(c). That section does not require solicitation but it does require substantially the same filings (in accordance with Commission rules) as if there *were* a solicitation.

Regulation 14C, which generally parallels Regulation 14A, requires the filing and transmittal of an "information statement." And the problem of *partial* solicitation is met by simply requiring that those holders that do not receive a proxy statement be given an information statement under Regulation 14C.[131]

When the information statement relates to an annual meeting at which directors are to be elected, there is a stockholders' report rule (14c-3(a)) that corresponds to Rule 14a-3(b). And there is a fraud rule (14c-6) that precisely parallels Rule 14a-9. On the other hand, there is no rule comparable to Rule 14a-7 with respect to security holder lists or the mailing of non-board literature by the issuer. And, aside from the requirement in Item 5 of Schedule 14C that an appropriate statement be made whenever any security holder entitled to vote has submitted a proposal with notice of his intention to present it for action at the meeting, there is nothing

[130] Sec. Ex. Act Rel. 23,847, 37 SEC Dock. 39 (1986). The principal difference between the practices of broker-dealers and banks in this area is that banks frequently deposit beneficial owners' securities with other banks for safekeeping. See id. at 91-92.

[131] Rule 14c-2.

in Schedule 14C comparable to the stockholder proposal rule (14a-8).

During fiscal 1977 (the last year for which there are published figures) the Commission received only 149 information statements as compared with 5832 proxy statements (of which 14 were non-board).[132] The relatively small number of information statements is accounted for by the number of small companies that do not hold annual meetings (notably some of the mining companies on the Salt Lake Stock Exchange) and those that have only debt securities registered (particularly public utility subsidiaries whose equity securities are owned by their parents). Moreover, the Commission has used its exemptive authority in §12(h) to issue a number of orders exempting from §14(c).

9. Enforcement of the Proxy Rules and Status of Action Taken by Means of Proxies Illegally Solicited[133]

In the overwhelming majority of cases the proxy literature is cleared, without question of formal enforcement, through the same process of examination and letter of comment that is used under the 1933 Act.[134] However, when management or a security holder is adamant in refusing to comply with the rules as the Commission construes them, there is no administrative procedure quite like the stop order proceeding under the 1933 Act. The Commission may investigate. It may use its statutory power to "publish information concerning * * * violations."[135] It may institute appropriate administrative proceedings of a disciplinary nature when the offender happens to be a registered broker-dealer or investment adviser or an exchange or NASD member or an associate of such a person, as it may when some other statutory provision or Commission rule has been violated.[136] It may even use a violation of §14(a) as a basis for delisting the security or it may ask the Attorney General

[132] 43 SEC Ann. Rep. 107 (1977).

[133] For convenience this section will not refer separately to §14(c).

[134] In 1978 the Commission announced that its staff normally would not review investment company proxy material that was limited to an uncontested election of directors, ratification of an auditor's selection, and continuation of an investment advisory contract. Inv. Co. Act Rel. 10,447, 15 SEC Dock. 1310 (1978).

[135] §21(a).

[136] Sec. Ex. Act §§15(b)(4)(D), 19(h)(2)(A)-(B), 19(h)(3); Inv. Adv. Act §§203(e)(4), 203(f).

to prosecute willful violations. And since the Insider Trading Sanctions Act or 1984 it may order compliance pursuant to §15(c)(4).[137] Presumably, however, the Commission's principal weapon will continue to be the statutory action for injunction.[138]

In the real world all these statutory sanctions have been dwarfed by the courts' implication of *private* actions for violation of the rules. We leave that development until the chapter on civil liability, in which we consider the implication of private actions generally. But the quantum of relief is relevant also to SEC injunctive actions. And there is no reason to believe that the relief that a court of equity may grant is any different in the two situations (except for the possibility of awarding damages to private plaintiffs). Consequently the scope of relief in litigation under the proxy rules generally will be explored at this point.

A literal reading of the court's injunctive power would justify restraining only continued or threatened *solicitation* in violation of the proxy rules, since it is the solicitation and not the use of the proxies that is unlawful. But the court's power does not stop there. Once the court's jurisdiction is properly invoked, it has all the inherent powers of a court of equity. Indeed, under §12(2) of the 1933 Act, which makes fraudulent sellers of securities liable to their buyers for rescission or damages, the Supreme Court early sustained a complaint for an accounting, appointment of a receiver, and an injunction *pendente lite.* Pointing out that §22(a) of the 1933 Act gave specified courts jurisdiction "of all suits in equity and actions at law brought to enforce any liability or duty created by" the Act (and as to this §27 of the 1934 Act is identical), the Court stated:

> The power *to enforce* implies the power to make effective the right of recovery afforded by the Act. And the power to make the right of recovery effective implies the power to utilize any of the procedures or actions normally available to the litigant according to the exigencies of the particular case. If petitioners' bill states a cause of action when tested by the customary rules governing suits

[137] See p. 441 supra. The Commission had previously used §15(c)(4) to reach §14(a) violations to the extent that Form 10-K either permitted or required the incorporation of material from the proxy statement by reference. Playboy Enterprises, Inc., Sec. Ex. Act Rel. 17,059, 10 SEC Dock. 916, 925 n. 9 (1980); Form 10-K, Gen. Instr. G(3). It had also obtained by consent the broad range of ancillary relief that has become commonplace in consent injunction cases (see p. 1006 infra). E. g., Hycel, Inc., Sec. Ex. Act Rel. 14,981, 15 SEC Dock. 315 (1978); Spartek, Inc., Sec. Ex. Act Rel. 15,567, 16 SEC Dock. 1094 (1979).

[138] §21(e).

> of such character, the Securities Act authorizes maintenance of the suit, providing the bill contains the allegations the Act requires. That it does not authorize the bill in so many words is no more significant than the fact that it does not in terms authorize execution to issue on a judgment recovered under Section 12(2).[139]

In Chafee prose, "As it is the function of a factory to produce goods, so it is the function of courts to produce justice, and they should feel free to use for that object all or any of the means which long custom and legislation have placed at their disposal."[140]

Accordingly, since equity will not suffer an offender to enjoy the fruits of his illegal action, the courts have enjoined the *use* of proxies obtained through illegal solicitation.[141] This is no more than equity has done quite apart from statute when proxies have been obtained by misrepresentation.[142] And this is where the Rubicon is crossed, in the sense that the statutory text with its reference to enjoining *violations* is left behind. For §14(a), as already noted, does not (in the criminal sense) prohibit the *use* of proxies illegally solicited. Thus, the difference between enjoining the use of the proxies in voting on something like a merger and enjoining consummation of the merger itself once the proxies have been voted is a difference of degree. Indeed, the Supreme Court, though cautioning that nothing in the statutory policy "requires the court to unscramble a corporate transaction merely because a violation occurred," recognized that "Possible forms of relief will include setting aside the merger * * *."[143] And that recognition logically applies to any *lesser* relief.[144]

Clearly the plaintiff will find it harder to arouse the chancellor's conscience as he proceeds from point *A* (injunction against further solicitation in literal violation of the rules) to *B* (injunction against use of the proxies for, say, the approval of a merger) to *C* (injunction against consummation of the merger) to *D* (putting Humpty to-

[139] Deckert v. Independence Shares Corp., 311 U. S. 282, 288 (1940).

[140] Chafee, Some Problems of Equity (1950) 148.

[141] E. g., Henwood v. SEC, 298 F. 2d 641 (9th Cir. 1962), *cert. denied*, 371 U. S. 814; Studebaker Corp. v. Gittlin, 360 F. 2d 692 (2d Cir. 1966).

[142] E g., Campbell v. Loew's, Inc., 36 Del. Ch. 563, 134 A. 2d 852 (Ch. 1957); Berendt v. Bethlehem Steel Corp., 108 N. J. Eq. 148, 151, 154 Atl. 321, 322 (Ch. 1931); Jackson v. Munster Bank, Ltd., 13 L. R. Ir. 118, 134, 137 (Ch. 1884).

[143] Mills v. Electric Auto-Lite Co., 396 U. S. 375, 386 (1970), infra p. 945.

[144] Yamamoto v. Omiya, 564 F. 2d 1319, 1323-24 (9th Cir. 1977). In Allyn Corp. v. Hartford National Corp., CCH Fed. Sec. L. Rep. ¶98,646 at 93,007 (D. Conn. 1982), the court enjoined the consummation of a merger until corrected proxy materials were made available.

gether again after consummation of the merger, which is to say in "legal English," restoration of the *status quo ante*). And no American case has yet gone the whole way.[145] For one thing, the further along the chain one gets, the more the court is likely to have to consider the rights of innocent third persons. But it is all a matter of judicial discretion, not jurisdiction. And, of course, state law can be only persuasive, not binding.[146] There is precedent in the antitrust divestiture cases.[147] And the Supreme Court has said: "In devising retrospective relief for violation of the proxy rules, the federal courts should consider the same factors that would govern the relief granted for any similar illegality or fraud. One important factor may be the fairness of the terms of the merger."[148] This includes the possibility of monetary relief.[149]

All this is not to say that every illegally solicited proxy is *ipso facto* invalid so as automatically to void the election or any other action taken by its use. Violation of the proxy rules should stand on the same footing as any other illegality or fraud that might induce a court under appropriate circumstances to invalidate a corporate election or to grant other equitable relief. Thus, a violation consisting of the distribution of the proxy statement on the ninth rather than the tenth day after filing, or the failure to file a piece of follow-up literature in advance, should presumably be insufficient to set aside the vote, whether or not it should suffice for equitable relief *before* the use of the proxies. On the other

[145]But see Fogler v. Norcan Oils, Ltd., 47 W. W. R. 257, 261, 43 D. L. R. 2d 508, 512 (Alta. 1964), *rev'd on other grounds* sub nom. Norcan Oils, Ltd. v. Fogler, 49 W. W. R. 321, 46 D. L. R. 2d 630 (Sup. Ct. Can. 1964), where approval of an amalgamation of two companies was set aside because the proxy statement had not disclosed sufficient information to enable shareholders "to judge of the fairness and propriety of the scheme." Cf. Wright v. Heiser Corp., 560 F. 2d 236, 252-54 (7th Cir. 1977), *cert. denied*, 434 U. S. 1066, *on remand*, 802 F. Supp. 503 (N. D. Ill. 1980), a 10b-5 case in which the court did unravel past transactions, including a charter amendment that increased the authorized number of common shares and a pledge.

[146]J. I. Case Co. v. Borak, 377 U. S. 426 (1964), infra p. 926.

[147]E. g., United States v. E. I. duPont de Nemours & Co., 366 U. S. 316, esp. at 328-31 (1961).

[148]Mills v. Electric Auto-Lite Co. 396 U.S. 375, 386 (1970), infra p. 945. But fairness does not *preclude* relief, because that would bypass the stockholders. Id. at 381.

[149]Id. at 388-89. In Gerstle v. Gamble-Skogmo, Inc., 478 F. 2d 1281 (2d Cir. 1973), the court affirmed a judgment for restitutional damages and an accounting with respect to a consummated merger. See also Ohio Drill & Tool Co. v. Johnson, 498 F. 2d 186, 192-93 (6th Cir. 1974); cf. Swanson v. American Consumer Industries, Inc., 475 F. 2d 516, 519-21 (7th Cir. 1973) (Rule 10b-5 in a merger context). The causation element in cases of this type is discussed in the civil liability chapter. See p. 955 infra.

hand, a proxy obtained by means of a material misstatement or an omission to state a material fact is quite a different animal.

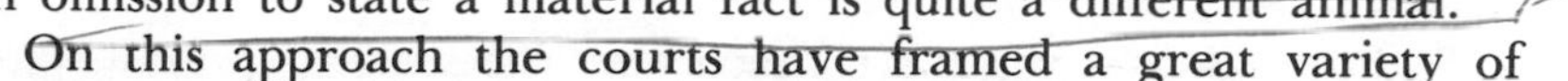

On this approach the courts have framed a great variety of judgments. For example:

In the *Transamerica* case, where the company was found to have illegally excluded stockholder proposals from its proxy statement, the court enjoined the meeting (except for the purpose of electing directors) and ordered resolicitation.[150]

Another court thought that merely requiring the defendant committee to distribute a correction was not the relief best calculated to protect investors, because it would place the onus on the stockholders to revoke their proxies, which they could always do anyway. Accordingly, the court declared the proxies void, adjourned the meeting to permit ample time for resolicitation, and spelled out precisely the corrective statement to be included in the next piece of proxy material.[151]

In a case in which a voting trust had been extended in violation of the proxy rules, the court rescinded the extension.[152]

Even in England, where circulars, though not required, normally do accompany the notice of meeting if anything other than ordinary business is to be transacted, Professor Gower says that "there have been many cases in which resolutions have been set aside on the ground that they were passed as a result of a 'tricky' circular."[153]

[150] SEC v. Transamerica Corp., 67 F. Supp. 326 (D. Del. 1946), *modified and aff'd,* 163 F. 2d 511 (3d Cir. 1947), *cert. denied,* 332 U. S. 847, supra p. 471.

[151] Central Foundry Co. v. Gondelman, 166 F. Supp. 429, 446 (S. D. N. Y. 1958), *modified* sub nom. SEC v. Central Foundry Co., 167 F. Supp. 821 (S. D. N. Y. 1958). The court ordered that the opposition committee clearly state in the next piece of proxy material, *inter alia,* that the resolicitation had become necessary because of the court's determination in an action brought by the company and the SEC that the committee's earlier solicitations, written and oral, had been materially misleading and unlawful. See also Gladwin v. Medfield Corp., CCH Fed. Sec. L. Rep. ¶95,013 (M. D. Fla. 1975), *modified on other grounds and aff'd,* 540 F. 2d 1266 (5th Cir. 1976), where management's violation of Rule 14a-9 resulted in the court's ordering a new election.

[152] Reserve Life Ins. Co. v. Provident Life Ins. Co., 499 F. 2d 715, 726 (8th Cir. 1974).

[153] L. Gower, The Principles of Modern Company Law (4th ed. 1979) 536; see, e. g., Baillie v. Oriental Telephone & Electric Co., Ltd., [1915] 1 Ch. 503 (C. A.) (suit to set aside ratification of directors' remuneration from subsidiary and to enjoin company and directors from acting thereon for failure to disclose very large amount of remuneration that had been received); Prudential Assurance Co., Ltd., v. Newman Industries, Ltd. (No. 2), [1980] 3 W. L. R. 543, [1980] 2 All E. R. 841 (Ch.).

And these cases are echoed in the United States altogether apart from the SEC laws.[154]

So far as election cases are concerned, the remedy in most states is an action in the nature of *quo warranto*, and the United States District Courts may not issue any of the extraordinary legal writs that are not ancillary to jurisdiction otherwise acquired.[155] But the fact that the federal courts have not reviewed elections as a matter of historic equity is simply a reflection of the fact that there was no need for them to do so until the proxy rules came along. There is no inherent reason why federal equity should not act when there is no adequate *federal* remedy at law.[156]

The courts must simply be careful, when enjoining the use of proxies unlawfully solicited, to avoid disfranchisement of the innocent security holders who gave the violator their proxies. The solution is to order a postponement of the meeting, unless it is postponed voluntarily, in order to permit resolicitation.[157] In its actions against insurgents, the Commission has sometimes made the company a nominal defendant solely for this purpose.[158] And, in private actions in which the company or members of the management are plaintiffs rather than defendants, the court can either condition the granting of relief on a postponement of the meeting or, for that matter, simply enjoin the plaintiff or plaintiffs, as parties to the litigation, from holding the meeting or taking a vote until there has been time for resolicitation.[159]

[154] See, e. g., Lonergan v. Crucible Steel Co. of America, 37 Ill. 2d 599, 229 N. E. 2d 536 (1967); cf. Smith v. Van Gorkom, 488 A. 2d 858, 890 (Del. 1985); see Annot., Misrepresentation in Proxy Solicitation — State Cases, 10 A. L. R. 4th 1287 (1983).

[155] United States *ex rel.* Wisconsin v. First Federal Savings & Loan Assn., 248 F. 2d 804 (7th Cir. 1957); cf. Marshall v. Crotty, 185 F. 2d 622, 626-27 (1st Cir. 1950) (mandamus). The only exception is the District Court for the District of Columbia, which inherited an independent jurisdiction with respect to the prerogative writs from the Maryland common law. Kendall v. United States *ex rel.* Stokes, 12 Pet. 524, 619-20 (U. S. 1838).

[156] Equity reviewed an election for violation of the proxy rules in Dillon v. Berg, 326 F. Supp. 1214 (D. Del. 1971), *aff'd per curiam,* 453 F. 2d 876 (3d Cir. 1971); see also Dillon v. Scotten, Dillon Co., 335 F. Supp. 566 (D. Del. 1972) (declaratory judgment); cf. Stern v. South Chester Tube Co., 390 U. S. 606 (1968), where the Court held that the federal courts had diversity jurisdiction to enforce a stockholder's right under state law to inspect the corporation's books and records even though the state statute labeled the right of action "mandamus."

[157] E. g., Kennecott Copper Corp. v. Curtiss-Wright Corp., 584 F. 2d 1195, 1202 (2d Cir. 1978).

[158] E. g., SEC v. May, 134 F. Supp. 247 (S. D. N. Y. 1955), *aff'd,* 229 F. 2d 123 (2d Cir. 1956).

[159] E. g., Central Foundry Co. v. Gondelman, 166 F. Supp. 429, 435, 447

So far as preliminary relief is concerned — and here proxy and tender offer cases should be to some extent interchangeable —the courts are torn by conflicting considerations. On the one hand, as Chief Justice Burger said *obiter* in a tender offer case, quoting Judge Friendly's observation, "in corporate control contests the stage of preliminary injunctive relief, rather than post-contest lawsuits, 'is the time when relief can best be given.' "[160] On the other hand, "Experience seems to demonstrate that * * * the grant of a temporary injunction on antitrust grounds at the behest of a target company spells the almost certain doom of a tender offer."[161] The chancellor inevitably has a great deal of discretion.[162]

E. TENDER OFFERS

1. The Phenomenon

Tender offers — with the possible exception of insider trading, much of which in fact occurs in connection with tender offers — have been the "hottest" subject in the legal world of corporations and securities for two decades. And unlike the proxy area, where there is virtually no state law, the law of tender offers is bifurcated. Looked at from the point of view of the target company, it is largely traditional state corporation law, mostly adaptation of the common law duties of loyalty and care (although we shall notice the states' attempts, only partly successful, to get into the act through legislation affecting both tender offeror and target). Looked at from the point of view of the tender offeror, the law is part of the SEC scheme of things, largely but not entirely disclosure-oriented.

There are two ways to capture control of an unwilling target company: proxy contests and tender offers. And, as the age of

(S. D. N. Y. 1958), *modified* sub nom. SEC v. Central Foundry Co., 167 F. Supp. 821 (S. D. N. Y. 1958).

[160] Piper v. Chris-Craft Industries, Inc., 430 U. S. 1, 42 (1977), infra p. 931.

[161] Missouri Portland Cement Co. v. Cargill, Inc., 498 F. 2d 851, 870 (2d Cir. 1974), *cert. denied*, 419 U. S. 833; Jewelcor, Inc. v. Pearlman, 397 F. Supp. 221, 252 (S. D. N. Y. 1975) (in a proxy contest shareholders will misinterpret a preliminary injunction as a determination of improper conduct); cf. Schmidt v. Enertec Corp., 598 F. Supp. 1528, 1530-31 (S. D. N. Y. 1984), a tender offer case under §14(e) (infra p. 527), where one of the court's reasons for denying a preliminary injunction requiring the tender offeror to make certain disclosures was that the offeror might well withdraw his offer.

[162] Compare, e. g., Sonesta Int'l Hotels Corp. v. Wellington Associates, 483 F. 2d 247, 250 (2d Cir. 1973) (§14(e) injunction *granted*), with Sherman v. Posner, 266 F. Supp. 871, 873-74 (S. D. N. Y. 1966) (§14(a)).

conglomerates got to the 1960s and the supply of willing merger partners seemed to be dwindling, expansionist-minded managements on this side of the ocean discovered that the British were onto a good thing in their preference for the "takeover bid" (or "tender offer," to use the more common American term) rather than the proxy fight: (1) It was relatively cheaper, because the expenditures, which could be very heavy in a proxy fight, resulted in an investment as well as purchase of control. (2) If the tender offer was not successful, the defeated offeror might well be able to dispose of its block of stock without any loss — sometimes, indeed, at a profit — to the target company or to some larger aggregate into which an initially worried and latterly relieved management of the target company had arranged a merger. (3) The offer could be limited to a fixed period of time, so that the resultant speed with which the entire transaction could take place was an influential factor both in preventing the build-up of management defenses and in curbing the expenses of acquiring control. (4) If the offeror was confident of management opposition and did not wish to seek its cooperation, secrecy enabled it to catch the management by surprise. (5) Until 1968, except for certain provisions of the Holding Company and Investment Company Acts that regulate purchases of securities,[1] there was no federal regulation remotely comparable to the proxy rules.

An *exchange* tender offer, of course, has always had to be registered under the 1933 Act, and the prospectus must contain detailed information about the business and financial condition of both companies involved — although the Commission has no choice, when the management of the target company is uncooperative, but to permit the offeror to use the most recent data filed with the Commission by the target. But in the case of a *cash* offer the only potential pitfalls before the 1968 legislation were the fraud and insider trading provisions of Rule 10b-5 and §16.

Gradually, therefore, the Americans have taken over the British takeover. Even the British term "takeover" is gradually replacing the American "tender offer," although technically the American term is broader because not all tender offers seek control.

Tender offers may be made for cash or for paper (typically convertible debentures) or both.[2] There were a number of reasons for preferring cash aside from avoidance of 1933 Act registration, with

C. 7E [1]Holding Co. Act §§9, 10; Inv. Co. Act §23(c); see 6 Loss 3647-49.

[2]See Austin, Tender Offer Update: 1978-1979, 15 Mergers & Acquisitions (No. 2) 13, 14 (1980).

an important saving in time as well as money: limitation of the interest deduction on "corporate acquisition indebtedness" by the Tax Reform Act of 1969;[3] accounting reforms that favored the "purchase" over the "pooling" method;[4] and the question of valuation of the offered paper, with its invitation to litigation. But perhaps the most significant development with respect to cash offers was their new "respectability." That is to say, the surprise takeover was labeled "unethical" as long as it was linked with the classic raid aimed at liquidation, but its image changed so that corporate managers and financial executives came to view it as a legitimate procedure for corporate expansion.[5]

This development has produced a great body of both law and practice,[6] which is nothing if not rich in financial slang:[7]

"Black knight": a third company that comes in to spoil an offer that the target *favors.*

"Crown jewels": the target's most valuable or significant assets.

"Front-end loaded" or "two-tier" deal: typically a cash offer that produces control, followed by acquisition of the remaining equity, generally at a lower price for debt or equity securities of the acquiring company.

[3] 83 Stat. 487. This made it harder for "mice" to acquire "elephants" by offering large amounts of their convertible debentures, on which the interest would be fully deductible, in exchange for common stock, on which the mouse would pay income tax only to the extent of 15 percent of dividends received from its elephant subsidiary.

[4] See Acctg. Ser. Rel. 130 (1972).

[5] Increasingly proxy fights are being waged in connection with tender offers, as part of strategies to spur change. See 18 Sec. Reg. L. Rep. 441 (1986), summarizing a study of proxy fights by the Investor Responsibility Research Center. See also, Lowenstein, Pruning Deadwood in Hostile Takeovers: A Proposal for Legislation, 83 Colum. L. Rev. 249, 264-65 (1983); Schwartz and Tillman, Proxy Contest Developments, 16 Rev. Sec. Reg. 789 (1983) (review of 1982-83 proxy season contests — some of them of a new variety, called by the writers the "bust-up proposal" proxy fight, that seeks to put pressure on the board to sell or liquidate the company). Some of these more recent proxy fights have involved shareholders' merely "precatory" requests (such as by-law amendments to require the appointment of a special board committee to make recommendations with respect to the appropriate management response to any proposed tender offer) as well as charter amendments designed to implement proposed "shark-repellent" efforts. See Bialkin, Proxy Contests, in Practising Law Institute, Fifteenth Annual Institute on Securities Regulation (1984) c. 12.

[6] See A. Fleischer, Tender Offers: Defenses, Responses, and Planning (1983); M. Steinberg (ed.), Tender Offers: Developments and Commentaries (1985) (a symposium); Jacobs, Hostile Tender Offers: A Selected Bibliography, 41 N. Y. C. B. A. 390 (1986); R. Ferrara, M. Brown, and J. Hall, Takeovers: Attack and Survival: A Strategist's Manual (1987).

[7] On the origins of some of this jargon, see Gilson, The Case Against Shark Repellent Amendments: Structural Limitations on the Enabling Concept, 34 Stan. L. Rev. 775, 775-76 (1982).

"Golden parachute": a special employment agreement with a target officer affording certain financial assurance in the event of a change in control.

"Greenmail": the purchase of a substantial block of target securities by an unfriendly suitor with the primary purpose of coercing the target into repurchasing the block at a premium.[8]

"Grey knight": a competing offeror no more acceptable to target management than the original offeror.

"Junk bonds": high yield, unrated, or low-rated bonds issued privately (largely to institutional investors eager for high returns) by a tender offeror to finance the offer; a device that, by avoiding dependence on traditional bankers, makes it possible for corporate "mice" to go after corporate "elephants."[9]

"Lock-up": in its broadest sense, any aspect of an acquisition transaction that is designed to preclude or at least inhibit or deter competition by any third party, for example, an option or agreement to buy unissued or treasury shares or the crown jewels, a merger agreement, an agreement for liquidated damages in the event of failure to consummate an acquisition, or an option or stock

[8] See SEC, Office of the Chief Economist, The Impact of Targeted Share Repurchases (Greenmail) on Stock Prices, CCH Fed. Sec. L. Rep. ¶83,713 (1984); Note, Greenmail: Targeted Stock Repurchases and the Management-Entrenchment Hypothesis, 98 Harv. L. Rev. 1045 (1985); Pin v. Texaco, Inc., 793 F. 2d 1448 (5th Cir. 1986), *rehearing en banc denied,* 797 F. 2d 977 (5th Cir. 1986).

It has been suggested that the "greenmailer" might be liable both (1) as aider and abettor of the target directors' breach of their fiduciary duty to the shareholders, and (2) as having committed a breach of his own fiduciary duty to the target's shareholders that he undertook and then abandoned. Heckmann v. Ahmanson, 168 Cal. App. 3d 119 (1985). But see Macey and McChesney, A Theoretical Analysis of Corporate Greenmail, 95 Yale L. J. 13, 16 (1985), where it is argued that "there is insufficient reason (theoretical or empirical) for any change in the law." In BFGoodrich Co., Sec. Ex. Act Rel. 22,792, 34 SEC Dock. 1263 (1986), the Commission found deficiencies in the company's annual report and proxy statement because of misstatements and omissions with respect to greenmail payment.

[9] See Congressional Research Service, The Role of High Yield Bonds (Junk Bonds) in Capital Markets and Corporate Takeovers: Public Policy Implications, Com. Print 99-W, House Com. on Energy & Commerce, 99th Cong., 1st Sess. (1985); Bleakley, The Power and the Perils of Junk Bonds, N. Y. Times, Apr. 14, 1985, p. F1, col. 4; SEC, Office of the Chief Economist, Noninvestment Grade Debt As a Source of Tender Offer Financing (1986), severely criticized in Lowenstein, Taking Issue with the SEC: Three New Reasons to Fear Junk Bonds, N. Y. Times, Aug. 24, 1986, p. F1; Comptroller of the Currency Bank Bul. 85-12, CCH Fed. Banking L. Rep. ¶49,108 (cautioning national banks). More recently some investment banking firms have been making "bridge" loans themselves with a view to recovering their money through their later underwriting of "junk bonds" issued by the tender offeror. See Sterngold, Can Salomon Brothers Learn to Love Junk Bonds?, N. Y. Times, Nov. 16, 1986, §3, p. 1. On application of the Federal Reserve margin requirements, see infra.

purchase agreement between a white knight and one or more principal shareholders.[10]

"Pac-man defense": a case where the quarry becomes the pursuer, or "I'll eat you before you eat me."[11] The Wall Street Journal of September 27, 1985, carried an Orlin cartoon that showed a television news broadcaster saying: "In New York today, two conglomerates gobbled each other up and disappeared without a trace."

"Poison pill": This term refers generally to preferred stock, rights, warrants, options, or debt instruments that an actual or potential target company distributes to its security holders. These instruments are designed to deter non-negotiated takeovers by conferring certain rights on shareholders upon the occurrence of a "triggering event," such as a tender offer or third party acquisition of a specified percentage of stock. These rights usually have little value until the triggering event occurs, but may subsequently become quite expensive for any party to redeem or purchase. In July 1986 the SEC invited comment on whether there should be a governmental response (at either federal or state level) to the proliferation of "poison pill" plans.[12]

"Shark repellent" or "porcupine" provisions: defensive steps such as amendment of the target's articles in an attempt to ward off

[10] See Nathan, Lock-Ups and Leg-Ups: The Search for Security in the Acquisitions Marketplace, in Practising Law Institute, Thirteenth Annual Institute on Securities Regulation (1982) c. 1; Note, Lock-Up Options: Towards a State Law Standard, 96 Harv. L. Rev. 1068 (1983); Herzel, Colling, and Carlson, Misunderstanding Lock-Ups, 14 Sec. Reg. L. J. 150 (1986); cf. Bialkin, The Use of Standstill Agreements in Corporate Transactions, Practising Law Institute, supra, c. 2.

[11] Martin Marietta Corp. v. Bendix Corp., 549 F. Supp. 623, 625 (D. Md. 1982), *rev'd on other grounds,* 690 F. 2d 558 (6th Cir. 1982). The term was invented in that opinion and is discussed in Mott, Pac-Man Tender Offers, [1983] Duke L. J. 116.

[12] Sec. Ex. Act Rel. 23,486, 36 SEC Dock. 230, 234 (1986). See Note, Protecting Shareholders Against Partial and Two-Tiered Takeovers: The "Poison Pill" Preferred, 97 Harv. L. Rev. 1964 (1984); Atkins, Takeover Defense, in Practising Law Institute, Fifteenth Annual Institute on Securities Regulation (1984) c. 11 (discussing "children's strength" and "adult dosage poison pills"); Chittur, Wall Street's Teddy Bear: The "Poison Pill" As a Takeover Defense, 11 J. Corp. L. 25 (1985).

Recent SEC staff studies, after finding and describing five types of pills that have evolved, conclude that their adoption has not been well received by the capital markets. SEC, Office of the Chief Economist, The Economics of Poison Pills, CCH Fed. Sec. L. Rep. ¶83,971 (1986); SEC, Office of the Chief Economist, The Effects of Poison Pills on the Wealth of Target Shareholders (1986). Indeed, nearly half of the thirty takeover attempts studied were defeated. Id. at 41. And the increasing number of "pill" proposals are being resisted by institutional investors. See Anders, Institutional Holders Irked by "Poison Pill," Wall St. J., Mar. 10, 1987, p. 6.

potential offers by going over to staggered boards or adopting supermajority voting requirements for mergers and the like.

"White knight": a third company that the target persuades to merge with it or to make a competing offer that it hopes will lead to a combination more to its liking.

Moreover, a galaxy of defenses has been developed from the "shark repellent" provisions just mentioned to selecting a "white knight" whose business will give the target an antitrust argument against the tender offer, and including redeployment of assets by restructuring the target's capitalization or selling a division of the business or effecting a partial liquidation or making a tender offer for the target's own shares.[13] As Judge Friendly put it with his usual felicity: "Drawing Excalibur from a scabbard where it would doubtless have remained sheathed in the face of a friendly offer, the target company typically hopes to obtain a temporary injunction

[13] See Schmults and Kelly, Cash Take-Over Bids — Defense Tactics, 23 Bus. Law. 115 (1967); Reuben and Elden, How to Be a Target Company, 23 N. Y. L. S. L. Rev. 423 (1978); Kreiger and Overlock, Developments in Tender Offer and Takeover Defense, in Practising Law Institute, Sixteenth Annual Institute on Securities Regulation (1984) c. 8; Saparoff and Hemond, Defensive Measures in REIT Takeovers, 17 Rev. Sec. Reg. 924 (1984). For an enumeration of defensive measures, with an indication of the disclosure they require in proxy materials looking toward their adoption, see Sec. Ex. Act Rel. 15,230, 15 SEC Dock. 1311 (1978). For a case study of a contested tender offer, together with a discussion of developments of both offensive and defensive tactics, see Freund, Jacobs, Katcher, and Chapnick, Case Study of a Contest: TWA, in Practising Law Institute, Seventeenth Annual Institute on Securities Regulation (1986) c. 9.

Almost 80 percent of the Standard & Poor's 500 companies had adopted some form of antitakeover measure by early 1986. Investor Responsibility Research Center, Antitakeover Charter Amendments: A Directory of Major American Corporations (1985).

The specific forms of "shark repellents" (antitakeover amendments) have changed considerably over the past decade or so in response to new takeover techniques as well as shareholder resistance toward amendments designed primarily to entrench incumbent management. The popularity of these recent antitakeover amendments has increased dramatically since the invention of the "fair price" amendment, which typically requires supermajority voting approval by shareholders for transfers of managerial control that are triggered by "two-tier" offers, with provision for waiver of the requirement either in the board's discretion or on the offeror's agreeing to pay a "fair price" for all purchased shares. SEC, Office of the Chief Economist, Shark Repellents and Stock Prices: The Effects of Antitakeover Amendments Since 1980 (July 24, 1985) 1. Whereas antitakeover amendments passed before 1980 had only a trivial effect on equity value according to this study, a sample for the period January 1979 through May 1985 reflected an average loss of 1.31 percent. But "fair price" amendments had very little effect on stock value, while supermajority, authorized preferred, and classified board amendments had substantial negative effects on stock value. Id. at 3-5.

which may frustrate the acquisition since the offering company may well decline the expensive gambit of a trial or, if it persists, the long lapse of time could so change conditions that the offer will fail even if, after a full trial and appeal, it should be determined that no antitrust violation has been shown."[14]

It has been claimed that these anti-takeover amendments "are a waste of time and are probably counter-productive";[15] indeed, 85 percent of all tender offers during the twelve months beginning July 1, 1978, were completely or partially successful,[16] although this includes a great many offers that were friendly either *ab initio* or by virtue of a beefed-up price or the intervention of a "white knight."[17] Indeed, there has been much controversy with respect to the propriety, as a matter of corporation law, of a target's taking *any* defensive measures to prevent its stockholders' receiving the benefit of a higher price for their shares resulting from the prospect of higher earnings when the offeror and target companies are combined (the favorite word here is "synergy"). Neither side claims to have *proved* that a "no-action rule" either does or does not maximize the wealth of investors and society.[18] The debate goes on, sharp-

[14] Missouri Portland Cement Co. v. Cargill, Inc., 498 F. 2d 851, 854 (2d Cir. 1974), *cert. denied,* U. S. 883.

[15] Flom, in Leiman, Recent Developments in Tender Offers: Defensive Tactics, in Practising Law Institute, Tenth Annual Institute on Securities Regulation (1979) c. 15 at 293-94; see also Cary, Corporate Devices Used to Insulate Management from Attack, 25 Bus. Law. 839 (1970).

[16] Austin, loc. cit. supra p. 498 n. 2.

[17] See Freund and Greene, Substance over Form S-14: A Proposal to Reform SEC Regulation of Negotiated Acquisitions, 36 Bus. Law. 1483, 1486-87 (1981), which discusses the fortuitous regulatory disparities between negotiated cash tender offers and negotiated cash mergers.

[18] In favor of target management's adopting a *laissez faire* position, see Easterbrook and Fischel, The Proper Role of a Target's Management in Responding to a Tender Offer, 94 Harv. L. Rev. 1161 (1981) (analysis in terms of "efficient market theory"); cf. Gilson, A Structural Approach to Corporations: The Case Against Defensive Tactics in Tender Offers, 33 Stan. L. Rev. 819, 879 (1981); Gilson, The Case against Shark Repellent Amendments: Structural Limitations on the Enabling Concept, 34 Stan. L. Rev. 775 (1982).

Contra: Lipton, Takeover Bids in the Target's Boardroom, 35 Bus. Law. 101 (1979); Lipton, Takeover Bids in the Target's Boardroom: A Response to Professors Easterbrook and Fischel, 55 N. Y. U. L. Rev. 1231 (1980); see also Steinbrink, Management's Response to the Takeover Attempt, 28 Case W. Res. L. Rev. 882 (1978) (the "knee jerk" opposition to a takeover attempt, whatever the price, has gone out of style, id. at 887); cf. Bebchuk, The Case for Facilitating Competing Tender Offers, 95 Harv. L. Rev. 1028 (1982) (disagreeing with Easterbrook and Fischel, supra, to the extent of maintaining that the facilitation of *competing bids* is desirable for both target stockholders and society).

ened by the continual development of new stratagems on both sides.[19] And it is reflected in the cases.[20]

There are at least three models, which do not evoke the same

[19]See Easterbrook and Fischel, Auctions and Sunk Costs in Tender Offers, 35 Stan. L. Rev. 1, 21 (1982); Bebchuk, The Case for Facilitating Competing Tender Offers: A Reply and Extension, 35 Stan. L. Rev. 23, 49 (1982); Gilson, Seeking Competitive Bids Versus Pure Passivity in Tender Offer Defense, 35 Stan. L. Rev. 51, 66 (1982); Riger, On Golden Parachutes — Ripcords or Rip-offs?, Some Comments on Special Termination Agreements, 3 Pace L. Rev. 15, 39 (1982) ("a small parting gift of corporate moneys without support in contract or corporate law"); Lipton and Brownstein, Takeover Responses and Directors' Responsibilities — An Update, 40 Bus. Law. 1403 (1985); Oesterle, Target Managers As Negotiating Agents for Target Shareholders in Tender Offers: A Reply to the Passivity Thesis, 71 Corn. L. Rev. 53 (1985); SEC, Office of the Chief Economist, Shareholder Wealth Effects of Ohio Legislation Affecting Takeovers (1987) (the new Ohio statute was accompanied by a drop in share prices of Ohio firms of roughly 2 percent).

For an essay that "reflects a willingness to challenge not only the abusive defenses, but also takeover bids themselves," see Lowenstein, Pruning Deadwood in Hostile Takeovers: A Proposal for Legislation, 83 Colum. L. Rev. 249, 251 (1983) (proposing legislation to permit shareholders to decide for themselves whether to approve management's proposed response and observing that they would have a vote on a merger). For a proposed set of rules designed to ensure undistorted choice and equal treatment, see Bebchuk, Toward Undistorted Choice and Equal Treatment in Corporate Takeovers, 98 Harv. L. Rev. 1693 (1985).

In general, see Practising Law Institute, Thirteenth Annual Institute on Securities Regulation (1982) cc. 1-10; R. Winter, M. Stumpf, and G. Hawkins, Shark Repellents and Golden Parachutes: A Handbook for the Practitioner (1983); ABA Committee on Corporate Laws, Guidelines for Directors: Planning for and Responding to Unsolicited Tender Offers, 41 Bus. Law. 209 (1985). In Dynamics Corp. of America v. CTS Corp., 794 F. 2d 250, 253 (7th Cir. 1986), *rev'd on other grounds* sub nom. CTS Corp. v. Dynamics Corp. of America, 107 S. Ct. 1637 (1987), Judge Posner cites as exemplars of the view that takeovers are bad: Scherer, Takeovers: Present and Future Dangers, Brookings Rev. (Winter-Spring 1986) 15; and as exemplars of the other pole, that all resistance is bad: Ginsburg and Robinson, The Case Against Federal Intervention in the Market for Corporate Control, Brookings Rev. (Winter-Spring 1986) 9.

Professor Coffee has concluded, after an exhaustive study, that, "if one believes that the current level of takeover activity exerts an influence that is, on balance, desirable (as this Article would tentatively conclude), it does not follow that more is better." Coffee, Regulating the Market for Corporate Control: A Critical Assessment of the Tender Offer's Role in Corporate Governance, 84 Colum. L. Rev. 1145, 1294 (1984). And the February 1985 Economic Report of the President concluded (c. 6, p. 192) that "the current state of knowledge strongly indicates that further Federal regulation of the takeover process, particularly insofar as it would make takeovers more costly, would be poor economic policy."

On the particular problems faced by trustees of employee benefit plans that own shares of a target company, see Tauber and Prendergast, Employee Benefit Plans in Takeovers, 16 Rev. Sec. Reg. 937 (1983). Because of these problems, "a general trend seems to be developing toward giving participants the power to decide whether or not the shares of employer/target stock held for their benefit under a plan should be tendered, rather than leaving that decision with

emotional response toward the one side or the other: (1) "The

---

either independent or in-house trustees." Id. at 937. The article discusses also ERISA complications.

[20]In Panter v. Marshall Field & Co., 646 F. 2d 271, 293-95 (7th Cir. 1981), *cert. denied,* 454 U. S. 1092, the court applied the common law business judgment rule to permit a series of defensive acquisitions designed to create antitrust problems for a tender offeror. See also Johnson v. Trueblood, 629 F. 2d 287 (3d Cir. 1980), *cert. denied,* 450 U. S. 999; Treadway Companies v. Care Corp., 638 F. 2d 357 (2d Cir. 1980); Jewel Companies, Inc. v. Pay Less Drug Stores Northwest, Inc., 741 F. 2d 1555 (9th Cir. 1984); Enterra Corp. v. SGS Associates, 600 F. Supp. 678 (E. D. Pa. 1985) ("standstill agreement"); Horwitz v. Southwest Forest Industries, 604 F. Supp. 1130 (D. Nev. 1985) ("poison pill"); Crown Zellerbach Corp. v. Goldsmith, 609 F. Supp. 187, 188 (S. D. N. Y. 1985) (a "high stakes game of 'chicken' "); Asarco, Inc. v. Holmes à Court, 611 F. Supp. 468 (D. N. J. 1985); GAF Corp. v. Union Carbide Corp., 624 F. Supp. 1016 (S. D. N. Y. 1985) (high interest debt securities containing covenants to protect their credit value that restricted for various periods the sale in any year of more than 25 percent, or in certain circumstances 5 percent, of the whole); Turner Broadcasting System, Inc. v. CBS, Inc., 627 F. Supp. 901 (N. D. Ga. 1985); Unocal Corp. v. Mesa Petroleum Co., 493 A. 2d 946 (Del. 1985) (target's two-tier self-tender, see Supp. p. 512 infra, that excluded stockholder making a hostile tender offer); Moran v. Household Int'l, Inc., 500 A. 2d 1346 (Del. 1985) ("poison pill preferred" came within business judgment rule); Revlon, Inc. v. MacAndrews & Forbes Holdings, Inc., 506 A. 2d 173 (Del. 1986) ("poison pill"); Harvard Industries, Inc. v. Tyson, — F. Supp. — , CCH Fed. Sec. L. Rep. ¶93,064 (E. D. Mich. 1986) (same).

The SEC filed an *amicus curiae* brief in the *Moran* appeal, in which it argued that this "most potent defense yet devised to tender offers" would "virtually eliminate hostile tender offers in addition to deterring proxy contests, so that the effect would be to entrench management at the expense of the shareholders' right to determine who should manage the company." Brief at 1-2. But see Hertzberg, Poison Pill Defense No Longer Is Seen As a Sure Way to Repel Hostile Suitors, Wall St. J., Oct. 31, 1985, p. 20, col. 3.

Contrast Norlin Corp. v. Rooney, Pace, Inc., 744 F. 2d 255 (2d Cir. 1984) (preliminary injunction against target's voting new shares issued to a wholly owned subsidiary and a newly created employee stock option plan); Unilever Acquisition Corp. v. Richardson-Vicks, Inc., 618 F. Supp. 407 (S. D. N. Y. 1985); Hanson Trust, PLC v. ML SCM Acquisition, Inc., 781 F. 2d 264 (2d Cir. 1986) (a "crown jewel" lock-up option under which a Merrill Lynch entity could buy two businesses from target on acquisition of one-third of target's stock by a third person was not approved in the independent directors' informed business judgment); Dynamics Corp. of America v. CTS Corp., 794 F. 2d 250, 257 (7th Cir. 1986), *rev'd sub. nom.* CTS Corp. v. Dynamics Corp. of America, — S. Ct. — (the tender offer "was not evaluated in a cool, dispassionate, and thorough fashion"); Amalgamated Sugar Co. v. NL Industries, 644 F. Supp. 1229 (S. D. N. Y. 1986) ("poison pill" held *ultra vires* under New Jersey law); Frantz Mfg. Co. v. EAC Industries, 501 A. 2d 401, 408 (Del. 1985) ("corporate action which seeks to undo a takeover bid *after* control has already passed to another group is not protected by the business judgment rule"); Revlon, Inc. v. MacAndrews & Forbes Holdings, Inc., supra (business judgment rule does not protect an asset "lock-up" option extended to foreclose further bidding in an active bidding situation); Edelman v. Freuhauf Corp., 798 F. 2d 882, 885 (6th Cir. 1986) (under Michigan law, board "unreasonably preferred incumbent management in the

rationale * * *, at least in a conventional, friendly deal, is to protect the parties in this newly avaricious world against the possibility that, notwithstanding their agreement to consummate a transaction, some third party may try to relieve them of that transaction." (2) The initial bidder in a *hostile* tender offer, recognizing the risk of losing out to a third-party bidder (frequently a "white knight") or to a defense of some sort, wants to enhance the possibilities of success before starting. (3) A target company, in order to induce a "white knight" to enter the bidding contest with the aggressor, needs to "put something on the table," like an agreement to sell some stock at a bargain price or to give the "white knight" the target company's "crown jewel" or an option on a division.[21]

There is controversy, too, with respect to the position of a bank that in one way or another serves both sides. The few holdings thus far reflect a judicial reluctance to interfere, at least in the absence of a bank's actually relaying confidential information it received from a client that is a putative target to another client that is a putative tender offeror.[22] But the SEC has recommended legislation with respect to investment bankers, financial advisers, and securities analysts as well as banks that are engaged to advise a tender offeror after having obtained material nonpublic information from the target company.[23]

---

bidding process — acting without objectivity and requisite loyalty to the corporation"); AC Acquisitions Corp. v. Anderson, Clayton & Co., 519 A. 2d 103 (Del. Ch. 1986).

In Brown v. Ferro Corp., 763 F. 2d 798 (6th Cir. 1985), *cert. denied,* 106 U. S. 344, the court held that a shareholder's challenge to a "golden parachute" agreement did not present a constitutional case or controversy when there had been no change of control.

In general, see Oesterle, The Negotiation Model of Tender Offer Defenses and the Delaware Supreme Court, 72 Corn. L. Rev. 117 (1986).

On the limited usefulness of §14(e) (infra p. 527) in this area, see Schreiber v. Burlington Northern, Inc., 472 U. S. 1 (1985), infra Supp. p. 529.

[21] Bialkin and Kramer, Lock-Ups, Proxy Contests, Counter-Tenders, and Other Acquisition Techniques, in Practising Law Institute, Fourteenth Annual Institute on Securities Regulation (1983) c. 14 at 191-92.

[22] Humana, Inc. v. American Medicorp, Inc., 445 F. Supp. 613 (S. D. N. Y. 1978); Washington Steel Corp. v. TW Corp., 602 F. 2d 594 (3d Cir. 1979); see Note, Regulating the Use of Confidential Information in Tender Offer Financing: A Common Law Solution, 55 N. Y. U. L. Rev. 838 (1980); Note, Bank Financing of Hostile Acquisitions of Corporate Law Customers, 31 Case W. Res. L. Rev. 132 (1981). Both notes recommend a "Chinese wall." See also Sec. Ex. Act Rel. 17,120, 20 SEC Dock. 1241, 1252 (1980). That concept is discussed in another connection at pp. 752-54 infra.

[23] See SEC Report on Tender Offer Laws, S. Com. on Banking, Housing & Urban Affairs, 96th Cong., 2d Sess. (Com. Print 1980) 15-45.

2. The Regulatory Scheme

Oddly, apart from Congress's borrowing in 1933 from the British prospectus provision, tender offers are the one area of securities regulation in which the British acted before the Americans. As we have seen, they experienced the phenomenon earlier. And there seems to have been an explosion of regulation of one kind or another throughout the capitalist world.[24] But the British, with their traditional skepticism about anything approaching an SEC,[25] rely on self-regulation. As early as 1959 a committee of various City groups that had been set up at the suggestion of the Governor of the Bank of England produced a concise code of recommended rules of conduct for "take-over bids."[26] And a Panel on Take-overs and Mergers, created in 1968 with an independent Chairman and Deputy Chairman appointed by the Governor of the Bank of England, administers a Code of "principles" and "rules."[27]

[24]See A. Vice, The Strategy of Takeovers: A Casebook of International Practice (1971); P. Anisman, Takeover Bid Legislation in Canada: A Comparative Analysis (1974); Tan, The Singapore Code on Takeovers and Mergers: An Introduction, 44 Malaya L. J. lxviii (1975); M. Weinberg and M. Blank, Takeovers and Mergers (4th ed. 1977) (United Kingdom); Macgregor, Takeovers Revisited, 95 S. Af. L. J. 329 (1978); Santow, Defensive Measures Against Company Takeovers, 53 Aust. L. J. 374 (1979); Lépine, The French General Philosophy Concerning the Transfer of Controlling Interests and the New Takeover Bid Rule, in L. Gower, L. Loss, and A. Sommer (co-chairmen), New Trends in Company Law Disclosure (1980) 269; Carvalhosa, The Brazilian Experience with Respect to Tender Offers, 3 J. Comp. L. & Sec. Reg. 103 (1981); Tatsuta, in Loss, Yazawa, and Banoff (eds.), Japanese Securities Regulation (1983) 172-91; Wtterwulghe, Takeover Bids in Belgium, 5 J. Comp. Bus. & Capital Market L. 41 (1984); J. Courtright, Securities Regulation of Take-Over Bids in Canada (1985); Howard, Current Takeover Law, 15 Melbourne U. L. Rev. 31 (1985); Sappideen, Takeover Bids and Target Shareholder Protection: The Regulatory Framework in the United Kingdom, United States and Australia, 8 J. Comp. Bus. & Cap. Market L. 281 (1986).

[25]See Report of Committee to Review the Functioning of Financial Institutions ("Wilson Report"), Cmd. 7937 (1980) §§1199, 1411. This view is by no means unanimous. See L. Gower, Principles of Modern Company Law (4th ed. 1979) 365. (Professor Gower there recommended "a smaller (poor man's) S. E. C." — which, under the Financial Services Act 1986, 1986 Acts c. 60, infra n. 27, now exists as the Securities and Investments Board.)

[26]See Queensbury Rules for Bids, 193 Economist 440 (1959).

[27]For a history of the Code and Panel written by its Deputy Chairman, see A. Johnson, The City Take-Over Code (1980). Initially the Panel was not expected to become a "self-regulatory organisation" under the Financial Services Act 1986, 1986 Acts c. 60, with its Securities and Investments Board. But even before that Act became fully operative, political pressure stemming from a restrictive practices (antitrust) investigation that adduced evidence of a massive effort to boost the target's share price during a takeover bid impelled the Government to announce that it would consider including takeover rules in the regulations being drafted by the SIB, and that the Government would also

Congress finally acted in 1968 by adding §§13(d)-(e) and 14(d)-(f) to the 1934 Act, and these sections (collectively known as the Williams Act) were amended into their present form in 1970.

Section 14(d)(1) makes it unlawful for any person "to make a tender offer for, or a request or invitation for tenders of," any class of equity security registered under §12 (or within the insurance company exemption in §12(g)(2)(G) or issued by a closed-end investment company registered under the Investment Company Act), if consummation of the offer would make that person the beneficial owner of more than 5 percent of the class,[28] unless he files with the Commission, concurrently with the first publication of the offer or its first transmission to security holders, whatever information the Commission may prescribe by rule. The five-day advance filing that would have been required in the bill as introduced was abandoned on the ground that "prior review was not necessary and in some cases might delay the offer when time was of the essence."[29] Supplementary soliciting material must be filed and sent to the issuer concurrently with its transmission to security holders, and the con-

review the possibility of putting Government regulators on the Panel. Wall St. J., Jan. 29, 1987, p. 33. Moreover, the 1986 Act inherits three sections on takeovers from the Companies Act 1985. 1985 Acts c. 6, §§428-30; 1986 Acts c. 60, §172 and Sch. 12. In Regina v. Panel on Take-Overs and Mergers, [1987] 1 All E. R. 564, 580 (Q. B.), where a losing takeover bidder alleged that the winning bidder had violated the Code, the Court of Appeal held that that "remarkable body" was not "above the law," but that the court's role was limited to considerations of "illegality," "rationality," or "procedural impropriety" (the last of these including "fundamental unfairness").

[28] The figure was dropped to 5 percent from the original 10 percent in 1970.

[29] S. Rep. No. 550, 90th Cong., 1st Sess. (1967) 4. However, the 1933 Act's strictures on offers must, of course, be observed in the case of a paper tender offer; the 1968 exemption from §14(d) for offers pursuant to a 1933 Act registration was deleted in the 1970 amendments although the similar exemption in §13(d)(6)(A) remained. Moreover, §7A of the Clayton Act, added by the Hart-Scott-Rodino Antitrust Improvements Act of 1976, applies if (1) either the tender offeror or the target has $100 million and the other has $10 million in sales or assets, and (2) the offering company would end up with 15 percent of the voting securities or $15 million of assets; and, when those two circumstances are present, the offering company must file a premerger notification with the Federal Trade Commission and the Assistant Attorney General in charge of the Antitrust Division fifteen or thirty days before any purchase of target stock, depending on whether or not the offer is for cash. The Government may waive the waiting period, and it may also extend the period within limits in order to accommodate its request for additional material. 15 U. S. C. §18a; see S. Axinn, B. Fogg, and N. Stoll, Acquisitions Under the Hart-Scott-Rodino Antitrust Improvements Act (1979). Apparently, for one reason or another, the Hart-Scott-Rodino Act has not turned out to be the significant impediment to market accumulation programs that at one time was anticipated. See Banner and Volk, The Large-Scale Open-Market Purchase Program, in Practising Law Institute, Fourteenth Annual Institute on Securities Regulation (1983) c. 17 at 241-42.

tents of any such material are again subject to the Commission's rules.

Section 14(d)(4) authorizes the Commission to regulate any solicitation or recommendation to holders to accept or reject a tender offer. This authorizes the Commission not only to specify the information to be included in any recommendation, whether by the management or others and whether in favor of or in opposition to a tender offer, but also to regulate (1) solicitations by broker-dealers, who are often compensated for shares tendered as a result of their activities, and (2) the activities of persons who make competing tender offers or seek to influence investors' decisions on a single tender offer.[30]

A new antifraud provision, §14(e), makes it unlawful for *any* person to make any untrue statement of a material fact (a half-truth being included as in the fraud provisions generally), "or to engage in any fraudulent, deceptive, or manipulative acts or practices," in connection with any tender offer or any solicitation in opposition to or in favor of a tender offer. This section, in the tradition of the general fraud provisions of the 1933 and 1934 Acts, applies to all securities without regard to registration.[31]

As with the scheme of proxy regulation, neither the statutory provisions nor the rules are limited to disclosure. So far as substantive provisions — which amount to federal corporation law — are concerned:

[30] S. Rep. No. 550, 90th Cong., 1st Sess. (1967) 9; H. R. Rep. No. 1711, 90th Cong., 2d Sess. (1968) 10.

[31] L. P. Acquisition Co. v. Tyson, 772 F. 2d 201, 208-09 (6th Cir. 1985). "In effect [§14(e)] applies Rule 10b-5 both to the offeror and to the opposition — very likely, except perhaps for any bearing it may have on the issue of standing, only a codification of existing case law." Electronic Specialty Co. v. International Controls Corp., 409 F. 2d 937, 940-41 (2d Cir. 1969). But there is a "bug" here. Section 14(e), alone of all the SEC fraud provisions that are not grounded on a registration requirement that is itself conditioned on some use of the mails or interstate commerce, is silent with respect to these assumed prerequisites to federal jurisdiction. It may be that the world of securities is so impregnated with interstate commerce that it is no longer constitutionally necessary to tie every prohibition, directly or indirectly, to use of the mails or interstate facilities, at least when some such use is pleaded and proved in the particular case. Cf. Perez v. United States, 402 U. S. 146 (1971) ("loan sharking" activities). But the omission in §14(e) was apparently inadvertent. Even if the Commission itself is careful in its own cases to allege and prove either (1) some use of the mails or interstate facilities or (2) the target company's registration, there is always the possibility that plaintiffs in private actions will not do so. And, in any event, it is not a foregone conclusion that the severability clause in §33 will save the section's constitutionality, though it should. For an essay in support of the contention that §14(e), despite its literal breadth, should be interpreted to apply only to tender offers within §14(d), see Conard, Tender Offer Fraud: The Secret Meaning of Subsection 14(e), 40 Bus. Law. 87 (1984).

Section 14(d)(5) permits persons who have tendered to withdraw within the first seven days after the tender offer or more than sixty days afterwards unless the Commission prescribes otherwise by rule or order. The Commission has in fact extended the period by rule to the entire offering period.[32] And the legislative reports contemplated the Commission's acting by order when, for example, shareholders might need more than seven days to assess correcting material that had been circulated or when the required approval of some regulatory authority might not be obtainable within the sixty days.[33]

Another of the Commission's suggestions — a *pro rata* acceptance requirement in the event of an overacceptance — is reflected in §14(d)(6). The Senate committee was persuaded by the testimony of the New York Stock Exchange, based on its own experience, to limit the *pro rata* requirement to shares offered during the first ten days of the offer, with an additional ten-day period in the event of an increase in price.[34] Nevertheless, and despite the absence of rulemaking authority in §14(d)(6), the Commission has used its fraud-prevention authority under §14(e) not only to extend the proration requirement to the life of the tender offer[35] but also to require all tender offers to be open for at least twenty business days plus ten business days after notice of any increase or decrease in the percentage of the class of securities being sought or the price or the dealer's soliciting fee.[36]

It startles a bit to see the §14(e) authority used in this way when Congress was careful to supply specific time periods for both withdrawal and proration purposes. On that account (and also on the

[32] Rule 14d-7.

[33] S. Rep. at 10 and H. R. Rep. at 10, supra p. 509 n. 30.

[34] S. Rep. at 4-5, supra p. 509 n. 30. For many years the Exchange has prohibited partial offers on a first-come, first-served basis. N. Y. Stock Ex. Listed Company Manual 311.03.

[35] Rule 14d-8. In Pryor v. United States Steel Corp., 794 F. 2d 52 (2d Cir. 1986), *cert. denied*, 107 S. Ct. 445, decided before the Commission extended the proration period to the life of the offer, the court held that offerors were not free to extend the proration deadline *after it had expired* when the effect was to diminish the numbers of shares purchased from those who had tendered before the deadline.

[36] Rule 14e-1. There is customarily a "protect" or "protection" — commonly of eight days during large tender offers — during which securities of the target company may be delivered to the offeror's depository *after* expiration of the offer in accordance with letters of transmittal or guarantees of delivery or other documentation (such as telegrams, facsimile transmissions, or letters from eligible institutions) submitted *before* expiration. Sec. Ex. Act Rel. 10,581, 29 SEC Dock. 822, 824 n. 19 (1984).

merits for Chairman Shad) two of the five Commissioners dissented from the adoption of the proration rule.[37]

The sixty-day withdrawal provision is construed administratively as not applying to the extent that the offeror has purchased the deposited securities, notwithstanding the practice of leaving the offer open for a considerable time in order to pick up odds and ends.

The Senate committee also referred to the abuse of "short tendering." In order to permit acceptance by brokers on behalf of shareholders who are away or otherwise not in a position to deposit their certificates, tender offers commonly provide that the certificates need not be deposited if a bank or a member firm of an exchange guarantees that they will be delivered on demand or at a specified time in the event of acceptance. As a result of this practice, a broker who estimated that only half of the shares tendered would be accepted on a *pro rata* basis could tender twice as many shares as he owned without depositing them. But the committee thought that the Commission had adequate power under the existing antifraud provisions to deal with the problem. And in 1968 the Commission adopted a new Rule 10b-4, which declares it a "manipulative or deceptive device or contrivance" for any person (1) to tender for his own account any security that he does not own or (2) to tender or guarantee the tender of any security on behalf of another person unless (A) the security is in the possession of the person making the tender or giving the guarantee or (B) the latter person has reason to believe that the former owns the security and, as soon as possible without undue inconvenience or expense, will deliver it to the latter. Ownership is defined as in Rule 10a-1, the rule on short sales.[38] And special provision is made for convertible securities and rights.[39]

The SEC's Advisory Committee on Tender Offers, in its 1983 Report of Recommendations, strongly endorsed continuation of Rule 10b-4, suggesting that it be extended to hedged tendering (the tendering of shares that are owned followed by a sale of a part of those shares in the market) as well as multiple tendering (tendering the same shares to more than one offeror).[40] In 1984 the Commission amended Rule 10b-4 to effectuate the first proposal by requir-

[37] Sec. Ex. Act Rel. 19,336, 26 SEC Dock. 1445, 1447-49 (1982). In San Francisco Real Estate Investors v. Real Estate Investment Trust of America, 692 F. 2d 814, 817 (1st Cir. 1982), the court held that, although the "ten-day deadline of §14(d)(6) * * * was not necessarily immutable," it had been enlarged by the District Court without specific reason.

[38] See p. 650 infra.

[39] See Sec. Ex. Act Rel. 8321 (1968).

[40] Id. at 47-49.

ing that all tendering shareholders be "net long" the amount of securities tendered at the end of the proration period, or on the last day securities may be tendered for acceptance by lot when that method for acceptance is used.[41] And the next year the Commission adopted a further amendment that was designed to prohibit hedged tendering through the use of call options.[42]

Section 14(d)(7) incorporates into the statute the Commission's further proposal that persons who have already tendered before an increase in the offering price must receive the same price as those who tender after the increase.[43] But there is no comparable provision with respect to a *decrease* at a later stage of a tender offer. This has made possible the "two-tier" or "front-end-loaded" offer, which comes in a number of varieties[44] — although there was a dramatic decrease in the number of such offers when the advent of "junk bonds" provided a ready means of financing purely cash offers.

With limited exceptions, the Commission took the position from the beginning "that (i) a tender offer must be extended to all holders of the class of securities which is the subject of the offer (the 'all holders requirement'); and (ii) all such holders must be paid the highest consideration offered under the tender offer (the 'best-price' rule)."[45] But the courts held that there was no "all-holders" rule under the statute,[46] and that the business judgment rule protected

[41] Sec. Ex. Act Rel. 20,799, 30 SEC Dock. 142 (1984). In Merrill Lynch, Pierce, Fenner & Smith, Inc. v. Bobker, 808 F. 2d 930 (2d Cir. 1986), the court held that arbitrators' nonenforcement of the "net long" provision did not meet the "manifest disregard of the law" test for upsetting an arbitral award.

[42] Sec. Ex. Act Rel. 21,782, 32 SEC Dock. 713 (1985). The technique is to require tendering persons to exclude from their "net long positions" any shares underlying standardized call options written after announcement of the tender offer.

[43] In Missouri Portland Cement Co. v. Cargill, Inc., 498 F. 2d 851, 874 (2d Cir. 1974) *cert. denied*, 419 U. S. 883, the court said that §14(d)(7) made it misleading for the target company to say that the offeror might raise its price if it did not get all the stock it wanted at its initial price. In Brill v. Burlington Northern, Inc., 590 F. Supp. 893, 898-900 (D. Del. 1984), the court held (1) that there had been two separate tender offers with two separate proration pools, so that the proration provisions of §14(d)(6) had not been violated, and (2) that "golden parachutes" were collateral agreements to which §14(d)(7) did not apply.

[44] In general, see Fogelson and Kapp, The Emergence of Proration Pools and Two-Tier Offers As Desired Structures for Acquisitions, in Practising Law Institute, Fourteenth Annual Institute on Securities Regulation (1983) c. 13; Lederman, Tender Offer Bidding Strategy, 17 Rev. Sec. Reg. 917 (1984); SEC, Office of the Chief Economist, The Economics of Any-or-All, Partial, and Two-Tier Tender Offers (1985).

[45] Sec. Ex. Act Rel. 22,198, 33 SEC Dock. 762 (1985).

[46] Unocal Corp. v. Pickens, 608 F. Supp. 1081 (C. D. Cal. 1985).

the directors' decision under Delaware law.[47] Thereupon the Commission in July 1986 concurrently adopted both "all-holders" and "best-price" rules.[48] This was shortly followed by a "concept release" in which the Commission solicited comment on some sort of self-governance exemption to the "all-holders" rule, as well as other provisions of the tender offer rules, that would permit stockholders and directors to decide for themselves whether they require the protections of the tender offer provisions.[49]

So far as the "best-price" rule is concerned, there is a nice question that is reminiscent of the "integration" problem that we met with respect to certain exemptions under the 1933 Act:[50] Since §14(d)(7) applies only when the price is increased "before the expiration of" the offer, and the rule applies only "during such tender offer," what if an offeror announces a new offer at a higher price immediately after the expiration of the original offer. Are there one or two offers? In one case, involving an increase in the number of shares covered, the answer was one.[51] And in an analogous situation an issuer's acquisition of 25 percent of its stock by five private purchases and one market purchase within hours after announcement of termination of the tender offer managed to escape the statutory scheme altogether, even though the issuer's large market purchases were in competition with a hostile tender offer that complied with the statute.[52]

[47] Unocal Corp. v. Mesa Petroleum Corp., 493 A. 2d 946 (Del. 1985).

[48] Rules 13e-4(f)(8), 14d-10, adopted by Sec. Ex. Act Rel. 23,421, 36 SEC Dock. 95 (1986). The "all-holders" provision extends to both record and beneficial owners. Id. at 101 n. 35.

The Commission sought to minimize the impact of the "all-holders" rule on otherwise constitutionally valid state blue sky laws by permitting the offeror to offer an alternative form of consideration (normally cash) to holders in a state in which the offer is prohibited by administrative or judicial action after a good faith effort to register, or to exclude holders in that state altogether. Id. at 101-04.

[49] Sec. Ex. Act Rel. 23,486, 36 SEC Dock. 230 (1986).

[50] See pp. 278-79 supra.

[51] McDermott, Inc. v. Wheelabrator-Frye, Inc., 649 F. 2d 489 (7th Cir. 1980).

[52] Hanson Trust PLC v. SCM Corp., 774 F. 2d 47 (2d Cir. 1985) (tender offeror's acquisition of 25 percent of target's stock by five private purchases and one market purchase within hours after announcement of termination of the tender offer); see also SEC v. Carter Hawley Hale Stores, Inc., 760 F. 2d 945, 953 (9th Cir. 1985), supra Supp. p. 519 n. 80 (although target's large market purchases were in competition with a hostile tender offer that complied with the statute); Maynard Oil Co. v. Deltec Panamerica, S. A., 630 F. Supp. 502, 505-06 (S. D. N. Y. 1985). But cf. Brill v. Burlington Northern, Inc., 590 F. Supp. 893, 898-900 (D. Del. 1984), supra p. 512 n. 43. In *Hanson*, supra, the court was guided by the "needs" test of SEC v. Ralston Purina Co., 346 U. S. 119 (1953), supra p. 318.

Finally, §14(f) is aimed at the practice, to the extent it is permitted by state law,[53] of using the authority of directors to fill vacancies so as to have the entire board resign *seriatim* upon a shift of control. On the theory that the disclosures required by the proxy rules should be made before a new board is installed pursuant to a private agreement for a transfer of control even though the ownership of a majority of the shares makes it unnecessary to solicit proxies, and consistently with the new §14(c) that was added in the 1964 amendments,[54] the new §14(f) requires the issuer in such a case to file with the Commission before any new director takes office, and transmit to all holders of record who would be entitled to vote at a meeting for election of directors, information substantially equivalent to the information that would be required by §14(a) or §14(c) if the directors were to be elected at a meeting of shareholders.[55]

Section 14(d)-(f) is complemented by §§13(d) and 13(e), which are directed, respectively, to (1) the period *before* a potential tender offer and (2) issuer tender offers for their own shares.

Under §13(d)(1) any person who *after acquiring* the beneficial ownership of an equity security registered under §12 (or issued by an insurance company or a closed-end investment company as in §14(d)(1)) becomes the beneficial owner of more than 5 percent of the class must send to the issuer and to each exchange on which the security is traded and also file with the SEC — all within ten days after the acquisition — whatever information the Commission may by rule prescribe with respect to such matters as (A) the background and identity of the buyers, (B) the source and amount of the consideration used, together with a description of any borrowing (except that the name of any bank lending in the ordinary course of business is to be kept confidential on request), (C) any plans to liquidate the issuer, sell its assets, merge it, or make any other major change in its structure if the purpose of the purchases or prospective purchases is to acquire control, (D) the number of shares that the buyer and each associate own beneficially or have a right to acquire, and (E) any contracts or arrangements with any person concerning any securities of the issuer, including transfers, joint ventures, loan or option arrangements, puts or calls, guaran-

[53] See R. Clark, Corporate Law (1986) §11.4.2.

[54] See p. 490 supra.

[55] See Rule 14f-1; Ratner, Section 14(f): A New Approach to Transfers of Corporate Control, 54 Corn. L. Rev. 65 (1968). Presumably the courts will develop a federal "*de facto* director" doctrine with respect to directors who assume office without compliance with the section.

tees, division of losses or profits, or giving or withholding of proxies. These disclosures are altogether apart from the ownership reports required by §16(a). Moreover, a new §13(d)(2) authorizes the Commission to adopt rules with respect to amendments to the statement filed in the event of material changes — an authority that goes not only to the form and content of the amendments but also to the time of transmission.[56] But there is nothing to prevent making significant additional acquisitions during the ten-day period, and to that extent preserving the element of surprise.[57]

Section 13(e)(1) makes it unlawful for an issuer to "self-tender," that is to say, to buy any of its own equity securities in contravention of the Commission's rules adopted to define, and "to prescribe means reasonably designed to prevent," practices that are "fraudulent, deceptive, or manipulative." The rules under §13(e) may require the issuer to furnish whatever information the Commission considers necessary or material with respect to such matters as the reasons for the purchase, the source of the funds, the number of shares to be purchased, the price, and the method of purchase. Moreover, a purchase by or for any person in a control relationship with the issuer, or a purchase "subject to control of the issuer or any such person," is considered (subject to rulemaking authority to define and exempt) a purchase by the issuer. In contrast to §14(e), however, §13(e) applies only to an issuer that has a class of registered equity securities or that is a closed-end investment company registered under the 1940 Act. The bill as passed by the Senate was amended before enactment to make it clear that the Commission may not regulate issuers' repurchases apart from the prevention of fraud — a concept borrowed from §15(c)(2), part of the over-the-counter broker-dealer complex.[58]

Apart from the Williams Act provisions but closely related to §13(d) is §13(g), which resulted from the Commission's 1976 report on beneficial ownership[59] and was adopted by the Domestic and

[56] The determination whether an amendment is filed "promptly" as required by Rule 13d-2 is "based on all of the facts and circumstances surrounding both prior disclosures by the filing person and the material changes which trigger the obligation to amend." Cooper Laboratories, Inc., Sec. Ex. Act Rel. 22,171, 33 SEC Dock. 647, 651 (1985).

[57] The Commission has expressed its concern with respect to the practice. Sec. Ex. Act Rel. 16,420, 18 SEC Dock. 1293, 1304 (1979).

[58] See p. 707 infra. But the Commission does not view its §13(e) authority as limited to requiring disclosure. Sec. Ex. Act Rel. 17,222, 21 SEC Dock. 212, 217 (1980).

[59] See p. 488 n. 124 supra.

Foreign Investment Disclosure Act of 1977.[60] Section 13(g) was designed to close some gaps in §13(d): it applies to every person who "is" a 5 percent beneficial owner, regardless of when he achieved that status or of the exemptions in §13(d)(6) for acquisitions made pursuant to a 1933 Act registration statement or totaling not more than 2 percent of the class in twelve months. It would have been simpler, of course, to amend §13(d). And the Commission has done the next best thing by adopting a single reporting regulation denominated D-G.[61]

Permeating the legislative history of all the Williams Act paraphernalia is the "extreme care" that was taken "to avoid tipping the balance of regulation either in favor of management or in favor of the person making the takeover bid."[62] In principle, "The incumbent management has no protected interest in remaining in power."[63] But, just as not all tender offerors are "raiders" or "pirates," not all managements are "stodgy old fools."[64]

[60] 91 Stat. 1498 (1977). This statute is flavored by the concurrent adoption of the Foreign Corrupt Practices Act, which added §30A to the 1934 Act. See pp. 154-55 supra.

[61] Sec. Ex. Act Rel. 15,348, 16 SEC Dock. 228 (1978). Concurrently with the adoption of §13(g), Congress in §13(h) directed the Commission to report with respect to the effectiveness of the ownership reporting requirements contained in the 1934 Act and the desirability of modifying the 5 percent threshold used in §§13(d)(1) and 13(g). The Commission submitted a report in 1980 that concluded that the existing reporting requirements in §§13, 14, and 16 were "effective in accomplishing [their] purposes" and that no further legislation was necessary. Report of the Securities and Exchange Commission on Beneficial Ownership Reporting Requirements Pursuant to Section 13(h) of the Securities Exchange Act of 1934 (1980) 8, 39, 66-68.

[62] S. Rep. No. 550, 90th Cong., 1st Sess. (1967) 3; H. R. Rep. No. 1711, 90th Cong., 2d Sess. (1968) 4; Rondeau v. Mosinee Paper Co., 422 U. S. 49, 58-59 (1975).

[63] General Time Corp. v. American Investors Fund, Inc., 283 F. Supp. 400, 403 (S. D. N. Y. 1968), *aff'd* sub nom. General Time Corp. v. Talley Industries, Inc., 403 F. 2d 159 (2d Cir. 1968), *cert. denied,* 393 U. S. 1026.

[64] We are told that the reaction of one official of a company that was subject to a takeover bid was: "This type of maneuver, which has been rampant in England, is, in my opinion, a wholly unfair and even an un-American approach." Mundheim, Why the Bill on Tender Offers Should Not Be Passed, 1 Institutional Investor 24 (May 1967). See generally Brudney, A Note on Chilling Tender Solicitations, 21 Rutgers L. Rev. 609 (1967); Jarrell and Bradley, The Economic Effects of Federal and State Regulations of Cash Tender Offers, 23 J. L. & Econ. 371 (1980).

3. Definitions and Exemptions

a. "Beneficial Owner," "Class," and "Group"

"Beneficial owner" is elaborately defined in Rule 13d-3 in terms basically of "voting power" and "investment power." The definition is quite different from the comparable definition under §16(a),[65] where the emphasis is on the economic incidence of ownership rather than the ability to shift control.[66]

The three reporting provisions themselves, in identical language, define "class" to exclude securities held by or for the issuer or a subsidiary[67] and provide that two or more persons acting as a partnership "or other group" for the purpose of acquiring, holding, or disposing of securities are considered a "person."[68] It has been variously held that the post-1968 formation of a group is an acquisition by the group "person" from the members of the group, so that the group must file under §13(d)(1) (and presumably §13(g)(1)) within ten days after its members agree to act together even though no member has acquired any security between 1968 and that time;[69] at the other extreme, that there is no acquisition by the group in such a case;[70] and, in the middle, that the duty to report is touched off only when the group *later* agrees to act in concert "to acquire additional shares," but that, once it is shown that a group has agreed to pursue a common objective and that a member has *thereafter* acquired additional shares, that acquisition creates a rebuttable presumption that the acquisition was pursuant to an agreement as of

[65] See p. 569 infra.

[66] Beneficial ownership may be disclaimed. Rule 13d-4. "Normally a registered representative of a broker-dealer will not be deemed to beneficially own common stock held in non-discretionary accounts of customers. However, in certain limited situations where a registered representative has or shares the *de facto* power to direct the voting or disposition of the securities in customer accounts, the registered representative may be deemed to beneficially own securities held by customers in non-discretionary accounts." Harvey Katz, Sec. Ex. Act Rel. 20,893, 30 SEC Dock. 417, 420 (1984).

[67] §§13(d)(4), 13(g)(4), 14(d)(3).

[68] §§13(d)(3), 13(g)(3), 14(d)(2). See Note, Group Formation Under Section 13(d) of the Securities Exchange Act of 1934, 33 Case W. Res. L. Rev. 72 (1982).

[69] GAF Corp. v. Milstein, 453 F. 2d 709 (2d Cir. 1971), *cert. denied,* 406 U. S. 910. The same court later distinguished the case of a *management* group created to stave off a tender offer: "Since the Exchange Act contains a specific provision governing the disclosures required of a target company's management, it would be pointless to superimpose requirements found in another section, which does not deal specifically with management disclosures." Corenco Corp. v. Schiavone & Sons, Inc., 488 F. 2d 207, 218 (2d Cir. 1973).

[70] Ozark Air Lines, Inc. v. Cox, 326 F. Supp. 1113 (E. D. Mo. 1971).

the acquisition date to acquire securities in furtherance of the group's objective.[71] The Commission has codified the first of these views by rule.[72]

In any event, a mere relationship (family, personal, or business) among individuals or entities does not create a group "person." There must be an agreement to act in concert,[73] though that agreement, obviously, need not be in writing.[74]

Query: Once there is a group "person," how does a member dissociate himself? Would it suffice simply to report that fact in a new filing? If the group refuses to make such a filing, could the ex-member do so, though he alone had never filed before? Wouldn't his filing be a self-serving statement? Would he have to go so far as to get rid of his stock?

b. "Tender Offer"

It is odd that, with everything in §14(d)-(f) turning on the existence of a "tender offer," that term is defined by neither statute nor rule. A *release* accompanying amendments to the very first preliminary rules referred to an exclusion (which must have been excised before the adoption of the amendments) of "offers to no more than ten security holders during any period of twelve months."[75] But no such exclusion has ever been adopted. And in 1976, after its tender offer hearings,[76] the Commission said that a definition was neither appropriate nor necessary in view of "the dynamic nature of these transactions and the need * * * to remain flexible."[77] In

[71] Bath Industries, Inc. v. Blot, 427 F. 2d 97, 108-10 (7th Cir. 1970).

[72] Rule 13d-5(b). But see Portsmouth Square, Inc. v. Shareholders Protective Committee, 770 F. 2d 866, 872 (9th Cir. 1985) ("Congress did not intend section 13(d) to apply to shareholders who attempt to raise funds for a lawsuit challenging the validity of existing corporate stock").

[73] Texasgulf, Inc. v. Canada Development Corp., 366 F. Supp. 374, 403 (S. D. Tex. 1973). Although parallel purchasing may evidence an agreement to act in concert, such purchasing to be persuasive would have to involve relatively large amounts of stock over a short period of time. Moreover, the mere sharing of certain information provides little support for a "group" conclusion. K-N Energy, Inc. v. Gulf Interstate Co., 607 F. Supp. 756 (D. Colo. 1983).

[74] SEC v. Savoy Industries, Inc., 587 F. 2d 1149, 1163 (D. C. Cir. 1978), *cert. denied,* 440 U. S. 913; Wellman v. Dickinson, 682 F. 2d 355, 362-63, *cert. denied* sub nom. Dickinson v. SEC, 460 U. S. 1069 (2d Cir. 1982).

[75] Sec. Ex. Act Rel. 8392 (1968).

[76] See Sec. Ex. Act Rel. 11,003, 5 SEC Dock. 115 (1974); Sec. Ex. Act Rel. 11,088, 5 SEC Dock. 406 (1974).

[77] Sec. Ex. Act Rel. 12,676, 10 SEC Dock. 143, 145 (1976); see also Sec. Ex. Act Rel. 15,548, 16 SEC Dock. 973, 980 (1979).

this state of affairs case law has pretty well settled a number of propositions:

It is clear that the concept is not limited to the classic page in the Wall Street Journal that confronts a surprised chief executive officer over his breakfast coffee. The Commission is on record[78] that "the term is to be interpreted flexibly and applies to special bids;[79] purchase resulting from widespread solicitations by means of mailings, telephone calls and personal visits; and any transaction where the conduct of the person seeking control causes pressures to be put on shareholders similar to those attendant to a conventional tender offer." And that is about as good a generalization concerning the case law as any.[80] We are reminded that there is no "constitutional requirement that the legislative standards be translated by the Commission into formal and detailed rules of thumb prior to their application in a particular case."[81] Moreover, although *hostile* offers formed the immediate catalyst for the Williams Act, a tender offer is no less a tender offer because it is unopposed by the target; for "there is no reason to assume that the danger [of the stockholders'

[78] Sec. Ex. Act Rel. 12,676, 10 SEC Dock. 143, 145 (1976); see generally Zuckerman v. Franz, 573 F. Supp. 351, 358 (S. D. Fla. 1983); Note, The Developing Meaning of "Tender Offer" Under the Securities Exchange Act of 1934, 86 Harv. L. Rev. 1250 (1973).

[79] See also Sec. Ex. Act Rel. 16,112, 18 SEC Dock. 67, 71 (1979). This refers to a special stock exchange procedure for filling bids for blocks too large to be filled in the regular auction market. See 2 Loss c. 7F, esp. at 1238-39.

[80] See Cattlemen's Investment Co. v. Fears, 343 F. Supp. 1248, 1251-52 (W. D. Okla. 1972) (alleged "active and widespread solicitation of public shareholders in person, over the telephone and through the mails" seems designed even more than a general newspaper advertisement to force a shareholder into making a hurried investment decision); S-G Securities, Inc. v. Fuqua Investment Co., 466 F. Supp. 1114, 1126-27 (D. Mass. 1978) ("(1) a publicly announced intention by the purchaser to acquire a substantial block of the stock of the target company for purposes of acquiring control thereof; and (2) a subsequent rapid acquisition by the purchaser of large blocks of stock through open market and privately negotiated purchases").

But cf. University Bank & Trust Co. v. Gladstone, 574 F. Supp. 1006 (D. Mass. 1983) ("record falls short of establishing the high-pressure, take-it-or-leave-it, rapid accumulation of stock that normally signals a tender offer"). In SEC v. Carter Hawley Hale Stores, Inc., 760 F. 2d 945, 950-52 (9th Cir. 1985), the court preferred the eight-factor test suggested by the Commission in Wellman v. Dickinson, 475 F. Supp. 783, 823-24 (S. D. N. Y. 1979), *aff'd on other grounds*, 682 F. 2d 355 (2d Cir. 1982), *cert. denied* sub nom. Dickinson v. SEC, 460 U. S. 1069, over the test in *S-G Securities*, supra, which it considered "vague and difficult to apply."

[81] Wellman v. Dickinson, 475 F. Supp. 783, 826 (S. D. N. Y. 1979), *aff'd on other grounds*, 682 F. 2d 355 (2d Cir. 1982), *cert. denied* sub nom. Dickinson v. SEC, 460 U. S. 1069, quoting from American Power & Light Co. v. SEC, 329 U. S. 90, 106 (1946).

being misled by the offeror or the target's management] will be lessened when both are on the same side of the fence."[82]

On the other hand, a tender offer does not result *merely* from unsolicited market purchases[83] or privately negotiated transactions at premium prices[84] or both.[85] This legitimates the "creeping tender offer" practice whereby the proposed tender offeror accumulates just under 5 percent and *then* makes its tender offer. But this may not be true with respect to *issuer* tender offers[86] or someone's purchases either to *block* a tender offer or to cement an existing control position.[87]

On the question of what changes create a new "tender offer," it was the staff's view before the 1986 adoption of the "best-price" rule that a decrease in the price or the number of shares (the statute in §14(d)(7) refers only to increases), or the offeror's bringing a partner in during the offer, required the offeror to terminate its existing offer, return all shares, and start a new offer with new time periods.[88] But the "best-price" rule, as we have seen,[89] brought a reversal of that position.

Statutory mergers and consolidations are not tender offers.[90] Nor is an issuer's purchase under a statutory appraisal procedure when

[82] Smallwood v. Pearl Brewing Co., 489 F. 2d 579, 598 (5th Cir. 1974), *cert. denied*, 419 U. S. 873.

[83] See City Investing Co. v. Simcox, 633 F. 2d 56, 61 n. 11 (7th Cir. 1980) (dictum that no court has so held); Sec. Ex. Act Rel. 16,385, 18 SEC Dock. 1092, 1095 (1979). Support is lent to this conclusion by the impossibility of applying the withdrawal, proration, and equal price provisions of §14(d)(5)-(7) to market purchases.

[84] Kennecott Copper Corp. v. Curtiss-Wright Corp., 584 F. 2d 1195, 1206-07 (2d Cir. 1978); Rand v. Anaconda Ericsson, Inc., 794 F. 2d 843, 848 (2d Cir. 1986), *cert. denied*, 107 S. Ct. 579.

[85] Brascan, Ltd. v. Edper Equities, Ltd., 477 F. Supp. 773, 789 (S. D. N. Y. 1979); Energy Ventures, Inc. v. Appalachian Co., 587 F. Supp. 734 (D. Del. 1984); see also cases cited supra p. 513 n. 52.

[86] See Kerr, Corporate Stock Repurchases — Substantive Trading Restrictions, in Practising Law Institute, Sixth Annual Institute on Securities Regulation (1975) 3, 29.

[87] See Lipton in Law, Lipton, and Flom, Take-Over Bids: Recent Developments, in Practising Law Institute, Seventh Annual Institute on Securities Regulation (1976) 181, 208.

[88] See Greene, Developments in Offense, in Practising Law Institute, Sixteenth Annual Institute on Securities Regulation (1984) c. 10 at 136-39; cf. Brill v. Burlington Northern, Inc., 590 F. Supp. 893, 898-900 (D. Del. 1984), supra p. 512 n. 43.

[89] See p. 513 supra.

[90] Sec. Ex. Act Rel. 16,385, 18 SEC Dock. 1092, 1097 (1979). This is true also when the merger contains a cash option feature. Sec. Ex. Act Rel. 14,699, 14 SEC Dock. 894, 899-900 (1978), followed in Beaumont v. American Can Co., 621 F. Supp. 484, 500 (S. D. N. Y. 1985), *aff'd on other grounds*, 797 F. 2d 79 (2d Cir. 1986). The second (merger) step in a two-tier tender offer has never been considered part of the tender offer for purposes of §14(d)(7).

preemptive rights are eliminated.[91] And the absence of "a statutory checklist of features" led the Second Circuit to apply a "rule of reason" so as to conclude that an announcement in the Wall Street Journal that professed not to be a tender offer, and that stated that tenders could be made only after stockholders had received a printed offer, fell short of being a tender offer.[92]

The Commission has abandoned two attempts at an objective solution. One was a proposed rule, published in 1979, that would have supplied a two-tier definition — partly objective, partly subjective: *either* (1) one or more offers to buy (or solicitations of offers to sell) more than 5 percent of a single class, directed to more than ten persons during any forty-five-day period (other than market offers at market prices without solicitation or unusual brokers' commissions or dealers' markups), *or* (2) dissemination of an offer in a widespread manner, and with a premium in excess of the greater of 5 percent or $2 above market, without "a meaningful opportunity to negotiate the price and terms."[93] The other proposal — a legislative solution that the Commission submitted to Congress in 1980,[94] only to say four years later that it was giving the matter further study[95] — would simply have required that any purchases in excess of 10 percent of a company's shares be made through a public tender offer.

c. Exemptions

There are no exemptions from §13(e) or 14(e), although both sections give the Commission authority to exempt by rule.

Section 13(d)(6) exempts offers to buy in consideration of securities registered under the 1933 Act. In addition, both that section and §14(d)(8), apart from giving the Commission rulemaking authority to exempt, afford automatic exemptions for (1) acquisitions up to 2 percent of the class in a twelve-month period and (2) issuer acquisitions of their own equity securities. But the Commission

[91] Leighton v. American Telephone & Telegraph Co., 397 F. Supp. 133 (S. D. N. Y. 1975).

[92] Corenco Corp. v. Schiavone & Sons, Inc., 488 F. 2d 207, 216 (2d Cir. 1973). The court referred by analogy to Rules 134 and 135 under the 1933 Act. See pp. 99, 107 supra.

[93] Sec. Ex. Act Rel. 16,385, 18 SEC Dock. 1092, 1108 (1979); see also Code §202(166)(A).

[94] S. 1388, 96th Cong. 2d Sess. (1980).

[95] H. R. Rep. No. 98-1028, 98th Cong., 2d Sess. (1984) 12.

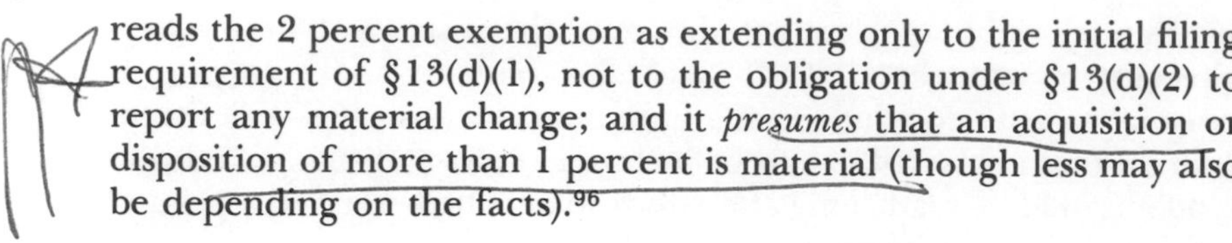

reads the 2 percent exemption as extending only to the initial filing requirement of §13(d)(1), not to the obligation under §13(d)(2) to report any material change; and it *presumes* that an acquisition or disposition of more than 1 percent is material (though less may also be depending on the facts).[96]

4. The Rules

Since the late 1970s there has been a veritable orgy of rulemaking under the Williams Act provisions as the Commission has replaced its temporary rules with an elaborate regulatory structure and as the tender offer practices have rapidly evolved. Portions of the scheme — for example, the definition of "beneficial owner" in Rule 13d-3 — have already been touched on. Our endeavor here is to present the "big picture" in inevitably summarized and incomplete form.

Regulation D-G, adopted under §§13(d) and 13(g), consists of Rules 13d-1 to 13d-7. And Rule 13d-1 requires the filing of Schedule 13D or 13G as the case may be.[97]

Rule 13e-1 prohibits a target company from buying any of its equity securities during another's tender offer unless it files a statement (and within the past six months has sent or given its equity security holders the substance of the information) with respect to such data as the manner and purpose of the purchases and the source of funds to be used.

There is no Rule 13e-2. A proposed rule under that number that would have imposed both disclosure requirements and substantive purchasing limitations on issuers' stock repurchases was ultimately adopted in different form as Rule 10b-18.[98]

Rule 13e-3 is directed at the "going private" phenomenon. There are ways of "going private" other than by the issuer's or an affiliate's buying up the publicly held stock — notably the "reverse split" and the "freezeout."[99] The Supreme Court aborted an attempt to make a Rule 10b-5 violation out of "a breach of fiduciary duty by majority

[96] Sec. Ex. Act Rel. 17,353, 21 SEC Dock. 775, 779 (1980). There are also exemptions in some of the rules.

[97] For a collection of staff views, see Sec. Ex. Act Rel. 16,623, 19 SEC Dock. 807 (1980).

[98] See p. 867 infra.

[99] This refers to the procedure, available under the laws of many states, whereby those in control initiate a merger into a corporate shell that they own and require public holders to take cash or a newly created debt security. But see, e. g., Bryan v. Brock & Blevins Co., Inc., 490 F. 2d 563 (5th Cir. 1974),

stockholders, without any deception, misrepresentation, or nondisclosure."[100] But the Commission has tried its hand by way of Rule 13e-3.

In early 1975 the Commission, in giving notice of a public investigation and rulemaking proceeding, suggested alternative versions of a rule: both versions would have turned on "fair value," but, in addition, one would have required two independent valuations and the other a valid business purpose.[101] In adopting Rule 13e-3 more than four years later, the Commission expressed the belief that the fairness question should be deferred until there was an opportunity to determine the efficacy of the new rule.[102] And the Commission also abandoned the idea of valid business purpose. But Schedule 13E-3 requires a statement whether the issuer or affiliate filing the schedule "reasonably believes that the Rule 13e-3 transaction is fair or unfair to unaffiliated security holders," with a discussion in reasonable detail of the enumerated factors on which the belief with respect to fairness is based.[103]

A "Rule 13e-3 transaction" is defined as (1) a purchase of an equity security by the issuer or an affiliate, (2) a tender offer for an equity security made by the issuer or an affiliate, or (3) a solicitation subject to Regulation 14A or 14C in connection with a merger or similar transaction, sale of assets to an affiliate, or reverse stock split involving the purchase of fractional interests, if in any such case the transaction has a reasonable likelihood or purpose of causing either (a) termination of reporting obligations by bringing the number of record holders below 300 or (b) a class of equity securities to be neither listed nor authorized to be quoted on an interdealer quotation system.[104]

---

cert. denied, 419 U. S. 844 (Georgia law); Singer v. Magnavox Co., 380 A. 2d 969 (Del. 1977).

In general, see Am. B. Assn., Com. on Corp. Laws, Guidelines on Going Private, 37 Bus. Law. 313 (1981); A. Borden, Going Private (1982). On the incidental problems that arise as a matter of corporation law, see Brudney, A Note on "Going Private," 61 Va. L. Rev. 1019 (1975); Note, Going Private, 84 Yale L. J. 903 (1975).

[100] Santa Fe Industries, Inc. v. Green, 430 U. S. 462 (1977), infra p. 804. But cf., e. g., Goldberg v. Meridor, 567 F. 2d 209, *cert. denied,* 434 U. S. 1069 (2d Cir. 1977) (alleged nondisclosure to stockholders when all the directors were part of the alleged deceit); Healey v. Catalyst Recovery of Pa., Inc., 616 F. 2d 641 (3d Cir. 1980).

[101] Sec. Ex. Act Rel. 11,231, 6 SEC Dock. 250 (1975).

[102] Sec. Ex. Act Rel. 16,075, 17 SEC Dock. 1449, 1451 (1979).

[103] Sch. 13E-3, Item 8. See Howing Co. v. Nationwide Corp., 625 F. Supp. 146 (S. D. Ohio 1985).

[104] Rule 13e-3(a)(3). For a collection of staff views on the rule, see Sec. Ex. Act Rel. 17,719, 22 SEC Dock. 783 (1981). Although §13(e) is restricted to "an

The next rule, 13e-4, applies to issuer tender offers generally.[105] And we have noticed the 1986 insertion of "all-holders" and "best-price" rules. If Rule 13e-3 applies by its terms, Rule 13e-4 continues to apply as well. Moreover, even when both those rules apply, that does not exclude Rule 13e-1.[106] Schedule 13E-4 resembles Schedule 14D-1.

Aside from the rules under §13(d)-(e), the Commission adopted a whole new set of rules under §14(d)-(e) effective in January 1980.[107] They are, unhappily, both long — 16 two-column pages in the SEC

---

issuer which has a class of equity securities registered pursuant to section 12 of this title, or which is a closed-end investment company registered under the Investment Company Act of 1940," Rule 13e-3(c)(1) extends to an issuer (or its affiliate) within §15(d). *Query* whether the Commission's reliance on §10(b) for this extension (Sec. Ex. Act Rel. 14,185, 13 SEC Dock. 839, 847 (1982)) is justified in the face of a §13(e) that is as restricted as it is.

It has been held that "conclusionary allegations of a 'reasonable likelihood' probably suffice to withstand a motion to dismiss a claim under Rule 13e-3," and that the mere possibility that the company may list its stock on another exchange or over the counter does not preclude violation of the rule. Shamrock Associates v. Horizon Corp., 632 F. Supp. 566, 572 (S. D. N. Y. 1986). Moreover, the "reasonable likelihood" must be determined without regard to the tender offeror's own purchase, which the target cannot control. Maynard Oil Co. v. Deltec Panamerica, S. A., 630 F. Supp. 502, 505-07 (S. D. N. Y. 1985).

On the Wisconsin "going private" regulation, Wis. Ad. Code §SEC 6.05, which was modeled on proposed SEC Rule 13e-3A, Sec. Ex. Act Rel. 5567, 6 SEC Dock. 250 (1975), see Comment, Regulation of Going Private Transactions in Wisconsin and the Effect of *Edgar* v. *MITE*, [1983] Wis. L. Rev. 689.

[105]The rule was adopted by Sec. Ex. Act Rel. 16,112, 18 SEC Dock. 67 (1979). And in Sec. Ex. Act Rel. 19,988, 28 SEC Dock. 423 (1983), the Commission amended the rule (with a companion amendment to 13e-3) in order to except tender offers by issuers to buy shares from their securityholders (other than participants in a stock purchase, dividend reinvestment, or similar plan) who own a specified number of shares below 100 as of a specified date before the announcement of the offer. "In light of their limited purpose and the fact that they are not characterized by large premiums or significant market impact, Odd-lot Offers present minimal potential for fraud and manipulation." Id. at 423.

On an analysis of the economic effect on target shareholders of defensive target repurchases of its stock, it has been contended that defensive purchases generate substantial pressure on target shareholders to sell in much the same manner as other tender offers create pressure to tender to the outside offeror. Bradley and Rosenzweig, Defensive Stock Repurchases, 99 Harv. L. Rev. 1378 (1986). For a critique of that article, see Gordon and Kornhauser, Takeover Defense Tactics: A Comment on Two Models, 96 Yale L. J. 295 (1986). For replies, see Bradley and Rosenzweig, Defensive Stock Repurchases and the Appraisal Remedy, 96 Yale L. J. 322 (1986); McChesney, Assumptions, Empirical Evidence, and Social Science Method, 96 Yale L. J. 339 (1986); Macey, Takeover Defense Tactics and Legal Scholarship: Market Forces Versus the Policymaker's Dilemma, 96 Yale L. J. 342 (1986). See also p. 502 n. 13 supra.

[106]Maynard Oil Co. v. Deltec Panamerica, S. A., 630 F. Supp. 502, 505 (S. D. N. Y. 1985).

[107]Sec. Ex. Act Rel. 16,384, 18 SEC Dock. 1053 (1979).

Docket — and complex. We shall have to settle for a few highlights:

(1) One way that a cash tender offer "commences" is by *any* public announcement that identifies the offeror and the target and states the amount, class, and price range, *unless* within five business days the offeror either (a) publicly reneges or (b) files a Schedule 14D-1, *hands* it to the target and any other offeror that has filed a Schedule 14D-1, and telephones specified information and mails a copy of the schedule to every exchange on which the security is traded (as well as NASDAQ[108] if the security is quoted there); and in the latter event (that is to say, if the offeror acts as in (b)) the date of commencement is the date that specified information is first published or sent to security holders.[109] The effect of this peculiar on-again-off-again formula — as well as, one suspects, its purpose — is to buttress the Commission's preemption argument with respect to those state tender offer statutes that impose a post-filing waiting period and sometimes a hearing procedure before a tender offer may be made.[110]

(2) Rule 14d-5 is a stockholder list rule modeled on Rule 14a-7.[111]

(3) Neither the target company nor specified persons connected with it may do any soliciting or recommending without filing a "recommendation statement" on Schedule 14D-9 and circulating copies as specified. There is an exception, however, for a "stop, look, and listen" communication in which the target may request holders to wait up to ten business days for the target's views.[112]

(4) In any event, the target, within ten business days, *must* publish or give security holders a reasoned statement to the effect that it recommends acceptance or rejection, is remaining neutral, or is unable to take a position.[113]

The same day that these new §14(d)-(e) rules were adopted, the

[108]See p. 600 infra.

[109]Rule 14d-2. The rule uses the term "bidder," which is defined in Rule 14d-1(b)(1) to mean "any person who makes a tender offer or on whose behalf a tender offer is made" (except for an issuer making a "self-tender"). The defined term does not include (1) majority shareholders without evidence of financial participation or (2) commercial lenders that provide funds to finance a tender offer. Revlon, Inc. v. Pantry Pride, Inc., 621 F. Supp. 804, 814, 817 (D. Del. 1985).

[110]See pp. 533-39 infra. The conflict "is so direct and substantial as to make it impossible to comply with both sets of requirements as they presently exist." Sec. Ex. Act Rel. 16,384, 18 SEC Dock. 1053, 1060 (1979).

[111]See p. 466 supra.

[112]Rule 14d-9.

[113]Rule 14e-2. Rule 14e-3, an insider trading rule, is discussed later. See p. 759 infra.

Commission invited comment on still further proposals and questions, including the need for rules with respect to the impact of defensive charter amendments on tender offer practice and interested investors.[114] And in 1986 came the "all-holders" and "best-price" rules.[115]

Finally, the Commission has used its §10(b) authority to adopt two rules that relate to tender offers: Rule 10b-4, which we have already noticed, to prohibit "short tenders,"[116] and Rule 10b-13, which prohibits a person making a cash tender offer or exchange offer for *any* equity security (whether or not registered) from buying or arranging to buy any such security (or any other security that is immediately convertible into any such security) outside the tender or exchange offer — a practice sometimes called buying "alongside" the tender offer.[117] The latter rule is made inapplicable to purchases pursuant to stock option plans within specified sections of the Internal Revenue Code. And the Commission reserves an *ad hoc* exemptive authority.

5. Content of the Schedules

As with respect to other filings,[118] it has been held that the Williams Act filing requirements impose a duty to file truthfully and completely.[119]

[114]Sec. Ex. Act Rel. 16,385, 18 SEC Dock. 1092 (1979).

[115]Rule 14d-10, supra p. 513.

[116]See p. 511 supra.

[117]See Swanson v. Wabash, Inc., 577 F. Supp. 1308, 1317 (N. D. Ill. 1983) (the rule would be violated if some shareholders received "a *real* benefit not accorded to other shareholders" (italics added)); Pryor v. United States Steel Corp., 591 F. Supp. 942, 960-61 (S. D. N. Y. 1984), *aff'd in part and rev'd in part on other grounds,* 794 F. 2d 52 (2d Cir. 1986), *cert. denied,* 107 S. Ct. 445 (SEC did not intend "that any deviation, however minor, from the terms of a tender offer in the purchase of shares, would constitute a violation of 10b-13"); City National Bank v. American Commonwealth Financial Corp., 801 F. 2d 714 (4th Cir. 1986) (one's status as a party to an executory contract to buy stock in the future does not immunize him from the rule); Burack, When Buying Rights Is Wrong: Purchases of Target Company Stock During Exchange Offers and Mergers, 33 Bus. Law. 605 (1978).

Rule 10b-13 was adopted also under §§13(e) and 14(e). Sec. Ex. Act Rel. 8712 (1969).

[118]See pp. 433-34 supra.

[119]GAF Corp. v. Milstein, 453 F. 2d 709, 720 (2d Cir. 1971), *cert. denied,* 406 U. S. 910; SEC v. Savoy Industries, Inc., 587 F. 2d 1149, 1165 (D. C. Cir. 1978), *cert. denied,* 440 U. S. 913. "A person or group filing a Schedule 13D may not use 'investment' as a catch-all purpose when the plans for implementing another purpose or purposes are indefinite or undeveloped." K-N Energy, Inc. v. Gulf Interstate Co., 607 F. Supp. 756 (D. Colo. 1983).

Rules 14d-4(c) and 14d-6(d) — together with Rules 13e-4(d)(2) and 13e-4(e)(2)

As with respect to the proxy statement,[120] it is the Commission's position, too, that "Disclosure of material facts is not limited to the specific requirements of" the schedules.[121] For there is always §14(e) as there is Rule 14a-9. It follows that a tender offeror's financial statements of one kind or another might be "material" even if not specifically required by the appropriate schedule.[122] Schedule 14D-1 — as well as Schedules 13E-3 and 13E-4 with respect to issuer tender offers — now refers specifically to financial data of one kind or another.[123] This moots the question to a large extent — but not entirely, because Schedule 14D-1 requires "adequate" financial information only when the offeror is not a natural person and its financial condition is "material" to target stockholders,[124] and Schedule 13E-4 likewise contains the "material" modifier. There is thus some rubber left. Financial information may be material under the circumstances even in the case of a cash offer, particularly if it is a partial offer.[125]

6. False or Misleading Statements [§14(e)]

Section 14(e) is beginning to rival Rule 10b-5 as the subject of litigation.[126] It would not be an exaggeration to say that there has

---

with respect to issuer tender offers — specifically require material changes to be promptly disclosed to security holders. For a statement designed to clarify the Commission's view "that a waiver of a minimum share condition is a material change," and to reiterate the Commission's view that the rules require that material changes "be disseminated in a manner reasonably calculated to inform security holders of such changes and with sufficient time for security holders to absorb such new information," see Sec. Ex. Act Rel. 24,296, 38 SEC Dock. 17, 18-19 (1987).

[120] See p. 464 supra.

[121] Sch. 14D-1, Item 10(f); Sec. Ex. Act Rel. 13,787, 12 SEC Dock. 1256, 1264 n. 22 (1977).

[122] For a review of the cases, see Prudent Real Estate Trust v. Johncamp Realty, Inc., 599 F. 2d 1140 (2d Cir. 1979). But this is limited to "such additional information as may be necessary to make the disclosures required by other items not materially misleading." Weinberger v. Rio Grande Industries, Inc., 519 A. 2d 116, 124-25 (Del. Ch. 1986).

[123] Sch. 13E-3, Item 14; Sch. 13E-4, Item 7; Sch. 14D-1, Item 9.

[124] "The facts and circumstances concerning the tender offer, particularly the terms of the tender offer, may influence a determination as to whether disclosure of financial information is material. However, once the materiality requirement is applicable, the adequacy of the financial information will depend primarily on the nature of the bidder." Sch. 14D-1, Item 9, Instr. 1.

[125] Life Investors, Inc. v. AGO Holding, N. V., CCH Fed. Sec. L. Rep. ¶98,356 at 92,194 (8th Cir. 1981).

[126] See Lowenstein, Section 14(e) of the Williams Act and Rule 10b-5 Comparisons, 71 Geo. L. J. 1311 (1983).

hardly been a contested tender offer in which both sides have not hurled §14(e) thunderbolts at each other.

The section does not track Rule 14a-9, the proxy fraud rule, as closely as it might. For example, it is an open question whether the "solicitation" of §14(e) is as broad as the "solicit" of §14(a).[127] But much of what has been said in the discussion of Rule 14a-9 applies equally here. For example:

(1) *Standard of disclosure:* Judge Friendly cautioned in the first appellate opinion on the Williams Act that tender offers, like proxy contests, generally are contests. "Congress intended to assure basic honesty and fair dealing, not to impose an unrealistic requirement of laboratory conditions that might make the new statute a potent tool for incumbent management to protect its own interests against the desires and welfare of the stockholders."[128] At the same time, the tender offeror may not look to the target to remedy its own disclosure deficiencies.[129] So far as antitrust implications are concerned, all that is required is "the disclosure of basic facts so that outsiders may draw upon their own evaluated experience in reaching their own investment decisions with knowledge equal to that of the insiders."[130]

(2) *Materiality:* There is no reason to believe that materiality does not have the same meaning in the two contexts.[131]

(3) *Scienter:* Section 14(e), though not quite as broad as Rule 14a-9,[132] is, like §17(a) of the 1933 Act and unlike Rule 10b-5, a statute and not a rule. Therefore, the Supreme Court's construction of §17(a) should govern so as to conclude that scienter (whatever its meaning) is required by the "fraudulent" and "deceptive" clause of §14(e), which more or less tracks §17(a)(1) of the 1933 Act and

[127] See Sargent v. Genesco, Inc., 492 F. 2d 750, 769 (5th Cir. 1974). See also p. 455 supra.

The application of §14(e) does not have to await an actual tender offer. SEC v. Gaspar, CCH Fed. Sec. L. Rep. ¶92,004 at 90,979 (S. D. N. Y. 1985), and cases cited.

[128] Electronic Specialty Co. v. International Controls Corp., 409 F. 2d 937, 948 (2d Cir. 1969). See also Data Probe Acquisitions Corp. v. Datatab, Inc., 722 F. 2d 1, 5-6 (2d Cir. 1983), *cert. denied*, 465 U. S. 1052: "The disclosure required by the Act [specifically Rule 14e-2] is not a rite of confession or exercise in common law pleading." In the proxy context, see p. 479 supra.

[129] Sonesta Int'l Hotels Corp. v. Wellington Associates, 483 F. 2d 247, 255 (2d Cir. 1973).

[130] Gulf & Western Industries, Inc. v. Great Atlantic & Pacific Tea Co., 476 F. 2d 687, 697 (2d Cir. 1973).

[131] Electronic Specialty Co. v. International Controls Corp., 409 F. 2d 937, 948 (2d Cir. 1969); see also TSC Industries, Inc. v. Northway, Inc., 426 U. S. 438 (1976), supra p. 480.

[132] See p. 478 supra.

§10(b) of the 1934 Act, but not by the untrue statement clause, which *precisely* tracks §17(a)(2).[133]

(4) *Plaintiff need not be a buyer or seller:* It has been held that there is no basis for applying to §14(e) the requirement under Rule 10b-5 that the plaintiff be a buyer or seller.[134]

(5) *"Manipulative":* In *Schreiber v. Burlington Northern, Inc.*, the Court concluded unanimously (except for the nonparticipation of Justices Powell and O'Connor) that the term "manipulative" in §14(e) required misrepresentation or nondisclosure of the acts complained of. This, the Court held, was consistent with both the common law concept of manipulation as affecting market activity by means of practices such as wash sales and rigged prices[135] and the earlier holding in *Santa Fe Industries, Inc.* v. *Green*[136] that §10(b) did not cover mismanagement without some sort of misrepresentation. Consequently Schreiber's withdrawal of a hostile tender offer in favor of an offer negotiated with the target did not amount to a "manipulative" distortion of the market as long as everything was fully disclosed.[137]

[133] Aaron v. SEC, 446 U. S. 680 (1980), infra p. 783. Scienter is *not* required with respect to §13(d)(1), or presumably §14(d)(1). SEC v. Savoy Industries, Inc., 587 F. 2d 1149, 1167 (D. C. Cir. 1978). In Pryor v. United States Steel Corp., 591 F. Supp. 942, 955 (S. D. N. Y. 1984), *aff'd in part and rev'd in part on other grounds,* 794 F. 2d 52 (2d Cir. 1986), *cert. denied,* 107 S. Ct. 445, the court, while expressing reservations about applying its scienter view under Rule 10b-5 to the misstatement portion of §14(e), nevertheless did so on an *in pari materia* approach as between §14(e) and Rule 10b-5. See also Connecticut National Bank v. Fluor Corp., 808 F. 2d 957, 961 (2d Cir. 1987). But in Caleb & Co. v. E. I. duPont de Nemours & Co., 599 F. Supp. 1468 (S. D. N. Y. 1984), the court distinguished *Pryor* with respect to an action brought not directly under §14(e) but under Rule 14e-1, which flatly requires a tender offeror to pay or return the deposited securities promptly after the termination or withdrawal of the offer; the court reasoned that the activity prohibited by a *rule* under §14(e) need not be itself fraudulent as long as the rule was reasonably designed to *prevent* fraud. There is also a dictum to the same effect in Schreiber v. Burlington Northern, Inc., 472 U. S. 1, — n. 11 (1985), infra p. 707 n. 23. See generally p. 786 infra.

[134] Pryor v. United States Steel Corp., 591 F. Supp. 942, 954 (S. D. N. Y. 1984), *aff'd in part and rev'd in part on other grounds,* 794 F. 2d 52 (2d Cir. 1984), *cert. denied,* 107 S. Ct. 445. See p. 792 infra.

[135] 472 U. S. 1, 7 (1985), citing the text at pp. 845-50.

[136] 430 U. S. 462 (1977), infra p. 804.

[137] See also, e. g., Data Probe Acquisition Corp. v. Datatab, Inc., 722 F. 2d 1 (2d Cir. 1983), *cert. denied,* 465 U. S. 1052 (certain options granted to a prospective merger partner during the course of a tender offer, the practical effect being to guarantee that exercise of the options would result in the target's acquisition through a merger no matter how many outstanding shares were tendered, were not a manipulative device under §14(e)); Gearhart Industries, Inc. v. Smith Int'l, Inc., 741 F. 2d 707, 724 (5th Cir. 1984) ("springing" warrants); Biechele v. Cedar Point, Inc., 747 F. 2d 209 (6th Cir. 1984) (neither an add-on agreement nor a standstill agreement was a "manipulative" device under

(6) *"Fraudulent":* Although §14(e) adds "fraudulent" to the "manipulative or deceptive" of §10(b), the two sections have been treated *in pari materia.*[138]

(7) *Causation:* In *Schreiber,* where the plaintiff alleged that the target management and the tender offeror had entered into undisclosed and deceptive agreements in connection with the *second* offer but the complaint sought redress only in connection with the cancellation of the *first* offer, the Court held that the allegedly deceptive acts "bear no possible causal relationship to [the plaintiff's] alleged injuries."[139]

7. Enforcement

What has been said with respect to enforcement of the proxy rules — the absence of an effective administrative sanction, the quantitative primacy of private litigation, and the breadth of the courts' ancillary jurisdiction with respect to the scope of relief — applies here *mutatis mutandis.*[140] And we shall similarly explore the

---

the circumstances); Radol v. Thomas, 772 F. 2d 244, 255 (6th Cir. 1985) (two-tier tender offer), *cert. denied,* 106 U. S. 3272; Pin v. Texaco, Inc., 793 F. 2d 1448 (5th Cir. 1986), *rehearing en banc denied,* 797 F. 2d 977 (5th Cir. 1986).

On the *Schreiber* case and the meaning of "manipulative" in §§10(b) and 14(e), see Poser, Stock Market Manipulation — Corporate Control Transactions, 40 U. Miami L. Rev. 671 (1986). Judge Poser observes that the Court in *Schreiber* ignored *Santa Fe*'s qualifying language to the effect that "nondisclosure is *usually* essential to the success of a manipulative scheme" (italics supplied). He also perceptively discusses several questions that *Schreiber* leaves open: What is the nature of the misrepresentation or nondisclosure that is a requisite for manipulation? Does a failure to reveal the motives or possible consequences of the defendant's actions provide the necessary nondisclosure? What is the nature of the intent that must be proved? Does it differ for different kinds of manipulation? What does "manipulative" add to "deceptive" anyway if the former requires deceit?

For a criticism of *Schreiber* concluding that broad federal legislation is needed to limit the uses of certain tender offer defenses, see Fiflis, Of Lollypops and Law — A Proposal for a National Policy Concerning Tender Offer Defenses, 19 U. Cal. Davis L. Rev. 303 (1986). For a suggestion that the state law approach "promises to be more fruitful than *ex cathedra* pronouncements on 'manipulation' have been," see Note, Lock-Up Options: Toward a State Law Standard, 96 Harv. L. Rev. 1068, 1081-82 (1983).

In any event, *Schreiber* should not govern §9(a)(2), the principal antimanipulation section (see p. 853 infra), which presumably does not require deception beyond the falsification of market appearance created by the trading.

[138] Golub v. PPD Corp., 576 F. 2d 759 (8th Cir. 1978); Panter v. Marshall Field & Co., 646 F. 2d 271, 282 (7th Cir. 1981), *cert. denied,* 454 U. S. 1082; Mobil Corp. v. Marathon Oil Co., 669 F. 2d 366 (6th Cir. 1984), *cert. denied,* 455 U. S. 982.

[139] 472 U. S. at 13.

[140] See pp. 491-97.

scope of relief here, because that is relevant to SEC as well as private actions, leaving the question of implying private actions to the chapter on civil liability.

In *Rondeau* v. *Mosinee Paper Corp.*, an action for injunction under §13(d), the Supreme Court held that the plaintiff must "satisfy the traditional prerequisites of extraordinary equitable relief by establishing irreparable harm" notwithstanding "the fact that [he] is pursuing a cause of action which has been generally recognized to serve the public interest."[141] The defendant filed a Schedule 13D more than two months late, but did so as soon as he learned of the 1970 amendment that reduced the §13(d) figure from 10 to 5 percent. That is to say, the violations were inadvertent and the defendant took immediate steps to rectify them.

This case must not be read too broadly. The Chief Justice took pains to point out:

> Because this case involves only the availability of injunctive relief to remedy a §13(d) violation following compliance with the reporting requirements, it does not require us to decide whether or under what circumstances a corporation could obtain a decree enjoining a shareholder who is currently in violation of §13(d) from acquiring further shares, exercising voting rights, or launching a takeover bid, pending compliance with the reporting requirements.[142]

This seems to refute any categorical requirement that the Commission in its own injunctive actions must show "irreparable harm" as distinct from "equity," which gets down to whether the defendant's past conduct indicates — under all the circumstances and not merely in view of the time that has elapsed since the last violation — that there is a reasonable likelihood of further violation in the future. For SEC injunctions are creatures of statute. As the Supreme Court said in *Hecht Co.* v. *Bowles,* which was relied upon in the *Rondeau* case, "the standards of the public interest, not the requirements of private litigation, measure the propriety and need for injunctive relief in these cases."[143] But *query.*

[141] 422 U. S. 49, 61, 65 (1975); see also Gulf Corp. v. Mesa Petroleum Co., 582 F. Supp. 1110, 1116 (D. Del. 1984) (any suggestion that company's February publications would affect shareholder decisions at the annual meeting in May was "too speculative"); MacFadden Holdings, Inc. v. JB Acquisition Co., 802 F. 2d 62, 67 (2d Cir. 1986) (courts must "exercise care so not to impede the informed choice of the shareholders of a target company").

[142] 422 U. S. at 59 n. 9.

[143] 321 U. S. 331; cf. SEC v. Capital Gains Research Bureau, Inc., 375 U. S. 180, 192 (1963); see generally SEC v. American Board of Trade, Inc., 751 F. 2d 529 (2d Cir. 1984); see also 3 Loss 1975-80; 6 id. 4109-17; p. 72 n. 3 supra; Pitt and Markham, SEC Injunctive Actions, 6 Rev. Sec. Reg. 955 (1973), an

At any rate, when the plaintiff establishes that some relief is appropriate, there is a great variety of precedent to choose from.[144] To proceed once more by way of example:

Under §13(d) one formula restrains further purchases until a corrected schedule has been filed,[145] and perhaps for a period of thirty days or so thereafter.[146] The courts, while conceiving of the possibility of divestiture or disfranchisement, seem to regard those remedies as rather harsh.[147]

Relief under §14(d)-(e) has included extension of the depositing security holders' statutory right to withdraw,[148] preliminary restraint against transferring or hypothecating deposited shares in order to permit their return if it should ultimately be ordered,[149] and requiring both sides to start over when both have violated.[150]

---

essay by two SEC staff members that takes objection to the somewhat softer line in Mathews, SEC Civil Injunctive Actions, 5 Rev. Sec. Reg. 969 (1972). The court's discretion is particularly broad with respect to preliminary relief.

[144] See Porter and Hyland, Rondeau v. Mosinee Paper Co. and the Williams Act Injunction, 59 Marq. L. Rev. 743 (1976). The authors enumerate five basic forms of preliminary relief and four of permanent. Id. at 745-46, 762. See, e. g., SEC v. General Refractories Co., 400 F. Supp. 1248, 1260 (D. D. C. 1975), where the court froze certain assets by way of preliminary relief against the likelihood of an ultimate disgorgement of illicit benefits. On the difficulties of framing appropriate relief once the tender offer has been consummated, see Hamilton, Some Reflections on Cash Tender Offer Legislation, 15 N. Y. L. F. 269, 292 (1969). On ancillary relief, see p. 1004 infra.

[145] General Aircraft Corp. v. Lampert, 556 F. 2d 90 (1st Cir. 1977).

[146] Kirsch Co. v. Bliss & Laughlin Industries, Inc., 495 F. Supp. 488, 502 (W. D. Mich. 1980); cf. Rule 13d-1(b)(3)(ii), applied in Jacobs v. Pabst Brewing Co., 549 F. Supp. 1068, 1079-80 (D. Del. 1982). But cf. Corenco Corp. v. Schiavone & Sons, Inc., 488 F. 2d 207 (2d Cir. 1973) (court concluded that a "cooling off" period would not be justified on the facts); Chromalloy American Corp. v. Sun Chemical Corp., 611 F. 2d 240, 248-49 (8th Cir. 1979) (no ninety-day injunction against purchases while information was disseminated to public).

[147] Bath Industries, Inc. v. Blot, 427 F. 2d 97 (7th Cir. 1970); Raybestos-Manhattan, Inc. v. Hi-Shear Industries, Inc., 503 F. Supp. 1122, 1126, 1133 (E. D. N. Y. 1980); cf. Kirsch Co. v. Bliss & Laughlin Industries, Inc., 495 F. Supp. 488, 502-06 (W. D. Mich. 1980) (no rescission offer). In SEC v. Scott, 565 F. Supp. 1513, 1537 (S. D. N. Y. 1983), *aff'd per curiam* sub nom. SEC v. Cayman Islands Reinsurance Corp., 734 F. 2d 118 (2d Cir. 1984), the court, though ordering disgorgement against one of the defendants, denied an injunction largely because "the grave collateral consequences of an injunction" against a broker-dealer "would result in punishing [him] instead of merely deterring him." See also Gearhart Industries, Inc. v. Smith Int'l, Inc., 741 F. 2d 707 (5th Cir. 1984).

[148] Butler Aviation Int'l, Inc. v. Comprehensive Designers, Inc., 425 F. 2d 842 (2d Cir. 1970).

[149] North American Car Corp. v. Flying Tiger Corp., CCH Fed. Sec. L. Rep. ¶92,757 (N. D. Ill. 1970).

[150] Cauble v. White, 360 F. Supp. 1021 (E. D. La. 1973).

8. State Legislation

Beginning with a Virginia statute that became effective in March 1968,[151] about five months before the federal provisions, some thirty-five states soon adopted their own tender offer statutes.[152] Those acts varied a great deal: in the presence or absence of an advance filing requirement or a hearing provision, in their standards as between disclosure and substantive tests, and in their selection of one or more of a number of criteria by way of establishing contact with the particular state (incorporation or doing business or having a "principal" business or substantial assets in the state).[153] But it seems fair to say that, in contrast to the federal provisions, all the state statutes, to a greater or lesser degree, were motivated toward protecting local industry against tender offers.[154] The great majority of them, for example, excluded "friendly" tender offers from their restrictions.

After a considerable number of constitutional attacks under the Supremacy and Commerce Clauses had been mounted in both federal and state courts, most of them successfully, the Supreme Court in 1982 threw out the Illinois statute.[155] But so many flowers bloomed among the seven opinions — partly because four Justices thought the case was moot — as to make this case less than altogether definitive.

In the first place, the only decision that was able to muster a majority of five (and that only because Justice Powell, though in the moot camp, concurred on this one point in view of the decision of a majority to reach the merits) was that the Illinois statute violated the Commerce Clause because the burden it imposed on interstate commerce through its *incidental* regulation was "excessive in light

[151] Va. L. 1968, c. 119.

[152] All the statutes are collected in CCH Blue Sky L. Rep. For a detailed chart of the then thirty-three statutes, see Bartell, State Takeover Laws: A Survey, in Practising Law Institute, Ninth Annual Institute on Securities Regulation (1978) App. B. The North American Securities Administrators Association (*not* the National Conference of Commissioners on Uniform State Laws) approved a "Uniform Take-Over Act" in October 1981. CCH NASAA Rep. §§4601 et seq.

[153] See Langevoort, State Tender-Offer Legislation: Interests, Effects, and Political Competency, 62 Corn. L. Rev. 213 (1977).

[154] The writer has elsewhere paid his compliments to the first Ohio legislation by calling it "shockingly one-sided, with all the onus on the take-over bidder and none on the management of the target company." Loss, Foreword to Symposium, Controlling Corporate Takeover Bids: State Regulation and the Ohio Approach, 21 Case W. Res. L. Rev. 605, 609, 611 (1970).

[155] Edgar v. MITE Corp., 457 U. S. 624 (1982); see also Telvest, Inc. v. Bradshaw, 697 F. 2d 576 (4th Cir. 1983) (Virginia statute).

of the local interests the Act purports to further."[156] There was no majority for the anterior proposition that the statute "*directly* regulates transactions which take place across state lines, even if wholly outside the State of Illinois,"[157] and even if the tender offer would not affect a single Illinois stockholder.

The preemption decision was joined in only by Chief Justice Burger and Justices Blackmun and White, who identified three provisions that "upset the careful balance struck by Congress":[158] (1) the twenty-day waiting period that applied to the offeror but not to the target; (2) the hearing provisions, which introduced extended delay; and (3) the state's passing on the substantive fairness of the offer.[159]

It does not follow, of course, that the six Justices who did not join in the preemption holding disagreed with it. Only Justice Stevens — with whom Justice Powell agreed generally — went out of his way to limit his concurring opinion by stating that he was not persuaded "that Congress' decision to follow a policy of neutrality in its own legislation is tantamount to a federal prohibition against state legislation designed to provide special protection for incumbent management."[160] The other four justices simply did not address the question — three (Justices Brennan, Marshall, and Rehn-

[156] 457 U. S. at 640. Those who favored this view noted the complete statutory exemption of the tender offer that the target had made for its own shares — a distinction that "is at variance with Illinois' asserted legislative purpose, and tends to undermine appellant's justification for the burdens the statute imposes on interstate commerce." Id. at 644. And they brushed aside the argument of state interest in regulating the internal affairs of domestic corporations (the target was incorporated in Illinois) by observing that "Tender offers contemplate transfers of stock by stockholders to a third party and do not themselves implicate the internal affairs of the target company." Id. at 645. Besides, the statute applied also to foreign corporations with their principal place of business in other states if Illinois stockholders owned 10 percent of the class of equity securities subject to the offer.

[157] Id. at 641 (italics supplied). More recently the Supreme Court has disfavored any "supposedly precise division between 'direct' and 'indirect' effects on interstate commerce," noting that the trend is to "look in every case to 'the nature of the state regulation involved, the objective of the state, and the effect of the regulation upon the national interest in the commerce.' " Arkansas Electric Cooperative Corp. v. Arkansas Public Service Commission, 461 U. S. 375, 379 (1983), quoting from Illinois Gas Co. v. Public Service Co., 314 U. S. 498, 505 (1942).

[158] 457 U. S. at 634.

[159] The events in the litigation preceded the promulgation of Rule 14d-2(b), supra p. 525. Id. at 636 n. 11. And there was "no contention that it would be impossible to comply with both the provisions of the Williams Act and the more burdensome requirements of the Illinois law. The issue thus is * * * whether the Illinois Act frustrates the objectives of the Williams Act in some substantial way."

[160] Id. at 655.

quist) because they thought the case was moot and the fourth (Justice O'Connor) because the holding of invalidity under the Commerce Clause made it unnecessary, she thought, to reach the preemption issue. Consequently the preemption question was left open, and even the Commerce Clause holding remained subject to distinction with respect to statutes of narrower scope.

A number of other state statutes then fell under *MITE*'s Commerce Clause argument.[161] Still others failed almost uniformly to survive the Supremacy Clause.[162] And soon there developed a second generation of state statutes that attack the tender offer process through regulation of the internal affairs of domestic corporations *after completion* of the tender offer, so that they are much closer to "corporation law" than to "securities regulation."[163]

These states are of various types, and some states have adopted more than one kind. In Ohio, for example, acquisitions of control-

[161] Martin Marietta Corp. v. Bendix Corp., 690 F. 2d 558, 565-68 (6th Cir. 1982) (Michigan statute); Telvest, Inc. v. Bradshaw, 697 F. 2d 576 (4th Cir. 1983) (Virginia statute); Mesa Petroleum Co. v. Cities Service Co., 715 F. 2d 1425 (10th Cir. 1983) (Oklahoma statute); Sharon Steel Corp. v. Whaland, 124 N. H. 1, 466 A. 2d 919 (1983) (New Hampshire statute, almost identical with Illinois's, one justice dissenting on the ground that *Sharon Steel* involved large open-market purchases rather than a formal tender offer as in *MITE*); Newell Co. v. Connolly, 624 F. Supp. 126, CCH Fed. Sec. L. Rep. ¶92,367 (D. Mass. 1985).

[162] The First Circuit reversed a preemption holding with respect to the Massachusetts statute — which it characterized as involving far less conflict with the federal law than the statutes involved in the appellate preemption decisions — and remanded for consideration of the Commerce Clause question in the light of the *MITE* case, which had been decided while the appeal was pending. Agency Rent-A-Car, Inc. v. Connolly, 686 F. 2d 1029 (1st Cir. 1982). But every other Circuit Court case to consider a preemption attack has come out the other way. Great Western United Corp. v. Kidwell, 577 F. 2d 1256 (5th Cir. 1978), *rev'd on other grounds* sub nom. Leroy v. Great Western United Corp., 443 U. S. 173 (1979); MITE Corp. v. Dixon, 633 F. 2d 486 (7th Cir. 1980), *aff'd on other grounds* sub nom. Edgar v. MITE Corp., 457 U. S. 624 (1982); Kennecott Corp. v. Smith, 637 F. 2d 181 (3d Cir. 1980), *on remand*, 507 F. Supp. 1206 (D. N. J. 1981); National City Lines, Inc. v. LLC Corp., 687 F. 2d 1122 (8th Cir. 1982); L. P. Acquisition Co. v. Tyson, 772 F. 2d 201 (6th Cir. 1985) (Michigan statute was preempted but did not violate the Commerce Clause); see also Icahn v. Blunt, 612 F. Supp. 1400 (W. D. Mo. 1985) (Missouri statute *held* unconstitutional under both clauses); Esmark, Inc. v. Strode, 639 S. W. 2d 768 (Ky. 1981). Indeed, Justices Brennan and Marshall joined Justice White's preemption dissent in Leroy v. Great Western United Corp., 443 U. S. 173, 190 (1970).

[163] See Profusek and Gompf, State Takeover Legislation after *MITE*: Standing Pat, Blue Sky, or Corporation Law Concepts?, 7 Corp. L. Rev. 3 (1983) ("there can and should be a role for significant state regulation of nationwide takeover bids"); Block, Barton, and Roth, State Takeover Statutes: The "Second Generation," 13 Sec. Reg. L. J. 332 (1986).

ling interests must be approved by the disinterested stockholders.[164] In Maryland a successful tender offeror that intends a "business combination" must either obtain supermajority approval from the disinterested stockholders (as well as all stockholders) or pay a "fair price" to those non-tendering stockholders who are forced into the combination.[165] And the Pennsylvania Business Corporation Law has been amended to permit the directors and officers to "consider the effects of any action upon employees, suppliers and customers of the corporation, communities in which offices * * * are located and all other pertinent factors," to disfranchise interested shareholders in approving certain transactions, and to force 30 percent owners of a class of voting stock registered under the 1934 Act to offer to buy out all other shareholders at a price that, in effect, includes the highest premium paid to accumulate the 30 percent.[166]

For a while it was all "sound and fury, signifying nothing." The second generation seemed to be as unconstitutional as the first, under one clause or the other or both.[167] Then in 1987 the Su-

[164]See Kreider, Fortress Without Foundation? Ohio Takeover Act II, 52 U. Cin. L. Rev. 108 (1983).

[165]See Scriggins and Clarke, Takeovers and the 1983 Maryland Fair Price Legislation, 43 Md. L. Rev. 266 (1984).

[166]See Newlin and Gilmer, The Pennsylvania Shareholder Protection Act: A New State Approach to Deflecting Corporate Takeover Bids, 40 Bus. Law. 111 (1984); see also Note, The Constitutionality of the New York Security Takeover Disclosure Act: An Analysis After *Edgar* v. *MITE Corp.*, 48 Albany L. Rev. 239 (1983); Comment, Securities Regulation: The Validity of North Carolina's Tender Offer Disclosure Act, 19 Wake Forest L. Rev. 267 (1983).

In late 1985 New York enacted a different type of statute that regulates tender offers for New York corporations (if they have their principal executive offices and "significant business operations" within the state and at least 10 percent of the voting stock is owned beneficially by residents) by (1) prohibiting any person that buys 20 percent or more of a corporation's stock from "engaging in any business combination" with the corporation for five years without the board's approval *before* the acquisition of the 20 percent, (2) permitting 20 percent purchases thereafter only with the consent of a majority of disinterested stockholders *or* payment of the same amount to all stockholders in accordance with a statutory formula, (3) requiring 5 percent offerors to make certain information public, and (4) for good measure, outlawing "greenmail" (defined as the purchase of 10 percent or more of a company's stock at a price above market without the occurrence of both directors and stockholders, unless the company offers to buy from all holders or the offer is limited to stock beneficially owned for more than two years). N. Y. L. 1985, c. 915, enacting Bus. Corp. L. §§513(e), 912, and amending the Security Takeover Disclosure Act.

[167]Dynamics Corp. of America v. CTS Corp., 794 F. 2d 250 (7th Cir. 1986), *rev'd* sub nom. CTS Corp. v. Dynamics Corp. of America, 107 S. Ct. 1637 (Indiana statute; both clauses); see also Newell Co. v. Connolly, 624 F. Supp. 126 (D. Mass. 1985) (Commerce Clause); Fleet Aerospace Corp. v. Holderman, 796 F. 2d 135 (6th Cir. 1986), *vacated* sub nom. Ohio v. Fleet Aerospace Corp., 107 S. Ct. 1949 (Ohio statute; same); APL Limited Partnership v. Van Dusen Air, Inc., 17 Sec. Reg. L. Rep. 1672 (8th Cir. 1985) (Minnesota statute; same);

preme Court sustained the Indiana Control Shares Acquisitions

---

Gelco Corp. v. Coniston Partners, — F. Supp. — (D. Minn. 1986), CCH Fed. Sec. L. Rep. ¶93,067 at 95,304-08, *vacated as moot,* 811 F. 2d 414 (8th Cir. 1987) (later version of same statute; same); Terry v. Yamashita, 643 F. Supp. 161 (D. Hawaii 1986) (Commerce Clause with dictum on preemption).

See also Mesa Partners II v. Unocal Corp., 607 F. Supp. 624 (W. D. Okla. 1985), where the court applied the Commerce Clause to defeat Oklahoma's third attempt at legislation. The focus of the first two statutes was the protection of shareholders through adequate disclosure. Seagram & Sons, Inc. v. Marley, CCH Fed. Sec. L. Rep. ¶98,246 (W. D. Okla. 1981); Mesa Petroleum Co. v. Cities Service Co., 715 F. 2d 1425 (10th Cir. 1983), supra p. 535 n. 161. By contrast, the statute involved in *Mesa Partners II* purported to be directed at the protection of energy resource assets. But the court found that the legislation was "so riddled with exemptions, exceptions, and limitations," in addition to its time periods' being carefully tailored to coincide with the time limitations of the Williams Act, that the statute did not "realistically seem to be structured with conservation as its main goal."

But cf. Cardiff Acquisitions, Inc. v. Hatch, 751 F. 2d 906 (8th Cir. 1984), where the court sustained a revised Minnesota Take-Over Act (predecessor to the one in *APL,* supra) under both Commerce and Supremacy Clauses for the most part, because its scope was limited to Minnesota shareholders of companies with a substantial nexus there. The fact that state officials might require disclosures in addition to those under the Williams Act was not regarded as fatal so long as the disclosures were "purely factual," not "judgmental" in nature, not inconsistent with the Williams Act, and not unduly burdensome to interstate commerce.

See generally Sargent, Do the Second-Generation State Takeover Statutes Violate the Commerce Clause?, 8 Corp. L. Rev. 3 (1984).

Cf. p. 449 n. 1, supra (state proxy regulation). And for an exploration of the possibility of applying the common law tort remedy of interference with a prospective economic advantage (or with a contract once a tender offer has been accepted), see Lowenstein, Tender Offer Litigation and State Law, 63 N. C. L. Rev. 493 (1985).

Under the Code preemption would be complete except for (1) a "regulated industry" and (2) "the law of any State in which (A) the registrant to whose security holders the tender offer is directed has its principal place of business and (B) more than 50 percent of the record or beneficial holders of its outstanding voting securities holding more than 50 percent of those securities are residents." These exceptions should be well within the limits of the Constitution.

The "regulated industry" exception "is designed to make the section inapplicable to provisions on acquisitions that are found in the insurance or banking or other specialized statutes." 2 Code 978. On the Insurance Holding Company System Regulatory Act Model Bill, approved by the National Association of Insurance Commissioners in 1969, [1969] 2 NAIC Proc. 737, and since adopted in almost every state, see Kennedy, State Insurance Commissioner Involvement in Takeovers of Insurers: An Overview of Procedures and Some Constitutional Considerations, 17 Forum 374 (1981); see also Note, State Regulation of Tender Offers for Insurance Companies After *Edgar* v. *MITE,* 51 Ford. L. Rev. 943 (1983). For citations to the state statutes, see id. at 944 n. 8. With respect to regulated industries generally, see Silberman, Kezsbom, and Sacks, Disputed Tender Offers in Regulated Industries, 8 J. Corp. L. 461 (1983).

The cases are in conflict on the question whether the McCarran-Ferguson Act (supra p. 206) precludes preemption of the special state tender offer legislation with respect to insurance companies. *Yes:* Professional Investors Life Ins. Co., Inc. v. Roussel, 528 F. Supp. 391 (D. Kan. 1981); John Alden Life Ins.

Chapter of the Business Corporation Law under both clauses.[168] The statute — subject to a particular corporation's opting out by amendment of its articles or by-laws — covers any Indiana corporation that has (1) at least 100 shareholders, (2) its principal place of business or office or substantial assets in the state, *and* (3) either more than 10 percent of its shareholders resident in the state *or* more than 10 percent of its shares owned by residents *or* 10,000 resident shareholders.

The act focuses on the acquisiton of "control shares," an event that occurs whenever voting power (but for the operation of the act) would equal any of three thresholds: 20, 33⅓, or 50 percent. The acquiring entity has no voting rights without the approval of a majority of the preexisting disinterested shareholders.

Justice Powell, for a majority of six, distinguished Justice White's plurality opinion in *MITE* on the preemption point. He noted that the federal statute, if construed to preempt any state statute that might limit or delay the free exercise of power after a successful tender offer, "would pre-empt a variety of state corporate laws of hitherto unquestioned validity," such as staggered term and cumulative voting statutes.[169]

With respect to the Commerce Clause, the decisive factor for the majority was "the fact that state regulation of corporate governance is regulation of entities whose very existence and attributes are a product of state law."[170] And "it is well within the State's role as overseer of corporate governance" to offer shareholders collectively the opportunity to determine whether there should be a change of control.[171]

Co. v. Woods, CCH Fed. Sec. L. Rep. ¶98,617 (D. Idaho 1981). *Contra:* National City Lines, Inc. v. LLC Corp., 524 F. Supp. 906 (W. D. Mo. 1981) *aff'd on other grounds,* 687 F. 2d 1122 (8th Cir. 1982); Gunter v. Ago Int'l B. V., 533 F. Supp. 86 (N. D. Fla. 1981). A fifth court has followed the Commission's suggestion (see its brief as *amicus curiae* in *John Alden,* supra) that the two regulatory systems can be harmonized so long as only the taking down of the shares and their payment, but not the offer itself, are conditioned on approval by the insurance authorities — this on the theory that the tender offer process itself is not the "business of insurance" within the McCarran-Ferguson Act. Sun Life Group, Inc. v. Standard Life Ins. Co. of Ind., CCH Fed. Sec. L. Rep. ¶97,314 (S. D. Ind. 1980). On the meaning of that phrase, see SEC v. National Securities, Inc., 393 U. S. 453 (1969); Group Life & Health Ins. Co. v. Royal Drug Co., Inc., 440 U. S. 205 (1979).

[168] CTS Corp. v. Dynamics Corp., 1075 S. Ct. 1637 (1987).

[169] Id. at 1647.

[170] Id. at 1649.

[171] Id. at 1651. Justice White, dissenting, was joined with respect to the preemption holding by Justices Blackmun and Stevens. Justice Scalia concurred in the judgment.

It seems safe to predict a wave of state statutes on the Indiana model. The cost of federalism sometimes comes high.

9. Legislative Proposals

Tender offers are an emotional subject, and many bills of all sorts have been introduced.[172] The SEC's Advisory Committee on Tender Offers, in a Report of Recommendations (July 1983) that contained fifty recommendations for changes in legislation and rules, was of the view that "there is insufficient basis for concluding that takeovers are either per se beneficial or detrimental to the economy or the securities markets in general, or to issuers or their shareholders, specifically,"[173] and that takeover regulations "should aim to achieve a reasonable balance while at the same time protecting the interests of shareholders and the integrity and efficiency of the markets."[174]

Professor (now Judge) Easterbrook and Gregg A. Jarrell, an economist, strongly dissented, calling the report "essentially a plea for more regulation."[175] Starting from the position that "tender offers benefit shareholders of both bidders and targets,"[176] they called the "common attacks on tender offers one reads in the popular press * * * so much hogwash."[177] And they proposed the termination of all federal regulation of tender offers except the *MITE* decision.

In March 1984 the Commission in an open meeting endorsed most of the recommendations (some with modifications) and rejected others as an undue intrusion into state corporation law (for example, a recommendation that federal law forbid the use of charter or by-law provisions that erect high barriers to a change of control,

[172] See esp. Senator d'Amato's proposed Tender Offer Reform Act of 1985, S. 1907, 99th Cong., 1st Sess. (1985).

[173] Id. at xvii; see also id. at 7.

[174] Id. at xviii.

[175] Id. at 70.

[176] Id. at 71.

[177] Id. at 73. Justice Goldberg filed a separate statement in which he suggested, *inter alia,* that tender offers should be submitted to an independent person or institution selected by the SEC for evaluation of fairness to shareholders of both companies and "whether, in economic terms, the public interest is protected." Id. at 122, 127; see also Goldberg, Regulation of Hostile Tender Offers: A Dissenting View and Recommended Reforms, 43 Md. L. Rev. 225 (1984).

For a critique of the advisory committee report — "rather small fruit for so important an undertaking" — see Lowenstein, Regulation of Tender Offers: A Critical Comment, 16 Rev. Sec. Reg. 829 (1983). The author of that essay is particularly critical because of the committee's failing to come to grips with two central issues: the function of the tender offer, and the regulation of target company defenses.

and a requirement that acquisitions of more than 20 percent be by tender offer).[178]

In September 1984 the House Committee on Energy and Commerce reported out a bill to (1) amend §14 of the 1934 Act so as to limit the use of certain tactics in tender offers and other contests for corporate control, as well as to close certain regulatory gaps, (2) amend §13 to require persons who acquire more than 5 percent of an issuer's securities to report the acquisition and certain other information before making additional purchases, as well as to disclose the impact of the acquisition on affected communities and employees of the issuer, and (3) amend §7[179] to provide uniform margin requirements in transactions involving the acquisitions of securities of certain United States corporations by foreign persons when the acquisitions are financed by foreign lenders.[180] The report stated that, although the committee intended to conduct a comprehensive review of the tender offer regulatory scheme in the next Congress, it had decided to proceed on a partial basis in order to remedy certain abuses and gaps that demanded immediate attention.

The Commission opposed three of the bill's proposals — the community impact concept, the forty-day minimum offering period, and the failure to qualify or limit the kinds of tender offers that would trigger the restrictions on defensive tactics. It concluded, therefore, that the legislation would upset the balance between bidders and targets to the detriment of the markets and the interests of shareholders.[181] The Administration opposed on different grounds: that the bill "would work to the disadvantage of the investing public by reducing the frequency of corporate takeover bids and increasing the volume of wasteful takeover related litigation," and that the bill would also "intrude unnecessarily into state law and constitute an unwarranted step toward imposition of a substantive federal corporation law." The Office of Management and Budget had previously stated that the Cabinet Council on Economic Affairs opposed new federal regulation of both tender offers and tender offer defenses. Although the Council agreed, according to the OMB memorandum, that there were abusive tactics by target managements, "top priority should be given to avoiding any first steps toward a federal corporation law."[182]

[178] See CCH Fed. Sec. L. Rep. No. 1064 (Mar. 21, 1984).
[179] See pp. 652 et seq. infra.
[180] H. R. Rep. No. 98-1028 on H. R. 5693, 98th Cong., 2d Sess. (1984).
[181] Id. at 8-9.
[182] 16 Sec. Reg. L. Rep. 1546 (1984).

Thus far the only relevant legislation in recent years is a provision in the Internal Revenue Code that specifies new tax rules for "golden parachutes."[183]

Altogether it would be difficult to think of another area in the securities world in which there is so much dissension in all quarters — among legislators, judges, regulators, practicing and academic lawyers, investment bankers, economists, and corporate executives.

F. INSIDER TRADING

1. Introduction

The last of the provisions activated by registration under the 1934 Act is §16, which has to do with insider trading.

"Prior to the enactment of the Securities Exchange Act," the Commission has said, "profits from 'sure thing' speculation in the stocks of their corporations were more or less generally accepted by the financial community as part of the emolument for serving as a corporate officer or director notwithstanding the flagrantly inequitable character of such trading."[1] The 1934 report of the Senate Banking and Currency Committee stated:

> Among the most vicious practices unearthed at the hearings before the subcommittee was the flagrant betrayal of their fiduciary duties by directors and officers of corporations who used their positions of trust and the confidential information which came to them in such positions, to aid them in their market activities. Closely allied to this type of abuse was the unscrupulous employment of inside information by large stockholders who, while not directors and officers, exercised sufficient control over the destinies of their companies to enable them to acquire and profit by information not available to others.[2]

In one case described in the committee's report on the bill, "the president of a corporation testified that he and his brothers controlled the company with a little over 10 percent of the shares; that shortly before the company passed a dividend, they disposed of their holdings for upward of $16 million and later repurchased them for

[183] §280G.

C. 7F [1] 10 SEC Ann. Rep. 50 (1944).

[2] Stock Exchange Practices, S. Rep. No. 1455, 73d Cong., 2d Sess. (1934) 55.

about $7 million, showing a profit of approximately $9 million on the transaction."[3]

It was in order to "bring these practices into disrepute and encourage the voluntary maintenance of proper fiduciary standards" that §16 was enacted.[4] And it reflects a variety of approaches:

(1) Section 16(a) provides that every officer or director of a company with an equity security registered under §12, as well as every person "who is directly or indirectly the beneficial owner of more than 10 per centum of any class of any equity security" so registered, shall file with the Commission, and also any exchange on which the security is listed, an initial report of his holdings of *all* the issuer's equity securities and a further report within ten days after the close of each calendar month in which there has been any change in his holdings. The factor that touches off the reporting requirement is the registration of an *equity* security. If a particular company has only its common stock registered, §16 applies also to its preferred. But the section does not apply to any of the securities — even equity securities — of a company that has only a nonconvertible bond issue registered. Similarly, a 10 percent owner of an *unregistered* equity security who is neither a director nor an officer is not subject to §16 even with respect to equity securities that are registered.[5]

This is pure disclosure, except that §16(a) serves the further function of facilitating the enforcement of §16(b).

(2) Section 16(b) — a nice example of "native American radicalism" — has a sting:[6]

> For the purpose of preventing the unfair use of information which may have been obtained by such beneficial owner, director, or officer by reason of his relationship to the issuer, any profit realized by him from any purchase and sale, or any sale and purchase, of any equity security of such issuer (other than an exempted security) within any period of less than six months, unless such security was acquired in good faith in connection with a debt previously contracted, shall inure to and be recoverable by the issuer, irrespective of any intention on the part of such beneficial owner, director, or

[3] S. Rep. No. 792, 73d Cong., 2d Sess. (1934) 9.

[4] H. R. Rep. No. 1383, 73d Cong., 2d Sess. (1934) 13. All of §16 is incorporated in §30(f) of the Investment Company Act, and §16(a)-(b) is reflected in §17(a)-(b) of the Holding Company Act.

[5] Abrams v. Occidental Petroleum Corp., 450 F. 2d 157, 160 n. 6 (2d Cir. 1971), *aff'd on other grounds* sub nom. Kern County Land Co. v. Occidental Petroleum Corp., 411 U. S. 582 (1973).

[6] See Arrow Distributing Corp. v. Baumgartner, 783 F. 2d 1274, 1277 (5th Cir. 1986), quoting the text, *amended per curiam on other grounds,* — F. 2d —(5th Cir. 1986), *rehearing denied;* CCH Fed. Sec. L. Rep. ¶92,791 (5th Cir. 1986).

officer in entering into such transaction of holding the security purchased or of not repurchasing the security sold for a period exceeding six months. Suit to recover such profit may be instituted at law or in equity in any court of competent jurisdiction by the issuer, or by the owner of any security of the issuer in the name and in behalf of the issuer if the issuer shall fail or refuse to bring such suit within sixty days after request or shall fail diligently to prosecute the same thereafter; but no such suit shall be brought more than two years after the date such profit was realized. This subsection shall not be construed to cover any transaction where such beneficial owner was not such both at the time of the purchase and sale, or the sale and purchase, of the security involved, or any transaction or transactions which the Commission by rules and regulations may exempt as not comprehended within the purpose of this subsection.[7]

(3) Whereas conduct within §16(b), though it may be expensive, is not *unlawful* in the criminal sense — or even in the sense of permitting injunctive relief at the instance of the SEC — §16(c) does prohibit short sales by §16 insiders. This contrasts with §10(a), under which short sales in general are simply subject to SEC rule-making.

It is interesting that the only explicit answer of Congress to the insider trading problem was §16, not some sort of provision (along the lines of the vast jurisprudence that ultimately developed under Rule 10b-5) for civil liability to the other party to an insider's transaction. It is interesting, too, that §16(b) and Rule 10b-5 are at opposite jurisprudential poles on the objective-subjective or predictability-fairness continuum. That must be borne in mind as we examine both provisions — §16(b) here because of its being an integral part of the §16 scheme and Rule 10b-5 in the chapters on fraud and civil liability.

[7]Cf. Societas Europaea §5, as submitted to EEC Council, [1970] 2 Bul. Eur. Comms. (Supp. to Bul. No. 8). Otherwise, there is apparently nothing quite like §16(b) in the Canadian and European statutes. Japan, which inherited all of §16 as part of the postwar reception of American law, kept §16(b) but repealed §16(a)! Whether on that account or because of cultural differences, there was said a few years ago to have been only one §16(b) action in Japan, an unreported case that arose from an internal management conflict. See Tatsuta, Enforcement of Japanese Securities Legislation, 1 J. Comp. Corp. L. & Sec. Reg. 95, 112 (1978); see also Tatsuta, Proxy Regulation, Tender Offers, and Insider Trading, in L. Loss, M. Yazawa, and B. Banoff (eds.), Japanese Securities Regulation (1983) c. 8.

On tolling the statute of limitations pending the filing of the required reports, see p. 415 n. 29 supra.

On both the statute of limitations and the demand requirement, see Annot., Time for Bringing Suit to Recover Insider Short-Swing Profits Under §16(b) of the Securities Exchange Act of 1934, 67 A. L. R. Fed. 849 (1984).

The basic premise of the entire SEC attack on insider trading, under both provisions, has been sharply challenged by able economists. Professor Manne argues (1) that the exploitation and sale of valuable information are necessary as a method of compensating entrepreneurs, so as to guarantee the uninterrupted flow of entrepreneurial abilities into American business enterprise; (2) that no one is really hurt when insiders market valuable information; and (3) that, far from there having been any economic demonstration of the evils of insider trading, it is a good thing.[8] It has been contended, in short, that "speculative trading by insiders may be beneficial in an 'economic' sense."[9] Needless to say, however, the economists are not of one persuasion.[10] And the grievous defect of

[8] H. Manne, Insider Trading and the Stock Market (1966); see also Hetherington, Insider Trading and the Logic of the Law, [1967] Wis. L. Rev. 720; Demsetz, Perfect Competition, Regulation, and the Stock Market, in H. Manne (ed.), Economic Policy and the Regulation of Corporate Securities (1968) 11-16; Note, The Efficient Capital Market Hypothesis, Economic Theory and the Regulation of the Securities Industry, 29 Stan. L. Rev. 1031 (1977), supra p. 34 n. 26; Carlton and Fischel, The Regulation of Insider Trading, 35 Stan. L. Rev. 857, 861 (1983) ("allowing the practice may be an efficient way to compensate corporate managers"); Moran, Insider Trading in the Stock Market: An Empirical Test of the Damage to Outsiders (Center for the Study of American Business, Washington U., Working Paper No. 89, July 1984) ("insider trading harms no one and improves the performance of the stockmarket," so that "insiders' profits are not outsiders' losses but evidence of more efficient resource allocation"); cf. Easterbrook, Insider Trading As an Agency Problem, in J. Pratt and R. Zeckhauser, Principals and Agents; The Structure of Business (1985) c. 4. For a more moderate, though dubious, view about it all, see Herman, Equity Funding, Inside Information, and the Regulators, 21 U. C. L. A. L. Rev. 1 (1973).

[9] Wu, An Economist Looks at Section 16 of the Securities Exchange Act of 1934, 68 Colum. L. Rev. 260, 269 (1968).

[10] See Mendelson, The Economics of Insider Trading Reconsidered, 117 U. Pa. L. Rev. 470 (1969); Cox, Insider Trading and Contracting: A Critical Response to the "Chicago School," [1986] Duke L. J. 628. For a debate between Professor Manne, who is a lawyer-economist, and some of his lawyer colleagues, see Painter, Book Rev., 35 Geo. Wash. U. L. Rev. 146 (1966); Schotland, Unsafe at Any Price: A Reply to Manne, *Insider Trading and the Stock Market*, 53 Va. L. Rev. 1425 (1967); Manne, Insider Trading and the Law Professors, 23 Vand. L. Rev. 547 (1970); Ferber, The Case Against Insider Trading: A Response to Professor Manne, 23 Vand. L. Rev. 621 (1970); Manne, A Rejoinder to Mr. Ferber, 23 Vand. L. Rev. 627 (1970).

See also Insider Trading, A Report by Justice (British Section of Int'l Commission of Jurists, 1972) ¶(3), which, referring to the Manne thesis, concluded: "Nevertheless, we think 'insider trading' is wrong and ought to be illegal." And the 1985 ABA Task Force on Insider Trading was persuaded that there were still persuasive reasons for continuing insider trading regulation even "in a marketplace dominated by large institutions, ready availability of research information, and instantaneous communication." Am. B. Assn. Committee on Federal Regulation of Securities, Report of the Task Force on Regulation of Insider Trading, Part I: Regulation Under the Antifraud Provisions of the Securities Exchange Act of 1934, 41 Bus. Law. 223, 227-28 (1985).

the strictly economic arguments against insider trading regulation is their apparent scorn for the moral or public opinion factor, which is relegated to the "it's just not right" propositions.[11] This overlooks the fact that it is important for the markets, as it is for the courts, not merely to do equity but to *appear* to do equity. Why should the public enter the market if the rules of the game make it perfectly legitimate for insiders (and their friends and business associates) to play with marked cards?[12]

At any rate, whatever the merit of the economic arguments, the insider trading regulatory structure that is in place requires analysis. And, far from that structure's withering away, its underlying philosophy (to be sure, more along the 10b-5 than along the 16(b) model) is spreading. In the United Kingdom, after a Labor Government had concluded in 1973 that it was essential to insure by legislation, "as far as practically possible, that the market operates freely on the basis of equality between buyer and seller,"[13]

[11] H. Manne, Insider Trading and the Stock Market (1966) 15, and c. n. 42; see Arrow Distributing Corp. v. Baumgartner, 783 F. 2d 1274, 1280 (5th Cir. 1986), quoting the text, *amended per curiam on other grounds,* — F. 2d — (5th Cir. 1986), *rehearing denied,* CCH Fed. Sec. L. Rep. ¶92,791 (5th Cir. 1986). For a summary of the arguments against insider trading, see Carlton and Fischel, The Regulation of Insider Trading, 35 Stan. L. Rev. 857, 872-82 (1983). The public concern is reflected in the Insider Trading Sanctions Act of 1984, infra p. 1008. Again in January 1986 the United States Parole Commission voted unanimously to more than double the minimum prison time before eligibility for parole so that persons convicted of trading illegally on inside information should be treated like persons convicted of mail or wire fraud, forgery, or other white collar crimes. 18 Sec. Reg. L. Rep. 141 (1986).

[12] The justifications that have been advanced for the attack on insider trading under Rule 10b-5 (see c. 9B infra) apply equally here: A variation of the "fair play" rationale there suggested is that, if the public is loathe to play an unfair game, the markets will suffer and the efficient allocation of capital will be impeded. Under the "informed market" rationale the prohibition of insider trading removes an incentive to *delay* the release of corporate information. There is also the "business property" theory. As to all these, see Scott, Insider Trading: Rule 10b-5, Disclosure and Corporate Privacy, 9 J. Legal Stud. 801 (1980). Most recently still another perspective has been suggested: that the prohibition of insider trading may enhance business decision-making in large corporations. See Haft, The Effect of Insider Trading Rules on the Internal Efficiency of the Large Corporation, 80 Mich. L. Rev. 1051 (1982). "It is important that we not lose sight of the moral underpinnings of the law in our concern for its economic consequences." Flaumm v. Eberstadt, 814 F. 2d 1169, 1182 (7th Cir. 1987) (Cudahy, J., concurring).

[13] Company Law Reform, Cmd. 5391 (1973) §15.

a Conservative Government, while eschewing civil liability, criminalized insider trading in the Companies Act 1980.[14]

[14] 1980 Acts c. 22, §§68-73, now Company Securities (Insider Dealing) Act 1985, 1985 Act. c. 8, as amended by Financial Services Act 1986, 1986 Acts c. 60, §§173-78. See L. Gower, Principles of Modern Company Law (4th ed., Supp. 1980) 636-38. "* * * after a long and agonizing gestation, a viable embryo has emerged which, if it does nothing else, will provide a fertile source of examination questions for years to come." Ibid. On the first few British cases, see 4 Co. Law. 117 (1983).

In general, see P. Anisman, Insider Trading Legislation for Australia: An Outline of the Issues and Alternatives (1986) (a detailed critique, prepared for the National Companies and Securities Commission's Working Party on Insider Trading, of the present law and proposals for change in Australia, Canada, the United Kingdom, and the United States); see also K. Hopt and M. Will, Europäisches Insiderrecht (1973) (the German language seems not to have a word with the precise connotation of "insider"); Loss (ed.), Multiple Approaches — Corporate Insiders (1976) (edited transcript of an Anglo-American-Franco-German conference); Commission Recommendation of 25 July 1977 Concerning a European Code of Conduct Relating to Transactions in Transferable Securities, 20 Off. J. Eur. Communities, No. L 212/37, 77/534 EEC (1977) ¶9; B. Rider and L. Ffrench, The Regulation of Insider Trading (1979) (worldwide treatment).

On individual countries, see, e. g., A. Yoran, Insider Trading in Israel and England (1972); Pillai, Insider Trading in Singapore and Malaysia, 16 Malaya L. Rev. 333 (1974); R. Baxt, H. Ford, G. Samuel, and C. Maxwell, An Introduction to the Securities Industry Codes (Australia, 2d ed. 1982) c. 14; Hawes, Lee, and Robert, Insider Trading Law Developments: An International Analysis, 14 L. & Pol. in Int'l Bus. 335 (1982) (France, United Kingdom, and United States); T. Dingledey, Insider-Handel und Strafrecht (1983); Tunc, The Reform of French Insider Trading Law, 4 Co. Law. 205 (1983); Rosenbaum, Simmonds, Simpson, and Vaidila, Corporate and Investment Attitudes Towards Insider Trading in Canada, 8 Can. Bus. L. J. 485 (1984); Patterson, Insider Trading and Business Ethics, [1984] N. Z. L. J. 369; Wallace, Who Is Subject to the Prohibition Against Insider Trading: A Comparative Study of American, British and French Law, 15 Sw. U. L. Rev. 217 (1985); Blum, The Regulation of Insider Trading in Germany, 7 Nw. J. Int'l L. & Bus. 507 (1986).

The last bastion is tottering if it has not fallen. In early 1985, at the demand of the banking authorities, the Swiss Government published a draft law that makes insider trading on stock exchanges a criminal offense and also allows Swiss authorities to supply information to foreign regulators about alleged insider trading by Swiss banks. 17 Sec. Reg. L. Rev. 797 (1985). The purpose was to free Swiss banks of banking secrecy rules under the terms of a 1977 treaty with the United States to provide information about clients being investigated by American regulatory authorities. See N. Y. Times, Jan. 15, 1982, p. D2, col. 6; 14 Sec. Reg. L. Rep. 104 (1982); N. Y. Times, Jan. 3, 1983, p. D1, col. 4 (action by Swiss banks); Note, Banking Secrecy and Insider Trading: The U. S.-Swiss Memorandum of Understanding on Insider Trading, 23 Va. J. Int'l L. 605 (1983); Fedders, U. S. Capital Markets: Obtaining Evidence Abroad, 18 Int'l Law. 89 (1984) ("waiver by conduct" proposal), with responses in symposium, 6 J. Comp. Bus. & Cap. Market L. 307 (1984); see generally Comment, Recent Developments in Insider Trading Through Swiss Bank Accounts: An End to the "Double Standard," 5 Nw. J. Int'l L. & Bus. 658 (1983); Hawes, Swiss Insider Trading Bill Brings Lively Debate, Legal Times, July 16, 1984, p. 19.

The first request pursuant to the treaty resulted after three years in the largest insider trading case ever settled by the Commission to that time. The

So far as the Code is concerned, the Reporter and his advisers considered the several grounds that some had advanced for abandoning §16(b): "(a) that it is needlessly arbitrary to the point of being quixotic; (b) that it has acted as a trap for the unwary; (c) that the Commission has made insufficient use of its exemptive authority; and (d) that, most of all, the jurisprudence that has developed under Rule 10b-5 (and that is being codified in large part) has rendered obsolete the concept of *automatic* recapture of *certain* short-term profits of *certain* insiders."[15] Instead, on the theory that §16(b) "has a symbolic significance that must be, and deserves to be, recognized," the Code codifies the most important areas of the §16(b) jurisprudence, polishing the rough diamond a bit in the process without derogating from the basic genius of the section, and with the expectation that the Commission will "use its expanded rule-making authority in order to play a greater quasi-legislative role in this area than it has in the past."[16]

2. From the "Objective" to the "Subjective"

Section 16(b) was described by the Administration's spokesman in the 1934 hearings as a "crude rule of thumb."[17] Consequently, a showing of an actual unfair use of inside information is not required for recovery; the preamble of the section was intended merely as an aid to constitutionality, as well as a guide to the Commission

defendants, who included a Lebanese businessman residing in Europe, a Kuwaiti businessman, and an Iraqi living in London, agreed to disgorge $7.8 million in profits from trading in Santa Fe International Corporation securities with knowledge of insider information with respect to merger discussions between Santa Fe and Kuwait Petroleum Corporation. SEC v. Certain Unknown Purchasers, CCH Fed. Sec. L. Rep. ¶91,951 (S. D. N. Y. 1986).

For a collection of cases and materials on foreign secrecy laws, see ALI-ABA, The Face of Insider Trading: *Chiarella, Dirks* and Beyond (1983) 231-311.

[15] 2 Code 751.

[16] 2 id. 751-52.

[17] 15 Stock Exchange Practices, Hearings Before S. Com. on Banking & Currency, 73d Cong., 2d Sess. (1934) 6557 (testimony of Thomas G. Corcoran). This characterization was approved in Booth v. Varian Associates, 334 F. 2d 1, (1st Cir. 1964), *cert. denied,* 379 U. S. 961. Later characterizations afford counsel a choice of rhetoric: "an extremely crude rule of a most deformed and misshapen thumb" [Provident Securities Co. v. Foremost-McKesson, Inc., 331 s in F. Supp. 787, 792 (N. D. Cal. 1971), *aff'd,* 506 F. 2d 601 (9th Cir. 1974), *aff'd* sub nom. Foremost-McKesson, Inc. v. Provident Securities Co., 423 U. S. 232 (1976)] or (if one is in a more benign mood) "a placid inlet in the chaotic sea of securities law — a statute designed for easy application" [Cummings v. Commissioner, 506 F. 2d 449, 452 (2d Cir. 1974), *cert. denied,* 421 U. S. 913].

in the exercise of its rulemaking authority.[18] By the same token, no estoppel flows from the fact that the defendant acquired the stock pursuant to an incentive stock option plan initiated by the company,[19] or sold the stock at the issuer's suggestion.[20] The statute uses the corporation as an instrument — perhaps an unwilling one — to effectuate its policy.[21] This being so, the Second Circuit has held that the rights of the company and its innocent stockholders cannot be defeated by attempting to prove that the real party in interest was the plaintiff's attorney, whose sole motive was to obtain a fee, although it did add the caveat that "A showing of misconduct is naturally pertinent to the determination of an appropriate fee."[22] As the District Court later pointed out with evident distaste in awarding a fee in the same case, Congress apparently "regards public policy against proved and repeated violations of fiduciary responsibility by corporate officers at the expense of the public more detrimental to public good than the violation of generally accepted ethics by attorneys."[23]

[18] Smolowe v. Delendo Corp., 136 F. 2d 231, 235 (2d Cir. 1943), *cert. denied,* 320 U. S. 751; Emerson Electric Co. v. Reliance Electric Co., 434 F. 2d 918 923-24 (8th Cir. 1970), *aff'd on other grounds* sub nom. Reliance Electric Co. v Emerson Electric Co., 404 U. S. 418 (1972).

[19] Jefferson Lake Sulphur Co. v. Walet, 104 F. Supp. 20, 23-24 (E. D. La 1952), *aff'd* sub nom. Walet v. Jefferson Lake Sulphur Co., 202 F. 2d 433 (5th Cir. 1953), *cert. denied,* 346 U. S. 820; cf. Lockheed Aircraft Corp. v. Campbell 110 F. Supp. 282 (S. D. Cal. 1953) (stock acquired as part of company policy to compensate executives for a drastic salary cut); Sonics Int'l, Inc. v. Johnson, 38' F. Supp. 741, 744 (N. D. Tex. 1975). *Contra:* Consolidated Engineering Corp v. Nesbit, 112 F. Supp. 112 (S. D. Cal. 1951), *order denying intervention rev'd* sub nom. Pellegrino v. Nesbit, 203 F. 2d 463 (9th Cir. 1953).

[20] Magida v. Continental Can Co., Inc., 231 F. 2d 843 (2d Cir. 1956), *cert. denied,* 351 U. S. 972; Roth v. Fund of Funds, Ltd., 405 F. 2d 421, 422-23 (2d Cir. 1968), *cert. denied,* 394 U. S. 975 (sale to issuer at its suggestion); Texa Int'l Airlines v. National Airlines, Inc., 714 F. 2d 533, 536-38 (5th Cir. 1983), *cert. denied,* 465 U. S. 1054. The issuer cannot waive its rights. Kay v. ScienTe Corp., 719 F. 2d 1009, 1014 (9th Cir. 1983). Cf. Reece Corp. v. Walco Nationa Corp., 565 F. Supp. 158 (S. D. N. Y. 1983) (court rejected argument that ther was no profit on resale to issuer at premium over purchase price because pre mium was in consideration of defendant's covenant not to attempt a takeove of the issuer).

[21] Blau v. Lamb, 314 F. 2d 618, 619-20 (2d Cir. 1963), *cert. denied,* 375 U. S 813. The "inure to" phrase in §16(b) suggests also the concept of a constructiv trust. See 5 Scott, Trusts (3d ed. 1967) §505; cf. Diamond v. Oreamuno, 2 N. Y. 2d 494, 248 N. E. 2d 910 (1969), infra p. 582.

[22] Magida v. Continental Can Co., Inc., 231 F. 2d 843, 848 (2d Cir. 1956 *cert. denied,* 351 U. S. 972. "If there has been a violation of N. Y. Penal La §274 as alleged, offenders are liable to its criminal sanction. But the publi policy of New York cannot nullify this federally created right * * * ." 231 F 2d at 848.

[23] Magida v. Continental Can Co., Inc., 176 F. Supp. 781, 783 (S. D. N. Y 1956). The Second Circuit held in its first §16(b) opinion that the plaintiff wa

On the other hand, the "crude rule of thumb" works two ways. An insider who holds for six months or more before selling does not become liable under §16(b), no matter how much proof is adduced of unfair resort to nonpublic information:[24]

> Congress recognized * * * that §16(b) would not correct all the practices thought to be evil; obviously the six month limitation alone "let many fish out of the net" since the tax laws tend to encourage a holding period longer than six months. * * * One can speculate on whether the moral or ethical values are altered by the passage of 24 hours but the statute makes an honest if not honorable man out of the insider in that period.[25]

As we have been reminded by the Supreme Court, "Liability cannot be imposed simply because the investor structured his transaction with the intent of avoiding liability under §16(b)."[26] There is also no guarantee against evasion by mutual "back-scratching" of insiders in different corporations, or by trading through relatives or friends. Provisions in the early drafts making unlawful the improper disclosure of confidential information by insiders, and providing that any profit made by any person to whom such unlawful disclosure was made should inure to the issuer, were deleted, "pre-

---

entitled to reimbursement for reasonable counsel fees from the sum recovered, on the analogy of the rule in stockholders' or creditors' representative actions, and that, "Since in many cases such as this the possibility of recovering attorney's fees will provide the sole stimulus for the enforcement of §16(b), the allowance must not be too niggardly." Smolowe v. Delendo Corp., 136 F. 2d 231, 241 (2d Cir. 1943), *cert. denied*, 320 U. S. 751. This risk of champerty led this writer to suggest that Congress consider substituting the SEC as plaintiff. 2 Loss 1053-54. But he sadly yields to Professor Cary's rejoinder to the effect that §16(b) "is an appropriate vehicle for the corporate gadfly." Cary, Book Rev., 75 Harv. L. Rev. 857, 861 (1962). When the chips were down, the writer did not consider it practical to push his suggestion as Reporter for the Code.

[24] Arrow Distributing Corp. v. Baumgartner, 783 F. 2d 1274, 1282 (5th Cir. 1986), quoting the text, *amended per curiam on other grounds*, — F. 2d — (5th Cir. 1986), *rehearing denied*, CCH Fed. Sec. L. Rep. ¶92,791 (5th Cir. 1986).

[25] Adler v. Klawans, 267 F. 2d 840, 845 (2d Cir. 1959); see also B. T. Babbitt, Inc. v. Lachner, 332 F. 2d 255, 258 (2d Cir. 1964) (interval of six months and one day). The six-month test has been explained on the ground that "Improper use of inside information by corporate insiders is most likely to occur in short-term, in-and-out trading" and that "Congress sought to minimize misuse of confidential information without unduly discouraging *bona fide* long-term investment." Blau v. Max Factor & Co., 342 F. 2d 304, 308 (9th Cir. 1965), *cert. denied*, 382 U. S. 892.

[26] Reliance Electric Co. v. Emerson Electric Co., 404 U. S. 418, 422 (1972), infra p. 563 n. 58. In Sterman v. Ferro Corp., 785 F. 2d 162 (6th Cir. 1985), an issuer rebuying its shares paid the seller the precise amount of the seller's 16(b) liability, and the seller delivered a check in that amount to the issuer.

sumably because the burden of proof made enforcement unfeasible."[27]

At the same time, the provision's very simplicity has undoubtedly had a substantial deterrent effect.[28] Since the elements of the action are so simple, the defendant is apt to find that he has no practicable alternative but to pay up; "the liability is, as a practical matter, inexorable."[29] Consequently the number of reported decisions is probably no criterion of the total amount of short-term profits recaptured or, once the section became well known, simply foregone.[30] Conversely, although there have been quite a few reported cases, they all involved some legal question that counsel obviously thought was worth the expense of a defense. For "There is no rule so 'objective' ('automatic' would be a better word) that it does not require some mental effort in applying it on the part of the person or persons entrusted by law with its application."[31]

Witness the "subjective-objective" clash that sharply divided the Supreme Court in *Kern County Land Co.* v. *Occidental Petroleum Corp.*:[32]

[27] Smolowe v. Delendo Corp., 136 F. 2d 231, 236 (2d Cir. 1943), *cert. denied,* 320 U. S. 751. In Blau v. Lehman, 368 U. S. 403, 411-12 (1962), infra p. 566, the Court pointed to this history in answer to a policy argument directed to evasion.

[28] See Whiting v. Dow Chemical Co., 523 F. 2d 680, 689 (2d Cir. 1975).

[29] Anderson v. Commissioner, 480 F. 2d 1304, 1308 (7th Cir. 1973).

[30] See Arrow Distributing Corp. v. Baumgartner, 783 F. 2d 1274, 1278 (5th Cir. 1986), quoting the text, *amended per curiam on other grounds,* — F. 2d — (5th Cir. 1986), *rehearing denied,* CCH Fed. Sec. L. Rep. ¶92,791 (5th Cir. 1986).

[31] Blau v. Lamb, 363 F. 2d 507, 520 (2d Cir. 1966), *cert. denied,* 385 U. S. 1002. For the SEC staff's views on 151 enumerated questions of interpretation that have arisen under §16(a) and (b), see Sec. Ex. Act Rel. 18,114, 23 SEC Dock. 856 (1981).

Since §16(a) requires the filing of a report whenever there is a change of beneficial ownership, it is self-evident that not every transaction reported under §16(a) can be the basis of liability under §16(b). Chemical Fund, Inc. v. Xerox Corp., 377 F. 2d 107, 112 (2d Cir. 1967). But the converse does not follow. In order that "Section 16(b) liability should not be predicated upon any transactions which are not subject to the reporting requirements of Section 16(a)" (Sec. Ex. Act Rel. 4801 (1953)), the Commission adopted Rule 16a-10: "Any transaction which has been or shall be exempted by the Commission from the requirements of section 16(a) shall, in so far as it is otherwise subject to the provisions of section 16(b), be likewise exempted from section 16(b)." See Adler v. Klawans, 267 F. 2d 840, 847 (2d Cir. 1959).

With respect to questions of jurisdiction, venue, procedure, and statute of limitations under §16(b), see 2 Loss 1044-58; 5 id. 3006-21. Section 16(b) merely *resembles* a derivative action in some respects, but it is a statutory action with its own procedural attributes. Dottenheim v. Murchison, 227 F. 2d 737 (5th Cir. 1955), *cert. denied,* 351 U. S. 919. Therefore, the contemporaneous ownership requirement of Rule 23.1 of the Federal Rules of Civil Procedure does not apply. Ibid. With respect to statute of limitations, see p. 415 supra.

[32] 411 U. S. 582 (1973).

Unquestionably, one or more statutory purchases occur when one company [Occidental], seeking to gain control of another [Old Kern], acquires more than 10% of the stock of the latter through a tender offer made to its shareholders. But is it a §16(b) "sale" when the target of the tender offer defends itself by merging into a third company [Tenneco] and the tender offeror then exchanges his stock for the stock of the surviving company and also grants an option to purchase the latter stock that is not exercisable within the statutory six-month period? This is the question before us in this case.

I

* * *

* * * By the terms of the option agreement, the option could not be exercised prior to December 9, 1967, a date six months and one day after expiration of Occidental's tender offer. On June 2, 1967, within six months of the acquisition by Occidental of more than 10% ownership of Old Kern, Occidental and Tenneco Corp. executed the option. * * *

The Old Kern-Tenneco merger plan was presented to and approved by Old Kern shareholders at their meeting on July 17, 1967. Occidental refrained from voting its Old Kern shares, but in a letter read at the meeting Occidental stated that it had determined prior to June 2 not to oppose the merger and that it did not consider the plan unfair or inequitable. Indeed, Occidental indicated that, had it been voting, it would have voted in favor of the merger.

* * *

The option granted by Occidental on June 2, 1967, was exercised on December 11, 1967. * * * Occidental's total profit was $19,506,419.22 on the shares obtained through its tender offer.

* * *

II

* * *

Although traditional cash-for-stock transactions that result in a purchase and sale or a sale and purchase within the six-month, statutory period are clearly within the purview of §16(b), the courts have wrestled with the question of inclusion or exclusion of certain "unorthodox" transactions.[24] The statutory definitions of "pur-

[24] The term, see 2 L. Loss, Securities Regulation 1069 (2d ed. 1961), has been applied to stock conversions, exchanges pursuant to mergers and other corporate reorganizations, stock reclassifications, and dealings in options, rights,

chase" and "sale" are broad and, at least arguably, reach many transactions not ordinarily deemed a sale or purchase. In deciding whether borderline transactions are within the reach of the statute, the courts have come to inquire whether the transaction may serve as a vehicle for the evil which Congress sought to prevent — the realization of short-swing profits based upon access to inside information[26] — thereby endeavoring to implement congressional objectives without extending the reach of the statute beyond its intended limits. The statute requires the inside, short-swing trader to disgorge all profits realized on all "purchases" and "sales" within the specified time period, without proof of actual abuse of insider information, and without proof of intent to profit on the basis of such information. Under these strict terms, the prevailing view is to apply the statute only when its application would serve its goals. "[W]here alternative constructions of the terms of §16(b) are possible, those terms are to be given the construction that best serves the congressional purpose of curbing short-swing speculation by corporate insiders." *Reliance Electric Co.* v. *Emerson Electric Co.,* 404 U. S., at 424. See *Blau* v. *Lamb,* 363 F. 2d 507 (C. A. 2 1966), *cert. denied,* 385 U. S. 1002 (1967). Thus, "[i]n interpreting the terms 'purchase' and 'sale,' courts have properly asked whether the particular type of transaction involved is one that gives rise to speculative abuse." *Reliance Electric Co.* v. *Emerson Electric Co.,* supra, at 424 n. 4.

* * * [28]

III

* * * [The exchange did not] involve a "sale" of Old Kern shares within the meaning of §16(b) * * *, for we think it totally

and warrants. Cf. Kay v. ScienTex Corp., 719 F. 2d 1009, 1013 (9th Cir. 1983), where the court used the "possibility of abuse" approach to hold that, although it was doubtful whether an overissuance of stock accomplished entirely without participation by the recipient presented an opportunity for abuse, the defendant had caused the overissuance to himself.

[26] Several decisions have been read as to apply a so-called "objective" test in interpreting and applying §16(b). [Citations omitted.] Under some broad language in those decisions, §16(b) is said to be applicable whether or not the transaction in question could possibly lend itself to the types of speculative abuse that the statute was designed to prevent. By far the greater weight of authority is to the effect that a "pragmatic" approach to §16(b) will best serve the statutory goals. [Citations omitted.]

[28] * * * Although Occidental did not exchange its Old Kern shares until December 11, 1967, it is not contended that that date, rather than the date on which Occidental became irrevocably bound to do so, should control. Similarly, although the option was not exercised until December 11, 1967, no liability is asserted with respect to that event, because it occurred more than six months after Occidental's last acquisition of Old Kern stock.

unrealistic to assume or infer from the facts before us that Occidental either had or was likely to have access to inside information, by reason of its ownership of more than 10% of the outstanding shares of Old Kern, so as to afford it an opportunity to reap speculative, short-swing profits from its disposition within six months of its tender-offer purchases.

* * * There is no basis for finding that, at the time the tender offer was commenced, Occidental enjoyed an insider's opportunity to acquire information about Old Kern's affairs.

It is also wide of the mark to assert that Occidental, as a sophisticated corporation knowledgeable in matters of corporate affairs and finance, knew that its tender offer would either succeed or would be met with a "defensive merger." If its takeover efforts failed, it is argued, Occidental knew it could sell its stock to the target company's merger partner at a substantial profit. Calculations of this sort, however, whether speculative or not and whether fair or unfair to other stockholders or to Old Kern, do not represent the kind of speculative abuse at which the statute is aimed, for they could not have been based on inside information obtained from substantial stockholdings that did not yet exist. Accepting both that Occidental made this very prediction and that it would recurringly be an accurate forecast in tender-offer situations, we nevertheless fail to perceive how the fruition of such anticipated events would require, or in any way depend upon, the receipt and use of inside information. If there are evils to be redressed by way of deterring those who would make tender offers, §16(b) does not appear to us to have been designed for this task.

* * *

The possibility that Occidental had, or had the opportunity to have, any confidential information about Old Kern before or after May 11, 1967 [the day after Occidental became a 10+ percent owner], seems extremely remote. * * *

There is, therefore, nothing in connection with Occidental's acquisition of Old Kern stock pursuant to its tender offer to indicate either the possibility of inside information being available to Occidental by virtue of its stock ownership or the potential for speculative abuse of such inside information by Occidental. Much the same can be said of the events leading to the exchange of Occidental's Old Kern stock for Tenneco preferred, which is one of the transactions that is sought to be classified a "sale" under §16(b). The critical fact is that the exchange took place and was required pursuant to a merger between Old Kern and Tenneco. That merger was not engineered by Occidental but was sought by Old Kern to frustrate the attempts of Occidental to gain control of Old Kern. Occidental obviously did not participate in or control the negotiations or the agreement between Old Kern and Tenneco. [Citations omitted.] Once agreement between those two companies crystallized, the course of subsequent events was out of Occidental's hands. Old Kern needed the consent of its stockholders, but as it turned out, Old Kern's management had the necessary votes without the affirmative vote of Occidental. * * * Occidental, although registering its opinion that the merger would be beneficial to Old Kern shareholders, did not in fact vote at the stockholders' meeting at which merger approval was obtained. Under California law, its abstention was tantamount to a vote against approval of the merger. * * *

* * * We do not suggest that an exchange of stock pursuant to a merger may never result in §16(b) liability. But the involuntary nature of Occidental's exchange, when coupled with the absence of the possibility of speculative abuse of inside information, convinces use that §16(b) should not apply to transactions such as this one.

IV

Petitioner also claims that the Occidental-Tenneco option agreement should itself be considered a sale, either because it was the kind of transaction the statute was designed to prevent or because the agreement was an option in form but a sale in fact. But the mere execution of an option to sell is not generally regarded as a "sale." [Citations omitted.] And we do not find in the execution of the Occidental-Tenneco option agreement a sufficient possibility for the speculative abuse of inside information with respect to Old Kern's affairs to warrant holding that the option agreement was itself a "sale" within the meaning of §16(b). The mutual advantages of the arrangement appear quite clear. * * * Motivations like these do not smack of insider trading; and it is not clear to us, as it was not to the Court of Appeals, how the negotiation and execution of the option agreement gave Occidental any possible opportunity to trade on inside information it might have obtained from its position as a major stockholder of Old Kern. * * *

Neither does it appear that the option agreement, as drafted and executed by the parties, offered measurable possibilities for speculative abuse. * * * Thus, the option, by its very form, left Occidental with no choice but to sell if Tenneco exercised the option, which it was almost sure to do if the value of Tenneco stock remained relatively steady. On the other hand, it is difficult to perceive any speculative value to Occidental if the stock declined and Tenneco chose not to exercise its option. * * *

The option, therefore, does not appear to have been an instrument with potential for speculative abuse, whether or not Occidental possessed inside information about the affairs of Old Kern. In addition, the option covered Tenneco preference stock, a stock as yet unissued, unregistered, and untraded. It was the value of this stock that underlay the option and that determined whether the option would be exercised, whether Occidental would be able to profit from the exercise, and whether there was any real likelihood of the exploitation of inside information.

Nor can we agree that we must reverse the Court of Appeals on the ground that the option agreement was in fact a sale because the premium paid was so large as to make the exercise of the option almost inevitable, particularly when coupled with Tenneco's desire to rid itself of a potentially troublesome stockholder. * * *

Justice Douglas, with whom Justices Brennan and Stewart concurred, dissented:[33]

The Court, in resorting to an *ad hoc* analysis of the "possibility for the speculative abuse of inside information," charts a course for the interpretation of §16(b) of the Securities Exchange Act of 1934, 15 U. S. C. §78p(b), that in my mind undermines the congressional purpose. * * *

* * *

The majority takes heart from those decisions of lower federal courts which endorse a "pragmatic" approach to §16(b). Many involved the question whether a conversion of one security of an issuer into another security of the same issuer constituted a purchase or a sale. It would serve no purpose to parse their holdings because, as Louis Loss describes, they have a "generalization-defying nature."[14] In 1966 the Securities and Exchange Commission exercised its exemptive power under §16(b) to adopt Rule 16b-9, which under specified conditions excludes a conversion from the operation of §16(b). This rule will relieve the courts of much of the burden that has developed from *ad hoc* analyses in this narrow area. But, by sanctioning the approach of these cases, the majority brings to fruition Louis Loss' prophecy that they will "continue to rule us from their graves,"[16] for henceforth they certainly will be applied by analogy to the area of mergers and other consolidations.

Thus, the courts will be caught up in an *ad hoc* analysis of each transaction, determining both from the economics of the transaction and the *modus operandi* of the insider whether there exists the possibility of speculative abuse of inside information. * * * Section 16(b), because of the six-month limitation, allows some to escape who have abused their inside information. It should not be surpris-

[33] 411 U. S. at 611-13.
[14] 5 L. Loss, Securities Regulation 3029 (Supp. to 2d ed. 1969).
[16] 5 L. Loss, Securities Regulation 3029 (Supp. to 2d ed. 1969).

ing, given the objective nature of the rule, if some are caught unwillingly.

(1) The Second Circuit promptly held "that whether the tender offeror quits fighting when the defensive merger is announced [as in *Kern*] or continues to fight in the hope of winning, his exchange of stock on the merger after he has been defeated is not *ipso facto* a 'sale' for §16(b) purposes."[34] But the Seventh Circuit quite properly distinguished *Kern* where an unsuccessful tender offeror sold to a third person.[35] And a divided Fourth Circuit, in considering whether there was a merger-*purchase* rather than a merger-sale, took into account, in applying the possibility of abuse test, only premerger events (as distinct from the defendant's access to corporate information after the merger); in its view the Supreme Court considered events all the way to the second of the two transactions sought to be matched only because the merger there *was* the second transaction.[36]

(2) Although the adjective "unorthodox" that this writer coined to describe merger and other cases lending themselves to a "possibility of abuse" analysis is itself orthodox enough, it has become something of a term of art.[37] It cannot be overemphasized that it is of no more relevance than in routine cash transactions to consider whether inside information was in fact used. But it does seem to be of considerable consequence to consider whether the circumstances were such that the defendant could possibly have obtained an advantage over the public generally that did not already exist. *Cessante ratione legis, cessat et ipsa lex.*

(3) Justice Douglas was quite correct in reminding the majority that the Court had taken an *objective* approach in the *Reliance Electric* case, where (as he did not point out) the Court had held for the *defendant* in deciding that a 10+ percent holder who sold down to

[34] American Standard, Inc. v. Crane Co., 510 F. 2d 1043, 1055 (2d Cir. 1974), *cert. denied,* 421 U. S. 1000; cf. Pay Less Drug Stores v. Jewell Companies, Inc., 579 F. Supp. 1396 (N. D. Cal. 1984).

[35] Allis-Chalmers Mfg. Co. v. Gulf & Western Industries, Inc., 527 F. 2d 335 (7th Cir. 1975), *cert. denied,* 423 U. S. 1078, 424 U. S. 928; see also Texas Int'l Airlines v. National Airlines, Inc., 714 F. 2d 533, 539-40 (5th Cir. 1983), *cert. denied,* 465 U. S. 1054 (distinguishing *Kern* where an unsuccessful tender offeror sold for *cash* to its rival just before the rival's merger with the target); Super-Stores, Inc. v. Reiner, 737 F. 2d 962 (11th Cir. 1984).

[36] Gold v. Sloan, 486 F. 2d 340 (4th Cir. 1973), *cert. denied,* 419 U. S. 873.

[37] See 2 Loss 1069. On the §16(b) treatment of (1) conversions, mergers, reclassifications, and other exchanges, (2) rights and other options, and (3) gifts, see 2 id. 1066-84; 5 id. 3027-47. That material reads as of 1969, but the analysis should still be helpful.

9.96 percent and then sold the rest of his holdings in a separate transaction, both transactions occurring within less than six months after the defendant's purchase, was not liable with respect to the second sale. A completely reliable lodestar in these cases is hard to find. But can one justify simply taking whichever approach, "objective" or "subjective," gives the case to the plaintiff?

(4) When the market price of a common stock rises above the redemption price of a callable and convertible preferred, the market considers them to be equivalents. And, when the preferred is called and a director converts along with everybody else and shortly thereafter sells the common on the market, the transactions that *should* be paired are not the conversion-purchase and market sale of common,[38] but the purchase of *preferred* and sale of common.[39] For the first pairing would have all the significance of a change of a ten dollar bill into two fives, whereas the purchase and sale in the second pairing could just as readily be based on inside information as (a) a cash purchase and cash sale of common or (b) a cash purchase and cash sale of preferred. Yet covering the first pairing might make it harder, logically, to cover the second. *Query*: Would the *Kern* dissenters cover *both* configurations?

(5) The scant authority on the question of matching a purchase of one security against a sale of another is not conclusive.[40] But, when the Commission in 1966 adopted Rule 16b-9 by way of *exempting* any acquisition or disposition involved in a conversion, it made the exemption inapplicable to the extent that the insider buys

[38] See Ferraiolo v. Newman, 259 F. 2d 342, 346 (6th Cir. 1958), *cert. denied*, 359 U. S. 927.

[39] In Gund v. First Fla. Banks, Inc., 726 F. 2d 682 (11th Cir. 1984), the court saw nothing unorthodox to prevent the matching of market sales of convertible debentures against market purchases of the conversion stock, even though allegedly the two securities were not traded in relation to each other.

[40] In American Standard, Inc. v. Crane Co., 510 F. 2d 1043, 1057-63 (2d Cir. 1974), *cert. denied*, 421 U. S. 1000, the court refused to match a cash purchase of the merged company's shares against a sale of shares of the surviving company. But in Bershad v. McDonough, 428 F. 2d 693, 697 n. 5 (7th Cir. 1970), *cert. denied*, 400 U. S. 992, the court matched a sale of an option against a prior purchase of the underlying security, stating: "Certainly the interest of simple application of the prohibitions of Section 16(b) does not carry so far as to facilitate evasion of that provision's function by formalistic devices." See also Blau v. Lamb, 363 F. 2d 507, 525 (2d Cir. 1966), *cert. denied*, 385 U. S. 1002 (dictum that under the circumstances the purchase of convertible preferred might be treated as a purchase of common under the statutory definition of "purchase" as including "any contract to buy * * * "); Chemical Fund, Inc. v. Xerox Corp., CCH Fed. Sec. L. Rep. ¶91,653 at 95,419 (W. D. N. Y. 1966), *rev'd on other grounds*, 377 F. 2d 107 (2d Cir. 1967) (court without discussion matched purchases of convertible debentures against sales of common); Gund v. First Fla. Banks, Inc., 726 F. 2d 682 (11th Cir. 1984), supra n. 39.

(or sells) one of the securities and sells (or buys) the other (otherwise than in the conversion itself or in a transaction exempted by any other rule) within a period of less than six months that includes the date of conversion.[41] The Commission has thus hedged against the possibility that a court might *decline* to match transactions in convertible and conversion securities.

(6) The Code's successor to §16(b) exempts a conversion or merger-like transaction, as well as a share-for-share exchange involving two companies, if the defendant proves that he "*did* not use" (not *could* not have used) inside information.[42] But, on the ground of greater potentiality for abuse, the Code also *covers* the two-security situation in the context not only of conversions but also of warrants, merger-like transactions, voting trust certificates, and certificates of deposit for securities "unless the defendant proves that under the circumstances he *could* not have been advantaged by the use of" insider information.[43]

3. "Profit Realized"

In the absence of any hint in the statute on how the "profit realized" is to be calculated when there are more than one pair of transactions, the 1943 opinion of the Second Circuit in *Smolowe* v. *Delendo Corp.*,[44] has reigned supreme.[45] In Judge Clark's words:

> * * * Analysis will show that the income tax rules cannot apply

[41] Sec. Ex. Act Rel. 7826 (1966).

[42] §1714(h)(1); 2 Code 755-56.

[43] §1714(g); 2 Code 754-55.

[44] 136 F. 2d 231, *cert. denied,* 320 U. S. 751.

[45] See, e. g., Arrow Distributing Corp. v. Baumgartner, 783 F. 2d 1274, 1278 (5th Cir. 1986), *amended per curiam on other grounds,* — F. 2d — (5th Cir. 1986), *rehearing denied,* CCH Fed. Sec. L. Rep. ¶92,791 (5th Cir. 1986). A single District Court judge who ventured to disagree was reversed, though he found one vote on appeal. Western Auto Supply Co. v. Gamble-Skogmo, Inc., 231 F. Supp. 456, 460-61 (D. Minn. 1964), *rev'd,* 348 F. 2d 736, 742-43 (8th Cir. 1965), *cert. denied,* 382 U. S. 987.

In Gund v. First Fla. Banks, Inc., 726 F. 2d 682, 687-88 (11th Cir. 1984), which involved market sales of convertible debentures and market purchases of the conversion stock, the court affirmed the District Court's use by analogy of a method of computation patterned after Rule 16b-6, which limits the recoverable profit in long-term option cases to the difference between the proceeds of sale of the stock and the lowest market price within six months on either side of the sale. Although that method yielded a slightly different result from the profit calculated under the *Smolowe* rule, the court found either method to be consistent with the language and purpose of the statute.

In Morales v. Lukens, Inc., 593 F. Supp. 1209, 1213-14 (S. D. N. Y. 1984), three sales at different prices that were part of a settlement of an unsuccessful tender offer were treated as one transaction, whose *average* price governed.

> without defeating the law almost completely. Under the basic rule of identifying the stock certificate, the large stockholder, who in most cases is also an officer or director, could speculate in long sales with impunity merely by reason of having a reserve of stock and upon carefully choosing his stock certificates for delivery upon his sales from this reserve. Moreover, his profits from any sale followed by a purchase would be practically untouchable, for the principle of identity admits of no gain without laboring proof of a subjective intent — always a nebulous issue — to effectuate the connected phases of this type of transaction. In consequence the statute would be substantially emasculated. We cannot ascribe to it a meaning so inconsistent with its declared purpose.
>
> Once the principle of identity is rejected, its corollary, the first-in, first-out rule, is left at loose ends. At best it is a rule of convenience designed originally to hit marginal trading without shares in hand and supplementing the principle of identity. Its rationalization is the same as that for the identification rule, for which it operates as a presumptive principle; and it has no other support. If we reject one, we reject the other and for like reasons. * * *
>
> Another possibility might be the striking of an average purchase price and an average sale price during the period, and using these as bases of computation. What this rule would do in concrete effect is to allow as offsets all losses made by such trading. * * *
>
> * * * We must suppose that the statute was intended to be thorough-going, to squeeze all possible profits out of stock transactions, and thus to establish a standard so high as to prevent any conflict between the selfish interest of a fiduciary officer, director, or stockholder and the faithful performance of his duty. [Citations omitted.] The only rule whereby all possible profits can be surely recovered is that of lowest price in, highest price out — within six months — as applied by the district court.

Eight years later the Second Circuit reasserted the lowest-in-highest-out formula after independent analysis in awarding a judgment of some $300,000 although the defendant's trading during various six-month periods had resulted in a loss of more than $400,000.[46] Observing that this "crushing" liability "should certainly serve as a warning, and may prove a deterrent,"[47] Judge Learned Hand referred[48] to "the doctrine which has been law since the days of the

[46] Gratz v. Claughton, 187 F. 2d 46 (2d Cir. 1951), *cert. denied,* 341 U. S. 920. The loss of $400,000 is mentioned in App. to Defendant-Appellant's Brief, p. 29, and in Adler v. Klawans, 267 F. 2d 840, 847-48 (2d Cir. 1959).

[47] Gratz v. Claughton, 187 F. 2d at 52. This was quoted in Texas Int'l Airlines v. National Airlines, Inc., 714 F. 2d 533, 541 n. 16 (5th Cir. 1983), *cert. denied,* 465 U. S. 1052.

[48] 187 F. 2d at 51-52.

'Chimney Sweeper's Jewel Case,'[49] that when damages are at some unascertainable amount below an upper limit and when the uncertainty arises from the defendant's wrong, the upper limit will be taken as the proper amount." It might have been more apt to recall the condemned prisoner who, when asked if he had any last words before the noose was pulled, replied: "Yes, sir, this sure is gonna teach me a lesson."

More specifically, the calculation proceeds as follows:

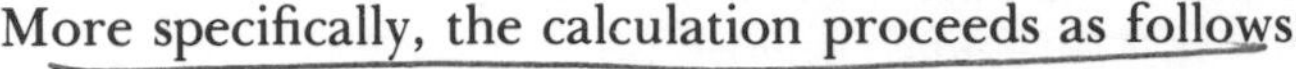

> Listed in one column are all the purchases made during the period for which recovery of profits is sought. In another column is listed all of the sales during that period. Then the shares purchased at the lowest price are matched against an equal number of the shares sold at the highest price within six months of such purchase, and the profit computed. After that the next lowest price is matched against the next highest price and that profit is computed. Then, the same process is repeated until all the shares in the purchase column which may be matched against shares sold for higher prices in the sales column have been matched off. Where necessary to accurate computation it would seem proper to split a larger denomination or lot of shares in order to match off part of the lot against an equal amount on the other side. The gross recovery is the sum of the profits thus determined.[50]

But "obviously no transaction can figure in more than one equation."[51] That is to say, if there is a purchase of 100 shares on February 1 followed by a sale of 100 shares on March 1 and another purchase of 100 shares on April 1, the sale on March 1 can be matched against either purchase (the plaintiff, of course, will pick the one at the lower price) but not both. On the other hand, if the case were the same except that 200 shares were sold on March 1, presumably 100 of that figure could be matched against the February 1 purchase and the other 100 against the April 1 purchase.

It is equally obvious that several different six-month periods may be included in the same lawsuit, with the above calculation applied to each period separately, as long as the two-year statute of limitations has not expired. And it is at least arguable that the periods may overlap as long as no transaction is used more than once. For example, if a director were to buy 100 shares at 4 on February 1, sell 100 at 6 on April 1, sell another 100 at 5 on June 1, and buy

[49] Armory v. Delamirie, 1 Strange 505, 93 Eng. Reprint 664 (K. B. 1722).

[50] Rubin and Feldman, Statutory Inhibitions upon Unfair Use of Corporate Information by Insiders, 95 U. Pa. L. Rev. 468, 482-83 (1947).

[51] Gratz v. Claughton, 187 F. 2d 46, 52 (2d Cir. 1951), *cert. denied*, 341 U. S. 920.

100 at 3 on September 1, a court might well match the lowest purchase (September 1) against the highest sale (April 1) and the next lowest purchase (February 1) against the next highest sale (June 1) although the entire period in which the formula were thus applied would have exceeded six months.

The amount of damages awarded is computed net after brokerage commissions and transfer taxes on all transactions that figured in the computation.[52] The same logic permits the deduction of expenses incurred in effecting transactions otherwise than in the usual way.[53] Whether the defendant should be charged with dividends (or interest on convertible debt securities) that he received, or *credited* with dividends or interest that he *failed* to receive because his transactions were sale-purchase rather than purchase-sale, is a question that does not yet permit of a general answer.[54] This is

[52] Falco v. Donner Foundation, Inc., CCH Fed. Sec. L. Rep. ¶90,612 (S. D. N. Y. 1953), *rev'd on other grounds,* 208 F. 2d 600 (2d Cir. 1953).

[53] Blau v. Mission Corp., 212 F. 2d 77, 82 (2d Cir. 1954), *cert. denied,* 347 U. S. 1016; Arkansas La. Gas Co. v. W. R. Stephens Investment Co., Inc., 141 F. Supp. 841 (W. D. Ark. 1956); Texas Int'l Airlines v. National Airlines, Inc., 714 F. 2d 533, 541-42 (5th Cir. 1983), *cert. denied,* 347 U. S. 1052 (court allowed deduction of brokerage commissions and transfer taxes, but not "nontransactional expenses" not incidental to the purchase and sale, including interest costs related to margin loans and various legal and investment banking fees); Morales v. Lukens, Inc., 593 F. Supp. 1209, 1215-16 (S. D. N. Y. 1984); Herrmann v. Steinberg, 812 F. 2d 63 (2d Cir. 1987).

But cf. Oliff v. Exchange Int'l Corp., 449 F. Supp. 1277, 1302 (N. D. Ill. 1978), *aff'd on other grounds,* 669 F. 2d 1162 (7th Cir. 1980), *cert. denied,* 450 U. S. 915 (court rejected argument that amount of judgment should be reduced by expenses, including reasonable attorney's fees, with respect to probate court proceedings on the sale side); Lane Bryant, Inc. v. Hatleigh Corp., 517 F. Supp. 1196, 1202 (S. D. N. Y. 1981) (court refused to consider administrative overhead expenses and interest on loans with which defendant had made the purchases, as well as office overhead and litigation costs).

[54] See Adler v. Klawans, 267 F. 2d 840, 848 (2d Cir. 1959); Western Auto Supply Co. v. Gamble-Skogmo, Inc., 348 F. 2d 736, 744 (8th Cir. 1965), *cert. denied,* 382 U. S. 987; Blau v. Lamb, 363 F. 2d 507, 528 (2d Cir. 1966), *cert. denied,* 385 U. S. 1002; Allis-Chalmers Mfg. Co. v. Gulf & Western Industries, Inc., 372 F. Supp. 570, 588-89 (N. D. Ill. 1974), *rev'd in part on other grounds,* 527 F. 2d 335 (7th Cir. 1975), *cert. denied,* 423 U. S. 1078; Champion Home Builders Co. v. Jeffress, 385 F. Supp. 245, 250 (E. D. Mich. 1974); Cutler-Hammer, Inc. v. Leeds & Northrop Co., Inc., 469 F. Supp. 1021, 1024 (E. D. Wis. 1979); Morales v. Lukens, Inc., 593 F. Supp. 1209, 1215 (S. D. N. Y. 1984) (dividend need not be disgorged unless it was manipulated).

Cf. Morales v. Consolidated Oil & Gas, Inc., CCH Fed. Sec. L. Rep. ¶98,796 (S. D. N. Y. 1982), where the court held that profits must be computed without regard to the "incentive income" provisions of §83 of the Internal Revenue Code, whose application to the defendant's purchase by way of a stock option would have resulted in a loss. "In determining the profits to be disgorged it should not be necessary for a court to inquire into an insider's tax bracket, annual income, deductions, etc., matters which are extraneous to the adminis-

true, too, with respect to the question whether interest will be allowed from the time of realization of profit. More often than not, probably, it is awarded, often without discussion. But some courts have been led to deny interest by the Supreme Court's statement, in a case in which interest had been denied by both lower courts, "that it did not think the denial was either so unfair or so inequitable as to require us to upset it." In a situation of this sort, the Court reminded, "interest is not recovered according to a rigid theory of compensation for money withheld, but is given in response to considerations of fairness."[55]

4. MEASUREMENT OF THE SIX-MONTH PERIOD

Since the statute refers to "any period of less than six months," the profit realized from a purchase on January 1 and a sale on June 30 would not be recoverable. As Judge Dimock put it — citing Blackstone, who might have been surprised to be told that he would be making law under the Securities Exchange Act of 1934 — the statutory period of "less than six months" means "six months minus one full period from midnight to midnight since the law does not take into account fractions of a day." The phrase "for a period exceeding six months" later on in §16(b) was regarded "as a mere referential inaccuracy which cannot prevail over the language used by Congress in creating the cause of action."[56]

5. CHANGE OF STATUS

Whatever its rationale — perhaps on the theory that substantial stockholders as such are less likely than directors or officers to have access to inside information unless they are long-term investors — the last sentence of §16(b) excludes "any transaction where such beneficial owner was not such both at the time of the purchase and sale, or the sale and purchase, of the security involved." This, the Supreme Court has held, excludes the purchase that makes a person

tration of §16(b)." Id. at 94,080. Cf. Randall v. Loftsgaarden, 106 S. Ct. 3143 (1986), infra p. 886.

[55] Blau v. Lehman, 368 U. S. 403, 414 (1962).

[56] Stella v. Graham-Paige Motors Corp., 132 F. Supp. 100, 104 (S. D. N. Y. 1955), *remanded on other grounds,* 232 F. 2d 299 (2d Cir. 1956), *cert. denied,* 352 U. S. 831; see also Colonial Realty Corp. v. MacWilliams, 381 F. Supp. 26 (S. D. N. Y. 1974), *aff'd per curiam,* 512 F. 2d 1187 (2d Cir. 1975), *cert. denied,* 423 U. S. 867.

corporated, functions corresponding to those performed by the foregoing officers." The General Counsel of the Commission early expressed the opinion

> that an assistant would be an "officer" if his chief is so inactive that the assistant is really performing his chief's functions. However, an assistant, although performing some functions which might be those of his chief, would not be an "officer" so long as these duties were under the supervision of his chief. Temporary absence or brief vacation of an officer during which an assistant performs the officer's duties would not constitute the assistant an "officer."[65]

A Second Circuit dictum cast doubt on the validity of the Commission's definition; the court preferred a more subjective, statute-oriented test in terms of accessibility to inside information.[66] But a proposed revision of the rule in those terms met an unfavorable response.[67] And there is now some authority in support of the rule's validity.[68]

The most recently announced administrative view is as follows:

> Generally, it is not difficult to identify a company's principal officers by their traditional titles and functions. However, an employee who does not possess a title may nevertheless be an officer because of the significant functions he performs; similarly, an employee who holds a title may nonetheless not be an officer because his functions and duties are insignificant, despite his formal position. The staff generally takes the view that anyone holding an appropriate title is an officer for purposes of Section 16(a).[69]

[65] Sec. Ex. Act Rel. 2687 (1940).

[66] Colby v. Klune, 178 F. 2d 872 (2d Cir. 1949).

[67] Sec. Ex. Act Rels. 4718, 4754 (1952).

[68] Lockheed Aircraft Corp. v. Rathman, 106 F. Supp. 810 (S. D. Cal. 1952); Lockheed Aircraft Corp. v. Campbell, 110 F. Supp. 282 (S. D. Cal. 1953).

[69] Sec. Ex. Act Rel. 18,114, 23 SEC Dock. 856, 860-61 (1981). In Merrill Lynch, Pierce, Fenner & Smith, Inc. v. Livingston, 566 F. 2d 1119, 1122 (9th Cir. 1978), involving an "Account Executive" who was one of some 350 "Executive Vice Presidents," the court held: "The title 'Vice President' does no more than raise an inference that the person who holds the title has the executive duties and the opportunities for confidential information that the title implies. The inference can be overcome by proof that the title was merely honorary and did not carry with it any of the executive responsibilities that might otherwise be assumed." The same court later emphasized that "officer" status was determined "by the title [held], with a very limited exception applicable only where the title is essentially honorary or ceremonial." National Medical Enterprises, Inc. v. Small, 680 F. 2d 83, 84 (9th Cir. 1982). For a discussion of the then eight decided cases — there has been none since — see Comment, Section 16(b) of the Securities and [*sic*] Exchange Act of 1934: Is a Vice President an Officer?, 58 Neb. L. Rev. 733 (1979).

b. "Director" [§3(a)(7)]

The statute itself defines the term "director" to mean "any director of a corporation or any person performing similar functions with respect to any organization, whether incorporated or unincorporated." This is broad enough to cover a trustee of a Massachusetts trust or of a voting trust, or a member of a committee that issues certificates of deposit. It also extends to an "honorary" director who plays no role with respect to policy issues and has no access to insider information.[70] Presumably, since the Commission's definition of "officer" is modeled on this statutory definition of "director," much the same considerations govern.

The big question here is whether one who "deputizes" another to be a director is himself a director and, if so, what it takes to "deputize." In a 1962 case, *Blau* v. *Lehman,* the Supreme Court stated: "No doubt Lehman Brothers, though a partnership, could for purposes of §16 be a 'director' of Tide Water and function through a deputy * * *."[71] But the Court thought there was no deputization on the facts. Seven years later, in *Feder* v. *Martin Marietta Corp.,* the Supreme Court's dictum became a square holding in the Second Circuit through what the court called "a legal fiction."[72] The action was to recover §16(b) profits in the purchase and sale of Sperry Rand Corporation stock by Martin Marietta Corporation on the theory that Martin had deputized Bunker, its President and Chief Executive officer, to serve on the Sperry board. And the court had this to say:[73]

> * * * the validity of the deputization theory, presumed to be valid here by the parties and by the district court, is unquestionable. Nevertheless, the situations encompassed by its application are not as clear. The Supreme Court in *Blau* v. *Lehman* intimated that the issue of deputization is a question of fact to be settled case by case and not a conclusion of law. See 368 U. S. at 408-409. Therefore, it is not enough for appellant to show us that inferences to support appellant's contentions should have been drawn from the evidence. Id. at 409. Rather our review of the facts and inferences found by the court below is imprisoned by the "unless clearly erroneous" standard. Fed. R. Civ. P. 52(a). In the instant case, applying that standard, though there is some evidence in the record to support the trial court's finding of no deputization, we, upon considering

[70] Fort Worth National Corp., CCH Fed. Sec. L. Rep. ¶78,309 (letter 1971).
[71] 368 U. S. 403, 409.
[72] 406 F. 2d 260, 262-63 (2d Cir. 1969), *cert. denied,* 396 U. S. 1036; see also Lewis v. Dekcraft Corp., CCH Fed. Sec. L. Rep. ¶94,620 at 96,202 (S. D. N. Y. 1974).
[73] 406 F. 2d at 263-66.

the entire evidence, are left with the definite and firm conviction that a mistake was committed. * * *

Bunker served as a director of Sperry from April 29, 1963 to August 1, 1963, when he resigned. During the period December 14, 1962 through July 24, 1963, Martin Marietta accumulated 801,300 shares of Sperry stock of which 101,300 shares were purchased during Bunker's directorship. Between August 29, 1963 and September 6, 1963, Martin Marietta sold all of its Sperry stock. Plaintiff seeks to reach, on behalf of the Sperry Rand Corporation, the profits made by Martin Marietta from the 101,300 shares of stock acquired between April 23 and August 1, all of which, of course, were sold within six months after purchase.

The district court, in determining that Bunker was not a Martin deputy, made the following findings of fact to support its decision. (1) Sperry initially invited Bunker to join its Board two and a half months before Martin began its accumulation of Sperry stock; (2) Bunker turned down a second offer by Sperry at a time when Martin already held 400,000 shares of Sperry stock; (3) Sperry, not Martin, took the initiative to encourage Bunker to accept the directorship; (4) no other Martin man was ever mentioned for the position in the event Bunker absolutely declined; and (5) Bunker's fine reputation and engineering expertise was the prime motivation for Sperry's interest in him. In addition, the testimony of the only two witnesses who testified at trial, Mr. Bunker and a Mr. Norman Frost, a Sperry director and its chief counsel, were fully believed and accepted as truthful by the court. We assume all of the foregoing findings have a basis of fact in the evidence, but we find there was additional, more germane, uncontradicted evidence, overlooked or ignored by the district court, which we are firmly convinced require us to conclude that Martin Marietta was a "director" of Sperry Rand.

First and foremost is Bunker's testimony that as chief executive of Martin Marietta he was "ultimately responsible for the total operation of the corporation" including personal approval of all the firm's financial investments, and, in particular, all of Martin's purchases of Sperry stock. As the district court aptly recognized, Bunker's control over Martin Marietta's investments, coupled with his position on the Board of Directors of Sperry Rand, placed him in a position where he could acquire inside information concerning Sperry and could utilize such data for Martin Marietta's benefit without disclosing this information to any other Martin Marietta personnel. Thus, the district court's findings that Bunker "never disclosed inside information relevant to investment decisions" and that the "information that he obtained while a director 'simply wasn't germane to that question at all' " are not significant. 286 F. Supp. at 946. Nor are these findings totally supported by the evidence. Bunker's testimony revealed that while he was a Sperry director three Sperry officials had furnished him with information relating to the "short-range outlook" at Sperry, and, in addition, Bunker admitted discussing Sperry's affairs with two officials at Martin Marietta and participating in sessions when Martin's investment in Sperry was reviewed. Moreover, an unsigned document concededly originating from the Martin Marietta files, entitled "Notes on Exploratory Investment in Sperry Rand Corporation," describing the Sperry management, evaluating their abilities, and analyzing the merit of Sperry's forecasts for the future, further indicates that Martin Marietta may have benefited, or intended to benefit, from Bunker's association with Sperry Rand.

In contrast, in *Blau* v. *Lehman,* supra, where Lehman Brothers was the alleged "director," the Lehman partner exercised no power of approval concerning the partnership's investment; was not consulted for advice; had no advance knowledge of Lehman Brothers' intention to purchase the stock of the corporation of which he was a member of the board of directors; and never discussed the operating details of that corporation's affairs with any member of Lehman Brothers. 368 U. S. at 406. * * *

It appears to us that a person in Bunker's unique position could act as a deputy for Martin Marietta even in the absence of factors indicating an intention or belief on the part of both companies that he was so acting. We do not hold that, without more, Bunker's control over Martin Marietta, * * * or the possibility that inside information was obtained or disclosed, mandates that Bunker was Martin's deputy. However, additional evidence detailed hereafter which indicates that the managements of Sperry Rand and of Martin Marietta intended that Bunker should act as Martin's deputy on the Sperry Board, and believed he was so acting, lends valuable support to our factual conclusion.

* * *

* * * the Board of Directors of Martin Marietta formally consented to and approved Bunker's directorship of Sperry prior to Bunker's acceptance of the position. * * *

Finally, Bunker's testimony clearly established that the Martin Marietta Corporation had representatives or deputies who served on the boards of other corporations. * * *

This leaves a number of questions:

(1) Was Bunker's mistake that he asked permission?

(2) If a *corporation* can be a "director" of another corporation, there is no reason to assume that a partnership (as in *Blau* v. *Lehman*) or an individual who "deputizes" cannot be. One may guess, however, that no "director by deputization" has ever filed a §16(a) report or signed a 1933 Act registration statement as a "director."

(3) Is it conceivable — let alone likely — that Congress contemplated a director by "deputization" when it defined the term to include "any person performing similar functions" to those of a "director of a *corporation*" and defined "person" in §3(a)(9) to include a "partnership"?[74] Is this not the sort of wooden reading of statutes that the courts have so often disapproved? Is it not much more likely that the quoted language was directed simply to trustees of business trusts and active general partners?

The Code's definition of "director" specifically excludes "a person who deputizes another person to be a director" on the ground that the theory is "out of harmony with the spirit" of §16(b).[75] That is to say, this area, unlike the area of mergers and so on, seems more appropriate for an "objective" approach. It seems significant in this respect that early drafts of what became §16(b) not only would have made it unlawful for any of the specified insiders to disclose any confidential information regarding registered securities, but also would have extended to all profits received by *anyone*, insider or not, "to whom such unlawful disclosure" had been made.[76]

c. Beneficial Ownership

Throughout §16 there is the question of determining who is a 10+ percent "beneficial owner," a phrase that Mr. Corcoran told the Senate committee in 1934 was "the broadest term you can have."[77] In addition, whereas the criterion under §16(b) is whether there have been a "purchase and sale," the criterion under §16(a) for all three types of insiders is beneficial ownership, direct or indirect. Changes in beneficial ownership must be reported whether they result from a purchase or a sale or a gift or any other event. Record ownership alone is of no consequence.

Although the Act does not define "beneficial ownership," there are a number of rules and releases with respect to various relationships:

(i) *Family relationships:* Intrafamily bookkeeping arrangements are not conclusive. In 1966 the Commission restated the applicable

[74] The 1975 amendments substituted the word "company."
[75] §202(40); 2 Code 752.
[76] Blau v. Lehman, 368 U. S. 403, 412 (1962).
[77] 15 Stock Exchange Practices, Hearings Before S. Com. on Banking & Currency, 73d Cong., 2d Sess. (1934) 6556.

principles as enunciated in a 1935 interpretation of its General Counsel:[78]

> Generally a person is regarded as the beneficial owner of securities held in the name of his or her spouse and their minor children. Absent special circumstances such relationship ordinarily results in such person obtaining benefits substantially equivalent to ownership, e. g., application of the income derived from such securities to maintain a common home, to meet expenses which such person otherwise would meet from other sources, or the ability to exercise a controlling influence over the purchase, sale, or voting of such securities. Accordingly, a person ordinarily should include in his reports filed pursuant to section 16(a) securities held in the name of a spouse or minor children as being beneficially owned by him.
>
> A person also may be regarded as the beneficial owner of securities held in the name of another person, if by reason of any contract, understanding, relationship, agreement, or other arrangement, he obtains therefrom benefits substantially equivalent to those of ownership. Accordingly, where such benefits are present such securities should be reported as being beneficially owned by the reporting person. Moreover, the fact that the person is a relative or relative of a spouse and sharing the same home as the reporting person may in itself indicate that the reporting person would obtain benefits substantially equivalent to those of ownership from securities held in the name of such relative. Thus, absent countervailing facts, it is expected that securities held by relatives who share the same home as the reporting person will be reported as being beneficially owned by such person.
>
> A person also is regarded as the beneficial owner of securities held in the name of a spouse, minor children or other person, even though he does not obtain therefrom the aforementioned benefits of ownership, if he can vest or revest title in himself at once, or at some future time [the 1935 opinion had added at this point, "without payment of other than a nominal consideration"].

This 1966 release marked no sharp departure from the published interpretation of 1935 — with its dual approach in terms of a "benefits" test and a "right to recapture" test — except for the statement that, "absent countervailing facts," a person might be considered to derive "benefits substantially equivalent to those of ownership" from the mere fact that his (or his spouse's) relative (presumably of any degree) shared his home. This was apparently designed to correct the impression on the part of many practitioners at that time that one spouse did not have benefits substantially

[78] Sec. Ex. Act Rel. 175 (1935); Sec. Ex. Act Rel. 7793 (1966), corrected by Sec. Ex. Act Rel. 7824 (1966).

equivalent to those of ownership as far as the other's securities were concerned unless the first spouse had not merely some economic benefit from them but also control over their purchase or sale.

Surely the proverbial case of the wealthy (and perhaps hostile) mother-in-law who moves in with her daughter is a "countervailing fact." The norm with which the release deals, though the rebuttable presumption it creates is not so limited, is the insider's wife (for simplicity we shall make the husband rather than the wife the insider) or minor child. And, even before the 1966 release, the obvious course — as simple as it was prudent — was to include the wife's and minor children's securities with the husband's (except in the event of a divorce or separation or, *perhaps* since the 1966 release, a clear case in which the wife had always been the "moneyed" member of the family in her own right) together with a disclaimer.[79]

There are only a few reported opinions in point. In what is perhaps the closest case, a director of Dow Chemical Company whose wife was a Dow heiress was held to be the beneficial owner of his wife's Dow stock under the harmonious family circumstances, so as to match her sales against his later exercise of an option financed by using the proceeds of her sale, which he borrowed from her at 7 percent interest.[80]

(ii) *Partnerships:* A partnership that is a 10+ percent beneficial owner for its own account must report regardless of whether reports are filed by the partners. Moreover, an individual partner must report as well if he is an officer or director of the issuer, or if his indirect interest in the security through the partnership (together

[79] This is permitted by Rule 16a-3.

[80] Husband and wife filed joint tax returns and had the same financial advisers. She used his gift tax exclusion. He contributed virtually his entire salary to living expenses. But she was primarily responsible for the style in which they lived, which included the cost of their children's education and maintaining a vacation home. Whiting v. Dow Chemical Co., 523 F. 2d 680 (2d Cir. 1975).

See also Blau v. Potter, CCH Fed. Sec. L. Rep. ¶94,115 (S. D. N. Y. 1973) (judgment for defendant); Altamil Corp. v. Pryor, 405 F. Supp. 1222 (S. D. Ind. 1975); Whittaker v. Whittaker Corp., 639 F. 2d 516 (9th Cir. 1981), *cert. denied,* 454 U. S. 1030 (director felt free to manage his aged mother's assets as his own); but cf. CBI Industries, Inc. v. Horton, 682 F. 2d 643 (7th Cir. 1982) (distinguishing *Whiting* and *Whittaker* as involving the required "direct pecuniary benefit to the insider").

Not surprisingly, the federal policy in §16(b) has been held to prevail over the local community property law, so that the husband (or presumably the wife if she is an insider) is liable for the entire amount of the profit and not merely half. Jefferson Lake Sulphur Co. v. Walet, 104 F. Supp. 20, 25 (E. D. La. 1952), *aff'd on lower court's "fuller discussion" of the point* sub nom. Walet v. Jefferson Lake Sulphur Co., 202 F. 2d 433, 434 (5th Cir. 1953), *cert. denied,* 346 U. S. 820.

with the amount of the security of which he is otherwise directly or indirectly the beneficial owner) exceeds 10 percent, or if he is the beneficial owner of 10+ percent of some other class of registered equity security of the same issuer.[81] When a partner reports, he must state the entire amount owned by the partnership, though he may elect to disclose the extent of his interest in the partnership and its transactions.[82]

Absent "deputization," and on the assumption that a partnership buys and sells without the advice or concurrence of the partner who is a director, the partner-director is liable only for his *pro rata* share of the firm's profit.[83] But, however innocent himself, he cannot avoid all liability by disclaiming his interest in the firm's profit.[84]

(iii) *Holding companies:* Concerning the question of indirect beneficial ownership through a holding company that is itself a 10+ percent beneficial owner, the Commission's General Counsel expressed the view in 1938 that "no consideration need be given by the owner of stock in a holding company to the holdings of that company, except in a case where the holding merely provides a medium through which one person, or several persons in a small group, invest or trade in securities, and where such company has no other substantial business."[85] But a 1981 release seems to tighten up a bit when it considers any "control person of a closely held company" to be "the beneficial owner of all securities held by that company."[86]

[81] Op. Gen. Counsel, Sec. Ex. Act Rel. 1965 (1938); Sec. Ex. Act Rel. 18,114, 23 SEC Dock. 856, 863 (1981).

[82] Form 3, Instr. 10; Form 4, Instr. 10.

[83] Blau v. Lehman, 368 U. S. 403 (1962).

[84] Blau v. Lehman, 286 F. 2d 786 (2d Cir. 1960), *aff'd on other grounds,* 368 U. S. 403 (1962).

[85] Op. Gen. Counsel, Sec. Ex. Act Rel. 1965 (1938).

[86] Sec. Ex. Act Rel. 18,114, 23 SEC Dock. 856, 863 (1981). See generally Boston & Me. R. R. Co. v. Hillman, CCH Fed. Sec. L. Rep. ¶90,813 (S. D. N. Y. 1957); Blau v. Lamb, 242 F. Supp. 151, 161 (S. D. N. Y. 1965), *aff'd in part and rev'd in part,* 363 F. 2d 507 (2d Cir. 1966), *cert. denied,* 385 U. S. 1002; Morales v. Colt Industries, Inc., CCH Fed. Sec. L. Rep. ¶93,569 (S. D. N. Y. 1972); Popkin v. Dingman, 366 F. Supp. 534, 541 (S. D. N. Y. 1973); Margolies v. Rea Bros., PLC, CCH Fed. Sec. L. Rep. ¶99,261 (S. D. N. Y. 1983) (director-shareholder who exercised control over the company did not realize direct pecuniary benefit from trades executed by the company).

In Kay v. ScienTex Corp., 719 F. 2d 1009, 1015 n. 5 (9th Cir. 1983), the court stated *obiter* that in the case of a sole stockholder it "need not pause over the question of whether the acquisition of stock by a corporation is also an acquisition by that corporation's insiders for purposes of 16(b)."

Query whether the "controlling person" liability of §20(a) (infra p. 1011) extends to §16(b). In *Margolies* (supra) the court held not, referring to (1) the inconsistency between the "good faith" defense in §10(a) and the strict liability of §16(b) and (2) the internal completeness of §16(b)'s "statutory scheme."

The Commission does have a rule that no report is required of any person with respect to his indirect interest in portfolio securities held by a holding or investment company registered under the 1935 or 1940 Act, a "pension or retirement plan holding securities of an issuer whose employees generally are the beneficiaries of the plan," or a business trust with more than twenty-five beneficiaries.[87]

(iv) *Trusts [Rule 16a-8]:* About the only simple statement one can safely make about the many different kinds of trust situations is that "beneficial ownership" within the meaning of §16 "must be construed in context and is not necessarily identical with similar concepts in other contexts such as tax law, nor does it depend solely upon the form in which the trust is established."[88] But Rule 16a-8 is reasonably straightforward:

Beneficial ownership for purposes of §16(a) is considered to flow from any one of three relationships to a trust:[89] (1) a trustee when either he or members of his immediate family have a vested interest in the income or corpus of the trust; (2) an owner of a vested beneficial interest in a trust; and (3) a settlor of a trust who has the power to revoke the trust without obtaining the consent of all the beneficiaries.

In addition, the trust and the trustees as such are required to file reports when the trust is a 10+ percent beneficial owner; this, in effect, treats the trust "entity" as the beneficial owner, for which in practice reports are normally filed by the trustee. However, except in so far as the *trust* as a beneficial owner is concerned, the rule

[87]Rule 16a-8(g). See Tomlinson, The Application of Section 16(b) to Tax-Qualified Employee Benefit Plans, 33 Stan. L. Rev. 231 (1981).

[88]Sec. Ex. Act Rel. 4720 (1952).

[89]So far as §16(b) is concerned, presumably Rule 16a-10 forestalls its application when Rule 16a-8 makes it clear that the person is *not* a beneficial owner. But it does not follow that a person declared to be a beneficial owner by the rule will be so treated for purposes of 16(b). See Sec. Ex. Act Rels. 4801 (1953), 7824 (1966); CBI Industries, Inc. v. Horton, 682 F. 2d 643 (7th Cir. 1982). In Marquette Cement Mfg. Co. v. Andreas, 239 F. Supp. 962, 967 (S. D. N. Y. 1965), where the defendant was himself beneficiary of one of the trusts of which he was trustee and was also sole trustee of eighteen other trusts of which for the most part members of his family were beneficiaries, the court held him liable only *pro rata* under Blau v. Lehman (supra p. 566), saying that Rule 16a-8 had "only slight significance in assessing insider liability under Section 16(b)." Whether the defendant held a beneficial interest in the stock of the other trusts was considered a question of fact to be determined from all the evidence. His normal interest in seeing that members of his family were well and comfortable did not bring him within §16(b). All the trusts were *bona fide* and irrevocable except the one for his benefit, and all but that one were for the benefit of individuals with recognizably different interests from his. Cf. Colan v. Monumental Corp., 713 F. 2d 330 (7th Cir. 1983) (option holder's being a "beneficial owner" of the underlying stock for §16(a) purposes does not carry over to §16(b)).

provides an exemption with respect to any obligation that would otherwise be imposed solely by reason of ownership as a *settlor* or *beneficiary* when (1) less than 20 percent in market value of the trust's securities having a readily ascertainable market value (determined as of the end of the trust's preceding fiscal year) consists of equity securities with respect to which reports would otherwise be required, or (2) the ownership, acquisition, or disposition of the securities by the trust is made without the settlor's or beneficiary's prior approval.[90]

d. "Equity Security" [§3(a)(11)]

Section 3(a)(11) defines "equity security," in substance, to mean any stock or any security that carries a right to acquire stock, whether by conversion or otherwise, with rulemaking authority to add any security "of similar nature." Until the 1964 amendments, this term was significant *only* with respect to §16. With the use of the term in §12(g)(1) discriminating in favor of issuers of unlisted *non-equity* securities, the Commission in 1965 adopted Rule 3a11-1 to flesh out the statutory definition:[91]

> The term "equity security" is hereby defined to include any stock or similar security, certificate of interest or participation in any profit sharing agreement, preorganization certificate or subscription, transferable share, voting trust certificate or certificate of deposit for an equity security, limited partnership interest, interest in a joint venture, or certificate of interest in a business trust; or any security convertible, with or without consideration, into such a security, or carrying any warrant or right to subscribe to or purchase such a security; or any such warrant or right.

Even before this rule, voting-trust certificates and certificates of deposit were considered to be equity securities whenever the underlying securities were.[92] Hence 10+ percent owners of registered instruments of these types, as well as committee members, voting trustees, and any other persons whose position with the issuer of the instruments corresponds to an officer or director of a corporation, are subject to §16. Moreover, since beneficial ownership of these certificates involves beneficial ownership of the underlying security, persons who beneficially own more than 10 percent of the

[90] See also Rule 16a-8(g). And there is more. See Sec. Ex. Act Rel. 18,114, 23 SEC Dock. 856, 864, 878-82 (1981).

[91] Sec. Ex. Act Rel. 7581 (1965).

[92] See Rule 16a-2(a), infra p. 578, text at n. 94.

underlying security (both directly and through beneficial ownership of one of these instruments), as well as officers and directors of the issuer of the underlying security, are subject to §16 with respect to changes in their beneficial ownership of the certificates as well as of the underlying security. This assumes that the underlying security is registered. If so, it is immaterial whether or not the certificates issued against them are registered as well.

Treasury stock is an "equity security" even though it is expressly included in the definition of "security" and not specifically mentioned in the definition of "equity security."[93] And presumably a warrant to subscribe to a convertible bond would be an equity security, though twice removed. *Query* the status of income bonds and the hybrid instruments.

e. "Class"

We have already considered the definition of "class" in connection with §12(g) registration. But it has a fillip in the §16 context so far as convertible debt securities are concerned.

In the first case to construe "class" in the §16 context, the corporation had two series of cumulative preferred stock and the defendant owned more than 10 percent of the smaller series but not more than 10 percent of both combined. The two series differed in that they had been listed fourteen months apart, they had different dividend rates, redemption prices, and sinking-fund provisions, they were redeemable separately, and a two-thirds vote of the particular series was required for any charter amendment adversely affecting its holders. But neither series was preferred over the other with respect to dividends or liquidation; the par value was the same; on a default in four quarterly dividends, the preferred as a class had the right to elect one-third of the directors; the articles themselves referred to the preferred as a class with provision for its issuance in "series"; and they referred also to a second preferred as a separate class with series, thus unequivocally distinguishing between different classes and different series. Applying the normal distinction between "class" and "series" in corporation law, and pointing out that most of the states specifically provide for the

[93] Walet v. Jefferson Lake Sulphur Co., 202 F. 2d 433, 435 (5th Cir. 1953), *cert. denied*, 346 U. S. 820.

division of "classes" into "series," the Second Circuit concluded that there was but a single "class."[94]

In 1967, however, the same court, disagreeing with the SEC's position as *amicus curiae,* held that convertible debentures were not themselves a "class of any equity security," but were equity securities only in the sense that the class consists of the common stock augmented as to any beneficial holding in question by the number of shares into which the debentures owned by the particular person are convertible.[95] The *holding* of the case was that a 10+ percent owner of the debentures was not liable for any profit resulting from the matching of purchases of debentures against sales of common stock within less than six months when the defendant had never owned as much as 10 percent of the class under the court's construction. Judge Lumbard found nothing in the legislative history to indicate that the owners of debentures as such ought to be considered "insiders," and saw "no reason whatever to believe that any holder of any Convertible Debentures would, by reason of such holding, normally have any standing or position with the officers, directors or large stockholders of a company so that such holder of Debentures would be the recipient of any inside information."[96] Moreover, the court pointed to the anomaly whereby the defendant, able to command less than 3 percent of the common stock on a hypothetical conversion of all its debentures, would touch off §16 under the Commission's view although a holder of 9 percent of the common would not.

The opinion is persuasive. But the anomaly that concerned the court is built into the statute: if (altogether apart from convertibility) a company has twenty times as much Class A stock as Class B Stock, the 11 percent holder of B stock (if it is registered) activates §16 even though the 1 percent holder of A stock, with a far greater

[94] Ellerin v. Massachusetts Mutual Life Ins. Co., 270 F. 2d 259, 261 (2d Cir. 1959). Cf. Rule 12d1-1(d): "If a class of security is issuable in two or more series with different terms, each such series shall be deemed a separate class for the purposes of this regulation." Cf. also Sec. Ex. Act §15(d), 4th sentence: "For the purposes of this subsection, the term 'class' shall be construed to include all securities of an issuer which are of substantially similar character and the holders of which enjoy substantially similar rights and privileges." These two provisions, as the court observed, are expressly made applicable only for their own peculiar purposes.

[95] Chemical Fund, Inc. v. Xerox Corp., 377 F. 2d 107 (2d Cir. 1967). See also Foremost-McKesson, Inc. v. Provident Securities Co., 423 U. S. 232, 236 n. 5 (1976), involving a purchase and sale of a convertible debenture, where the Court stated merely: "The owner of debentures convertible into more than 10% of a corporation's registered common stock is a beneficial owner within the meaning of the Act."

[96] Chemical Fund, Inc. v. Xerox Corp., 377 F. 2d 107, 111 (2d Cir. 1967).

equity in the company, does not. And the opinion does leave a number of perplexing questions. There are convertible debentures and convertible debentures. One that is fully protected against dilution[97] and that is traded in the market will be considered by the market to be the substantial equivalent of the common stock, and will rise in price with the common if the market price of the common, on adjustment for the conversion ratio, exceeds the call price of the debentures. We have earlier noticed the desirability of being able to match a purchase (or sale) of the one security against a sale (or purchase) of the other in such a situation.[98] And that would not be easy if the two were considered separate "classes" — though §16(b) is not explicit to the effect that the purchase and sale must be of the same "class," and the section *might* be applied to the purchase and sale of different "classes" that were nevertheless substantially similar. At any rate, when conversion of debentures is *not* economical, it is their senior position and fixed interest claim that give them value. At least in that situation, the debentures, until converted, would seem *a fortiori* to be a different "class" of security from the common if a convertible *preferred* (which is indubitably an "equity security" even apart from the convertibility feature) is ever a different "class" from the common;[99] and surely the court is not saying that a convertibility feature automatically makes the preferred and common the same "class."

Presumably, too (apart from the arbitrage exemption in §16(e) in the event of simultaneous transactions), the matching would have been sustained if the defendant *had* owned enough of the debentures (either alone or together with holdings of common stock) to make it a 10+ percent owner of the single class, or if the defendant had been an officer or director. Indeed, the court's single-class approach should greatly facilitate matching in such a case. And it is even clearer that any such person would be liable for profits from short-term trading in the debentures themselves. Again, since the "class," in the court's view, is augmented by the number of shares into which the beneficial holding in question is convertible, not the number of shares into which all outstanding debentures are con-

[97] On what constitutes full protection, see Posner, Developments in Federal Securities Regulation, 22 Bus. Law. 645, 664 n. 68 (1967).

[98] See p. 557 supra.

[99] But see American Standard, Inc. v. Crane Co., 346 F. Supp. 1153, 1161 (S. D. N. Y. 1972), *rev'd on other grounds,* 510 F. 2d 1043 (2d Cir. 1974), *cert. denied,* 421 U. S. 1000, a case in which a hypothetical conversion on the *Chemical Fund* rationale resulted in a holding of *more* than 10 percent of the common. The court refused to distinguish a convertible preferred from a convertible debenture on the contention that every preferred is *per se* an "equity security."

vertible, one does not come to the case of the person who owns more than 10 percent of the *common stock* alone but less than 10 percent of the common as augmented by the shares into which outstanding debentures are convertible.[100] But what of the short-term trader in convertible debentures (or preferred) who is neither officer nor director and who owns more than 10 percent of the convertible debentures (or preferred) alone but not more than 10 percent of the "class" in the court's sense? And what of the occasional convertible debentures that have voting rights?

In 1968, in the wake of the *Chemical Fund* case, the Commission recognized the result of that case by adopting a rule to the effect that, for the purpose of determining whether a person is a 10+ percent beneficial owner, he is considered to be the beneficial owner of securities of the class that he has the right to acquire "through the exercise of presently exercisable options, warrants or rights or through the conversion of presently convertible securities."[101] But the Commission has not read *Chemical Fund* as requiring any change in its traditional position that a person who apart from the formula of that case is a beneficial owner of more than 10 percent of a registered security convertible into an equity security (or of a class of stock purchase warrants) is required to file reports under §16(a).[102]

Conversion complexities aside, other questions are determined by an older rule:[103] A class of a given security is considered to consist of the total amount outstanding, exclusive of any securities of the class held by the issuer itself or a subsidiary. However, in the case of voting-trust certificates or certificates of deposit for equity securities, the class of certificates is considered to consist of the entire amount issuable for the class of equity securities that may be deposited, regardless of how many have in fact been deposited.[104]

[100] Jennings and Marsh put this intriguing *query*: "Suppose a corporation has outstanding 1,000,000 shares of listed common stock and an outstanding debenture issue which is convertible into 500,000 shares of common stock, although none of it has been converted. A owns 110,000 shares of common stock, and he purchases and sells common stock within a period of six months. Under the Chemical Fund rationale, is he subject to liability under Section 16(b) as a *10% holder* of a registered security?" R. Jennings and H. Marsh, Securities Regulation Cases and Materials (6th ed. 1987) 1418.

[101] Rule 16a-2(b); Sec. Ex. Act Rel. 8325 (1968). Securities subject to such rights or conversion privileges are considered for the purpose of computing the percentage of the class owned by the particular person, but not for the purpose of computing the percentage owned by any other person. Ibid.

[102] Sec. Ex. Act Rel. 8202 (1967); Sec. Ex. Act Rel. 18,114, 23 SEC Dock. 856, 868, 873 and n. 57 (1981).

[103] Rule 16a-2(a).

[104] See Chemical Fund, Inc. v. Xerox Corp., 377 F. 2d 107, 110 (2d Cir. 1967), supra p. 576; United States v. Guterma, 281 F. 2d 742, 748-49 (2d Cir.

f. "Purchase" and "Sale" [§§3(a)(13), 3(a)(14)]

In contrast to the 1933 Act, with its elaborate definitions of "sale" and "offer" and no definition at all of "purchase," §§3(a)(13) and 3(a)(14) of the 1934 Act contain parallel language on "purchase" and "sale." But they are not really definitions. All we are told is that ("unless the context otherwise requires") the two terms "include" contracts to buy "or otherwise acquire," or to sell "or otherwise dispose of." Nevertheless, the First Circuit, in reading the bonus clause of the 1933 Act into §2(a)(14), saw "no reason to believe that Congress intended, one year after the passage of the Securities Act, to dilute the concept of 'sale' in the Securities Exchange Act."[105]

Nice questions have been litigated with respect to fixing the time of the "purchase" and "sale" for purposes of determining the six-month period as well as computing the profit. And there is the related question of when beneficial ownership starts and stops for purposes of determining when a person who is not an officer or director must file reports under §16(a), as well as determining when any of the persons covered by §16(a) has had a change in his beneficial ownership. The criteria in the two cases, however, are not necessarily the same. The broker's or dealer's confirmation would ordinarily seem determinative in fixing the dates of *purchase and sale*. On the other hand, the opinion was early expressed by the Commission's General Counsel that *beneficial ownership* is acquired

1960), *cert. denied,* 364 U. S. 871 ("class" does not include unissued shares reserved for exercise of options or conversion rights).

[105] Lawrence v. SEC, 398 F. 2d 276, 280 (1st Cir. 1968); see also Dasho v. Susquehanna Corp., 380 F. 2d 262, 266 (7th Cir. 1967), *cert. denied* sub nom. Bard v. Dasho, 389 U. S. 977. But cf. SEC v. Sterling Precision Corp., 393 F. 2d 214, 217-18 (2d Cir. 1968), where Judge Friendly said in holding that a redemption was not a "purchase" under §17(a)(2) of the Investment Company Act, which does not define the term:

> "Purchase" is not a peculiarly technical term and "[a]fter all, legislation when not expressed in technical terms is addressed to the common run of men and is therefore to be understood according to the sense of the thing, as the ordinary man has a right to rely on ordinary words addressed to him." Addison v. Holly Hill Fruit Products, Inc., 322 U. S. 607, 618 (1944). A party asserting that a word in a statute should be given a meaning different from what it has in the speech of common men or, in this instance, the common speech of lawyers, has the burden of showing that context or evident purpose requires this.

Cf. also Northland Capital Corp. v. Silver, 735 F. 2d 1421, 1426 n. 5 (D. C. Cir. 1984). For a detailed review of the legislative history of §3(a)(14), see Chemical Bank v. Arthur Andersen & Co., 726 F. 2d 930, 940 n. 17 (1984), *cert. denied,* 469 U. S. 884. On "purchase" and "sale" in the Rule 10b-5 context, see Supp. pp. 800-01, new par. (12), infra.

or divested when the insider "takes a firm commitment" for the purchase or sale of the security.[106]

This is no longer true so far as options (and convertible securities) are concerned. There, as we have seen, there is a rule for reporting purposes to the effect that a person is considered the beneficial owner of securities that he has a right to acquire through the exercise of currently exercisable options.[107] For §16(b) purposes, however, it is the "established rule * * * that the mere granting of an option to purchase is not a sale [or a purchase]."[108]

Can the date of purchase or sale ever be fixed at a time *later* than the date of an option's exercise? In an unusual option case in which it was agreed between the company and an officer that he should be obligated to pay the price specified in the option upon his mailing of notice of exercise, but that payment and delivery might be postponed until the termination of employment, title to remain in the company and the officer to have no rights as a stockholder pending payment, the court held that the purchase had occurred upon the officer's sending of notice. Consequently there was no purchase, at the time of payment and delivery some three years later, that could

[106] Op. Gen. Counsel, Sec. Ex. Act Rel. 116 (1935), cited in Stella v. Graham-Paige Motors Corp., 232 F. 2d 299, 301 n. 2 (2d Cir. 1956), *cert. denied,* 352 U. S. 831; see Arrow Distributing Corp. v. Baumgartner, 783 F. 2d 1274, 1279-81 (5th Cir. 1986), *amended per curiam on other grounds,* — F. 2d — (5th Cir. 1986), *rehearing denied,* CCH Fed. Sec. L. Rep. ¶92,791 (5th Cir. 1986). In Sterman v. Ferro Corp., 785 F. 2d 162, 167 (6th Cir. 1985), the court held that even a firm commitment standing alone might not suffice and that the critical date was when the buyer had "incurred an irrevocable liability," which required board action.

In Portnoy v. Revlon, Inc., 650 F. 2d 895 (7th Cir. 1981), the court held that an insider holding shares in a merged company had not "sold" on execution of the merger agreement even though the necessary votes were sure, because a number of significant conditions remained with respect to tax rulings, accounting opinion on pooling of interests, maximum number of dissenting shares, employment agreements, and non-competition undertaking. See also Colan v. Cutler-Hammer, Inc., CCH Fed. Sec. L. Rep. ¶92,806 (N. D. Ill. 1986), *aff'd per curiam,* 812 F. 2d 357 (7th Cir. 1987).

The question of fixing the date of sale has arisen in other contexts. See p. 299 n. h supra (§3(a)(ii)); p. 989 infra (statute of limitations).

[107] Rule 16a-2(b), supra p. 578, text at n. 91.

[108] Abrams v. Occidental Petroleum Corp., 450 F. 2d 157, 164 (2d Cir. 1971), *aff'd on other grounds* sub nom. Kern County Land Co. v. Occidental Petroleum Corp., 411 U. S. 582 (1973), supra p. 550. But cf. Bershad v. McDonough, 428 F. 2d 693 (7th Cir. 1970), *cert. denied,* 400 U. S. 992, which the *Abrams* court characterized as a case where "the 'option' [which was held to be essentially a firm sale with a delayed payment provision] was accompanied by a wink of the eye." Cf. also Pay Less Drug Stores v. Jewel Companies, Inc., 579 F. Supp. 1396, 1399-1400 (N. D. Cal. 1984) (attempted exercise of option and subsequent favorable settlement of contract action constituted a "purchase" on date that transfer would have taken place if there had not been a breach of contract).

be matched against a sale less than six months before that time. The court conceded that "The inclusion of executory transactions does not import the exclusion of executed ones." But that, the court said, cannot "justify finding two 'purchases' where in fact but one exists." Judge Clark stated that speculation was the only vice within the purview of §16(b), and the court held as it did on the ground that the important factor was the insider's "firm assurance that a fixed quantity [of stock] can be acquired or disposed of at a fixed price" rather than "who has title or possession or who can vote the stock or receive dividends."[109]

7. Exemptions

(1) Section 16(a)-(c) does not apply to an "exempted security."[110] In addition, §16(b) authorizes the Commission to exempt "transactions" by rule, and §12(h) authorizes exemption, by rule *or order,* from all of §16.[111]

(2) Section 16(b) by its own terms does not apply if the security "was acquired in good faith in connection with a debt previously contracted."[112]

(3) Section 16(d) added a marketmaker exemption from §16(b) in 1964.[113]

[109] Blau v. Ogsbury, 210 F. 2d 426, 427 (2d Cir. 1954); see also Freeman v. Decio, 584 F. 2d 186, 200 (7th Cir. 1978) (defendant "bought" optioned stock when he exercised his option and made payment, not five years later, when certain restrictions lapsed and the certificates were delivered); Riseman v. Orion Research, Inc., 749 F. 2d 915 (1st Cir. 1984); Lewis v. Bradley, 599 F. Supp. 327 (S. D. N. Y. 1984); but cf. Booth v. Varian Associates, 334 F. 2d 1 (1st Cir. 1964), *cert. denied,* 379 U. S. 961; Newmark v. RKO General, Inc., 425 F. 2d 348 (2d Cir. 1970), *cert. denied,* 400 U. S. 854.

[110] See §3(a)(12), supra p. 442; with respect to foreign securities exempted by Rule 3a12-3, see Supp. p. 77 supra.

[111] See p. 428 supra.

[112] See Smolowe v. Delendo Corp., 136 F. 2d 231, 239 (2d Cir. 1943), *cert. denied,* 310 U. S. 751; Park & Tilford, Inc. v. Schulte, 160 F. 2d 984, 987 (2d Cir. 1947), *cert. denied,* 332 U. S. 761; Rheem Mfg. Co. v. Rheem, 295 F. 2d 473, 475 (9th Cir. 1961); Booth v. Varian Associates, 334 F. 2d 1, 5-6 (1st Cir. 1964), *cert. denied,* 379 U. S. 961.

[113] See Painter, Section 16(d) of the Securities Exchange Act: Legislative Compromise or Loophole?, 113 U. Pa. L. Rev. 358 (1965). In C. R. A. Realty Corp. v. Tri-South Investments, 738 F. 2d 73 (2d Cir. 1984), the court (1) agreed with the SEC's position that common stock trading came within the exemption, on a "market equivalence" theory, if incident to the firm's marketmaking in the issuer's convertible debentures, and (2) held that marketmaking status could be established despite interruptions in the firm's appearance in the over-the-counter "sheets" and without the firm's so identifying itself when it did appear in the "sheets."

(4) Section 16(e) (which was §16(d) until the present §16(d) was added) has always exempted "foreign or domestic arbitrage transactions" from all of §16 unless made in contravention of Commission rules. The Commission has adopted a rule that, in substance, subjects arbitrage by officers or directors, but not by 10+ percent stockholders, to §§16(a) and 16(b), with a complete exemption from §16(c).[114]

(5) All these *statutory* provisions aside, the Commission has used its §16(b) authority to exempt "transactions," as well as its §3(a)(12) rulemaking authority to define "exempted securities," in order to adopt a considerable number of *rules* that exempt from one or more provisions in §16(a)-(c).[115] The most frequently amended and litigated of these exemptive rules is Rule 16b-3, which exempts certain transactions under employee benefit plans from §16(b).

8. The Common Law

It is wise once in a while — especially when dealing with a body of occasionally esoteric federal law — to return to our Mother, the Common Law. For it turns out that the lady has a remarkable resilience.

There is a leading case, *Diamond* v. *Oreamuno,* decided by the New York Court of Appeals in 1969.[116] Chief Judge Fuld wrote:

> Upon this appeal from an order denying a motion to dismiss the complaint as insufficient on its face, the question presented — one of first impression in this court — is whether officers and directors

[114]Rule 16d-1; see Falco v. Donner Foundation, Inc., 208 F. 2d 600, 604 (2d Cir. 1953); Lewis v. Dakraft Corp., CCH Fed. Sec. L. Rep. ¶94,620 (S. D. N. Y. 1974).

[115]On the relationship of these two grants of authority, see Kornfeld v. Eaton, 217 F. Supp. 671, 679 (S. D. N. Y. 1963), *aff'd,* 327 F. 2d 263 (2d Cir. 1964). In general, see Greene v. Dietz, 247 F. 2d 689 (2d Cir. 1957) (arising under an earlier version of the rule, but still relevant with respect to the extent of the Commission's exemptive authority); Cohn, Stock Appreciation Rights and the SEC: A Case of Questionable Rulemaking, 79 Colum. L. Rev. 66 (1979); Kailer, Shareholder Approval of Employee Stock Purchase Plans, 17 Rev. Sec. Reg. 869 (1984). In Sec. Ex. Act Rel. 19,756, 27 SEC Dock. 1105 (1983), the Commission announced its non-acquiescence in the holding in Colema Realty Corp. v. Bibow, 555 F. Supp. 1030 (D. Conn. 1983), to the effect that an amendment to an existing stock option plan permitting the delivery of stock already owned in payment for the exercise of a stock option conferred material benefits on option holders and required shareholder approval in order to retain the exemption. See Whitson, Cashless Exercises of Employee Stock Options, 16 Rev. Sec. Reg. 900 (1983).

[116]24 N. Y. 2d 494, 248 N. E. 2d 910.

may be held accountable to their corporation for gains realized by them from transactions in the company's stock as a result of their use of material inside information.

The complaint was filed by a shareholder of Management Assistance, Inc. (MAI) asserting a derivative action against a number of its officers and directors to compel an accounting for profits allegedly acquired as a result of a breach of fiduciary duty. It charges that two of the defendants — Oreamuno, chairman of the board of directors, and Gonzalez, its president — had used inside information, acquired by them solely by virtue of their positions, in order to reap large personal profits from the sale of MAI shares and that these profits rightfully belong to the corporation. Other officers and directors were joined as defendants on the ground that they acquiesced in or ratified the assertedly wrongful transactions.

MAI is in the business of financing computer installations through sale and lease back arrangements with various commercial and industrial users. * * * As a result of a sharp increase by IBM of its charges for such [maintenance] service, MAI's expenses for August of 1966 rose considerably and its net earnings declined from $262,253 in July to $66,233 in August, a decrease of about 75%. This information, although earlier known to the defendants, was not made public until October of 1966. Prior to the release of the information, however, Oreamuno and Gonzalez sold off a total of 56,500 shares of their MAI stock at the then current market price of $28 a share.

After the information concerning the drop in earnings was made available to the public, the value of a share of MAI stock immediately fell from the $28 realized by the defendants to $11. * * *

* * *

It is well established, as a general proposition, that a person who acquires special knowledge or information by virtue of a confidential or fiduciary relationship with another is not free to exploit that knowledge or information for his own personal benefit but must account to his principal for any profits derived therefrom. (See, e. g., *Byrne* v. *Barrett,* 268 N. Y. 199.) This, in turn, is merely a corollary of the broader principle, inherent in the nature of the fiduciary relationship, that prohibits a trustee or agent from extracting secret profits from his position of trust.

* * *

It is true that the complaint before us does not contain any allegation of damages to the corporation but this has never been considered to be an essential requirement for a cause of action founded on a breach of fiduciary duty. (See, e. g., *Matter of People [Bond & Mtge. Guar. Co.]*, 303 N. Y. 423, 431; *Wendt* v. *Fischer*, 243 N. Y. 439, 443; *Dutton* v. *Willner*, 52 N. Y. 312, 319.) This is because the function of such an action, unlike an ordinary tort or contract case, is not merely to *compensate* the plaintiff for wrongs committed by the defendant but, as this court declared many years ago (*Dutton* v. *Willner*, 52 N. Y. 312, 319, supra), "to *prevent* them, by removing from agents and trustees all inducement to attempt dealing for their own benefit in matters which they have undertaken for others, or to which their agency or trust relates." (Emphasis supplied.)

Just as a trustee has no right to retain for himself the profits yielded by property placed in his possession but must account to his beneficiaries, a corporate fiduciary, who is entrusted with potentially valuable information, may not appropriate that asset for his own use even though, in so doing, he causes no injury to the corporation. The primary concern, in a case such as this, is not to determine whether the corporation has been damaged but to decide, as between the corporation and the defendants, who has a higher claim to the proceeds derived from the exploitation of the information. In our opinion, there can be no justification for permitting officers and directors, such as the defendants, to retain for themselves profits which, it is alleged, they derived solely from exploiting information gained by virtue of their inside position as corporate officials.

In addition, it is pertinent to observe that, despite the lack of any specific allegation of damage, it may well be inferred that the defendants' actions might have caused some harm to the enterprise. Although the corporation may have little concern with the day-to-day transactions in its shares, it has a great interest in maintaining a reputation of integrity, an image of probity, for its management and in insuring the continued public acceptance and marketability of its stock. When officers and directors abuse their position in order to gain personal profits, the effect may be to cast a cloud on the corporation's name, injure stockholder relations and undermine public regard for the corporation's securities. * * *

* * *

Although no appellate court in this State has had occasion to pass upon the precise question before us, the concept underlying the present cause of action is hardly a new one. (See, e. g., Securities Exchange Act of 1934 (48 U. S. Stat. 881), §16(b); U. S. Code, tit. 15, §78p, subd. [b]; *Brophy* v. *Cities Serv. Co.*, 31 Del. Ch. 241; Restatement, 2d, Agency, §388, comment *c;* Israels, A New Look at Corporate Directorship, 24 Business Lawyer 727, 732 et seq.; Note, 54 Cornell L. Rev. 306, 309-312.) Under Federal law (Securities Exchange Act of 1934, §16[b]), for example, it is conclusively presumed that, when a director, officer or 10% shareholder buys and sells securities of his corporation within a six-month period, he is trading on inside information. * * *

* * *

Although the provisions of section 16(b) may not apply to all cases of trading on inside information, it demonstrates that a derivative action can be an effective method for dealing with such abuses which may be used to accomplish a similar purpose in cases not specifically covered by the statute. In *Brophy* v. *Cities Serv. Co.* (31 Del. Ch. 241, supra), for example, the Chancery Court of Delaware allowed a similar remedy in a situation not covered by the Federal legislation. One of the defendants in that case was an employee who had acquired inside information that the corporate plaintiff was about to enter the market and purchase its own shares. On the basis of this confidential information, the employee, who was not an officer and, hence, not liable under Federal law, bought a large block of shares and, after the corporation's purchases had caused the price to rise, resold them at a profit. The court sustained the complaint in a derivative action brought for an accounting, stating that "[p]ublic policy will not permit an employee occupying a position of trust and confidence toward his employer to abuse that relation to his own profit, regardless of whether his employer suffers a loss" (31 Del. Ch. at p. 246). And a similar view has been expressed in the Restatement, 2d, Agency (§388, comment *c*):

> c. *Use of confidential information.* An agent who acquires confidential information in the course of his employment or in violation of his duties has a duty * * * to account for any profits made by the use of such information, although this does not harm the principal. * * * So, if [a corporate officer] has "inside" information that the corporation is about to purchase or sell securities, or to declare or to pass a dividend, profits made by him in stock transactions undertaken because of his knowledge are held in constructive trust for the principal.

In the present case, the defendants may be able to avoid liability to the corporation under section 16(b) of the Federal law since they had held the MAI shares for more than six months prior to the sales. Nevertheless, the alleged use of the inside information to dispose of their stock at a price considerably higher than its known value constituted the same sort of "abuse of a fiduciary relationship" as is condemned by the Federal law. Sitting as we are in this case as a court of equity, we should not hesitate to permit an action to prevent any unjust enrichment realized by the defendants from their allegedly wrongful act.

* * *

* * * the defendants acknowledge that the facts asserted constitute a violation of rule 10b-5. The remedies which the Federal law provides for such violation, however, are rather limited. * * *

In view of the practical difficulties inherent in an action under the Federal law, the desirability of creating an effective common law remedy is manifest. "Dishonest directors should not find absolution from retributive justice," Ballantine observed in his work on Corporations ([rev. ed., 1946], p. 216), "by concealing their identity from their victims under the mask of the stock exchange." There is ample room in a situation such as is here presented for a "private Attorney General" to come forward and enforce proper behavior on the part of corporate officials through the medium of the derivative action brought in the name of the corporation. (See, e. g., *Associated Ind.* v. *Ickes,* 134 F. 2d 694, 704; *Cherner* v. *Transitron Electronic Corp.,* 201 F. Supp. 934, 936.) Only by sanctioning such a cause of action will there be any effective method to prevent the type of abuse of corporate office complained of in this case.

There is nothing in the Federal law which indicates that it was intended to limit the power of the States to fashion additional remedies to effectuate similar purposes. Although the impact of Federal securities regulation has on occasion been said to have created a "Federal corporation law," in fact, its effect on the duties and obligations of directors and officers and their relation to the corporation and its shareholders is only occasional and peripheral. The primary source of the law in this area ever remains that of the State which created the corporation. * * *

Nor should we be deterred, in formulating a State remedy, by the defendants' claim of possible double liability. Certainly, as already indicated, if the sales in question were publicly made, the likelihood that a suit will be brought by purchasers of the shares is quite remote. But, even if it were not, the mere possibility of such a suit is not a defense nor does it render the complaint insufficient. It is not unusual for an action to be brought to recover a fund which may be subject to a superior claim by a third party. If that be the situation, a defendant should not be permitted to retain the fund for his own use on the chance that such a party may eventually appear. A defendant's course, if he wishes to protect himself against double liability, is to interplead any and all possible claimants and bind them to the judgment (CPLR 1006, subd. [b]).

In any event, though, no suggestion has been made either in brief or on oral argument that any purchaser has come forward with a claim against the defendants or even that anyone is in a position to advance such a claim.[1] As we have stated, the defendants' assertion

[1] In the absence of any such appearance by adverse claimants, we need not now decide whether the corporation's recovery would be affected by any amounts which might have to be refunded by the defendant to the injured purchasers.

> that such a party may come forward at some future date is not a basis for permitting them to retain for their own benefit the fruits of their allegedly wrongful acts. For all that appears, the present derivative action is the only effective remedy now available against the abuse by these defendants of their privileged position.

This case confounded those lawyers who had relegated *Brophy*, the 1949 Delaware Chancery case cited by the court,[117] to the indiguity of a "sport." It does seem surprising that it took twenty years for another square holding like *Brophy* to find its way into the law reports. Nevertheless, *Diamond* indicates — as a commentator put it who confused the Common Law Mother's sex but was blessed with a deft pen — that, "Like the fertile octogenarian, state law has made a belated comeback."[118] The New York court, understandably, found satisfaction in observing that *its* writ was not limited to specified types of insiders, or to publicly held companies, or to in-and-out (or out-and-in) transactions within a specified interval.

Indeed, it may be contended with considerable cogency that a director who knows that *another* director is buying or selling securities on the basis of confidential information may incur liability for failure to prevent his colleague's action, since a trustee has an obligation to prevent a co-trustee from violating their joint trust.[119] Or the same result might be reached on another line of reasoning: Since it is the corporation that has a cause of action against a fiduciary who uses confidential information for his own profit, it is the obligation of each director to protect that corporate asset or he will be liable for failure to do so.

Soon the Second Circuit, applying a nonexistent Florida law, carried *Diamond* a step further by holding the president's "tippees" (one of whom was a "tippee" thrice removed) on a "common enterprise" theory, reenforced by the rule that one who knowingly participates in a breach of fiduciary obligation is liable jointly and

[117] In Davidge v. White, 377 F. Supp. 1084, 1089-90 (S. D. N. Y. 1974), the court denied a motion to dismiss under Delaware law on the ground that the *Brophy* principle applied even when the defendant had resigned as a director before he finished selling. See also Thomas v. Roblin Industries, Inc., 520 F. 2d 1393, 1399 (3d Cir. 1975) (dictum).

[118] 55 Va. L. Rev. 1520, 1533 (1969).

[119] It was on this line of reasoning that the Court in Mosser v. Darrow, 341 U. S. 267 (1951), surcharged a Chapter X trustee under general equitable principles for profits derived by two employees from trading in securities of the debtor's subsidiaries although he had considered their services indispensable and had expressly agreed that they could continue to trade and there was no hint of personal profit on his part.

severally with the fiduciary.[120] But this thrust forward also planted the seed of something like a counterrevolution. For the Supreme Court remanded with instructions to certify the question of Florida law to the Florida Supreme Court under Florida's reception statute.[121] And the Florida court disavowed not only *Diamond*'s extension but also *Diamond* itself.[122] Since then the Seventh Circuit has said no under Indiana law [123] and the District Court for New Jersey has said yes under New Jersey law.[124]

On this background, one may hazard the guess that the future lies with *Diamond* rather than its rivals. There is authority for the proposition that directors of an investment company are in breach of their fiduciary duty when they trade in *portfolio* securities.[125] And

[120]Schein v. Chasen, 478 F. 2d 817 (2d Cir. 1973), *vacated* sub nom. Lehman Bros. v. Schein, 416 U. S. 386 (1974); but cf. Frigitemp Corp. v. Financial Dynamics Fund, Inc., 524 F. 2d 275, 278-79 (2d Cir. 1975) (*Diamond* and *Schein* were distinguished under New York law where plaintiff alleged only that defendants had entered into a "special relationship" with the company by receiving confidential information in connection with their purchase of its debentures); Walton v. Morgan Stanley & Co., Inc., 623 F. 2d 796 (2d Cir. 1980) (same result under Delaware law where investment banker for acquiring company used information obtained in confidence from friendly target to buy target stock for its own account).

[121]Lehman Brothers v. Schein, 416 U. S. 386 (1974).

[122]Schein v. Chasen, 313 So. 2d 739 (Fla. 1975).

[123]Freeman v. Decio, 584 F. 2d 186 (7th Cir. 1978). Actually the *Freeman* court held that the defendants had traded on mere guesses as to the company's economic future rather than on inside information. 584 F. 2d at 199. For a detailed analysis of these cases, see Wimberley, Corporate Recovery of Insider Trading Profits at Common Law, 8 Corp. L. Rev. 197 (1985).

[124]In re ORFA Securities Litigation, 654 F. Supp. 1449, CCH Fed. Sec. L. Rep. ¶93,225 (D. N. J. 1987).

[125]McMenomy v. Ryden, 276 Minn. 55, 148 N. W. 2d 804 (1967); Cambridge Fund, Inc. v. Abella, 501 F. Supp. 598, 631 (S. D. N. Y. 1980) (Del. law); cf. SEC v. Midwest Technical Development Corp., CCH Fed. Sec. L. Rep ¶91,252 (D. Minn. 1963). The 1970 amendments added §17(j) to the Investment Company Act in order to subject these practices to SEC rulemaking on a fraud-prevention basis. And in 1980 the Commission adopted Rule 17j-1 in order (*inter alia*) to require registered investment companies, their advisers, and their principal underwriters to adopt written codes of ethics, which are specifically mentioned in §17(j), and to require "access persons" (as defined) to report their transactions to their investment companies, advisers, or principal underwriters. Inv. Co. Act Rel. 11,421, 21 SEC Dock. 488 (1980).

there are signs of movement in the less volatile British courts.[126]

[126]See cases cited in L. Gower, Principles of Modern Company Law (4th ed. 1979) 595 n. 65. Thirty-five years ago Professor Gower cited the *Brophy* case in support of the view he had long held that principles of agency law are sufficiently elastic to enable a company to recover from its director any profit that he has made on share dealings as a result of the misuse of confidential information, although he added that no English company had yet had the temerity to make such a claim. Gower, Investor Protection in the U. S. A., 15 Mod. L. Rev. 446, 453 (1952). See also Beck, The Saga of Peso Silver Mines: Corporate Opportunity Reconsidered, 49 Can. B. Rev. 80 (1971); Beck, The Quickening of Fiduciary Obligation: *Canadian Aero Services* v. *O'Malley*, 53 Can. B. Rev. 771 (1975).

CHAPTER 8

MARKET REGULATION

A. STRUCTURE OF THE MARKETS

The structure of the securities markets has been insightfully described by Professor Norman S. Poser, whose experience as both key SEC official and Executive Vice President of the American Stock Exchange before his happy ascent to Academe uniquely qualifies him to tell the story.[1] Current annotations are supplied by the present writer.

It is generally believed that the securities markets serve an important economic purpose; they provide a mechanism by which business enterprises obtain equity capital and long-term debt from the public. These markets may be divided into two distinct parts: the new-issue markets, in which companies typically issue securities to the public through syndicates of dealers and underwriters; and the trading markets, in which these securities may be bought and sold after they have been issued.

The economic function of the trading markets is to create liquidity — a market characteristic that enables investors to dispose of or purchase securities at a price reasonably related to the preceding price. For the sale of a new issue of securities to succeed, prospective purchasers must have a reasonable assurance of liquidity in the market for the security. Thus, the success of new-issue markets is dependent on the effectiveness of trading markets. In addition, since trading markets are a price setting mechanism, they facilitate

C. 8A [1] Poser, Restructuring the Stock Markets: A Critical Look at the SEC's National Market System, 56 N. Y. U. L. Rev. 881 (1981), copyright 1981 by New York University Law Review and reprinted from the December 1981 issue of the Review with permission of the editors and of Professor Poser.

the use of securities as collateral for loans, determine the price at which a company is able to issue additional securities, and establish a basis for the valuation of securities for taxation and other purposes. * * *

* * * The trading markets consist of ten stock exchanges[a] and the over-the-counter market, a structure that came into existence by an evolutionary process, substantially free of government regulation.[b] During the nineteenth century, stock exchanges were organized in various parts of the country and served as loci for the trading of securities; the stock exchanges were supplemented by a loosely organized "over-the-counter" market, in which brokers and dealers executed transactions in their offices, in coffee houses, and in other public places. The evolution of these markets was affected only minimally by the advent of federal securities regulation in the 1930's. This legislation was designed to protect investors from market abuses rather than to alter the structure of the markets. The growth, combination, and attrition of particular stock exchanges and the over-the-counter market that had occurred prior to the enactment of the Exchange Act continued in the years that followed.

A. THE STOCK EXCHANGES

A stock exchange provides a place and organized rules and procedures for buying and selling securities that have been admitted to trading. Only members may trade on a stock exchange floor, either for their own accounts or for customers. Since each stock exchange has a limited number of members, a stock exchange membership, or "seat," has a value, and there is a market for exchange seats.

There is no bar to a company's listing its securities on more than one stock exchange.[c] * * *

The securities of a company may also be traded on a stock exchange even though the company has not applied to the stock exchange for a listing and actually opposes being listed. This occurs

[a]Ed.: Section 5 of the 1934 Act requires all exchanges to be registered with the SEC as "national securities exchanges" — one of the several categories of "self-regulatory organizations" (see c. 8C infra) — unless they are exempted.

[b]Ed.: The over-the-counter market is not an "exchange." Dorfman v. First Boston Corp., 336 F. Supp. 1089, 1097 (E. D. Pa. 1972). Nor is a dealer that matches sales with purchases for its own account. LTV Federal Credit Union v. UMIC Gov't Securities, Inc., 523 F. Supp. 819, 834 (N. D. Tex. 1981), *aff'd on opinion below,* 704 F. 2d 199 (5th Cir. 1983), *cert. denied,* 464 U. S. 852.

[c]Ed.: On the listing requirements, see p. 429 supra.

when a stock exchange on its own initiative admits the company's securities to "unlisted" trading. Since 1934, the granting of such "unlisted trading privileges" has been subject to the approval of the SEC, which has broad discretion as to whether or not to grant applications. For many years, the Commission's policy has been to grant applications by stock exchanges for unlisted trading privileges freely if the class of securities is already listed on another exchange. This SEC policy has made it possible for many securities to be traded on more than one stock exchange (i. e., to be "dually traded").[d]

[d]ED.: All trading, on or off exchanges, started as "unlisted" trading, in the sense that brokers and dealers needed no "by your leave" from an issuer in order to make a market in its outstanding securities. It took time for exchanges to become established and to develop to the point where they were able to exact the filing of listing applications, with certain conditions, from issuers that sought the prestige and advantages of an exchange market. At the same time, the exchanges were reluctant to surrender their unlisted trading. Indeed, except for the New York Stock Exchange (the "Big Board"), most of the exchanges would have had difficulty surviving in 1934 with only listed trading. It was not until 1910 that the New York Stock Exchange abolished its unlisted department, in accordance with the recommendation made the year before in the report of the committee that had been appointed by Governor Hughes of New York to investigate speculation in securities and commodities. J. Meeker, The Work of the Stock Exchange (rev. ed. 1930) 72; Report of the Governor's Committee on Speculation in Securities and Commodities (N. Y. 1909), reprinted in W. Van Antwerp, The Stock Exchange from Within (1913) 415. And in 1934 even the New York Curb Exchange (now the American Stock Exchange), the second largest exchange, was trading 1689 securities unlisted as compared with only 374 that were listed. Stock Exchange Regulation, Hearings Before House Com. on Int'l & For. Commerce on H. R. 7852 and H. R. 8720, 73d Cong., 2d Sess. (1934) 374.

It was quite natural, therefore, that the Curb should lead the attack, in which most of the smaller exchanges joined, against the proposal of the original 1934 bills to solve the problem of unlisted trading by abolishing it outright. Id. at 367 et seq., 511. As a result, §12(f) of the statute as enacted in 1934 directed the Commission to study the problem and report to Congress with its recommendations by January 3, 1936. See SEC, Report on Trading in Unlisted Securities upon Exchanges (1936). And §12(f), as amended in 1936, again in 1964, and mostly recently in 1975, today specifies three types of unlisted trading, the first two of which have remained fairly constant from the beginning:

(A) Securities that were traded unlisted before July 1, 1964 (originally March 1, 1934), are automatically "grandfathered" in. The theory in 1934 was that the Curb and the regional exchanges should be able to survive the gradual attrition of their unlisted issues as a result of liquidations and mergers and so on while they were building up their listed departments. That theory proved sound, to the extent that §902 of the Code deletes the "grandfather" treatment (subject to the Commission's general exemptive authority) in view of the small number of "unlisted only" issues left: only 38 issues of 37 companies as of September 1, 1978, of which 12 were §12(g) companies and 7 had their common stock listed with unlisted trading privileges for their preferred. 1 Code 365-66.

(B) The second category consists of dually traded securities — those listed on one exchange and admitted to unlisted trading on another with the Commis-

The markets maintained by the stock exchanges are known as

sion's approval under a "fair and orderly markets" test. See Ludlow Corp. v. SEC, 604 F. 2d 704 (D. C. Cir. 1979). Since listing on the first exchange means full registration, the Commission has acted almost routinely in this area. See Midwest Stock Exchange, Sec. Ex. Act Rel. 16,422, 18 SEC Dock. 1323 (1979) (910 securities).

(C) With the enactment of §12(g) in 1964, the logic of the second category should apply as well to over-the-counter as to listed securities as long as they are registered. But, far from creating a third category of unlisted trading based on §12(g) registration, Congress in 1964 deleted the third category based on §15(d) reporting (see p. 436 supra) that had existed as virtually a dead letter since 1936. It took eleven years and the force of the 1975 amendments for the §12(g) logic to prevail, so that the Commission may today extend unlisted trading privileges to any security registered under §12 if it makes a series of specified findings related (*inter alia*) to competitive factors, "fair and orderly markets," and development of a national market system. Pacific Resources, Inc., Sec. Ex. Act Rel. 17,584, 22 SEC Dock. 283 (1981). (The issuer's consent is not required, although it may petition the Commission under §12(f)(4) for *termination* of unlisted trading privileges.) But the Commission characterized the *Pacific Resources* case, where the stock was concurrently *delisted* on the issuer's application, as a "limited exception to its general policy" of deferring action in Clause (C) cases pending further developments in a national market system. Id. at 284. See c. 8F infra.

In Xonics, Inc., Sec. Ex. Act Rel. 19,609, 27 SEC Dock. 563 (1983), the Commission denied unlisted trading privileges because it was "unable to determine that the national market system has evolved to such an extent as to make the grant of UTP appropriate in the context of non-reported securities not listed on an exchange." Id. at 566. *Pacific Resources* was distinguished as involving a "reported security," that is to say, one reported by the Consolidated Tape Association, which requires that the security be listed on the New York or American Stock Exchange, or that it be admitted to unlisted trading privileges on a regional exchange *and* substantially meet the American Stock Exchange listing standards. See also Triton Group, Ltd., Sec. Ex. Act Rel. 20,084, 28 SEC Dock. 784 (1983).

Finally, in September 1985 the Commission announced its policy to extend unlisted trading privileges in National Market System securities (see pp. 696-97 infra) on certain conditions, including (1) the Commission's approval of a plan submitted by the exchanges and the NASD to consolidate the relevant exchange and over-the-counter quotations and transaction reports, and (2) "the exchange's providing NASDAQ [see p. 600 n. 47 infra] marketmakers access to the exchange market in the subject securities to the same extent that NASDAQ market makers provide access to their OTC trading facilities." Sec. Ex. Act Rel. 22,412, 33 SEC Dock. 1435, 1448 (1985). The Commission proceeded cautiously, initially limiting each exchange to 25 securities.

Among the reasons given for the Commission's action were these:

> Since enactment of the 1975 Amendments enhancements to the original NASDAQ system in conformance with the development of the NMS have altered the conditions in which OTC stocks trade and have made OTC trading of these securities more compatible with exchange trading. The dissemination in 1980 of the NASDAQ best bid and offer to registered representatives and the investing public in place of a representative bid and ask has improved the usefulness of OTC quotation information.
>
> In addition, the initiation in April 1982 of last sale reporting for OTC securities designated as NMS Securities * * * has increased the market information available for these OTC securities. Market makers are required to report their trades in NMS Securities on a gross basis within 90

"auction" markets because buy and sell orders are executed at a central location at the best available price. Typically, an investor who wishes to buy or sell an exchange-listed security will give the order to an exchange member who, acting as a broker (i. e., agent), executes the order on the floor of the exchange and receives a commission as compensation.[e] Most of these orders are either "market" orders, which require the broker to execute the order promptly at the best available price, or "limit" orders, which require the broker to buy at or below or sell at or above the stated (limit) price. It is possible, then, for the orders of a buying customer and a selling customer, each represented by a broker, to meet on the floor of an exchange without the intervention of a professional dealer (i. e., one who trades for his own account). In 1971, however, forty-five percent of all share volume on the New York Stock Exchange involved a member firm's buying or selling for its own account on one side of the trade; the remaining fifty-five percent represented customers' orders executed without the participation of a member acting as principal.

Specialist units (or specialists), which compose a category of exchange member firms separately registered with the exchange, play a unique and important role in the trading process. When a stock has been admitted to trading, the exchange "allocates" it to a particular specialist. During trading hours, the specialist remains at a particular location, or "post," on the trading floor of the exchange, and any member who wishes to trade in a stock, either for his own

---

seconds of execution, providing a real-time indication of trading conditions. There are now over 1000 NMS Securities.

Id. at 1436.

In addition, in Midwest Stock Exchange, Inc., Sec. Ex. Act Rel. 19,621, 27 SEC Dock. 617, 618 n. 4 (1983), where the Commission granted unlisted trading privileges to a stock never listed, it cited the length of time that it had been traded pursuant to Rule 12a-5, a "temporary" exemption from registration of securities of the same issuer added to or substituted for securities admitted to unlisted trading privileges, as well as the public availability of last sale information. But it cautioned that in the future it intended to treat applications in 12a-5 cases in accordance with the standards applicable to over-the-counter securities with no preexisting trading market.

In recent years, at least, the Commission has used Clause (C) to extend unlisted trading privileges in a Clause (A) case to another exchange. See Philadelphia Stock Exchange, Inc., Sec. Ex. Act Rel. 19,823, 27 SEC Dock. 1344 (1983), referring simply to the security as "registered on another national securities exchange," which is technically correct under §12(f)(6), although it was traded only on an unlisted basis.

[e] Ed.: Legend has it that the first specialist was a member of the New York Stock Exchange who broke his leg in the 1870s, whereupon he took up a position at the spot where Western Union stock was traded and handled orders there for other members.

account or for the account of a customer, will go to the post of the specialist in that stock. All trading in the stock takes place at that location.

Exchange transactions in a given stock may be executed between two brokers standing in the trading "crowd" at the post or between a broker and a specialist. The specialist may trade for his own account or for a customer's account. If an order cannot be executed readily at a price reasonably close to the price of the preceding sale (i. e., if a customer cannot be found for the other side of a transaction at such price), the exchange rules require the specialist to buy or sell the securities for his own account. The specialist, using his own capital, thus offsets temporary imbalances between supply and demand by making bids to buy stock and offers to sell stock. His role is essentially passive, in that he buys or sells when approached by an exchange member. For example, a specialist may bid for a stock at a price of fifty and offer stock at a price of fifty and one-half. In that case he will buy when requested to do so at fifty and he will sell at fifty and one-half. His profit is the fifty-cents-per-share difference between the bid and the offer.

The specialist also acts as a broker, handling for other brokers limit orders that cannot be executed at the current market price. Typically, a broker holding a customer's limit order to buy at a price below the current market price (or to sell above the current market price) will leave the order with the specialist. If the market moves down (or up) to the customer's limit, the specialist will execute the order for the customer and will receive a portion of the commission paid by the customer. The aggregate of limit orders held by a specialist in a particular stock is known as his "book." Exchange rules "protect" customers' orders left on the book against an inferior execution. Thus, if a customer's buy order at a price of twenty-five is on the book, no transaction may take place on that exchange at a price lower than twenty-five before that customer's order is executed. * * *

All exchange transactions, whether or not a specialist participates, are immediately reported to an exchange employee for transmission to the ticker tape and to data reporting services, which electronically disseminate reports of completed transactions to subscribers. Prices and volume of completed stock exchange transactions are summarized daily in the financial press.[f]

[f]Ed.: In Sec. Ex. Act Rel. 23,768, 36 SEC Dock. 1138 (1986), the SEC, in order to encourage retail broker-dealers to affiliate with specialists, approved rules of the New York and American Stock Exchanges that permit a member organization affiliated with a specialist or specialist unit to trade, and engage in specified other activities, in specialty securities. But the Commission emphasized

In 1979, over 99.6% of the dollar amount of trading on U. S. stock exchanges occurred on six stock exchanges, the New York [NYSE], American [Amex], Midwest, Pacific, Philadelphia, and Boston stock exchanges.[23] Although these stock exchanges have identical legal statuses since all are registered with the SEC as national securities exchanges, they have very different characteristics and economic functions.

1. The New York Stock Exchange

The NYSE is the dominant stock exchange, and its dominance is perhaps the key determinant of the structure of the securities markets. In 1979, its 374 member firms that do business directly with the public comprised only fifteen percent of all broker-dealer firms doing business with the public and yet accounted for ninety percent of the total assets and eighty-five percent of the gross revenues of such broker-dealer firms. Since most NYSE member firms doing business with the public are also members of the Amex and one or more of the regional stock exchanges, the various exchanges cannot be thought of as separate entities in the sense of distinct groups of firms competing with each other. On the other hand, many of the broker-dealers that act as specialists on the Amex and most of the specialists on the regional exchanges are not members of the NYSE.

The NYSE also is dominant in terms of companies whose shares are traded on it. The 1,915 companies whose securities were listed on the NYSE as of September 30, 1980 include most of the largest industrial and commercial enterprises in the United States. As of December 31, 1979, the value of all common stocks listed on the NYSE was $960.6 billion, compared to $57.8 billion for stocks listed on the Amex and $3.9 billion for stocks exclusively listed on other exchanges. Similarly, the NYSE dwarfs the other stock exchanges in terms of trading activity. In 1979, the NYSE accounted for

---

that these proposals were "critically dependent on the creation of effective internal controls, so-called Chinese Walls, to eliminate" potential conflicts resulting from combination of the unique position of a primary market specialist with the retail distribution networks and investment banking relationships of a large retail firm. Sec. Ex. Act Rel. 22,396, 33 SEC Dock. 1355, 1363, esp. n. 22 (1985) (proposal release).

At year-end 1986 the New York Stock Exchange, after a study of concentration in the specialist business, concluded that it was not unduly concentrated but adopted a procedure designed "to permit proposed combinations which neither have an adverse impact on market quality nor result in an undue concentration." N. Y. Stock Ex. Special Membership Bul., Dec. 14, 1986.

[23] See [1979-1980] SEC Ann. Rep. 126. The other four registered securities exchanges are the Chicago Board Options Exchange and the Cincinnati, Intermountain (in Salt Lake City), and Spokane Stock Exchanges. The Intermountain, though registered, is inactive.

83.65% of total dollar volume of trading on U.S. stock exchanges, the Amex 6.93%, and the regional exchanges 9.42%.

2. The American Stock Exchange

The Amex, having lower listing standards than those of the NYSE, generally serves as a market for the securities of smaller, newer companies than those listed on the NYSE. As of September 30, 1980, there were 1,034 companies with stocks traded on the Amex. Many Amex-listed companies, when they meet the more stringent NYSE listing requirements, transfer their listings to the latter exchange. Until 1976, rules of the NYSE and Amex prohibited their respective members from dealing on the exchange in any securities listed on the other exchange; in addition, Amex rules provided for automatic delisting of any security whose listing was transferred to the NYSE.

Despite repeal of these rules, there is virtually no trading on the Amex in securities listed on NYSE. Few companies whose securities are listed on the Amex choose to remain listed on that exchange after obtaining a NYSE listing, presumably because they believe that concentration of all trading in a single market will produce more liquidity for their shares. Moreover, the Amex, not wishing to enter into direct competition with its powerful neighbor, has an informal policy of not actively seeking listings or unlisted trading privileges in NYSE-listed securities. Finally, NYSE member firms, many of which are also Amex members, have been unwilling to direct to the Amex any portion of their customers' orders in securities listed on both exchanges. Unlike the four regional exchanges, then, the Amex is not a derivative market, but is, rather, a "primary" market (i. e., the principal market for the securities that are admitted to trading) established on a much smaller scale than the NYSE.

3. The Regional Exchanges

The Midwest (MSE), Pacific (PSE), Philadelphia (Phlx), and Boston (BSE) stock exchanges are known as regional exchanges. Although the regional exchanges began their existence as primary markets for the securities of companies of local geographic interest, most trading on the regional exchanges since the 1930's has been in securities whose primary market is the NYSE or, to a lesser extent, the Amex. Despite their concentration in NYSE and Amex issues, the regional exchanges account for only a small percentage of the total trading in shares listed on these two primary markets. In 1980, approximately ten percent of the total share volume in stocks listed on the NYSE represented regional exchange transactions, while the corresponding figure for Amex-listed issues was only about two percent. Dual trading is thus of great importance to the regional exchanges, but the regional exchanges are relatively minor factors in the trading of securities of national importance. The markets for listed stocks thus comprise a high concentrated industry that is dominated by the NYSE and its member firms.

The regional exchanges, like the NYSE and Amex, use the specialist system. The method of trading stocks whose primary market is the NYSE or Amex, however, differs substantially from the trading system in the primary markets. These differences reflect the fact that the regional exchange markets in these stocks are derivative markets. According to a study conducted by the SEC in the 1960's, the prices at which transactions were executed on the regional exchanges normally were based on the prices in the primary markets. Although regional exchange specialists participated as dealers in the overwhelming majority of all transactions, typically they did not publish quotations competing with those on the primary markets; instead, "[a] variety of special arrangements have been developed * * * by which a customer may be enabled to receive a price substantially equivalent to that in the primary market * * *." Because of these characteristics, the secondary markets that were made on the regional exchanges did not tend to affect the primary market prices of dually traded securities. It is essential to keep in mind this role of the regional exchanges as derivative markets when considering the proposal to establish an NMS [National Market System].[g]

B. THE OVER-THE-COUNTER MARKET

The over-the-counter (OTC) market is the residual securities market. All transactions that do not take place on a stock exchange are said to be executed in the OTC market. Like their counterparts in the securities exchanges, brokers and dealers trading in the OTC market are required to register with the SEC, but they need not become stock exchange members. In practice, most broker-dealers serving the public are members of the National Association of Securities Dealers (NASD), a national securities association registered with the SEC.

A broad spectrum of securities is traded OTC, including government and corporate bonds and shares of various industrial and commercial enterprises. Common stocks traded solely OTC tend to

[g]ED.: See c. 8F infra.

represent smaller and newer companies than those listed on stock exchanges. Additionally, there is some OTC trading in securities that are traded on one or more stock exchanges; such trading is referred to as the "third market." In 1980, third market transactions represented just over two percent of all trading in NYSE-listed stocks and one percent of all trading in Amex-listed stocks. The proposal for an NMS contemplates that the OTC market, including the third market, will be an integral part of the system.

OTC transactions are usually executed over the telephone by broker-dealers in their offices.[h] If an investor wishes to buy an OTC security, the broker-dealer handling his account may sell him the security as principal out of the broker-dealer's inventory. If the broker-dealer does not own the security [which is the usual case], he will buy the security from a "market maker" in that security and sell the security to his customer, acting either as an agent and charging a commission, or as a principal and charging a markup to the customer.[45] A market maker is a broker-dealer who holds himself out "as being willing to buy and sell [a] security for his own account on a regular or continuous basis."[46] Market makers' quotations in the 2,700 most active OTC securities are made through the National Association of Securities Dealers Automated Quotations (NASDAQ), a computerized quotations system operated by the NASD.[47]

[h] ED.: Dealers' counters have gone the way of the grocers'. "Over-the-telephone" would be a more accurate description. Indeed, the German term is precisely that: *Telefonhandel.*

[45] * * * This works the same way when a customer sells a security, except that the broker charges a markdown rather than a markup.

[46] [Sec. Ex. Act §3(a)(38); see Jaksich v. Thomson McKinnon Securities, Inc., 582 F. Supp. 485, 493 n. 8 (S. D. N. Y. 1984), quoting the text.]

[47] NASDAQ, inaugurated in 1971, displays continuously updated price quotations (i. e., bids and offers) on a real-time basis on cathode ray terminals located in subscribers' offices. There are three kinds of terminals, designated as Levels I, II, and III. Market makers use Level III terminals, consisting of a cathode ray tube ("CRT") screen and a keyboard. Using the keyboard, a market maker can enter, change, or cancel any bid or offer for any stock in which he makes a market. All current bids and offers entered by market makers in that stock are shown on the CRT screen. Level II terminals, used by brokers and dealers who do not act as market makers, provide the same information as Level III terminals but do not permit inputting of bids and offers. Thus, any firm subscribing to the NASDAQ system can see at a glance which market maker in any NASDAQ-quoted stock is disseminating the highest bid and the lowest offer. Level I terminals, which are used by salespeople of brokerage firms, show only a "representative" bid and offer in each NASDAQ-quoted stock and provide both salesperson and customer with an approximate idea of the price at which a security can be bought or sold. When a brokerage firm receives an order from a customer to buy (or sell) a stock that is quoted in the NASDAQ system, it checks the Level II or III screen to ascertain the market maker quoting the best

There are several important differences between the stock exchanges and the OTC market. First and most obvious, each stock exchange provides a central place for trading where all customers' buy and sell orders meet and the highest buy order is matched against the lowest sell order in an auction-type process; the OTC market, on the other hand, is a decentralized market in which transactions are negotiated among broker-dealers and between broker-dealers and their customers. Second, unlike the stock exchanges, the OTC market provides no way for the orders of a buying customer and a selling customer to meet directly; in virtually every OTC transaction, there is a professional dealer who participates by buying or selling for his own account. The OTC market is therefore known as a "dealer" market.

A third significant difference between the two types of markets is that although there is typically only one specialist allocated to a particular stock on any given stock exchange, it is common for there to be several market makers (sometimes as many as thirty) in a particular OTC stock. A fourth difference is that the specialist at his central location on the exchange floor is in a position to see and participate in all trading, whereas the OTC market maker in his office can become a participant in trading only by issuing competitive quotations that will induce other broker-dealers to trade with him. Finally, the OTC market, unlike the stock exchanges, does

---

current offer (or bid). The firm then telephones the market maker and executes the transaction with him. In doing so, the brokerage firm will either act as an agent for its customer and charge the customer a commission, or as a principal and purchase the security for its own account and immediately resell at a price markup to the customer who placed the order. * * *

["Since its commencement in 1971, NASDAQ has matured into a major securities market * * *." Sec. Ex. Act Rel. 20,264, 28 SEC Dock. 1263, 1265 (1983). Monthly share volume for the first half of 1983 was about three-quarters that of the New York Stock Exchange and nearly seven times larger than the American Stock Exchange. Id. at 1265 n. 4.

On December 17, 1984, the NASD's "Small Order Execution System" went into effect, linking 450 market makers in 750 locations around the country in a mainframe computer located in Connecticut. "When a broker pushes the button, the computer instantly finds the best price available from listings provided by traders in advance and executes the trade within three seconds, 10 times faster than a manual execution. * * * SOES will begin automating 25 of the most active over-the-counter stocks and then phase in all [NASD] national market system stocks over a six-month period." Ross, Full Automation Near in Securities Trading, Wash. Post, Nov. 15, 1984, p. F4. Initially the maximum order size in the system is 500 shares. CCH NASD Manual ¶2451(a)7; see generally id., ¶¶2451-70.

On the National Daily Quotation Service, which is published by the National Quotation Bureau, Inc., a private business corporation that long antedated NASDAQ and ultimately became a subsidiary of Commerce Clearing House, Inc., in 1963, see 5 Loss 3317-27.]

not have a ticker tape showing the price and volume of completed transactions as they occur. OTC stock tables appearing in the newspapers provide the daily volume of activity and the bids and offers of market makers, but not the prices of completed transactions.[i]

B. BROKER-DEALER REGISTRATION

1. THE REGISTRATION REQUIREMENT

We have already noted the original §15 and the 1936 amendment that, among other things, codified the Commission's rules on broker-dealer registration.[1] As it now reads, §15(a)(1) requires the registration of any broker or dealer that wants to "effect any transactions in, or to induce or attempt to induce the purchase or sale of, any security (other than an exempted security or commercial paper, bankers' acceptances, or commercial bills)."[2] Before the 1975 amendments this section applied only to transactions "otherwise than on a national securities exchange" — which is to say, over the counter — on the theory that the Commission already had some control over members of registered exchanges. But most member firms registered anyway, if only because they also effect some transactions over the counter. And the over-the-counter limitation was eliminated in 1975.[3]

Registration and withdrawal forms (BD and BDW) have been adopted by the SEC, the North American Securities Administrators Association, and virtually all the states for use by the states and the

[i]ED.: Despite all these differences between the Exchange and over-the-counter markets, the Texas State Securities Board — logically enough — has held that the NASDAQ system is an "organized stock exchange" for purposes of applying for the Texas exemption from registration of securities listed on "any recognized and responsible stock exchange as defined in the 1934 Act approved by the Commissioner." NASD, Inc., CCH Blue Sky L. Rep. ¶72,211 (Tex. St. Sec. Bd. 1985).

C. 8B [1]See pp. 409-10 supra.

[2]See generally N. Wolfson, R. Phillips, and T. Russo, Regulation of Brokers, Dealers and Securities Markets (1977); E. Weiss, Registration and Regulation of Brokers and Dealers (1965).

[3]The Commission, however, has exempted a specialist's block purchases and sales off the floor when the transactions are approved by the exchange and effected under its rules to help the specialist to maintain a fair and orderly market.

self-regulatory organizations as well as the SEC in both broker-dealer registration and withdrawal.[4]

Within 45 days after the filing of an "application" (not, be it noted, a "registration statement"), the Commission must either grant registration or institute denial proceedings, and any proceedings must be concluded within 120 days of filing.[5] Before 1975 there were no qualifications to be met.[6] In effect, any person who had managed to stay clear of a securities violation had a right to become registered or to be associated with a registered firm.[7] Today §15(b)(7) imposes "operational capability" standards on all registered broker-dealers; requires that they and their natural person associates meet Commission-imposed standards of "training, experience, competence, and * * * other qualifications"; and specifically authorizes the Commission to administer tests to any or all classes of broker-dealers and their associates. But the Commission, after proposing a set of minimum qualifications for all registered broker-dealers and their associates,[8] is relying on the NASD and the exchanges to develop and administer examinations for their respective members together with their associates.[9]

For administrative purposes the Commission applies the entity theory to all registrants and applicants for registration, whether they are organized as corporations or partnerships or in some other

[4] Sec. Ex. Act Rel. 20,406, 29 SEC Dock. 249 (1983). A complementary purpose of the revisions was to make the forms compatible with the NASAA/NASD Central Registration Depository, which has been developed in two phases. Phase I, which established a system for broker-dealers' *representatives* to register with the states and the self-regulaory organizations, was substantially operational by year-end 1983. And the SEC anticipates that eventually all broker-dealers will file through the Depository rather than directly with the Commission. The Depository is designed to permit the filing of a single form, whose data will go into the central computer, and copies will simply be filed elsewhere. Sec. Ex. Act Rel. 23,374, 35 SEC Dock. 1216, 1219 (1986).

[5] The Commission may extend the 120 days for a period up to 90 more days. §15(b)(1).

[6] On the special provisions for non-SEC broker-dealers that were in effect from 1964 to 1975, see pp. 623-24 infra.

[7] The grounds for denial were the same as those for revocation or other discipline of broker-dealers already registered — grounds that were themselves extended somewhat in 1975. See pp. 630-33 infra.

[8] Sec. Ex. Act Rel. 13,629, 12 SEC Dock. 1017 (1977).

[9] A great deal of uniformity has developed among the examinations administered by the NASD, the exchanges, and most of the states. Sec. Ex. Act Rel. 13,629, 12 SEC Dock. 1017, 1021 n. 22 (1977). Section 15(b)(7), as enacted in 1975, authorizes the Commission to cooperate with the exchanges and the NASD in devising and administering tests, and to require that *their* tests be passed even though they might be more stringent than the Commission's requirements, which were regarded as a floor. For a history of the several examination requirements, see id. at 1018-21.

form. Consistently with that theory, the Commission does not separately register partners, officers, directors, and the like. And, unlike virtually all the state statutes, the 1934 Act does not call for a new registration annually, or require the separate registration of salesmen, or contain any bonding provision.

2. Definitions of "Broker" and "Dealer" [§§3(a)(4), 3(a)(5)]

Unlike the artificial definition of "dealer" in §2(12) of the 1933 Act to include a broker, the 1934 Act defines the two terms separately and in accordance with the normal distinction between agent and principal. Section 3(a)(4) defines a "broker" as "any person engaged in the business of effecting transactions in securities for the account of others." Section 3(a)(5) defines a "dealer" as "any person engaged in the business of buying and selling securities for his own account, through a broker or otherwise"; and, to be on the safe side, it specifically excludes "any person insofar as he buys or sells securities for his own account, either individually or in some fiduciary capacity, but not as a part of a regular business."

a. What Constitutes a "Business"

The phrase "engaged in the business" is common to both definitions, with the adjective "regular" modifying the word "business" in the second part of the "dealer" definition. With or without the adjective, the phrase connotes a certain regularity of participation in purchasing and selling activities rather than a few isolated transactions.[10] But there is no requirement that the purchase and sale of securities be a person's *principal* business or the principal source of his income. It may be a small percentage of his business. A large firm that handles securities, commodities, and perhaps real estate and insurance may do more securities business than a small firm that is exclusively a broker-dealer in securities.

A similar question has been before the Supreme Court under §32 of the Banking Act of 1933,[11] under which the Board of Governors of the Federal Reserve System removed certain persons as directors of a national bank on the ground that they were employees

[10] See Conroy v. Andeck Resources '81 Year-End, Ltd., 137 Ill. App. 3d 375, 387-88, 484 N. E. 2d 525, 534-35 (1985) (state statute).

[11] 48 Stat. 194 (1933), 49 Stat. 709 (1935), 12 U. S. C. §78.

of a firm "primarily engaged" in the underwriting of securities. The firm, Eastman Dillon & Co., had ranked ninth among the ninety-four leading investment bankers in its participation in bond underwritings in 1943 and for a time during that year had ranked first. Nevertheless, for an indefinite period only about 15 percent of its total transactions, in both number and market value of the securities, had consisted of underwriting; and during its preceding two and one-half fiscal years the portion of its total gross income attributable to underwriting had been only 26, 32, and 39 percent, compared with 42, 47, and 40 percent from brokerage. Pointing out that §32 would apply to no one if "primarily" were construed to mean more than half, the Court read it to mean "essentially" or "fundamentally." "One might as well say," Justice Douglas remarked, "that a professional man is not 'primarily engaged' in his profession though he holds himself out to serve all comers and devotes substantial time to the practice but makes the greater share of his income on the stock market."[12] The case is, of course, stronger under the 1934 Act because of the absence of the word "primarily."

There is likewise nothing in the concept of a "business" to preclude a person from being a broker or dealer because he handles, with regularity, only a single issue of securities.[13] In principle, therefore, an issuer selling and buying its own securities with sufficient regularity might itself be a "dealer." Although there might be peculiar circumstances that would justify this position, the Commission has apparently considered that no purpose would be served by requiring the ordinary open-end investment company, which is continually issuing and redeeming its securities, to register under §15 of the 1934 Act as well as under the 1933 and 1940 Acts. Moreover, the Commission has not required the registration of trust companies whose business is substantially confined to the investment of trust funds even though transactions of purchase and sale are effected as an incident of that activity.[14]

b. The Dealer-Trader Distinction

One aspect of the "business" concept is the matter of drawing the line between a "dealer" and a trader — an ordinary investor who buys and sells for his own account with some frequency. This

[12] Board of Governors of Federal Reserve System v. Agnew, 329 U. S. 441, 446-47 (1947).

[13] Cf. Fogel v. Chestnutt, 533 F. 2d 731, 750-52 (2d Cir. 1975) (investment adviser placing buy and sell orders for investment company's portfolio).

[14] Cf. Sec. Ex. Act Rel. 11,742, 8 SEC Dock. 82 (1975).

question does not arise so far as a "broker" is concerned, since the ordinary investor does not effect transactions for the account of others. But when do a person's trading activities make him a "dealer"?

There is no ready distinction. However, a dealer has characteristic attributes: He ordinarily tries to obtain a regular clientele. He is apt to transact a substantial portion of his business directly with investors rather than with other dealers or through exchange members, although there are "marketmakers" who trade principally with other professionals. A dealer ordinarily holds himself out as one engaged in buying and selling securities at a regular place of business. And his business (except when he participates in underwriting) is ordinarily characterized by a regular turnover, whereas a trader's transactions are generally more irregular in both volume and time. A trader, on the other hand, does not handle other people's money or securities; he does not "make a market"; and he does not furnish the services that are usually provided by dealers, such as quoting the market, rendering incidental investment advice, extending or arranging for the extension of credit, and lending securities to customers. Needless to say, a person does not have to exhibit all or any given number of these dealer characteristics in order to be considered a dealer.[15]

c. Officials or Salesmen of an Issuer Making a Direct Distribution

Under the state statutes other than the Uniform Securities Act an issuer distributing its securities directly to the public without the intervention of a broker or dealer is sometimes defined as a "dealer" itself, as we have seen.[16] This is not true under the 1934 Act, because such an issuer, even if it is considered to be engaged in the "business" of *selling* securities, does not do any *buying* as required by the definition. However, since buying is not an element of the definition of "broker," the question remains whether the individual officials or employees who do the actual selling for the issuer are themselves required to register. In the states they frequently have

[15] Eastside Church of Christ v. National Plan, Inc., 391 F. 2d 357, 361-62 (5th Cir. 1968), *cert. denied* sub nom. Church of Christ v. National Plan, Inc., 393 U. S. 913, *judgment for plaintiff on remand aff'd* sub nom. McGregor Blvd. Church of Christ v. Walling, 428 F. 2d 401 (5th Cir. 1970); Conroy v. Andeck Resources '81 Year-End, Ltd., 137 Ill. App. 3d 375, 387-88, 484 N. E. 2d 525, 534-35 (1985) (state statute).

[16] See p. 17 supra.

to register as salesmen but not, ordinarily, as brokers. Whether they have to register with the SEC as brokers is a question of fact in each case, depending on much the same considerations that determine whether they are "servants" or "independent contractors" at common law.

This remains true despite the Commission's adoption of an elaborate "safe harbor" rule in 1985, which is specific that no presumption of violation of §15(a) arises from failure to meet its conditions.[17]

The rule first defines "associated person of an issuer" — that is to say, the category of persons eligible to sail into the harbor — to include any natural person who is a partner, officer, director, or employee not only of the issuer but also of (1) a corporate general partner of a limited partnership that is the issuer, (2) a company or partnership that is in a control relationship with the issuer, or (3) an investment adviser to an issuer that is a registered investment company. The harbor is extended to the partnership case because most partnerships issuing securities are in fact controlled solely by one or more corporate general partners.

Three preliminary conditions must be satisfied in order to gain the harbor: the associated person may not (1) be subject to a statutory disqualification, (2) receive commissions or transaction-based compensation in connection with the sale of the issuer's securities, or (3) be an associated person of a broker of dealer.

All three of those conditions satisfied, the rule further requires compliance with *any* of three additional conditions:

(1) The associate must restrict his participation in one of four ways: offering and selling (a) to various financial institutions and intermediaries such as registered broker-dealers, (b) securities exempted by §§3(a)(7), 3(a)(9), and 3(a)(10) of the 1933 Act, (c) in connection with reorganizations, reclassifications, and acquisitions "made pursuant to a plan submitted for the approval of security holders who will receive securities of the issuer," or (d) pursuant to a pension, profit-sharing, or similar employee benefit plan as well as a dividend reinvestment plan.

(2) The associate must primarily perform substantial duties for the issuer otherwise than in connection with securities transactions; may not have been a broker or dealer or an associated person of a broker or dealer within the preceding twelve months; and (with special provision for "shelf offerings" under the 1933 Act's Rule 415) may not have participated in selling on behalf of an issuer

[17] Sec. Ex. Act Rel. 22,172, 33 SEC Dock. 652 (1985).

within the preceding twelve months other than in reliance on the first and third of these alternative conditions.

(3) The associate must limit his conduct to "passive" sales efforts.

The test for determining whether associates are "underwriters" within the meaning of the 1933 Act may be different; for an associate might be considered a person who "sells for" the issuer within the contemplation of §2(11) of the 1933 Act without being "engaged in the business" of selling securities for purposes of §3(a)(5) of the 1934 Act.[18]

d. Banks

Both definitions exclude banks. The term "bank" as defined in §3(a)(6) does not include a nonbanking holding company or a subsidiary or other affiliate of a bank. Nor, literally, does it include a foreign bank.[19] But the Commission has regarded properly supervised American branches and agencies of foreign banks to be "banks" as defined in §3(a)(2) of the 1933 Act.[20]

In 1985 the Commission — referring to the changes in banks' brokerage and related promotional activities from merely providing existing customers with accommodation services to activities functionally indistinguishable from those offered by registered broker-dealers — adopted Rule 3b-9 to exclude from the term "bank" as used in the definitions of "broker" and "dealer" any bank that "(1) publicly solicits brokerage business for which it receives transaction-related compensation * * *; (2) directly or indirectly receives transaction-related compensation for providing brokerage services for

[18]The Commission has ruled that an insurance company must register as a broker-dealer if it distributes variable annuities representing interests in a separate account. "Since the insurance company engages in the purchase and sale of its own portfolio securities, will make purchases and sales of securities for the portfolio of the Separate Account, and will distribute the variable annuity interests of which it and the Separate Account are co-issuers [see p. 209 n. 15 supra], the insurance company would be a 'broker' as defined in Section 3(a)(4) of the Act as well as a 'dealer' as defined in Section 3(a)(5) of the Act." Sec. Ex. Act Rel. 8389 (1968). A substantial number of insurance companies (usually their brokerage affiliates) are registered. But, whatever the validity of the "broker" interpretation, the "dealer" interpretation seems to say too much in the light of the administrative line that the Commission has always drawn between dealers and active traders. See p. 605 supra. Although mutual funds, universities, and other institutional investors likewise engage in the purchase and sale of securities for their portfolios, the Commission has never suggested that they are "dealers" on that account alone.

[19]United States v. Weisscredit Banca Commerciale e d'Investimenti, 325 F. Supp. 1384, 1390-92 (S. D. N. Y. 1971).

[20]Sec. Act Rel. 6661, 36 SEC Dock. 746 (1986), supra p. 271 n. 2.

trust, managing agency or other accounts to which the bank provides advice * * *; or (3) deals in or underwrites securities."[21] But the District of Columbia Circuit, relying substantially on the systematic oversight to which banks were already subjected, invalidated the rule despite the Commission's argument of regulatory coherence.[22]

e. Finders and Investment Advisers

Although a pure finder may "induce the purchase or sale of" a security within the meaning of §15(a), he is not normally a "broker" because he effects no transactions. He merely brings buyer and seller together.[26] Nor is an investment adviser ordinarily a "broker," whether or not he is registered under the Investment Advisers Act. He may even place orders with brokers or dealers for his clients' accounts as long as he receives no special compensation for that service. The question becomes close when his total compensation is based on individual transactions.

3. Exemptions

Section 15(a) does not apply to a broker or dealer "whose business is exclusively intrastate" or to any transaction in "an exempted security[27] or commercial paper, bankers' acceptances, or commercial bills."

a. Exclusively Intrastate Business

If all the broker's or dealer's securities activities and customers are confined to a single state, he need not register. This precludes

[21] Sec. Ex. Act Rel. 22,205, 33 SEC Dock. 807 (1985). The rule did not require the bank itself to register if the designated activities were conducted by a subsidiary or affiliate, which is the normal practice. Moreover, the rule codified the staff no-action positions whereby a bank was not required to register as a separate broker-dealer if it entered into a so-called "networking" arrangement with a registered broker-dealer to provide brokerage services. There were also a number of exemptions.

[22] American Bankers Assn. v. SEC, 804 F. 2d 739 (D. C. Cir. 1986).

[26] But the emphasis is on "pure." See SEC, Final Report on Bank Securities Activities (1977) 53-54, 101-02; Augustine and Fass, Finder's Fees in Security and Real Estate Transactions, 35 Bus. Law. 485 (1980).

[27] See p. 422 supra.

him, for example, from selling even once as underwriter for an out-of-state issuer[28] or as broker for an out-of-state customer.[29] And this is equally true with respect to his selling to or buying for an out-of-state customer.[30] He may not even offer his customers securities acquired on a stock exchange or mutual fund shares, since those securities are continually moving in the stream of interstate commerce.[31] However, as long as the buying and selling customers are all in the same state, the issuers of the securities need not be local companies.[32] And the exemption is not destroyed by sending the securities to out-of-state transfer agents. Nor is it necessary that the *market* in the securities dealt in be exclusively or predominantly intrastate. That was the test under the rules adopted by the Commission pursuant to the original §15, but it was dropped in the 1936 amendment of the statute.[33]

The intrastate exemption is eliminated in the Code, as it would have been in the bill that passed the Senate in connection with the 1964 amendments.[34] The Code's comments repeat the reasons given at that time:

> (a) The scope of the exemption is very narrow and only a small number can avail themselves of it. (b) Intrastate broker-dealers are subject to X15(c)(1)-(3), so that the Commission has responsibility for their conduct in important respects without adequate means to discharge that responsibility; it is anomalous that they are subject to the capital requirements without being required to keep records in order to show how much capital they have; as a result, the Com-

[28] Professional Investors, Inc., 37 SEC 173, 175-76 (1956).

[29] Whitehall Corp., 38 SEC 259, 271 (1958).

[30] Capital Funds, Inc., 42 SEC 245, 249 (1964), *aff'd* sub nom. Capital Funds, Inc. v. SEC, 348 F. 2d 582 (8th Cir. 1965).

[31] See SEC Legislation, 1963, Hearings Before Subcom. of S. Com. on Banking & Currency on S. 1642, 88th Cong., 1st Sess. (1963) 388.

[32] The SEC advised the Senate committee in 1963: "In order to qualify for the exclusively intrastate exemption, a broker-dealer must not only deal with customers who are exclusively within the State, but he must deal exclusively in securities originating in the State." Ibid. The Commission, it is understood, did not mean to imply that the issuer always had to be a local company. The reference may have been to something like the "coming to rest" concept in the hands of local *buying* customers. See E. Weiss, Registration and Regulation of Brokers and Dealers (1955) 14-15. That is to say, a resident who buys out-of-state securities with a view to distribution and resells them to a dealer in the state destroys the dealer's intrastate exemption, presumably on the theory that the dealer has been made a step in the distribution of an out-of-state issue.

[33] Sec. Ex. Act Rel. 721 (1936).

[34] The House committee deleted the repeal provision on the ground of lack of demonstrated need, fortified by the false ground of preemption. H. R. Rep. No. 1418, 88th Cong., 2d Sess. (1964) 12. But there would have been no more preemption than there is today with *inter*state broker-dealers — which is to say, none at all.

> mission must devote a disproportionate amount of time and effort to fraud investigations involving intrastate firms. (c) They often involve themselves in inadvertent violations of X15(a)(1) by overstepping the bounds of the exemption. (d) When they do observe those restrictions, they are limited in the securities they can recommend and sell to customers. (e) If the Commission is to have the authority to suspend for a limited period, a broker or dealer should not be able to ameliorate a suspension by conducting an intrastate business.[35]

To these reasons the Code's comments add two more: the "critically important * * * limitation of SIPC protection[36] to customers of *registered* broker-dealers," and the fact that "many states have no broker-dealer inspection programs."[37]

b. Combination of Exemptions

The intrastate exemption is destroyed by effecting an *inter*state transaction even in an *exempted* security. For the *entire* business of the broker-dealer must be exclusively intrastate. It follows also from the Commission's construction of the intrastate exemption that a broker-dealer relying on it may not effect a transaction on an exchange in another state even though he places the order through a member of that exchange with an office in his own state. Nor may he effect a transaction on an exchange even in the *same* state if the security is in fact sold to or purchased from a person *outside* the state. Since one cannot ordinarily tell who the other party will be in an exchange transaction, a broker-dealer relying on the intrastate exemption is precluded, in effect, from engaging in exchange transactions altogether.[38]

4. Government Securities

Because §15(a) from the beginning did not apply to an "exempted security," which has always been defined to include obligations issued or guaranteed by the United States Government,[39] broker-dealers who handled only government paper did not have

[35] 1 Code 324.
[36] See p. 38 supra.
[37] 1 Code 325.
[38] Professional Investors, Inc., 37 SEC 173, 175-76 (1956).
[39] §3(a)(12).

to register. There are 40 primary dealers, which report to the Federal Reserve Bank of New York on a daily, monthly, and annual basis, as well as an unknown number of secondary dealers, whose government securities transactions are largely unregulated although some of them report to the Bank on a monthly basis. Those firms operate in a market that dwarfs — in a ratio of 15 to 1 — the annual dollar volume of trading in all the exchange and over-the-counter markets.[40]

In April 1985 the SEC, under Congressional pressure to respond to "the widely publicized failures of several small government securities dealers" during the preceding seven years, invited comment on government (and agency) securities markets and dealers in order to determine, in consultation with the Treasury and the Federal Reserve, whether the recent failures pointed to legislative or regulatory initiatives.[41] A subsequent SEC report to Congress outlined a legislative proposal, which the other federal agencies supported.[42] And this eventuated in the Government Securities Act of 1986 generally effective July 25, 1987, which added a new §15C, with complementary provisions and amendments elsewhere.[43]

Instead of creating a new self-regulatory organization to parallel the Municipal Securities Rulemaking Board, as the earlier House-passed bill would have done,[44] §15C gives the rulemaking authority to the Secretary of the Treasury in consultation (except for emergencies) with the SEC and the Federal Reserve. This authority extends to such matters as financial responsibility, custody and use

[40] Sec. Ex. Act Rel. 21,959, 32 SEC Dock. 1336 (1985).

[41] Ibid.

[42] SEC, Regulation of the Government Securities Market (Report to Subcom on Telecommunications, Consumer Protection & Finance, H. R. Com. on Energy & Commerce, June 20, 1985).

[43] 100 Stat. 3208 (1986); see S. 1416 and S. Rep. No. 99-426 (1986). Instead of a conference report, a joint floor statement of the two committees was inserted in the Congressional Record by way of legislative history. 132 Cong. Rec S5795-800 (daily ed., Oct. 9, 1986).

The definition of "exempted security" has always included securities issued or guaranteed by government *corporations* as designated by the Treasury. §3(a)(12) And the Government Securities Act, which is about to be examined, revised the definition to include all "government securities," a newly defined term that encompasses not only (1) securities issued by Treasury-designated corporations [§3(a)(42)(B)] but also (2) securities issued or guaranteed by *any* corporation designated by name in a statute as exempt securities within the SEC statute [§3(a)(42)(C)] and (3) for purposes of §15C (as well as §17A) any option on an exempted security (other than an option that is traded on an exchange or for which quotations are disseminated through, in effect, NASDAQ) [§3(a)(42)(D) But issuers in the (B) and (C) categories are excluded from the definitions of "government securities broker" and "government securities dealer." §§3(a)(44 3(a)(45).

[44] H. R. 2032 and H. R. Rep. No. 99-258 (1985). See p. 627 infra.

of customers' securities, recordkeeping, financial reporting, and transfer and control of government securities subject to repurchase agreements and in similar transactions.[45] But all government securities brokers or dealers not already registered (as ordinary broker-dealers or municipal securities dealers) must register with the SEC.

"Financial institutions" — defined to mean domestic or foreign banks or federally insured savings and loan associations[46] — need not register. But they, along with government securities broker-dealers already registered, must file with the "appropriate regulatory agency" (which is to say, the SEC or the particular bank or savings and loan regulator)[47] a notice of their status as "government securities brokers" or "government securities dealers";[48] and a bank, though not a "broker" or "dealer" *per se,* achieves "government securities broker" status if it is "regularly engaged in the business of effecting transactions in government securities for the account of others"[49] and achieves "government securities dealer" status if it is engaged "as part of a regular business" in "buying and selling securities for its own account other than in a fiduciary capacity."[50]

The Treasury may classify and may also exempt by rule or order. But the legislative history indicates that there should be no exemption for primary dealers as a class.[51] And the Treasury is to consider the sufficiency of existing laws and rules before imposing new rules. In addition, the NASD is authorized to promulgate rules with respect to fraudulent advertising of government securities.[52]

Administrative discipline rests with the SEC (as well as the exchanges and the NASD under the usual SEC oversight) so far as broker-dealers are concerned, and with the bank (or savings and loan) regulators so far as financial institutions are concerned.[53]

The appropriate regulatory agency has a visitatorial power. And

[45] See also p. 707 n. 23 infra. [9An.p.11] A "sunset" provision terminates the power on October 1, 1991, without effect on rules previously adopted.

[46] §3(a)(46).

[47] §3(a)(34).

[48] The SEC promulgates the forms for registration as well as these notices when filed by registered broker-dealers. And the Federal Reserve (after consultation with the SEC as well as the other bank and savings and loan regulators) does so with respect to notices filed by "financial institutions."

[49] §3(a)(43).

[50] §3(a)(44). Note the legislative solution in this context of the bank problem that the Commission tried unsuccessfully to solve through rulemaking so far as ordinary broker-dealers are concerned. See p. 608 supra.

[51] 132 Cong. Rec. S15799 (daily ed., Oct. 9, 1986).

[52] This is understood to be directed toward advertisements of yields available on GNMAs.

[53] §§3(a)(48), 15A(f)(2), 15A(g)(4), 15C(c).

membership in an exchange or a national securities association (the NASD) is compulsory except for financial institutions. But the SEC (after consultation with the Treasury) may exempt from that requirement by rule or order.

Title II of the statute requires the Treasury to establish standards by rule for the safeguarding and use of customer securities held by a non-dealer "depository institution"[54] in a fiduciary or similar capacity. But the Treasury is required also to exempt depository institutions that are subject to adequate regulation by an appropriate regulatory authority.

Since government securities are not "exempted securities" for purposes of §17A,[55] government securities clearing agencies must register with the SEC.

Finally, the statute mandates no fewer than four studies:[56]

(1) The Treasury, the SEC, and the Federal Reserve are to evaluate the effectiveness of rules promulgated under the statute in effectuating its purposes, and are to provide Congress by October 1, 1990, with their recommendation on extension of the Treasury's rulemaking authority as well as any other appropriate recommendations.

(2) The Comptroller General is to make a similar study and recommendations.

(3) The Comptroller General is also required (in consultation with the Federal Reserve, the Treasury, and the SEC) to study trading in the secondary market for government securities, including the availability of quotations and brokers' services, and to report to Congress not later than six months after enactment of the statute.[57]

(4) The SEC is to study (in consultation with the Treasury and the bank regulators) the use made of the exemption contained in §3(a)(2) of the 1933 Act for securities guaranteed by banks (typically by means of standby letters of credit). This study was agreed to in place of an amendment to the 1933 Act — appended to the unrelated Government Securities Act during its progression through Congress — that would have created an exemption for certain securities guaranteed by insurance policies. The study is to focus on competition between banks and insurance companies.[58]

[54] 31 U. S. C. §9110(e)(1).

[55] §3(a)(12)(B)(i).

[56] Government Securities Act §§103-05.

[57] For a report on a joint hearing by the four agencies, as well as a fuller description of the government securities market, see 19 Sec. Reg. L. Rep. 191 (1987).

[58] In Sec. Act Rel. 6688, 37 SEC Dock. 774 (1987), the Commission solicited comment as a step in this study. "Financial guarantees first gained widespread

C. GOVERNMENTAL *VERSUS* SELF-REGULATION

1. The Philosophy

At best, direct regulation of a complex business through the machinery of government — even with the advantages that the administrative process offers over traditional enforcement by grand jury investigation and criminal prosecution — divides black from white with a buzz saw when the many variations of gray call for a surgeon's scalpel. Although appropriate provisions on registration and fraud prevention furnish an indispensable foundation for an adequate system of control, they must be supplemented by regulation on an ethical plane in order "to protect the investor and the honest dealer alike from dishonest and unfair practices by the submarginal element in the industry" and "to cope with those methods of doing business which, while technically outside the area of definite illegality, are nevertheless unfair both to customer and to decent competitor, and are seriously damaging to the mechanism of the free and open market."[1] And regulation of the *ethics* of an industry means a substantial degree of *self*-regulation, properly supervised by government.

Witness the early symbiosis between the Commission under the chairmanship of William O. Douglas and the New York Stock Exchange. In late 1937, after negotiations with the exchanges on their voluntary reorganization had broken down, Mr. Douglas gave a statement to the press in which he stressed the importance of reaching an early decision on where to draw the line between the two kinds of regulation:

> Ideally, of course, it would be desirable to have all national securities exchanges so organized and so imbued with the public interest that it would be possible and even desirable to entrust to them a great deal of the actual regulation and enforcement within their own field, leaving the government free to perform a supervisory or residual role. * * *
>
> At the present time, however, I have doubts as to the desirability, from the standpoint of the public interest, of assigning to exchanges

---

acceptance in the 1970s to insure payment of principal and interest on municipal bonds. Since that time, they have been used to back issues of corporate bonds, commercial paper, limited partnerships, and debt securities backed by assets including mortgages, automobile loans, and credit card receivables.)" Id. at 775.

C. 8C [1] S. Rep. No. 1455 at 3 and H. R. Rep. No. 2307 at 4, 75th Cong., 3d Sess. (1938).

> such a vital role in the nation's economic affairs, before they adopt programs of action designed to justify their existence solely upon their value as public market places. I have always regarded the exchanges as the scales upon which that great national resource, invested capital, is weighed and evaluated. Scales of such importance must be tamper-proof, with no concealed springs — and there must be no laying on of hands. * * * Such an important instrument in our economic welfare * * * must be surrounded by adequate safeguards. Yet it is also obvious that such restrictions must be consistent with the profit motive, which in final analysis is and must remain the driving force in our economy.
>
> * * *
>
> Operating as private-membership associations, exchanges have always administered their affairs in much the same manner as private clubs. For a business so vested with the public interest, this traditional method has become archaic.[2]

Elsewhere Douglas expressed his philosophy as

> letting the exchanges take the leadership with Government playing a residual role. Government would keep the shotgun, so to speak, behind the door, loaded, well oiled, cleaned, ready for use but with the hope it would never have to be used.[3]

The New York Stock Exchange responded by appointing a com mittee to study the need of reorganization. The committee's repor of January 1938 recognized the public nature of the exchanges anc provided a plan for a modern administrative organization. But Wal Street seems to be synonymous with drama. Six weeks later, befor any action could be taken, one of the most spectacular incidents i the financial history of the United States focused the country's at tention on the state of the Exchange housekeeping. The firm o Richard Whitney & Co. was suspended by the Exchange for insol vency and Whitney himself was soon on his way to Sing Sing fo grand larceny. Whitney was a former president and a pillar of th Exchange. An investigation disclosed that his firm had been insol vent for at least three and a half years, largely as a result of hi personal speculations in ventures "involving such widely divers products as applejack, peat humus, and mineral colloids."[4] To rais funds for these ventures, Whitney had begun misappropriating customer's securities as far back as 1926, and his misappropriation

[2] Douglas, Democracy and Finance (J. Allen, ed. 1940) 64-65.
[3] Id. at 82.
[4] 10 SEC Ann. Rep. 37 (1944).

had become a steady practice by 1936, extending even to securities of the Exchange's gratuity fund, of which he was a trustee. Many persons high in the administration of the Exchange were aware of Whitney's financial difficulty for a considerable time before his suspension, but the "unwritten code of silence" protected him until, as in a detective thriller, the accident of a groundless rumor led to the discovery of his embezzlement.[5] The Commission immediately began an investigation, during which public hearings were held from time to time during the months of April through June.[6]

In March 1938 the Exchange voted a radically revised constitution, which became effective in May. It provided for a paid nonmember president, executive staffs to carry out functions formerly conducted by the governors sitting as committee members, direct representation of the public on the board of governors, increased representation of Exchange firms doing business with the public, and a greatly simplified administrative structure. Similar reorganizations had been effected earlier the same year by the then Detroit and Chicago Stock Exchanges, and the New York Curb Exchange (now the American Stock Exchange) followed early in 1939.[7]

The year 1938 also saw the implementation of the mixed regulatory philosophy when Congress in the Maloney Act added §15A to the 1934 Act in order to provide for the registration of one or more "national securities associations" that would perform for the over-the-counter market the same self-regulatory function performed by the "national securities exchanges." As each of the legislative committees then put it:

> The committee believes that there are two alternative programs by which this problem [of adequate regulation of the over-the-counter market] could be met. The first would involve a pronounced expansion of the organization of the Securities and Exchange Commission; the multiplication of branch offices; a large increase in the expenditure of public funds; an increase in the problem of avoiding the evils of bureaucracy; and a minute, detailed, and rigid regulation of business conduct by law. It might very well mean expanding the present process of registration of brokers and dealers with the Commission to include the proscription not only of the dishonest, but also of those unwilling or unable to conform to rigid standards of financial responsibility, professional conduct, and technical profi-

[5] 1 SEC, In the Matter of Richard Whitney (1938) 181-82.

[6] The Commission published its three-volume report on November 1, 1938. SEC, In the Matter of Richard Whitney (1938).

[7] See 4 SEC Ann. Rep. 20 (1938); 5 id. 37 (1939).

> ciency.[8] The second of these alternative programs, which the committee believes distinctly preferable to the first, is embodied in S. 3255. This program is based upon cooperative regulation, in which the task will be largely performed by representative organizations of investment bankers, dealers, and brokers, with the Government exercising appropriate supervision in the public interest, and exercising supplementary powers of direct regulation. In the concept of a really well organized and well-conducted stock exchange, under the supervision provided by the Securities Exchange Act of 1934, one may perceive something of the possibilities of such a program.[9]

In short, as Senator Maloney of Connecticut emphasized, the scheme is not so much self-regulation as "cooperative regulation."[10]

The idea is encapsulated in the provision in §§6(b)(5) and 15A(b)(6) that has always conditioned registration as a "national securities exchange" or a "national securities association" on its

[8] Congress was to do substantially this in 1975, as we have seen. See p. 603 supra.

[9] S. Rep. No. 1455 at 3-4 and H. R. Rep. No. 2307 at 4-5, 75th Cong., 3d Sess. (1938).

[10] 83 Cong. Rec. 4451 (1938). A philosophy of governmentally supervised self-regulation permeates the far-reaching legislation recently enacted in the United Kingdom. Financial Services Act 1986, 1986 Acts c. 60; see L. Gower, Review of Investor Protection: Report: Part I, Cmd. 9125 (1984) esp. c. 60; Dep't of Trade & Industry, Financial Services in the United Kingdom: A New Framework for Investor Protection, Cmd. 9432 (1985) esp. §§16.4, 16.5; L. Gower, Review of Investor Protection: Report: Part II (1985) (commenting on developments since Part I, supra, and the White Paper's differences from Part I). The role of government should be "to provide the grit which enables the oyster to produce the pearl of effective self-regulation." Gower, supra, Part I, at 10. For a discussion of all three documents, see Pimlott, The Reform of Investor Protection in the U. K. — An Examination of the Proposals of the Gower Report and the U. K. Government's White Paper of January, 1985, 7 J. Comp. Bus. & Capital Market L. 141 (1985).

The Act contemplates governmental recognition of a series of functionally organized "self-regulatory organisations" (defined in §8) and "professional bodies" (defined in §16). Although the contemplated regulations are essentially statutory, their monitoring is to be largely undertaken by these agencies acting under the surveillance of a recognized body answerable to the Government and, through it, to Parliament.

The Government is represented in the statute by the Secretary of State, but the Act contemplates his transferring any or all of his functions to the Securities and Investments Board Limited ("SIB"), which is not otherwise described. §§114-15. Prospective "self-regulatory organisations" and "professional bodies" will apply to the SIB for recognition. §§9-11, 17-20.

The Act also creates a Financial Services Tribunal consisting of three members nominated by the Secretary of State or the SIB from a panel of ten or more persons who are either lawyers appointed by the Lord Chancellor or others appointed by the Secretary of State or the SIB. The Tribunal's function is to review adverse administrative action. §§96-101. And it may be assumed that the courts will retain a limited degree of *judicial* review. See Regina v. Panel on Take-Overs and Mergers, [1987] 1 All E. R. 564, supra p. 508 n. 27.

having rules designed "to promote just and equitable principles of trade."[11] The 1975 amendments, which greatly enlarged the statute, altered the mix somewhat away from self-regulation.[12] But the statutory scheme continues to give the Commission considerable discretion in drawing the line between self-regulation and direct governmental supervision.

[11]See N. Y. Stock Ex. Const., Art. I, §2(a), CCH N. Y. Stock Exchange Guide ¶1002; NASD Rules of Fair Practice, Art. III, §1, CCH NASD Manual ¶2151. In Todd v. SEC, 557 F. 2d 1008, 1013 (3d Cir. 1977), the court sustained the NASD rule against a charge of vagueness. Some of these rules of the NASD are patterned after the Commission's fraud and disclosure rules. Indeed, the NASD has uniformly considered — and properly so in the SEC's view — that violations of the statutes and the Commission's rules on fair dealing and fraud constitute conduct inconsistent with "just and equitable principles of trade" and hence violations of Article III, §1. Valley Forge Securities Co., Inc., 41 SEC 486, 488 (1963); see CCH NASD Manual ¶2152.

Other NASD strictures are more specific. One of the most significant is its "suitability" requirement, which will be considered later in connection with the emergent role of the SEC itself in that area. NASD Rules of Fair Practice, Art. III, §2, id., ¶2152. Another, for example, prohibits the payment of any reward to an employee of another firm without that firm's consent. Art. III, §10, id., ¶2160; see H. C. Keister & Co., 43 SEC 164, 166-71 (1966).

The NASD has also issued a number of significant "interpretations" of Article III, §1, dealing with such matters as the review of corporate financing (CCH NASD Manual ¶2151.02) and the "free riding" problem with respect to "hot issues" (id., ¶2151.06), where the aim is to assure a good faith offer to the public for a reasonable time at the prospectus price. On the latter subject, see 5 Loss 3455-61; Report of the Securities and Exchange Commission Concerning the Hot Issues Market (1984). On the NASD's mark-up policy, see p. 819 infra.

[12]See generally 2 SEC, Study of Unsafe and Unsound Practices of Brokers and Dealers (1971) c. 9, pp. 27-36. "Self-regulation," the Commission there said, "has worked, but not well enough." Id. at 27. For an assessment of the performance of the New York Stock Exchange and the NASD, see Securities Industry Study, H. R. Rep. No. 92-1519 (1972) ("Moss Report") 91-100. That report found the Commission frequently negotiating with the exchanges "as if they were coordinate sovereign bodies." Id. at 113. A concurrent report on the Senate side concluded: "The concept of industry self-regulation, subject to SEC oversight, is well-adapted to dealing with problems of conduct and ethics, but is not well-adapted to dealing with general economic questions involving competitive interrelationships among firms within the industry." Securities Industry Study, Report of Subcom. on Securities, S. Com. on Banking, Housing & Urban Affairs, 93d Cong., 1st Sess. (1973) 2-3.

For a critical analysis of what the author calls "the myth of self-regulation," see Miller, Self-Regulation of the Securities Markets: A Critical Examination, 42 Wash. & Lee L. Rev. 853, 855 (1985).

2. The Self-Regulatory Organizations

a. National Securities Exchanges

There are now four kinds of self-regulatory organizations.[13] The original 1934 Act contemplated only one, the national securities exchanges.

b. National Association of Securities Dealers

The second came in 1938 with the addition of §15A, which, as we have just seen, invented the "national securities association."

The resemblance of §15A to the 1933 National Industrial Recovery Act — as well as the genesis of the NASD in that short-lived statute — is not accidental. The NRA code of fair competition for investment bankers, which was approved by the President in November 1933, embraced all over-the-counter brokers and dealers. In March 1934 the President approved an amendment to the code that incorporated certain rules of fair practice. After the demise of the NRA in the spring of 1935, representatives of the industry discussed with the Commission the feasibility of a new organization that would undertake to perpetuate the objectives of the code by regulating brokers and dealers in a manner comparable to the exchanges' regulation of their members. The result was the formation in 1936 of the Investment Bankers Conference, Inc., as a Delaware nonprofit corporation. And the Conference and the Commission jointly sponsored the bill that became the Maloney Act. That act was approved June 25, 1938. In the summer of 1939 the Investment Bankers Conference, Inc., became the National Association of Securities Dealers, Inc., also a Delaware nonprofit corporation. On August 7, 1939, after a public hearing, the Commission found that the NASD satisfied the statutory standards and granted its application for registration.[14] No other association has ever applied for registration.

[13] See Smythe, Government Supervised Self-Regulation in the Securities Industry and the Antitrust Laws: Suggestions for an Accommodation, 62 N. C. L. Rev. 475 (1984); see also pp. 621-22, 689-90 infra.

[14] National Assn. of Securities Dealers, Inc., 5 SEC 627 (1939). It is interesting, on this background, that no constitutional attack was made on §15A until the early 1950s, when the challenge received short shrift. In the light of the statutory provisions concerning the Commission's power to disapprove the NASD's rules according to reasonably fixed standards, as well as the Commission's review of any disciplinary action, the Second Circuit saw no merit in

An interesting technique was used to get the great bulk of the over-the-counter broker-dealer community to put their heads in the lion's mouth by subjecting themselves to the risks and expense of an additional regulatory and disciplinary system. First of all, the leaders of the industry — the major underwriting firms that had been active in the Conference — favored the scheme. Secondly, the proponents, in effect, got an antitrust exemption inserted into the statute. Section 15A(i) as enacted in 1938 (now §15A(e)(1) as amended technically in 1975) provides:

> The rules of a registered securities association may provide that no member thereof shall deal with any nonmember professional * * * except at the same prices, for the same commissions or fees, and on the same terms and conditions as are by such member accorded to the general public

And §15A(n) provided:

> If any provision of this section is in conflict with any provision of any law of the United States in force on the date this section takes effect, the provision of this section shall prevail.

It is these two subsections that afforded the NASD an exemption from the antitrust laws[15] and that, according to the Commission, made it "virtually impossible for a dealer who is not a member of the NASD to participate in a distribution of important size."[16] For the rules of the Association not only require members to treat non-member brokers and dealers the way they do members of the public, but also forbid members to "join with any non-member broker or dealer in any syndicate or group contemplating the distribution to the public of any issue of securities or any part thereof."[17] It is doubtful whether more than a few hundred of the Association's

---

contention that §15A involved an unconstitutional delegation of power to the NASD. R. H. Johnson & Co. v. SEC, 198 F. 2d 690, 695 (2d Cir. 1952), *cert. denied,* 344 U. S. 855; see also First Jersey Securities, Inc. v. Bergen, 605 F. 2d 690, 697 (3d Cir. 1979), *cert. denied* sub nom. First Jersey Securities, Inc. v. Biunno, 444 U. S. 1074; Sorrell v. SEC, 679 F. 2d 1323 (9th Cir. 1982).

[15] See United States v. Socony-Vacuum Oil Co., Inc., 310 U. S. 150, 227 n. 60 (1940); National Assn. of Securities Dealers, Inc., 19 SEC 424, 478 n. 9 (1945); but cf. Harwell v. Growth Programs, Inc., 451 F. 2d 240, 245-47 (5th Cir. 1971), *modifed per curiam*, 459 F. 2d 461 (5th Cir. 1972), *cert. denied* sub nom. NASD v. Harwell, 409 U. S. 876.

[16] National Assn. of Securities Dealers, Inc., 19 SEC 424, 441 (1945).

[17] NASD Rules of Fair Practice, Art. III, §25, CCH NASD Manual ¶2175. In its opinion granting the NASD's application for registration, the Commission did not comment on the extension of this rule beyond the literal language of §15A(i) (now §15A(e)(1)). National Assn. of Securities Dealers, Inc., 5 SEC 627, 632 (1939).

members engage in underwriting. But, entirely apart from underwriting, members may give each other the benefit of special discounts in ordinary trading that they do not give to the general public and hence may not give to nonmember brokers and dealers. And there is the distribution of investment company shares to be considered.[18]

Congress deleted §15A(n) in the 1975 amendments, apparently on the theory that it should be left to the courts to prick out the extent to which an antitrust exemption is to be implied from §15A(e)(1). But everybody seems to be proceeding on the assumption that an exemption survives. Although the Supreme Court said in 1963 that "Repeal [of the antitrust laws] is to be regarded as implied only if necessary to make the Securities Exchange Act work, and even then only to the minimum extent necessary,"[19] it carefully left open the antitrust question as applied to §15A, with its provision for Commission "jurisdiction and ensuing judicial review for scrutiny of a particular exchange ruling."[20] And the Commission later embraced that distinction.[21]

In 1945 the NASD emulated the major exchanges by requiring the registration with itself of members' representatives.[22] And in 1956 it instituted an elementary written examination requirement for all members and representatives, which has been developed since.[23]

[18] No member may purchase any security of an open-end investment company from a nonmember underwriter at a discount, and no member underwriter may sell any such security to a nonmember broker-dealer at a discount. NASD Rules of Fair Practice, Art. III, §26(c), CCH NASD Manual ¶2176. Section 22(d) of the Investment Company Act provides, with exceptions, that, if a redeemable security of a registered investment company's issue "is being currently offered to the public by or through an underwriter, no principal underwriter of such security and no dealer shall sell any such security to any person except a dealer, a principal underwriter, or the issuer, except at a current public offering price described in the prospectus." For a detailed discussion of the legislative and administrative history of §22(d), see Inv. Co. Act Rel. 13,183, 27 SEC Dock. 974, 980-89 (1983).

[19] Silver v. New York Stock Exchange, 373 U. S. 341, 357 (1963).

[20] Id. at 358 n. 12.

[21] C. A. Benson & Co., Inc., 42 SEC 107, 112 (1964); cf. Gordon v. New York Stock Exchange, Inc., 422 U. S. 659 (1975) (fixed stock exchange commissions); see also Austin Municipal Securities, Inc. v. NASD, Inc., 757 F. 2d 676, 694-96 (5th Cir. 1985) ("Congress necessarily repealed the antitrust laws insofar as those laws condemn actions required to be undertaken in the effectuation of NASD disciplinary process").

[22] See National Assn. of Securities Dealers, Inc., 20 SEC 508 (1945), *petition for review denied per curiam,* 4 SEC Jud. Dec. 669 (2d Cir. 1946).

[23] See p. 603 n. 9 supra. In Exchange Services, Inc., Sec. Ex. Act Rel. 22,245, 33 SEC Dock. 929, 931 (1985), the SEC held that a member's "order takers" were engaged in the member's securities business and did not perform merely clerical or ministerial functions so as to be excluded from the examination requirement.

"Over the years," the then Chairman of the SEC said in 1975, speaking of both the NASD and the exchanges, "the Commission has had a sort of love-hate relationship with these self-regulators."[24] For they are, after all, only half self-regulatory organizations. And, apart from the inevitable lack of universal harmony even in that capacity, they are half trade associations. "Finlandized" to an extent they may be; but they are not SEC satellites.

At any rate, the Commission, in connection with the events leading to the 1964 amendments, was concerned that a significant number of registered broker-dealers was avoiding the self-regulation component of the statutory scheme by simply not joining the NASD. So just as §12(g) attacked the discrepancy between the exchange and over-the-counter markets as far as the *disclosure*-oriented provisions (§§12, 13, 14, and 16) are concerned, a series of amendments of §§15 and 15A was designed to put the two markets more nearly on the same level as far as the *regulatory* features of the statute are concerned. But a number of investment companies objected strenuously to the principle of compulsory membership in any trade association.[25] In the event, they outsmarted themselves. As the then Chairman of the SEC later indicated, some of the investment company lobbyists had not anticipated the suggestion of the Chairman of the House Commerce Committee that the alternative was direct SEC regulation on an *ethical* plane.[26]

That is what eventuated in the form (as renumbered and amended in 1975) of new §15(b)(8) and (9) — which the industry promptly dubbed the "SECO provisions" (pronounced "see-co") by way of referring to those broker-dealers that were subject to the "SEC only." Roughly paralleling §15A as concurrently amended in 1964 and again in 1975, they gave the Commission a considerable amount of unwanted authority, which, went among other things, to the adoption of rules designed "to promote just and equitable principles

[24]Garrett, The Markets: Nationalization or Centralization? (address before N. Y. Chamber of Commerce & Industry, New York, Mar. 20, 1975) 11.

Under §17 of the Commodity Exchange Act, 7 U. S. C. §21, which was added in 1974 on the model of §15A of the Securities Exchange Act, the National Futures Association is functioning as a "registered futures association" along the lines of the NASD. See [1984] CFTC Ann. Rep. 70. With respect to Government securities, see p. 612 infra. And the NASD may be on the way toward acting as a self-regulatory organization for investment advisers who are its members, and ultimately perhaps for all advisers. See 18 Sec. Reg. L. Rep. 565 (1986). On the Japanese Securities Dealers Association, see L. Loss, M. Yazawa, and B. Banoff (eds.), Japanese Securities Regulation (1983) 99-103.

[25]H. R. Rep. No. 1418, 88th Cong., 2d Sess. (1964) 3.

[26]W. Cary, Politics and the Regulatory Agencies (1967) 108-10.

of trade" and "to remove impediments to and perfect the mechanism of a free and open market."

All this, of course, represented a step backward from the 1938 decision to leave the regulation of ethics to the industry itself in the first instance. And, quite apart from regulatory philosophy, it created anomalies. To be sure, the Commission was inevitably placed in the "ethics business" when the original §15A gave it jurisdiction to review NASD disciplinary proceedings for violation of its ethical strictures. But under the SEC regime a willful violation of the SECO rules was quite literally a *felony* under the penalty provision, §32(a), which covers "any rule or regulation" of the Commission under the Act.

For these reasons those who worked on the Code would have preferred to abandon the SECO concept. But under all the circumstances, including some constitutional doubts that had been expressed, the Code makes no significant change.[27] Then in 1983, with no particular fuss, Congress amended §15(b)(8)-(9) to make it unlawful for any registered broker or dealer to effect any transaction in a security (other than an exempted security or commercial paper) unless he is a member of a national securities association (which today means the NASD) or effects transactions solely on an exchange of which he is a member, with authority in the Commission conditionally or unconditionally to exempt any broker or dealer or class. Very little was said except for a reference to efficiency and equality of regulation.[28]

A metamorphosis of ethics into law nevertheless persists at the state blue sky level. One of the grounds for administrative discipline of a broker-dealer or investment adviser under §204(a)(2)(G) of the Uniform Securities Act is a finding that he "has engaged in dishonest or unethical practices in the securities business." And the North American Securities Administrators Association has adopted statements of policy spelling out in considerable detail what constitutes "unethical practice" on the part of investment advisers and broker-dealers.[29]

[27] §905(c).

[28] See H. R. Rep. No. 98-106, 98th Cong., 1st Sess. (1983) 24-25. Rule 15b9-1 exempts a broker-dealer that (1) is an exchange member, (2) carries no customer accounts, and (3) has annual gross income from over-the-counter transactions of not more than $1000.

[29] CCH NASAA Rep. ¶1402.

c. Registered Clearing Agencies

One response to the "back office" or "paper crunch" crisis of the late 1960s and early 1970s — when more than a hundred broker-dealers were forced to close their doors or merge not because of too little but because of too much business — was the Commission's being put for the first time into the business of regulating the securities transfer and clearance processes, a subject previously left to state law. In a new §17A Congress, in recognition (*inter alia*) of new data processing and communications techniques, directed the Commission to use its authority "to facilitate the establishment of a national system for the prompt and accurate clearance and settlement of transactions in securities (other than exempted securities)."[30] This more or less parallels the direction in the new §11A (which we examine later) to "facilitate the establishment of a national market system."[31]

Section 17A requires the registration not only of transfer agents[32] but also of clearing agencies.[33] The latter give us our third category of self-regulatory organizations.[34] The relationship with the Com-

[30] §17A(a)(2).

[31] §11A(a)(2); see c. 8F infra.

[32] §17A(c); Rule 17Ac2-1. See SEC v. Netelkos, 597 F. Supp. 724, 725 S. D. N. Y. 1984) (issuer's failure to register when acting as its own transfer gent); Guttman, Federal Regulation of Transfer Agents, 34 Am. U. L. Rev. 81 (1985).

[33] §17A(b). "Clearing agency" as elaborately defined in §3(a)(23) goes well eyond the old-fashioned clearing agency that exchanges envelopes to "any erson, such as a securities depository, who (i) acts as a custodian of securities n connection with a system for the central handling of securities whereby all ecurities of a particular class or series of any issuer deposited within the system re treated as fungible and may be transferred, loaned, or pledged by bookeeping entry without physical delivery of securities certificates, or (ii) otherwise ermits or facilitates the settlement of securities transactions or the hypotheca-ion or lending of securities without physical delivery of securities certificates." ndeed, Congress made a bow toward the "certificateless society" by directing he Commission to use its authority (without further statutory specification) "to nd the physical movement of securities certificates" in connection with settle-nents among brokers and dealers. §17A(e). And until Nirvana is achieved, 12(l) authorizes the Commission to regulate both the form (that is to say, hether bearer or, in the non-SEC sense, registered) and the format (that is to ay, the style) of registered securities. See SEC, Division of Market Regulation, taff Report: Progress and Prospects: Depository Immobilization of Securities nd Use of Book-Entry Systems (1985).

[34] The National Securities Clearing Corporation, the result of a merger of hree clearing agencies that were wholly owned subsidiaries of the New York tock Exchange, the American Stock Exchange, and the NASD, was granted egistration in January 1977. National Securities Clearing Corp., Sec. Ex. Act el. 13,163, 11 SEC Dock. 1448 (1977), *aff'd and remanded* sub nom. Bradford ational Clearing Corp. v. SEC, 590 F. 2d 1085 (D. C. Cir. 1978), *on remand*

mission here is modeled basically on that of the exchanges and the NASD. But, because so many transfer agents and clearing agencies are banks, a political compromise (reminiscent of the 1964 adoption of §12(i) with respect to the registration of bank securities) split jurisdiction between the SEC and the federal bank regulators (the Comptroller of the Currency for national and District of Columbia banks, the Board of Governors of the Federal Reserve System for state member banks, and the Federal Deposit Insurance Corporation for nonmember banks that it insures) with respect to transfer agents and clearing agencies that are banks.[35]

(1) Bank transfer agents (but not bank clearing agencies) register with their bank regulators rather than the SEC.

(2) With respect to both categories, however, the Commission has a broader rulemaking authority (anything "in furtherance of the purposes" of the statute) than the bank regulators (just "the safeguarding of securities and funds").[36] This, of course, recognizes the essentiality of all transfer agents' playing in accordance with the same rules if there is to be a national clearance and settlement system.

(3) Again with respect to both bank clearing agencies and bank transfer agents, the Commission and the bank regulators are enjoined to cooperate with each other as well as with state banking

---

sub nom. National Securities Clearing Corp., Sec. Ex. Act Rel. 17,562, 22 SEC Dock. 129 (1981). This agency controls by far the preponderance of the market.

In Sec. Ex. Act Rel. 20,221, 28 SEC Dock. 1175 (1983), the Commission in a lengthy release announced the full registration of nine clearing agencies, thus culminating "eight years of cooperative efforts by the securities industry and the Commission to put in place central portions of the National System." In Sec. Ex. Act Rel. 24,046, 37 SEC Dock. 711 (1987), the Commission granted temporary registration to the MBS Clearing Corporation, a wholly owned subsidiary of the Midwest Stock Exchange, which provides clearing agency services for mortgage-backed securities issued or guaranteed by the Federal National Mortgage Corporation, or the Government National Mortgage Association.

[35] It does this by an incredibly complex definition of "appropriate regulatory agency" in §3(a)(34), which the Code manages to condense from six long paragraphs to twenty lines. §202(5); see also §202(12) (definition of "bank regulator").

[36] §17A(d)(1); Rules 17Ad-1 to 17Ad-8. See also Rules 17Ad-9 to 17Ad-13, adopted and summarized in Sec. Ex. Act Rel. 19,860, 28 SEC Dock. 68 (1983) on the maintenance of accurate security holder files and the safeguarding of funds and securities by registered transfer agents. In Sec. Ex. Act Rel. 20,581, 29 SEC Dock. 822 (1984), the SEC adopted Rule 17Ad-14 to require a registered transfer agent acting as a tender agent for a bidder (that is to say, as a depository in connection with a cash tender offer, or as an exchange agent in connection with a registered exchange offer) to establish with all qualified securities depositories special accounts for the book-entry movement of tendered securities between that agent and depository participants. A "qualified" depository is a registered clearing agency that has an automated tender offer processing program approved by the Commission pursuant to §19(b).

authorities;[37] and the bank regulators are given "primary responsibility" with respect to inspections and enforcement.[38] They also play a role with respect to registration applications by bank clearing agencies,[39] their rule changes,[40] and (as we shall see) disciplinary proceedings.[41]

d. Municipal Securities Rulemaking Board

Until 1975 the Commission had nothing to do with state or municipal securities (generically "municipals") except for some of the fraud provisions. For they have always been exempted from registration by §3(a)(2) of the 1933 Act and §§3(a)(12) and 12(a) of the 1934 Act; and municipal broker-dealers and investment advisers were exempted by §§15(a)(1) and 15A(f) of the 1934 Act and §§202(a)(11)(E) of the Advisers Act. Indeed, §3(a)(2) is the only exemption in the 1933 Act that carries over to §12(2), on civil liability, though not to §17(a),[42] and municipal securities are likewise exempted from the over-the-counter broker-dealer fraud prevention rules under §15(c)(2), though not from the narrower authority in §15(c)(1) to "define" fraudulent practices.

The 1975 amendments did not disturb this scheme so far as securities registration[43] and the fraud provisions are concerned. But they extended the SEC's jurisdiction to municipal *dealers* in a new §15B. Here again, the banks — which have never been kept out of the municipal securities business by the banking laws and, insofar as those laws permit them to act as brokers (not dealers) in securities generally, have always been excluded from the definition of "broker" (and, for that matter, "dealer") — did not relish the prospect of SEC regulation of their municipal securities activities.

So, once more, there was a jurisdictional compromise. All mu-

[37] §17A(d)(3)(A). See, e. g., SEC and Office of the Comptroller of the Currency v. Fraser, Litig. Rel. 10,512, 31 SEC Dock. 325 (D. D. C. 1984) (consent injunction against violating specified rules of both agencies by filing false financial data).

[38] §17A(d)(3)(A)(ii).

[39] §19(a)(2).

[40] §19(b)(4).

[41] See pp. 633-34 infra.

[42] See §§4 (introduction), 17(c).

[43] The so-called Tower Amendment added §15B(d) apparently to make this clear. But the language raises more questions than it answers. See Code §1105, 1 Code 442-43. On the more recent legislative efforts to put municipal financing under some sort of SEC jurisdiction, see Seligman, The Municipal Disclosure Debate, 9 Del. J. Corp. L. 647 (1985).

nicipal dealers, including banks, must register with the SEC.[44] But, instead of giving the Commission rulemaking authority with respect to practices in the municipal securities business (outside the fraud areas of §§10(b) and 15(c)(1)), Congress created the Municipal Se-

[44](1) The interrelation of the definitions of "broker," "dealer," "municipal broker," and "municipal dealer" is confusing. See 1 Code 159-60:

> (1) X3(a)(4) and 3(a)(5), which were not amended in 1975, define "broker" and "dealer" in terms of any "person" other than a bank. X3(a)(30) defines "municipal securities dealer" in terms of "any person" *including* a bank (that is not trading as a fiduciary). And X3(a)(31) defines "municipal securities broker" to mean a "broker" in municipals. As a result, one who uses the statute must remember (a) that any provision applicable to a "broker" includes a municipal broker; (b) that, on the other hand, a bank, not being a "broker," is not a "municipal securities broker"; (c) that a *non*bank "municipal securities dealer" comes within the term "dealer" wherever it is used, though a *bank* municipal dealer does not; and (d) that a "municipal securities dealer," as distinct from a "dealer," *may* be a bank.
>
> The Code attempts to achieve greater comprehensibility without substantive change by making the four definitions mutually exclusive (that is to say, limiting the definitions of "broker" and "dealer" in §§202(16) and 202(34) to nonmunicipals) and defining "municipal broker," without reference to the definition of "broker," in terms of any "person" other than a bank. So far as the definition of "municipal dealer" (§202(99)) is concerned, that term is used only when it is meant to cover both bank and nonbank municipal dealers; otherwise this draft refers to a "bank municipal dealer" or a "nonbank municipal dealer" (terms that do not have to be defined since their definitions are implicit in §202(99)).
>
> As a result, it is necessary under the Code to remember only that a bank is not a "broker," "dealer" or "municipal broker" but *can* be a "municipal dealer."

(2) One may also wonder why it is that registration is required only of bank municipal *dealers,* not bank municipal *brokers.* This follows from the fact that banks, under the 1975 amendments, are not "municipal securities brokers" because they are excluded from the definition of "broker," which is used in the §3(a)(31) definition of "municipal securities broker." To refer once more to the Code's comments (1 Code 323):

> The arguments against requiring the registration of bank municipal brokers are these:
>
> (i) The problems that led to the regulation of municipals in the 1975 amendments did not concern bank activities as brokers.
>
> (ii) Since banks do not have to register as "brokers" insofar as they effect brokerage transactions in *industrial* securities, it would seem odd to require them to register as *municipal* brokers. Indeed, the banks might well oppose registration as municipal brokers for fear that that requirement would be the entering wedge to their registration as brokers and their subjection in that capacity to the SEC unrelieved by the Municipal Board.
>
> (iii) The Glass-Steagall Act prohibits banks from acting only as dealers, not as brokers, with an exception from the dealer prohibition so far as municipals are concerned. So in a sense it is logical here to require banks to register only insofar as they come within that exception. The Code preserves existing law in this respect by excluding banks from the definition of "municipal broker."

curities Rulemaking Board. This fourth of the self-regulatory organizations differs from the other three in that it has no members (or, as in the case of the clearing agencies, "participants"). It is purely a rulemaking agency. But to that extent its relationship to the Commission follows roughly the established pattern.

The Board consists of fifteen members appointed initially by the Commission for two-year terms and thereafter by the incumbents for terms specified in the Board's rules.[45] The Board is neatly (and neutrally) divided into thirds — with five members representing bank municipal brokers and dealers, five representing non-bank municipal brokers and dealers, and five persons not associated with a broker, dealer, or municipal dealer, at least two of the last group functioning as "public representatives" (one for municipal issuers and one for municipal security investors).[46]

The rules that the Board is required to adopt apply equally to bank and non-bank municipal dealers *and brokers.* And they have to do with such matters as qualifications (including tests), the promotion of "just and equitable principles of trade," periodic inspections, the form and content of quotations, recordkeeping, and the Board's fees and charges. The Board's rules are enforced by the NASD.[47] But violation of the Board's rules, unlike the rules of the other self-regulatory organizations, is *unlawful;* for §15B(c)(1) provides that "no broker, dealer, or municipal securities dealer shall * * * effect any transaction in * * * any municipal security in contravention of any rule of the Board."[48]

[45] The rules specify a three-year term, with the terms of one-third of the Board expiring each year and a prohibition against reelection. MSRB Rule A-3(c), CCH MSRB Manual ¶3011.

[46] Section 15B was amended in 1983. The original disqualification of a public representative from being associated with a broker, dealer, or municipal dealer prevented virtually all property/casualty insurance brokers from serving; for an insurance company is commonly part of a holding company that has a subsidiary selling variable annuities through a registered broker-dealer formed solely for the purpose. The amendment permits one who is associated indirectly with a broker or dealer to serve on the Board if the broker or dealer is not a municipal broker or dealer. The amendment also permits advisers who sell mutual funds to their clients through a registered broker-dealer affiliate to serve. At the same time, the committee said it would be concerned "if, as a result of the revised eligibility criteria, public representatives were drawn exclusively from firms representing institutional investors or municipal securities issuers." H. R. Rep. No. 98-106, 98th Cong., 1st Sess. (1983) 26.

[47] §§15A(b)(7), 19(g)(1).

[48] Accordingly, violations of rules of the Municipal Board (like the other self-regulatory organization rules) are expressly covered by the injunctive provision. §21(e). Any constitutional question presented by making it unlawful to violate a rule of a self-regulatory organization is avoided by the Commission's §19(b)(1)-(2) authority over self-regulatory organization rules, especially the provision in

3. Qualifications and Discipline

We have already noticed the qualifications for *becoming* one of the self-regulatory organizations. Here we shall examine the qualifications for membership in an exchange or the NASD or participation in a clearing agency, as well as the machinery for disciplining the self-regulatory organizations themselves, their officials, members, members' associates, and participants. All this, again, is manifested at two levels: the governmental (action by the SEC or one of the bank regulators) and the self-regulatory (action by an exchange, the NASD, or a clearing agency). So far as those three self-regulatory organizations are concerned, they may be both *discipliners* and *disciplined.*

(1) Under §15(b)(4) the Commission is required to discipline any registered broker-dealer if it finds in a quasi-judicial administrative proceeding that the respondent or an associate (A) has "willfully"[49]

---

§19(b)(2) that conditions the effectiveness of all rules and changes on the Commission's approval. See 1 Code 441.

In general, Part VII of the Code integrates today's separate registration provisions for broker-dealers and municipal dealers in §§15 and 15B of the 1934 Act, as well as investment advisers under the Advisers Act, so that a single registration form will do for all three categories.

With respect to Government securities, see p. 612 supra.

[49]This word is a much abused legal workhorse, which appears not only in most of the disciplinary provisions but also in all the SEC statutes' penal provisions and in a few miscellaneous sections. See 2 Code 874-76. Its meaning depends on statutory context. United States v. Murdock, 290 U. S. 389, 394-95 (1933). In the §15(b)(4) context it has been held to mean "no more than that the person charged with the duty knows what he is doing." Hughes v. SEC, 174 F. 2d 969, 977 (D. C. Cir. 1949); Arthur Lipper Corp. v. SEC, 547 F. 2d 171, 180 (2d Cir. 1976), *rehearing en banc denied,* 551 F. 2d 915 (2d Cir. 1977), *cert. denied,* 430 U. S. 1009; Edward J. Mawod & Co. v. SEC, 591 F. 2d 588, 596 (10th Cir. 1978); Steadman v. SEC, 603 F. 2d 1126, 1135 (5th Cir. 1979), *aff'd on other grounds,* 450 U. S. 91 (1981).

The term may well mean something more in the criminal context. See Tager v. SEC, 344 F. 2d 5, 8 (2d Cir. 1965). But see State v. Fries, 214 Neb. 874, 337 N. W. 2d 398 (1983), and cases cited, where the courts adopted the "aware of what he was doing" test for criminal blue sky purposes. See also State v. Bilbrey, 349 N. W. 2d 1 (N. D. 1984).

In general, see Hawes and Sherrard, Reliance on Advice of Counsel As a Defense in Corporate and Securities Cases, 62 Va. L. Rev. 1, 82-93 (1976).

The Code abandons the term in favor of a new phrase, "without reasonable justification or excuse," for the disciplinary provisions (on the theory that that language directs attention to *conduct* rather than state of mind) and the then pending Criminal Code's "intentionally or recklessly" for the penal provisions. Inevitably, however — and it is just as well —both phrases "leave room for some play as applied to varying substantive provisions, depending on their relative technicality and perhaps other factors." 2 Code 878, citing United States v. Crosby, 294 F. 2d 928 (2d Cir. 1961), *cert. denied* sub nom. Mittelman v. United States, 368 U. S. 984; see generally 5 Loss 3368-73. In Trans World Airlines,

made or caused a material misstatement in any application for registration, required report, or proceeding with respect to registration under the statute (or has omitted a material fact required to be stated in such an application or report), (B) has been convicted of a specified securities or commodities or similar offense within ten years before applying for registration or while registered,[50] (C) "is" (*not* "has ever been") subject to an injunction (permanent or temporary) entered by "any court of competent jurisdiction" (presumably including a state or even a foreign court) with respect to specified securities or commodities or similar conduct, (D) "has willfully violated" any provision of the 1933 or 1934 or either 1940 Act, the Commodity Exchange Act, the rules under one of those Acts, or the rules of the Municipal Board, or "is unable to comply with any such provision," (E) has "willfully" aided or procured any such violation by another person, or "has failed reasonably to supervise" a person subject to his suspension who commits such a violation,[51] or (F) is subject to a Commission order barring or suspending the respondent from being associated with a broker or dealer.

Clause (D) is the most significant in the sense that it empowers the Commission to litigate in its own forum. Consequently, if it appears in court at all, it is there not as an ordinary plaintiff that has to sustain the burden of proof in a District Court but as a quasi-judicial tribunal responding to a petition to review its order in a Court of Appeals, where it not only enjoys the benefit of the sub-

Inc. v. Thurston, 469 U. S. 111 (1985), the Court construed "willful" in the double damages provision of the Age Discrimination in Employment Act of 1967, in view of the punitive purpose of that provision, to mean that "the employer * * * knew or showed reckless disregard for the matter of whether its conduct was prohibited."

[50] The imposition of a sanction under §15(b)(4) for a conviction involving the same conduct is not precluded by principles of *res judicata.* A. J. White & Co. v. SEC, 556 F. 2d 619, 624 (1st Cir. 1977), *cert. denied,* 434 U. S. 969. Nor does it constitute double jeopardy. Walter H. T. Seager, Sec. Ex. Act Rel. 20,831, 30 SEC Dock. 252, 253 (1984).

[51] There is a safe harbor provision with respect to Clause (E). "Effective supervision by broker-dealers and their supervisory employees is a critical element in the regulatory scheme." Thomson McKinnon Securities, Inc., Sec. Ex. Act Rel. 20,908, 30 SEC Dock. 488, 489 (1984). The registrant had failed to establish procedures designed to prevent and detect the primary violations found by the Commission, and in some instances its designated supervisors had failed to follow established firm procedures. See also Prudential-Bache Securities, Inc., Sec. Ex. Act Rel. 22,755, 34 SEC Dock. 1094 (1986); Shearson Lehman Brothers, Inc., Sec. Ex. Act Rel. 23,640, 36 SEC Dock. 754, 759 (1986) ("a system of supervisory procedures which rely solely on the branch manager is insufficient").

The references to the Commodity Exchange Act in Clauses (B)-(E) were added by the (unrelated) Insider Trading Sanctions Act of 1984 (infra Supp. p. 1008).

stantial evidence rule on questions of fact but also is given considerable deference with respect to choice of sanction.[52]

Although the Commission is *required,* not merely authorized, to act in these cases, the six bases for action are softened by being conditioned on a further finding that the particular sanction is "in the public interest." This gives the Commission a good deal of discretion, which is increased by the wide choice of sanctions, from censure to revocation of registration. In between those extremes the Commission may also choose to "place limitations on the [respondent's] activities, functions, or operations" or enter a suspension up to twelve months; and in consent cases (which represent the great bulk of proceedings in recent years) the Commission has been imaginative in fashioning conditions to govern the respondent's future operations.[53]

The Commission's duty under §15(b)(4) to act against the broker or dealer himself (or itself), whether for his (or its) own derelictions or those of an associate, is complemented by a duty under §15(b)(6) to proceed directly against an associate or one seeking to become an associate. If the Commission makes any of the (A)-(E) findings

[52]American Power & Light Co. v. SEC, 329 U. S. 90, 112 (1946); Seaton v. SEC, 670 F. 2d 309 (D. C. Cir. 1982). This is not to say that the sanction is immune from review for harshness. Beck v. SEC, 413 F. 2d 832 (6th Cir. 1969), *bar order reaff'd on remand* sub nom. Commonwealth Securities Corp., Sec. Ex. Act Rel. 8720 (1969), *rev'd* sub nom. Beck v. SEC, 430 F. 2d 673 (6th Cir. 1970) (the bar order was held to be punitive, not remedial); Arthur Lipper Corp. v. SEC, 547 F. 2d 171, 183-84 (2d Cir. 1976), *rehearing en banc denied,* 551 F. 2d 915 (2d Cir. 1977), *cert. denied,* 430 U. S. 1009.

Even in fraud cases it is now settled that the ordinary preponderance of the evidence standard of proof applies, and that violations need not be proved by "clear and convincing evidence" as in some types of proceedings. Steadman v. SEC, 450 U. S. 91 (1981) (administrative proceeding); Herman & MacLean v. Huddleston, 459 U. S. 375, 387-90 (1983), infra p. 975 (private action). But this last case does not weaken the requirement in Rule 9(b) of the Federal Rules of Civil Procedure that fraud be pleaded with particularity. Summers v. Lukash, 562 F. Supp. 737 (E. D. Pa. 1983).

[53]See, e. g., Hibbard & O'Connor Securities, Inc., Sec. Ex. Act Rel. 12,344, 9 SEC Dock. 411 (1976) (certain stock to be placed in a voting trust satisfactory to SEC with a view to insuring election of three outside directors satisfactory to SEC). For a collection of cases on the factors that the Commission considers under the "public interest" phrase, see O'Leary v. SEC, 424 F. 2d 908, 910 (D. C. Cir. 1970); see also Steadman v. SEC, 603 F. 2d 1126, 1140 (5th Cir. 1979), *aff'd,* 450 U. S. 91 (1981). For a study of the disparities in sanctions, see Ewick, Redundant Regulation: Sanctioning Broker-Dealers, 7 L. & Policy 421 (1985).

Rule of Practice 29 sets forth the procedures to be followed by persons barred by Commission order who thereafter submit an application for consent to associate, or to change the terms and conditions of association, with a registered broker, dealer, municipal securities dealer, investment adviser, or investment company. For a discussion of the Commission's readmission procedure, see Sec. Ex. Act Rel. 11,267, 6 SEC Dock. 346 (1975).

specified in §15(b)(4) with respect to the associate, together with a "public interest" finding, it may enter a censure or limitation-of-activities order or suspend (up to twelve months) or bar the respondent from being associated with a broker or dealer. This is the kind of suspension or bar order that, under §15(b)(4)(F), may result without more in sanctions against a *broker or dealer* who seeks to employ the suspended or barred person.[54]

(2) The Commission is given similar directions with respect to municipal dealers and their associates, with concurrent jurisdiction in the appropriate bank regulator when the municipal dealer is a bank.[55]

(3) There are similar disciplinary and consultation provisions also

[54]Section 15(b)(6) is not limited to proceeding against persons associated with *registered* broker-dealers, though other provisions [e. g., §§15(b)(7), 17(c)(1)(A)] *are* so limited. John Kilpatrick, Sec. Ex. Act Rel. 23,251, 35 SEC Dock. 914, 917 (1986). It has also been the SEC's longstanding interpretation that it has jurisdiction under §15(b)(6) to bring proceedings against persons who *were* associated with a broker-dealer when they committed the alleged violation. The 1975 amendment of former §15(b)(7), now (6), to remove the authority to proceed against "any person," regardless of whether he or it had ever engaged in the securities business or had any apparent intention of doing so, did not change this despite the reference to persons associated or seeking to become associated with a broker-dealer; for it would allow persons who had violated while in the securities business to avoid administrative sanctions by leaving and stating that they had no intention of returning. Id. at 918.

Altogether apart from the Exchange Act, §14(b) of the Securities Investor Protection Act makes it unlawful for any broker or dealer for whom a trustee has been appointed (or for whom a "direct payment procedure" has been initiated) to engage in business as a broker or dealer "unless the Commission otherwise determines in the public interest." The Commission may also bar, or suspend for any period, any officer, director, general partner, 10 percent holder of voting securities, or controlling person of any such broker or dealer from being associated with a broker or dealer if, after appropriate notice and opportunity for hearing, the Commission determines that such a bar or suspension is in the public interest. The Commission has read this as requiring proof of negligence or nonfeasance, but that will suffice without a finding of violation of a substantive provision of law. Carrol P. Teig, 46 SEC 615, 622 (1976); Dirks v. SEC, 802 F. 2d 1468 (D. C. Cir. 1986) (not unconstitutionally void for vagueness).

[55]§§15B(c)(2)-(5). Before one agency begins an investigation or proceeding with respect to a bank (or an associate), it must notify and consult with the other agency. §15B(c)(6). This extends not only to violation of §15B or the Board's rules but also, so far as Commission action is concerned, beyond to the Commission's fraud rules under §15(c)(1) or (2) and, so far as the appropriate bank regulator's action is concerned, to any Commission rule with respect to municipal securities or dealers.

With respect to both broker-dealers and municipal dealers, there are also withdrawal, cancellation, and *pendente lite* suspension provisions. §§15(b)(5), 15B(c)(3).

with respect to transfer agents, except that only the appropriate bank regulator may proceed against a transfer agent that is a bank.[56]

(4) Next there is a group of provisions with respect to action by the Commission or the appropriate bank regulator, as the case may be, against a self-regulatory organization itself (other than the Municipal Board), or an officer, director, or member (or member's associate) of a stock exchange or the NASD, or a participant in a clearing agency, or a member or employee of the Municipal Board.[57] In some of these cases it is sufficient to prove only a violation of a self-regulatory organization rule as distinct from a rule of the Commission. It should be understood, of course, that revoking the registration of the New York Stock Exchange would be the financial equivalent of dropping the H-bomb.

(5) Finally, at the level of the self-regulatory organizations themselves (other than the Municipal Board) as *doers* in the business of discipline rather than *done to:*[58]

First, their rules must provide for sanctions similar to those that may be imposed by the Commission[59] if (1) in the case of an exchange or the NASD, a member or associate violates the 1934 Act, the Commission's rules under that Act, or the rules of the exchange or association as the case may be, (2) in the case only of the NASD, a member or associate violates the rules of the Municipal Board, or (3) in the case of a clearing agency, a participant violates the agency's rules.[60]

[56] §§17A(c)(3), 17A(d)(2) and (3). Cf. also §11A(b)(6) with respect to "securities information processors" (infra pp. 692-93).

[57] §§15B(c)(8), 19(h).

[58] At both levels, since the proceedings are instituted to protect the public interest rather than to redress private wrongs, it is unnecessary to show that any customer was in fact misled. Wall St. West, Inc. v. SEC, 718 F. 2d 973, 975 (10th Cir. 1983).

[59] See pp. 630-31 supra.

[60] §§6(b)(6), 15A(b)(7), 17A(b)(3). On the extent to which NASD investigatory and disciplinary action is "governmental action," see Note, Governmental Action and the National Association of Securities Dealers, 47 Ford. L. Rev. 585 (1979).

The misconduct of an exchange member firm's employee need not occur at the member firm in order to be subject to the exchange's disciplinary authority. Vincent Musso, Sec. Ex. Act Rel. 21,135, 30 SEC Dock. 1103 (1984) ("moonlighting" activities by accountant employed full time by member firm). So far as associates are concerned, §§6(b)(6) and 15A(b)(7) are narrower than §15(b)(4) (supra p. 630) in that they do not (expressly at least) authorize the Commission to discipline a member, broker, or dealer for an associate's conduct, as §15(b)(4) does, but merely require the rules of an exchange or association to provide that "its members [and their associates] shall be appropriately disciplined for violations * * *." The contrast invites argument that the objects of self-regulatory organization discipline for associates' violations are to be only the associates and not the members with whom they are associated. This is not to say that a

Secondly, an exchange or the NASD *may* deny membership in the first instance to any person who is subject to a "statutory disqualification" and bar any such person from becoming an associate of a member; a clearing agency *may* deny participation to such a person; and these several self-regulatory organizations *must* do so when the Commission directs.[61] A person is subject to a "statutory disqualification" if, in general, one of the grounds exists for subjecting him to direct disciplinary action by the Commission or he has been found to be a cause of such disciplinary action against a broker, dealer, or municipal dealer.[62]

A final disciplinary or denial or bar order entered by a self-regulatory organization is reviewable by the Commission or the appropriate bank regulator.[63] Although the hearing may consist solely of the record before the self-regulatory organization and argument, the Commission normally reviews the self-regulatory organization's findings of violation *de novo* rather than on a "substantial evidence" basis. The Commission may not *increase* a sanction imposed by a self-regulatory organization. And the Commission's (or bank regulator's) final order, if adverse, is reviewable in an appropriate Court of Appeals like any other final order, which is to say, on a "substantial evidence" basis.[64]

The doctrine of exhaustion of administrative remedies normally prevents short-circuiting this procedure by way of an action for injunction or damages against the self-regulatory organization or its officers.[65] Indeed, the self-regulatory organizations, their disciplinary officers, and (in their prosecutory role) staff members enjoy "absolute" (as distinct from "qualified") immunity for action taken within the scope of their duties.[66]

---

member who participates in the violation might not be found to have violated as an aider and abettor. But it *is* to say that notions of liability on a *respondeat superior* basis, or as a controlling person under §20(a), do not necessarily carry over from private damage actions to self-regulatory organizations discipline. See pp. 1016-22 infra.

[61] §§6(c)(2), 15A(g)(2), 17A(b)(4)(A).

[62] §3(a)(39).

[63] §19(d)-(f). There is no stay pending administrative review unless ordered by the agency. §19(d)(2). And "in the absence of extraordinary circumstances" the Courts of Appeals are without jurisdiction to order a stay after a Commission denial. Allan v. SEC, 577 F. 2d 388, 391 (7th Cir. 1978); Waco Financial, Inc. v. SEC, CCH Fed. Sec. L. Rep. ¶98,220 (6th Cir. 1981) *semble*.

[64] §25.

[65] First Jersey Securities, Inc. v. Bergen, 605 F. 2d 690 (3d Cir. 1979), *cert. denied* sub nom. First Jersey Securities, Inc. v. Biunno, 444 U. S. 1074; Merrill Lynch, Pierce, Fenner & Smith, Inc. v. NASD, Inc., 616 F. 2d 1363 (5th Cir. 1980).

[66] Austin Municipal Securities, Inc. v. NASD, Inc., 757 F. 2d 676, 686-94 (5th Cir. 1985).

Apart from its authority to review self-regulatory organizations' disciplinary actions, the Commission exercises a supervisory role with respect to their rules. With a few qualifications, a proposed rule change may not become effective unless the Commission approves it on a finding that it "is consistent with the requirements of this title and the rules and regulations thereunder applicable to such organization."[67] The Commission may also "abrogate, add to, and delete from" the rules of a self-regulatory organization to the extent that "the Commission deems necessary or appropriate to insure the fair administration of the self-regulatory organization, to conform its rules to requirements of this title and the rules and regulations thereunder applicable to such organization, or otherwise in furtherance of the purposes of this title."[68]

The Commission has not yet used this latter authority. The language is very broad. *Query* whether it would extend to rewriting the listing rules of the New York Stock Exchange or the rules of the NASD by imposing, for example, a one-share-one-vote rule.[69]

D. SUBSTANTIVE REGULATION

1. Protection of Customers' Funds and Securities

The 1934 Act contains a number of provisions, in the nature of substantive regulation, that are designed to protect customers' funds and securities in the hands of broker-dealers:[1]

a. Recordkeeping and Reports

A registered broker, dealer, municipal dealer, or transfer agent, as well as a self-regulatory organization, must make and keep whatever records, and disseminate whatever reports, the Commission's

[67] §19(b)(2).
[68] §19(c).
[69] See p. 465 supra. Cf. Van Gemert v. Boeing Co., 520 F. 2d 1373 (2d Cir. 1975), *cert. denied,* 423 U. S. 947 (New York Stock Exchange listing agreement and section of Company Manual were considered "rules" whose violation might give rise to civil liability).

C. 8D [1] It has been suggested that the federal securities laws established two types of investor protection — information and market regulation — and that the SEC has warmly accepted its former mandate at the expense of the latter. Werner, The SEC As a Market Regulator, 70 Va. L. Rev. 755 (1984).

rules prescribe.[2] Registered clearing agencies and transfer agents are subject to further recordkeeping and reporting requirements laid down by either the Commission or the appropriate bank regulator, as the case may be.[3] And those registered clearing agencies, transfer agents, and municipal dealers that are banks must file copies of their SEC reports with their bank regulators and vice versa.[4]

b. Financial Reports

A registered broker or dealer must file balance sheets and income statements (normally audited) with the Commission annually, together with whatever additional financial information the Commission prescribes by rule, and send copies of its balance sheets and any supplemental financial information to its customers.[5]

In late 1975, after a study by a Commission-appointed Report Coordinating Group, the Commission adopted the FOCUS report (an acronym for a financial and operational combined uniform single report).[6] That report replaced a number of SEC and self-regulatory organization forms and reports. Denominated Form X-17A-5 after the Commission's previous annual report form for broker-dealers, the FOCUS report and a highly articulated Rule 17a-5 together specify who files, and sends to customers, what, and when.[7]

c. Financial Responsibility

SECURITIES EXCHANGE ACT RELEASE NO. 18,417: NET CAPITAL REQUIREMENTS FOR BROKERS AND DEALERS

24 SEC Dock. 594

Securities and Exchange Commission, 1982

* * *

Capital standards based upon liquidity for brokers and dealers have been in effect since at least 1934 when the Securities Exchange

[2] §17(a)(1). This section extends also to "securities information processors." See pp. 692-93 infra. And the Municipal Board has a parallel rulemaking duty with respect to the records of municipal brokers and municipal dealers. §15B(b)(2)(G).

[3] §17(a)(2)-(3).

[4] §17(c)(1)-(2).

[5] §17(e); Rule 17a-5.

[6] Sec. Ex. Act Rel. 11,935, 8 SEC Dock. 808 (1975); see also Sec. Ex. Act Rel. 10,612, 3 SEC Dock. 423 (1974).

[7] See also Rules 17a-10, 17a-11.

Act was adopted. Section 8(b) of the original act made it unlawful for a member of a national securities exchange to allow "in the ordinary course of business as a broker" its aggregate indebtedness to all other persons to exceed such percentage of the net capital employed in the business (but not exceeding in any case 2000%) as the Commission may by rules prescribe as necessary or appropriate. The primary purpose of this section was to prevent a broker from operating on a "shoe-string." Because of inherent limitations in the wording of Section 8(b), it never was more than a general standard of conduct for the securities business.

In 1938, Congress enacted Section 15(c)(3) of the Securities Exchange Act which authorized the Commission to adopt financial responsibility standards for brokers and dealers. In 1942, the Commission adopted Rule X-15C3-1 which incorporated the aggregate indebtedness standards of Section 8(b). The rule exempted from coverage members of national securities exchanges whose rules and practices imposed minimum capital requirements more comprehensive than those of the Commission. In succeeding years, the Commission was generally satisfied with the financial responsibility program.[a] During the years 1967-1970, however, the securities industry underwent an unprecedented financial and operational crisis. That crisis is extensively detailed in the Commission's Study of Unsafe and Unsound Practices of Brokers and Dealers[4] which the Commission was called upon to prepare for the Congress under Section 11(h) of the Securities Investor Protection Act of 1970. Referring to the operational crisis of the late 1960's, the Study exposed the structural weaknesses of an industry which could not withstand "the stresses and strains placed upon it by events of virtual hurricane force."[5] Out of this period emerged a number of legislative and administrative proposals designed to prevent recurrence of the resulting problems.

The first major development was the passage of the Securities Investor Protection Act of 1970, which was designed to give investors who dealt with brokers and dealers additional protections for their funds and securities, in the event of the insolvency of a broker

[a]ED.: In 1961 the Fifth Circuit called Rule 15c3-1 "one of the most important weapons in the Commission's arsenal to protect investors." Blaise d'Antoni & Associates, Inc. v. SEC, 289 F. 2d 276, 277 (5th Cir. 1961), *rehearing denied,* 290 F. 2d 688 (5th Cir. 1961), *cert. denied,* 368 U. S. 899. See also Rules 15c3-1a to 15c3-1d.

[4]See Securities and Exchange Commission, Study of Unsafe and Unsound Practices of Brokers and Dealers, H. R. Doc. No. 92-231, 92d Cong., 1st Sess. (1971).

[5]Id. at 11.

or dealer. Therein Congress provided additional authority to the Commission to adopt rules relating to the acceptance of custody and use of customer securities and the carrying and use of customers' deposits and credit balances. Pursuant to this authority, the Commission adopted Rule 15c3-3, which requires a broker or dealer to have and maintain possession or control of all fully-paid and excess margin securities carried by it for the account of customers and to use customers' funds or customer-related funds only in "safe" areas of its business related to financing customer transactions and to deposit in a separate bank account any such funds not so used.[b]

In the meantime the Commission also adopted Rule 17a-13, which requires quarterly counts of securities by brokers and dealers in their possession or control, in order to establish a minimum standard as to the location of securities for brokers and dealers. The Commission also improved its early-warning system to require a broker or dealer to report immediately any net capital violation or the lack of current books and records. The Commission, in addition, revised its reporting provisions to provide for more detailed surveillance of brokers and dealers and to coordinate effectively the examination programs of the Commission and the self-regulatory organizations.

Finally, the Commission, responding to Congressional concern, substantially reformed its net capital rule. The Commission eliminated the exemption in its prior net capital rule for all members of national securities exchanges and made virtually all registered brokers and dealers subject to the Commission's capital requirements.[6] The reformed rule continued the basic liquidity concept under which the securities industry had operated for many years. That concept requires a firm to have and maintain designated minimum amounts of liquid assets in relation to its aggregate indebtedness. In addition, the Commission introduced an alternative method to measure the capital adequacy of brokers and dealers. The alternative method

[b]ED.: See generally Sec. Ex. Act Rel. 11,094, 5 SEC Dock. 448 (1974); Sec. Ex. Act Rel. 11,497, 7 SEC Dock. 241 (1975); Sec. Ex. Act Rel. 17,208, 21 SEC Dock. 139 (1980). See also Sec. Ex. Act Rel. 17,209, 21 SEC Dock. 162 (1980); A. G. Becker Paribas, Inc., Sec. Ex. Act Rel. 20,492, 29 SEC Dock. 545 (1983). Under an earlier version of §15(c)(3) the Commission had adopted also Rule 15c3-2 to prohibit a broker's or dealer's use of a customer's free credit balances in the operation of his business unless he has established adequate procedures for reporting to the customer at specified intervals with respect to the amount due, with notice that the funds are not segregated, may be used in the broker's or dealer's business, and are payable on demand. Sec. Ex. Act Rel. 7325 (1964).

[6]Section 15(c)(3) of the Act was amended by the Securities Acts Amendments of 1975 to require the Commission, by September 1, 1975, to establish minimum financial responsibility requirements for all brokers and dealers.

linked the capital requirement of a broker or dealer to its customer related business as measured by the requirement of Rule 15c3-3. These reforms were significant steps in the Commission's continuing efforts to structure its rules to provide adequate protection for customers' assets while recognizing the industry's need for flexibility in efficiently allocating capital resources.

The Commission's present net capital rule requires that a broker's or dealer's "aggregate indebtedness" never be more than 1500% of its "net capital," as those terms are defined in the rule. Net capital essentially means the net worth of a broker or dealer reduced by prescribed percentages of the market value of securities owned by the broker or dealer ("haircuts") and reduced by other assets not readily convertible into cash, but including certain subordinated debt, i. e., net liquid assets. Aggregate indebtedness includes all the money liabilities of a broker or dealer, except certain specifically described items. In essence, the rule requires a broker or dealer to cover each dollar of its liabilities with not less than one dollar and six and two-thirds cents of liquid assets [i. e., 100 ÷ 15].

The alternative method of computing net capital requires a broker or dealer to maintain minimum net capital equal to the greater of $100,000 or 4% of aggregate debit items computed in accordance with the Formula for Determination of Reserve Requirements for Brokers and Dealers under Rule 15c3-3 ("Reserve Formula"), 17 C. F. R. 240.15c3-3a. The debit items in the Reserve Formula represent monies owed the broker or dealer in relation to customer transactions. The alternative method is founded on the concept that if the debit items in the Reserve Formula can be liquidated at or near their contract values, these assets, along with any cash required to be on deposit under the net capital rule, will be sufficient to satisfy all customer-related liabilities (which are represented as credit items in the Reserve Formula). As an additional safeguard, election of the alternative method requires a firm to reduce by 3% its aggregate debit items to provide, in essence, a bad debt reserve of firm capital to assure adequate resources to pay customer claims. Election of the alternative also requires that operational charges (stock record differences and suspense account items) be reflected in the Reserve Formula after seven business days, rather than after 30 business days, as permitted for those firms which have not elected the alternative method. These limitations, whether under the basic or the alternative method, allow a firm to increase its customer commitments only insofar as its net capital can support the increases.[c]

[c] ED.: In January 1985 the Commission solicited comments on a broad range

d. Hypothecation of Customers' Securities

Section 8(b) of the 1934 Act (which was §8(c) before the 1975 amendments)[8] authorizes the Commission by rule to prohibit the hypothecation or arranging for the hypothecation of

> any securities carried for the account of any customer under circumstances (1) that will permit the commingling of his securities without his written consent with the securities of any other customer, (2) that [regardless of consent] will permit such securities to be commingled with the securities of any person other than a *bona fide* customer, or (3) that [again regardless of consent] will permit such securities to be hypothecated, or subjected to any lien or claim of the pledgee, for a sum in excess of the aggregate indebtedness of such customers in respect of such securities.

Although §8 applies only to "any member of a national securities exchange, or any broker or dealer who transacts a business in securities through the medium of any such member," §15(c)(2) authorizes the Commission by rule to "define, and prescribe means

---

of questions in connection with its reexamination of the scope, adequacy, and necessity of the financial responsibility rules. Sec. Ex. Act Rel. 21,651, 32 SEC Dock. 329 (1985). And it concurrently issued a report. SEC, Directorate of Economic and Policy Analysis, Study on the Financing and Regulatory Capital Needs of the Securities Industry (1985).

For a detailed discussion of Rule 15c3-3 and the Securities Investor Protection Act (supra p. 38), see Bloomenthal and Salcito, Customer Protection from Brokerage Failures: The Securities Investor Protection Corporation and the SEC, 54 U. Colo. L. Rev. 161 (1983). The adoption of Rule 15c3-3 really shifted the focus of the Commission's financial responsibility program from merely assuring liquidity to providing more direct protection for customer funds and securities. See Molinari and Kibler, Broker-Dealers' Financial Responsibility Under the Uniform Net Capital Rule — A Case for Liquidity, 72 Geo. L. J. 1 (1983). On the "special reserve bank account for the exclusive benefit of customers," see Joseph J. Balint, Sec. Ex. Act Rel. 20,950, 30 SEC Dock. 629, 630 (1984).

The way the reserve formula works is this:

> Under the Rule, a broker-dealer is required to make a weekly computation (or in certain cases a monthly computation), as of the close of business Friday, to determine how much money it is holding which is either customer money or money obtained from the use of customer securities (i. e., formula debits). If the credits exceed the debits, the broker-dealer must deposit the excess by Tuesday morning in a Reserve Bank Account. If the debits exceed the credits, no deposit is necessary.
>
> One of the purposes of the Reserve Formula is to ensure that customers' funds held by a broker-dealer are deployed only in areas of the broker-dealer's business related to servicing its customers (i. e., debit items in the Reserve Formula) or, to the extent that the funds are not deployed in these limited areas, that they are deposited in a Reserve Bank Account.

Sec. Ex. Act Rel. 22,499, 34 SEC Dock. 266, 267 (1985), adopting the most recent amendments to the rule.

[8] The Commission's rule is still numbered 8c-1.

reasonably designed to prevent, such acts and practices as are fraudulent [or] deceptive" in connection with transactions effected by *any* broker or dealer *otherwise than on an exchange.* The Commission, therefore, covered all situations by adopting two identical sets of rules, one under each section.[9]

In 1966, in the light of the development of centralized systems for the handling and delivery of securities through the use of automated procedures, the Commission added paragraph (g) to each rule to provide that the hypothecation of customers' securities held by a clearing corporation (or other subsidiary organization of an exchange or of the NASD) or by a custodian bank pursuant to a central system in which the customers' securities are commingled with others does not of itself constitute a prohibited commingling.[10]

Even apart from statute, a broker is guilty of a conversion when, without his customer's consent, he hypothecates his customer's securities for loans in excess of the customer's indebtedness to him or commingles his securities with those of the broker or other customers.[11] And there may be legislation or blue sky rules[12] in a

[9] Rules 8c-1, 15c2-1. For a general description of these rules, see Sec. Ex. Act Rel. 2690 (1940), reprinted in 2 Loss 1193-99.

[10] Sec. Ex. Act Rel. 7896 (1966). For the exemption to be applicable, the custodian, in general, must agree to deliver the securities that it holds as directed by the system and not to assert any claim, right, or lien against the securities; the system must have safeguards for the handling, transfer, and delivery of securities; it must provide fidelity bond coverage of employees and agents of the clearing corporation or other subsidiary organization; and it must contain provision for periodic examination by independent public accountants. The exemption applies only after the Commission finds this agreement and these safeguards and provisions, as well as any amendments of them, to be adequate for the protection of investors. Ibid.

[11] See Lefever, Stockbrokers' Rehypothecation of Customers' Securities As Constituting Conversion in Pennsylvania, 13 Temp. L. Q. 312 (1939); Turner v. Schwarz, 140 Md. 465, 117 Atl. 904 (1922); Sproul v. Sloan, 241 Pa. 284, 88 Atl. 501 (1913); but see Stein v. Broder, 8 N. J. Misc. 357, 150 Atl. 194 (Sup. Ct. 1930), *aff'd per curiam,* 107 N. J. L. 536, 154 Atl. 768 (1931). Of course, when an insolvent broker or dealer, in connection with his customers' buy orders, accepts their fully paid securities for safekeeping with the intention of converting them to his own use — or accepts their securities as collateral for margin loans with the intention of selling (or hypothecating) the securities for more than the balances due from those customers and converting the proceeds to his own use — he commits a fraud. SEC v. Lawson, 24 F. Supp. 360 (D. Md. 1938).

In view, however, of Blue Chip Stamps v. Manor Drug Stores, 421 U. S. 723 (1975), infra p. 792, it does not follow from these cases that a customer who has not bought or sold a security, within the definitions of those terms to include a contract to purchase or sell (see pp. 800-01 infra) has a private right of action under Rule 10b-5. Smith v. Chicago Corp., 566 F. Supp. 66, 68-69 (N. D. Ill. 1983); Bosio v. Norbay Securities, Inc., 599 F. Supp. 1563, 1566-67 (E. D. N.

particular state. The New York General Business Law contains a provision that is in some respects more strict than §8(b) of the 1934 Act and in other respects less strict. Whereas Clause (1) of §8(b) does not attach to a hypothecation when there is no commingling, New York makes it a felony to pledge or dispose of a security under any circumstances unless the broker has a lien on the security or some special property in it or obtains the customer's consent. Again, whereas Clause (3) of §8(b) speaks in terms of the aggregate indebtedness of all customers and makes the customer's consent irrelevant, the comparable New York provision prohibits the hypothecation of a *particular* customer's securities for more than the amount of the broker's lien on those *particular* securities *unless the customer consents.*[13]

e. Inspection

Section 17(b) subjects all the records of registered brokers, dealers, municipal dealers, and transfer agents, as well as the self-regulatory organizations, to "reasonable periodic, special, or other examinations" by the Commission and the bank regulators, as the case may be.[14] Although the Commission has never had the facilities to inspect all these persons at fixed intervals, even with the increased selectivity permitted by the increasing cooperation among the SEC, the NASD, the exchanges, and the states, the inspection program is one of the most important implements in the detection

Y. 1985); Crummere v. Smith Barney, Harris Upham & Co., Inc., 624 F. Supp. 751 (S. D. N. Y. 1985).

[12] See Cal. Ad. Code, Tit. 10, c. 3, Rule 260.216.8, CCH Blue Sky L. Rep. ¶12,189.

[13] N. Y. Gen. Bus. Law §339-e, which replaced N. Y. Penal Law §956 in 1967. Although this provision is less strict than §8(b)(3) in that the customer can consent, it is stricter in that under §8(b)(3), theoretically, a broker-dealer owed $100,000 in margin accounts by all customers could hypothecate one customer's securities for that sum even though that one customer owed a much lesser amount. For an application of §339-e, see Passman v. Oliphant, 77 Misc. 2d 431, 353 N. Y. S. 2d 117 (Sup. Ct. 1974), *rev'd*, 46 A. D. 2d 878, 362 N. Y. S. 2d 18 (1st Dept. 1974). For an application of the former §956, see, e. g., People v. Atwater, 229 N. Y. 303, 128 N. E. 196 (1920); see also In re Salmon Weed & Co., Inc., 53 F. 2d 335 (2d Cir. 1931), where the court, influenced by that provision, held that a broker's unauthorized pledge of a customer's securities for a greater amount than the original loan was a conversion *ipso facto* without any tender or demand on the customer's part, and therefore limited the broker's claim against the customer's estate in bankruptcy to the difference between the customer's debt in his margin account and the damages for conversion.

[14] This extends also to "securities information processors." See p. 693 infra.

and prevention of violations not only of the recordkeeping and capital rules but also of the 1933 and 1934 Acts and the Commission's rules generally by broker-dealers.

Broker-dealer inspections are conducted as a matter of routine by accountants in the Commission's Regional Offices. Sometimes they are limited to particular phases of a firm's operation, such as its financial condition or its method of handling particular accounts. They are made on a surprise basis. And they are of three kinds: (1) routine inspections, (2) inspections for cause, which are usually limited to the subject matter of a customer's complaint; and (3) oversight inspections of self-regulatory organization members, which include a review of the latest inspection by the self-regulatory organization with a view to determining whether its inspection program is thorough and effective.

These inspections are designed not only to ferret out violations but also to educate those inspected in the legal requirements. In addition, they provide information that is useful in determining the need for new regulations or amendments to existing rules. Accordingly, most of the infractions that are discovered result in corrective measures on the basis of purely informal cautioning by the Commission's Regional Offices.

A number of provisions are directed to the multiregulator and multimembership problems:

(1) The Commission and the appropriate bank regulator are to consult with respect to their inspections of municipal dealers, transfer agents, and clearing agencies that are banks with a view to avoiding unnecessary duplication of regulation.[15]

(2) With respect to a member of more than one self-regulatory organization, the Commission, by rule or order, may relieve any of the self-regulatory organizations in question of any responsibility to inspect or receive reports or carry out other specified regulatory functions. And it may also allocate rulemaking authority when it is shared by two or more self-regulatory organizations.[16]

(3) A Commission rule implements the former authority.[17] Another rule invites the self-regulatory organizations to propose plans for allocating regulatory responsibilities.[18] And any lacuna in an effective plan will be filled by Commission direction.[19]

[15] §§17(b), 17(c)(3).

[16] §17(d)(1).

[17] Rule 17d-1, adopted by Sec. Ex. Act Rel. 12,532, 9 SEC Dock. 450 (1976

[18] Rule 17d-2, adopted by Sec. Ex. Act Rel. 12,935, 10 SEC Dock. 807 (1976 See Sec. Ex. Act Rel. 15,191, 15 SEC Dock. 1163 (1978), *amended,* Sec. Ex. Ac

One's failure to permit an authorized inspection is a violation of law that may activate the usual disciplinary, injunctive, and criminal sanctions. Moreover, it has been held in mandatory injunction actions that the inspection power does not constitute an unreasonable search and seizure within the Fourth Amendment and that, since a registered broker-dealer's books and records are held subject to the Commission's examination, even an individual registrant may not refuse to make his books and records available to the Commission on the ground that their production might tend to incriminate him.[20]

2. Short Sales

a. Pre-SEC Legal Status of Short Sales

The 1934 report of the Senate investigation described the mechanics of the modern short sale:

> Short selling is a device whereby the speculator sells stock which he does not own, anticipating that the price will decline and that he will thereby be enabled to "cover," or make delivery of the stock sold, by purchasing it at the lesser price. If the decline materializes, the short seller realizes as a profit the differential between the sales price and the lower purchase or covering price.
>
> An order is given to a broker to sell the stock short, and the order is executed on the floor of the exchange and recorded in precisely the same manner as any other order to sell. The purchaser is altogether unaware whether he is buying from a short seller or an actual owner of stocks. The seller is required to make delivery of the stocks he has sold within the period limited by the rules of the exchange. Since he has no shares to deliver, he must obtain them somewhere. The usual practice is for the broker executing

Rel. 15,723, 17 SEC Dock. 262 (1979) (plan filed by NASD in conjunction with four regional exchanges).

[19] Rule 17d-2(g).

[20] United States v. Kaufman, 429 F. 2d 240, 247 (2d Cir. 1970), *cert. denied* sub nom. Burns v. United States, 400 U. S. 925; see also SEC v. Olsen, 243 F. Supp. 338, 339 (S. D. N. Y. 1965), *contempt adjudication aff'd*, 354 F. 2d 166 (2d Cir. 1965) (Inv. Adv. Act). In Marshall v. Barlow's, Inc., 436 U. S. 307 (1978), the Court held that an inspection without a warrant under §8(a) of the Occupational Safety and Health Act of 1970, 29 U. S. C. §657(a), was an unreasonable search and seizure. But it referred to certain industries, like liquor and firearms, with "such a history of government oversight that no reasonable expectation of privacy * * * could exist for a proprietor over the stock of such an enterprise." 436 U. S. at 313. And it left the question to be decided statute by statute, emphasizing that "we base today's opinion on the facts and law concerning OSHA." 436 U. S. at 322.

the sale to borrow the stock on his customer's behalf. Usually, it is borrowed from another broker. There must be deposited with the lender of the stock the market value of the stock loaned, and the amount of this deposit varies with changes in the price of the security. If the market price rises, the deposit must be increased; and, conversely, if the market price drops, the borrower of the stock may request the return of the difference between the amount which he has deposited and the then market value of the stock. In brief, the lender is entitled at all times to have on deposit a sum equivalent to the market value of the stock. The broker uses the borrowed stock to make delivery to the person who has purchased from his customer, the short seller. Later, when the short seller covers, his broker purchases the stock in the market and delivers it to the lender. When the borrowed stock is returned, the lender repays the sum which is on deposit with him and the transaction is closed.

Where the stock borrowed is in demand, a premium is exacted by the lender for the loan of the stock. This premium at times may be substantial. * * *

In a "flat loan," the stock is loaned without the payment of interest or premium. A loan that is "flat" in the first instance may change to a loan on interest or a loan on premium when there is a change in rate.

Where a lender is also a broker, he generally lends the securities of his customers who have authorized him to do so. In the absence of agreement to the contrary, customers whose securities are loaned receive no part of any premium paid for the loan — that is retained by their broker. Nor do they participate in the interest earned on the funds deposited with their broker when he loans their stock — that also he keeps.[21]

[21] Stock Exchange Practices, Report of Com. on Banking & Currency, S. Rep. No. 1455, 73d Cong., 2d Sess. (1934) 50-51. Until the 1960s securities lending was done between broker-dealers as an accommodation. But charges began to be imposed on loans when the increased trading volume of the 1960s and early 1970s increased the demand for securities loans. And in the early 1970s broker-dealers began to turn to institutional holders to meet the growing demand. Securities are now borrowed to cover not only short sales but also "fails" (securities sold but not available for delivery) as well as option and arbitrage positions.

Speculation is only one of the motivations for short selling. Among the nonspeculative kinds of short selling are the so-called technical short sale (for example, by arbitrageurs, specialists, and odd-lot dealers), the hedging short sale, the short sale for tax purposes, and the sale "against the box." 2 SEC, Report of Special Study of Securities Markets, H. R. Doc. No. 95, 88th Cong., 1st Sess. (1963) 247, 249-51.

The Senate report had this to say about the last device: "A type of sale not technically a short sale, but similar in nature, is a sale 'against the box.' In such a transaction, the seller owns and possesses stock which he can deliver but which for some reason he prefers not to deliver. This is a device which can be employed by corporate officials and insiders who desire to sell their corporation's

Daniel Drew, one of the nineteenth century financial buccaneers, was the author of the jingle:

> He that sells what isn't his'n,
> Must buy it back or go to prison.[22]

This bit of doggerel expresses the feeling — which seems to have been shared by legislators in different ages and different lands — that the very idea of a person's selling something he does not own, in the hope of buying it back later at a lower price, is essentially immoral. The result is that short selling has been a favorite whipping boy, both when it has deserved to be and when it has not.

More than three centuries ago the Dutch first banned short selling and then subjected it to special taxation, but both schemes were ignored and in time the laws were repealed. Napoleon attacked the practice in 1802 by requiring actual delivery of securities and making short sales of public securities criminal, but these regulations were not too strictly enforced and in 1885 the French law was changed.[23] On June 17, 1864, in the closing days of the Civil War, Congress prohibited short sales of gold. In those days gold was traded on the New York Stock Exchange like a commodity because the large amounts of paper money had driven it out of circulation. But the law was repealed on July 2 after a two-week increase in the price of 100 gold dollars from about 200 paper dollars to almost 300.[24] Germany enacted a stringent Exchange Law in 1896. This act, among other things, prohibited all future dealings in grain and in mining and industrial stocks and permitted such dealings in other securities only between persons who entered their names on an "Exchange Register."[25] The statute had been favored by the agrarians on the theory that short selling was responsible for the low agricultural prices, and the act was designed to stop speculation by

---

stock short without disclosing such short selling. Like the ordinary short seller, he borrows stock for the purpose of making delivery. It is contended by stock-exchange authorities that a sale 'against the box' is not a short sale, since the customer need not buy the stock back but may make delivery from the securities in his box. It is plain, however, that when a person initially makes a sale 'against the box' but subsequently changes his mind, there is nothing to prevent him from covering in the open market. In such case he is indistinguishable from any other short seller." Stock Exchange Practices, supra, at 52.

[22] See B. White, The Book of Daniel Drew (1910) 180.

[23] See J. Flynn, Securities Speculation (1934) 266-70; J. Meeker, Short Selling (1932) 205-07, 217-21; Stevens, The Utility of Speculation in Modern Commerce, 7 Pol. Sci. Q. 419, 419-20 (1892).

[24] 13 Stat. 132, 344 (1864); J. Meeker, Short Selling (1932) 232-34; J. Eames, The New York Stock Exchange (1894) c. 24, New York Gold Exchange.

[25] Börsengesetz, RGB (1896) Nr. 15, Art. 4, §50.

the general public. But the law was full of loopholes and was substantially amended in 1908.[26]

In England Sir John Barnard's "act to prevent the infamous practice of stock-jobbing," passed in 1734, voided puts and calls, as well as all contracts to sell "public securities" when the seller did not have possession or legal or beneficial ownership, and subjected persons participating in such transactions to fine.[27] But as early as 1838 short sales were held to be legal.[28] Then the act was repealed in 1860.[29] And in 1893 a law, which is still on the books, was passed specifically authorizing short sales.[30]

Essentially this same legislative pattern has been repeated in many of the American states. For example, a New York statute of 1813 prohibited short sales of stock and United States or state bonds.[31] This act was modified in 1830[32] and repealed in 1858 in favor of a provision (now in the General Obligation Law) that specifically authorizes short sales.[33] Today the courts' touchstone in distinguishing between gambling contracts on the one hand and short sales of securities (or commodity futures contracts or contracts to sell securities "when issued") on the other hand is whether there was an intent to deliver when the contract was made rather than merely to adjust price differences later.[34]

This was the status of the short sale when in early 1932 the Senate resolved to determine to what extent the "bear raiders"

[26] Börsengesetz, RGB (1908) Nr. 27. The 1908 law remained on the books until the Nazi regime. See U. S. Treasury Dept., Office of the General Counsel, Germany — Preliminary Report on Selected Financial Laws, Decrees and Regulations — Corporate Securities, Dividends and Profits (1944). See generally J. Meeker, German Regulation of Stock Exchanges 1896-1908, 15 Stock Exchange Practices, Hearings Before S. Com. on Banking & Currency, 73d Cong., 2d Sess. (1934) 7159-65.

[27] 7 Geo. 2, c. 8, §VIII (1734).

[28] Hibblewhite v. McMorine, 5 M. & W. 462, 151 Eng. Reprint 195 (Ex. 1838), cited with approval in Clews v. Jamieson, 182 U. S. 461, 489 et seq. (1901), infra n. 34.

[29] 23 Vict., c. 28 (1860).

[30] "The goods which form the subject of a contract of sale may be either existing goods, owned or possessed by the seller, or goods to be manufactured or acquired by the seller after the making of the contract of sale, in this Act called 'future goods.'" Sale of Goods Act 1893, 56 & 57 Vict., c. 71, §5(1).

[31] 2 L. 1813, p. 187, §18.

[32] 1 Rev. Stat. (2d ed. 1836) *710, §6.

[33] L. 1858, c. 134, modified by L. 1897, c. 417, §22, later Pers. Prop. Law §33(1), now Gen. Oblig. Law §5-1101; see also UCC §2-105(2).

[34] Hurd v. Taylor, 181 N. Y. 231, 73 N. E. 977 (1905); cf. Clews v. Jamieson, 182 U. S. 461, 489 et seq. (1901) (sale of securities for future delivery, with a dictum on short sales). But see p. 242 supra, as applied to futures trading in securities indexes (see pp. 232, 241 n. 35, 241 n. 37), where there is nothing to deliver.

were preventing recovery.[35] The Banking and Currency Committee found in its 1934 report:

> Few subjects relating to exchange practices have been characterized by greater differences of opinion than that of short selling. The proponents of short selling contend that it is a necessary feature of an open market for securities; that in a crisis short sellers are useful in maintaining an orderly market; and that their activities serve as a cushion to break the force of a decline in the price of stocks. Its opponents assert that short selling unsettles the market, forces liquidation, depresses prices, accelerates declines, and has no economic value or justification.[36]

Apparently finding it impossible to discover where the truth lay between the extreme views that had been expressed, Congress in §10(a) simply placed the practice of short selling in registered securities under the plenary rulemaking authority of the Commission.[37]

[35] President Hoover is said to have been convinced that the stock market situation was primarily due to the "bear raids" of short sellers, who were canceling out his measures for halting the panic, and in March 1932 the Senate passed a resolution calling for an investigation by its Banking and Currency Committee. Nor was Hoover alone. "It is of more than passing interest," Mr. John T. Flynn observed at the time, "that the blaze of popular wrath against the Exchange flamed up not when people found themselves stripped of their life's savings in the disorderly declines of 1929 and 1930, but later in 1931 when the notion got about that the decline was the work of a group of wicked bear raiders — professional speculators — who by selling short were driving prices lower and preventing recovery." J. Flynn, Security Speculation (1934) 216. At any rate, it was the 1932 Senate resolution — bolstered by a second resolution very early in the Roosevelt Administration containing a new set of teeth with a harder bite — that led to the first securities statutes. S. Res. 56, 73d Cong., 1st Sess. (1933); see also S. Res. 97, 73d Cong., 1st Sess. (1933). Both are set out in Stock Exchange Practices, Report of S. Com. on Banking & Currency, S. Rep. No. 1455, 73d Cong., 2d Sess. (1934) 2-3. For a popular account of the investigation, see F. Pecora, Wall Street Under Oath (1939).

[36] Stock Exchange Practices, Report of S. Com. on Banking & Currency, S. Rep. No. 1455, 73d Cong., 2d Sess. (1934) 50.

[37] The same section applies to the use or employment of any "stop-loss order" in connection with a registered security. "A stop-loss order is an order to buy or sell a stated amount of a security at the market if and when a transaction occurs at a designated price. The purpose of such an order may be to limit the loss on an open commitment; to safeguard a profit on an open commitment; or to insure the making of a new commitment when a specified price level is reached." SEC, Report on the Feasibility and Advisability of the Complete Segregation of the Functions of Dealer and Broker (1936) 26. But the Commission has never implemented that portion of §10(a) by rule.

The SEC Acts contain three other provisions on short selling by certain persons. Section 16(c) of the Exchange Act and §30(f) of the Investment Company Act, which prohibit short sales by certain types of corporate insiders, have already been noticed. See pp. 542 n. 4, 543 supra. In addition, §12(a)(3) of the Investment Company Act gives the Commission rulemaking power (which it has

b. SEC Short-Selling Rules

Effective in 1938 — and as since amended partly in response to the evolving National Market System — there are three short-selling rules:

Rule 3b-3 defines "short sale":

> The term "short sale" means any sale of a security which the seller does not own or any sale which is consummated by the delivery of a security borrowed by, or for the account of, the seller. A person shall be deemed to own a security if (1) he or his agent has title to it; or (2) he has purchased, or has entered into an unconditional contract, binding on both parties thereto, to purchase it but has not yet received it; or (3) he owns a security convertible into or exchangeable for it and has tendered such security for conversion or exchange; or (4) he has an option to purchase or acquire it and has exercised such option; or (5) he has rights or warrants to subscribe to it and has exercised such rights or warrants: Provided, however, That a person shall be deemed to own securities only to the extent that he has a net long position in such securities.

Rule 10a-1, subject to a number of exceptions of a technical sort, prohibits a short sale (1) *below* the last sale price or (2) *at* the last sale price unless that price is above the next preceding different price; and each exchange may elect whether short sales are to be governed by this "tick test" in terms of its own market or any market in the composite "transaction reporting system."[38] In other words, after sales at 49⅞ and 50 an indefinite number of short sales may be effected at 50; but, after sales at 49⅞ and 49¾, the minimum price at which a short sale may be effected is 49⅞.[39]

The third rule, Rule 10a-2, has to do with covering transactions. If on the due date of delivery of a security sold pursuant to an order marked "long" the member has not received the security from the customer, he must cover the open position unless he knows or has been informed by the seller either (1) that the security is in transit to him, or (2) that the seller owns the security, that it is then impracticable to deliver it and that it will be delivered as soon as possible without undue inconvenience or expense.[40]

---

never exercised) to regulate short sales of any securities by registered investment companies except in connection with underwritings in which they participate.

[38] Both New York exchanges have elected the second alternative.

[39] Every sale order must be marked "long" or "short." Rule 10a-1(b) to (d); see Naftalin & Co., Inc. v. Merrill Lynch, Pierce, Fenner & Smith, Inc., 469 F. 2d 1166, 1172 n. 5 (8th Cir. 1972).

[40] See Edwards & Hanly v. Wells Fargo Securities Clearance Corp., 602 F. 2d 478, 486 (2d Cir. 1979), *cert. denied,* 444 U. S. 1045. The rule does not in so

Beginning in 1975 the Commission repeatedly questioned whether the great increase in sophistication of the regulatory framework since 1938, together with the evolution of a central market system, might not permit detection of destructive short selling by the Commission or the self-regulatory organizations without complex federal regulation of each short sale.[41] In 1977 the Commission held a public investigation and rulemaking proceeding on the question.[42] But in 1980 the Commission announced an apparent consensus among those who commented that the "tick test" was working well and should not be modified.[43]

For four decades the rules did not apply to the over-the-counter market, in part because last sale reports were not available. With the implementation in 1975 of a consolidated reporting system for transactions in listed securities both on the exchanges and in the over-the-counter market, the Commission extended the rule to over-the-counter transactions in reported securities.[44] But in 1985, concurrently with its move to extend unlisted trading privileges in National Market System securities,[45] as well as its allowing listed securities not included in the consolidated transaction reporting system to be designated as National Market System securities,[46] the Commission proposed amendments,[47] which it adopted in 1986,[48] to exclude transactions in National Market System securities from the rules until resolution of the question of over-the-counter short sale regulation.

These rules seem pretty well to have taken the caffeine out of the short sale. Nevertheless, Representative Sabath, inveighing against the evils of short selling, introduced a bill in May 1947 that would have levied a 5 percent tax on all short sales of stocks or commodities — thus completing the circle begun by his Dutch predecessors of three centuries ago.[49]

many words require that the position be covered. It prohibits delivery with a borrowed security or failure to deliver on the due date. This leaves no alternative but covering.

[41] Sec. Ex. Act Rel. 11,276, 6 SEC Dock. 378, 381 n. 4 (1975); see also Sec. Ex. Act Rel. 11,468, 7 SEC Dock. 150, 154 (1975); Sec. Ex. Act Rel. 12,384, 9 SEC Dock. 495, 496 (1976).

[42] Sec. Ex. Act Rel. 13,091, 11 SEC Dock. 1229 (1976).

[43] Sec. Ex. Act Rel. 17,347, 21 SEC Dock. 781 (1980).

[44] Sec. Ex. Act Rel. 22,127, 33 SEC Dock. 622, 626-27 (1985). With respect to "reported securities," see p. 692 infra.

[45] See p. 593 n.d, 7th par., supra.

[46] See p. 697 n. 39.

[47] Sec. Ex. Act Rel. 22,414, 33 SEC Dock. 1456 (1985).

[48] Sec. Ex. Act Rel. 22,975, 35 SEC Dock. 199 (1986).

[49] H. R. 3593, 80th Cong., 1st Sess. (1947). No hearings were held.

3. Credit Regulation

a. The Statutory Credit Provisions and Their Philosophy [§7]

Section 7(a) directs the Board of Governors of the Federal Reserve System to prescribe rules from time to time "with respect to the amount of credit that may be initially extended and subsequently maintained" on any nonexempted security.

Section 7(c) makes it unlawful for an exchange member, broker, or dealer, "directly or indirectly, to extend or maintain credit or arrange for the extension or maintenance of credit to or for any customer" on any nonexempted security in contravention of the Board's rules. It is unlawful likewise for any member, broker, or dealer to extend or maintain credit, or arrange for its extension or maintenance, on any collateral *other than* securities, or without collateral at all, except insofar as the Board's rules may permit (A) the maintenance for a limited period of credit initially extended in conformity with its rules and (B) the extension or maintenance of credit for some purpose other than purchasing or carrying securities. Acting primarily under §7(c), the Board adopted Regulation T.[50]

Section 7(d) authorizes the Board to adopt similar rules governing the extension or maintenance of credit by any person not covered by §7(c) when the purpose of the credit is to purchase or carry a security. But it exempts, among other things, not only a loan on an exempted security but also "a loan by a bank on a security other than an equity security." Under this section the Board adopted Regulation U, applicable only to banks, and (in 1968) Regulation G, applicable to certain lenders not covered by Regulation T or U.

The Act and its legislative history indicate that the credit provi-

[50]Section 7 as a whole does not apply to exempted securities. Here as elsewhere in the Act it is the SEC rather than the Board that has the authority to define "exempted securities." §3(a)(12), supra p. 422. The Commission has exempted from the §7(c) prohibition against extension of credit on unregisteredsecurities (1) those exempted from registration by Rule 12a-5, the "temporary" exemption of substituted or additional securities, and (2) securities traded on an exempted exchange. Rules 7c2-1, 12a-5. These two categories of securities are treated, in effect, as if they were registered for purposes of §7(c). Apart from §7, however, the New York Stock Exchange imposes its own margin requirements (see p. 665 infra) of 5 percent of principal amount on positions in Government bonds and 15 percent of principal amount or 25 percent of market (whichever is lower) on positions in other exempted securities (for the most part state and municipal bonds), unless in either case the Exchange reduces the requirement on written application with respect to a particular issue. N. Y. Stock Ex. Rule 431(c)(2), CCH N. Y. Stock Ex. Guide ¶2431.

sions rest on three separate philosophies, which are not altogether consistent:

(1) The statute itself speaks in terms of "preventing the excessive use of credit for the purchase or carrying of securities." So does the House report:

> The main purpose [of the credit provisions] is to give a Government credit agency an effective method of reducing the aggregate amount of the nation's credit resources which can be directed by speculation into the stock market and out of other more desirable uses of commerce and industry — to prevent a recurrence of the pre-crash situation where funds which would otherwise have been available at normal interest rates for uses of local commerce, industry, and agriculture, were drained by far higher rates into security loans and the New York call market.[51]

(2) The report of the Senate Banking and Currency Committee's investigation, on the other hand, says that the margin provisions are also intended "to protect the margin purchaser by making it impossible for him to buy securities on too thin a margin."[52] As Chairman Rayburn of the House Commerce Committee put it in language no less forceful for its mixed metaphor: "A reasonably high margin requirement is essential so that a person cannot get in the market on a shoe string one day and be one of the sheared lambs when he wakes up the next morning."[53]

(3) At the same time, Congress apparently had in mind also that the Board's powers would be used to prevent undue market fluctuations and help stabilize the economy generally, because it directed the Board to adopt for its initial rules a formula based on the nature of past price movements of the collateral.

b. The Federal Reserve Formulas and Percentages

In the early and most recent years, at least, the chief emphasis seems to have been placed on this third philosophy. Although there

[51] H. R. Rep. No. 1383, 73d Cong., 2d Sess. (1934) 8; see Naftalin & Co., Inc. v. Merrill Lynch, Pierce, Fenner & Smith, Inc., 469 F. 2d 1166, 1180 (8th Cir. 1972) (§7 "is more concerned with the regulation of macro-economic conditions"); Bennett v. United States Trust Co. of N. Y., 770 F. 2d 308, 312-13 (2d Cir. 1985), *cert. denied,* 106 S. Ct. 800.

[52] Stock Exchange Practices Report of S. Com. on Banking & Currency, S. Rep. No. 1455, 73d Cong., 2d Sess. (1934) 11. The House report refers to this as "a by-product of the main purpose." H. R. Rep. No. 1383, 73d Cong., 2d Sess. (1934) 8.

[53] 78 Cong. Rec. 7700 (1934).

is no statutory requirement that the margin be the same for lenders of all types, the Board has never differentiated. Since November 1974 the margin requirement has stood at 50 percent of current market value.[54] But it has oscillated between 40 percent and, for a period of more than a year beginning in January 1945, 100 percent. "While it was recognized," Board Chairman Eccles stated shortly after that "dry" interval, "that margin requirements would have only a minor influence in combatting general inflation, the Board nevertheless felt that it should do what it could to curb inflationary

[54]This means that one who buys 100 shares of a "margin security" at $100 must put up either $5000 in cash or $10,000 of other "margin securities," which at 50 percent of their market value equals the required $5000 deposit. See Jacksich v. Thomson McKinnon Securities, Inc., 582 F. Supp. 485, 493 (S. D. N. Y. 1984), citing the text.

Regulation T defines "margin security" to mean "any registered security, OTC margin stock, OTC margin bond, or any security issued by either an open-end investment company or unit investment trust" registered under the 1940 Act. §2(o). An "OTC margin stock" is any over-the-counter equity security that the Board "has determined has the degree of national investor interest, the depth and breadth of market, the availability of information respecting the security and its issuer, and the character and permanence of the issuer to warrant being treated like an equity security traded on a national securities exchange." Reg. T, §2(s); Reg. U, §2(j); Reg. G, §2(k). And an "OTC margin bond" is an over-the-counter debt security that meets three requirements: (1) at least $25 million principal amount was outstanding at the time of the original issue; (2) the issue was registered under the 1933 Act and the issuer either files reports under the 1934 Act or is an insurance company within §12(g)(2)(G) of that Act; (3) the lending broker or dealer "has a reasonable basis for believing that the issuer is not in default on interest or principal payments."

There are some 3100 "OTC margin stocks" on the list that the Board publishes from time to time. See CCH Fed. Sec. L. Rep. ¶22,256. On the requirements for inclusion in the list, see Reg. T, §17; Reg. U, §7; Reg. G, §6. In 1984 the Board amended all these regulations in order automatically to permit brokers and dealers to lend on over-the-counter securities designated for trading in the National Market System portion of NASDAQ. See p. 600 supra. The Board observed that, unlike other securities traded in the over-the-counter market, "last sale" reporting was required of National Market System securities, which were included in the System under two sets of criteria developed by the NASD with the approval of the SEC. See pp. 696-97 infra. There were 1050 stocks then traded in the System. All this is without interruption of the Board's practice of continuing from time to time to publish its list of *other* over-the-counter margin stocks.

Notwithstanding all this, the only test when an exempt security or a registered nonconvertible debt security or an "OTC margin bond" is purchased (or deposited in a margin account with a broker-dealer to secure the purchase of another security) — or when a "nonmargin stock" (see p. 657 par. (2), infra) is purchased (or so deposited with a bank or other lender) — is "good faith loan value." Reg. T, §18(b); Reg. U, §8(b); Reg. G, §7(b). This means, the Board has said, that the maximum loan value of any such collateral "should be the amount which the bank would customarily lend on such collateral if that were the only collateral for the loan." 24 Fed. Res. Bul. 1042 (1938).

developments brought about by speculative activity in the stock markets."[55]

c. Extension of Credit by Brokers and Dealers [Reg. T]

Regulation T reflects the fact that purchases of securities, like purchases of any merchandise, may be effected either for cash or on credit. A customer who buys securities for cash pays the broker or dealer outright the full amount of the purchase price. On the other hand, a customer who buys on credit pays only part of the purchase price in cash and receives an extension of credit from the broker or dealer for the unpaid balance; usually the broker or dealer in turn uses the customer's securities so purchased as collateral for bank loans to finance the balance of the purchase price, as we have seen in our examination of the SEC's rehypothecation rules.[56] Under Regulation T, purchases for cash are usually made in "cash accounts" (there are also six special purpose accounts), and credit purchases are made in "margin" accounts. The usual credit purchases are treated in §4 of the regulation, cash purchases in §8.

Section 4(a) starts with the premise that "All transactions not specifically authorized for inclusion in another account shall be recorded in the margin account." Section 4(c)(3) goes on to provide that "A margin call shall be satisfied within 7 business days after the margin deficiency was created or increased." The broker or dealer may obtain an extension from a national securities exchange or the NASD. But, when this is not done, he is required by §4(d) to liquidate an appropriate amount of securities.

[55]Eccles, Readjustment of Margin Requirements, 33 Fed. Res. Bul. 149, 149-50 (1947). Professor Friend concluded in 1982: "The empirical evidence on the impact of margin regulation on market efficiency is conflicting * * *." Friend, Economic and Equity Aspects of Securities Regulation (Rodney L. White Center for Financial Research, Wharton School, U. Pa., Working Paper No. 7-82, 1982) 34-35.

[56]See p. 641 supra. On the technique, the justification, and the economic function of margin trading, see Twentieth Century Fund, Inc., The Security Markets (1935) c. 9. For an economic analysis of the claim that speculation aids in directing the flow of savings into those industries in which the need for additional funds is greatest, see id., c. 10. For a comprehensive discussion of security credit generally, see J. Bogen and H. Krooss, Security Credit: Its Economic Role and Regulation (1960). For a technical discussion of all the margin rules, together with related bookkeeping procedures and practices as of November 21, 1983, see R. Rittereiser, Margin Regulations and Practices (2d ed., J. Geelan, 1983).

A cash account may be used, under §8(a), to

> (1) buy for or sell to any customer any security if: (i) there are sufficient funds in the account; or (ii) the creditor accepts in good faith the customer's agreement that the customer will promptly make full cash payment for the security before selling it and does not contemplate selling it prior to making such payment;
>
> (2) buy from or sell for any customer any security if: (i) the security is held in the account; or (ii) the creditor accepts in good faith the customer's statement that the security is owned by the customer or the customer's principal, and that it will be promptly deposited in the account.[57]

Normally, if full cash payment is not obtained within seven business days after the date of purchase, §8(b) requires the broker or dealer "promptly" to cancel or otherwise liquidate the transaction. But that is simply an outside period. The privilege of using a cash account is conditioned on acceptance "in good faith" of the customer's agreement that he will "promptly make full cash payment." And that does not give the broker or dealer the privilege of automatically delaying collection for seven business days.

One of the other special accounts is a "nonsecurities credit account," which is used for transactions in commodities or foreign exchange or for extensions of "secured or unsecured nonpurpose credit."[58] But every extension of credit (except in a commodity or foreign exchange transaction) is considered to be for the purpose of buying or carrying or trading in securities unless the broker or dealer "accepts in good faith from the customer a written statement that it is not purpose credit"; and "good faith" means that the broker or dealer "shall be aware of the circumstances surrounding the extension of credit and shall be satisfied that the statement is truthful."[59]

Although §7(a) of the Act directs the Board to require the *maintenance* of certain margins as well as their initial deposit, no margin calls are required after the initial deposit, no matter how much the market falls. Regulation T, however, specifically saves the right of the broker or dealer to call for additional collateral of any description for his own protection, as well as the right of the exchanges to adopt more stringent rules on both initial extension and mainte-

[57] Paragraph (2) reflects the fact that Regulation T normally applies the same 50 percent margin requirement to short sales.

[58] Reg. T, §9(a).

[59] Id., §§2(u), 9(b); see Naftalin & Co., Inc. v. Merrill Lynch, Pierce, Fenner & Smith, Inc., 469 F. 2d 1166, 1175 (8th Cir. 1972); SEC v. Packer, Wilbur & Co., 498 F. 2d 978, 981 n. 1 (2d Cir. 1974).

nance, and the exchanges do have maintenance requirements, as we shall see.[60]

d. Extension of Credit by Banks [Reg. U]

Section 7(d) of the Act and Regulation U are more restricted in scope than §7(c) and Regulation T, although the gap was narrowed by the amendment of Regulation U concurrently with the adoption of Regulation G in early 1968 and then by the amendment of §7 itself in mid-1968 together with subsequent amendments of the regulation:

(1) Although §7(d) authorizes the Board to regulate extensions of credit "by any person not subject to subsection (c)" as long as he lends "in the ordinary course of his business," the credit provisions of Regulation U have always applied only to banks.[61]

(2) Although §7(d) extends to *any* bank loan for the purpose of purchasing or carrying *any* security, except a loan "on a security other than an equity security," Regulation U applies only to extensions of credit on "margin stock" for the purpose of purchasing or carrying "margin stock";[62] and that term is defined to mean any exchange-traded stock, an "OTC margin stock," a debt security convertible into, or carrying a right to purchase, a margin stock, any such right itself, and most investment company securities.[63]

(3) Until 1968, §7(c) gave no loan value whatever to unregistered securities and §7(d), by contrast, was silent on the question. The 1934 legislative hearings reveal several reasons for the distinction between brokers and banks so far as the eligibility of unregistered securities for credit is concerned. On the one hand, brokers were prohibited from extending credit on unregistered securities because, their market value being usually indefinite, the lenders could

[60] See p. 665 infra.

[61] With respect to foreign banks, see p. 608 supra; pp. 659-61 infra.

[62] Reg. U, §1(b).

[63] Reg. U, §2(h). On the definition of "OTC margin stock," see p. 654 n. 54 supra.

Until March 31, 1982, Regulation U applied more broadly to extensions of credit on *any* stock for the purpose of purchasing or carrying "margin stock." The reason for the pre-1982 limitation to loans collateralized by stock of some kind was to avoid subjecting banks to the administrative burden of determining the purpose of all their loans regardless of collateral, particularly since it was assumed that most persons who finance their stock purchases at the bank tend in fact to pledge stock as collateral. See Solomon and Hart, Recent Developments in the Regulation of Securities Credit, in Practising Law Institute, Second Annual Institute on Securities Regulation (1971) 167, 174.

otherwise evade the margin restrictions with respect to registered securities by extending credit on a package of registered and unregistered securities and overvaluing the latter. On the other hand, it was thought that banks (which in any event were subject to an additional check by virtue of periodic bank examinations) would handle loans on unregistered securities as a purely commercial matter, so that they would be less apt to engage in similar practices.[64]

As of July 29, 1968, on the recommendation of the SEC's "Special Study,"[65] and with everybody's blessing, §§7(a), 7(c), and 7(d) were amended to delete all the restrictions to "registered" securities. And the Board's regulations have been appropriately accommodated to certain over-the-counter securities, as we have seen.[66]

(4) Section 7(d), unlike §7(c), gives the Board an exemptive authority, which it has used — although the Board has achieved much the same result under Regulation T through the pre-1983 "special miscellaneous account" and its successors.

(5) Banks' stock-collateralized loans, in the nature of things, may be made for purposes altogether unrelated to the purchasing or carrying of securities — so-called nonpurpose loans. To make sure that Regulation U is complied with unless a loan secured by "margin stock" is clearly "nonpurpose," the bank must obtain a statement executed on the Board's Form U-1 by both the borrower and a duly authorized officer of the bank before the credit is extended (except that this requirement does not apply in connection with routine loans to brokers and dealers, in view of their regulation by the SEC, as well as certain exempted loans). The statement must affirmatively describe the purpose of the loan, and it must be accepted by the officer in good faith.[67]

The "carrying" as distinct from the "purchasing" part of §7(d) of the Act is defined to include "credit that enables a customer to maintain, reduce, or retire indebtedness originally incurred to purchase a security that is currently a margin stock."[68]

[64] 15 Stock Exchange Practices, Hearings Before S. Com. on Banking & Currency, 73d Cong., 2d Sess. (1934) 6473-74; Stock Exchange Regulation, Hearing Before House Com. on Int. & For. Commerce on H. R. 7852 and H. R. 8720, 73d Cong., 2d Sess. (1934) 92, 687; see also 4 SEC, Report of Special Study of Securities Markets, H. R. Doc. No. 95, 88th Cong., 1st Sess. (1963) 18-19.

[65] 4 id. at 22-23, 38-39.

[66] See p. 654 n. 54, 657 supra.

[67] Reg. U, §2(c); Serzysko v. Chase Manhattan Bank, 290 F. Supp. 74 (S. D. N. Y. 1968), *aff'd per curiam,* 409 F. 2d 1360 (2d Cir. 1969), *cert. denied,* 396 U. S. 904.

[68] Reg. U, §2(c); Serzysko v. Chase Manhattan Bank, 290 F. Supp. 74, 83 (S. D. N. Y. 1968), *aff'd per curiam,* 409 F. 2d 1360 (2d Cir. 1969), *cert. denied,* 396 U. S. 904; see Solomon and Hart, Simplicity v. Effectiveness: Trade-Offs in

e. Extension of Credit by Persons Other Than Brokers, Dealers, or Banks [Reg. G]

The "Special Study" confirmed the existence of a group of unregulated moneylenders (or "factors," as they are sometimes called) that financed the purchase or carrying of securities, either intermittently or regularly.[69] As early as 1959 the Board codified a 1946 interpretation[70] by adopting §3(q) of Regulation U. That section applied Regulation U to credit extended to any customer that was not subject to Regulation T or U and that was engaged, "principally, or as one of the customer's important activities," in the business of extending credit (which is to say, relending) for the purpose of purchasing or carrying margin stocks.[71]

In 1968 the Board hit the problem head on by adopting Regulation G. Unlike the two older regulations, this one necessarily begins with a registration requirement. As the regulation now reads, every person who "in the ordinary course of business" and during any calendar quarter extends or maintains $100,000 or more of credit secured by any "margin stock,"[72] or who has $500,000 or more of such credit outstanding at any time during the quarter, must register within thirty days after the end of the quarter.[73]

Lenders under Regulation G, like banks under Regulation U, are subject to whatever margin requirements the Board sets from time to time, and thus far it has specified the same figures as for Regulations T and U.[74]

f. Obtaining of Credit by Persons Other Than Brokers or Dealers [Reg. X]

Until 1971 nothing in the 1934 Act affected *borrowers* other than brokers or dealers.[75] And, particularly when domestic credit was tight, borrowers went to foreign banks. Although arguably a for-

---

Regulating Credit to "Carry" Securities, 25 Mercer L. Rev. 415, esp. at 418 (1974).

[69] SEC, Report of Special Study of Securities Markets, H. R. Doc. No. 95, 88th Cong., 1st Sess. (1963) 5-6.

[70] 32 Fed. Res. Bul. 874 (1946).

[71] See 45 Fed. Res. Bul. 485 (1959); Cooper v. North Jersey Trust Co. of Ridgewood, N. J., Inc., 226 F. Supp. 972, 976 (S. D. N. Y. 1964).

[72] The Regulation G definition of "margin stock" (§2(i)) is identical with the Regulation U definition (§2(h)), supra p. 654 n. 54.

[73] Reg. G, §3(a)(1).

[74] Id., §7.

[75] With respect to brokers and dealers, see p. 661 infra.

eign bank (at least one not present in and regulated in the United States) is not a "bank,"[76] and therefore *could* be a "broker" or "dealer" whose *lending* would be subject to Regulation T,[77] principles of territoriality would preclude applicability of the regulation.[78] Indeed, Regulation U specifically exempts "Any credit extended outside the United States."[79]

This foreign gap was substantially narrowed in 1970, when Congress added §7(f) to the 1934 Act in order to make it unlawful for any "United States person" (as defined), or any foreign person controlled by or acting for or with a United States person, to "obtain, receive, or enjoy" credit from *any* lender *anywhere* "for the purpose of (A) purchasing or carrying United States securities [as defined], or (B) purchasing or carrying within the United States of any other securities," if the loan would have been prohibited had it occurred in a lender's place of business in the United States.[80] The Board has implemented §7(f) by adopting Regulation X, which contains explanations of and exemptions from the statutory provisions.[81]

Despite all this, a bill passed by the House in 1981, as well as another reported out in 1984, would further approach the limits of territoriality by extending §7(f) beyond any "United States person" to *any* person.[82] But, whereas the earlier bill would have extended the margin provisions to foreign lenders as well as borrowers, the later bill referred only to foreign borrowers, which is to say, those persons that actually effect transactions in securities issued by United

[76] See p. 608 n. 18 supra.

[77] United States v. Weisscredit Banca Commerciale e d'Investimenti, 325 F. Supp. 1384, 1390-92 (S. D. N. Y. 1971).

[78] Metro-Goldwyn-Mayer, Inc. v. Transamerica Corp., 303 F. Supp. 1354, 1357-58 (S. D. N. Y. 1969). The court relied not only on §30(b) of the 1934 Act — to the effect that (subject to rulemaking authority that the SEC has never exercised) the Act does not apply to any person "insofar as he transacts a business in securities without the jurisdiction of the United States" — but also, with respect to Regulation G, on the absence of a Federal Reserve district in which the foreign bank might register. See p. 659 supra.

[79] Reg. U, §6(c).

[80] 84 Stat. 1124 (1970).

[81] The Board revised Regulation X, with effect in January 1984, as part of its general overhaul of the margin regulations. The major changes were the exclusion of purely domestic borrowings already regulated by margin rules applicable to lenders, and an increase in the exemption for margin credit obtained by United States persons residing abroad from $5000 to $100,000.

[82] H. R. Rep. No. 97-258 on H. R. 4145, 97th Cong. 2d Sess. (1984); H. R. Rep. No. 98-1028 on H. R. 5693, 98th Cong. 2d Sess. (1984).

States companies. These bills reflect the fear of foreign takeovers of American industry.[83]

g. Broker-Dealer Borrowing [§8(a)]

Almost inevitably, once a broker or dealer becomes a lender he must also "a borrower be." The Board's authority in §7(c) over the *lending* activities of brokers and dealers is complemented by its authority in §8(a) over their *borrowing* activities. Insofar as their borrowing is collateralized by securities of customers — whether the same margin customers to whom the brokers or dealers extend credit or customers whose fully paid securities the brokers or dealers are holding in safekeeping — §8(a) is also the reverse side of the coin of which the obverse is the Commission's hypothecation rules.

Section 8(a) makes it unlawful for any exchange member, or any broker or dealer who is registered or does business through a member, to borrow "in the ordinary course of business as a broker or dealer" on any nonexempted registered security except (1) from or through a member bank of the Federal Reserve System, (2) from a nonmember bank that has filed with the Board an agreement to comply with all the provisions of the Exchange Act, the Federal Reserve Act, and the Banking Act of 1933 that are applicable to member banks and that relate to the use of credit to finance transactions in securities,[84] or (3) in accordance with whatever rules the Board prescribes to permit loans between such brokers and dealers "or to permit loans to meet emergency needs." The Board has implemented Clause (3) of this section by adopting a provision of Regulation T that in substance permits one broker or dealer to borrow from another on the same terms on which Regulation T permits the second broker or dealer to lend.[85]

[83]See Sullivan, Application of Margin Rules to Tender Offers by Foreign Investors, 8 N. C. J. Int'l L. & Com. Reg. 17 (1982). As we have seen (supra p. 660 n. 81), the Board has since moved in the other direction.

[84]The Board may terminate any such agreement, after notice and opportunity for hearing, for the bank's failure to comply with the provisions of the agreement or of the designated statutes. Willful violation of the agreement subjects the bank to the penalties provided for violations of rules prescribed under the Exchange Act. And for this one purpose §8(a) gives the Board the same authority to investigate and obtain injunctions as the Commission has generally under §21.

[85]Reg. T, §15(a)(13); see also id., §11 (broker-dealers' *lending* to other broker-dealers); Reg. U, §5 (special purpose loans to broker-dealers).

h. Arranging for Others to Extend Credit

Both §7(c) and §7(d) of the statute give the Board rulemaking authority not only with respect to extending credit but also with respect to *arranging* for the extension of credit. And what is now §13 of Regulation T has long provided, in substance and with exceptions, that a broker or dealer may not arrange for credit to be given a customer except on the same conditions on which he could himself extend the credit; as amended effective February 15, 1982, this section excludes credit that results from "investment banking services" (as defined). But, apart from the 1959 adoption of the former §3(q) of Regulation U with respect to bank loans to significant relenders,[86] Regulation U contained no similar provision on "arranging" until the amendments of early 1968. The SEC's "Special Study" found evidence that United States banks did in fact arrange loans with foreign banks for their domestic customers.[87] And in 1968 provisions similar to §7(a) of Regulation T were accordingly inserted in both Regulations U and G.[88]

In 1986 the Commission adopted Rule 3a12-9 to exempt from the "arranging" provisions of §7(c), on certain conditions, securities of certain "direct participation programs" with mandatory deferred payments — which is to say, tax shelter programs with tax-flow consequences, typically limited partnerships or some investment contracts. But there is no exemption from the prohibition against the direct extension of credit by the broker-dealer, nor may he arrange for the extension of credit beyond the deferred payment itself.[89] Under the Board's previous interpretations — which are not affected by the exemption — Regulation T applied to public offerings but not to private placements of these programs. The SEC's exemption does not, of course, affect private placements pursuant to the Board's earlier interpretation.[90]

There has been a fair amount of litigation on what constitutes "arranging."[91]

[86] See p. 659 supra.

[87] 4 SEC, Report of Special Study of Securities Markets, H. R. Doc. No. 95, 88th Cong., 1st Sess. (1963) 31.

[88] Reg. U, §3(a)(3); Reg. G, §3(d).

[89] Sec. Ex. Act Rel. 22,979, 35 SEC Dock. 245 (1986). The exemption extends also to §11(d)(1) (infra p. 667).

[90] 58 Fed. Res. Bul. 398 (1972).

[91] Sutro Bros. & Co., 41 SEC 443, 456 (1963); see also, e. g., Pearlstein v. Scudder & German, 429 F. 2d 1136, 1140-41 (2d Cir. 1970), *cert. denied,* 401 U. S. 1013; Shull v. Dain, Kalman & Quail, Inc., 561 F. 2d 152, 160-61 (8th Cir. 1977). On the Board's view that a broker's or dealer's installment sale of limited partnership interests within §5 of the 1933 Act involves an arrangement

i. Unconventional Extensions of Credit

There is space here only to note the inevitable clash between a technical set of retail securities credit regulations and the emergence of many types of unconventional but widely marketed securities, not to mention the financing needs connected with the corporate acquisition movement.[92] For example:

(1) The Board has ruled that Regulation T does *not* apply to a dealer's extension of credit to a corporation in connection with the retirement of its own stock.[93]

(2) The Board's staff, on the other hand, has taken the position that a private placement of a debt issue to finance the purchase of securities is an extension of credit, distinguishing a *public* offering only by a pragmatic reference to custom and concern about damage to the bond market.[94]

(3) The question with respect to tender offers ultimately turns on the facts of each case.[95] But in January 1986 the Board adopted a controversial "interpretative rule" under Regulation G whereby debt securities issued by a shell corporation that is used as an acquisition vehicle for purchasing stock of a target company are presumed to be "indirectly secured" by the stock to be acquired so as to be subject to margin regulation. This interpretation does not extend to a number of general types of acquisition transactions in which its rationale does not apply: a guarantee of the debt securities by the shell's parent or another company with substantial non-margin stock assets or cash flow, and either an agreed-upon or a short-form merger. Moreover, although the interpretation as proposed would have applied equally whether the debt securities were privately placed or publicly distributed, the Board decided to consider the question whether buyers of publicly issued debt securities should be treated as lenders for purposes of margin rules in the context of

---

of credit subject to Regulation T, see Hensley and Rothwell, Regulation T and Public Offerings of Limited Partnerships: Time for a Change, 39 Bus. Law. 543 (1984).

[92] See Hart and Homer, Some Credit Aspects of Unconventional Securities, 25 Mercer L. Rev. 395 (1974); The Impact of the Federal Reserve Margin Regulations on Acquisition Financing, A Program by the [American Bar Association] Committee on Developments in Business Financing, 35 Bus. Law. 517 (1980).

[93] 48 Fed. Res. Bul. 1589 (1962).

[94] See Karmel, The Investment Banker and the Credit Regulations, 45 N. Y. U. L. Rev. 59, 74 (1970). With respect to public offerings, see Revlon, Inc. v. Pantry Pride, Inc., 621 F. Supp. 804, 814-15 (D. Del. 1985).

[95] Shull v. Dain, Kalman & Quail, Inc., 561 F. 2d 152, 161 (8th Cir. 1977), *cert. denied*, 434 U. S. 1086; see generally Schwartz and Kelley, Bank Financing of Corporate Acquisitions — The Cash Tender Offer, 88 Banking L. J. 99 (1971).

formal amendments to Regulation G.[96] The SEC had ample Administration company in attacking the proposal: The Board's authority was questioned by the Departments of Justice, the Treasury, Commerce, and Labor, as well as the Office of Management and Budget and the Council of Economic Advisers; and the interpretation was adopted by a vote of three to two.[97]

(4) The SEC has adopted an exemptive rule, on certain conditions, for a broker's or dealer's arranging credit on an "investment contract security involving the direct ownership of specified residential real property."[98]

(5) In order to facilitate the growth of a forward trading market for mortgage-backed securities, the Secondary Mortgage Market Enhancement Act of 1984 authorizes depository institutions to invest in any "mortgage related security," as defined in a new §3(a)(41) of the 1934 Act. In that connection the 1984 statute added §7(g) and amended §8(a) in the 1934 Act[99] in order to reflect the need for delayed delivery (up to 180 days after purchase or whatever shorter period is designated by Federal Reserve rule). The statute also exempts these mortgage-related securities (as well as first-lien notes exempted by §4(5) of the 1933 Act) from the state blue sky laws to the same extent as an obligation issued or guaranteed by the United States or any of its agencies or instrumentalities[100] unless a particular state reimposes a registration requirement within seven years.[101]

j. Enforcement

Although the promulgation of margin rules is the function of the Board, their enforcement is assigned to the SEC along with the other provisions of the Exchange Act generally. All the statutory

[96] 12 Code Fed. Regs. §207.112; Fed. Res. Rels., Dec. 6, 1985, Jan. 10, 1986.

[97] In the event, the rule was found to have only a slight impact on the practice to which it was directed: the use of "junk bonds" (see p. 500 supra) in tender offering financing. See Investor Responsibility Research Center, Inc., Junk Bonds and Tender Offer Financing, discussed in 19 Sec. Reg. L. Rep. 166-67 (1987). See also 18 Sec. Reg. L. Rep. 32-34 (1986).

[98] Rule 3a12-5; see generally Hart, Securities Regulation of Real Estate Developments — Financing Arrangement Considered As an Extension of Credit, 35 Ohio St. L. J. 300 (1974).

[99] There was a corresponding amendment to §11(d)(1). See p. 667 infra.

[100] See p. 271 supra.

[101] §106, 15 U. S. C. §77r-1, enacted as part of the 1984 statute, not the Exchange Act.

sanctions (administrative, injunctive, and criminal) apply without qualification to violations of §§7 and 8(a) and of the Board's credit regulations.[102]

Regulation T is enforced primarily through the Commission's routine inspections of registered brokers and dealers and by the exchanges' and NASD's inspection and disciplining of their members.

The Commission in practice leaves the policing of Regulation U to the federal and state bank examining authorities under an arrangement whereby substantial violations are to be brought to the Commission's attention. But even with respect to banks any injunctive proceedings must be brought in the Commission's name under §21(e).

The matter of implied civil liability of violating lender to borrower, as well as enforceability of a violating lender's contract, is considered in the chapter on civil liability.

k. Margin Requirements of the Exchanges and the NASD

The margin rules of the exchanges and the NASD themselves are subject, like all their rules, to the jurisdiction of the SEC, not the Board.[103] But the Commission has never used this indirect margin authority, perhaps because the exchanges' rules go further than the Board's. For example:

(1) The most significant difference is a strict maintenance requirement, which on the New York Stock Exchange has been for many years (with some exceptions) 25 percent of all securities "long" in the account.[104]

An exchange member must comply, of course, with the margin requirements of both his exchange and the Board. For purposes of illustrating the interrelation of the two requirements, let us assume the present "T" margin requirement of 50 percent. Let us assume further that a New York Stock Exchange member buys 100 shares of stock for a customer when the market is 100. The customer

[102] In a criminal prosecution based in part on Regulation T, the constitutionality of §7 of the Act and the validity of the regulation were sustained on appeal. United States v. McDermott, 131 F. 2d 313 (7th Cir. 1942), *cert. denied,* 318 U. S. 765. But see United States v. Van de Carr, 343 F. Supp. 993 (C. D. Cal. 1972), infra, p. 668, text at n. 114 (directed verdict under Reg. U).

[103] Sec. Ex. Act §§19(b)(1)-(3), 19(c).

[104] N. Y. Stock Ex. Rule 431(c)-(e), CCH N. Y. Stock Ex. Guide ¶2431; Sec. Ex. Act Rel. 24,144, 37 SEC Dock. 997 (1987). The maintenance margin for securities "short" in the account varies with the market price of the stock; and it is different for bonds. With respect to exempted securities, see p. 652 n. 50 supra.

deposits $5000 in cash or margin securities with a market value of $10,000 (or an appropriate combination of cash and securities) in order to meet the Board's 50 percent initial margin requirement. The market ultimately falls to 66⅔, so that the stock that was bought is worth $6666.67. The member is not required to call for additional margin, although he may wish to do so for his own protection,[105] because the customer still has an equity in the account of $1666.67 ($6666.67, the current market value, minus the debt of $5000), which is 25 percent of the current market value ($6666.67). The market then falls to 65, giving the shares a value of $6500. No matter how much the market declines, Regulation T does not require any margin calls if there are no withdrawals. But at this point the customer's equity is only $1500, and it has to be brought up to $1625 (25 percent of the new market value) in order to comply with the Exchange's maintenance requirement. This may be done by depositing either $125 in cash or securities in such an amount ($166.67) that the equity in the account ($1666.67) will be 25 percent of the market value of all the securities in the account ($6666.67).

(2) The New York Stock Exchange also has an *initial* margin rule that requires the deposit of cash equal to the cost of the security, or cash or securities reflecting an equity in the account of at least $2000. And withdrawals of cash or securities are not permitted from any account that has a debit balance, short position, or commitments unless the equity will be at least $2000 or the amount specified in the maintenance requirement, whichever is greater.[106]

(3) "Substantial additional margin must be required in all cases where the securities carried * * * are subject to unusually rapid or violent changes in value, or do not have an active market on a National Securities exchange, or where the amount carried is such that the position cannot be liquidated promptly."[107]

(4) In early 1987 the Commission approved a comprehensive revision, which, among other things, (1) lowered maintenance requirements for government, municipal, and certain nonconvertible corporate debt securities, (2) permitted member firms to extend more credit on control and restricted securities (at the price of specified net capital deductions), and (3) for the first time required

[105] It is said that most firms have "house" maintenance requirements of their own that are usually higher than the Stock Exchange margin, and that vary from account to account depending on the kind of securities held as collateral and other factors. Solomon and Hart, Recent Developments in the Regulation of Securities Credit, 20 J. Pub. L. 172-73 (1971).

[106] Rule 431(b), CCH N. Y. Stock Ex. Guide ¶2431.

[107] Rule 431(f)(1), CCH N. Y. Stock Ex. Guide ¶2431.

member firms to establish procedures for reviewing the credit extended to customers, to formulate margin requirements, and to consider whether requirements higher than those imposed by the rule are appropriate for particular customers.[108]

The NASD has a set of more or less similar rules, from which members of the leading exchanges are exempted.[109]

1. Extension of Credit on New Issues [§11(d)(1)]

The Exchange Act contains one other credit provision in §11(d)(1). That section is not a part of the scheme of credit control by the Board of Governors of the Federal Reserve System. It is part of the treatment of the general problem of segregation of the functions of broker and dealer.[110] As the House committee described the section, it

> strikes at one of the greatest potential evils inherent in the combination of the broker and dealer function in the same person, by assuring that he will not induce his customers to buy on credit securities which he has undertaken to distribute to the public.[111]

The section does this by making it unlawful, in substance, for a person who is *both* a broker *and* a dealer to extend, maintain, or arrange for credit "to or for a customer on any security (other than an exempted security) which was a part of a new issue in the distribution of which he participated as a member of a selling syndicate or group within thirty days prior to such transaction."[112]

Unfortunately, §11(d)(1) — however laudable its purpose — has been one of the most troublesome provisions of the 1934 Act to construe. As is apparent from its language, it raises many of the interpretative problems with which the Commission and the public

[108] Sec. Ex. Act Rel. 24,144, 37 SEC Dock. 997 (1987).

[109] Rules of Fair Practice, Art. III, §30 and App. A, CCH NASD Manual ¶¶2180, 2180A.

[110] See 2 Loss c. 7D.

[111] H. R. Rep. No. 1383, 73d Cong., 2d Sess. (1934) 22; see also S. Rep. No. 792, 73d Cong., 2d Sess. (1934) 12. As the House committee put it when the section was amended in 1954: "The apparent purpose was to provide that new issues would be initially placed with investors rather than with speculators." H. R. Rep. No. 1542, 83d Cong., 2d Sess. (1954) 15.

[112] See A. J. White & Co. v. SEC, 556 F. 2d 619, 623-24 (1st Cir. 1977), *cert. denied*, 434 U. S. 969; Lowell H. Listrom & Co., Inc. v. SEC, 803 F. 2d 938, 941 (8th Cir. 1986); Lowell H. Listrom & Co., Inc., Sec. Ex. Act Rel. 23,769, 36 SEC Dock. 1150, 1151-52 (1986). Rule 11d1-1 affords a number of exemptions. But the section is fully applicable to intrastate offerings. Sec. Ex. Act Rel. 21,495, 31 SEC Dock. 916, 919 (1984).

have had to struggle under the prospectus provision of the 1933 Act, along with some peculiar difficulties of its own. And the Code deletes it, both because it has long since lost its broker-dealer-segregation motif and "because any *raison d' être* that survives is the avoidance of 'share-pushing' by persons engaged in distributions, and the Commission is given ample authority to attack that problem both by direct rule * * * and by using its enhanced rulemaking authority with reference to exchanges and the NASD."[113]

m. Proposals for Change

The margin regulations — and it must be emphasized that what has been presented here is a condensed and simplified version with many qualifications omitted — are not among the most happily drafted in the securities regulatory structure. In a 1972 case the court wondered whether anybody "could ever be an 'expert' in the maze of conflicting, contradictory and confusing regulations issued by the Federal Reserve Board, enforced by the Securities and Exchange Commission, and attempted to be used here as bases for this criminal prosecution."[114]

The Code[115] assayed a "major overhaul of the credit provisions * * * designed to facilitate understanding of a technical area rather than to make significant changes of substance."[116] Toward this end the Code's Reporter enjoyed the expert and enthusiastic assistance of key members of the Board's staff. And as of March 31, 1984, the regulations themselves underwent a "general overhaul * * * aimed at bringing them up to date with current circumstances in the securities markets, reducing regulatory burden, and simplifying and clarifying the language."[117] Then, in late 1982, the Board announced a more ambitious staff study, in cooperation with the staffs of the SEC and the CFTC, because of the changes since 1934 in the structure of financial markets and the development of markets for financial futures and options, which operate under a differ-

[113] 1 Code 417.

[114] United States v. Van de Carr, 343 F. Supp. 993, 1011 n. 28 (C. D. Cal. 1972).

[115] §917.

[116] 1 Code 414.

[117] Fed. Res. Rel. (Jan. 18, 1982).

ent framework from the cash markets on which they are based.[118] The report, published in late 1984,[119] raised basic questions:

With particular reference to new futures and options instruments and the security-commodity dichotomy,[120] the report stated:[121]

> Margins in the new markets for options based on stock indexes unquestionably are subject to federal regulation. The Federal Reserve has asserted that, at least, margins on stock-related futures fall within its jurisdiction. Whether the new futures contracts and new option contracts calling for the delivery of these futures are subject to federal jurisdiction has been questioned, however. The futures exchanges, citing a long history in which the Congress has considered and rejected imposing federal regulation over futures margins, say that they are not so subject. The issue has not been tested in the courts. Whatever the present legalities of the matter, however, the new contracts traded on options exchanges and the futures and options contracts traded on the futures exchanges perform roughly equivalent functions and offer similar risk-return opportunities. Because they can serve as close substitutes for leveraged trading in common stocks for some important purposes, their existence and the present regulatory scheme raise questions about whether the objectives sought by the Congress when it enacted securities credit regulation are still being adequately served.

The report then examined the objectives of security margin regulation:[122]

(1) The "diversion of credit" concern of 1934, the report stated, reflects a false impression of the basic economic nature of the transactions involved, in that "the trading of corporate shares involves only the transfer of ownership of claims on existing assets, and thus it does not absorb the real savings of the economy. If the buyer of shares borrows to make the purchase, the funds he employs are transferred to the seller, who then reinvests the proceeds: the funds involved in the stock purchase do not disappear."[123] Besides, "margin credit is a far smaller part of total credit outstanding today, so that any diversion that occurs necessarily would be of negligible proportions."[124]

[118] Fed. Res. Rel. (Oct. 21, 1982).

[119] A Review and Evaluation of Federal Margin Regulations, A Study by the Staff of the Board of Governors of the Federal Reserve System (Dec. 1984), of which c. 1, Introduction and Summary of Conclusions, is reprinted in CCH Fed. Sec. L. Rep. ¶83,728.

[120] See c. 3K supra.

[121] At 4-5.

[122] See p. 653 supra.

[123] A Review, etc., op. cit. supra n. 119, at 9.

[124] Id. at 10.

(2) So far as the protection of investors is concerned, the report conceded that "Relatively high margins do tend to protect investors against the risks associated with highly leveraged positions in securities," but observed that that aspect of margin regulation was "very uneven at present, with leveraging opportunities far greater in the derivative markets than in the underlying equities market."[125]

(3) With respect to the role of credit in destabilizing stock prices, the report suggested countervailing considerations: the widely accepted "random walk" theory,[126] and evidence suggesting that in any event credit-financed trading "may not have an important influence on the behavior of stock prices."[127]

(4) The report considered also a fourth objective, which "was not a central focus of the writers of securities credit legislation a half century ago: protection of brokers — or of the market mechanism more generally."[128] There the report referred to "an obvious trade-off that individual brokerage firms, associations of firms that have formed an exchange, and other institutions (such as banks) must make between safety, on the one hand, and volume of business on the other."[129] And, although "By and large the record shows that, in those cases, in which firms and exchanges have made such choices without government oversight, they have done so in a way that provided adequate protection for the firms involved,"[130] the Board's transmittal letter concluded that "the primary purpose of margin regulation today should be to ensure the integrity of the marketplace, in large part by seeing that there are adequate protections against significant credit loss for brokers, banks, and other lenders."[131]

With respect to the *administration* of margin regulation, the report recommended that, if it were concluded that margin requirements above those needed to protect brokers and other lenders as well as the integrity of the marketplace were no longer needed, consideration should be given to returning authority to the private sector. This might be done in a variety of ways, such as assigning responsibility to the self-regulatory organizations, perhaps with one

[125] Id. at 11.

[126] See the reference to the "Efficient Capital Market Hypothesis" at pp. 33-34 supra.

[127] A Review, etc., op. cit. supra p. 669 n. 119, at 14.

[128] Id. at 6.

[129] Id. at 7.

[130] Ibid.

[131] Letter from Federal Reserve Chairman Volcker to Senator Helms (Jan. 11, 1985).

or more government agencies (or a council of the Federal Reserve, the SEC, and the CRTC) playing some role.[132]

Concurrently Secretary of the Treasury Regan urged Congress either to abolish margin regulation entirely or to look to the exchanges and the NASD; and Chairman Shad of the SEC supported at least the delegation idea, subject to the Commission's oversight or veto, although abolition "warrants careful consideration."[133] And the 1984 Bush report recommended that margin responsibility for options on financial instruments other than individual equity securities should be shifted from the Board to the appropriate securities exchanges, subject to SEC veto. This much would codify existing practice.[134]

E. INVESTMENT ADVISERS

1. Registration

The emergence of investment advisers as an independent occupation or profession did not occur until after the First World War. But the brief supplemental report on investment advisers that the Commission filed as an incident of its investment trust study[1] found sufficient evidence of abuse by the fringe operators in this new field to persuade the Senate Banking and Currency Committee to state in 1940:

> Not only must the public be protected from the frauds and misrepresentations of unscrupulous tipsters and touts, but the *bona fide* investment counsel must be safeguarded against the stigma of the activities of these individuals. Virtually no limitations or restrictions exist with respect to the honesty and integrity of individuals who may solicit funds to be controlled, managed, and supervised. Persons who may have been convicted or enjoined by courts because of perpetration of securities fraud are able to assume the role of investment advisers. Individuals assuming to act as investment advisers at present can enter profit-sharing contracts which are nothing more than "heads I win, tails you lose" arrangements. Contracts with investment advisers which are of a personal nature may be

[132] A Review, etc., op. cit. supra p. 669 n. 119, at 22-26.

[133] Letter from Secretary Regan to Chairman Volcker (Dec. 6, 1984); letter from Chairman Shad to Chairman Volcker (Jan. 3, 1985).

[134] Blue Print for Reform: The Report of the Task Force on Regulation of Financial Services (1984) 92-93.

C. 8E [1] SEC, Investment Counsel, Investment Management, Investment Supervisory, and Investment Advisory Services (1939).

> assigned and the control of funds of investors may be transferred to others without the knowledge or consent of the client.[2]

The result was the enactment of the Investment Advisers Act of 1940 as Title II of the bill of which Title I was the Investment Company Act.[3] For twenty years this statute was little more than a continuing census of the Nation's investment advisers. But it was substantially tightened by a series of amendments in 1960, fifteen years after the Commission had first urged such action in a special report to Congress,[4] and was again amended in the Investment Company Amendments Act of 1970 and the Securities Acts Amendments of 1975.

The 1975 amendments were designed essentially to conform the registration and disciplinary *procedures* more closely to those concurrently prescribed in the same legislation for broker-dealers.[5] But there are still differences, notably (1) provision for the filing of a registration application by "any person who presently contemplates becoming an investment adviser," (2) specification of the contents of the application for registration as an adviser, whereas the contents of the broker-dealer application are left entirely to the Commission, and (3) the absence of any prescribed qualifications or financial responsibility provisions for registration as an adviser.[6] Otherwise what has been said with respect to broker-dealer registration and disciplinary procedures applies equally here.

In 1985 the SEC revised Form ADV, the investment adviser registration application form, in order to make it a uniform form identical to that adopted by the North American Securities Administrators Association.[7] The Commission stated that uniform requirements for amendments and annual reports would also be developed, in addition to a central registration system (like the Central Registration Depository maintained by the NASD) under which an adviser would file a single form whose information would be transmitted electronically to the Commission and all states in which

[2] S. Rep. No. 1775, 76th Cong., 3d Sess. (1940) 21-22.

[3] For an exhaustive study of the statute, see T. Frankel, The Regulation of Money Managers: The Investment Company Act and the Investment Advisers Act (4 vols. 1978-80). On a broader front — covering also the Employee Retirement and Income Security Act (ERISA), pension plans, and bank and insurance company activities — see H. Bines, The Law of Investment Management (1978).

[4] SEC, Protection of Clients' Securities and Funds in Custody of Investment Advisers (1945), summarized in Inv. Adv. Act Rel. 39 (1945).

[5] See pp. 630-33 supra.

[6] Inv. Adv. Act §203(c), (e), (f), (h). There is no *pendente lite* suspension provision.

[7] Inv. Adv. Act Rel. 991, 34 SEC Dock. 425 (1985).

the adviser was registering.[8] Part II of the form may be used as the disclosure document required by the "brochure rule."[9]

2. Definition of "Investment Adviser"

The critical definition, of course, is that of "investment adviser":

> "Investment adviser" means any person who, for compensation, engages in the business of advising others, either directly or through publications or writings, as to the value of securities or as to the advisability of investing in, purchasing, or selling securities, or who, for compensation and as part of a regular business, issues or promulgates analyses or reports concerning securities; but does not include (A) a bank, or any bank holding company as defined in the Bank Holding Company Act of 1956 which is not an investment company, (B) any lawyer, accountant, engineer, or teacher whose performance of such services is solely incidental to the practice of his profession; (C) any broker or dealer whose performance of such services is solely incidental to the conduct of his business as a broker or dealer and who receives no special compensation therefor; (D) the publisher of any *bona fide* newspaper, news magazine or business or financial publication of general and regular circulation, (E) any person whose advice, analyses, or reports relate to no securities other than securities which are direct obligations of or obligations guaranteed as to principal or interest by the United States, or securities issued or guaranteed by corporations in which the United States has a direct or indirect interest which shall have been designated by the Secretary of the Treasury, pursuant to section 3(a)(12) of the Securities Exchange Act of 1934, as exempted securities for the purposes of that Act; or (F) such other persons not within the intent of this paragraph, as the Commission may designate by rules and regulations or order.[10]

a. In General

This definition is broad enough to cover every person who for compensation gives advice as to securities, from the highest grade

[8] Id. at 426.

[9] See p. 683 infra. Among the few substantive changes in the previous Form ADV was the addition of new items to identify advisers holding themselves out as engaged in financial planning services and to tailor items of the form in order to obtain information about those activities. Id. at 432. For a detailed statement of staff interpretative positions regarding the form, as well as other reporting and disclosure requirements, see Inv. Adv. Act Rel. 1000, 34 SEC Dock. 906 (1985).

[10] §202(a)(11).

investment counselor who renders personalized service to the publisher of the lowliest tipster sheet. Quite clearly the definition does not cover a person who merely advises issuers with respect to a tender offer[11] or the value of their own securities generally; for there is nothing to indicate that Congress intended that the Advisers Act should regulate investment banking functions. It is equally clear, on the other hand, that the reports referred to in the definition do not necessarily have to analyze specific securities; it is enough that the person advises with respect to the desirability of investing in the securities markets rather than another medium like commodities or gold or real estate. Whether a professional *appraiser* is an investment adviser depends on whether he performs the purely ministerial functions of checking the various financial services to determine market prices, or whether he actually makes an independent judgment of value by examining the financial reports of issuers or preparing comparative charts or the like.[12]

This much said, a considerable gray area survives the exclusions in Clauses (A)-(F):

(1) What about persons who provide advisory services as a component of other financially related services — for example, financial or pension consultants or sports or entertainment representatives, as distinct from the lawyers and brokers and others whose advisory services are equally incidental but who are specifically excluded by Clauses (B) and (C)?[13] With respect to the rapidly growing breed of "financial planners" particularly:

> The staff has interpreted the definition of investment adviser to include persons who advise clients either directly or through publications or writings concerning the relative advantages and disadvantages of investing in securities in general as compared to other investment media.
>
> * * *
>
> * * * However, a person whose principal business is providing financial services other than investment advice would not be re-

[11] Goldman Sachs & Co. v. Hydrometals, Inc., CCH Fed. Sec. L. Rep. ¶96,534 (N. Y. Sup. Ct. 1978).

[12] For a discussion of the extent to which the statutory scheme of the Advisers Act applies to the range of computer-related services, see Langevoort, Information Technology and the Structure of Securities Regulation, 98 Harv. L. Rev. 747, 793-803 (1985).

[13] See Zinn v. Parrish, 644 F. 2d 360 (7th Cir. 1981) (isolated screening of stock recommendations as agent for a football player was considered incidental to the agent's principal duty of negotiating football contracts); Dan King Brainard, Inv. Adv. Act Rel. 892, 29 SEC Dock. 268, 273 (1983) (market timing services); see generally Inv. Adv. Act Rel. 770, 23 SEC Dock. 556, 559 (1981).

garded as being *in the business* of giving investment advice if, as part of his service, he merely discusses in general terms the advisability of investing in securities in the context of, for example, a discussion of economic matters or the role of investments in securities in a client's overall financial plan.[14]

(2) Should a person who is engaged in the business of finding advisers for others be considered to be an adviser himself on the theory that he is advising his clients to invest in the securities recommended by the adviser he selects? Possibly, though the reasoning requires a bit of a stretch.[15]

(3) When a limited partnership is organized for the purpose of investing in securities — a so-called hedge fund that provides a pass-through tax shelter and would be an investment company except for the exclusion in §3(c)(1) of the Investment Company Act of issuers that have fewer than a hundred security holders and do not make a public offering — is the general partner an investment adviser to the limited partners? The Second Circuit has said yes, citing (1) the limited partners' reliance on monthly reports in determining whether or not to withdraw their funds and (2) the fact that the general partners' compensation depended in part on profit and capital gains.[16] But suppose those two factors or at least the second is absent and the general partner limits himself to the day-to-day management of the firm, relying on an outside adviser who either (a) recommends or (b) is given authority to decide what and when to buy and sell. Indeed, even without an outside adviser — which should be a relatively easy case — it has not been suggested that the president of an internally managed *corporate* investment company should be considered to be an investment adviser to his stockholder "clients." In the case of a trust, it has been held that the trustee does not advise the trust corpus but acts as principal; that is to say, the trustee himself embodies the trust.[17]

A further complication, and a question apparently left open by the Second Circuit: If the general partner *is* an adviser, does he have a single client, the firm, in which event he could come within the §203(b)(3) exemption in terms of fewer than fifteen clients,[18]

[14] Id. at 558, 559.

[15] Ibid.

[16] Abrahamson v. Fleschner, 568 F. 2d 862, 869-70 (2d Cir. 1977), *cert. denied,* 436 U. S. 913; see Hacker and Rotunda, SEC Registration of Private Investment Partnerships After *Abrahamson* v. *Fleschner*, 78 Colum. L. Rev. 1471 (1978).

[17] Selzer v. Bank of Bermuda, Ltd., 385 F. Supp. 415, 420 (S. D. N. Y. 1974). In Wang v. Gordon, 715 F. 2d 1187 (7th Cir. 1983), the court distinguished *Abrahamson* on the ground that the case before the court involved a real estate partnership rather than a securities investment partnership.

[18] See p. 682 infra.

or is each limited partner a client? This latter question is addressed in a "safe harbor" rule that specifies certain situations in which the limited partnership rather than each limited partner is counted as a client of the general partner when he is in fact acting as investment adviser to the firm.[19]

(4) In parent-subsidiary situations in which the adviser subsidiary is undercapitalized, or dependent on the parent's personnel or office facilities or research data for the practical ability to render advice, is the question of the parent's status as an adviser to be determined by the usual veil-piercing factors? Or does §208(d) — to the effect that it is unlawful for any person to do "indirectly, or through or by any other person," anything it would be unlawful for him to do directly — sharpen the veil-piercing dagger?[20] Does such a provision add anything anyway under modern concepts of statutory construction?

b. What Constitutes a "Business"

What has been said with reference to the term "business" as used in the definitions of "broker" and "dealer" under the Exchange Act applies equally here.[21] But there is one significant point peculiar to the definition of "investment adviser": Registration is not required simply because one is the author or publisher of a book, pamphlet, or article that "does not contain recommendations, reports, analyses, or other advisory information relating to specific securities or issuers" and is not one of a series intended to be supplemented.[22]

c. Exclusions

(i) *Certain professional persons:* Of course, a lawyer or accountant or engineer or a teacher of any kind *can* be an investment adviser if the advice he renders is not solely incidental to the practice of his profession. Much of what will be said in a moment with reference to the exclusion of certain brokers and dealers by Clause (C) is

[19] Rule 203(b)(3)-1, proposed by Inv. Adv. Act Rel. 956, 32 SEC Dock. 740 (1985), and adopted by Inv. Adv. Act Rel. 983, 33 SEC Dock. 948 (1985).

[20] See Inv. Adv. Act Rel. 353 (1972).

[21] See p. 604 supra.

[22] Inv. Adv. Rel. 563, 11 SEC Dock. 1500 (1977). The staff there abandoned the further condition that the publication not contain any "formulae or guidelines."

equally applicable here. Arguably, however, it is not essential that every advisory client of the lawyer be a legal client as well if the lawyer does not hold himself out to the public as an investment adviser and is first and foremost a lawyer whose advisory services are "solely incidental" to his law practice generally.

(ii) *Publishers:* It is sometimes a close question whether an individual who writes advisory material for a newspaper or other periodical is an employee or an independent contractor. However, the spirit of Clause (D) would seem to cover even the author of a syndicated financial column.[23] In the absence of a comparable exemption for radio and television stations, there is some question whether the stations, or the producers of the programs, may not come within the definition if they broadcast programs of investment advice. The fact that their compensation comes from the sponsor rather than the listeners is not necessarily decisive.[24]

This area is complicated by First Amendment considerations, particularly since the Supreme Court's recent recognition of the availability of some degree of constitutional protection for commercial speech.[25] When the New York Attorney General had earlier sought, under the substantially similar language in the Martin Act,[26] to examine the books and papers of a corporation that was registered with the SEC as an investment adviser and that had published a book by one Darvas, a professional dancer, entitled How I Made $2,000,000 in the Stock Market, the Attorney General had prevailed in the Court of Appeals without any discussion of free speech.[27] And the Second Circuit, in similarly allowing the SEC to investigate a daily publication that reprinted broker-dealers' market letters, had held that the "*bona fide*" phrase in Clause (D) should not be construed as if the sole issue was the number of "the usual indicia of a newspaper." Rather, the phrase refers to "those publications which seem to deviate from customary newspaper activities to such an extent that there is a likelihood that the wrongdoing which the Act was designed to prevent has occurred." And the court thought it was "not necessary to enlarge the category of '*bona fide*' newspapers

[23] See Loomis, The Securities Exchange Act of 1934 and the Investment Advisers Act of 1940, 28 Geo. Wash. L. Rev. 214, 245 n. 97 (1959).

[24] Ibid.

[25] Virginia State Board of Pharmacy v. Virginia Citizens Consumer Council, 425 U. S. 748 (1976); see Schoeman, Subscription Advisers, Blue Sky Registration and the First Amendment, 33 Bus. Law. 249 (1977). For a collection of Supreme Court cases on commercial speech outside the SEC field, see Jesse Rosenblum, Inv. Adv. Act Rel. 913, 30 SEC Dock. 692, 696 (1984).

[26] N. Y. Gen. Bus. Law, Art. 23-A, §359-eee(a).

[27] Matter of Attorney-General of the State of N. Y. (Darvas), 10 N. Y. 2d 108, 176 N. E. 2d 402 (1961), *cert. denied*, 368 U. S. 947.

into an exclusion for all publications which could conceivably be brought within the term 'typical newspaper' in order to avoid the 'seeds of a constitutional controversy' * * *."[28]

The Second Circuit, writing in 1970, guessed wrong. For in 1985, in *Lowe* v. *SEC,*[29] a bare majority of the Supreme Court stretched to avoid the First Amendment question for which certiorari had been granted by holding that newsletters and a chart service that "contained general commentary about the securities and bullion markets, reviews of market indicators and investment strategies, and specific recommendations for buying, selling, or holding stocks and bullion"[30] came within the publisher's exclusion. Three other Justices (one did not sit) disagreed on the interpretation of the exclusion but reached the same result on constitutional grounds. A few excerpts will convey the flavor of the fairly lengthy majority opinion:

> The exclusion itself uses extremely broad language that encompasses any newspaper, business publication, or financial publication provided that two conditions are met. The publication must be "*bona fide,*" and it must be "of regular and general circulation." Neither of these conditions is defined, but the two qualifications precisely differentiate "hit and run tipsters" and "touts" from genuine publishers. Presumably a "*bona fide*" publication would be genuine in the sense that it would contain disinterested commentary and analysis as opposed to promotional material disseminated by a "tout." Moreover, publications with a "general and regular" circulation would not include "people who send out bulletins from time to time on the advisability of buying and selling stocks," [citation omitted], or "hit and run tipsters." * * * [31]
>
> * * *
>
> * * * The mere fact that a publication contains advice and comment about specific securities does not give it the personalized character that identifies a professional investment adviser. Thus, petitioners' publications do not fit within the central purpose of the Act because they do not offer individualized advice attuned to any specific portfolio or to any client's particular needs. On the contrary, they circulate for sale to the public at large in a free, open

[28] SEC v. Wall St. Transcript Corp., 422 F. 2d 1371, 1378-79 (2d Cir. 1970), *cert. denied,* 398 U. S. 958; see also SEC v. C. R. Richmond & Co., 565 F. 2d 1101, 1107 (9th Cir. 1977); SEC v. Wall St. Transcript Corp., 454 F. Supp. 559 (S. D. N. Y. 1978) (the exclusion applied under Second Circuit's test).

[29] 472 U. S. 181.

[30] Id. at 185.

[31] Id. at 206.

> market — a public forum in which typically anyone may express his views.[32]
>
> * * * In light of the legislative history, this phrase ["*bona fide*"] translates best to "genuine"; petitioners' publications meet this definition: they are published by those engaged solely in the publishing business and are not personal communications masquerading in the clothing of newspapers, news magazines, or financial publications. * * *[33]
>
> * * * To the extent that the chart service contains factual information about past transactions and market trends, and the newsletters contain commentary on general market conditions, there can be no doubt about the protected character of the communications * * *. * * * As long as the communications between petitioners and their subscribers remain entirely impersonal and do not develop into the kind of fiduciary, person-to-person relationships that were discussed at length in the legislative history of the Act and that are characteristic of investment adviser-client relationships, we believe the publications are, at least presumptively, within the exclusion and thus not subject to registration under the Act.[34]

(1) The majority opinion seems forced. Justice White's concurring opinion calls it "improvident."[35] As he observes, the majority view makes the exclusion virtually eat up the rule.

(2) Paradoxically, the majority opinion's interpretative approach entails a more radical result than the concurring opinion's constitutional approach. For the latter opinion leaves it open to the Commission to enforce the antifraud provisions of §206, whereas the majority's exclusion from the definition would presumably leave *Lowe*-type advisers completely immune from the Act (unless, presumably, they were "hit and run tipsters" or "touts").

(3) Congress is free, of course, to overrule *Lowe* by clarifying the language of the publisher's exclusion. The general tenor of the majority opinion indicates that the Court would be likely to find a First Amendment impediment if it could not avoid the question. But in an earlier case involving a lawyer's person-to-person solicitation of business it did say:

> Numerous examples could be cited of communications that are regulated without offending the First Amendment, such as the exchange of information about securities, *SEC* v. *Texas Gulf Sulphur Co.,* 401 F. 2d 833 (CA2 1968), *cert. denied,* 394 U. S. 976 (1969),

[32] Id. at 208.
[33] Id. at 208-09.
[34] Id. at 210.
[35] Id. at 211.

> [or] corporate proxy statements, *Mills v. Electric Auto-Lite Co.*, 396 U. S. 375 (1970) * * *.[36]

(4) Meanwhile the constitutional question must be considered open.[37]

(5) *Query* the status of the earlier cases by way of interpretation of the publisher's exclusion.[38]

(iii) *Brokers and dealers:* Two related questions are presented under Clause (C): the meaning of "solely incidental" and what constitutes "special compensation."

So far as the first phrase is concerned, it is the administrative view that a broker or dealer whose business consists *almost exclusively* of managing discretionary accounts is an investment adviser.[39]

With respect to the meaning of "special compensation," the Commission's General Counsel early stated:

> Clause (C) of Section 202(a)(11) amounts to a recognition that brokers and dealers commonly give a certain amount of advice to their customers in the course of their regular business, and that it would be inappropriate to bring them within the scope of the Investment Advisers Act merely because of this aspect of their business. On the other hand, that portion of clause (C) which refers to "special compensation" amounts to an equally clear recognition that a broker or dealer who is specially compensated for the rendition of advice should be considered an investment adviser and not be excluded from the purview of the Act merely because he is also engaged in effecting market transactions in securities. It is well known that many brokers and dealers have investment advisory departments which furnish investment advice for compensation in the same manner as does an investment adviser who operates solely in

[36] Ohralik v. Ohio State Bar Assn., 436 U. S. 447, 456 (1978).

[37] In SEC v. Suter, 732 F. 2d 1294, 1299 (7th Cir. 1984), a pre-*Lowe* case in which the lower court had prohibited the distribution of any publication discussing the securities markets unless a copy was contemporaneously sent to the SEC, the court could not say that that restriction was "broader than reasonably necessary to prevent the deception."

[38] See pp. 677-78 supra. Cf. SEC v. Wall St. Publishing Institute, Inc., 591 F. Supp. 1070, 1078 (D. D. C. 1984), *stay granted*, CCH Fed. Sec. L. Rep. ¶91,635 (D. C. Cir. 1984), where the court quoted from Jack Sonner (letter avail. Mar 11, 1983):

> It is our view that a provider of information relating to securities will be deemed neither to furnish investment advice nor to issue or promulgate an analyses [*sic*] or report concerning securities when the information provided is readily available in its raw state, the categories of information are not highly selective, and the information provided is not organized or presented in a manner which suggests the purchase, holding, or sale of any security or securities.

[39] Inv. Adv. Act Rel. 640, 15 SEC Dock. 1211, 1212 (1978).

> an advisory capacity. The essential distinction to be borne in mind in considering borderline cases * * * is the distinction between compensation for advice itself and compensation for services of another character to which advice is merely incidental.[40]

This approach is equally applicable in principle to dealers as well as brokers, except that, since dealers do not ordinarily disclose their profits or spreads, it is more difficult as a practical matter to determine whether the profit or spread in a particular case is greater because of the amount of incidental investment advice rendered. Similar problems have resulted from the "unbundling" of rates and the discounting that followed the abolition of fixed stock exchange commissions in 1975. It would be fatal, not surprisingly, for a firm to make two general fee schedules available whose difference is attributable primarily to the presence or absence of investment advice. But the staff does not consider that there is "special compensation" merely because, for example, a "full service" firm charges higher rates than a "discount" firm, or a firm negotiates different fees with different clients for similar transactions.[41]

Frequently brokers and dealers distribute to their customers reports or analyses concerning specific securities or securities of certain types. It is understood to be the administrative construction that a broker or dealer does not receive "special compensation" for such pamphlets when he charges no more than the cost of *printing* and *distributing* them. Manifestly, however, there would be nothing left of the "no special compensation" restriction if a broker or dealer could charge any of the cost of *preparing* the pamphlet and still avoid registration as an investment adviser. When a broker or dealer distributes a pamphlet prepared *by another person,* he may likewise charge not more than the cost of the pamphlet to him and the postage.

When a broker or dealer thus acts as a conduit for the distribution of reports or analyses prepared by others and charges *more* than the cost and postage, the question whether it is he who "issues or promulgates" the analyses or reports within the meaning of the definition depends on other considerations. If the identity of the author is disclosed and the broker or dealer does not adopt the analyses or reports as his own by adding his own name — for example, when a broker or dealer merely distributes the Standard and Poor's reports on specific securities to his customers — he would

[40] Op. Gen. Counsel, Inv. Adv. Act Rel. 2 (1940); see also Inv. Adv. Act Rel. 626, 14 SEC Dock. 946 (1978).

[41] Id. at 950-51.

not seem to be a person who "issues or promulgates" the reports. On the other hand, when the reports, although prepared by a third person, are issued under the sole name of a broker or dealer, he would seem to come within the definition. When he merely adds his own name to that of the author, there is room for argument.[42]

(iv) *Commission's power to exclude:* There have been a number of orders excluding, typically, professional trustees[43] and family corporations rendering advice solely to their stockholders.[44]

3. Exemptions

Apart from a plenary exemptive authority by rule or order in §206A, which was inserted in the 1970 amendments, §203(b) contains three exemptions from the registration requirement:

> (1) any investment adviser all of whose clients are residents of the State within which such investment adviser maintains his or its principal office and place of business, and who does not furnish advice or issue analyses or reports with respect to securities listed or admitted to unlisted trading privileges on any national securities exchange;
>
> (2) any investment adviser whose only clients are insurance companies; or
>
> (3) any investment adviser who during the course of the preceding twelve months has had fewer than fifteen clients and who neither holds himself out generally to the public as an investment adviser nor acts as an investment adviser to any [registered investment company or "business development company" within §54 of the Investment Company Act]. * * *

The only problems of any substance are raised by the third clause: The maximum of fourteen applies to the total number of clients during the past twelve months rather than the number at any one time. On the other hand, the term "clients" refers presumably to paying clients, so that a broker or dealer who renders advice to his customers generally and hence is excluded from the definition of "investment adviser" can charge a few customers for his advice and still come within this exemption.

So far as the second condition of the exemption is concerned,

[42] Whether the *author* of reports must register depends on (1) whether he is an employee or independent contractor, and (2) the exemption granted by §203(b)(3) (infra).

[43] Augustus P. Loring, Jr., 11 SEC 885 (1942).

[44] Pitcairn Co., 29 SEC 186 (1949).

the important consideration, as with respect to the 1933 Act exemption for transactions "not involving any public offering," is the number of persons whom the adviser is willing to accept as clients rather than the number of actual clients. In other words, an adviser with only one client, or none at all, may not describe himself as an investment adviser in his letterheads or literature or list himself in the classified section of the telephone book. Under the language of the exemption, it is difficult for a person "to start from scratch" and build up to a maximum of fourteen clients without holding himself out generally to the public as an investment adviser. He would have to restrict himself to a small predetermined group of persons and demonstrate an unwillingness to accept other clients. As a practical matter, this exemption is used for the most part by persons who, for compensation, advise members of their families or close friends.

4. Regulatory Provisions

a. Recordkeeping, Reports, and Inspection

The 1960 amendments supplied the original statute's lack of any provision comparable to §17(a) of the 1934 Act, which gives the Commission authority to inspect the books and records of registered brokers and dealers, to prescribe what books and records shall be kept, and to require the filing of reports.[45] The rules prescribe certain records and reports.[46] And a so-called brochure rule requires advisers (with certain exceptions) to deliver a specified "disclosure statement" with respect to their background and business practices to every client or prospective client initially, and thereafter to offer annually in writing to deliver a current disclosure statement on request without charge.[47]

A visitatorial power has always raised more delicate questions with respect to those investment advisers who do personalized counseling than with respect to broker-dealers because of "the personal details of a client's life which the adviser keeps on file to assist management of a portfolio."[48] Even the original statute prohibited the Commission from making public the facts ascertained during an

[45] See pp. 636-37, 643-45 supra.

[46] Rules 204-1, 204-2.

[47] Rule 204-3; for staff interpretations of the statement, see Inv. Adv. Act Rel. 1000, 34 SEC Dock. 906, 907-08 (1985).

[48] S. Rep. No. 1760, 86th Cong., 2d Sess. (1960) 6.

investigation — or, indeed, the fact that an investigation was being conducted — except in a subpoena-enforcement or injunctive proceeding or a public hearing under the statute or in the event of a resolution or request from either House of Congress.[49] And this provision was extended by the 1960 amendments so that it applies equally to examinations under the visitatorial power that was then added and also prohibits the members and employees of the Commission from disclosing, except to each other or with the Commission's approval, any information obtained as the result of an examination or investigation. The staff is thus "under a duty of nondisclosure similar to that of a bank examiner."[50]

b. Profit-Sharing [§205(1)]

Investment advisers compensate themselves in a number of ways. Those who for the most part give continuous advice on the basis of the individual needs of each client generally charge a fixed fee or a fee computed at a certain percentage of the aggregate value of the assets managed. Some scale their rates according to the size of the fund supervised. And those whose services consist only of uniform publications charge fixed subscription prices. With one exception, any basis of compensation may be used as long as it is not so vague as to amount to a fraudulent practice. That exception is a prohibition against compensation based on "a share of capital gains upon or capital appreciation of the funds or any portion of the funds of the client"; and that exception is itself subject to several exceptions, which were enlarged in the 1970 amendments and again in the Small Business Investment Incentive Act of 1980 to permit certain performance or incentive fees in advisory contracts with investment companies and "business development companies."[51]

The purpose was "to prohibit arrangements for contingent compensation to investment advisers based on profit-sharing arrangements with clients which encourage advisers to take undue risks with the funds of clients"[52] — or, as the Senate committee put it, arrangements of the "heads I win, tails you lose" variety.[53] It seems clear from this statement of legislative purpose that the prohibition

[49] §210(b).

[50] S. Rep. No. 1760, 86th Cong., 2d Sess. (1960) 7.

[51] §205(1); Rules 205-1, 205-2; see Inv. Co. Act Rel. 7130 (1972) ("Survey of Investment Company Incentive Fee Arrangements").

[52] H. R. Rep. No. 2639, 76th Cong., 3d Sess. (1940) 29.

[53] S. Rep. No. 1775, 76th Cong., 3d Sess. (1940) 22.

cannot be evaded by any "satisfaction or your money back" arrangements, or by means of purported gratuities that bear any relation to the amount of capital gains or appreciation.[54]

A fee based on dividend and interest income, however, is not precluded.[55] Moreover, §205 itself contains limited exemptions. And in late 1985 the Commission adopted a general exemption, Rule 205-3, that permits performance fees (with some qualifications) if (1) the client has at least $500,000 under the management of the adviser, or the adviser reasonably believes the client has a net worth of at least $1 million; (2) the adviser's compensation is based on a formula that includes realized capital losses and under certain circumstances unrealized capital depreciation; (3) the performance period is at least a year; (4) the adviser discloses certain information to the client; and (5) the adviser reasonably believes that the contract represents an arm's-length arrangement and that the client, alone or together with the client's independent agent, understands the performance fee contract and its risks.[56]

c. Assignment of Advisory Contracts [§205(2)]

Section 205 prohibits any advisory contract that "fails to provide, in substance, that no assignment of such contract shall be made by the investment adviser without the consent of the other party to the contract." And the statute contains a broad definition of "assignment" to include "any direct or indirect transfer or hypothecation of an investment advisory contract by the assignor or of a controlling block of the assignor's outstanding voting securities by a security holder of the assignor."[57]

[54] Inv. Adv. Act Rel. 721, 20 SEC Dock. 89, 90-91 n. 13 (1980).

[55] Inv. Adv. Act Rel. 721, 20 SEC Dock. 89 n. 5 (1980).

[56] In general, see Schultz, Performance-Based Fees Under the Investment Advisers Act of 1940, 39 Bus. Law. 521 (1984).

[57] §202(a)(1); to the same effect, see Inv. Co. Act §2(a)(4), construed in Willheim v. Murchison, 342 F. 2d 33 (2d Cir. 1965), *cert. denied,* 382 U. S. 840. The definition goes on to provide that, "if the investment adviser is a partnership, no assignment of an investment advisory contract shall be deemed to result from the death or withdrawal of a minority of the members of the investment adviser having only a minority interest in the business of the investment adviser, or from the admission to the investment adviser of one or more members who, after such admission, shall be only a minority of the members and shall have only a minority interest in the business." Moreover, Rule 202(a)(1) 1, adopted by Inv. Adv. Act Rel. 1034, 36 SEC Dock. 651 (1986), provides that a transaction that does not result in a charge of "actual control" is not deemed an "assignment."

On the other hand, §205(2) is supplemented by §205(3), which requires the

Section 205(2) obviously rules out any indefinite consent to future assignments when the contract is entered into; otherwise the section could easily be rendered nugatory. Moreover, it has been the administrative policy to resolve any doubts in favor of the client in view of the "delicate fiduciary nature of an investment advisory relationship."[58] In a sense, §205(2) merges into §206, the general fraud provision.[59] For example, if a new partnership were formed and the name of a former partner were retained in the firm after he had dropped out, a careful explanation should be made to each client. Again, whether or not fee-splitting amounts to a partial assignment of the contract, it would seem to be a fraudulent and deceptive practice for the adviser to fail to disclose the fact that anyone other than an employee shares in his fee or furnishes advice that he automatically passes on to his client.

d. Use of the Title, "Investment Counsel" [§208(c)]

At the urging of the branch of the industry that renders continuous investment advice on a personalized basis, there was inserted after the introduction of the original bill a provision, §208(c), that, as amended in 1960, makes it unlawful for any registered investment adviser to "represent that he is an investment counsel or to use the name 'investment counsel' as descriptive of his business unless (1) his or its principal business consists of acting as investment adviser and (2) a substantial part of his or its business consists of rendering investment supervisory services."[60] The term "investment supervisory services" is defined to mean "the giving of continuous advice as to the investment of funds on the basis of the individual needs of each client."[61] The criterion for the use of the descriptive term "investment counsel" is thus the continuity and personalized nature of the advice rather than how conservative or speculative it is.

---

advisory contract "to provide, in substance, that the investment adviser, if a partnership, will notify the other party to the contract of any change in the membership of such partnership within a reasonable time after such change."

[58] See SEC v. Capital Gains Research Bureau, Inc., 375 U. S. 180, 191 n. 38 (1963).

[59] See p. 837 infra.

[60] There is also a complementary provision in §210(c) that protects "any investment adviser engaged in rendering investment supervisory services" against disclosure to the Commission of "the identity, investments, or affairs of any client" except as necessary or appropriate in a particular proceeding or investigation to enforce the statute.

[61] §202(a)(13).

5. Proposals for Change

The Advisers Act is no exception to the gales of change that seem to be blowing — from one direction or another — in the SEC field generally.

The Code[62] attacks the most serious defect that remains in the statute: the absence of any educational or other qualifications for registration as an investment adviser notwithstanding the ability of that occupation to "cause havoc unless engaged in by those with appropriate background and standards."[63]

[62]See 1 Code 326, 330.

[63]Marketlines, Inc. v. SEC, 384 F. 2d 264, 267 (2d Cir. 1967), *cert. denied*, 390 U. S. 947. Registrations early became effective for "booking agents, dress designers in Hollywood, dentists and real estate people, physicians, physicists, hotel managers, salesmen of floor wax, [and] a manager of a surgical supply house." See Schenker, The S. E. C. Looks at Investment Advisers, 3 Inv. Counsel Annual 6, 11 (1941); see also 7 SEC Ann. Rep. 34 (1941). Mr. Schenker, who was Chief Counsel of the Investment Trust Study and the first Director of the Commission's former Investment Company Division, told also of one flowery application — withdrawn after investigation — that turned out to have been filed by a convict who was doing a "bit" in a Wisconsin jail for assault with intent to rob and murder and wanted to use his registration as an investment adviser in an attempt to persuade the parole board that he had a business he could go into as soon as he was released. Schenker, supra, at 14. Murder is not a disqualification under §203(e)(2), though burglary would be! See Michael D. Marant, Inv. Adv. Act Rel. 1056, 37 SEC Dock. 767 (1987), where the Commission in a proceeding against an applicant who was serving a life sentence for first degree murder, alleged not the conviction but a failure to make adequate disclosure in the registration form.

The report of the "Special Study" tells the story, simultaneously hilarious and hair-raising, of the new publication entitled The Trading Floor that appeared on several newsstands in downtown New York City on May 21, 1962, selling for $.50 and advertised as a daily investment advisory service that would recommend eleven new stocks in each issue. The publisher and entire staff turned out to be a nineteen-year-old who had held seven different jobs during the eighteen months after he had dropped out of college. His "major source" of information was two cousins who he said were "fanatically interested in the stock market and * * * send away for all this free advice." One cousin was a twenty-year-old college student and the other a fourteen-year-old high school freshman. The mastermind's mother helped him collate and staple the pages after he had run them off on a mimeograph machine in the kitchen of their Brooklyn apartment. It is perhaps anticlimactic to add that his registration was withdrawn. 1 SEC, Report of Special Study of Securities Markets, H. R. Doc. No. 95, 88th Cong., 1st Sess. (1963) 147-48.

It is not even certain that the Commission could do anything about professed astrologers, one or two of whom have registered in the past. A 1966 news story quoted a Washington seeress whose predictions on the basis of "psychic information" had been widely publicized as saying: "So many people have come to me in the past two weeks that I just can't count them. I can help many of these people. It depends on the psychic atmosphere and whether God really wants them to know." Wall St. J., May 16, 1966, p. 1, col. 4. But what of the sun spot theorists? The same story quotes the chairman of the advisory committee

The Code also reflects a novel approach to the "mini-account," that is to say, the investment management services that many investment advisers (and some broker-dealers, banks, and bank affiliates) have developed in recent years for persons with as little as $5000 or even $1000 to invest. Whereas today this evolving investment medium is in a state of limbo because of the necessity of an all-or-nothing approach — either full registration under the Securities and Investment Company Acts or no regulation at all apart from the fraud provisions, which are themselves applicable only if there is a "security" — the Code offers a new scheme by way of regulation of the investment advisers (including for this purpose banks).[64]

Code reforms aside, the Commission in 1980 requested comment with respect to the issues it should consider in the course of a study of the Advisers Act, including the possibility of establishing one or more self-regulatory organizations.[65] And in June 1986 the Commission submitted to Congress a proposal to "clarify" the definition of "investment adviser" in light of the *Lowe* case.[66]

F. A NATIONAL MARKET SYSTEM

1. The Concept

When Congress, in the Securities Acts Amendments of 1975, directed the Commission in the new §11A of the 1934 Act "to use its authority * * * to facilitate the establishment of a national mar-

of an investment counsel firm as saying that because of a historical pattern in sun spots "an important stock market peak may lie some one to four years hence," and a research partner of a New York Stock Exchange member firm as saying: "I believe the market reacts to atmospheric or cosmic influences, but I've never seen any theory refined enough to accurately predict the stock market."

[64]See 1 Code 396-407; cf. Small Account Investment Management Services, Report of the Advisory Committee on Investment Management Services for Individual Investors (1973), reprinted in Fixed Rates and Institutional Membership, Hearings on S. 470 and S. 488 Before Subcom. on Securities, S. Com. on Banking, Housing & Urban Affairs, 93d Cong., 1st Sess. (1973) 474, 476-77.

[65]Inv. Adv. Act Rel. 717, 19 SEC Dock. 1195 (1980).

[66]See Lee, The Effects of *Lowe* on the Application of the Investment Advisers Act of 1940 to Impersonal Investment Advisory Publications, 42 Bus. Law. 507, 549-50 (1987).

ket system for securities,"[1] it bestowed on that agency a role that, wanted or not, was clearly unwonted: that of coaxer, encourager, prodder, midwife, what have you, toward the *industry's* development of the disparate exchange and over-the-counter markets into some sort of unelucidated "national market system"("NMS").[2]

Actually the antecedents of the NMS are found further back: in the major exchanges' fixed commission structure, which allowed no quantity discounts on even the largest institutional orders and prohibited rebates to nonmembers; in their restricting membership to persons engaged in the securities business; and in their "offboard trading" rules, which (with certain exceptions) prohibited members from executing transactions over the counter in securities trade or the particular exchange.[3]

Although the SEC and antitrust orbits had occasionally crossed from the relatively early days of the Commission,[4] both the Commission and the New York Stock Exchange "stood up and took notice" when the Supreme Court decided *Silver* v. *New York Stock Exchange* in 1963.[5] Nonmember brokers complained that the Exchange had cut their wire connections with several members. The

[C]. 8F [1] §11A(a)(2).

[2] Professor Poser (see p. 591 supra), painting a picture of the stage *circa* late 1981 in the evolutionary process, was not only dubious of the endeavor's desirability but also critical of a certain wishywashiness in the Commission's handling of its task. Poser, Restructuring the Stock Markets: A Critical Look at the SEC's National Market System, 56 N. Y. U. L. Rev. 883 (1981); see also Werner, The SEC As a Market Regulator, 70 Va. L. Rev. 755, 773-78 (1984). For a decidedly more favorable appraisal, see J. Seligman, The Transformation of Wall Street (1982) c. 12 *passim*; see also Calvin, The National Market System: A Successful Adventure in Industry Self-Improvement, 70 Va. L. Rev. 785 (1984); Seligman, The Future of the National Market System, 10 J. Corp. L. 79 (1984) (critical of the Commission for not carrying out the legislative mandate more vigorously). In general, see L. Feller, M. Fitterman, and R. Colby, The National Market System: A Selective Outline of Significant Events 1971-1983 (paper by former and current SEC staff members, 1983); Allen, A National Market System for Stock Trading: A Review of Developments and Issues (Congressional Research Service, Library of Congress, Rep. No. 85-28E, 1985).

The critical releases are Sec. Ex. Act Rel. 9484 (1972), Statement on the Future Structure of the Securities Markets; Sec. Ex. Act Rel. 14,416, 14 SEC Dock. 31 (1978), Development of a National Market System (a status report); Sec. Ex. Act Rel. 15,671, 17 SEC Dock. 24 (1979), Development of a National Market System (another status report).

[3] See Harman, The Evolution of the National Market System — An Overview, 33 Bus. Law. 2275, 2277 (1978). In 1941 the Commission invalidated such a New York Stock Exchange rule so far as trading on a regional exchange was concerned. Former Rule 394, now Rule 390, CCH N. Y. Stock Ex. Guide ¶2390; Rules of New York Stock Exchange, 10 SEC 270 (1941).

[4] The story is told to 1969 in 5 Loss 3153-86. See also pp. 621–22 supra.

[5] 373 U. S. 341 (1963).

case did not involve rates, membership, or offboard trading. But the Court held that an antitrust exemption would be implied "only if necessary to make the Securities Exchange Act work, and even then only to the minimum extent necessary";[6] this raised the spectre that the exchanges' commission rate and other restrictive rules might be subject to antitrust attack, both public and private. Moreover, the Court later held that, in determining whether a particular stock exchange action was exempted from antitrust coverage, the Court would examine whether the SEC had power to review such action and, if so, whether it had actually exercised oversight;[7] this, of course, gave the SEC considerable leverage.

"*Silver* furnished the legal setting for the collapse of the NYSE's market system; economic developments in the securities markets brought on the actual collapse."[8] Managers of the rapidly growing institutional portfolios found ways of appropriating the "fat" in the commissions on large transactions. For example, an investment company manager would direct the executing broker to share the commission with other broker-dealers who had sold shares of the investment company or provided research or other services to the company or its manager. This, in turn, motivated the regional exchanges to amend their rules in order to permit such "give-ups" to any broker-dealer registered with the SEC. The result was an increase in the business of both the regional exchanges and the third market (an over-the-counter market in exchange-listed securities by nonmembers), and resulted in "market fragmentation."

In 1970, after public hearings, the SEC began to phase out the fixed commission structure.[9] And on May 1, 1975 — "May Day" to the brokerage community — all commissions paid by public customers became subject to negotiation.[10]

Meanwhile the Commission in 1971 proposed — rather casually in a letter transmitting to Congress its Institutional Study Investment Report — "the creation of a strong central market system for securities of national importance, in which all buying and selling interest in these securities could participate and be represented under a competitive regime."[11] And without waiting for legislation

[6] Id. at 357.

[7] Gordon v. New York Stock Exchange, 422 U. S. 659 (1975) (Court sustained fixed commissions). Indeed, it is not clear that *actual* oversight is essential to antitrust immunity. See United States v. NASD, 422 U. S. 694, 721-22 (1975)

[8] Poser, supra p. 689 n. 2, at 898.

[9] See Sec. Ex. Act Rel. 9007 (1970); Sec. Ex. Act Rel. 9079 (1971).

[10] Rule 19b-3, adopted by Sec. Ex. Act Rel. 11,203, 6 SEC Dock. 147 (1975)

[11] 8 SEC, Institutional Investor Study Report, H. R. Doc. No. 92-64 (1971 xxiv.

the Commission in 1972 began to implement the National Market System ("NMS") idea. The legislative mandate took form later in the Securities Acts Amendments of 1975, whose initial focus was quite different, as we have seen.[12]

The §11A that was then added to the 1934 Act simply directed the Commission "to use its authority * * * to facilitate the establishment of a national market system for securities,"[13] with no more guidance than the recitation of five qualities that the securities markets should have:

> (i) economically efficient execution of securities transactions;
> (ii) fair competition among brokers and dealers, among exchange markets, and between exchange markets and markets other than exchange markets;
> (iii) the availability to brokers, dealers, and investors of information with respect to quotations for and transactions in securities;
> (iv) the practicability of brokers executing investors' orders in the best market; and
> (v) an opportunity, consistent with the provisions of clauses (i) and (iv) of this subparagraph, for investors' orders to be executed without the participation of a dealer.[14]

Apart from the NMS, the 1975 amendments did deal with the three restrictive rules of the New York Stock Exchange:

(1) Even though the SEC's rule eliminating fixed commissions had become effective a month earlier, Congress in §6(e) double-locked the door (with minor exceptions).

(2) Section 6(c) threw exchange membership open to any qualified broker-dealer. But the exchanges may continue to limit the number of members.[15] In addition, §11(a) prohibits exchange

[12] See p. 36-37 supra.

[13] §11A(a)(2).

[14] §11A(a)(1)(C).

[15] An exchange may not decrease the number of memberships below the number in effect on May 1, 1975. The Commission may amend the rules of an exchange to increase (but not to decrease) or to remove any limitation on number. The New York Stock Exchange created a category of "physical access" members as one of several means to increase access consistently with the goals of the 1975 legislation. Physical access memberships carry most of the basic rights of equity memberships except that they are for a fixed term of one year and entail no equity interest in the Exchange itself in the event of liquidation. In New York Stock Exchange, Inc., Sec. Ex. Act Rel. 19,520, 27 SEC Dock. 283 (1983), the Commission approved a rule change to limit the number of physical access members on the Exchange to twenty-four and establish a new fee structure. The Commission observed that there had never been a demand for more than that number. There are also as many "electronic access" members as the Board of Directors determines from time to time. Const., Art. II, §1, 2 CCH N. Y. Stock Ex. Guide ¶1051.

members from effecting exchange transactions for their own accounts, accounts of associated persons, or accounts for which they exercise investment discretion, subject to certain exemptions and any further exemptions that the SEC may make by rule.

(3) The offboard trading problem was left to the Commission to solve, though within tight time limits reflecting a sense of urgency. The statute simply directs the Commission to review all relevant rules and promptly amend any that impose "a burden on competition which does not appear to the Commission to be necessary or appropriate in furtherance of the purposes of this chapter."[16]

Finally, §11A(b) requires the registration of a new breed called "securities information processors."[17]

2. Elements of the NMS

"In its efforts to implement the NMS," as Professor Poser analyzes the complex, "the SEC has identified six major 'elements,' some of which are facilities that can be regarded as components of the NMS, and others that are changes in the regulations governing the securities markets."[18]

a. The Consolidated Tape

The first solid step in the implementation of the NMS started as early as 1972 with a rule that required every exchange and the NASD to file a plan for the collection, processing, and dissemination of *completed transactions* in securities traded on an exchange.[19] The rule also prohibited the exchanges and the NASD from publishing such reports on a current and continuing basis without a plan declared effective by the Commission.

In 1973 five of the principal exchanges filed a joint plan,[20] which called for two ticker networks: Network A disseminates price and

[16] §11A(c)(4)(A).

[17] The term is defined in §3(a)(22). On the display of transaction reports, last sale data, and quotation information by securities information processors, see Rule 11Ac1-2.

[18] Poser, supra p. 591 n. 2, at 916. There is room here for only a skeletal treatment of each of the six elements, which are fully considered in Professor Poser's article.

[19] Rule 17a-15, later redesignated 11Aa3-1.

[20] See Sec. Ex. Act Rel. 15,250, 15 SEC Dock. 1355, 1356 n. 11 (1978). In 1981 the joint plan idea was formalized in Rule 11Aa3-2.

volume information concerning transactions in all NYSE-listed stocks, whether executed on the NYSE, on a regional exchange, or in the third market. Network B does so not only for all stocks traded on the American Stock Exchange but also for certain stocks traded only on one or more of the participating regional exchanges. All this information is made available through interrogation devices that securities information processors furnish to their subscribers. The plan is administered by an unincorporated association called the Consolidated Tape Association.

b. The Composite Quotation System

A model for displaying the *bids* and *offers* of competing specialists and marketmakers in a format that would enable a broker to ascertain the highest bid and lowest offer anywhere has proved harder to achieve. A "Quote Rule," which required the exchanges and the NASD to collect quotations from their specialists and marketmakers for reported securities (those covered by the consolidated tape), and to make these quotations available to quotation vendors, finally became effective on August 1, 1978.[21] But by February 1981 the Commission announced that its hopes had not been fully realized.[22] And the next year the Commission amended the rule to permit regional exchange specialists and third marketmakers, under specified circumstances, to disseminate quotations on a voluntary, rather than mandatory, basis.[23]

c. Market Linkage Systems

The consolidated tape and the composite quotation system point to the "best execution" market. But somehow the order must still get there. And this, as a practical matter, requires a computerized system capable of routing orders automatically.

The principal exchanges opposed a Commission proposal that the exchanges and the NASD promptly implement a "common message switch" that would route orders directly from brokers' or dealers'

[21] Rule 11Ac1-1, adopted by Sec. Ex. Act Rel. 14,416, 14 SEC Dock. 31 1978).

[22] Sec. Ex. Act Rel. 17,583, 22 SEC Dock. 269, 271 (1981).

[23] Sec. Ex. Act Rel. 18,482, 24 SEC Dock. 876 (1982).

offices to any qualified market,[24] for they feared that "such a facility would, in effect, bypass the stock exchanges by placing the switching mechanism that would form the heart of the NMS in a 'neutral' central computer."[25] This reaction persuaded the Commission to support instead the less radical idea of developing a linkage of the floors of the two New York exchanges and four others (Boston, Midwest, Pacific, and Philadelphia) through a facility called the Intermarket Trading System ("ITS"):

> The primary function of the ITS is to link the participating market centers by routing messages between them so that participants in one market center can communicate with participants in other market centers in order to purchase or sell stock. * * * The ITS enables brokers and specialists who are physically present in one market center to transmit electronically their own orders or their customers' orders in an ITS Stock to another market center. * * * This is accomplished by the entry of a "commitment to trade" into a computer terminal located on the floor of a participating market center.
>
> A commitment to trade identifies the destination market center, provides the necessary clearing data, specifies whether the commitment is a buy or sell, and indicates the number of shares involved and the price at which the security is to be executed. * * *
>
> An order, i. e., a "commitment to trade," initiated by an originating market center by entry into a computer terminal is delivered or queued for delivery to the destination market center's output terminal in a matter of seconds. * * * Assuming that the commitment is transmitted correctly, the broker or market-maker in the destination market center then has the following options: (1) the commitment can be allowed to expire; (2) the commitment can be cancelled; (3) the commitment can be accepted; or (4) an administrative message can be sent.
>
> A commitment to trade entered into the system is a firm obliga-

[24] Sec. Ex. Act Rel. 14,416, 14 SEC Dock. 31, 39 (1978); Sec. Ex. Act Rel. 15,671, 17 SEC Dock. 24, 35 (1979).

[25] See Poser, supra p. 591 n. 2, at 923.

A fully automated market — the "black box" understandably dreaded by the exchange community — has been functioning on an experimental basis for almost a decade as the National Securities Trading System of the Cincinnati Stock Exchange. See SEC, Directorate of Economic and Policy Analysis, A Report on the Operation of the Cincinnati Stock Exchange National Securities Trading System 1978-1982 (1982). But the system has seen little use. The Merrill Lynch firm alone accounted for about 75 percent of total volume, and it withdrew in 1983 because trading was so skimpy. Wall St. J., July 13, 1983, p. 2, col. 2.

In late 1984 the first fully automated commodity futures market — Intex, the International Futures Exchange (Bermuda) Ltd. — began operating. The organizers are reported to have selected Bermuda because the CFTC had indicated that it would take many years before it could rule on so innovative a trading system. N. Y. Times, Dec. 10, 1984, p. D4, col. 3.

tion for a fixed period of time on the part of its originator to buy or sell the specified security. If a commitment to trade is accepted by a broker or specialist at the receiving market center, a short message is entered into the system and the system quickly reports an execution back to the originating market center. If a commitment is not accepted during the designated time period, the commitment is automatically cancelled. A commitment to trade may also be manually rejected within the designated time period. In that event, the cancellation is reported back to the originating market.[26]

Meanwhile, in 1979, the NASD had announced plans to enhance NASDAQ by developing a "computer assisted execution system" (CAES) that would permit automatic execution of orders against the quotations published by over-the-counter marketmakers.[27] And in 1981 the NASD also proposed that an Automated Interface (AI) be developed between CAES and ITS "to permit automated execution of commitments sent from participating exchanges and to permit marketmakers participating in the enhanced NASDAQ to efficiently route commitments to exchange markets for execution there."[28] Thereupon the Commission ordered the six ITS participating exchanges and the NASD to act jointly in planning, developing, and operating the AI. Under the order, the AI would become operational on a pilot basis by March 1, 1982, and fully operational by September 1, 1982.[29] But the pilot marriage was somewhat forcibly consummated in May 1982, after the Commission on its own motion had adopted appropriate amendments to the ITS plan in the absence of complete agreement between plan participants and the NASD.[30]

d. Nationwide Protection of Limit Orders

Limited orders entrusted to a specialist are protected by exchange rules against execution at an inferior price.[31] But this pro-

[26] SEC Directorate of Economic and Policy Analysis, A Report on the Operation of the Intermarket Trading System: 1978-1981 (1982) 5-8.

[27] Sec. Ex. Act Rel. 17,516, 21 SEC Dock. 1519, 1527-28 (1981).

[28] Id. at 1522.

[29] Sec. Ex. Act Rel. 17,744, 22 SEC Dock. 845 (1981); see also Sec. Ex. Act Rel. 18,536, 24 SEC Dock. 1079 (1982) (status report).

[30] Sec. Ex. Act Rel. 18,713, 25 SEC Dock. 243 (1982). For a history of the off-board trading problem, see Sec. Ex. Act Rel. 20,074, 28 SEC Dock. 748 (1983). For critiques of the Commission's record in this area, see Poser, supra p. 591 n. 2, at 931-44; Macey and Haddock, Shirking at the SEC: The Failure of the National Market System, [1985] U. Ill. L. Rev. 315.

[31] These are orders to buy at a price below, or to sell at a price above, the current market.

tection does not extend to other exchanges. The difficulties of achieving the Commission's aim of nationwide protection of limit orders are partly technical and partly rooted, once again, in the exchange community's fear that it will be replaced by a monstrous "black box" that automatically spews out executions.[32] So this objective of the NMS has so far proved elusive.

e. Elimination of Off-Board Trading Systems

In September 1975 the Commission submitted a report to Congress in which it concluded that off-board trading rules did impose burdens on competition.[33] Shortly thereafter the Commission adopted Rule 19c-1, which invalidated all restrictions on exchange members' execution of agency transactions for customers in the third market.[34] And in June 1980 the Commission's Rule 19c-3 extended that treatment to all transactions (including those executed as principal or in-house agency crosses) in stocks that became listed after April 26, 1979 (the date the rule had been published for comment), or that were then traded in an exchange but did not remain listed.[35] But all this still leaves the New York Stock Exchange's offboard trading rule operative to prevent its members from acting as third-market dealers in most listed stocks.

f. Qualified Securities

Section 11A contemplates that the NMS will include only "qualified securities," to be so designated by the Commission.[36] In 1981 the Commission adopted a qualification rule,[37] which, as amended in 1987, designates as "National Market System Securities" all securities listed on one of the New York exchanges or solely on a regional exchange that substantially meets the New York listing criteria, as well as those over-the-counter securities that meet the

[32] The acronym here is CLOB, for "consolidated limit order book."

[33] Sec. Ex. Act Rel. 11,628, 7 SEC Dock. 762 (1975); see also Sec. Ex. Act Rel. 13,662, 12 SEC Dock. 947, 956 (1977).

[34] Sec. Ex. Act Rel. 11,942, 8 SEC Dock. 756 (1975).

[35] Sec. Ex. Act Rel. 16,888, 20 SEC Dock. 334 (1980); see SEC Directorate of Economic and Policy Analysis and Division of Market Regulation, A Monitoring Report on the Operation and Effect of Rule 19c-3 Under the Securities Exchange Act of 1934 (1981).

[36] §§11A(a)(1)(D), 11A(a)(2).

[37] Rule 11Aa2-1, adopted by Sec. Ex. Act Rel. 17,549, 22 SEC Dock. 22 (1981).

criteria contained in the NASD's Transaction Reporting Plan.[38] And those criteria were concurrently amended to include certain corporate governance standards.[39]

Notwithstanding all this activity, one is left with the impression that the goals stated by the SEC in the 1970s remain largely unfulfilled, and that business and technological developments seem to have a greater impact on market structure than governmental efforts.

[38] Sec. Ex. Act Rel. 24,625, 38 SEC Dock. 952 (1987).
[39] Sec. Ex. Act Rel. 24,633, 38 SEC Dock. 945 (1987).

CHAPTER 9

"FRAUD" AND MANIPULATION

A. COMMON LAW AND SEC "FRAUD"

1. The Weapons in the Federal Arsenal

Before the Securities Act of 1933 there was no way for the federal government to deal with securities frauds except by criminal prosecution for violating the mail fraud statute[1] or for conspiring to violate it,[2] or by the Postmaster General's administratively entering a so-called "fraud order" whereby all mail directed to the respondent or his agent was returned to the sender.[3]

All these remedies remain.[4] And they are used. Indeed, the mail

C. 9A [1] "Whoever, having devised or intending to devise any scheme or artifice to defraud, or for obtaining money or property by means of false or fraudulent pretenses, representations, or promises, * * * for the purpose of executing such scheme or artifice or attempting so to do, places in any post office or authorized depository for mail matter, any matter or thing whatever to be sent or delivered by the Postal Service, or takes or receives therefrom, any such matter or thing, or knowingly causes to be delivered by mail according to the direction thereon, or at the place at which it is directed to be delivered by the person to whom it is addressed, any such matter or thing, shall be fined not more than $1,000 or imprisoned not more than five years, or both." 18 U. S. C. §1341. See generally Comment, Survey of the Law of Mail Fraud, [1975] U. Ill. L. F. 237. There is a parallel statute on fraud by interstate or foreign "wire, radio, or television communications." 18 U. S. C. §1343.

[2] 18 U. S. C. §371.

[3] As the statute now reads, "Upon evidence satisfactory to the Postal Service that any person is engaged in conducting a scheme or device for obtaining money or property through the mails by means of false representations," the Service may also forbid the payment of any money order or postal note made out to the person and return the money. 39 U. S. C. §3005(a). The constitutionality of the statute has been sustained. Donaldson v. Read Magazine, Inc., 333 U. S. 178 (1948); see also Public Clearing House v. Coyne, 194 U. S. 497 (1904); Lynch v. Blount, 330 F. Supp. 689 (S. D. N. Y. 1971), *aff'd per curiam*, 404 U. S. 1007 (1972) (notwithstanding the 1968 amendment that made it unnecessary to show scienter or intent to defraud).

[4] In Edwards v. United States, 312 U. S. 473, 483-84 (1941), the Court held that §17(a) of the 1933 Act had not repealed the mail fraud statute with respect to securities.

fraud statute has been applied to certain breaches of fiduciary duty, as by an agent's obtaining secret profits.[5] But the 1933 Act, aside from requiring the registration of new offerings and certain secondary distributions under §5, included a general antifraud provision (§17(a)) and a limited sort of antitouting provision (§17(b)).[6] Section 17(a) creates three separate offenses:

> It shall be unlawful for any person in the offer or sale of any securities by the use of any means or instruments of transportation or communication in interstate commerce or by the use of the mails, directly or indirectly —
>
> (1) to employ any device, scheme, or artifice to defraud, or

[5]United States v. Buckner, 108 F. 2d 921, 926 (2d Cir. 1940), *cert. denied,* 309 U. S. 669 (scheme by protective committee to defraud bondholders in course of supposed efforts to secure favorable legislation by Philippine Government); United States v. Groves, 122 F. 2d 87 (2d Cir. 1941), *cert. denied,* 314 U. S. 670 (officer's secret profit on purchase of company's stock and resale to company); United States v. Bryza, 522 F. 2d 414 (7th Cir. 1975), *cert. denied,* 426 U. S. 912 (buying agent's accepting kickbacks from suppliers); cf. United States v. Bush, 522 F. 2d 641 (7th Cir. 1975), *cert. denied,* 424 U. S. 977 (city employee's failure to disclose his interest in a company to which the city awarded a contract); United States v. Von Barta, 635 F. 2d 999 (2d Cir. 1980), *cert. denied,* 450 U. S. 998; United States v. Bronston, 658 F. 2d 920 (2d Cir. 1981), *cert. denied,* 456 U. S. 915; United States v. Newman, 664 F. 2d 12, 19-20 (2d Cir. 1981).

But cf. Epstein v. United States, 174 F. 2d 754, 767-68 (6th Cir. 1949) (whether a breach of trust is an active fraud depends upon what the particular breach consists of, and it is not enough to show that directors of Company *A* profited from other companies that sold commodities to *A* and that they did not disclose the relationship, there being no proof of overreaching); United States v. Lemire, 720 F. 2d 1327 (D. C. Cir. 1983), *cert. denied,* 467 U. S. 1226 (not every breach of a fiduciary duty of some sort constitutes a "scheme to defraud" under the wire fraud statute).

Although these are not securities cases, there is no reason why the principle should not apply in a securities context. But *query* the whole line of cases in the light of the Supreme Court's holding in Santa Fe Industries, Inc. v. Green, 430 U. S. 462 (1977), infra p. 803, that a breach of fiduciary duty by majority stockholders (or presumably anyone else) without any deception, misrepresentation, or nondisclosure is not 10b-5 fraud. *Query* also the impact of the rejection of the "intangible rights" theory of mail fraud in *Gray* v. *United States,* 107 S. Ct. 2875 (1987).

In general, see Wang, Recent Developments in the Federal Law Regulating Stock Market Inside Trading, 6 Corp. L. Rev. 291, 308-13 (1983); Coffee, The Metastasis of Mail Fraud: The Continuing Story of the "Evolution" of a White-Collar Crime, 21 Am. Crim. L. Rev. 1 (1983). Observing that "Under the 'intangible rights' doctrine, a public or private fiduciary can be prosecuted on the theory that his conduct has deprived his beneficiaries of their right to his honest and faithful services,' " Professor Coffee suggests that "the case for statutory reform is strong." Id. at 3.

[6]On §17(b), see United States v. Amick, 439 F. 2d 351, 364-65 (7th Cir. 1971), *cert. denied,* 404 U. S. 823; SEC v. Wall St. Publishing Institute, Inc., 591 F. Supp. 1070, 1088-89 (D. D. C. 1984), *stay granted,* CCH Fed. Sec. L. Rep. ¶91,635 (D. C. Cir. 1984).

(2) to obtain money or property by means of any untrue statement of a material fact or any omission to state a material fact necessary in order to make the statements made, in the light of the circumstances under which they were made, not misleading, or

(3) to engage in any transaction, practice, or course of business which operates or would operate as a fraud or deceit upon the purchaser.[7]

This section marked an advance over the mail fraud statute in a number of respects: (1) It is specifically tailored to the securities field. (2) The 1933 Act affords the civil remedy of injunction, thus making it possible to nip certain types of fraud in the bud rather than to rely exclusively on criminal prosecution after the deed.[8] (3) Clause (2) does not refer to "fraud" as such but speaks in terms of material misstatements and half-truths. The entire section, however, refers to fraud or misrepresentation "in the offer or sale of any securities." It is perhaps arguable that this does not limit the application of the section to cases of fraud by *sellers* as distinct from fraud by *buyers* of securities — that it was intended merely to make it clear that §17(a), in contrast to the mail fraud statute, is restricted to the securities field. But the Commission has never sought to apply §17(a) except against fraudulent *sellers.*[9]

[7]Since the three clauses of §17(a) are in the disjunctive, United States v. Naftalin, 441 U. S. 768, 774 (1979), the Government or the Commission need not prove a violation of all three, United States v. Strand, 617 F. 2d 571 (10th Cir. 1980), *cert. denied,* 449 U. S. 841, and an indictment that charges all three in separate counts is not duplicitous, United States v. Amick, 439 F. 2d 351, 359 (7th Cir. 1971), *cert. denied,* 404 U. S. 823. But this is not to say that there may be three convictions for a single offense pleaded under all three clauses. United States v. Greenberg, 30 F. R. D. 164, 169-70 (S. D. N. Y. 1962).

Moreover, mail fraud and §17(a) counts are commonly joined in the same indictment, and this is permissible. United States v. Tallant, 547 F. 2d 1291, 1299 (5th Cir. 1977), *cert. denied,* 434 U. S. 889. But under the majority view consecutive sentences are improper when the convictions arose out of a single fact pattern. United States v. Reed, 639 F. 2d 896, 903-06 (2d Cir. 1981), and cases cited.

[8]§20(b). Section 17(a) does not itself create a crime any more than §5 does. But, apart from the injunctive remedy, any person who "willfully" violates *any* provision of the 1933 Act commits a crime under §24, in addition to subjecting himself or itself to administrative disciplinary proceedings under the 1934 Act if he or it is registered with the Commission in certain capacities or is an associate of a person so registered. See pp. 630-34 supra. The 1934 Act (see §§32(a), 21(e)) and the other statutes follow the same pattern.

[9]This includes the "man bite dog" case of the *customer* who defrauds his *broker* by selling short with no intention to deliver if the market goes up; for the purposes of the Act go beyond the protection of investors to the achieving of "a high standard of business ethics * * * *in every facet of the securities industry.*" United States v. Naftalin, 441 U. S. 768, 775 (1979), quoting from SEC v.

In 1934 the Securities Exchange Act added two relevant provisions, §§9(a)(4) and 10(b). The former, part of the §9 attack on market *manipulation,* makes it unlawful for any "dealer or broker, or other person selling or offering for sale or purchasing or offering to purchase the security, to make, regarding any security registered on a national securities exchange, for the purpose of inducing the purchase or sale of such security, any statement which was at the time and in the light of the circumstances under which it was made, false or misleading with respect to any material fact, and which he knew or had reasonable ground to believe was so false or misleading." Section 9(a)(4) is self-operative but limited to registered securities. Section 10(b), on the other hand, is an omnibus section that is not so limited but is not self-operative either:

> It shall be unlawful for any person, directly or indirectly, by the use of any means or instrumentality of interstate commerce or of the mails, or of any facility of any national securities exchange —
>
> * * *
>
> (b) To use or employ, in connection with the purchase or sale of any security registered on a national securities exchange or any security not so registered, any manipulative or deceptive device or contrivance in contravention of such rules and regulations as the Commission may prescribe as necessary or appropriate in the public interest or for the protection of investors.

The potentialities of §10(b) — and the most illustrious of its progeny, Rule 10b-5, which we shall examine at some depth — were not appreciated for some years, as we shall see. But the Commission has developed a gaggle of other rules under §10(b): Rules 10b-1, 10b-2, 10b-3, 10b-6, and 10b-18, on manipulation;[10] 10b-4 and 10b-13, on short tendering and buying "alongside" a tender offer;[11] 10b-7 and 10b-8, on market stabilization;[12] 10b-9, which imposes certain restrictions on "all-or-none" offerings;[13] 10b-10, the confir-

---

Capital Gains Research Bureau, Inc., 375 U. S. 180, 186-87 (1963) (the ellipsis and italics are the Court's); see also United States v. Tager, 788 F. 2d 349, 354 (6th Cir. 1986).

[10] See c. 9D infra.

[11] See pp. 511, 526 supra.

[12] See p. 859 infra.

[13] See SEC v. Blinder, Robinson & Co., CCH Fed. Sec. L. Rep. ¶99,491 (10th Cir. 1983), *cert. denied*, 469 U. S. 1108; Rooney, Pace, Inc., Sec. Ex. Act Rel. 23,763, 36 SEC Dock. 1133 (1986). Cf. Rule 15c2-4, infra p. 708.

mation rule;[14] 10b-16, on disclosure of credit terms in margin transactions;[15] and 10b-17, on untimely announcements of record dates for dividends and other specified events.

In 1936 the Exchange Act was amended by adding what is the present §15(c)(1), then §15(c). As amended in 1975, that section provides that

> No broker or dealer shall make use of the mails or of any means or instrumentality of interstate commerce to effect any transaction in, or to induce the purchase or sale of, any security (other than commercial paper, bankers, acceptances, or commercial bills) otherwise than on a national securities exchange of which it is a member by means of any manipulative, deceptive, or other fraudulent device or contrivance.

There is a similar prohibition with respect to municipal dealers so far as municipal securities are concerned, except that there is no reference to exchange trading because it is virtually nonexistent. And the section concludes:

> The Commission shall, for the purposes of this paragraph, by rules and regulations define such devices or contrivances as are manipulative, deceptive, or otherwise fraudulent.

[14]See p. 704 n. 20 infra. The term "customer" in the rule encompasses a subscriber in a "best efforts" underwriting. Lowell H. Listrom & Co., Inc. v. SEC, 803 F. 2d 938, 940 (8th Cir. 1986).

In Sec. Ex. Act Rel. 19,687, 27 SEC Dock. 874 (1983), the Commission amended Rule 10b-10 to provide an exception from the immediate delivery requirement for transactions in shares of certain investment companies that attempt to maintain a constant net asset value. The amendments also require disclosure to investors of certain yield and call feature information in connection with transactions in debt securities other than municipals.

In Ettinger v. Merrill Lynch, Pierce, Fenner & Smith, Inc., — F. Supp. —, CCH Fed. Sec. L. Rep. ¶93,102 (E. D. Pa. 1986), the court seemed to assume, without noticing the point, that the exemption of marketmakers' transactions from the confirmation rule's requirement of disclosure of mark-ups or markdowns (Rule 10b-10(a)(8)(i)(A)) carried over to the "shingle theory" (infra p. 811), to the effect that *excessive* spreads violate the fraud provisions.

[15]This reflects the exemption of brokers' margin loans from the disclosure requirement of the Truth in Lending Act, 15 U. S. C. §1603(2), on the legislative assumption that the Commission would adopt an appropriate rule. Sec. Ex. Act Rel. 8773 (1969).

In Abeles v. Oppenheimer & Co., Inc., 597 F. Supp. 532, CCH Fed. Sec. L. Rep. ¶92,517 (N. D. Ill. 1986), the court held that a deposit of money with a broker in connection with the purchase of GNMA forwards did not involve an extension of credit under Rule 10b-16, since there was no debt obligation to pay the purchase price due and owing on the trade date and the deposit was not part of a financing arrangement but was more akin to a performance bond or earnest money deposit designed to insure performance of an obligation at a future date.

This section differs in substance from §10(b) in a number of respects: (1) Although it directs the Commission to adopt rules of definition, the first portion of the section is literally self-operative, whereas §10(b) is not operative in the absence of specific rules. (2) It is limited to over-the-counter transactions, whereas §10(b) is not.[16] (3) It is limited to transactions by brokers or dealers (or, since 1975, municipal dealers). However, like §10(b) and unlike §17(a), it covers fraud in the purchase as well as the sale of securities.

There are eight rules, all of them in form definitions of the term "manipulative, deceptive, or other fraudulent device or contrivance" as used in §15(c)(1) of the Act. Rule 15c1-1 simply defines "customer" and "completion of the transaction" as used in this series of rules. And Rule 15c1-2 is a general antifraud provision that is modeled on Clauses (2) and (3) of §17(a) of the 1933 Act, except that the portion comparable to Clause (2) applies only when the "statement or omission is made with knowledge or reasonable grounds to believe that it is untrue or misleading."[17] The other six rules are particularizations of Rule 15c1-2,[18] although the Commission was careful to provide in that rule that they are not exhaustive.[19]

Rule 15c1-3, in substance, prohibits a broker-dealer from representing that his registration indicates that the Commission has passed on his financial standing or conduct or the merits of any security or transaction.

[16]Section 15(c)(1) does cover over-the-counter transactions in securities traded on an exchange notwithstanding the intimation to the contrary in Gilman v. Shearson/American Express, Inc., 577 F. Supp. 492, 496 (D. N. H. 1983).

[17]In full text:

> (a) The term "manipulative, deceptive, or other fraudulent device or contrivance," as used in section 15(c)(1) of the Act, is hereby defined to include any act, practice, or course of business which operates or would operate as a fraud or deceit upon any person.
>
> (b) The term "manipulative, deceptive, or other fraudulent device or contrivance," as used in section 15(c)(1) of the Act, is hereby defined to include any untrue statement of a material fact and any omission to state a material fact necessary in order to make the statements made, in the light of the circumstances under which they are made, not misleading, which statement or omission is made with knowledge or reasonable grounds to believe that it is untrue or misleading.

[18]William I. Hay, 19 SEC 397, 408 n. 15 (1945).

[19]"The scope of this rule shall not be limited by any specific definitions of the term 'manipulative, deceptive, or other fraudulent device or contrivance' contained in other rules adopted pursuant to section 15(c)(1) of the act." Rule 15c1-2(c).

Rules 15c1-5 and 15c1-6[20] are complementary. The former requires any broker or dealer "controlled by, controlling, or under common control with, the issuer of any security" to disclose the existence of control to his customer before entering into any purchase or sale contract. Rule 15c1-6 requires a *broker* who is acting for a customer or for both sides, as well as a *dealer* who is to receive a fee from a customer for rendering advice, to give his customer written notification, at or before the completion of the transaction, whenever he "is participating or is otherwise financially interested" in "the primary or secondary distribution" of the security being bought or sold.

Rule 15c1-7 contains two requirements in connection with discretionary accounts. Immediately after effecting any transaction with or for a discretionary account, the broker or dealer must make a record of the customer's name, the name, amount, and price of the security, and the date and time of the transaction. And transactions may not be "excessive in size or frequency in view of the financial resources and character" of the account. The latter prohibition is directed at the "churning" of customers' accounts. Here again, however, this rule is but a partial particularization of Rule 15c1-2. Even though Rule 15c1-7 applies only when the broker or dealer has been "vested" with discretionary power, the Commission has repeatedly held that the "churning" of customers' accounts may violate Rule 15c1-2, as well as §17(a)(3) of the 1933 Act, "whenever the broker or dealer is in a position to determine the volume and frequency of transactions by reason of the customer's willingness to follow the suggestions of the broker or dealer and he abuses the customer's confidence by overtrading."[21]

[20] The former Rule 15c1-4 was a confirmation rule, which in the late 1970s gave way to Rule 10b-10 because §15(c)(1) is limited to over-the-counter transactions. Sec. Ex. Act Rel. 13,508, 12 SEC Dock. 299 (1977).

[21] Norris & Hirshberg, Inc., 21 SEC 865, 890 (1946), *aff'd* sub nom. Norris & Hirshberg, Inc. v. SEC, 177 F. 2d 228 (D. C. Cir. 1949); see also, e. g., Russell L. Irish, 42 SEC 735 (1965), *aff'd* sub nom. Irish v. SEC, 367 F. 2d 637 (9th Cir. 1966), *cert. denied*, 386 U. S. 911; Hecht v. Harris, Upham & Co., 430 F. 2d 1202, 1206-07 (9th Cir. 1970); Fey v. Walston & Co., Inc., 493 F. 2d 1036 (7th Cir. 1974); Carras v. Burns, 516 F. 2d 251 (4th Cir. 1975); Miley v. Oppenheimer & Co., Inc., 637 F. 2d 318 (5th Cir. 1981).

Litigation over churning seems to be increasing: One does not have to be a broker or dealer to be guilty of churning. The fiduciary obligations that an investment manager owes to an investment company and the control it exercises over investments are as great as those of a broker. Armstrong v. McAlpin, 699 F. 2d 79, 90 (2d Cir. 1983).

"Churning, in and of itself, may be a deceptive and manipulative device under section 10(b), the scienter required by section 10(b) [see p. 774 infra] being

Rule 15c1-8, in effect, prohibits purported "market offerings" (as distinct from "fixed price offerings") unless the broker or dealer knows or has reasonable ground to believe that a market exists other

---

implicit in the nature of the conduct." Id. at 91.

There can be no churning without control over the account. M & B Contracting Corp. v. Dale, 795 F. 2d 531 (6th Cir. 1986). And it is improper to instruct a jury that the requisite degree of "control" is established when a client routinely follows his broker's recommendations, since that is only one element of control, not the determinative factor. The proper instruction on "churning" emphasizes the many factors suggesting control. Tiernan v. Blythe, Eastman, Dillon & Co., 719 F. 2d 1 (1st Cir. 1983). For an enumeration of those factors, see Nunes v. Merrill Lynch, Pierce, Fenner & Smith, Inc., 635 F. Supp. 1391, 1393-94 (D. Md. 1986).

An investor who wanted frequent trading of the sort his broker consummated cannot establish churning. Thompson v. Smith Barney, Harris Upham & Co., 709 F. 2d 1413 (11th Cir. 1983). That is to say, "the excessive trading element of a churning case is not established unless the frequency of the trades was unrelated to the customer's objectives." Follansbee v. Davis, Skaggs & Co., Inc., 681 F. 2d 673, 676 (9th Cir. 1982).

Although the churning plaintiff who determines not to present expert evidence proceeds at some risk, such evidence is not a legal prerequisite to going to the jury. Costello v. Oppenheimer & Co., Inc., 711 F. 2d 1361, 1369 (7th Cir. 1983). But in Shad v. Dean Witter Reynolds, Inc., 799 F. 2d 525 (9th Cir. 1986), the court reversed for failure to allow expert testimony on churning.

On the causation element, see Hatrock v. Edward D. Jones & Co., 750 F. 2d 767, 773 (9th Cir. 1984), infra Supp. p. 928 n. 125.

Failure to calculate the turnover ratio is not fatal, since the ratio is not determinative. Mauriber v. Shearson/American Express, Inc., 567 F. Supp. 1231, 1237-38 (S. D. N. Y. 1983).

Indeed, "Considering the nature of an action for churning, it appears that no consistently appropriate measure of damages exists, but that different theories of recovery may be proper in different cases, depending upon the particular facts of each case." Nunes v. Merrill Lynch, Pierce, Fenner & Smith, Inc., 635 F. Supp. 1391, 1396 (D. Md. 1986) (no damages when plaintiff made a profit).

On methods of computing turnover, as well as measuring damages in private actions, see Note, Churning by Securities Dealers, 80 Harv. L. Rev. 869, 875-76, 883-85 (1967); see also Code §§1606, 1717; Winer v. Patterson, 644 F. Supp. 898 (D. N. H. 1986) (lost profits minus excess commissions in order to avoid double recovery).

On the peculiarities of churning listed options, see Poser, Options Account Fraud: Securities Churning in a New Context, 39 Bus. Law. 571 (1984):

> Because of the complexity of listed options and the variety of ways in which they may be used, mathematical measurements of the amount of trading are considerably less useful in options cases in order to reach a determination as to whether the broker has acted inconsistently with his duty to his customer. In several recent options churning cases, federal courts have abandoned the traditional measurements of churning. Instead, the inquiry as to whether the broker's conduct toward his customer was fraudulent tends to focus on the riskiness of the particular strategy used and the ability and willingness of the customer to assume the risks.

Id. at 572. This article contains also an excellent description of the elements of traditional churning, together with a collection of cases. Id. at 576-85. Churning often turns on "suitability." See p. 829 infra.

than that made or controlled by him or a related person. It is noteworthy that Rules 15c1-7 and 15c1-8, alone among the broker-dealer fraud rules under §15(c)(1), go beyond the disclosure philosophy. This is particularly evident in the case of Rule 15c1-7.

Rule 15c1-9 prohibits the use of any *pro forma* financial statement — that is, a statement "purporting to give effect to the receipt and application of any part of the proceeds from the sale or exchange of securities" — unless the underlying assumptions are clearly set forth as part of the caption of the statement.

As part of the Maloney Act amendment that added §15A in 1938,[22] Congress enacted the present §15(c)(2), which is similar to §15(c)(1) except that (1) it does not apply to an "exempted security," (2) it covers "fictitious quotations" as well as fraudulent, deceptive, or manipulative practices, and (3) it directs the Commission by rule to "prescribe means reasonably designed to prevent" such practices and quotations as well as to define them. The Supreme Court has stated that the same language as borrowed in §14(e) gives the Commission "latitude to regulate nondeceptive activities as a 'reasonably designed' means of preventing manipulative acts, without suggesting any change in the meaning of the term 'manipulative' itself."[23]

Like §15(c)(1), §15(c)(2) has a first sentence that on its face is self-operative; and a proscription of "fictitious quotations" would seem specific enough even for a criminal prosecution without the emendation afforded by rules. Nevertheless, the Commission, in arguing to the Supreme Court that §206(4) of the Investment Advisers Act, which was modeled on §15(c)(2), was not self-operative, stated that the Commission had "for many years interpreted" §15(c)(2) that way.[24] And the Commission has seldom if ever instituted any action under either §15(c)(1) or §15(c)(2) without pleading a specific rule, of which there are now eight under §15(c)(2). Three of them we have already noticed: Rule 15c2-1, on hypothecation of customers' securities;[25] 15c2-8, on delivery of preliminary

[22] See p. 620 supra.

[23] Schreiber v. Burlington Northern, Inc., 472 U. S. 1, 11 n. 11 (1985). Section 15C(b)(2)(A), added to the 1934 Act by the Government Securities Act of 1986 (supra p. 611), provides, again on the model of §15(c)(2) but with changes, that the Treasury's rules under §15C shall "be designed to prevent fraudulent and manipulative acts and practices * * *." One wonders why the draftsman courted needless litigation by omitting the word "reasonably" before "designed" as well as the word "deceptive."

[24] Petition for Cert., p. 19, SEC v. Capital Gains Research Bureau, Inc., 375 U. S. 180 (1963).

[25] See p. 624 n. 9 supra.

and final prospectuses;[26] and Rule 15c2-11, which, in effect, prohibits quotations without specified information.[27] The other five rules are 15c2-2, on broker-dealers' pre-dispute arbitration agreements with their customers;[28] 15c2-3, a postwar rule that prohibits trading in German securities without validation; 15c2-4, on handling the proceeds of non-firm-commitment underwritings;[29] 15c2-5, which calls for certain credit and other information going beyond the prospectus in connection with the joint selling of mutual fund shares and life insurance;[30] and 15c2-7, on the identification of quotations submitted to an interdealer quotation system.

With §10(b) non-self-operative, the combination of §17(a) of the 1933 Act and §§9(a)(4), 15(c)(1), and 15(c)(2) of the 1934 Act did not cover fraud in the *purchase* of securities by persons *other than* (1) brokers and dealers acting over the counter or (2) persons buying registered securities for the purpose of inducing their purchase by others. This was a serious gap, because an issuer itself, or an officer or director or principal stockholder, could buy in its securi-

[26] See p. 128 n. 19 supra.

[27] In late 1984 the Commission found that, although the rule "has helpec somewhat to minimize the problem of manipulative trading in the securities o reactivated shell corporations, the Rule as presently structured does not adequately achieve its more general purpose of preventing arbitrary quotes fo certain thinly traded securities," largely because of fundamental changes in the structure and practices of the over-the-counter market. Sec. Ex. Act Rel. 21,470 31 SEC Dock. 797, 798 (1984). The Commission accordingly amended the rul in a number of respects, *inter alia,* creating an exception for NASDAQ-quote securities and subjecting unpriced entries to the rule. Then in April 1985 th Commission initiated a cost-benefit study, soliciting comment and date on th rule as amended. Sec. Ex. Act Rel. 21,914, 32 SEC Dock. 1091 (1985).

[28] See p. 1030 n. 107 infra.

[29] See Eastside Church of Christ v. National Plan, Inc., 391 F. 2d 357, 36 (5th Cir. 1968), *cert. denied* sub nom. Church of Christ v. National Plan, Inc 393 U. S. 913, *judgment for plaintiff on remand aff'd* sub nom. McGregor Blvd Church of Christ v. Walling, 428 F. 2d 401 (5th Cir. 1970); United States v Koss, 506 F. 2d 1103, 1110 (2d Cir. 1974), *cert. denied,* 421 U. S. 911; Lowe H. Listrom & Co., Inc., Sec. Ex. Act Rel. 22,689, 34 SEC Dock. 872, 873 (1985 *aff'd on other grounds* sub nom. Lowell H. Listrom & Co., Inc. v. SEC, 803 F. 2 938 (8th Cir. 1986). Cf. Rule 10b-9, supra p. 702.

"It is well established that undisclosed purchases by underwriters or thei affiliates, arranged for the purpose of closing an unsuccessful 'all-or-none' o 'part-or-none' offering, are fraudulent." Brock Lippitt, Sec. Ex. Act Rel. 23,49 36 SEC Dock. 277 (1986) (affirmance of NASD order based on a violation c Rule 15c2-4 as unethical conduct). And purchases that are not ratified befor the expiration date do not reflect *bona fide* sales. Rooney, Pace, Inc., Sec. E Act Rel. 23,763, 36 SEC Dock. 1133 (1986). But that result does not follo merely from the fact that the buyer, after reading the prospectus that he g with the confirmation after the expiration date, immediately resold the share Id. at 1135 n. 7.

[30] See Lellock v. Paine, Webber, Jackson & Curtis, Inc., CCH Fed. Sec. L Rep. ¶99,440 (W. D. Pa. 1983).

ties by fraudulent practices without being touched by federal authority except for criminal prosecution under the mail or wire fraud statute or the entry of a mail fraud order. In the revision program of 1941 the Commission and the securities industry jointly suggested an amendment to extend §17(a) to the purchase as well as the sale of securities.[31] When this program fell casualty to Pearl Harbor, the Commission in May 1942 hit upon a solution to the problem that from hindsight appears exceedingly simple and obvious. Acting under §10(b), which had been in the Exchange Act from the beginning, the Commission adopted Rule 10b-5 (originally designated X-10B-5), which merely borrows the language of §17(a), except for the reference in Clause (2) to *obtaining money or property by means of* an untrue statement or half-truth, and applies it "in connection with the purchase or sale of any security":

> It shall be unlawful for any person, directly or indirectly, by the use of any means or instrumentality of interstate commerce, or of the mails, or of any facility of any national securities exchange,
>
> (1) to employ any device, scheme, or artifice to defraud,
>
> (2) to make any untrue statement of a material fact or to omit to state a material fact necessary in order to make the statements made, in the light of the circumstances under which they were made, not misleading, or
>
> (3) to engage in any act, practice, or course of business which operates or would operate as a fraud or deceit upon any person, in connection with the purchase or sale of any security.[32]

Aside from these provisions and rules relating to purchases or sales, there are a number of others that are more specialized: We have already noticed Rule 14a-9, the proxy fraud rule, together with its analogue, Rule 14c-6, when an "information statement" is used.[33] We have noticed also §§14(e) and 13(e) of the 1934 Act,

[31] Investment Bankers Assn. et al., Report on the Conferences with the SEC and Its Staff on Proposals for Amending the Securities Act of 1933 and the Securities Exchange Act of 1934 (1941) 167.

[32] In one respect §10(b) and the rule may be *narrower* than §17(a), which reads "in the *offer or sale*" — an incident of the 1954 amendment of §5 to permit offers during the waiting period (see p. 95 supra) — in contrast with the "sale" of Rule 10b-5. See Blue Chip Stamps v. Manor Drug Stores, 421 U. S. 723, 732-34 (1975), infra p. 792, see also People v. Riley, 708 P. 2d 1359, 1365 (Colo. 1985) (Colorado version of Rule 10b-5).

The rule has been held not to be unconstitutionally vague. United States v. Persky, 520 F. 2d 283, 287 (2d Cir. 1975); see also Speed v. Transamerica Corp., 99 F. Supp. 808, 831-32 (D. Del. 1951) (rejecting arguments of vagueness and delegation as "shop worn").

[33] See pp. 477-86, 490 supra.

with respect to tender offers and issuer repurchases.[34] In addition, §17(j) of the Investment Company Act, on the model of the rule-making provision in §15(c)(2) of the Exchange Act, authorizes the Commission to "define, and prescribe means reasonably designed to prevent, * * * fraudulent, deceptive or manipulative acts" by persons in specified relationships to registered investment companies in connection with their portfolio securities;[35] and §206 of the Advisers Act is a cross, so far as investment advisers are concerned, between the language of 1933 Act §17(a)(1) and (3) and 1934 Act §10(b), with the addition of rulemaking authority along the lines of 1934 Act §15(c)(2).[36]

This cacophony — which characterizes not only the substantive language but also the jurisdictional references to use of the mails or interstate commerce[37] — has resulted in much wasteful litigation. Virtually every proceeding, public or private, is based alternatively on as many of these provisions and rules as may be applicable, for fear of missing a pearl here or there. Accordingly, the integration of all these "fraud" provisions into basically a single section is one of the major reforms proposed by the Code. In the words of the commentary:

> Sections 202(61) and 202(96) define "fraudulent act" and "misrepresentation" basically in the language of the respective portions of §17(a) — which was borrowed in Rule 10b-5 — but with special provision in §202(96)(B) for estimates and projections. These definitions, together with the definitions of "fact" and "material" in §§202(55) and 202(92), make it possible in a single brief section (§1602(a)) to cover all of today's fraud provisions with respect to purchases, sales, proxy solicitations, tender requests and investment advice. There is a limited duty to correct (§1602(b)). These provisions are self-operative. But §1614(a) gives the Commission rulemaking authority (along the lines, for example, of X15(c)(2)) not only to define, but also to "prescribe means reasonably designed to prevent," conduct in violation of Part XVI ("Fraud, Misrepresentation, and Manipulation") generally.[38]

[34] See pp. 509, 515 supra. On the rules under these sections, see pp. 522-26 supra.

[35] These rules may require registered investment companies and their investment advisers and principal underwriters to adopt codes of ethics. And Rule 17j-1, *inter alia,* has implemented that authority.

[36] The rules under §206 are described infra pp. 837-40.

[37] Ink has been spilled over the difference, if any, between the "in interstate commerce" of 1933 Act §17(a) and the "of interstate commerce" of 1934 Act §10(b). See p. 94 supra.

[38] 1 Code xlv.

Far from tidying up the SEC fraud scene, however, Congress cluttered it further with Chapter 96 of the Criminal Code,[39] entitled Racketeer Influenced and Corrupt Organizations ("RICO"), which was adopted as Title IX of the Organized Crime Control Act of 1970.[40]

The RICO statute makes it unlawful, *inter alia,* for "any person through a pattern of racketeering activity * * * to acquire or maintain, directly or indirectly, any interest in or control of any enterprise which is engaged in, or the activities of which affect, interstate or foreign commerce."[41] It defines "pattern of racketeering activity" to require "at least two acts of racketeering activity [usually called "predicate acts"], one of which occurred after the effective date of this chapter and the last of which occurred within ten years (excluding any period of imprisonment) after the commission of a prior act of racketeering activity";[42] and "racketeering activity" is defined to include "fraud in the sale of securities."[43]

How the last phrase got into the definition — whose fourth category couples it with bankruptcy fraud and offenses involving dangerous drugs — is no more clear than what "fraud" means in this context. The closest reference in the legislative history is (in the testimony of J. Edgar Hoover) to "thefts of securities from brokerage houses," in a number of which "close associates and relatives of La Cosa Nostra figures are known to be involved."[44]

The critical term is "pattern." The Supreme Court has held that, although the statute "requires" at least two "racketeering" acts, two may not suffice; that is to say, two isolated acts are not a "pattern."[45] And a single continuing scheme does not provide the "continuity" essential to a "pattern."[46] Whether the two predicate acts must be related is a question that has split the courts.[47]

[39] 18 U. S. C. §§1961-68.

[40] 84 Stat. 922.

[41] 18 U. S. C. §1962(b).

[42] 18 U. S. C. §1961(5).

[43] 18 U. S. C. §1961(1)(D). This does not exclude fraud in the purchase. Lickhalter v. System Development Corp., CCH Fed. Sec. L. Rep. ¶91,459 (C. D. Cal. 1984).

[44] S. Rep. No. 617, 91st Cong., 1st Sess. (1969) 77; see also 39 SEC Ann. Rep. 89 (1973).

[45] Sedima, S. P. R. L. v. Imrex Co., Inc., 473 U. S. 479, 496 n. 14 (1985), infra pp. 923-24.

[46] Superior Oil Co. v. Fulmer, 785 F. 2d 252 (8th Cir. 1986); cf. United States v. Weisman, 624 F. 2d 1118, 1124 n. 5 (2d Cir. 1980), *cert. denied,* 449 U. S. 871 (nine counts of securities fraud under §17(a) of the 1933 Act were a single predicate crime because they were "out of the same episode").

[47] *Yes:* United States v. Starnes, 644 F. 2d 673, 678 (7th Cir. 1981), *cert. denied,* 454 U. S. 826; United States v. Brooklier, 685 F. 2d 1208, 1222 (9th

2. The Relation Between SEC "Fraud" Concepts and Common Law Deceit

Statutes build on the common law and, especially when statutes are new, judges and lawyers who are trained in the common law are apt to look to it for guidance.[48] This is not the place for a detailed discussion of the common law tort action of deceit,[49] or of its criminal analogue in the false pretenses statutes that go back to George II.[50] At the same time, it is impossible to describe the statutory fraud concepts that have developed under the securities laws without some brief summary of what has gone before — a summary that, because of its generalization and the great number of common law jurisdictions, must be taken *cum grano salis.*

The hornbook "elements" of deceit — which, it must be remembered, was not consciously or especially molded for the flotation of securities — are six in number: There must be (1) a false representation of (2) a material (3) fact; (4) the defendant must know of the falsity (this kind of knowledge is called scienter) but make the statement nevertheless for the purpose of inducing the plaintiff to rely on it; and (5) the plaintiff must justifiably rely on it and (6) suffer damage as a consequence. The enumeration of these elements suggests the questions that have arisen and that in large measure carry over to the SEC Acts:

(1) It would seem to be a relatively simple matter to determine whether a representation is true or false. But what of ambiguous statements — those that are true in one sense but false in another? And what of statements that are literally true but convey a different impression to the average person? Or half-truths — statements that are true as far as they go but are misleading because of the absence

---

Cir. 1982), *cert. denied,* 459 U. S. 1206. *Contra:* United States v. Weisman, 624 F. 2d 1118, 1122-23 (2d Cir. 1980), *cert. denied,* 449 U. S. 871; United States v. Bright, 630 F. 2d 804, 830 n. 47 (5th Cir. 1980).

See generally United States v. Turkett, 452 U. S. 576 (1981) ("enterprise" encompasses both legitimate and illegitimate enterprises); 1 M. Steinberg and R. Ferrara, Securities Practice: Federal and State Enforcement (1985) c. 6. RICO also has a civil side. See p. 923 infra. And twenty-four states together with Puerto Rico have their own RICO statutes, which are set out in CCH RICO Business Disputes Guide and summarized in CCH Blue Sky L. Rep. ¶6605. See, e. g., State *ex rel.* Corbin v. Pickrell, 136 Ariz. 589, 667 P. 2d 1304 (1983).

[48] See Doll v. James Martin Associates (Holdings), Ltd., 600 F. Supp. 510, 526 (E. D. Mich. 1984).

[49] See Restatement (Second) of Torts, Div. 4, Deceit, esp. c. 22, Misrepresentation and Nondisclosure Causing Pecuniary Loss; Green, Deceit, 16 Va. L. Rev. 749 (1930).

[50] 30 Geo. 2, c. 24 (1757); see Note, The Crime of False Pretenses in the Context of Commercial Credit Transactions, 65 Yale L. J. 887 (1956).

of pertinent qualifications? Or an omission to make any express representation at all when there is an implied representation of fair dealing or when a fiduciary relationship imposes an affirmative duty to speak?

(2) A fact is material if "a reasonable man would attach importance to its existence or nonexistence in determining his choice of action in the transaction in question."[51] But there is still ample room for argument on the facts of particular cases and typically the question will be for the fact finder.

(3) What is a statement of fact as distinguished from an expression of opinion — for example, a statement of value or mere "puffing"? Or as distinguished from a statement of law — for example, that a corporation is empowered to do certain things? Or as distinguished from a forecast or promise — for example, that certain dividends will be earned or that the proceeds of an issue of securities will be applied to certain purposes?[52]

(4) The fourth element, scienter, has been stated here in its most rigorous aspect. But it has been variously defined to mean everything from knowing falsity with an implication of *mens rea,* through the various gradations of recklessness, down to such nonaction as is virtually equivalent to negligence or even liability without fault (and were better treated as creating a distinct species of liability not based on intent).[53]

(5) There is always the question whether the plaintiff relied on the false representation complained of or on something quite unrelated — perhaps a tip from a third person.[54]

[51] Restatement (Second) of Torts §538(2)(a); see Shores v. Sklar, 647 F. 2d 462, 468 (5th Cir. *en banc* 1981), *cert. denied,* 459 U. S. 1102.

[52] See Kripke, Rule 10b-5 Liability and "Material" "Facts," 46 N. Y. U. L. Rev. 1061, 1070-75 (1972); Luce v. Edelstein, 802 F. 2d 49, 55 (2d Cir. 1986) ("making a specific promise to perform a particular act in the future while secretly intending not to perform that act," but "Such a promise * * * must encompass particular action and be more than a generalized promise to act as a faithful fiduciary").

[53] "Where a party innocently misrepresents a material fact by mistake * * * such representation will support an action for fraud." Stein v. Treger, 182 F. 2d 696, 699 (D. C. Cir. 1950), and cases cited; see also, e. g., Mears v. Accomac Banking Co., Inc., 160 Va. 311, 321, 168 S. E. 740, 743 (1933). It is said that a majority of the states now permit actions on the basis of negligent or sometimes innocent misrepresentation. See Prosser, Handbook of the Law of Torts (4th ed. 1971) 699-714. "There has * * * been a growing recognition by common-law courts that the doctrines of fraud and deceit which developed around transactions involving land and other tangible items of wealth are ill-suited to the sale of such intangibles as advice and securities, and that accordingly, the doctrines must be adapted to the merchandise in issue." SEC v. Capital Gains Research Bureau, Inc., 375 U. S. 180, 194 (1963). For The American Law Institute's view, see Restatement (Second) of Torts §552C.

[54] On the concept of *justifiable* reliance, see pp. 874 n. 12, 957 infra. In List

(6) Finally there are all the questions of causation in which the law of torts abounds.[55]

In effect, the charge of deceit (as least in those jurisdictions that have not substantially watered down the concept of scienter) is an accusation of thievery. In 1889 the House of Lords was so concerned with its implications that it could not bring itself to hold that gentlemen respected in the business community could be guilty of deceit because of a false statement in a prospectus however unreasonable their belief in the statement's truth.[56] The immediate reaction of Parliament was to pass the Directors' Liability Act of 1890, as we shall see when we come to the chapter on Civil Liability. But in the last century the courts in both England and the United States have considerably softened the common law of deceit — the degree of liberalization varying, of course, with the jurisdiction. Thus, apart from the watering down of the scienter concept, there is ample precedent for holding that false statements on legal matters are actionable. And at this point it is almost obligatory to quote Lord Bowen's observation that "The state of a man's mind is as much a fact as the state of his digestion."[57]

Perhaps nowhere is this liberalization more noticeable than it is with respect to what constitutes a false representation. It is now quite clear that a half-truth is as bad as an outright lie. Thus, in 1932 a British court sent Lord Kylsant to prison because his steamship line had issued a prospectus that had *truthfully* stated its average net income for the past ten years and its dividends for the past seventeen, but had deliberately *concealed* the fact that its earnings during the first three of the ten years had been greatly augmented by World War I as compared with the seven lean years that followed.[58] This was a criminal prosecution rather than a deceit ac-

---

v. Fashion Park, Inc., 340 F. 2d 457, 462 (2d Cir. 1965), *cert. denied* sub nom. List v. Lerner, 382 U. S. 811, a case under Rule 10b-5, the court contrasted materiality and reliance by stating that reliance requires that the *individual plaintiff* must have acted upon the fact misrepresented, whereas materiality requires that a *reasonable person* would have so acted. The court added, however, that care must be taken to distinguish the requirement that a reasonable person would have *believed* the fact misrepresented, since there is a marked trend away from that common law requirement.

[55] See 1 Code 61-62, Comment (5).

[56] Derry v. Peek, 14 A. C. 337 (1889).

[57] Edington v. Fitzmaurice, 29 Ch. D. 459, 483 (1885). The Restatement of Torts (Second) has it that "One who fraudulently makes a misrepresentation of fact, opinion, intention or law for the purpose of inducing another to act or refrain from action in reliance upon it, is subject to liability to the other in deceit for pecuniary loss caused to him by his justifiable reliance upon the misrepresentation." §525; see esp. Comment d; see also id., §§539, 544, 545.

[58] Rex v. Kylsant, 23 Cr. App. R. 83, [1932] 1 K. B. 442.

tion. The Larceny Act of 1861, under which it was brought, made it a misdemeanor for a director to make "any written statement or account which he shall know to be false in any material particular" with intent to induce any person to advance property to his company.[59] It is not surprising, therefore, that the same view should prevail in common law deceit. In 1941, for example, the Supreme Court of the United States, applying Iowa law in a deceit case involving an allegedly misleading prospectus, approved the view of The American Law Institute to the effect (in the Court's paraphrase) that "a statement of a half truth is as much a misrepresentation as if the facts stated were untrue."[60] A lay Englishman managed to capture the thought very well:

> That a lie which is half a truth is ever the blackest of lies,
> That a lie which is all a lie may be met and fought with outright,
> But a lie which is part a truth is a harder matter to fight.[61]

At the same time there is still no common law liability in deceit for complete nondisclosure as distinguished from a half-truth, unless the one party to a business transaction "by concealment or other action intentionally prevents the other from acquiring material information,"[62] or the one party is under a duty to the other to exercise reasonable care to disclose the matter in question "because of a fiduciary or other similar relation of trust and confidence between them."[63] So far as a fiduciary is concerned, however, the courts have posed

> an affirmative duty of "utmost good faith, and full and fair disclosure of all material facts," as well as an affirmative obligation "to employ reasonable care to avoid misleading" his clients.[64]

[59] 24 & 25 Vict., c. 96, §84.

[60] Equitable Life Ins. Co. of Iowa v. Halsey, Stuart & Co., 312 U. S. 410, 424-26 (1941).

[61] Tennyson, The Grandmother, Stanza 8.

[62] Restatement (Second) of Torts §550.

[63] Id., §551(2)(a). Some would have it that, "under the modern law of misrepresentation, the existence of a duty to disclose is not limited to situations involving preexisting fiduciary relationships." See Anderson, Fraud, Fiduciaries, and Insider Trading, 10 Hofstra L. Rev. 341, 351 (1982).

[64] SEC v. Capital Gains Research Bureau, Inc., 375 U. S. 180, 194 (1963). Indeed, fraud in equity rather than law

> properly includes all acts, omissions and concealments which involve a breach of legal or equitable duty, trust, or confidence, justly reposed, and are injurious to another, or by which an undue and unconscientious advantage is taken of another.

Id. at 194, quoting Moore v. Crawford, 130 U. S. 122, 128 (1888), which in turn quoted 1 Story, Equity Jurisprudence (13th ed. 1886) §187.

Now there are superimposed on this common law background the several antifraud provisions of the SEC statutes. It is obvious from the language that some of the basic problems are the same — what is false, what is a fact, what is material. Because of the legislative background it seems reasonable to assume at the very least that the most liberal common law views on these questions should govern under the statutes.[65] The antifraud provisions are part of a statutory scheme that resulted from a finding that securities are "intricate merchandise"[66] and a congressional determination that the public interest demanded legislation that would recognize the gross inequality of bargaining power between the professional securities firm and the average investor. "The essential objective of securities legislation is to protect those who do not know market conditions from the overreachings of those who do."[67]

The fact is that the courts have repeatedly said that the fraud provisions in the SEC Acts, as well as the mail fraud statute, are not limited to circumstances that would give rise to a common law action for deceit.[68] How much further the statutes go is difficult to say definitely. The courts have traditionally refused, whether at common law deceit or under securities laws, to define fraud with specificity. Were any hard and fast rule to be laid down as to what constitutes fraud under the blue sky law, the Oregon court has said, "a certain class of gentlemen of the 'J. Rufus Wallingford' type — 'they toil not neither do they spin' — would lie awake nights endeavoring to conceive some devious and shadowy way of evading the law. It is more advisable to deal with each case as it arises."[69]

[65]See Burger, C. J., in Chiarella v. United States, 445 U. S. 222, 228 n. 10 (1980); see also SEC v. Capital Gains Research Bureau, Inc., 375 U. S. 180, 195 (1963): "Congress intended the Investment Advisers Act of 1940 to be construed like other securities legislation 'enacted for the purpose of avoiding frauds,' not technically and restrictively, but rather flexibly to effectuate its remedial purposes." In thus indulging in the game of labels, however, Justice Goldberg overlooked the more realistic approach of a distinguished predecessor. See Jackson, J., in SEC v. C. M. Joiner Leasing Corp., 320 U. S. 344, 350-53 (1943), supra p. 186, at p. 190.

[66]H. R. Rep. No. 85, 73d Cong., 1st Sess. (1933) 8.

[67]Charles Hughes & Co., Inc. v. SEC, 139 F. 2d 434, 437 (2d Cir. 1943), *cert. denied,* 321 U. S. 786; see also Hall v. Geiger-Jones Co., 242 U. S. 539, 552 (1917).

[68]See e. g., Charles Hughes & Co., Inc. v. SEC, 139 F. 2d 434, 437 (2d Cir. 1943), *cert. denied,* 321 U. S. 786; Harris v. American Investment Co., 523 F. 2d 220, 224 (8th Cir. 1975), *cert. denied,* 423 U. S. 1054. Under the mail fraud statute, see, e. g., United States v. Groves, 122 F. 2d 87, 90 (2d Cir. 1941), *cert. denied,* 314 U. S. 670.

[69]State v. Whiteaker, 118 Ore. 656, 661, 247 Pac. 1077, 1079 (1926). It was on this approach that §401(d) of the Uniform Securities Act was drafted to provide merely that " 'Fraud,' 'deceit,' and 'defraud' are not limited to common-

Nevertheless, certain propositions are reasonably clear. Whether to this extent the SEC Acts go beyond common law fraud depends upon the particular common law jurisdiction:

(1) It has been the law under the mail fraud statute ever since a Supreme Court decision in 1896[70] that "to promise what one does not mean to perform or to declare an opinion as to future events which one does not hold is a fraud."[71] On this approach the Commission regards valuations, geological reports, and the like, although they may be expressions of opinion, as based on implied representations that appropriate standards have been followed; hence a failure to observe those standards by one who is held out as an expert involves a misrepresentation of fact.[72] An accountant's report is likewise regarded as a material fact.[73] And estimates or statements of prospects are regarded as involving misrepresentations of fact if they are lacking in foundation.[74] The same thing may be true with respect to a misstatement of a point of law.[75]

All this is to say that there is no longer much room for judicial predilection in drawing the line between misrepresentation and "puffing"; for the "puffing" concept in the securities context has all but gone the way of the dodo. One still sees occasional characterizations of loose talk as "puffing."[76] But it is not the kind of

---

law deceit." See Loss, Commentary on the Uniform Securities Act (1976) 93-94.

[70] Durland v. United States, 161 U. S. 306, 313-14 (1896). The mail fraud statute has since been amended to cover "false promises" specifically.

[71] E. g., United States v. Grayson, 166 F. 2d 863, 866 (2d Cir. 1948); cf. Burns v. Paddock, 503 F. 2d 18, 23 (7th Cir. 1974); but cf. Marx & Co., Inc. v. Diners' Club, Inc., 550 F. 2d 505, 514-15 (2d Cir. 1977), *cert. denied*, 434 U. S. 861 (the general nature of predictions about a possible takeover precluded their being representations of fact).

[72] E. g., Haddam Distillers Corp., 1 SEC 37, 42 (1934); Intermountain Petroleum, Inc., 38 SEC 538, 544 (1958).

[73] Cornucopia Gold Mines, 1 SEC 364, 367 (1936).

[74] E. g., American Kid Co., 1 SEC 694, 699 (1936); Marx v. Computer Sciences Corp., 507 F. 2d 485 (9th Cir. 1974); Eisenberg v. Gagnon, 766 F. 2d 770, 775-76 (3d Cir. 1985), *cert. denied* sub nom. Wasserstrom v. Eisenberg, 106 S. Ct. 343. The Commission's former antipathy to forecasts *per se* (see pp. 162-64 supra) applied only with respect to prospectuses and proxy statements. The text statement here presumably applies today to forecasts in those media as it has always applied to forecasts in other media.

[75] Byron v. United States, 273 Fed. 769, 772-73 (9th Cir. 1921), *cert. denied*, 257 U. S. 653 (mail fraud statute).

[76] E. g., in Campo v. Shearson Hayden Stone, Inc., CCH Fed. Sec. L. Rep. ¶97,517 at 97,726 (S. D. N. Y. 1980), the court considered a statement that the plaintiff "could make a lot of money if he invested in options" to be, "at worst, an example of brokers' 'puffing' which does not rise to the level of an actionable wrong under the federal securities laws." See also Zerman v. Ball, 735 F. 2d 15, 20-21 (2d Cir. 1984) (the advertising slogan, "When E. F. Hutton Talks, People Listen," is not a representation of fact); Newman v. L. F. Rothschild,

rhetoric that is likely to appeal, at least to the Commission, which has said:

> The concept of "puffing" is derived from the doctrine of *caveat emptor* and arises primarily in the sale of tangibles where it appears that examination by the purchaser may offset exaggerated statements and expressions of opinion by the salesman. It can have little application to the merchandising of securities.[77]

The judge put it all very succinctly in a common law deceit case involving the sale of insurance when he said: "Buyer beware' lingers now only in the argument of the lawyers."[78]

(2) We have already noticed the Supreme Court's 1976 definition of materiality in the context of Rule 14a-9, the proxy fraud rule, as a fact with respect to which "there is a substantial likelihood that a reasonable shareholder would consider it important in deciding how to vote,"[79] and we have observed that that definition has been followed in other contexts.[80] Nevertheless, the learning of some of the earlier cases under Rule 10b-5 presumably survives by way of indicating what sort of evidence will satisfy the Supreme Court's test:

(a) In the *Texas Gulf Sulphur* case, where the question was whether inside buyers should have disclosed that preliminary drilling for copper and other minerals had produced one or more rich cores, a majority of the Second Circuit *en banc* emphasized that the test of materiality assumed a *reasonable* man, not merely a "prudent" or "conservative" investor.[81]

Unterberg, Towbin, 651 F. Supp. 160, 163 (S. D. N. Y. 1986) ("I'm the best in the business"). On "puffing" in proxy contests, see p. 479 supra.

[77] B. Fennekohl & Co., 41 SEC 210, 216 (1962). As the Commission put it with commendable restraint in another proceeding:

> In his testimony Pollock [an employee of the broker-dealer] characterized himself as a "sales promotionist." He went on to define this term as follows: "Have you watched TV programs sir? Do they huff, do they puff? This is sales promotion." It is clear to us that Pollock completely misconceived the role of a writer of securities sales literature.

Fred L. Carvalho, 41 SEC 620, 622 n. 2 (1963).

[78] Knox v. Anderson, 159 F. Supp. 795, 806 (D. Hawaii 1958), *aff'd* sub nom. Anderson v. Knox, 297 F. 2d 702 (9th Cir. 1961), *cert. denied,* 370 U. S. 915.

[79] TSC Industries, Inc. v. Northway, Inc. 426 U. S. 438, 449 (1976), supra p. 480.

[80] See p. 482 supra.

[81] SEC v. Texas Gulf Sulphur Co., 401 F. 2d 833, 849 (2d Cir. 1968), *cert. denied* sub nom. Coates v. SEC and Kline v. SEC, 394 U. S. 976 ("speculators and chartists * * * are also 'reasonable' investors"); Lehigh Valley Trust Co. v. Central National Bank of Jacksonville, 409 F. 2d 989, 992-93 (5th Cir. 1969) (transaction between banks); Carroll v. First National Bank of Lincolnwood, 413

(b) Presumably by way of extrapolation of the basic "reasonable man" test, a number of opinions have described as "material" those facts "which in reasonable and objective contemplation might affect the value of the corporation's stock or securities."[82] And that means market value when there is a market.[83]

(c) Precedent in the securities field also mirrors the common law view that a matter is material if "the maker of the representation knows or has reason to know that its recipient regards or is likely to regard the matter as important * * * although a reasonable man would not so regard it."[84] For the securities laws "were enacted for the very purpose of protecting those who lack business acumen."[85] Hence "the monumental credulity of the victim is no shield for the accused."[86] But this is not to say that omissions to state material facts are justified by the investor's being a person of financial sophistication.[87]

F. 2d 353, 357 (7th Cir. 1969), *cert. denied,* 396 U. S. 1003 (brokers are protected); Wheat v. Hall, 535 F. 2d 874, 876 (5th Cir. 1976). But "It is not a violation of any securities law to fail to disclose a result that is obvious even to a person with only an elementary understanding of the stock market." Zerman v. Ball, 735 F. 2d 15, 21 (2d Cir. 1984), and cases cited.

[82] E. g., Kohler v. Kohler Co., 319 F. 2d 634, 642 (7th Cir. 1963). This "economic materiality" test does not include information "material not to the value of the *shares,* but to the [nuisance] value of the *shareholders'* [bargaining] *position.*" Grigsby v. CMI Corp., 590 F. Supp. 826, 832 (N. D. Cal. 1984), *aff'd,* 765 F. 2d 1369 (9th Cir. 1985).

[83] But, while lack of market movement on the release of accurate information is persuasive evidence of immateriality, it is not so conclusive as to warrant dismissal of an item that may or may not "be a coordinate in the 'matrix.' " State Teachers Retirement Board v. Fluor Corp., 566 F. Supp. 945, 950 (S. D. N. Y. 1973).

The Code defines "material" in the Supreme Court's language, but, with respect to an "insider's" *failure* to disclose as distinct from a misstatement or half-truth, coins a new phrase, "fact of special significance"; and a fact is "of special significance" if "(A) in addition to being material it would be likely on being made generally available to affect the market price of a security to a significant extent, or (B) a reasonable person would consider it especially important under the circumstances in determining his course of action in the light of such factors as the degree of its specificity, the extent of its difference from information generally available previously, and its nature and reliability." §§202(56), 202(92)(A). See p. 724 infra. However, the version of the Code approved by the Commission requires the plaintiff to plead and prove only materiality, affording a *defense* (except in SEC injunctive and disciplinary actions) of lack of special significance.

[84] Restatement (Second) of Torts §538(2)(b); cf. Code §202(92)(B).

[85] United States v. Monjar, 47 F. Supp. 421, 425 (D. Del. 1942), *aff'd,* 147 F. 2d 916 (3d Cir. 1944), *cert. denied,* 325 U. S. 859; Norris & Hirshberg, Inc. v. SEC, 177 F. 2d 228, 233 (D. C. Cir. 1949) ("the investing and usually naive public").

[86] Deaver v. United States, 155 F. 2d 740, 744-45 (D. C. Cir. 1946), *cert. denied,* 329 U. S. 766 (mail fraud statute).

[87] Rogen v. Ilikon Corp., 361 F. 2d 260, 266 (1st Cir. 1966). That is "only

(d) Thus far there has been a good deal of speculation but no square decision on the question whether failure to disclose the insider's identity is itself a violation of the rule. Invariably nondisclosure of identity has been accompanied by a failure to reveal other material facts. All that can be safely said in the present state of the law, therefore, is that an insider cannot be certain that failure to disclose his identity will *not* be considered a violation of Rule 10b-5, or at the very least will not be more likely to lead the courts to find a violation when the nondisclosure of identity is considered in connection with all the other circumstances.

(e) The mere fact that otherwise material negotiations (as for a merger or a patent-licensing contract) have not yet been consummated does not *preclude* a finding of materiality.[88] But it is harder to fix the point affirmatively at which materiality attaches.[89] There is general agreement that *premature* disclosure of merger negotiations that are inherently fluid may be more misleading than secrecy[90] — not to mention the danger of derailment. But that is a

---

one factor to be considered in determining the overall reasonableness of [the plaintiff's] reliance * * * ." Nye v. Blyth Eastman Dillon & Co., 588 F. 2d 1189, 1197 (8th Cir. 1978); see also *Texas Gulf Sulphur* and other cases cited supra p. 718, par. (a). But the same court that decided *Texas Gulf Sulphur* stated a few years later: "The securities laws were not enacted to protect sophisticated businessmen from their own errors of judgment." Hirsch v. du Pont, 553 F. 2d 750, 763 (2d Cir. 1977); see also IIT v. Vencap, Ltd., 519 F. 2d 1001, 1011-12 (2d Cir. 1975).

The Commission tried a pseudo-mathematical formula in Raymond L. Dirks, Sec. Ex. Act Rel. 17,480, 21 SEC Dock. 1401, 1408 n. 32 (1981), citing cases, *aff'd* sub nom. Dirks v. SEC, 681 F. 2d 824, 842-44 (D. C. Cir. 1982), *rev'd on other grounds,* 463 U. S. 646 (1983):

> The probability-magnitude test weighs the likelihood that an event will occur against its magnitude if it should occur. The market impact test weighs the actual impact on the market of disclosure of the information in question. These tests are, however, merely serviceable objective methods for making the factual determination mandated by [TSC Industries, Inc. v. Northway, Inc., 426 U. S. 438 (1976)], and they have been regularly employed since *Texas Gulf Sulphur. Northway* did not disapprove these tests, and courts have continued to use them.

[88] Rogen v. Ilikon Corp., 361 F. 2d 260, 266-67 (1st Cir. 1966), *rev'g* 250 F. Supp. 112, 116 (D. Mass. 1966); SEC v. Shapiro, 494 F. 2d 1301, 1306 (2d Cir. 1974); SEC v. Geon Industries, Inc., 531 F. 2d 39, 47-48 (2d Cir. 1976); SEC v. Mize, 615 F. 2d 1046, 1054-55 (5th Cir. 1980), *cert. denied,* 449 U. S. 901. For a collection of cases where 10b-5 claims have withstood attack although the alleged omissions or misrepresentations concerned unadjudicated legal liabilities for violations of the law, see Grossman v. Waste Management, Inc., CCH Fed. Sec. L. Rep. ¶99,530 at 97,066 (N. D. Ill. 1983), *stay denied,* CCH Fed. Sec. L. Rep. ¶99,548 (N. D. Ill. 1984).

[89] For a good analysis of materiality from the "gleam in the eye" stage to consummation, see Fleischer, in Symposium, Insider Trading in Stocks, 21 Bus. Law. 1009, 1017 (1966).

[90] Staffin v. Greenberg, 672 F. 2d 1196, 1206 (3d Cir. 1982); Reiss v. Pan

generalization. The appellate courts are split on the meaning of "premature." To the Third Circuit and others it refers to a time before "fundamental agreement on the *price and structure* of a merger."[91] To the Sixth Circuit it means that, although there is no absolute duty to disclose ongoing merger talks, such a duty does arise if the company chooses to make a public statement that would be false or misleading without disclosure of the discussions.[92] Since the company in the latter case made three "no corporate development" statements while engaged in talks that ultimately led to its acquisition by another company, what the court said about the lack of a disclosure duty in the absence of a published statement is dictum and what it *held* was simply the classic proposition that a company that speaks at all must speak the truth.[93]

The Commission has expressed its disagreement with the Third Circuit's view:

> * * * an issuer that wants to prevent premature disclosure of nonpublic preliminary merger negotiations can, in appropriate circumstances, give a "no comment" response to press inquiries concerning rumors or unusual market activity. A "no comment" response would not be appropriate where, *inter alia,* the issuer has made a statement that has been rendered materially false or misleading as a result of subsequent events or market rumors are attributable to leaks from the issuer.[94]

American World Airways, Inc., 711 F. 2d 11 (2d Cir. 1983); Starkman v. Marathon Oil Co., 772 F. 2d 231, 242-43 (6th Cir. 1985), *cert. denied,* 106 S. Ct. 1195; see also Revlon, Inc. v. Pantry Pride, Inc., 621 F. Supp. 804 (D. Del. 1985).

[91] Greenfield v. Heublein, Inc., 742 F. 2d 751, 756 (3d Cir. 1984), *cert. denied,* 469 U. S. 1215; Flamm v. Eberstadt, 814 F. 2d 1169 (7th Cir. 1987); see also Guy v. Duff & Phelps, Inc., 628 F. Supp. 252 (N. D. Ill. 1985). But cf. Harnett v. Ryan Hanes, Inc., 496 F. 2d 832, 838 (3d Cir. 1974) (drawing the line at "inchoate ideas, musings as it were"); Paul v. Berkman, 620 F. Supp. 638 (W. D. Pa. 1985) (*Staffin,* supra p. 720 n. 90, and *Greenfield* were distinguished in a *sale of assets* context).

Failure to agree is not the "negative equivalent of an agreement in principle." Greenfield v. Heublein, supra, at 758. At the same time, the "price and structure" threshold does not preclude a finding of materiality when the reasons for that standard disappear because of the absence of a market. Michaels v. Michaels, 767 F. 2d 1185, 1196 (7th Cir. 1985), *cert. denied,* 106 S. Ct. 797. This is not to say that a more subjective standard of materiality applies when the corporation is closely held — though that may cause the "total mix" of information available to the reasonable stockholder to be different. Id. at 1196-97; see also Grigsby v. CMI Corp., 765 F. 2d 1369, 1373 (9th Cir. 1985); Jordan v. Duff & Phelps, Inc., 815 F. 2d 429 (7th Cir. 1987).

[92] Levinson v. Basic, Inc., 786 F. 2d 741 (6th Cir. 1986), *cert. granted* sub nom. Basic, Inc. v. Levinson, 107 S. Ct. 1284.

[93] See 786 F. 2d at 746; Schlanger v. Four-Phase Systems, Inc., 582 F. Supp. 128 (S. D. N. Y. 1984); Carnation Co., Sec. Ex. Act Rel. 22,214, 33 SEC Dock. 874, 877 (1985).

[94] Id. at 877 n. 6.

But *query* whether a "no comment" may not sometimes be a comment, especially if the company previously issued denials in response to prior inquiries about the same rumor.[95]

(3) Clause (2) of §17(a) of the 1933 Act, as well as the comparable clauses in Rules 10b-5 and 15c1-2, is specifically aimed at half-truths.[96] But those provisions are still limited to half-truths as distinct from complete omissions to disclose anything. They do not require the seller "to state every fact about stock offered that a prospective purchaser might like to know or that might, if known, tend to influence his decision."[97] In the next sections of this chapter we shall notice the development of special fraud doctrines based on *implied* representations in certain circumstances. But otherwise Clause (2) of §17(a), with its requirement that some statement be made, may not go so far in some cases as Clauses (1) and (3), under which a scheme to defraud may perhaps more readily be based upon silence when there is a duty to speak.[98]

(4) There is another respect in which Clause (2) of §17(a) is narrower than Clauses (1) and (3). It is a specific element of the offense under Clause (2) that the seller actually "obtain money or property by means of" the false statement or half-truth.[99] By con-

[95] Flamm v. Eberstadt, 1169, F. 2d 1178-79 (7th Cir. 1987), and cases cited. See SEC, SEC Roundtable: Market Rumors and Trading Halts (1986). "Although brokers are not liable for the conveyance of rumors as such [citation omitted], their representation of rumor as verified fact may violate state and federal securities laws as a misrepresentation of material fact." Hatrock v. Edward D. Jones & Co., 750 F. 2d 767, 774 (9th Cir. 1984).

In the context of the tender offer provisions, the Commission has tried to navigate the minefield by requiring disclosure of any negotiation that is under way or is being undertaken and that relates, among other things, to a tender offer or a transfer of a material amount of assets. Sch. 14D-9, Item 7(a). The instruction to the schedule recognizes that negotiations can occur before an agreement in principle, and allows targets to withhold the "possible terms of any transaction or the parties thereto * * * if in the opinion of the Board of Directors * * * such disclosure would jeopardize continuation of such negotiations." But that does not relieve the target of the duty to disclose the *fact* of negotiations; once they ripen into an agreement in principle, that becomes an event that must be disclosed. Id., Item 7(b). See Revlon, Inc., Sec. Ex. Act Rel. 23,320, 35 SEC Dock. 1148, 1152 (1986).

[96] Hughes v. SEC, 174 F. 2d 969, 976 (D. C. Cir. 1949); Myzel v. Fields, 386 F. 2d 718, 733 (8th Cir. 1967), *cert. denied*, 390 U. S. 951.

[97] Otis & Co. v. SEC, 106 F. 2d 579, 582 (6th Cir. 1939). Nor is it sufficient "to assert vaguely that a false and misleading impression was created." In re Union Carbide Class Action Securities Litigation, 648 F. Supp. 1322, 1326 (S. D. N. Y. 1986), CCH Fed. Sec. L. Rep. ¶93,021. On the duty to correct statements that are discovered to be misleading or that are rendered misleading by subsequent events, see 2 Code 650-55. See also p. 737 n. 57 infra.

[98] E. g., List v. Fashion Park, Inc., 340 F. 2d 457, 462 (2d Cir. 1965), *cert. denied* sub nom. List v. Lerner, 382 U. S. 811. See p. 786 infra.

[99] This is not true of the second clause of Rule 10b-5, which omits the words, "to obtain money or property by means of," that appear in Clause (2) of §17(a).

trast, Clause (3) refers to a transaction, practice, or course of business that operates "or would operate" as a fraud or deceit upon the purchaser. And it is clear that the establishment of a "scheme * * * to defraud" under Clause (1) is not dependent on proof that any victim suffered actual loss. In other words, it is irrelevant whether the scheme succeeded or failed.[100]

(5) The extent to which the SEC "fraud" provisions require scienter — as well as what it means when it is required — is considered in connection with the Rule 10b-5 saga, to which we now turn.

B. CORPORATE "INSIDERS"

1. Insiders' Purchases at Common Law

Rule 10b-5, like §17(a) of the Securities Act, is not limited to corporate insiders — however that term may be defined. The rule may be invoked whenever any person — insider or outsider — indulges in fraudulent practices, misstatements, or half-truths in connection with the purchase or sale of securities. However, it is in the application of Rule 10b-5 to *purchases* by *corporate insiders* that most of the special problems have arisen. The typical pattern is a purchase by a corporate insider, or by the issuer itself, without disclosure of relevant financial data or other information that indicates that the security is worth considerably more than it appears to be worth on the basis of market value or whatever information may be available to the seller. We start with another obeisance to the common law and then examine the changes that have been produced by Rule 10b-5.

The courts are divided on the common law duty of disclosure owed by an officer or director in purchasing the stock of his corporation. Under the view that is usually described as the "majority" or "strict" rule ("loose" might be a better characterization), officers and directors have a fiduciary obligation only *to the corporation* and to the stockholders in their dealings *with or on behalf of the corporation*; hence as individuals they may trade in the securities of the corporation without any affirmative obligation of disclosure as long as there is no misrepresentation or half-truth or active concealment by

[100] United States v. Amick, 439 F. 2d 351, 366 (7th Cir. 1971), *cert. denied*, 404 U. S. 823; United States v. Pollack, 534 F. 2d 964, 971 (D. C. Cir. 1976), *cert. denied*, 429 U. S. 924; cf. State v. McCall, 101 N. M. 32, 677 P. 2d 1068 (1984) (state law).

word or deed.[1] Under the so-called minority or fiduciary rule — which is followed in a few of the more agrarian states and approved by most commentators — corporate insiders are held to fiduciary standards in their dealings with stockholders and hence must make full disclosure of all material facts.[2] And a number of jurisdictions take an in-between position, imposing liability for nondisclosure by insiders through application of the so-called "special circumstances" doctrine enunciated by the Supreme Court in 1909 in *Strong* v. *Repide.* The Court there held that a controlling stockholder and general manager of a corporation was guilty of fraud in purchasing the holdings of a minority stockholder without disclosure of the then current status of negotiations for the sale of the corporation's property because, on a consideration of all the factors and particularly the insider's position and consequent special knowledge of the company, "it became the duty of the defendant, acting in good faith, to state the facts before making the purchase."[3]

C. 9B [1]A leading case for this view is Carpenter v. Danforth, 52 Barb. 581 (N. Y. Sup. Ct. 1868). This is also the English view. Percival v. Wright, [1902] 2 Ch. 421. But thirty-five years ago there was said to be "more judicial authority than is generally realized" for a development in England similar to the American development at common law whereby additional facts may convert a director into a quasi-trustee for the stockholders. See Gower, Investor Protection in the U. S. A., 15 Mod. L. Rev. 446, 452-53 (1952), citing Allen v. Hyatt, 30 T. L. R. 444 (P. C. 1914). And Parliament finally criminalized insider trading in some detail in the Companies Act 1980. 1980 Acts c. 22, §§68-75, now Company Securities (Insider Dealing) Act 1985, 1985 Acts c. 8, as amended by Financial Services Act 1986, 1986 Acts c. 60, §§173-78. But Percival v. Wright, which has had a remarkable career for a *nisi prius* case, remains unreversed despite repeated legislative proposals going back at least to the Jenkins Report of 1962. Board of Trade, Report of the Company Law Amendment Committee, Cmd. 1749 (1962) §§86-89, 99(b). Indeed, its principle was reflected in the 1980 Companies Act, 1980 Acts c. 6, §46(2), now §309(2) of the consolidated Companies Act 1985, 1985 Acts c. 22.

But see Coleman v. Myers, [1977] 2 N. Z. L. R. 297. In Gadsden v. Bennetto, 9 D. L. R. 719 (Man. 1913), the court — in a case strikingly reminiscent of Strong v. Repide, 213 U. S. 419 (1909), infra though without citing it —distinguished *Percival* and *Carpenter.* But there was very little discussion. And the case is not cited in the leading English or Canadian treatises. (For this reference the present writer is indebted to Anisman, Insider Trading Under the Canada Business Corporations Act, in McGill University Faculty of Law, Meredith Memorial Lectures, Canada Business Corporations Act (1975) 151, 163.)

On insider trading in other countries, see p. 546 n. 14 supra.

[2]Oliver v. Oliver, 118 Ga. 362, 45 S. E. 232 (1903); Stewart v. Harris, 69 Kan. 498, 77 Pac. 277 (1904); Jacobson v. Yaschik, 249 S. C. 577, 584-85, 155 S. E. 2d 601, 605 (1967).

[3]Strong v. Repide, 213 U. S. 419, 431 (1909). Since this case came up from the Philippines, the Supreme Court was applying civil law, but it indicated that

This is the dialectic — which, of course, an advocate can never afford to ignore. In actual results the old "majority" rule has substantially merged into the "special circumstances" doctrine,[4] which in turn is scarcely distinguishable from the so-called minority rule. Although one does not begin in the "majority" or "special circumstances" jurisdictions with the premise that insiders are fiduciaries, the "special circumstances" doctrine is manifestly based on the existence of a relationship between director and stockholder that is different from the relationship between arm's-length traders. In *Strong* v. *Repide* the "special circumstances" were found in the fact that the defendant had been entrusted with the negotiations to sell the corporate assets; but certainly if he had not been a director he never would have had an affirmative duty to make disclosure. In other jurisdictions, similarly, the "special circumstances" are commonly no more substantial. Thus, the Michigan court described them in 1925 as any "fact or condition enhancing the value of the stock, known by the officer or officers, not known by the stockholder, and not to be ascertained by an inspection of the books."[5]

It seems fair to conclude from all this that the so-called majority view is gradually giving way to the generally growing attitude of responsibility of corporate insiders — the development of a status of "trusteeship" in a nontechnical sense. Very likely a more pronounced evolution of the common law toward the "minority" view was aborted by the onslaught of Rule 10b-5, as so often happens when legislation comes on the scene.[6]

---

the common law rule was the same. Under Erie v. Tompkins, of course, this opinion is no longer binding on the federal courts in diversity cases.

[4]See Arlinghaus v. Ritenour, 622 F. 2d 629, 636 (2d Cir. 1980), *cert. denied*, 449 U. S. 1013, and New York cases cited.

[5]Buckley v. Buckley, 230 Mich. 504, 508, 202 N. W. 955, 956 (1925).

An Illinois case indicates that there may be a greater common law duty to disclose when an insider buys for the account of the issuer than when he buys for his own account. In sustaining a complaint that alleged constructive fraud, the court relied on both Strong v. Repide, 213 U. S. 419 (1909), and Oliver v. Oliver, 118 Ga. 362, 45 S. E. 232 (1903), supra p. 24 nn. 2, 3, and distinguished various Illinois cases on the ground that they had involved purchases by officers *for their own accounts.* Whatever the position of a director when he acts in his individual capacity with a stockholder, the court held, he occupies the position of a trustee for each individual stockholder when he acts *for the company.* Northern Trust Co. v. Essaness Theatres Corp., 348 Ill. App. 134, 108 N. E. 2d 493 (1952); see also Fleetwood Corp. v. Merisch, 404 N. E. 2d 38, 46 (Ind. App. 1980). *Contra:* Gladstone v. Murray Co., 314 Mass. 584, 50 N. E. 2d 958 (1943). Cf. Jordan v. Global Natural Resources, Inc., 564 F. Supp. 59, 68 (S. D. Ohio 1983): "We have engaged in extensive research and have found nothing to indicate that a fiduciary relationship exists between a corporation and its shareholders." See also p. 739 n. 60 infra.

[6]For a fuller discussion of the common law, see Seligman, The Reformulation

2. Introduction to Rule 10b-5

The 10b-5 story tempts the pen. For it is difficult to think of another instance in the entire *corpus juris* in which the interaction of the legislative, administrative rulemaking, and judicial processes has produced so much from so little. What is more remarkable is that the whole development was unplanned. Like the British Empire, which Eamon de Valera called "A domain created in a moment of world absent-mindedness,"[7] it just happened. One has his choice of figures of speech: Chief Justice Rehnquist's "judicial oak which has grown from little more than a legislative acorn";[8] Professor Painter's reference to the medieval alchemist's "universal solvent" that was so potent it dissolved every container employed to hold it;[9] the present writer's occasional reference to the rule as "a horse of dubious pedigree but very fleet of foot."

We have already noticed the gap left by §17(a) of the 1933 Act and §§9(a)(4), 15(c)(1), and 15(c)(2) of the 1934 Act: fraud in a *purchase* unless effected (1) by a *broker or dealer over the counter* or (2) by any person buying a *registered* security for the purpose of inducing its purchase by others. We have noticed also the abortive 1941 attempt to extend §17(a) to the purchase side and the 1942 resort to §10(b) by the adoption of Rule 10b-5.

Section 10(b) itself has been characterized by the Supreme Court as a "catch-all."[10] If that is not perfectly obvious from the provision's juxtaposition in the statute — following, as it does, a number of provisions in §§9 and 10(a) designed to curb or regulate such practices as market manipulation, trading in puts and calls, short selling, and "stop loss orders" — one need only refer to the Administration's spokesman's apt characterization of the somewhat broader version that was §9(c) of the original 1934 bills: "Subsection (c) says, 'Thou shalt not devise any other cunning devices.' "[11]

As for the adoption of the rule, the present writer recalls very well the account given by Mr. Milton V. Freeman, for many years a distinguished member of the District of Columbia Bar, because the writer was "at the creation" as his junior:

---

of Federal Securities Law Concerning Nonpublic Information, 73 Geo. L. J. 1083, 1091-1103 (1985).

[7] E. Brussell (ed.), Dictionary of Quotable Definitions (1970) 59.

[8] Blue Chip Stamps v. Manor Drug Stores, 421 U. S. 723, 737 (1975).

[9] Painter, The Use of Rule 10b-5 in Derivative Actions, in V. Nordin (ed.), Emerging Federal Securities Law: Potential Liability (1969) c. 3 at 37.

[10] Ernst & Ernst v. Hochfelder, 425 U. S. 185, 203 (1976).

[11] Thomas G. Corcoran in Stock Exchange Regulation, Hearings Before House Com. on Int'l. & For. Commerce, 73d Cong., 2d Sess. (1934) 115.

> It was one day in the year [1942], I was sitting in my office in the S. E. C. building in Philadelphia and I received a call from Jim Treanor who was then the Director of the Trading and Exchange Division. He said, "I have just been on the telephone with Paul Rowen," who was then the S. E. C. Regional Administrator in Boston, "and he has told me about the president of some company in Boston who is going around buying up the stock of his company from his own shareholders at $4.00 a share, and he has been telling them that the company is doing very badly, whereas, in fact, the earnings are going to be quadrupled and will be $2.00 a share for this coming year. Is there anything we can do about it?" So he came upstairs and I called in my secretary and I looked at Section 10(b) and I looked at Section 17, and I put them together, and the only discussion we had there was where "in connection with the purchase or sale" should be, and we decided it should be at the end.
>
> We called the Commission and we got on the calendar, and I don't remember whether we got there that morning or after lunch. We passed a piece of paper around to all the commissioners. All the commissioners read the rule and they tossed it on the table, indicating approval. Nobody said anything except Sumner Pike who said, "Well," he said, "we are against fraud, aren't we?" That is how it happened.[12]

Here is the administrative rulemaking process reacting to the legislative process. The Commission got what it wanted: a handle for investigating and obtaining injunctive relief against insiders who were buying their companies' stock. The writer can vouch that nobody at the Commission table gave any indication that he was remotely thinking of civil liability.[13] That was the function of the Third Branch, aided and abetted, to be sure, by the Commission's frequent appearances as *amicus curiae*. And the courts have responded with such gusto that there are now two multivolume treatises devoted primarily to Rule 10b-5.[14]

Although the volume of private litigation has thus dwarfed the proceedings initiated by the Commission, we leave most questions that are unique to private actions (for example, reliance and causation) to the next chapter, on Civil Liability. In this chapter the existence of a private right of action for violation of the rule is

[12] Am. B. Assn., Section of Corp., Banking & Bus. Law, Conference on Codification of the Federal Securities Laws, 22 Bus. Law. 793, 921-23, esp. at 922 (1967).

[13] See id. at 922.

[14] A. Bromberg and L. Lowenfels, Securities Fraud and Commodities Fraud (1979); A. Jacobs, Litigation and Practice Under Rule 10b-5 (2d ed. 1981); see also 3 Loss 1445-74, 1757-97; 6 id. 3556-3647, 3864-3925; W. Painter, The Federal Securities Code and Corporate Disclosure (1979) cc. 3-8.

assumed, and we include private cases basically for their learning on the substantive law.

That law, of course, is federal: the "federal common law" of which Judge Friendly and others have spoken as forming a penumbra around every federal statute.[15] In theory the courts are merely construing a statute and rule. But, when the statute and rule are, like §10(b) and Rule 10b-5, virtually as vague as the Due Process Clause, the law is surely as much judge-made as is the classic common law of the states. *Erie* is of no consequence. Precedents under state law have whatever weight the federal courts want to give them. Indeed, when the state courts do have to interpret the SEC statutes and rules — although the 1934 Act, alone of the series, gives the federal courts exclusive jurisdiction — *they* must look to the *federal* law: a process that some writers have called "*reverse Erie*."[16]

It is this emancipation from state law that undoubtedly accounts for "the 10b-5 revolution." For most judges in the second half of the twentieth century seem to view the "majority" rule at common law — a rule that holds a director to the standard of a fiduciary when he is dealing with the corporation, which is only a *persona ficta*, a ghost, but not when he is dealing with the flesh-and-blood persons who are his constituents — as a monument to the ability of lawyers and judges to hypnotize themselves with their own fictions.

We shall notice something of a counterrevolution as the Supreme Court belatedly awoke in the 1970s to the rapid growth of the oak tree under the tender nursing of the lower courts. But close analysis reveals that those cases are not cataclysmic. One may still cry, "*Viva la revolución*."

It is a revolution, nevertheless, that has progressed to the point,

[15] Friendly, In Praise of *Erie* — and of the New Federal Common Law, 19 Record A. B. C. N. Y. 64 (1964), reprinted with minor changes, 39 N. Y. U. L. Rev. 383 (1964); see also Friendly, The Gap in Lawmaking — Judges Who Can't and Legislators Who Won't, 63 Colum. L. Rev. 787 (1963); Note, Exceptions to *Erie* v. *Tompkins*: The Survival of Federal Common Law, 59 Harv. L. Rev. 966 (1946); Field, Sources of Law: The Scope of Federal Common Law, 99 Harv. L. Rev. 881 (1986). In McClure v. Borne Chemical Co., 292 F. 2d 824, 834 (3d Cir. 1961), *cert. denied*, 368 U. S. 939, Judge Biggs said: "It can be fairly said that the Exchange Act, of which sections 10(b) and 29(b) are parts, constitutes far-reaching federal substantive corporation law." See also Rekant v. Dresser, 425 F. 2d 872, 879-80 (5th Cir. 1970). But cf. Burks v. Lasker, 441 U. S. 471, 478 (1979) ("Congress has never indicated that the entire corpus of state corporation law is to be replaced simply because plaintiff's cause of action is based upon" the Investment Company Act); Texas Industries, Inc. v. Radcliff Materials, Inc., 451 U. S. 630, 640-47 (1981).

[16] Cf. Local 174, Int'l. Brotherhood of Teamsters v. Lucas Flour Co., 369 U. S. 95, 102 (1962) (state court must apply federal law under Labor Management Relations Act §301(a)); International Union, United Automobile Workers of America v. Hoosier Cardinal Corp., 383 U. S. 696 (1966).

in the view of an American Bar Association committee, where Congress "should confront the basic policy question of what uses of informational advantage are to be forbidden, rather than leaving the law primarily to case-by-case development under" Rule 10b-5. Further regulation through the rulemaking process, while useful, would have an uncertain statutory basis, the committee's report stated, to the extent that it departs from the fraud bases of §§10(b) and 14(e).[17] The report accordingly suggested alternative statutes. Both, departing from the fraud-based framework of §10(b), would directly regulate trading and tipping regardless of whether the conduct might be characterized as "fraud." The first is rooted in the Federal Securities Code, but takes into account subsequent judicial developments. The second is a shorter and simpler approach that would leave considerably more to interpretation.[18]

3. "Disclose or Abstain"

It does not seem too much to say today that the "minority" or "trusteeship" view at common law has become, thanks to Rule 10b-5, the law of the land. Two early cases set the pattern:

The first judicial pronouncement on the rule (apart from a passing reference by the Second Circuit)[19] came in *Kardon* v. *National Gypsum Company,* a case in which a father and son sued two brothers for an accounting of profits allegedly resulting from the defendants' purchase of the plaintiffs' stock in violation of the rule. These four persons were the sole stockholders, officers, and directors, and they had owned the outstanding stock in equal portions. The plaintiffs charged a conspiracy between the defendants and a third company to which the defendants had sold the bulk of the corporate assets pursuant to an agreement made before their purchase of the plaintiffs' stock. There was some dispute whether the defendants had expressly stated in purchasing the shares that there was no agreement to sell the corporate assets. Judge Kirkpatrick found for the plaintiffs on the question of fact but held that they were entitled to an accounting in any event.[20]

[17] Am. B. Assn., Committee on Federal Regulation of Securities, Report of the Task Force on Regulation of Insider Trading, Part I: Regulation Under the Antifraud Provisions of the Securities Exchange Act of 1934, 41 Bus. Law. 223, 225 (1986).

[18] Id. at 225-26, 253-57.

[19] Baird v. Franklin, 141 F. 2d 238, 244 (2d Cir. 1944), *cert. denied,* 323 U. S. 737.

[20] Kardon v. National Gypsum Co., 73 F. Supp. 798 (E. D. Pa. 1947).

At about the same time Judge Leahy decided *Speed* v. *Transamerica Corporation.*[21] Transamerica, as majority stockholder of Axton-Fisher Tobacco Company, had inside information that the cash realization value of Axton-Fisher's large tobacco inventory was far greater than the "average cost" book value set forth in its published financial statements, which did not reveal the enormous increase in the market value of the tobacco. This information was not made available to the minority stockholders. Intending to capture the enhanced value of this inventory by merging, dissolving, or liquidating the company, Transamerica purchased most of the minority-held stock directly from its holders. The price it paid was in excess of the current market but far below the redemption or liquidating value of the shares. It then caused Axton-Fisher to sell some of its tobacco, distribute the rest to its stockholders by means of warehouse receipts, and dissolve. These were the facts that Judge Leahy ultimately found.

First, one Geller, who had sold his stock to Transamerica, brought a common law deceit action against Transamerica based on diversity of citizenship. Finding that both Delaware and Kentucky, the charter state, followed the so-called majority view, Judge Leahy granted summary judgment for the defendant on the ground that it had not been guilty of misrepresentation or active concealment and had been under no duty to say anything about the appreciation of the tobacco inventory.[22]

Then one Speed and others brought a similar action based also on Rule 10b-5, and the court held that the complaint alleged a violation of the rule.[23] This was in 1947. Four years and twenty-three briefs later, Judge Leahy found for the plaintiffs in an exhaustive opinion in which he stated:

> The rule is clear. It is unlawful for an insider, such as a majority stockholder, to purchase the stock of minority stockholders without disclosing material facts affecting the value of the stock, known to the majority stockholder by virtue of his inside position but not known to the selling minority stockholders, which information would have affected the judgment of the sellers.[24]

[21] 71 F. Supp. 457 (D. Del. 1947).

[22] Geller v. Transamerica Corp., 53 F. Supp. 625 (D. Del. 1943), *aff'd per curiam,* 151 F. 2d 534 (3d Cir. 1945), *petition for leave to fill bill of review based on discovery of new matter denied,* 63 F. Supp. 248 (D. Del. 1945).

[23] Speed v. Transamerica Corp., 71 F. Supp. 457 (D. Del. 1947).

[24] Id., 99 F. Supp. 808, 828-29 (D. Del. 1951), *reaff'd on later motions,* 100 F. Supp. 461, 463 (D. Del. 1951), 103 F. Supp. 47 (D. Del. 1952), *opinion on damages,* 135 F. Supp. 176 (D. Del. 1955), *modified,* 235 F. 2d 369 (3d Cir. 1956).

Here, then, is proof positive of the utility of Rule 10b-5. For it enabled Speed to stay in court, and ultimately to obtain a very substantial judgment, whereas Geller's common law action arising out of the same purchase had been dismissed.[25]

But *is* the rule clear? One may applaud the result as an overdue reform in American corporation law while conceding that there is a good deal of *ipse dixit* in the cases so far as the underlying basis of the affirmative duty to disclose is concerned. Judge Kirkpatrick in *Kardon* said simply:

> Under any reasonably liberal construction, these provisions [§10(b) and Rule 10b-5] apply to directors and officers who, in purchasing the stock of the corporation from others, fail to disclose a fact coming to their knowledge by reason of their position, which would materially affect the judgment of the other party to the transaction.[26]

And Judge Leahy in *Transamerica* went on to say only this:

> The duty of disclosure stems from the necessity of preventing a corporate insider from utilizing his position to take unfair advantage of the uninformed minority stockholders. It is an attempt to provide some degree of equalization of bargaining position in order that the minority may exercise an informed judgment in any such transaction. Some courts have called this a fiduciary duty while others state it is a duty imposed by the "special circumstances." One of the primary purposes of the Securities Exchange Act of 1934 was to outlaw the use of inside information by corporate officers and prin-

[25] The force of this contrast is not weakened by the fact that Judge Leahy in his opinion on the merits, purporting (not too convincingly) to distinguish the *Geller* case, reinstated the common law deceit count on which he had originally granted summary judgment to the defendant. Speed v. Transamerica Corp., 99 F. Supp. 808, 828 (D. Del. 1951), supra p. 730 n. 24. For the dismissal of Geller's action would have been the last chapter if Speed had not joined a count under the rule in his suit. Nor can the teaching of *Kardon* and *Speed* be wished away on the ground that neither went to appeal and the *Kardon* language with respect to nondisclosure was *obiter* to boot. For there are square appellate holdings to the effect that "total nondisclosure" (that is to say, the absence of any significant communication bearing on value except for offer and acceptance) can violate Rule 10b-5. SEC v. Texas Gulf Sulphur Co., 401 F. 2d 833 (2d Cir. 1968), *cert. denied* sub nom. Coates v. SEC and Kline v. SEC, 394 U. S. 976; List v. Fashion Park, Inc., 340 F. 2d 457, 461-62 (2d Cir. 1965), *cert. denied* sub nom. List v. Lerner, 382 U. S. 811. See also Chiarella v. United States, 445 U. S. 222, 226-30 (1980), infra p. 755; cf. Affiliated Ute Citizens of Utah v. United States, 406 U. S. 128 (1972), infra p. 959.

[26] 73 F. Supp. at 800.

> cipal stockholders for their own financial advantage to the detriment of uninformed public security holders.[27]

Indeed, Judge Leahy reacted with some impatience to the defendant's attempt to pin the plaintiff down among the three clauses of the rule. Though relying primarily on Clauses (1) and (3), he emphasized that the three clauses "are mutually supporting and not mutually exclusive," so that an insider's breach of his disclosure obligation "can be viewed as a violation of all three subparagraphs."[28]

After four decades or so of building, there is little one can add to the underpinnings. Nevertheless there are three mutually supporting theories:

(1) At least when the insider's identity is not hidden, and in the absence of countervailing representations, Clause (2) of the rule may be invoked on the basis of an implied representation flowing from the insider's fiduciary obligation,[29] or at any rate from the "special

[27] 99 F. Supp. at 828-29; see also Kohler v. Kohler Co., 319 F. 2d 634, 638 (7th Cir. 1963); SEC v. Texas Gulf Sulphur Co., 401 F. 2d 833, 848 (2d Cir. 1968), *cert. denied* sub nom. Coates v. SEC and Kline v. SEC, 394 U. S. 976.

[28] 99 F. Supp. at 829. On the mutually supporting nature of the three clauses, see also Cady, Roberts & Co., 40 SEC 907, 913 (1961), infra p. 740, at p. 744; List v. Fashion Park, Inc., 240 F. 2d 457, 462 (2d Cir. 1965), *cert. denied* sub nom. List v. Lerner, 382 U. S. 811; Harris v. Union Electric Co., 787 F. 2d 355 (8th Cir. 1986), *cert. denied,* 107 S. Ct. 94.

[29] See Connelly v. Balkwill, 174 F. Supp. 49, 59 (N. D. Ohio 1959), *aff'd per curiam,* 279 F. 2d 685 (6th Cir. 1960). This theory wears a bit thin (1) as applied to *debt* securities, or (2) even with respect to stock when the insider *sells* to one not already a stockholder. It begs the question, of course, to observe that §10(b) and the rule apply universally. But they do, for what it is worth. And the securities cases reflect judicial impatience with any buyer-seller distinction so far as duty to disclose is concerned. SEC v. Murphy, 626 F. 2d 633, 652 n. 23 (9th Cir. 1980); cf. Gratz v. Claughton, 187 F. 2d 46, 49 (2d Cir. 1951), *cert. denied,* 341 U. S. 920.

With respect to insiders' sales, Judge Learned Hand's observation in the *Gratz* case, infra p. 745 n. 23, was quoted approvingly in Chiarella v. United States, 445 U. S. 222, 227 n. 8 (1983), infra p. 755. See also Kingstone v. Oceanography Development Corp., CCH Fed. Sec. L. Rep. ¶96,387 at 93,348 (S. D. N. Y. 1978) (court said simply that, "as an officer, [the defendant] owed the plaintiff a fiduciary duty to disclose material facts despite the fact that the plaintiff was *not yet a bondholder*" (italics supplied)); cf. Fausett v. American Resources Management Corp., 542 F. Supp. 1234, 1236-40 (D. Utah 1982) (alleged misrepresentations by issuer after plaintiff's *short* sale and before covering).

The same liberality, however, has not marked the case of the *option* trader, where again it is hard to find a fiduciary relationship. Laventhall v. General Dynamics Corp., 704 F. 2d 407 (8th Cir. 1983), *cert. denied,* 464 U. S. 846 (company trading in its own securities had no disclosure duty to a plaintiff holding options to buy company stock); see also O'Connor & Associates v. Dean Witter Reynolds, Inc., 529 F. Supp. 1179, 1184-85 (S. D. N. Y. 1981) (option trader has no equity interest in the corporation, and the corporation is not "run for his benefit"). But *individual* insiders who trade in options stand in a different

circumstances" that satisfied the Supreme Court in pre-*Erie* and pre-SEC days, that the insider has performed his duty and has not withheld any material inside information.

(2) On the analogy of certain developments in the field of broker-dealer fraud concepts that will be examined later in this chapter,[30] the insider's offer to buy at a fixed price might be considered to constitute an implied representation, again under Clause (2), that within reasonable limits the stated price represents the insider's judgment of the value of the security.[31]

(3) Since §10(b) is part of a statute designed to raise the morals of the marketplace, and in view of the consensus that the SEC fraud provisions are not limited to common law deceit,[32] perhaps the most honest approach is to say simply that the insider's action may be considered a scheme to defraud by misleading or overreaching, or an act, practice, or course of business that would so operate to defraud public security holders.[33]

Whatever the theory, one cannot cavil with the results of the relatively small number of nondisclosure cases that have survived defendants' motions for summary judgment and subsequent settlement negotiations to go to final judgment for the plaintiffs on the merits: for example, a contract to sell the company's assets;[34] a several-fold increase in basic inventory value;[35] a rich ore strike;[36]

---

position. Bianco v. Texas Instruments, Inc., 627 F. Supp. 154, 158-61 (N. D. Ill. 1985). And, of course affirmative misrepresentations are another matter. In re Digital Equipment Corp. Securities Litigation, 601 F. Supp. 311, 315 (D. Mass. 1984).

All this seems to have been solved so far as options are concerned by §20(d) of the 1934 Act as amended by the Insider Trading Sanctions Act of 1984. See p. 1010 infra.

[30] See p. 811 infra.

[31] Judge Leahy did find in *Transamerica:* "In making an offer of 33⅓% above the current market price, defendant impliedly represented that the price offered was a fair price at that time." 99 F. Supp. at 843.

[32] See p. 716 supra.

[33] "* * * the Act is violated when directors with inside information purchase stock without full disclosure. Such conduct constitutes engaging in an 'act, practice, or course of business which * * * would operate as a fraud.' " Kardon v. National Gypsum Co., 83 F. Supp. 613, 614 (E. D. Pa. 1947) (the ellipsis is the court's).

[34] Kardon v. National Gypsum Co., 73 F. Supp. 798, 800 (E. D. Pa. 1947), supra p. 729.

[35] Speed v. Transamerica Corp., 99 F. Supp. 808 (D. Del. 1951), supra p. 730 and n. 21.

[36] SEC v. Texas Gulf Sulphur Co., 401 F. 2d 833 (2d Cir. 1968), *cert. denied* sub nom. Coates v. SEC and Kline v. SEC, 394 U. S. 976.

a plan by the buyers to sell shares at a much higher price;[37] large installment land sales.[38] Indeed, all these cases could fit quite readily under a "special circumstances" approach if that rubric were to mark the limits of the 10b-5 disclosure obligation. As the Second Circuit has stated, "An insider's duty to disclose information or his duty to abstain from dealing in his company's securities arises only in 'those situations which are essentially extraordinary in nature and which are reasonably certain to have a substantial effect on the market price of the security if [the extraordinary situation is] disclosed.' "[39]

Note the statement of the duty in the alternative: "to disclose * * * or * * * abstain." In end result, since conflict is inevitable between the director's 10b-5 duty to the other party to the transaction to disclose material facts and the common law duty he will often have to the company *not* to make premature disclosure, the director has no viable alternative but to abstain.[40]

If the insider nevertheless does choose the disclosure alternative, he must also conjure with the proposition that merely telling the SEC just before trading normally does not suffice.[41] The time required for the market to digest the information varies with the circumstances.[42]

Moreover, it is the Commission's view that the mere *possession* of material information is the test without the necessity of the plaintiff's showing that the insider trading was conducted on the *basis* of the information in question.[43] A number of cases use language that

[37] Ross v. Licht, 263 F. Supp. 395, 409 (S. D. N. Y. 1967). See also p. 755 n. 91 infra. But cf. Grigsby v. CMI Corp., 765 F. 2d 1369 (9th Cir. 1985) (parent company buying minority shares in a subsidiary did not have to disclose negotiations for sale of the parent).

[38] Baumel v. Rosen, 283 F. Supp. 128 (D. Md. 1968), *rev'd on other grounds*, 412 F. 2d 571 (4th Cir. 1969), *cert. denied*, 396 U. S. 1037.

[39] SEC v. Texas Gulf Sulphur Co., 401 F. 2d 833, 848 (2d Cir. 1968), *cert. denied* sub nom. Coates v. SEC and Kline v. SEC, 394 U. S. 976, quoting from Fleischer, Securities Trading and Corporate Information Practices: The Implications of the Texas Gulf Sulphur Proceeding, 51 Va. L. Rev. 1271, 1289 (1965) (brackets are the court's). It is on this theory that the Code defines "fact of special significance" as one that is a bit more than "material." See p. 719 n. 85 supra.

[40] Oliver v. Oliver, 118 Ga. 362, 368, 45 S. E. 232, 234 (1903); Cady, Roberts & Co., 40 SEC 907, 911 (1961); Rogen v. Ilikon Corp., 361 F. 2d 260, 268 (1st Cir. 1966); SEC v. Texas Gulf Sulphur Co., 401 F. 2d 833, 848 (2d Cir. 1968), *cert. denied* sub nom. Coates v. SEC and Kline v. SEC, 394 U. S. 976.

[41] Dirks v. SEC, 463 U. S. 646, 661 n. 21 (1983).

[42] See 4 Loss 3605-09; see also p. 749 n. 79 infra.

[43] See Insider Trading Sanctions and SEC Enforcement Legislation, Hearing on H. R. 559 Before Subcom. on Telecommunications, Consumer Protection, & Finance, Serial No. 98-33, 98th Cong., 1st Sess. (1983) 48-49; 15 Sec. Reg. L. Rep. 1820 (1983) (report of address by Daniel Goelzer, SEC General Coun-

seems to look the other way.[44] But there seems to be no case[45] that turns on the point. And when there is no question that the inside information was actually used in trading — which is normally the case — it seems natural to speak in terms of not trading "on" or "on the basis of" the information without necessarily implying that possession alone would not suffice. The very difficulty of establishing actual use of inside information points to possession as the test. So does the application of Rule 10b-5 to insiders' dissemination of false information without their trading at all.[46] The situation when one person in an organization knows a piece of inside information while a colleague trades in ignorance of the information is part of the "Chinese wall" problem.[47] In the event, Congress in the Insider Trading Sanctions Act of 1984 opted for the "possession" test.[48]

There is no insoluble conflict here between federal and state law — no occasion for invocation of the Supremacy Clause. If your duty to the company requires you not to make premature disclosure of negotiations or other material information that Rule 10b-5 requires you to disclose when you trade, just don't trade. After all, there is nothing in Holy Writ that requires the insider to buy or sell. And it would be a strange rule of fiduciary conduct that yielded to a plea of conflict of interest, especially a conflict so readily avoidable. When the issuer itself wants to buy or sell its own securities, it has a choice: desist or disclose. But, when the buyer or seller is an insider rather than the company itself, the *only* solution is not to trade on inside information. For it is neither his role nor his responsibility to disseminate corporate information to the public; that is a corporate function.

The leading exchanges have played a significant role in alleviating the problem by expecting their listed companies to "release quickly * * * any news or information which might reasonably be expected to materially affect the market for [the] securities"[49] and to make "a frank and explicit announcement" if "rumors or unusual

---

sel); Sterling Drug, Inc., Sec. Ex. Act Rel. 14,675, 14 SEC Dock. 824, 827 (1978).

[44] E. g., Investors Management Co., Inc., 44 SEC 633, 641, 646-47 (1971) (one of the elements of a violation is that "the information be a factor in [the insider's] decision to effect the transaction," though its possession creates a rebuttable presumption that it was a factor); see also cases cited in Hearing, supra p. 734 n. 43, at 285 n. 64.

[45] *Pace* Investors Management Co., Inc., 44 SEC 633, 647 n. 28 (1971).

[46] See p. 736 infra.

[47] See p. 752 infra.

[48] See p. 1008 infra. See also Rule 14e-3(a), infra p. 759 (applicable to certain persons in "possession" of information with respect to a tender offer).

[49] CCH N. Y. Stock Ex. Listed Company Manual 202.05; see also id. at 202.06.

market activity indicate that information on impending developments has leaked out."[50] In 1965 the New York Stock Exchange went so far as to recommend a series of quite stringent guidelines that might be followed by insiders to avoid any conflict-of-interest criticism when they want to buy or sell.[51] But there is no escaping the conclusion that a person who may want to trade — especially if he is a broker-dealer — has to think twice before becoming a director or other insider.[52]

Are insiders safe, then, if they simply refrain from trading when there is material information undisclosed? Or might they be held to have violated the rule by causing the company not to release material information that, if available, would presumably have affected the market price? Short of a Supreme Court holding, there is no doubt that a company and its responsible insiders can violate the rule by disseminating *false* information, whether in a report or a press release or a director's speech or in any other way, even though neither the company nor any insider does any trading. In the *Texas Gulf Sulphur* case, which involved a misleadingly unfavorable press release with respect to a tremendous ore strike in Ontario, the Second Circuit, concluding that "It does not appear to be unfair to impose upon corporate management a duty to ascertain the truth of any statements the corporation releases to its shareholders or to the investing public at large," held that the rule "is violated whenever assertions are made * * * in a manner reasonably calculated to influence the investing public, e. g., by means of the financial media * * *, if such assertions are false or misleading or are so incomplete as to mislead irrespective of whether the issuance of the release was motivated by corporate officials for ulterior purposes."[53]

[50] Id. at 202.03.

[51] N. Y. Stock Ex., The Corporate Director and the Investing Public (1965) 12-13; CCH N. Y. Stock Ex. Listed Company Manual 309.

[52] Compare the discussion of the "Chinese wall," infra p. 752.

[53] SEC v. Texas Gulf Sulphur Co., 401 F. 2d 833, 861-63 (2d Cir. 1968), *cert. denied* sub nom. Coates v. SEC and Kline v. SEC, 394 U. S. 976; see also Herskowitz v. Nutri/System, Inc., — F. Supp. — , — , CCH Fed. Sec. L. Rep. ¶92,829 at 94,037 (E. D. N. Y. 1986) (even if false release is to be followed by a proxy statement); but cf. Etshokin v. Texasgulf, Inc., 612 F. Supp. 1212, 1217 (N. D. Ill. 1984), *summary judgment for defendants,* 612 F. Supp. 1220 (N. D. Ill. 1985).

In Sec. Act Rel. 6504, 29 SEC Dock. 792 (1984), the Commission cautioned that "The antifraud provisions of the federal securities laws apply to all company statements that can reasonably be expected to reach investors and the trading markets, whoever the intended primary audience." And in Howard Bronson & Co., Sec. Ex. Act Rel. 21,138, 30 SEC Dock. 1113 (1984), the Commission expressed its concern regarding the promotional efforts of public relations firms

But both the Commission[54] and the courts[55] have recognized the propriety of *temporarily withholding* material information from the market when there are good business reasons, so long as neither the issuer nor insiders trade.

Whether there is a *greater* duty to disclose to the marketplace by way of correcting an earlier statement that has become misleading in a material respect presents a harder question. The Commission "believes that, depending on the circumstances, there is a duty to correct statements made in any filing * * * if the statements either have become inaccurate by virtue of subsequent events, or are later discovered to have been false and misleading from the outset, and the issuer knows or should know that persons are continuing to rely on all or any material portion of the statements."[56] Moreover, the cases, though by no means conclusive, point to a general duty to correct.[57]

---

on behalf of issuers with publicly held securities.

The Second Circuit made one concession in *Texas Gulf:* "that if corporate management demonstrates that it was diligent in ascertaining that the information it published was the whole truth and that such diligently obtained information was disseminated in good faith, Rule 10b-5 would not have been violated." 401 F. 2d at 862. See the discussion of scienter, infra p. 774.

[54] Investors Management Co., Inc., 44 SEC 633, 646 (1971); see Ferber (SEC Solicitor), Duties of Disclosure of Corporate Insiders, 34 U. Mo. Kan. City L. Rev. 222, 223 (1966).

[55] Dolgow v. Anderson, 438 F. 2d 825, 829 (2d Cir. 1970); cf. Financial Industrial Fund, Inc. v. McDonnell Douglas Corp., 474 F. 2d 514 (10th Cir. 1973), *cert. denied,* 414 U. S. 874 (judgment against issuer *rev'd*). In Staffin v. Greenberg, 672 F. 2d 1196, 1204 (3d Cir. 1982), the court said that its attention had not been called to any case "which imposed any duty of disclosure under the Federal Securities Laws on a corporation which is *not* trading in its own stock and which has *not* made a public statement." See also Roeder v. Alpha Industries, Inc., 814 F. 2d 22, 26-28 (1st Cir. 1987).

[56] Sec. Act Rel. 6084, 17 SEC Dock. 1048, 1054 (1979); see also Sec. Ex. Act Rel. 8995 (1970) (a company that has complied with the reporting requirements "still has an obligation to make full and prompt announcement of facts regarding the company's financial condition"); National Telephone Co., Inc., Sec. Ex. Act Rel. 14,380, 13 SEC Dock. 1393 (1978) (a report of an investigation into the activities of the company's outside directors). Cf. p. 478 n. 96 supra. The duty is, if anything, more acute since the advent of "shelf registration" and integrated disclosure (supra pp. 136, 146).

[57] See SEC v. Shattuck Denn Mining Corp., 297 F. Supp. 470, 475-76 (S. D. N. Y. 1968) (failure to correct press release); Butler Aviation Int'l, Inc. v. Comprehensive Designers, Inc., 425 F. 2d 842, 843 (2d Cir. 1970) *semble* (same); Thomas v. Duralite Co., 386 F. Supp. 698, 715 (D. N. J. 1974), *aff'd as to liability and rev'd and remanded as to damages,* 524 F. 2d 577 (3d Cir. 1975); Ross v. A. H. Robins Co., Inc., 465 F. Supp. 904, 908 (S. D. N. Y. 1979), *rev'd on other grounds,* 607 F. 2d 545 (2d Cir. 1979), *cert. denied,* 446 U. S. 946 (failure to correct prospectus and annual reports to stockholders); Greenfield v. Heublein, Inc., 742 F. 2d 751, 758 (3d Cir. 1984), *cert. denied,* 469 U. S. 1215 (dictum).

With respect to accountants, cf. Fischer v. Kletz, 266 F. Supp. 180, 189-94 (S. D. N. Y. 1967) (accountant's failure to disclose later discovered falsity of

It has been suggested, however, that the mere presence of rumors or of publicly circulating inaccuracies concerning the issuer does not require a response from the issuer, although a response may become necessary when the issuer is the source of the inaccuracies or is responsible for their dissemination.[58] And the time frame within which any general disclosure question is relevant is substantially narrowed by the "management discussion and analysis" required in annual and quarterly reports filed with the Commission.[59] The ultimate analysis comes down to the truism that, the more frequent and complete the disclosures in Exchange Act reports or otherwise, the less is the exposure under Rule 10b-5 — which was never intended as more than a *residual* antifraud mechanism.

4. "Insiders" and "Tippees"

When Congress specifically addressed itself to inside trading in §16, it spoke of directors, officers, and 10+ percent beneficial owners. In the §10(b) area, where there is no evidence that Congress was thinking of insiders specifically, we do not have any comparable pre-packaging. It has, therefore, been up to the courts to decide

---

financial statements certified for inclusion in annual report filed with SEC); United States v. Natelli, 527 F. 2d 311, 319 (2d Cir. 1975), *cert. denied*, 425 U. S. 934; Hirsch v. du Pont, 553 F. 2d 750, 761 (2d Cir. 1977) (dictum); Sharp v. Coopers & Lybrand, 83 F. R. D. 343, 346-47 (E. D. Pa. 1979); Summer v. Land & Leisure, Inc., 571 F. Supp. 380, 386 (S. D. Fla. 1983); Reingold v. Deloitte Haskins & Sells, 599 F. Supp. 1241, 1257-59 (S. D. N. Y. 1984).

[58] Sheffey, Securities Law Responsibilities of Issuers to Respond to Rumors and Other Publicity: Reexamination of a Continuing Problem, 57 Notre Dame Law. 755 (1982); see Electronic Specialty Co. v. International Controls Corp., 409 F. 2d 937, 949 (2d Cir. 1969); Elkind v. Liggett & Myers, 635 F. 2d 156, 162-64 (2d Cir. 1980); State Teachers Retirement Board v. Flour Corp., 654 F. 2d 843, 850 (2d Cir. 1981); Plessey Co., PLC v. General Electric Co., PLC, 628 F. Supp. 477, 491-93 (D. Del. 1986); Schwartz v. Novo Industries, A/S, 658 F. Supp. 795 (S. D. N. Y. 1987).

The exchanges, as we have seen, have their own requirements, both with respect to timely disclosure of material news developments and with respect to responding to rumors.

See generally Schneider and Hammerman, The Obligation to Disclose and Issuer Relations with the Investment Community, in Practising Law Institute, Fifteenth Annual Institute on Securities Regulation (1984) c. 15; Block, Barton, and Garfield, Affirmative Duty to Disclose Material Information Concerning Issuer's Financial Condition and Business Plans, 40 Bus. Law. 1243 (1985).

[59] Reg. S-K, Item 303; in general, see Olson and Wheat, Disclosure Problems of Troubled Companies, in Practising Law Institute, Fourteenth Annual Institute on Securities Regulation (1983) c. 11 at 137; Wander and Schwartzman, Timely Disclosure, 17 Rev. Sec. Reg. 861 (1984); Wander, Timeliness, in Practising Law Institute, Fifteenth Annual Institute on Securities Regulation (1984) c. 1.

precisely what persons should have an affirmative obligation to disclose; and that group one loosely calls "insiders."

In connection with its codification of a good deal of the 10b-5 jurisprudence, §1603(b) of the Code defines "insider" in a manner thought to represent existing case law:

> For purposes of section 1603, "insider" means (1) the issuer, (2) a director or officer of, or a person controlling, controlled by, or under common control with, the issuer, (3) a person who, by virtue of his relationship or former relationship to the issuer, knows a material fact about the issuer or the security in question that is not generally available, or (4) a person who learns such a fact from a person within section 1603(b) (including a person within section 1603(b)(4)) with knowledge that the person from whom he learns the fact is such a person, unless the Commission or a court finds that it would be inequitable, on consideration of the circumstances and the purposes of this Code (including the deterrent effect of liability), to treat the person within section 1603(b)(4) as if he were within section 1603(b)(1), (2), or (3).

More specifically:

First: "Certainly directors and officers are insiders."[60]

Second: Controlling persons are almost invariably directors except when they are corporations. But, when they are not, there is no reason to treat them any differently from directors or officers.[61]

Third: In *Texas Gulf Sulphur* Judge Bonsal agreed that the "insider" concept extends for purposes of Rule 10b-5 to any employees "who are in possession of material undisclosed information obtained

[60] Ross v. Licht, 263 F. Supp. 395, 409 (S. D. N. Y. 1967). And "There appears to be no valid reason why the duty to make full disclosure should be any less stringent upon the issuing corporation itself than upon an officer or director buying for his own account." Kohler v. Kohler Co., 208 F. Supp. 808, 820 (E. D. Wis. 1962), *aff'd*, 319 F. 2d 634, 638 (7th Cir. 1963). For a collection of common law cases on issuer repurchases, see 3 Loss 1448 n. 8. In Starkman v. Marathon Oil Co., 772 F. 2d 231, 238 (6th Cir. 1985), *cert. denied*, 106 S. Ct. 1195, the court correctly conditioned Rule 10b-5's affirmative disclosure obligation on the existence of a "duty to speak," but *assumed* without discussion that a tender offeror's target had no such duty to its own stockholders.

[61] Speed v. Transamerica Corp., 71 F. Supp. 457 (D. Del. 1947) (on motion for summary judgment), 99 F. Supp. 808 (D. Del. 1951) (on the merits); Cochran v. Channing Corp., 211 F. Supp. 239, 242 (S. D. N. Y. 1962); Kohler v. Kohler Co., 319 F. 2d 634, 637-38 (7th Cir. 1963) (court found no violation on the facts); Schoenbaum v. Firstbrook, 268 F. Supp. 385, 395 n. 5 (S. D. N. Y. 1967) (dictum), *modified on other grounds en banc*, 405 F. 2d 215 (2d Cir. 1968), *cert. denied* sub nom. Manley v. Schoenbaum, 395 U. S. 906; see also Kuehnert v. Texstar Corp., 286 F. Supp. 340, 344 (S. D. Tex. 1968), *aff'd*, 412 F. 2d 700 (5th Cir. 1969) ("major stockholders").

in the course of their employment."[62] And the Eighth Circuit has approved an instruction that "An insider is a person who because of his position or intimate association with a corporation has greater knowledge of the financial affairs of the corporation."[63] We explore later whether this is broad enough to cover the outside consultant, such as a law firm and *its* employees.[64]

Fourth: Whatever duty of disclosure Rule 10b-5 imposes on any of the persons so far mentioned could be readily bypassed if the same duty were not held to devolve at least on their spouses, members of their immediate families, and family trusts.[65]

Fifth: The courts having come this far on the slippery slope, they could hardly ignore the friend or acquaintance who is given information from an insider that he knows to be nonpublic — in short, the "tippee."[66] Analysis of that concept lends itself best to a historical treatment. The first published opinion was one issued by the Commission itself in 1961:

tippee held liable - tinted as well as Cady

IN THE MATTER OF CADY, ROBERTS & CO.

Securities and Exchange Commission, 1961
40 SEC 907

By CARY, Chairman.

This is a case of first impression and one of signal importance in our administration of the Federal securities acts. It involves a selling broker who executes a solicited order and sells for discretionary accounts (including that of his wife) upon an exchange. The crucial question is what are the duties of such a broker after receiving

[62] SEC v. Texas Gulf Sulphur Co., 258 F. Supp. 262, 279 (S. D. N. Y. 1966), *aff'd in part and rev'd in part*, 401 F. 2d 833 (2d Cir. 1968), *cert. denied* sub nom. Coates v. SEC and Kline v. SEC, 394 U. S. 976; see also Bianco v. Texas Instruments, Inc., 627 F. Supp. 154, 163 (N. D. Ill. 1985).

[63] Myzel v. Fields, 386 F. 2d 718, 739 (8th Cir. 1967), *cert. denied,* 390 U. S. 951; see also Cady, Roberts & Co., 40 SEC 907, 912 (1961), infra.

[64] See pp. 768-69, 772 infra.

[65] In *Texas Gulf Sulphur* the Court of Appeals treated sales made in the name of insiders' wives as having been made by the insiders, noting simply that another treatment would be "unrealistic." 401 F. 2d at 841 n. 4.

[66] "Professor Louis Loss invented the convenient term 'tippee' for those who receive tips from insiders. In his * * * Securities Regulation in the USA, Professor Loss in 1969 said: 'Having some respect for the English language, he does pray his readers, for at least a decent interval, not to join elements of the press in dropping the quotation marks' (vol. vi, p. 3561). Perhaps the decent interval can now be regarded as having elapsed." A. Johnson, The City Take-Over Code (1980) 156 n. 1.

nonpublic information as to a company's dividend action from a director who is employed by the same brokerage firm.

* * * The respondents [Cady, Roberts & Co. ("registrant") and Gintel (a partner)] have submitted an offer of settlement which essentially provides that the facts stipulated by respondents shall constitute the record in these proceedings for the purposes of determining the occurrence of a willful violation of the designated antifraud provisions [§17(a) of the 1933 Act and Rule 10b-5] * * *.

* * *

On the morning of November 25, the Curtiss-Wright directors, including J. Cheever Cowdin ("Cowdin"), then a registered representative of registrant, met to consider, among other things, the declaration of a quarterly dividend. The company had paid a dividend, although not earned, of $.625 per share for each of the first three quarters of 1959. The Curtiss-Wright board * * * approved a dividend for the fourth quarter at the reduced rate of $.375 per share. At approximately 11:00 A. M., the board authorized transmission of information of this action by telegram to the New York Stock Exchange. The Secretary of Curtiss-Wright immediately left the meeting room to arrange for this communication. There was a short delay in the transmission of the telegram because of a typing problem and the telegram, although transmitted to Western Union at 11:12 A. M., was not delivered to the Exchange until 12:29 P. M. It had been customary for the company also to advise the Dow Jones News Ticker Service of any dividend action. However, apparently through some mistake or inadvertence, the Wall Street Journal was not given the news until approximately 11:45 A. M., and the announcement did not appear on the Dow Jones ticker tape until 11:48 A. M.

Sometime after the dividend decision, there was a recess of the Curtiss-Wright directors' meeting, during which Cowdin telephoned registrant's office and left a message for Gintel that the dividend had been cut. Upon receiving this information, Gintel entered two sell orders for execution on the Exchange, one to sell 2,000 shares of Curtiss-Wright stock for 10 accounts, and the other to sell short 5,000 shares for 11 accounts. Four hundred of the 5,000 shares were sold for three of Cowdin's customers. According to Cowdin, pursuant to directions from his clients, he had given instructions to Gintel to take profits on these 400 shares if the stock took a "run-up." These orders were executed at 11:15 and 11:18 A. M. at 40¼ and 40⅜, respectively.

When the dividend announcement appeared on the Dow Jones tape at 11:48 A. M., the Exchange was compelled to suspend trading in Curtiss-Wright because of the large number of sell orders. Trading in Curtiss-Wright stock was resumed at 1:59 P. M. at 36½, ranged during the balance of the day between 34⅛ and 37, and closed at 34⅞.

VIOLATION OF ANTIFRAUD PROVISIONS

So many times that citation is unnecessary, we have indicated that the purchase and sale of securities is a field in special need of regulation for the protection of investors. To this end one of the major purposes of the securities acts is the prevention of fraud, manipulation or deception in connection with securities transactions. Consistent with this objective, Section 17(a) of the Securities Act, Section 10(b) of the Exchange Act and Rule 10b-5, issued under that Section, are broad remedial provisions aimed at reaching misleading or deceptive activities, whether or not they are precisely and technically sufficient to sustain a common law action for fraud and deceit. Indeed, despite the decline in importance of a "Federal rule" in the light of *Erie R. Co.* v. *Tompkins,* the securities acts may be said to have generated a wholly new and far-reaching body of Federal corporation law.[10]

Section 17(a) and Rule 10b-5 * * * are not intended as a specification of particular acts or practices which constitute fraud, but rather are designed to encompass the infinite variety of devices by which undue advantage may be taken of investors and others.

Section 17 and Rule 10b-5 apply to securities transactions by "any person." Misrepresentations will lie within their ambit, no matter who the speaker may be. An affirmative duty to disclose material information has been traditionally imposed on corporate "insiders," particularly officers, directors, or controlling stockholders. We, and the courts have consistently held that insiders must disclose material facts which are known to them by virtue of their position but which are not known to persons with whom they deal and which, if known, would affect their investment judgment. Failure to make disclosure in these circumstances constitutes a violation of the anti-fraud provisions. If, on the other hand, disclosure prior

[10] As was stated in McClure v. Borne Chemical Co., Inc., 292 F. 2d 824, 834 (C. A. 3, 1961):

> * * * It can be said fairly that the Exchange Act, of which Sections 10(b) and 29(b) are parts, constitutes far reaching Federal substantive corporation law.

to effecting a purchase or sale would be improper or unrealistic under the circumstances, we believe the alternative is to forego the transaction.

The ingredients are here and we accordingly find that Gintel willfully violated Sections 17(a) and 10(b) and Rule 10b-5. We also find a similar violation by the registrant, since the actions of Gintel, a member of registrant, in the course of his employment are to be regarded as actions of registrant itself. It was obvious that a reduction in the quarterly dividend by the Board of Directors was a material fact which could be expected to have an adverse impact on the market price of the company's stock. The rapidity with which Gintel acted upon receipt of the information confirms his own recognition of that conclusion.

We have already noted that the anti-fraud provisions are phrased in terms of "any person" and that a special obligation has been traditionally required of corporate insiders, e. g., officers, directors and controlling stockholders. These three groups, however, do not exhaust the classes of persons upon whom there is such an obligation. Analytically, the obligation rests on two principal elements; first, the existence of a relationship giving access, directly or indirectly, to information intended to be available only for a corporate purpose and not for the personal benefit of anyone, and second, the inherent unfairness involved where a party takes advantage of such information knowing it is unavailable to those with whom he is dealing. In considering these elements under the broad language of the anti-fraud provisions we are not to be circumscribed by fine distinctions and rigid classifications. Thus our task here is to identify those persons who are in a special relationship with a company and privy to its internal affairs, and thereby suffer correlative duties in trading in its securities. Intimacy demands restraint lest the uninformed be exploited.

The facts here impose on Gintel the responsibilities of those commonly referred to as "insiders." He received the information prior to its public release from a director of Curtiss-Wright, Cowdin, who was associated with the registrant. Cowdin's relationship to the company clearly prohibited him from selling the securities affected by the information without disclosure. By logical sequence, it should prohibit Gintel, a partner of registrant.[17] This prohibition extends

[17] See 3 Loss, Securities Regulation 1450-1 (2d ed., 1961). Cf. Restatement, Restitution, Section 201(2) (1937). Although Cowdin may have had reason to believe that news of the dividend action had already been made public when he called registrant's office, there is no question that Gintel knew when he received

not only over his own account, but to selling for discretionary accounts and soliciting and executing other orders. In somewhat analogous circumstances, we have charged a broker-dealer who effects securities transactions for an insider and who knows that the insider possesses non-public material information with the affirmative duty to make appropriate disclosures or dissociate himself from the transaction.[18]

The three main subdivisions of Section 17 and Rule 10b-5 have been considered to be mutually supporting rather than mutually exclusive. Thus, a breach of duty of disclosure may be viewed as a device or scheme, an implied misrepresentation, and an act or practice, violative of all three subdivisions.[19] Respondents argue that only clause (3) may be applicable here. We hold that, in these circumstances, Gintel's conduct at least violated clause (3) as a practice which operated as a fraud or deceit upon the purchasers. Therefore, we need not decide the scope of clauses (1) and (2).

We cannot accept respondents' contention that an insider's responsibility is limited to existing stockholders and that he has no special duties when sales of securities are made to non-stockholders. This approach is too narrow. It ignores the plight of the buying public — wholly unprotected from the misuse of special information.

Neither the statutes nor Rule 10b-5 establishes artificial walls of responsibility. Section 17 of the Securities Act explicitly states that it shall be unlawful for any person in the offer or sale of securities to do certain prescribed acts. Although the primary function of Rule 10b-5 was to extend a remedy to a defrauded seller, the courts and this Commission have held that it is also applicable to a defrauded buyer. There is no valid reason why persons who *purchase* stock from an officer, director or other person having the responsibilities of an "insider" should not have the same protection afforded by disclosure of special information as persons who *sell* stock to them. Whatever distinctions may have existed at common law based on the view that an officer or director may stand in a fiduciary relationship to existing stockholders from whom he purchases but not to members of the public to whom he sells, it is clearly not

---

the message that the information was not yet public and was received from a director.

[18] Hughes & Treat, 22 S. E. C. 623, 626 (1946); Fry v. Schumaker, 83 F. Supp. 476, 478 (E. D. Pa. 1947). Cf. William I. Hay, 19 S. E. C. 397, 406-09 (1945); R. D. Bayly & Co., 19 S. E. C. 773, 784 (1945); Alexander Smith, 22 S. E. C. 13, 18 (1946).

[19] Speed v. Transamerica Corp., 99 F. Supp. 808, 829 (D. Del. 1951).

appropriate to introduce these into the broader anti-fraud concepts embodied in the securities acts.[23]

Respondents further assert that they made no express representations and did not in any way manipulate the market, and urge that in a transaction on an exchange there is no further duty such as may be required in a "face-to-face" transaction.[24] We reject this suggestion. It would be anomalous indeed if the protection afforded by the anti-fraud provisions were withdrawn from transactions effected on exchanges, primary markets for securities transactions. If purchasers on an exchange had available material information known by a selling insider, we may assume that their investment judgment would be affected and their decision whether to buy might accordingly be modified. Consequently, any sales by the insider must await disclosure of the information.

* * *

Respondents argue that any requirement that a broker-dealer in exchange transactions make disclosure of "adverse factors disclosed by his analysis" would create uncertainty and confusion as to the duties of those who are constantly acquiring and analyzing information about companies in which they or their clients are interested.

[23] As Judge Learned Hand has stated in the context of Section 16(b) of the Exchange Act:

> For many years a grave omission in our corporation law had been its indifference to dealings of directors or other corporate officers in the shares of their companies. When they bought shares they came literally within the conventional prohibitions of the law of trusts; yet the decisions were strangely slack in so deciding. When they sold shares, it could indeed be argued that they were not dealing with a beneficiary, but with one whom his purchase made a beneficiary. That should not, however, have obscured the fact that the director or officer assumed a fiduciary relation to the buyer by the very sale; for it would be a sorry distinction to allow him to use the advantage of his position to induce the buyer into the position of a beneficiary although he was forbidden to do so once the buyer had become one.

Gratz v. Claughton, 187 F. 2d 46, 49 (C. A. 2 1951), *cert. denied,* 341 U. S. 920 (1951). [See also Chiarella v. United States, 445 U. S. 222, 227 n. 8 (1980), infra p. 755.]

[24] It is interesting to note that earlier attacks on the applicability of Rule 10b-5 rested on the contention that it applied only to exchange transactions or other transactions on an organized security market. The courts have rejected these attempts to narrow the broad applicability of the rule. Matheson v. Armbrust, 284 F. 2d 670 (C. A. 9 1960), *cert. denied,* 365 U. S. 870 (1961); Fratt v. Robinson, 203 F. 2d 627 (C. A. 9 1953).

Furthermore, it is claimed, substantial practical difficulties would be presented as to the manner of making disclosures.

There should be no quandary on the facts here presented. While there may be a question as to the materiality and significance of some corporate facts and as to the necessity of their disclosure under particular circumstances, that is not this case. Corporate dividend action of the kind involved here is clearly recognizable as having a direct effect on the market value of securities and the judgment of investors. Moreover, knowledge of this action was not arrived at as a result of perceptive analysis of generally known facts, but was obtained from a director (and associate) during the time when respondents should have known that the board of directors of the issuer was taking steps to make the information publicly available but before it was actually announced.

Furthermore, the New York Stock Exchange has recognized that prompt disclosure of important corporate developments, including specifically dividend action, is essential for the benefit of stockholders and the investing public and has established explicit requirements and recommended procedures for the immediate public release of dividend information by issuers whose securities are listed on the Exchange. The practical problems envisaged by respondents in effecting appropriate disclosures in connection with transactions on the Exchange are easily avoided where, as here, all the registered broker-dealer need do is to keep out of the market until the established procedures for public release of the information are carried out instead of hastening to execute transactions in advance of, and in frustration of, the objectives of the release.

Finally, we do not accept respondents' contention that Gintel was merely carrying out a program of liquidating the holdings in his discretionary accounts — determined and embarked upon prior to his receipt of the dividend information. In this connection, it is further alleged that he had a fiduciary duty to these accounts to continue the sales, which overrode any obligations to unsolicited purchasers on the Exchange.

The record does not support the contention that Gintel's sales were merely a continuance of his prior schedule of liquidation. * * * Moreover, while Gintel undoubtedly occupied a fiduciary relationship to his customers, this relationship could not justify any actions by him contrary to law.[31] Even if we assume the existence

[31] "But to say that a man is a fiduciary only begins analysis; it gives direction to further inquiry, to whom is he a fiduciary? What obligation does he owe as a fiduciary?" S. E. C. v. Chenery Corporation, 318 U. S. 80, 85-86 (1943). In the circumstances, Gintel's relationship to his customers was such that he would

of conflicting fiduciary obligations, there can be no doubt which is primary here. On these facts, clients may not expect of a broker the benefits of his inside information at the expense of the public generally. * * *

* * *

Judicial recognition of the tippee concept was not long in following.[67] Indeed, there is nothing radical about it. So long as the concept is limited to one who knew, or at least should reasonably have inferred, that he was being given an inside tip, treating him as if he stood in the shoes of the tipper does no violence to common law tradition. "Where a fiduciary in violation of his duty to the beneficiary communicates confidential information to a third person, the third person, if he had notice of the violation of duty, holds upon a constructive trust for the beneficiary any profit which he makes through the use of such information."[68] And persons who knowingly join with a fiduciary in transactions constituting a breach of his duty become jointly and separately liable for the profits.[69]

But, if "tippees" are to be held liable, the next question is *which* "tippees." There are many variables. There is a scale running

---

have a duty not to take a position adverse to them, not to take secret profits at their expense, not to misrepresent facts to them, and in general to place their interests ahead of his own. [See Frankel, Fiduciary Law, 71 Calif. L. Rev. 795 (1983).]

[67] E. g., Ross v. Licht, 263 F. Supp 395, 410 (S. D. N. Y. 1967). Indeed, it has been suggested that "Tipping because it involves a more widespread imbalance of information presents an even greater threat to the integrity of the marketplace than simple insider trading." Fridrich v. Bradford, 542 F. 2d 307, 327 n. 12 (6th Cir. 1976) (concurring opinion), *cert. denied,* 429 U. S. 1053.

There may be difficulties, however, in proving by circumstantial evidence that the alleged tippee is in fact a tippee. E. g., in SEC v. Materia, CCH Fed. Sec. L. Rep. ¶99,583 at 97,283 (S. D. N. Y. 1983), *aff'd on other grounds,* 745 F. 2d 197, *cert. denied,* 471 U. S. 1053 (2d Cir. 1984), with respect to certain transactions by the estranged wife of a financial printer's employee, there was failure of proof that she "knew or by reason of recklessness failed to use [her] reason to know that the information was non-public and had been obtained improperly."

[68] Restatement of Restitution §201(2). On the notice point, cf. SEC v. Monarch Fund, 608 F. 2d 938 (2d Cir. 1979). Of course, "Realistically, it may be hard to envision a tippee inquiring of the donor goose as to where she came upon the golden eggs and whether they have been offered to everyone. To question the goose may render her barren in the future." Note, Scienter and Rule 10b-5, 69 Colum. L. Rev. 1057, 1071 (1969). But see pp. 662-70 infra.

[69] Jackson v. Smith, 254 U. S. 586, 588-89 (1921); Mosser v. Darrow, 341 U. S. 267, 272 (1951); Irving Trust Co. v. Deutsch, 73 F. 2d 121, 123, 125 (2d Cir. 1934), *cert. denied,* 294 U. S. 708.

from the director of Corporation *X* who gives a tip to his good friend in a similar position with Corporation *Y* — perhaps on an express or implied "I'll scratch your back and you scratch mine basis[70] — to the director who feels in an expansive mood while he is having a manicure. There is the studied eavesdropper, or the briber, or perhaps in this day and age the wiretapper, or the representative of the news media who upon hearing an important announcement from a company calls his broker before he calls his office *versus* the barber or the taxi driver or the caddy who by chance overhears a bit of corporate news. There is the direct as against the indirect tippee — the tippee's tippee, in a progression that can go on indefinitely.[71] There is what might be called the specific tip as opposed to the general tip. Obviously, to take these last two classifications alone, (1) a director's statement to his best friend that his corporation is about to consummate a merger that should double the price of the stock stands at the opposite extreme from (2) the case of the stranger to the corporation who is told by his secretary that she was told by the corporation's geologist that if she had any extra cash it might not be a bad idea to buy some of the stock; and in between there are many gradations.

Under any reasonable view of the tippee concept, a person who picks up private information in the course of business negotiations with a corporation — perhaps negotiations to buy the corporation's assets or the management's stock — should normally be treated like a tippee of the second corporation as long as that information remains private.[72] So, too, a broker who buys on behalf of an insider and who has knowledge of inside information would seem to be under the same obligation to disclose as the insider who purchases directly.[73] And, of course, a dealer who is himself a director or officer or controlling person of the issuer of the securities in which he trades has an insider's obligation to make full disclosure of material facts.[74] Since these facts may sometimes concern secret processes or plans that the legitimate business interests of the corporation dictate should not be disclosed, a broker or dealer who becomes a

[70] On the "backscratching syndrome," cf. SEC v. Lund, 570 F. Supp. 1397 (C. D. Cal. 1983).

[71] Cf. SEC v. Platt, 565 F. Supp. 1244, esp. the table at 1262 (W. D. Okla. 1983).

[72] Van Alstyne, Noel & Co., 43 SEC 1080 (1969); SEC v. Shapiro, 494 F. 2d 1301 (2d Cir. 1974) ("corporate marriage broker").

[73] List v. Fashion Park, Inc., 340 F. 2d 457, 461 (2d Cir. 1965), *cert. denied* sub nom. List v. Lerner, 382 U. S. 811; Myzel v. Fields, 386 F. 2d 718, 739 (8th Cir. 1967), *cert. denied,* 390 U. S. 957. Of course, the broker's principal would be liable even if the broker were innocent.

[74] Freeman v. Decio, 584 F. 2d 186, 200 (7th Cir. 1978).

corporate insider must assume the risk that his duty to the corporation may sometimes prevent him from making a market in its securities. This has long been the case under common law agency principles, presumably, so far as concerns an insider-broker's acting as *agent* for a customer in the purchase or sale of his corporation's securities.[75]

There is also the matter of pricking out a line between the financial analyst who draws correct inferences solely on the basis of his expert analytical powers and his colleague whose analysis is reinforced by a visit to the corporation's plant. Presumably even an insider is under no obligation to give the ordinary investor the benefit of his superior financial analysis.[76] "Even though a shrewd guess by an insider is often worth fifty accounting statements, it would be highly unfair to make him publicize his guess and then to hold him responsible if it turns out to be wrong."[77] Nevertheless, a broker or other person who has determined through his own financial analysis that "A security is ripe for purchase or sale may find that receipt of certain information regarding that security will bar him from taking action without disclosure, even though the inside information serves only to confirm an independently reached decision."[78] Consequently, prudent corporate counsel will advise the officers not to speak at financial analyst societies' luncheons unless the press is present, or to grant exclusive press interviews unless the newspaper or other news medium has a sufficient circulation to make it reasonable to consider that publication will have been achieved.[79]

[75] Black v. Shearson, Hammill & Co., 266 Cal. App. 2d 362, 368, 72 Cal. Rptr. 157, 161 (1968).

[76] Kohler v. Kohler Co., 208 F. Supp. 808, 827 (E. D. Wis. 1962), *aff'd on other grounds*, 319 F. 2d 634 (7th Cir. 1963); Arber v. Essex Wire Corp., 490 F. 2d 414, 421 (6th Cir. 1974), *cert. denied*, 419 U. S. 830; Feldman v. Simkins Industries, Inc., 679 F. 2d 1299, 1304 (9th Cir. 1982).

[77] Comment, The Prospects for Rule X 10B-5: An Emerging Remedy for Defrauded Investors, 59 Yale L. J. 1120, 1148 (1950).

[78] Note, Broker Silence and Rule 10b-5: Expanding the Duty to Disclose, 71 Yale L. J. 736, 745 (1962).

[79] "Whenever managers and analysts meet elsewhere than in public, there is a risk that the analysts will emerge with knowledge of material information which is not publicly available." Elkind v. Liggett & Myers, Inc., 635 F. 2d 156, 165 (2d Cir. 1980).

As we shall see (infra pp. 768-69), the Supreme Court seems to treat analysts more liberally. And it has been reported that some corporate executives do hold private meetings with groups of analysts without even issuing a press release afterwards. Wall St. J., Dec. 17, 1986, p. 25, col. 4.

When information becomes generally available is, of course, a separate question. Certainly not the moment a release is handed to the press. "Before insiders may act upon material information, such information must have been

That is to say, types of tippees aside, it is now quite clear that Rule 10b-5 falls on the nontrading tipper as well as the trading tippee. In *Texas Gulf Sulphur* the Commission, faced with a choice

---

effectively disclosed in a manner sufficient to insure its availability to the investing public." SEC v. Texas Gulf Sulphur Co., 401 F. 2d 833, 854 (2d Cir. 1968), *cert. denied* sub nom. Coates v. SEC and Kline v. SEC, 394 U. S. 976. In that case both courts expressed the hope that the Commission would use its expertise in order to adopt a rule that would "provide some predictability of certainty for the business community." 401 F. 2d at 854 n. 18; 258 F. Supp. at 289. But the Commission has not done so. And unofficial rules of thumb have run from "waiting for the morning newspaper to carry the information" or "for fifteen minutes after the tape runs" (2 A. Bromberg and L. Lowenfels, Securities Fraud and Commodities Fraud (1979) 190.3, quoted in Billard v. Rockwell Int'l Corp., 526 F. Supp. 218, 220 (S. D. N. Y. 1981)) to twenty-four hours after publication of a release in a national medium or forty-eight hours when publication is not so widespread (American Stock Exchange Disclosure Policies (1970) 16-17). The Code provides: "A fact is 'generally available' one week (or any other period prescribed by Commission rule) after it is disclosed by means of a filing or press release or in any other manner reasonably designed to bring it to the attention of the investing public. Otherwise the burden of proving that a fact is 'generally available' is on the person who so asserts." §202(64).

But what if the news item is not significant enough for what has been called the Wall Street Journal's policy of "selective revelation"? This leaves the insider in something like the position of a principal who seeks to protect himself against the apparent authority of a discharged agent. One does the best he can. If there are local newspapers or appropriate trade publications, he might consider paid advertisements or a letter to stockholders or distribution of a release to dealers known to have an interest in the security. See American Stock Exchange Disclosure Policies (1970) 13; Report of the Industrial Issuers Advisory Committee to the SEC (1972) ¶17. But in the last analysis the burden here is on the insider.

It has been said that the best rule for determining whether information is "in the public domain" is that "a public disclosure of information relieves the duty to disclose if it is reasonable to conclude that the plaintiff should have been made aware of the fact as a result of that disclosure." Powell v. American Bank & Trust Co., 640 F. Supp. 1568, 1579 (N. D. Ind. 1986), and cases cited.

In any event, whatever may be the effective moment of disclosure, the critical time to which it is related is not when the insider's order is executed but when it is placed. "Otherwise, insiders would be able to 'beat the news' * * * by requesting in advance that their orders be executed immediately after the dissemination of a major news release but before outsiders could act on the release." SEC v. Texas Gulf Sulphur Co., 401 F. 2d at 853 n. 17. It follows, on the other hand, that knowledge acquired *after* the parties are committed to each other does not affect the bargain. Radiation Dynamics, Inc. v. Goldmuntz, 464 F. 2d 876, 890-91 (2d Cir. 1972); Sundstrand Corp. v. Sun Chemical Corp., 553 F. 2d 1033, 1050 (7th Cir. 1977), *cert. denied*, 434 U. S. 875; Brooks v. Land Drilling Co., 574 F. Supp. 1050, 1054 (D. Colo. 1983); Jefferies & Co. v. United Mo. Bank of Kansas City, N. A., CCH Fed. Sec. L. Rep. ¶99,257 at 96,146 (W. D. Mo. 1983); Grigsby v. CMI Corp., 590 F. Supp. 826, 830-31 (N. D. Cal. 1984), *aff'd on other grounds*, 765 F. 2d 1369 (9th Cir. 1985), and cases cited. But cf. Goodman v. Epstein, 582 F. 2d 388, 412-13 (7th Cir. 1978), *cert. denied*, 440 U. S. 939 (a series of potential investment decisions); Currie v. Cayman Resources Corp., 595 F. Supp. 1364, 1376 (N. D. Ga. 1984).

of seeking injunctive and restitutional relief[80] against certain tippees, who were not insiders but who *had* been unjustly enriched, or against their tippers, who had not received any direct benefit from the tippees' purchases but who *were* insiders, the Commission apparently decided that the tipper was the more likely prospect for the first sally into court. And it won a ruling that one of the defendants had violated by tipping.[81]

Having held the "tippee" to be a violator of Rule 10b-5 in *Cady, Roberts & Co.* and having persuaded the Second Circuit in *Texas Gulf Sulphur* that the "tipper" had violated as well, the Commission next brought an administrative proceeding against the Merrill Lynch firm in which it combined both these theories. The firm and certain of its personnel having consented to various suspensions and censures, the Commission found that the firm had disclosed to twelve institutional and other large customers certain nonpublic information, obtained in connection with its proposed underwriting of a

[80] This case is also a bellwether with respect to the Commission's practice of seeking various kinds of restitution or disgorgement of profits. SEC v. Texas Gulf Sulphur Co., 446 F. 2d 1301 (2d Cir. 1971), *on remand,* 331 F. Supp. 671 (S. D. N. Y. 1971); SEC v. Manor Nursing Centers, Inc., 458 F. 2d 1082, 1103-06 (2d Cir. 1972), *on remand,* CCH Fed. Sec. L. Rep. ¶93,359 (S. D. N. Y. 1972); SEC v. Shapiro, 494 F. 2d 1301, 1309 (2d Cir. 1974); SEC v. Materia, 745 F. 2d 197, 200-01 (2d Cir. 1984), *cert. denied,* 471 U. S. 1053. The theory is deterrence rather than compensation. And the relief is ancillary to the court's equity jurisdiction. See pp. 1004-11 infra.

In *Texas Gulf Sulphur* the court ordered the tipper to disgorge not only his own profits but also those realized by his tippees, who were not parties. 446 F. 2d at 1308. That case was distinguished in SEC v. Gaspar, CCH Fed. Sec. L. Rep. ¶92,004 at 90,981 (S. D. N. Y. 1985), where the tippee (and subtippees) had been made parties and had consented to disgorge their profits. "To permit disgorgement twice for a single trader's profits," the court thought, "would appear more in the nature of a penalty than remedial relief."

[81] SEC v. Texas Gulf Sulphur Co., 401 F. 2d 833, 852 (2d Cir. 1968), *cert. denied* sub nom. Coates v. SEC and Kline v. SEC, 394 U. S. 976; cf. Mosser v. Darrow, 341 U. S. 267 (1951); see 2 Code 666, Comment (6). If tipping itself is an illegal act, it must be on some sort of aiding and abetting or conspiracy or criminal attempt theory.

Nice questions arise if the "tipper" is to be held for the "tippee's" gains. For example:

(1) Would the corporation itself then be liable to a market seller because it had done nothing to prevent its directors and other insiders from taking advantage of inside information? We have already noticed a suggestion that a director who knows that *another* director is buying securities on the basis of confidential information may incur a liability for failure to prevent his colleague's action, since a trustee has an obligation to prevent a co-trustee from violating their joint trust. See p. 587 supra.

(2) If both tipper and tippee are liable, will there be a contribution? Or will the two be treated as joint tortfeasors with neither in a superior position? See p. 1035 infra.

debenture offering, concerning a precipitate drop in the earnings of Douglas Aircraft Co., Inc.; that some of those customers had thereafter sold Douglas stock, either long or short, before public disclosure of the information; and that during that period the broker-dealer had effected purchases of Douglas stock on behalf of other customers without telling them what it had told the twelve large customers.[82] The same incident resulted in a Second Circuit decision that held Merrill Lynch liable as tipper to persons who had bought Douglas stock in the market during the same period.[83]

In accepting Merrill Lynch's offer of settlement of the administrative proceeding, the Commission, with appropriate words of caution and a reminder that prompt public dissemination was the best preventive, took into account the firm's erection of what has come to be known as a "Chinese wall" between its underwriting division and its retail personnel.[84] And the custom has spread among not only multiservice securities houses but also commercial banks, which face the same problem when their loan departments obtain inside information of value to their trust departments. But how effective is the "wall"? In the first place, particularly in the case of smaller

[82] Merrill Lynch, Pierce, Fenner & Smith, Inc., 43 SEC 933 (1968); see also Investors Management Co., Inc., 44 SEC 633 (1971) (proceeding against the sellers in the same case).

[83] Shapiro v. Merrill Lynch, Pierce, Fenner & Smith, Inc., 495 F. 2d 228 (2d Cir. 1974); see also State Teachers Retirement Board v. Flour Corp., 654 F. 2d 843, 854-55 (2d Cir. 1981). The question of liability to *whom* and for *how much* is considered in the next chapter. See pp. 965-75 infra.

In Dirks v. SEC, 681 F. 2d 824 (D. C. Cir. 1982), *rev'd on other grounds*, 463 U. S. 646 (1983), infra p. 762, Judge Wright held that a broker-dealer's analyst-employee who had passed on bearish information that he had received as tippee had violated Rule 10b-5 as aider and abettor of *his* tippees' illegal sales. *Query:* Doesn't the aiding and abetting run in the other direction — from tippee (the secondary violator) to tipper (the primary violator in his fiduciary capacity)? In Chiarella v. United States, 445 U. S. 222, 230 n. 12 (1980), the Court stated: "The tippee's obligation has been viewed as arising from his role as a participant after the fact in the insider's breach of a fiduciary duty." See also cases cited supra pp. 751-52, nn. 81-83; United States v. Newman, 664 F. 2d 12 (2d Cir. 1981), infra p. 758 n. 107.

[84] Merrill Lynch, Pierce, Fenner & Smith, Inc., 43 SEC 933, 938 (1968). See also Rule 14e-3(b), infra p. 759. The term turned up in the British Licensed Dealers (Conduct of Business) Rules 1983, which defined "Chinese Wall" as one might expect by way of creating an exception from the requirement that a licensed dealer disclose any "material interest" in a proposed transaction to his customer. S. I. 1983 No. 585, §§2, 8. But the 1985 White Paper stated: "The Government are not convinced that total reliance can be placed on Chinese Walls because they restrict flows of information and not the conflicts of interest themselves." Dep't of Trade & Industry, Financial Services in the United Kingdom: A New Framework for Investor Protection, Cmd. 9432 (1985) §7.4. And a former General Counsel of the SEC said of a Chinese wall provision that he would call it a Swiss cheese provision. 16 Sec. Reg. L. Rep. 643 (1984).

banks whose lending and trust officers are in continual contact, will juries be convinced that the "wall" is not porous? And, even if a securities firm's "wall" is found to be airtight, that very quality will inevitably result in its salesmen's innocently "bulling" to "widows and orphans" stock that they would not touch if they knew what the underwriting personnel knew. Surely it cannot be assumed that agency law would not attribute the underwriting personnel's knowledge to the firm — how else can a corporation or other firm "know" *anything?* — and the *firm* is thus selling stock (the salesmen being only its agents) with respect to which the *firm* as tippee has material information of a "bearish" nature. A firm that followed the Merrill Lynch model soon learned that these are not academic questions:

The "schoolmaster" was *Slade* v. *Shearson, Hammill & Co., Inc.,*[85] a case on all fours with *Merrill Lynch.* There were two consolidated class actions brought against the firm by buyers of the stock in question. The District Court, observing that the firm had voluntarily entered into fiduciary relationships with both the issuer and its customers, distinguished *Merrill Lynch* as standing for "no more than the proposition that a banker who receives inside information from an investment banking client cannot reveal same 'to favored customers.' "[86] The Court of Appeals permitted an interlocutory appeal, but then followed the highly unusual course of remanding the case without any decision in view of the factual questions involved and the failure of the parties together with the several *amici* (including the SEC) to agree in "spelling out the legal questions that are here involved and which it is suggested we answer in the abstract."[87] This leaves the District Court's opinion standing as if there had been no attempt at review.

At the moment, in short, the problem defies clear solution. The Commission's suggestion of a "restricted list" is bound to create rumors. Customer gives *A,* a representative of Firm *X,* an order to buy. *A* says, "Sorry, that security is on our restricted list." "Why?" "I can't say." "But Firm *Y* next door is trading the stock." "Sorry, I can't explain." Nevertheless, many multiservice firms use a restricted list as a supplement to a "wall" in order to avoid any appearance of impropriety. "For example," an officer of one of these firms has said, "it does not make good sense to issue a sell recom-

[85] 517 F. 2d 398 (1974).

[86] CCH Fed. Sec. L. Rep. ¶94,329 at 95,131-32 (S. D. N. Y. 1974); cf. Black v. Shearson, Hammill & Co., Inc., 266 Cal. App. 2d 362, 368, 72 Cal. Rptr. 157, 161 (1968).

[87] 517 F. 2d at 402.

mendation, even innocently, about the stock of an issuer for which you are about to launch a tender offer."[88]

A determined effort to draft for the Code a "Chinese wall" provision that would preclude liability in certain instances floundered on the difficulties here expounded. But, in connection with a provision to the effect that questions of imputation of an agent's knowledge to his principal should be governed by federal common law, the Code directs the courts and the Commission to consider, when it is the fact, that the principal has established either a wall or (as some firms have done) procedures "reasonably designed * * * to prevent transactions in and recommendations concerning securities of the [particular] issuer."[89] This reliance on the common law technique to prick out a line was preferred over some sort of "safe harbor" approach, because "it gives the courts sufficient flexibility to consider, in developing the law in this area, not only the particular factual configuration but also the type, purpose and 'morality' of the specific procedures that have been adopted."[90]

5. Fitting *Chiarella* and *Dirks* into the 10b-5 Grid

All the cases, real and hypothetical, so far discussed fall within the classic pattern of insider-*cum*-tippee. Now consider three models:

(1) The president of Company *A,* which uses widgets in its own manufacturing, buys heavily into Company *B,* a widget manufacturer with which he has had no previous relationship, after deciding to give Company *B* a large order for widgets.

(2) A law clerk to a Supreme Court justice, knowing that an opinion will be coming down within a week to the effect that the antitrust laws do not require General Motors to split up, buys.

[88] Harmon, The Chinese Wall, in Practising Law Institute, Twelfth Annual Institute on Securities Regulation (1981) c. 24 at 426. Another problem with relying solely on a "wall" is that Rule 10b-6 (infra p. 862) prohibits purchases during a distribution without regard to whether market personnel have knowledge of the distribution. See generally Lipton and Masur, The Chinese Wall Solution to the Conflict Problems of Securities Firms, 50 N. Y. U. L. Rev. 459 (1975); Varn, The Multi-service Securities Firm and the Chinese Wall: A New Look in the Light of the Federal Securities Code, 63 Neb. L. Rev. 197 (1984).

[89] §202(86)(C)(ii).

[90] 1 Code 149. Nevertheless, variations of the "Chinese wall" have been adopted not only by the SEC under §14(e) (Rule 14e-3, infra pp. 759-60), but also by the Comptroller of the Currency (12 Code Fed. Regs. §9.7(d)) and the Board of Governors of the Federal Reserve System (policy statement, 43 Fed. Reg. 12,755, 12,756 (1978)). See also p. 760 n. 113 infra; p. 596 n. f supra.

(3) An employee of a financial printing firm that is hired by a tender offeror manages to deduce the identity of the target company, whose stock he buys.

These three cases are similar to each other, as well as to the cases previously discussed, in that each buyer has a significant informational advantage. They are also similar to each other, but different from the cases previously discussed, in that none of the buyers is either an insider of the *issuer* or such an insider's tippee.[91] The company president's nonpublic information is self-created; the law clerk's comes from his public office; and the printer's comes from the wrong company (the tender offeror, not the target whose shares he buys).

The printer's case is *Chiarella* v. *United States.*[92] The Second Circuit, in affirming the printer's conviction, held that "*Anyone* — corporate insider or not — who regularly receives material nonpublic information may not use that information to trade in securities without incurring an affirmative duty to disclose."[93] A divided Supreme Court reversed, Justice Powell writing for the majority:[94]

> * * * administrative and judicial interpretations have established that silence in connection with the purchase or sale of securities may operate as a fraud actionable under §10(b) despite the absence of statutory language or legislative history specifically addressing the legality of nondisclosure. But such liability is premised upon a duty to disclose arising from a relationship of trust and confidence between parties to a transaction. Application of a duty to disclose prior

[91] Cases of this type are sometimes characterized as involving "market information." See generally Fleischer, Mundheim, and Murphy, An Initial Inquiry into the Responsibility to Disclose Market Information, 121 U. Pa. L. Rev. 798 (1973). This is a confusing phrase as so used, because "there is no reason in either principle or the case law to distinguish * * * between material information that is intrinsic to the company (for example, a major mineral discovery) and market information that will not affect the company's assets or earning power (for example, information received by the president from a large brokerage firm's analyst who has interviewed him to the effect that the firm is about to publish a favorable report on the company together with a 'buy' recommendation)." 2 Code 657, cited in Dirks v. SEC, 463 U. S. 646, 656-57 n. 15 (1983); see also Chiarella v. United States, 445 U. S. 222, 240-41 n. 1 (dissenting opinion of Burger, C. J., the majority's one-sentence observation the other way, id. at 235, being clearly dictum); Zweig v. Hearst Corp., 594 F. 2d 1261, 1266-67 (9th Cir. 1979), infra pp. 761-62; Moss v. Morgan Stanley, Inc., 719 F. 2d 5, 11 n. 9 (2d Cir. 1983), *cert. denied* sub nom. Moss v. Newman, 465 U. S. 1025 (italics are the court's), quoting from Barry, The Economics of Outside Information and Rule 10b-5, 129 U. Pa. L. Rev. 1307, 1309-10 n. 11 (1980): "*The important factor is not the type of information,* so long as it is material, *but its source.*"

[92] 445 U. S. 222 (1980).

[93] United States v. Chiarella, 588 F. 2d 1358, 1365 (2d Cir. 1978).

[94] 445 U. S. at 230-31, 234-35.

to trading guarantees that corporate insiders, who have an obligation to place the shareholder's welfare before their own, will not benefit personally through fraudulent use of material nonpublic information.

In this case the petitioner was convicted of violating §10(b) although he was not a corporate insider and he received no confidential information from the target company. * * * The jury simply was told to decide whether petitioner used material nonpublic information at a time when "he knew other people trading in the securities market did not have access to the same information."

* * *

* * * Section 10(b) is aptly described as a catchall provision, but what it catches must be fraud. When an allegation of fraud is based upon nondisclosure, there can be no fraud absent a duty to speak. We hold that a duty to disclose under §10(b) does not arise from the mere possession of nonpublic market information. * * *

One cannot cavil with this holding in the present state of the law, which requires analysis in terms of fraud. The Commission itself did not espouse market egalitarianism before the *Texas Gulf Sulphur* case in 1968, where the Second Circuit referred to the rule as "based in policy on the justifiable expectation of the securities marketplace that all investors trading on impersonal exchanges have relatively equal access to material information," and went on to say that "anyone in possession of material inside information must either disclose it to the investing public, or * * * must abstain from trading * * *."[95] But that language must be read in the context of a case involving classic insiders and their tippees.

[95] SEC v. Texas Gulf Sulphur Co., 401 F. 2d 833, 848 (2d Cir. 1968), *cert. denied* sub nom. Coates v. SEC and Kline v. SEC, 394 U. S. 976. Contrast Cady, Roberts & Co., 40 SEC 907, 911 (1961), supra p. 740. For a legislative egalitarian proposal, see Seligman, The Reformulation of Federal Securities Law Concerning Nonpublic Information, 73 Geo. L. J. 1083 (1985). Professor Brudney has advanced another theory, which falls somewhat short of egalitarianism: that there should be a universal ban on trading by persons who obtain material, nonpublic information through "unerodable informational advantages" — which is to say, advantages that normally arise because of a person's position giving access to information not legally available to public investors however diligent. Brudney, Insiders, Outsiders and Informational Advantages Under the Federal Securities Laws, 93 Harv. L. Rev. 322 (1979). It has also been suggested that the wrong associated with insider trading has to do with "self-dealing and breach of fiduciary duty toward the corporation or shareholders and clients as a group, rather than with misrepresentation or deception of individual investors," and that the Court in *Chiarella* "appears simply to be playing games with [common law misrepresentation] doctrine in order to limit liability without articulating the reasons why liability should be limited in just that way." Anderson, Fraud,

Yet one intuitively would like to cover the printer's and law clerk's cases, if not the two-company "widget" model. The British solution when Parliament criminalized insider trading in the Companies Act 1980 was to cover the two-company situation and the "public servant" (the law clerk in our model) in so many words.[96] But this sort of particularization invites argument by negative implication when novel schemes come along. And at the purely criminal level there are other federal statutes available in this country.[97]

The Code suggested an alternative that would not necessarily require legislation: a new judicially created category of "quasi-insider," who would not be an insider but would be treated as if he were. The Code's technique for accomplishing this — apart from extending the Commission's rulemaking power to *prevent* fraudulent practices from §15(c)(2) of the 1934 Act and other provisions to the Code's fraud part generally — is not to attempt to extend §1603, the partial codification of the affirmative duty to speak under Rule 10b-5, beyond insiders (including their tippees) on some theory of "market egalitarianism." Instead the Code invites the courts to fall back on the residual §1602(a)(1), which basically repeats Rule 10b-5, "to the extent that a sufficiently egregious or shocking or offensive case of trading while silent *cannot* be rationalized on an 'insider' analysis."[98]

This "quasi-insider" idea met with the Second Circuit's favor in *Chiarella.*[99] And Chief Justice Burger, in a dissenting opinion in which Justices Blackmun and Marshall joined, cited the Code's "quasi-insider" concept favorably.[100] But he shifted the emphasis a bit by observing that "These quasi-insiders share the characteristic that their informal advantage is obtained by conversion and not by legitimate economic activity that society seeks to encourage."[101] This

Fiduciaries, and Insider Trading, 10 Hofstra L. Rev. 341, 373, 376 (1982); see also Dooley, Enforcement of Insider Trading Restrictions, 66 Va. L. Rev. 1 (1980).

[96] 1985 Acts c. 22, §§68(2), 69, now Company Securities (Insider Dealing) Act 1985, 1985 Acts c. 8, §§1(2), 2, as amended by Financial Services Act 1986, 1986 Acts c. 60, §173.

[97] United States v. Peltz, 433 F. 2d 48 (2d Cir. 1970), *cert. denied,* 401 U. S. 955 (conspiracy to defraud the Government by trading on basis of information about proposed litigation obtained from an SEC employee); United States v. Keane, 522 F. 2d 534, 544-51 (7th Cir. 1975), *cert. denied,* 424 U. S. 976 (mail fraud statute).

[98] 2 Code 663. Cf. Blyth & Co., Inc., 43 SEC 1037 (1969) (traders in broker-dealer's Government bond department got advance information from Federal Reserve Bank employee of terms of new Government issues).

[99] 588 F. 2d at 1366.

[100] 445 U. S. at 242 n. 3.

[101] Ibid.

seems to reflect the Government's alternative theory that the defendant's breach of duty to his employer's customer (the tender offeror) supported a §10(b) conviction for fraud perpetrated upon both the offeror company and the market sellers — that is to say, that Chiarella "breached a duty to the acquiring corporation."[102]

This quotation is from the majority opinion. The Burger and Blackmun-Marshall dissenting opinions, as well as the Brennan concurring opinion, speak in terms of "misappropriation" or "conversion" of the inside information.[103] When there is in fact a fiduciary duty to a third person, the two locutions may be treated as synonymous. But the "misappropriation" concept is broader in the sense that it covers the defendant who obtains nonpublic information without violating any duty owed either to the issuer or to any other person (apart from the societal duty not to commit crimes) — which is to say, the defendant who resorts to practices like industrial espionage or outright thievery of corporate documents. And there is nothing in *Chiarella* that would preclude a holding that that sort of conduct suffices.[104] The problem is to draw the line between that kind of malefactor and the person who cannot help overhearing an executive "blabbermouth" in an elevator or a taxi.[105]

In any event, the majority in *Chiarella* declined to rule on the Government's alternative theory because it had not been submitted to the jury. But the theory was approved by four Justices (the three dissenters and Justice Brennan in his concurring opinion), and the other five in *Bateman Eichler, Hill Richards, Inc.* v. *Brenner* joined an opinion stating that they "also have noted that a tippee may be liable [under Rule 10b-5] if he otherwise 'misappropriate[s] or illegally obtain[s] the information.' "[106] The theory has also been endorsed by the Second Circuit for criminal purposes,[107] though not for private actions.[108]

[102] Id. at 235.

[103] 445 U. S. at 245; see Aldave, Misappropriation: A General Theory of Liability for Trading on Nonpublic Information, 13 Hofstra L. Rev. 101 (1984).

[104] The Chief Justice's dissenting opinion in *Chiarella* quoted eminent academic authority: "Any time information is acquired by an illegal act it would seem that there should be a duty to disclose that information." Keeton, Fraud — Concealment and Non-Disclosure, 15 Tex. L. Rev. 1, 25-26 (1930).

[105] Cf. SEC v. Switzer, 590 F. Supp. 756 (W. D. Okla. 1984).

[106] 472 U. S. 299, 313 n. 22 (1985). The opinion quoted from *Dirks* (463 U. S. at 665), although all that Justice Powell said there was: "Nor did Dirks misappropriate or illegally obtain the information about Equity Funding." See Pollack, J., in SEC v. Tome, 638 F. Supp. 596, 620-22 (S. D. N. Y. 1986).

[107] United States v. Newman, 664 F. 2d 12 (2d Cir. 1981), *conviction aff'd without published opinion,* 722 F. 2d 729 (2d Cir. 1983), *cert. denied,* 464 U. S. 863. In *Newman,* employees of investment banking firms allegedly tipped Newman (the only person before the court) and other co-conspirators with respect

Meanwhile the Commission, without waiting for a judicial test of that theory, resorted to its rulemaking authority in §14(e)[109] to get at *tender offerors'* tippees who buy *target companies'* stock. Once a person "has taken a substantial step or steps to commence" a tender offer, Rule 14e-3[110] prohibits any such tippee (as well as the offeror itself) from trading in target securities until "a reasonable time" after public disclosure of any material information he may have with

---

to proposed mergers and acquisitions. The court reversed the dismissal of an indictment on the ground that Newman had aided and abetted the employees' duty of loyalty to their employers, thus defrauding not only the investment banking firms but also *their* clients. See also SEC v. Materia, 745 F. 2d 197 (2d Cir. 1984), *cert. denied,* 471 U. S. 1053 (a *Chiarella*-type case in which the court followed *Newman*); United States v. Reed, 601 F. Supp. 685 (S. D. N. Y. 1985), *rev'd on other grounds,* 773 F. 2d 477 (2d Cir. 1985) (if it could be proved that a criminal defendant, with inside merger information given in confidence by his father, a director of the company to be merged, bought options on that company's stock in breach of a confidential relationship that existed between them under the circumstances, it would not matter whether the father actually suffered the injuries that could have resulted from defendant's activities); cf. Rothberg v. Rosenbloom, 771 F. 2d 818 (3d Cir. 1985); see also People v. Florentino, 456 N. Y. S. 2d 638 (N. Y. C. Cr. Ct. 1982) (the first criminal prosecution under N. Y. Martin Act §352-c for insider trading).

In United States v. Carpenter, 791 F. 2d 1024 (2d Cir. 1986), *cert. granted,* 107 S. Ct. 666 — where a writer of the Wall Street Journal's "Heard on the Street" column gave several persons advance information on the content of his columns and shared in their resulting trading profits — the court concluded that the existence of wronged third parties in *Newman* and *Materia* (the employer's investment banking clients and printing customers) was not an essential element. *Carpenter* is different, because the alleged violation did not hinge on any information emanating from either a classic or a temporary insider but from an "insider" that did not even intend to trade on the basis of the information, the Wall Street Journal. The defendant still "stole" the information — to use Chief Justice Burger's characterization (445 U. S. at 245) — but is it the kind of theft or breach of duty that is property within the scope of the insider trading laws? Judge Miner, dissenting, stated: "Knowledge of publication dates simply is not the special securities-related knowledge implicated in the misappropriation theory." 791 F. 2d at 1037.

Proving the use of inside information sometimes requires intricate detective work. See SEC v. Musella, 578 F. Supp. 425 (S. D. N. Y. 1984) (similar to *Newman,* supra, except that defendant was a law firm's office manager rather than a printer's employee).

[108] Moss v. Morgan Stanley, Inc., 719 F. 2d 5 (2d Cir. 1983), *cert. denied* sub nom. Moss v. Newman, 465 U. S. 1025; see Phillips, Insider Trading Liability After *Dirks,* 16 Rev. Sec. Reg. 841, 845-46 (1983) (the duty-to-a-third-person theory is fundamentally at odds with *Santa Fe,* infra p. 803).

[109] See p. 509 supra.

[110] The validity of Rule 14e-3 was sustained in O'Connor & Associates v. Dean Witter Reynolds, Inc., 529 F. Supp. 1179, 1190-93 (S. D. N. Y. 1981). The court there held also (1) that trading on the basis of nonpublic information concerning an impending tender offer satisfied the rule's phrase, "in connection with a tender offer," and (2) that the fact that no tender offer had actually become effective did not bar the application of §14(e). Id. at 1191-93.

respect to the tender offer and the source of that information.[111] But an exception is made for a non-natural person that shows that (1) the individuals within the organization that made the investment decision did not in fact know the information in question *and* (2) the organization

> had implemented one or a combination of policies and procedures, reasonable under the circumstances, taking into consideration the nature of the person's business, to ensure that individual(s) making investment decision(s) would not violate [the rule], which policies and procedures may include, but are not limited to, (i) those which restrict any purchase, sale and causing any purchase and sale of any such security or (ii) those which prevent such individual(s) from knowing such information.[112]

Clause (ii), of course, refers to the "Chinese wall." And Clause (i) contemplates restricted lists. The Commission cautioned:

> Depending on the circumstances, it may be appropriate to advise customers of its [the organization's] use of the Chinese Wall, because the institution would not be using all information that it had received to the benefit of a particular customer. There is also a danger that the Chinese Wall may not be fully effective in all instances and that information may pass through the wall. In that regard, other informal procedures are often used in conjunction with and to supplement the Chinese Wall at times when the institution has material, nonpublic information but before the information is appropriate for public release or to cause placement of the security on a strict list. This "watch list" procedure enables the institution to monitor trading activity to determine whether any leaks in the Chinese Wall have occurred.[113]

[111] Rule 14e-3(a). Examples of a "substantial step" presumably include such actions as a board resolution or the arranging of financing or the preparation of tender offer material, or possibly an offeror's purchase of 5 percent of a target's stock after negotiations have broken off but before a public tender offer is announced.

The prohibition applies also to tippees from the target companies whose stock they trade (as well as the targets themselves). Ibid. These are classic 10b-5 situations in any event. In addition, the rule prohibits *tipping per se.* Rule 14e-3(d).

[112] Rule 14e-3(b).

[113] Sec. Ex. Act Rel. 17,120, 20 SEC Dock. 1241, 1252 (1980). See pp. 751-54 supra. The House committee report on the Insider Trading Sanctions Act of 1984 (see p. 1008 infra) blessed the "Chinese Wall" in these words:

> The Committee also believes it appropriate that if an adviser to an investment company directed trades on behalf of the investment company while in possession of material nonpublic information, the adviser, and not the investment company shareholders, should be subject to the triple

Presumably this use of the rulemaking authority in §14(e) to make a potential felon out of not only the prospective tender offeror's president but also his personal secretary who buys target stock, while leaving the president free to buy for the prospective tender offeror itself before any announcement is made, finds its explanation in the "free 5 percent" provision in §13(d). There is an inherent anomaly, however, that goes beyond Rule 14e-3 to the Commission-advocated misappropriation theory under Rule 10b-5: The president of Company *B* who buys Company *A* stock without disclosing his intention to cause *B* to give a huge order for widgets to *A* is safe so far as Rule 10b-5 is concerned, thanks to *Chiarella*. But, once more, his poor secretary had better watch out; for the secretary's purchase of *A* stock would violate a fiduciary duty owed to his or her "boss."

(3) *Query,* next, whether *Chiarella* leaves anything of "scalping" cases like *Zweig* v. *Hearst Corp.,*[114] where Rule 10b-5 was applied with respect to a newspaper columnist's practice of buying shares of companies that he expected to discuss favorably. The court analyzed the case in terms of the defendant's failure to disclose his ownership. But it did cite the Supreme Court's decision in *SEC* v. *Capital Gains Research Bureau, Inc.,*[115] where the "scalper" was an investment adviser who made recommendations in monthly reports to subscribers. To be sure, an investment adviser — even the publisher of a tipster sheet — is a fiduciary.[116] But more important, arguably, is the language of the underlying statute in the *Capital Gains* case: §206 of the Advisers Act contains "fraud" language comparable to Clauses (1) and (3) of Rule 10b-5 but no prohibition of misstatements or half-truths along the lines of Clause (2). A *Zweig*

---

penalty as a direct violator.

Insider Trading Sanctions Act of 1983, H. R. Rep. No. 98-355, 98th Cong., 1st Sess. (1983) 11. The Commission's suggestion of an amendment to the bill to incorporate the Commission's rule was not adopted. Insider Trading Sanctions Act of 1983, Hearing on H. R. 559 Before Subcom. on Securities, S. Com. on Banking, Housing & Urban Affairs, 98th Cong., 2d Sess. (1984) 12.

[114] 594 F. 2d 1261 (9th Cir. 1979). See Note, The First Amendment and "Scalping" by a Financial Columnist: May a Newspaper Article Be Commercial Speech?, 57 Ind. L. J. 131 (1981).

[115] 375 U. S. 180 (1963). In Santa Fe Industries, Inc. v. Green, 430 U. S. 462, 471 n. 11 (1977), infra p. 803, where the Court was talking not of scienter but of the relationship of nondisclosure to "fraud," it observed that the references in *Capital Gains* to fraud in the "equitable" sense of the term were premised on the recognition that Congress intended the Advisers Act to establish federal fiduciary standards for advisers. See also Aaron v. SEC, 446 U. S. 680, 691-95 (1980), infra p. 783.

[116] When the "scalper" is a broker or dealer, resort might be had also to the "shingle" theory (infra p. 811).

type of case might, therefore, have a better chance of surviving *Chiarella* if it were analyzed in terms of a fraudulent "act" or "scheme" rather than a failure to disclose.[117]

We now move from "insider" to "tippee." More specifically, we have to explore the Supreme Court's teaching in *Dirks* v. *SEC*[118] by way of measuring its departure from previous thinking about tippees. Once again Justice Powell wrote, this time for a majority of six (Justices Blackmun, Brennan, and Marshall dissenting):

> I
>
> In 1973, Dirks was an officer of a New York broker-dealer firm who specialized in providing investment analysis of insurance company securities to institutional investors. On March 6, Dirks received information from Ronald Secrist, a former officer of Equity Funding of America. Secrist alleged that the assets of Equity Funding, a diversified corporation primarily engaged in selling life insurance and mutual funds, were vastly overstated as a result of fraudulent corporate practices. Secrist also stated that various regulatory agencies had failed to act on similar charges made by Equity Funding employees. He urged Dirks to verify the fraud and disclose it publicly.
>
> Dirks decided to investigate the allegations. He visited Equity Funding's headquarters in Los Angeles and interviewed several officers and employees of the corporation. The senior management denied any wrongdoing, but certain corporation employees corroborated the charges of fraud. Neither Dirks nor his firm owned or traded any Equity Funding stock, but throughout his investigation he openly discussed the information he had obtained with a number of clients and investors. Some of these persons sold their holdings of Equity Funding securities, including five investment advisers who liquidated holdings of more than $16 million.
>
> * * *
>
> During the two-week period in which Dirks pursued his investigation and spread word of Secrist's charges, the price of Equity

[117] On fraud by deed, see 2 Code 661-62; p. 768 infra. Cf. United States v. Winans, 612 F. Supp. 827 (S. D. N. Y. 1985) (Wall Street Journal writer). In any event, such activity is "conduct inconsistent with just and equitable principles of trade" within the meaning of the rules of the exchanges and the NASD. In Smith Barney, Harris Upham & Co., Inc., Sec. Ex. Act Rel. 21,242, 31 SEC Dock. 209 (1984), the Commission affirmed the American Stock Exchange's finding of such conduct where a member organization had effected options transactions for its own account before its research recommendation with respect to the underlying stock had been disseminated to its public customers.

[118] 463 U. S. 646 (1983).

Funding stock fell from $26 per share to less than $15 per share. This led the New York Stock Exchange to halt trading on March 27. Shortly thereafter California insurance authorities impounded Equity Funding's records and uncovered evidence of the fraud. Only then did the Securities and Exchange Commission (SEC) file a complaint against Equity Funding and only then, on April 2, did the Wall Street Journal publish a front-page story based largely on information assembled by Dirks. Equity Funding immediately went into receivership.

The SEC began an investigation into Dirks' role in the exposure of the fraud. After a hearing by an administrative law judge, the SEC found that Dirks had aided and abetted violations of §17(a) of the Securities Act of 1933 [and Rule 10b-5], by repeating the allegations of fraud to members of the investment community who later sold their Equity Funding stock. The SEC concluded: "Where 'tippees' — regardless of their motivation or occupation — come into possession of material 'information that they know is confidential and know or should know came from a corporate insider,' they must either publicly disclose that information or refrain from trading." 21 SEC Docket, 1401, 1407 (1981) (footnote omitted) (quoting Chiarella v. United States, 445 U. S. 222, 230 n. 12 (1980)). Recognizing, however, that Dirks "played an important role in bringing [Equity Funding's] massive fraud to light," 21 SEC Docket, at 1412, the SEC only censured him.

Dirks sought review in the Court of Appeals for the District of Columbia Circuit. The court entered judgment against Dirks "for the reasons stated by the Commission in its opinion." * * *

* * *

III

* * * Unlike insiders who have independent fiduciary duties to both the corporation and its shareholders, the typical tippee has no such relationships.[14] In view of this absence, it has been unclear how a tippee acquires the *Cady, Roberts* duty to refrain from trading on insider information.

[14] Under certain circumstances, such as where corporate information is revealed legitimately to an underwriter, accountant, lawyer, or consultant working for the corporation, these outsiders may become fiduciaries of the shareholders. The basis for recognizing this fiduciary duty is not simply that such persons acquired nonpublic corporate information, but rather that they have entered into a special confidential relationship in the conduct of the business of the enterprise and are given access to information solely for corporate purposes. [Citations omitted.] When such a person breaches his fiduciary relationship, he may be treated more properly as a tipper than a tippee. [Citation omitted.] For such a duty to be imposed, however, the corporation must expect the outsider to keep the disclosed nonpublic information confidential, and the relationship at least must imply such a duty.

A

The SEC's position, as stated in its opinion in this case, is that a tippee "inherits" the *Cady, Roberts* obligation to shareholders whenever he receives inside information from an insider. * * *

This view differs little from the view that we rejected as inconsistent with congressional intent in *Chiarella*. * * *

* * * We reaffirm today that "[a] duty [to disclose] arises from the relationship between parties * * * and not merely from one's ability to acquire information because of his position in the market." 445 U. S., at 232-233, n. 14.

Imposing a duty to disclose or abstain solely because a person knowingly receives material nonpublic information from an insider and trades on it could have an inhibiting influence on the role of market analysts, which the SEC itself recognizes is necessary to the preservation of a healthy market. It is commonplace for analysts to "ferret out and analyze information," 21 SEC, at 1406, and this often is done by meeting with and questioning corporate officers and others who are insiders. And information that the analysts obtain normally may be the basis for judgment as to the market worth of a corporation's securities. The analyst's judgment in this respect is made available in market letters or otherwise to clients of the firm. It is the nature of this type of information, and indeed of the markets themselves, that such information cannot be made simultaneously available to all of the corporation's stockholders or the public generally.

B

The conclusion that recipients of inside information do not invariably acquire a duty to disclose or abstain does not mean that such tippees always are free to trade on the information. The need for a ban on some tippee trading is clear. Not only are insiders forbidden by their fiduciary relationship from personally using undisclosed corporate information to their advantage, but they may not give such information to an outsider for the same improper purpose of exploiting the information for their personal gain. See 15 U. S. C. §78t(b) (making it unlawful to do indirectly "by means of any other person" any act made unlawful by the federal securities laws). Similarly, the transactions of those who knowingly participate with the fiduciary in such a breach are "as forbidden" as transactions "on behalf of the trustee himself." * * * the tippee's duty to disclose or abstain is derivative from that of the insider's duty. * * *

Thus, some tippees must assume an insider's duty to the shareholders not because they receive inside information, but rather because it has been made available to them *improperly*.[19] And for Rule

[19] The SEC itself has recognized that tippee liability properly is imposed only

10b-5 purposes, the insider's disclosure is improper only where it would violate his *Cady, Roberts* duty. Thus, a tippee assumes a fiduciary duty to the shareholders of a corporation not to trade on material nonpublic information only when the insider has breached his fiduciary duty to the shareholders by disclosing the information to the tippee and the tippee knows or should know that there has been a breach.[20] * * * Tipping thus properly is viewed only as a means of indirectly violating the *Cady, Roberts* disclose-or-abstain rule.

C

In determining whether a tippee is under an obligation to disclose or abstain, it thus is necessary to determine whether the insider's "tip" constituted a breach of the insider's fiduciary duty. All disclosures of confidential corporate information are not inconsistent with the duty insiders owe to shareholders. * * * [T]he test is whether the insider personally will benefit, directly or indirectly, from his disclosure. Absent some personal gain, there has been no breach of duty to stockholders. And absent a breach by the insider, there is no derivative breach. * * *

* * * [T]he initial inquiry is whether there has been a breach of duty by the insider. This requires courts to focus on objective criteria, i. e., whether the insider receives a direct or indirect personal benefit from the disclosure, such as a pecuniary gain or a reputational benefit that will translate into future earnings. * * * There are objective facts and circumstances that often justify such an inference. For example, there may be a relationship between the insider and the recipient that suggests a quid pro quo from the latter, or an intention to benefit the particular recipient. The elements of fiduciary duty and exploitation of nonpublic information also exist when an insider makes a gift of confidential information

---

in circumstances where the tippee knows, or has reason to know, that the insider has disclosed improperly inside corporate information. In *Investors Management Co.*, supra, the SEC stated that one element of tippee liability is that the tippee knew or had reason to know "that [the information] was non-public and had been obtained *improperly* by selective revelation or otherwise." 44 SEC, at 641 (emphasis added). Commissioner Smith read this test to mean that a tippee can be held liable only if he received information in breach of an insider's duty not to disclose it. Id., at 650 (concurring in the result).

[20] Professor Loss has linked tippee liability to the concept in the law of restitution that "'[w]here a fiduciary in violation of his duty to the beneficiary communicates confidential information to a third person, the third person, if he had notice of the violation of duty, holds upon a constructive trust for the beneficiary any profit which he makes through the use of such information.'" 3 L. Loss, Securities Regulation 1451 (2d ed. 1961) (quoting Restatement of Restitution §201(2) (1937)). * * *

to a trading relative or friend. The tip and trade resemble trading by the insider himself followed by a gift of the profits to the recipient.

Dirks on its facts is a sport — all principle (from the SEC's point of view) and no "sex." The Commission would have been well advised to use its prosecutor's discretion, as it did with respect to Dirks's principal informant,[119] in order to close the file. Even so, the Commission seems to have snatched a considerable measure of victory from the jaws of defeat.

In reversing the District of Columbia Circuit's affirmance of the Commission's censure,[120] the Supreme Court held first that, "Unlike insiders who have independent fiduciary duties to both the corporation and its shareholders, the typical tippee has no such relationships."[121] His status derives from the inside tipper. Consequently a plaintiff must show that the tipper acted "*improperly*" (the italics are Justice Powell's), which is to say, that he tipped for "personal gain."[122]

Secondly, with this proof of the *tipper's* motive out of the way, the *tippee* still does not violate unless *he* "knows or should know that there has been a breach" of the tipper's fiduciary duty.[123]

The second holding is all but implicit in the older cases, to the extent that the tippee must "know or have reason to know that [the information] was non-public and had been obtained improperly by selective revelation or otherwise," and that the information must be "a factor in his decision to effect the transaction."[124] This proposition is simply a manifestation of the broader principle that "the transactions of those who knowingly participate with the fiduciary in [his] breach are 'as forbidden' as transactions 'on behalf of the

[119] Raymond L. Dirks, Sec. Ex. Act Rel. 17,480, 21 SEC Dock. 1401, 1402 (1981). In contrast to Dirks's censure, the reluctant Wall Street Journal reporter ultimately got a Pulitzer Prize.

[120] Dirks v. SEC, 681 F. 2d 824 (D. C. Cir. 1982). A footnote in the Commission's memorandum in opposition to *certiorari* stated that the Solicitor General was of the view that the holding below was in conflict with Chiarella v. United States, 445 U. S. 222 (1980).

[121] 445 U. S. at 653, supra p. 763.

[122] Id. at 662, supra p. 765.

[123] Ibid.; see also Bateman Eichler, Hill Richards, Inc. v. Berner, 472 U. S. 299 n. 21 (1985); State Teachers Retirement Board v. Flour Corp., 592 F. Supp. 592 (S. D. N. Y. 1984).

[124] Investors Management Co., Inc., 44 SEC 633, 641 (1971). There the respondents, with one exception, did not meet the burden of showing that the information in question was *not a factor.* More recently the Commission has been taking the position that *mere possession* of inside information while trading is enough. See pp. 734-35, supra.

trustee himself.' "[125] As a practical matter, we shall see, proof of the defendant's knowledge of a breach of the tipper's fiduciary duty should not often be an obstacle.

The *first* holding — which goes to the impropriety of the *tipper's* conduct — is an extension of prior law. But it, too, turns out on examination to be quite limited.

Take first the case where, in Justice Powell's words, "corporate information is revealed legitimately to an underwriter, accountant, lawyer, or consultant working for the corporation."[126] Under the old dispensation, which treated tippers and tippees alike, these people were considered to be tippees. Under the new, as stated in a footnote 14 that is destined for fame, "when such a person breaches his fiduciary relationship, he may be treated more properly as a tipper than a tippee."[127]

The result is the same, except that the Court's approach creates a problem of drawing the line around the note 14 category; for the Court's enumeration of these "outsiders" become "insiders" could hardly have been meant to be exclusive. And, if an *outside* accountant or lawyer may become a fiduciary of the shareholders, this must be true *a fortiori* of a *house* accountant or lawyer — or, for that matter, any employee, such as the personal secretary of one of these note 14 "insiders."[128]

Note 14 aside, when dealing with the proof required in the case of one who indubitably *is* a tippee under the Court's lexicon, we find the Court going out of its way to list a number of "objective facts and circumstances that often justify * * * an inference" that the tipper received a "direct or indirect personal benefit from the disclosure, such as a pecuniary gain or a reputational benefit that will translate into future earnings."[129] The Powell opinion expounds on this:

> For example, there may be a relationship between the insider and the recipient that suggests a quid pro quo from the latter, or an intention to benefit the particular recipient. The elements of fidu-

[125] 463 U. S. at 659.

[126] Id. at 655 n. 14. See SEC v. Tome, 638 F. Supp. 596, 621 (S. D. N. Y. 1986).

[127] 463 U. S. at 655. Justice Powell added: "For such a duty to be imposed, however, the corporation must expect the outsider to keep the disclosed nonpublic information confidential, and the relationship at least must imply such a duty."

[128] Bianco v. Texas Instruments, Inc., 627 F. Supp. 154, 163-64 (N. D. Ill. 1985). Analogy suggests itself from the attorney-client privilege, which binds the attorney's secretary to the same degree as the attorney.

[129] 463 U. S. at 664.

ciary duty and exploitation of nonpublic information also exist when an insider makes a gift of confidential information to a trading relative or friend. The tip and trade resemble trading by the insider himself followed by a gift of the profits to the recipient.[130]

This is pretty broad language. The tip-for-reward and the tip-from-friendship describe the two classic cases. With the former undoubtedly broad enough to cover mutual back-scratching between two corporate executives who exchange nonpublic information about their respective companies, and with consultants and the like transmuted by the Court from tippees to tippers, it does not seem too much to speculate that the Court's examples may cover most tips in practice.[131]

If this is so, the primary gainer of the *Dirks* case is the financial analyst. For the analyst category is very likely the prime example of the tip that is *not* given for either friendship or personal gain.[132]

Under the traditional view, as epitomized in the Commission's opinion, the Commission "recognized that an analyst may utilize non-public, inside information which in itself is immaterial in order

[130] Ibid.

[131] The House committee report on the Insider Trading Sanctions Act of 1984 (see p. 1008 infra) — expressing the belief that, "if the *Dirks* decision is properly and narrowly construed by the courts, the Commission's insider trading program will not be adversely affected" — observed that, according to a report by Commission officials soon after the *Dirks* decision, a review of the thirty-four insider trading cases brought by the Commission in the preceding two years revealed that only one case might have been affected by the decision. The Committee nevertheless directed the Commission to monitor the effects of *Dirks* for at least two years and to report back annually. Insider Trading Sanctions Act of 1983, H. R. Rep. No. 98-355, 98th Cong., 1st Sess. (1984) 14-15. The first such report concluded, on a detailed analysis of judicial interpretations during the two years after *Dirks,* that "the decision has not adversely affected, to a significant degree, the Commission's enforcement program against insider trading." Report of the SEC to the House Committee on Energy and Commerce on *Dirks* v. *SEC* (1985) 3-4.

In SEC v. Platt, 565 F. Supp. 1244 (W. D. Okla. 1983), *on the merits,* Litig. Rel. 10,320, 30 SEC Dock. 243 (W. D. Okla. 1984), the University of Oklahoma football coach, who claimed that he had merely overheard information while sitting near the issuer's former president at a track meet, was exonerated, along with six other defendants who had allegedly been tipped by the coach or his tippees, for the Commission's failure to prove that the former president had intentionally disclosed the information.

[132] This assumes that the insider does not act improperly by favoring a particular analyst out of friendship or with donative intent, or perhaps by exacting a bribe for the "scoop." Presumably there is nothing wrong *per se* with the insider's consistently confining his disclosures to one or two analysts out of many in the community.

to fill in 'interstices in analysis,' "[133] although "such 'tidbits' of inside information 'may assume heightened significance when woven by the skilled analyst into the matrix of knowledge obtained elsewhere,' thereby creating material information."[134] But, despite the utility of the analyst's role, he had "no special license to ignore the insider trading proscriptions of the federal securities laws."[135]

By contrast, the Court's paean to the analyst [136] startles; for there are analysts and analysts. The Court's very reference to "clients of the firm" indicates that it was thinking of analysts employed by broker-dealer or investment advisory firms, which do normally publish market letters. But, apart from such a "classic" analyst's calling his broker before he goes into print, what of the analyst who is employed by a single institutional investor, to which alone his analytical powers and his information are made available? Or the analyst who tips spouse or friend, or perhaps a few favored clients who would be expected to reward him suitably in the future?[137] The Court was aware of the fact that Dirks had revealed his information selectively to five advisory firms.[138]

All this is a part of the larger problem of inside information given for a *proper* purpose to a person who makes *improper* use of it. This variation on the theme has already been adjudicated in a post-*Dirks* case, in which the chief executive officer of Company *A* gave nonpublic information for a proper corporate purpose to a friend who was chief executive officer of Company *B*, on whose board the officer of *A* sat, and the officer of *B* knew or should have known that

[133] 21 SEC Dock. at 1409, quoting from Investors Management Co., Inc., 44 SEC 633, 646 (1971). See generally Comment, An Examination of Investment Analyst Liability Under Rule 10b-5, [1984] Ariz. St. L. J. 129.

[134] 21 SEC Dock. at 1409, quoting from SEC v. Bausch & Lomb, Inc., 565 F. 2d 8, 9, 14 (2d Cir. 1977).

[135] 21 SEC Dock. at 1406; see also p. 749 supra.

[136] Cf. Chiarella v. United States, 445 U. S. 222, 233 n. 16 (1980), where the Court was similarly impressed with the fact that Congress specifically exempted exchange specialists and certain other market professionals from the prohibition in §11(a)(1) of the 1934 Act against a member's trading on the exchange for his own account — an exemption similarly based on the social utility of those professionals' contribution to a fair and orderly market.

[137] Financial journalists, too, perform a socially useful function. But (like broker-dealers and investment advisers) they may not "scalp" — which is to say, buy just before publication of a bullish column (or market letter) or sell just before publication of a bearish column (or market letter). SEC v. Capital Gains Research Bureau, Inc., 375 U. S. 180 (1963); Zweig v. Hearst Corp., 594 F. 2d 1261 (9th Cir. 1979). See pp. 761-62 supra. And what about arbitrageurs? Do they not promote market efficiency?

[138] 21 SEC Dock. at 1405. At *some* point, surely, one's status as an analyst will not prevent his being regarded as an ordinary tippee — as, for example, when he bribes an employee of the issuer to give him nonpublic information that he plans to use for himself or a favored client.

the information was confidential. The District Court simply considered *B*'s officer to be a "temporary insider" within *Dirks's* note 14.[139]

Other "proper purpose" cases, however, are not so readily soluble. The Court mentioned, for example, a 1980 case in the Second Circuit involving an acquirer's investment banker that traded on information obtained in the course of negotiations with a friendly target management later turned hostile.[140] And what of the issuer's supplier, or customer, who in negotiating a large supply or purchase contract is apt to learn a good deal about the orders for future delivery that are on the issuer's books?

Other questions remain to intrigue Bench and Bar in further litigation:

What must be established in an action against a tippee's tippee — a tippee once (or further) removed?[141] In a post-*Dirks* case in which an insider tipped a broker who then tipped a customer, the Supreme Court indicated that the customer would be liable for insider trading only if he knew or should have known that the insider had acted improperly.[142] The difficulty is that the second tippee is likely not even to know who the initial tipper was. And yet it would be odd if recovery were to be easier against a remote tippee than against an immediate tippee.[143]

What, next, of the tipper's liability for the tippee's profit when the tippee did not know of the tipper's breach of his fiduciary duty?

[139] SEC v. Lund, 570 F. Supp. 1397 (C. D. Cal. 1983).

[140] 463 U. S. at 662 n. 22; Walton v. Morgan Stanley & Co., 623 F. 2d 796 (2d Cir. 1980). The Supreme Court did not mention that *Walton* was a common law case of the Diamond v. Oreamuno type, 24 N. Y. 2d 494, 248 N. E. 2d 910 (1969), supra p. 582, in which recovery of profits was sought on behalf of the company rather than the other party to the transaction. Cf. also Frigitemp Corp. v. Financial Dynamics Fund, 524 F. 2d 275, 278-79 (2d Cir. 1975) (another *Diamond*-type case, in which defendants got information from the issuer in negotiation for a private placement in which it was hoped they would join).

[141] The configuration is not unknown. See Schein v. Chasen, 478 F. 2d 817 (2d Cir. 1973), *vacated on other grounds* sub nom. Lehman Bros. v. Schein, 416 U. S. 386 (1974), where the court held a tippee *thrice* removed from the company's president.

[142] Bateman Eichler, Hill Richards, Inc., v. Berner, 472 U. S. 299, 311 n. 21 (1985), infra p. 1034.

[143] In Schick v. Steiger, 583 F. Supp. 841, 847 (E. D. Mich. 1984), where a first generation tippee (T1) interposed the defense of *in pari delicto* to an action against him by *his* tippee (T2), the court held that, although T1 as a tippee within *Dirks* had a duty to disclose or abstain, it was "not so clear * * * that *Dirks* imposed on defendant [T1] the duty not to selectively disclose the information," and therefore T2 "did not acquire the insider's [tipper's] duty to disclose or refrain from trading."

If the *tippee* is not liable in that kind of case, it would seem odd to hold the *tipper. Sed quaere.*

Again a very large question on which neither the majority nor the dissenting opinion in *Dirks* touched concerns allocation of the burden of going forward. So far as the insider's motive is concerned, it is not beyond conceit — since the relevant facts are apt to be better known to defendant than to plaintiff — that the plaintiff who alleges and proves a tip from an "insider" will be held to have established a *prima facie* case that shifts to the defendant the burden of going forward with evidence negativing the insider's impropriety. Similarly, when an action is brought against an analyst (or an insider as the analyst's tipper), it is at least arguable that the defendant should go forward with evidence that the analyst used the inside information in some legitimate way — perhaps that he made a reasonable effort to make it available as simultaneously as possible (in Justice Powell's words) "to all of the corporation's stockholders or the public generally."[144]

Despite all the questions left by both *Chiarella* and *Dirks,* they are great steps forward in securities regulation:

First: All four of the opinions in *Chiarella* recognized an affirmative duty on the part of insiders to disclose material information when trading in their corporation's securities — which as a practical matter means to abstain from trading, since it is not their corporate function to disclose. And this follows also from *Dirks* to the extent that it recognizes tippee liability as derivative from the liability of an inside tipper. In time, if there had been no Rule 10b-5, this might have come about at common law. But the Supreme Court in pre-*Erie* days went as far only as imposing a disclosure obligation when there are "special circumstances."[145] Although some state courts watered that concept down to something little more than "materiality," as recently as 1946 Ballantine referred to the "so-called majority rule" in terms of not imposing any fiduciary duty on directors to shareholders individually as distinct from the corporation.[146] The states espousing the contrary view were decidedly a minority.[147] There was also a particular problem with respect to transactions on a stock exchange.[148] And in England the 1902 *nisi prius* case of Percival v. Wright[149] reigns supreme. In this country, however, it seems safe to say that what is the minority view at

[144]463 U. S. at 659.

[145]Strong v. Repide, 213 U. S. 419 (1909), supra p. 724.

[146]Ballantine, Corporations (rev. ed. 1946) 212.

[147]Id. at 213.

[148]Goodwin v. Agassiz, 283 Mass. 358, 186 N. E. 659 (1933).

[149][1902] 2 Ch. 421, supra p. 724 n. 1.

common law has become the law of the land through the alchemy of Rule 10b-5.

Second: The insider's affirmative obligation to "disclose or abstain" applies equally to open market and face-to-face transactions.[150] And it has been extended to cover insiders' sales as well as their purchases although market sales are not necessarily made to persons who are already stockholders. The majority opinion in *Chiarella* adverted to this obstacle *en passant,* stating simply that the Commission "embraced the reasoning of Judge Learned Hand that 'the director or officer assumed a fiduciary relation to the buyer by the very sale; for it would be a sorry distinction to allow him to use the advantage of his position to induce the buyer into the position of a beneficiary although he was forbidden to do so once the buyer had become one.' "[151]

Third: The affirmative obligation extends beyond insiders to their consultants and the other persons specified in *Dirks*'s note 14, as well as similar persons and (probably) all employees. Moreover, it is altogether possible that *Dirks*'s limitations will not exclude most tippees as things are done in "the real world."

Fourth: Perhaps most important of all (as we shall notice later)[152] is the Court's recognition of private actions under Rule 10b-5.

All this is no small thing to have developed from a §10(b) that was described in 1934 as saying, "Thou shalt not devise any other cunning devices."[153] Indeed, Chief Justice Rehnquist's reference to "a judicial oak which has grown from little more than a legislative acorn"[154] falls short, if anything, of describing one of the most dramatic examples in the entire American *corpus juris* of the growth of law through the interaction of the legislative, administrative, and judicial processes.

Nevertheless, Congress still sits. With full appreciation of the advantages of the common law's *ad hoc* technique, it still seems clear that the 10b-5 jurisprudence has developed to the point where it cries out for the kind of philosophic consistency that only studied legislation can provide. The Insider Trading Sanctions Act of 1983 goes little further than providing for a civil penalty, in the court's

[150] The Court so stated in Superintendent of Insurance of the State of N. Y. v. Bankers Life Ins. Co., 404 U. S. 6, 10 (1971).

[151] 445 U. S. at 227 n. 8, quoting from Gratz v. Claughton, 187 F. 2d 46, 49 (2d Cir. 1951), *cert. denied,* 341 U. S. 920. *Query* (for the same lack of fiduciary relationship) the similar difficulties with the fiduciary theory in the case of insider trading in debt securities and in options. See Supp. p. 732 n. 29 supra.

[152] See p. 955 infra.

[153] See p. 726 supra.

[154] Ibid.

discretion, up to three times the defendant's profit. That legislation — its merit here assumed — will not do the trick.[155] On the contrary, the House Committee perhaps too readily followed the Commission's lead in turning aside suggestions that the new penalty provision should be accompanied by specific language defining the scope of the violation.

A broader legislative approach, going beyond patchwork, is overdue. The Code leaves a number of questions "to further judicial development as not ripe for codification."[156] Nevertheless, it does codify the greater part of the 10b-5 area, with appropriate changes, on twenty-five enumerated points;[157] and this is apart from the advantages flowing from that area's being part of an integrated document.

Although a codification addressed to Congress need not, of course, follow the Supreme Court — that is one of the exhilarating rewards of a code's draftsman — the Code needs to be reexamined in the light of more recent Supreme Court decisions, notably *Chiarella* and *Dirks.*[158] And it may be that the legislative approach ought not to be limited to a fraud rubric — that certain undesirable practices in the area should simply be prohibited the way wash sales and certain short sales are prohibited.

This is basically the approach taken by an American Bar Association committee in 1985. Its report suggested alternative statutes. Both, departing from the fraud-based framework of §10(b), would directly regulate trading and tipping regardless of whether the conduct might be characterized as "fraud." The first is rooted in the Code, but takes into account subsequent judicial developments. The second is a shorter and simpler approach that would leave considerably more to interpretation.[159]

With the recent scandals, as well as the imminence (at this writ-

[155] See Supp. p. 1008, end, infra. "The legislation does not change the underlying substantive law of insider trading as reflected in judicial and administrative holdings." H. R. Rep. No. 98-335, 98th Cong., 1st Sess. (1983) 13.

[156] 2 Code 659.

[157] 2 id. 656-59; see also 2 id. 659-67 and Code §1603.

[158] Neither case had been decided before the Code's approval by the ALI in 1978, but *Chiarella* was decided between that time and the SEC's approval in 1980.

[159] Am. B. Assn., Committee on Federal Regulation of Securities, Report of the Task Force on Regulation of Insider Trading, Part I: Regulation Under the Antifraud Provisions of the Securities Exchange Act of 1934, 41 Bus. Law. 223, 225-26, 253-57 (1985). Cf. N. Y. Bus. Corp. L. §1609(b), enacted in 1985 as part of the Security Takeover Disclosure Law (supra p. 536 n. 166).

ing) of a Supreme Court ruling on the misappropriation theory,[160] it is likely that the 100th Congress will see considerable activity in the allied fields of insider trading and tender offers.

6. Scienter

Whatever scienter may mean in common law deceit,[161] it has been held that intent is essential to a "scheme to defraud" under §17(a)(1) of the 1933 Act, as it is under the mail and wire fraud statutes.[162] But "The law is settled that no amount of honest belief that the enterprises would ultimately make money for the stockholders can excuse or justify false representations" in the sale of securities.[163] This kind of "good faith" argument — which Lord Chief Justice Hewart analogized to "the excuse of the office boy who takes a half-crown from the till because he has a good thing for the Grand National"[164] — is quite different from the defense of good faith in the sense that the defendant had reasonable ground to believe that his statements were true.[165]

Moreover, intent (or scienter) being subjective, it must often "be inferred from a series of seemingly isolated acts and instances which have been * * * aptly designated as badges of fraud."[166] It has been inferred also "where the lack of knowledge consists of ignorance of facts which any ordinary person under similar circumstances should have known."[167] In short, intent to defraud in the

[160] See esp. SEC v. Boesky, Litig. Rel. 11,288,37 SEC Dock. 66 (S. D. N. Y. 1986), supra p. 1010 n. 25. The pending case in United States v. Carpenter, 791 F. 2d 1024 (2d Cir. 1986), *cert. granted*, 107 S. Ct. 666, supra p. 758 n. 107.

[161] See pp. 808-12 supra.

[162] Troutman v. United States, 100 F. 2d 628, 632 (10th Cir. 1938), *cert. denied*, 306 U. S. 649; Rice v. United States, 149 F. 2d 601 (10th Cir. 1945).

[163] Foshay v. United States, 68 F. 2d 205, 210 (8th Cir. 1933), *cert. denied*, 291 U. S. 674, and cases cited (mail fraud statute); Frank v. United States, 220 F. 2d 559, 564 (10th Cir. 1955) (also §17(a)); United States v. Painter, 314 F. 2d 939, 943 (4th Cir. 1963), *cert. denied*, 374 U. S. 831 (mail and wire fraud statutes); United States v. Diamond, 430 F. 2d 688, 691 (5th Cir. 1970) (mail fraud statute).

[164] Rex v. Bishirgian, [1936] 1 All E. R. 586, 594 (C. C. A.).

[165] Frank v. United States, 220 F. 2d 559, 564-65 (10th Cir. 1955).

[166] Nassan v. United States, 126 F. 2d 613, 615 (4th Cir. 1942) (mail fraud statute); see also Deaver v. United States, 155 F. 2d 740, 744 (D. C. Cir. 1946), *cert. denied*, 329 U. S. 766 (same); Walters v. United States, 256 F. 2d 840, 84[illegible] (9th Cir. 1958), *cert. denied*, 358 U. S. 833; United States v. Vandersee, 279 F. 2d 176, 179 (3d Cir. 1960), *cert. denied*, 364 U. S. 943.

[167] Stone v. United States, 113 F. 2d 70, 75 (6th Cir. 1940); see also Irwin v. United States, 338 F. 2d 770, 774 (9th Cir. 1964), *cert. denied*, 381 U. S. 91[illegible] (mail fraud statute); United States v. Meyer, 359 F. 2d 837, 839 (7th Cir. 1966).

context of §17(a)(1) and the mail and wire fraud statutes has taken on a coloration of recklessness.[168]

These softening precedents as to intent and scienter were made primarily in the context of criminal prosecutions under §17(a) or the mail fraud statute or both. So far as criminal prosecutions under §17(a) are concerned, the element of willfulness alone in §24, the penal provision, presumably requires (whatever it may mean in other contexts) knowledge of the falsity (or recklessness with respect to the truth of the matter) if nothing else. But the rationale of these holdings should apply with at least equal force to injunction actions or other civil cases based on Clause (1) of §17(a) or its counterparts in the fraud rules.[169]

This leaves the question — to which we turn next — of the applicability of this learning to *civil* actions under §17(a) generally, as well as Rule 10b-5 and the other fraud provisions. The full flavor of the leading case requires the quotation of substantial excerpts of the opinions:

ERNST & ERNST v. HOCHFELDER

Supreme Court of the United States, 1976
425 U. S. 185

MR. JUSTICE POWELL delivered the opinion of the Court.

* * *

I

Petitioner, Ernst & Ernst, is an accounting firm. From 1946 through 1967 it was retained by First Securities Company of Chicago (First Securities), a small brokerage firm and member of the Midwest Stock Exchange and of the National Association of Securities Dealers, to perform periodic audits of the firm's books and records. * * *

Respondents were customers of First Securities who invested in

---

cert. denied, 385 U. S. 837; United States v. Seasholtz, 435 F. 2d 4, 8 (10th Cir. 1970) (mail fraud statute).

[168] See United States v. Henderson, 446 F. 2d 960, 966 (8th Cir. 1971), *cert. denied,* 401 U. S. 991 ("reckless disregard" of the facts); United States v. Mackay, 491 F. 2d 616, 623 (10th Cir. 1973), *cert. denied,* 416 U. S. 972, 419 U. S. 1047 (mail fraud statute); United States v. Boyer, 694 F. 2d 58 (3d Cir. 1982).

[169] SEC v. Glass Marine Industries, Inc., 208 F. Supp. 727, 742-43 (D. Del. 1962).

a fraudulent securities scheme perpetrated by Leston B. Nay, president of the firm and owner of 92% of its stock. Nay induced the respondents to invest funds in "escrow" accounts that he represented would yield a high rate of return. * * * In fact, there were no escrow accounts as Nay converted respondents' funds to his own use immediately upon receipt. These transactions were not in the customary form of dealings between First Securities and its customers. The respondents drew their personal checks payable to Nay or a designated bank for his account. No such escrow accounts were reflected on the books and records of First Securities, and none was shown on its periodic accounting to respondents in connection with their other investments. Nor were they included in First Securities' filings with the Commission or the Exchange.

This fraud came to light in 1968 when Nay committed suicide, leaving a note that described First Securities as bankrupt and the escrow accounts as "spurious." Respondents subsequently filed this action for damages against Ernst & Ernst * * *. The complaint charged that Nay's escrow scheme violated §10(b) and Commission Rule 10b-5, and that Ernst & Ernst had "aided and abetted" Nay's violations by its "failure" to conduct proper audits of First Securities. As revealed through discovery, respondents' cause of action rested on a theory of negligent nonfeasance. * * * The practice principally relied on was Nay's rule that only he could open mail addressed to him at First Securities or addressed to First Securities to his attention, even if it arrived in his absence. Respondents contended that if Ernst & Ernst had conducted a proper audit, it would have discovered this "mail rule." The existence of the rule then would have been disclosed in reports to the Exchange and to the Commission by Ernst & Ernst as an irregular procedure that prevented an effective audit. This would have led to an investigation of Nay that would have revealed the fraudulent scheme. Respondents specifically disclaimed the existence of fraud or intentional misconduct on the part of Ernst & Ernst.

* * *

We granted certiorari to resolve the question whether a private cause of action for damages will lie under §10(b) and Rule 10b-5 in the absence of any allegation of "scienter" — intent to deceive, manipulate, or defraud.[12] 421 U. S. 909 (1975). We conclude that it will not and therefore we reverse.

[12] Although the verbal formulations of the standard to be applied have varied,

* * *

A

Section 10(b) makes unlawful the use or employment of "any manipulative or deceptive device or contrivance" in contravention of Commission rules. The words "manipulative or deceptive" used in conjunction with "device or contrivance" strongly suggest that §10(b) was intended to proscribe knowing or intentional misconduct. See *SEC* v. *Texas Gulf Sulphur Co.*, 401 F. 2d 833, 868 (C. A. 2 1968) (Friendly, J., concurring), *cert. denied* sub nom. *Coates* v. *SEC*, 394 U. S. 976 (1969); Loss, Summary Remarks, 30 Bus. Law. 163, 165 (Special Issue 1975). * * *

In its *amicus curiae* brief, however, the Commission contends that nothing in the language "manipulative or deceptive device or contrivance" limits its operation to knowing or intentional practices. * * * The argument simply ignores the use of the words "manipulative," "device," and "contrivance" — terms that make unmistakable a congressional intent to proscribe a type of conduct quite different from negligence. Use of the word "manipulative" is especially significant. It is and was virtually a term of art when used in connection with securities markets. It connotes intentional or willful conduct designed to deceive or defraud investors by controlling or artificially affecting the price of securities.

---

several Courts of Appeals have held in substance that negligence alone is sufficient for civil liability under §10(b) and Rule 10b-5. Other Courts of Appeals have held that some type of scienter — i. e., intent to defraud, reckless disregard for the truth, or knowing use of some practice to defraud — is necessary in such an action. But few of the decisions announcing that some form of negligence suffices for civil liability under §10(b) and Rule 10b-5 actually have involved only negligent conduct. [Citations in this paragraph are omitted.]

In this opinion the term "scienter" refers to a mental state embracing intent to deceive, manipulate or defraud. In certain areas of the law recklessness is considered to be a form of intentional conduct for purposes of imposing liability for some act. We need not address here the question whether, in some circumstances, reckless behavior is sufficient for civil liability under §10(b) and Rule 10b-5.

Since this case concerns an action for damages we also need not consider the question whether scienter is a necessary element in an action for injunctive relief under §10(b) and Rule 10b-5. Cf. SEC v. Capital Gains Research Bureau, 375 U. S. 180 (1963).

* * *

C

The 1933 and 1934 Acts constitute interrelated components of the federal regulatory scheme governing transactions in securi ties. * * *

* * *

The structure of the Acts does not support the Commission's argument. * * * The express recognition of a cause of action premised on negligent behavior in §11 stands in sharp contrast to the language of §10(b), and significantly undercuts the Commission's argument.

We also consider it significant that each of the express civil remedies in the 1933 Act allowing recovery for negligent conduct, see §§11, 12(2), 15, 15 U. S. C. §§77k, 77*l*(2), 77*o*, is subject to significant procedural restrictions not applicable under §10(b). Section 11(e) of the 1933 Act, for example, authorizes the court to require a plaintiff bringing a suit under §11, §12(2), or §15 thereof to post a bond for costs, including attorneys' fees, and in specified circumstances to assess costs at the conclusion of the litigation. Section 13 specifies a statute of limitations of one year from the time the violation was or should have been discovered, in no event to exceed three years from the time of offer or sale, applicable to actions brought under §11, §12(2), or §15. * * *

* * *

D

We have addressed, to this point, primarily the language and history of §10(b). The Commission contends, however, that subsections (b) and (c) [(1) and (3)] of Rule 10b-5 are cast in language which — if standing alone — could encompass both intentional and negligent behavior. * * *

* * * The rulemaking power granted to an administrative agency charged with the administration of a federal statute is not the power to make law. Rather, it is " 'the power to adopt regulations to carry into effect the will of Congress as expressed by the statute.' " [Citations deleted.] Thus, despite the broad view of the Rule advanced by the Commission in this case, its scope cannot

exceed the power granted the Commission by Congress under §10(b).

* * *

MR. JUSTICE STEVENS took no part in the consideration or decision of this case.

MR. JUSTICE BLACKMUN, with whom MR. JUSTICE BRENNAN joins, dissenting.

* * *

* * * It seems to me however, that an investor can be victimized just as much by negligent conduct as by positive deception, and that it is not logical to drive a wedge between the two, saying that Congress clearly intended the one but certainly not the other.

* * *

The majority opinion in *Ernst & Ernst* is puzzling, and it leaves as many questions as it answers:

(1) Insofar as it construes the "manipulative or deceptive device or contrivance" of §10(b) as requiring that some sort of scienter element be read into Rule 10b-5, the opinion is profoundly correct. The western Circuits that read Clause (2) literally as requiring only proof of a misstatement or a half-truth were not sufficiently sensitive to the fact that they were dealing with a *rule,* which must be construed against the enabling provision of the statute.[170] Consequently, just as the courts will construe a *statute* if at all possible so as to avoid holding it *unconstitutional,* they should construe a *rule* if at all possible so as to avoid holding it *ultra vires.* With respect, it is no answer to say, as Justice Blackmun did following the SEC's contention as *amicus curiae,* that "an investor can be victimized just as much by negligent conduct as by positive deception."[171] A pedestrian fatally hit by a negligent driver is just as dead as if the driver had been roaring drunk, but that does not convict the negligent driver of manslaughter.

(2) It is necessary, therefore, that "some sort of watered-down

[170] See, e. g., Ellis v. Carter, 291 F. 2d 270 (9th Cir. 1961).

[171] 425 U. S. at 216, supra (Blackmun, J.); id. at 198, supra p. 777 (description of SEC's reasoning by Powell, J.).

scienter element" be read into Clause (2).[172] But why — in construing a fraud provision that was designed to *raise* the standards of securities trading, and that the courts have repeatedly interpreted as not limited to circumstances that would amount to common law deceit[173] — did the majority opinion reach back in history to the strictest common law definition: not merely knowing falsity but "intent to deceive, manipulate, or defraud"?[174]

(3) What is even more strange is that the Court did not have to define scienter at all. All it had to hold was that *negligence* did *not* suffice; for negligence is all that was alleged.[175] Indeed, one might persuasively argue that the *ratio decidendi* is even more limited: that, whatever may be the degree of culpability contemplated by Rule 10b-5 with respect to a *primary* violator, an accounting firm is not *secondarily* liable for mere negligence.[176] Therefore, as law students are taught to read cases, all the talk about the meaning of scienter is interesting but *obiter* — although it is easier for an academic than for a lower court judge to say that in the face of the majority opinion as a whole.

(4) What has just been said *is* reflected to an extent in a footnote — the famous note 12, with its invitation to the lower federal courts to consider whether "recklessness" might not suffice "in some

[172]3 Loss 1766; 6 id. 3884. There is no difficulty in finding scienter on the part of a corporation even though it "clearly must derive from the states of mind of those acting on behalf of the corporation." Naye v. Boyd, — F. Supp. —, — , CCH Fed. Sec. L. Rep. ¶92,979 at 94,807 (W. D. Wash. 1986).

[173]See p. 712 supra.

[174]In common law deceit, as the Supreme Court stated *obiter* in SEC v. Capital Gains Research Bureau, Inc., 375 U. S. 180, 192 n. 39 (1963), an action for injunction under §206 of the Investment Advisers Act, "the intent which must be established need not be an intent to cause injury to the client"; all that is required is proof that the defendant intended action in reliance on the truth of the misrepresentation. That is to say, intent to *cause harm* is of no importance at common law except with respect to the issue of punitive damages; the intent to deceive or mislead or convey a false impression that is implicit in the scienter concept goes simply to the matter of belief, or absence of belief, that the representation is true. Prosser and Keeton on the Law of Torts (5th ed. 1984) 740.

[175]See Aaron v. SEC, 446 U. S. 680, 690 (1980), infra p. 783; United States v. Chiarella, 588 F. 2d 1358, 1370-71 (2d Cir. 1978), *rev'd on other grounds* sub nom. Chiarella v. United States, 445 U. S. 222 (1980).

[176]See SEC v. Coffey, 493 F. 2d 1304, 1315-16 (6th Cir. 1974), *cert. denied,* 420 U. S. 908; see also p. 781 infra; cf. Code §1724(b). In Robinson v. Heilman, 563 F. 2d 1304, 1308 (9th Cir. 1977), the court held that *Hochfelder* was equally applicable to a direct participant — though, "the closer the relationship of the person charged to the corporation and the greater his participation in the transactions attacked, the easier it will be to prove the requisite scienter."

circumstances" after all.[177] That leaves the question of interpreting "reckless." Several Circuits have followed the rather strict approach taken by the Seventh Circuit in 1977: "In view of the Supreme Court's analysis in *Hochfelder* of the statutory scheme of implied private remedies and express remedies, the definition of 'reckless behavior' should not be a liberal one lest any discernible distinction between 'scienter' and 'negligence' be obliterated for these purposes. We believe 'reckless' in these circumstances comes closer to being a lesser form of intent than merely a greater degree of ordinary negligence."[178]

At the same time, there is authority that *Hochfelder* did not "establish a standard of specific intent to defraud,"[179] except that liability as an aider and abettor "requires something closer to an actual intent to aid in a fraud, at least in the absence of some special relationship with the plaintiff that is fiduciary in nature";[180] that the plaintiff need not prove knowledge of *illegality*;[181] and that reckless-

[177] The invitation has been accepted. Coleco Industries, Inc. v. Berman, 567 F. 2d 569, 574 (3d Cir. 1977); Rolf v. Blyth, Eastman Dillon & Co., Inc., 570 F. 2d 38, 46 (2d Cir. 1978) (at least when defendant owed a fiduciary duty); McLean v. Alexander, 599 F. 2d 1190, 1197 (5th Cir. 1979); Hackbart v. Holmes, 675 F. 2d 1114 (9th Cir. 1982); Dirks v. SEC, 681 F. 2d 824, 844 (D. C. Cir. 1982), *rev'd on other grounds*, 463 U. S. 646 (1983) ("the overwhelming rule in the Courts of Appeals").

[178] Sanders v. John Nuveen & Co., Inc., 554 F. 2d 790, 793 (7th Cir. 1977); see also Pegasus Fund, Inc. v. Laraneta, 617 F. 2d 1335, 1340-41 (9th Cir. 1980); Broad v. Rockwell Int'l Corp., 614 F. 2d 418, 440 (5th Cir. *en banc* 1981); G. A. Thompson & Co. v. Partridge, 636 F. 2d 945, 961 (5th Cir. 1981) ("severe recklessness"). In Reiss v. Pan American World Airways, Inc., 711 F. 2d 11, 14 (2d Cir. 1983), the court said: "To prove *scienter*, more than a conscious failure to disclose must be shown. Rather, there must be proof that the nondisclosure was intended to mislead." See also Wechsler v. Steinberg, 733 F. 2d 1054 (2d Cir. 1984).

But questions of intent "are usually inappropriate for disposition on summary judgment." Id. at 1058. Cf. Sunstrand Corp. v. Sun Chemical Corp., 553 F. 2d 1033, 1044 (7th Cir. 1977), *cert. denied*, 434 U. S. 875 (in holding that reckless *non*disclosure suffices, court considered it "highly inappropriate to construe the Rule 10b-5 remedy to be more restrictive in substantive scope than its common law analogs").

See generally Milich, Securities Fraud Under Section 10(b) and Rule 10b-5: Scienter, Recklessness, and the Good Faith Defense, 11 J. Corp. L. 179, 200 (1986).

[179] United States v. Chiarella, 588 F. 2d 1358, 1370 (2d Cir. 1978), *rev'd on other grounds* sub nom. Chiarella v. United States, 445 U. S. 222 (1980).

[180] Edwards & Hanly v. Wells Fargo Securities Clearance Corp., 602 F. 2d 478, 485 (2d Cir. 1979); Ross v. Bolton, 639 F. Supp. 323 (S. D. N. Y. 1986) (since clearing broker does not owe a fiduciary duty to owners of the securities that pass through its hands, the scienter requirement scales upward to "something closer to an actual intent to aid in a fraud").

[181] Arthur Lipper Corp. v. SEC, 547 F. 2d 171, 180-81 (2d Cir. 1976), *re-*

ness connotes "carelessness approaching indifference"[182] (one might say "negligence plus" rather than the Seventh Circuit's "intent minus"). Moreover, a professional (or a person who has greater access to information) has an obligation to disclose data indicating that the opinion or forecast may be doubtful, and failure to investigate further may support an influence that he had no genuine belief that he had the information on which the opinion could be predicated.[183]

About all that can be said with confidence is that "the standard falls somewhere between intent and negligence."[184]

(5) *Query* whether the reference in Rule 15c1-2(b) to a "statement or omission [that] is made with knowledge or reasonable grounds to believe that it is untrue or misleading" adequately reflects — phrased as it is in the alternative — the §15(c)(1) test in terms of "any manipulative, deceptive, or other fraudulent device or contrivance."

For a while the Commission fought a rear-guard action in reliance on *Hochfelder's* expressly leaving the scienter question open in in-

---

hearing en banc denied, 551 F. 2d 915 (2d Cir. 1977); SEC v. Falstaff Brewing Corp., 629 F. 2d 62, 76-77 (D. C. Cir. 1980).

[182] Hoffman v. Estabrook & Co., Inc., 587 F. 2d 509, 516 (1st Cir. 1978); see also Bell v. Cameron Meadows Land Co., 669 F. 2d 1278, 1282-83 (9th Cir. 1982).

[183] Eisenberg v. Gagnon, 766 F. 2d 770, 776 (3d Cir. 1985), *cert. denied* sub nom. Wasserstrom v. Eisenberg, 106 S. Ct. 343.

[184] Mansbach v. Prescott, Ball & Turben, 598 F. 2d 1017, 1025 n. 36 (6th Cir. 1979). "One who deliberately tips information which he knows to be material and non-public to an outsider who may reasonably be expected to use it to his advantage has the requisite *scienter.* This action amounts to knowing misconduct." Elkind v. Liggett & Myers, Inc., 635 F. 2d 156, 167 (2d Cir. 1980).

At any rate, it is clear that in proving *scienter* "circumstantial evidence can be more than sufficient." Herman & MacLean v. Huddleston, 459 U. S. 375, 390 n. 30 (1983).

There is authority that failure to profit personally from the fraudulent scheme (corrupt payments abroad) does not preclude scienter. Cramer v. General Telephone & Electronics Corp., 582 F. 2d 259, 273 (3d Cir. 1978). There is also contrasting authority that investment of one's own money tends to negative scienter since it "belies any known or obvious danger." Hoffman v. Estabrook & Co., Inc., 587 F. 2d 509, 517 (1st Cir. 1978).

In White v. Abrams, 495 F. 2d 724, 735 (9th Cir. 1974), the Ninth Circuit, two years before *Hochfelder,* had developed a "flexible duty" concept under which the scope of the defendant's duty to disclose would vary on the basis generally of five factors: "the relationship of the defendant to the plaintiff, the defendant's access to the information as compared to the plaintiff's access, the benefit that the defendant derives from the relationship in making his investment decisions and the defendant's activity in initiating the securities transaction in question." The Ninth Circuit considers that, "Although *White v. Abrams* has been overruled insofar as it contemplated liability without scienter, its approach to the duty question is otherwise good law." Kidwell *ex rel.* Penfold v. Meikle, 597 F. 2d 1273, 1294 (9th Cir. 1979); Mirotznick v. Sensey, Davis & McCormick, 658 F. Supp. 932, CCH Fed. Sec. L. Rep. ¶93,137 (W. D. Wash. 1986). *Query.*

junctive actions.[185] Then in 1980 the Supreme Court in *Aaron* v. *SEC* (Justices Blackmun, Brennan, and Marshall dissenting once more) stuck to its *Hochfelder* guns so far as Rule 10b-5 is concerned.[186] But, the defendant being a seller rather than a buyer, the Commission's action was based also on §17(a) of the 1933 Act. Justice Stewart's opinion made three points:

(1) "In our view, the rationale of *Hochfelder* ineluctably leads to the conclusion that scienter is an element of a violation of §10(b) and Rule 10b-5, regardless of the identity of the plaintiff or the nature of the relief sought."[187]

(2) But the three clauses of §17(a) require disparate results:

> The language of §17(a) strongly suggests that Congress contemplated a scienter requirement under §17(a)(1), but not under §17(a)(2) or §17(a)(3). The language of §17(a)(1), which makes it unlawful "to employ any device, scheme, or artifice to defraud," plainly evinces an intent on the part of Congress to proscribe only knowing or intentional misconduct. * * *
>
> By contrast, the language of §17(a)(2), which prohibits any person from obtaining money or property "by means of any untrue statement of a material fact or any omission to state a material fact," is devoid of any suggestion whatsoever of a scienter requirement. As a well-known commentator has noted, "[t]here is nothing on the face of Clause (2) itself which smacks of scienter or intent to defraud." 3 L. Loss, Securities Regulation 1442 (2d ed. 1961). * * *
>
> Finally, the language of §17(a)(3), under which it is unlawful for any person "to engage in any transaction, practice, or course of business which *operates* or *would operate* as a fraud or deceit," (emphasis added) quite plainly focuses upon the effect of particular conduct on members of the investing public, rather than upon the culpability of the person responsible. * * *

(3) This brought the Court to the injunctive provisions of the two statutes:

> * * * with respect to those provisions such as §17(a)(2) and §17(a)(3), which may be violated even in the absence of scienter, nothing on the face of §20(b) or §21(d) purports to impose an in-

[185] 425 U. S. at 193 n. 12; see SEC v. Coven, 581 F. 2d 1020 (2d Cir. 1978).

[186] "The term 'scienter' is used throughout this opinion, as it was in Ernst & Ernst v. Hochfelder, 425 U. S. 185, 194, n. 12, to refer to 'a mental state embracing intent to deceive, manipulate, or defraud.' We have no occasion here to address the question, reserved in *Hochfelder*, ibid., whether, under some circumstances, scienter may also include reckless behavior." 446 U. S. at 714 n. 5.

[187] The Court distinguished SEC v. Capital Gains Research Bureau, Inc., 375 U. S. 180 (1963), infra p. 840, an injunction action under the fraud provision of the Advisers Act.

dependent requirement of scienter. And there is nothing in the legislative history of either provision to suggest a contrary legislative intent.

This is not to say, however, that scienter has no bearing at all on whether a district court should enjoin a person violating or about to violate §17(a)(2) or §17(a)(3). In cases where the Commission is seeking to enjoin a person "*about* to engage in any acts or practices which . . . *will* constitute" a violation of those provisions, the Commission must establish a sufficient evidentiary predicate to show that such future violation may occur. See *SEC* v. *Commonwealth Chemical Securities, Inc.*, 574 F. 2d 90, 98-100 (C. A. 2 1978) (Friendly, J.); 3 L. Loss, Securities Regulation, at 1976. An important factor in this regard is the degree of intentional wrongdoing evident in a defendant's past conduct. See *SEC* v. *Wills,* 472 F. Supp. 1250, 1273-1275 (D. C. 1978). Moreover, as the Commission recognizes, a district court may consider scienter or lack of it as one of the aggravating or mitigating factors to be taken into account in exercising its equitable discretion in deciding whether or not to grant injunctive relief. * * *

(1) This fragmented result in *Aaron* reflects the fragmentation of the fraud provisions as they stand. The case is, therefore, eloquent testimony to the necessity of the integration that would be effected by the Code.[188]

(2) Meanwhile the Commission, of course, will simply plead under Clauses (2) and (3) of §17(a), as it normally has done anyhow in suing sellers. More significant is the non-scienter "out" afforded private plaintiffs if buyers should be given access to §17(a) at all in view of their express (and in some respects more limited) rights of action under §§11 and 12(2). It is a very substantial "if" in this writer's view. Nevertheless, substantial judicial authority permits private actions under §17(a).[189]

(3) Any tightening of federal fraud law bespeaks closer attention to the state blue sky laws. That is particularly true with respect to scienter. First of all, insofar as an action under state law is considered to require scienter, the state courts (or the federal courts in applying state law) might well give the term a more modern reading than it received in *Hochfelder,* especially if the common law of deceit in the particular state incorporates a relatively relaxed construction of the term.[190] Secondly, §101 of the Uniform Securities Act is a

[188] See p. 710.

[189] See pp. 977-78 infra.

[190] See p. 713 supra. Militating in the other direction is §415 of the Uniform Securities Act: "This act shall be construed * * * to coordinate the interpretation * * * of this act with the related federal regulation."

virtual carbon copy of Rule 10b-5 except that it is, of course a statute like §17(a), without the limiting language of §10(b), not a rule. And, although §410(h) forecloses private actions for violation of §101,[191] a number of states have adopted the Uniform Act without that aspect of §410(h).[192] In those states, under the Supreme Court's reasoning in *Aaron,* Clause (2) of §101 should not require scienter at all.[193]

(4) On the one hand, a literal reading of §17(a)(2) and (3) does not require even negligence; at least under §17(a)(2), any misstatement of a material fact would do, however innocent.[194] On the other hand, it cannot be assumed that *Aaron* dispenses with scienter under §17(a)(2) and (3) so far as liability on an aider and abettor or a conspiracy basis is concerned.[195]

(5) *Query:* Should a court consider disgorgement of profits by way of ancillary relief in an injunctive action[196] in which there is no proof of scienter?

(6) Finally, to go back to *Hochfelder* as well as *Aaron,* to what extent does their teaching carry over to the more specialized fraud sections and rules?[197]

So far as Rule 14a-9 is concerned, §14(a) has none of the limiting language of §10(b). Even so, the Sixth Circuit, in an opinion reminiscent of the Cardozo prose that has indoctrinated generations of torts students,[198] held that scienter had to be shown in order to

[191] See 3 Loss 1649 n. 100; Loss, Commentary on the Uniform Securities Act (1976) 8.

[192] See 6 Loss 3798 n. 100.

[193] Sprangers v. Interactive Technologies, Inc., 394 N. W. 2d 498 (Minn. App. 1986); Kittilson v. Ford, 93 Wash. 2d 223, 608 P. 2d 264 (1980); cf. Pottern v. Bache Halsey Stuart, Inc., 41 Colo. App. 451, 589 P. 2d 1378 (1978), where the court held that a previous judgment for the defendant under Rule 10b-5 was not *res judicata* with respect to an action under Colorado's equivalent of §12(2) because that section did not require scienter.

[194] But cf. Shidler v. All American Life & Financial Corp., 775 F. 2d 917, 927 (8th Cir. 1985), where the court held that a "strict liability rule [that] would impose liability for fully innocent misstatements" without negligence "is too blunt a tool to ferret out the kind of deceptive practices Congress sought to prevent in enacting section 14(a)."

[195] The point was queried in Pharo v. Smith, 621 F. 2d 656, 674 (5th Cir. 1980).

[196] See p. 751 n. 80 supra.

[197] See p. 863 n. 92 infra.

[198] Ultramares Corp. v. Touche, 255 N. Y. 170, 174 N. E. 441 (1931). That case's limitation of accountants' liability for negligence to their clients has been weakened in recent years, at least with respect to members of a class whose reliance is foreseen. See Restatement (Second) of Torts §552; Fiflis, Current Problems of Accountants' Responsibilities to Third Parties, 28 Vand. L. Rev. 31, esp. at 101-13 (1975). But in Credit Alliance Corp. v. Arthur Andersen & Co., 65 N. Y. 2d 536, 483 N. E. 2d 110 (1985), the New York Court of Appeals

recover against accountants.[199] But the Third Circuit has applied a negligence standard in a case involving "outside" directors.[200]

What then about 1934 Act §15(c)(1) and (2), with respect to over-the-counter broker-dealer fraud, 1934 Act §§14(e)[201] and 13(e), with respect to tender offers and issuer repurchases, and Advisers Act §206? None of those sections echoes the second clause of §17(a), except that §14(e) does so an alternative to the §10(b) formula. Otherwise the 1934 Act sections follow basically the §10(b) formula, and §206 does so as an *alternative* to the language of the *first* and *third* clauses of §17(a). We consider in the next chapter whether private actions may be based at all on certain of these sections.[202] But to whatever extent there may be private plaintiffs, and in any event so far as SEC injunctive actions are concerned, presumably *Hochfelder* and *Aaron* apply with respect to the 1934 Act sections.[203] The answer under §206 is not clear. There is lower court authority applying *Aaron* to §206(1) (modeled on Clause (1) of §17(a)) though not to §206(2) (modeled on Clause (3)).[204] But the Court in *Aaron* distinguished the *Capital Gains* case.[205]

7. Violation of Rule 10b-5 by Nonverbal Acts

Although the second clause's misstatement and half-truth language, without any "fraud" or "deceit" terminology, makes that

---

stuck to its *Ultramares* guns as qualified by Glanzer v. Shepard, 233 N. Y. 236, 135 N. E. 2d 275 (1922), which allowed a negligence action against public weighers because the plaintiff's intended reliance on the information directly transmitted by the weighers to the plaintiff as the primary user of the information created a relationship "so close as to approach that of privity." 65 N. Y. 2d at 546, 483 N. E. 2d at 115. For collections of cases both ways in other states, see 65 N. Y. 2d at 546 n. 7, 483 N. E. 2d at 114-15 n. 7; see also p. 903 n. 65 infra.

[199] Adams v. Standard Knitting Mills, Inc., 623 F. 2d 422 (6th Cir. 1980); see also Gerstle v. Gamble-Skogmo, Inc., 478 F. 2d 1281, 1300-01 (2d Cir. 1973) (pre-*Hochfelder* dictum).

[200] Gould v. American-Hawaiian Steamship Co., 535 F. 2d 761 (3d Cir. 1976); but see Gerstle v. Gamble-Skogmo, Inc., 478 F. 2d 1281, 1300-01 (2d Cir. 1973) (dictum).

[201] See p. 509 supra.

[202] See pp. 913, 939-41, 952-54, 988 infra.

[203] In Lowenschuss v. Kane, 520 F. 2d 255, 268 n. 10 (2d Cir. 1975), the Second Circuit, which applied a recklessness type of scienter requirement under Rule 10b-5 in those pre-*Hochfelder* days, referred to the culpability standard of §14(e) as "unsettled" in the light of the three opinions by the panel (two of whom were the same) that had sat in Chris-Craft Industries, Inc. v. Piper Aircraft Corp., 480 F. 2d 341 (2d Cir. 1973), *cert. denied*, 414 U. S. 910.

[204] SEC v. National Executive Planners, Ltd., 503 F. Supp. 1066, 1074 (M. D. N. C. 1980).

[205] 446 U. S. at 693-95.

clause broader *prima facie* than the first and third clauses even apart from the question of scienter, the Supreme Court observed fifteen years ago that the first and third clauses were not restricted by the language of the second, and that the defendants' *activities* (indeed, their silence under circumstances giving them a duty to speak) "disclose, within the very language of one or the other of those [clauses], a 'course of business' or a 'device, scheme or artifice' that operated as a fraud upon the * * * sellers."[206] That is to say, "deception [under Rule 10b-5] may take the form of nonverbal acts."[207]

Indeed, when liability under Rule 10b-5 is based on nondisclosure rather than a false statement or a half-truth, it comes close to a matter of semantics (or a lawyer might prefer to say the advocate's choice of rhetoric) whether to say that liability is grounded philosophically on silence that certain activity of the insider makes misleading or on that activity itself. At any rate, there is no dearth of cases.[208] Sometimes the two themes are intertwined, as in a case where the "defendants not only failed to disclose a material fact (the true reason for the cut in the dividend rate) but were themselves responsible for its very existence."[209]

Essentially under this heading, there are several "man bite dog" cases in which customers were held to have defrauded their brokers — notably a criminal case in the Supreme Court involving a short-selling customer who had no intent to deliver if the market went up.[210] It follows, moreover, that the fraud need not relate to

[206] Affiliated Ute Citizens of Utah v. United States, 406 U. S. 128, 153 (1972).

[207] O'Neill v. Maytag, 339 F. 2d 764, 768 (2d Cir. 1964) (dictum); see also Harris v. Union Electric Co., 787 F. 2d 355 (8th Cir. 1986), *cert. denied,* 107 S. Ct. 94.

[208] E. g., Herbert L. Honohan, 13 SEC 754, 755, 757-58 (1943) (in tender of non-listed bonds to sinking funds, broker-dealer submitted bids based on inside information purchased from employee of corporate trustee); Richard K. Fudge, 30 SEC 334 (1949) (partner and employee of broker-dealer firm defrauded holders of assessable shares by inducing prospective bidders to refrain from entering competitive bids at public delinquent assessment sale); Kavit v. A. L. Stamm & Co., CCH Fed. Sec. L. Rep. ¶91,915 (S. D. N. Y. 1967) (broker-dealer's unauthorized short sale); Pittsburgh Terminal Corp. v. Baltimore & Ohio R. R. Co., 680 F. 2d 933, 941-42 (3d Cir. 1982), *cert. denied* sub nom. Price v. Pittsburgh Terminal Corp., 459 U. S. 1056; for additional cases, see 2 Code 661-62; cf. also pp. 857-59 infra (over-the-counter manipulation); p. 705 infra ("churning"). Insofar as these are principal-agent rather than buyer-seller cases, they should survive Blue Chip Stamps v. Manor Drug Stores, 421 U. S. 723 (1975), infra p. 792. See pp. 799-800 infra.

[209] Cochran v. Channing Corp., 211 F. Supp. 239, 243 (S. D. N. Y. 1962).

[210] United States v. Naftalin, 441 U. S. 768 (1979); see also A. T. Brod & Co. v. Perlow, 375 F. 2d 393 (2d Cir. 1967) (customers entered purchase or sale orders with the intention of defaulting in payment or delivery if the market went down or up, as the case might be, before the settlement date); Walling v. Beverly Enterprises, Inc., 476 F. 2d 393 (9th Cir. 1973) (entering into a reorganization agreement without unconditional intent to perform it); Mansbach v.

the investment value of the securities.[211] Thus, where a widow had been induced by the defendant and his co-conspirators to sell certain securities and other property worth $124,000 in return for a deed to 125 acres of land represented to be worth $150,000 but afterward discovered to be worth only $12,500, the Ninth Circuit not only applied Rule 10b-5 to fraud with respect to the value of the consideration given for the security rather than the value of the security itself, but also exercised pendent jurisdiction over the entire scheme on a finding that there was a single cause of action involving a single fraudulent scheme to defraud the plaintiff of her property, non-securities as well as securities.[212]

8. Scope of Rule 10b-5

a. The Rule's Universality

In its first case involving a private action under Rule 10b-5, the Supreme Court "read §10(b) to mean that Congress meant to bar deceptive devices and contrivances in the purchase or sale of securities whether conducted in the organized markets or [as in that case] face-to-face."[213]

So far as face-to-face transactions are concerned, the seminal *Kardon* case was on its facts as extreme as any case could be in this respect: Although the two plaintiffs and two defendants were the sole stockholders, and all four were directors, Judge Kirkpatrick stated that he could not agree "that two men who have acquired ownership of the stock of a corporation are not investors merely because they own half of the total issue."[214]

Prescott, Ball & Turben, 598 F. 2d 1017, 1026-27 (6th Cir. 1979) (improper executions by broker as well as refusal to return customer's fully paid bonds); Rooney, Pace, Inc. v. Reid, 605 F. Supp. 158 (S. D. N. Y. 1985).

[211] Mansbach v. Prescott, Ball & Turben, 598 F. 2d 1017, 1026 (6th Cir. 1979); Cooper v. North Jersey Trust Co. of Ridgewood, N. J., Inc., 226 F. Supp. 972, 978 (S. D. N. Y. 1964); Glickman v. Schweickart & Co., 242 F. Supp. 670, 674 (S. D. N. Y. 1965).

[212] Errion v. Connell, 236 F. 2d 447 (9th Cir. 1956); see also AVC Nederland B. V. v. Atrium Investment Partnership, 740 F. 2d 148, 158 n. 17 (2d Cir. 1984), and cases cited. But cf. Saxe v. E. F. Hutton & Co., Inc., 789 F. 2d 105, 108 (2d Cir. 1986) (liquidation of a stock trading account for reinvestment in a commodities account, where the only misrepresentations alleged related to the commodity futures that plaintiff would invest in, was not fraud "in connection with" the sale inherent in the liquidation); cf. also Supp. p. 790 n. 219 infra.

[213] Superintendent of Ins. of the State of N. Y. v. Bankers Life & Casualty Co., 404 U. S. 6, 12 (1971).

[214] Kardon v. National Gypsum Co., 69 F. Supp. 512, 514 (E. D. Pa. 1946); to the same effect, see also, e. g., SEC v. Texas Gulf Sulphur Co., 401 F. 2d

So far as market transactions are concerned, there are problems — to be considered in the next chapter on Civil Liability —of determining who are eligible plaintiffs and fixing their damages, particularly when insiders have traded in silence. But those problems are not insuperable, as we shall see. And, of course, it "would be anomalous indeed if the protection afforded by the antifraud provisions were withdrawn from transactions affected on exchanges, primary markets for securities transactions."[215] Moreover, in principle, it would be an odd rule of fiduciary conduct that permitted an insider to avoid his affirmative disclosure obligation by hiding behind the mask of the stock exchange. Surely an insider could not escape that obligation by trading offboard through an agent for an undisclosed principal.[216] And what is a stock exchange if not an aggregation of agents trading for undisclosed principals?[217]

The plaintiff does, of course, have to prove that the prohibited conduct was effected, in the language of §10(b), "by the use of any means or instrumentality of interstate commerce or of the mails or of any national securities exchange." But it is "well established" that "the jurisdictional hook need not be large to fish for securities law violations."[218]

b. "In Connection with a Purchase or Sale"

The requirement of both section and rule that the prohibited conduct be "in connection with the purchase or sale of any security" is not the least difficult aspect of the 10b-5 complex to tie down. A

833, 848 (2d Cir. 1968), *cert. denied* sub nom. Coates v. SEC and Kline v. SEC, 394 U. S. 976; Spector v. L Q Motor Inns, Inc., 517 F. 2d 278 (5th Cir. 1975) (transfer of eighteen shares as part of a divorce settlement). But see Judge Posner's concurring opinion in Trecker v. Scag, 679 F. 2d 703, 710-11 (7th Cir. 1982): while conceding that an incidental intrastate telephone call created federal jurisdiction over "a spat between two shareholders of a closely held corporation," he suggested that "perhaps we should not have jurisdiction" that displaces "state substantive law and state court jurisdiction in an area remote from any federal concern that might arise from federal regulation of the securities markets," a result that "could not have been foreseen by the framers of the Securities Exchange Act."

[215] Cady, Roberts & Co., 40 SEC 907, 914 (1961).

[216] See Strong v. Repide, 213 U. S. 419 (1909), supra p. 724 n. 3.

[217] More precisely the principals are *partially* disclosed; for (specialists aside) they know that their brokers are not buying or selling for their own accounts.

[218] Lawrence v. SEC, 398 F. 2d 276, 278 (1st Cir. 1968); SEC v. United Financial Group, Inc., 474 F. 2d 354, 356-57 (9th Cir. 1973); United States v. Jones, 712 F. 2d 1316 (9th Cir. 1983), *cert. denied* sub nom. Webber v. United States, 464 U. S. 986; see 3 and 6 Loss c. 9F; see also pp. 93-94 supra. There are nevertheless limitations. See United States v. Maze, 414 U. S. 395 (1974).

good deal of the difficulty is traceable to Justice Douglas's reference in the first Supreme Court case (involving a complex fraud in which an insurance company was bought with its own assets) to the plaintiff's having "suffered an injury as a result of deceptive practices touching its sale of securities as an investor."[219]

The Douglas opinion has led to analysis of the "connection" requirement in terms of causation:

> While it may be that *Bankers Life* suggests that the "connection" element of §10(b) is not precisely the same as causation, since the bond sale only *made possible* the accomplishment of the fraud as opposed to having *caused* it, the two concepts are similar to one another. This is so because both the "connection" and "causation" principles speak to the degree of proximity required between a misrepresentation and a securities transaction.[220]

[219] Superintendent of Ins. of the State of N. Y. v. Bankers Life & Casualty Co., 404 U. S. 6, 12-13 (1971); see also cases cited in Natowitz v. Mehlman, 567 F. Supp. 942 (S. D. N. Y. 1983); Abrams v. Oppenheimer Government Securities, Inc., 737 F. 2d 582, 593 (7th Cir. 1984) (the "requirement amounts to some nexus but not necessarily a direct and close relationship"); Wilsmann v. Upjohn Co., 775 F. 2d 713 (6th Cir. 1985), *cert. denied,* 106 S. Ct. 2893; Shapiro v. Merrill Lynch & Co., 634 F. Supp. 587, 595 (S. D. Ohio 1985) (plaintiff need not establish "a close temporal connection between a specific fraudulent statement or omission and a specific purchase or sale"); SEC v. Drysdale Securities Corp., 785 F. 2d 38 (2d Cir. 1986), *cert. denied* sub nom. Essner v. SEC, 106 S. Ct. 2894; Pross v. Katz, 784 F. 2d 455 (2d Cir. 1986) (a securities transaction entailed as an integral step the fraudulent securing of blank signature pages for purposes of a later conversion); First Federal Savings & Loan Assn. of Pittsburgh v. Oppenheim, Appel, Dixon & Co., 629 F. Supp. 427, 439-42 (S. D. N. Y. 1986); Jabend, Inc. v. Four-Phase Systems, Inc., 631 F. Supp. 1339 (W. D. Wash. 1986); SEC v. Warner, 652 F. Supp. 647, 650-51 (S. D. Fla. 1987) (the phrase may be broader than the "in" of Sec. Act §17(a)).

But cf. Chemical Bank v. Arthur Andersen & Co., 726 F. 2d 930 (1984), *cert. denied,* 469 U. S. 484 (although a pledge of a subsidiary's stock to support parent-guaranteed notes that were not themselves "securities" (see p. 165 n. 1 supra) was a "sale," it was not enough to allege a misstatement with respect to the financial condition of the parent); Head v. Head, 759 F. 2d 1172, 1175-76 (4th Cir. 1985); Rand v. Anaconda-Ericsson, Inc., 794 F. 2d 843, 847 (2d Cir. 1986), *cert. denied,* 107 S. Ct. 579; DMI Furniture, Inc. v. Brown, Kraft & Co., 644 F. Supp. 1517 (C. D. Cal. 1986) (accountant hired by an acquiring company did not act "in connection with" the sale of stock, since it performed a function not contemplated by the SEC disclosure system). Judge Van Graafeiland's dissenting opinion in *Chemical Bank* seems more persuasive in concluding: "Because there was only one fraudulent scheme, so long as the district court has acquired jurisdiction of a portion of it that clearly is securities related, there is no reason why the court should not be permitted to dispose of the entire action." 726 F. 2d at 947. Both that opinion and *Drysdale,* supra, cited Errion v. Connell, 236 F. 2d 447, 454 (9th Cir. 1956), supra p. 228.

[220] Ketchum v. Green, 557 F. 2d 1022, 1029 (3d Cir. 1977), *cert. denied,* 434 U. S. 94 (italics are the court's); Liberty National Ins. Co. v. Charter Co., 734 F. 2d 545, 555 (11th Cir. 1986).

But this should not preclude the rule's application merely because the alleged fraud concerned the trading of securities generally rather than the value of a particular security.[221]

Actually there is no reason to believe that Justice Douglas's use of "touching" was anything more than his variation of "in connection with" as a matter of literary style.[222] Certain things, however, are reasonably clear.

First: As stated in the Code's commentary:

> No change is intended in the interpretation of "in connection with." For example, nothing in the Code is inconsistent with any of the learning (though uncodified) of *Superintendent of Insurance* v. *Bankers Life & Casualty Co.*, 404 U. S. 6 (1971): (A) that "the fact that creditors of the defrauded corporate buyer or seller of securities may be the ultimate victims does not warrant disregard of the corporate entity" (404 U. S. at 12); and (B) that misappropriation of the proceeds of a sale of securities may be a fraudulent act creating liability for the misappropriator if "the seller was duped into believing that it, the seller, would receive the proceeds" (404 U. S. at 9), even though the sale is for full value and the misappropriator is neither a buyer nor a seller.[223]

Second: A fraud is not "in connection with" a purchase or sale if the purchaser or seller was aware of the facts when he bought or sold.[224]

Third: The rule may be violated by feeding misinformation into the marketplace, or even withholding information too long, without any buying or selling. This we have already noticed.[225]

[221] Arrington v. Merrill Lynch, Pierce, Fenner & Smith, Inc., 651 F. 2d 615 (9th Cir. 1981) (failure to disclose risks of margin trading); Angelastro v. Prudential-Bache Securities, Inc., 764 F. 2d 939, 943-46 (3d Cir. 1985), *cert. denied*, 106 S. Ct. 267 (misrepresentations concerning interest on margin accounts); Gaudette v. Panos, 644 F. Supp. 826, 832-33 (D. Mass. 1986). *Contra:* SEC v. Wall St. Publishing Institute, Inc., 591 F. Supp. 1070, 1088 (D. D. C. 1984), *stay granted*, CCH Fed. Sec. L. Rep. ¶91,635 (D. D. C. 1984) (fraud in sale of investment advisory services); Shamir v. Kidder, Peabody & Co., CCH Fed. Sec. L. Rep. ¶91,505 at 98,539 (S. D. N. Y. 1984) (misrepresentation as to expertise of broker's representative); Corbey v. Grace, 605 F. Supp. 247, 252 (D. Minn. 1985) (misrepresentation regarding operation of a margin account).

[222] Chemical Bank v. Arthur Andersen & Co., 726 F. 2d 930, 942 (2d Cir. 1984), *cert. denied*, 469 U. S. 884, quoting the text; In re Financial Corp. of America Shareholders Litigation, 796 F. 2d 1126, 1130 (9th Cir. 1986), citing the text.

[223] 2 Code 660.

[224] Shivers v. AMERCO, 670 F. 2d 826, 829-30 (9th Cir. 1982).

[225] See pp. 736 supra. In Heit v. Weitzen, 402 F. 2d 909 (2d Cir. 1968), the court held that the "in connection with" clause was satisfied by complaints in two related actions by market buyers against the same issuer and its directors (together with the issuer's controlling stockholder and auditor in one of the

Fourth: The *plaintiff,* however, does have to be a buyer or seller. This proposition goes back to the Second Circuit's 1952 decision in *Birnbaum* v. *Newport Steel Corp.,*[226] to the effect that public stockholders could not complain that those in control had sold out at a favorable price without giving the plaintiffs the same opportunity. Twenty-three years later the Supreme Court in *Blue Chip Stamps* v. *Manor Drug Stores*[227] approved the *Birnbaum* principle in a different factual context. Blue Chip, pursuant to an antitrust judgment, registered an offering to retailers like Manor that had used Blue Chip's stamps. Manor complained that it had been misled into *not* buying by an overly pessimistic prospectus. Justice Rehnquist (as he then was) wrote for a majority of six (Justices Blackmun, Douglas, and Brennan dissenting). A few excerpts from the lengthy opinion will give some of its flavor:

* * *

> While the damages suffered by purchasers and sellers pursuing a §10(b) cause of action may on occasion be difficult to ascertain, *Affiliated Ute Citizens* v. *United States,* 406 U. S., at 155, in the main such purchasers and sellers at least seek to base recovery on a demonstrable number of shares traded. In contrast, a putative plaintiff, who neither purchases nor sells securities but sues instead for intangible economic injury such as loss of a noncontractual opportunity to buy or sell, is more likely to be seeking a largely conjectural and speculative recovery in which the number of shares involved will depend on the plaintiff's subjective hypothesis. * * *

* * *

> The principal express nonderivative private civil remedies, created by Congress contemporaneously with the passage of §10(b), for violations of various provisions of the 1933 and 1934 Acts are by their terms expressly limited to purchasers or sellers of securities. * * * It would indeed be anomalous to impute to Congress an intention to expand the plaintiff class for a judicially implied cause

---

cases) alleging the dissemination of financial statements that had overstated the issuer's net assets and past and prospective income because of the failure to disclose substantial, recoverable overcharges by the issuer on governmental contracts. Although the judge below had considered the alleged scheme as directed primarily toward the Government notwithstanding the possibility of an incidental market impact, the appellate court held that the "ulterior motive" was irrelevant as long as the false information had been circulated to a large segment of the investing public, and that it was of no consequence that none of the defendants had been engaged in buying or selling.

[226] 193 F. 2d 461 (2d Cir. 1952).

[227] 421 U. S. 723 (1975).

of action beyond the bounds it delineated for comparable express causes of action.

* * * it would be disingenuous to suggest that either Congress in 1934 or the Securities and Exchange Commission in 1942 foreordained the present state of the law with respect to Rule 10b-5. It is therefore proper that we consider, in addition to the factors already discussed, what may be described as policy considerations when we come to flesh out the portions of the law with respect to which neither the congressional enactment nor the administrative regulations offer conclusive guidance.

* * *

There has been widespread recognition that litigation under Rule 10b-5 presents a danger of vexatiousness different in degree and in kind from that which accompanies litigation in general.

* * *

We believe that the concern expressed for the danger of vexatious litigation which could result from a widely expanded class of plaintiffs under Rule 10b-5 is founded in something more substantial than the common complaint of the many defendants who would prefer avoiding lawsuits entirely to either settling them or trying them. These concerns have two largely separate grounds.

The first of these concerns is that in the field of federal securities laws governing disclosure of information even a complaint which by objective standards may have very little chance of success at trial has a settlement value to the plaintiff out of any proportion to its prospect of success at trial so long as he may prevent the suit from being resolved against him by dismissal or summary judgment. The very pendency of the lawsuit may frustrate or delay normal business activity of the defendant which is totally unrelated to the law suit. * * *

Congress itself recognized the potential for nuisance or "strike" suits in this type of litigation, and in Title II of the 1934 Act amended §11 of the 1933 Act to provide that:

> In any suit under this or any other section of this title the court may, in its discretion, require an undertaking for the payment of the costs of such suit, including reasonable attorney's fees. §206(d), 48 Stat. 881, 908.

* * *

The potential for possible abuse of the liberal discovery provisions of the Federal Rules of Civil Procedure may likewise exist in this type of case to a greater extent than they do in other litigation. * * *

Without the *Birnbaum* rule, an action under Rule 10b-5 will turn largely on which oral version of a series of occurrences the jury may decide to credit, and therefore no matter how improbable the allegations of the plaintiff, the case will be virtually impossible to dispose of prior to trial other than by settlement.

* * * The fact of purchase of stock and the fact of sale of stock are generally matters which are verifiable by documentation, and do not depend upon oral recollection, so that failure to qualify under the *Birnbaum* rule is a matter that can normally be established by the defendant either on a motion to dismiss or on a motion for summary judgment.

* * *

The second ground for fear of vexatious litigation is based on the concern that, given the generalized contours of liability, the abolition of the *Birnbaum* rule would throw open to the trier of fact many rather hazy issues of historical fact the proof of which depended almost entirely on oral testimony. * * *

* * *

* * * Plaintiff's proof would not be that he purchased or sold stock, a fact which would be capable of documentary verification in most situations, but instead that he decided *not* to purchase or sell stock. Plaintiff's entire testimony could be dependent upon uncorroborated oral evidence of many of the crucial elements of his claim, and still be sufficient to go to the jury. * * * In the absence of the *Birnbaum* doctrine, bystanders to the securities marketing process could await developments on the sidelines without risk, claiming that inaccuracies in disclosure caused nonselling in a falling market and that unduly pessimistic predictions by the issuer followed by a rising market caused them to allow retrospectively golden opportunities to pass.

Blue Chip was not the apocalypse that some in the Commission and the academic world believed it was, at least initially. For one thing, *Birnbaum* had reigned virtually supreme at the appellate level for twenty-three years.[228] The cascade of 10b-5 litigation during

[228] The only discordant voice in the appellate courts was Eason v. General Motors Acceptance Corp., 490 F. 2d 654 (7th Cir. 1973), *cert. denied,* 416 U. S. 960. But there is always the possibility in the *Blue Chip* factual configuration of recovery at common law. Holloway v. Forsyth, 226 Mass. 358, 115 N. E. 48[illegible]

that period confirmed the utility of the buy-sell requirement as *some* means to keep the little rule from taking over a large slice of the corporation law universe. And there is no gainsaying that a grant of standing to a plaintiff who had not changed his position would be, in most factual configurations if not that in *Birnbaum* or *Blue Chip,* an "invitation to fraud," as Justice Powell stated in his concurring opinion.[229]

What is disturbing to many is not the holding but the tone of the majority opinion as a possible harbinger of the demise or crippling of Rule 10b-5 — as if all the harms, in Justice Blackmun's words, "were unknown to lawsuits taking place in America's courthouses every day."[230] Is a majority of the Court determined drastically to roll back the whole development of a "federal corporation law"?[231] Or will *Blue Chip* and later 10b-5 cases turn out to be simply another example of the pendulum phenomenon that has characterized so much legal doctrine?

Recent history is hard to write. We have already noticed the Court's strict scienter approach in *Hochfelder* and *Aaron.* And we shall soon consider the Court's unwillingness to expand the rule's "fraud" concept in another sense.[232] But all these cases together leave the rule intact for fraudulent acts or statements known to be false (or, probably, false statements made with reckless disregard as to truth or falsity) in connection with *any* purchase or sale of *any* security by *any* person to *any* person — not to mention cases of insiders (and probably most tippees') silence.

Meanwhile *Blue Chip* puts heavy weight on what constitutes a "sale" or "purchase" within the meaning of the rule. The lower courts in the period between *Birnbaum* and *Blue Chip,* while almost uniformly following the Second Circuit — and principally the Sec-

---

(1917) (plaintiffs refrained from selling in reliance on defendant's misrepresentations).

[229] 421 U. S. at 761.

[230] Id. at 769.

[231] The Second Circuit has referred to Justice Rehnquist's language with reference to the settlement value of 10b-5 complaints in construing the requirement in Rule 9(b) of the Federal Rules of Civil Procedure that fraud be pleaded with particularity. Decker v. Massey-Ferguson, Ltd., 681 F. 2d 111, 114 (2d Cir. 1982). On Rule 9(b) in the SEC context, see Note, Pleading Securities Fraud Claims with Particularity Under Rule 9(b), 97 Harv. L. Rev. 1432 (1984); Comment, Pleading Constructive Fraud in Securities Litigation — Avoiding Dismissal for Failure to Plead Fraud with Particularity, 33 Emory L. J. 517 (1984). The rule does not attach to §11 of the 1933 Act. In re LILCO Securities Litigation, 625 F. Supp. 1500 (E. D. N. Y. 1986). But it does apply when Rule 10b-5 is pleaded as a predicate offense in a RICO action (see p. 710-11 supra). International Data Bank, Ltd. v. Zepkin, 812 F. 2d 149 (4th Cir. 1987).

[232] Santa Fe Industries, Inc. v. Green, 430 U. S. 462 (1977), infra p. 804.

ond Circuit itself — did put a high gloss on those critical terms. How much of that gloss still shines?

(1) Our analysis in Chapter 4A of the term "sale" in §2(3) of the 1933 Act cannot be applied blindly in the 10b-5 context, because, as we have noticed elsewhere,[233] §§3(a)(13) and 3(a)(14) of the 1934 Act do not really define "purchase" and "sale." But we have noticed also that there is authority for looking to the 1933 Act definition in construing the 1934 Act on an *in pari materia* approach.[234]

(2) In stockholders' derivative actions it is the corporation, not the plaintiff, that must have bought or sold.[235]

(3) As long as *somebody* bought or sold, *Blue Chip* should not affect criminal[236] or SEC injunctive[237] (or administrative) actions.

(4) The Second Circuit did not apply its own *Birnbaum* ruling in private injunctive actions — as where stockholders complained that insiders had manipulated the market and kept dividends down in order to force the other stockholders to sell out cheaply, although the plaintiffs themselves had not sold.[238] *Query* whether the Supreme Court will be more amenable to recognizing such an exception from *Blue Chip* in injunctive actions than it was in *Aaron* with respect to an exception from the scienter requirement of *Hochfelder*. Arguably the context here goes only to standing, not to violation as in the scienter context.

(5) It is quite well established that, although one does not ordinarily speak of an *issuance* of stock as a "sale" because there is

[233] See p. 579 supra.

[234] Ibid.

[235] Herpich v. Wallace, 430 F. 2d 792 (5th Cir. 1970) (a company is a "purchaser" entitled to damages for harmful acts already committed in furtherance of a merger plan not yet consummated). On the same rationale, it should suffice that there was a purchase or sale by the plaintiff's decedent or, if a 10b-5 claim is assignable, the plaintiff's assignor. But cf. SIPC v. Vigman, 803 F. 2d 1513 (9th Cir. 1986) (SIPC cannot sue as subrogee of the broker's customers that it made whole); Citron v. Rollins Environmental Services, Inc., 644 F. Supp. 733, 737-38 (D. Del. 1986) (plaintiff's standing as buyer does not pass to defendant as third-party plaintiff).

[236] United States v. Newman, 664 F. 2d 12, 17 (2d Cir. 1981), *cert. denied*, 464 U. S. 863.

[237] SEC v. National Securities, Inc., 393 U. S. 453 (1969), cited in Blue Chip Stamps v. Manor Drug Stores, 421 U. S. 723, 751 n. 14 (1975).

[238] Mutual Shares Corp. v. Genesco, Inc., 384 F. 2d 540 (2d Cir. 1967); see also Kahan v. Rosenstiel, 424 F. 2d 161 (3d Cir. 1970); Liberty National Ins. Holding Co. v. Charter Co., 734 F. 2d 545, 557 (11th Cir. 1984).

Contra: Cowin v. Bresler, 741 F. 2d 410, 424-25 (D. C. Cir. 1984). In Doll v. James Martin Associates (Holdings), Ltd., 600 F. Supp. 510, 522 (E. D. Mich. 1984), the plaintiff failed in his attempt to extend *Birnbaum*'s exception beyond "prophylactic relief." And "The federal securities laws do not give one who has suffered no injury a commission to act as a private attorney general to enforce the laws, nor a warrant to invoke remedies of no benefit to himself." Packer v. Yampol, 630 F. Supp. 1237, 1241 (S. D. N. Y. 1986).

nothing to be sold until the issuance has occurred, an issuance does involve a "sale" or "purchase" for purposes of Rule 10b-5.[239] This, as we shall see, opens up a good deal of the corporate mismanagement area to federal law as long as the other elements of Rule 10b-5 are present;[240] for many, if not most, derivative actions involve a security transaction to which the corporation is a party.

(6) The "forced seller" in a "short-form merger" is a "seller" under the rule.[241] And this is true *a fortiori* with respect to an ordinary merger in which the stockholders have a vote; on this point there is Supreme Court precedent antedating *Blue Chip.*[242] This means that Rule 10b-5 is available to attack proxy literature for a merger when Rule 14a-9, the proxy fraud rule, is unavailable because the security is not registered.[243] It follows in turn that a state appraisal remedy, even though it may be exclusive as a matter of state law, cannot preclude resort to the federal actions.[244]

(7) In connection with the 1933 Act we have noticed the uncertainty whether a liquidating dividend payable in securities is a "sale."[245] In the 10b-5 context, the Fifth Circuit has applied the "forced sale" concept to liquidations on the theory that the nature of the shareholder's investment "has been fundamentally changed from an interest in a going enterprise into a right solely to a payment of money for his shares."[246] The same court has reaffirmed

[239] Hooper v. Mountain States Securities Corp., 282 F. 2d 195 (5th Cir. 1960); Ruckle v. Roto American Corp., 339 F. 2d 24 (2d Cir. 1964); Rochelle v. Marine Midland Grace Trust Co. of N. Y., 535 F. 2d 523, 527-28 (9th Cir. 1976) (debentures).

[240] See pp. 801-09 infra.

[241] Vine v. Beneficial Finance Co., Inc., 374 F. 2d 627 (2d Cir. 1967); Herskowitz v. Nutri/System, Inc., — F. Supp. — , — , CCH Fed. Sec. L. Rep. ¶92,829 at 94,036 (E. D. N. Y. 1986); cf. Mayer v. Oil Field Systems Corp., 721 F. 2d 59, 65 (2d Cir. 1983).

[242] SEC v. National Securities, Inc., 393 U. S. 453 (1969). But cf. Rathborne v. Rathborne, 683 F. 2d 914 (5th Cir. 1982) (parent corporation's transfer of assets to a newly organized and wholly owned subsidiary in exchange for subsidiary's stock was a mere "transfer between corporate pockets"); Mosher v. Kane, 784 F. 2d 1385, 1389 (9th Cir. 1986); Rand v. Anaconda-Ericsson, Inc., 794 F. 2d 843 (2d Cir. 1986), *cert. denied,* 107 S. Ct. 579 (the "forced sale" theory falls far short of converting any fraudulent conduct resulting in a corporate bankruptcy into securities fraud); Bold v. Simpson, 802 F. 2d 314, 320 (8th Cir. 1986), citing the text (promoter's conversion of plaintiff's interest in a ranching lease). See generally Annot., "Forced Seller" for Purposes of Maintenance of Civil Action Under §10(b) * * * and SEC Rule 10b-5, 59 A. L. R. Fed. 10 (1982).

[243] "The fact that there may well be some overlap is neither unusual nor unfortunate." SEC v. National Securities, Inc., 393 U. S. 453, 468 (1969).

[244] Austell v. Smith, 634 F. Supp. 326, 330 (W. D. N. C. 1986).

[245] See pp. 250-52 supra.

[246] Dudley v. Southeastern Factor & Finance Corp., 446 F. 2d 303 (5th Cir. 1971), *cert. denied* sub nom. McDaniel v. Dudley, 404 U. S. 858. So, too, with

this view since *Blue Chip*, concluding that "The forced seller doctrine does not undermine the policy objectives of" that case.[247] On the other hand, just *before Blue Chip* the Fifth Circuit, again, *rejected* a contention that the issuance of new shares in a refinancing plan had so diluted the plaintiffs' position as to make them "forced sellers."[248]

(8) A redemption of convertible debentures in order to prevent conversions and dilution of voting control has been held to be a "purchase." As a result of the redemption, the Second Circuit *en banc* stated, the controlling stockholder "was acquiring the bondholders' rights to obtain common stock by conversion and thereby reducing the outstanding rights to interests in the equity securities of the corporation to the same extent as though it had purchased common shares on the open market."[249] In any event, there can

---

respect to the liquidation of a limited partnership. Feldberg v. O'Connell, 338 F. Supp. 744 (D. Mass. 1972).

[247] Alley v. Miramon, 614 F. 2d 1372, 1385-86 (5th Cir. 1980); see also Garner v. Pearson, 374 F. Supp. 591 (M. D. Fla. 1974) (plaintiffs, as liquidators of a bank, could sue as forced sellers where they alleged that as a result of defendants' fraudulent scheme the assets of the bank had been plundered and were reduced to a mere claim for a portion of its remaining assets in the liquidation proceedings); Federal Deposit Ins. Corp. v. Kerr, 637 F. Supp. 828 (W. D. N. C. 1986).

In Falls v. Fickling, 621 F. 2d 1362 (5th Cir. 1980), the court applied the "forced seller" doctrine to a person whose stock had been bought at a sheriff's sale.

[248] Sargent v. Genesco, Inc., 492 F. 2d 750, 765 (5th Cir. 1974); see also Arnesen v. Shawmut County Bank, N. A., 504 F. Supp. 1077 (D. Mass. 1980) (Supreme Court's "policy to confine Rule 10b-5 within manageable limits" dictates a narrow interpretation of the "forced seller" doctrine as inapplicable in the absence of a formal liquidation even though a bank's foreclosure left minority shareholders with valueless stock in a company that had ceased its active existence); Rodriguez Cádiz v. Mercado Jiménez, 579 F. Supp. 1176 (D. P. R. 1983); Batchelder v. Northern Fire Lites, Inc., 630 F. Supp. 1115, 1120 (D. N. H. 1986); SIPC v. Vigman, 803 F. 2d 1513 (9th Cir. 1986) (not every SIPC liquidation that satisfies customers' claims with cash is a "forced sale").

[249] Drachman v. Harvey, 453 F. 2d 722, 737 n. 2 (2d Cir. *en banc* 1972). The court distinguished SEC v. Sterling Precision Corp., 393 F. 2d 214, 217-18 (2d Cir. 1968), supra p. 579 n. 105, on the ground that "sale" had a broader meaning in the Exchange Act than in the Investment Company Act. Cf. Foltz v. U. S. News & World Report, Inc., 627 F. Supp. 1143, 1159-60 (D. D. C. 1986) (even though defendant had an option to buy back each employee's stock, former employee who asserts that he would have deferred retirement pending a hoped-for increase in the value of his holdings states a 10b-5 claim). But cf. Trecker v. Scag, 747 F. 2d 1176 (7th Cir. 1984), *cert. denied*, 471 S. Ct. 1066 (company's failure to tell a redeeming shareholder that it was negotiating to sell the redeemed stock was not a material omission, since shareholder had already decided to redeem his shares before negotiations began and under state law could not change that decision after learning of the negotiation).

be no doubt that persons who do convert are both sellers and purchasers.[250]

(9) Quite clearly a pledgor is a "seller" and a pledgee is a "purchaser."[251]

(10) As long as the plaintiff is a buyer or seller, nothing in *Blue Chip* requires that he buy *from* or sell *to* the defendant rather than buying or selling *through* the defendant as broker.[252] We have seen

[250] See p. 263 supra.

[251] Rubin v. United States, 449 U. S. 424 (1981), supra p. 249. In our analysis of the 1933 Act we have noticed cases where the *pledgor* violated §5 or 17(a). See pp. 249, 259 supra. In Dopp v. Franklin National Bank, 374 F. Supp. 904 (S. D. N. Y. 1974), the pledgor alleged that the defendant *pledgee* had violated Rule 10b-5 by promising the plaintiff a right of first refusal without disclosing negotiations to sell to others. And "courts have recognized the standing of defaulting pledgors * * *, with only a partial right to the proceeds of the sale of their stock, to sue as 'sellers' under Rule 10b-5 when their stock is sold to pay off the loan against which the stock was pledged." Madison Consultants v. Federal Deposit Ins. Corp., 710 F. 2d 57, 61 (2d Cir. 1983), citing cases; see also Mansbach v. Prescott, Ball & Turben, 598 F. 2d 1017, 1028-30 (6th Cir. 1979).

[252] Principal *versus* agent (broker): Hecht v. Harris, Upham & Co., 430 F. 2d 1202 (9th Cir. 1970), and other "churning" cases cited supra p. 705 n. 21; Nye v. Blyth, Eastman Dillon & Co., Inc., 588 F. 2d 1189 (8th Cir. 1978) (*Blue Chip* question was not raised); cf. SEC v. Fifth Avenue Coach Lines, Inc., 435 F. 2d 510, 517-18 (2d Cir. 1970) (controlling persons, without full disclosure to entire board, caused their corporation to sell valuable stock owned by it to another corporation they knew could not pay for it).

Agent (broker) *versus* principal: A. T. Brod & Co. v. Perlow, 375 F. 2d 393, 397 (2d Cir. 1967), supra p. 787 n. 210; Carroll v. First National Bank of Lincolnwood, 413 F. 2d 353, 356-57 (7th Cir. 1969), *cert. denied,* 396 U. S. 1003; cf. United States v. Peltz, 433 F. 2d 48, 53 (2d Cir. 1970), *cert. denied,* 401 U. S. 955.

There have been cases also of beneficiary *versus* trustee or executor. James v. Gerber Products Co., 483 F. 2d 944 (6th Cir. 1973); Kirshner v. United States, 603 F. 2d 234, 240-41 (2d Cir. 1978); cf. Norris v. Wirtz, 719 F. 2d 256 (7th Cir. 1983), *cert. denied,* 466 U. S. 929 (court regarded beneficiary as a "seller" where her prior approval was required for trustee's sales of trust stock to close corporations that he controlled); Margaret Hall Foundation, Inc. v. Atlantic Financial Management, Inc., 572 F. Supp. 1475 (D. Mass. 1983) (similar).

But cf. Canut v. Lyons, 450 F. Supp. 26 (C. D. Cal. 1977) (issuer's receiver cannot recover against individuals allegedly responsible for false offering circulars, because issuer, though a seller, received the benefit of any violations); Baker v. Heller, 571 F. Supp. 419 (S. D. Fla. 1983) (same); O'Brien v. Continental Ill. National Bank & Trust Co., 593 F. 2d 54 (7th Cir. 1979) (failure of bank trustee or agent with sole investment discretion to disclose information about transactions to plaintiff beneficiary or principal did not satisfy the "connection" requirement; plaintiff's allegation of bank's buying high risk securities to protect its own interest as a commercial lender went simply to breach of fiduciary duty); Congregation of the Passion, Holy Cross Province v. Kidder, Peabody & Co., Inc., 800 F. 2d 177 (7th Cir. 1986) (plaintiff that gave an investment adviser full authority had no 10b-5 action against executing brokers). The "churning" cases alone (supra p. 705 n. 21) demonstrate that this last case says too much if it

that an insider may be liable to a market buyer or seller without the insider's having traded at all.[253] The case where a broker defrauds his customer without the customer's buying or selling — by "bucketing" a buy order, for example[254] — is hostile to a literal reading of *Blue Chip*. But, arguably, it is not inconsistent with *Blue Chip*'s philosophy; for "the principal-agent (or similar) relationship affords at least as close a nexus as does the buyer-seller relationship."[255]

(11) On the "contract to buy" and "contract to sell" language in the definitions of "purchase" and "sale,"[256] a divided court has applied the common law concept that there can be no contract without a manifestation of mutual assent.[257] But this "does not prevent a court from finding a purchase where there was an appar-

---

stands for the proposition that discretionary authority always precludes a 10b-5 violation.

Whether or not the beneficiary of a trust whose trustee buys or sells can proceed against the *trustee,* he has standing as buyer or seller against the *seller* or *buyer.* Haber v. Kobrin, CCH Fed. Sec. L. Rep. ¶99,259 at 96,162 (S. D. N. Y. 1983); Gross v. Diversified Mortgage Investors, 431 F. Supp. 1080, 1093 (S. D. N. Y. 1977), *aff'd without published opinion,* 636 F. 2d 1201 (2d Cir. 1980). This should apply equally to the principal-agent relationship. The representative of an estate of a decedent who bought or sold likewise has standing. Miller v. Merrill Lynch, Pierce, Fenner & Smith, Inc., 572 F. Supp. 1180, 1183 (N. D. Ga. 1983). So does an indenture trustee as representative of the bondholders who bought. In re Washington Public Power System Securities Litigation, 623 F. Supp. 1466, 1483-84 (W. D. Wash. 1985). But cf. Prudential Ins. Co. of America v. BMC Industries, Inc., 655 F. Supp. 710, CCH Fed. Sec. L. Rep. ¶93,120 (S. D. N. Y. 1987).

A legatee as such, or a donee, is not a buyer or seller of securities bought from or sold to the estate by the testator or donor; but the legatee will ultimately inherit the *estate's* cause of action, and the donee can take an assignment from the donor. Rose v. Arkansas Valley Environmental & Utility Authority, 562 F. Supp. 1180, 1188-90 (W. D. Mo. 1983); but cf. In re Saxon Securities Litigation, 644 F. Supp. 465 (S. D. N. Y. 1985).

Some of these cases preceded *Blue Chip*. But it must be remembered that *Blue Chip* simply endorsed the widely followed *Birnbaum* case.

[253] See p. 736 supra.

[254] Silverman v. Bear, Stearns & Co., 331 F. Supp. 1334 (E. D. Pa. 1971) (delayed execution in broker's interest); cf. Stockwell v. Reynolds & Co., 252 F. Supp. 215 (S. D. N. Y. 1965) (court sustained a complaint that alleged that plaintiffs had been induced to defer market sales by the fraudulent representations of a broker-dealer and ultimately had sold at a greater loss). But cf. Smith v. Chicago Corp., 566 F. Supp. 66 (N. D. Ill. 1983) (broker's failure to execute purchase orders and misappropriation of funds from customer's accounts).

[255] 2 Code 736. Cf. SIPC v. Vigman, 803 F. 2d 1513, 1519 (9th Cir. 1986) (a broker's "unauthorized purchase or sale of securities with the customer's assets * * * may be attributed to the customer for purposes of satisfying the *Birnmbaum* rule").

[256] §§3(a)(13), 3(a)(14), supra p. 579.

[257] Northland Capital Corp. v. Silver, 735 F. 2d 1421 (D. C. Cir. 1984) (plaintiff sued to recapture funds placed in escrow before aborted closing).

ent manifestation of mutual assent that was negated by a party's misrepresentation."[258] Moreover, the existence of a contract is not precluded by a delayed delivery provision or the contract's pertaining to "when issued" securities.[259] Nor is a "sale" precluded by the fact that the contract is never fully performed, or that the stock delivery is conditional.[260]

c. Corporate Mismanagement: The "New Fraud" Theory and Its Demise

Two seemingly self-evident, but not readily reconcilable, propositions have been repeated in judicial utterances: (1) Congress "did not seek to regulate transactions which constitute no more than internal corporate mismanagement."[261] (2) The mere fact that the sale or purchase transaction "was part of a broader scheme of corporate mismanagement" does not preclude an action under Rule 10b-5.[262]

It fell to the Second Circuit's lot to explore these outer frontiers of the rule in a series of parries and thrusts that ultimately produced another visit from the Supreme Court. The story is best told chronologically:

In *Ruckle,*[263] a 1964 case, a director who represented more than

[258] Id. at 1429 n. 14; see also Mullen v. Sweetwater Development Corp., 619 F. Supp. 809, 816 (D. Colo. 1985) (plaintiffs, as parties to a contract for the sale of stock whose validity is uncertain, have standing under Rule 10b-5 when the reason for the contract's questionable validity also forms the basis for the claim).

[259] Abrams v. Oppenheimer Government Securities, Inc., 737 F. 2d 582, 587 (7th Cir. 1984).

[260] Yoder v. Orthomolecular Nutrition Institute, Inc., 751 F. 2d 555, 559 (2d Cir. 1985); Mosher v. Kane, 784 F. 2d 1385, 1389 n. 5 (9th Cir. 1986) (the "aborted purchaser seller doctrine"); Sulkow v. Crosstown Apparel, Inc., 807 F. 2d 33 (2d Cir. 1986) (stock was never issued); cf. Brooks v. Land Drilling Co., 564 F. Supp. 1518, 1523-24 (D. Colo. 1983) (court found a sale even though the two boards had agreed to rescind the merger agreement); Brennan v. EMDE Medical Research, Inc., 652 F. Supp. 255 (D. Nev. 1986) (preemptive rights are contracts to purchase, so that plaintiff who fails to exercise rights because of a violation of Rule 10b-5 has standing).

The person who is induced to *defer* selling is no better off, however, than the person who (as in *Blue Chip* itself) is induced not to buy. Gurley v. Documation, Inc., 674 F. 2d 253 (4th Cir. 1982); Baum v. Phillips, Appel & Walden, Inc., 648 F. Supp. 1518, 1525-1526 (S. D. N. Y. 1986).

[261] Superintendent of Ins. of the State of N. Y. v. Bankers Life & Casualty Co. 404 U. S. 6, 12 (1971); see also Birnbaum v. Newport Steel Corp., 193 F. 2d 461, 464 (2d Cir. 1952) (using the phrase, "*fraudulent* mismanagement").

[262] Herpich v. Wallace, 430 F. 2d 792, 808 (5th Cir. 1970); Schlick v. Penn-Dixie Cement Corp., 507 F. 2d 374, 380 (2d Cir. 1974).

[263] Ruckle v. Roto American Corp., 339 F. 2d 24 (2d Cir. 1964).

half the voting stock, but somehow had let control evade or escape him, brought a derivative action against his six fellow directors, who constituted the corporation's officers, alleging that they had sought to perpetuate their control, among other ways, by having the board approve the issuance of some 75,000 treasury shares that were to be resold to the president or voted as he directed. The plaintiff alleged that the defendants had withheld the latest financial statements from the board, had arbitrarily ascribed a $3 value to the shares, and had approved several transactions involving the stock without disclosing pertinent facts to the entire board. Reversing a dismissal, the Second Circuit held that it was possible under Rule 10b-5 for a corporation to be defrauded by a majority of its directors "or even the entire board."[264]

Only a few weeks later, in *O'Neill*,[265] the same court distinguished *Ruckle*. *O'Neill* was a derivative action by a National Airlines stockholder against all nine of the National directors and Pan American complaining that the two companies had eliminated their cross-ownership (as ordered by the Civil Aeronautics Board) at an unfavorable ratio that cost National $1 million on the basis of market prices. The plaintiff's theory was that the National directors had caused National to pay a premium in order to get rid of a Pan American threat to their control. The panel split. The two who sat in both cases, Judges Lumbard and Marshall, distinguished *Ruckle* because of the allegation there of the withholding of the company's most recent financial statement. Judge Hays, the only Judge who had *not* sat in *Ruckle*, dissented without opinion.

The next case, *Schoenbaum*,[266] culminated in a rehearing *en banc*. A derivative complaint on behalf of Banff Oil against all its directors and a company called Aquitaine alleged that Aquitaine, after winning control of Banff through a tender offer, had put three directors on its eight-person board, which had then caused Banff to sell stock to Aquitaine at a market price that did not reflect an oil strike on Banff's properties. The court denied the defendants' motion for summary judgment by a vote of seven to three. Judge Hays, for the majority, said simply that Aquitaine had "exercised a controlling

[264] To the effect that there is no conceptual difficulty in carrying through with the fiction that a corporation is a separate "person" that can be defrauded by a majority or even all of its directors, see also Condon v. Richardson, 411 F. 2d 489, 491-92 (7th Cir. 1969); Shell v. Hensley, 430 F. 2d 819 (5th Cir. 1970); Goldberg v. Meridor, 567 F. 2d 209, 215 (2d Cir. 1977), *cert. denied*, 434 U. S. 1069, infra pp. 805-07.

[265] O'Neill v. Maytag, 339 F. 2d 764 (2d Cir. 1964).

[266] Schoenbaum v. Firstbrook, 405 F. 2d 215 (2d Cir. *en banc* 1968), *cert. denied* sub nom. Manley v. Schoenbaum, 395 U. S. 906.

influence over the issuance to it of treasury shares of Banff for a wholly inadequate consideration," and that this violated the third clause of the rule — to which he added that "Aquitaine and the directors of Banff were guilty of deceiving the stockholders of Banff (other than Aquitaine)."[267] The opinion cited *Ruckle* but not *O'Neill*.

The case could be rationalized on the basis of the parent buyer's nondisclosure of the oil strike to "the corporation" as represented by the stockholders in the absence of a disinterested majority of directors.[268] And it was later so read.[269] On the other hand, since the majority opinion was *not* specifically analyzed in terms of failure to disclose the inadequate consideration, some commentators found in *Schoenbaum* a "new fraud" theory of Rule 10b-5: that inadequate (some said "grossly unfair") price coupled with controlling influence was enough to establish a violation regardless of disclosure.[270]

Usually there will be little if any difference in end result, whichever theory is followed; for to say that an insider may not buy from (or sell to) his company at an unfair price without disclosing the unfairness to an *independent* board (or, in the absence of an independent board, to the *stockholders*, typically by means of a proxy statement cleared by the SEC) is to say as a practical matter that he may not buy (or sell). In any event, the next Second Circuit case resulted in the demise of a doctrine that probably never was. The case got to the Supreme Court as *Santa Fe Industries, Inc.* v. *Green*.[271]

Santa Fe, which had acquired 95 percent of the stock of Kirby Lumber Corp., effected a "short-form merger" under Delaware law. The plaintiffs, instead of pursuing their statutory appraisal remedies in the Delaware Court of Chancery, sued in federal court under Rule 10b-5 to set aside the merger or recover what they

[267] 405 F. 2d at 219-20.

[268] See Pappas v. Moss, 393 F. 2d 865, 869 (3d Cir. 1968). Should the procedure of a stockholder vote be too clumsy, the answer — as in the case of the insider whose duty to the corporation requires him to remain silent with respect to facts that he would have to disclose under Rule 10b-5 if he bought or sold in the market (see p. 734 supra) — is that there is no compulsion on the directors to go through with the particular transaction. And, even if the interested directors own or can influence the holders of enough shares to obtain ratification regardless of disclosure, it still does not follow that disclosure is nugatory; for, apart from the fact that the very requirement of disclosure may counter directors' over-acquisitive instincts, it may prompt a derivative action or an injunction, which is in fact what was done in both *Ruckle* and *O'Neill* after the facts had come to light. See p. 807 infra.

[269] Popkin v. Bishop, 464 F. 2d 714 (2d Cir. 1972).

[270] See, e. g., Note, The Controlling Influence Standard in Rule 10b-5 Corporate Mismanagement Cases, 86 Harv. L. Rev. 1007 (1973).

[271] 430 U. S. 462 (1977).

claimed to be the fair value of their shares, which was $772 as contrasted with an allegedly "fraudulent appraisal" of $125 and a Santa Fe offer of $150.

A divided Court of Appeals held "that a complaint alleges a claim under Rule 10b-5 when it charges, in connection with a Delaware short-form merger, that the majority has committed a breach of its fiduciary duty to deal fairly with minority shareholders by effecting the merger without any justifiable business purpose."[272] Further: "Whether full disclosure has been made is not the crucial inquiry since it is the merger and the undervaluation which constituted the fraud, and not whether or not the majority determines to lay bare their real motives. If there is no valid corporate purpose for the merger, then even the most brazen disclosure of that fact to the minority shareholders in no way mitigates the fraudulent conduct."[273]

The Supreme Court reversed. Leaning heavily on the logic behind the Court's scienter holding in *Ernst & Ernst* v. *Hochfelder,*[274] Justice White stated for the majority (Justice Brennan dissenting):

> * * * the claim of fraud and fiduciary breach in this complaint states a cause of action under any part of Rule 10b-5 only if the conduct alleged can be fairly viewed as "manipulative or deceptive" within the meaning of the statute.
>
> * * *
>
> It is our judgment that the transaction, if carried out as alleged in the complaint, was neither deceptive nor manipulative and therefore did not violate either §10(b) of the Act or Rule 10b-5.
>
> As we have indicated, the case comes to us on the premise that the complaint failed to allege a material misrepresentation or material failure to disclose. * * *
>
> * * *
>
> It is also readily apparent that the conduct alleged in the complaint was not "manipulative" within the meaning of the statute. "Manipulation" is "virtually a term of art when used in connection with securities markets." *Ernst & Ernst,* 425 U. S., at 199. The term refers generally to practices, such as wash sales, matched or-

[272]Green v. Santa Fe Industries, Inc., 533 F. 2d 1283, 1289 (2d Cir. 1976).
[273]Id. at 1292.
[274]425 U. S. 185 (1976), supra p. 775.

ders, or rigged prices, that are intended to mislead investors by artificially affecting market activity. * * *

* * *

* * * Absent a clear indication of congressional intent, we are reluctant to federalize the substantial portion of the law of corporations that deals with transactions in securities, particularly where established state policies of corporate regulation would be overridden.[275]

The Supreme Court's reversal was no surprise — indeed, the Second Circuit denied a rehearing *en banc* because it was "confident" that a grant of *certiorari* was "inevitable"[276] — for this time the panel that sat dispelled "any lingering doubt" that in its view it was sufficient to allege that the "majority has committed a breach of its fiduciary duty to deal fairly with minority shareholders by effecting [a Delaware short-form] merger without any justifiable business purpose."[277] As Judge Moore remarked, this would "override and nullify" the short-form merger statutes of three-quarters of the states.[278] He might have gone further and said that the majority opinion came "very close to holding that the Delaware law is a device to defraud."[279] Oddly enough, the venerable Judge Medina, writing in his ninetieth year, did not mention his bitter "what is the world coming to?" dissent in *Schoenbaum,* in which he had viewed the majority opinion as "nothing short of a standing invitation to blackmail and extortion."[280]

In any event, the Supreme Court's decision was not the last word. Six months later a sharply divided panel of the Second Circuit concluded in *Goldberg* v. *Meridor*[281] that *Santa Fe* did not overrule

[275] See also Kademian v. Ladish Co., 792 F. 2d 614 (7th Cir. 1986); Loengard v. Santa Fe Industries, Inc., 639 F. Supp. 673 (S. D. N. Y. 1986) (N. Y. Gen. Bus. L. §352-c); Gochnauer v. A. G. Edwards & Sons, Inc., 810 F. 2d 1042 (11th Cir. 1987). Moreover, if a breach of a fiduciary duty by itself does not make out a federal claim, failure to perform an implied promise not to commit a breach of such a duty does not violate federal law; otherwise any fiduciary breach could be converted into a federal action by the simple allegation that the fiduciary had promised to perform his duties and then failed to do so. Pross v. Katz, 784 F. 2d 455, 457-58 (2d Cir. 1986). But cf. Luce v. Edelstein, 802 F. 2d 49 (2d Cir. 1986).

[276] Green v. Santa Fe Industries, Inc., 533 F. 2d 1309 (2d Cir. 1976).

[277] Id., at 1283, 1287, 1291.

[278] Id. at 1299.

[279] Dyer, An Essay on Federalism in Private Actions Under Rule 10b-5, [1976] Utah L. Rev. 7, 9.

[280] 405 F. 2d at 221.

[281] 567 F. 2d 209 (2d Cir. 1977).

Schoenbaum. A derivative action on behalf of UGO charged that its parent, Maritimecor, had caused it to issue shares to the parent for all its assets and liabilities in an unfair transaction and on the basis of nondisclosure or misleading disclosure of material facts that were known to all the directors. Judge Friendly stated for the majority:

> The problem with the application of §10(b) and Rule 10b-5 to derivative actions has lain in the degree to which the knowledge of officers and directors must be attributed to the corporation, thereby negating the element of deception. * * *
>
> * * * [There is no requirement that there be] one virtuous or ignorant lamb among the directors in order for liability to arise under §10(b) or Rule 10b-5 on a deception theory as to securities transactions with a controlling stockholder.
>
> * * *
>
> *Schoenbaum,* then, can rest solidly on the now widely recognized ground that there is deception of the corporation (in effect, of its minority shareholders) when the corporation is influenced by its controlling shareholder to engage in a transaction adverse to the corporation's interests (in effect, the minority shareholders' interests) and *there is nondisclosure or misleading disclosures as to the material facts of the transaction* (italics supplied). Assuming that, in light of the decision in *Green,* the existence of "controlling influence" and "wholly inadequate consideration" — an aspect of the *Schoenbaum* decision that perhaps attracted more attention, see 405 F. 2d at 219-20 — can no longer alone form the basis for Rule 10b-5 liability, we do not read *Green* as ruling that no action lies under Rule 10b-5 when a controlling corporation causes a partly owned subsidiary to sell its securities to the parent in a fraudulent transaction and fails to make a disclosure or, as can be alleged here, makes a misleading disclosure. * * *
>
> * * * The nub of the matter is that the conduct attacked in *Green* did not violate the " 'fundamental purpose' of the Act as implementing a 'philosophy of full disclosure,' " 430 U. S. at 478; the conduct here attacked does.
>
> Defendants contend that even if all this is true, the failure to make a public disclosure or even the making of a misleading disclosure would have no effect, since no action by stockholders to approve the UGO-Maritimecor transaction was required. * * *
>
> * * * When, as in a derivative action, the deception is alleged to have been practiced on the corporation, even though all the directors were parties to it, the test [of materiality] must be whether the facts that were not disclosed or were misleadingly disclosed to the shareholders "would have assumed actual significance in the

deliberations" of reasonable and disinterested directors or created "a substantial likelihood" that such directors would have considered the "total mix" of information available to have been "significantly altered." * * *

Beyond this Goldberg and other minority shareholders would not have been without remedy if the alleged facts had been disclosed. * * *

The availability of injunctive relief if the defendants had not lulled the minority stockholders of UGO into security by a deceptive disclosure, as they allegedly did, is in sharp contrast to *Green,* where the disclosure following the merger transaction was full and fair, and, as to the pre-merger period, respondents accepted "the conclusion of both courts below that under Delaware law they could not have enjoined the merger because an appraisal proceeding is their sole remedy in the Delaware courts for any alleged unfairness in the terms of the merger," fn. 14. * * *

(1) The appellate courts have read *Goldberg* as requiring more than mere nondisclosure of impure motive or culpability.[282]

(2) The *Goldberg* case has attracted a following.[283] But there is disagreement whether its reference to the "availability of injunctive relief if the defendants had not lulled the minority stockholders of UGO into security by a deceptive disclosure"[284] requires proof that an action for injunction under state law would have been won,[285] or merely that such an action was "available" and that the facts shown make out a *prima facie* case for relief,[286] or that there was a "reasonable probability" of success.[287] The first and third of those views require a trial within a trial.

[282] Alabama Farm Bureau Mutual Casualty Co., Inc. v. American Fidelity Life Ins. Co., 606 F. 2d 602, 610 (5th Cir. 1979); Panter v. Marshall Field & Co., 646 F. 2d 271, 291 (7th Cir. 1981); Atchley v. Qonaar Corp., 704 F. 2d 355, 358 (7th Cir. 1983).

[283] In addition to the cases about to be cited, see Kas v. Financial General Bankshares, Inc., 796 F. 2d 508 (D. C. Cir. 1986).

[284] 567 F. 2d at 220.

[285] Kidwell *ex rel.* Penfold v. Merkle, 597 F. 2d 1273, 1294 (9th Cir. 1979); Madison Consultants v. Federal Deposit Ins. Corp., 710 F. 2d 57 (2d Cir. 1983); Mayer v. Oil Field Systems Corp., 721 F. 2d 59, 67 (2d Cir. 1983), citing the text. The Ninth Circuit also thought that the proper inquiry on the materiality question was what would have been considered significant by a reasonable shareholder, not by a reasonable director as stated in *Goldberg.* 597 F. 2d at 1293 n. 10.

[286] Alabama Farm Bureau Mutual Casualty Co., Inc. v. American Fidelity Life Ins. Co., 606 F. 2d 602, 614 (5th Cir. 1979).

[287] Healey v. Catalyst Recovery of Pa., Inc., 616 F. 2d 641, 648 (3d Cir. 1980). In Lockspeiser v. Western Md. Co., 768 F. 2d 558 (4th Cir. 1985), the court stated: "Considering materiality in terms of the availability of injunctive relief is not the exclusive way to test the materiality of omissions from proxy

(3) The Seventh Circuit seems to have brought fairness back in (with the burden of going forward on the defendant) as a limitation on the *Goldberg* rule when there *is* nondisclosure.[288]

(4) *Goldberg* does produce an anomaly with its rationale that a state law remedy for breach of fiduciary duty, far from foreclosing a 10b-5 action, is precisely the foundation for a theory of deception in that inadequate disclosure lulls stockholders into foregoing their state law remedies. As Judge Aldisert put it in a dissenting opinion, "Thus, rather than aiding plaintiffs under federal law who have no state remedy, the majority's formulation provides federal relief to plaintiffs who have state remedies, but denies federal relief to plaintiffs who have no state remedy!"[289]

(5) We have already observed that Rule 10b-5 may be violated through nonverbal acts by reference to the first and third clauses, which in some respects are broader than the second.[290] Although the Code endorses *Santa Fe,* its commentary does say that "it may be assumed that there is a grey area in which 'unfairness' if gross enough may merge into 'fraud.' "[291]

---

materials involving a squeeze merger." On these several approaches, see Comment, Causation in Rule 10b-5 Actions for Corporate Mismanagement, 48 U. Chi. L. Rev. 936 (1981).

[288] Wright v. Heizer Corp., 560 F. 2d 236, 255-56 (7th Cir. 1977). For another limitation on *Goldberg,* see Abbey v. Control Data Corp., 603 F. 2d 724, 731 (8th Cir. 1979), where the court, citing *Santa Fe,* stated: "Illegal foreign payments clearly involve state law questions of breach of fiduciary duties. They should not be dealt with under the general disclosure provisions of the federal securities laws where it is apparent, as here, that the nondisclosure of such payments had little, if any, impact on the plaintiffs dealings in the corporation's stock."

[289] Healey v. Catalyst Recovery of Pa., Inc., 616 F. 2d 641, 658 (3d Cir. 1980). Arthur Borden of the New York Bar has coined the phrase "sue fact doctrine" to describe the group of cases stemming from *Goldberg,* a doctrine that he calls "judicial casuistry": "The 'sue fact' doctrine holds that Rule 10b-5 requires the disclosure not only of information relevant to an *investment decision* but also information relevant to a *decision to sue* under state law, whenever such law provides a remedy to the shareholder. * * * A 'sue fact' is, in general, a fact which is material to a sue decision. A 'sue decision' is a decision by a shareholder whether or not to institute a representative or derivative suit alleging a state-law cause of action." Borden, "Sue Fact" Rule Mandates Disclosure to Avoid Litigation in State Courts, in H. Schlagman and N. Hirsch (eds.), SEC '82 (L. J. Seminars-Press 1982) 201, 204, 206; see also Gelb, Rule 10b-5 and *Santa Fe* — Herein of Sue Facts, Shame Facts, and Other Matters, 87 W. Va. L. Rev. 189 (1984-85).

[290] See pp. 786-87 supra.

[291] 2 Code 662. For an essay concluding that "*Santa Fe's* distinction between fraud (including 'constructive fraud' concepts) and fiduciary duty is, as a practical matter, untenable," see Langevoort, Fraud and Deception by Securities Professionals, 61 Tex. L. Rev. 1247, 1248 (1983). The difficulty, the author of that essay suggests, is that labeling the misconduct as fraud or breach of fiduciary duty is of little consequence so far as the common law is concerned, because for

(6) The *Santa Fe* limitation has been applied to §14(e) and Rule 14a-9 (with respect to tender offers and proxy solicitations) because of their similarity of purpose to Rule 10b-5.[292]

(7) Urged on perhaps by Professor Cary's "race to the bottom" criticism of the Delaware Supreme Court,[293] that court and other state courts have reacted to *Santa Fe*'s reminder that questions of fairness, business purpose, and breach of fiduciary duty in "squeeze-out" mergers are matters of state law.[294]

9. Relation to §16(b)

Query: Since both §16(b) and Rule 10b-5 apply to trading by corporate insiders, does either have to yield to the other because of the possibility of double liability? Suppose, for example, that an insider purchases a listed equity security without disclosing secret information and sells within six months at a handsome profit. Is he liable both to the seller under Rule 10b-5 (or by way of common law deceit) and to the corporation under §16(b)? The question has not arisen. But it would seem strange if the seller's rights could be cut off at any time within six months by a second transaction with which he had nothing to do — a transaction effected by the very party responsible for his loss.[295] Indeed, if it was a sale-purchase sequence, or a purchase-sale sequence in which the insider did not

---

most purposes a common law court need not distinguish the two doctrines. Id. at 1252.

[292]Golub v. PPD Corp., 576 F. 2d 759 (8th Cir. 1978); see also In re Sunshine Mining Co. Securities Litigation, 496 F. Supp. 9, 11 (S. D. N. Y. 1979). See Schreiber v. Burlington Northern, Inc., 472 U. S. 1 (1985), supra p. 529. The *Santa Fe* limitation has been applied also to §§12(2) and 17(a) of the 1933 Act. Doll v. James Martin Associates (Holdings), Ltd., 600 F. Supp. 510, 526 (E. D. Mich. 1984).

[293]Cary, Federalism and Corporate Law: Reflections upon Delaware, 83 Yale L. J. 663 (1974).

[294]Singer v. Magnavox Co., 380 A. 2d 969 (Del. 1977); see also Bryan v. Brock & Blevins Co., Inc., 490 F. 2d 563 (5th Cir. 1974) (Georgia law); Perl v. IU Int'l Corp., 61 Hawaii 622, 639-40, 607 P. 2d 1036, 1046 (1980); Berkowitz v. Power/Mate Corp., 135 N. J. Super. 36, 342 A. 2d 566 (1975). For a summary of later Delaware cases, see Nathan and Sternberg, State Law Implications in Going Private Transactions, 2 Legal Notes & Viewpoints, No. 2, p. 31 (1982). In Weinberger v. UOP, Inc., 457 A. 2d 701 (Del. 1983), the Delaware Supreme Court abandoned the business purpose test. See generally Steinberg and Londahl, The New Law of Squeeze-Out Mergers, 621 Wash. U. L. Q. 351 (1984).

[295]Cf. Schur v. Salzman, 50 A. D. 2d 781, 377 N. Y. S. 2d 82 (1st Dept. 1975), where a §16(b) payment was credited against damages in a later derivative action against the same defendant for profits resulting from his sell-out in breach of his fiduciary duty.

sell *all* his stock, the insider buyer who had violated 10b-5 would in effect get a rebate on his purchase price by sharing indirectly as a stockholder in the recovery pursuant to §16(b).

The insider who had paid the seller first, by way of judgment or settlement, might be in a better position to defend against a §16(b) action on the ground that the payment had destroyed his profit.[296] On the other hand, it might be argued that there is no reason to read the word "profit" in §16(b) to mean net after deduction of losses in a lawsuit, since this would, in effect, confine §16(b) to *innocent* transactions.[297] There is no absolute rule of law precluding double liability. In *Diamond* v. *Oreamuno,* the common law action that has been considered in connection with our examination of §16(b), the New York Court of Appeals was not "deterred, in formulating a State remedy, by the defendants' claim of possible double liability."[298] Indeed, if an insider tried hard enough to put his neck in a noose, one could conjure up the horror of *treble* liability: (1) to his company under §16(b), (2) to his sellers for misrepresentation or nondisclosure having a "bearish" effect, and (3) to his *buyers* for misrepresentation (or nondisclosure if he was under a duty to disclose) having a "bullish" effect.

C. BROKERS, DEALERS, AND INVESTMENT ADVISERS

Section 17(a) of the 1933 Act, Rule 10b-5, and §9(a)(4) of the 1934 Act, as well as the proxy and tender offer fraud provisions (Rule 14a-9 and §14(e)), apply to broker-dealers along with everybody else.[1] But over-the-counter brokers-dealers, as we have al-

[296] *Query* whether this approach might be carried so far as to give the insider an action to recover what he had paid the company under §16(b) to the extent of what he later paid the seller or buyer. *Query* also whether, if the company should make such a repayment voluntarily, another action would lie under §16(b), or perhaps a derivative action against the directors generally for waste of corporate assets.

[297] Baumel v. Rosen, 283 F. Supp. 128, 145 (D. Md. 1968), *aff'd in part and rev'd in part on other grounds,* 412 F. 2d 571 (4th Cir. 1969), *cert. denied,* 396 U. S. 1039.

[298] 24 N. Y. 2d 494, 504, 248 N. E. 2d 910, 915 (1969), supra p. 582; cf. McCandless v. Furlaud, 296 U. S. 140, 167 (1935). The interpleader suggestion made in *Diamond* presents jurisdictional problems.

C. 9C [1] Recently, indeed, an appellate court, in holding that a broker-dealer-employed analyst who was both tippee and tipper had violated Rule 10b-5 as aider and abettor of *his* tippees' trading, stated that the analyst had obligations to the SEC and the public "completely independent" of any acquired under the

ready noticed, are subject *in addition* to §15(c)(1) and (2) of the 1934 Act and a batch of rules under those provisions.[2] Moreover, a number of special fraud concepts have been developed in connection with brokers and dealers.

1. THE "SHINGLE" THEORY

In 1939 the Commission held for the first time, in the course of an administrative proceeding against a broker-dealer, that it was a fraud under §17(a) of the 1933 Act and Rule 15c1-2[3] for a dealer to sell securities to a customer without disclosing that the price bore no relation to the current market.[4] After a series of such cases,[5] one, *Charles Hughes & Co., Inc.* v. *SEC,* got to the Second Circuit by way of judicial review of a revocation order.[6] As Judge Charles E. Clark related the facts:

> The customers were almost entirely single women or widows who knew little or nothing about securities or the devices of Wall Street. * * * [Two employees of the firm] worked their way so completely into [one Mrs. Furbeck's] confidence that she virtually placed complete control of her securities portfolio in their hands. Every few days one or the other would have another "marvelous" buy — one that was definitely "beyond the usual" — and she would add it to her collection, selling a more reputable security in order to finance the transaction.

10b-5 doctrine with respect to tipping, because the 1934 Act subjects registered broker-dealers and their associates "to myriad duties not imposed on corporate officers or other members of the general public." Dirks v. SEC, 681 F. 2d 824, 840 (D. C. Cir. 1982), *rev'd on other grounds,* 463 U. S. 646 (1983), the Court expressly stating that it was not passing on this "novel theory," id. at 657 n. 16.

[2] See pp. 703-08 supra. Although those provisions are limited to brokers and dealers, presumably an employee or other person may violate them as an accessory and hence become a principal under the federal aider and abettor statute. 18 U. S. C. §2. Apparently there have been no criminal prosecutions against persons other than brokers or dealers under §15(c)(1); for it is simpler to rely on Rule 10b-5 on the purchase side and §17(a) on the sale side. But the Commission has found officers and salesmen guilty of violating §15(c)(1) in administrative proceedings. E. g., Richard K. Fudge, 30 SEC 334, 338 n. 11 (1949); Naftalin & Co., Inc., 41 SEC 823, 832 (1964). It has also used the aider and abettor statute as a basis for injunction. E. g., SEC v. Barraco, 438 F. 2d 97 (10th Cir. 1971). But cf. Gilbert v. Bagley, 492 F. Supp. 714, 732 (M. D. N. C. 1980) (private action). These administrative and injunctive practices of the Commission were codified in 1960 with respect to the Advisers Act. §§203(e)(5), 209(e).

[3] See p. 704 supra. Rule 10b-5 was not yet a gleam in the eye.

[4] Duker & Duker, 6 SEC 386 (1939).

[5] See 10 SEC Ann. Rep. 74 n. 56 (1944).

[6] 139 F. 2d 434 (2d Cir. 1943), *cert. denied,* 321 U. S. 786.

> The prices which Mrs. Furbeck and other customers paid for the securities purchased in this manner ranged from 16.1 to 40.9 per cent over market value. In addition, most of the transactions involved little or no risk for petitioner, because an order was usually confirmed before it bought the securities that it was selling. * * * It is unchallenged * * * that at no time did either Stillman or Armstrong reveal the true market price of any security to Mrs. Furbeck or the fact that petitioner's profits averaged around twenty-five per cent. * * *

The legal analysis that followed, far from indicating concern over a substantial extension of common law fraud concepts, displayed judicial indignation:

> There is evidence in the record to show a threefold violation of §17(a) of the Securities Act, *viz.*, the obtaining of money "by means of any untrue statement of a material fact"; the "omission to state a material fact" necessary to make statements actually made not misleading; and the engaging in a course of business which operates "as a fraud or deceit upon the purchaser." It is true that the only specific evidence of false statements of a material fact is that of Mrs. Furbeck that the sales price was under the market price, and, as we have noted, these statements were denied by the salesmen. Although the Commission has neglected to make any finding of fact on this point, we need not remand for a specific finding resolving this conflict, for we feel that petitioner's mark-up policy operated as a fraud and deceit upon the purchasers, as well as constituting an omission to state a material fact.
>
> An over-the-counter firm which actively solicits customers and then sells them securities at prices as far above the market as were those which petitioner charged here must be deemed to commit a fraud. It holds itself out as competent to advise in the premises, and it should disclose the market price if sales are to be made substantially above that level. Even considering petitioner as a principal in a simple vendor-purchaser transaction (and there is doubt whether, in several instances at least, petitioner was actually not acting as broker-agent for the purchasers, in which case all undisclosed profits would be forfeited), it was still under a special duty, in view of its expert knowledge and proffered advice, not to take advantage of its customers' ignorance of market conditions. The key to the success of all of petitioner's dealings was the confidence in itself which it managed to instill in the customers. Once that confidence was established, the failure to reveal the mark-up pocketed by the firm was both an omission to state a material fact and a fraudulent device. When nothing was said about market price, the natural implication in the untutored minds of the purchasers was that the price asked was close to the market. The law of fraud knows no difference

between express representation on the one hand and implied misrepresentation or concealment on the other. *Strong* v. *Repide*, 213 U. S. 419, 430;[7] *United States* v. *Brown*, 2 Cir., 79 F. 2d 321, *certiorari denied* 296 U. S. 650. "The best element of business has long since decided that honesty should govern competitive enterprises, and that the rule of caveat emptor should not be relied upon to reward fraud and deception." *Federal Trade Commission* v. *Standard Education Society*, 302 U. S. 112, 116.

We need not stop to decide, however, how far common-law fraud was shown. For the business of selling investment securities has been considered one peculiarly in need of regulation for the protection of the investor. "The business of trading in securities is one in which opportunities for dishonesty are of constant recurrence and ever present. It engages acute, active minds, trained to quick apprehension, decision and action." *Archer* v. *Securities and Exchange Commission*, 8 Cir., 133 F. 2d 795, 803, *certiorari denied* 319 U. S. 767. * * * Had we been in doubt on the matter we should have given weight to these rulings as a consistent and contemporaneous construction of a statute by an administrative body. * * * But we are not content to rest on so colorless an interpretation of this important legislation.

The essential objective of securities legislation is to protect those who do not know market conditions from the overreachings of those who do. Such protection will mean little if it stops short of the point of ultimate consequence, namely, the price charged for the securities. Indeed, it is the purpose of all legislation for the prevention of fraud in the sale of securities to preclude the sale of "securities which are in fact worthless, or worth substantially less than the asking price." *People* v. *Federated Radio Corp.*, 244 N. Y. 33, 40, 154 N. E. 655, 658.[8] If after several years of experience under this highly publicized legislation we should find that the public cannot rely upon a commission-licensed broker not to charge unsuspecting investors 25 per cent more than a market price easily ascertainable by insiders, we should leave such legislation little more than a snare and a delusion. We think the Commission has correctly interpreted its responsibilities to stop such abusive practices in the sale of securities.

This has nothing to do with any agency obligation. The theory is that even a dealer at arm's length impliedly represents when he hangs out his shingle that he will deal fairly with the public. It is an element of that implied representation, the theory goes, that his prices will bear some reasonable relation to the current market unless he discloses to the contrary. Therefore, charging a price that

[7] See p. 724 supra.
[8] See p. 16 supra.

does not bear such a relation is a breach of the dealer's implied representation and works a fraud on the customer. Just as the doctrine is not an aspect of agency or brokerage law, it has nothing to do with limiting the amount of the dealer's profit — except, of course, when his own purchase is substantially contemporaneous with his sale. If a dealer buys a security at $10 and holds onto it until the market hits $20, he is perfectly free to take his profit of 100 percent and a bit more. Conversely, if he buys a security at $10 and is unlucky enough to stay with it until the market falls to $5, it is fraudulent for him without disclosure to sell it at a price not reasonably related to the current market of $5 notwithstanding that he will suffer a loss.

Of course, just as the "abstain or disclose" principle under Rule 10b-5 normally means "abstain," so here. For who will trade with a dealer that states he will charge (or pay) a price that is unreasonable in relation to current market? Furthermore, the theory suffers more than a little from question-begging. If I am allowed to state the major premise of my syllogism, I shall march inexorably to the conclusion I want. And Judge Clark got carried away a bit when he stated in a later case that the broker-dealer "implicitly *warrants* the soundness of statements of stock value."[9] For the theory clearly does not extend to non-negligent errors of fact, much less of analysis or opinion. Quite the contrary, the scienter requirement of Rule 10b-5 presumably extends to the shingle theory whether the plaintiff relies on that rule or on Rule 15c1-2.[10]

By now — one may add "happily" — the shingle theory not only is unchallenged but has been considerably refined.

Thus, the Commission has made it clear that a violation exists when unreasonable prices are charged in individual transactions; that in computing mark-ups on sales to customers the dealer may not deduct self-imposed losses sustained in purchases from them as part of the scheme to induce the switching of securities and maintain customers' confidence; and that a dealer may not "avoid the onus which attaches to the practice of gouging customers in individual transactions by pointing to the over-all percentage of profits he has extracted."[11] Nor is a violation precluded by the existence of large

[9] Kahn v. SEC, 297 F. 2d 112, 115 (2d Cir. 1961) (concurring opinion, italics supplied); see also SEC v. N. A. R. & D. Corp., 424 F. 2d 63, 84 (2d Cir. 1970).

[10] See pp. 703-04 supra.

[11] Trost & Co., Inc., 12 SEC 531, 535 (1942); Maryland Securities Co., Inc., 41 SEC 836, 838 (1964) (NASD case). Because many of the Commission's opinions by way of review of NASD disciplinary orders for violation of the NASD's own philosophy on reasonable spreads (infra pp. 819-20) are equally appropriate

selling expenses[12] or the fact that the customer's financial position was improved.[13] Not surprisingly, the Commission has applied the same approach in the slightly different context of failure to disclose lower market transactions when affecting a *distribution* of securities, whether under a Securities Act registration statement[14] or under a prospectus for an unregistered offering.[15]

Moreover, the potentialities of the "shingle" theory are not necessarily exhausted by using it as a basis for an implied representation of pricing reasonably related to the market. Since a dealer impliedly

---

in the present context, some of those cases will be cited here with a "cf." and the distinguishing signal, "NASD case."

[12]Morris Luster, 36 SEC 298, 300 (1955).

[13]E. H. Rollins & Sons, Inc., 18 SEC 347, 371 (1945). One can go on: Evidence of sales by other dealers at comparable prices is not a defense; at most it creates a conflict in the evidence. Associated Securities Corp. v. SEC, 293 F. 2d 738, 741 (10th Cir. 1961). It is no defense that in sales to employees of the issuer the price was specified by them. Wesco & Co., 43 SEC 8, 9 n. 3 (1966) (NASD case). Nor is it a defense that a sale is short, with whatever risk that entails. Investment Service Co., 41 SEC 188, 196 (1962), *aff'd* sub nom. Barnett v. United States, 319 F. 2d 340 (8th Cir. 1963). Mark-ups on government and municipal securities, like those on corporate debt securities, are usually smaller than those on equities. Sec. Ex. Act Rel. 24,368, 38 SEC Dock. 158, 160 (1987). And the established mark-up rules and policies of the Commission, the NASD, and the Municipal Securities Rulemaking Board apply fully to transactions in zero-coupon securities (debt securities that do not pay interest before maturity and are sold, therefore, at a substantial discount). Id. at 158.

[14]Cristina Copper Mines, Inc., 33 SEC 397, 401-02 (1952). This was a stop-order opinion under the 1933 Act, so that it did not even involve a broker-dealer respondent.

[15]Indiana State Securities Corp., 38 SEC 118 (1957). An underwriter impliedly represents "that he has met the standards of his profession in his investigation of the issuer." Sanders v. John Nuveen & Co., Inc., 524 F. 2d 1064, 1070 (7th Cir. 1975). So, too, a dealer who recommends the purchase of mutual fund shares violates the fraud provisions if he fails to disclose that substantial savings in sales load would be available through the purchase of additional shares or the combination of purchases to equal or exceed the break-point amount. Russell L. Irish, 42 SEC 735, 740-42 (1965), *aff'd* sub nom. Irish v. SEC, 367 F. 2d 637 (9th Cir. 1966), *cert. denied*, 386 U. S. 911. And cf. United States v. Bronson, 145 F. 2d 939 (2d Cir. 1944), where the court confirmed the conviction of a mining promoter under §17(a) and the mail fraud statute for distributing treasury stock on the market without disclosing that the price exceeded the net return to the corporate treasury plus a fair commission.

Rule 10b-10(a)(8)(i), the confirmation rule (see p. 704 n. 20 supra), which requires disclosure of any mark-up or mark-down in certain "riskless" transactions (see p. 820 n. 36 infra) in an equity security by a non-marketmaker, does not act as a "safe harbor" against more complete disclosure under the fraud provisions generally. Krome v. Merrill Lynch & Co., Inc., 637 F. Supp. 910, 915-16 (S. D. N. Y. 1986). Vacated in part on other grounds, 110 F. R. D. 693 (S. D. N. Y. 1986).

represents that he will execute only authorized transactions on behalf of customers, the effecting of unauthorized transactions violates the fraud provisions.[16] Since trade custom requires a dealer to consummate transactions with customers promptly unless there is a clear understanding or indication to the contrary, it is a fraud to fail to disclose to customers whose orders and payments are accepted that the dealer has no intention of filling their orders promptly but intends to use their funds in his other business activities.[17] Since a selling dealer impliedly represents that the buyer will have clear title to securities he buys for cash, it is fraudulent not to state that the securities were pledged without authority from the customer.[18] Since a dealer impliedly represents that he is able to meet his obligations as they mature, it is fraudulent for him to accept customers' funds or securities while insolvent; on this basis the Commission almost routinely shuts down broker-dealers that are discovered (usually through a routine inspection) to be insolvent or undercapitalized[19] by moving for a preliminary injunction (sometimes an *ex parte* restraining order) under the fraud provisions and asking the court to appoint a receiver by way of ancillary relief.[20] It is likewise an incident of the representation of fair dealing that the dealer will disclose any substantial long or short position or

[16] First Anchorage Corp., 34 SEC 299 (1952).

[17] Ned J. Bowman Co., 39 SEC 879, 883 (1960); DeMarco v. Edens, 390 F. 2d 836, 840 (2d Cir. 1968) (§12(2) judgment on ground of underwriter's failure to disclose that it would neither remit proceeds to issuer nor deliver stock to plaintiffs); cf. Investment Service Co., 41 SEC 188, 197-98 (1962), *aff'd* sub nom. Barnett v. United States, 319 F. 2d 340, 344-45 (8th Cir. 1963). It is a fraud to accept an order to sell "at the earliest possible date" and to fail to execute it with due diligence, other sales having been effected at a higher price after receipt of the first order). Sec. Ex. Act Rel. 8363 (1968).

[18] Richard A. Sebastian, 38 SEC 865, 868-69 (1959).

[19] See Rule 15c3-1, supra p. 638.

[20] E. g., SEC v. Alan F. Hughes, Inc., 461 F. 2d 974, 981-83 (2d Cir. 1972); Tcherepnin v. Franz, 485 F. 2d 1251, 1256 (7th Cir. 1973), *cert. denied* sub nom. McGurren v. Ittelson, 415 U. S. 918; SEC v. Bartlett, 422 F. 2d 475 (8th Cir. 1970); SEC v. Investors Security Corp., 560 F. 2d 561, 567 (3d Cir. 1977); SEC v. Wencke, 577 F. 2d 619, 623 (9th Cir. 1978), *cert. denied,* 439 U. S. 964. In SEC v. Heritage Trust Co., 402 F. Supp. 744 (D. Ariz. 1975), the court at first denied a receivership, whereupon the company issued a newsletter stating: "GOOD NEWS — WE WON — WE BEAT THE S. E. C. ! ! * * * ." Thereupon, on renewal of the motion, the court found that "The purpose and content of that newsletter was a blatant attempt to mislead defendants' investors," and appointed a receiver. Id. at 753. On the breadth of such a receiver's authority, see SEC v. Hardy, 803 F. 2d 1034 (9th Cir. 1986).

Since the Securities Investor Protection Act of 1970 (supra p. 38) it has been the Commission's practice to move for appointment of a temporary receiver until the SIPC applies for appointment of a liquidating trustee. E. g., SEC v. Baron & Co., Inc., Litig. Rel. 5250 (D. N. J. 1971).

other bias that may affect his recommendations.[21] And an oil royalty dealer impliedly represents that his selling price is reasonably related not only to the current wholesale price — as is true of dealers in securities generally — but also to reasonable estimates of the oil recoverable from the tract underlying the royalty interest.[22]

Notwithstanding all this, it does not detract from the landmark character of the *Hughes* opinion to say that it does not answer all the questions posed by the "shingle" theory:

First: Although the court considered the Hughes firm "as a principal in a simple vendor-purchaser transaction," it referred to its "special duty, in view of its expert knowledge and proffered advice, not to take advantage of its customers' ignorance of market conditions."[23] In most of the cases there has been some similar element of advice and of disparity in the degree of knowledge of market conditions possessed by dealer and customer. But the Commission has indicated "that the fundamental principle underlying these cases is that any person, regardless of his knowledge of the matter or his access to market information, is entitled to rely on the implied representation, made by a registered dealer in securities, that customers will be treated fairly."[24] And it would seem that the doctrine should likewise apply regardless of the amount of solicitation or advice on the part of the dealer. For the doctrine is founded on the supreme importance of market value in the purchase and sale

[21] See p. 825 infra. In Chasins v. Smith, Barney & Co., 438 F. 2d 1167 (2d Cir. 1970), the court, without specific mention of the shingle theory, held that a dealer's failure to disclose a conflict resulting from his status as a marketmaker had violated Rule 10b-5. Although the opinion was rewritten to tie it down to the circumstances of the case, the Supreme Court in Affiliated Ute Citizens of Utah v. United States, 406 U. S. 128, 153 (1972), held, without express qualification, that the first and third clauses of Rule 10b-5 required marketmakers' status to be disclosed in connection with "sales their activities produced." Disclosure of marketmaker status by a broker-dealer acting for his own account with respect to an equity security is now required by the confirmation rule. Rule 10b-10(a)(8)(ii).

So long as a broker adequately discloses its status to its customer, however, it is not a fraudulent practice for the firm to sell securities to its customers as principal while it is acting as a marketmaker. Pross v. Baird Patrick & Co., Inc., 585 F. Supp. 1456 (S. D. N. Y. 1984), and cases cited. Cf. Shivangi v. Dean Witter Reynolds, Inc., 107 F. R. D. 313 (S. D. Miss. 1985) (failure to disclose account executive's extra compensation in marketmaking principal trades above normal agency commission).

[22] SEC v. LeDone, Litig. Rel. 394 (S. D. N. Y. 1947) (consent injunction); but cf. United States v. Grayson, 166 F. 2d 863 (2d Cir. 1948) (difficulties of proof); Klein v. SEC, 224 F. 2d 861 (2d Cir. 1955) (*inter alia,* NASD's failure to object to 50 percent mark-ups after an earlier inspection created an interpretation on which the firm reasonably relied).

[23] 139 F. 2d at 437.

[24] United Securities Corp., 15 SEC 719, 727 (1944).

of securities — intangibles that have no intrinsic use value.[25] The doctrine thus has an affinity to the holdings that it is a fraud for a dealer to sell without disclosing that he has manipulated the market or otherwise dominated it.[26]

Second: How does one ascertain the market that is so important in the pricing of transactions when there are no published quotations? The *Hughes* case, where quotations *were* available, looked also to the dealer's own substantially contemporaneous cost. And gradually, as the concept of substantially contemporaneous cost has been refined, it has come to be preferred even when current, independent asked prices are available.[27] Of course, if there is no market and the dealer has held the security for some time before selling it, there is nothing for the *Hughes* doctrine to operate on. But over-the-counter dealers normally do not carry any substantial inventory, whether for lack of capital or to avoid risk. Typically the dealer buys a security for his own account only after he has obtained an order from a customer.

Third: It is customary for dealers in the over-the-counter market

[25] The Supreme Court has referred to securities as "the equivalent of money." Geddes v. Anaconda Copper Mining Co., 254 U. S. 590, 598 (1921). Indeed, intrinsic or other value will be generally considered in the case of securities only when there is no market value. Cf. Virginia v. West Virginia, 238 U. S. 202, 212-13 (1915) (establishing value in deceit action).

[26] On manipulation, see c. 9D infra. On market domination, see Norris & Hirshberg, Inc., 21 SEC 865, 874-82 (1946), *aff'd* sub nom. Norris & Hirshberg, Inc. v. SEC, 177 F. 2d 228 (D. C. Cir. 1949); Jack W. Pagel, Sec. Ex. Act Rel. 22,280, 33 SEC Dock. 1003 (1985), *aff'd* sub nom. Pagel, Inc. v. SEC, 803 F. 2d 942 (8th Cir. 1986) (abuse of underwriter's power to dominate the market by controlling wholesale pricing to such an extent as to preclude an independent, competitive market from arising is manipulation). Cf. the cases, supra p. 817 n. 21, on disclosure of "marketmaker" status under certain circumstances.

[27] Managed Investment Programs, 37 SEC 783, 786 (1957) (NASD case); J. A. Winston & Co., 42 SEC 62, 68-69 (1964). This will not work, however, in the case of a marketmaker. For a marketmaker typically buys from other dealers at or around its bid and sells to other dealers at or around its offering price, so that using its cost as a basis for computing mark-ups might compel it to charge retail prices that are less than its wholesale offering prices, and that would impair market liquidity by deterring marketmakers from taking the risk of maintaining a market. Normally, therefore, a marketmaker's mark-ups are computed on the basis of its actual contemporaneous sales to other dealers or its contemporaneous offering prices. On the other hand, when the marketmaker dominates the market, using its own offering prices would give it unrestricted latitude; and so in that situation the Commission uses either (1) contemporaneous prices charged by that or other marketmakers in actual sales to other dealers or (2) contemporaneous and representative asked quotations of other marketmakers. Peter J. Kisch, Sec. Ex. Act Rel. 19,005, 25 SEC Dock. 1242, 1246-47 (1982); Alstead, Dempsey & Co., Inc., Sec. Ex. Act Rel. 20,825, 30 SEC Dock. 208 (1984). The use of *quotations* is "problematic" in the case of obscure securities with limited interdealer trading activity, because "They often show wide spreads between the bid and asked prices and are likely to be subject to negotiation." Id. at 210.

to take lower spreads on the purchase side than they do on the sale side. Indeed, in shifting a customer from one security into another they frequently act as agent in disposing of the old security for the customer and as principal in selling him the new. Nevertheless, if a dealer should *purchase* a security from a customer at a price not reasonably related to the current market (or, in the absence of a market, at a price not reasonably related to the price received by the dealer on substantially contemporaneous resale), his failure to disclose that fact would clearly violate the *Hughes* doctrine.[28]

Fourth: This leaves the most critical question of all — precisely what spread is reasonable in relation to whatever base is used. The Commission has carefully refrained from fixing any arbitrary standards, presumably for fear that the maximum spread would tend to become the minimum in all cases. It is necessary to consider the entire business conduct of a particular firm rather than one or a half-dozen isolated transactions or even (as we have seen) the *average* mark-up.[29] Percentages are particularly unreliable when the gross dollar amount of a particular transaction is relatively small. Nevertheless, the mark-up may be excessive even with securities selling at very low unit prices.[30] And, despite the uncertainty, the Commission's application of the *Hughes* doctrine has apparently eliminated the more shocking mark-ups.

In this endeavor the Commission's work has been supplemented by the NASD in what is a good example of the alliance of law and ethics that it was the purpose of §15A to encourage. The NASD has always had a rule to the effect that a member trading as principal with a customer "shall buy or sell at a price which is fair, taking into consideration all relevant circumstances, including market conditions with respect to [the] security at the time of the transaction, the expense involved, and the fact that he is entitled to a profit."[31] In a 1943 survey the Association found that 47 percent of its members' over-the-counter transactions had been effected at a gross spread over the current market of not more than 3 percent and 71 percent of the transactions at a gross spread of not more than 5 percent.[32] As a result, the Board of Governors adopted an interpretation of its basic rule against unethical conduct:

[28] Associated Securities Corp., 40 SEC 10, 14-17 (1960), *stay denied* sub nom. Associated Securities Corp. v. SEC, 283 F. 2d 773 (10th Cir. 1960).

[29] See pp. 814-15 supra.

[30] J. A. Winston & Co., Inc., 42 SEC 62, 69 (1964).

[31] NASD Rules of Fair Practice, Art. III, §4, CCH NASD Manual ¶2154.

[32] The trend since has been steadily downward.

> It shall be deemed conduct inconsistent with just and equitable principles of trade for a member to enter into any transaction with a customer in any security at any price not reasonably related to the current market price of the security.[33]

This is in substance the *Hughes* doctrine, except that it is stated without reference to disclosure. Disclosure will not always obviate a violation of rules of ethics. Nevertheless, the Commission has held, the degree of disclosure made must be considered along with all other pertinent circumstances in judging the reasonableness of the mark-ups and the ethics of the transactions.[34] In short, "there is no hard and fast '5 percent rule.' "[35]

The need for the "shingle" theory in the mark-up area is reduced to the extent that disclosure of dealers' over-the-counter spreads is available. But that was long in coming.[36] And, of course, there are the other areas in which the theory operates.

[33]CCH NASD Manual ¶2154, esp. at 2056. The Commission rejected a contention that this interpretation, with its accompanying instructions, amounted to a 5 percent "rule" that was illegal because it had neither been submitted to a vote of the membership nor been filed with the Commission; and it found that there were adequate safeguards in the statute against improper use of the policy thus established. National Assn. of Securities Dealers, Inc., 17 SEC 459 (1944). There is also a judicial holding that "The statement of the 5% policy establishes sufficient guidelines" to overcome a due process argument. Handley Investment Co. v. SEC, 354 F. 2d 64, 66 (10th Cir. 1965). But cf. Fox v. Neff, CCH Blue Sky L. Rep. ¶71,839 (Tenn. Ch. 1981), where the court held that a statutory reference to "variations from current market prices as, in light of all circumstances[,] are unconscionable" was too vague to support revocation of a salesman's license, although he had participated in at least 45 transactions involving markups or markdowns of more than 5 percent and the Commissioner had followed the NASD's 5 percent guide (which the court referred to as "a subjective test").

[34]Herrick, Waddell & Co., Inc., 25 SEC 437 (1947).

[35]Samuel B. Franklin & Co. v. SEC, 290 F. 2d 719, 725 (9th Cir. 1961), *cert. denied,* 368 U. S. 889.

Municipal bonds are exempted from §15A and therefore from the NASD's rules. But they have always been subject to the statutory fraud provisions and the shingle theory. Crosby & Elkin, Inc., Sec. Ex. Act Rel. 17,709, 22 SEC Dock. 772, 775 (1981). See p. 627 supra.

[36](1) Traditionally the quotations that were available to the public were adjusted. See 5 Loss 3317-34.

(2) The development of a national market system produced last sale data for those over-the-counter securities that are "NMS securities" (see pp. 696-97 supra). For an account of that development, see Sec. Ex. Act Rel. 21,708, 32 SEC Dock. 495, 497 (1985).

(3) On the confirmation front, the Commission in its former Rule 15c1-4, adopted in 1937, followed common law agency precept in requiring disclosure of execution price and brokerage commission only in agency transactions. Then in 1978 the Commission required the inclusion of mark-ups (or markdowns on dealers' *purchases*) in non-marketmaker's riskless principal transactions (see p. 828 infra). Finally, in 1985 the Commission extended the current confirmation

2. "Now I'm a Principal, Now I'm an Agent"

a. Disclosure Required of a Dealer Occupying a Fiduciary Position

Concurrently with the development of the "shingle" theory that culminated in the Second Circuit's opinion in the *Hughes* case, the Commission began exploring the status of a broker-dealer who, although purporting to act as principal rather than agent, places himself in a position of trust and confidence with his customer.[37] Such a broker-dealer, the Commission declared, is under a much stricter obligation than merely to refrain from taking excessive mark-ups over the current market. His duty as a fiduciary selling his own property to his principal, or buying from his principal for his own account, is to make a scrupulously full disclosure of every element of his adverse interest in the transaction. Like the "shingle" theory, this doctrine culminated in a Commission opinion that was sustained on judicial review.[38] Oddly, the broker-dealer here too was named Hughes.[39]

Arleen Hughes registered with the Commission both as a broker-dealer and as an investment adviser. Each of her clients signed a "Memorandum of Agreement" specifying that she was to act in all transactions as both investment adviser and principal except as otherwise agreed. The contract included an elaborate schedule of rates and charges applicable to each transaction, and it specified maximum spreads that would be added to a so-called base price when the firm sold securities to a client or bought them from a client. There was no allegation of unreasonable spreads.

Judge Champ Clark stated for the District of Columbia Circuit:

---

rule, 10b-10, to elicit, in "any other case of a [principal] transaction in a reported security, the trade price reported in accordance with an effective transaction reporting plan, the price to the customer in the transaction, and the difference, if any, between the reported trade price and the price to the customer"; and the term "reported security" is defined in Rule 11Aa3-1 to mean "any listed equity security or non-listed national market system security for which a transaction reporting plan with respect to transactions in such security is required to be filed." Sec. Ex. Act Rel. 22,396, 33 SEC Dock. 1355, 1376 (1985).

[37] Allender Co., Inc., 9 SEC 1043, esp. at 1053-55 (1941); William J. Stelmack Corp., 11 SEC 601, esp. at 617-21 (1942); Lawrence R. Leeby, 13 SEC 499, 505-09 (1943).

[38] Arleen W. Hughes, 27 SEC 629 and 952 (1948), *aff'd* sub nom. Hughes v. SEC, 174 F. 2d 969 (D. C. Cir. 1949).

[39] Stranger still, both firms were operated by women. And, if one is interested in statistical probabilities, still another coincidence might be noted: Both opinions were written by judges named Clark.

In the vast majority of transactions between this petitioner and her clients, petitioner concededly acted as a fiduciary. The record shows clearly that, except for a few isolated instances, petitioner acted simultaneously in the dual capacity of investment adviser and of broker and dealer. In such capacity, conflicting interests must necessarily arise. When they arise, the law has consistently stepped in to provide safeguards in the form of prescribed and stringent standards of conduct on the part of the fiduciary. More than 100 years ago the Supreme Court set forth this principle as follows:

> In this conflict of interest, the law wisely interposes. It acts not on the possibility, that, in some cases, the sense of that duty may prevail over the motives of self-interest, but it provides against the probability in many cases, and the danger in all cases, that the dictates of self-interest will exercise a predominant influence, and supersede that of duty.[12]

But the Commission in this case did not, and we in turn do not, base the validity of the revocation order upon common law principles of fraud or deceit. [Citing Sec. Act §17(a) and Sec. Ex. Act §§10(b) and 15(c)(1) and the rules thereunder.] * * *

It cannot now be doubted that, as respondent points out, the securities field, by its nature, requires specialized and unique legal treatment. * * *

* * * The Commission found that petitioner failed to disclose to her clients (1) the best price at which the securities could be purchased for the clients in the open market in the exercise of due diligence and (2) the cost to petitioner of the securities sold by her to her clients. In no less than three places in the above-quoted statutes and regulations we find that, "any omission to state a material fact necessary in order to make the statements made, in the light of the circumstances under which they were made, not misleading," is expressly made unlawful. These quoted words as they appear in the statute can only mean that Congress forbid not only the telling of purposeful falsity but also the telling of half-truths and the failure to tell the "whole truth." These statutory words were obviously designed to protect the investing public as a whole whether the individual investors be suspicious or unsuspecting. The best price currently obtainable in the open market and the cost to registrant are both material facts within the meaning of the above-quoted language and they are both factors without which informed consent to a fiduciary's acting in a dual and conflicting role is impossible.

Petitioner strongly urges that she has fully and completely fulfilled any disclosure requirement by the insertion in the Memorandum of Agreement (entered into with each of her clients since 1943)

[12][Michoud v. Giròd, 4 How. 503, 555 (U. S. 1846).] * * *

> of the clause that the "Company, when acting as investment adviser, shall act as Principal in every such transaction, except as otherwise agreed," and that, in any event, petitioner has always stood ready to provide any further information which her clients desired. The clause inserted in the Memorandum of Agreement does not even approach the minimum disclosure requirements. In the first place, it is certainly doubtful whether petitioner's clients either knew of or understood the legal effect of the technical language inserted in fine print in the printed document which each client signed when he or she first became a client of petitioner. Secondly, even assuming, as urged by amici, that *all* of petitioner's clients are persons of more than average experience and intelligence with regard to the conceded intricacies of securities transactions, an assumption which is at best dubious in view of the present record, their full knowledge that petitioner either sold them securities she then owned or bought securities in her own name and then resold them to the clients cannot be considered sufficient knowledge to enable the clients to give their informed consent. * * * It is not enough that one who acts as an admitted fiduciary proclaim that he or she stands ever ready to divulge material facts to the ones whose interests she is being paid to protect. Some knowledge is prerequisite to intelligent questioning. This is particularly true in the securities field. Readiness and willingness to disclose are not equivalent to disclosure. The statutes and rules discussed above make it unlawful to omit to state material facts irrespective of alleged (or proven) willingness or readiness to supply that which has been omitted.[40]

The teaching, of course, is considerably older: "No man can serve two masters * * * ."[41] And it applies equally to any person who stands in a fiduciary relation toward another, whether he be trustee, executor, administrator, lawyer, officer, director, invest-

[40] The court rejected the arguments in an *amicus curiae* brief for 120 of the petitioner's 175 clients to the effect that the clients had a full understanding of the memorandum and were altogether satisfied. Since the Commission's order satisfied the prerequisites for revocation, "the revocation is proper even if one, or none, of the particular clients here involved has been misled or has suffered injury." 174 F. 2d at 974.

[See also Chasins v. Smith, Barney & Co., Inc., 438 F. 2d 1167 (2d Cir. 1970); cf. Campbell v. Shearson/American Express, Inc., CCH Fed. Sec. L. Rep. ¶92,303 at 92,064 (E. D. Mich. 1985); but cf. Avern Trust v. Clarke, 415 F. 2d 1238, 1239-40 (7th Cir. 1969), *cert. denied,* 397 U. S. 963.]

[41] Matt. 6:24; see Tisdale v. Tisdale, 2 Sneed 596, 608, 64 Am. Dec. 775, 783 (Tenn. 1855). This maxim, the Supreme Court has observed, "is especially pertinent if one of the masters happens to be economic self-interest." United States v. Mississippi Valley Generating Co., 364 U. S. 520, 549 (1961); see also SEC v. Capital Gains Research Bureau, Inc., 375 U. S. 180, 196 n. 50 (1963).

ment adviser, or broker.[42] The law has always looked with such suspicion upon a fiduciary's dealing with his beneficiary for his own account without scrupulously fair disclosure of his adverse interest that it permits the beneficiary at any time to set aside the transaction without proving actual abuse or damage.[43]

What the *Arleen Hughes* case does is to say that such conduct amounts to a violation of the fraud provisions of the securities laws.[44] More than that, the opinion spells out precisely what disclosure is required in this type of case.

First, there must be a clear statement of the fiduciary's capacity and his actual cost (or, in the case of a purchase from a client, the fiduciary's resale price when known). This much the law has traditionally required of a fiduciary on pain of having the transaction set aside.[45] In addition, however, the Commission's opinion recognized the obvious fact that in the securities field there is another criterion of adverse interest that is usually a good deal more significant. That criterion is the current market price — the best available bid or offer, as the case may be, that the fiduciary is able to discover in the exercise of reasonable diligence.[46] Of course, it is not essential to disclose the best available market price unless it is more favorable than the price at which the fiduciary proposes to buy from or sell to his client. Furthermore, disclosure of cost and

[42] Hotchkiss v. Fischer, 136 Kan. 530, 537, 16 P. 2d 531, 534 (1932); Tate v. Williamson, L. R. 1 Eq. 528, 537 (1866), *aff'd,* L. R. 2 Ch. 55 (1866); G. Bower, The Law Relating to Actionable Non-disclosure (1915) §§320, 408; 3 J. Pomeroy, Equity Jurisprudence (5th ed. 1941) §956a.

[43] Robertson v. Chapman, 152 U. S. 673, 681 (1894).

[44] Compare the mail fraud cases cited supra p. 700 n. 5. The same point had earlier been made in Op. Dir. Trading & Ex. Div., Sec. Ex. Act Rel. 3653, Inv. Adv. Act Rel. 40 (1945). That opinion was qualified by the Commission thirty years later, as we shall see (infra pp. 842-43). But the story is best told chronologically.

[45] Old Dominion Copper Mining & Smelting Co. v. Bigelow, 188 Mass. 315, 320-21, 74 N. E. 653, 658 (1905), *aff'd on other grounds,* 225 U. S. 111 (1912); Norris v. Beyer, 124 N. J. Eq. 284, 286-87, 1 A. 2d 460, 461 (1938); Allender Co., Inc., 9 SEC 1043, 1054 (1914).

[46] The fact situations that have been dealt with by the courts have related for the most part to unique properties rather than properties having a readily ascertainable market value, and generally relief has been based on failure to disclose the fact that the fiduciary was selling for his own account or to disclose the amount of his cost or profit. However, even in these situations the courts have recognized that the fiduciary is under a duty to obtain or dispose of the property for his principal at the best price discoverable in the exercise of reasonable diligence. Doyen v. Bauer, 211 Minn. 140, 147, 300 N. W. 451, 455 (1941); Berkeley Sulphur Springs v. Liberty, 10 N. J. Misc. 1067, 1069, 162 Atl. 191, 192 (Ch. 1932); Van Dusen v. Bigelow, 13 N. D. 277, 283, 100 N. W. 723, 724-25 (1904); Ridgeway v. McGuire, 176 Ore. 428, 433, 158 P. 2d 893, 895-96 (1945).

market will normally be the same when the fiduciary effects an approximately contemporaneous transaction with another dealer to offset a transaction with a client. However, when the fiduciary has held a security in inventory for some time before selling it to a client, the fiduciary's cost, although still significant, is of secondary importance, and disclosure of cost alone without disclosure of current market may be positively misleading. Suppose, for example, that the fiduciary paid 50 for a security in inventory and is charging the client 20, but the current market is 10; disclosure of cost alone would indicate that the client is getting a bargain, whereas in fact he is being cheated.

The Commission also spelled out in some detail how the required disclosure of capacity and market might be made. The nature and extent of disclosure with respect to capacity will vary with the particular client involved. In some cases use of the term "principal" itself may suffice. In others a more detailed explanation will be required. In all cases, however, the burden is on the firm that acts as fiduciary to make certain that the client understands that the firm is selling its own securities. In disclosing market price, when it is more favorable than cost, the firm must make certain that the quotations it furnishes to clients are reliable and truly indicative of the current market.

All this, of course, is aside from the duty the agent always has to disclose to his principal all facts "which he should realize have or are likely to have a bearing upon the desirability of the transaction from the viewpoint of the principal."[47] It is understood to be the administrative construction, for example, that one incident of this duty is that a broker or investment adviser who solicits or recommends purchases or sales must disclose the existence (though not necessarily the amount) of any long or short position of the firm, or any partner, officer, director or member of their immediate families, or any employee assuming responsibility for the recommendation, if the position is substantial in relation to the total resources and holdings of the firm or any such individual.[48] Any other

[47] Restatement (Second) of Agency §390, Comment a. The obligation of fair dealing is not diminished because a statutory prospectus or offering circular has been or is to be delivered, since the information in those documents furnishes background against which the salesman's representations may be tested. J. P. Howell & Co., Inc., 43 SEC 325, 329 (1967), *aff'd* sub nom. Vanasco v. SEC, 395 F. 2d 349 (2d Cir. 1968).

[48] Brennan v. Midwestern United Life Ins. Co., 286 F. Supp. 702, 707 (N. D. Ind. 1968), *aff'd on other grounds,* 417 F. 2d 147 (7th Cir. 1969), *cert. denied,* 397 U. S. 989; Prawer v. Dean Witter Reynolds, Inc., 626 F. Supp. 642, 643-44 (D. Mass. 1985); see CCH N. Y. Stock Ex. Guide ¶2472.40(2)(iii).

bias of the firm or of any such individual must likewise be disclosed. And, on the theory of an implied representation of fair dealing, the same duty is considered to apply even to a *dealer* who does any recommending or soliciting. Again, a broker, as well as a dealer who recommends or solicits purchases or sales, must be careful to avoid conflicts of interest between different classes of customers. All this is under penalty of violating the fraud provisions.[49]

b. Determination of Fiduciary Status

Unfortunately there is no touchstone for determining when a dealer assumes the obligation of a fiduciary. Sometimes, as in the *Arleen Hughes* case itself, the answer is easy: A firm that is registered as an investment adviser, and that admittedly renders investment advice with respect to the same transactions in which it purports to act as principal, can hardly deny its fiduciary status. Nor can a firm that is specifically vested with discretionary authority.[50] But take a

[49] A broker's fiduciary duty to his customer is not affected by the presence of an investment adviser. Rolf v. Blyth, Eastman Dillon & Co., Inc., 570 F. 2d 38, 45 n. 10 (2d Cir. 1978), *cert. denied,* 439 U. S. 1039.

The common law recognizes that an agent who deals with his principal on his own account in regard to the subject matter of his employment may be excused from his disclosure obligation when the principal has manifested that he either knows all material facts in connection with the transaction or does not care to know them. Restatement (Second) of Agency §390 and Comment b; see also id., §389, Comments b, d. Presumably, however, at least so far as the antifraud provisions of the securities laws are concerned, any sort of waiver or "advance ratification" on the part of a fiduciary's client will be construed very strictly, particularly in the case of a relatively unsophisticated investor. Section 14 of the 1933 Act and §29(a) of the 1934 Act provide that any waiver of compliance with any provision of the statute or of the Commission's rules is "void." At the very least these sections indicate a congressional feeling that by and large the professional broker-dealer and the investor do not bargain on a par with each other. Cf. id., §390, Comment a: "If the principal has limited business experience, an agent cannot properly fail to give such information merely because the principal says he does not care for it; the agent's duty of fair dealing is satisfied only if he reasonably believes that the principal understands the implications of the transaction."

For a legal-sociological analysis of various mechanisms for resolving what sociologists would call the broker's status-set and role-set conflicts, see Levin and Evan, Professionalism and the Stockbroker, 21 Bus. Law 337 (1966). These mechanisms are said to be segregation of statuses, regulatory and self-regulatory structures, and professionalization.

[50] Norris & Hirshberg, Inc., 21 SEC 865, 883-85 (1946), *aff'd* sub nom. Norris & Hirshberg, Inc. v. SEC, 177 F. 2d 228 (D. C. Cir. 1949). Discretionary authority is basically inconsistent with the firm's buying or selling for its own account; for it no longer has a genuinely discretionary power in so far as it obtains the customer's informed consent to each transaction. Rule 15c1-7, supra p. 705, prohibits excessive trading by any "broker or dealer * * * with or for

broker-dealer firm that simply buys and sells securities as principal, rendering the incidental investment advice that is well-nigh universal in the industry (except for discount brokers) and without which it could hardly operate. The Commission emphasized in the *Arleen Hughes* case that "it is not intended that the disclosure requirements, which we have found applicable to registrant, be imposed upon broker-dealers who render investment advice merely as an incident to their broker-dealer activities unless they have by a course of conduct placed themselves in a position of trust and confidence as to their customers."[51] When, then, does a firm cross the line from the first *Hughes* doctrine to the second?

The fact that the firm confirms as principal is not conclusive as to the relationship of the parties.[52] Nor, on the other hand, does

---

any customer's account" as to which he has discretionary power. But the Commission has denied that this language contemplates that a dealer may hold discretionary power and trade for his own account. "The rule is intended to be broad in coverage and to include excessive activity even by a dealer — whether he has procured adequate consent to act as a dealer or is violating his duties. The attempt to make of Rule [15c1-7] a license to permit fiduciaries to violate their duties is utterly beyond the purpose and spirit of that rule." Norris & Hirshberg, Inc., supra, at 885; Paine, Webber, Jackson & Curtis, Inc. v. Adams, — Colo. — , 718 P. 2d 508 (1986) (account's status as nondiscretionary does not *per se* defeat a common law claim for breach of fiduciary duty).

[51] 27 SEC at 639. Cf. Inv. Adv. Act §202(a)(11)(C), supra p. 680; cf. also Caravan Mobile Home Sales, Inc. v. Lehman Brothers Kuhn Loeb, Inc., 769 F. 2d 561 (9th Cir. 1985) (a non-discretionary account with a brokerage firm did not create a fiduciary relationship that would impose a post-purchase disclosure duty to advise investors of adverse developments); Lefkowitz v. Smith Barney, Harris Upham & Co., Inc., 804 F. 2d 154, 155 (1st Cir. 1986) (even against a broker, who is not a fiduciary under Massachusetts law in the case of a "simple stockbroker-customer relationship," allegations of customer's "minimal knowledge of investments and blind reliance upon his broker are not sufficient for a proper pleading of fiduciary duty").

[52] Twomey v. Mitchum, Jones & Templeton, Inc., 262 Cal. App. 2d 690, 715, 69 Cal. Rptr. 222, 240 (1968); Birch v. Arnold & Sears, Inc., 288 Mass. 125, 192 N. E. 591 (1934); Porter v. Wormser, 94 N. Y. 431, 447 (1884); Norris & Hirshberg, Inc. v. SEC, 177 F. 2d 228, 233 n. 10 (D. C. Cir. 1949) *semble;* Allender Co., Inc., 9 SEC 1043, 1054-55 (1941); J. Logan & Co., 41 SEC 88, 98-99 (1962), *aff'd per curiam* sub nom. Hersh v. SEC, 325 F. 2d 147 (9th Cir. 1963), *cert. denied,* 377 U. S. 937.

It is not improper for a broker-dealer to act on one occasion as agent for a customer and on another occasion as principal, as long as the relationship is agreed to by the customer at or before the completion of each transaction. G. Alex Hope, 7 SEC 1082, 1083 (1940). But an agent must make a clean break with his principal if he wants to shift to a principal-and-principal basis in future dealings, and it is his burden to prove that he brought the change "to the attention of his principal in such a manner as to avoid all chance of misunderstanding." Smokeless Fuel Co. v. Western United Corp., 19 F. 2d 834, 836 (4th Cir. 1927). When the relationship from the start has been that of *broker* and customer, the mere sending of a confirmation reading "We confirm purchase from you" does not change the relationship to one of *dealer* and customer.

the absence of inventory when the firm solicits a customer to buy establish an agency relationship. In a 1946 opinion, in which the language was not too happily chosen, the Commission did indicate that in such circumstances a firm would normally be considered an agent.[53] There was no disputing the firm's capacity in the particular case. One customer was a ninety-year-old widow, and the other was a spinster ten years her junior. However, there was considerable furor about the Commission's broad language. Taken literally, it would have put a very substantial segment of the over-the-counter industry on an agency basis in view of the practice of many firms to sell before they buy. The fact is that a securities dealer, like any other type of merchant, does not become an agent for his customer *merely* because he tries to sell merchandise that he does not own at the time.[54] And the Commission soon made it clear that it had no intention of establishing such a rule of thumb.[55] But, as we have seen, disclosure of spread in these riskless transactions is now required with respect to equity securities by the confirmation rule (unless the broker-dealer is acting as a marketmaker), the theory being that they are in many respects equivalent to agency transactions.[56]

The determination of a broker-dealer's capacity in a particular transaction must depend on all the circumstances, including the degree of sophistication of the parties and the course of conduct

---

Hence, when a broker buys in for his own account securities pledged as collateral by a customer, he is guilty of conversion and the transaction is voidable at the customer's option, unless the broker sustains the burden of proving that the customer knew and consented to the broker's purchase for his own account. Johnson v. Winslow, 155 Misc. 170, 279 N. Y. Supp. 147 (Sup. Ct. 1935), *aff'd per curiam,* 246 App. Div. 800, 285 N. Y. Supp. 1075 (1st Dept. 1936), *aff'd per curiam,* 272 N. Y. 467, 3 N. E. 2d 872 (1936). For a discussion of what constitutes adequate disclosure of capacity in the confirmation, see Bates and Douglas, Secondary Distribution of Securities — Problems Suggested by *Kinney* v. *Glenny,* 41 Yale L. J. 949, 985-94 (1932).

[53] Oxford Co., Inc., 21 SEC 681, 692-93 (1946).

[54] See Douglas and Bates, Stock "Brokers" As Agents and Dealers, 43 Yale L. J. 46, 60-61 (1933); Bates and Douglas, Secondary Distribution of Securities — Problems Suggested by *Kinney* v. *Glenny,* 41 Yale L. J. 949, 980-81 (1932). For a summary of the legal relationship between customer and broker and the standards of behavior whose violation gives rise to rights and duties *inter se,* see id. at 964-72.

[55] See the present writer's address before the Stock Brokers' Associates of Chicago and the former Chicago Stock Exchange, in his then capacity as Chief Counsel to the Commission's Division of Trading and Exchanges, The SEC and the Broker-Dealer, Mar. 16, 1948, reprinted with annotations in 1 Vand. L. Rev. 516, 529-30 (1948). The *Oxford* case was ignored by the Commission in the *Arleen Hughes* case, although about half the transactions there represented solicited, non-position trading.

[56] Rule 10b-10(a)(8)(i)(A), supra p. 820 n. 36.

between them.[57] The law must operate on the habits of people. Typically there is no express meeting of the minds as to the nature of the relationship. The two *Hughes* doctrines really blur into each other, to the point where a finding of fraud is occasionally based on violation of the two doctrines in the alternative. Indeed, the Commission in recent years seems to have deemphasized *Hughes II*, incorporating a good deal of it into *Hughes I*[58] — which may not be the wisest policy, as the author has had occasion to say elsewhere in suggesting that

> the Commission would be likely to find firmer ground under its collective feet if it were to talk in terms of *Hughes II* when the circumstances warranted — and to take the relatively small step of extending the "reasonable basis" and "suitability" doctrines [infra pp. 829-37] to agents, including manufactured agents of the *Hughes II* type — rather than attempting to construe the statutory fraud provisions as imposing a greater fiduciary obligation on principals than the common law imposes on agents.[59]

3. Duty to Investigate and the Suitability Doctrine

More recently, in an evolution from ethical precept to law that is still incomplete, the Commission (with some help from the courts) has been refining its "shingle" and "fair dealing" concepts into something that approaches a "suitability" requirement — an obligation on the part of the dealer to recommend only securities that are suitable to the needs of the particular customer.

The development began as an attack on the evils of high-pressure selling, mainly via the long-distance telephone — which is to say, the "boiler room," so called because of the high pressure generated in the selling effort. The term has appeared in the judicial literature for at least five decades.[60] And Judge Friendly has given us a colorful description of a typical "boiler room" operation:

[57] In Value Line Fund, Inc. v. Marcus, CCH Fed. Sec. L. Rep. ¶91,523 at 94,967-68, 94,973 (S. D. N. Y. 1965), the court held that a firm acting as principal in form might be an agent in substance, at least for purposes of finding the privity between the firm's selling principal and the buyer that is required by §12 of the 1933 Act.

[58] Contrast Russell L. Irish, 42 SEC 735 (1965), *aff'd* sub nom. Irish v. SEC, 367 F. 2d 637 (9th Cir. 1966), *cert. denied*, 386 U. S. 911, with Mason, Moran & Co., 35 SEC 84 (1953).

[59] Loss, Book Rev., 18 J. Legal Ed. 238, 241-42 (1965).

[60] United States v. Rollnick, 91 F. 2d 911, 915 (2d Cir. 1937).

> The process would begin by sending to persons on various occupational lists, "such as doctors, plumbers, anything you want," which Kimball owned or would purchase, "teaser letters" describing the bright financial future afforded by low-priced stocks. These were followed by sales literature touting some particular stock. Next would come a telephone call from a salesman called an "opener," who "would try and sell the prospect as much or as little as he could." This would be followed by more mail relating the "good news about the company," and then by the knock-out blow, a call from a "high-pressure salesman," colorfully characterized as a "loader," who would "try and increase the purchase of the stock."[61]

In the Commission's view, "boiler rooms" fell under the ban of the fraud provisions on alternate theories: (1) because those provisions "contemplate at the least, that recommendations of a security made to proposed purchasers shall have a reasonable basis and that they shall be accompanied by disclosure of known or easily ascertainable facts bearing upon the justification for the representation,"[62] and (2) because of *failure* to *disclose* to customers "the lack of adequate financial information or caution them as to the risk involved in purchasing the stock without such information."[63]

[61] United States v. Ross, 321 F. 2d 61, 64 (2d Cir. 1963), *cert. denied,* 375 U. S. 894; see also J. Logan & Co., 41 SEC 88, 89-91 (1962), *aff'd* sub nom. Hersh v. SEC, 325 F. 2d 147 (9th Cir. 1963), *cert. denied,* 377 U. S. 937.

[62] Best Securities, Inc., 39 SEC 931, 933-34 (1960); see also Mac Robbins & Co., Inc., 41 SEC 116, 119 (1962), *aff'd* sub nom. Berko v. SEC, 316 F. 2d 137 (2d Cir. 1963); Green v. Jonhop, Inc., 358 F. Supp. 413, 419 (D. Ore. 1973). Neither "blind faith in the issuer's self-serving assurances" nor the defendant's own investment and loss are a defense. Richard C. Spangler, Inc., 46 SEC 238 (1976). But a broker who has neither solicited the order nor recommended the security "has a minimal duty, if any at all, to investigate the purchase and disclose material facts to a customer." Canizaro v. Kohlmeyer & Co., 370 F. Supp. 282, 289 (E. D. La. 1974), *aff'd per curiam,* 512 F. 2d 484 (5th Cir. 1975); see also Lefkowitz v. Smith Barney, Harris Upham & Co., Inc. 804 F. 2d 154 (1st Cir. 1986), supra p. 827 n. 5; Quincy Co-operative Bank v. A. G. Edwards & Sons, Inc., 655 F. Supp. 78, 86 (D. Mass. 1986), CCH Fed. Sec. L. Rep. ¶92,958 at 94,683-84 (broker's obligation to investigate and disclose "increases in direct proportion to the degree of his participation in the sale"). And when the Commission published a proposed "boiler room" rule in 1962 — which it withdrew as unnecessary three years later — it inserted an exemption for "isolated transactions not a part of any concentrated sales effort by the broker-dealer." Sec. Ex. Act Rels. 6885 (1962), 7517 (1965).

[63] B. Fennekohl & Co., 41 SEC 210, 215, 217 (1962). See also Sec. Act Rel. 4445 (1962). "Where public information concerning the company is not available from the Commission or standard research sources, the extent of inquiry required to reasonably assure the broker or dealer that the proposed transaction complies with applicable legal requirements will be correspondingly greater." Sec. Act Rel. 5168 (1971). And an unseasoned company needs more investigation than one that is well established. Merrill Lynch, Pierce, Fenner & Smith, Inc., Sec. Ex. Act Rel. 14,149, 13 SEC Dock. 646 (1977). In general, see Brud-

So far as salesmen are concerned, they may not rely blindly on information furnished by the broker-dealer by whom they are employed, or by the issuer, especially if the broker-dealer has an underwriter's responsibility and more especially in the case of a promotional issue.[64] In a pair of "boiler room" cases involving two salesmen who were held to be causes of the revocation of their employer's registration as a broker-dealer, the Second Circuit, after initially remanding to the Commission for further findings,[65] ultimately added its *imprimatur* to the Commission's statement:

> Whatever may be a salesman's obligation of inquiry, or his right to rely on information provided by his employer, where securities of an established issuer are being recommended to customers by a broker-dealer who is not engaged in misleading and deceptive high-pressure selling practices, * * * there can be little, if any, justification for a claim of reliance on literature furnished by an employer who is engaged in a fraudulent sales campaign.[66]

Meanwhile the NASD had always had a rule on its books, dating from the Investment Bankers Code of NRA days:

> In recommending to a customer the purchase, sale, or exchange of any security, a member shall have reasonable grounds for believing that the recommendation is suitable for such customer upon the basis of the facts, if any, disclosed by such customer as to his other security holding and as to his financial situation and needs.[67]

And the New York Stock Exchange's "know your customer" rule[68] — which has been called "the eleventh commandment of Wall Street"[69] — is being pulled in the same direction, although its requirement of "due diligence to learn the essential facts relative to

---

ney, Origins and Limited Applicability of the "Reasonable Basis" or "Know Your Merchandise" Doctrine, in Practising Law Institute, Fourth Annual Institute on Securities Regulation (1973) c. 9.

[64] Hanly v. SEC, 415 F. 2d 589, 595-97 (2d Cir. 1969) (review of administrative proceeding); SEC v. N. A. R. & D. Corp., 424 F. 2d 63, 84 (2d Cir. 1970) (injunction); Franklin Savings Bank v. Levy, 551 F. 2d 521, 527 (2d Cir. 1977) (§12(2) defense).

[65] Kahn v. SEC, 297 F. 2d 112 (2d Cir. 1961); Berko v. SEC, 297 F. 2d 116 (2d Cir. 1961).

[66] Mac Robbins & Co., Inc., 41 SEC 116, 128-29 (1962), *aff'd* sub nom. Berko v. SEC, 316 F. 2d 137, 142-43 (2d Cir. 1963).

[67] Rules of Fair Practice, Art. III, §2, CCH NASD Manual ¶2152.

[68] Rule 405, CCH N. Y. Stock Ex. Guide ¶2405; see also Am. Stock Ex. Rule 411, CCH Am. Stock Ex. Guide ¶9431.

[69] Surgil v. Kidder, Peabody & Co., Inc., 63 Misc. 2d 473, 477, 311 N. Y. S. 2d 157, 162 (Civ. Ct. 1970), *rev'd on other grounds*, 69 Misc. 2d 213, 329 N. Y. S. 2d 993 (Sup. Ct. 1971).

every customer [and] every order" seems more designed to protect the member firm than the customer.[70]

In the *Greenberg* case in 1960, where the broker-dealer had not raised (or at least had not stressed) before the NASD the restriction of the duty under the language of the rule to cases where the relevant facts have been disclosed to the broker by the customer, the Commission in effect read that limitation out of the rule:

> The clear purpose of the Rule would be defeated if it were construed as permitting a broker or dealer to engage in a practice of recommending low price speculative securities to unknown customers —a practice which by its nature involves a high probability that the recommendation will not be suitable to at least some of the persons solicited — without any knowledge of or attempt to obtain information concerning the customer's other security holdings, his financial situation, and his needs so as to be in a position to judge the suitability of the recommendation.[71]

The NASD's interpretation, on the other hand, gives effect to the words "if any" by not requiring the broker-dealer "to assume any responsibility until the customer objectively demonstrates his reliance on the superior skill and knowledge of the broker-dealer by supplying him with financial information about himself."[72] And the Special Study's recommendation that "Greater emphasis should be given by the Commission and the self-regulatory bodies to the concept of 'suitability' of particular securities for particular customers"[73] received a cold reception from the industry.[74]

[70] See N. Y. Stock Ex. M. F. Educ. Circ. 234 (1968): "An important purpose of this rule is to protect the firm against loss or rule violation due to unethical actions of customers." See also 1 SEC, Report of Special Study of Securities Markets, H. R. Doc. No. 95, 88th Cong., 1st Sess. (1963) 316, where President Funston of the Exchange is said to have expressed the view in the text.

[71] Gerald M. Greenberg, 40 SEC 133, 137-38 (1960). In Eugene J. Erdos, Sec. Ex. Act Rel. 20,376, 29 SEC Dock. 180, 182 n. 10, 183 (1983), *aff'd* sub nom. Erdos v. SEC, 742 F. 2d 507 (9th Cir. 1984), the Commission stated further that recommendations were not rendered suitable merely because they might "result in profits to customers" (quoting from CCH NASD Manual ¶2152 at 2051), and that whether the *customer* "considered the transactions in her account suitable is not the test." Moreover, the court cited *Greenberg* approvingly.

[72] Mundheim, Professional Responsibilities of Broker-Dealers: The Suitability Doctrine, [1965] Duke L. J. 445, 458; see 1 SEC, Report of Special Study of Securities Markets, H. R. Doc. No. 95, 88th Cong., 1st Sess. (1963) 311-12; Parsons v. Hornblower & Weeks-Hemphill Noyes, 447 F. Supp. 482, 495 (M. D. N. C. 1977), *aff'd per curiam*, 571 F. 2d 203 (4th Cir. 1978).

[73] 1 SEC, Report of Securities Markets, H. R. Doc. No. 95, 88th Cong., 1st Sess. (1963) 329.

[74] 1 Investor Protection, Hearings Before Subcom. of House Com. on Int. & For. Commerce on H. R. 6789, H. R. 6793, S. 1642, 88th Cong., 1st Sess. (1963) 394, 471; 2 id. 686, 690 (1963-64).

Since the early 1960s all concerned have been living with a compromise. The NASD in 1964 adopted a set of guidelines on "Fair Dealing with Customers."[75] And a year earlier the New York Stock Exchange — whose members normally, of course, have the fiduciary obligation that the law imposes on an agent — adopted certain "guideposts" for *written* communications with the public, one of which has to do with recommendations:

> A recommendation (even though not labeled as a recommendation) must have a basis which can be substantiated as reasonable.
>
> When recommending the purchase, sale or switch of specific securities, supporting information must be provided or offered.[76]

This compromise, however, goes more to the "duty to investigate" or "know your merchandise" concept than to "know your customer" or "suitability." In any event, it cannot be assumed that a broker-dealer's effecting a transaction on the basis of an unsuitable recommendation is a violation of the general fraud rules, at least outside (1) the "boiler room" context, where by hypothesis the relationship to customers is such that there can be no basis for believing that *any* recommendation is suitable or unsuitable, and (2) perhaps the situation where the broker-dealer is acting as agent or pseudo-agent, though even the law of agency does not impose a duty under all circumstances to make affirmative inquiry. Nevertheless, there are enough cases (though there is still a paucity of square holdings) to indicate that a subtle shift from ethics to law may be in process.[77] And this is apart from the extent to which the

[75] CCH NASD Manual ¶2152.

[76] Rule 472.40(1), CCH N. Y. Stock Ex. Guide ¶2472.(40); see also N. Y. Stock Ex. P. R. & R. I. Circ. 5 (1964) 2 (what is a "reasonable" basis for a recommendation is a matter of interpretation dependent on the circumstances, but the usual primary or secondary research sources would normally be considered reasonable). An undated publication of the Exchange entitled "Supervision and Management of Registered Representatives and Customer Accounts" adds: "Like a doctor or a lawyer, the representative should determine pertinent facts concerning the client's situation prior to giving advice." P. 7.

[77] A number of Commission decisions point in that direction, albeit by way of dictum or under extraordinary circumstances. Herbert R. May, 27 SEC 814, 824 (1948); Ramey Kelly Corp., 39 SEC 756, 759 (1960); Powell & McGowan, Inc., 41 SEC 933, 935 (1964).

In SEC v. Rabinowitz, Litig. Rel. 2444 (D. Ariz. 1962), a "spread" case in which the Commission got a preliminary injunction, it pleaded partly on a theory of "contravention of high standards of commercial honor and just and equitable principles of trade."

In Merrill Lynch, Pierce, Fenner & Smith, Inc. v. Bocock, 247 F. Supp. 373, 376-77 (S. D. Tex. 1965), apparently a common law case involving a short sale, the court cited the NASD rule in support of its conclusion that the plaintiff was

suitability idea is already reflected in the SEC structure — going

---

a "suitable person."

By 1967, after citing "boiler room" cases and others indiscriminately with respect to the duty to make reasonable inquiry, the Commission was able to say flatly that, when the record clearly established a scheme to defraud in the sale of a speculative security by means of a high-pressure campaign involving the recurring use of the same basic fraudulent representations and predictions, the legal principles were the same whether or not there was a specific finding of the existence of a "boiler-room." James De Mammos, 43 SEC 333, 337 (1967), *aff'd* sub nom. De Mammos v. SEC, 2d Cir., Dock. No. 31,469, Oct. 13, 1967.

In Hecht v. Harris, Upham & Co., 283 F. Supp. 417, 428-31 (N. D. Cal. 1968), *aff'd on this point and modified on other grounds*, 430 F. 2d 1202 (9th Cir. 1970), the court's finding of estoppel on the part of the plaintiff — a widow who was "neither as 'dumb' in matters of brokerage accounts as plaintiff's counsel contends or as plaintiff, herself, made herself appear to be on the stand, nor * * * as smart, experienced, or informed as defendants' counsel would make her out to be" — made it unnecessary for the court to decide whether there might be liability for violation of the "suitability" rule of the NASD and the "know your customer" rule of the New York Stock Exchange. But the court thought that those rules "may in any event be considered as expressions of the industry itself concerning what constitutes proper conduct, the violation of which under certain circumstances may amount to fraud." 283 F. Supp. at 433.

In Twomey v. Mitchum, Jones & Templeton, Inc., 262 Cal. App. 2d 690, 721-22, 69 Cal. Rptr. 222, 244 (1968), a common law action, the court stated in following certain guidelines that had been suggested for the NASD:

> It may be asserted that the proposed guidelines are merely ethical standards and should not be a predicate for civil liability. Good ethics should not be ignored by the law. It would be inconsistent to suggest that a person should be defrocked as a member of his calling, and yet not be liable for the injury which resulted from his acts or omissions.

In Plunkett v. Dominick & Dominick, Inc., 414 F. Supp. 885, 896 (D. Conn. 1976), the court without elucidation referred to the NASD suitability rule as imposing duties "identical to what is at least imposed at common law."

In Michael Batterman, 46 SEC 304 (1976), a consent case, the Commission expressed its particular concern with respect to the suitability of option transactions for particular customers. See also Smith Barney, Harris Upham & Co., Sec. Ex. Act Rel. 21,813, 32 SEC Dock. 766, 768 (1985).

In Delporte v. Shearson, Hammill & Co., Inc., 548 F. 2d 1149 (5th Cir. 1977), the court found a margin account to be unsuitable, but the plaintiff's signature on the margin agreement was forged.

Perhaps most significantly, in Clark v. John Lamula Investors, Inc., 583 F. 2d 594 (2d Cir. 1978), the court held that, under the circumstances, violation of the NASD rule coupled with the scienter finding required by *Hochfelder* amounted to a violation of Rule 10b-5. Although the charge to the jury was limited to "the circumstances," proof of scienter in this context should normally present no great obstacle. See also Mauriber v. Shearson/American Express, Inc., 567 F. Supp. 1231, 1237 (S. D. N. Y. 1983); In re Catanella & E. F. Hutton & Co. Securities Litigation, 583 F. Supp. 1388, 1405 (E. D. Pa. 1984) (knowing purchase of unsuitable security for a discretionary account); Platsis v. E. F. Hutton & Co., CCH Fed. Sec. L. Rep. ¶91,963 at 90,803 n. 2 (W. D. Mich. 1985); Levin v. Shearson Lehman/American Express, Inc., CCH Fed. Sec. L. Rep. ¶92,080 (S. D. N. Y. 1985) (failure to *disclose* lack of suitability); Clark v. Kidder, Peabody & Co., 636 F. Supp. 195, 198 (S. D. N. Y. 1986) (since unsuitable purchase itself is the proscribed act, customer need not allege a *representation*

back to the Supreme Court's "self-fending" concept in the *Ralston Purina* case, which finds expression also in Rule 506(b)(2)(ii), the private offering rule.[78]

Finally — and oddly — it was a common law deceit action involving the sale of insurance rather than securities that gave the Commission the greatest aid and comfort. In a case coming up from Hawaii, the Ninth Circuit held that an insurance agent who had induced the plaintiff to purchase excessive amounts of bank-financed insurance was liable because of his false representation that what he was selling "was a suitable program for plaintiff and his family and fitted his needs."[79]

This evaluation (whether planned or not) has not gone unchallenged: At common law even a business *agent* (let alone a dealer acting as principal) "represents that he has the knowledge which is standard for the profession in which he is employed; there is, however, no representation that his knowledge is complete and accu-

---

of suitability).

On the other hand, the court held in Xaphes v. Merrill Lynch, Pierce, Fenner & Smith, Inc., 632 F. Supp. 471, 481 (D. Me. 1986), that failure of the firm's review procedures with respect to suitability was of no practical import as long as there would have been a finding of suitability even if all relevant information about the customer had been properly reviewed.

The uniform limited offering exemption adopted in 1982 by the North American Securities Administrators Association contains a "reasonable inquiry" suitability condition, but with a presumption of suitability if the investment does not exceed 10 percent of the investor's net worth. It is not stated whether the presumption is rebuttable. CCH NASAA Rep. ¶6201, §D1. For other suitability rules under the blue sky laws, see Baker and Lawrence, Actions Against Broker-Dealers for the Sale of Unsuitable Securities, 13 Stetson L. Rev. 283 (1984). See also CCH NASAA Rep. ¶2604 (oil and gas programs), discussed in Strahota, Oil and Gas Program Offerings, 17 Rev. Sec. Reg. 811 (1984); CCH NASAA Rep. ¶3603 (real estate programs).

In the United Kingdom the 1985 White Paper apparently referred to law, not merely ethics, in stating: "The Government believe that — in line with existing good market practice in the United Kingdom and the United States of America — investment businesses should take account of the expertise, needs and resources of the customer before recommending a particular transaction." Dep't of Trade & Industry, Financial Services in the United Kingdom: A New Framework for Investor Protection, Cmd. 9432 (1985) §7.14.

[78] See p. 318 supra; on the concept as applied in various special situations (e. g., Rule 15c2-5, supra p. 708), see Roach, The Suitability Obligations of Brokers: Present Law and the Proposed Federal Securities Code, 29 Hastings L. J. 1067, 1073-1119 (1978).

[79] Anderson v. Knox, 297 F. 2d 702, 705 (9th Cir. 1961), *cert. denied,* 370 U. S. 915; cf. Steadman v. McConnell, 149 Cal. App. 2d 334, 308 P. 2d 361 (1957); Hardt v. Brink, 192 F. Supp. 879 (W. D. Wash. 1961). It has been claimed that the *Anderson* case has not in fact been followed. Leatherberry, Remedies for the Buyer or Beneficiary of an Unsuitable Life Insurance Plan, 32 Rutgers L. Rev. 431, 447 (1979).

rate."[80] Moreover, there is the question of how much investigation and actual knowledge will satisfy the obligation once it is imposed. For the duty (as the Commission sees it) to inquire into the financial resources of the customer goes beyond the implied warranty of fitness for a particular purpose that is imposed by §2-315 of the Uniform Commercial Code when the seller of goods has reason to know the particular purpose for which the goods are acquired and the buyer relies on the seller's skill or judgment in selecting or furnishing goods that are suitable for the purpose. Will the broker-dealer be held to the standard of "a prudent man in the management of his own property" as under §11 of the 1933 Act? "From a practical standpoint, the broker-dealer trading in an issue or participating in the sale of a small number of shares, as distinguished from being engaged in a major distribution of such securities, could not afford to make an investigation of the type required to be made by a principal underwriter of an issue."[81]

On the other hand, the common law does not set the outer limits of the SEC fraud provisions.[82] And the suitability doctrine has been well rationalized by Dean Mundheim in terms of "risk threshold":

> A suitability doctrine imposes a responsibility on the broker-dealer to take the risk threshold of his customers into account when he recommends or sells securities to them. * * * The broker-dealer may discharge his responsibility under the suitability doctrine by informing the customer of the risk aspects of the transaction in a way which will enable the customer, in light of his individual capabilities, to relate these risks to his risk threshold and thus make his own determination of suitability. If under these circumstances the customer wishes to purchase the security, the broker-dealer can sell it to him even though he does not think it is within the customer's risk threshold.
>
> * * *
>
> If the customer refuses to furnish the broker-dealer with information sufficient to determine the customer's risk threshold, the

[80] Restatement (Second) of Agency §10, Comment c; see also id., §379, which speaks simply of the care and skill that are "standard in the locality for the kind of work which [the agent] is employed to perform."

[81] Kennedy, in Symposium, Current Problems of Securities Underwriters and Dealers, 18 Bus. Law. 27, 76-77 (1962).

[82] See p. 716 supra.

> broker-dealer should not be required to prevent the customer from purchasing securities which are beyond his risk threshold.[83]

As for the question of what constitutes a recommendation, the only time when the broker-dealer is clearly relieved of a suitability duty is when his only relationship with the customer is that of an order clerk; in the intermediate cases between the order clerk situation, where reliance is clearly absent, and the recommendation to an inexperienced customer, where reliance is clearly present, there should be (Dean Mundheim suggests) a presumption of reliance, which, however, the broker-dealer should be free to rebut.[84] He also proposes an NASD guideline on suitability that would suggest ways to handle some of the common but troublesome cases — like the "sweet trusting widow" who turns out to be "a greedy old lady."[85]

4. Fraud by Investment Advisers

Section 206 of the Investment Advisers Act makes it unlawful for any investment adviser, by use of the mails or interstate facilities, directly or indirectly "(1) to employ any device, scheme, or artifice to defraud any client or prospective client;[86] (2) to engage in any transaction, practice, or course of business which operates as a fraud or deceit upon any client or prospective client; * * * [or] (4) to engage in any act, practice, or course of business which is fraudulent, deceptive, or manipulative," with rulemaking authority under Clause (4), as in §15(c)(1) of the 1934 Act, to "define, and prescribe

[83] Mundheim, Professional Responsibilities of Broker-Dealers: The Suitability Doctrine, [1965] Duke L. J. 445, 449-50.

[84] Id. at 450, 472-73.

[85] Id. at 472-79; see, e. g., Scott R. Serfling, Sec. Ex. Act Rel. 21,297, 31 SEC Dock. 380 (1984). For an analysis of the great many variations that go into a determination of suitability, see Bines, Setting Investment Objectives: The Suitability Doctrine — Part II, 4 Sec. Reg. L. J. 418 (1977). For an examination of the economists' "portfolio concept" of risk suitability and a suggestion of a way of using that theoretical model to provide additional substantive content to the legal standards, see Cohen, The Suitability Rule and Economic Theory, 80 Yale L. J. 1604 (1971); but cf. Note, The Regulation of Risky Investments, 83 Harv. L. Rev. 603, 624 (1970): "The law conceives of risk as the risk of capital loss associated with particular securities rather than with the portfolio as a whole."

[86] "Client" means client, not a business partner or associate. Brooks v. Black, — F. Supp. —, — n. 1, CCH Fed. Sec. L. Rep. ¶92,532 at 93,185 n. 1 (D. Mass. 1986) (dictum).

means reasonably designed to prevent, such acts, practices, and courses of business as are fraudulent, deceptive, or manipulative."[87]

The first two clauses are modeled on §17(a)(1) and (3) of the 1933 Act; the substantive portion of the fourth clause is modeled on §10(b) of the 1934 Act; and the rulemaking authority is modeled on §15(c)(2) of the 1934 Act.[88] Consequently, everything that has been said thus far in this chapter applies with equal force to investment advisers *mutatis mutandis.* In other words, Arleen Hughes's course of business violated §206(1) and (2) of the Advisers Act as well as the fraud provisions of the 1933 and 1934 Acts.[89] Section 206, however, can be violated without a securities transaction;[90] indeed, when there is a securities transaction, §206 is hardly needed.

There are three rules under §206(4), with a fourth in the offing:

The first, Rule 206(4)-1, is an advertising rule, which defines "advertisement" to include any communication, addressed to more than one person,

> which offers (1) any analysis, report, or publication concerning securities, or which is to be used in making any determination as to when to buy or sell any security, or which security to buy or sell, or (2) any graph, chart, formula, or other device to be used in making any determination as to when to buy or sell any security, or which security to buy or sell, or (3) any other investment advisory service with regard to securities.

This definition has been considered broad enough to cover advisory material, as well as so-called "progress reports," designed to induce subscriptions.[91]

[87] On §206(3), see p. 842 infra. Section 206(4), together with the rulemaking authority, was added in 1960. Since it is not expressly limited to "clients" like the first three clauses, it might be construed to cover fraudulent advice to a non-securities client with respect to something like gold.

[88] See pp. 805-06 supra.

[89] The Commission's proceeding was based solely on the 1933 and 1934 Acts, because it then had no power to proceed against a person's registration either as a broker-dealer or as an investment adviser for violation of §206 of the Advisers Act.

[90] Ronald B. Donati, Inc., Inv. Adv. Act Rels. 666, 683, 16 SEC Dock. 1081 (1979), 17 SEC Dock. 1215 (1979) (respondent consented to a finding that it had violated §206 by persuading its clients to guarantee its bank loans and ultimately to post their securities as collateral without disclosing its deteriorating financial condition and other outstanding loans).

[91] SEC v. C. R. Richmond & Co., 565 F. 2d 1101, 1105 (9th Cir. 1977); Spear & Staff, Inc., 42 SEC 549, 555-56 (1965); SEC v. Wall St. Publishing Institute, Inc., 591 F. Supp. 1070, 1087 (D. D. C. 1984), *stay granted,* CCH Fed. Sec. L. Rep. ¶91, 635 (D. C. Cir. 1984). In H. I. Glass & Co., Inv. Adv. Act Rel. 1003, 34 SEC Dock. 1028 (1985), the Commission found a violation of Rule 206(4)-1 on the part of a registered adviser who had not informed his clients of his

In announcing the adoption of the rule, the Commission stated that

> it should be borne in mind that investment advisers are professionals and should adhere to a stricter standard of conduct than that applicable to merchants, securities are "intricate merchandise," and clients or prospective clients of investment advisers are frequently unskilled and unsophisticated in investment matters.[92]

Accordingly, the cases stress that advisers' conduct "must be measured from the viewpoint of a person unskilled and unsophisticated in investment matters";[93] that advertisements may be "deceptive and misleading in their over-all effect even though it might be argued that, when narrowly and literally read, no single statement of a material fact was false";[94] and that brochures must not overstate "the amounts and probabilities of gains" and understate "the risks and speculative elements involved."[95]

Rule 206(4)-2 requires advisers who have custody or possession of funds or securities of clients to segregate their securities, hold them in safekeeping, and set up a separate trust account in a bank for the funds belonging to each client. Among other conditions in the rule, the adviser must send each client, at least quarterly, an itemized statement of the funds and securities in his custody or possession and all debits, credits, and transactions in the account during the period; and at least once each calendar year the funds and securities must be verified by an independent public accountant in a surprise examination.

Rule 206(4)-3 prohibits cash payments for the solicitation of clients except under specified circumstances and conditions.[96]

---

executing their transactions through a broker-dealer firm pursuant to an oral agreement whereby 40 percent of the brokerage commissions would go to pay the adviser's expenses.

[92] Inv. Adv. Act Rel. 121 (1961); see also Inv. Adv. Act Rels. 113 (1961) (original proposal), 119 (1961) (amended proposal); Stanford Investment Management, Inc., 43 SEC 864, 867 (1968), and cases cited.

[93] SEC v. C. R. Richmond & Co., 565 F. 2d 1101, 1104-05 (9th Cir. 1977).

[94] Spear & Staff, Inc., 42 SEC 549, 553 (1965).

[95] Stanford Investment Management, Inc., 43 SEC 864 (1968); see also T. J. Holt & Co., Inc., Inv. Adv. Act Rel. 254 (1969). In general, see Marketlines, Inc., 43 SEC 267, 268-70 (1967), *aff'd* sub nom. Marketlines, Inc. v. SEC, 384 F. 2d 264 (2d Cir. 1967), *cert. denied*, 390 U. S. 947; Paul K. Peers, Inc., 42 SEC 539 (1965); Clover Capital Management, Inc., CCH Fed. Sec. L. Rep. ¶73,378 (letter, Oct. 28, 1986) (use of model or actual results is no longer considered fraudulent *per se*, but specified practices are inappropriate).

[96] The Commission cautioned in adopting the rule that it should not be taken as an indication that it was proper to use clients' *brokerage* to pay referral fees. Inv. Adv. Act Rel. 688, 17 SEC Dock. 1293, 1294 n. 4 (1979). See also Sec.

In late 1986 the Commission proposed a Rule 206(4)-4, which would codify the long-standing interpretation that §206 requires an adviser to disclose to clients (1) material facts with respect to a financial condition "that is reasonably likely to impair the ability of the adviser to meet contractual commitments to clients" and (2) a "legal or disciplinary event that is material to an evaluation of the adviser's integrity or ability to meet" those commitments.[97]

The great case under the Advisers Act is *SEC* v. *Capital Gains Research Bureau, Inc.*, decided by the Supreme Court in 1963.[98] In six instances the advisory firm took a long position in a listed stock on the New York Stock Exchange shortly before sending its approximately 5000 subscribers one of its "Special Recommendations" or "Special Bulletins" containing a financial analysis of the particular company without disclosing the firm's position or intention. In each case there was a small market rise and the firm within a few days sold its stock at a profit. There was also one instance of a short position followed by converse activity. The practice is known on Wall Street as "scalping." In a broad opinion (perhaps unduly broad in some of its language) Justice Goldberg stated for the Court (only Justice Harlan dissenting):

(1) "The Investment Advisers Act of 1940 * * * reflects a congressional recognition 'of the delicate fiduciary nature of an investment advisory relationship,' as well as a congressional intent to eliminate, or at least to expose, all conflicts of interest which might incline an investment adviser — consciously or unconsciously — to render advice which was not disinterested. It would defeat the manifest purpose of the Investment Advisers Act of 1940 for us to hold, therefore, that Congress, in empowering the courts to enjoin any practice which operates 'as a fraud or deceit,' intended to require proof of intent to injure and actual injury to clients."[99]

(2) This conclusion is not in derogation of the common law of fraud. "Even in a damage suit between parties to an arms-length transaction, the intent which must be established need not be an

---

Ex. Act §28(e), interpreted in Sec. Ex. Act Rel. 23,170, 35 SEC Dock. 703 (1986).

[97] Inv. Adv. Act Rel. 1035, 36 SEC Dock. 793 (1986).

[98] 375 U. S. 180 (1963).

[99] Id. at 191-92. On the first sentence of this paragraph, see also Transamerica Mortgage Advisors, Inc. v. Lewis, 444 U. S. 11, 17 (1979), infra pp. 913-14 ("§206 establishes 'federal fiduciary standards' "); SEC v. Wall St. Publishing Institute, Inc., 591 F. Supp. 1070, 1084-85 (D. D. C. 1984), *stay granted,* CCH Fed. Sec. L. Rep. ¶91, 635 (D. C. Cir. 1984) (*inter alia,* misleading masthead on "Stock Market Magazine").

intent to cause injury to the client, as the courts below seem to have assumed."[100]

(3) The content of common law fraud has not remained static, and it also has a broader meaning in equity than at law in that an intention to defraud or misrepresent is not a necessary element in equity.[101]

(4) "We cannot assume that Congress, in enacting legislation to prevent fraudulent practices by investment advisers, was unaware of these developments in the common law of fraud. Thus, even if we were to agree with the courts below that Congress had intended, in effect, to codify the common law of fraud in the Investment Advisers Act of 1940, it would be logical to conclude that Congress codified the common law 'remedially' as the courts had adapted it to the prevention of fraudulent securities transactions by fiduciaries, not 'technically' as it has traditionally been applied in damage suits between parties to arms-length transactions involving land and ordinary chattels."[102]

(5) The legislative history indicates that the omission of something like Clause (2) of §17(a) of the 1933 Act "does not seem significant."[103] Clause (2) was included in §17(a), part of a statute that was the first experiment in federal securities regulation, "out of an abundance of caution."[104] "It soon became clear, however, that the courts, aware of the previously outlined developments in the common law of fraud, were merging the proscription against nondisclosure into the general proscription against fraud, treating the former, in effect, as one variety of the latter."[105] In 1940 Congress presumably "deemed a specific proscription against nondisclosure surplusage."[106]

(6) The legislative history of the 1960 amendment of §206 that gave the Commission authority to adopt rules defining and designed to prevent fraudulent practices offers no indication "that Congress intended such rules to substitute for the 'general and flexible' antifraud provisions which have long been considered necessary to control 'the versatile inventions of fraud-doers.' "[107]

(7) The argument that the advice was "honest" in the sense that it was believed to be sound is but another way of putting the re-

[100] 375 U. S. at 195.
[101] Id. at 193-94.
[102] Id. at 195.
[103] Id. at 197.
[104] Id. at 198.
[105] Ibid.
[106] Id. at 199.
[107] Ibid.

jected argument that the elements of technical common law fraud — particularly intent — must be established before an injunction requiring disclosure may be ordered. The Advisers Act was "directed not only at dishonor but also at conduct that tempts dishonor."[108]

Query how much of this will turn out to survive *Aaron,* the 1980 decision that requires scienter in an injunction action under Rule 10b-5.[109] The Court there distinguished *Capital Gains* on the basis essentially of "the delicate fiduciary nature of an investment advisory relationship" and the disparate legislative history of §§10(b) and 206. But, once more, the question is how much to make of the difference in *tone* between the two opinions.

It remains to consider §206(3), which makes it unlawful for an adviser,

> acting as principal for his own account, knowingly to sell any security to or purchase any security from a client, or acting as broker for a person other than such client, knowingly to effect any sale or purchase of any security for the account of such client, without disclosing to such client in writing before the completion of such transaction the capacity in which he is acting and obtaining the consent of the client to such transaction.[110]

In the *Arleen Hughes* case the Commission by way of dictum adopted the same position that had been previously announced in a staff opinion, to the effect that the written disclosure must be made and the consent obtained "before the completion of each transaction of purchase or sale."[111] The Commission added the thought that this provision, apart from requiring that the disclosure be made in writ-

[108] Id. at 200, quoting from United States v. Mississippi Valley Generating Co., 364 U. S. 520, 549 (1961). Dishonor in this field, nevertheless, is a virus that defies immunization. The Special Study found evidence of "scalping" among both brokers and investment advisers. 1 SEC, Report of Special Study of Securities Markets, H. R. Doc. No. 95, 88th Cong., 1st Sess. (1963) 372.

The matter of "scalping" aside, the Commission has also made it clear that Clauses (1) and (2) of §206 are violated by the dissemination of unverified tips, since advisers have at least as great a duty as broker-dealers to use a high degree of care in order to ensure accurate and adequate representations with respect to securities they discuss in printed advisory material. Anne C. Robin, 41 SEC 634, 637 (1963).

[109] Aaron v. SEC, 446 U. S. 680 (1980), supra p. 783.

[110] Written consent, though advisable, is not required. Rule 206(3)-2 provides a nonexclusive method for compliance with §206(3) in connection with an "agency cross-transaction," which is to say, a transaction in which a person acts as adviser in relation to a transaction in which the adviser, or an affiliate, acts as broker for both the advisory client and the other side. See Inv. Adv. Act Rel. 881, 28 SEC Dock. 1034 (1983).

[111] Arleen W. Hughes, 27 SEC 629, 641 n. 17 (1948), *aff'd on other grounds* sub nom. Hughes v. SEC, 174 F. 2d 969 (D. C. Cir. 1949); Op. Dir. Trading & Ex. Div., Inv. Adv. Act Rel. 40 (1945).

ing, was merely declaratory of the common law. The opinions of the Commission and the court also demonstrate that Clause (3) does not define the full measure of the disclosure obligation of an adviser who seeks to trade with his own clients. Therefore, when §206(3) goes on to provide that it does not apply "to any transaction with a customer of a broker or dealer if such broker or dealer is not acting as an investment adviser in relation to such transaction," it does not exclude the applicability of the other three clauses and of the fraud provisions in the 1933 and 1934 Acts.[112]

In 1975 the Commission adopted an exemptive rule, 206(3)-1, in recognition of the fact that the abolition of fixed stock exchange commissions created a §206(3) problem for broker-dealers who "unbundled" their advisory services. The rule exempts advisers who are registered broker-dealers with respect to the providing "of certain impersonal investment advisory services as to which the benefits of the Section 206(3) protections, because of the nature of the relationship between the investment adviser and the client in those situations, are far outweighed by the administrative difficulties and the costs involved in compliance with Section 206(3)."[113] In that connection the Commission recalled that §206(3) did not exclude any other fraud provision that might be applicable, but it modified the 1945 staff opinion[114] that had preceded the *Arleen Hughes* case "in light of the investment advisory business as it has evolved to the present time" by stating that the duty to disclose any particular facts (including cost and market) "will depend both upon the materiality of such facts in each situation and upon the degree of the client's trust and confidence in and reliance on the investment adviser with respect to the transaction."[115]

D. THE "FREE MARKET" CONCEPT

1. A Classic Portrait of Market Manipulation

Related to the field of fraud — but not altogether a part of it as a matter of legal analysis — is the matter of market manipulation.

[112] Ibid.

[113] Inv. Adv. Act Rel. 470, 7 SEC Dock. 686 (1975).

[114] Op. Dir. Trading & Ex. Div., Inv. Adv. Act Rel. 40 (1945), supra p. 842 n. 111.

[115] Inv. Adv. Act Rel. 470, 7 SEC Dock. 686, 687 (1975); Note to Rule 206(3)-1.

The practice is probably as old as the securities markets.[1] And — perhaps because the tragedy involved in some of the notorious market pools has been mixed with an element of drama — there is a substantial literature on the classic manipulation techniques.[2] The practices of the typical "bull" pools of the years before the SEC have been described in this "simplified composite picture":[3]

> * * * The group first secures an option to purchase at a price higher than the then market quotation a large block of a stock which possesses actual or potential market appeal[12] and an easily controllable floating supply. It is the task of the pool manager and operator to raise the market price above the option price, and, if the supply on the market remains constant,[14] this can be accomplished only by increasing the demand. The most effective manner of inducing others to purchase is to have a favorable ticker tape record which indicates to prospective purchasers that others consider the security to be underpriced. The manager opens a number of accounts with various brokers and, fortified by a knowledge of the condition of the market obtained from the book of a specialist, enters both buying and selling orders with a preponderance of the former so that the price is made to rise slowly upon an increasing volume of transactions. In the cruder form of operation many of these transactions will be washed sales in which the operator is both buyer and seller

C. 9D [1] In 1903 it was estimated that roughly a third of all the trading on the New York Stock Exchange represented manipulation, a third represented members' floor trading, and a third represented actual buying and selling by pools and public. S. Pratt, The Work of Wall Street (1903) 48.

[2] See, e. g., Twentieth Century Fund, Inc., The Security Markets (1935) c. 13; Stock Exchange Practices, Report of Com. on Banking & Currency, S. Rep. No. 1455, 73d Cong., 2d Sess. (1934) 30-55; J. Flynn, Security Speculation (1934) cc. 5, 6.

[3] Comment, Market Manipulation and the Securities Exchange Act, 46 Yale L. J. 624, 626-28 (1937).

[12] Since the success of the manipulative venture depends on the ability of the operator to induce the public to purchase the security, the probabilities of a profitable outcome are enhanced if the stock is one which may easily be played up to the trader's imagination. Thus, the radio securities in 1929, the liquor stocks in 1933, and the aircraft securities in 1934 all lent themselves to manipulation. * * * [As a matter of fact, a pool that operated in Libbey-Owens-Ford Glass Co. in June 1933 was materially aided by a popular delusion that the company made glass bottles, so that the stock was a Repeal stock. Actually the company made no bottles at all. It was confused with Owens-Illinois Glass Co. See Stock Exchange Practices, Report of Com. on Banking & Currency, S. Rep. No. 1455, 73d Cong., 2d Sess. (1934) 36-37.]

[14] In actual practice the supply is diminished. The operator may drive down the price to touch off stop-loss orders and cause weak holders of the stock to sell, thereby enabling him to purchase more readily. He also contracts with large holders of the stock in order that their holdings may be kept off the market for a suitable period of time. Thus, supply is decreased as well as demand stimulated, and the pool attains its mark-up in price by attacking both sides of the market.

of the same stock; in others known as matched orders he enters orders to sell with the knowledge that some confederate is concomitantly entering orders to purchase the same amount of stock at the same price. As the price slowly rises, a complex publicity apparatus is set into motion to aid the stimulation of demand: The directors of the corporation whose stock is being manipulated, who may be members of the pool, issue favorable, but not wholly true, statements concerning the corporation's prospects; brokers, likewise interested in the operations, advise customers through market letters and customers' men to purchase the stock; subsidized tipster sheets and financial columnists in the daily papers tell glowingly of the corporation's future; "chisellers," "touts," and "wire-pluggers" are employed to disseminate false rumors of increased earnings or impending merger. As the market price passes the option price, the operator exercises his option and, increasing his sales over purchases, carefully unloads upon the public the optioned stock as well as that acquired in the process of marking up the price. But the operator does not necessarily rest with this gain. If he is able to distribute his holdings, he may sell short, and the stock, priced at an uneconomically high level and bereft of the pool's support, declines precipitately. As it approaches its normal quotation the pool covers its short position, thereby profiting both from the rise which it has engineered and the inevitable reaction.

2. Manipulation Before the SEC

It is of the essence of the economic function of a securities exchange that it be a free market — free of the artificiality of manipulation (the laying of hands on the scales) as it is free of the unfairness of insider trading (playing cards with a marked deck). If the Americans have been well ahead of the British in the unceasing struggle against insider trading, the British took the lead in the largely successful fight against manipulation.[4]

The first English manipulation case was *Rex* v. *de Berenger,* decided by the King's Bench in 1814. The Allies were hoping for a speedy end to the war. Many rumors were current, mostly favorable. As each gained credence stocks rose, only to fall when confirmation failed. On the morning of February 21, 1814, a man dressed in a military uniform arrived in Winchester from Dover, scattering French gold among the postillions. He had let it be known on the

[4] In general, see Berle, Liability for Stock Market Manipulation, 31 Colum. L. Rev. 264 (1931); Berle, Stock Market Manipulation, 38 Colum. L. Rev. 393 (1938); Comment, Regulation of Stock Market Manipulation, 56 Yale L. J. 509 (1947).

way that he bore glorious news: Napoleon had been killed and the Allies were at Paris. Shortly afterwards two other men dressed as French Loyalist officers arrived with similar tidings, to disappear forthwith. Stocks immediately rose and, of course, fell again when this rumor proved to be as unfounded as the others. This time, however, the Stock Exchange investigated with success. The first traveler, who had called himself du Bourg, turned out to be de Berenger, a Prussian subject who had sought employment as an instructor of sharpshooters from Admiral Sir Alexander Cochrane. It was at the house of the Admiral's nephew that de Berenger had alighted upon arriving in Winchester. The younger Cochrane was a gallant naval captain who had made a fortune under the prize system and had gone into the stock market. As the market rose with the rumor of Napoleon's death, he and a number of friends sold their holdings and made large profits. The Stock Exchange was determined to prosecute, and Cochrane, de Berenger and seven others were convicted of a conspiracy to raise the price of public Government funds and other Government securities without just cause and with intent to injure the public who might buy such securities on February 21.

Moving in arrest of judgment, the defendants argued that a conspiracy to raise the price of Government funds was not a crime in the absence of some collateral object giving it a criminal character, "as if it had been shewn that on that day the defendants were possessed of certain shares in the funds, and intended to sell them, and thereby, by raising the price, to cheat the particular persons who should become purchasers; or if the indictment had alleged that it was the day on which the commissioners for reducing the national debt were wont to purchase, and that the defendants did it with intent to enhance the price of such purchases."[5] As a matter of fact, it was argued, "the higher the price of the public funds, the better for the country, because the higher the state of public credit."[6] But a unanimous court overruled these objections. It was not necessary to show either that the Government as such had been injured or that the defendants had benefited. Both the means used and the object sought were wrong. The essence of the matter is that the public has a right that a natural market should not be tampered with. As Lord Ellenborough put it:

A public mischief is stated as the object of this conspiracy; the

[5] Rex v. de Berenger, 3 Maule & S. 67, 70, 105 Eng. Reprint 536, 537 (K. B. 1814).

[6] Ibid.

conspiracy is by false rumours to raise the price of the public funds and securities; and the crime lies in the act of conspiracy and combination to effect that purpose, and would have been complete although it had not been pursued to its consequences, or the parties had not been able to carry it into effect. The purpose itself is mischievous, it strikes at the price of a vendible commodity in the market, and if it gives it a fictitious price, by means of false rumours, it is a fraud levelled against all the public, for it is against all such as may possibly have any thing to do with the funds on that particular day. It seems to me also not to be necessary to specify the persons, who became purchasers of stock, as the persons to be affected by the conspiracy, for the defendants could not, except by a spirit of prophecy, divine who would be the purchasers on a subsequent day. The excuse is, that it was impossible they should have known, and if it were possible, the multitude would be an excuse in point of law. But the statement is wholly unnecessary, the conspiracy being complete independantly of any persons being purchasers. I have no doubt it must be so considered in law according to the cases.[7]

Thus there became established in Great Britain, as a matter of criminal law, the concept of a free and open public market. And near the end of the century that concept was applied to a case of manipulation by means of trading alone, without the dissemination of false rumors. "I can see no substantial distinction," Lord Lopes said in *Scott* v. *Brown,* "between false rumours and false and fictitious acts."[8]

[7]3 Maule & S. at 72-73, 105 Eng. Reprint at 538; see also Regina v. Aspinall, 1 Q. B. D. 730 (1876), *aff'd,* 2 Q. B. D. 48 (C. A. 1876). For an interesting account of this case, with emphasis upon Lord Cochrane's part in it, see F. Birkenhead, Famous Trials of History (2d ed. 1926) 193-204. Some of the background facts related in the text are found in this account rather than in the court's opinion. For the latest of several reviews of the case — which concludes, unlike several earlier biographies of Cochrane, that he was clearly guilty — see H. Cecil, A Matter of Speculation: The Case of Lord Cochrane (1965). Guilty or not, Cochrane — who served a term in prison, was forced to leave the Navy, and saw his banner of the Order of the Bath unscrewed from its place in Westminster Abbey to be literally kicked out of the Chapel and down the steps — was not only reelected posthaste to the House of Commons, where he made fierce attacks on the judge in his case, Lord Ellenborough, but also lived to help liberate Chile, Peru, and Brazil, to receive a "free pardon" in 1832 from William IV, to be restored to the Navy List in the rank he would have held if he had never left it, and to be considered for employment in the Crimean War when he was nearly eighty. Appropriately enough, he was also buried in the Abbey (though, lest the matter be overdone, without a public funeral). See also W. Tute, Cochrane: A Life of Admiral the Earl of Dundonald (1965).

[8]Scott v. Brown, Doering, McNab & Co., [1892] 2 Q. B. 724, 730, 61 L. J. (N. S.) 738, 741 (C. A.). That case was an unsuccessful rescission action against a broker who had agreed to buy certain shares on the Exchange for the plaintiff

The pre-SEC cases in the United States followed much the same trend, although in some respects they did not go so far and in other respects they went further. As in England, the cases arose in three contexts — criminal prosecution, litigation between manipulators, and litigation between investor and manipulator.

The criminal attack on manipulation came under the mail fraud statute and special state legislation, primarily in New York. In 1933 Judge Woolsey in the Southern District of New York wholeheartedly adopted the open market theory in overruling a demurrer to an indictment under the mail fraud and conspiracy statutes. The defendants bribed customers' men to tout the stock, "washed" the stock among ninety-one accounts, and put out false statements with respect to the company's earnings. Without regard to this evidence of conventional fraud, Judge Woolsey, after reviewing the English law beginning with the *de Berenger* case, held squarely that the manipulative trading itself was fraudulent.[9] The Second Circuit, in affirming the conviction that followed, sustained the indictment on the narrow ground of the allegations concerning touting, wash sales, and false statements. Consequently, the court held that it "need not enter into a general discussion of the lawfulness of stock 'pools,'

---

with the sole purpose, as the court found, of creating trading on the Exchange at a premium in order to mislead the public as to the market and to induce public buying. Sir Frederick Pollock referred to the case as a modern version of the "well-known legal legend * * * of a highwayman coming into equity for an account against his partner." 9 L. Q. Rev. 105 (1893). But Scott v. Brown contains a dictum to the effect that a third person induced to buy from the manipulators at an unfair price may sue any or all of them for damages. [1892] 2 Q. B. at 734, 61 L. J. (N. S.) at 743. This is supported by the cases to the extent that the plaintiffs have been able to work out a contract or trust relationship with the defendants. E. g., Barry v. Croskey, 2 J. & H. 1, 70 Eng. Reprint 945 (Ch. 1861). Otherwise, however, the British courts have been reluctant to adopt the free market concept. As a result, plaintiffs purchasing on the open market have been unable to surmount the hurdles of reliance and privity, as is so often the case in common law deceit actions. E. g., Salaman v. Warner, 64 L. T. R. (N. S.) 598, 7 T. L. R. 431 (Q. B. 1891), *aff'd*, 65 L. T. R. (N. S.) 132, 7 T. L. R. 484 (C. A. 1891). On the English cases generally, see Moore and Wiseman, Market Manipulation and the Exchange Act, 2 U. Chi. L. Rev. 46, 57-65 (1934).

Interesting analogies, whose influence may be noticed in the common law manipulation cases, are afforded by the early English statutory crimes (borrowed from the Roman law) of engrossing, regrating, and forestalling. 5 & 6 Edw. 6, c. 14 (1551-52). Engrossing resembled the modern practice of cornering the supply. Forestalling consisted of intercepting the seller on his way to the market and buying his wares to keep them off the market. Regrating was the process of producing an artificial scarcity by buying up goods in the market and reselling them in or near the same market. See 3 Wharton, Criminal Law and Procedure (1957) c. 45, esp. §1193; Mason, Monopoly in Law and Economics, 47 Yale L. J. 34, 38-39 (1937).

[9] United States v. Brown, 5 F. Supp. 81, 85 (S. D. N. Y. 1933).

as the Judge did below."[10] At the same time, it did not overrule the District Court's holding to the effect that interference with a free and open market by manipulative trading is itself fraudulent. And substantially the same results have been reached under various provisions formerly in the New York Penal Law and now in the General Business Law.[11]

So far as litigation between manipulators is concerned, before the mid-1930s there was no American case of manipulation by trading alone, like *Scott* v. *Brown*. The courts refused to enforce contracts in the extreme cases of corners,[12] or contracts to effect fictitious transactions[13] or for the touting of securities.[14] But otherwise neither the defendants nor the courts seem to have raised the question of illegality or public policy in litigation between pool members.[15] Then in the late 1930s two courts — perhaps influenced by the passage of the SEC statutes, although both cases were decided at common law — went even further than *Scott* v. *Brown* in that they refused to enforce contracts for "stabilization" or "pegging," which (as we shall see) is a relatively benign form of manipulation.[16]

In the context of litigation between a third party and one of the manipulators, the American cases have followed much the same pattern as the British. Contracts of sale between manipulators and innocent persons have been held voidable upon proof of manipulation.[17] However, the right of an open market purchaser to re-

[10] Id., 79 F. 2d 321, 323 (2d Cir. 1935), *cert. denied* sub nom. McCarthy v. United States, 296 U. S. 650; see also Harris v. United States, 48 F. 2d 771 (9th Cir. 1931); Goddard v. United States, 86 F. 2d 884 (10th Cir. 1936). Judge Woolsey's opinion in *Brown* was cited favorably in Schreiber v. Burlington Northern, Inc., 472 U. S. 1, 7 n. 4 (1985) (see p. 529 supra), which cited the text without citing *Brown's* subsequent history.

[11] N. Y. Gen. Bus. Law §§339 to 339-h For references to similar statutes in a number of other states that have stock exchanges, see Moore and Wiseman, Market Manipulation and the Exchange Act, 2 U. Chi. L. Rev. 46, 66 n. 85 (1934).

[12] Sampson v. Shaw, 101 Mass. 145 (1869). A corner is a purchase of more than the available supply of a security (or commodity) with the intention of forcing settlement from short sellers at the purchaser's figure.

[13] Livermore v. Bushnell, 5 Hun 285 (N. Y. App. Div., 1st Dept. 1875).

[14] Ridgely v. Keene, 134 App. Div. 647, 119 N. Y. S. 451 (2d Dept. 1909).

[15] For a collection of such cases, see Moore and Wiseman, Market Manipulation and the Exchange Act, 2 U. Chi. L. Rev. 46, 69-70 (1934).

[16] Harper v. Crenshaw, 82 F. 2d 845 (D. C. Cir. 1936), *cert. denied*, 298 U. S. 685; Bigelow v. Oglesby, 302 Ill. App. 27, 36, 23 N. E. 2d 378, 382 (1939).

[17] Willcox v. Harriman Securities Corp., 10 F. Supp. 532 (S. D. N. Y. 1933); Singleton v. Harriman, 152 Misc. 323, 272 N. Y. Supp. 905 (Sup. Ct. 1933), *aff'd per curiam*, 241 App. Div. 857, 271 N. Y. S. 996 (1st Dept. 1934); Scherer v. Zacks, [1952] 4 D. L. R. 503, [1952] O. W. N. 341 (Ont. High Ct.). On the other hand, the courts have held buyers to their contracts when they *knew* that their sellers were rigging the market or when they were *in pari delicto*. In re

cover against market manipulators seems to be quite a different matter.[18]

3. Manipulation of the Exchange Markets Under the SEC Statutes

As in the general field of fraud, the supervention of the SEC statutes in no sense derogates from the body of common and statutory law that has been developed independently of those Acts. The function of the SEC statutes has been to give a greater degree of definiteness to the concept of manipulation and to supply an enforcement and preventive mechanism. The problem of manipulation was attacked by Congress in a number of ways — by specific prohibitions, by giving the Commission rulemaking authority in certain areas, and by a general prohibition against any trading for a manipulative purpose. As we shall see, the statutory scheme is a blend of fraud theories and the open market concept developed in the English and American cases.

First of all, there are the basic fraud provisions — §17(a) of the 1933 Act and §§10(b) and 15(c)(1) and (2) of the 1934 Act —which, like the mail fraud statute, have been used in the attack on certain types of manipulative practices. In fact, §§10(b), 15(c)(1), and 15(c)(2) use the *word* "manipulative," which, the Supreme Court has said *obiter*, is "virtually a term of art" reflecting Congress's intention "to prohibit the full range of ingenious devices that might be used to manipulate securities prices."[19] Moreover, some of the rules under these sections have a distinctly antimanipulative flavor — for example, Rule 15c1-8, which prohibits broker-dealers in certain circumstances from offering securities at a price represented as being related to the market price unless an independent market exists.[20]

Next, Congress in §9 of the Exchange Act outlawed a series of specific manipulative practices. Section 9(a)(1) prohibits wash sales and matched orders[21] when the purpose is to create "a false or misleading appearance of active trading in any security registered on a national securities exchange, or a false or misleading appear-

---

B. Solomon & Co., 268 Fed. 108 (2d Cir. 1920); Bacciocco v. Transamerica Corp., 2 Cal. App. 2d 595, 38 P. 2d 417 (1934).

[18]See Moore and Wiseman, Market Manipulation and the Exchange Act, 2 U. Chi. L. Rev. 46, 70-72 (1934).

[19]Santa Fe Industries, Inc. v. Green, 430 U. S. 462, 477 (1977), supra p. 803.

[20]See also Rules 10b-2, 10b-6, infra pp. 862-63.

[21]See pp. 844-45 supra.

ance with respect to the market for any such security."[22] And §9(a)(3)-(5) contains a series of prohibitions against manipulation of the market (again in registered securities) by false statements, rumors, or paid touts.[23]

In addition, §9(b)-(d) gives the Commission rulemaking authority with respect to the acquisition, endorsement, and guarantee of any put, call, or other option or privilege, as well as the effecting of transactions in connection with which any such option or privilege is outstanding. We have already noted the manipulation-prone history of these instruments in considering whether they are "securities."[24] A 1959-61 staff report[25] discussed, *inter alia,* the Put and Call Brokers and Dealers Association, organized in 1934 to represent the interests of put and call broker-dealers during the legislative hearings. That report found: "The attitude of the Association has always been that it will police its members and it has been most willing to adopt recommendations made from time to time by the Commission's staff."[26] Whether on that account or because the other antimanipulative weapons have worked well enough so that there would be no point in needlessly hampering the legitimate use of options, there are no option rules of an antimanipulative nature in effect under §9.[27] This, of course, does not preclude a violation

[22] The specific purpose requirement has been given a stringent reading. Harold T. White, 3 SEC 466, 510 (1938); Southern Brokerage Co. v. Cannarsa, 405 S. W. 2d 457, 461-62 (Tex. Civ. App. 1966), *cert. denied,* 386 U. S. 1004. Thus, there is nothing illegal about the sale and immediate repurchase of a security in order to establish a capital gain and obtain the benefit of a higher cost base for tax purposes. Again, the mere "crossing" of orders is not itself illegal. "Where a broker has both an order to buy and an order to sell at the same price, the transaction can be consummated by the crossing of these orders in accordance with the protective provisions of the exchange rules." Michael J. Meehan, 2 SEC 588, 606 (1937).

[23] Although all of §9 is limited to securities registered on a national securities exchange, it is not altogether correct to speak of §9 as coextensive with manipulation of the exchange markets. On the one hand, it applies to over-the-counter manipulation of registered securities — that is, those that are either listed or admitted to unlisted trading privileges. Charles C. Wright, 3 SEC 190, 213 (1938), *rev'd on other grounds* sub nom. Wright v. SEC, 112 F. 2d 89 (2d Cir. 1940), order *reinstated on remand,* 12 SEC 100 (1942), *aff'd* sub nom. Wright v. SEC, 134 F. 2d 733 (2d Cir. 1943). On the other hand, §9 does not apply to exempted securities even when they are traded on an exchange, §9(f); on the definition of "exempted securities," §3(a)(12), see p. 422 supra. There the attack on manipulation is made on the same basis as it is with respect to securities that are traded solely in the over-the-counter market.

[24] See pp. 233-34 supra.

[25] SEC, Div. of Trading & Exchanges, Report on Put and Call Options (1961).

[26] Id at 100.

[27] The Commission did adopt a Rule 9b-1 in 1973 to require the filing by exchanges of plans regulating transactions in options. Sec. Ex. Act Rel. 10,552, 3 SEC Dock. 224 (1973). But after the 1975 statutory amendments the Com-

of §9(a) when transactions in connection with an option are involved.[28] Moreover, we have already noticed §9(g), added as part of the codification of the SEC-CFTC "treaty," which gives the Commission rulemaking power with respect to "any put, call, straddle, option, or privilege on any security, certificate of deposit, or group or index of securities * * *, or any put, call, straddle, option or privilege entered into on a national securities exchange related to foreign currency (but not, with respect to any of the foregoing, an option on a contract for future delivery)."[29] And there are various exchange rules governing options.[30]

It is too early to say whether the revolution in this field with the creation of the Chicago Board Options Exchange in 1974 will give rise to new problems of manipulation. One of the concerns expressed by the Commission in initiating the study that led to the 1978 report[31] related to "the ability of self-regulatory organizations to detect price manipulations of options and their underlying securities."[32]

---

mission repealed the rule because its procedures were largely duplicated by the new §19(b) and Rule 19b-4, with respect to the filing of self-regulatory organizations' rule changes generally. Sec. Ex. Act Rel. 11,604, 7 SEC Dock. 652, 655 (1975). On the altogether different Rule 9b-1 adopted in 1982 — basically a disclosure rule of the 1933 Act type — see p. 235 supra.

[28] Harold T. White, 3 SEC 466, 535-37 (1938).

[29] See pp. 240, 241 n. 37 supra.

[30] See e. g., N. Y. Stock Ex. Rules 77, 96, 102, 105, 424, CCH N. Y. Stock Ex. Guide ¶¶2077, 2096, 2102, 2105, 2424.

[31] Report of the Special Study of the Options Markets to the Securities and Exchange Commission, House Com. Print 96-IFC3, 96th Cong., 1st Sess. (1978).

[32] Sec. Ex. Act Rel. 14,056, 13 SEC Dock. 366, 372 (1977). See J. Newman & Co., Sec. Ex. Act Rel. 14,384, 13 SEC Dock. 1401 (1978) (option manipulation case); cf. Shultz v. SEC, 614 F. 2d 561 (7th Cir. 1980) (circular trading by CBOE marketmaker in violation of exchange rules).

In late 1973, in connection with the commencement of listed options trading on the Chicago Board Options Exchange, the SEC adopted Rule 12a-6 to exempt the underlying listed stocks from §12(a) registration if certain conditions were met. Sec. Ex. Act Rel. 10,123, 1 SEC Dock. No. 12, p. 4 (1973). The purpose of the rule was to relieve the option-trading exchanges of the need to register the underlying stocks pursuant to §12(a) (or to apply for unlisted trading privileges), but only when the particular exchange had provided for comparable disclosure with respect to both securities and did not seek to establish trading markets in the underlying stocks.

In May 1985 the Commission amended Rule 12a-6 to extend the exemption to over-the-counter stocks if quotation information was disseminated through NASDAQ. Sec. Ex. Act Rel. 22,025, 33 SEC Dock. 14 (1985). The Commission concurrently announced its conditional agreement in principle with proposals by the option-trading exchanges to change their own rules in order to permit a pilot program in side-by-side marketmaking in the six most active securities designated as National Market System securities pursuant to Rule 11Aa2-1(b)(1) (see pp. 696-97 supra). Sec. Ex. Act Rel. 22,026, 33 SEC Dock. 18 (1985). This was made subject to Commission determinations that grants of unlisted trading

Finally, these specific provisions in §9 are complemented by §9(e), a provision on civil liability that will be considered in the next chapter, and a general provision in §9(a)(2), which has led the attack on manipulation of the exchange markets:

> It shall be unlawful for any person, directly or indirectly, by the use of the mails or any means or instrumentality of interstate commerce, or of any facility of any national securities exchange, or for any member of a national securities exchange * * * [i] To effect, alone or with one or more other persons, a series of transactions in any security registered on a national securities exchange [ii] creating actual or apparent active trading in such security or raising or depressing the price of such security, [iii] for the purpose of inducing the purchase or sale of such security by others.

The object of §9(a)(2) — which the Commission has termed "the very heart of the act"[33] — is to outlaw not only pool operations, but "every other device used to persuade the public that activity in a security is the reflection of a genuine demand instead of a mirage."[34] This accounts for the general language of the section. And the bracketed numbers here added indicate the three elements that must be proved.

(i) One who initiates a transaction "effects" it even though he acts as agent for another;[35] and the phrase, "alone or with one or more other persons," embraces considerably more than the idea of a common plan or conspiracy. The word "series" is satisfied by as

---

privileges and the practice of exchange side-by-side trading in the pilot stocks would be consistent with the Act and the creation of adequate equity and options audit trails.

Most recently, in late 1985, the Commission having announced its readiness to grant unlisted trading privileges in certain National Market System securities (Sec. Ex. Act Rel. 22,412, 33 SEC Dock. 1435 (1985), supra Supp. p. 593 n. d), it published another considered release in which it discussed the comments on the May options release and denied a petition by the NASD for reconsideration of that release (Sec. Ex. Act Rel. 22,439, 34 SEC Dock. 95 (1985)). The Commission expressed its continued belief that "allowing side-by-side marketmaking in the OTC market but not on exchanges * * * would subject exchanges to unfair competitive disadvantages." Id. at 97.

[33] SEC, Report on Proposals for Amendments to the Securities Act of 1933 and the Securities Exchange Act of 1934, H. R. Com. Print, Com. on Int. & For. Commerce, 77th Cong., 1st Sess. (1941).

[34] Stock Exchange Practices, Report of Com. on Banking & Currency, S. Rep. No. 1455, 73d Cong., 2d Sess. (1934) 54. Both these quotations were repeated in Crane Co. v. Westinghouse Air Brake Co., 419 F. 2d 787, 794 (2d Cir. 1969), *cert. denied,* 400 U. S. 822.

[35] S. Rep. No. 792, 73d Cong., 2d Sess. (1934) 17; Op. Gen. Counsel, Sec. Ex. Act Rel. 605 (1936); Michael J. Meehan, 2 SEC 588, 605, 616 (1937) (transactions for discretionary account).

few as three purchases;[36] perhaps even two would suffice. And the Commission has held that the term "transactions" has a broader meaning than "purchases or sales" — that in an auction market the mere placing of bids, even though they are not met by sellers, "may be as effective an influence on price as a completed sale," since the result would normally be to force other bidders to raise their bids.[37]

(ii) So far as the type of prohibited activity is concerned, there do not seem to be any reported cases without a price change, but it is clear that the creation of trading and changing the price are alternative requirements.[38] It seems apparent, moreover, that, when §9(a)(2) talks of "raising or depressing the price * * * for the purpose of inducing the purchase or sale of such security by others," it means raising the price for the purpose of inducing purchases or depressing the price for the purpose of inducing sales.[39] Even a small price change suffices.[40] And the price of a security may be raised without raising the bid. *Following* the market too closely on a rise with either purchases or bids may be just as instrumental in creating a price rise. The obvious effect of promptly putting a new floor under the market each time it goes up as the result of an independent purchase or bid is to exhaust the supply of securities that may be offered at lower levels and thus to force others to raise their bids.[41]

(iii) Most of the litigation under §9(a)(2), not surprisingly, has involved the troublesome requirement of showing a purpose to *induce others* to buy or sell.[42]

The dictum in *Rex* v. *de Berenger* that "raising or lowering the price of the public funds is not per se a crime"[43] finds expression in the legislative reports underlying the Exchange Act. "If a person is merely trying to acquire a large block of stock for investment, or desires to dispose of a big holding," the House report says, "his

[36] Kidder, Peabody & Co., 18 SEC 559, 568 (1945).

[37] Id. at 568-70; Gob Shops of America, Inc., 39 SEC 92, 101 (1959).

[38] United States v. Stein, 456 F. 2d 844, 850 (2d Cir. 1972).

[39] For an instance of the latter practice (a "bear raid"), see Financial Investments Corp., Sec. Ex. Act Rel. 10,834, 4 SEC Dock. 354 (1974).

[40] Kidder, Peabody & Co., 18 SEC 559, 571 (1945) (1/2 point on a $50 stock); United States v. Stein, 456 F. 2d 844, 846 (2d Cir. 1972), *cert. denied,* 408 U. S. 922.

[41] Sec. Ex. Act Rel. 17,222, 21 SEC Dock. 212, 230 n. 65 (1980).

[42] The Code, as amended after discussions with the Commission, substitutes "for the purpose of raising or depressing the price." §1609(c).

[43] 3 Maule & S. 67, 74, 105 Eng. Reprint 536, 539 (K. B. 1814).

knowledge that in doing so he will affect the market price does not make his action unlawful."[44]

For the rest, the precise theoretical definition of "purpose" — whether there is any distinction between "purpose" and "intent" in the criminal sense — may be left to the metaphysicians.[45] It is more fruitful to consider what evidence has sufficed to prove purpose in specific cases under §9(a)(2). "Since it is impossible to probe into the depths of a man's mind," the Commission has said, "it is necessary in the usual case (that is, absent an admission) that the finding of manipulative purpose be based on inferences drawn from circumstantial evidence."[46] In short, a *motive* to manipulate, when joined with the requisite series of transactions, *prima facie* establishes the manipulative *purpose* and shifts to the accused the burden of going forward with the evidence.[47]

The motive might be an option to purchase a substantial amount of the security at a price above the current market,[48] or a desire to obtain more than the current market price for a block of stock that the manipulator plans to distribute either as owner or as best-efforts underwriter[49] or that is left in an underwriter's hands after a "sticky" offering,[50] or to get rid of a "white elephant,"[51] or to make more attractive a security pledged as collateral for a bank loan that the

[44] H. R. Rep. No. 1383, 73d Cong., 2d Sess. (1934) 20; Frigitemp Corp. v. Financial Dynamics Fund, 524 F. 2d 275, 277 n. 1 (2d Cir. 1975); Alabama Farm Bureau Mutual Casualty Co., Inc. v. American Fidelity Life Ins. Co., 606 F. 2d 602, 615 n. 12 (5th Cir. 1979).

[45] See Cook, Act, Intention, and Motive in the Criminal Law, 26 Yale L. J. 645 (1917). At the hearings, the terms were said to be synonymous. See 15 Stock Exchange Practices, Hearings Before S. Com. on Banking & Currency, 73d Cong., 2d Sess. (1934) 6510.

[46] Federal Corp., 25 SEC 227, 230 (1947). In the oft quoted language of United States v. Allis, 73 Fed. 165, 171 (C. C. E. D. Kan. 1893): "The intent with which an act is done is often more clearly and conclusively shown by the act itself than by any words or explanations of the actor. Thus, if you found a stranger leading your horse, saddled and bridled, from your barn, in the night, without your permission, and he should explain to you that he did not intend to steal him, but was simply leading him out for exercise, you would undoubtedly infer his intent from his act rather than from his words."

[47] Alabama Farm Bureau Mutual Casualty Co., Inc. v. American Fidelity Life Ins. Co., 606 F. 2d 602, 616 (5th Cir. 1979).

[48] Charles C. Wright, 3 SEC 190, 206 (1938), *rev'd on other grounds* sub nom. Wright v. SEC, 112 F. 2d 89 (2d Cir. 1940), *order reinstated on remand*, 12 SEC 100 (1942), *aff'd* sub nom. Wright v. SEC, 134 F. 2d 733 (2d Cir. 1943).

[49] Federal Corp., 25 SEC 227 (1947).

[50] Halsey, Stuart & Co., Inc., 30 SEC 106, 109, 112-14, 124 (1949).

[51] R. J. Koeppe & Co. v. SEC, 95 F. 2d 550 (7th Cir. 1938).

borrower is being pressed to repay or reduce,[52] or to further[53] or defeat[54] a tender offer.

The *evidence* of purpose might be an option to buy successive blocks at stepped-up rates,[55] or the pattern of trading.[56] Again, the series of purchases may be coupled with devices of one sort or another to reduce or "dry up" the overhanging supply of the security (such as agreements with large holders to withhold their securities from the market),[57] or the sending out of misleadingly "bullish" literature,[58] or paying touts to recommend the security,[59] or guaranteeing purchasers against loss,[60] or arranging for the issuer to declare a dividend at a critical juncture in the manipulation.[61]

Immediate resale of the shares purchased by the manipulator is not an indispensable element of the offense,[62] but it is "of great *evidentiary weight* in determining the *purpose* with which the buying was undertaken."[63] Indeed, the Commission has held that, in the absence of a satisfactory explanation, an inference of manipulative purpose arises from the mere fact that "one who has purchased stock in a series of transactions and raised its price disposes of the stock before the true effect of his purchases has been dissipated by other market factors."[64] For this reason, the Commission's General Counsel has advised that a person who effects a series of transactions raising the price of a security for the *bona fide* purpose of acquiring

[52] Op. Gen. Counsel, Sec. Ex. Act Rel. 3056 (1941).

[53] Davis v. Pennzoil Co., 438 Pa. 194, 207-08, 264 A. 2d 597, 603 (1970) (by increasing the price of the offeror's stock).

[54] Crane Co. v. Westinghouse Air Brake Co., 419 F. 2d 787, 792-99 (2d Cir. 1969), *cert. denied,* 400 U. S. 822 (by increasing the price of the target's stock).

[55] United States v. Minuse, 114 F. 2d 36 (2d Cir. 1940).

[56] R. J. Koeppe & Co. v. SEC, 95 F. 2d 550, 552 (7th Cir. 1938) (frequently effecting the opening and closing transactions of the day); United States v. Minuse, 114 F. 2d 36 (2d Cir. 1940) (wash sales and matched orders); F. S. Johns & Co., Inc., 43 SEC 124, 136 n. 14 (1966), *aff'd* sub nom. Dlugash v. SEC, 373 F. 2d 107, 109 (2d Cir. 1967), and *per curiam* sub nom. Winkler v. SEC, 377 F. 2d 517 (2d Cir. 1967) ("reaching" for the security by bidding more than necessary); Crane Co. v. Westinghouse Air Brake Co., 419 F. 2d 787, 793-95 (2d Cir. 1969), *cert. denied,* 400 U. S. 822 ("painting the tape" by buying virtually all the shares traded on a given day, or buying on the exchange so as to establish a "print" on the tape and selling for the most part over the counter so as to minimize publicity and also reduce the "floating supply").

[57] Aurelius F. DeFelice, 29 SEC 595 (1949).

[58] United States v. Minuse, 114 F. 2d 36 (2d Cir. 1940).

[59] Ibid.

[60] Ibid.

[61] Collins v. United States, 157 F. 2d 409 (9th Cir. 1946).

[62] Federal Corp., 25 SEC 227, 231 (1947).

[63] Op. Gen. Counsel, Sec. Ex. Act Rel. 3056 (1941).

[64] Thornton & Co., 28 SEC 208, 223 (1948), *aff'd per curiam* sub nom. Thornton v. SEC, 171 F. 2d 702 (2d Cir. 1948).

a supply that he will be able to dispose of at a profit if a further increase materializes *from other causes* should take care, before making any sales either on or off the exchange, "to permit a sufficient period of time to elapse from [the] time of his last purchase to make sure that the effect of his purchases on the market will have been dissipated, and the market will have found a level (whether above, below, or at, his last purchase price) which is its own independent level, created by outside factors of supply and demand and unaffected by his own activities."[65] It is impossible to tell in advance how much time will be required for the effect of a buyer's purchases to be dissipated. The answer will depend, among other things, on the character of the market, the length of time during which the buying activities continued, their pattern, the extent of the market rise, and the size of the floating supply. The period may be weeks or months. If the purchases dried up virtually the entire supply, it is difficult to say when a resale may be effected without creating an inference that the purchases had a manipulative purpose.

4. Manipulation of the Over-the-Counter Market Under the SEC Statutes

The field of manipulation is no exception to the pre-1964 lopsidedness of the Exchange Act so far as the specificity of regulation of the exchange and over-the-counter markets is concerned. In contrast to the relatively elaborate structure of §9 that Congress erected to deal with manipulation of the market for securities registered on exchanges, the only statutory bases for dealing with the manipulation of unregistered securities are the general antifraud provisions of the 1934 Act — which specifically refer, as we have noticed, to "manipulative" as well as "deceptive" practices — together with §17 of the 1933 Act. Nevertheless, consistently with the legislative intention that the Commission should use its administrative powers to place the regulation of the two markets on a par so far as practicable, it has managed to put over-the-counter manipulation beyond substantially the same pale as manipulation of the exchange markets.

In the *Barrett* case, the first over-the-counter manipulation proceeding, the Commission concluded, after a reference to §9(a)(2):

> We think that there is no reasonable distinction in this respect between manipulation of over-the-counter prices and manipulation of

[65] Op. Gen. Counsel, Sec. Ex. Act Rel. 3056 (1941).

> prices on a national securities exchange, and that both are condemned as fraudulent by the Securities Exchange Act and, in fact, were fraudulent at common law. * * * We believe that the Securities Exchange Act contemplates that Section 15(c)(1) affords to the over-the-counter market at least as great a degree of protection against manipulation or attempted control as is afforded to the exchange market by Section 9(a).[66]

Even when §9 applies, it has been repeatedly held both by the Commission and by the courts that there is a violation of the antifraud provisions when securities are in fact sold at manipulated prices without *disclosure* of the manipulation.[67] So, too, in the *Barrett* case the Commission did not rely solely on the pseudo-9(a)(2) application of §15(c)(1). It fortified its holding with a reference to its long line of decisions to the effect that,

> when a security is sold "at the market," the failure to disclose to purchasers the fact that the market price has been artificially inflated by the sellers' manipulation is an omission to state a material fact and constitutes a fraud on the purchasers.[68]

Whereas this application of the antifraud provisions is essentially ancillary to §9(a)(2) in the exchange cases, it is perhaps more proper in the over-the-counter cases, where there is no specific 9(a)(2) language, to take the further step of proving nondisclosure and thus bring the manipulation more nearly within the conventional fraud theories. Since nondisclosure of a manipulation is usually, if not invariably, essential to its success,[69] this is of little practical consequence. The fact is that in the more recent cases the Commission

[66] Barrett & Co., 9 SEC 319, 328 (1941); see also SEC v. Management Dynamics, Inc., 515 F. 2d 801, 810 (2d Cir. 1975).

Rule 10b-5 and §15(c)(1) are *broader* than §9 in the sense that they contain no purpose requirement. And, of course, the first and third clauses of both the rule and §17(a) must not be overlooked in this context. United States v. Charnay, 537 F. 2d 341 (9th Cir. 1976), *cert. denied,* 429 U. S. 1000.

[67] Coplin v. United States, 88 F. 2d 652, 661-64 (9th Cir. 1973), *cert. denied,* 301 U. S. 703; Thornton & Co., 28 SEC 208, 224 (1948), *aff'd per curiam* sub nom. Thornton v. SEC, 171 F. 2d 702 (2d Cir. 1948); Carroll v. United States 326 F. 2d 72, 76-77 (9th Cir. 1963); United States v. Hayutin, 398 F. 2d 944, 949 (2d Cir. 1968), *cert. denied,* 393 U. S. 961; Davis v. Pennzoil Co., 438 Pa 194, 208, 264 A. 2d 597, 604 (1970). Most of these cases involved offerings represented to be "at the market." See Rule 15c1-8, supra p. 706. But the Commission has held that "The market price level prior to and during the commencement of a secondary [or presumably primary] distribution is an extremely important fact to prospective purchasers, whether the offering be at a fixed price or at the market." Kidder, Peabody & Co., 18 SEC 559, 571 (1945).

[68] Barrett & Co., 9 SEC 319, 329 (1941).

[69] See Santa Fe Industries, Inc. v. Green, 430 U. S. 462, 477 (1977) (dictum).

has been de-emphasizing the 9(a)(2) approach, although it has never been abandoned.[70]

Although a few large-scale manipulations were detected in the early years of the Commission's history, the Commission was able by 1950 to express the belief that manipulation was no longer "an appreciable factor in our markets."[71] Eleven years later the Chairman referred to "evidences of a substantial amount of manipulation."[72] And in April 1967 the American Stock Exchange announced that, in cooperation with the SEC and the United States Attorney's office, it was conducting an investigation of trading into certain listed stocks "which may have been influenced by alleged manipulative activities." There were rumors of underworld involvement, with "talk of entrapment employing prostitutes and incriminating photographs."[73] It does seem fair to say, however, that in recent years attempts to manipulate have become more subtle and complex. And, in large measure, whatever success the Commission has had in this field has been due to the continual improvement in its procedures (as well as the exchanges') for the systematic surveillance of the markets.

5. Stabilization

There is one further provision, §9(a)(6), which acts as a limitation on §9(a)(2) in that it excludes certain types of manipulation ("any series of transactions for the purchase and/or sale of any security registered on a national securities exchange for the purpose of pegging, fixing, or stabilizing the price of such security") from the general prohibition and subjects them to the Commission's rule-making authority.

Stabilization, which is a generic term, has been described by the Commission as "that process whereby the market price of a security is pegged or fixed for the limited purpose of preventing or retarding a decline in contemplation of or during a public offering of securi-

[70] E. g., Gob Shops of America, Inc., 39 SEC 92, 98, 101 (1959).
[71] 16 SEC Ann. Rep. 37 (1950).
[72] Securities Markets Investigation, Hearings Before Subcom. of House Com. on Int. & For. Commerce on H. J. Res. 438, 87th Cong., 1st Sess. (1961) 33.
[73] Wall St. J., Apr. 24, 1967, p. 32, col. 1.

ties."[74] The sudden glut tends to destabilize the market. So usually the syndicate managers reserve the right to stabilize on behalf of syndicate members and during the life of the syndicate. Not infrequently the agreement among underwriters limits the maximum position resulting from stabilizing purchases to a fixed percentage of the amount of securities being offered. When the security is traded on an exchange, a bid for a stated amount of the security is normally placed with the specialist, and it is followed by additional bids for stated amounts if necessary. The result is that the market price of the security is supported or stabilized by absorbing, to the extent of the amounts specified in the bids, all sell orders that meet the bids and are not taken up by others. Moreover, the general publicity given to stabilizing purchases on the ticker tape and in the other reporting media — where they are never distinguished from nonstabilizing purchases — has a secondary stabilizing effect in that nobody is likely to sell in the over-the-counter market or on another exchange at a price materially less than the last reported price on the exchange on which the stabilization is being conducted. When the security to be stabilized is not traded on an exchange, one or more bids are normally placed with various dealers known to be active in the security.[75]

In either case, if the selling pressure gets too heavy to permit the constant "pegging" of the market, the syndicate bid is usually dropped to successively lower levels or it may have to be withdrawn altogether. For the same reason, stabilization cannot be used as a practical matter to stem a market or economic trend of any real significance. On the other hand, in the case of a particularly successful issue, stabilization is unnecessary because the market usually takes care of itself. Thus, as the Commission has observed, "stabilizing is regarded as necessary only in the case of issues which are neither notable successes nor notable failures."[76]

The statute itself recognizes, by placing the provision on stabilization in a section labeled "Prohibition Against Manipulation of Security Prices," that stabilization is a form of manipulation. Indeed, it would hardly lie in the mouth of a person who is stabilizing the price of a security as a means of facilitating its distribution to deny that his transactions are "for the purpose of inducing the

[74] Sec. Ex. Act Rel. 4163 (1948).

[75] Since the word "manipulative" as used in §§10(b) and 15(c)(1) has never had any precise meaning it seems obvious that those sections incorporate the policy reflected in §9(a)(6) of leaving it largely to the Commission to distinguish between stabilization and unlawful manipulation in the over-the-counter market.

[76] Sec. Ex. Act Rel. 2446 (1940).

purchase * * * of such security by others." But Congress found that the evidence as to the value of stabilizing operations was "far from conclusive."[77] And so it authorized the Commission, as the Senate committee put it, "to prescribe such rules as may be necessary or appropriate to protect investors and the public from the vicious and unsocial aspects of these practices."[78] The Commission thus inherited the problem that the English courts had tackled forty years earlier.[79]

In the early years the Commission proceeded in a gingerly fashion. For people do not relish even benign tumors. In a 1940 "Statement of the SEC on the Regulation of Pegging, Fixing and Stabilizing of Security Prices," Commissioner Healey, who favored outright prohibition of stabilization as an interference with free markets, rejected the argument of necessity: "This is about equivalent to saying the distributor cannot induce the public to buy unless he is allowed to fool the public. The reasoning employed would almost justify taking the public's money by force if the corporation needing it had a maturity to meet."[80] And the majority seemed not too comfortable in recognizing that stabilization "is now an integral part of the American system of fixed price security distribution" that is essential for the purpose of "preserving the ready flow of capital into industry" — that "in the field of stabilizing it is faced with an existing condition, not a theory."[81]

In this state of affairs the Commission gradually developed an "SEC common law" of stabilization (Chairman Demmler called it a "folklore") through informal and unpublished rulings of its staff, to the point where the jumble was codified into Rule 10b-7 in 1955, with the concurrent adoption of Rule 10b-6 (to be considered in

[77] H. R. Rep. No. 1383, 73d Cong., 2d Sess. (1934) 10; see also id. at 21.

[78] Stock Exchange Practices, Report of Com. on Banking & Currency, S. Rep. No. 1455, 73d Cong., 2d Sess. (1934) 55.

[79] Six years after Scott v. Brown, supra p. 847, one of the judges who had sat in that case distinguished it and enforced a contract by which jobbers on the Exchange had made a market at a "fair price" while the defendant had distributed a block of stock. Sanderson & Levi v. British Westralian Mine & Share Corp., 43 Sol. J. 45 (Q. B. 1898), *aff'd*, London Times, July 19, 1899, p. 4, col. 1 (C. A.), reprinted in United States v. Brown, 5 F. Supp. 81, 90 n. 1 (S. D. N. Y. 1933), *aff'd,* 79 F. 2d 321 (2d Cir. 1935), *cert. denied* sub nom. McCarthy v. United States, 296 U. S. 650; see also Masterson v. Pergament, 203 F. 2d 315, 335 (6th Cir. 1953), *cert. denied,* 346 U. S. 832. But cf. the *Harper* and *Bigelow* cases, supra 849 n. 16.

[80] Sec. Ex. Act Rel. 2446 (1940).

[81] Demmler, How Shall We Amend the SEC Acts?, 178 Com. & Fin. Chron. 2381, 2438 (1953).

the next section) and Rule 10b-8 (on rights offerings).[82] One's expectation of complexity in an area of this sort is not disappointed on an examination of the rule. But its core is a command that "no person shall (i) begin to stabilize a security at a price higher than the highest current independent bid price for such security or (ii) raise the price at which he is stabilizing" or (iii) stabilize at a price above the current distribution price.[83] There is also a series of exemptions "to provide for unusual situations which may fall within the literal language of a rule but can be demonstrated not to be comprehended within its purpose,"[84] together with disclosure requirements.[85]

6. PROHIBITION OF TRADING DURING DISTRIBUTION [RULE 10b-6]

By 1943 the administrative view had become sufficiently established to warrant publication of a release to the effect that the limitations on stabilization could not be avoided by an underwriter's effecting purchases through its "trading" department, even though that department operated independently of the firm's retail distributing organization.[86] And the general doctrine limiting the trading

[82] Sec. Ex. Act Rel. 5194 (1955). These rules were adopted under §10(b) because of the limitations of §9(a)(6) to registered securities.

Those who looked the gift horse in the mouth thought at first that they saw a risk that the promulgation of anything more than perhaps a statement of policy on the subject would destroy in large measure the elasticity of the informal system of control with which they had learned to live. See Foshay, Market Activities of Participants in Securities Distributions, 45 Va. L. Rev. 907, 919 (1959).

[83] Rule 10b-7(j)(1) and (5). In practice, the stabilizing bid is entered at a price below the current market in order to avoid potential short sellers' bombarding the bid. N. Y. Stock Ex. letter, Oct. 11, 1974, attached to Sec. Ex. Act Rel. 11,051, 5 SEC Dock. 277, 283 (1974). On Rule 10b-7 generally, see Klein, Stabilizing Securities Prices, 5 Sec. Reg. L. J. 13 (1977); Williams, Current Developments Under Exchange Act Rule 10b-7, in Practising Law Institute, Ninth Annual Institute on Securities Regulation (1979) c. 14.

[84] Sec. Ex. Act Rel. 5194 (1955).

[85] Rule 10b-7(k) and (l); see also Rule 17a-2; Reg. S-K, Item 502(d). In Sec. Ex. Act Rel. 20,155, 28 SEC Dock. 960 (1983), the Commission amended Rule 17a-2 to eliminate the requirement that participants in an offering that is stabilized file reports of their transactions, including stabilizing transactions, in the offered securities. Instead information concerning stabilizing transactions must be retained by the syndicate manager.

[86] Op. Dir. Trading & Ex. Div., Sec. Ex. Act Rel. 3505 (1943); see also Op. Gen. Counsel, Sec. Ex. Act Rel. 3056 (1941); Halsey, Stuart & Co., Inc., 30 SEC 106, 123-25 (1949); S. T. Jackson & Co., Inc., Sec. Ex. Act Rel. 4459 (1950) 30 n. 51.

activity of underwriters was codified into Rule 10b-6 as a complement to the stabilization rule in 1955.

The rule prohibits any person who is participating in a "distribution," whether acting alone or with others, from bidding for or buying for any account in which he has a beneficial interest (or attempting to induce any other person to buy) any security that is the subject of the distribution, or any security of the same class and series, or any right to purchase any such security.[87] When Rules 10b-6, 10b-7, and 10b-8 are viewed together, Rule 10b-6 is the central rule that prohibits *all* bidding or purchasing subject to a series of exemptions.[88] Its purpose is "to protect the integrity of the secondary trading market as an independent pricing mechanism and thereby enhance investor confidence in the marketplace."[89]

"Where the rule applies, its prohibition is absolute."[90] This manipulation *per se* approach, with its corollary that the defendant need not be shown to have "actually intended to defraud the marketplace through his purchases,"[91] has been held not to survive the scienter requirement.[92] But *query* whether these cases are correct in reject-

[87]The Commission interprets the rule as including officers and directors of the issuer in a distribution. SEC v. Burns, 816 F. 2d 471, 475-76 (9th Cir. 1987).

See also the much older Rule 10b-2, which in general prohibits a person who is interested in a distribution from paying compensation to a second person for soliciting a third person to buy the security on an exchange. The concept underlying these overlapping rules — "that buying (or inducing purchases) during a distribution is manipulation *per se* without regard to any sort of purpose requirement as in X9(a)(2)" (2 Code 677) — was considered sufficiently basic to warrant statutory codification into a single §1609(d). See generally 2 Code 677-81; Lewis, Overview of Rules 10b-2 and 10b-6, in Practising Law Institute, The 10b Series of Rules (Corp. Prac. Tr. Ser. 21, 1975) c. 9 at 279-80.

[88]Two of the exemptions are for transactions permitted by Rules 10b-7 and 10b-8. At the same time, those two rules are not *merely* exemptions from Rule 10b-6. In form, they contain their own prohibitions with their own exemptions. Consequently, a transaction that is not permitted by Rule 10b-7 or 10b-8 violates one or the other of those rules and, as a result of the destruction of the exemptions from Rule 10b-6, the latter rule as well. Goldstein v. Regal Crest, Inc., 62 F. R. D. 571, 575 (E. D. Pa. 1974).

Another significant exemption applies when the distribution is to the employees or shareholders of an issuer or subsidiary pursuant to a "bonus, profit-sharing, pension, retirement, thrift, savings, incentive, stock purchase, stock ownership, stock appreciation, stock option, dividend reinvestment or similar plan." Rule 10b-6(c)(4).

[89]Sec. Ex. Act Rel. 24,003, 37 SEC Dock. 602, 603 (1987).

[90]Jaffee & Co. v. SEC, 446 F. 2d 387, 391 (2d Cir. 1971).

[91]Ibid.

[92]Chemetron Corp. v. Business Funds, Inc., 682 F. 2d 1149, 1164 n. 39 (5th Cir. 1982), *rehearing denied*, 689 F. 2d 190 (5th Cir. 1982), *vacated on other grounds*, 460 U. S. 1007 (1983); Robertson v. Dean Witter Reynolds, Inc., 749 F. 2d 530, 540 (9th Cir. 1984) (*Hochfelder* requires scienter for all §10(b) rules); SEC v. Burns, 816 F. 2d 471, 474 (9th Cir. 1987); cf. SEC v. Mick Stack Asso-

ing the Commission's argument that the specific acts proscribed by Rule 10b-6 are inherently manipulative or deceptive.[93] Indeed, *query* whether an independent scienter element is not redundant as applied to provisions like the first and third clauses of §10(b) — since scienter is implicit in their "fraud" and "deceit" language — as distinct from a provision like the second clause, which speaks in terms of an "untrue statement" or "omission."

A key question, obviously, goes to the meaning of "distribution" in this context, which the rule defines in a way that "substantially reflects current decisional law":[94]

> For purposes of this section only, the term "distribution" means an offering of securities, whether or not subject to registration under the Securities Act of 1933, that is distinguished from ordinary trading transactions by the magnitude of the offering and the presence of special selling efforts and selling methods.[95]

On the one hand, the term is not limited to its meaning in §2(11) of the 1933 Act, the definition of "underwriter"; for one thing, the absence of control is irrelevant.[96] On the other hand, not every distribution that is registerable under the 1933 Act comes within Rule 10b-6. In 1975, before defining the term in the rule itself, the Commission had overruled its earlier view to the contrary,[97] stating that it could result in unnecessary disruption of the trading markets, particularly when a specialist or other marketmaker had acquired registered shares in the performance of his normal func-

---

ciates, Inc., 675 F. 2d 1148, 1150 n. 1 (10th Cir. 1982) (Rule 10b-13, supra p 526). On the scienter requirement, see p. 794 supra.

Robertson involved Rule 10b-16 (supra p. 703 n. 15), on disclosure of credit terms in margin transactions. And it has been argued *against* a scienter requirement in that context that, since Congress created a private right of action without scienter under the Truth in Lending Act and exempted broker-dealers in contemplation of "substantially similar" requirements to be imposed by Commission rule, it must have anticipated an analogous remedy. Haynes v. Anderson & Strudwick, Inc., 508 F. Supp. 1303, 1321 (E. D. Va. 1981).

[93] In Edward J. Mawod & Co. v. SEC, 591 F. 2d 588, 595 (10th Cir. 1979), the court noted "that the wash sale and matched order are per se manipulative and are so regarded in the *Ernst & Ernst* scheme of things," citing Ernst & Ernst v. Hochfelder, 425 U. S. 185, 206 (1976).

[94] Sec. Ex. Act Rel. 19,565, 27 SEC Dock. 432, 435 (1983). See Bruns Nordeman & Co., 40 SEC 652, 660 (1961); Schraufnagel v. Broadwall Securities Corp., CCH Fed. Sec. L. Rep. ¶91,827 at 95,849 (S. D. N. Y. 1966).

[95] Rule 10b-6(c)(5).

[96] SEC v. American Beryllium & Oil Corp., 303 F. Supp. 912, 916 (S. D N. Y. 1969).

[97] Jaffee & Co., Sec. Ex. Act Rel. 8866 (1970), *aff'd in relevant part and vacated on other grounds* sub nom. Jaffee & Co. v. SEC, 446 F. 2d 387 (2d Cir. 1961).

tions.[98] It has also been said — a point reminiscent of some of the 1933 Act exemptions — that, at least under certain circumstances, a distribution cannot be considered complete "until the shares came to rest in the hands of public investors."[99]

For the rest, there are provisions on when the trading prohibition begins and when it ends; and the answers vary depending on whether the person that wants to trade is an issuer or other distributor, an underwriter or "prospective underwriter," a broker or dealer, or another participant in the distribution.

The rule is specific that

> The distribution of a security (1) which is immediately exchangeable for or convertible into another security, or (2) which entitles the holder thereof immediately to acquire another security, shall be deemed to include a distribution of such other security within the meaning of this rule.[100]

One effect of Clause (2) is, at least arguably, to prevent an exchange tender offeror from buying the target's securities for which the offeror's securities are exchangeable. But the substantial codification of this interpretation by the adoption of Rule 10b-13 in 1969[101] makes its validity "of secondary importance."[102] And, as part of the deregulatory mood that in late 1982 produced a safe harbor rule numbered 10b-18,[103] the Commission concurrently exempted

[98] Collins Securities Corp., Sec. Ex. Act Rel. 11,766, 8 SEC Dock. 250, 256 (1975), *remanded on other grounds* sub nom. Collins Securities Corp. v. SEC, 562 F. 2d 820 (D. C. Cir. 1977). In Oppenheimer & Co., Inc., Sec. Ex. Act Rel. 16,817, 20 SEC Dock. 58, 59 n. 7 (1980), the Commission stated that *Collins* did not alter the definition in *Bruns,* supra p. 864 n. 94.

[99] Mayo & Co., Inc., 41 SEC 944, 947 (1964); R. A. Holman & Co., Inc. v. SEC, 366 F. 2d 446, 449 (2d Cir. 1966), *amended on rehearing,* 377 F. 2d 665 (2d Cir. 1967), *cert. denied,* 389 U. S. 991. A distribution continues when an underwriter withholds part of an offering in proprietary or nominee accounts and later sells those securities to the public after trading has begun. SEC v. Blinder, Robinson & Co., CCH Fed. Sec. L. Rep. ¶99,491 (10th Cir. 1983), *cert. denied,* 469 U. S. 1108. However, *customers'* reselling in the aftermarket on being solicited to do so by the underwriter does not extend the period of that underwriter's "distribution." Wall St. West, Inc., Sec. Ex. Act Rel. 20,557, 29 SEC Dock. 751, 752 (1984).

[100] Rule 10b-6(b).

[101] Sec. Ex. Act Rel. 8595 (1969).

[102] Piper v. Chris-Craft Industries, Inc., 430 U. S. 1, 43 n. 30 (1977). The 10b-6 provisions may extend to one or two situations not covered by 10b-13. See Goolrick, Purchases on the Market of Target Company Stock, 26 Bus. Law. 457, 467-71 (1970); Wheat, Trading Activity in Exchange Offers: Some Possible Pitfalls, in Practising Law Institute, Second Annual Institute on Securities Regulation (1971) 291.

[103] See p. 867 infra.

purchases during what it called a "technical" distribution:[104] that is to say,

> bids for or purchases of any security of an issuer, any security of the same class and series as such security, or any security immediately convertible into, or exchangeable or exerciseable for, any such security solely because the issuer or a subsidiary of such issuer *has outstanding* securities which are immediately convertible into, or exchangeable or exerciseable for, such security [italics supplied].[105]

The rule, it bears repeating, is complex.[106] And it was not rendered less so by the adoption of Rule 415, the "shelf registration" rule.[107] Initially the Commission followed the historical interpretation that preceded the rule's codification and extension of the prior practice with respect to "shelf" registrations: the "single distribution position," which subjected *every* "shelf" shareholder to Rule 10b-6 whenever *any* of them took shares off the shelf. But that approach required an unwieldy coordination effort among a sometimes large number of otherwise unrelated shareholders. And it was abandoned in a 1986 interpretation that applies the rule's restrictions to an individual shareholder only when he himself is offering or selling securities off the shelf (unless he is a defined "affiliate" of, or acting in concert with, the issuer or another "shelf" shareholder).[108]

The latest series of amendments came in January 1987. Among other things, they define the rule's applicability to certain persons who are affiliated with participants in a distribution, allow participants to exercise throughout the distribution period standardized call options written before they became participants, and codify the Commission's position that a participant may rely on the rule's exceptions only if the contemplated transactions are not made for manipulative purposes.[109]

[104]Sec. Ex. Act Rel. 19,244, 26 SEC Dock. 868, 876 (1982).

[105]Rule 10b-6(f).

[106]On the relationship between Rule 10b-6 and Rules 137-39 under the 1933 Act (supra pp. 100-01), see Sec. Ex. Act Rel. 21,332, 31 SEC Dock. 454, 458-59 (1984). For a more detailed discussion of the entire manipulation-stabilization area — which has not erupted with the same rigor as most of the SEC volcanos in the past two decades — see 3 and 6 Loss c. 10A-B.

[107]See p. 136 supra.

[108]Sec. Ex. Act Rel. 23,611, 36 SEC Dock. 595 (1986).

[109]Sec. Ex. Act Rel. 24,003, 37 SEC Dock. 602 (1987).

7. The Safe Harbor [Rule 10b-18]

SECURITIES EXCHANGE ACT RELEASE NO. 19,244: PURCHASES OF CERTAIN EQUITY SECURITIES BY THE ISSUER AND OTHERS; ADOPTION OF SAFE HARBOR

26 SEC Dock. 868 (1982)

The Commission has considered on several occasions since 1967 he issue of whether to regulate an issuer's repurchases of its own ecurities. The predicates for this effort have been twofold: First, nvestors and particularly the issuer's shareholders should be able o rely on a market that is set by independent market forces and ıot influenced in any manipulative manner by the issuer or persons losely related to the issuer. Secondly, since the general language f the anti-manipulative provisions of the federal securities laws ffers little guidance with respect to the scope of permissible issuer narket behavior, certainty with respect to the potential liabilities or issuers engaged in repurchase programs has seemed desirable.

The most recent phase of this proceeding is proposed Rule 13e-, which was published for public comment on October 17, 1980.[2] This rule would have imposed disclosure requirements and substanive purchasing limitations on an issuer's repurchases of its common nd preferred stock. These restrictions, which generally would have mited the time, price, and volume of purchases, also would have een imposed on certain persons whose purchases could be deemed o be attributable to the issuer. In addition, the issuer, its affiliates, nd certain other persons would have been subject to a general ntifraud provision in connection with their purchases of the issuer's ommon and preferred stock.

The Commission has recognized that issuer repurchase programs re seldom undertaken with improper intent, may frequently be of ubstantial economic benefit to investors, and, that, in any event, ndue restriction of these programs is not in the interest of inves-rs, issuers, or the marketplace. Issuers generally engage in re-urchase programs for legitimate business reasons and any rule in is area must not be overly intrusive. Accordingly, the Commission as endeavored to achieve an appropriate balance between the goals escribed above and the need to avoid complex and costly restric-ons that impinge on the operation of issuer repurchase programs.

In light of these considerations, and based on the extensive public les developed in this proceeding, the Commission has determined

[2] [Sec. Ex. Act Rel. 17,222, 21 SEC Dock. 212 (1980).]

that it is not necessary to adopt a mandatory rule to regulate issuer repurchases. Accordingly, the Commission has today withdrawn proposed Rule 13e-2, and, as discussed in this release, is amending Rule 10b-6 to eliminate most issuer repurchase regulation under that rule. In lieu of direct regulation under Rule 10b-6 and proposed Rule 13e-2, the Commission has determined that a safe harbor is the appropriate regulatory approach to offer guidance concerning the applicability of the anti-manipulative provisions of Rule 10b-5 and Section 9(a)(2) to issuer repurchase programs. New Rule 10b-18 reflects this determination.

The Commission wishes to stress, however, that the safe harbor is not mandatory nor the exclusive means of effecting issuer purchases without manipulating the market. As a safe harbor, new Rule 10b-18 will provide clarity and certainty for issuers and broker-dealers who assist issuers in their repurchase programs. If an issuer effects its repurchases in compliance with the conditions of the rule, it will avoid what might otherwise be substantial and unpredictable risks of liability under the general anti-manipulative provisions of the federal securities laws.[5] * * *

The Commission emphasizes that no affirmative inference should be drawn that bids for or purchases of an issuer's stock by persons to which the safe harbor is not explicitly available, or with respect to securities other than the issuer's common stock, should be made in accordance with the safe harbor. The safe harbor is not intended to define the appropriate limits to be observed by those persons not covered by the safe harbor nor the appropriate limits to be observed by anyone when purchasing securities other than common stock. In addition, the safe harbor is not the exclusive means by which issuers and their affiliated purchasers may effect purchases of the issuer's stock in the marketplace. Given the greatly varying characteristics of the markets for the stock of different issuers, there may be circumstances under which an issuer could effect repurchases outside of the guidelines that would not raise manipulative concerns. This is especially the case in the context of the uniform volume guide

[5] Paragraph (b) of the rule provides that any issuer and its affiliated purchaser could not be held liable under the antimanipulative provisions of Section 9(a)(2) of the Act or Rule 10b-5 under the Act solely by reason of the number of brokers or dealers used, and the time, price, and amount of bids for or purchases of common stock of the issuer, if such bids or purchases are effected in compliance with all of the conditions of paragraph (b) of the rule. Of course, Rule 10b-18 is not a safe harbor from violations of Rule 10b-5 which may occur in the course of an issuer repurchase program but which do not entail manipulation. * * *

lines, which cannot easily reflect those varying market characteristics. * * * In order to make it clear that Rule 10b-18 is not the exclusive means to effect issuer repurchases, paragraph (c) of the rule provides that no presumption shall arise that an issuer or affiliated purchaser has violated Section 9(a)(2) or Rule 10b-5 if the purchases do not meet the conditions of paragraph (b).

* * *

The rule applies only to "a purchase of common stock of an issuer by or for the issuer or any affiliated purchaser of the issuer" (a term defined in terms of control) subject to a number of exceptions. The conditions go to the use of a single broker or dealer and the timing, price, and volume of purchases.[110]

[110] On Rule 10b-18 generally, see Feller and Chamberlin, Issuer Repurchases, 7 Rev. Sec. Reg. 993 (1984); Lewis, Relaxation of Trading Restrictions, in Practising Law Institute, Fifteenth Annual Institute on Securities Regulation (1984) c. 16.

CHAPTER 10

CIVIL LIABILITY

Persons injured in securities transactions are frequently able to choose among (and under modern alternative pleading to combine) a substantial number of private rights of action. They may be grouped into three categories — (A) actions at common law or in equity, (B) actions, express and implied, under the state blue sky laws, and (C) actions, express and implied, under the federal securities statutes. About two-thirds of the blue sky laws specifically save the nonstatutory rights and remedies;[1] and (the tender offer area aside)[2] there is no question of supersedure so far as the SEC statutes are concerned, because the 1933, 1934, and 1939 Acts specifically save all other rights and remedies and there is no reason to assume a federal-state conflict so far as the other statutes are concerned.[3]

C. 10 [1]See Unif. Sec. Act §410(h).

[2]See pp. 533-39 supra.

[3]The reorganization exemptions in the bankruptcy statute expressly preempt the blue sky laws. 11 U. S. C. §§364(f), 1145(a), supra pp. 286 n. 29, 288 n. 33; see also Commodity Exchange Act, 7 U. S. C. §2, supra pp. 235-36, 242; Interstate Commerce Act, 49 U. S. C. §11361(a).

"The ultimate effectiveness of the federal remedies, when the defendants are not prone to settle, may depend in large measure on the applicability of the class action device." 3 Loss 1819. This statement has been repeatedly quoted by the courts. E. g., Esplin v. Hirschi, 402 F. 2d 94, 101 (10th Cir. 1968), *cert. denied,* 394 U. S. 928; Green v. Wolf Corp., 406 F. 2d 291, 295 (2d Cir. 1968), *cert. denied,* 395 U. S. 977; Blackie v. Darrack, 524 F. 2d 891, 903 (9th Cir. 1975), *cert. denied,* 429 U. S. 816. And there have been many class actions under the SEC statutes, mostly involving Rule 10b-5.

With respect to the much rarer *defendants'* class action in the securities field, see In re Victor Technologies Securities Litigation, 102 F. R. D. 53, 61-65 (N. D. Cal. 1984); Akerman v. Oryx Communications, Inc., 609 F. Supp. 363, 374-77 (S. D. N. Y. 1984), *class certification dismissed as unappealable,* 810 F. 2d 344 (2d Cir. 1987); In re Consumers Power Co. Securities Litigation, 105 F. R. D. 583, 611-15 (E. D. Mich. 1985). In the last of these cases, which involved classes on both sides, there were three defendant classes consisting of 83-121 members of three underwriting syndicates, and the court designated the managing underwriter as the provisional representative of the classes with instructions to convene meetings of the three syndicates and allow their members to decide whether some other party should be substituted. The intricacies of the

A. COMMON LAW AND EQUITABLE LIABILTIES

The remedies at common law and in equity are breach of warranty, rescission (both by way of an affirmative action seeking restitution and by way of defense to an action on the contract) and the tort action of deceit. The last of these has already been considered to some extent in the discussion of the "substantive law" of fraud.[1] Suffice it here to include a brief synopsis of those remedies, subject to a strong *caveat* by reason of the necessary generalization, and to consider a few matters (such as the question of the measure of recovery) that are more appropriate here.[2]

1. Breach of Warranty

Breach of warranty is the most limited of all nonstatutory remedies in the securities field. The Uniform Commercial Code is explicit that the term "goods" in Article 2 (Sales) does not include "investment securities and things in action."[3] Moreover, Article 8 (Investment Securities) provides that "A person by transferring a certificated security to a purchaser for value warrants only that: (a) his transfer is effective and rightful; (b) the security is genuine and has not been materially altered; and (c) he knows no fact which might impair the validity of the security."[4] Consequently the only warranties implied from the mere sale are a warranty of title and a warranty that the stock or bond is a general security of the kind it purports to be on its face; there is no implied warranty of quality or value.

To make matters even worse, a plaintiff relying on this remedy may find that the parol evidence rule (if otherwise applicable in the particular jurisdiction) will be invoked against him to exclude consideration of any promises, and probably representations as well, not contained in the written contract (if there is a written contract that may be considered an "integration" of the parties' previous

---

class action must be left to the writers on civil procedure. See generally Banoff and DuVal, The Class Action As a Mechanism for Enforcing the Federal Securities Laws: An Empirical Study of the Burdens Imposed, 31 Wayne L. Rev. 1 (1984).

C. 10A [1] See pp. 712-15 supra.

[2] For a synthesis of the various remedies for misrepresentation, see Prosser and Keeton on the Law of Torts (5th ed. 1984) c. 18 and §105.

[3] §2-105(1); but cf. Agar v. Orda, 264 N. Y. 248, 191 N. E. 479 (1934), discussed in UCC — Official Text (9th ed. 1978) 41.

[4] §8-306(2).

negotiations). The parol evidence rule is not applicable to deceit actions, or to rescission actions based on the promisor's conscious falsity.[5] But the hapless plaintiff at common law who pursues his remedy in deceit may avoid the parol evidence pitfall only to run into the scienter hurdle.[6]

2. RESCISSION (INCLUDING DEFENSE TO ACTION ON CONTRACT)

Although all the common law and equitable remedies reveal, to a greater or lesser degree, the fact that they were not developed with particular reference to the idiosyncrasies of securities trading, rescission (legal and equitable insofar as there may still be vestiges of the historical distinction)[7] is the simplest of the nonstatutory remedies when it is available. This includes the defensive employment of the law of rescission in resisting a seller's action for breach of contract, as well as its use by the buyer offensively in an action for restitution. And the principles are the same whether it is the buyer or the seller who is the person offended, although most of the cases (understandably enough) involve rescission actions by the buyer for return of the purchase price, or actions by the seller for breach of contract. For convenience, therefore, the discussion here will proceed (unless otherwise stated) from the point of view of the buyer alone.

The elements of rescission, in a nutshell, are "misrepresentation" of a "material" "fact" on which the buyer justifiably "relied." The buyer need not show any causal connection between the misrepresentation and his damage; indeed, he need not even show that he has been damaged. Nor is the knowledge or intent of the seller relevant. However, unless the buyer can prove that the misrepresentation was intentional, he must worry about what is "material" and also, perhaps, about whether the court will regard it as equitable to grant restitution when the security has suffered a severe depreciation in market value.[8] In any event, whether the misstatement was intentional, negligent, or altogether innocent, there is the problem of distinguishing between a statement of "fact" on the one hand

[5] 9 Wigmore, Evidence (Chadbourn ed. 1981) §§2423, 2439.

[6] Cabot v. Christie, 42 Vt. 121, 1 Am. Rep. 313 (1869).

[7] For a summary of the historical distinction, see Prosser and Keeton on the Law of Torts (5th ed. 1984) §94, §105 at 729-30.

[8] The law is not clear on this point. See Restatement of Restitution §69, esp. the caveat, and §142, esp. the caveat and Comment c.

and an expression of "opinion" or a "forecast" or a statement of "law" or "value" on the other. Moreover, the buyer, though escaping the obstacles of causation and scienter that he faces in a deceit action, meets rescission's own prerequisites of "privity" between the parities and ability to restore the seller to the *statute quo.*[9] Problem children of the latter element are the difficulties of "tender," "laches," "waiver," and "ratification."

Rescission or cancellation is not the only remedy that equity has to give in cases of fraud — or what is paradoxically labeled "equitable fraud," that is, such conduct as will support an equitable rescission suit.[10] In a proper case the plaintiff may also obtain reformation, specific performance of the bargain as represented, or a receivership, or he may have a constructive trust declared or be awarded any other appropriate relief within the comprehensive powers of equity to grant.[11]

3. Deceit

Deceit has the same elements as a rescission so far as misrepresentation of a material fact and reliance are concerned.[12] In addition, the buyer must prove causation (that he suffered damage as a consequence of his reliance on the misrepresentation) and scienter. The latter element, as we have seen, has been variously defined.[13] Ever since 1789 there has been no absolute requirement of privity as there is in rescission.[14] It is thus possible to hold third parties in a deceit action — but only if the plaintiff is one to whom, or to

[9]The better rule is that, in the case of fungibles like securities, the buyer need not restore the identical pieces of paper but may substitute a like amount of other pieces. Id., §66(4) and Comment e. There is a certain amount of flexibility here. "Courts have recognized that the restoration need not be exact for rescission to be proper." Harman v. Diversified Medical Investments Corp., 524 F. 2d 361, 364 (10th Cir. 1975).

[10]See People v. Federated Radio Corp., 244 N. Y. 33, 154 N. E. 655 (1926).

[11]3 Pomeroy, Equity Jurisprudence (5th ed. 1941) §910; Deckert v. Independence Shares Corp., 311 U. S. 282 (1940).

[12]On "justifiable" reliance in the deceit context and its relation to contributory negligence, which the better reasoned cases have rejected as a defense applicable to intentional deceit, see Prosser and Keeton on the Law of Torts (5th ed. 1984) 750-53; see also Restatement (Second) of Torts §§540-41.

[13]See p. 713 supra.

[14]Pasley v. Freeman, 3 D. & E. (3 Term. Rep.) 51, 100 Eng. Reprint 450 (K. B. 1789).

influence whom, the third party made the representation.[15] There is always the question, too, whether the defendant (a director or officer, for example) actively participated in the making of the representation by his corporation.[16]

4. MEASURE OF DAMAGES

In rescission there is no problem of computing damages. Either the plaintiff can restore the defendant to the *status quo ante* or he has no action of rescission at all (or no rescission-based defense to an action on the contract).

In an action for breach of warranty the recognized measure of damages is the so-called loss-of-bargain rule. That rule is codified in the Uniform Commercial Code as "the difference at the time and place of acceptance between the value of the goods accepted and the value they would have had if they had been as warranted, unless special circumstances show proximate damages of a different amount"[17] — in short, value as warranted minus value at delivery. The theory is that the plaintiff should not only be made whole, as he would if he got the difference between actual purchase price and value at delivery, but should have the benefit he bargained for.

A majority of the states apply the same loss-of-bargain or warranty measure of damages in deceit.[18] However, the English courts and some of the states have followed the so-called tort measure or out-of-pocket rule, under which the buyer is limited to the difference between the purchase price and the value at the time of delivery.[19] Whereas the "warranty rule" gives the buyer the benefit of

[15] Restatement (Second) of Torts §531; cf. also id., §533 (representation made through a third person). Thus, when the directors of a corporation make a false statement in a prospectus published to induce subscriptions to its bonds, the representation is made to every purchaser of bonds, but not to persons who in reliance on the prospectus buy the corporation's *stock*, whether in the open market or from the corporation itself or even from one of the directors. Id., §531, Comment d. Cf. Peek v. Gurney, L. R. 6 H. L. 377, 403 (1873).

[16] See Note, The Liability of Directors and Officers for Misrepresentation in the Sale of Securities, 34 Colum. L. Rev. 1090 (1934).

[17] §2-714(2).

[18] Prosser and Keeton on the Law of Torts (5th ed. 1984) 768; see Spencer Companies, Inc. v. Armonk Industries, Inc., 489 F. 2d 704, 706 (1st Cir. 1973).

[19] Peek v. Derry, L. R. 37 Ch. Div. 541 (C. A. 1887), *rev'd on other grounds* sub nom. Derry v. Peek, 14 A. C. 337 (1889); Reno v. Bull, 226 N. Y. 546, 124 N. E. 144 (1919) (corporate stock). This was also the pre-*Erie* federal rule. Smith v. Bolles, 132 U. S. 125 (1889) (mining corporation stock); Sigafus v. Porter, 179 U. S. 116 (1900).

his bargain, the "tort rule" is intended merely to make him whole.[20]

Actually few states have applied either rule consistently. And the usual statements of the measures of damages need a good deal of tailoring for securities cases. For example, the New York Court of Appeals, which had apparently wedded itself to the tort measure in *Reno* v. *Bull*,[21] found it necessary to obtain at least a limited divorce a few short years later when it was confronted with a case involving a bond that the defendant brokerage firm had recommended, and that he had been informed was being purchased, as an *investment*. In such circumstances, the court held, the value of the bond need not be determined by the market at the time of the purchase; for that would result in *no* damages. Instead, the value at the time of purchase could be determined in the light of the subsequent history of the issuer, an oil company that because of its unsound financial condition was unable to withstand a period of distress and was forced into liquidation. Hence damages were computed at $980 per bond (the price paid), with interest from the date of payment, less the trivial amount of $5.85 received on liquidation, less the interest received by the plaintiff.[22] Substantially this rule appears to have been adopted in the Restatement (Second) of Torts. That is, when there is a widespread belief in misrepresentations similar to those

[20]The American Law Institute initially favored the tort rule (§549), but the Restatement (Second) of Torts allows benefit-of-the-bargain damages if they are "proved with reasonable certainty":

> (1) The recipient of a fraudulent misrepresentation is entitled to recover as damages in an action of deceit against the maker the pecuniary loss to him of which the misrepresentation is a legal cause, including
> (a) the difference between the value of what he has received in the transaction and its purchase price or other value given for it; and
> (b) pecuniary loss suffered otherwise as a consequence of the recipient's reliance upon the misrepresentation.
> (2) The recipient of a fraudulent misrepresentation in a business transaction is also entitled to recover additional damages sufficient to give him the benefit of his contract with the maker, if these damages are proved with reasonable certainty.

However, the tort measure "must of necessity be adopted where the defendant is a third party who has made no contract with the plaintiff." Prosser and Keeton on the Law of Torts (5th ed. 1984) 768. And a further complication is presented when in a warranty-rule jurisdiction the value-if-the-warranty-were-true is hard to prove, so that the court is induced to look to the price paid as some evidence of it. Morrell v. Wiley, 119 Conn. 578, 178 Atl. 121 (1935). When that is done, both rules reach the same result.

[21]226 N. Y. 546, 124 N. E. 144 (1919).

[22]Hotaling v. A. B. Leach & Co., Inc., 247 N. Y. 84, 159 N. E. 870 (1928). See 2 Harper, James, and Gray, The Law of Torts (2d ed. 1986) §7.15; Note, Measure of Damages in Action for Fraud in the Sale of Corporate Securities, 23 Minn. L. Rev. 205 (1939).

made to the plaintiff, as often happens in the case of sales of securities, value is determined after the discovery of the fraud, when the price ceases to be fictitious.[23]

B. BLUE SKY LAWS

Blue sky civil liability — which shows signs of a revival in the wake of the recent restriction of the 10b-5 remedy[1] — comes in a variety of shapes and sizes, and not infrequently two or more provisions are found in a single jurisdiction:

[23] §54, Comment c. This comment is further qualified when the plaintiff has sold before anyone has discovered the falsity. There his loss is the difference between the price paid and the price received on resale. When the plaintiff discovers the falsity sometime after the general public, the value is fixed by the market price at the time of his own discovery. Still another qualification: one who retains securities in reliance on a particular representation cannot recover any loss that was in no way due to the falsity of that representation but was caused by some subsequent unrelated event. Ibid. In short, "causation" survives this distillation of the measure-of-damages formula.

C. 10B [1] For example:

(1) Section 415 of the Uniform Securities Act provides that "This act shall be so construed as to effectuate its general purpose to make uniform the law of those states which enact it and to coordinate the interpretation and administration of this act with the related federal regulation." That section merely expresses "a general statement of legislative policy," not a requirement. Draftsmen's commentary to §415, in Loss, Commentary on the Uniform Securities Act (1976) 165. But this has been quite effective in practice. See, e. g., Shermer v. Baker, 2 Wash. App. 845, 848, 472 P. 2d 589, 592 (1970); Lane v. Midwest Bancshares Corp., 337 F. Supp. 1200, 1209 (E. D. Ark. 1972); Specialized Tours, Inc. v. Hagen, 392 N. W. 2d 520, 535 (Minn. 1986) (court was persuaded by §415 to follow the *Landreth* case (supra p. 197) in rejecting the "sale of business" doctrine, though it would have held otherwise if "writing on a clean slate").

(2) We have already noticed the possibility of a weaker scienter requirement at common law than under Rule 10b-5, or perhaps none at all. See p. 713 supra. So, too, with respect to blue sky fraud. See Silverberg v. Paine, Webber, Jackson & Curtis, Inc., 710 F. 2d 678, 690 (11th Cir. 1983), a case under the Florida version of Rule 10b-5, where the court followed Merrill Lynch, Pierce, Fenner & Smith, Inc. v. Byrne, 320 So. 2d 436, 440 (Fla. App. 1975), stating that it was "especially hesitant to overturn a state court's interpretation of a state law where the law has been interpreted so as to provide more stringent protection for the citizens of the state than the parallel federal statute provides to persons seeking remedies under federal law."

(3) Section 410(b) of the Uniform Act (infra p. 678, n. 3) and comparable provisions elsewhere may enable a plaintiff to reach additional defendants.

(4) Attorneys' fees might be more readily awarded. See Melton v. Unterreiner, 575 F. 2d 204, 209 (8th Cir. 1978) (Missouri law).

(5) The punitive damages that are foreclosed under the Securities Exchange Act of 1934, at least (see p. 973 infra), might be available in some states.

See generally Comment, Maryland Statutory and Common Law Remedies for Misrepresentation in Securities Transactions, 13 U. Balt. L. Rev. 574 (1984).

(1) Consistently with the aim of furthering federal-state coordination as well as uniformity, the draftsmen of the Uniform Securities Act closely modeled §410(a) on §12 of the Securities Act of 1933.[2] Thus, §410(a)(1) imposes civil liability on a person who offers or sells a security in violation of specified registration and other provisions, and §410(a)(2) imposes civil liability for sales by means of fraud or misrepresentation. Much of the analysis of §410(a) can accordingly be left for the subsequent discussion of §12.

At the same tme, the remainder of §410, in light of the experience under the state statutes and §12, incorporates a number of features that are not found in the federal statute: a detailed specification of those *prima facie* liable under §410(b) along with the seller;[3] specific provisions on prejudgment tender and on survivability on both sides; a ban on the enforceability of any illegal contract;[4] and, in addition to a flat two-year statute of limitations running from the contract of sale, a bar against suit

> (1) if the buyer received a written offer, before suit and at a time when he owned the security, to refund the consideration paid together with interest at six percent per year from the date of payment, less the amount of any income received on the security, and he failed to accept the offer within thirty days of its receipt, or (2)

[2] See pp. 883-95 infra. In a princely gesture toward federal-state coordination, Florida, a non-uniform state, has simply incorporated the federal remedies "for the purchasers or sellers of securities." Fla. Stat. (1981) §517.241(3).

[3] The list includes "Every person who directly or indirectly controls a seller liable under subsection (a), every partner, officer, or director of such a seller, every person occupying a similar status or performing similar functions, every employee of such a seller who materially aids in the sale, and every broker-dealer or agent who materially aids in the sale." In Foster v. Jesup & Lamont Securities Co., Inc., 482 So. 2d 1201 (Ala. 1986), the court held that the "materially aids" of the Uniform Act was broader than the "substantial factor" interpretation of §12(2).

The statutory language covers an employer. Todaro v. E. F. Hutton & Co., Inc., CCH Blue Sky L. Rep. ¶71,957 at 70,413 (E. D. Va. 1982). But an auditor is not *per se* an agent. Jenson v. Touche, Ross & Co., 335 N. W. 2d 720, 729 (Minn. 1983). With respect to the activities that might bring a lawyer within this kind of language, see Black & Co., Inc. v. Nova-Tech, Inc., 333 F. Supp. 468 (D. Ore. 1971); Adams v. American Western Securities, Inc., 265 Ore. 513, 510 P. 2d 838 (1973); Annot., Attorney's Preparation of Legal Document Incident to Sale of Securities As Rendering Him Liable Under State Securities Regulation Statutes, 62 A. L. R. 3d 252 (1975).

[4] It is quite clear from the official comment to this provision, which is §410(f) and is roughly similar to §29(b) of the 1934 Act, that it applies only to sellers' actions to *enforce* illegal contracts. See Loss, Commentary on the Uniform Securities Act (1976) 150. Nevertheless, at least two courts have read the provision as barring an action for *rescission* by a buyer with knowledge, allegedly, of the failure to register the securities. Hayden v. McDonald, 742 F. 2d 423, 430 (8th Cir. 1984) (Unif. Sec. Act); Dunn v. Bemor Petroleum, Inc., 680 S. W. 2d 304 (Mo. App. 1984).

> if the buyer received such an offer before suit and at a time when he did not own the security, unless he rejected the offer in writing within thirty days of its receipt.[5]

The Uniform Act forecloses implied actions, although that provision has been deleted in some states.[6]

(2) The typical pattern before the Uniform Act was — and it still is in the nonuniform states — some sort of provision voiding all or specified types of illegal contracts, almost universally with a specific right of rescission in favor of the buyer and usually with an enumeration of the persons liable as well as specification of the measure of recovery.

(3) The Uniform Act followed the existing pattern in authorizing the administrator by rule (a) to require registered broker-dealers (as well as their agents) and investment advisers to post surety bonds in amounts up to $10,000 and (b) to determine the conditions of the bonds.[7] A bond must provide for suit thereon with respect to causes of action under §410 and, if the administrator requires by rule or order, with respect to nonstatutory actions. In addition, a few nonuniform states, in an elusive search for riskless investment, require surety bonds in connection with *the registration of securities.*[8]

(4) The only states with no civil liability provisions of any type (not even broker-dealer bonding requirements) are New York and Rhode Island. With rare exceptions, however, the courts generally, on one basis or another, have recognized implied rights of action for rescission of illegal sales. Indeed, some of the best known of the early blue sky cases were decisions to the effect that sales made in violation of the statutes were either "void" or "voidable," without benefit of statutory declaration to that effect.[9]

[5] See In the Matter of Van Dyke, CCH Blue Sky L. Rep. ¶71,955 (7th Cir. 1984); Dixon v. Oppenheimer & Co., Inc., 739 F. 2d 165 (4th Cir. 1984).

[6] §410(h); see 1 and 4 Loss c. 11B n. 100. One result of the deletion is the possibility of an implied action for violation of §101, which substantially repeats Rule 10b-5 and thus covers fraud in connection with the purchase as well as the sale of a security. See In re Catanella Securities Litigation, 583 F. Supp. 1388, 1439 (E. D. Pa. 1984); Hammerman v. Peacock, 607 F. Supp. 911, 918 (D. D. C. 1985); Comment, State Blue Sky Laws: An Alternative to the Federal Securities Laws and State Common Law in Third-Party Accountant Malpractice Cases, 57 Temp. L. Q. 601, 642-52 (1984). On the complications created by the deletion of §410(h), see Naye v. Boyd, CCH Fed. Sec. L. Rep. ¶92,979 (W. D. Wash. 1986).

[7] §202(e).

[8] E. g., Ga. Code §10-5-6(b).

[9] E. g., Kneeland v. Emerton, 280 Mass. 371, 183 N. E. 155 (1932); Drees v. Minnesota Petroleum Co., 189 Minn. 608, 250 N. W. 563 (1933); Pennicard v. Coe, 124 Ore. 423, 263 Pac. 920 (1928). *Contra:* Eaton v. Coal Par of W. Va., Inc., 580 F. Supp. 572, 577-78 (S. D. Fla. 1984) (Florida law).

Paradoxically one of the few cases in modern times to reject an implied rescission remedy was in Rhode Island.[10] The New York courts do not imply private actions for failure to file the required "state notice,"[11] or under the fraud provisions,[12] on the ground that the legislative purpose in both cases was merely to facilitate the Attorney General's enforcement powers. But the courts *have* recognized private actions under §1204 of the New York Insurance Law, with respect to the unlicensed public sale of insurance company securities,[13] as well, it would seem, as the section on registration of real estate securities.[14]

(5) There are also the state RICO statutes to be considered.[15]

C. SEC CIVIL LIABILITY: AN INTRODUCTION

Superimposed on this array of liabilities at common law and under the state legislation are the civil liabilities under the six SEC statutes of 1933-40. Apparently concluding that the older liabilities were a good deal richer in quantity than in quality, Congress inserted one or more specific liability provisions in each of the Acts except the Advisers Act, especially the first two. And the courts

[10] Coastal Finance Corp. v. Coastal Finance Corp. of North Providence, 387 A. 2d 1373, 1378 (R. I. 1978) (very little discussion). Cf. Penn-Allen Broadcasting Co. v. Taylor, 389 Pa. 490, 497, 133 A. 2d 528, 532 (1957), decided before Pennsylvania's adoption of the Uniform Act, where the court enforced an issuer's contract against a subscriber's defense that the plaintiff had improperly received an exemption as a "dealer."

[11] Sajor v. Ampol, Inc., 275 N. Y. 125, 9 N. E. 2d 803 (1937).

[12] Gen. Bus. Law §§339-a, 352-c; CPC Int'l, Inc. v. McKesson Corp., 120 A. D. 2d 221, 507 N. Y. S. 2d 984 (1st Dept. 1986).

[13] See pp. 18-19 supra.

[14] Gen. Bus. Law §352-e. In Coolidge v. Kaskel, 16 N. Y. 2d 559, 208 N. E. 2d 780 (1965), the court sustained the defendants' objection to class action status without considering whether there was a cause of action at all. See also In re Cohen's Will, 51 F. R. D. 167 (S. D. N. Y. 1970). And in Steingart v. 21 Associates, Inc., 31 Misc. 2d 212, 215, 220 N. Y. S. 276, 279 (Sup. Ct. 1961), the court, in dismissing the *vendor's* defense and counterclaim, stated without elucidation: "The remedy for a violation of section 352-e * * * is a prosecution by the Attorney-General and/or a civil suit by the investors, but only against those responsible for the misleading prospectus."

On the tender requirement, ratification and related defenses, and officers' and directors' liability (express and implied), see 3 Loss 1672-82; 6 id. 3817-20.

[15] See pp. 710-11 supra, p. 923 infra; Milner, A Civil RICO Bibliography, 21 Cal. W. L. Rev. 409 (1986). Not all of them include civil liability provisions. On the other hand, a substantial number include violations of the blue sky law (at least fraud violations) as a predicate offense. There is also an interesting federal-state connection in that some of the provisions, by incorporating the federal RICO definitions, make mail and wire fraud predicate acts under state law.

have also implied additional liabilities under certain provisions of the SEC statutes.

As a Court of Appeals put it in an early case,[1]

> The purpose of the civil liability provisions of the first Act was to broaden the law of deceit. In that branch of the law of torts there had raged one of those controversies that delight lawyers and disgust laymen. It had its inception in the famous case of *Derry* v. *Peek*[2] and stemmed from a 19th Century English Court's conservative reluctance to believe ill of the tycoons of its day.

The effects of that classic case can be seen most vividly in §11 of the 1933 Act, which was modeled on provisions of the English Companies Act derived from the Directors' Liability Act, 1890, an act passed by Parliament within a year after the House of Lords in *Derry* had demonstrated the impotence of the common law deceit action in the realm of securities.[3] Section 11, particularly, is thus a good deal closer to the English law, with its similar disclosure philosophy, than it is to the blue sky statutes in this country. This makes available a body of relatively close judicial precedent — not only in the British courts but also in the courts of Commonwealth countries whose prospectus provisions were likewise borrowed from England's — which should not be overlooked by the American practitioner.

There are three civil liability provisions in the 1933 Act. Section 11, in the case of *registered* securities, subjects the issuer and numerous other persons to liability for damages when the registration statement is materially misleading or defective. Section 12(1) imposes liability for rescission or damages upon anyone who offers or sells a security in violation of the registration or prospectus provisions of §5. Section 12(2) imposes liability for rescission or damages upon anyone who offers or sells any security, *whether or not registered or exempt from registration*, by means of a material misstatement. In addition, §15 imposes liability on any person who "controls" a person liable under §11 or §12, subject to a special defense of innocence. A statute of limitations is prescribed in §13. Section 22 gives the state and federal courts concurrent jurisdiction over "all suits in equity and actions at law brought to enforce any liability

C. 10C [1] Rosenberg v. Hano, 121 F. 2d 818, 819 (3d Cir. 1941).

[2] 14 A. C. 337 (1889), supra p. 3.

[3] 53 & 54 Vict., c. 64. That statute was later incorporated in the Companies Act, and it was from the Companies Act, 1929, that the draftsmen of the 1933 Act borrowed it. 19 & 20 Geo. 5, c. 23, §37. The successor provision now in effect is in the Companies Act, 1985, 1985 Acts c. 6, §§67-69.

or duty created by" the Act[4] and gives private plaintiffs the same privileges of wide choice of venue and nationwide (really worldwide) service of process in the federal courts that the Commission enjoys in its own actions.

Writing about these provisions in 1933 — with remarkable foresight as it turned out — Professor Shulman concluded: "Once the policy questions as to the objectives of the Act are answered, there is little in the civil liability provisions which, in a less scientific and less systematic manner, could not or would not have been quietly developed over a period of years by courts on the basis of their own common-law precedents."[5] Certainly events have allayed the fears expressed by some well-informed persons at the time that the new liabilities would constitute an undue threat to free investment.[6]

First we shall consider the specific liabilities by categories. Then we shall look at the development of the implied liabilities. And, finally, we shall discuss a number of matters — such as secondary liability, ancillary relief, the class action device, *in pari delicto* and related defenses, indemnification, and security for costs — that are common to several or all of these liabilities.

[4] This is true of all the SEC statutes except the 1934 Act (which has given rise to most of the private actions) and, since December 1970, §36(b)(5) of the Investment Company Act (infra pp. 985-86). Since there is no explanation in the legislative history for singling out those areas, and the exclusive jurisdiction gives rise to serious problems (of personal jurisdiction, *res judicata,* and collateral estoppel) when the proxy rules, for example, are urged by way of defense or replication in state court proceedings (see 2 Loss 977-1001; 5 id. 2950-58), the Code, with a few exceptions, provides for concurrent jurisdiction, but without the non-removal provisions found in the 1933 and other Acts. §1822(a); see 2 Code 942-44; for the venue and service provisions, see §1822(b)-(i).

On the due process implications of nationwide service of process, see GRM v. Equine Investment & Management Group, 596 F. Supp. 307, 312-19 (S. D. Tex. 1984), and cases cited; Reingold v. Deloitte Haskins & Sells, 599 F. Supp. 1241 (1984), and cases cited; Paulson Investment Co., Inc. v. Norbay Securities, Inc., 603 F. Supp. 615 (D. Ore. 1984). With respect to venue, the burden of transferring a federal securities case under §1404(a) of the Judicial Code has been held to be no higher than in other types of civil actions. Minstar, Inc. v. Laborde, 626 F. Supp. 142, 149 (D. Del. 1985).

[5] Shulman, Civil Liability and the Securities Act, 43 Yale L. J. 227, 253 (1933).

[6] See Douglas and Bates, The Federal Securities Act of 1933, 43 Yale L. J. 171 (1933); Dean, The Federal Securities Act: I, 8 Fortune 50 (Aug. 1933); Seligman, Amend the Securities Act, 153 Atl. Monthly 370 (Mar. 1934); Ballantine, Amending the Federal Securities Act, 20 A. B. A. J. 85 (1934).

D. VIOLATION OF REGISTRATION OR PROSPECTUS PROVISIONS OF THE 1933 ACT [§12(1)]

1. Elements of the Action

Section 12(1) can afford to be brief when it provides that "Any person who offers or sells a security in violation of section 5 shall be liable to the person purchasing such security from him," because the liability is virtually absolute.[1] The theory, of course, is deterrence, not restitution. The plaintiff need allege and prove only (1) that the defendant was a seller;[2] (2) that the mails or some means of transportation or communication in interstate commerce was used, not just in connection with the offering of the security generally but in the offer or sale to the particular plaintiff;[3] (3) that the defendant failed to comply with either the registration or the prospectus requirement;[4] (4) that the action is not barred by the statute of limitations; and (5) that adequate tender was made when the plaintiff is seeking rescission.

The only defense then available to the defendant is to allege and prove that the particular security or transaction was exempt from §5. The seller's intent and his knowledge of the violation, though they may be relevant to an administrative or criminal proceeding or perhaps even a Commission action for injunction based on the violation, are entirely irrelevant in an action under §12(1).[5] Nor is

C. 10D [1] White Lighting Co. v. Wolfson, 68 Cal. 2d 336, 355, 438 P. 2d 345, 356-57 (1968); Swenson v. Engelstad, 626 F. 2d 421, 424 n. 5 (5th Cir. 1980).

[2] The built-in privity requirement is discussed infra p. 1017 as part of the general problem of secondary liability.

[3] Aid Auto Stores, Inc. v. Cannon, 525 F. 2d 468, 470 (2d Cir. 1975).

[4] On burden of going forward, see pp. 274-75 supra.

[5] Wonneman v. Stratford Securities Co., CCH Fed. Sec. L. Rep. ¶91,034 at 93,459 (S. D. N. Y. 1961) (even if president and sole stockholder of defendant company believed in good faith on the basis of an opinion of counsel that the securities were exempt, "that does not negative the knowledge he admittedly had of the facts giving rise to the liability of [the company] * * * and thus, does not absolve him from liability"); Hill York Corp. v. American Int'l Franchises, Inc., 448 F. 2d 680, 694 n. 19 (5th Cir. 1971); Smith v. Manausa, 385 F. Supp. 443, 451 (E. D. Ky. 1974), *modifed and aff'd on other grounds,* 535 F. 2d 353 (6th Cir. 1976) (advice of counsel is no defense); SEC v. Holschuh, 694 F. 2d 130, 137 n. 10 (7th Cir. 1982) (court in injunctive action held good faith was "not relevant to whether there has been a primary violation of the registration requirements," but did not consider its bearing on equity to enjoin). Even "reliance upon a statement made by the corporation commissioner to the effect that no permit was necessary" has been held no defense under the California statute.

ultra vires a defense for a corporation.[6] And, when there are separate transactions, there is no reason why the plaintiff cannot choose to rescind only those that have been unprofitable.[7]

2. Illegal Offer

What if an illegal offer is followed by a legal sale? Suppose, in other words, that the seller either "beats the gun" in violation of §5(c) or makes a preeffective or posteffective offer in violation of §5(b)(1), but the actual *sale* is made after the effective date and a proper prospectus accompanies or precedes the confirmation or the security (whichever is sent first) in full compliance with §5(b). Of course, the offeree can have no recourse if he does not buy, whatever action may be taken against the offeror for the violation by way of public enforcement. But what if he does buy?

Whatever doubt there may once have been as to the applicability of §12(1) to illegal offers was resolved when the original definition of "sale" was split into separate definitions of "sale" and "offer" in 1954, with the incidental amendment of §12(1) to refer to any person "who offers or sells a security in violation of section 5" so as "to preserve the effect of the present law" by not excluding the newly permissible preeffective offers from liabilities under §12.[8] Although the result "may appear to be harsh," Congress "made altogether clear that an offeror of a security who had failed to follow one of the allowed paths could not achieve absolution simply by returning to the road of virtue before receiving payment."[9] But the Code follows the minority view in order to make a sale possible in such a case without giving the buyer a put.[10] Authority under the blue sky laws is divided.[11]

Boss v. Silent Drama Syndicate, 82 Cal. App. 109, 113, 255 Pac. 225, 227 (1927); but cf. Bartlett v. Suburban Estates, Inc., 12 Cal. 2d 527, 86 P. 2d 117 (1939).

[6] Stadia Oil & Uranium Co. v. Wheelis, 251 F. 2d 269, 276 (10th Cir. 1957).

[7] Piantes v. Hayden-Stone, Inc., 30 Utah 2d 110, 112, 514 P. 2d 529, 530 (1973), *cert. denied,* 415 U. S. 995 (Utah Unif. Sec. Act); Dixon v. Oppenheimer & Co., Inc., 739 F. 2d 165 (4th Cir. 1984) (Virginia Unif. Sec. Act).

[8] S. Rep. No. 1036 at 18 and H. R. Rep. No. 1542 at 26, 83d Cong., 2d Sess. (1954).

[9] Diskin v. Lomasney & Co., 452 F. 2d 871, 876 (2d Cir. 1971), supra p. 102, at p. 105.

[10] §1702(a)(1); 2 Code 692, Comment (7).

[11] For plaintiff: United Bank & Trust Co. v. Joyner, 40 Ariz. 229, 11 P. 2d 829 (1932); California Western Holding Co. v. Merrill, 7 Cal. App. 2d 131, 46 P. 2d 175 (1935). *Contra:* Bauer v. Bond & Goodwin, Inc., 285 Mass. 117, 118 N. E. 708 (1934); Christensen v. Dean Witter Reynolds, Inc., CCH Blue Sky L. Rep. ¶72,045 at 70,612 (D. Minn. 1984).

3. Illegal Delivery

Section 5 has separate subdivisions directed to offers and sales on the one hand and to deliveries after sale on the other. Section 12(1), however, makes no specific reference to delivery; it imposes liability in so many words only upon a person who "offers or sells" in violation of §5. Suppose, then, that a person does not violate §5(a)(1) or §5(b)(1) or §5(c) because he makes no use of the mails or interstate facilities in *offering* or *selling* the securities, but he does violate §5(a)(2) or §5(b)(2) because he uses the mails to *deliver* an unregistered security, or a registered security not accompanied or preceded by a statutory prospectus. Is such a person liable under §12(1)?

Before this question came to be squarely litigated, the Second Circuit said by way of dictum, in an action under §12(2), that "we cannot doubt that the liability (under [§12(1)]) was intended to embrace all transactions made unlawful by section 5." The court thought it was "inconceivable" that Congress intended to impose civil liability on a person who violated the one half of §5 but not on a person who violated the other half.[12] So far as the contrast in the language of §§5 and 12(1) is concerned, the court merely pointed out that §2 itself makes the statutory definitions applicable "unless the context otherwise requires." The court held that §2(3), with its reference to any "disposition" of a security, defined the term "sale" broadly enough to include a delivery after sale, and Judge Swan concluded: "In section 5 where the draftsman differentiated between use of the mails to sell and use of the mails for delivery after sale, the context requires a narrower definition of the term 'sell,' but there is nothing in section 12 to require the definition to be so narrowed."[13]

Under this view, in short, §12(1) is construed as if it referred to "any person who violates section 5." This was obviously the statutory purpose. There are now several square holdings to that effect.[14] And the Code extends to "a person who sells or confirms a sale of a security, delivers a security after sale, or accepts payment

[12] Schillner v. H. Vaughan Clarke & Co., 134 F. 2d 875, 878 (2d Cir. 1943), infra p. 893. This was before the 1954 amendments, when there were only §§5(a) and 5(b).

[13] Ibid.

[14] Dupler v. Simmons, 163 F. Supp. 535, 540-42 (D. Wyo. 1958), *appeal dismissed by stipulation* sub nom. Simmons v. Dupler, 268 F. 2d 217 (10th Cir. 1959); Repass v. Rees, 174 F. Supp. 898, 903 (D. Colo. 1959); Value Line Fund, Inc. v. Marcus, CCH Fed. Sec. L. Rep. ¶91,523 at 94,969 (S. D. N. Y. 1965) (use of mails to confirm); Nicewarner v. Bleavins, 244 F. Supp. 261, 265 (D. Colo. 1965) (use of mails to correct error in royalty instrument).

for a security in violation of" the registration and prospectus provision.[15]

4. MEASURE OF DAMAGES

It seems clear in statutory context that, when the plaintiff in §12 no longer owns the security, damages are to be measured so as to result in the substantial equivalent of rescission — namely, the difference between the purchase price and the plaintiff's resale price, plus interest, and less any income or return of capital (with interest) that the plaintiff received on the security.[16] Obviously, too, the plaintiff is entitled to restoration of the entire purchase price without deduction for the defendant's selling commission.[17] And the rate of interest is determined not by reference to local statutes but in accordance with the equitable considerations of the particular case.[18]

The Supreme Court has recently held that "§12(2) does not authorize an offset of tax benefits received by a defrauded investor against the investor's rescissionary recovery, either as 'income received' or as a return of 'consideration,' and that this is so whether or not the security in question is classified as a tax shelter."[19]

[15] §1702(a)(1).

[16] Randall v. Loftsgaarden, 106 S. Ct. 3143, 3149 (1986), citing the text; see also Cady v. Murphy, 113 F. 2d 988, 991 (1st Cir. 1940), *cert. denied*, 311 U. S. 705; Code §1702(d)(1). In Foster v. Financial Technology, Inc., 517 F. 2d 1068, 1071 (9th Cir. 1975), the court held that forbearance to institute an action on a franchise matter constituted consideration in a bilateral contract for the sale of securities and that its reasonable value was recoverable. In general, see Todaro v. E. F. Hutton & Co., CCH Blue Sky L. Rep. ¶71,957 at 70,414 (E. D. Va. 1982) (Virginia Unif. Sec. Act). On Rule 10b-5, see pp. 967-75 infra.

[17] Stadia Oil & Uranium Co. v. Wheelis, 251 F. 2d 269, 276 (10th Cir. 1957).

[18] Johns Hopkins University v. Hutton, 297 F. Supp. 1165, 1229 (D. Md. 1968), *aff'd in part and rev'd in part on other grounds*, 422 F. 2d 1124 (4th Cir. 1970).

[19] Randall v. Loftsgaarden, 106 S. Ct. 3143 (1986). In Torres v. Borzelleca, 641 F. Supp. 541 (E. D. Pa. 1986), this holding was extended to deny damages constituting the difference in the tax credits promised from a tax shelter and the tax credits actually received.

E. MISSTATEMENT OR OMISSION IN SALE OF SECURITIES

1. Generally [§12(2)]

a. Elements of the Action

Since §12(2) is not too happily drafted, it is best not to attempt a paraphrase:

> Any person who offers or sells a security (whether or not exempted by the provisions of section 3, other than paragraph (2) of subsection (a) thereof), by the use of any means or instruments of transportation or communication in interstate commerce or of the mails, by means of a prospectus or oral communication, which includes an untrue statement of a material fact or omits to state a material fact necessary in order to make the statements, in the light of the circumstances under which they were made, not misleading (the purchaser not knowing of such untruth or omission), and who shall not sustain the burden of proof that he did not know, and in the exercise of reasonable care could not have known, of such untruth or omission, shall be liable to the person purchasing such security from him, who may sue either at law or in equity in any court of competent jurisdiction, to recover the consideration paid for such security with interest thereon, less the amount of any income received thereon, upon the tender of such security, or for damages if he no longer owns the security.

To start with what is clearest, the section applies to all sales of securities, whether or not registered and whether or not the particular security or transaction is exempted from §5,[1] with one exception: securities exempted under §3(a)(2), which in substance are those of the federal, state, and local governments, banks, and interests in certain bank common trust funds and tax-exempt plans. When the seller is the issuer itself or an underwriter and the security

C. 10E [1] Although the first parenthetical phrase of §12(2) refers only to securities exempted by §3 and not to transactions exempted by §4, this is a mere happenstance of drafting. The introductory clause of §3 creates an exemption from "the provisions of this title" "Except as hereinafter expressly provided," whereas the introductory clause of §4 exempts only from "The provisions of section 5." See Hill York Corp. v. American Int'l Franchises, Inc., 448 F. 2d 680, 695 (5th Cir. 1971).

is registered, there is some overlap between §§12(2) and 11.[2] But, so far as the ultimate investor is concerned in the orthodox distribution, §12(2) is vital even when there is registration; for the ordinary dealer, whether or not a member of the selling group, is not covered by §11.

Section 12(2) can perhaps best be analyzed and evaluated by comparing it with common law (or equitable) rescission, from which it was adapted; if the differences between rescission and deceit are kept in mind,[3] the comparison will indicate the contrasts between §12(2) and deceit as well. It must be remembered, of course, that the buyer's meat is the seller's poison.

Rescission and §12(2) are *substantially the same* in that both require the buyer to prove a "misrepresentation" of "fact."[4] It may be assumed that the common law concern over the distinction between what is "fact" on the one hand and forecast or promise or opinion or law on the other is substantially carried over. There is every reason in the general policy of the Act, of course, for applying the most progressive common law view on those questions. There is even more reason, in view of the express reference to omissions, to expunge any lingering distinction between outright lies and half-truths. And the Second Circuit has held that "the standards of disclosure required of a registered company are equally applicable [under §12(2)] to the prospectus of an unregistered company";[5] that the court "need not find that the prospectus contained untrue statements" if it was "misleading"; and that "Availability elsewhere of truthful information cannot excuse untruths or misleading omissions in the prospectus."[6] At the same time, §12(2) does not impose

[2] The purchaser of a registered security, whether from the issuer directly or from an underwriter or dealer, presumably cannot rescind the transaction under §12(2) and at the same time retain his status as a security holder in order to sue for damages under §11. In re Gap Stores Securities Litigation, 79 F. R. D. 283, 307 (N D. Cal. 1978). But "it is reasonable to assume that the plaintiff may pursue both remedies to judgment, electing his choice at the last possible moment." Ibid.

[3] See pp. 873-75 supra.

[4] *Query*: Is the parol evidence rule an obstacle in making such proof? We have seen that in common law deceit actions, as well as rescission actions based on the seller's conscious falsity, the rule presents no obstacle. See pp. 872-73 supra. But §12(2) covers negligent as well as intentional misstatements.

[5] Dale v. Rosenfeld, 229 F. 2d 855, 857 (2d Cir. 1956); DeMarco v. Edens, 390 F. 2d 836, 840-41 (2d Cir. 1968).

[6] Dale v. Rosenfeld, 229 F. 2d 855, 858 (2d Cir. 1956).

A California state court has held in an action under §12(2) that an issuer offering securities in California impliedly represents that a permit has been obtained under the California blue sky law, and that the omission to state that a permit has not been obtained creates a liability under §12(2). Leven v. Legarra, Los Angeles Daily J., Dec. 23, 1949, p. 1, col. 3 (Cal. Super. Ct.), *aff'd*

liability for omissions *per se* — although here again the section presumably goes at least as far as the common law in imposing an affirmative duty to speak in special situations, as when the seller occupies a fiduciary relationship to the buyer; in such cases the "statements" referred to in the section take the form (as we have seen) of implied representations flowing from the special circumstances.[7]

The *advantages* that §12(2) affords the buyer as compared with common law rescission are several:

(1) He does not have to prove "reliance" on the misstatement or omission; he must show only that he did not know of it, which is presumably a lesser burden.[8] The common law rule that contributory negligence is no defense[9] carries over to §12(2).[10] And the

without reference to federal law, 103 Cal. App. 2d 319, 229 P. 2d 383 (1951). This holding apparently goes back to Mary Pickford Co. v. Bayly Bros., Inc., 12 Cal. 2d 501, 519, 86 P. 2d 102, 111 (1939), where the court stated, referring to the Corporate Securities Act: "Whenever, therefore, an issuer or underwriter of securities offers them for sale to the public, he impliedly represents that the applicable provisions of law have been complied with. The falsity of that representation may give rise to an action either for breach of warranty or for fraud depending upon the culpability of the seller in the particular transaction." See also Elzarian v. Wiser, 216 Cal. App. 506, 31 Cal. Rptr. 126 (1963) (violation of terms of permit); Korber v. Lehman, 41 Misc. 2d 568, 569-70, 245 N. Y. S. 2d 830, 831-32 (Sup. Ct. 1963) (§12(2)); Pennebaker v. Kimble, 126 Ore. 317, 325, 269 Pac. 981, 983-84 (1928).

These cases, if they are sound, create an interesting bridge between the state and federal statutes. In effect, any buyer who has a state cause of action for failure to comply with the state statute automatically has a federal cause of action under §12(2) (if the mails or facilities of interstate commerce are used) unless the seller expressly states that the security has not been qualified under the state statute. But is this not too facile? On the same reasoning why does not the implied representation go also to registration under the federal act? If so, almost every 12(1) action can be transformed into a 12(2) action. Although normally a private plaintiff would be foolish to prefer §12(2) over §12(1), the same logic would seem to transform every violation of the registration or prospectus provisions of §5 (when the seller did not disclose the violation) into a violation of the fraud provisions of §17(a). That grates. See Rotstein v. Reynolds & Co., 359 F. Supp. 109 (N. D. Ill. 1973); Ingenito v. Bermec Corp., 376 F. Supp. 1154, 1176-77 (S. D. N. Y. 1974); cf. Thiele v. Davidson, 440 F. Supp. 585, 589 (M. D. Fla. 1977), *aff'd mem.*, 612 F. 2d 578 (5th Cir. 1980).

The phenomenon is reminiscent of the equally questionable movement in the other direction — from §12(2) to §12(1) — on the theory that a defective prospectus is no §10 prospectus at all. See p. 113 supra.

[7] See pp. 811-20 supra.

[8] Johns Hopkins University v. Hutton, 422 F. 2d 1124, 1129-30 (4th Cir. 1970); Gilbert v. Nixon, 429 F. 2d 348, 356-57 (10th Cir. 1970); Hill York Corp. v. American Int'l Franchises, Inc., 448 F. 2d 680, 695 (5th Cir. 1971); Alton Box Board Co. v. Goldman, Sachs & Co., 560 F. 2d 916, 919 n. 3 (8th Cir. 1977); Wigand v. Flo-Tek, Inc., 609 F. 2d 1028, 1034 (2d Cir. 1979).

[9] See p. 874 n. 12 supra.

[10] American Bank & Trust Co. in Monroe v. Joste, 323 F. Supp. 843, 847 (W. D. La. 1970).

plaintiff, however sophisticated, has no duty to investigate beyond applying his general knowledge.[11]

Inevitably, to be sure, some element of reliance (which is subjective) is inherent in the concept of materiality (which is an objective, "reasonably prudent person" concept).[12] But, especially since Congress left §12(2) alone when it amended §11 in 1934 to require proof of reliance in some circumstances, that element should not be permitted to come in the back door by way of a definition of materiality.

This legislative history also argues against reading something like a reliance (or causation) requirement into the statutory reference to a sale "by means of" a misleading prospectus or oral communication.[13] At the same time, that phrase presumably saves the seller who uses a misleading "preliminary prospectus" during the waiting period from being liable under §12(2) to the buyer who saw only

[11] Hill York Corp. v. American Int'l Franchises, Inc., 448 F. 2d 680, 696 (5th Cir. 1971); Wigand v. Flo-Tek, Inc., 609 F. 2d 1028, 1034 (2d Cir. 1979); Sanders v. John Nuveen & Co. ["Sanders IV"], 619 F. 2d 1222, 1229 (7th Cir. 1980), *cert. denied,* 450 U. S. 1005. Compare the discussion (infra p. 957) of the plaintiff's duty under Rule 10b-5. Compare also the rule in common law deceit to the effect that the recipient of a fraudulent misrepresentation "is justified in relying upon its truth, although he might have ascertained the falsity of the representation had he made an investigation," unless "he knows that it is false or its falsity is obvious to him." Restatement (Second) of Torts §§540-41.

[12] Gilbert v. Nixon, 429 F. 2d 348, 356-57 (10th Cir. 1970).

[13] In Sanders v. John Nuveen & Co. ("Sanders IV"), 619 F. 2d 1222, 1225 (7th Cir. 1980), *cert. denied,* 450 U. S. 1005, the court held that the "by means of" language did not require proof that the plaintiff had ever received the misleading prospectus; that the causal connection contemplated by §12(2) was an open-market theory (cf. p. 962 infra with respect to Rule 10b-5); and that "Thus, it is enough that the seller sold by means of a misleading prospectu[s] securities of which those purchased by the plaintiff were a part." See also Klein v. Computer Devices, Inc., 591 F. Supp. 270, 277 (S. D. N. Y. 1984), quoting the text, *reargument on other grounds,* 602 F. Supp. 837 (S. D. N. Y. 1985). The *Sanders* court expressed some concern about the application of its open-market theory to the extent that §12(2) covered oral communications, since "Spoken words lack continuing vitality and are unlikely to affect the general market price of a security," but left that problem for another day. 619 F. 2d at 1227; cf. Jackson v. Oppenheim, 533 F. 2d 826, 830 n. 8 (2d Cir. 1976). To the effec[t] that proof of causation is not necessary, see also Hill York Corp. v. American Int'l Franchises, Inc., 448 F. 2d 680, 696 (5th Cir. 1971); Adalman v. Baker Watts & Co., 807 F. 2d 359 (4th Cir. 1986). But cf. Alton Box Board Co. v. Goldman, Sachs & Co., 560 F. 2d 916, 924 (8th Cir. 1977), where the cour[t] held that, although the plaintiff need not prove reliance, "some causal relationship between the misleading representation and the sale must be shown"; the court went on to hold, however, that that had been established as a matter of law from the defendant's failure to investigate the credit worthiness of the Penn Central notes that it had sold. Ibid.; see also Barnes v. Resources Royalties, Inc., 795 F. 2d 1359, 1366 n. 9 (8th Cir. 1986); Brooks v. Land Drilling Co., 574 F. Supp. 1050, 1054 (D. Colo. 1983).

the corrected final prospectus. The case of the buyer who saw the misleading "preliminary prospectus" is more difficult, because the 1954 addition of the words "offers or," as an incident of the split of the original definition of "sale" into separate definitions of "sale" and "offer," must be given some meaning. Yet it does not seem necessary to follow here the categorical §12(1) approach that grounds liability on an illegal offer followed by a legal sale.[14] In §12(1) there is no alternative to that reading except to disregard both the addition of the words "offers or" in 1954 and the general realization that there is often no other effective sanction for "beating the gun." But it is possible in §12(2) to give meaning to both phrases —"offers or" and "by means of" — by grounding liability on the use of a misleading prospectus or other document that was corrected before the sale *unless it is clear that the correction was brought to the buyer's attention before he bought.* If this analysis is correct — and this is another area of SEC law that is *terra incognita* — it indicates the advisability of emphasizing the correction, perhaps to the extent of sending a separate letter along with the final prospectus.

(2) The second respect in which the buyer is better off under §12(2) than in a common law rescission action is that, if he is not in a position to tender the security for rescission because he no longer owns it, he may obtain damages. Indeed, whereas from the point of view of the common law tender requirement the buyer may weaken his position by reselling, there is if anything the reverse question under §12(2) whether the buyer may not be under a *duty* to resell in order to mitigate damages after he learns of the misstatement or omission.[15]

(3) Section 12(2) permits the buyer to pierce the privity requirement that normally prevails in common law rescission to the extent of reaching (as we shall see) controlling persons under §15, "sellers" who are agents rather than principals, and others who participate in the sale more or less in the criminal aider and abettor sense.[16]

(4) The final advantage that §12(2) affords the buyer is the right to sue in a federal court, without at the same time losing access to

[14]See p. 884 supra.

[15]In Monetary Management Group of St. Louis, Inc. v. Kidder, Peabody & Co., Inc., 604 F. Supp. 764, 767-68 (E. D. Mo. 1985), the court held for purposes of §12(2) (presumably §12(1) as well) (1) that a buying agent was a *purchaser* and hence a proper plaintiff, and (2) that whether such a purchaser was an *owner* within the meaning of the last few words of §12 depended on whether he "possesses sufficient control or authority to effectuate a tender."

[16]See pp. 1017-22 infra; Klein v. Computer Devices, Inc., 591 F. Supp. 270, 277 (S. D. N. Y. 1984), quoting the text, *reargument on other grounds,* 602 F. Supp. 837 (S. D. N. Y. 1985).

his local state court. He may pick his forum with due regard to strategic, geographical, and other considerations. If he picks the federal court, he has a broad choice of venue, with the privilege of nationwide service of process, and he need not comply with the usual $10,000 requirement, and the defendant cannot remove.

So far the buyer has both his common law cake and his statutory icing. But the icing may be too rich for his blood:

(1) The most important concession that §12(2) makes to the *seller* is to give him a defense, which he does not have in common law rescission, if he can "sustain the burden of proof that he did not know, and in the exercise of reasonable care could not have known, of such untruth or omission." Obviously having in mind common law deceit with its scienter element rather than rescission, the House Committee report on the bill that became the Securities Act justified this "shift in the burden of proof[17] as both just and necessary, inasmuch as the knowledge of the seller as to any flaw in his selling statements or the failure of the seller to exercise reasonable care are matters in regard to which the seller may readily testify, but in regard to which the buyer is seldom in a position to give convincing proof."[18]

(2) Since this defense in effect limits §12(2) to *intentional* or *negligent* misstatements or omissions, and since the buyer need not prove the materiality of *intentional* misstatements in order to obtain restitution in the absence of statute, the reference in §12(2) to materiality is another respect in which the buyer who can prove an intentional misstatement or omission is given no favor by the statutory action.

(3) Again, the buyer is faced with a much shorter statute of limitations under §12(2) than in a nonstatutory action, where all he may have to worry about is laches and in any event the local statute of limitations usually is considerably longer.

(4) Finally, the dependence of §12(2) on use of the mails or interstate facilities has on occasion been the buyer's nemesis and relegated him to his common law or state statutory remedies.[19]

[17] Wilko v. Swan, 346 U. S. 427, 431 (1953) (dictum).

[18] H. R. Rep. No. 85, 73d Cong., 1st Sess. (1933) 9, 23-24.

[19] Another problem has been raised but never decided. Section 12(2) refers to anyone who offers or sells a security "by means of a prospectus or oral communication." Section 2(10)(a) provides that in certain circumstances supplementary selling literature accompanying or following the statutory prospectus "shall not be deemed a prospectus." What, then, if the seller uses the statutory prospectus, which tells the truth and the whole truth, but sends supplementary literature containing a pack of lies along with or after the official prospectus? The question has not been litigated. Although a Victorian court might have

b. Use of the Mails or Interstate Facilities

We have noticed the question under §12(1) whether there is liability when the mails are used only in making delivery.[20] A similar question has arisen under §12(2). More precisely, the question there is whether the mails must be used in making the misrepresentation or whether it suffices to prove an oral misrepresentation (not made by interstate telephone) and use of the mails or interstate facilities in making delivery or in some other aspect of the transaction.

In the case in the Second Circuit that we have already noticed because of the court's arguing by analogy to §12(1), there was an oral misrepresentation followed by the mailing of the securities from Philadelphia to Rome, New York. The court took the broad view, reasoning partly from the premise that the word "sells" must have the same meaning in both parts of §12 and that (as we have already seen) it must be taken to include "delivers" if §12(1) is not to be limited to violations of only one part of §5. The narrow construction, the court thought, was not "the inevitable, or even the most natural, meaning of the statutory language" of §12(2). That construction "would render the phrase 'oral communication' of most limited application because the section would then reach only interstate telephone calls or conversations where the parties might be talking across a state line."[21]

This view has been followed[22] except in the Seventh Cir-

---

considered itself helpless, it seems hard to believe that many judges today would so exalt a "drafting bug" over the clear legislative intention as to deny recovery. The obvious escape, once more, is that §2 defines various terms, including "prospectus," "unless the context otherwise requires." In §12(2) the context most certainly requires that supplementary selling literature be considered a "prospectus." Some support for this construction is found in the 1954 amendment of §2(10)(a). See p. 114 n. 48 supra. Actually it would have been better to amend §12(2) itself than to insert the parenthetical language in §2(10)(a); for the latter solution invites an *expressio unius* argument to the effect that supplementary literature *other than* a §10(b) summary prospectus is *not* a "prospectus" for purposes of §12(2). Even so, however, the clearly manifested statutory purpose in §12(2) should prevail over an argument drawn purely from the words of the statute. See Code §1703(a)-(b). Section 410(a)(2) of the Uniform Securities Act avoids the question by referring simply to any person who "offers or sells a security by means of any untrue statement * * *."

[20] See p. 885 supra.

[21] Schillner v. H. Vaughan Clarke & Co., 134 F. 2d 875, 877 (2d Cir. 1943).

[22] Blackwell v. Bentsen, 203 F. 2d 690 (5th Cir. 1953), *cert. dismissed,* 347 U. S. 925 (1954); Creswell-Keith Inc. v. Willingham, 264 F. 2d 76, 82 (8th Cir. 1959) (mails were used only in *buyer's* remittances of checks to defendant's creditors as part of the purchase price); cf. Fratt v. Robinson, 203 F. 2d 627, 633-34 n. 20 (9th Cir. 1953) (distinguishing the question under Rule 10b-5, the

cuit.[23] And, although §12(2) is not a model of draftsmanship, the language seems to favor the Second Circuit's view. What is more important, there is no justification in the background of the statute for assuming that Congress regarded the jurisdictional language of §12(2) as anything more than a constitutional necessity.[24] As we have seen, it is perfectly clear that a violation of the mail fraud statute and of §17(a) and the other SEC fraud provisions can be made out without showing that the mails were used in making the misrepresentation. It seems odd, as the Eighth Circuit observed, to withhold civil liability under §12(2) for a fraud that could put the defendant in jail under §17(a) or the mail fraud statute.[25]

These are old cases, of no great importance now that the intrastate telephone suffices.[26] The broadest reading of §12(2), however, requires — as with §12(1)[27] — *some* use of the mails or interstate facilities in connection with the sale *to the particular plaintiff*.[28]

c. Defense of Reasonable Care

The statutory defense requires the defendant to prove "that he did not know, and in the exercise of reasonable care could not have known," of the untruth or omission.[29] There is not much law on

court referred to *Schillner*, supra p. 893 n. 21, as having "the best reasoning in support").

[23] Kemper v. Lohnes, 173 F. 2d 44, 46 (7th Cir. 1949).

[24] Creswell-Keith, Inc. v. Willingham, 264 F. 2d 76, 80 (8th Cir. 1959).

[25] Ibid.; see pp. 93-94 supra.

[26] See pp. 93-94, 789 supra.

[27] See p. 883 supra.

[28] Larson v. Tony's Investments, Inc., CCH Fed. Sec. L. Rep. ¶92,578 at 98,648 (M. D. Ala. 1970); Franklin Savings Bank v. Levy, 406 F. Supp. 40, 42 (S. D. N. Y. 1975), *rev'd on other grounds*, 551 F. 2d 521 (2d Cir. 1977). Thus there is no reason to suppose that a buyer who receives a prospectus without use of the mails may rescind because another buyer (with respect to whom the mails *were* used) failed to receive one. See Schneider and Zall, Section 12(1) and the Imperfect Exempt Transaction: The Proposed I & I Defense, 28 Bus. Law. 1011, 1021 (1973).

[29] For an analysis of the various "due care" locutions under the existing statutes and the Code, together with a table that charts the Code's provisions with their respective sources (if any) in existing law, see 1 Code 134-49. The locution in §1703(f), successor to §12(2), requires the defendant to prove merely that "he reasonably did not believe that there was a misrepresentation." And §202(131) defines "reasonably" to require "reasonable care," adding that "the questions whether reasonable care requires an investigation or inquiry and, if

how this defense may be established. The Second Circuit, speaking *obiter,* has said that the defendant must show that he "could not have known" of the omission, not merely that "he had used reasonable care" to avoid or correct it: "It is true that in some cases evidence of steps taken to avoid or correct an omission in a communication would negate reasonable knowledge that an omission existed. * * * But reasonable effort to extinguish ignorance does not necessarily prove reasonable unawareness of continued ignorance."[30] Presumably one may rely on SEC filings at least while they are relatively fresh. The key word is "reasonable."

---

so, its extent are left to construction in context and in the light of the circumstances." All this is subject to §1704(g):

> In determining what constitutes reasonable investigation and reasonable ground for belief * * *, the standard of reasonableness is that required of a prudent man under the circumstances in the conduct of his own affairs. Relevant circumstances include, with respect to a defendant other than the registrant, (1) the type of registrant, (2) the type of defendant, (3) when the defendant is an officer, the office held, (4) when the defendant is an officer, director, or proposed director, (A) the presence or absence of another relationship to the registrant, and (B) reasonable reliance on officers (or other officers when the defendant is an officer), employees, and other whose duties would reasonably be expected to give them knowledge of the particular facts (in light of the functions and responsibilities of the particular defendant with respect to the registrant and the filing), (5) when the defendant is an underwriter, the type of underwriting arrangement and the role of the particular defendant as an underwriter, and (6) whether, with respect to a fact or document incorporated by reference, the particular defendant had any responsibility for the fact or document at the time of the filing from which it was incorporated.

On Clause (6), see Rule 176(h), supra p. 149 n. 8.

[30] Jackson v. Oppenheim, 533 F. 2d 826, 829 n. 7 (2d Cir. 1976). For additional treatments of the defense, see Murphy v. Cady, 30 F. Supp. 466, 468-69 (D. Me. 1939), *aff'd on other grounds* sub nom. Cady v. Murphy, 113 F. 2d 988 (1st Cir. 1940), *cert. denied,* 311 U. S. 705; First Trust & Savings Bank of Zanesville, Ohio v. Fidelity-Philadelphia Trust Co., 214 F. 2d 320 (3d Cir. 1954), *cert. denied,* 348 U. S. 856; DeMarco v. Edens, 390 F. 2d 836, 841-43 (2d Cir. 1968); Gilbert v. Nixon, 429 F. 2d 348 (10th Cir. 1970).

Query Sanders v. John Nuveen & Co., 524 F. 2d 1064 (7th Cir. 1975), *on later appeal,* 619 F. 2d 1222 (7th Cir. 1980), where the court equated an underwriter's §12(2) duty of care in the sale of §3(a)(3)-exempted commercial paper to an underwriter's duty with respect to a false registration statement under §11 (infra p. 896). Indeed, the court referred to the defendant's failure to verify the audited financial statements or to review the auditor's work papers — steps that are not required even by §11(b)(3)(C) (infra pp. 899-900).

With respect to measure of damages, what has been said under §12(1) (supra p. 886) applies equally to §12(2). With respect to privity, see pp. 1011-24 infra.

2. Misstatement or Omission in Registration Statement [§11]

a. Elements of the Action

Section 11 was the *bête noire* that was going to stifle legitimate financing — and that did not produce a substantial recovery for thirty years. But before we examine the scant litigation history we must have a look at the elements of the action.[31]

(i) *Plaintiffs:* Suit may be brought by any person who acquired a *registered* security, whether in the process of distribution or in the open market.[32] All he must prove is that "any part of the registration statement, when such part became effective, contained an untrue statement of a material fact or omitted to state a material fact required to be stated therein or necessary to make the statements therein not misleading."[33] The plaintiff is spared any concern about reliance (at least insofar as it is divorced from materiality) unless he bought after the issuer had made generally available to its security holders an earnings statement covering a period of at least a year beginning after the effective date; but even then "reliance may be established without proof of the reading of the registration statement by such person."[34] And, instead of the plaintiff's having to

[31] Section 11 was made less harsh in a number of respects concurrently with the passage of the 1934 Act. On the political background of the 1934 amendments, see M. Parrish, Securities Regulation and the New Deal (1970) 186-98.

[32] See Klein v. Computer Devices, Inc., 591 F. Supp. 270, 275 (S. D. N. Y. 1984), citing the text, *reargument on other grounds,* 602 F. Supp. 837 (S. D. N. Y. 1985).

[33] §11(a). Since the "preliminary prospectus" under Rule 430 is not part of an effective registration statement, deficiencies in it cannot give rise to §11 liability if they are corrected before the effective date. The expanded "tombstone ad" under Rule 134 is not filed as part of the registration statement at all. And §10(b) specifically excludes the "summary prospectus" under Rule 431 from §11 liability.

The application of the phrase "when such part became effective" to a "shelf" registration under Rule 415 (supra pp. 136-42) "that incorporates by reference an annual report on form 10-K and one or more quarterly reports on form 10-Q (which were filed before the effective date) and a form 10-Q or 8-K filed thereafter will be quite difficult. The difficulty will be compounded in the case of an underwriter that becomes such after the effective date [see p. 897 n. 39 infra]." See Williams, Problems in the Application of the 1933 Act and Rules Thereunder to Shelf Offerings, in Practising Law Institute, Fourteenth Annual Institute on Securities Regulation (1983) c. 9 at 119.

[34] §11(a), last par. This limited reliance requirement was added in 1934. Commentators had pointed out that the shift of the burden of proof to the defendant filled a long felt need particularly during the early life of the security, when the registration statement is an important conditioner of the market; but after a substantial time, they observed, there is less justification for so weighting

prove causation, damages are reduced to the extent that the *defendant* proves that they did not result from his misconduct[35] — what might be called "comparative causation with a reverse twist."[36]

(ii) *Defendants:* There is a wide variety of potential defendants:[37] (1) every person who signed the registration statement, which is to say under §6(a), the issuer itself, "its principal executive officer or officers, its principal financial officer, its comptroller or principal accounting officer," and in the case of a foreign or territorial issuer "its duly authorized representative in the United States";[38] (2) every person who was a director (or person performing similar functions) of the issuer or a partner in the issuer "at the time of the filing of the part of the registration statement with respect to which his liability is asserted"; (3) every person who with his consent was named in the statement as about to assume any such position;[39] (4) every accountant, engineer, appraiser, or other expert named in the statement with his consent, but only to the extent of liability concerning any part of the statement or any related report or valuation prepared or certified by him;[40] and (5) every underwriter.[41] In

---

the scales in the investor's favor, because the information in the registration statement then becomes outmoded and discounted by many other factors. See Douglas and Bates, The Federal Securities Act of 1933, 43 Yale L. J. 171, 176 (1933); H. R. Rep. No. 1838, 73d Cong., 2d Sess. (1934) 41.

In Sec. Act Rel. 6485, 28 SEC Dock. 1146 (1983), the Commission adopted Rule 158 in order to define the critical terms, "earning statement," "made generally available to its security holders," and "effective date of the registration statement" for purposes of the last paragraph of §11(a). In view of the integrated disclosure system, the information in the "earning statement" may be contained in multiple documents.

[35] §11(e).

[36] See Collins v. Signetics Corp., 605 F. 2d 110, 114 (3d Cir. 1979). In Feit v. Leasco Data Processing Equipment Corp., 332 F. Supp. 544, 586 (E. D. N. Y. 1971), the court took judicial notice of "the very drastic general decline in the stock market in 1969" and adjusted the damage figure accordingly. See also Akerman v. Oryx Communications, Inc., 810 F. 2d 336 (2d Cir. 1987) (defendants' summary judgment *aff'd* on a finding that they had carried their burden of proving that the decline was caused by other factors); cf. Rolf v. Blyth, Eastman Dillon & Co., Inc., 637 F. 2d 77, 84 (2d Cir. 1980), *on remand,* CCH Fed. Sec. L. Rep. ¶98,201 at 91,414-15 (S. D. N. Y. 1981) (Rule 10b-5).

[37] §11(a)(1)-(5).

[38] *Query* the holding that a principal financial officer who does not sign is not liable even though his not signing was a breach of duty. Ahern v. Gaussoin, 611 F. Supp. 1465, 1481 (D. Ore. 1985).

[39] If any person who has not signed the registration statement is named in it as about to become a director, his written consent must be filed with the registration statement unless the registrant files a verified statement giving the reasons for omitting such a consent and establishing that obtaining it "is impracticable or involves undue hardship on the registrant." Rule 438.

[40] On the limitation to the "expertized" material, see Ahern v. Gaussoin, 611 F. Supp. 1465, 1482 (D. Ore. 1985). Moreover, when the Commission in 1982 permitted disclosure of security ratings for debt and preferred stocks by nation-

addition, §15 reaches anyone whom the plaintiff can show to be in control of any of these persons.[42]

(iii) *Defenses:* The issuer's liability is absolute with but one exception: it has the defense, available to all defendants, of showing that the plaintiff knew of the untruth or omission at the time of his acquisition of the security.[43] For other defendants an elaborate series of reasonable care *defenses* is substituted for scienter:[44]

(A) The defendant might establish that before the effective date of the part of the registration statement in question, or upon becoming aware of its effectiveness, he had taken appropriate steps to sever all his described connections with the issuer and had advised the issuer and the Commission that he had taken such action and would not be responsible for that part of the statement and (when it was the fact) had given reasonable public notice that that part of the statement had become effective without his knowledge.[45]

---

ally recognized statistical rating organizations, it adopted Rule 436(g) to exclude such ratings from §11(a)(4). Sec. Act Rel. 6383, 24 SEC Dock. 1262, 1282 (1982).

[41] "If any person becomes an underwriter with respect to the security after the part of the registration statement with respect to which his liability is asserted has become effective, then for the purposes of [his liability] such part of the registration statement shall be considered as having become effective with respect to such person as of the time when he became an underwriter." §11(d).

[42] See p. 1011 infra. Even when a registration statement is filed in connection with a secondary distribution by a person in a control relationship with the issuer, that person is not liable under §11 directly. He is liable only under §15, since he need not sign the registration statement.

[43] Before the new bankruptcy statute of 1978 there was confusion with respect to the impact of this strict liability of the issuer on the status of stockholder plaintiffs under §11 (or §12(2) or Rule 10b-5) vis-à-vis creditors of the issuer (who might or might not be holders of debt securities with their own rights under §11) when the issuer is insolvent. See Slain and Kripke, The Interface Between Securities Regulation and Bankruptcy — Allocating the Risk of Illegal Securities Issuance Between Securityholders and the Issuer's Creditors, 48 N. Y. U. L. Rev. 261 (1973); Huff, The Defrauded Investor in Chapter X Reorganizations: Absolute Priority v. Rule 10b-5, 50 Am. Bankr. L. J. 197 (1976). Now 11 U. S. C. §510(b) is categorical:

> Any claim for recission [*sic*] of a purchase or sale of a security of the debtor or of an affiliate or for damages arising from the purchase or sale of such a security shall be subordinated for purposes of distribution to all claims and interests that are senior or equal to the claim or interest represented by such security.

See In re Amarex, Inc., CCH Fed. Sec. L. Rep. ¶92,375 (W. D. Okla. 1985); Davis, The Status of Defrauded Securityholders in Corporate Bankruptcy, [1983] Duke L. J. 1.

[44] For an analysis of the subtle distinctions between these defenses and the due care defense in §12(2), see Folk, Civil Liabilities Under the Federal Securities Acts: The *BarChris* Case — Part II — The Broader Implications, 55 Va. L. Rev. 199, 207-16 (1969).

[45] §11(b)(1)-(2).

(B) A nonexpert defendant (which is to say a director, officer, or underwriter), as well as an expert sued on his "expertized" portion of the registration statement, might establish that "he had, after reasonable investigation, reasonable ground to believe and did believe, at the time such part of the registration statement became effective," that it was true and complete.[46] And the standard of reasonableness was changed in 1934 — largely for psychological reasons, so it seems — from "that required of a person occupying a fiduciary relationship" to "that required of a prudent man in the management of his own property."[47]

This is substantially the standard adopted in the Restatement (Second) of Trusts[48] and applied under the English Companies Act; the English courts recognize that a director may rely on clerks and other competent persons for information concerning the business,[49] but do not regard reliance on the statements of promoters or approval of the prospectus by other directors as a defense.[50] Indeed, even under the original "fiduciary" standard, the conference report on the bill that became the Securities Act recognized that a fiduciary need not "individually perform every duty imposed upon him," but may delegate to others "the performance of acts which it is unreasonable to require that the fiduciary shall personally perform," especially "where the character of the acts involves professional skill or facilities not possessed by the fiduciary himself."[51]

(C) A nonexpert defendant sued on an "expertized" portion of

[46] §11(b)(3)(A)-(B). This is the basis for the so-called due diligence obligation (see p. 903 infra), which is not a requirement at all but just a defense. On the due diligence process, see Lovejoy, Initial Public Offerings: The Due Diligence Process and Blue Sky Problems, in Practising Law Institute, Thirteenth Annual Institute on Securities Regulation (1982) c. 22; id., App. C, Outline of the Due Diligence Process and Blue Sky Problems; Fitzsimmons, Due Diligence, in K. Bialkin and W. Grant (eds.), Securities Underwriting: A Practitioner's Guide (1985) c. 8. On the evolution of the process, without which "the intent of the statute could not have been achieved," see J. Auerbach and S. Hayes, Investment Banking and Diligence: What Price Deregulation?, (1986) c. 4, esp. at 82. Rule 176 enumerates some of the relevant circumstances in determining whether or not a person (other than the issuer) meets the standard of §11(c).

[47] §11(c). "The amendment to section 11(c) removes possible uncertainties by substituting for the present language the accepted common law definition of the duty of a fiduciary." H. R. Rep. No. 1838, 73d Cong., 2d Sess. (1934) 41.

[48] §174.

[49] Stevens v. Hoare, 20 T. L. R. 407 (Ch. 1904) (Directors' Liability Act, 1890).

[50] Adams v. Thrift, [1915] 2 Ch. 21 (C. A.); see also Bundle v. Davies, [1932] N. Z. L. R. 1097, 1099 (Sup. Ct.). Both *Stevens*, supra n. 49, and *Adams* were cited approvingly in Lanza v. Drexel & Co., 479 F. 2d 1277, 1297 (2d Cir. *en banc, obiter,* 1973). And *Adams* was followed in Escott v. BarChris Construction Corp., 283 F. Supp. 643, 688 (S. D. N. Y. 1968).

[51] H. R. Rep. No. 152, 73d Cong., 1st Sess. (1933) 26.

the registration statement has a somewhat readier, double negative defense: that "he had no reasonable ground to believe and did not believe, at the time such part of the registration statement became effective, that the statements therein were untrue or that there was an omission to state a material fact required to be stated therein or necessary to make the statements therein not misleading * * *."[52]

b. "Expertising"

To what extent may officers, directors, and underwriters legitimately mitigate their burden of due care under §11 by relying on experts? Certainly not to the extent of all or substantially all of the registration statement. Section 7, as implemented by the Commission's rules, requires the manually signed consent of any expert named as having prepared or certified any part of the registration statement or a report or valuation for use in connection with the registration statement.[53] This whole machinery obviously was intended for such parts of the registration statement as the financial data, appraisers' valuations, engineers' reports, the opinion of counsel as to the legality of the issue, and the like. The Commission will not permit the central data in the registration statement — the description of the business, the promotional history, the underwriting arrangements, and so on — to be "expertized."[54] In fact, the Com-

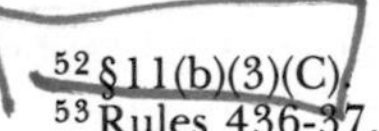

[52] §11(b)(3)(C).

[53] Rules 436-37.

[54] As Judge McLean put it in Escott v. BarChris Construction Corp., 283 F Supp. 643, 683 (S. D. N. Y. 1968):

> To say that the entire registration statement is expertised because some lawyer prepared it would be an unreasonable construction of the statute. Neither the lawyer for the company nor the lawyer for the underwriters is an expert within the meaning of Section 11.

See also In re Flight Transportation Corp. Securities Litigation, 593 F. Supp 612, 616 (D. Minn. 1984) (*held* also, rendering legal advice to an underwrite does not automatically "expertise" the registration statement); Seidel v. Publi Service Co. of N. H., 616 F. Supp. 1342, 1361 (D. N. H. 1985) (court denie motion to dismiss a complaint that alleged that the lawyer defendants wer "experts" with respect to the company's legal proceedings).

Although a lawyer normally prepares the bulk of the registration statement he is an "expert" only with respect to his required opinion on the legality o the issue. But lawyers' opinions sometimes cover a variety of other question like the validity of a title or a patent. See A. Jacobs, Opinion Letters in Securitie Matters (1980). On lawyers' liability as *lawyers* under §11 and Rule 10b-5, se Small, An Attorney's Responsibilities Under Federal and State Securities Laws Private Counselor or Public Servant?, 61 Calif. L. Rev. 1189 (1973); Cheek Counsel Named in a Prospectus, 6 Rev. Sec. Reg. 939 (1973).

mission has indicated that even when an expert may be properly employed — indeed, is essential, as in the case of independently prepared financial statements — management may not rely blindly on the expert's work; for "The fundamental and primary responsibility for the accuracy of information filed with the Commission and disseminated among the investors rests upon management."[55]

In *Escott* v. *BarChris Construction Corp.*, the court sitting without a jury, although it concluded (1) that one of the outside directors believed that certain figures that had been audited by a national accounting firm were correct because he had confidence in the firm and had no reasonable ground to believe otherwise, and (2) that a young lawyer who had become secretary and a director could likewise rely on those figures, found also (3) that the corporation's treasurer and chief financial officer, who had reason to believe that those same figures were incorrect, "could not shut his eyes to the facts and rely on [the accounting firm] for that portion," and (4) that the controller, a relatively minor figure in the company, had nevertheless failed to establish his defense because he was familiar with the issuer's books as its financial officer.[56]

c. Comparison with Common Law Actions and §12(2)

How does this elaborate structure of §11 compare with the common law actions and §12(2)?

So far as proving a "misstatement" of a "material" "fact" is concerned, they would all seem to be alike except that materiality need not be shown in the case of a *required* statement. The novel aspect of materiality under §11 is that, no matter whether the plaintiff purchased a day or a year after the effective date of the particular part of the registration statement complained of, materiality is reckoned as of that one date.[57]

[55] Interstate Hosiery Mills, Inc., 4 SEC 706, 721 (1939); United States v. Erickson, 601 F. 2d 296, 305 (7th Cir. 1979), *cert. denied*, 444 U. S. 979. The English courts have taken a similar view in denying company officials the defense that statements in the prospectus were phrased or omitted under legal advice. Shepheard v. Broome, [1904] A. C. 342, 347, *aff'g* Broome v. Speak, [1903] 1 Ch. 586 (C. A.); but see Adams v. Thrift, [1915] 2 Ch. 21, 24 (C. A.). In general, see Hawes and Sherrard, Reliance on Advice of Counsel As a Defense in Corporate and Securities Cases, 62 Va. L. Rev. 1, 11-22 (1976).

[56] 283 F. Supp. 643, 685-87 (S. D. N. Y. 1968).

[57] This creates a problem of currency for the accountant's audit figures. In Escott v. BarChris Construction Corp., 283 F. Supp. 643, 697-704 (S. D. N. Y. 1968), the court held that the purpose of a so-called "S-1 review" after the date of the balance sheet was to ascertain whether any material change had occurred

Reliance, which is required in both common law actions but not as such under §12(2), is back in §11 subject to the one-year provision; and causation, which is an element of deceit but not of §12(2), is likewise back in §11 to the extent that *lack* of causation is at least a partial affirmative defense.[58] Anyway, neither reliance nor causation is entirely banished as long as materiality is in issue; much of this is dialectic. Whereas §12(2) requires the *purchaser* to prove that he did *not* know of the particular untruth or omission, §11 makes the purchaser's knowledge a matter of affirmative defense. One searches vainly for the rationale of this kind of distinction.

Scienter, the hobgoblin of both common law deceit and Rule 10b-5, is foreign to the vocabulary of §11 just as in the case of common law rescission and §12(2). Although the parties must conjure with the substitute concepts of reasonable investigation and reasonable ground for belief, the new standards sound more in negligence than in fraud. The requirement of reasonable investigation and reasonable ground to believe, the House Committee said, "throws upon originators of securities a duty of competence as well as innocence which the history of recent spectacular failures overwhelmingly justifies."[59] This is not to say that all participants in the process of distribution were intended to be held to the identical burden of investigation. The House Committee recognized that "The duty of care to discover varies in its demands upon participants in security distribution with the importance of their place in the scheme of distribution and with the degree of protection that the public has a right to expect."[60] But it was recognized also, and intended, that there would be a minimum duty of investigation upon all directors that would "have a direct tendency to preclude persons from acting as nominal directors while shirking their duty to know and guide the affairs of the corporation" and "result in persons retiring from many boards and confining their efforts to a few boards where they will actually direct."[61]

---

in the issuer's financial position that should be disclosed in order to prevent the balance sheet figures from being misleading; that this did not amount to a complete audit; that the accountant's *program* for the review had conformed to generally accepted auditing standards, but that the actual review had not; that there were enough danger signals in the materials that the accountant had examined to require some further investigation on his part; and that the accountant had not sustained the defense under §11(b). The court held also that the plaintiffs could not take advantage of any undertakings or representations in the accountant's "comfort letter" to the underwriters. 283 F. Supp. at 698.

[58] See p. 897 n. 36 supra.

[59] H. R. Rep. No. 85, 73d Cong., 1st Sess. (1933) 9.

[60] Ibid.

[61] S. Rep. No. 47, 73d Cong., 1st Sess. (1933) 5.

Not surprisingly, the chief executive officer and the other "inside" (management) directors have a greater burden than "outside" directors,[62] to the point where Judge Weinstein was "led to the conclusion that liability will lie in practically all cases of misrepresentation."[63] But the extent to which participating underwriters may rely on the principal underwriters to make a reasonable investigation is still not altogether clear. It has been suggested that participating underwriters may delegate their duties to the managing underwriter as long as he himself makes an appropriate investigation.[64] On the other hand, a Commission release would require each participant to "satisfy himself that the managing underwriter makes the kind of investigation the participant would have performed if he were the manager."[65]

In practice, the principal underwriters traditionally arranged sometime during the waiting period for a "due diligence meeting" attended by representatives of the issuer, its counsel, the underwriters and their counsel, the accountant, and any other experts. Everybody was thus afforded an opportunity to exercise "due diligence" by asking questions.[66] But the practice is in a state of flux.

[62] Escott v. BarChris Construction Corp., 283 F. Supp. 643, 684 (S. D. N. Y. 1968).

[63] Feit v. Leasco Data Processing Equipment Corp., 332 F. Supp. 544, 578 (E. D. N. Y. 1971). A lawyer-director may be so deeply involved in a particular case as to become an insider. Id. at 576.

[64] Folk, Civil Liabilities Under the Federal Securities Acts: The *BarChris* Case, Part I — Section 11 of the Securities Act of 1933, 55 Va. L. Rev. 1, 56-58 (1969).

[65] Sec. Act Rel. 5275 (1972) 12; see In re Gap Stores Securities Litigation, 79 F. R. D. 283, 299-302 (N. D. Cal. 1978). The question was left open in Escott v. BarChris Construction Corp., 283 F. Supp. 643, 697 n. 26 (S. D. N. Y. 1968), because the lead underwriter itself had failed to establish its due diligence. Contrast Competitive Associates, Inc. v. International Health Sciences, Inc., CCH Fed. Sec. L. Rep. ¶94,966 at 97,337 (S. D. N. Y. 1975), where the lead underwriter's successful defense "inured to the benefit of all the underwriters," though some were not present at the "due diligence meeting."

One of the circumstances going to the question of reasonable investigation under the Code is "the type of underwriting arrangement [and] the role of the particular defendant as an underwriter." §1704(g)(6), borrowed in Rule 176(g). This clause is "designed to permit discrimination, for example, * * * between ordinary and 'technical' underwriters, and between managing underwriters and members of the underwriting group. At the same time, Clause (6) is not intended entirely to relieve conventional underwriters other than managing underwriters of the duty to investigate regardless of obstacles that the issuer may put in the way of their access." 2 Code 714. Underwriters, it has been said, "must play devil's advocate." Feit v. Leasco Data Processing Equipment Corp., 332 F. Supp. 544, 582 (E. D. N. Y. 1971).

[66] In general, see Symposium, Current Problems of Securities Underwriters and Dealers, 18 Bus. Law. 27, 37-42 (1962), with a checklist for underwriters' investigation at 90-91. Of course, the "due diligence" meeting must not be used

We have noticed the exacerbation of the general due diligence problem with the trend toward incorporation by reference from 1934 Act filings, as well as the Commission's borrowing of the Code's solution.[67] And new practices will also have to evolve in the light of the new "shelf rule."[68]

Unlike §12, §11 presents no problem of use of the mails or the channels of interstate commerce. Constitutionality is afforded by conditioning registration on the use of those instrumentalities.

It is in its assault on the citadel of privity that §11 marks its greatest departure from precedent. In the first place, §11 increases the number of potential plaintiffs by considerably broadening the common law exception to the extent that it permits the ultimate investor to sue both the issuer and the underwriter notwithstanding a chain of title from issuer to underwriter to dealer to investor, and gives the same right of action even to a buyer in the open market, all without the plaintiff's proving that the misrepresentation was addressed to or intended to influence *him.*[69] In the second place, the section increases the number of potential *defendants* insofar as it covers officers, directors, and experts.

On the latter score the "revolutionary" change that Chief Judge Cardozo (as he then was) referred to in the famous *Ultramares* case[70]

---

to whip up the interest of salesmen or there is likely to be a violation of §5. For this reason, the managing underwriter would be wise to screen attendance so as to limit the audience to underwriters.

[67] See p. 149 n. 8 supra; Greene, Determining the Responsibility of Underwriters Distributing Securities Within an Integrated Disclosure System, 56 Notre Dame Law. 755 (1981); Committee on Federal Regulation of Securities, Am. B. Ass'n, Current Issues and Developments in the Duties and Liabilities of Underwriters and Securities Dealers, 33 Bus. Law. 335, esp. at 350 (1977) (for an approach varying with the circumstances).

[68] Rule 415, supra pp. 136-42. It should be significant in this respect that the Commission has said that a court would not expect the accountant's investigation in connection with a short-form registration of a seasoned company to be the same as would be reasonable in connection with an initial public offering. Sec. Act Rel. 6383, 24 SEC Dock. 1262, 1296 n. 101 (1982).

[69] The open-market buyer, however, must be able to trace his particular securities to the registration statement when it covered additional securities of an outstanding class. This is a nonsensical, but unavoidable, result of a statutory scheme that registers not *classes* but *units* of securities. Barnes v. Osofsky, 373 F. 2d 269 (2d Cir. 1967); Klein v. Computer Devices, Inc., 591 F. Supp. 270, 273 n. 7 (S. D. N. Y. 1984), quoting the text, *reargument on other grounds,* 602 F. Supp. 837 (S. D. N. Y. 1985); Abbey v. Computer Memories, Inc., 634 F. Supp. 870 (N. D. Cal. 1986). In Kirkwood v. Taylor, 590 F. Supp. 1375 (D. Minn. 1984), the court rejected three proferred methods of tracing.

[70] Ultramares Corp. v. Touche, 255 N. Y. 170, 187, 174 N. E. 441, 447 (1931), supra pp. 785-86 n. 120. The common law has not stood still since. There is now respectable precedent that goes beyond directly *foreseen* users of the financial information, as, for example, in Haddon View Investment Co. v. Coopers & Lybrand, 70 Ohio St. 2d 154, 436 N. E. 2d 212 (1982), to the

has now been "wrought by legislation" as he said it would have to be. Section 11 goes as far in protecting purchasers of securities as the New York Court of Appeals there refused to go at common law in protecting creditors who had relied on a certified balance sheet negligently prepared by accountants for an insolvent borrower. Indeed, it goes further in putting the burden on the accountant (or other expert) to show affirmatively that he made a reasonable investigation and had reasonable ground to believe and did believe that the "expertized" statements were true and that there was no omission of a material fact.

Section 11 had originally referred to damages, without definition, as a substitute for rescission. Obviously, in that context, it meant what it does today in §12: the difference between purchase price and resale price (with interest) less any income or return of capital received by the buyer on the security. As amended in 1934, however, §11(e) incorporates a modified "tort measure" of damages — in the main, purchase price less value at the time of *suit* rather than *delivery*.[71] Section 11(g) limits the amount that may be recovered to the price at which the security was offered to the public;[72] this primarily limits the plaintiff who purchased in the open market rather than in the course of the distribution. When the security has been disposed of in the open market before suit, the measure of damages is purchase price less resale price (with no mention of interest or of deducting income received on the security as in §12). If the market goes up *pending suit* and the security is disposed of before judgment, the defendant gets the benefit of the increase over the value at the time of suit; but, if the market goes *down* and the security is disposed of pending suit, the plaintiff still gets only the difference between the purchase price and the value at the time of suit. In other words, it is to the plaintiff's advantage not to hold

---

foreseeable. H. Rosenblum, Inc. v. Adler, 93 N. J. 324, 461 A. 2d 138 (1983); Citizens State Bank v. Timm, Schmidt & Co., 113 Wis. 2d 376, 335 N. W. 2d 361 (1983); JEB Fasteners, Ltd. v. Marks, Bloom & Co., [1981] 3 All E. R. 389, *aff'd on other grounds,* [1983] 1 All E. R. 583 (C. A.). See Brodsky and Swanson, The Expanded Liability of Accountants for Negligence, 12 Sec. Reg. L. J. 252 (1984); Ebke, In Search of Alternatives: Comparative Reflections on Corporate Governance and the Independent Auditor's Responsibilities, 79 Nw. U. L. Rev. 663 (1984).

[71] The reference to "value" at time of suit notwithstanding the use of the term "price" for most of the calculations indicates that market price on the date of suit does not necessarily govern. But the burden is on the plaintiff to show that the defendant's statements had "artificially" inflated the market price. Grossman v. Waste Management, Inc., 589 F. Supp. 395, 416 (N. D. Ill. 1984).

[72] See also §11(e), 1st parenthetical clause.

the security after filing suit if he wants to be sure of being made whole.[73]

d. Litigation History

The 30,000 registration statements filed during the first thirty-five years of the SEC's history resulted in two adjudicated recoveries together with six reported decisions approving settlements of class actions.[74] The first substantial recovery did not come until 1963, in *Cherner* v. *Transitron Electronic Corp.*, and that case taxed the resources of the judicial process.[75] An allegation that the registration statement falsely disavowed any patent claims against the issuer resulted in a pretrial settlement of $5.3 million, which was approved

[73] An underwriter who does not receive preferential treatment over other underwriters has his aggregate liability limited, so far as all suits brought against him under §11 are concerned, to the total offering price of that part of the issue underwritten by him and actually distributed; otherwise, at least in theory, the aggregate liability is unlimited, since an indefinite number of successive purchasers can recover their trading losses (limited only by the provision that the plaintiff's purchase price cannot exceed the public offering price of the security) unless the defendant proves that they were not due to the misstatement or omission complained of.

This provision of §11(e) has led to the holding that an underwriter cannot be held as an aider and abettor under §12(2) (see p. 1016 infra) "merely by performing the functions of a typical lead underwriter." Klein v. Computer Devices, Inc., 602 F. Supp. 837, 840 (S. D. N. Y. 1985). On the other hand, since the preferential treatment must come "from the issuer" under §11(e) in order for the underwriter to be liable *in solido*, the clause is routinely evaded by having the managing underwriter's extra fee come from the members of the underwriting group. For that reason, and because extending the preferential language to cover that practice would create a severe problem under the capital rules, the clause in question is deleted in the Code. See 2 Code 730, comment.

This clause was one reason for the transition from joint to several underwriting. Assume an issue offered to the public for $1 million and underwritten equally by ten firms. The value of the securities has declined by $500,000 by the time a misstatement is discovered in the registration statement. If the underwriting was joint, each firm is liable for the entire $500,000, subject to its right of contribution (see p. 1036 infra). If the underwriting was several, on the other hand, each firm's initial liability is only $100,000, which is the amount of his underwriting participation. Note, however, that even when the underwriting is several each firm's maximum liability initially is not merely 10 percent of the *total liability* or $50,000. It will work out that way after contribution if all the underwriters are sufficiently solvent, but initially each firm is liable up to $100,000 to any one or more plaintiffs, whether or not they can trace title back to that firm.

For a good analysis of the measure of damages, see Feit v. Leasco Data Processing Equipment Corp., 332 F. Supp. 544, 584-88 (E. D. N. Y. 1971). On indemnification and contribution, see p. 1035 infra.

[74] 6 Loss 3826.

[75] 221 F. Supp. 48 (D. Mass. 1963).

in January 1963. The court appointed a special master, together with an electronic data processing corporation as assistant special master, and the court was not able to approve the master's final report until November 1965 and to discharge him finally until October 1968. More than 33,000 claims were approved by the master, for total "recognized losses" of $42.7 million within the meaning of the settlement agreement. The settlement fund, which had been paid in Treasury bills, earned income of about $330,000, which more than paid the total counsel fees of some $275,000. But total administration costs came to some $860,000, leaving just under $4.5 million for distribution. Ultimately claimants got 10.51 percent of their recognized losses. A total of 1777 claims were disapproved, including 143 after hearing.[76]

In terms of leading cases that went to judgment on the merits, *Cherner* was followed by *Escott* v. *BarChris Construction Co.* in 1968,[77] the first considered opinion on the several defenses, and *Feit* v. *Leasco Data Processing Equipment Corp.* in 1971.[78]

In *BarChris* Judge McLean concluded that the defense had not been established by any of the defendants: the chief executive officer, the president, the vice president, the treasurer and chief financial officer, the controller, a young lawyer who had become secretary and a director, two outside directors, a lawyer-director who had prepared the registration statement, the underwriters, and the accountants.[79]

In the process, the court held that the liability of *officers and directors* did not depend on whether or not they had read the registration statement or, if they had, whether or not in view of their very limited education they had understood what they had read; that an officer who must have known that the registration statement was untrue in part "was not entitled to sit back and place the blame on the lawyers for not advising him about it";[80] that §11 imposed liability in the first instance on a director, no matter how new he was, so that his general reliance on the assurance of the principal officers in answer to his general inquiries in the nature of a credit check did not establish the defense of reasonable diligence; that the issuer's lawyer, though sued as a director rather than for malpractice in his professional capacity, nevertheless had to establish more

[76] Id., Civ. No. 61-857-W, Report of Special Master with Respect to Proposed Final Distribution, D. Mass., Oct. 1, 1965; see Transitron: One for the Books, 67 Fortune 191 (Mar. 1963).

[77] 283 F. Supp. 643 (S. D. N. Y. 1968).

[78] 332 F. Supp. 544 (E. D. N. Y. 1971).

[79] With respect to the accountants, see pp. 904-05 n. 52 supra.

[80] 283 F. Supp. at 685.

in the way of reasonable investigation than could fairly be expected of a director who had had no connection with the writing of the registration statement; and that, although this did not require the lawyer-director to make an independent audit of the figures supplied to him by his client, it was not unreasonable to require him to check matters easily verifiable by way of testing oral information against the original written record.

With respect to the *underwriter* defendants, the court held that they were just as responsible for false statements as the company so far as the Securities Act was concerned, particularly because prospective investors rely on the reputation of the underwriters; that, consequently, it was no more sufficient than in the case of the lawyer who had prepared the registration statement merely to ask questions, to obtain answers that would be thought satisfactory if true, and to let it go at that, without seeking to ascertain from the records whether the answers were in fact true and complete; that, even if it were assumed *arguendo* that a *director* might rely on information furnished to him by the officers without independently verifying it, the *underwriters* could not be so trusting with respect to information received from the issuer's officers, whose position was in a sense adverse to their own; that otherwise the inclusion of underwriters in §11 would afford investors no additional protection; that the underwriters must "make some reasonable attempt to verify the data submitted to them" instead of relying solely on the issuer's officers or counsel; and that the principal underwriter was bound by its own counsel's failure to make a reasonable investigation.[81]

The surprising thing about *BarChris* — where just about everything that could go wrong did go wrong with a bowling alley manufacturer after the bowling bubble had deflated — is the very surprise on the part of elements of the securities Bar at discovering that §11 meant what Congress had said thirty-five years before. More than a thousand lawyers, accountants, and investment bankers flocked from all over the country to the Waldorf-Astoria in New York, which had to turn even more away for lack of space, to attend a two-day "National Institute" on the *BarChris* case sponsored by the American Bar Association's Section of Corporation, Banking and Business Law.[82] The present writer was hard put to it to find words of wisdom to utter as the keynote speaker:[83]

> I don't find anything new in the opinion, in principle. Let me run through it quickly.

[81] Id. at 692-97.
[82] 24 Bus. Law. 523 (1969).
[83] Loss, The Opinion, 24 Bus. Law. 527 (1969).

We are told at page 40 that a prospectus can be literally true and yet false by implication. Well, there is nothing new about that. That's true even in common law deceit.

Then a few pages later, around page 43, there is some talk about what "material" means. I shall have a little more to say about that a little later, but I do want to point out, by way of negativing some of the shockwaves from this opinion, that the judge made almost as many negative findings as he did affirmative findings on what was material in the particular case.

At page 47 we learn that we cannot "expertise," if I may use a bastard word, the whole registration statement. Certainly we lawyers ought to breathe a sigh of relief about that, because you know who would be the "experts."

We then read something about the defenses that are applicable to the signers of the registration statement and the directors, and we are told that they must investigate. We are told that they must not rely blindly on others. In the case of the president and the executive vice president and the vice president in this case, and the treasurer and the comptroller, it seems to me a plaintiff could not have wanted a case that was more open and shut on the facts as they were painted by the judge. Anyway, these are findings of fact on a very long record, so I see nothing startling in those pages.

At page 52 there are some references to the young lawyer who was house counsel. Well, he found himself in a tough position. I might say I have often doubted the wisdom of law firms' making young lawyers secretaries, or assistant secretaries, of corporate clients.

Then we have some learning at pages 53 to 56 about the outside directors who were held liable. There the court goes all the way back to an English opinion, *Adams* v. *Thrift*, [1915] 1 Ch. 557, *aff'd*, [1915] 2 Ch. 21, which held that a director who knew nothing about the prospectus and who had not even read it, but who had simply relied on the statement of the managing director that it was "all right," was liable for its untrue statements.

Next we are told at page 66 that the underwriter is just as liable as the issuer, subject to the underwriter's statutory defense, and that the underwriter can no more rely solely on the issuer's officers and counsel than can the outside directors. Surely, there is nothing new in that, as a matter of principle, to anybody who has ever looked at Section 11.

As far as accountants are concerned, I agree entirely with what Mr. Sommers says in his outline, that virtually all the instances of lack of due diligence that the court found involved simple mistake rather than errors in judgment. And, anyway, here again there were findings both ways, findings of fact on a very long record.

We are told at page 77 that, so far as the S-1 review is concerned, the accountant must not disregard danger signals. Again, there is nothing startling there.

To back up a few pages to around 56 — the case of Mr. Grant, the lawyer who was a director and who did most of the work on the registration statement — that case is to me a bit stickier. But first I must emphasize, as the court did, that he was not liable as a lawyer. He was held liable as a director. I find it hard to quarrel with the holding at page 57 that, so far as the nonexpertised portion of the registration statement is concerned, the director who is a lawyer and who did most of the work on the registration statement has a somewhat greater burden by way of establishing his defense than the other directors. * * * To me it is one of the most interesting aspects in the case, perhaps because it strikes closest to home.

Here again, I have often wondered, I must say, why it is that lawyers are so anxious to be directors. It has always seemed to me that there are many reasons why a lawyer should not want to be a director. Surely as general counsel he can attend the board meetings without being a director. Insofar as he is a director, he has to some extent a fool for a client — he becomes that much more emotionally attached to his client — and it may just possibly be that this case will persuade some lawyers that it is the better part of valor not to become a director of a corporate client. If this gentleman had not been a director, any liability he might have had would have been purely of the common law variety for malpractice. It would not have been a Section 11 liability at all. It is, of course, a matter of taste; I don't suggest remotely that there is anything unprofessional about a lawyer's being a director.

Be that as it may — again I must acknowledge that I haven't read the record, and we must bear in mind that this case has not been appealed but, I take it, has been settled — surely every experienced lawyer knows how essential it is to cross-examine his own witnesses severely, quite apart from the SEC field. *A fortiori* that is true in the context of Section 11. And, although it is easy to be a Monday morning quarterback, a lawyer hardly makes a reasonable investigation, whether he is acting for the issuer or for the underwriter, if he doesn't read the basic agreements, like the factoring agreement in this case, or if he doesn't follow up on absent minutes, as the court found was not done in this case. So, here again, I see nothing in principle to be excited about.

In general, I simply don't see anything to quarrel with as a matter of principle. The press and a good part of the Bar in this country tend not infrequently to discover profound truths a few decades after they have been writ large in our statute book. It has been thirty-five years since Congress determined in this country that directors are supposed to direct so far as registration statements are concerned. What would have been really surprising, I suggest to you, would have been a contrary decision. It is a little bit like imagining the consequences of the Supreme Court's having decided *Brown* v. *Board of Education* the *other* way ten years ago.

We must remember that the basic philosophy of the '33 and '34 Acts — I emphasize the word "philosophy" — is that as nearly as possible everybody should be on a par in trading in a security. We know that it is not possible, but that is the guiding spirit of this legislation. * * *

You may quarrel, if you like, with that philosophy. But there is no doubt that that is the philosophy of the statute. So I suggest to you, gentlemen, that the real question in the case and the *raison d'être* of this institute are not questions of principle. They are practical questions: What do you do as counsel for the company, as counsel for the underwriter, as counsel for the accountants, and so on, in the light of this opinion and in the light of Section 11 generally?

Since on that score I would defer to most of the people in this room, let me now take the broader look that I earlier said I would like to take and get away from the opinion as such, which others are going to discuss for the next two days.

First, though, I do want to negative any suggestion that the opinion answers all the legal questions under Section 11 — and I don't think one can fairly criticize the court for not answering questions that in the context of the case simply were not raised.

One question that one could speculate about is this: Does the court's treatment of the lawyer-director indicate that perhaps inside directors generally will be held to a higher standard under Section 11 than outside directors? Section 11 makes no distinction between one director and another. But I suppose that, if the director who happens as a lawyer to prepare the registration statement is held to a higher standard of care (or, rather, is given a tougher defense to have to prove) than the other directors and if you have a large board, and three nonlawyer members are delegated to be primarily responsible for working with counsel, who is not himself a director, one could argue (I am not saying that it is right, but one could argue) that those three directors are held to a higher standard because they were delegated the primary responsibility for working with counsel who was preparing the registration.

We all know what the contrary argument would be. It would be based on the fact that Section 11 doesn't distinguish between one director and another. That would have been the argument, I suppose, if *BarChris* had gone up on appeal.

Nevertheless, if *BarChris* is right, I suggest that perhaps there are distinctions between inside directors and outside directors. I suppose, on the same assumption, it might be argued that the ordinary director is entitled to rely more on outside counsel than on one who is himself a director. If that is so, it may be not only that the lawyer himself, in the light of *BarChris*, will now have an extra motivation not to go on the board, but also that the other directors will prefer to have registrations prepared by lawyers who are not themselves directors, so that, if they are sued, they will be able to say, "Well, we didn't rely on a fellow director. We relied on a lawyer. This is a complicated matter. And what would you have us do, particularly those of us who are outside directors? What are we supposed to do?" Indeed, what *should* an outside director do? I have heard some people criticize *BarChris* for not telling us what an outsider should have to do. Well, it doesn't tell us. But, of course, all the court had to decide in this particular case was that what the directors did was not enough. We don't know what would be enough in another case. Well, there are many other questions that one could talk about. But to me the really surprising thing about *BarChris* is that it took so long for it to come along—that it took so long generally for Section 11 to get off the ground. * * *

So far as the *Feit* case is concerned — a case that grew out of an exchange tender offer for the stock of an insurance company without adequate disclosure in the registration statement of the substantial possibility of the issuer's gaining control of some $100 million of assets not required for operating the target company — perhaps Judge Weinstein's scholarly opinion will be best remembered for teaching non-insurance lawyers the meaning of "surplus surplus": that "portion of surplus not required in insurance operations."[84]

F. VOIDABILITY PROVISIONS

Section §29(b) of the Exchange Act and its counterparts in the Holding Company, Investment Company, and Investment Advisers Acts provide — subject to the apparently congenital disability in these closely related statutes to draft any two comparable provisions quite the same — that every contract made in violation of the statute or any rule thereunder, as well as every contract whose performance would involve such a violation, is "void" as regards the rights of (1) any violator and (2) any person, not a party to the contract, who acquires any right thereunder with actual knowledge of the facts resulting in the violation.[1]

Several propositions are clear: (1) Notwithstanding the word

[84] Feit v. Leasco Data Processing Equipment Corp., 332 F. Supp. 544, 550 (E. D. N. Y. 1971).

C. 10F [1] Holding Co. Act §26(b); Inv. Co. Act §47(b); Inv. Adv. Act §215(b). The Investment Company Act was amended in 1980 to go over to the Code model (§1722(c)) in terms of whether enforcement or non-enforcement of the contract "would produce a more equitable result."

"void," such a contract is voidable, not void.[2] (2) Only a party to the contract can use one of these provisions.[3] (3) Although state law governs in general the rights and duties of sellers and purchasers of goods, "the effect of illegality under a federal statute is a matter of federal law * * * even in diversity actions in the federal courts after" *Erie.*[4]

That leaves two questions: the *extent* to which those provisions can be used by a non-violating party (1) defensively (against the violator's attempt to enforce the contract) or (2) offensively (to get restitution after the contract has been performed). And, happily, the Supreme Court has spoken quite broadly on both points. The case involved the voidability provision of the Advisers Act. And Justice Stewart wrote for a Court that was unanimous on this point:

> By declaring certain contracts void, §215 by its terms necessarily contemplates that the issue of voidness under its criteria may be litigated somewhere. At the very least Congress must have assumed that §215 could be raised defensively in private litigation to preclude the enforcement of an investment adviser's contract. But the legal consequences are typically not so limited. A person with the power to avoid a contract ordinarily may resort to a court to have the contract rescinded and to obtain restitution of consideration paid. See *Deckert* v. *Independence Corp.*, 311 U. S. 282, 289; S. Williston, Contracts §1525 (3d ed. 1970); J. Pomeroy, Equity Jurisprudence §§881 and 1092 (4th ed. 1918). And this Court has previously recognized that a comparable provision, §29(b) of the Securities Exchange Act of 1934, 15 U. S. C. §78cc(b), confers a "right to rescind" a contract void under the criteria of the statute. *Mills* v. *Electric Auto-Lite Co.*, 396 U. S. 375, 388. Moreover, the federal courts in general have viewed such language as implying an equitable cause of action for rescissions or similar relief. E. g., *Kardon* v. *National Gypsum Co.*, 69 F. Supp. 512, 514 (E. D. Pa. 1946); see 3

[2] Mills v. Electric Auto-Lite Co., 396 U. S. 375, 386-88 (1970).

[3] Natkin v. Exchange National Bank, 342 F. 2d 675, 676-77 (7th Cir. 1965); Greater Iowa Corp. v. McLendon, 378 F. 2d 783, 792 (8th Cir. 1967); Regional Properties, Inc. v. Financial & Real Estate Counseling Co., 678 F. 2d 552, 559-60 (5th Cir. 1982); but cf. Cameron v. Outdoor Resorts of America, Inc., 608 F. 2d 187, 195 (5th Cir. 1979), *modified on other grounds,* 611 F. 2d 105 (5th Cir. 1980) (assignee of investment contract who had taken from the seller in good faith and without knowledge of Rule 10b-5 violation could foreclose on buyers' defaulted mortgage notes).

[4] Kelly v. Kosuga, 358 U. S. 516, 519 (1959) (antitrust case); General Life of Mo. Investment Co. v. Shamburger, 546 F. 2d 774, 783 n. 15 (8th Cir. 1976); Rothberg v. Rosenbloom, 808 F. 2d 252, 254 n. 2 (3d Cir. 1986), *cert. denied* sub nom. Rosenbloom v. Rothberg, 107 S. Ct. 1895. *Contra:* Bankers Life & Casualty Co. v. Bellanca Corp., 288 F. 2d 784 (7th Cir. 1961), *cert. denied,* 368 U. S. 827.

L. Loss, Securities Regulation 1758-1759 (2d ed. 1961). Cf. *Blue Chip Stamps* v. *Manor Drug Stores*, 421 U. S. 723, 735.

For these reasons we conclude that when Congress declared in §215 that certain contracts are void, it intended that the customary legal incidents of voidness would follow, including the availability of a suit for rescission or for an injunction against continued operation of the contract, and for restitution. * * *[5]

In the earlier *Mills* case — under Rule 14a-9 of the 1934 Act, the proxy fraud rule — the Supreme Court did not read §29(b) as requiring that the (resulting) merger be set aside simply because

the merger agreement is a "void" contract. This language establishes that the guilty party is precluded from enforcing the contract against an unwilling innocent party, but it does not compel the conclusion that the contract is a nullity, creating no enforceable rights even in a party innocent of the violation. The lower federal courts have read §29(b), which has counterparts in the Holding Company Act, the Investment Company Act, and the Investment Advisers Act, as rendering the contract merely voidable at the option of the innocent party. [Citations omitted.] See also 5 Loss, supra at 2925-2926 (Supp. 1969); 6 id., at 3866. This interpretation is eminently sensible. The interests of the victim are sufficiently protected by giving him the right to rescind; to regard the contract as void where he has not invoked that right would only create the possibility of hardships to him or others without necessarily advancing the statutory policy of disclosure.[6]

Moreover, even an innocent party has no right to insist on setting aside the merger at all costs. "In short, in the context of a suit such as this one, §29(b) leaves the matter of relief where it would be under *Borak* without specific statutory language — the merger should be set aside only if a court of equity concludes, from all the circumstances, that it would be equitable to do so."[7]

Although the 1933 and 1939 Acts have no comparable provision, a buyer should nevertheless have a defense of violation of §5 or §17. For, at least under the 1933 Act, there would be little point in giving the seller an action on his contract only to have the buyer put things *in statu quo ante* by counterclaiming or bringing his own

[5] Transamerica Mortgage Advisors, Inc. v. Lewis, 444 U. S. 11, 18-19 (1979).

[6] Mills v. Electric Auto-Lite Co., 396 U. S. 387-88 (1970).

[7] Id. at 388. But *query* Bassler v. Central National Bank in Chicago, 715 F. 2d 308 (7th Cir. 1983), where the court read the *Transamerica* case as not meaning to hold that the voidability provision alone created a private remedy without "other and independent clues to Congressional intent to create a private remedy," and accordingly rejected a private right of action for violation of Regulation U based on the bank's failure to obtain a non-purpose statement.

action under §11 or §12.[8] And, as is generally held under the blue sky laws,[9] expiration of the statute of limitations for an action by the buyer should not be a bar to his asserting the violation defensively.[10]

It by no means follows, however, that *all* contracts involving a violation of the Securities Act are unenforceable. The Supreme Court spoke to this point in *A. C. Frost & Co.* v. *Coeur d'Alene Mines Corp.*, decided in 1941.[11] But the case did not involve an attempt to enforce an illegal sale contract against a reluctant buyer. Quite the contrary, an underwriter's assignee sued an issuer for breach of an option contract on treasury shares given by the issuer to the plaintiff's assignor. After some of the optioned shares had been sold by the issuer for the plaintiff's account (as authorized by a modification of the contract), the issuer repudiated the contract because the shares had not been registered. Reversing the Idaho court, the Supreme Court stated through Justice McReynolds:

> No provision of the Act declares that in the absence of registration, contracts in contemplation of or having relation to a public offering shall be void. * * *
>
> Although the challenged contract bears no evidence of criminality and is fair upon its face, we are asked to apply a sanction beyond that specified [in §12(1)] by declaring it null and void because of relationship to a public offering. The basis for this demand is a supposed federal public policy which requires such annulment in order to secure observance, effectuate the legislative purpose and prevent noxious consequences.
>
> Courts have often added a sanction to those prescribed for an offense created by statute where the circumstances fairly indicated this would further the essential purpose of the enactment; but we think where the contrary definitely appears — actual hindrance indeed of that purpose — no such addition is permissible. The latter situation is beyond the reason which supports the doctrine now relied upon.
>
> Here the clear legislative purpose was protection of innocent purchasers of securities. They are given definite remedies inconsistent

[8]See Garfield v. Strain, 320 F. 2d 116, 119 (10th Cir. 1963).

[9]Mechanics Loan & Savings Co. v. Mathers, 185 Ga. 501, 195 S. E. 429 (1938); Midwest Management Corp. v. Stephens, 291 N. W. 2d 896, 905-06 (Iowa 1980); Zehring v. Foster, 184 Kan. 599, 399 P. 2d 331 (1959).

[10]Cf. United States v. Western Pacific R. R., 352 U. S. 59, 72-73 (1956). A contrary argument might be based on the federal rule (see p. 991 infra) that, when the very statute that creates the cause of action also contains a limitation period, the statute of limitations not only bars the remedy but also destroys the liability. See Lamb v. Young, 250 Ore. 228, 441 P. 2d 616 (1968) (blue sky law).

[11]312 U. S. 38 (1941).

with the idea that every contract having relation to sales of unregistered shares is absolutely void; and to accept the conclusion reached by the supreme court below would probably seriously hinder rather than aid the real purpose of the statute.

* * *

The rule that contracts in contravention of public policy are not enforceable came under discussion in *Steele* v. *Drummond,* 275 U. S. 199 and *Twin City Co.* v. *Harding Glass Co.,* 283 U. S. 353, 356, 357. In the latter the opinion declares, the principle "should be applied with caution and only in cases plainly within the reasons on which that doctrine rests. It is only because of the dominant public interest that one who, like respondent, has had the benefit of performance by the other party will be permitted to avoid his own promise."

The protean basis underlying this doctrine has often been stated thus — No one can lawfully do that which tends to injure the public or is detrimental to the public good. If it definitely appears that enforcement of a contract will not be followed by injurious results, generally, at least, what the parties have agreed to ought not to be struck down.[12]

If this is a hard case that made bad law, the Commission must share the blame. For it advocated the result reached, and Justice McReynolds quoted from its brief as *amicus curiae*:

It is obvious that the purposes of the Act would be defeated by any judicial doctrine which prevented the issuing corporation from recovering from the underwriter, and putting to the intended use in its business, the money invested by the public in the issuer. And it would be anomalous to rest such an injury to the investors upon the fact that the transactions in which the securities were distributed violated the Act, which was designed to protect those investors. Compare Sections 11 and 12 which, by implication, permit a purchaser to affirm a sale in violation of the Act. It can scarcely be assumed that any court would render such an unfortunate decision. Yet this would be the logical consequence of applying literally the broad language used by the Supreme Court of Idaho in stating the proposition that the courts will not lend their aid to the parties to a contract that is prohibited by law or is against public policy.

It appears to us to be entirely immaterial whether in such a case,

[12] Id. at 41-44 (1941); see also Judson v. Buckley, 130 F. 2d 174, 179-80 (2d Cir. 1942), *cert. denied,* 317 U. S. 679; Wood v. Reznik, 248 F. 2d 549, 552 (7th Cir. 1957) (recovery of broker's commission for effecting an illegal sale); Fuller v. Dilbert, 244 F. Supp. 196, 213-14 (S. D. N. Y. 1965), *aff'd per curiam* sub nom. Righter v. Dilbert, 358 F. 2d 305 (2d Cir. 1966); cf. Mathers Fund, Inc. v. Colwell Co., 564 F. 2d 780 (7th Cir. 1977).

> the agreement is labelled "void" or the parties are held to be "in pari delicto." These labels, as often is the case, merely state the conclusion reached, but do not aid in solution of the problem. The ultimate issue is whether the result in the particular case would effectuate or frustrate the purposes of the Act.[13]

The Commission showed insufficient faith in the Supreme Court's ability to distinguish when necessary in subsequent cases. The result reached in the *Frost* case was hardly required in order to protect future issuers against double-crossing underwriters in the hypothetical situation posed by the Commission. Indeed, enforcement of the contract would not be essential in order to avoid doing violence to the public interest even in the Commission's hypothetical case; for the buyers would clearly have an action against the underwriter under §12(2), and probably nonstatutory remedies as well. One cannot quarrel with the Court's rejection of a formalistic determination whether to enforce contracts made in violation of the act. But, granted that there should be an inquiry in each case to decide whether enforcement or nonenforcement of the contract would better promote the purposes of the statute, why encourage violations by enforcing illegal contracts between two guilty parties when no public interest is involved? Only a year after the *Frost* case the Commission again filed a brief as *amicus curiae* in which it stated that on the facts of the *Frost* case it would recommend nonenforcement.[14]

The question did not arise again until 1952, when the Second Circuit decided *Kaiser-Frazer Corp.* v. *Otis & Co.* This was an issuer's action for breach of an underwriting agreement. Agreeing with the underwriter's defense that the registration statement contained false and misleading statements, the court held that the contract was illegal and unenforceable. "We cannot blind ourselves," Judge Clark said, "to the fact that the sale of this stock by Kaiser-Frazer, though, insofar as the particular contract was concerned, [it] was a sale only to the underwriters, was but the initial step in the public offering of the securities which would necessarily follow. The prospectus, which has been found to have been misleading, formed an integral part of the contract and the public sale of the stock by the underwriter was to be made and could only have been made in reliance on that prospectus."[15]

[13] A. C. Frost & Co. v. Coeur d'Alene Mines Corp., 312 U. S. 38, 43 n. 2 (1941).

[14] Judson v. Buckley, 130 F. 2d 174, 179-80 (2d Cir. 1942), *cert. denied*, 317 U. S. 679.

[15] 195 F. 2d 838, 844 (2d Cir. 1952), *cert. denied*, 344 U. S. 856.

The court's conclusion seems unexceptionable enough if the materiality of the misstatement is assumed. Indeed, since it was a condition of the contract that the registration statement be accurate, the court did not have to reach the question of illegality except in determining compliance with the condition. But the failure to mention the *Frost* case, together with the Supreme Court's denial of *certiorari* notwithstanding the argument in the petition directed to the *Frost* case, leaves the law here in something less than a satisfactory state. It is understood, for example, that, for a while at least after the *Kaiser-Frazer* opinion, some law firms qualified their opinions to their underwriting clients with respect to the enforceability of the usual indemnity and warranty clauses against the issuer. Their fear was that, when an underwriter had been held accountable in damages to a purchaser under §11 because of his failure to sustain the burden of proof under that section, his rights under those clauses might not be recognized if it were shown later that the registration statement contained a material misstatement or omitted to state a material fact, even though the underwriter had completed the distribution and paid for the securities in full and there was no evidence of his having joined with the issuer in intentionally or knowingly perpetrating the misrepresentation.

The *Kaiser-Frazer* case seems distinguishable in this context under the doctrine that a lawful bargain is not invalidated by a collateral or remote bargain or act that is illegal.[16] This is an area of the law in which so much depends on the public policy underlying the particular statute, as well as the question of who is suing whom for what, that generalization from holdings in other statutory contexts is risky. With that caveat, however, it is worth pointing out that the Supreme Court seems to have followed the "remote act" doctrine under the antitrust laws:

> As a defense to an action based on contract, the plea of illegality based on violation of the Sherman Act has not met with much favor in this Court. This has been notably the case where the plea has been made by a purchaser in an action to recover from him the agreed price of goods sold. * * *
>
> * * *
>
> * * * Past the point where the judgment of the Court would itself be enforcing the precise conduct made unlawful by the Act, the courts are to be guided by the overriding general policy, as Mr.

[16] 6 Corbin, Contracts (1951) §1529; Restatement (Second) of Contracts §184.

Justice Holmes put it, "of preventing people from getting other people's property for nothing when they purport to be buying it."[17]

One may hazard the guess that, when a seller sues a buyer for breach of an executory contract whose enforcement would violate §5 or §17 of the Securities Act, *Kaiser-Frazer* rather than *Frost* will carry the day.[18] On the other hand, when the seller has already delivered the securities in violation of §5, or after a sale that violates §5 or §17(a), the court may be expected to be somewhat concerned about the general policy that was so pungently expressed by Justice Holmes.[19]

In this state of affairs, the Code conditions enforceability, as well as denial of rescission of a consummated contract, on a showing that such action "would produce a more equitable result" and "would not be inconsistent with the purposes of" the Code.[20]

G. MISCELLANEOUS STATUTORY LIABILITIES

First: The voidability provisions in all six Acts except those of 1933 and 1939 have their offensive as well as their defensive side, in that they are one of the bases of the implied liabilities that we discuss in the next subchapter. In that sense implied actions are really semi-express.

Second: We have already examined the provisions on recapture of short-term trading in §16(b) of the 1934 Act together with §17(b) of the 1935 Act and §30(f) of the Investment Company Act.[1]

Third: Under §9(e) of the 1934 Act any person "who willfully participates in any act or transaction" in violation of the remainder of §9, the manipulation section,[2] is liable "to any person who shall

[17] Kelly v. Kosuga, 358 U. S. 516, 518, 520-21 (1959), quoting from dissenting opinion in Continental Wall Paper Co. v. Louis Voigt & Sons Co., 212 U. S. 227, 271 (1909); see also Lyons v. Westinghouse Electric Corp., 222 F. 2d 184, 187-88 (2d Cir. 1955), *cert. denied* sub nom. Walsh v. Lyons, 350 U. S. 825.

[18] See General Life of Mo. Investment Co. v. Shamburger, 546 F. 2d 774, 783-85 (8th Cir. 1976); Byrnes v. Faulkner, Dawkins & Sullivan, 550 F. 2d 1303, 1313 (2d Cir. 1977).

[19] Cf. Bankers Life & Casualty Co. v. Bellanca Corp., 288 F. 2d 784 (7th Cir. 1961), *cert. denied,* 368 U. S. 827; Goldman v. Bank of the Commonwealth, 467 F. 2d 439, 447 (6th Cir. 1972); Occidental Life Ins. Co. of N. C. v. Pat Ryan & Associates, Inc., 496 F. 2d 1255, 1266-67 (4th Cir. 1974), *cert. denied,* 419 U. S. 1023.

[20] §1722(c).

C. 10G [1] See c. 7 F supra.

[2] See p. 850 supra.

purchase or sell any security at a price which was affected by such act or transaction" for "the damages sustained as a result of any such act or transaction." There is a contribution provision comparable to that in §11(f) of the 1933 Act,[3] except that it is not expressly limited to situations where the plaintiff in contribution was not guilty of fraud and the defendant in contribution was.

It is small wonder that §9(e) has been a dead letter so far as producing recoveries is concerned. For, aside from its ignoring privity of contract between plaintiff and defendant as does §11 of the 1933 Act, it is no bargain:

(1) Although §9(e), apart from some of the substantive provisions in §9(a)-(d), does not require proof of scienter and does not specifically refer to "reliance," it does not shift the burden on causation to the defendant as §11(e) does. Quite the contrary, §9(e) contains a causation requirement that may be stricter than the burden the plaintiff would face in a common law deceit action based on the defendant's manipulation.[4] It is not only that damages are limited to those "sustained as a result" of the manipulation; the plaintiff must also show that he bought or sold "at a price which was affected by" the manipulation.[5] Presumably this language does not import anything analogous to the "comparative negligence" rule. In other words, once the plaintiff shows that he has bought or sold "at a price which was affected by" the illegal activity, it is at least arguable that the damages he has "sustained as a result" of that activity do not have to be prorated according to the extent to which the price was affected by that activity as distinct from the extent to which it may have been affected by ordinary market movements — a fanciful subject for speculation at best. But even this is by no means certain. And except in the cruder cases of manipulation — which are not apt to recur as long as the SEC walks its beat — it may be no mean trick to demonstrate, in addition to the *fact* of the wash sales or other illegal activity, that that activity affected the price at which the plaintiff bought or sold. With all the factors that determine stock market prices, the plaintiff will be particularly hard put to sustain this burden if he bought or sold some months after the manipulation complained of, when its lingering effects may have become intermingled with many other market determinants.

[3] See p. 1036 infra.

[4] On manipulation at common law, see pp. 845-50 supra.

[5] See Chemetron Corp. v. Business Funds, Inc., 682 F. 2d 1149, 1157 (5th Cir. 1982), *vacated and remanded on other grounds,* 460 U. S. 1007 (1983), *on remand,* 718 F. 2d 725 (5th Cir. 1983), *cert. denied* sub nom. Bintliff v. Chemetron Corp., 460 U. S. 1013.

(2) Apart from this double-barreled problem of causation, the plaintiff must prove also that the defendant "willfully" participated in the manipulation. Ordinarily, on the assumption that there is any proof that the defendant participated at all in the manipulation, this requirement should not cause much trouble in view of the loose way the courts have interpreted "willfully" even in criminal cases and in broker-dealer revocation proceedings under the 1934 Act.[6] But it is some indication of the legislative approach to §9(e) that it is the only civil liability provision in any of the six statutes that contains the "willfully" requirement.

(3) The only apparent advantage that §9(e) offers in comparison with §§11 and 12(2) of the Securities Act — aside from the privity requirement in §12(2) — is that there is no express reference to the plaintiff's knowledge of the manipulation. Because actual cases if they ever arise will most likely present infinite factual variations, there is not much point in speculating whether this apparent advantage is a thing of substance.

(4) There is no measure of damages specified in §9(e), or anywhere else in the 1934 Act, and the question has not yet been litigated. Presumably the answer will be found in the "tort measure" traditionally favored by the federal courts.[7]

[6] See p. 640 n. 39 supra.

[7] A few of the cases under §9(e) are worth mention.

In Rosenberg v. Hano, 121 F. 2d 818 (3d Cir. 1941), the plaintiff was an elderly and semi-retired lawyer who spent some of his leisure time in the customers' room of the defendant brokerage firm. On the representation, allegedly, of a customers' man that a certain whiskey stock was going to advance 15 points as the result of a deal made with the editor of a tipster sheet, the plaintiff bought 100 shares. When the stock declined, as the court put it, "our 'investor' fled for protection and restitution to the legislation designed, as he thought, for such as he." "In his eagerness," the court added, "he does not seem to have given much thought to either its philosophy or its terms." Id. at 819. The court held that the plaintiff's remedy, if any, was under §12(2) of the 1933 Act, as to which the statute of limitations had run.

In Fischman v. Raytheon Mfg. Co., 188 F. 2d 783, 788 (2d Cir. 1951), the court held that common stockholders, whose cause of action under §11 of the 1933 Act had been dismissed because the registration statement on which they claimed to have relied covered only the issuer's preferred stock, should be permitted to amend (if they could) by alleging facts showing that the defendants had deliberately used the registration statement for the purpose of fraudulently inducing the purchase of common stock sold by the defendants, in violation of §9(a)(4) of the 1934 Act.

In In re Penn Central Securities Litigation, 347 F. Supp. 1327, 1343 (E. D. Pa. 1972), *modified on other grounds,* 357 F. Supp. 869 (E. D. Pa. 1973), *aff'd on other grounds,* 494 F. 2d 528 (3d Cir. 1974), the court held that the plaintiff must be a buyer or seller, not a mere holder.

In Crane Co. v. American Standard, Inc., 603 F. 2d 244, 251-53 (2d Cir. 1979), the court held that a tender offeror's claim for loss of an opportunity to control the target was not within the scope of §9(e), since the price at which the

Fourth: Section 18 of the 1934 Act (together with its satellites in §16(a) of the 1933 Act and §323(a) of the 1939 Act) is a very much attenuated §11. It imposes liability on any person who makes or causes to be made in any application or report or document filed under the 1934 Act or any rule under that Act — and there are many such papers — any statement that "was at the time and in the light of the circumstances under which it was made false or misleading with respect to any material fact."[8] The Second Circuit has construed this section as applicable to any document filed with a national securities exchange, even though it is not filed also with the Commission.[9] There is the same double-barreled causation requirement as in §9(e): The liability runs to anyone who buys or sells "at a price which was affected by such statement" and it is for "damages caused by" reliance on the statement.[10] For good measure, there is a specific reliance requirement, together with a requirement that the plaintiff not know the statement is false or misleading when he buys or sells; and there is not even a provision, as in §11 of the 1933 Act, that reliance may be established without proof of the plaintiff's reading of the particular document. The capstone is a provision letting the defendant off if he proves "that he acted in good faith and had no knowledge that such statement was false or misleading." Aside from the shift in the burden of proof to the defendant, this seems to be first cousin to scienter. And there is a contribution provision as in §9(e).[11]

Except for avoiding any question that the person making the false statement or causing it to be made can be sued by the buyer or seller notwithstanding the absence of privity between them, it is hard to see what advantage §18 gives the investor that he does not have in common law deceit, where (if he has a right of action at all)

---

offeror's stock in the target was sold was not "affected by the alleged manipulation."

[8] A specific reference to omissions in this section was removed in conference as surplusage in view of the fact that a statement obviously may be misleading because of a material omission." H. R. Rep. No. 1838, 73d Cong., 2d Sess. (1934) 36; cf. id. at 32 (§9(a)(4)).

[9] Fischman v. Raytheon Mfg. Co., 188 F. 2d 783, 788 (2d Cir. 1951), supra 921 n. 7. The court held that the plaintiffs should be permitted to amend so as to allege (if they could) that the registration statement or prospectus had been filed with a national securities exchange, in which event §18(a) would apply.

[10] See Hoover v. Allen, 241 F. Supp. 213, 223-25 (S. D. N. Y. 1965).

[11] In an action under §323(a) the Ninth Circuit held (1) that federal law governed the assignment of claims, and (2) that investors who had bought convertible debentures from class members who had bought directly from the issuer did not automatically become assignees of those members' federal cause of action against the indenture trustee, because §323(a) did not extend to indirect buyers. In re Nucorp Energy Securities Litigation, 772 F. 2d 1486 (9th Cir. 1985).

he might at least be able to avoid proving, under traditional concepts of causation and reliance, that he had bought or sold at a price affected by the false statement. At common law, whether a particular document filed with a government agency is intended for the public at large is a question of construction of the particular statute.[12]

The Code, after a section on false registration statements and offering statements that reflects §11, blends §18 and aspects of the jurisprudence under Rule 10b-5 into a section on civil liability for other false filings.[13]

Fifth: Lurking in the wings — and perhaps panting with anticipation of a career to rival Rule 10b-5's — is "RICO" (the chapter of the Criminal Code on Racketeer Influenced and Corrupt Organizations), whose criminal aspect has already been noticed.[14] Any person who proves injury "in his business or property" by reason of a violation may obtain treble damages and costs (including a reasonable attorney's fee).[15] And the District Courts may enter divestiture orders, dissolve or reorganize an enterprise, and impose "reasonable restrictions on the future activities of any person."[16] This statute may prove particularly useful when the plaintiff anticipates difficulty in establishing a "sale" of a "security."

In July 1985 a bare majority of the Supreme Court foiled an apparent attempt by a number of Second Circuit judges to put boundaries around the extremely broad language of RICO.[17] The Court held that a private action was not conditioned on (1) an

[12] Restatement (Second) of Torts §536.

[13] For the sake of completeness:

Section 305(d) of the 1939 Act makes §§11 and 12 of the 1933 Act and §323 of the 1939 Act itself (the provision modeled on §18 of the 1934 Act) inapplicable to "statements in or omissions from any analysis" of indenture provisions required by the 1939 Act. Section 309(d) of the 1939 Act withholds liability on the part of a trustee under a qualified indenture on account of its failure to comply with the statute. See also Trust Ind. Act §305(a), last sentence.

There is also a fidelity bond rule for larceny and embezzlement by officers and employees of registered management investment companies with access to securities or funds. Inv. Co. Act Rule 17g-1.

On Inv. Co. Act §36(b), see pp. 985-86 infra

Finally, §33 of the Investment Company Act requires that, whenever certain actions have been settled with court approval or final judgment has been entered on the merits, every registered investment company that was a party to the action, as well as every "affiliated person" who was a defendant, shall within thirty days transmit copies of the record to the Commission for its use in connection with any report or study that it may make of lawsuits of investment companies or companies generally.

[14] Crim. Code c. 96, 18 U.S.C. §§1961-68, supra p. 711.

[15] Id., §1964(c).

[16] Id., §1964(a).

[17] See pp. 710-11 n. 4 supra.

earlier criminal conviction, or (2) proof of a racketeering injury different from the injury caused by predicate acts like securities fraud.[18]

The 1984 Bush report proposed to amend RICO "to insure that its civil liability provisions are not misused by private parties in litigation involving financial institutions."[19] And the great variety of bills that were introduced expired with the adjournment of Congress in October 1986.[20]

H. IMPLIED LIABILITIES

1. Theory and Scope: Seven Decades of Supreme Court History

Until a number of recent Supreme Court cases, most of this rich structure of express liabilities, especially in the 1933 and 1934 Acts, was quite overshadowed by the wide recognition of implied liabilities. After a historical exegesis of theory and scope culminating in those cases — not all of them involving the SEC statutes by any means — we shall try to ascertain the present status of the most important implied liabilities in the light of the Supreme Court's teaching.

The idea of implying civil liabilities from the violation of statutes is an old one. Lord Campbell applied the doctrine 130 years ago in construing an 1844 statute that subjected shipowners who did

[18]Sedima, S. P. R. L. v. Imrex Co., Inc., 473 U. S. 479 (1985); see also American National Bank & Trust Co. of Chicago v. Haroco, Inc., 473 U. S. 606 (1985).

[19]Blueprint for Reform: The Report of the Task Force on Regulation of Financial Services (1984) 95.

[20]In general, see CCH, RICO: Business Disputes and the "Racketeering" Laws, Federal and State (1984); Buraff Publications, Civil RICO Report; Andrews Publications, Inc., Racketeering Litigation Reporter; Long, Treble Damages for Violations of the Federal Securities Laws: A Suggested Analysis and Application of the RICO Civil Cause of Action, 85 Dick. L. Rev. 201 (1981); Note, Civil RICO: The Temptation and Impropriety of Judicial Restrictions, 45 Harv. L. Rev. 1101 (1982).

On the civil side of the state RICO statutes, see M. Steinberg and R. Ferrara, Securities Practice: Federal and State Enforcement (1985) c. 6; Milner, A Civil RICO Bibliography, 21 Cal. W. L. Rev. 409 (1986).

At the state level it is also quite common to find unfair and deceptive trade practices statutes, along the lines of the Federal Trade Commission legislation, which are generally held not to apply to securities. See Russell v. Dean Witter Reynolds, Inc., 200 Conn. 172, 510 A. 2d 972 (1986), and cases cited. *Contra:* Preston v. Kruezer, 641 F. Supp. 1163, 1168-69, (N. D. Ill. 1986).

not keep certain medicines aboard to a penalty of £20 for each default, to be paid in part to any common informer and for the rest to the Seaman's Hospital Society.[1] Although the court sustained a demurrer to an injured seaman's first count, which pleaded (without reference to the statute) what would today be called unseaworthiness in admiralty law, a second count that alleged noncompliance with the statute was held to give the plaintiff an action; for "in every case, where a statute enacts, or prohibits a thing for the benefit of a person, he shall have a remedy * * * for the recompence of a wrong done to him contrary to the said law."[2]

The text writers on the law of torts tend to discuss the doctrine in terms of negligence cases: Since the "reasonably prudent man" of the law of negligence — who, of course, is presumed to know the law — does not commit crimes, his violating the speed limit when he hits a pedestrian is negligence *per se*, or at least, in a substantial minority of American courts, "evidence of negligence."[3]

C. 10H [1] 7 & 8 Vict., c. 112, §18.

[2] Couch v. Steel, 3 E. & B. 402, 411, 118 Eng. Rep. 1193, 1196 (Q. B. 1854), cited in Texas & Pacific Ry. Co. v. Rigsby, 241 U. S. 33, 40 (1916), and in Greater Iowa Corp. v. McLendon, 378 F. 2d 783, 789-90 (8th Cir. 1967). *Couch* is the last, not the first, of a line of English tort cases going back at least to the beginning of the eighteenth century. H. Street, The Law of Torts (6th ed. 1976) 265 n. 4. Indeed, the lineage may be much more ancient. Lord Campbell described the Statute of Westminster 2, 13 Ed. 1, c. 50 (1385), as giving "a remedy by action on the case to all who are aggrieved by the neglect of any duty created by statute." 3 E. & B. at 411, 118 Eng. Rep. at 1196. It may be that looseness has been bred, as Dean Thayer said (Thayer, Public Wrong and Private Action, 27 Harv. L. Rev. 317, 331 (1914)), by Lord Campbell's unqualified quotation of the statement in Comyns' Digest that "in every Case, where a Statute enacts, or prohibits a Thing for the Benefit of a Person, he shall have a Remedy upon the same Statute for the Thing enacted for his Advantage, or for the Recompence of a Wrong done to him contrary to the said Law." 1 Com. Dig. 248 (1762). But, if it be assumed that Lord Campbell was a poor historian, his error seems to have been legitimated by time, at least (as we shall soon see) by many American courts as well as The American Law Institute. *Communis error facit jus.*

Oddly enough, although the English-invented doctrine has flowered in America, it has been considerably qualified by the English courts except with respect to industrial welfare legislation. See Williams, The Effect of Penal Legislation in the Law of Tort, 23 Mod. L. Rev. 233 (1960). However, the Law Commissions in a 1969 report recommended a statutory provision to the effect that "the breach of an obligation is intended to be actionable at the suit of any person who by reason of that breach suffers or apprehends damage, unless a contrary intention is expressly stated." Law Commission (No. 21) and Scottish Law Commission (No. 11), The Interpretation of Statutes (1969) ¶38. And it is worthy of note that the civil law is said to impose liability much more broadly than the common law. See Newman, Breach of Statute As the Basis of Responsibility in the Civil Law, 27 Can. B. Rev. 782, esp. at 797-802 (1949).

[3] In general, see 3 Harper, James, and Gray, The Law of Torts (2d ed. 1986)

The doctrine, however, is not limited to negligence cases.[4] The Restatement (Second) of Torts puts it this way:

> When a legislative provision protects a class of persons by proscribing or requiring certain conduct but does not provide a civil remedy for the violation, the court may, if it determines that the remedy is appropriate in furtherance of the purpose of the legislation and needed to assure the effectiveness of the provision, accord to an injured member of the class a right of action, using a suitable existing tort action or a new cause of action analogous to an existing tort action.[5]

The Supreme Court's decisions in the past twenty years and more have gone through several stages, not marked by clear boundaries. The first — which might be called the "ebullient stage" — was marked by a case involving Rule 14a-9, the proxy fraud rule under the 1934 Act, as it applied to a corporate merger, and it was the

---

§17.6. For a number of different philosophical approaches, see Thayer, Public Wrong and Private Action, 27 Harv. L. Rev. 317, 320 (1914); Lowndes, Civil Liability Created by Criminal Legislation, 16 Minn. L. Rev. 361, 369 (1932); Morris, The Role of Criminal Statutes in Negligence Actions, 49 Colum. L. Rev. 21 (1949); Foy, Some Reflections on Legislation, Adjudication, and Implied Private Actions in the State and Federal Courts, 71 Corn. L. Rev. 501 (1986).

In 1916 the Supreme Court recognized an action by an intrastate railroad employee for violation of the Safety Appliance Acts, although only *interstate* employees were given an express right of action:

> A disregard of the command of the statute is a wrongful act, and where it results in damage to one of the class for whose especial benefit the statute was enacted, the right to recover the damages from the party in default is implied, according to a doctrine of the common law * * *. This is but an application of the maxim, *Ubi jus ibi remedium.*

Texas & Pacific Ry. v. Rigsby, 241 U. S. 33, 39-40 (1916); but cf. Moore v. Chesapeake & Ohio R. R., 291 U. S. 205 (1934). On the possible limitation of the *Moore* case, see 2 Loss 990-92.

[4]See Tunstall v. Brotherhood of Locomotive Firemen & Enginemen, 323 U. S. 210, 213 (1944) (injunction and damage action against a labor union "which is derived from the duty imposed by the Railway Labor Act" on the union to represent all employees in the craft regardless of race); Reitmeister v. Reitmeister, 162 F. 2d 691, 694 (2d Cir. 1947) (wiretapping provision of Communications Act of 1944); Fitzgerald v. Pan American World Airways, Inc., 229 F. 2d 499, 501 (2d Cir. 1956) (statute prohibiting discrimination by air carriers). In the last of these cases the court relied on two of its own decisions under the SEC statutes. Goldstein v. Groesbeck, 142 F. 2d 422 (2d Cir. 1944), *cert. denied*, 323 U. S. 727 (1935 Act); Fischman v. Raytheon Mfg. Co., 188 F. 2d 783 (2d Cir. 1951); see also Baird v. Franklin, 141 F. 2d 238, 244-45 (2d Cir. 1944), *cert. denied*, 323 U. S. 737 (Sec. Ex. Act §6(b), requiring exchanges to discipline members for unethical conduct); but cf. Huffington v. Enstar Corp., 589 F. Supp. 624 (S. D. Tex. 1984) (1935 Act).

[5]§874A; see also §§285(a), 286-88C.

first implication of a private action by the Supreme Court under the SEC statutes.[6] Justice Clark wrote for a unanimous Court:

> * * * We consider only the question of whether §27 of the Act authorizes a federal cause of action for rescission or damages to a corporate stockholder with respect to a consummated merger which was authorized pursuant to the use of a proxy statement alleged to contain false and misleading statements violative of §14(a) of the Act. * * *
>
> * * *
>
> It appears clear that private parties have a right under §27 to bring suit for violation of §14(a) of the Act. Indeed, this section specifically grants the appropriate District Courts jurisdiction over "all suits in equity and actions at law brought to enforce any liability or duty created" under the Act. * * * the causal relationship of the proxy material and the merger are questions of fact to be resolved at trial, not here. * * *
>
> While the respondent contends that his Count 2 claim is not a derivative one, we need not embrace that view, for we believe that a right of action exists as to both derivative and direct causes.
>
> * * * While [the legislative history] makes no specific reference to a private right of action, among its chief purposes is "the protection of investors," which certainly implies the availability of judicial relief where necessary to achieve that result.
>
> * * * Private enforcement of the proxy rules provides a necessary supplement to Commission action. As in antitrust treble damage litigation, the possibility of civil damages or injunctive relief serves as a most effective weapon in the enforcement of the proxy requirements. * * *
>
> We, therefore, believe that under the circumstances here it is the duty of the courts to be alert to provide such remedies as are necessary to make effective the congressional purpose. * * * It is for the federal courts "to adjust their remedies so as to grant the necessary relief" where federally secured rights are invaded. "And it is also well settled that where legal rights have been invaded, and a federal statute provides for a general right to sue for such invasion, federal courts may use any available remedy to make good the wrong done." *Bell* v. *Hood*, 327 U. S. 678, 684 (1946). Section 27 grants the District Courts jurisdiction "of all suits in equity and actions at law brought to enforce any liability or duty created by this title * * *." In passing on almost identical language found in the Securities Act of 1933, the Court found the words entirely sufficient to fashion a remedy to rescind a fraudulent sale, secure restitution

[6] J. I. Case Co. v. Borak, 377 U. S. 426 (1964).

and even to enforce the right to restitution against a third party holding assets of the vendor. *Deckert* v. *Independence Shares Corp.*, 311 U. S. 282 (1940). This significant language was used:

> The power *to enforce* implies the power to make effective the right of recovery afforded by the Act. And the power to make the right of recovery effective implies the power to utilize any of the procedures or actions normally available to the litigant according to the exigencies of the particular case. At 288. [Citations deleted.]

Nor do we find merit in the contention that such remedies are limited to prospective relief. This was the position taken in *Dann* v. *Studebaker-Packard Corp.*, 288 F. 2d 201 * * *. But we believe that the overriding federal law applicable here would, where the facts required, control the appropriateness of redress despite the provisions of state corporation law, for it "is not uncommon for federal courts to fashion federal law where federal rights are concerned." *Textile Workers* v. *Lincoln Mills,* 353 U. S. 448, 457 (1957). * * *

Moreover, if federal jurisdiction were limited to the granting of declaratory relief, victims of deceptive proxy statements would be obliged to go into state courts for remedial relief. And if the law of the State happened to attach no responsibility to the use of misleading proxy statements, the whole purpose of the section might be frustrated. Furthermore, the hurdles that the victim might face (such as separate suits, as contemplated by *Dann* v. *Studebaker-Packard Corp.*, supra, security for expenses statutes, bringing in all parties necessary for complete relief, etc.) might well prove insuperable to effective relief.

The result is eminently sound. But the opinion disappointed:

(1) To consider it "clear" without discussion that a private action under the proxy rules *is* one "brought to enforce any liability or duty created by" the Act within the meaning of §27 is to beg the question. For, as the Court later made plain,[7] §27 simply confers jurisdiction on the District Courts to hear actions created expressly or by implication elsewhere in the statute.

(2) The treble damage actions that the opinion refers to as "a most effective weapon" are, of course, expressly provided for in the antitrust laws.

(3) All that the *Deckert* case stands for — as well as the other restitution or divestiture cases that are cited in the opinion — is that historic equity jurisprudence gives the federal courts very broad

[7] See Touche Ross & Co. v. Redington, 442 U. S. 560, 577 (1979), infra p. 934.

authority to grant relief that is ancillary to an action expressly created.

In short, the Court reached the right result not for the wrong reason but for no reason at all. It would have been much easier to write an opinion in terms of the tort doctrine. Yet, inexplicably, the Court did not so much as mention that concept. This, with respect, is the opinion's greatest fault. For, if the Court really meant to hold that aid to enforcement was itself an independent basis of civil liability — as some commentators assumed — the implications not only for the extension of implied liability, but also for the type of proof required in contrast to a tort-based rationale, were considerable. On this account alone it was fairly predictable that the Court one day would have to rationalize *Borak* in more traditional terms. As Justice Harlan put it in his concurring opinion six years later in a case in which the Court implied an action for violation of the Fourth Amendment by a federal agent acting under color of authority:

> * * * the exercise of judicial power involved in *Borak* simply cannot be justified in terms of statutory construction * * *; nor did the *Borak* Court purport to do so. * * * The notion of "implying" a remedy, therefore, as applied to cases like *Borak,* can only refer to a process whereby the federal judiciary exercises a choice among *traditionally available* judicial remedies according to reasons related to the substantive social policy embodies in an act of positive law.[8]

A few months later the Court finally decided a case under the then twenty-eight-year-old Rule 10b-5. By that time Justice Douglas was able to content the Court with the statement: "It is now established that a private right of action is implied under §10(b)."[9] In sum, whereas *Borak* gave us an opinion without a workable *ratio decidendi,* the 10b-5 case gave us a decision without an opinion. So much for the Court's "ebullient" stage!

What might be called the "back to orthodoxy" stage that was heralded by the Harlan concurring opinion soon evolved into what might be called the "shift of presumption" stage. Indeed, in the very Fourth Amendment case in which Justice Harlan concurred,

[8] Bivens v. Six Unknown Named Agents of the Federal Bureau of Narcotics, 403 U. S. 388, 402 n. 4 (1971); see also Wyandotte Transportation Co. v. United States, 389 U. S. 191, 201-08 (1967), where Justice Fortas cited the Restatement (Second) of Torts.

[9] Superintendent of Ins. of the State of N. Y. v. Bankers Life & Casualty Co., 404 U. S. 6, 13 n. 9 (1971). The earlier case of Tcherepnin v. Knight, 389 U. S. 332 (1967), though brought under Rule 10b-5, came to the Court only on the question whether a "security" was involved.

Chief Justice Burger dissented, stating: "Legislation is the business of the Congress, and it has the facilities and competence for that task — as we do not."[10] This was followed by cases in which the Court rejected private actions to enjoin the discontinuance of passenger service under the "Amtrak" Act[11] and to compel the Securities Investor Protection Corporation to take action against a financially troubled broker-dealer under the Securities Investor Protection Act.[12]

There were also other skirmishes, all leading to a unanimous opinion in 1975 — *Cort* v. *Ash*[13] — that seemed designed as a definitive guide to Bench and Bar. Rejecting a stockholder's implied action against directors for violation of a criminal statute that prohibited corporate contributions in connection with Presidential elections,[14] Justice Brennan stated for a Court that was unanimous as in *Borak*:

> In determining whether a private remedy is implicit in a statute not expressly providing one, several factors are relevant. First, is the plaintiff "one of the class for whose *especial* benefit the statute was enacted," *Texas & Pacific R. Co.* v. *Rigsby,* 241 U. S. 33, 39 (1916) (emphasis supplied) — that is, does the statute create a federal right in favor of the plaintiff? Second, is there any indication of legislative intent, explicit or implicit, either to create such a remedy or to deny one? See, e. g., *National Railroad Passenger Corp.* v. *National Railroad Passengers,* 414 U. S. 453, 458, 460 (1974) (*Amtrak*). Third, is it consistent with the underlying purposes of the legislative scheme to imply such a remedy for the plaintiff? See, e. g., *Amtrak,* supra; *Securities Investor Protection Corp.* v. *Barbour,* 421 U. S. 412, 423 (1975); *Calhoon* v. *Harvey,* 379 U. S. 134 (1964). And finally, is the cause of action one traditionally relegated to state law, in an area basically the concern of the States, so that it would be inappropriate to infer a cause of action based solely on federal law? See *Wheeldin* v. *Wheeler,* 373 U. S. 647, 652 (1963); cf. *J. I. Case Co.* v. *Borak,* 377 U. S. 426, 434 (1964); *Bivens* v. *Six Unknown Federal Narcotics Agents,* 403 U. S. 388, 394-395 (1971); id., at 400 (Harlan, J., concurring in judgment).

[10] Bivens v. Six Unknown Named Agents of the Federal Bureau of Narcotics, 403 U. S. 388, 412 (1971).

[11] 45 U. S. C. §547; National R. R. Passenger Corp. v. National Assn. of R. R. Passengers, 414 U. S. 453 (1974).

[12] Securities Investor Protection Corp. v. Barbour, 421 U. S. 412 (1975).

[13] 422 U. S. 66 (1975).

[14] 18 U. S. C. §610.

* * *

* * * Here, there was nothing more than a bare criminal statute, with absolutely no indication that civil enforcement of any kind was available to anyone.

We need not, however, go so far as to say that in this circumstance a bare criminal statute can *never* be deemed sufficiently protective of some special group so as to give rise to a private cause of action by a member of that group. For the intent to protect corporate shareholders particularly was at best a subsidiary purpose of §610, and the other relevant factors all either are not helpful or militate against implying a private cause of action.

* * *

* * * We are necessarily reluctant to imply a federal right to recover funds used in violation of a federal statute where the laws governing the corporation may put a shareholder on notice that there may be no such recovery.

* * * In *Borak,* the statute involved was clearly an intrusion of federal law into the internal affairs of corporations; to the extent that state law differed or impeded suit, the congressional intent could be compromised in state-created causes of action. In this case, Congress was concerned, not with regulating corporations as such, but with dulling their impact upon federal elections.

Two years later the Court, in a case under §14(e) of the 1934 Act[15] and Rule 10b-6[16] that turned essentially on standing rather than implied liability, relied largely on its *Cort* v. *Ash* analysis to reject an implied action for damages by Chris-Craft Industries, Inc., the loser of two competing tender offerors for the stock of Piper Aircraft Corporation, against the winner, Bangor Punta Corporations.[17] Chief Justice Burger stated for a majority of six:

The reasoning of [the proxy and 10b-6] holdings is that, where congressional purposes are likely to be undermined absent private enforcement, private remedies may be implied in favor of the particular class intended to be protected by the statute. * * *

[15] See p. 527 supra.

[16] See p. 862 supra.

[17] Piper v. Chris-Craft Industries, Inc., 430 U. S. 1, 42 n. 28, 47 n. 33 (1970). See pp. 952-54 infra.

> * * *
>
> The legislative history * * * shows that the sole purpose of the Williams Act was the protection of investors who are confronted with a tender offer. * * * We find no hint in the legislative history * * * that Congress contemplated a private cause of action for damages by one of several contending offerors against a successful bidder or by a losing contender against the target corporation.
>
> * * *
>
> Our conclusion as to the legislative history is confirmed by the analysis in *Cort* v. *Ash,* 422 U. S. 66 (1975). * * *
>
> What we have said thus far suggests that, unlike *J. I. Case Co.* v. *Borak,* supra, judicially creating a damages action in favor of Chris-Craft is unnecessary to ensure the fulfillment of Congress' purposes in adopting the Williams Act. * * *
>
> Although we reserve judgment on the broader standing issues arising under Rule 10b-6, we hold that, in the context of these cases, Chris-Craft is without standing to sue for damages on account of Bangor's alleged Rule 10b-6 violations. * * * as the issues have been framed, Chris-Craft did not come to the courts in the posture of a hoodwinked investor victimized by market manipulation; its complaint, as we noted, is that it lost a chance to gain control of a corporation, a claim beyond the bounds of the specific concern of Rule 10b-6.

Two years after *Piper,* a non-SEC case (*Cannon* v. *University of Chicago*)[18] that came out the other way on a *Cort* analysis shattered the unanimity of the *Cort* Court. Six Justices implied a private right of action under §901(a) of Title IX of the Education Amendments of 1972, which prohibits discrimination on the basis of sex under any education program receiving federal assistance.

With respect to the second *Cort* factor, Justice Stevens for the majority recognized that the legislative history of a statute that does not expressly create or deny a private right of action will typically be silent or ambiguous. "Therefore, in situations such as the present one 'in which it is clear that federal law has granted a class of persons certain rights, it is not necessary to show an intention to *create* a private right of action, although an explicit purpose to *deny* such cause of action would be controlling.' "[19] Here, the opinion continued, the drafters of Title IX explicitly assumed that it would be interpreted to grant a private right of action as Title VI (with

[18] 441 U. S. 677 (1979).
[19] Id. at 694, quoting from Cort v. Ash, 422 U. S. 66, 82 (1975).

respect to race) had been during the preceding eight years. Even so: "When Congress intends private litigants to have a cause of action to support their statutory rights, the far better course is for it to specify as much when it creates those rights."[20]

Justice Rehnquist, though joining the Stevens opinion, was much more pointed in a concurring opinion in which Justice Stewart joined: After expressing his agreement with the view of the Stevens opinion that Congress intended to lean on the courts with respect to civil rights actions, Justice Rehnquist stated: "It seems to me that the factors to which I have here briefly adverted apprise the lawmaking branch of the Federal Government that the ball, so to speak, may well now be in its court. Not only is it 'far better' for Congress to so specify when it intends private litigants to have a cause of action, but for this very reason this Court in the future should be extremely reluctant to imply a cause of action absent such specificity on the part of the Legislative Branch."[21]

This attack on *Cort*'s four-part analysis was as nothing compared with the dissenting opinion of Justice Powell. Whereas Justices White and Blackmun also dissented, questioning the minor premise of the syllogism as it were, Justice Powell squarely attacked the major premise, concluding that *Cort* was an unconstitutional encroachment on the separation of powers:

> * * * as mounting evidence from the courts below suggests, and the decision of the Court today demonstrates, the mode of analysis we have applied in the recent past cannot be squared with the doctrine of the separation of powers. The time has come to reappraise our standards for the judicial implication of private causes of action.
>
> * * *
>
> In recent history, the Court has tended to stray from the Art. III and separation-of-power principle of limited jurisdiction. This, I believe, is evident from a review of the more or less haphazard line of cases that led to our decision in *Cort* v. *Ash,* 422 U. S. 66 (1975). The "four factor" analysis of that case is an open invitation to federal courts to legislate causes of action not authorized by Congress. It is an analysis not faithful to constitutional principles and should be rejected. Absent the most compelling evidence of affirmative congressional intent, a federal court should not infer a private cause of action.

[20] 441 U. S. at 717.
[21] Id. at 718.

* * *

> * * * In the four years since we decided *Cort,* no less than 20 decisions by the Courts of Appeals have implied private actions from federal statutes. [Citations omitted.] It defies reason to believe that in each of these statutes Congress absentmindedly forgot to mention an intended private action. * * *[22]

Here, then, are several members of the Court who seem to be denigrating three of the four *Cort* factors in favor of the second, which goes to legislative intent. And the two cases that follow indicate that, although *Cort* may yet have a long "half-life," its four-factor analysis is already passé.

In the next securities case, *Touche Ross & Co.* v. *Redington,*[23] the Court concluded that a broker's customers had no implied action for damages against the broker's auditors for alleged misstatements contained in the reports required under §17(a) of the 1934 Act.[24] The Court's opinion (from which only Justice Marshall dissented, Justice Powell not participating) was delivered by Justice Rehnquist:

> The question of the existence of a statutory cause of action is, of course, one of statutory construction. [Citations deleted.] SIPC's argument in favor of implication of a private right of action based on tort principles, therefore, is entirely misplaced. * * * Instead, our task is limited solely to determining whether Congress intended to create the private right of action asserted by SIPC and the Trustee. * * *

* * *

> The intent of §17(a) is evident from its face. Section 17(a) is like provisions in countless other statutes that simply require certain regulated businesses to keep records and file periodic reports to enable the relevant governmental authorities to perform their regulatory functions. * * *

* * *

> * * * Obviously, then, when Congress wished to provide a private damages remedy, it knew how to do so and did so expressly. [Citing §§9(e), 16(b), 18(a), 20.]

[22] Id. at 730, 731, 741-42.
[23] 442 U. S. 560 (1979).
[24] See p. 637 supra. The firm had been taken over by SIPC, which joined the trustee in suing.

> * * * It is true that in *Cort* v. *Ash*, the Court set forth four factors that it considered "relevant" in determining whether a private remedy is implicit in a statute not expressly providing one. But the Court did not decide that each of these factors is entitled to equal weight. The central inquiry remains whether Congress intended to create, either expressly or by implication, a private cause of action. Indeed, the first three factors discussed in *Cort* — the language and focus of the statute, its legislative history, and its purpose, see 422 U. S., at 78 — are ones traditionally relied upon in determining legislative intent. * * *
>
> * * *
>
> The reliance of SIPC and the Trustee on §27 is misplaced. Section 27 grants jurisdiction to the federal courts and provides for venue and service of process. It creates no cause of action of its own force and effect; it imposes no liabilities. * * * We do not now question the actual holding of that case, but we decline to read the opinion so broadly that virtually every provision of the Securities Acts gives rise to an implied private cause of action. E. g., *Piper* v. *Chris-Craft Industries, Inc.*, supra.
>
> * * * To the extent our analysis in today's decision differs from that of the Court in *Borak*, it suffices to say that in a series of cases since *Borak* we have adhered to a stricter standard for the implication of private causes of action, and we follow that stricter standard today. *Cannon* v. *University of Chicago*, supra, at 688-709. The ultimate question is one of congressional intent, not one of whether this Court thinks that it can improve upon the statutory scheme that Congress enacted into law.

Note the correction of *Borak*'s erroneous reading of §27, the jurisdictional provision, as creating a cause of action of its own force and effect.

Note also the relegation of three of the four *Cort* factors — a process begun in *Cannon* — to a negative role. Apparently they may not, even as a troika, carry the day unless "Congress intended to create, either expressly or by implication, a private cause of action." We shall have a bit more to say about legislative intent after we examine the next case, *Transamerica Mortgage Advisors, Inc.* v. *Lewis*.[25] The Court was unanimous, as we have seen,[26] that the voidability provision in §215 of the Investment Advisers Act could be used to obtain rescission. But Justices White, Brennan, Marshall,

[25] 444 U. S. 11 (1979).
[26] See p. 913 supra.

and Stevens dissented from the further holding that there was no implied action for *damages* for violation of §206, the general fraud provision of that statute.[27]

Justice Stewart's majority opinion began with "the language of the statute itself,"[28] and, referring to the injunctive, criminal, and administrative remedies, in effect applied the *expressio unius* maxim without resort to the Latin incantation. The dissenting opinion, by contrast, stressed the resemblance of §§206 and 215 to §§10(b) and 29(b) of the 1934 Act.

There have been other Supreme Court cases, mostly negative[29] — including, notably, a commodities fraud case, *Merrill Lynch, Pierce, Fenner & Smith, Inc.* v. *Curran,*[30] which introduced a new note (Justice Stevens writing for the majority in a five-four decision):

> Prior to the comprehensive amendments to the CEC [Commodity Exchange Act] enacted in 1974, the federal courts routinely and consistently had recognized an implied private cause of action on behalf of plaintiffs seeking to enforce and to collect damages for violation of provisions of the CEA or rules and regulations promulgated pursuant to the statute. The routine recognition of a private

[27] "Where rescission is awarded, the rescinding party may of course have restitution of the consideration given under the contract, less any value conferred by the other party. See 5 A. Corbin, Contracts §1114 (1964). Restitution would not, however, include compensation for any diminution in the value of the rescinding party's investment alleged to have resulted from the adviser's action or inaction. Such relief could provide by indirection the equivalent of a private damage remedy that we have concluded Congress did not confer." 444 U. S. at 24 n. 14. See also pp. 940-41 infra.

[28] 444 U. S. at 16.

[29] E. g., Davis v. Passman, 442 U. S. 228 (1979) (*Cort* analysis does not apply to actions based directly on the Constitution, in this case an allegation of sex-based discrimination by a Congressman in violation of the Fifth Amendment); Carlson v. Green, 446 U. S. 14 (1980) (Court extended *Bivens*, supra p. 929, to Eighth Amendment's proscription of cruel and unusual punishment); Kissinger v. Reporters Committee for Freedom of the Press, 445 U. S. 136 (1980) (no action under Federal Records Act of 1950, as supplemented by Records Disposal Act, or Freedom of Information Act); Universities Research Assn. v. Coutu, 450 U. S. 754 (1981) (no employee action for back wages under Davis-Bacon Act, with respect to federal construction contracts); Northwest Airlines, Inc. v. Transport Workers Union of America, 451 U. S. 77 (1981), infra p. 1040 (no statutory or federal common law allows federal courts to fashion contribution among violators of Equal Pay Act of 1963 and Title VII of Civil Rights Act of 1964); California v. Sierra Club, 451 U. S. 287 (1981) (no action for violation of requirement in §10 of Rivers and Harbors Appropriations Act of 1899 that any obstruction to navigable capacity be authorized by Congress); Texas Industries, Inc. v. Radcliff Materials, Inc., 451 U. S. 630 (1981), infra p. 1040 (no statutory or federal common law allows federal courts to fashion contribution among antitrust violators); Middlesex County Sewerage Authority v. National Sea Clammers Assn., 453 U. S. 1 (1981) (no action for violation of Federal Water Pollution Control Act and Marine Protection, Research, and Sanctuaries Act of 1972).

[30] 456 U. S. 353 (1982).

remedy under the CEA prior to our decision in *Cort* v. *Ash* was comparable to the routine acceptance of an analogous remedy under the Securities Exchange Act of 1934.[31]

As for *Cort* v. *Ash:*

In view of our construction of the intent of the legislature there is no need for us to "trudge through all four of the factors when the dispositive question of legislative intent has been resolved." See *California* v. *Sierra Club,* 451 U. S., at 301 (Rehnquist, J., concurring in the judgment).[32]

Justice Powell together with Chief Justice Burger and Justices Rehnquist and O'Connor, in a sharp dissent, considered this new approach "incompatible with our constitutional separation of powers";[33] observed (as did the majority opinion) that "modern federal regulatory statutes tend to be exceedingly complex";[34] referred to the "severe and growing burden on the lower federal courts";[35] and lamented:

* * * Fewer than a dozen district courts wrongly create a remedy in damages under the CEA; Congress fails to correct the error; and congressional silence binds this Court to follow the erroneous decisions of the district courts and courts of appeals.

With one subsequent SEC case, *Herman & MacLean* v. *Huddleston*[36] — which is set out later because it involved the question whether the established right of action under Rule 10b-5 applied in the face of an express remedy for the same conduct under §11 of the 1933 Act — all the Supreme Court cases that are directly in point under the SEC statutes have been referred to here, as well as the most significant non-SEC cases. *Query* where all this leaves the matter of implied liability under the securities legislation:

(1) It seems fairly clear that *Cort,* though still used, has been weakened, at least to the extent that the third and fourth factors (consistency with the statutory scheme and impact on state law) are irrelevant unless the second factor (legislative intent) — together perhaps with the first (whether the plaintiff is a member of a class meant to be especially benefited)[37] — points to an affirmative conclusion.

[31] Id. at 379. This theme is repeated in Herman & MacLean v. Huddleston, 459 U. S. 375, 380, infra pp. 975-76.

[32] 456 U. S. at 388.

[33] Id. at 395.

[34] Id. at 408.

[35] Id. at 409 n. 17.

[36] 459 U. S. 375 (1983), infra p. 975.

[37] California v. Sierra Club, 451 U. S. 287, 297 (1981).

(2) It is difficult to quarrel with legislative intent as the ultimate determinant. After all, that criterion — perhaps better phrased more objectively as statutory purpose — is the key to all statutory construction. The trouble is that, in the ordinary case in which a statute makes no mention of a civil remedy, "the obvious conclusion can only be that when the legislature said nothing about it, they either did not have the civil suit in mind at all, or deliberately omitted to provide for it."[38] But that assumption concedes too much. History, after all, has vindicated Lord Coke and not James I.[39] Legislative intention in the literal, lay sense is one thing, and the growth of the common law (including the *Erie*-resistant "federal common law" that surrounds federal statutes) by the interaction of judges' decisions upon legislation is another.[40] The statutory tort doctrine, more or less as expounded in the Restatement,[41] is now an accepted part of American law. Consequently, if the silence of the statute does not justify the conclusion that the legislature affirmatively "intended" that there should be a private remedy, neither does it justify the conclusion that Congress had the contrary "intention." There is no need, as Dean Thayer wrote more than seventy years ago, for the court to try to discover "supposed legislative intent." "The legislature is to be credited with meaning just what it said — that the conduct forbidden is an offense against the public, and that the offender shall suffer certain specified penalties for his offense. Whether his offense shall have any other legal consequence has not been passed on one way or the other as a question of legislative intent, but is left to be determined by the rules of law."[42]

All this is to say (now that the Supreme Court has spoken) that, although legislative intent is currently "the name of the game," the

[38] Prosser, Handbook of the Law of Torts (4th ed. 1971) 191.

[39] "Then the King said that he thought the Law was founded upon reason, and that he and others had reason as well as the judges: To which it was answered by me, that * * * causes which concerned the life, or inheritance, or goods, or fortunes of his Subjects; they are not to be decided by natural reason, but by the artificial reason and judgment of Law, which Law is an act which requires long study and experience * * *." Prohibitions del Roy, 12 Rep. 63, 64-65 (1608).

[40] The theme has been developed in a number of well-known essays. Landis, Statutes and the Sources of Law, in Harv. Legal Essays (1934) 213; Pound, Common Law and Legislation, 21 Harv. L. Rev. 383 (1908); Stone, The Common Law in the United States, 50 Harv. L. Rev. 4, esp. at 12-16 (1936).

[41] See p. 926 supra.

[42] Thayer, Public Wrong and Private Action, 27 Harv. L. Rev. 317, 320 (1914); see also 2 Harper, James, and Gray, The Law of Torts (2d ed. 1986) 614-15 (modern cases in the United States make little use of the "discredited reasoning" from legislative intention); Taylor v. Bear Stearns & Co., 572 F. Supp. 667, 671 (N. D. Ga. 1983), quoting the text.

statutory tort doctrine (the first *Cort* factor) should be considered along with legislative intent, or at least as a significant factor in determining legislative intent. That is where a majority of the Court now seems to be, with the other two *Cort* factors ignored except as brakes on the first two.

(3) Suppose Congress wants civil liability but prefers to delegate the job of working out the nuances to the courts. For example, both of the legislative reports on the Small Business Investment Incentive Act of 1980[43] emphasized the value of private rights of action as a necessary adjunct to the SEC's enforcement efforts as well as providing a compensatory function, and made it plain that the courts were expected to recognize private rights of action under the legislation, since they "would be consistent with and further Congress' intent in enacting [the particular] provision, and * * * such actions would not improperly occupy an area traditionally the concern of state law."[44] So, even under Justice Powell's constitutional view a formula exists for affording judicial flexibility without at the same time offending Article III. That view — which (with respect) is weakened by its ignoring the statutory tort doctrine's roots in the judge-made law well before 1787[45] — seems to have picked up three more Justices.[46]

(4) The Latin maxims resist burial. Justice White complained in his dissenting opinion in the case under the Advisers Act:

> The Court concludes that because the Act expressly provides for SEC enforcement proceedings, Congress must not have intended to create private rights of action. This application of the oft-criticized maxim *expressio unius est exclusio alterius* ignores our rejection of it in *Cort* v. *Ash,* 422 U. S., at 82-83, n. 14, in the absence of specific support in the legislative history for the proposition that express statutory remedies are to be exclusive.[47]

However convenient a role maxims play by way of affording "the

[43] See p. 306 supra.

[44] H. R. Rep. No. 96-1341; 28-29, 96th Cong., 1st Sess. (1979) S. Rep. No. 96-958 14 (1980).

[45] See p. 924 supra, 96th Cong., 2d Sess. (1980).

[46] Id. at 397. For endorsements of the Powell view, see Stewart and Sundstein, Public Programs and Private Rights, 95 Harv. L. Rev. 1193 (1982); Brown, Of Activism and *Erie* — The Implication Doctrine's Implications for the Nature and Role of the Federal Courts, 69 Iowa L. Rev. 617 (1984); Maher and Maher, Statutorily Implied Federal Causes of Action After *Merrill Lynch:* How Sad It Is; How Simple It Could Be, 88 Dick. L. Rev. 593 (1984). But see Creswell, The Separation of Powers Implications of Implied Rights of Action, 34 Mercer L. Rev. 973 (1983).

[47] Transamerica Mortgage Advisors Inc. v. Lewis, 444 U. S. 11, 29 n. 6.

verbal tools of accepted rhetoric for use in court,"[48] they are no more than a substitute for legal reasoning, worthy perhaps of being sprinkled throughout an opinion as a chef sprinkles spice after his culinary creation has been completed. Maxims not only tyrannize, as Justice Jackson observed. They also are self-defeating: in this very context of determining when to imply civil liability from violation of a criminal statute, a comment in the Restatement (Second) of Torts puts it:

> Resort is sometimes made to maxims of statutory construction. Here, as in other instances, however, these maxims point in opposite directions and therefore prove to be inconclusive. One maxim is *Ubi ius ibi remedium,* suggesting that if the legislation created a right it must have been intended to create an adequate remedy to enforce that right. Opposed to this is the maxim, *Expressio unius exclusio alterius est,* suggesting that if the legislation called for a criminal penalty the civil liability must have intentionally been omitted, or if one section calls for civil liability and another does not it must have been intended that there would be no civil liability under the second section.[49]

Four years after *Transamerica* Justice Marshall echoed this thought for a unanimous Court — dare one say finally? — when he said in *Herman & MacLean,* recalling Justice Jackson's response to argument from maxims in the *Joiner* case,[50] "We also reject application of the maxim of statutory construction, *expressio unius est exclusio alterius.*"[51]

(5) The Advisers Act case makes it crystal clear that the voidability provisions in the 1934, 1935, and 1940 Acts may be used by the innocent party offensively to achieve rescission, not merely defensively to avoid enforcement of the contract.[52] This is at least

[48] Ballantine, Corporations (rev. ed. 1946) 313, quoting Llewellyn.

[49] §874A, Comment c.

[50] SEC v. C. M. Joiner Leasing Co., 320 U. S. 344, 350 (1943), supra p. 178.

[51] 459 U. S. at 387 n. 23.

[52] However, only an investment advisory contract can be voided under the *Transamerica* case; and only an adviser and its clients (or prospective clients) are proper parties in a private action. Paul S. Mullin & Associates, Inc. v. Bassett, 632 F. Supp. 532 (D. Del. 1986).

It does not follow, moreover, that the innocent party may seek a declaratory judgment under §29(b). Such an action does not arise under federal law for purposes of 28 U. S. C. §1331. Skelly Oil Co. v. Phillips Petroleum Co., 339 U. S. 667 (1950). This is because the underlying coercive version of the suit would be a state action to enforce a contract against which §29(b) would be merely a federal defense; and such a suit does not arise under federal law by virtue of the rule in Louisville & Nashville R. R. v. Mottley, 211 U. S. 149 (1908).

two-thirds or three-quarters of a loaf, and one whose aroma seemed pleasing to all nine of the then Justices. Indeed, it is arguable even in the face of *Transamerica* that §29(b) of the 1934 Act makes the *whole* loaf available — damages as well as rescission — because it alone of the four voidability provisions contains a statute of limitations, inserted in 1936 along with the enactment of what is now §15(c)(1), with respect to the voiding of any contract for violation of that section "in any action maintained in reliance on" §29(b).[53] In any event, it should not be overlooked that rescission, or a rescission measure of damages, is all that §12 of the 1933 Act allows. And, although the voidability provisions *ex hypothesi* require a contract, their restitution rationale makes causation irrelevant.[54] It may be too much to say that the Advisers Act and Commodity Exchange Act cases and *Herman & MacLean* herald what might be called a new "Lazarus stage." But surely the last chapter in the history of the Court's struggle with implied liabilities is yet to be written.[55]

(6) The *approach* of *Borak* does seem quite dead, except perhaps in cases based on civil rights legislation or directly on the Constitution.[56] But the *holding* of *Borak* was "grandfathered" in by *Touche Ross & Co.* v. *Redington.*[57] So were the 10b-5 cases, although the

---

Query rescissory damages (see p. 969, par. (6), infra), which arguably are closer to rescission than to damages. See p. 936 n. 27 supra.

[53] See, e. g., Geismar v. Bond & Goodwin, Inc., 40 F. Supp. 876 (S. D. N. Y. 1941). *Contra:* Corbey v. Grace, 605 F. Supp. 247, 250 (D. Minn. 1985); cf. Bassler v. Central National Bank in Chicago, 715 F. 2d 308 (7th Cir. 1983), supra p. 914 n. 7. The courts are divided on the question whether the statute of limitations applies to damage as well as rescission actions. *Yes*: Newburger, Loeb & Co., Inc. v. Gross, 365 F. Supp. 1364, 1372 (S. D. N. Y. 1973). *No*: Douglass v. Glenn E. Hinton Investments, Inc., 440 F. 2d 912 (9th Cir. 1971).

[54] Regional Properties, Inc. v. Financial & Real Estate Consulting Co., 678 F. 2d 552, 559 (5th Cir. 1982). The court held also that §29(b) of the 1934 Act could be invoked by persons other than investors. Id. at 561.

[55] See, e. g., Krome v. Merrill Lynch & Co., Inc., 637 F. Supp. 910, 918-20 (S. D. N. Y. 1986) (various Inv. Co. Act provisions, including NASD rules under §22 with respect to excessive sales loads).

[56] *Borak* was cited in Cannon v. University of Chicago, 441 U. S. 677, 711 (1979), and Herman & MacLean v. Huddleston, 459 U. S. 375, 380 n. 9 (1983), infra p. 975. And in Bateman Eichler, Hill Richards, Inc. v. Berner, 472 U. S. 299, 310 (1985), Justice Brennan quoted *Borak* for a unanimous Court: "* * * we repeatedly have emphasized that implied private actions provide 'a most effective weapon in the enforcement' of the securities laws and are 'a necessary supplement to Commission action.'" See Ashford, Implied Cause of Action Under Federal Laws: Calling the Court Back to *Borak,* 79 Nw. U. L. Rev. 227 (1984).

[57] 442 U. S. 560, 577 (1979). *Borak* involved Rule 14a-9, the proxy fraud rule. In Haas v. Wieboldt Stores, Inc., 725 F. 2d 71 (7th Cir. 1984), the court followed *Borak* under Rule 14a-7, the proxy rule with respect to shareholder

proxy rules could readily have been distinguished as displacing virtually no state law.[58] At the same time, a majority of the Court was unwilling to extend *Borak*'s holding to the closely related form of corporate warfare by tender offer rather than by proxy, at least when the plaintiff is outside looking in. And, as we saw in the last chapter, the Court has been narrowing Rule 10b-5 as a matter of substantive coverage.

(7) Certainly the old talk about implying a private right of action "unless the legislation evidences a contrary intention"[59] is no longer justified. The lower courts have "got the message" that the burden of the argument now goes the other way. Nevertheless, there has been some foot-dragging. For example, the District of Columbia Circuit, in applying the *Cort* tests to conclude that nothing in §11 or 12(2) of the 1933 Act or §18 of the 1934 Act precluded resort to Rule 10b-5, stated:

> If Congress had spoken plainly enough, the task would be simple. The quest, therefore, is not necessarily for evidence that Congress specifically intended to imply a private right of action, but rather for indications whether Congress meant to deny such a remedy. This was the thrust of *Transamerica.*[60]

Judge Friendly probably captured the present state of affairs best in his opinion in one of the commodity cases that the Supreme Court recently affirmed, when he said that *Cort* should be read "in light of the later *caveat* in *Touche Ross & Co.* v. *Redington,* 442 U. S. 560, 575 (1979), that the basic inquiry is always to plumb the intent of Congress, that the *Cort* factors are simply inquiries helpful in that endeavor, and that satisfaction of one or more of the *Cort* factors

---

lists (see p. 466 supra). See also New York City Employees' Retirement System v. American Brands, Inc., 634 F. Supp. 1382, 1385-86 (S. D. N. Y. 1986) (Rule 14a-8, the stockholder proposal rule). But in Rauchman v. Mobil Corp., 739 F. 2d 205 (8th Cir. 1984), the court expressed "substantial reservations" about the existence of a private action under Rule 14a-8, although it was able to assume an affirmative answer because it found against the plaintiff on the merits.

[58] " * * * a private right of action under Section 10(b) of the 1934 Act and Rule 10b-5 has been consistently recognized for more than 35 years. The existence of this implied remedy is simply beyond peradventure." Herman & MacLean v. Huddleston, 459 U. S. 375, 380 (1983), infra p. 975.

[59] Brown v. Bullock, 194 F. Supp. 207, 224 (S. D. N. Y. 1961), *aff'd en banc*, 294 F. 2d 415 (2d Cir. 1961) (Inv. Co. Act).

[60] Wachovia Bank & Trust Co. v. National Student Marketing Corp., 650 F. 2d 342, 352 (D. C. Cir. 1980), *cert. denied* sub nom. Peat, Marwick, Mitchell & Co. v. Wachovia Bank & Trust Co., 452 U. S. 954. The Supreme Court later reached the same result with respect to §11. Herman & MacLean v. Huddleston, 459 U. S. 375 (1983), infra p. 975. But that does not detract from what the court said in *Wachovia Bank.*

will not alone carry the day."[61] To this he later added, with reference to "the recent triad" of *Cannon, Redington,* and *Transamerica:*

> We do think, however, that the rumors about the death of the implied cause of action which have been circulating in the wake of these decisions — an attitude strongly reflected in the dissent — are exaggerated, at least as far as previously enacted statutes are concerned, and that the effect of the decisions is simply to emphasize that the ultimate touchstone is congressional intent and not judicial notions of what would constitute wise policy.[62]

We must now examine those civil liabilities that were most commonly implied before the recent Supreme Court cases and try to ascertain their present status in the light of those cases.

2. Proxy Rules

An earlier chapter has explored the quantum of relief available on a showing of violation of the proxy rules, since there is no reason to suppose that the answer turns (except for the possibility of award-

[61] Leist v. Simplot, 638 F. 2d 283, 302 n. 20 (2d Cir. 1980), *aff'd* sub nom. Merrill Lynch, Pierce, Fenner & Smith, Inc. v. Curran, 456 U. S. 353 (1982). But cf. Daily Income Fund, Inc. v. Fox, 464 U. S. 523, 530 (1984), infra p. 986 n. 253, where the Court enumerated all four factors in *denying* an implied right of action for an investment company under §36(b) of the Investment Company Act.

[62] 638 F. 2d at 316. In Liberty National Ins. Holding Co. v. Charter Co., 734 F. 2d 545, 561 n. 35 (11th Cir. 1984), Judge Tjoflat stated that "implying the existence and limits of a private right of action is a judicial practice which, like virtually all other judicial practices, floats on a sea of fluid judicial precedent that may shift with the tides." And it has been suggested that "the Supreme Court's refusal to imply private rights of action is not truly based on the concerns for federalism that the Court has articulated, but rather on more substantive grounds"; that "the invocation of federalism rhetoric may also be a reflection of the individual political preferences of the members of the Court"; and that "the Court's articulated rationale cannot explain its opinions." Anderson, The Meaning of Federalism: Interpreting the Securities Exchange Act of 1934, 70 Va. L. Rev. 813, 821 (1984). For a reply, see Kitch, A Federal Vision of the Securities Laws, 70 Va. L. Rev. 857 (1984).

When the question is whether a private right of action should be implied from violation of a *rule* of the Commission, the Third Circuit has suggested a two-fold inquiry: (1) Does the enabling statute properly permit the implication of a private right of action? "To this determination, the method of analysis developed by the Supreme Court is fully applicable." (2) If the first hurdle is surmounted, should a private right of action be implied from the particular rule? At this stage, "inquiry should focus on whether granting private parties the ability to bring suit under the rule will further the substantive purposes of the enabling statute" — language reminiscent of *Borak.* Angelastro v. Prudential-Bache Securities, Inc., 764 F. 2d 939, 947 (3d Cir. 1985), *cert. denied,* 106 S. Ct. 267.

ing damages to a private plaintiff) on whether the plaintiff is a private person or the Commission itself.[63] We examine here a number of questions that arise only in private actions.

a. Standing

Since *Borak* it is clear that the corporation itself has standing to sue, which means that stockholders may also sue derivatively. This view is consistent with the administrative approach of neutrality in proxy contests — a position firmly grounded on legislative history. The Senate report on the bill that became the 1934 Act is more specific here than it is on most of the statutory provisions:

> It is contemplated that the rules and regulations promulgated by the Commission will protect investors from promiscuous solicitation of their proxies, on the one hand, by irresponsible outsiders seeking to wrest control of a corporation away from honest and conscientious corporation officials, and, on the other hand, by unscrupulous corporate officials seeking to retain control of the management by concealing and distorting facts.[64]

It is less clear whether a stockholder has standing to sue nonderivatively when he has not himself given a proxy to the defendant. In most of the cases (including *Borak*) it can be inferred from the very hostility between the parties that the plaintiff did not give a proxy to anybody in the defendant's camp. And the private right of action is based not on any concept of the proxy attorney's violation of a fiduciary obligation to his principal, but on the premise that either side in a contested solicitation has a legitimate interest, in view of the statutory purpose, to cry "Foul" against the other.[65] So the answer should be "Yes."

[63] See pp. 491-97 supra. With respect to scienter, see pp. 785-86 supra. In general, see Painter, Civil Liability under the Federal Proxy Rules, 64 Wash. U. L. Q. 425 (1986).

[64] S. Rep. No. 1455, 73d Cong., 2d Sess. (1934) 77; see also Studebaker Corp. v. Gittlin, 360 F. 2d 692, 695 (2d Cir. 1966); Greater Iowa Corp. v. McLendon, 378 F. 2d 783, 795 (8th Cir. 1967). *Contra:* Cook United, Inc. v. Stockholders Protective Committee of Cook United, Inc., CCH Fed. Sec. L. Rep. ¶96,875 at 95,578 n. 1 (S. D. N. Y. 1979).

[65] See Dann v. Studebaker-Packard Corp., 288 F. 2d 201, 209-11 (6th Cir. 1961); Union Pacific R. R. v. Chicago & North Western Ry., 226 F. Supp. 400 (N. D. Ill. 1964); Clayton v. Skelly Oil Co., CCH Fed. Sec. L. Rep. ¶96,269 at 92,747-48 (S. D. N. Y. 1977); Lynch v. Fulks, CCH Fed. Sec. L. Rep. ¶97,831 (D. Kan. 1980); Hershfang v. Knotter, 562 F. Supp. 393, 398 (E. D. Va. 1983), *aff'd without published opinion*, 725 F. 2d 675 (4th Cir. 1984); Cowin v. Bresler, 741 F. 2d 410, 426-27 (D. C. Cir. 1984); Palumbo v. Deposit Bank, 758 F. 2d

b. Causation

Borak's admonition that "the causal relationship of the proxy material and the merger are questions of fact to be resolved at trial,"[66] together with the lower court cases on causation in the immediate wake of *Borak,* led the present writer to say that it was "apparent that causation has now become the critical question in this area."[67] But a second proxy case, *Mills* v. *Electric Auto-Lite Co.,*[68] which the Supreme Court decided within months after he made that statement, proved him a false prophet. Like *Borak, Mills* involved a merger allegedly accomplished through a false proxy statement.

Justice Harlan, speaking for all except Justice Black, first distinguished *Borak*'s relegating the causation question to the trial stage by stating:

> In the present case there has been a hearing specifically directed to the causation problem. The question before the Court is whether the facts found on the basis of that hearing are sufficient in law to establish petitioners' cause of action, and we conclude that they are.

He then continued:

> Where the misstatement or omission in a proxy statement has been shown to be "material," as it was found to be here, that determination itself indubitably embodies a conclusion that the defect was of such a character that it might have been considered important by a reasonable shareholder who was in the process of deciding how to vote. This requirement that the defect have a significant *propensity* to affect the voting process is found in the express terms of Rule 14a-9, and it adequately serves the purpose of ensuring that a cause of action cannot be established by proof of a defect so trivial, or so unrelated to the transaction for which approval is sought, that

113, 116 (3d Cir. 1985) ("one who alleges that he has been wrongfully ousted from a Board of Directors because management improperly persuaded other shareholders not to vote for him, has articulated an injury cognizable under §14(a)"); cf. Bradshaw v. Jenkins, CCH Fed. Sec. L. Rep. ¶99,719 (W. D. Wash. 1984), *reconsideration denied,* CCH Fed. Sec. L. Rep. ¶91,645 (W. D. Wash. 1984) (reliance is not essential as long as plaintiff is damaged).

Contra: Gaines v. Haughton, 645 F. 2d 761, 773-74 (9th Cir. 1981), *cert. denied*, 454 U. S. 1145; Summers v. Lukash, 562 F. Supp. 737, 741 (E. D. Pa. 1983); Recchion v. Westinghouse Electric Corp., 606 F. Supp. 889, 894 (W. D. Pa. 1985); cf. Textron, Inc. v. American Woolen Co., 122 F. Supp. 305, 307-10 (D. Mass. 1954).

[66] J. I. Case Co. v. Borak, 377 U. S. 426, 431 (1964), supra p. 927.

[67] 5 Loss 2933.

[68] 396 U. S. 375 (1970).

correction of the defect or imposition of liability would not further the interests protected by §14(a).

There is no need to supplement this requirement, as did the Court of Appeals, with a requirement of proof of whether the defect actually had a decisive effect on the voting. Where there has been a finding of materiality, a shareholder has made a sufficient showing of causal relationship between the violation and the injury for which he seeks redress if, as here, he proves that the proxy solicitation itself, rather than the particular defect in the solicitation materials, was an essential link in the accomplishment of the transaction. This objective test will avoid the impracticalities of determining how many votes were affected, and, by resolving doubts in favor of those the statute is designed to protect, will effectuate the congressional policy of ensuring that the shareholders are able to make an informed choice when they are consulted on corporate transactions. Cf. *Union Pac. R. Co.* v. *Chicago & N. W. R. Co.,* 226 F. Supp. 400, 411 (D. C. N. D. Ill. 1964); 2 L. Loss, Securities Regulation 962 n. 411 (2d ed. 1961); 5 id., at 2929-2930 (Supp. 1969).[69]

Query:

(1) Does materiality subsume causation always or only sometimes? In a merger case decided a few weeks *before Mills,* the Seventh Circuit held that a second proxy statement that was admittedly fair and complete had remedied any deficiencies in the original proxy statement.[72] And the Ninth Circuit has held that *Mills'* materiality-causation equation "is logically limited to situations in which shareholder approval was sought (and fraudulently secured) for a transaction requiring such approval, typically so-called 'fundamental corporate changes.' "[73] By contrast, directors' failure to disclose alleged misconduct (in that case questionable foreign payments) was not "the legal cause of the pecuniary loss to the corporation, if any," so long as there was no underlying transaction that required shareholder approval and the case was not one of self-dealing or fraud against the corporation.[74]

[69] A footnote at this point states: "We need not decide in this case whether causation could be shown where the management controls a sufficient number of shares to approve the transaction without any votes from the minority. * * * [citations deleted]." The opinion goes on to discuss the form of relief. See pp. 492-97 supra.

[72] Schy v. Susquehanna Corp., 419 F. 2d 1112, 1117 (7th Cir. 1970), *cert. denied,* 400 U. S. 826.

[73] Gaines v. Haughton, 645 F. 2d 761, 775 (9th Cir. 1981), *cert. denied,* 454 U. S. 1145.

[74] 645 F. 2d at 775; see also Weisberg v. Coastal States Gas Corp., 609 F. 2d 650 (2d Cir. 1979), *cert. denied,* 445 U. S. 951. There is authority, too, that the

(2) A number of courts have written in these cases in terms of "a showing of both *loss causation* — that the misrepresentations or omissions caused the economic harm — and *transaction causation* — that the violations in question caused the [shareholder] to engage in the transaction in question."[75] With all the confusion already inherent in the more traditional terms, "causation in fact" or "but for" causation (which is really reliance) and "legal cause,"[76] does adding two new terms advance the discourse? Are both new terms subsumed within "causation in fact," so as to leave room for the policy and foreseeability arguments traditionally associated with "causation at law"? Or are "transaction" and "loss" causation synonymous, respectively, with "causation in fact" and "legal causa-

---

Mills equation does not apply to an omission to include information affirmatively required by Rule 14a-3 if the omission does not violate Rule 14a-9. Ash v. GAF Corp., 546 F. Supp. 89 (E. D. Pa. 1982), and cases cited, *aff'd on other grounds,* 723 F. 2d 1090, 1094-95 (3d Cir. 1983). The court there held that a shareholder who claimed to have received his annual report late in violation of the proxy rules failed to show injury at all. Because he did not exercise his proxy or participate in the election, the report's tardy arrival had no effect on his voting rights. Nor did he prove that the delay had impaired the integrity of the uncontested election. Therefore, the court did not reach the issue of causation.

[75] Schlick v. Penn-Dixie Cement Corp., 507 F. 2d 374, 380 (2d Cir. 1974), *cert. denied,* 421 U. S. 976; Bennett v. U. S. Trust Co. of N. Y., 770 F. 2d 308, 313-14 (2d Cir. 1985), *cert. denied,* 106 S. Ct. 800 (failure to establish "loss causation").

[76] See 1 Code 57-63, comments to §202(19), which defines causation in traditional terms: "A loss is 'caused' by specified conduct to the extent that (A) the conduct was a substantial factor in producing the loss, and (B) the loss was of a kind that might reasonably have been expected to occur as a result of the conduct." The commentary has this to say:

> §202(19)(A): This is the language of "causation in fact" that Restatement (Second) of Torts §546 uses in stating the general rule on causation in deceit. As applied to the *fact* of causation alone, according to Prosser, no better test has been devised. Prosser, Torts 240, 248 (4th ed. 1971). The language makes it plain, for example, that, if the defendant's misrepresentation was a "substantial factor" in inducing the plaintiff to buy, the defendant is not absolved merely because other factors — for example, the plaintiff's having recently received a large inheritance or his having been counseled to diversify his portfolio — contributed to the result.
>
> §202(19)(B): To repeat, it does not follow that "but for" causation (as defined in "substantial factor" terms) should always establish liability. For "but for" is at most a rule of exclusion: if it is not satisfied, clearly there can be no causation, but, even if it *is* satisfied, policy considerations other than factual causation may preclude liability. See id. at 238-39. These are the considerations subsumed under the question-begging but useful term, "legal cause," which §202(19)(B) defines in the reasonable expectancy language of Restatement (Second) of Torts §548A — a test that, realistically, must be viewed as a general caveat that "but for" is not necessarily enough. * * *

tion"?[77] If so, why bother? If not, what is the difference? Judge Frankel, while he thought that the new labels "may prove eventually to be useful," was "not convinced at this time that the Circuit ought to be committed to their employment or to their still uncertain implications."[78]

(3) Whatever one calls the first step in the causation chain — why not simply "reliance"? — *Mills* is clear that, once the plaintiff has shown materiality, he "has made a sufficient showing of causal relationship between the violation and the injury for which he seeks redress if, as here, he proves that the proxy solicitation itself, rather than the particular defect in the solicitation materials, was an essential link in the accomplishment of the transaction."[79]

(4) What about the question, which *Mills* left open, whether causation could be shown when the management itself controls enough shares to approve the transaction?[80] A substantial number of cases now say it makes no difference.[81] The usual arguments are that the minority stockholders will be in a better position to protect their interests with full disclosure and that an unfavorable minority vote might influence the majority to modify or reconsider the transaction in question. In a case where the stockholders had no appraisal rights under state law because the stock was listed on the New York Stock Exchange, the court advanced two additional considerations: (1) the *market* would be informed; and (2) even "a rapacious controlling management" might modify the terms of the merger because it would not want to "hang its dirty linen out on the line and thereby expose itself to suit or Securities Commission or other action — in terms of reputation and future take-overs."[82]

[77] "The requirement of 'loss causation' derives from the common law tort concept of 'proximate causation.' " Manufacturers Hanover Trust Co. v. Drysdale Securities Corp., 801 F. 2d 13, 20 (2d Cir. 1986), *cert. denied* sub nom. Arthur Andersen & Co. v. Manufacturers Trust Co., 107 S. Ct. 952.

[78] Schlick v. Penn-Dixie Cement Corp., 507 F. 2d 374, 384 (2d Cir. 1974, concurring opinion), *cert. denied,* 421 U. S. 976.

[79] 396 U. S. at 385. But cf. Berg v. First American Bankshares, Inc., CCH Fed. Sec. L. Rep. ¶92,011 at 91,011-12 (D. D. C. 1985), *aff'd on other grounds,* 796 F. 2d 489 (D. C. Cir. 1986), where the court limited the *Mills* holding to class actions in which *somebody* (if not the plaintiff) was deceived.

[80] 396 U. S. at 385 n. 7.

[81] E. g., Cole v. Schenley Industries, Inc., 563 F. 2d 35, 40 (2d Cir. 1977); see also Popkin v. Bishop, 464 F. 2d 714, 720 (2d Cir. 1972) (Rule 10b-5); Selk v. St. Paul Ammonia Products, Inc., 597 F. 2d 635, 638 (8th Cir. 1979) (dictum); Cowin v. Bresler, 741 F. 2d 410, 428 n. 23 (D. C. Cir. 1984); cf. NUI Corp. v. Kimmelman, 765 F. 2d 399 (3d Cir. 1985), supra p. 449 n. 1.

[82] Schlick v. Penn-Dixie Cement Corp., 507 F. 2d 374, 384 (2d Cir. 1974), *cert. denied,* 421 U. S. 976. We shall have more to say about causation generally when we get to Rule 10b-5. See p. 955 infra.

c. Interrelation with State Law

In a unitary system of government we would be at the end of our problem. But, of course, the SEC proxy rules are superimposed on the state law governing proxies and shareholder meetings. The fact is, as a former Chairman of the Commission has written, that "The stuff of these controversies [under the SEC rules] is the sort of thing which courts have been adjudicating since corporate elections began. The injury to the complainant, real or fancied, may, and usually does, include substantive matters unrelated to the proxy rule violation."[83] In this the proxy rules are not atypical. We have it from a scholar who was a keen student of the federal courts that "legal problems repeatedly fail to come wrapped up in neat packages marked 'all-federal' or 'all-state.' "[84]

Since this is so, nobody will quarrel with the proposition that, ideally, whichever court adjudicates a controversy about a corporate election, or a merger or stock option plan or other extraordinary transaction that requires a vote of stockholders, should adjudicate the whole controversy, in both its state and its federal elements. This raises difficult problems concerning the relationship between federal and state courts. And the problems are only aggravated, not created, by the provision in §27 of the 1934 Act — the only such general provision in any of the SEC statutes — giving the United States District Courts "exclusive jurisdiction of violations of this title or the rules and regulations thereunder, and of all suits in equity and actions at law brought to enforce any liability or duty created by this title or the rules and regulations thereunder."[85]

There are many grounds on which either side may wish to enjoin or attack an election, or on which a stockholder may wish to enjoin or attack something like a merger or a stock option plan. Some of these grounds raise questions purely of state law: for example, proxies that have been forged, otherwise improperly signed, given by persons who are not stockholders of record, or revoked by later

[83] Demmler, Private Suits Based on Violation of the Proxy Rules, 20 U. Pitt. L. Rev. 587, 591 (1959).

[84] Hart, The Relations Between State and Federal Law, 54 Colum. L. Rev. 489, 498 (1954). It is characteristic of federal law that it "is generally interstitial in its nature. * * * Federal legislation * * * builds upon legal relationships established by the states, altering or supplanting them only so far as necessary for the special purpose. Congress acts, in short, against the background of the total *corpus juris* of the states in much the way that a state legislature acts against the background of the common law, assumed to govern unless changed by legislation." Hart and Wechsler, The Federal Courts and the Federal System (2d ed. 1973) 470-71.

[85] See also Inv. Co. Act §36(b)(5), infra pp. 985-86.

proxies. Other grounds raise questions purely of federal law: for example, soliciting orally without furnishing a proxy statement, or soliciting too early, or perhaps an opposition group's soliciting somewhat more than ten persons without filing a proxy statement at all. And at least one ground — probably the most important — raises questions of both federal and state law: soliciting on the basis of misleading or inadequate information.

Suppose, first, that a plaintiff with allegations in two or more of these three categories, or even the third alone, brings his action in a state court. He may be attacking an election in the traditional manner of a proceeding in the nature of *quo warranto,* or under a special statute,[86] or he may be seeking injunctive relief in equity (or perhaps a mandamus) before or during the meeting. In any event, he is met with the *defense* that *he,* the *plaintiff,* has violated the proxy rules and hence should be denied relief, whether as a matter of federal law that the state court must honor under the Supremacy Clause or as a matter of the state law relating to unclean hands. Still another plaintiff might base his case on state law but answer a defense of stockholder ratification, or anticipate the defense and include a replication-type allegation in his initial pleading, by claiming that the ratification is ineffective because of violation of the proxy rules. *Can* the state court decide the questions of violations and its effect? *Must* it? And is the *decision* of the highest state court reviewable by the Supreme Court of the United States if the court refuses to consider those questions? Or for error in interpreting the rules, or determining the effect of a violation, or both, if the court does consider those questions? Indeed, is a state court complaint that pleads a violation of the SEC rules removable to the federal court in the first place?

Suppose now that the plaintiff in our hypothetical case walks across the street to the federal court. Take first the simpler case in which there is diversity of citizenship. If the charter state has a special statute on review of elections, as in Delaware, is that statute within the "equitable remedial rights doctrine," in which event it cannot be applied by a federal court? Or is it essentially "substantive" within *Erie?* Or might it be both? Indeed, did the remedial rights doctrine survive the *Erie* holocaust in the first place — not to mention the merger of law and equity in the Federal Rules of Civil Procedure? If it did, and a statute on review of elections exists in the charter state, is it necessary to decide whether the statute is "substantive" or "remedial"? Or is the remedy supplied by the

[86] E. g., Del. Code, Tit. 8, §225.

historic equity jurisdiction of the federal courts? Does not this last question have to be faced in any event if the charter states does *not* have a statute of the Delaware type, since the plaintiff certainly cannot rely on the state *quo warranto* remedy in the federal court and there is no independent federal *quo warranto* jurisdiction?[87] Suppose next that there is no diversity of citizenship. On the assumption that the complaint states a non-frivolous claim under the proxy rules, will the federal court have "pendent jurisdiction" to consider those elements of the action that are based on state law? Will that be so even if the federal law count, say, is based on solicitation without delivery of a proxy statement and the state law count is based on forged proxies, so that there is no common evidence? If so, what of the defendant who has been brought into court through extraterritorial service of process under §27? And what of the purely federal-law plaintiff who is met with a state-law counterclaim?

If the plaintiff is to be faced with all these difficult questions when he chooses to bring the federal elements of his action into a state court or the state elements into a federal court, is his solution to bring two separate actions? Apart from the general undesirability of splitting causes of action, and the very practical problem that arises if neither the federal aspects of the action nor the state aspects, standing alone, affect enough votes to alter the outcome, this course immediately raises questions of *res judicata* or, at any rate, collateral estoppel.

These are problems so complex that one could wish that "judicial federalism" in the United States had developed along simpler lines. But the problems are there. They cannot be wished away. And they are anything but purely theoretical. Unfortunately, space limitations here preclude more than references to discussions elsewhere.[88]

One basic point should be made, however, if only because a very important court in the corporate world, the Supreme Court of Del-

[87] See p. 496 supra.

[88] There has not been too much movement here since Loss, The SEC Proxy Rules and State Law, 73 Harv. L. Rev. 1249 (1960), reprinted with insubstantial changes in 2 Loss 973-1019 and supplemented in 5 id. 2949-80. For more general surveys, see Note, Problems of Parallel State and Federal Remedies, 71 Harv. L. Rev. 513 (1958); Note, Exclusive Jurisdiction of the Federal Courts in Private Civil Actions, 70 Harv. L. Rev. 509 (1957). On a more fundamental level, no lawyer should approach this maze without reading Professor Hart's penetrating essay, The Relations Between State and Federal Law, 54 Colum. L. Rev. 489 (1954).

aware, overlooked it.[89] It is this: Even if it be assumed that §27 precludes a state court from entertaining an action insofar as relief is sought on the basis of alleged violation of the proxy rules, nothing in that section prevents a state court from considering questions under the proxy rules that are introduced by way of defense, and failure to do so would violate the Supremacy Clause.[90]

3. Tender Offers

We have already visited the matter of available relief for violation of the tender offer provisions, usually §14(e), since that question is not peculiar to private actions.[91] And much of what has just been said with respect to litigation under the proxy rules applies here *mutatis mutandis.*[92] The big question here is what implied liability, if any, survives *Piper,* where the Court expressly reserved its views on (1) whether either the target or its stockholders had standing and (2) whether a *tender offeror* might obtain injunctive relief as distinct from damages.[93]

[89] Standard Power & Light Corp. v. Investment Associates, Inc., 29 Del. Ch. 593, 606, 51 A. 2d 572, 579 (1947). But cf. Columbian Fuel Corp. v. Superior Court, 52 Del. 365, 374, 378, 158 A. 2d 478, 483, 485 (1960), *aff'd* sub nom. Pan American Petroleum Corp. v. Superior Court, 366 U. S. 656 (1961).

[90] See Pratt v. Paris Gas Light & Coke Co., 168 U. S. 255 (1897) (defense going to the validity of a patent); Lear, Inc. v. Adkins, 395 U. S. 653, 675-76 (1969) (state court jurisdiction assumed); Aetna State Bank v. Altheimer, 430 F. 2d 750, 754, 756 (7th Cir. 1970); Shareholders Management Co. v. Gregory, 449 F. 2d 326 (9th Cir. 1971); Birenbaum v. Bache & Co., 555 S. W. 2d 513, 514-15 (Tex. Civ. App. 1977).

So, too, when questions under the proxy rules are raised by way of replication. A stockholder, for example, brings a derivative action under state law seeking to enjoin the consummation of an executive stock option plan as a waste of corporate assets. The defendants plead shareholder ratification. The plaintiff — either in replication or, anticipating the defense, in his complaint — argues that the ratification is ineffective because of fraud or inadequate disclosure in soliciting proxies. See Eliasberg v. Standard Oil Co., 23 N. J. Super. 431, 92 A. 2d 862 (Ch. 1952), *aff'd per curiam,* 12 N. J. 467, 97 A. 2d 437 (1953); cf. American Well Works Co. v. Layne & Bowler Co., 241 U. S. 257, 259-69 (1916).

[91] See pp. 530-32 supra.

[92] With respect to scienter, see pp. 785-86 supra.

[93] Piper v. Chris-Craft Industries, Inc., 430 U. S. 1, 42 n. 28, 47 n. 33 (1977), supra p. 931. *Piper*'s withholding of standing from the tender offeror, at least with respect to damages, contrasts with the two-way standing under the proxy rules (see p. 944 supra), as the Stevens-Brennan dissent observed. 430 U. S. at 57-59. It is interesting, too, that an early proxy case in the Second Circuit denied standing to the *management* side. Howard v. Furst, 238 F. 2d 790 (2d Cir. 1956), *cert. denied,* 353 U. S. 937.

In Kalmanovitz v. G. Heileman Brewing Co., Inc., 769 F. 2d 152, 160 (3d Cir. 1985), the court held that in the context of *Piper* "a plaintiff who occupies

Several Circuits — one of them *since Piper* — have permitted *injunctive* actions by target companies.[94] The First Circuit, in a *pre-Piper* case, recognized target actions for damages as well, as has the Second Circuit in a *post-Piper* damage action by target stockholders under §14(d)(6), the proration provision.[95] The Second Circuit, in the first appellate opinion under the tender offer provisions, permitted *nontendering stockholders* to join the target company as plaintiffs;[96] stockholders who have tendered do not need §14(e), because they are classic sellers within Rule 10b-5. On the other hand, there is authority that target stockholders may not sue *their own company* for chilling the offer by misrepresenting the offeror's intentions, because the very fact that no offer was ever made precluded the required proof of reliance on misrepresentations made by target management.[97]

These holdings are presumably weakened to the extent that they

---

the dual roles of a very substantial tender offeror and merely a nominal target shareholder may be considered to be only an offeror for the purpose of judging his standing * * *."

[94] Electronic Specialty Co. v. International Controls Corp., 409 F. 2d 937 (2d Cir. 1969); Gulf & Western Industries, Inc. v. Great Atlantic & Pacific Tea Co., Inc., 476 F. 2d 687 (2d Cir. 1973); Smallwood v. Pearl Brewing Co., 489 F. 2d 579, 596 (5th Cir. 1974), *cert. denied*, 419 U. S. 873; Marathon Oil Co. v. Mobil Corp., 669 F. 2d 378 (6th Cir. 1981). In recent years, however, the courts have been more sensitive to the fact that "a delay of several days or a week to require an offeror to cure its disclosure defects could result in the temporary or even permanent lost opportunity to acquire the target company." Martin-Marietta Corp. v. Bendix Corp., 547 F. Supp. 533, 539-40 (D. Md. 1982).

[95] H. K. Porter Co. v. Nicholson File Co., 482 F. 2d 421 (1st Cir. 1973); cf. Pryor v. United States Steel Corp., 794 F. 2d 52, 57-58 (2d Cir. 1986), *cert. denied*, 107 S. Ct. 445.

[96] Electronic Specialty Co. v. International Controls Corp., 409 F. 2d 937 (2d Cir. 1969). The plaintiff, of course, "must show that he or she has been injured by retaining the stock instead of selling it at the premium offered by the tender offeror." Horowitz v. Pownall, 582 F. Supp. 665, 668 (D. Md. 1984).

Cf. Smallwood v. Pearl Brewing Co., 489 F. 2d 579, 596 (5th Cir. 1974), *cert. denied*, 419 U. S. 873; Beaumont v. American Can Co., 797 F. 2d 79, 84 (2d Cir. 1986) (non-tenderers to a self-tender offer had no standing under Rule 10b-13); Plaine v. McCabe, 797 F. 2d 713, 717-18 (9th Cir. 1986) (though preclusive effect had to be given to California Corporations Commissioner's finding that freeze-out merger price was fair, plaintiff might still prove that stockholders' negotiating position would have produced a higher amount if §14(e) had been complied with).

[97] Lewis v. McGraw, 619 F. 2d 192 (2d Cir. 1980), *cert. denied*, 449 U. S. 951; Panter v. Marshall Field & Co., 646 F. 2d 271 (7th Cir. 1981), *cert. denied*, 454 U. S. 1092; but cf. Lowenschuss v. Kane, 520 F. 2d 255 (2d Cir. 1975). *Panter* held also that there was no right of action on behalf of stockholders who had decided *not* to sell in the *market*.

On the possibilities here, and elsewhere in tender offer litigation, of the common law tort of interference with prospective economic advantage, see Lowenstein, Tender Offer Litigation and State Law, 63 N. C. L. Rev. 493 (1985).

rely, explicitly or implicitly, on the two-way standing in the proxy cases.[98] But the *Piper* Court, despite its disclaimer, almost invites target company or target stockholder actions when it observes that the preliminary injunctive stage is the time when relief can best be given;[99] for *somebody* must be the plaintiff. And, if the target or its stockholders or both may sue for injunctive relief, why not for damages as well? The Court's refusal to distinguish SEC injunctive actions and damage actions for purposes of the 10b-5 scienter requirement[100] furnishes some analogy, although the question there goes to substance rather than standing. Finally, there is District Court authority distinguishing *Piper* to permit the *offeror* to sue competitor for *injunctive relief.*[101]

So far as §13(d) is concerned, again there is appellate authority — some of it *post-Piper* — granting injunctive relief to the company and its stockholders.[102] On the other hand, some courts have rejected actions not only for damages[103] but also, since *Piper,* for injunctive relief.[104] Damage actions for false filings under §13(d) raise the question whether the exclusive remedy is not under §18.[105]

[98] See Liberty National Ins. Holding Co. v. Charter Co., 734 F. 2d 545, 568-71, esp. at 570 (11th Cir. 1984).

[99] 430 U. S. at 42.

[100] See p. 783 supra.

[101] Humana, Inc. v. American Medicorp, Inc., 445 F. Supp. 613 (S. D. N. Y. 1978). In Caleb & Co. v. E. I. duPont de Nemours & Co., 615 F. Supp. 96 (S. D. N. Y. 1985), *reargument granted on other grounds,* 624 F. Supp. 747 (S. D. N. Y. 1985), the court recognized a private action under the requirement in Rule 14e-1(c) that a tender offeror pay or return the deposited securities promptly after the termination or withdrawal of the offer.

[102] GAF Corp. v. Milstein, 453 F. 2d 709, 720-21 (2d Cir. 1971), *cert. denied,* 406 U. S. 910; Mosinee Paper Corp. v. Rondeau, 500 F. 2d 1011 (7th Cir. 1974), *rev'd on other grounds* sub nom. Rondeau v. Mosinee Paper Corp., 422 U. S. 49 (1975) (without considering question of private right of action, court ordered injunction, which Supreme Court reversed for lack of irreparable injury); General Aircraft Corp. v. Lampert, 556 F. 2d 90 (1st Cir. 1977), supra p. 532 n. 145; Chromalloy American Corp. v. Sun Chemical Corp., 611 F. 2d 240 (8th Cir. 1979) (relief *granted* without discussion of standing); Dan River, Inc. v. Unitex, Ltd., 624 F. 2d 1216 (4th Cir. 1980), *cert. denied,* 449 U. S. 1101; Indiana National Corp. v. Rich, 712 F. 2d 1180 (7th Cir. 1983); Gearhart Industries, Inc. v. Smith Int'l, Inc., 741 F. 2d 707, 714 (5th Cir. 1984); Portsmouth Square, Inc. v. Shareholders Protective Committee, 770 F. 2d 866, 871 n. 8 (9th Cir. 1985), and cases cited; HUBCO, Inc. v. Rappaport, 628 F. Supp. 345, 350-51 (D. N. J. 1985) (any right of action by issuer is limited to requiring defendant to file a corrected schedule).

[103] E. g., Myers v. American Leisure Time Enterprises, Inc., 402 F. Supp. 213 (S. D. N. Y. 1975), *aff'd without opinion,* 538 F. 2d 312 (2d Cir. 1976); Sanders v. Thrall Car Mfg. Co., 582 F. Supp. 945, 960 (S. D. N. Y. 1983), *aff'd per curiam,* 730 F. 2d 910 (2d Cir. 1984); see Note, Private Rights of Action for Damages Under Section 13(d), 32 Stan. L. Rev. 581 (1980).

[104] E. g., Leff v. CIP Corp., 540 F. Supp. 857 (S. D. Ohio 1982), citing cases both ways; Equity Oil Co. v. Consolidated Oil & Gas, Inc., 596 F. Supp. 507 (D.

4. RULE 10b-5

The Supreme Court is clearly disinclined to question implied liability for violation of Rule 10b-5, extending not merely to contractual rescission under §29(b) but to damages as well.[106] On that assumption a plaintiff's counsel who is not of the *cognoscenti* might conclude that all he needs to prove is (1) some use of the mails or interstate commerce and (2) an untrue statement of a material fact (or some activity within the first or third clause of the rule) in connection with (3) a purchase or sale of a security. But, if it is "cricket" for the federal courts to invent new torts or tort-like actions, it seems fair enough for them to invent reasonable restrictions on the new actions as common law judges a long time ago invented doctrines like materiality and scienter and reliance and causation in order to achieve a sense of balance.[107]

We have already gone into materiality and scienter, and we have also noticed that there is no privity requirement in private actions under Rule 10b-5.[108] We here examine reliance and causation and explore the measure of relief that is available to the successful plaintiff.

a. Reliance and Causation

As the Second Circuit put it in 1965, imposition of a reliance requirement is reasonable in a private action under Rule 10b-5,

---

Utah 1983), and cases cited; cf. Liberty National Ins. Holding Co. v. Charter Co., 734 F. 2d 545, 559-67 (11th Cir. 1984) (no issuer action for divestment of shares). The *Liberty* case was held in Florida Commercial Banks v. Culverhouse, 772 F. 2d 1513 (11th Cir. 1984), not to preclude *corrective* relief under §13(d), §14(d), or §14(e).

[105] See p. 922 supra. In Fisher v. Plessey Co., Ltd., CCH Fed. Sec. L. Rep. ¶99,246 (S. D. N. Y. 1983), the court on a *Cort* analysis permitted a §13(e) action by an investor against the company. In Kalmanovitz v. G. Heileman Brewing Co., Inc., 595 F. Supp. 1385, 1395 (D. Del. 1984), *aff'd*, 769 F. 2d 152, 160 (3d Cir. 1985), the court held categorically that "no private right of action for money damages exists under section 13(e)," but the plaintiff there, as in *Piper*, was a losing tender offeror. In Berg v. First American Bankshares, Inc., CCH Fed. Sec. L. Rep. ¶92,011 at 91,012-13 (D. D. C. 1985), *aff'd on other grounds*, 796 F. 2d 489 (D. C. Cir. 1986), where the plaintiffs were former stockholders in a "going private cash-out" merger, the court followed *Kalmanovitz* without noticing the point here made.

[106] See Herman & MacLean v. Huddleston, 459 U. S. 375 (1983), infra p. 975.

[107] Herpich v. Wallace, 430 F. 2d 792, 805 (5th Cir. 1970) ("courts have sought to construct workable limits to liability").

[108] See pp. 480-83, 734-38, 774 supra.

since the aim of the rule "is to qualify, as between insiders and outsiders, the doctrine of *caveat emptor* — not to establish a scheme of investors insurance."[109] Although abandonment of the reliance requirement would facilitate outsiders' proof of insiders' fraud and thus advance the purpose of the rule, that is "an inadequate reason for reading out of the rule so basic an element of tort law as the principle of causation in fact."[110] Civil actions differ from administrative proceedings under the rule, whose aim is to deter misconduct by insiders rather than to compensate their victims. There the fact that no harm actually results from the misconduct, because of the peculiar circumstances of the particular outsiders involved, is ordinarily irrelevant to the preventive purpose.

When the plaintiff rests his 10b-5 case on §29(b), it is arguable that reliance is no more an element of recovery than it is when an action is based on §12(2) of the 1933 Act or (normally) §11. But it cannot be assumed that the courts will not imply a reliance requirement in either event. Reliance is, of course, an element of traditional rescission for fraud.

Many cases have simply *assumed* that reliance is an element of a private action.[111] And there is no difficulty in conceptualizing reliance on an insider's *silence.* The test is not whether the plaintiff consciously had in mind the negative of the fact concealed but "whether the plaintiff would have been influenced to act differently than he did if the defendant had disclosed to him the undisclosed fact."[112]

On the other hand, "it is not necessary that plaintiff have relied

[109] List v. Fashion Park, Inc. 340 F. 2d 457, 463 (2d Cir. 1965), *cert. denied* sub nom. List v. Lerner, 382 U. S. 811.

[110] Ibid.; see also, e. g., Janigan v. Taylor, 344 F. 2d 781, 785-86 (1st Cir. 1965), *cert. denied,* 382 U. S. 879; Britt v. Cyril Bath Co., 417 F. 2d 433, 436 (6th Cir. 1969); Dopp v. Franklin National Bank, 461 F. 2d 873, 880 (2d Cir. 1972); Landy v. Federal Deposit Ins. Corp., 486 F. 2d 139, 170 (3d Cir. 1973), *cert. denied,* 416 U. S. 960; Clegg v. Conk, 507 F. 2d 1351 (10th Cir. 1974), *cert. denied,* 422 U. S. 1007; Harris v. American Investment Co., 523 F. 2d 220, 229 n. 7 (8th Cir. 1975), *cert. denied,* 423 U. S. 1054; Kiernan v. Homeland, Inc., 611 F. 2d 785 (9th Cir. 1980).

[111] E. g., Reed v. Riddle Airlines, 266 F. 2d 314, 319 (5th Cir. 1959); Texas Continental Life Ins. Co. v. Dunne, 307 F. 2d 242 (6th Cir. 1962). But see Siebel v. Scott, 725 F. 2d 995, 1000 (5th Cir. 1984), *cert. denied,* 467 U. S. 1242: "When a deceiving purchaser casts his net broadly and hauls in every fish, the reliance element in §10(b) is inferable if it appears that no plaintiff planned to sell his security before the defendant undertook fraudulently to induce the sales."

[112] List v. Fashion Park, Inc., 340 F. 2d 457, 463 (2d Cir. 1965), *cert. denied* sub nom. List v. Lerner, 382 U. S. 811; cf. Stier v. Smith, 473 F. 2d 1205 (5th Cir. 1973).

exclusively upon the defendants."[113] And the Second Circuit has foregone proof of reliance "in the limited instance when no volitional act is required and the result of a forced sale is exactly that intended by the wrongdoer."[114]

We have seen that the concept of *justifiable* reliance is in disfavor even with respect to common law deceit.[115] But, quite apart from the fact that the concept of materiality supplies something of the objective element,[116] the courts have shown a tendency to impose *some* sort of duty on the *plaintiff* — whether by speaking of *justifiable* reliance or by considering the plaintiff's due care to be an element of a violation of Rule 10b-5 (or, at least, lack of due care to be an affirmative defense).[117] Since a 10b-5 plaintiff must prove scienter, it would be odd to subject him to a greater duty of care than at common law, where "contributory negligence is not a defense to an intentional tort case of fraud."[118] At the same time, "a plaintiff

[113] Kohler v. Kohler Co., 208 F. Supp. 808, 824 (E. D. Wis. 1962), *aff'd on other grounds,* 319 F. 2d 634 (7th Cir. 1963) (italics supplied); see also cases cited supra p. 713 n. 87.

[114] Vine v. Beneficial Finance Co., Inc., 374 F. 2d 627, 635 (2d Cir. 1967), *cert. denied,* 389 U. S. 970; see also Mader v. Armel, 402 F. 2d 158, 162 (6th Cir. 1968), *cert. denied* sub nom. Young v. Mader, 394 U. S. 930.

[115] See c. 574 n. 12 supra.

[116] See List v. Fashion Park, Inc., 340 F. 2d 457, 462 (2d Cir. 1965), *cert. denied* sub nom. List v. Lerner, 382 U. S. 811. On the blurring of subjective reliance and objective materiality, see Titan Group, Inc. v. Faggen, 513 F. 2d 234, 239 (2d Cir. 1975), *cert. denied,* 423 U. S. 840; Thomas v. Duralite Co., Inc., 524 F. 2d 577, 584 (3d Cir. 1975).

[117] See Wheeler, Plaintiff's Duty of Due Care Under Rule 10b-5: An Implied Defense to an Implied Remedy, 70 Nw. U. L. Rev. 561 (1975). On due diligence as a separate element in a 10b-5 case, see Thompson v. Smith Barney, Harris Upham & Co., 709 F. 2d 1413, 1418 (11th Cir. 1983). For rejecting any duty of care as inappropriate to Rule 10b-5 litigation, see Sachs, The Relevance of Tort Law Doctrines to Rule 10b-5: Should Careless Plaintiffs Be Denied Recovery?, 71 Corn. L. Rev. 96 (1985); see also Gabaldon, Unclean Hands and Self-Inflicted Wounds: The Significance of Plaintiff Conduct in Actions for Misrepresentation Under Rule 10b-5, 71 Minn. L. Rev. 317 (1986).

It has been said to be "axiomatic that one insider cannot maintain a suit against another." Harnett v. Ryan Homes, Inc., 360 F. Supp. 878, 885 (W. D. Pa. 1973), *aff'd on other grounds,* 496 F. 2d 832 (3d Cir. 1974). But a plaintiff is not necessarily an "insider" because of his title in the corporate hierarchy. Rosenbloom v. Adams, Scott & Conway, Inc., 552 F. 2d 1336, 1338 (9th Cir. 1977).

[118] Holdsworth v. Strong, 545 F. 2d 687, 694 (10th Cir. 1976), *cert. denied,* 430 U. S. 955; see also Dupuy v. Dupuy, 551 F. 2d 1005, 1018 (5th Cir. 1977), *cert. denied,* 434 U. S. 911; Zobrist v. Coal-X, Inc., 708 F. 2d 1511 (10th Cir. 1983) (only when plaintiff's conduct "rises to a level of culpable conduct comparable to that of the defendant's will reliance be unjustifiable," and that means at least reckless behavior); Siebel v. Scott, 725 F. 2d 995, 1000 (5th Cir. 1984), *cert. denied,* 467 U. S. 1242 (plaintiff's due diligence obligation "is not applied stringently"); Morgan, Olmstead, Kennedy & Gardner, Inc. v. Schipa, 585 F. Supp. 245, 250 (S. D. N. Y. 1984); Teamsters Local 282 Pension Trust Fund v.

may not reasonably or justifiably rely on a misrepresentation where its falsity is palpable."[119] This mirrors the common law,[120] and is reflected in the Code.[121]

As with respect to reliance (causation in fact), the concept of legal causation is so integral a part of the law of torts generally that the courts have typically assumed the requirement in actions under Rule 10b-5.[122] But the cases do not agree on what the concept means.[123] Some speak in the "but for" terms of "causation in fact": "But for your misstatement," says the plaintiff, "I would not have bought."[124] Other cases, however, seem closer to requiring "legal cause."[125] And in most cases there is no indication one way or the other.

Angelos, 762 F. 2d 522, 527-29 (7th Cir. 1985); Xaphes v. Merrill Lynch, Pierce, Fenner & Smith, Inc., 600 F. Supp. 692, 695 (D. Me. 1985), citing the text; Manufacturers Hanover Trust Co. v. Drysdale Securities Corp., 801 F. 2d 13, 17 (2d Cir. 1986), *cert. denied* sub nom. Arthur Andersen & Co. v. Manufacturers Trust Co., 107 S. Ct.952; cf. Carroll v. First National Bank of Lincolnwood, 413 F. 2d 353, 358 (7th Cir. 1969), *cert. denied,* 396 U. S. 1003 (Rule 10b-5).

The court in *Zobrist* enumerated eight factors as determining whether reliance was justifiable:

> (1) the sophistication and expertise of the plaintiff in financial and securities matters; (2) the existence of long-standing business or personal relationships; (3) access to the relevant information; (4) the existence of a fiduciary relationship; (5) concealment of the fraud; (6) the opportunity to detect the fraud; (7) whether the plaintiff initiated the stock transaction or sought to expedite the transaction; and (8) the generality or specificity of the misrepresentations.

708 F. 2d at 1516.

[119] Holdsworth v. Strong, 545 F. 2d 687, 694 (10th Cir. 1976), *cert. denied,* 430 U. S. 955; Zobrist v. Coal-X, Inc., 708 F. 2d 1511, 1517 (10th Cir. 1983), supra p. 957 n. 118; Hamilton v. Harrington, 807 F. 2d 102, 107 n. 5 (7th Cir. 1986) (one who is "aware of a high probability of a fact may not rely on silence about that fact").

[120] See 2 Code 700-01.

[121] §§1703(e), 1704(e), 1705(e), 1707(e).

[122] E. g., Vine v. Beneficial Finance Co., Inc., 374 F. 2d 627, 635 (2d Cir. 1967), *cert. denied,* 389 U. S. 970; Mutual Shares Corp. v. Genesco, Inc., 384 F. 2d 540, 546 (2d Cir. 1967); Britt v. Cyril Rath Co., 417 F. 2d 433, 435-36 (6th Cir. 1969).

[123] See pp. 946-48 supra.

[124] E. g., Vine v. Beneficial Finance Co., Inc., 374 F. 2d 627, 635 (2d Cir. 1967), *cert. denied,* 389 U. S. 970; Chasins v. Smith, Barney & Co., Inc., 438 F. 2d 1167, 1172 (2d Cir. 1971) (defendant's failure to disclose that it was a marketmaker); Gottreich v. San Francisco Investment Corp., 552 F. 2d 866 (9th Cir. 1977).

[125] See pp. 964-65 infra. On the "transaction causation" and "loss causation" phraseology, see pp. 947-48 supra. Loss causation need not be proved in churning cases. Hatrock v. Edward D. Jones & Co., 750 F. 2d 767, 773 (9th Cir. 1984). Nor need it be proved when "the evil is not the price the investor paid for the security, but the broker's fraudulent inducement of the investor to purchase the security." Kafton v. Baptist Park Nursing Center, Inc., 617 F. Supp. 349 (D. Ariz. 1985).

Whereas the courts traditionally require proof of *reliance* in fraud cases whether the basis of the action is tort or restitution, the concept of *legal cause* is foreign to the law of restitution. In any event, the private action under §29(b), as we have seen,[126] is more express than implied. And there is authority that reliance may be dispensed with under that section.[127]

This was essentially the state of the 10b-5 law with respect to reliance and causation in 1972, when the Supreme Court, in *Affiliated Ute Citizens of Utah* v. *United States,*[128] applied to Rule 10b-5 what it had said two years earlier with respect to Rule 14a-9 in the *Mills* case:[129]

> Under the circumstances of this case, involving primarily a failure to disclose, positive proof of reliance is not a prerequisite to recovery. All that is necessary is that the facts withheld be material in the sense that a reasonable investor *might* have considered them important in the making of his decision. See *Mills* v. *Electric Auto-Lite Co.*, 396 U. S. 375, 384 (1970); *SEC* v. *Texas Gulf Sulphur Co.*, 401 F. 2d 833, 849 (C. A. 2 1968), *cert. denied* sub nom. *Coates* v. *SEC*, 394 U. S. 976 (1969); 6 L. Loss, Securities Regulation 3876-3880 (1969 Supp. to 2d ed. of Vol. 3); A. Bromberg, Securities Law, Fraud — SEC Rule 10b-5, §§2.6 and 8.6 (1967). This obligation to disclose and this withholding of a material fact establish the requisite element of causation in fact.[130]

It has been suggested that "the rationale for a presumption of causation in fact [which is to say, reliance] in cases like *Affiliated Ute*, in which no positive statements exist," is that "reliance as a practical matter is impossible to prove."[131] Certainly the holding — which is not limited to face-to-face transactions[132] — has an important ef-

[126]See p. 919 supra.

[127]Eastside Church of Christ v. National Plan, Inc., 391 F. 2d 357, 361-62 (5th Cir. 1968), *cert. denied* sub nom. Church of Christ v. National Plan, Inc., 393 U. S. 913; Regional Properties, Inc. v. Financial & Real Estate Consulting Co., 678 F. 2d 552, 558-59 (5th Cir. 1982).

[128]406 U. S. 128 (1972).

[129]Mills v. Electric Auto-Lite Co., 396 U. S. 375, 384-85 (1970), supra p. 945.

[130]406 U. S. at 153-54. The source of this holding as stated in *Mills* was not limited to omissions. See p. 396 U. S. at 384.

[131]Wilson v. Comtech Telecommunications Corp., 648 F. 2d 88, 93 (2d Cir. 1981). But see p. 956 supra.

[132]Shapiro v. Merrill Lynch, Pierce, Fenner & Smith, Inc. 495 F. 2d 228, 240 (2d Cir. 1974). *Contra:* Laventhall v. General Dynamics Corp., 704 F. 2d 407, 413 n. 4 (8th Cir. 1983), *cert. denied,* 464 U. S. 846. In any event, one can assume in face-to-face transactions that, had the information been disclosed, the plaintiff would have known of it. HSL, Inc. v. Daniels, CCH Fed. Sec. L. Rep. ¶99,557 at 97,196 (N. D. Ill. 1983).

fect on class actions.[133] But the holding is a bit soft around the edges.

First, although the holding is limited to "omissions" (nondisclosure) as distinct from "misrepresentations,"[134] the line between the two is fuzzy[135] and "The labels by themselves * * * are of little help."[136] The *Ute* presumption has been applied to half-truths[137] (which analytically are closer to lies than to nondisclosure). Moreover, in cases involving both misstatements and omissions, a number of courts, concerned that a dual instruction on burden of going forward might be confusing, have found refuge in the Supreme Court's reference to the circumstances in *Ute* as involving "primarily" a failure to disclose.[138]

Secondly, as with Rule 14a-9 and the *Mills* case, *Ute* by no means forecloses all consideration of reliance. Although the plaintiff need not prove reliance in "omission" cases, the courts have held that lack of reliance is a defense. In short, the effect of *Ute* is simply a

[133] See Cameron v. E. M. Adams & Co., 547 F. 2d 473, 477 (9th Cir. 1976); McNichols v. Loeb Rhoades & Co., Inc., 97 F. R. D. 331 (N. D. Ill. 1982) (investor would not be an adequate class representative in an action charging a brokerage firm with fraud on the market (see p. 962 infra), because he had a second claim based on individual misrepresentations made to him by a firm employee); Beebe v. Pacific Realty Trust, 99 F. R. D. 60, 68 (D. Ore. 1983) ("possibility of rebuttal * * * poses a major stumbling block to certification").

[134] Titan Group, Inc. v. Faggen, 513 F. 2d 234 (2d Cir. 1975), *cert. denied,* 423 U. S. 840; Chelsea Associates v. Rapanos, 527 F. 2d 1266, 1271 (6th Cir. 1975); Holdsworth v. Strong, 545 F. 2d 687 (10th Cir. 1976); Vervaecke v. Chiles, Heider & Co., Inc., 578 F. 2d 713, 717 (8th Cir. 1978).

[135] Blackie v. Barrack, 524 F. 2d 891, 906 (9th Cir. 1975), *cert. denied,* 429 U. S. 816; Little v. First Cal. Co., 532 F. 2d 1302, 1304 n. 4 (9th Cir. 1976); HSL, Inc. v. Daniels, CCH Fed. Sec. L. Rep. ¶99,557 at 97,195 (N. D. Ill. 1983) ("while there may be elements of misrepresentation, nondisclosure is still a major element"). But a misstatement cannot be transformed into an omission by alleging merely a failure to reveal the untruth of the statement made. Beck v. Cantor, Fitzgerald & Co., Inc., 621 F. Supp. 1547, 1556-57 (N. D. Ill. 1985).

[136] Wilson v. Comtech Telecommunications Corp., 648 F. 2d 88, 93 (2d Cir. 1981).

[137] Chris-Craft Industries, Inc. v. Piper Aircraft, Inc., 480 F. 2d 341 (2d Cir. 1973), *cert. denied,* 414 U. S. 910; Herbst v. International Telephone & Telegraph Corp., 495 F. 2d 1308 (2d Cir. 1974).

[138] Sharp v. Coopers & Lybrand, 649 F. 2d 175, 188 (3d Cir. 1981), *cert. denied,* 455 U. S. 938, quoting from Lewis v. McGraw, 619 F. 2d 192, 195 (2d Cir. 1980), *cert. denied,* 449 U. S. 951 (reliance will be presumed "only 'where it is logical' to do so"); Austin v. Loftsgaarden, 675 F. 2d 168, 178 n. 21 (8th Cir. 1982), *aff'd in part and rev'd in part en banc on other grounds after remand,* 768 F. 2d 949 (8th Cir. 1985), *rev'd on other grounds* sub nom. Randall v. Loftsgaarden, 106 S. Ct. 3143 (1986) (dictum); Cavalier Carpets, Inc. v. Caylor, 746 F. 2d 749 (11th Cir. 1984). In *Sharp* this approach resulted in applying *Ute* to both misstatements and omissions, and in *Cavalier Carpets* to neither.

shift in the burden of going forward on the reliance issue.[139] And, as the Fifth Circuit *en banc* held in *Shores* v. *Sklar*, the plaintiff's admission that he did not read or otherwise rely on the offering circular is enough to rebut the presumption.[140]

The court, however, limited this last holding — and the *Ute* presumption itself — to the *second* clause of Rule 10b-5, so that the plaintiff's not having read the offering circular did not defeat his claim of a fraudulent scheme to market bonds that was so pervasive that without it the bonds would never have entered the marketplace. The central purposes of the SEC statutes go far beyond disclosure to include "the promotion of free and honest markets." And it would have availed the plaintiff nothing to have read the circular. For the theory

> is not that he bought inferior bonds, but that the bonds he bought were fraudulently marketed. The securities laws allow an investor to rely on the integrity of the market to the extent that the securities it offers to him for purchase are entitled to be in the market place.[141]

[139] Rochez Bros., Inc. v. Rhoades, 491 F. 2d 402, 410 (3d Cir. 1973); Carras v. Burns, 516 F. 2d 251, 257 (4th Cir. 1975); Chelsea Associates v. Rapanos, 527 F. 2d 1266, 1271 (6th Cir. 1975); Sundstrand Corp. v. Sun Chemical Corp., 553 F. 2d 1033, 1048 (7th Cir. 1977); St. Louis Union Trust Co. v. Merrill Lynch, Pierce, Fenner & Smith, Inc., 562 F. 2d 1040 (8th Cir. 1977), *cert. denied*, 435 U. S. 925; Rifkin v. Crow, 574 F. 2d 256 (5th Cir. 1978); cf. Simon v. Merrill Lynch, Pierce, Fenner & Smith, Inc., 482 F. 2d 880 (5th Cir. 1973) (court distinguished *Ute* where plaintiff had made his own investment decisions and relied in no way on defendant's recommendations); Vohs v. Dickson, 495 F. 2d 607 (5th Cir. 1974).

For an analysis of what must be shown to rebut the reliance presumption, see Helman, Rule 10b-5 Omissions Cases and the Investment Decision, 51 Ford. L. Rev. 399 (1982). See also Black, Fraud on the Market: A Criticism of Dispensing with Reliance Requirements in Certain Open Market Transactions, 62 N. C. L. Rev. 435 (1984).

[140] Shores v. Sklar, 647 F. 2d 462, 468 (5th Cir. *en banc* 1981), *cert. denied*, 459 U. S. 1102. But cf. HSL, Inc. v. Daniels, CCH Fed. Sec. L. Rep. ¶99,557 at 97,196 (N. D. Ill. 1983) (even though plaintiff testified he had never read the annual and quarterly reports, "it may be inferred that had Playboy disclosed the information in its reports, it would have become known to the general public through the media"). Ibid.

[141] Shores v. Sklar, 647 F. 2d 462, 470-71 (5th Cir. *en banc* 1981), *cert. denied*, 459 U. S. 1102. The vote was 12 to 10, an elaborate dissent complaining that the majority was establishing "a new theory of recovery" under Rule 10b-5 that would effectively dispense with the reliance requirement, "at least where the security offered can be shown to be not 'entitled to be marketed.' " Id. at 486. Later the Third Circuit saw no reason why the theory could not be based on the second clause alone. Peil v. Speiser, 806 F. 2d 1154 (3d Cir. 1986).

A variation of the majority's theory rests on the integrity of the regulatory process with respect to the issuance of securities. Arthur Young & Co. v. United States District Court, 549 F. 2d 686, esp. at 695 (9th Cir. 1977), *cert. denied*,

This is a variation on the so-called "fraud on the market" theory, which is based on the feeding of false information into the marketplace and is thus a close relative of the "free market" concept that underlies the law of market manipulation.[142] Eight Circuits, beginning with *Blackie* v. *Barrack* in the Ninth Circuit, have now adopted the "fraud on the market" theory in some form, and none has rejected it.[143] But consider:

(1) As an alternative to reliance, the doctrine really adds nothing to *Ute*'s presumption of reliance from materiality in silence cases, except to give that presumption a stronger foundation with respect to market transactions (the transactions with the Ute Indians, it will be remembered, were face to face, with no active market) in terms of the efficient market hypothesis.

(2) This explains the Fifth Circuit's invention of the "fraudulently marketed" variation of the theory in order to cover the non-market, new issue situation in *Shores.*[144]

---

434 U. S. 829; T. J. Raney & Sons, Inc. v. Fort Cobb, Okla. Irrigation Fuel Authority, 717 F. 2d 1330 (10th Cir. 1983), *cert. denied* sub nom. Linde v. T. J. Raney & Sons, Inc., 465 U. S. 1026.

[142] See pp. 845-47 supra. In general, see Note, The Fraud-on-the-Market Theory, 95 Harv. L. Rev. 1143 (1982) (the efficient market hypothesis is the most persuasive rationale for the theory); Rapp, Rule 10b-5 and "Fraud-on-the-Market" — Heavy Seas Meet Tranquil Shores, 39 Wash. & Lee L. Rev. 861 (1982). For a dissenting view, see Black, Fraud on the Market: A Criticism of Dispensing with Reliance Requirements in Certain Open Market Transactions, 62 N. C. L. Rev. 435 (1984).

[143] Blackie v. Barrack, 524 F. 2d 891, 906 (9th Cir. 1975), *cert. denied,* 429 U. S. 816; Shores v. Sklar, 647 F. 2d 462, 468 (5th Cir. *en banc* 1981), *cert. denied,* 459 U. S. 1102; Panzirer v. Wolf, 663 F. 2d 365 (2d Cir. 1981), *vacated as moot* sub nom. Price Waterhouse v. Panzirer, 459 U. S. 1027 (1982); T. J. Raney & Sons, Inc. v. Fort Cobb, Okla. Irrigation Fuel Authority, 717 F. 2d 1330 (10th Cir. 1983), *cert. denied* sub nom. Linde v. T. J. Raney & Sons, Inc., 465 U. S. 1026; Lipton v. Documation, Inc., 734 F. 2d 740 (11th Cir. 1984), *cert. denied* sub nom. Peat, Marwick, Mitchell & Co. v. Lipton, 469 U. S. 1132; Levinson v. Basic, Inc., 786 F. 2d 741, 749-51 (6th Cir. 1986), *cert. granted* sub nom. Basic, Inc. v. Levinson, 107 S. Ct. 1284 (1987); Harris v. Union Electric Co., 787 F. 2d 355, 367 n. 9 (8th Cir. 1986); Peil v. Speiser, 806 F. 2d 1154 (3d Cir. 1986); see also, for a good analysis, Grossman v. Waste Management, Inc., 589 F. Supp. 395 (N. D. Ill. 1984).

But cf. Seiler v. E. F. Hutton & Co., Inc., CCH Fed. Sec. L. Rep. ¶91,632 at 99,207 n. 5 (D. N. J. 1984) ("the court seriously questions the relevance of a 'fraud-on-the-market' theory to a lawsuit against a stockholder rather than against the issuer of the stock"); Gibb v. Delta Drilling Co., 104 F. R. D. 59, 66-69, CCH Fed. Sec. L. Rep. ¶91,943 at 90,701-03 (N. D. Tex. 1985) (*Shores* excludes the broader doctrine of *Blackie*).

[144] See also T. J. Raney & Sons, Inc. v. Fort Cobb, Okla. Irrigation Fuel Authority, 717 F. 2d 1330 (10th Cir. 1983), *cert. denied* sub nom. Linde v. T. J. Raney & Sons, Inc., 465 U. S. 1026. With the theory presumably grounded in the efficient market hypothesis, the cases of an existing but thin market should be treated the same way. But the theory applies only to "efficient" markets.

(3) Even if it be assumed that the *Ute* rule itself is limited to *omissions,* the rationale of the "fraud on the market" theory, in its "pure" version as well as its *Shores* modification, is just as applicable logically to misstatements or half-truths.[145] Nevertheless, it is arguable that this proposition is even stronger with respect to the *Shores* modification because of the extra proof it requires.

(4) Both the reliance-from-materiality concept of *Ute* and "fraud on the market" are equally rebuttable so far as the second clause of Rule 10b-5 is concerned. It is not easy to conceive of how this might be done in an open market situation.[146] But *Blackie* identified two ways to do this: "1) by disproving materiality or by showing that an insufficient number of traders relied to inflate the stock's price, or 2) by proving that an individual plaintiff purchased despite knowledge of the falsity of defendant's representations, or that he would have, had he known of it."[147] "Though, as *Blackie* noted, this [second proposition] is a rather difficult burden to meet,[148] a defendant might help his own cause (though not necessarily establish it) by showing that the particular investor always does what his broker recommends, no matter what stock is involved."[149] And some courts have been satisfied with a showing that the investor relied "upon factors extraneous to the market."[150] But Judge Marshall concluded that reliance on a broker's or analyst's recommendation was not enough — that the defendant must show that the

---

Reingold v. Deloitte Haskins & Sells, 599 F. Supp. 1241, 1263 (S. D. N. Y. 1984).

[145] See Panzirer v. Wolf, 663 F. 2d 365, 367-68 (2d Cir. 1981), *vacated as moot* sub nom. Price Waterhouse v. Panzirer, 459 U. S. 1027 (1984).

[146] Little v. First Cal. Co., 532 F. 2d 1302, 1304 n. 3 (9th Cir. 1976). It has been suggested further:

> Acceptance of the logic of the fraud on the market theory * * * leads to the conclusion that there is no need in a securities fraud case for separate inquiries into materiality, reliance, causation, and damages. These inquiries are necessary in a face-to-face transaction where each party must make a subjective valuation of information provided by the other party, but irrelevant in open market transactions where the market price transmits all relevant information. The relevant inquiry in open market transactions should be whether the market price was in fact artificially affected by false information.

Fischel, Use of Modern Finance Theory in Securities Fraud Cases, 38 Bus. Law. 1, 13 (1982).

[147] Grossman v. Waste Management, Inc., 589 F. Supp. 395, 404 (N. D. Ill. 1984), citing Blackie v. Barrack, 524 F. 2d 891, 906 (9th Cir. 1975), *cert. denied,* 429 U. S. 816.

[148] 524 F. 2d 26 at 906-07 n. 22.

[149] Grossman v. Waste Management, Inc., 589 F. Supp. 395, 404 (N. D. Ill. 1984).

[150] Ibid., citing District Court cases.

decision to buy was based on factors "wholly" extraneous to the market.[151] And the Second Circuit has applied the "fraud on the market" theory to a plaintiff who relied not on market price but on an article in the Wall Street Journal.[152]

The "fraud on the market" theory aside, the *Ute* case does not affect considerations of *legal* causation. For neither *Ute* nor its predecessor, *Mills,* presented questions of "intervening" or multiple causes. Thus, when the market declines after the published rectification of a false earnings statement that was used in the sale of an electronics stock, the misrepresentation is not the "legal cause" of the buyer's loss, or at any rate not the *sole* legal cause, to the extent that a subsequent event that had no connection with or relation to the misrepresentation caused a market drop — for example, the suicide of the corporation's president, or a softening of the market in all electronics stocks, or a political assassination or invasion in some part of the world.[153]

In one case the Second Circuit referred to the "clear instructions on causation" below to the effect that the "misleading statement or omission played a substantial part in bringing about or causing the damage suffered by [the plaintiff] and that the damage was either a direct result or a reasonably foreseeable result of the misleading statement."[154] And in another case the same court, after calculating 10b-5 damages as the difference in the value of a mismanaged portfolio between the time the defendant broker began to aid and abet the adviser's fraud and the time of revocation of the adviser's trading authorization, reduced the resultant figure by the average percentage decline of the markets as a whole based on a common index such as Dow Jones or the Standard & Poor's 500.[155] The Ninth

[151] Id. at 406.

[152] Panzirer v. Wolf, 663 F. 2d 365 (2d Cir. 1981), *vacated as moot* sub nom Price Waterhouse v. Panzirer, 469 U. S. 1027 (1984).

[153] See St. Louis Union Trust Co. v. Merrill Lynch, Pierce, Fenner & Smith Inc., 562 F. 2d 1040 (8th Cir. 1977), *cert. denied,* 435 U. S. 925 (corporation, in exercising option to rebuy deceased stockholder's shares, need not disclose to executors information on a proposed public offering; for the purported "loss" was caused by the execution of the stock restriction and the death); Christo v. Safeguard Industries, Inc., CCH Fed. Sec. L. Rep. ¶99,494 (D. Minn. 1983) (any misrepresentations made by payee of a note in connection with foreclosure sale could not have caused loss of marker).

[154] Globus v. Law Research Service, Inc., 418 F. 2d 1276, 1291 (2d Cir. 1969), *cert. denied,* 397 U. S. 913; see also Bloor v. Carro, Spanbock, Londin, Rodman & Fass, 754 F. 2d 57 (2d Cir. 1985).

[155] Rolf v. Blyth, Eastman Dillon & Co., Inc., 570 F. 2d 38, 49 (2d Cir. 1978); see also Sundstrand Corp. v. Sun Chemical Corp., 553 F. 2d 1033, 1050 (7th Cir. 1977), *cert. denied,* 434 U. S. 875; In re Catanella Securities Litigation, 584 F. Supp. 1388, 1413-17 (E. D. Pa. 1984).

Circuit, on the other hand, in sustaining a claim that the misrepresentations caused the plaintiffs to make and hold investments in a declining market, met the defendants' argument that there was a general decline in stock prices by stating simply that the plaintiffs "relied on the misrepresentations; thus causation is adequately alleged."[156]

b. Relief Available[157]

The Code authorizes the court, within certain restrictions, to vary the prescribed measure of damages or definition of rescission on a showing that a different result "would be plainly more appropriate on consideration of such factors as the plaintiff's loss, the defendant's profit, and the deterrent effect of the particular type of liability."[158] By way of justifying that provision, the commentary states that

> there has been so much variation in the cases that it is tempting to conclude that "there is no law of damages under Rule 10b-5" — that the courts have taken an *ad hoc* approach and that, broadly using the common law out-of-pocket measure as an initial reference point, the appellate courts have exercised the discretion traditionally left to the trial courts in finding damages appropriate to the facts of the case.[159]

[156] Gottreich v. San Francisco Investment Corp., 552 F. 2d 866 (9th Cir. 1977). See Note, Rule 10b-5 Damage Computation: Application of Financial Theory to Determine Net Economic Loss, 51 Ford. L. Rev. 838 (1983).

[157] For the sake of simplicity, the plaintiff normally will be considered to be a seller rather than a buyer. See also p. 886 supra (Sec. Act §12).

[158] §1723(e).

[159] 2 Code 789, quoting from Note, Measurement of Damages in Private Actions Under Rule 10b-5, [1968] Wash. U. L. Q. 165, 179; see also Note, Insiders' Liability Under Rule 10b-5 for the Illegal Purchase of Actively Traded Securities, 78 Yale L. J. 864, 875-91 (1969); John R. Lewis, Inc. v. Newman, 446 F. 2d 800, 805 (5th Cir. 1971) ("federal courts may use any available remedy to make good the wrong done"); Nye v. Blyth Eastman Dillon & Co., 588 F. 2d 1189, 1198 (8th Cir. 1978), quoting from Garnatz v. Stifel, Nicolaus & Co., Inc., 559 F. 2d 1357, 1360 (8th Cir. 1977), *cert. denied,* 435 U. S. 951 (court's "function is to fashion the remedy best suited to the harm").

But see Easterbrook and Fischel, Optimal Damages in Securities Cases, 52 U. Chi. L. Rev. 611, 612 (1985):

> Our thesis is that things appear to be more chaotic than they are. Some fairly simple principles lead to intelligible rules of damages. These rules are not only elegant in theory but also applied in practice. The rhetoric that appears in opinions does not always track the analysis we supply, but neither do the courts' judgments follow their rhetoric.
>
> The principles we use are derived from the economics of sanctions.

First of all, like the plaintiff at common law in the case of a contract allegedly induced by fraud — and unlike the §12(2) plaintiff, who is restricted to rescission or a rescission measure of damages — the seller who proves a violation of Rule 10b-5 has the choice of undoing the bargain (when events since the transaction have not made rescission impossible) or holding the defendant to the bargain by requiring him to pay damages.[160] If the securities are still in existence and the plaintiff elects rescission, the defendant may presumably return the securities (together with any dividends or interest that he may have received on them) upon the plaintiff's repaying the amount the defendant originally paid him for them; or, since securities of the same class are fungible, the defendant should be permitted to pay the plaintiff the cash equivalent, at least when the securities are readily obtainable in the market.[161] In the latter event, the market price of the securities will presumably be computed as of the date of judgment.

Whether it is to the plaintiff's advantage to seek rescission or damages will naturally depend on the market action since the date of the transaction. If the plaintiff can prove that the security was worth 80 when he sold it to the defendant at 50, but the market when suit is brought has fallen to 40, obviously he will ask for damages rather than recission.[162]

[160] Randall v. Loftsgaarden, 106 S. Ct. 3143, 3153 (1986), citing the text (dictum, since the Court was able to *assume* that a rescissory recovery might sometimes be proper on a §10(b) claim and that this was such a case); see also Estate Counseling Service, Inc. v. Merrill Lynch, Pierce, Fenner & Smith Inc., 303 F. 2d 527, 531 (10th Cir. 1962); Rogen v. Ilikon Corp., 361 F. 2d 260, 268-69 (1st Cir. 1966); Myzel v. Fields, 386 F. 2d 718, 740-49 (8th Cir. 1967), *cert. denied*, 389 U. S. 951; Sackett v. Beaman, 399 F. 2d 884, 891 (9th Cir. 1968). The plaintiff who seeks rescission need not prove damages with the degree of particularity required in an action for damages. All he must establish is his injury. Holdsworth v. Strong, 545 F. 2d 687, 697 (10th Cir. *en banc* 1976).

[161] Baumel v. Rosen, 283 F. Supp. 128, 148 (D. Md. 1968), *aff'd in part and rev'd in part on other grounds*, 412 F. 2d 571 (4th Cir. 1969), *cert. denied*, 396 U. S. 1037; cf. Strong v. Repide, 213 U. S. 419, 421-22 (1909).

[162] The plaintiff's election is not absolute. An unequivocal demand for rescission will preclude a later action for damages under Rule 10b-5. Estate Counseling Service, Inc. v. Merrill Lynch, Pierce, Fenner & Smith, Inc., 303 F. 2d 527, 531-32 (10th Cir. 1962). And, "Where parties have the right to rescind they cannot delay the exercise of that right to determine whether avoidance or affirmance will be more profitable to them." Id. at 532; Chiodo v. General Waterworks Corp., 380 F. 2d 860, 867 (10th Cir. 1967), *cert. denied*, 389 U. S. 1004; Johns Hopkins University v. Hutton, 488 F. 2d 912, 915 n. 12 (4th Cir. 1973); see also Restatement of Restitution §64. That is to say, the plaintiff cannot play the market at the defendant's expense. It is not a matter of laches the courts in these cases do not mention any need to show prejudice in addition to delay. Guy v. Duff & Phelps, Inc., 628 F. Supp. 252, 257 (N. D. Ill. 1985) But cf. Myzel v. Fields, 386 F. 2d 718, 740-41 (8th Cir. 1967), *cert. denied*, 389

In the usual situation damages have been computed in accordance with the tort or out-of-pocket measure applied by the federal courts in common law fraud cases before *Erie.*[163] Normally that measure may be expected to yield the difference between the value of the security (not necessarily market value at the time of the defendant's purchase but presumably value at that time as judged in the light of the issuer's subsequent history) and the price paid the plaintiff for it (or the value of anything that the defendant may have given in exchange).[164] In the case of a close corporation, or when the market is thin, the court is not restricted to actual sales prices but may draw reasonable inferences.[165]

So much for the rule. Enter now the voracious exceptions:

(1) If the defendant buyer's profit on resale is greater than the tort measure, the plaintiff is entitled to the profit.[166] Once it is found that the defendant acquired the property by fraud and that the profit was the proximate consequence of the fraud, whether foreseeable or not, "it is more appropriate to give the defrauded party the benefit even of windfalls than to let the fraudulent party keep them.[167] The damages ceiling imposed by §28(a) in terms of

---

U. S. 951 ("rescissional damages"); Rogen v. Ilikon Corp., 361 F. 2d 260, 269 (1st Cir. 1966). On this point generally, see Randall v. Loftsgaarden, 106 S. Ct. 3143, 3155 (1986), citing the text.

[163] Affiliated Ute Citizens of Utah v. United States, 406 U. S. 128, 154-55 (1972); Randall v. Loftsgaarden, 106 S. Ct. 3143, 3152-53 (1986).

[164] In Levine v. Futransky, 636 F. Supp. 899 (N. D. Ill. 1986), the court held that the plaintiffs might be able to prove damages even though the profitable trust fund portfolios managed by the defendant exceeded the aggregate loss of the remaining portfolios; that is to say, it was not necessary to net the aggregate gains and aggregate losses.

[165] Affiliated Ute Citizens of Utah v. United States, 406 U. S. 128, 155 (1972); see also Holmes v. Bateson, 583 F. 2d 542, 563 (1st Cir. 1978); Glick v. Campagna, 613 F. 2d 31, 37 (3d Cir. 1979).

Whatever the measure of damages, in the case of a class action (see p. 871 n. 3 supra), those members who did not opt out or settle do not have their damages increased by reference to those who did opt out or settle. Kitchens v. U. S. Shelter, — F. Supp. — CCH Fed. Sec. L. Rep. ¶93,053 (D. S. C. 1986).

[166] Affiliated Ute Citizens of Utah v. United States, 406 U. S. 128, 155 (1972).

[167] Janigan v. Taylor, 344 F. 2d 781, 786 (1st Cir. 1965), *cert. denied,* 382 U. S. 879; see also Gould v. American-Hawaiian Steamship Co., 535 F. 2d 761, 782 (3d Cir. 1976); Siebel v. Scott, 725 F. 2d 995, 1002 (5th Cir. 1984), *cert. denied,* 467 U. S. 1242; but cf. Levine v. Seilon, Inc., 439 F. 2d 328, 334 (2d Cir. 1971); Simon v. New Haven Board & Carton Co., Inc., 516 F. 2d 303, 306 (2d Cir. 1975). There is authority for reducing the defendant's recoverable profit to reflect his own post-fraud efforts. Thomas v. Duralite Co., Inc., 524 F. 2d 577, 586 (3d Cir. 1975); Siebel v. Scott, supra; but cf. Rochez Bros., Inc. v. Rhoades, 491 F. 2d 402, 412 (3d Cir. 1973). Moreover, pointing to the Code, a split court sitting *en banc* held that the profit should be measured (as much by way of disgorgement in an SEC injunction action as in a private action) by the price "a reasonable time after public dissemination of the inside information."

"actual damages on account of the act complained of" does not foreclose a windfall recovery based on the defendant's benefit rather than the plaintiff's loss.[168] In *Randall* v. *Loftsgaarden,* the Court said it had "never interpreted §28(a) as imposing a rigid requirement that every recovery on an express or implied right of action under the 1934 Act must be limited to the net economic harm suffered by the plaintiff."[169]

(2) Although some courts have assumed that §28(a) *would* preclude the warranty measure of damages[170] that is the majority rule in common law deceit actions,[171] the Second Circuit has held that the "actual damages" of §28(a) could include benefit-of-the-bargain damages "when they can be established with reasonable certainty."[172] "Since the price paid by the successful offeror in a tender offer contest often exceeds the fair market value of the securities surrendered by the shareholders, defrauded shareholders of a target company would hardly ever, under the out-of-pocket measure of damages, have redress."[173]

(3) Consequential damages (which are "actual damages") are recoverable on top of everything else — for example, the plaintiff's cost of investigating the transaction before he entered into it.[174] And rescission does not preclude consequential damages for pre-

---

SEC v. MacDonald, 699 F. 2d 47, 55 (1st Cir. *en banc* 1983), *on remand,* 568 F. Supp. 111 (D. R. I. 1983), *aff'd per curiam,* 725 F. 2d 9 (1st Cir. 1984).

[168] Myzel v. Fields, 386 F. 2d 718, 748-49 (8th Cir. 1967), *cert. denied,* 389 U. S. 951. The courts have granted recovery also of fraudulent windfall profits reaped by fraudulent *sellers,* although they are harder to prove. Zeller v. Bogue Electric Mfg. Corp., 476 F. 2d 795, 801-03 (2d Cir. 1973), *cert. denied,* 414 U. S. 908; Ohio Drill & Tool Co. v. Johnson, 498 F. 2d 186, 190 (6th Cir. 1974); Hackbart v. Holmes, 675 F. 2d 1114, 1122 (10th Cir. 1982); but cf. Occidental Life Ins. Co. of N. C. v. Pat Ryan & Associates, Inc., 496 F. 2d 1255, 1265 (4th Cir. 1974), *cert. denied,* 419 U. S. 1023.

[169] 106 S. Ct. 3143, 3153 (1986).

[170] Estate Counseling Service, Inc. v. Merrill Lynch, Pierce, Fenner & Smith, Inc., 303 F. 2d 527, 533 (10th Cir. 1972); Kohler v. Kohler Co., 208 F. Supp. 808, 825 (E. D. Wis. 1962), *aff'd on other grounds,* 319 F. 2d 634 (7th Cir. 1963).

[171] See p. 875 supra.

[172] Osofsky v. Zipf, 645 F. 2d 107, 114 (2d Cir. 1981). But cf. Barrows v. Forest Laboratories, Inc., 742 F. 2d 54, 59 (2d Cir. 1984). A plaintiff cannot *rescind* a transaction and at the same time ask for the benefit of the bargain rescinded. Quintel Corp., N. V. v. Citibank, N. A., 596 F. Supp. 797, 803 (S. D. N. Y. 1984).

[173] Osofsky v. Zipf, 645 F. 2d 107, 114 (2d Cir. 1981).

[174] Esplin v. Hirschi, 402 F. 2d 94 (10th Cir. 1968), *cert. denied,* 394 U. S. 982; Madigan, Inc. v. Goodman, 498 F. 2d 233, 238-39 (7th Cir. 1974); see also Bowman & Bourdon, Inc. v. Rohr, 296 F. Supp. 847, 852 (D. Mass. 1969), *aff'd per curiam,* 417 F. 2d 780 (1st Cir. 1969); McLean v. Alexander, 449 F. Supp. 1251, 1268-70 (D. Del. 1978), *rev'd on other grounds,* 599 F. 2d 1190 (3d Cir. 1979).

rescission losses.[175] But "A plaintiff seeking consequential damages for fraud, at common law or under federal securities legislation, must establish the causal nexus with a good deal of certainty," varying "somewhat inversely with the depth of the fraud."[176] Under the familiar principle of mitigation of damages, a plaintiff cannot recover for his own failure to take reasonable steps to avoid further harm; at a point where a reasonable man would have taken protective action the chain of causation is broken.[177]

(4) Presumably §28(a) does not exclude the so-called "highest intermediate value" rule of damages when it would be appropriate. That is to say, the seller who can prove that "he probably would have made a sale while the [security] was at its highest point in value" within a reasonable time after the defendant's purchase in violation of Rule 10b-5 might well argue that that is the basis for measuring what his "actual damages" are.[178]

(5) In appropriate circumstances the plaintiff may obtain an accounting for profits.[179]

(6) The courts have granted "rescissory" (or "rescissional" or "rescissionary" or "restitutional") damages in various factual configurations,[180] sometimes doing their best to reconstruct the scena-

[175] Foster v. Financial Technology, Inc., 517 F. 2d 1068, 1072 (9th Cir. 1975).

[176] Zeller v. Bogue Electric Mfg. Corp., 476 F. 2d 795, 803 (2d Cir. 1973), *cert. denied*, 414 U. S. 908; see also Chris-Craft Industries, Inc. v. Piper Aircraft Corp., 516 F. 2d 172, 191 (2d Cir. 1975), *rev'd on other grounds* sub nom. Piper v. Chris-Craft Industries, Inc., 430 U. S. 1 (1977); James v. Meinke, 778 F. 2d 200, 205-06 (5th Cir. 1985), and cases cited.

[177] Foster v. Financial Technology, Inc., 517 F. 2d 1068, 1072 (9th Cir. 1975).

[178] See Restatement of Restitution §151, Comment c; Code §1723(e), Comment (1); cf. Fridrich v. Bradford, CCH Fed. Sec. L. Rep. ¶94,723 at 96,407 (M. D. Tenn. 1974), *rev'd on other grounds*, 542 F. 2d 307 (6th Cir. 1976), *cert. denied*, 429 U. S. 1053; but cf. Gerstle v. Gamble-Skogmo, Inc., 478 F. 2d 1281, 1305-06 (2d Cir. 1973).

[179] Kardon v. National Gypsum Co., 73 F. Supp. 798, 801-02 (E. D. Pa. 1947); Glick v. Campagna, 613 F. 2d 31 (3d Cir. 1979) (with rescission).

[180] Myzel v. Fields, 386 F. 2d 718, 740-41 (8th Cir. 1967), *cert. denied*, 389 U. S. 951; Chasins v. Smith Barney & Co., Inc., 438 F. 2d 1167, 1173 (2d Cir. 1971); Garnatz v. Stifel, Nicolaus & Co., Inc., 559 F. 2d 1357 (8th Cir. 1977), *cert. denied*, 435 U. S. 951; Rolf v. Blyth Eastman Dillon & Co., Inc., 570 F. 2d 38, 49 (2d Cir. 1978) ("gross economic loss on a portfolio-wide basis during a relevant period of time"); Austin v. Loftsgaarden, 675 F. 2d 168, 181 (8th Cir. 1982), *judgment after retrial aff'd in part and rev'd in part en banc on other grounds*, 768 F. 2d 949 (8th Cir. 1985), *rev'd on other grounds* sub nom. Randall v. Loftsgaarden, 106 S. Ct. 3143 (1986).

But cf. Huddleston v. Herman & MacLean, 640 F. 2d 534, 555 (5th Cir. 1981), *modified on other grounds*, 650 F. 2d 815 (5th Cir. 1981), *aff'd in part and rev'd in part on other grounds* sub nom. Herman & MacLean v. Huddleston, 459 U. S. 375 (1983). "A bank, unless it is acting as a broker or in a situation closely

rio as it would have been if everybody had acted properly.[181]

(7) So far we have not conjured with the complications created by the anonymity of market trading, where tracing shares to determine which were the subject of insiders' transactions would be (a) impossible and (b) in any event a lottery. If an insider buys 100 shares on the basis of a false press release or without *any* disclosure of "bullish" information — or if an insider who is responsible for a false press release does not trade at all — to whom is he liable for how much? If the *Texas Gulf Sulphur* defendants had been held liable to all those who had sold in the market during the five-month period between the mineral discovery and its truthful disclosure, Dean Ruder calculated that restitution damages would have exceeded $300 million.[182]

In *Shapiro* v. *Merrill Lynch,* the Second Circuit held that the defendant tippers were liable to all who had bought in the market "during the same period" when the tippees had sold. But, because the case had come up on an interlocutory appeal from an order denying the defendants' motion for judgment on the pleadings, the court was able to leave to the District Court on remand "the appropriate form of relief to be granted, including the proper measure of damages."[183]

analogous to that of a broker, is not within the category of parties against whom rescissional damages may be awarded." In re Letterman Bros. Energy Securities Litigation, 799 F. 2d 967, 972 (5th Cir. 1986), *rehearsing en banc denied,* 802 F. 2d 455 (5th Cir. 1986), *cert. denied,* Sub. nom. Letterman Bros. Energy Program 1980-2 v. BancTexas Dallas, N.A., 107 S. Ct. 1373. And a plaintiff who seeks a rescissionary measure of damages must act promptly. Feldman v. Pioneer Petroleum, Inc., 813 F. 2d 296, 310 n. 10 (10th Cir. 1987).

[181] Speed v. Transamerica Corp., 135 F. Supp. 176, 186-94 (D. Del. 1955), *modifed on another point and aff'd,* 235 F. 2d 369 (3d Cir. 1956); Opper v. Hancock Securities Corp., 250 F. Supp. 668, 676 (S. D. N. Y. 1966), *aff'd per curiam,* 367 F. 2d 157 (2d Cir. 1966); Gottlieb v. Sandia American Corp., 304 F. Supp. 980, 989-92 (E. D. Pa. 1969), *aff'd on this point and rev'd in part on other grounds,* 452 F. 2d 510 (3d Cir. 1971), *cert. denied* sub nom. Wechsler v. Gottlieb, 404 U. S. 938; John R. Lewis, Inc. v. Newman, 446 F. 2d 800, 805 (5th Cir. 1971); Pittsburgh Terminal Corp. v. Baltimore & Ohio R. R., 586 F. Supp. 1297, 1303 (W. D. Pa. 1984), *aff'd without opinion,* 760 F. 2d 260 (3d Cir. 1985), *cert. denied,* 106 S. Ct. 247; cf. Bird v. Ferry, 497 F. 2d 112 (5th Cir. 1974); Alley v. Miramon, 614 F. 2d 1372, 1387 (5th Cir. 1980). In general, see Thompson, The Measure of Recovery Under Rule 10b-5: A Restitution Alternative to Tort Damages, 37 Vand. L. Rev. 349 (1984).

[182] Ruder, Texas Gulf Sulphur — The Second Round, 63 Nw. U. L. Rev. 423, 428-29 (1968).

[183] Shapiro v. Merrill Lynch Pierce, Fenner & Smith, Inc., 495 F. 2d 228, 241 (2d Cir. 1974). In O'Connor & Associates v. Dean Witter Reynolds, Inc., 559 F. Supp. 800 (S. D. N. Y. 1983), the court applied the *Shapiro* rule to option trading despite the argument that buyers and sellers in the option market can be readily matched on the basis of trading records. The court said that the "same period" limitation was based primarily not on the matching difficulty but on the conclusion that the process would be fortuitous.

Several years later, in a case in which the defendants had not sold on the same day on which the insiders had bought, or even in the same month, and with no proof that the defendants' trading activities had had any impact on the market price, a majority of a Sixth Circuit panel disagreed with *Shapiro* and limited the *Ute* presumption of "causation" essentially to face-to-face transactions, so as to conclude that there was simply no "causation."[184] Judge Celebrezze, concurring in the result, would have allowed recovery by any plaintiffs (there were none) who had sold concurrently with any defendants' purchases.

The Second Circuit later followed Judge Celebrezze's approach:

> In *Shapiro,* 495 F. 2d at 237, this court held insider sellers subject to a duty to disclose only to those who purchased the stock "during the same period" as the insiders sales. To be sure, the district court on remand interpreted this language to refer to the period of time from the defendants' trades to the public disclosure of the insider information, *Shapiro* v. *Merrill Lynch, Pierce, Fenner & Smith, Inc.,* [1975-1976 Transfer Binder] Fed. Sec. L. Rep. (CCH) ¶95,377, at 98,878 (S D. N. Y. 1975), but the entire period in that case was only four days. To extend the period of liability well beyond the time of the insider's trading simply because disclosure was never made could make the insider liable to all the world. See *Shapiro,* 495 F. 2d at 239; *Globus* v. *Law Research Service, Inc.,* 418 F. 2d 1276, 1292 (2d Cir. 1969), *cert. denied,* 397 U. S. 913 (1970). Any duty of disclosure is owed only to those investors trading contemporaneously with the insider; non-contemporaneous traders do not require the protection of the "disclosure or abstain" rule because they do not suffer the disadvantage of trading with someone who has superior access to information. See *Fridrich* v. *Bradford,* 542 F. 2d 307, 326 (6th Cir. 1976) (Celebrezze, J., concurring), *cert. denied,* 429 U. S. 1053 (1977). * * * Because, in the instant case, Wilson purchased his Comtech stock approximately one month after appellees' sales, he did not trade contemporaneously with the insiders and he has no standing to sue on this claim.[185]

When there *is* standing under this test, the Second Circuit's rule is

> (1) to allow any uninformed investor, where a reasonable investor would either have delayed his purchase or not purchased at all if he had had the benefit of the tipped information, to recover any post-purchase decline in market value of his shares up to a reasonable

[184] Fridrich v. Bradford, 542 F. 2d 307 (6th Cir. 1976), *cert. denied,* 429 U. S. 1053.

[185] Wilson v. Comtech Telecommunications Corp., 648 F. 2d 88, 94-95 (2d Cir. 1981).

> time after he learns of the tipped information or after there is a public disclosure of it but (2) limit his recovery to the amount gained by the tippee as a result of his selling at the earlier date rather than delaying his sale until the parties could trade on in equal informational basis * * *. Should the intervening buyers, because of the volume and price of their purchases, claim more than the tippee's gain, their recovery (limited to that gain) would be shared *pro rata.*[186]

The court referred to this "disgorgement measure" as having "in substance been recommended by the Code."[187]

(8) On top of whatever monetary award is made, prejudgment interest may be awarded in the discretion of the court.[188] And in

[186]Elkind v. Liggett & Myers, Inc., 635 F. 2d 156, 172 (2d Cir. 1980); see also SEC v. MacDonald, 699 F. 2d 47, 52-55 (1st Cir. *en banc* 1983), *on remand,* 568 F. Supp. 111 (D. R. I. 1983), *aff'd per curiam,* 725 F. 2d 9 (1st Cir. 1984), infra Supp. p. 1009 end; State Teachers Retirement Board v. Fluor Corp., 566 F. Supp. 945, 953-54 (S. D. N. Y. 1983), *on later motions,* 589 F. Supp. 1268 (S. D. N. Y. 1984). In the first *State Teachers* opinion the court said that *Elkind*'s disgorgement measure would not work when there was a "laundry list" of omissions, so that it was impossible to isolate each item and project its effect on the market the day it became public. Reminding that the *Elkind* court itself had urged remedial flexibility, the *State Teachers* court observed that, although the retroactive valuation of stock traded during the period of nondisclosure seemed unnecessarily speculative in *Elkind,* it might nevertheless be appropriate in a case in which there was alleged to have been more than one tip.

For a critique of the *Elkind* case, see Friedman, Efficient Market Theory and Rule 10b-5 Nondisclosure Claims: A Proposal for Reconciliation, 47 Mo. L. Rev. 745 (1982).

[187]Elkind v. Liggett & Myers, Inc., 635 F. 2d 156, 172 (2d Cir. 1980); Code §§1603, 1703(b), 1708(b), 1711(j). The Code differs in several respects. For example, (1) it cuts off standing not when the insider or tippee stops trading as in *Elkind* but when the information in question becomes generally available as in *Shapiro,* and (2) it imposes arbitrary monetary ceilings in addition to a ceiling in terms of the defendant's profit. For a summary description of the Code scheme, see 1 Code xlix-l.

[188]*Granted, or remanded after denial:* E. g., Wessel v. Buhler, 437 F. 2d 279, 284 (9th Cir. 1971); Mitchell v. Texas Gulf Sulphur Co., 446 F. 2d 90, 106 (10th Cir. 1971), *cert. denied,* 404 U. S. 1004; Chris-Craft Industries, Inc. v. Piper Aircraft Corp., 516 F. 2d 172, 190 (2d Cir. 1975), *rev'd on other grounds* sub nom. Piper v. Chris-Craft Industries, Inc., 430 U. S. 1 (1977); Thomas v. Duralite Co., 524 F. 2d 577, 589 (3d Cir. 1975); Holmes v. Bateson, 583 F. 2d 542, 564 (1st Cir. 1978); Rolf v. Blyth, Eastman Dillon & Co., Inc., 637 F. 2d 77, 87 (2d Cir. 1980) ("compensatory," "customary in cases involving a breach of fiduciary duties," and "governed by fundamental considerations of fairness," even though defendant did not have the use of plaintiffs' money during the relevant period).

Denied, or remanded after grant: E. g., Norte & Co. v. Huffines, 416 F. 2d 1189, 1191-92 (2d Cir. 1969), *cert. denied* sub nom. Muscat v. Norte, 397 U. S. 989; Wolf v. Frank, 477 F. 2d 467, 479 (5th Cir. 1973), *cert. denied,* 414 U. S. 975; White v. Abrams, 495 F. 2d 724, 736 (9th Cir. 1974); cf. Occidental Life Ins. Co. of N. C. v. Pat Ryan & Associates, Inc., 496 F. 2d 1255, 1269 (4th Cir. 1974), *cert. denied,* 419 U. S. 1023.

With respect to the rate when interest is granted, see, e. g., Sanders v. John

appropriate circumstances all the ancillary remedies are available that equity traditionally recognizes. But it is clear that punitive or exemplary damages are precluded by the limitation in §28(a) to "actual damages."[189] It is clear, too, from the holdings to that effect, that §28(a) is not limited to the *express* liability provisions. But note:

(a) What about actions under §12(2), or (if they are permitted)[190] §17(a) of the 1933 Act, which has no provision comparable to §28(a)?[191]

(b) The very nonavailability of punitive damages, at least under Rule 10b-5, is an additional reason for adding a common law deceit count by way of pendent jurisdiction (or diversity jurisdiction when

---

Nuveen & Co., Inc. ("Sanders II"), 524 F. 2d 1064, 1075-76 (7th Cir. 1975). In Madigan, Inc. v. Goodman, 498 F. 2d 233, 240 (7th Cir. 1974), the court held that plaintiffs who sought more than the market rate "must prove with a good deal of certainty that they would have made a particular alternative investment that would have produced a higher return." In Wilsmann v. Upjohn Co., 572 F. Supp. 242, 245 (W. D. Mich. 1983), *vacated on other grounds,* 775 F. 2d 713 (6th Cir. 1985), *cert. denied,* 106 S. Ct. 2893, the court applied the Michigan statutory rate as "not unduly high," stating that, in addition, "the use of a standard rate prevents application of an *ad hoc* rate-setting system which could be used to penalize a defendant, rather than just to make the plaintiff whole." But federal law controls. Koehler v. Pulvers, 614 F. Supp. 829, 850 (S. D. Cal. 1985). The court there adopted the average rate for money market instruments and federal funds during the relevant period, which the plaintiff's actuary had set at 10.38 percent. Ibid.

[189] Myzel v. Fields, 386 F. 2d 718, 748 (8th Cir. 1967), *cert. denied,* 390 U. S. 951; Green v. Wolf Corp., 406 F. 2d 291, 302-03 (2d Cir. 1968), *cert. denied,* 395 U. S. 977; Richardson v. MacArthur, 451 F. 2d 35, 43 (10th Cir. 1971); Byrnes v. Faulkner, Dawkins & Sullivan, 550 F. 2d 1303, 1313 (2d Cir. 1977); Osofsky v. Zipf, 645 F. 2d 107, 111 (2d Cir. 1981) (even apart from §28(a)). But see p. 1008 infra (Insider Trading Sanctions Act).

[190] See pp. 977-80 infra.

[191] The only other SEC statute with a comparable provision is the Trust Indenture Act. §323(b). And the courts are divided under both §§12(2) and 17(a):

Punitive damages *permitted* under §12(2): Nagel v. Prescott & Co., 36 F. R. D. 445, 449 (N. D. Ohio 1964). *Contra*: Hill York Corp. v. American Int'l Franchises, Inc., 448 F. 2d 680, 697 (5th Cir. 1971); Salonin v. Spyro-Dynamics Corp., CCH Fed. Sec. L. Rep. ¶94,506 at 95,770 (S. D. N. Y. 1974).

Permitted under §17(a): Larson v. Tony's Investments, Inc., CCH Fed. Sec. L. Rep. ¶92,324 at 97,532 (M. D. Ala. 1968) (dictum); Klein v. Spear, Leeds & Kellogg, 306 F. Supp. 743, 751 (S. D. N. Y. 1969). *Contra*: Globus v. Law Research Service, Inc., 418 F. 2d 1276, 1283-87 (2d Cir. 1969), *cert. denied,* 397 U. S. 913 (the two statutes are *in pari materia*); deHaas v. Empire Petroleum Co., 435 F. 2d 1223, 1229-32 (10th Cir. 1970); Schaefer v. First National Bank of Lincolnwood, 326 F. Supp. 1186, 1193 (N. D. Ill. 1970), *aff'd in part and rev'd in part on other grounds,* 509 F. 2d 1287 (7th Cir. 1972), *cert. denied,* 425 U. S. 943; Burkhart v. Allson Realty Trust, 363 F. Supp. 1286, 1290 (N. D. Ill. 1973); Hatrock v. Edward D. Jones & Co., 750 F. 2d 767, 771 (9th Cir. 1984).

it exists).[192] Moreover, punitive damages on a common law claim will not preclude interest on the 10b-5 claim.[193]

(c) For "common law deceit" in the last paragraph, substitute "blue sky law."[194]

(d) Damages for mental distress are a species of "actual damages."[195] And they have been awarded not only in purely common law deceit cases[196] but also pursuant to pendent claims notwithstanding argument addressed to §28(a),[197] though not in 10b-5 actions themselves.[198]

(9) With respect to the non-offsetting of tax benefits received by the plaintiff, there is no reason to read §28(a) as impelling a differ-

[192]Young v. Taylor, 466 F. 2d 1329, 1337-38 (10th Cir. 1972); Falks v. Koegel, 504 F. 2d 702, 706-07 (2d Cir. 1974); Nye v. Blyth Eastman Dillon & Co., 588 F. 2d 1189, 1200 (8th Cir. 1978); Miley v. Oppenheimer & Co., 637 F. 2d 318, 330 (5th Cir. 1981); Hatrock v. Edward D. Jones & Co., 750 F. 2d 767, 771 (9th Cir. 1984); Aldrich v. Thomson McKinnon Securities, Inc., 756 F. 2d 243, 246 n. 3 (2d Cir. 1985); Nunes v. Merrill Lynch, Pierce, Fenner & Smith, Inc., 609 F. Supp. 1055, 1058-62 (D. Md. 1985), and cases cited; Gorgan v. Garner, 806 F. 2d 829 (8th Cir. 1986).

[193]Ibid.

[194]Punitive damages have been allowed. Allied Steel & Tractor Products, Inc. v. First National City Bank of N. Y., 54 F. R. D. 256 (N. D. Ohio 1971); Bateman v. Petro Atlas, Inc., CCH Blue Sky L. Rep. ¶71,463 at 68,522 (S. D. Tex. 1977) (court applied provision in Texas blue sky law that permitted punitive damages up to twice the actual damages when the representation or omission was proven to have been willfully made).

[195]Greitzer v. United States National Bank, 326 F. Supp. 762 (S. D. Cal. 1971). The court in Kimmel v. Peterson, 565 F. Supp. 476, 499 (E. D. Pa. 1983), found that the test in Restatement (Second) of Torts §46, Comment d, had not been satisfied:

> Liability has been found only where the conduct has been so outrageous in character, and so extreme in degree, as to go beyond all possible bounds of decency, and to be regarded as atrocious, and utterly intolerable in a civilized society. Generally, the case is one in which the recitation of facts to an average member of the community would arouse his resentment against the action, and lead him to exclaim "outrageous."

See also cases cited in 2 Code 787.

[196]Malandris v. Merrill Lynch, Pierce, Fenner & Smith, Inc., 447 F. Supp. 543 (D. Colo. 1977); cf. Anderson v. Knox, 297 F. 2d 702, 728-31 (9th Cir. 1961), *cert. denied,* 370 U. S. 915 (sale of unsuitable insurance policy).

[197]Ryan v. Foster & Marshall, Inc., 556 F. 2d 460, 464 (9th Cir. 1977); Martin v. Howard, Weil, Labouisse, Friedricks, Inc., 487 F. Supp. 503, 508 (E. D. La. 1980); LeCroy v. Dean Witter Reynolds, Inc., 585 F. Supp. 753 (E. D. Ark. 1984).

[198]Greitzer v. United States National Bank, 326 F. Supp. 762 (S. D. Cal. 1971); Emmons v. Merrill Lynch, Pierce, Fenner & Smith, Inc., 532 F. Supp. 480, 485 (S. D. Ohio 1982); Castro v. Paine, Webber, Jackson & Curtis, Inc., 99 F. R. D. 655 (D. P. R. 1984).

ent result under Rule 10b-5 from the negative conclusion reached by the Supreme Court under §12(2).[199]

c. Actions by Buyers [Herein Also of §17(a)]

May *buyers*, for whom Congress legislated specifically in §§11 and 12(2) of the 1933 Act, forego those express rights of action in favor of Rule 10b-5, and thus make an "end run" around the conditions and limitations of the express actions such as the short statute of limitations in §13 of the 1933 Act? Indeed, may buyers resort to an implied right of action under §17(a) of the 1933 Act?

In *Herman & MacLean* v. *Huddleston*, Justice Marshall, speaking for a unanimous Court (except for Justice Powell's non-participation), answered the first question in the affirmative:

> Although limited in scope, Section 11 places a relatively minimal burden on a plaintiff. In contrast, Section 10(b) is a "catchall" antifraud provision, but it requires a plaintiff to carry a heavier burden to establish a cause of action. * * *
>
> * * * It would be anomalous indeed if the special protection afforded to purchasers in a registered offering by the 1933 Act were deemed to deprive such purchasers of the protections against manipulation and deception that Section 10(b) makes available to all persons who deal in securities.
>
> While some conduct actionable under Section 11 may also be actionable under Section 10(b), it is hardly a novel proposition that the Securities Exchange Act and the Securities Act "prohibit some of the same conduct." *United States* v. *Naftalin*, 441 U. S. 768, 778 (1979) (applying Section 17(a) of the 1933 Act to conduct also prohibited by Section 10(b) of the 1934 Act in an action by the SEC). "The fact that there may well be some overlap is neither unusual nor unfortunate." Ibid., quoting *SEC* v. *National Securities, Inc.*, 393 U. S. 453, 468 (1969). In savings clauses included in the 1933 and 1934 Acts, Congress rejected the notion that the express remedies of the securities laws would preempt all other rights of action. [Citing Sec. Act §16 and Sec. Ex. Act §28(a).] * * *
>
> This conclusion is reinforced by our reasoning in *Ernst & Ernst* v. *Hochfelder*, supra, which held that actions under Section 10(b) require proof of scienter and do not encompass negligent conduct. In so holding, we noted that each of the express civil remedies in the 1933 Act allowing recovery for negligent conduct is subject to procedural restrictions not applicable to a Section 10(b) action. * * *
>
> This cumulative construction of the remedies under the 1933

[199] Randall v. Loftsgaarden, 106 S. Ct. 3143 (1986), supra p. 886.

> and 1934 Acts is also supported by the fact that, when Congress comprehensively revised the securities laws in 1975, a consistent line of judicial decisions had permitted plaintiffs to sue under Section 10(b) regardless of the availability of express remedies. * * * In light of this well-established judicial interpretation, Congress' decision to leave Section 10(b) intact suggests that Congress ratified the cumulative nature of the Section 10(b) action. See *Merrill Lynch, Pierce, Fenner & Smith, Inc.* v. *Curran,* — U. S. — , — (1982); *Lorillard* v. *Pons,* 424 U. S. 575, 580-581 (1978).
>
> A cumulative construction of the securities laws also furthers their broad remedial purposes. * * * The effectiveness of the broad proscription against fraud in Section 10(b) would be undermined if its scope were restricted by the existence of an express remedy under Section 11. Yet we have repeatedly recognized that securities laws combating fraud should be construed "not technically and restrictively, but flexibly to effectuate [their] remedial purposes." *SEC* v. *Capital Gains Research Bureau,* 375 U. S. 180, 195 (1963). [Citations deleted.] We therefore reject an interpretation of the securities laws that displaces an action under Section 10(b).[200]

Questions (as is so often the case) remain:

1. Clearly buyers and sellers should be treated alike, as they are in the Code. But the very first case that allowed a seller to sue his buyer for violation of Rule 10b-5 gave birth to a dilemma that soon made itself felt under present law. On the one hand, since §10(b) applies equally to sellers and buyers, may a buyer waive his express remedy under §11 or 12(2) of the 1933 Act and claim an implied remedy under Rule 10b-5 in order to avoid the short statute of limitations in §13 of the 1933 Act and the risk of having to pay his opponents' counsel fees as well as to post advance security for costs pursuant to §11(e)? The two statutes have been repeatedly held to be *in pari materia.*[201] And "special provisions prevail over general ones which, in the absence of the special provisions, would control."[202] On the other hand, is the cultivated pearl that is Rule 10b-5 to be limited to the seller, a relative stepchild of Congress, while the buyer, its favorite son, is relegated to whatever gleanings he can find in §11 or 12(2)?

[200] *Herman & MacLean* has been held to permit an action under §20(a) of the 1934 Act for violation of Rule 10b-5 although an action might have been brought under §15 of the 1933 Act as applicable to §12(2). In re Longhorn Securities Litigation, 573 F. Supp. 255, 268 (W. D. Okla. 1983). On §§20(a) and 15, which make controlling persons liable, see p. 1011 infra.

[201] E. g., Axelrod & Co. v. Kordich, Victor & Neufeld, 451 F. 2d 838, 843 (2d Cir. 1971).

[202] Missouri v. Ross, 299 U. S. 72, 76 (1936).

Judge Jerome Frank's solution was to allow the buyer to escape the strictures of §11 but only at the cost of proving fraud (scienter) under Rule 10b-5.[203] And that is essentially the rationale of *Herman & MacLean.*

2. *Query*: The only exempted securities to which §12(2) does not apply by its terms are those specified in §3(a)(2): municipals, banks, and interests in certain tax-exempt plans. Will buyers of those securities be permitted to escape that exemption by resorting to Rule 10b-5?[204]

3. Will §§17(a) of the 1933 Act support a private right of action? Justice Marshall's opinion was able to avoid that question.[205] If *anything* in the 1933 Act can be stated categorically, the answer should be no. In November 1933 Commissioner Landis of the Federal Trade Commission, who had played a prominent part in the drafting of the statute, stated in an address:

> The suggestion has been made on occasion that civil liabilities arise also from a violation of Section 17, the first subsection of which makes unlawful the circulation of falsehoods and untruths in connection with the sale of a security in interstate commerce or through the mails. But a reading of this section in the light of the entire Act leaves no doubt but that violations of its provisions give rise only to a liability to be restrained by injunctive action or, if wilfully done, to a liability to be punished criminally.[206]

The following passage has been frequently quoted by the lower courts:

> It is one thing to imply a private right of action under §10(b) or the other provisions of the 1934 act, because the specific liabilities created by §§9(e), 16(b) and 18 do not cover all the variegated activities with which that act is concerned. But it is quite another thing to add an implied remedy under §17(a) of the 1933 act to the detailed remedies specifically created by §§11 and 12. The 1933 act is a much narrower statute. It deals only with disclosure and fraud *in the sale* of securities. It has but two important substantive provisions, §§5 and 17(a). Noncompliance with §5 results in civil liability under

[203] Fischman v. Raytheon Mfg. Co., 188 F. 2d 783, 786-88 (2d Cir. 1951).

[204] See 3 Loss 1788-89.

[205] 459 U. S. at 378 n. 2.

[206] Landis, Liability Sections of Securities Act, 18 Am. Accountant 330, 331 (1933). See also Douglas and Bates, The Federal Securities Act of 1933, 43 Yale L. J. 171, 181-82 (1933), where the authors queried "whether the making of an act unlawful by the Act gives to purchasers an action of rescission on the grounds of illegality," but stated that it seemed clear by negative implication from §§11 and 12 that §17 probably does not enlarge the civil remedies of purchasers.

> §12(1). Faulty compliance results in liability under §11. And §17(a) has its counterpart in §12(2). It all makes a rather neat pattern. Within the area of §§5 and 17(a), §§11 and 12 (unlike §§9(e), 16(b) and 18 of the 1934 act) are all-embracing. This is not to say that the remedies afforded by §§11 and 12 are complete. But the very restrictions contained in those sections and the differences between them — for example, the fact that §11 but not §12 imposes liability on certain persons connected with the issuer without regard to their participation in the offering and the fact that §12(2) does not go so far in relation to §17(a) as §12(1) goes in relation to §5 — make it seem the less justifiable to permit plaintiffs to circumvent the limitations of §12 by resort to §17(a). Particularly is this so in view of the fact that §11, together with the statute of limitations in §13, was actually tightened in the 1934 amendments to the Securities Act.[207]

Judge Friendly, in his concurring opinion in *Texas Gulf Sulphur,* took the position that §17 was not intended to be the basis of any private actions; that, on the other hand, there seemed little practical point in denying a private action under §17 once it was established that a buyer had an action under Rule 10b-5, "with the important proviso that fraud, as distinct from mere negligence, must be alleged"; and that to go further "would totally undermine the carefully framed limitations imposed on the buyer's right to recover granted by §12(2) of the 1933 Act."[208]

Finally, in 1979, on a background of conflict of authority, the Second Circuit concluded flatly, with no analysis, that "the language of §17 is broad enough to imply a private right of action."[209]

[207] 3 Loss 1785; see, e. g., Dyer v. Eastern Trust & Banking Co., 336 F. Supp. 890, 904-05 (D. Me. 1971); Hill v. Der, 521 F. Supp. 1370, 1373-78 (D. Del. 1981); Bruns v. Ledbetter, 583 F. Supp. 1050, 1054 (S. D. Cal. 1984); In re Fortune Systems Securities Litigation, 604 F. Supp. 150, 156 (N. D. Cal. 1984); Mann v. Oppenheimer & Co., 517 A. 2d 1056, 1066 (Del. 1986). It is noteworthy, too, that §15 imposes liability on persons who control those liable under §11 or 12, without mention of §17.

[208] SEC v. Texas Gulf Sulphur Co., 401 F. 2d 833, 867-68 (2d Cir. 1968), *cert. denied* sub nom. Coates v. SEC and Kline v. SEC, 394 U. S. 976. And this view was widely followed. E. g., Sanders v. John Nuveen & Co., Inc., 554 F. 2d 790, 795-96 (7th Cir. 1977).

[209] Kirshner v. United States, 603 F. 2d 234, 241 (2d Cir. 1978); see also Newman v. Prior, 518 F. 2d 97, 99 (4th Cir. 1975); Daniel v. International Brotherhood of Teamsters, 561 F. 2d 1223, 1245 (7th Cir. 1977), *rev'd on other grounds* sub nom. International Brotherhood of Teamsters v. Daniel, 439 U. S. 551 (1979); Stephenson v. Calpine Conifers II, Ltd., 652 F. 2d 808, 815 (9th Cir. 1981). *Contra:* Shull v. Dain, Kalman & Quail, Inc., 561 F. 2d 152, 159 (8th Cir. 1971), *cert. denied,* 434 U. S. 1086; Landry v. All American Assurance Co., 688 F. 2d 381, 389-91 (5th Cir. 1982); Mann v. Oppenheimer & Co., 517 A. 2d 1056, 1063-66 (Del. 1986).

In Zerman v. Ball, 735 F. 2d 15, 20 (2d Cir. 1984), the court, rather strangely

It would be wrong to assume that §17(a) adds nothing to Rule 10b-5: Arguably §17(a), like Rule 10b-5, is not limited to §12's rescission measure of damages.[210] Indeed, there is no bar to punitive damages as there is under the 1934 Act.[211] The plaintiff is guaranteed access to a state court if he prefers it.[212] Section 17(a)'s "in the *offer* or sale" may be broader than §10(b)'s "in connection with the purchase or sale."[213] And — most importantly — the scienter that is required under Rule 10b-5 because of the "deceptive" language of §10(b) is not required under §17(a)(2) or (3).[214]

---

in light of *Kirshner,* seems to have treated the question as open. And in Yoder v. Orthomolecular Nutritional Institute, Inc., 751 F. 2d 555, 559 n. 3 (2d Cir. 1985), Judge Friendly, referring to the text's treatment (at pp. 977-78) and its characterization of *Kirshner* as being "with no analysis" as well as the Supreme Court's later reservation of the question, stated *obiter* that the *Kirshner* conclusion "may be open to reexamination."

The case against implication may be a *bit* stronger under Clauses (1) and (3) because of the lesser resemblance of their fraud language to §12(2) as compared with the misstatement language of Clause (2). See Dorfman v. First Boston Corp., 336 F. Supp. 1089, 1093-96 (E. D. Pa. 1972); Demoe v. Dean Witter & Co., 476 F. Supp. 275 (D. Alaska 1979) (just Clause (3)). In re Diasonics Securities Litigation, 599 F. Supp. 447, 462 (N. D. Cal. 1984), read the *Stephenson* language as limited to cases where fraud is alleged; and In re Fortune Systems Securities Litigation, 604 F. Supp. 150, 152-58 (N. D. Cal. 1984), considered that language to be dictum. See also Brabham v. Patenta N. V., 614 F. Supp. 568 (D. Ore. 1985).

[210] Dorfman v. First Boston Corp., 336 F. Supp. 1089, 1096 (E. D. Pa. 1972).

[211] See p. 973 supra. Nevertheless, *in pari materia* argues powerfully for extending the 1934 Act's ban to the 1933 Act. See Globus v. Law Research Service, Inc., 418 F. 2d 1276, 1283-87 (2d Cir. 1969), *cert. denied,* 397 U. S. 913; deHaas v. Empire Petroleum Co., 435 F. 2d 1223, 1229-32 (10th Cir. 1971).

[212] Compare Sec. Act §22(a) with Sec. Ex. Act §27.

[213] In Blue Chip Stamps v. Manor Drug Stores, 421 U. S. 723, 733-34 (1975), supra p. 792, the Court buttressed its point that the 10b-5 plaintiff must be a buyer or seller by pointing to this contrast. See Wulc v. Gulf & Western Industries, Inc., 400 F. Supp. 99 (E. D. Pa. 1975); Reid v. Madison, 438 F. Supp. 332 (E. D. Va. 1977); Doll v. James Martin Associates (Holdings), Ltd., 600 F. Supp. 510, 523-24 (E. D. Mich. 1984). This may be a way around *Blue Chip* if there is indeed a private action under §17(a) — a question that the *Blue Chip* Court expressly reserved (421 U. S. at 733 n. 6), presumably because the plaintiff had relied solely on Rule 10b-5.

[214] Aaron v. SEC, 446 U. S. 680 (1980), supra p. 783. In Hudson v. Capital Management Int'l, Inc., CCH Fed. Sec. L. Rep. ¶99,222 at 95,901 (N. D. Cal. 1982), *on reconsideration,* 565 F. Supp. 615, 625-27 (N. D. Cal. 1983), the court said that §17(a) civil liability "introduces a negligence standard into the realm of securities law unprotected by the procedural safeguards surrounding the other negligence actions. * * * This court finds this result absurd, but it is compelled by precedent to so rule." The court certified the case for interlocutory review, which the Ninth Circuit rejected. Thereupon the District Court reconsidered its previous ruling and decided that application of the analysis of legislative intent mandated by the Supreme Court compelled the conclusion that there was no private right of action under §17(a). See also Dannenberg v. Dorison, 603

This is perhaps the best reason for restricting §17(a) to public proceedings. For, unless the courts are willing to write §12(2)'s due care defense into §17(a), the result would seem to be the strict liability for misstatements that Congress imposed in only one case — the issuer when sued under §11.[215]

All this led to the statement in a 1974 case (and the confusion is certainly no less today): "It is the necessity of dealing with such issues, which cannot be resolved satisfactorily, that reflects the need for prompt enactment of the proposed federal securities code."[216]

4. What of §11's pale sister, §18 of the 1934 Act?[217] That section has been held not to preclude 10b-5 actions for false filings.[218] But implied actions — to the extent they are allowed at all under the tender offer provisions, §§13(d), 13(e), 14(d), and 14(e) — might meet a roadblock under §18 on the ground that none of them requires scienter as Rule 10b-5 does.[219] The Second Circuit has concluded that liability for negligent misstatements or omissions in violation of Rule 14a-9, the proxy fraud rule, is not inconsistent with §18, because §14(a) is specifically directed at proxy regulation and most documents within §18 are not distributed to stockholders for the purpose of inducing action.[220] But the Supreme Court, as we have seen, has taken a narrower view of implied actions with respect to tender offers than with respect to proxy solicitations.[221]

As Justice Marshall said in *Herman & MacLean*, "it is hardly a novel proposition that the Securities Exchange Act and the Securities Act 'prohibit some of the same conduct.' "[222] In the *Naftalin* case,[223] there cited, the Court applied §17(a) of the 1933 Act to "ordinary market trading" despite the contention that that was the

---

F. Supp. 1238, 1241 n. 5 (S. D. N. Y. 1985). *Contra:* Onesti v. Thomson McKinnon Securities, Inc., 619 F. Supp. 1262, 1266-67 (N. D. Ill. 1985).

[215] It was on this reasoning that the court in Baker v. Eagle Aircraft Co., 642 F. Supp. 1005 (D. Ore. 1986), implied a private right of action only under §17(a)(1).

[216] Crowell v. Pittsburgh & Lake Erie R. R., 373 F. Supp. 1303, 1310 (E. D. Pa. 1974).

[217] See p. 922 supra.

[218] Ross v. A. H. Robins Co., Inc., 607 F. 2d 545 (2d Cir. 1979); Wachovia Bank & Trust Co. v. National Student Marketing Corp., 650 F. 2d 342, 356-57 (D. C. Cir. 1980).

[219] Would-be §13(d) plaintiffs must also meet §18's purchaser or seller requirement. Myers v. American Leisure Time Enterprises, Inc., 402 F. Supp. 213 (S. D. N. Y. 1975), *aff'd without opinion,* 538 F. 2d 312 (2d Cir. 1976); W. A. Krueger Co. v. Kirkpatrick, Pettis, Smith, Polian, Inc., 466 F. Supp. 800, 803 (D. Neb. 1979).

[220] Gerstle v. Gamble-Skogmo, Inc., 478 F. 2d 1281, 1299 n. 18 (2d Cir. 1973).

[221] See pp. 953-54 supra.

[222] 459 U. S. at 383.

[223] United States v. Naftalin, 441 U. S. 768, 778 (1979).

province of Rule 10b-5 and that §17(a) should be limited to distributions. In the *National Securities* case,[224] also cited by Justice Marshall, the Court applied Rule 10b-5 to a merger of two insurance companies notwithstanding the inapplicability of the proxy rules because the companies did not then have any registered securities. Similarly, since it has long been clear that §17(a) did not *pro tanto* repeal the mail fraud statute,[225] dismissal of a §17(a) count for failure to allege a "security" surely would not prevent a mail fraud conviction for the same transaction. And it has been held that Rule 10b-5 can stand independently of the express civil liability provision in §9(e) of the 1934 Act for market manipulation in violation of §9(a)-(c).[226]

5. The clash between §11 and Rule 10b-5 caused the only bad split among the persons who produced the Code. With the Code's shift from securities to company registration and continuous reporting, some thought it would be anomalous to retain the Code's §11 successor, §1704, for the basic company registration statement and the occasional offering statement (today's registration statement) while the filed annual report (the "10-K"), which would be the Code's central disclosure document, would be subject only to the milder 10b-5 type of liability under Code §1705. Others objected to the necessity of practicing §11-type "due diligence" every year. The upshot was that the Institute took no position on the question and that the version of the Code that survived the subsequent negotiations with the Commission is a compromise that retains §11's multiple defendants, with the burden of going forward on them, but changes the defense from today's elaborate scheme based essentially on a negligence standard to proof of *lack of scienter*[227] and adds a new provision that simply makes it unlawful (without any civil liability) for a director to sign a filed annual report without "a reasonable investigation of its contents."[228]

5. Margin Rules

"There is something about the idea of allowing recovery to a customer who would have enjoyed greater profits as a result of the excessive credit he received if the market had moved in his favor —

[224] SEC v. National Securities, Inc., 393 U. S. 453, 468 (1969).
[225] Edwards v. United States, 312 U. S. 473, 483-84 (1941).
[226] Schaefer v. First National Bank of Lincolnwood, 509 F. 2d 1287, 1292 (7th Cir. 1975), *cert. denied,* 425 U. S. 943; Chemetron Corp. v. Business Funds, Inc., 718 F. 2d 725 (5th Cir. 1983).
[227] See 2 Code 703-18; 2 id. (2d Supp. 1981) 75-78.
[228] §2003(c)(4).

or who complains that the broker should have sold him out promptly when he did not pay in time — that causes the judicial gorge to rise."[229] Nevertheless, the Second Circuit was able to say by 1970 that "It has long been settled that a person for whom a broker [or presumably a bank or, under Regulation G, anybody else] has unlawfully arranged credit has a private right of action," whether in tort or under §29(b) of the 1934 Act.[230] And the 1970s produced a number of square appellate holdings.[231]

All this predated both the 1970 enactment of 7(f), which for the first time made it unlawful to *borrow* in violation of Federal Reserve rules,[232] and the Supreme Court's teaching in *Cort* v. *Ash*[233] and its sequelae.[234] All six Circuits to decide the question since are in the negative.[235]

Other possibilities remain. Section 29(b) — applied by the Supreme Court in *Transamerica*[236] — makes rescission (as distinct from damages) available both offensively[237] and defensively.[238] And a violation of the Federal Reserve rules is apt to entail a violation also of the margin rules, and perhaps other rules, of the particular stock exchange. On the assumption that neither a federal tort action nor

[229]See 2 Code 759 and cases cited.

[230]Junger v. Hertz, Neumark & Warner, 426 F. 2d 805, 806 (1970), *cert. denied,* 400 U. S. 880.

[231]See cases cited in 2 Code 759.

[232]See p. 660 supra.

[233]422 U. S. 66 (1975), supra p. 930.

[234]See pp. 931-37 supra.

[235]Bennett v. U. S. Trust Co. of N. Y., 770 F. 2d 308, 311-13 (2d Cir. 1985), *cert. denied,* 106 S. Ct. 800, and cases cited. See Comment, Civil Liability for Margin Violations — The Effect of Section 7(f) and Regulation X, 43 Ford. L. Rev. 93 (1964). For the opposite view, see Solomon and Hart, Recent Developments in the Regulation of Securities Credit, 20 J. Pub. L. 167, 209 (1971); Note, Regulation X and Investor-Lender Margin Violation Disputes, 57 Minn. L. Rev. 208 (1972). On the old cases' treatment of *in pari delicto,* measure of damages, and causation, see 2 Code 1154-56.

[236]Transamerica Mortgage Advisors, Inc. v. Lewis, 444 U. S. 11 (1979), supra p. 935. See Supp. p. 1052, end 1st sentence, supra.

[237]First Ala. Bancshares, Inc. v. Lowder, CCH Fed. Sec. L. Rep. ¶98,015 at 91,251-52 (N. D. Ala. 1981) (dictum); see also pp. 940-41 supra, p. 987 infra; but cf. Bassler v. Central National Bank in Chicago, 715 F. 2d 308 (7th Cir. 1983), supra p. 914 n. 7. This assumes privity of contract between plaintiff and defendant. In Natkin v. Exchange National Bank of Chicago, 342 F. 2d 675 (7th Cir. 1965), plaintiffs who delivered stock to one who used it as collateral in a loan transaction with a bank that allegedly violated Regulation U stated no cause of action against the bank on the basis of its wrongful conversion of the stock.

[238]Goldenberg v. Bache & Co., 270 F. 2d 675, 681 (5th Cir. 1959) (broker's counterclaim); In the Matter of Naftalin & Co., Inc. v. Merrill Lynch, Pierce, Fenner & Smith, Inc., 469 F. 2d 1166, 1180-82 (8th Cir. 1972); Johnson, Lane, Space, Smith & Co., Inc. v. Lenny, 129 Ga. App. 55, 198 S. E. 2d 923 (1973); Staley v. Salvesen, 35 Pa. D. & C. 2d 318, 321 (C. P. 1963).

an action under §29(b) would lie on the basis of the exchange rules themselves,[239] the borrower might bring an action *ex contractu* under state law "based on the contract between stockbroker and customer as affected by the federal statute and regulations."[240] That is to say the usages of the marketplace — which should certainly include the federal margin rules along with the rules and customs of the exchange — are an implied term of the contract[241] even if the contract establishing the margin account does not expressly provide (as it typically does) that the contract is subject to all applicable federal, state, and exchange rules.[242]

6. Self-Regulatory Organization Rules

Not long after the Second Circuit (speaking through Judge Friendly) left the door ajar in a 1966 case,[243] the Seventh Circuit flung it wide open in recognizing (at least *obiter*) an action for violation of the New York Stock Exchange's Rule 405, the "know your customer" rule, which it assumed was a rule required by the then §6 of the 1934 Act.[244] And the intervening two decades or so have produced cases both ways under a great variety of self-regulatory organization rules.[245]

[239] See pp. 983-85 infra.

[240] Goldenberg v. Bache & Co., 270 F. 2d 675, 680 (5th Cir. 1959). But the Fifth Circuit later declined to permit use of the exchange rules "by a knowing beneficiary [of the rules] as a dagger against his perhaps too lenient broker." McCormick v. Esposito, 500 F. 2d 620, 628 (5th Cir. 1974), *cert. denied*, 420 U. S. 912; see also Gordon v. duPont Glore Forgan, Inc., 487 F. 2d 1260 (5th Cir. 1973), *cert. denied*, 417 U. S. 946; cf. Meckel v. Continental Resources Co., 758 F. 2d 811, 818 (2d Cir. 1985) (debenture holders were not third-party beneficiaries of New York Stock Exchange Company Manual and issuer's listing agreement).

[241] See p. 1025 n. 87 infra.

[242] In Monetary Management Group of St. Louis, Inc. v. Kidder, Peabody & Co., Inc., 615 F. Supp. 1217, 1221-23 (E. D. Mo. 1985), the court sustained an action under §12(2) of the 1933 Act for misstating the eligibility of certain bonds for credit under Regulation T.

[243] Colonial Realty Corp. v. Bache & Co., 358 F. 2d 178 (2d Cir. 1966), *cert. denied*, 385 U. S. 817 (basic NYSE and NASD rules on ethical conduct).

[244] Buttrey v. Merrill Lynch, Pierce, Fenner & Smith, Inc., 410 F. 2d 135 (1969), *cert. denied*, 396 U. S. 838.

[245] *Pro:* Avern Trust v. Clarke, 415 F. 2d 1238, 1242 (7th Cir. 1969), *cert. denied*, 387 U. S. 963 (dictum on NASD suitability rule); SEC v. First Securities Co. of Chicago, 463 F. 2d 981, 988 (7th Cir. 1972), *cert. denied* sub nom. McKy v. Hochfelder, 409 U. S. 880 (NASD rule requiring members' supervision of their representatives); Landy v. FDIC, 486 F. 2d 139, 164-67 (3d Cir. 1973), *cert. denied*, 416 U. S. 960 (dictum *re* NYSE Rule 405); Van Gemert v. Boeing Co., 520 F. 2d 1373 (2d Cir. 1975), *cert. denied*, 423 U. S. 947 (violation of NYSE listing agreement and section of Company Manual); Hughes v. Dempsey-Tegeler & Co., Inc., 534 F. 2d 156, 173 (9th Cir. 1976), *cert. denied*, 429 U. S.

Nobody has suggested foreclosing *all* federal actions under self-regulatory organization rules, if only because of the sometimes fortuitous choice of quasi-legislator as between one of those bodies and the SEC; the readiest example, cited by Judge Friendly himself,[246] is the NYSE rule on the voting of "street name" stock, which apparently had caused the Commission to terminate a rulemaking proceeding of its own under §14(b) of the 1934 Act. On the other hand, Judge Friendly also drew attention to the consequences of too ready a recognition of federal actions in terms of (1) saddling the federal courts with garden-variety customer-broker suits, (2) the

---

896 (NYSE Constitution, Art. XIII, requiring suspension of member firm in unsafe condition, and Rule 325, the debt-capital ratio rule); Sacks v. Reynolds Securities, Inc., 593 F. 2d 1234, 1241-42 (D. C. Cir. 1978) (NYSE Rule 412 on transfer of accounts to another firm); Krome v. Merrill Lynch & Co., Inc., 637 F. Supp. 910, 917-18 (S. D. N. Y. 1986) (NASD rule pursuant to Inv. Co. Act §22, supra p. 50), *vacated in part on other grounds,* 110 F. R. D. 693 (S. D. N. Y. 1986).

Contra: Carras v. Burns, 516 F. 2d 251, 260 (4th Cir. 1975) (exchange margin maintenance rules were designed primarily to protect solvency of members); Hayden v. Walston & Co., Inc., 528 F. 2d 901 (9th Cir. 1975) (NASD rule requiring registration of representatives); Jablon v. Dean Witter & Co., 614 F. 2d 677 (9th Cir. 1980) (NASD suitability rule and NYSE "know your customer" rule); State Teachers Retirement Board v. Fluor Corp., 654 F. 2d 843, 852-53 (2d Cir. 1981) (NYSE Company Manual section requiring immediate announcement of unusual market activity); Redstone v. Goldman, Sachs & Co., Inc., 583 F. Supp. 74, 77 (D. Mass. 1983) (rules of Municipal Securities Rulemaking Board); Chapman v. Merrill Lynch, Pierce, Fenner & Smith, Inc., CCH Fed. Sec. L. Rep. ¶99,419 at 96,407-09 (D. Md. 1983) (court refused to imply action for violation of rules of NYSE and NASD even when fraud was alleged).

Cf. Sanders v. John Nuveen & Co., Inc., 554 F. 2d 790, 796-97 (7th Cir. 1977) (in holding that NASD rule requiring members' suspension of their representatives did not support a private action without a finding of fraud, court was "mindful of the admonition in *Colonial* [supra p. 983 n. 243] against adopting a simplistic all-or-nothing approach in deciding whether a private civil damage action exists"); Utah State University of Agriculture & Applied Science v. Bear, Stearns & Co., 549 F. 2d 164, 167-69 (10th Cir. 1977), *cert. denied,* 434 U. S. 890 (something "tantamount to fraud" must be shown for NASD suitability rule and NYSE "know your customer" rule to give rise to a private action); Shull v. Dain, Kalman & Quail, Inc., 561 F. 2d 152 (8th Cir. 1977), *cert. denied,* 434 U. S. 1086 (no action for breach of Chicago Mercantile Exchange rule without finding of fraud); Walck v. American Stock Exchange, Inc., 687 F. 2d 778, 788 (3d Cir. 1982), *cert. denied,* 461 U. S. 942 ("no basis for an inference that the Exchanges in their quasi-legislative capacity intended to subject *themselves* [italics supplied] to damages for non-enforcement"); Brawer v. Options Clearing Corp., 807 F. 2d 297 (2d Cir. 1986) (if private actions against exchange or clearinghouse for violation of §§6 and 17A exist at all, they require proof of fraud or bad faith).

[246] Colonial Realty Corp. v. Bache & Co., 358 F. 2d 178, 182 n. 4 (2d Cir. 1966), *cert. denied,* 385 U. S. 817.

outlawing of enforced arbitration,[247] and (3) the ousting of state courts because of the exclusive federal jurisdiction of §27.

As with respect to the Federal Reserve margin rules, there is the possibility also of the courts' considering applicable self-regulatory organization rules in measuring a member's duty in a common law action.[248]

7. Investment Company Act

Quite apart from restitutional possibilities under the voidability provision in §47(b) of the Investment Company Act,[249] liability has repeatedly been implied for violation of various provisions of that statute.[250] These holdings extended even to the original §36, which made nothing unlawful but simply authorized the appropriate District Court, at the instance of the Commission, to enjoin an investment company officer, director, or adviser (among others) from continuing to act in any of those capacities on a finding of "gross misconduct or gross abuse of trust."[251] The Second Circuit has held that this liability survives both (1) the 1970 addition of a

[247] This, of course, is no longer a consideration. See App. D infra.

[248] Mercury Investment Co. v. A. G. Edwards & Sons, 295 F. Supp. 1160 (S. D. Tex. 1969); Cash v. Frederick & Co., Inc., 57 F. R. D. 71, 78 (E. D. Wis. 1972); Piper, Jaffray & Hopwood, Inc. v. Ladin, 399 F. Supp. 292, 298 (S. D. Iowa 1975); Lange v. H. Hentz & Co., 418 F. Supp. 1376, 1383-84 (N. D. Tex. 1976); Miley v. Oppenheimer & Co., 637 F. 2d 318, 333 (5th Cir. 1981) (violation of NYSE and NASD suitability rules as one factor in determining whether account had been churned); Petrites v. J. C. Bradford & Co., 646 F. 2d 1033, 1034 n. 1 (5th Cir. 1981); Berk v. Oppenheimer & Co., Inc., CCH Fed. Sec. L. Rep. ¶99,603 at 97,371 (N. D. Ill. 1983); FDIC v. NASD, 582 F. Supp. 72, 74 (S. D. Iowa 1984), *aff'd per curiam*, 747 F. 2d 498 (8th Cir. 1984).

[249] See, e. g., Esplin v. Hirschi, 402 F. 2d 94, 103-04 (10th Cir. 1968), *cert. denied*, 394 U. S. 928. In Brown v. Bullock, 194 F. Supp. 207, 231-32 (S. D. N. Y. 1961), *aff'd*, 294 F. 2d 415 (2d Cir. 1961), §47(b) was applied to a "proxy contract." See also Mills v. Electric Auto-Lite Co., 396 U. S. 375, 387 (1970) (dictum).

[250] E. g., Taussig v. Wellington Fund, Inc., 313 F. 2d 472, 476 (3d Cir. 1963), *cert. denied*, 374 U. S. 806; Levitt v. Johnson, 334 F. 2d 815 (1st Cir. 1964), *cert. denied*, 379 U. S. 961; Meyer v. Oppenheimer Management Corp., 764 F. 2d 76, 85-88 (2d Cir. 1985). *Contra:* Brouk v. Managed Funds, Inc., 286 F. 2d 901 (8th Cir. 1961), *vacated pursuant to settlement*, 369 U. S. 424 (1962); M. J. Whitman & Co., Inc. Pension Plan v. American Financial Enterprises, Inc., 552 F. Supp. 17 (S. D. Ohio 1982), *aff'd on other grounds*, 725 F. 2d 394 (6th Cir. 1984). These are the only *contra* authorities, and the Eighth Circuit in Greater Iowa Corp. v. McLendon, 378 F. 2d 783 (8th Cir. 1967), stated *obiter* that *Brouk* was probably inconsistent with *Borak*, supra p. 927.

[251] E. g., Moses v. Burgin, 445 F. 2d 369, 373 (1st Cir. 1971), *cert. denied* sub nom. Johnson v. Moses, 404 U. S. 994.

§36(b),[252] which creates an express private right of action for a "breach of fiduciary duty" with respect to compensation,[253] and (2) *Transamerica*'s denial of damages (as distinct from rescission under §47(b)) for violation of the Advisers Act.[254] But questions of individual standing remain.[255]

[252]Tannenbaum v. Zeller, 552 F. 2d 402, 417 (2d Cir. 1977), *cert. denied* sub nom. F. Eberstadt & Co. v. Tannenbaum, 434 U. S. 934; Krinsk v. Fund Asset Management, Inc., 654 F. Supp. 1227, 1232 (S. D. N. Y. 1987) ("except where [the] claim amounts to nothing more than a claim for recoupment of excessive compensation such as Congress intended to be brought under §36(b)"). *Contra:* Tarlov v. Paine Webber Cashfund, Inc., 559 F. Supp. 429, 437 (D. Conn. 1983) (court also dismissed a count for rescission under §47 on the ground that §36(b) was intended to be exclusive). The original §36 became §36(a), which now refers to "a breach of fiduciary duty involving personal misconduct."

[253]See Galfand v. Chestnutt, 545 F. 2d 807 (2d Cir. 1976); Grossman v. Johnson, 674 F. 2d 115 (1st Cir. 1982), *cert. denied* sub nom. Grossman v. Fidelity Municipal Bond Fund, Inc., 459 U. S. 838.

In Daily Income Fund, Inc. v. Fox, 464 U. S. 523 (1984), the Court held that, since F. R. Civ. P. 23.1 governed a derivative action only if brought to enforce "a right of a corporation," and since §36(b) gave an express right of action only to the Commission or a security holder, not to the investment company itself, and since the *Cort* formula did not permit an *implied* right of action, a shareholder suing under §36(b) did not first have to make a demand on the directors.

Since a §36(b) action would have been considered as arising in equity before the 1935 merger of law and equity, there is no right to trial by jury. In re Gartenberg, 636 F. 2d 16 (2d Cir. 1980), *cert. denied* sub nom. Gartenberg v. Pollack, 451 U. S. 910; In re Evangelist, 760 F. 2d 27 (1st Cir. 1985).

In Schuyt v. Rowe Price Prime Reserve Fund, Inc., 622 F. Supp. 169 (S. D. N. Y. 1985), the court held that it was possible to join a claim under §20(a), the proxy provision, with a claim under §36(b).

[254]Transamerica Mortgage Advisors, Inc. v. Lewis, 444 U. S. 11 (1979), supra p. 913; see also S. Rep. No. 91-184 (1969) 16; H. R. Rep. No. 91-1382 (1969) 38.

[255]In General Time Corp. v. American Investors Fund, Inc., 283 F. Supp. 400, 401-02 (S. D. N. Y. 1968), *aff'd* sub nom. General Time Corp. v. Talley Industries, Inc., 403 F. 2d 159 (2d Cir. 1968), *cert. denied,* 393 U. S. 1026, the court held that a company that was the subject of a takeover bid by an investment company had no standing to assert violations of §§17(d) and 13(a)(3) of the Investment Company Act. As Judge Bryan there noticed (283 F. Supp. at 402 n. 4), there was an earlier case in which the court issued a preliminary injunction, at the instance of a corporation threatened with a takeover bid, against the defendant's violation of the registration provision of the Investment Company Act, but the question of standing was assumed without discussion. Natco Corp. v. Great Lakes Industries, Inc., 214 F. Supp. 185 (W. D. Pa. 1962), *remanded for dismissal, apparently pursuant to settlement,* CCH Fed. Sec. L. Rep. ¶91,236 (3d Cir. 1963). The appellate court in *General Time* expressly disavowed passing on the point. 403 F. 2d at 164. But the same panel soon acknowledged in a related appeal that its earlier decision "would better have been placed" on Judge Bryan's conclusion. SEC v. General Time Corp., 407 F. 2d 65, 71 (2d Cir. 1968), *cert. denied,* 393 U. S. 1026; see also Greater Iowa Corp. v. McLendon, 378 F. 2d 783 (8th Cir. 1967); Herpich v. Wallace, 430 F. 2d 792 (5th Cir. 1970) (no standing in stockholder of *portfolio* company); but cf. Independent

8. Miscellaneous Implied Liabilities

We have noticed the principal areas of implied liability under the SEC statutes. But other provisions have given rise to civil liability on one theory or another.[256] For example, the Fifth Circuit has twice applied §29(b) of the 1934 Act to broker-dealers doing business without registration in violation of §15(a).[257] The cases are in the affirmative under Rule 10b-16, the margin credit rule.[258] And we have earlier noticed the recent cases under the Trust Indenture Act[259] as well as the voidability provision of the Advisers Act.[260]

Investor Protective League v. SEC, 495 F. 2d 311 (2d Cir. 1974) (*non sequitur* that *only* investors in an investment company have standing).

[256] For a comprehensive list of cases both recognizing and rejecting implied liabilities, see 2 Code 775-79.

[257] Eastside Church of Christ v. National Plan, Inc., 391 F. 2d 357 (5th Cir. 1968), *cert. denied* sub nom. Church of Christ v. National Plan, Inc., 393 U. S. 913, *judgment for plaintiff on remand aff'd* sub nom. McGregor Blvd. Church of Christ v. Walling, 428 F. 2d 401 (5th Cir. 1970); Regional Properties, Inc. v. Financial & Real Estate Consulting Co., 678 F. 2d 552 (5th Cir. 1982), *after remand*, 752 F. 2d 178 (5th Cir. 1985); see also Davis v. Avco Corp., 371 F. Supp. 782, 789 (N. D. Ohio 1974).

Contra: SEC v. Seaboard Corp. (Admiralty Fund v. Hugh Johnson & Co., Inc.), 677 F. 2d 1301, 1309 (9th Cir. 1982); Bull v. American Bank & Trust Co., 363 F. Supp. 202, 207, CCH Fed. Sec. L. Rep. ¶92,545 (E. D. Pa. 1986). There is also a line of cases in the Southern District of New York that attempts to draw a distinction between an "unlawful contract" and an "unlawful transaction" that is "collateral or tangential" to the contract. Slomiak v. Bear Stearns & Co., 597 F. Supp. 676, 681-83 (S. D. N. Y. 1984); see also Drasner v. Thomson McKinnon Securities, Inc., 433 F. Supp. 485 (S. D. N. Y. 1977); Palmer v. Thomson & McKinnon Auchincloss, Inc., 474 F. Supp. 286, 291 (D. Conn. 1977); Zerman v. Jacobs, 510 F. Supp. 132 (S. D. N. Y. 1981), *aff'd on other grounds*, 672 F. 2d 901 (2d Cir. 1981); Rhoades v. Powell, 644 F. Supp. 645, 664 (E. D. Cal. 1986).

[258] Liang v. Dean Witter & Co., 540 F. 2d 1107, 1113 n. 25 (D. C. Cir. 1976) (dictum); Robertson v. Dean Witter Reynolds, Inc., 749 F. 2d 530, 534-39 (9th Cir. 1984); Angelastro v. Prudential-Bache Securities, Inc., 764 F. 2d 939, 948-50 (3d Cir. 1985), *cert. denied*, 106 S. Ct. 267; Finne v. Dain Bosworth, Inc., 648 F. Supp. 337 (D. Minn. 1986); Baum v. Phillips, Appel & Walden, Inc., 648 F. Supp. 1518, 1527 (S. D. N. Y. 1986).

Contra: Establissement Tomis v. Shearson, Hayden Stone, Inc., 459 F. Supp. 1355 (S. D. N. Y. 1980); cf. Greenblatt v. Drexel Burnham Lambert, Inc., 763 F. 2d 1352, 1358 n. 8 (11th Cir. 1985) (*dictum* that, since any cause of action existing under the rule could arise only under §10(b) of the statute, the only violations of the rule that could possibly create a private action would be those arising out of the purchase or sale of securities). Moreover, recognizing implied liability under Rule 10b-16 does not require that "courts should automatically imply a private action under every rule validly promulgated pursuant to section 10(b)." Robertson v. Dean Witter Reynolds, Inc., supra, at 537. "* * * the SEC might clearly intend to prohibit private actions under a particular rule." Ibid.

[259] See p. 37 n. 4 supra.

[260] See pp. 913-14, 940-41, 987 supra.

On the other hand, except apparently for only one 1963 case,[261] the courts have concluded that implication of a private action under §13(a) of the 1934 Act for false reports is precluded by §18(a).[262] And there are cases both ways under §15(c)(1) of the 1934 Act.[263]

All these affirmative cases, particularly those decided before the recent Supreme Court decisions, must be reassessed in the light of those holdings.[264]

I. STATUTES OF LIMITATIONS

1. Express Liabilities

a. The Prescribed Periods

Section 13 of the 1933 Act provides a double-barreled statute of limitations for all three civil liability provisions in that statute.[1] With

[261] Kroese v. Crawford, CCH Fed. Sec. L. Rep. ¶91,262 (S. D. N. Y. 1963).

[262] See 2 Code 776; cf. Eisenberger v. Spectex Industries, Inc., 644 F. Supp. 48 (E. D. N. Y. 1986) (§13(b)(2) requirement that certain issuers maintain books in conformity with accepted accounting criteria); cf. also p. 980 supra. In Westinghouse Credit Corp. v. Bader & Dufty, 627 F. 2d 221, 224 (10th Cir. 1980), the court held that one company had no standing to seek an injunction against another company's offering certain securities unless they were registered under §5 of the 1933 Act and §13(a) reports were filed simply because the plaintiff wanted to use the information to defend a state court action brought by the second company; for the reporting requirements were designed to protect the investing public. In ScienTex Corp. v. Kay, 689 F. 2d 879 (9th Cir. 1982), the court rejected an implied mandatory injunction action to require the filing of ownership reports under §16(a) of the 1934 Act.

[263] For a series of District Court cases implying liability under §15(c)(1), see 3 and 6 Loss, c. 11C n. 253; see also Speck v. Oppenheimer & Co., 583 F. Supp. 325, 330 (W. D. Mo. 1984). *Contra:* SEC v. Seaboard Corp. (Admiralty Fund v. Hugh Johnson & Co., Inc.), 677 F. 2d 1301, 1313-14 (9th Cir. 1982) (reference to §15 generally with very little discussion); Pierson v. Dean Witter Reynolds, Inc., 551 F. Supp. 497, 502-03 (C. D. Ill. 1982) (because §15(c)(1) is largely coterminous with §10(b), it would not further the purpose of the regulatory framework to allow an action under §15(c)(1)); Chapman v. Merrill Lynch, Pierce, Fenner & Smith, Inc., CCH Fed. Sec. L. Rep. ¶99,419 at 96,409 (D. Md. 1983); Wagman v. FSC Securities Corp., CCH Fed. Sec. L. Rep. ¶92,445 at 92,716 (N. D. Ill. 1985); Baum v. Phillips, Appel & Walden, Inc., 648 F. Supp. 1518, 1529 (S. D. N. Y. 1986), and cases cited; Roberts v. Smith Barney, Harris Upham & Co., Inc., 653 F. Supp. 406, 413-15 (D. Mass. 1987). The *contra* courts did not note the statute of limitations for §15(c)(1) actions in §29(b) (see p. 941).

[264] See Walck v. American Stock Exchange, Inc., 687 F. 2d 778, 786-88 (3d Cir. 1982), *cert. denied,* 461 U. S. 942, where the court rejected the holding in Baird v. Franklin, 141 F. 2d 238 (2d Cir. 1944), *cert. denied,* 323 U. S. 737, of an exchange's implied liability for violation of §6(b) of the 1934 Act (as it stood before the 1975 amendments) in failing to enforce its own rules. See also Gustafson v. Strangis, 572 F. Supp. 1154 (D. Minn. 1983) (no action against NASD).

C. 10I [1] That is to say, the one-year and three-year provisions are cumulative.

respect to §12(1) it is one year after the alleged violation of §5 and three years after the security was "*bona fide* offered to the public."[2] Presumably this means *first* offered to the public.[3] The courts are divided on the question whether the one-year period is subject to either the discovery rule or equitable tolling for fraudulent concealment.[4] In any event, the statute does not begin to run until whichever of the defendant's activities — offer, sale, or delivery by use of the mails or interstate commerce — occurred last.[5] And it seems clear that the private offering "integration" doctrine does not extend §13 to cover transactions otherwise barred.[6]

For §12(2) the period is "one year after the discovery of the untrue statement or the omission, or after such discovery should have been made by the exercise of reasonable diligence," and three years after the sale.[7] And the statute of limitations for §11 follows

---

Morley v. Cohen, 610 F. Supp. 798, 815, 817 (D. Md. 1985). Moreover, §13 rather than local law governs actions under the 1933 Act in state courts. Kleckley v. Hebert, 464 So. 2d 39 (La. App. 1985).

[2]Stewart v. Germany, 631 F. Supp. 236, 247-48 (S. D. Miss. 1986), and cases cited both ways on the facts. In the case of an installment sale the one-year period begins to run when the parties become committed. Lewis v. Schultz, CCH Fed. Sec. L. Rep. ¶92,363 at 92,318 (E. D. Ark. 1985); Holloway v. Combined Equities, Inc., 628 F. Supp. 59 (M. D. La. 1986); cf. p. 299 n. h supra.

[3]Morley v. Cohen, 610 F. Supp. 798, 816 (D. Md. 1985); In re National Mortgage Equity Corp. Mortgage Pool Certificates Securities Litigation, 636 F. Supp. 1138, 1167-68 (C. D. Cal. 1986), citing the text; Waterman v. Alta Verde Industries, Inc., 643 F. Supp. 797, 808-09 (E. D. N. C. 1986).

[4]For a collection of cases both ways, see McCullough v. Leede Oil & Gas, Inc., 617 F. Supp. 384, 386-88 (W. D. Okla. 1985). For recent non-tolling cases, see Platsis v. E. F. Hutton & Co., Inc., CCH Fed. Sec. L. Rep. ¶91,963 at 90,802 (W. D. Mich. 1985); In re National Mortgage Equity Corp. Mortgage Pool Certificates Securities Litigation, 636 F. Supp. 1138, 1166-67 (C. D. Cal. 1986); Erickson v. Kiddie, — F. Supp. — , — , CCH Fed. Sec. L. Rep. ¶92,889 at 94,311 (N. D. Cal. 1986).

[5]Doran v. Petroleum Management Corp., 576 F. 2d 91 (5th Cir. 1978); Folse v. Combined Equities, 592 F. Supp. 559 (W. D. La. 1984); Grannemann v. Shipley Energy Corp., CCH Fed. Sec. L. Rep. ¶99,726 at 97,964 (W. D. Okla. 1984); In re National Mortgage Equity Corp. Mortgage Pool Certificates Securities Litigation, 636 F. Supp. 1138, 1166 (C. D. Cal. 1986), citing the text. Drawing on letters of credit that are used to fund amounts due on notes is the equivalent of payment. Reid v. Walsh, 645 F. Supp. 685, 687 (M. D. La. 1986).

[6]Flinn Foundation v. Petro-Lewis Corp., CCH Fed. Sec. L. Rep. ¶92,449 (D. Colo. 1985); Sanders v. Robinson Humphrey/American Express, Inc., CCH Fed. Sec. L. Rep. ¶92,450 at 92,738 (N. D. Ga. 1985); Bresson v. Thomson McKinnon Securities, Inc., 641 F. Supp. 338, 343-44 (S. D. N. Y. 1986); cf. Hayden v. McDonald, 742 F. 2d 423, 437 (8th Cir. 1984) (Minn. Unif. Sec. Act); but cf. Kennedy v. Tallant, CCH Fed. Sec. L. Rep. ¶95,779 (S. D. Ga. 1976), *aff'd on other grounds,* 710 F. 2d 711, 716 n. 3 (11th Cir. 1983) (Rule 10b-5).

[7]On the question of fixing the date of the sale, see Hill v. Equitable Bank, N. A., 599 F. Supp. 1062, 1072-73 (D. Del. 1984); cf. pp. 579-81 supra (Sec. Ex. Act §16(b)). The magic moment is when the party enters into a binding commitment. Radiation Dynamics, Inc. v. Goldmuntz, 464 F. 2d 876, 890-91 (2d Cir. 1972) (Rule 10b-5). Hence an exchange of irrevocable letters of credit

the 12(2) formula with respect to the one-year period and the 12(1) formula with respect to the three-year period: one year after discovery, with the same "reasonable diligence" test, and three years after the security was "*bona fide* offered to the public."[8]

The standard under the one-year clauses applicable to §§11 and 12(2) is objective, requiring reasonable diligence on the part of the buyer.[9] And, as with §12(1), the three-year cutoffs are absolute,[10]

---

for partnership shares was a sale of partnership securities although the letters were not finally drawn until almost four years after the date of sale. Ackerman, Jablonski, Porterfield & De Ture v. Alhadeff, — F. Supp. — , — , CCH Fed. Sec. L. Rep. ¶92,756 at 93,683 (W. D. Wash. 1986). See also Amoroso v. Southwestern Drilling Multi-Rig Partnership, 646 F. Supp. 141 (N. D. Cal. 1986) (although contract was subject to certain contingencies). In the case of a purchase on a when-issued basis, the date of purchase is the later date of actual issuance. Nelson v. National Republic Bank of Chicago, CCH Fed. Sec. L. Rep. ¶91,481 at 98,396-97 (N. D. Ill. 1984); cf. Ambling v. Blackstone Cattle Co., Inc., 650 F. Supp. 170 (N. D. Ill. 1987) (date limited partnership was formed and plaintiffs received the interests for which they had previously paid).

[8] The respective periods in §11 were two and ten years instead of one and three in the original statute; they were cut down in the 1934 amendments. As a result, it is literally possible for the statute to expire before the purchaser acquires the security in the case of a very slow offering that may still be going on after three years! See LeCroy v. Dean Witter Reynolds & Co., 585 F. Supp. 753, 760 n. 6 (E. D. Ark. 1984); cf. Diskin v. Lomasney & Co., 452 F. 2d 871 (2d Cir. 1971).

When §24(e) of the Investment Company Act was amended in 1954 to permit the registration of additional securities of open-end investment companies to be effected by amending an earlier registration statement instead of filing a new one, and to require the filing of their supplemental prospectuses as posteffective amendments, it was provided in that section that for purposes of §13 "no such security shall be deemed to have been *bona fide* offered to the public prior to the effective date of the latest amendment filed pursuant to this subsection." S. Rep. No. 1036 at 21 and H. R. Rep. No. 1542 at 31, 83d Cong., 2d Sess. (1954). And we have noticed the Commission's perhaps dubious use of the undertaking technique in "shelf" registrations in an attempt to postpone the starting date of the limitations period from the effective date of the registration statement to the effective date of the posteffective amendment. See p. 140 supra; cf. First Multifund for Daily Income, Inc. v. United States, 602 F. 2d 332, 335-36 (Ct. Cl. 1979), *cert. denied*, 445 U. S. 916.

[9] Johns Hopkins University v. Hutton, 422 F. 2d 1124, 1130 (4th Cir. 1970). See also Rochambeau v. Brent Exploration, Inc., 79 F. R. D. 381, 387 (D. Colo. 1978), citing Gilbert v. Nixon, 429 F. 2d 348 (10th Cir. 1970), for the proposition that, "although Plaintiff is not under a duty to investigate, he must affirmatively plead that ascertainment of the facts could not with reasonable diligence have been made within the one-year period." These are all §12(2) cases, whose holding is equally applicable in principle to §11. In §12(1) cases there is no fraud to activate the federal tolling doctrine (see pp. 993-94 infra). Platsis v. E. F. Hutton & Co., Inc., CCH Fed. Sec. L. Rep. ¶91,963 at 90,802 (W. D. Mich. 1985); but cf. In re Gas Reclamation, Inc. Securities Litigation, 659 F. Supp. 493, 507, CCH Fed. Sec. L. Rep. ¶93,217 at 96,019 (S. D. N. Y. 1987) (fraudulent concealment of need to register).

[10] Summer v. Land & Leisure, Inc., 664 F. 2d 965, 968 (5th Cir. 1981); SEC v. Seaboard Corp. (Admiralty Fund v. Hugh Johnson & Co., Inc.), 677 F. 2d

although there are estoppel possibilities.[11] None of the SEC statutes contains a provision, common to many of the blue sky laws, permitting the seller substantially to reduce the limitation period by making a rescission offer.[12]

In §§9(e) and 18(c) of the 1934 Act (with respect to manipulation and false filings) the periods are (1) one year after discovery of "the facts constituting the violation" in the case of §9(e) or "the cause of action" in the case of §18(c) and (2) three years after the violation or the accrual of the cause of action. The statute of limitations in §29(b) for actions under §15(c)(1), we have already noticed, is similar to that for §9(e).[13] Although none of the three sections refers, as does §13 of the 1933 Act, to when "such discovery should have been made by the exercise of reasonable diligence," the Fifth Circuit ignored the contrast between the two statutes in reading a "reasonable diligence" requirement into the one-year discovery clause of §29(b).[14]

Since the liability of controlling persons under §15 of the 1933 Act and §20(a) of the 1934 Act[15] is derivative, those persons are subject to the same statutes of limitations as the controlled persons.[16]

b. Burden of Proof

It is the general rule in the federal courts that, when the very statute that creates the cause of action also contains a limitation period, the statute of limitations not only bars the remedy but also destroys the liability, and therefore the plaintiff must plead and

1301, 1308 (9th Cir. 1982); cf. Walck v. American Stock Exchange, Inc., 687 F. 2d 778, 791-92 (3d Cir. 1982), *cert. denied*, 461 U. S. 942 (Sec. Ex. Act §9(e), infra p. 991); Aldrich v. McCulloch Properties, Inc., 627 F. 2d 1036, 1042 (10th Cir. 1980) (Interstate Land Sales Full Disclosure Act).

[11] Katz v. Amos Treat & Co., 411 F. 2d 1046, 1055 (2d Cir. 1969). In a recent case both limitations periods were tolled by the filing of a defendant's class action against a group of underwriters, so that a time bar did not apply to an amended §11 complaint against those underwriters who had chosen to opt out of the class once a class was certified. In re Activision Securities Litigation, — F. Supp. — , CCH Fed. Sec. L. Rep. ¶92,998 at 94,898-99 (N. D. Cal. 1986).

[12] See pp. 1013-14 supra.

[13] See p. 941 supra. With respect to the statute of limitations in §16(b), see p. 415 supra.

[14] Goldenberg v. Bache & Co., 270 F. 2d 675, 681 (5th Cir. 1959).

[15] See p. 1011 infra.

[16] Herm v. Stafford, 663 F. 2d 669, 679 (6th Cir. 1981); Morley v. Cohen, 610 F. Supp. 798, 815, 818 (D. Md. 1985).

prove facts showing that he is within the statute.[17] This view has been consistently followed under the Securities Act.[18] So far as satisfying the burden is concerned, the facts in the decided cases are of course highly variegated.[19]

c. Laches

Does the doctrine of laches have any place with respect to the express liabilities? If the buyer discovers an untruth or §5 violation shortly after his purchase, may he wait until almost a full year has expired before tendering the security to the seller or reselling it on the market? This question lends itself to better discussion at a later point, after an analysis of the limitations problems with respect to the implied liabilities.[20]

2. Implied Liabilities

There is by hypothesis no statute of limitations for rights of action that have been invented by the courts; for there is no federal statute of limitations for civil actions generally. But "statutes of repose" are so basic an element of our jurisprudence — criminal as well as civil — that it would be unthinkable to be able to sue under Rule 10b-5, for example, without limit of time.[21] In this state of affairs resort must be had to a number of basic propositions that have been laid down by the Supreme Court:

(1) Where "Congress has not established a time limitation for a

[17] Cook v. Avien, Inc., 573 F. 2d 685, 695 (1st Cir. 1978). A limitation of this kind, moreover, must be applied in actions brought in state courts whether the state statute be longer or shorter. Brennan, J., concurring in McAllister v. Magnolia Petroleum Co., 357 U. S. 221, 228 (1958), and cases cited. Presumably state courts are equally bound to apply the federal rule of burden of proof even though the state rule puts the burden on the defendant. See 5 C. Wright and A. Miller, Federal Practice and Procedure (1979) §§1270-74.

[18] Pennsylvania Co. for Insurances on Lives & Granting Annuities v. Deckert, 123 F. 2d 979, 985 (3d Cir. 1941); Chambliss v. Coca-Cola Bottling Corp., 274 F. Supp. 401, 408 (E. D. Tenn. 1967), *aff'd per curiam,* 414 F. 2d 256 (6th Cir. 1969), *cert. denied,* 397 U. S. 916; Johns Hopkins University v. Hutton, 488 F. 2d 912, 915 n. 12 (4th Cir. 1973), *cert. denied,* 416 U. S. 916.

[19] E. g., Dale v. Rosenfeld, 229 F. 2d 855 (2d Cir. 1956); MacClain v. Bules, 275 F. 2d 431, 437 (8th Cir. 1960); Hoffman v. Estabrook & Co., Inc., 587 F. 2d 509, 518-19 (1st Cir. 1978). A conclusory statement does not suffice. Henry v. Kinney, CCH Fed. Sec. L. Rep. ¶91,806 at 90,071-72 (W. D. Okla. 1984).

[20] See pp. 1002-03 infra.

[21] Wilson v. Garcia, 471 U. S. 261, 271 (1985), quoting from Adams v. Woods, 2 Cranch 336, 341 (U. S. 1805).

federal cause of action, the settled practice has been to adopt a local time limitation as federal law if it is not inconsistent with federal law or policy to do so."[22] This rule is followed even though it often makes the result vary depending upon the state in which the action is brought, and even though, especially under a statute like the 1934 Act that provides for a broad choice of venue and nationwide service of process, it permits the plaintiff a considerable amount of forum-shopping.[23] Moreover, the same local statute will not necessarily be selected for all actions under a particular provision, say, Rule 10b-5. Although the Supreme Court has held that "a simple, broad characterization of all §1983 [civil rights] claims best fits the statute's remedial purpose,"[24] the Sixth Circuit has distinguished that decision in a RICO case where it held "that, as with most federal causes of action without incorporated periods of limitations, the selection of the applicable state limitations period in the individual case should be made on the basis of a characterization of the kind of factual circumstances and legal theories presented."[25]

(2) But an action for fraud cannot be barred, regardless of the local statute of limitations, as long as the plaintiff remains in igno-

[22] Wilson v. Garcia, 471 U. S. 261, 266-67 (1985). See also Holmberg v. Armbrecht, 327 U. S. 392, 395 (1946), and cases cited; for SEC cases, see, e. g., Ernst & Ernst v. Hochfelder, 425 U. S. 185, 210 n. 29 (1976) (dictum); Klein v. Bower, 421 F. 2d 338, 343 (2d Cir. 1970); Roberts v. Magnetic Metals Co., 611 F. 2d 450, 452 (3d Cir. 1979).

This includes any local "borrowing" statute. See, e. g., N. Y. CPLR §202 (applicable when the cause of action accrued outside the state and plaintiff is a nonresident); Sack v. Low, 478 F. 2d 360, 365 (2d Cir. 1973); Arneil v. Ramsey, 550 F. 2d 774, 779-80 (2d Cir. 1977); Industrial Consultants, Inc. v. H. S. Equities, Inc., 646 F. 2d 746, 747 (2d Cir. 1981), *cert. denied*, 454 U. S. 838; Brodsky, Statutes of Limitations, 12 Rev. Sec. Reg. 909 (1979). See also Lang v. Paine, Webber, Jackson & Curtis, Inc., 582 F. Supp. 1421, 1424-27 (S. D. N. Y. 1984) (discussion of *where* a cause of action "accrues" for purposes of applying the New York "borrowing" statute).

[23] H. L. Green Co., Inc. v. MacMahon, 312 F. 2d 650, 652 n. 3 (2d Cir. 1962, *leave to file pet. for cert. denied* sub nom. H. L. Green Co. v. United States Court of Appeals for the Second Circuit, 372 U. S. 928. However, although the distinction between a traditional limitation on the time for bringing suit and a time limitation on the right created may have some utility in certain areas of the law — for example, in conflict-of-laws cases when the choice is between the forum and the jurisdiction under whose laws the cause of action arose — that distinction should not be considered in determining the choice of statutes of limitations in Rule 10b-5 actions or the like. Berry Petroleum Co. v. Adams & Peck, 518 F. 2d 402, 407 (2d Cir. 1975).

[24] Wilson v. Garcia, 471 U. S. 261, 272 (1985).

[25] Silverberg v. Thomson McKinnon Securities, Inc., 787 F. 2d 1079, 1083 (6th Cir. 1986); see also Penturelli v. Spector Cohen Gadon & Rosen, 640 F. Supp. 867 (E. D. Pa. 1986) (Rule 10b-5). *Contra:* Friedlander v. Troutman, Sanders, Lockerman & Ashmore, 788 F. 2d 1500 (11th Cir. 1986) (court rejected claim-by-claim approach in favor of the blue sky two-year period as the one most appropriate statute).

rance of the fraud "without any fault or want of diligence or care on his part," "though there be no special circumstances or efforts on the part of the party committing the fraud to conceal it from the knowledge of the other party." "This equitable doctrine is read into every federal statute of limitation."[26]

(3) When suit is based on "a federally-created right * * * for which the *sole* remedy is *in equity*," the traditional equitable doctrine of laches alone governs the question whether the action is timely.[27] On the other hand, the federal equity doctrine does *not* prevail over the state statute of limitations even in equitable actions "when the jurisdiction of the federal court is concurrent with that of law or the suit is brought in aid of a legal right."[28]

This reference to state law makes for a great amount of utterly wasteful litigation. Since there are fifty-two jurisdictions and at least two statutes of limitations to choose from in each jurisdiction (for example, one for an action based on fraud, another in the blue sky law, and often a third residual statute) and five or six commonly implied actions under the SEC statutes (Rules 10b-5 and 14a-9, §14(e) of the 1934 Act, §36(a) of the Investment Company Act, and various rules of the self-regulatory organizations, not to mention rescission actions under the Investment Advisers Act pursuant to the *Transamerica* case), there are *at least* 500-odd possible answers (52 x 2 x 5). That is to say, if the Second Circuit today decides that New York's statute of limitations for fraud cases governs in a 10b-5 action, and tomorrow a 10b-5 case comes up from Connecticut, the court might decide that Connecticut's blue sky period is closer to 10b-5. And, if the next day a case comes to the Second Circuit from New York again, but it is a proxy case, the court will have to start afresh once more.

The *reductio ad absurdum* is marked by a 1977 case in which the District Court, properly holding that the statute of limitations that

[26] Holmberg v. Armbrecht, 327 U. S. 392, 397 (1946). There is also a line of cases holding that, "where an action is brought on behalf of an entity which has been defrauded by persons who completely dominated and controlled it, the statute of limitations is tolled as to the controlling wrongdoers during the period of their domination and control." Armstrong v. McAlpin, 699 F. 2d 79, 87 (2d Cir. 1983), and cases cited.

[27] Holmberg v. Armbrecht, 327 U. S. 392, 395 (1946) (italics are supplied).

[28] Russell v. Todd, 309 U. S. 280, 289 (1940) (dictum); Cope v. Anderson, 331 U. S. 461, 463-64 (1947); International Union, United Automobile Workers of America v. Hoosier Cardinal Corp., 383 U. S. 696, 703-05 (1966); see also Myzel v. Fields, 386 F. 2d 718, 742 (8th Cir. 1967), *cert. denied*, 389 U. S. 951 (fact that original prayer was for rescission or damages in alternative would not change applicability of state limitations statute as opposed to laches); Morgan v. Koch, 419 F. 2d 993, 996 (7th Cir. 1969).

would have governed the original actions continued to govern after their transfer to another forum by the Judicial Panel on Multidistrict Litigation, had to determine which state statute applied to each class of plaintiffs in a number of class actions.[29] All this is aside, moreover, from the great variation among the states in the limitation periods applicable to a given type of action, for example, one based on fraud. The result is that at one time or another the applicable period for just a 10b-5 action has been held to range from one year in Maryland to ten in Tennessee.[30]

The Code, of course, supplies a series of limitations for all actions, express or "implied."[31] Meanwhile, with the 1933 and 1934 Acts so closely related, why not look to *their* statutes of limitations by way of analogy rather than to a variant state law? Would it not be eminently more consistent with the overall statutory scheme to look to what Congress itself did when it was thinking specifically of private actions in securities cases rather than to a grab-bag of more or less analogous state statutes?

Two District Courts have turned back arguments directed to §13 by saying simply that that section does not apply to actions under §17(a) of the 1933 Act or Rule 10b-5, missing the point, of course, that the *state* statutes do not apply by their terms either but are simply applied *by analogy when there is no analogous statute of limitations at the federal level.*[32] And quite a few courts have looked wistfully to what the Fifth Circuit has considered "the logically appealing course of applying the period of limitations applicable to a similar cause of action expressly provided in the federal securities laws," while concluding that the rule of looking to state law was too definitely established.[33] Thus Judge Pollack, despite his own view that "Common sense and logic dictate" looking to the periods in the

[29] In re Clinton Oil Co. Securities Litigation, CCH Fed. Sec. L. Rep. ¶96,015 at 91,566-67 (D. Kan. 1977). But see p. 997 n. 40 infra.

[30] O'Hara v. Kovens, 625 F. 2d 15 (4th Cir. 1980), *cert. denied,* 449 U. S. 1124 (Maryland); Denny v. Performance Systems, Inc., CCH Fed. Sec. L. Rep. ¶93,387 (M. D. Tenn. 1971); but see Media General, Inc. v. Tanner, 625 F. Supp. 237, 246 (W. D. Tenn. 1985).

[31] §1727.

[32] Premier Industries, Inc. v. Delaware Valley Financial Corp., 185 F. Supp. 694 (E. D. Pa. 1960); Hendricks v. Flato Realty Investments, CCH Fed. Sec. L. Rep. ¶92,290 at 97,389 (S. D. Tex. 1968); see also Mosesian v. Peat, Marwick, Mitchell & Co., 727 F. 2d 873, 876 n. 5 (9th Cir. 1984), *cert. denied,* 469 U. S. 932 (statute of limitations in §18 does not apply to Rule 10b-5).

[33] McNeal v. Paine, Webber, Jackson & Curtis, Inc., 598 F. 2d 888, 892 (5th Cir. 1979); see also, e. g., Nickels v. Koehler Management Corp., 541 F. 2d 611, 614-15 (6th Cir. 1976), *cert. denied,* 429 U. S. 1074; Roberts v. Magnetic Metals Co., 611 F. 2d 450, 452 (3d Cir. 1979); Norris v. Wirtz, 818 F. 2d 1329, 1333 (7th Cir. 1987), quoting the text.

1933 and 1934 Acts, was deterred by Judge Learned Hand's caution thirty years earlier that it was not "desirable for a lower court to embrace the exhilarating opportunity of anticipating a doctrine which may be in the womb of time, but whose birth is distant."[34]

The Supreme Court has yet to speak in the SEC context. But there are utterances in other contexts negating any idea that a state limitations period is to be "mechanically applied * * * simply because a limitations period is absent from the federal statute." "State legislatures," the Court stated, "do not devise their limitations periods with national interests in mind, and it is the duty of the federal courts to assure that the importation of state law will not frustrate or interfere with the implementation of national policies. * * * State limitations periods will not be borrowed if their application would be inconsistent with the underlying policies of the federal statute."[35] The federal courts would not be engaging in a "drastic sort of judicial legislation" as they would be if they were to devise a uniform time limitation;[36] they would simply be deciding that the federal statutes afforded a better analogy than a reference to state law. And, for what it is worth, the commentators seem to be of one view.[37]

[34]Spector Motor Service, Inc. v. Walsh, 139 F. 2d 809, 823 (2d Cir. 1944) (L. Hand, J., dissenting); Mittendorf v. J. R. Williston & Beane, Inc., 372 F. Supp. 821, 830 n. 4 (S. D. N. Y. 1974).

[35]Occidental Life Ins. Co. v. Equal Employment Opportunity Commission, 432 U. S. 355, 367 (1977); see also McAllister v. Magnolia Petroleum Co., 357 U. S. 221 (1958) (a court may not apply a shorter period to a judicially created action for unseaworthiness than Congress prescribed for Jones Act negligence); International Union, United Automobile Workers of America v. Hoosier Cardinal Corp., 383 U. S. 696, 707 n. 9 (1966) ("an unusually short or long limitations period" under state law would raise questions). See esp. Justice Brennan's concurring opinion in *McAllister*, supra, to the effect that in Cope v. Anderson, 331 U. S. 461 (1947), supra p. 994 n. 28, "The state statutes were chosen by default." 357 U. S. at 228-29. See also DelCostello v. International Brotherhood of Teamsters, 402 U. S. 151, 169-71 (1983) (period for employee-union action was applied to employee-employer action).

[36]International Union, United Automobile Workers of America v. Hoosier Cardinal Corp., 383 U. S. 696, 703 (1966).

[37]See Schulman, Statutes of Limitation in 10b-5 Actions: Complication Added to Confusion, 13 Wayne L. Rev. 635 (1967); Israels, Book Rev., 77 Yale L. J. 1585, 1591-92 (1968); Martin, Statutes of Limitations in 10b-5 Actions: Which State Statute Is Applicable?, 29 Bus. Law. 443, 455 n. 91 (1974); Bromberg, Curing Securities Violations: Rescission Offers and Other Techniques, 1 J. Corp. L. 1, 9-10 (1975).

There *is* some precedent for considering the relatively brief federal periods in comparison with state law, as well as the absolute federal cutoffs, as one reason for preferring the shorter state blue sky period over the longer fraud period. Hitchcock v. deBruyne, 377 F. Supp. 1403, 1407 (D. Conn. 1974); Newman v. Prior, 518 F. 2d 97, 100 (4th Cir. 1975); Money v. Tallant, 397 F. Supp. 680,

As it is, fitting Rule 10b-5 into the existing doctrinal framework (the other implied liabilities will be ignored here for the sake of simplicity and also because Rule 10b-5 has been by far the most prolific breeder of litigation) is not easy.

(1) Can there ever be occasion under Rule 10b-5 to forgo state limitation law entirely in favor of the federal laches doctrine? Normally not. The typical action for damages is nothing more than a modified form of common law deceit. Even when the plaintiff seeks equitable rescission because the legal remedy is inadequate, the fact remains that alternative remedies do exist at law for violation of the rule. And, even in the case of a stockholder's derivative action on behalf of a corporation injured by a violation of the rule, it is only the derivative *remedy*, not the underlying "legal right," that is equitable.

(2) The Supreme Court has held that "the characterization of [the] action for the purpose of selecting the appropriate state limitations provision is ultimately a question of federal law," although "there is no reason to reject the characterization that state law would impose unless that characterization is unreasonable or otherwise inconsistent with national labor policy."[38] And Judge Friendly has said for the Second Circuit, in an action under the Clayton Act, that the court "looks first to federal law to determine the nature of the claim and then to state court interpretations of the statutory catalogue to see where the claim fits into the state scheme."[39]

(3) On the conflict-of-laws question of *which* state's limitation statute governs, that of the forum or that of the state where all the operative events occurred, it is not clear whether the choice of law should be made in accordance with *Erie* concepts or by operation of a different, federal conflict-of-laws rule.[40]

683-84 (N. D. Ga. 1975). But there is also authority favoring the longer fraud period as preferable in carrying out the federal policy. United Cal. Bank v. Salik, 481 F. 2d 1012 (9th Cir. 1973), *cert. denied*, 414 U. S. 1004; Berry Petroleum Co. v. Adams & Peck, 518 F. 2d 402, 409 (2d Cir. 1975).

The Insider Trading Sanctions Act of 1984 (infra p. 1008, end) imposes a five-year statute on the newly created action *by the Commission* for treble damages in insider trading cases. At this point, clearly, Congress must have been aware of the problem. *Query:* Does this have an impact either way on the argument here made that the courts in implied private actions should find their analogy in federal rather than state law?

[38] International Union, United Automobile Workers of America v. Hoosier Cardinal Corp., 383 U. S. 696, 706 (1966); see also Wilson v. Garcia, 471 U. S. 261, 269-70 (1985).

[39] Moviecolor, Ltd. v. Eastman Kodak Co., 288 F. 2d 80, 83 (2d Cir. 1961), *cert. denied*, 368 U. S. 821.

[40] See International Union, United Automobile Workers of America v. Hoosier Cardinal Corp., 383 U. S. 696, 705 n. 8 (1966); Hart and Wechsler, The

(4) With respect to the ultimate question of deciding which state statute of limitations is most nearly analogous to Rule 10b-5, the early cases rather uniformly followed (as have some recent ones) the period for actions grounded on "fraud,"[41] but more recent cases (with some exceptions) tend to favor the blue sky period.[42] The courts have worried a good deal about matching up Rule 10b-5 and the blue sky law with respect to scienter, which some Circuits did not require before the *Hochfelder* case.[43] In result, at least when the fraud period is applied, it is almost invariably longer than the federal period would be.[44]

Federal Courts and the Federal System (2d ed. 1973) 829. There are several 10b-5 cases in which the Ninth Circuit looked to the *lex loci delicti* without discussion of the choice of law. Fratt v. Robinson, 203 F. 2d 627, 634 (9th Cir. 1953); Errion v. Connell, 236 F. 2d 447, 455 (9th Cir. 1956); Turner v. Lundquist, 377 F. 2d 44, 46 (9th Cir. 1967); see also Hooper v. Mountain States Securities Corp., 282 F. 2d 195, 205 (5th Cir. 1960). But in accordance with modern conflicts doctrine, there is authority in class actions for picking a single limitation period by looking to such "significant contacts" as the state of incorporation, the corporation's principal place of business, and the place where the alleged fraud occurred. State Teachers Retirement Board v. Fluor Corp., 80 F. R. D. 142 (S. D. N. Y. 1978); Raymond v. Miller & Schroeder Municipals, Inc., CCH Fed. Sec. L. Rep. ¶99,714 (D. Minn. 1983).

[41] E. g., Fratt v. Robinson, 203 F. 2d 627, 635 (9th Cir. 1953); Aldrich v. McCulloch Properties, Inc., 627 F. 2d 1036, 1041 (10th Cir. 1980); Wood v. Combustion Engineering, Inc., 643 F. 2d 339 (5th Cir. 1981) (applying Texas's two-year fraud statute rather than its three-year blue sky statute, court did not "follow the practice of several other Circuits of making an inquiry into which state limitations period, independent of consideration of the substantive provisions of the corresponding state statute, best effectuates the purposes of Rule 10b-5"); Robuck v. Dean Witter & Co., Inc., 649 F. 2d 641, 644 (9th Cir. 1980); Sharp v. Coopers & Lybrand, 649 F. 2d 175, 1911-92 (3d Cir. 1981), *cert. denied,* 455 U. S. 938. *Wood,* supra, was reaffirmed by Corwin v. Marney, Orton Investments, 788 F. 2d 1063 (5th Cir. 1986), despite intervening amendments to the blue sky law that required neither reliance nor scienter.

[42] E. g., Berry Petroleum Co. v. Adams & Peck, 518 F. 2d 402 (2d Cir. 1975); Morris v. Stifel, Nicolaus & Co., Inc., 600 F. 2d 139 (8th Cir. 1979); Wachovia Bank & Trust Co. v. National Student Marketing Corp., 650 F. 2d 342, 346-48 (D. C. Cir. 1980), *cert. denied* sub nom. Peat, Marwick, Mitchell & Co. v. Wachovia Bank & Trust Co., 452 U. S. 954; White v. Sanders, 650 F. 2d 627 (5th Cir. 1981); Herm v. Stafford, 663 F. 2d 669 (6th Cir. 1981); Gurley v. Documation, Inc., 674 F. 2d 253, 258 (4th Cir. 1982); Teamsters Local 282 Pension Trust Fund v. Angelos, 815 F. 2d 452, 455-56 (7th Cir. 1987). For further collections of cases both ways, see Hill v. Der, 521 F. Supp. 1370, 1379-84 (D. Del. 1981); Block and Barton, Statute of Limitations in Private Actions Under Section 10(b) — A Proposal for Achieving Uniformity, 7 Sec. Reg. L. J. 374 (1980); Committee on Federal Legislation, The Need for the Enactment of Federal Statutes of Limitations to Govern Federal Rights of Action, 41 A. B. C. N. Y. 823 (1986).

[43] See, e. g., Charney v. Thomas, 372 F. 2d 97 (6th Cir. 1967); Diamond v. Lamotte, 709 F. 2d 1419, 1423 (11th Cir. 1983), *rehearing denied,* 716 F. 2d 914 (11th Cir. 1983); Currie v. Cayman Resources Corp., 595 F. Supp. 1364, 1375 (N. D. Ga. 1984).

[44] See Ernst & Ernst v. Hochfelder, 425 U. S. 185, 210 n. 29 (1976), supra p. 775.

(5) Even when the period of limitation has been determined, a surprising number of collateral issues may require decision before it can be said that a particular action is or is not barred: for example, when the action under Rule 10b-5 accrues,[45] when an action is deemed to be commenced, whether an amendment to a complaint relates back, when the period of limitation is tolled,[46] and the impact of changes in venue. Some of these questions seem rather uniformly to be referred to federal law, others to state law, and often the question of choice of law is either left in doubt or ignored.[47]

(6) With respect to the express rights of action in the SEC statutes, we have seen that the plaintiff has the burden of bringing himself within the particular statute of limitations.[48] But the case here is different. To be sure, Rule 8(c) of the Federal Rules of Civil Procedure, which makes the statute of limitations a matter of affirmative defense, covers only the matter of *pleading,* so that the *burden of proof* is referred to state law in diversity cases.[49] In federal question cases, however, where there is no reason to refer to state law except to find a limitation period, it seems more appropriate to

[45]See generally Moviecolor, Ltd. v. Eastman Kodak Co., 288 F. 2d 80, 83 (2d Cir. 1961), *cert. denied,* 368 U. S. 821; see also Sackett v. Beaman, 399 F. 2d 884, 891 (9th Cir. 1968); Norte & Co. v. Krock, CCH Fed. Sec. L. Rep. ¶92,295 at 94,409 (S. D. N. Y. 1968); Parrent v. Midwest Rug Mills, Inc., 455 F. 2d 123, 128 (7th Cir. 1972); Jennings v. Boenning & Co., 523 F. 2d 889 (3d Cir. *per curiam* 1975); Stull v. Bayard, 561 F. 2d 429 (2d Cir. 1977), *cert. denied,* 434 U. S. 1035; Vigman v. Community National Bank & Trust Co., 635 F. 2d 455, 458-59 (5th Cir. 1981); Kennedy v. Tallant, 710 F. 2d 711, 716 (11th Cir. 1983); Baron v. Allied Artists Pictures Corp., 717 F. 2d 105, 108 (3d Cir. 1983) (action for *damages* under the proxy rules accrued when merger was consummated, not when shareholder knew enough of the violation to seek an injunction, since it was not until consummation that the action could be successfully prosecuted in view of the fact that there was no actual injury until that event). In Levinger v. Shepard Niles Crane & Hoist Corp., 616 F. Supp. 21 (W. D. N. Y. 1985), the court followed the holding in Stull v. Bayard, supra, that the action accrued when the tender offer prospectus or proxy materials were mailed, not on the expiration date of the tender offer in *Stull* or the consummation date of the merger in *Levinger,* although the result in both cases was that the limitation period had expired.

[46]Under federal law commencement in a clearly inappropriate forum (here a 10b-5 action in a state court) does not equitably toll the statute. Silverberg v. Thomson McKinnon Securities, Inc., 787 F. 2d 1079, 1082 (6th Cir. 1986).

[47]See Developments in the Law: Statutes of Limitations, 63 Harv. L. Rev. 1177, 1266-67 (1950); Blume and George, Limitations and the Federal Courts, 49 Mich. L. Rev. 937, 950-62 (1951); Note, Federal Statutes Without Limitations Provisions, 53 Colum. L. Rev. 68, 71-72 (1953). Regardless of state law, "if a substantial part of a 10b-5 lawsuit is not time-barred, a federal court should entertain the entire action." Ferber v. Morgan Stanley Co., Inc., CCH Fed. Sec. L. Rep. ¶99,634 at 97,506 (E. D. Pa. 1984).

[48]See p. 991 supra.

[49]Cf. Palmer v. Hoffman, 318 U. S. 109, 117 (1943) (contributory negligence).

look to federal rather than state law in order to place the burden. And, when the right of action is judicially created, placing the burden of going forward on the defendant not only seems to follow by negative implication from the federal rule that puts the burden on the plaintiff when the very statute that creates the cause of action also contains a limitation period but also seems more consistent with Rule 8(c) than otherwise.[50] Even so, the federal courts "have placed the burden of proof on the plaintiffs when questions of limitations arise under §10(b) once the defendant has pleaded the statute of limitations."[51]

(7) When there is a federal statute of limitations that is silent on the point, it is always tolled while a reasonably diligent plaintiff remains in ignorance of any *fraud* that is an element of the cause of action.[52] This is true at law as it is in equity.[53] Moreover, although most state courts follow the same view,[54] the federal courts will apply the tolling doctrine in any event.[55] This is doctrinally sound. For, "when considering federal questions, federal courts should not be bound by the state's interpretation of the statute, as they are in diversity cases, but should adhere only to the period of

[50] In re Longhorn Securities Litigation, 573 F. Supp. 255, 266 (W. D. Okla. 1983); Currie v. Cayman Resources Corp., 595 F. Supp. 1364, 1374 (N. D. Ga. 1984). *Contra:* In Mooney v. Vitolo, CCH Fed. Sec. L. Rep. ¶92,116 at 96,549 (S. D. N. Y. 1967), the court, without discussion, directed that an amended complaint should "affirmatively plead facts which show that the statute of limitations has not run."

[51] Cook v. Avien, Inc., 573 F. 2d 685, 695 (1st Cir. 1978); General Builders Supply Co. v. River Hill Coal Venture, 796 F. 2d 8, 12 (1st Cir. 1986).

[52] Holmberg v. Armbrecht, 327 U. S. 392, 395, 397 (1946), supra p. 994 n. 26.

[53] Bailey v. Glover, 21 Wall. 342 (U. S. 1874); Tobacco & Allied Stocks, Inc. v. Transamerica Corp., 244 F. 2d 902, 1003 (3d Cir. 1957); Morgan v. Koch, 419 F. 2d 993, 997 (7th Cir. 1969). There is no similar doctrine that tolls the statute of limitations pending an SEC investigation, because private and enforcement proceedings under the SEC statutes are quite independent. Corson v. First Jersey Securities, Inc., 537 F. Supp. 1263, 1267 (D. N. J. 1982).

[54] See Dawson, Undiscovered Fraud and Statutes of Limitation, 31 Mich. L. Rev. 591 (1933); Errion v. Connell, 236 F. 2d 447, 455 (9th Cir. 1956); Vance v. National Realty Trust, CCH Fed. Sec. L. Rep. ¶95,004 (D. C. Cir. 1975); IIT v. Cornfeld, 619 F. 2d 909, 928-29 (2d Cir. 1980).

[55] Janigan v. Taylor, 344 F. 2d 781, 784 (1st Cir. 1965), *cert. denied,* 382 U. S. 879; Saylor v. Lindsley, 391 F. 2d 965, 970 (2d Cir. 1968); Vanderboom v. Sexton, 422 F. 2d 1233, 1240 (8th Cir. 1970); Aboussie v. Aboussie, 441 F. 2d 150, 156 (5th Cir. 1971), *rehearing on other grounds,* 446 F. 2d 56 (5th Cir. 1971); Schaefer v. First National Bank of Lincolnwood, 509 F. 2d 1287, 1298 (7th Cir. 1975), *cert. denied,* 425 U. S. 943; Newman v. Prior, 518 F. 2d 97, 100 (4th Cir. 1975); Hilton v. Mamaw, 522 F. 2d 588, 602 (9th Cir. 1975); State of Ohio v. Peterson, Lowry, Rall, Barber & Ross, 651 F. 2d 687, 691 (10th Cir. 1981), *cert. denied,* 454 U. S. 895.

time provided by the statute, since only that portion of federal law is lacking."[56]

A *caveat* must be entered here. The Supreme Court has held that in civil rights actions under §1983[57] the courts should look to state law on tolling as part of the incorporation of the state law of limitations, except only when the state tolling law is inconsistent with the federal policy underlying the cause of action.[58] Arguably these cases are distinguishable because of the express incorporation by §1988 of state law generally insofar as federal laws are inadequate.[59] This argument should appeal particularly in cases of active concealment — which did not figure in either of the Supreme Court cases — on the ground that there is more of a federal interest there. But one of these Supreme Court cases[60] has been followed with respect to Rule 10b-5 by the Seventh Circuit without the court's noticing the point.[61]

(8) What constitutes reasonable diligence on the plaintiff's part is itself a federal question.[62] The plaintiff need not show active concealment.[63] When there *is* active concealment, it tolls the statute of limitations in some courts until *actual* discovery by the plaintiff.[64] But, when there is no active concealment or the particular court does not recognize that doctrine, the plaintiff may not sit on his

[56]70 Harv. L. Rev. 566, 568 (1957); Wolf v. Frank, 477 F. 2d 467, 475 (5th Cir. 1973), *cert. denied,* 414 U. S. 975.

[57]42 U. S. C. §1983.

[58]Johnson v. Railway Express Agency, Inc., 421 U. S. 454 (1975); Board of Regents of the University of the State of N. Y. v. Tomanio, 446 U. S. 478 (1980); Wilson v. Garcia, 471 U. S. 261, 269 n. 17 (1985).

[59]See Silverberg v. Thomson McKinnon Securities, Inc., 787 F. 2d 1079, 1083 (6th Cir. 1986); see also Estate of Deering v. Deering, 646 F. Supp. 903, 908-09 (S. D. W. Va. 1986), where the point was discussed.

[60]Board of Regents of the University of the State of N. Y. v. Tomano, 446 U. S. 478 (1980).

[61]Suslick v. Rothschild Securities Corp., 741 F. 2d 1000, 1003 (7th Cir. 1984); Norris v. Wirtz, 818 F. 2d 1329 (7th Cir. 1987).

[62]Tobacco & Allied Stocks, Inc. v. Transamerica Corp., 143 F. Supp. 323, 329 (D. Del. 1956), *aff'd on other grounds,* 244 F. 2d 902 (3d Cir. 1957); Trecker v. Scag, 679 F. 2d 703, 706 (7th Cir. 1982).

[63]Bailey v. Glover, 21 Wall. 342, 348 (U. S. 1874).

[64]Tomera v. Galt, 511 F. 2d 504, 510 (7th Cir. 1975); see also Sperry v. Barggren, 523 F. 2d 708 (7th Cir. 1975). *Contra*: State of Ohio v. Peterson, Lowry, Rall, Barber & Ross, 651 F. 2d 687, 694 (10th Cir. 1981), *cert. denied,* 454 U. S. 895; Campbell v. Upjohn Co., 676 F. 2d 1122, 1126-28 (6th Cir. 1982). The statute is tolled *only* during the period of the potential defendants' concealment from the potential plaintiff. Suslick v. Rothschild Securities Corp., 741 F. 2d 1000, 1004 (7th Cir. 1984). For an essay in support of the proposition that the "actual discovery" notion should be rejected as undercutting the policies underlying the statute of limitations — and that concealment should be simply a factor in the diligence analysis — see Marcus, Fraudulent Concealment in Federal Court: Toward a More Disparate Standard?, 71 Geo. L. J. 829 (1983).

hands. He "must have exercised reasonable care and diligence in seeking to learn the facts which would disclose fraud."[65] The burden here is on the plaintiff once the defendant pleads the statute of limitations.[66] And the question is for the jury.[67] But the plaintiff is likely to satisfy the burden when (a) he shows his own lack of knowledge under §12(2) or whatever conduct is required of him under Rule 10b-5[68] or (b) he pleads the fraud with the particularity required by Rule 9(b) of the Federal Rules of Civil Procedure.[69]

(9) If the federal doctrine that *protects* the reasonably careful but unsuspecting plaintiff is read into the state statute of limitations, may a federal court under Rule 10b-5 also *bar* the plaintiff *before* the expiration of the statutory period if he was not reasonably diligent or, worse, if he is shown to have acquired actual knowledge of the fraud shortly after the transaction but to have waited several years before bringing suit? When a state statute of limitations applies to equitable as well as legal actions, it is clear that laches may still bar the federal plaintiff *in equity* before the expiration of the state statute[70] — at least when the state statute does not provide otherwise for the state courts and perhaps, since laches is a matter of federal equity jurisprudence,[71] even when it does.[72]

The fact remains, however, that laches is an equitable, not a legal,

[65] Morgan v. Koch, 419 F. 2d 993, 997 (7th Cir. 1969); see also deHaas v. Empire Petroleum Co., 435 F. 2d 1223, 1226 (10th Cir. 1970); Occidental Life Ins. Co. of N. C. v. Pat Ryan & Associates, Inc., 496 F. 2d 1255, 1268 (4th Cir. 1974), *cert. denied,* 419 U. S. 1023; Berry Petroleum Co. v. Adams & Peck, 518 F. 2d 402, 410 (2d Cir. 1975); Goldstandt v. Bear, Stearns & Co., 522 F. 2d 1265 (7th Cir. 1975); Koke v. Stifel, Nicolaus & Co., Inc., 620 F. 2d 1340 (8th Cir. 1980).

[66] Cook v. Avien, Inc., 573 F. 2d 685, 695 (1st Cir. 1978).

[67] Johns Hopkins University v. Hutton, 422 F. 2d 1124, 1131 (4th Cir. 1970), *reconsidered after remand,* 488 F. 2d 912 (4th Cir. 1973), *cert. denied,* 416 U. S. 916. There is, nevertheless, no impediment to the granting of summary judgment for the defendant, particularly when the plaintiff is the only person who would possibly be in possession of information sufficient to counter the inference of a lack of due diligence found in the plaintiff's depositions. Gieringer v. Silverman, 731 F. 2d 1272, 1279 (7th Cir. 1984).

[68] See pp. 889-90, 957-58 supra.

[69] Schaefer v. First National Bank of Lincolnwood, 509 F. 2d 1287, 1297 (7th Cir. 1975), *cert. denied,* 425 U. S. 943.

[70] Patterson v. Hewitt, 195 U. S. 309, 319 (1904); see Russell v. Todd, 309 U. S. 280, 288 n. 1 (1940); 2 Pomeroy, Equity Jurisprudence (5th ed. 1941) §419b.

[71] See p. 997 supra.

[72] Royal Air Properties, Inc. v. Smith, 312 F. 2d 210, 214 (9th Cir. 1962) (10b-5 action seeking a *legal* remedy); see also, e. g., Tobacco & Allied Stocks, Inc. v. Transamerica Corp., 143 F. Supp. 323, 327-28 (D. Del. 1956), *aff'd on other grounds,* 244 F. 2d 902 (3d Cir. 1957); Gordon v. Burr, 366 F. Supp. 156, 170-71 (S. D. N. Y. 1973), *aff'd in part and rev'd in part on other grounds,* 506 F. 2d 1080 (2d Cir. 1976).

doctrine. Therefore, although a *federal* statute of limitations will be extended to *protect* the reasonably diligent plaintiff suing on a fraud theory even in an action at *law* (unless the particular statute provides otherwise), it does not follow that a plaintiff who seeks a *legal* remedy on a federal cause of action within the period specified in the applicable statute of limitations, whether federal or state, should be barred under any circumstances short of the expiration of the statutory period.[73] The discovery doctrine at law was devised by the federal courts to protect victims of fraud, and the logical symmetry of using that exception *against* a plaintiff suing at law within the statutory period is only superficial.[74]

[73]Stevens v. Abbott, Proctor & Paine, 288 F. Supp. 836, 845 (E. D. Va. 1968); Norte & Co. v. Krock, CCH Fed. Sec. L. Rep. ¶92,295 at 94,410 (S. D. N. Y. 1968). Moreover, the doctrine of laches is not applicable merely because an action under Rule 10b-5 or the proxy rules is brought derivatively. Ibid.

[74]Cf. Myzel v. Fields, 386 F. 2d 718, 742 (8th Cir. 1967), *cert. denied,* 389 U. S. 951. In Jennings v. Boenning & Co., 352 F. Supp. 1000, 1006 (E. D. Pa. 1972), *rev'd on other grounds,* 482 F. 2d 1128 (3d Cir. 1973), *cert. denied,* 414 U. S. 1025, the court said that "the equitable doctrine of laches should be subordinated to the strong principles of public policy embodied in the Securities laws."

Conversely, in Gaudette v. Panos, 644 F. Supp. 826, 838 (D. Mass. 1986), the court applied the doctrine of "continuing wrong" in using the Massachusetts blue sky law for a 10b-5 case.

In general, with suggestions for escaping the quagmire, see Am. B. Assn. Committee on Federal Regulation of Securities, Report of the Task Force on Statute of Limitations for Implied Actions, 41 Bus. Law. 645 (1986).

A limitations question that is not directly relevant to Rule 10b-5, because it arises under the statutes of limitations governing the express actions, has been left for discussion here in the light of the federal-state analysis that has just been made: *If* laches may bar a plaintiff suing on a federal cause of action in equity before expiration of the appropriate state limitation period to which reference is made, might it have the same effect on a cause of action that is governed by a *federal* statute of limitations like §13 of the 1933 Act or §16(b), §9(e), §18(c), or §29(b) of the 1934 Act?

It need hardly be mentioned that the question must be approached as one of federal statutory construction. And the short answer Dean Shulman gave it in 1933 seems sound: "there being nothing in the section to the contrary, the buyer may do what he pleases so long as he brings suit within" the stipulated period. Shulman, Civil Liability and the Securities Act, 43 Yale L. J. 227, 246-47 (1933). It is one thing for a court of equity to apply the traditional doctrine of laches to an action whose outside limitation period is referred to state law. But we have seen that that is explained by simply not referring to state law beyond the point of necessity. That is to say, when Congress has not bothered to write its own limitation period, there is normally no evidence of a statutory purpose to exclude so basic an equitable doctrine as laches. But when Congress does prescribe a specific and relatively short statute of limitations for a federal action as it has done in the sections here specified — especially when it has rather uniformly provided that the action may be enforced "at law or in equity" as it has done in §12 of the 1933 Act and §§9(e), 16(b), and 18(a) of the 1934 Act — there is a strong inference that the prescribed limitation period is not to be cut short, whether in an action sounding in fraud or, *a fortiori*, in an action

J. MISCELLANEOUS ASPECTS OF CIVIL LIABILITY UNDER THE SEC STATUTES

There are a number of aspects of civil liability that are common to several or all of the federal actions:

1. Ancillary Relief

The Supreme Court early held that a plaintiff under §12(2) of the 1933 Act was not limited to a money judgment but could have the ancillary remedies traditionally available in a court of equity. The plaintiffs alleged fraud in the sale of unit trust installment certificates. The Court was unanimous:

> We think the Securities Act does not restrict purchasers seeking relief under its provisions to a money judgment. On the contrary, the Act as a whole indicates an intention to establish a statutory right which the litigant may enforce in designated courts by such legal or equitable actions or procedures as would normally be available to him. Undoubtedly any suit to establish the civil liability imposed by the Act must ultimately seek recovery of the consideration paid less income received or damages if the claimant no longer owns the security. §12(2). But §12(2) states the legal consequences of conduct proscribed by the Act; it does not purport to state the form of action or procedure the claimant is to employ.
>
> Moreover, in Section 22(a) specified courts are given jurisdiction "of all suits in equity and actions at law brought *to enforce* any liability or duty created by this subchapter." The power *to enforce* implies the power to make effective the right of recovery afforded by the Act. And the power to make the right of recovery effective implies the power to utilize any of the procedures or actions normally available to the litigant according to the exigencies of the particular case. If petitioners' bill states a cause of action when tested by the customary rules governing suits of such character, the Securities Act authorizes maintenance of the suit, providing the bill contains the allegations the Act requires. That it does not authorize the bill in so many words is no more significant than the fact that it does not in terms authorize execution to issue on a judgment recovered under §12(2).
>
> We are of the opinion that the bill states a cause for equitable relief. There are allegations that [the issuer] is insolvent, that its business is practically halted, that it is threatened with many law

under §12(1) of the 1933 Act for violation of §5. See Straley v. Universal Uranium & Milling Corp., 289 F. 2d 370 (9th Cir. 1961).

suits, that its assets are endangered, and that preferences to creditors are probable. There are prayers for an accounting, appointment of a receiver, an injunction *pendente lite*, and for return of petitioners' payments. * * *

The principle objects of the suit are rescission * * * and restitution * * *. That a suit to rescind a contract induced by fraud and to recover the consideration paid may be maintained in equity, at least where there are circumstances making the legal remedy inadequate, is well established. * * *

* * *

We hold that the injunction was a reasonable measure to preserve the status quo pending final determination of the questions raised by the bill. * * *[1]

Everything the Court said applies equally in principle to §§11 and 12(1) of the 1933 Act as well as all the other civil liabilities, express and implied, under the SEC statutes. A District Court followed this case in a §12(1) action in which holders of voting trust certificates issued without registration were granted restoration of the stock deposited.[2] The Eighth Circuit, relying simply on Rule 54(c) of the Federal Rules of Civil Procedure,[3] held in an action under §12(1) that the trial court had acted properly in (1) giving the plaintiffs a lien on certain property in the defendant's hands to ensure payment of the judgment; (2) giving the defendant who was a selling agent of the corporate defendant a similar lien if he should pay any part of the judgment, by way of ensuring his indemnification by his principal under the law of agency; and (3) impressing a

C. 10J [1] Deckert v. Independence Shares Corp., 311 U. S. 282, 287-90 (1940), *on remand*, 39 F. Supp. 592 (E. D. Pa. 1941), *rev'd on other grounds* sub nom. Pennsylvania Co. for Insurances on Lives & Granting Annuities v. Deckert, 123 F. 2d 979 (3d Cir. 1941); cf. United States v. E. I. du Pont de Nemours & Co., 366 U. S. 316, 323 (1961) (broad equity powers to fashion effective remedies in injunction suits under antitrust statutes).

[2] Corporation Trust Co. v. Logan, 52 F. Supp. 999 (D. Del. 1943); see also Kinsey v. Knapp, 154 F. Supp. 263 (E. D. Mich. 1957), *rev'd on other grounds* sub nom. Knapp v. Kinsey, 249 F. 2d 797 (6th Cir. 1957), *leave to file petition for cert. denied*, 356 U. S. 935.

[3] "Except as to a party against whom a judgment is entered by default, every final judgment shall grant the relief to which the party in whose favor it is rendered is entitled, even if the party has not demanded such relief in his pleadings."

trust for the plaintiffs' benefit upon the funds paid by them for drilling expenses.[4]

Injunctive relief has been regularly approved in private actions implied under Rule 10b-5, §14(e) (the tender offer fraud provision), and the Investment Company Act. We have also seen how far the courts have gone and might go in preventing violators of the proxy rules from enjoying the fruits of their illegality.[5] And we have noticed the appointment of receivers for insolvent or undercapitalized broker-dealers.[6] In all these areas there is no reason to distinguish between the SEC as plaintiff and private plaintiffs.

Perhaps the most dramatic use of the courts' ancillary jurisdiction has been in their ordering restitution or disgorgement of profits in SEC injunctive actions.[7] Disgorgement may be granted even when an injunction is denied[8] and even when a private action would have been barred by the *Blue Chip* doctrine.[9] The funds are usually

[4] Whittaker v. Wall, 226 F. 2d 868, 872-73 (8th Cir. 1955); cf. Speed v. Transamerica Corp., 135 F. Supp. 176, 187 (D. Del. 1955), *modified on other grounds and aff'd,* 235 F. 2d 369 (3d Cir. 1956).

[5] See pp. 491-97 supra.

[6] See p. 816 supra. There is also precedent

for appointing a "custodian" [Adelman v. CGS Scientific Corp., 332 F. Supp. 137, 147 (E. D. Pa. 1971)] or "special agent" to see to compliance with the reporting requirements [SEC v. Beisinger Industries Corp., 552 F. 2d 15 (1st Cir. 1977)] or "special fiscal agent" [Braasch v. Muscat, CCH Fed. Sec. L. Rep. ¶92,148 (S. D. N. Y. 1968), *vacated per curiam on other grounds,* 398 F. 2d 1022 (2d Cir. 1968); SEC v. Philip S. Budin & Co., Inc., CCH Fed. Sec. L. Rep. ¶93,088 (D. N. J. 1971)] or "escrow agent" [SEC v. Bennett & Co., 207 F. Supp. 919, 924-25 (D. N. J. 1962)] or "special counsel" [see cases cited infra p. 1068 nn. 8-12] or a "trustee" to oversee restitution [SEC v. Manor Nursing Centers, Inc., 458 F. 2d 1082, 1103-06 (2d Cir. 1972)]. See also SEC v. Vesco, 571 F. 2d 129 (2d Cir. 1978); Malhas v. Shinn, 597 F. 2d 28 (2d Cir. 1979).

2 Code 929-30, Comment (2). In SEC v. First Jersey Securities, Inc., Litig. Rel. 10,616, 31 SEC Dock. 1037 (S. D. N. Y. 1984), a consent case, the court appointed a "consultant" to review a broker-dealer firm's practices and supervisory procedures and report to the court with his recommendations, which would have to be fully implemented.

On the power to appoint receivers and require disgorgement generally, see SEC v. Wencke, 783 F. 2d 829, 837 n. 9 (9th Cir. 1986).

[7] See p. 751 n. 80 supra; Farrand, Ancillary Remedies in SEC Civil Enforcement Suits, 89 Harv. L. Rev. 1779 (1976); Mathews, Recent Trends in SEC Requested Ancillary Relief in SEC Level Injunctive Actions, 31 Bus. Law. 1323 (1976); Comment, Equitable Remedies in SEC Enforcement Actions, 123 U. Pa. L. Rev. 1188 (1975); SEC Civil Injunctive Actions, Program of the Committee on Federal Regulation of Securities, 30 Bus. Law. 1303 (1975); Dent, Ancillary Relief in Federal Securities Law: A Study in Federal Remedies, 67 Minn. L. Rev. 865 (1983); Krupp, Disgorgement, 10 Litig. 18 (1983).

[8] SEC v. Lund, 570 F. Supp. 1397, 1404 (C. D. Cal. 1983).

[9] SEC v. Tome, 638 F. Supp. 596, 626-27 (S. D. N. Y. 1986).

placed in escrow, to be applied to private judgments, with any balance going to the Treasury. The Treasury may also be the recipient to the extent it is not feasible to locate members of the public who were harmed.[10] But the courts exercise considerable discretion both in fixing the quantum of disgorgement and in deciding who gets it. In a *Chiarella*-type case, for example, where the defendant's inside information had come from the tender offeror whose printing he had been engaged in, the court required notice to be given to the printer's customer and the offeror and also referred to other potential recipients of the fund.[11]

All this is aside from the many consent injunctions in recent years that have provided for the appointment of directors[12] or special

[10]SEC v. Lund, 570 F. Supp. 1397, 1404 (C. D. Cal. 1983); see also SEC v. Blavin, 760 F. 2d 706, 711 (6th Cir. 1985) (investment adviser's disgorgement excluded subscribers' fees as well as defendant's trading profits); SEC v. Courtois, CCH Fed. Sec. L. Rep. ¶92,000 (S. D. N. Y. 1985).

[11]SEC v. Materia, CCH Fed. Sec. L. Rep. ¶99,583 at 97,284-85 (S. D. N. Y. 1983), *aff'd on other grounds,* 745 F. 2d 197 (2d Cir. 1984), *cert. denied,* 471 U. S. 1053.

In SEC v. Martin, CCH Fed. Sec. L. Rep. ¶99,508 (W. D. Wash. 1983), a consent case against an accountant, the defendant, because of his inability to pay all the money required to be disgorged, was allowed to satisfy the disgorgement order by turning over all his assets, except for some that a debtor in bankruptcy would ordinarily retain, to a receiver, who would present a distribution plan for judicial approval with a view to ultimate distribution to the defendant's creditors and those who had traded with him while he had been in possession of inside information.

In SEC v. Certain Unknown Purchasers of the Common Stock of, and Call Options for the Common Stock of Santa Fe Int'l Corp., CCH Fed. Sec. L. Rep. ¶99,424 (S. D. N. Y. 1983), an investor who had reduced his insider trading claim to judgment was not permitted to look to the profits that had been frozen in the SEC's injunction action. And in SEC v. Courtois, supra, where the court ordered the escrow fund to be paid into the Treasury, the court held that no seller was entitled to any part of the fund, but it left open the question whether the defendant was entitled to "equitable" consideration with respect to legal claims that might subsequently be asserted against him.

It is unsettled whether the Internal Revenue Service has a prior tax claim or whether, as the SEC contends, a constructive trust is imposed on the entire amount disgorged. See 7 Bus. Law. Update, No. 2, p. 1 (1986).

The House committee report on the Insider Trading Sanctions Act of 1984 (see p. 1008, end, infra) referred approvingly to ancillary jurisdiction by way of requiring "that independent directors be added to corporate boards, that audit committees be formed and that internal controls or procedures be modified to prevent the recurrence of violations." Insider Trading Sanctions Act of 1983, H. R. Rep. No. 98-355, 98th Cong., 1st Sess. (1983) 7.

[12]See Note, The SEC and Court-Appointed Directors: Time to Tailor the Director to Fit the Suit, 60 Wash. U. L. Q. 507 (1982). See also TBK Partners v. Luptak, — F. Supp. — , CCH Fed. Sec. L. Rep. ¶92,928 (E. D. Mich. 1986), which was *not* a consent case: on a showing that a corporation's major creditor would hold it in default if a receiver were appointed, the court ordered instead that the shareholder plaintiffs submit the names of two persons willing to sit on the board, one to participate on the audit committee, and that the parties should

counsel,[13] or that have barred defendants (not securities professionals) from acting as corporate directors or officers or being associated with publicly held companies for a period of years.[14]

On top of all this judge-made law, the Commission in 1982, recognizing "that current remedies do not provide sufficient deterrence" against insider trading notwithstanding its stepped-up efforts in recent years "to combat this threat to the securities markets," recommended additional legislation.[15] Congress responded by enacting the Insider Trading Sanctions Act of 1984,[16] which added a new §21(d)(2) to the 1934 Act: Whenever it appears to the Commission that

> any person has violated [the 1934 Act or the rules thereunder] by purchasing or selling a security while in possession of material non-public information in a transaction (i) on or through the facilities of a national securities exchange or from or through a broker or dealer, and (ii) which is not part of a public offering by an issuer of securities other than standardized options, the Commission may bring an action in a United States district court to seek, and the court shall have jurisdiction to impose, a civil penalty to be paid by such person, or any person aiding and abetting the violation of such person. The

---

jointly submit the name of an independent law firm to advise the board on specified matters.

[13]See pp. 1068-69 infra. In SEC v. Data Access Systems, Inc., CCH Fed. Sec. L. Rep. ¶98,779 (D. N. J. 1982), where a consent judgment permitted the defendants to seek the court's leave to refuse to implement specific recommendations of a "special agent," the court held that it would review recommendations only under a "clearly erroneous" test.

[14]SEC v. San Saba Nu-Tech, Inc., Litig. Rel. 10,531, 31 SEC Dock. 510 (D. D. C. 1984); SEC v. Florafax Int'l, Inc., Litig. Rel. 10,617, 31 SEC Dock. 1038 (N. D. Okla. 1984).

[15]SEC memorandum, CCH Fed. Sec. L. Rep. ¶83,259 (Sept. 27, 1982).

[16]98 Stat. 1264. The House bill (H. R. 559, 98th Cong.) was amended by the Senate and then enacted without either a Senate or a conference report. Consequently the legislative history consists of Insider Trading Sanctions and SEC Enforcement Legislation, Hearing on H. R. 559 Before Subcom. on Telecommunications, Consumer Protection, and Finance, House Com. on Energy & Commerce, 98th Cong., 1st Sess., Serial No. 98-33 (1983); Insider Trading Sanctions Act of 1983, H. R. Rep. No. 98-355, 98th Cong., 1st Sess. (1983), as modified by explanations by Senator D'Amato (130 Cong. Rec. S8912-14 (daily ed., June 29, 1984)) and Representative Dingell (130 Cong. Rec. H7757-58 (daily ed., July 25, 1984)); The Insider Trading Sanctions Act of 1983, Hearing on H. R. 559 Before Subcom. on Securities, S. Com. on Banking, Housing, & Urban Affairs, 98th Cong., 2d Sess. (1984).

See generally Brodsky, Insider Trading and the Insider Trading Sanctions Act of 1984: New Wine into New Bottles?, 41 Wash. & Lee L. Rev. 921 (1984); Langevoort, The Insider Trading Sanctions Act of 1984 and Its Effect on Existing Law, 37 Vand. L. Rev. 1273 (1984); Note, A Critique of the Insider Trading Sanctions Act of 1984, 71 Va. L. Rev. 455 (1985); Silver, Penalizing Insider Trading: A Critical Assessment of the Insider Trading Sanctions Act of 1984, [1985] Duke L. J. 960.

amount of such penalty shall be determined by the court in light of the facts and circumstances, but shall not exceed three times the profit gained or loss avoided as a result of such unlawful purchase or sale and shall be payable into the Treasury of the United States.

(1) "Profit gained" or "loss avoided" is defined as in the tort measure of damages that is at least the starting point under Rule 10b-5:[17] "the difference between the purchase or sale price of the security and the value of that security as measured by the trading price of the security a reasonable period after public dissemination of the nonpublic information." The House Committee report noted[18] that the First Circuit in *SEC* v. *MacDonald*[19] had rejected a Commission contention that the amount to be disgorged should be the entire profit, as measured by the difference between the purchase and sale prices of the security traded, even though the sale occurred many months after public disclosure of the inside information. The Commission's deterrence argument, in the committee's view, fell in the face of the treble damage provision. But the committee noted its non-endorsement of the *MacDonald* holding apart from actions under the new provision.[20]

(2) The aiding and abetting coverage is limited to "communicating material nonpublic information." It thus covers tippers even if they do not trade,[21] but not "broker-dealers and their registered representatives who do no more than execute trades for customers who are trading unlawfully."[22] And the section applies neither to controlling persons under §20(a)[23] nor (on any *respondeat superior* basis) to a violator's employer who is not otherwise liable. In the investment company area, the committee considered it "appropriate that if an adviser to an investment company directed trades on behalf of the investment company while in possession of material nonpublic information, the adviser, and not the investment company shareholders, should be subject to the triple penalty as a direct violator."[24]

(3) The new penalty is in addition to, not in substitution for,

[17] See p. 967 supra.

[18] H. R. Rep. No. 98-355, 98th Cong., 1st Sess. (1983) 11-12.

[19] 699 F. 2d 47, 52-55 (1st Cir. *en banc* 1983), *on remand*, 568 F. Supp. 111 (D. R. I. 1983), *aff'd per curiam*, 725 F. 2d 9 (1st Cir. 1984).

[20] H. R. Rep. No. 98-355, 98th Cong., 1st Sess. (1983) 12.

[21] Id. at 9.

[22] Id. at 10.

[23] See p. 1011 infra.

[24] Id. at 11.

injunction and disgorgement.[25] And payment of a penalty by one person does not immunize any other person.[26]

(4) The legislation does not change the underlying substantive case law of insider trading as reflected in judicial and administrative holdings.[27] Some suggested the addition of some sort of definition of the scope of the violation for purposes of the new provision (as well as 10b-5 cases generally). But Congress rejected this suggestion, which was opposed by the SEC, because (a) it believed that "the law with respect to insider trading is sufficiently well-developed at this time to provide adequate guidance," (b) a statutory definition would reduce flexibility, and (c) it was more advisable (as stated, the committee observed, in the commentary to the Code) to await further judicial development.[28]

(5) A new §20(d) provides:

> Wherever communicating, or purchasing or selling a security while in possession of, material nonpublic information would violate, or result in liability to any purchaser or seller of the security under any provision of this title, or any rule or regulation thereunder, such conduct in connection with a purchase or sale of a put, call, straddle, option, or privilege with respect to such security or with respect to a group or index of securities including such security, shall also violate and result in comparable liability to any purchaser or seller of that security under such provision, rule, or regulation.

(6) Rejecting the suggestion that liability be limited to those who "knowingly" cause the illegal transaction, the House committee stated that the legislation "is not intended to change current law with respect to the level of awareness required of a violator."[29]

(7) The committee disavowed any intention to "inhibit legitimate analytical activities."[30]

(8) The question of right to a jury trial in government and civil penalty actions was left to the Seventh Amendment.[31]

(9) For the new §19(d)(2) alone, there is a statute of limitations in terms of five years "after the purchase or sale," which is not to

[25] Id. at 8. See SEC v. Gafney, Litig. Rel. 10,725, 32 SEC Dock. 1265 (S. D. N. Y. 1985); SEC v. Ablan, Litig. Rel. 10,830, 33 SEC Dock. 988 (S. D. N. Y. 1985). In SEC v. Boesky, Litig. Rel. 11,288, 37 SEC Dock. 66 (S. D. N. Y. 1986), the defendant agreed to pay the equivalent of $100 million in cash and assets — half representing disgorgement of profits and half representing a civil penalty under the new statute.

[26] 130 Cong. Rec. S8913 (daily ed., June 29, 1984).

[27] H. R. Rep. No. 98-355, 98th Cong., 1st Sess. (1983) 13.

[28] Id. at 13-15.

[29] Id. at 9.

[30] Id. at 5.

[31] Id. at 16.

"be construed to bar or limit in any manner any action by the Commission or the Attorney General under any other provision of this title."

(10) The criminal provisions in §32(a) of the 1934 Act were amended by increasing the maximum fine under the statute generally from $10,000 to $100,000.

(11) There are indications in the House committee report that the committee favors the "breach of fiduciary duty to a third person" or misappropriation theory. An instance is the statement that, "for the purposes of the anti-fraud provisions, it does not matter whether the information about a corporation or its securities originates from inside or outside of the corporation."[32] — a statement not supported by the *Dirks* footnote that is cited for it.[33]

2. Secondary Liability

a. Controlling Persons

The 1933 and 1934 Acts provide, in somewhat different language, that anyone who "controls" a person liable thereunder is equally liable, subject to a special defense that varies in the two statutes.[34]

[32] Id. at 4; see also id. at 2.

[33] Dirks v. SEC, 463 U. S. 646, 656-57 n. 15 (1983).

Query: Is it fair for individual defendants to be thus pitted against the Government so far as private damages are concerned? Is it "cricket" to deprive defendants of a jury trial? And should the Commission be able, in effect, to obtain private relief without having to prove the reliance or causation that a private plaintiff would have to establish? See Katz and Nerheim, Injunctive Proceedings and Ancillary Remedies Under Federal Securities Statutes, in Practising Law Institute, The 10b Series of Rules (Corp. Prac. Tr. Ser. 21, 1975) 203-04. These questions must be considered in the light particularly of the availability of the class action.

[34] Sec. Act §15; Sec. Ex. Act §20(a). The unexplained difference in the defense is the more remarkable — and the more exasperating — in view of the fact that §15 of the 1933 Act as originally enacted contained no defense at all. The present defense was added by the 1934 amendments, which were part of the same bill that enacted the 1934 Act. See H. R. Rep. No. 1838, 73d Cong., 2d Sess. (1934) 42.

Four of the Acts also make it unlawful (somewhat tautologically) for any person to do indirectly, or cause to be done through another, what he may not do directly. Sec. Ex. Act §20(b); Holding Co. Act §27(a); Inv. Co. Act §48(a); Inv. Adv. Act §208(d). In SEC v. American Board of Trade, Inc., 593 F. Supp. 337, 341 (S. D. N. Y. 1984), *rev'd on other grounds,* 751 F. 2d 529 (2d Cir. 1984), the court referred to §48(a) of the Investment Company Act as "analogous" to the "controlling person" provisions of the 1933 and 1934 Acts.

So far as the meaning of "controls" is concerned, there is by now a fair amount of case law specifically directed to the concept of "control" in connection with civil liability. And, for the rest, we are relegated, in the absence of a statutory definition in the 1933 or 1934 Act, to the many considerations discussed in the chapter on control.[35]

For example, the partners of a New York broker-dealer firm were held liable, on a jury's finding of control, for a new California broker-dealer corporation's violations of Rule 10b-5 and the margin rules under §7 of the Exchange Act. The California corporation's president was a close friend of several of the partners of the New York firm, and two-thirds of the capital was provided by wives and relatives of those partners. The New York firm paid for a direct wire between the two offices. But it customarily paid for direct wires to its out-of-town correspondents. And neither its partners nor their wives and relatives ever interfered with the management of the California corporation.[36]

A number of propositions are reasonably clear:

(1) The control sections apply only to a person who was in control at the time the liability of the controlled person accrued, and not to a person who obtained control thereafter.[37]

(2) The defenses require some supervisory procedures and perhaps other precautionary measures, depending on the circum-

[35] C. 6 supra.

[36] Smith v. Bear, 237 F. 2d 79, 82 (2d Cir. 1956); see also, e. g., Hawkins v. Merrill Lynch, Pierce, Fenner & Beane, 95 F. Supp. 104, 123 (W. D. Ark. 1949) (nationwide brokerage firm *held* liable for Arkansas wire correspondent's violation of Rule 10b-5 and provisions on confirmations and financial reports); DeMarco v. Edens, CCH Fed. Sec. L. Rep. ¶91,856 at 95,934-36 (S. D. N. Y. 1966), *aff'd*, 390 F. 2d 836 (2d Cir. 1968); Myzel v. Fields, 386 F. 2d 718, 738-39 (8th Cir. 1967), *cert. denied*, 389 U. S. 951 (a controlling person who induced the conduct that violated Rule 10b-5 was liable even without knowledge of the specific wrongdoing if he was the intended beneficiary of the stock purchase); SEC v. First Securities Co. of Chicago, 463 F. 2d 981 (7th Cir. 1972), *cert. denied* sub nom. McKy v. Hochfelder, 409 U. S. 880 (broker-dealer corporation controlled its president); Hughes v. Dempsey-Tegeler & Co., Inc., CCH Fed. Sec. L. Rep. ¶94,133 at 94,550-51 (C. D. Cal. 1973), *aff'd on other grounds*, 534 F. 2d 156 (9th Cir. 1976), *cert. denied*, 429 U. S. 896 (stock exchange, in view of its directions to an undercapitalized member, controlled the member, but had the statutory defenses).

[37] Wittenberg v. Continental Real Estate Partners, Ltd., 478 F. Supp. 504 (D. Mass. 1979), *aff'd per curiam*, 625 F. 2d 5 (1st Cir. 1980). *Query* Metge v. Baehler, 762 F. 2d 621, 630-31 (8th Cir. 1985), *cert. denied*, Sub. nom. Metge v. Bankers Trust Co., 106 S. Ct. 798 and 832, where the court held that the plaintiff must prove (1) that the defendant *exercised* control over the corporation's operations *generally* and (2) that he had the *power* to control the *specific* transaction or activity on which the primary violation was predicated.

stances.[38] Thus, a newspaper publisher does not have the same duty to supervise a financial columnist[39] that a broker-dealer has to supervise its employees.[40]

(3) A controlling person who knows the underlying facts has no defense that he did not know that the interests involved were securities as a matter of law.[41]

(4) It is not necessary to join the allegedly controlled person.[42]

(5) Neither §15 nor §20(a) provides for contribution among controlling persons.[43]

(6) Sections 15 and 20(a) do not affect actions for injunction or disciplinary proceedings.[44]

[38]Richardson v. MacArthur, 451 F. 2d 35, 42 (10th Cir. 1971). In San Francisco-Okla. Petroleum Corp. v. Carstan Oil Co., Inc., 765 F. 2d 962, 965 (10th Cir. 1985), where the defendant attempted to sustain his burden by claiming he was a figurehead who had made no effort to learn what the corporation was doing, the court concluded that the testimony demonstrated that "he must have made a conscious effort not to know."

[39]Zweig v. Hearst Corp., 521 F. 2d 1129, 1132-35 (9th Cir. 1975), *cert. denied,* 423 U. S. 1025.

[40]Lorenz v. Watson, 258 F. Supp. 724, 732 (E. D. Pa. 1966); Henricksen v. Henricksen, 640 F. 2d 880, 888 (7th Cir. 1981), *cert. denied* sub nom. Smith Barney, Harris Upham & Co. v. Henricksen, 454 U. S. 1097; but cf. Sennott v. Rodman & Renshaw, 474 F. 2d 32, 39, 40 n. 5 (7th Cir. 1973), *cert. denied,* 414 U. S. 926 (broker-dealer firm's duty to control its partners, agents, and past employees extended only to their transactions involving the firm, and it could not have exercised bad faith with respect to transactions of which it had no knowledge).

In Bradshaw v. Van Houten, 601 F. Supp. 983 (D. Ariz. 1985), the court applied the "flexible duty" standard of White v. Abrams, 495 F. 2d 724 (9th Cir. 1974), to sustain a brokerage firm's defense.

In Davis v. Avco Financial Services, Inc., 739 F. 2d 1057, 1068 (6th Cir. 1984), *rehearing, and rehearing en banc, denied,* CCH Fed. Sec. L. Rep. ¶91,668 (6th Cir. 1984), *cert. denied,* 470 U. S. 1005, 472 U. S. 1012, the court listed the following considerations as pertinent in establishing the defense:

> (1) the quantum of decisional (planning) and facilitative (promotional) participation, such as designing the deal and contacting and attempting to persuade potential purchasers, (2) access to source data against which the truth or falsity of representations can be tested, (3) relative skill in ferreting out the truth * * *, (4) pecuniary interest in the completion of the transaction, and (5) the existence of a relationship of trust and confidence between the plaintiff and the alleged "seller."

[41]Hayden v. McDonald, 742 F. 2d 423, 438-39 (8th Cir. 1984) (Minnesota blue sky law).

[42]DeMarco v. Edens, 390 F. 2d 836, 840 (2d Cir. 1968); Kemmerer v. Weaver, 445 F. 2d 76, 78 (7th Cir. 1971).

[43]Shea v. Unger, CCH Fed. Sec. L. Rep. ¶91,558 (S. D. N. Y. 1965).

[44]SEC v. Coffey, 493 F. 2d 1304, 1318 (6th Cir. 1974), *cert. denied,* 420 U. S. 908; but cf. SEC v. Management Dynamics, Inc., 515 F. 2d 801, 812-13 (2d Cir. 1975). On the question whether §20(a) extends to §16(b), see p. 522 n. 86 supra.

(7) One who controls an aider and abettor[45] is covered though twice removed from the person primarily liable.[46] On the other hand, one cannot aid and abet a violation of one of the control provisions, because they are not substantive provisions that proscribe specified conduct.[47]

Less clear is the question — on which the Circuits are split — whether the control provisions are exclusive or whether principals are liable for the acts of their agents on common law agency concepts of *respondeat superior* without the statutory defenses.[48] The Code follows the majority view, which recognizes common law liability, so that the defenses are available only when the defendant controls as a holding company or in some other nonagency way.[49]

[45] See p. 1016 infra.

[46] Edwards & Hanly v. Wells Fargo Securities Clearance Corp., 458 F. Supp. 1110 (S. D. N. Y. 1978), *rev'd on other grounds,* 602 F. 2d 478 (2d Cir. 1979), *cert. denied,* 444 U. S. 1045.

[47] Bloor v. Carro, Spanbock, Londin, Rodman & Fass, 754 F. 2d 57 (2d Cir. 1985). Moreover, "In alleging the requisite 'substantial' assistance by the aider and abettor, the complaint must allege that the acts of the aider and abettor proximately caused the harm to the corporation on which the primary liability is predicated." Id. at 62.

[48] Contrast Musewicz, Vicarious Employer Liability and Section 10(b): In Defense of the Common Law, 50 Geo. Wash. L. Rev. 754 (1982), with Fitzpatrick and Carman, Respondeat Superior and the Federal Securities Laws: A Round Peg in a Square Hole, 12 Hofstra L. Rev. 1 (1983).

[49] §1724(a). In addition to the cases cited in 2 Code 792-93, Comment (3)(b), the following cases decidedly strengthen the majority view: Reyos v. United States, 431 F. 2d 1337, 1346-47 (10th Cir. 1970), *aff'd on this point and rev'd on other grounds* sub nom. Affiliated Ute Citizens of Utah v. United States, 406 U. S. 128, 154 (1972); Marbury Management, Inc. v. Kohn, 629 F. 2d 705, 712-17 (2d Cir. 1980), *cert. denied* sub nom. Wood, Walker & Co. v. Marbury Management, Inc., 449 U. S. 1011; Paul F. Newton & Co. v. Texas Commerce Bank, 630 F. 2d 1111, 1118-19 (5th Cir. 1980); Henricksen v. Henricksen, 640 F. 2d 880, 888 (7th Cir. 1981), *cert. denied* sub nom. Smith Barney, Harris Upham & Co. v. Henricksen, 454 U. S. 1097; Davis v. Avco Financial Services, Inc., 739 F. 2d 1057, 1066 (6th Cir. 1984), *rehearing, and rehearing en banc, denied,* CCH Fed. Sec. L. Rep. ¶91,668 (6th Cir. 1984), *cert. denied,* 470 U. S. 1005, 472 U. S. 1012; Xaphes v. Merrill Lynch, Pierce, Fenner & Smith, Inc., 600 F. Supp. 692, 695-96 (D. Me. 1985), citing the text; In re Atlanta Financial Management, Inc. Securities Litigation, 784 F. 2d 29 (1st Cir. 1986); Commerford v. Olson, 794 F. 2d 1319 (8th Cir. 1986).

Cf. Sharp v. Coopers & Lybrand, 649 F. 2d 175, 181-84 (3d Cir. 1981), *cert. denied,* 455 U. S. 938 (judgment against accounting firm was limited to the facts in recognition of the important services performed by accountants "in evaluating, synthesizing, and explicating complex financial data"); but cf. O'Connor & Associates v. Dean Witter Reynolds, Inc., 529 F. Supp. 1179, 1194 (S. D. N. Y. 1981) (insider trading, as distinct from a brokerage employee's misrepresentation designed to further the interests of his employer, is not "within the scope of employment").

The *Atlanta* case, supra, involved apparent authority, which the Court in American Society of Mechanical Engineers, Inc. v. Hydrolevel Corp., 456 U. S. 556, 565-70 (1982), applied under the antitrust laws, citing some of the SEC cases.

The commentary observes that the control provisions were aimed at the "dummy director" problem:

> There is no reason to assume that Congress contemplated a *lesser* liability than the law of agency would impose in the typical employer-employee case. Such liability may be based not only (i) on the *principal's* conduct in (for example) intentionally causing the agent's acts or failing properly to supervise [Restatement (Second) of Agency §§212-14] but also (ii) on vicarious concepts when the principal himself is quite innocent (id. §§257-58).[50]

In any event, the control provisions do not preclude "piercing the corporate veil" when that conclusion is justified under principles of corporation law.[51]

Finally, one can only *query* whether the scienter holding of *Hochfelder* in 10b-5 actions carries over to the controlling person if it is established that the controlled person acted with scienter. The question of secondary liability based on either §20(a) or *respondeat superior,* which is a vicarious, deeper pocket sort of liability, seems different from the question of secondary liability based on aiding and abetting, where the required degree of fault is greater, if anything, than it is with respect to the person primarily liable.[52] Sections 15 and 20(a), of course, have their own defenses. The Fifth Circuit required the defendant to show no more than lack of recklessness in the light of *Hochfelder.*[53] But other Circuits, without using "scienter" language, have required the *plaintiff* to show participation in the allegedly illegal activities (in some cases culpable participation) by way of establishing "control" in the first place.[54]

There is also the possibility, as against high-ranking corporate officers, of arguing that their action in behalf of the corporation is primary, so that holding the corporation liable does not require *respondeat superior.* Sharp v. Coopers & Lybrand, 649 F. 2d 175, 182 n. 8 (3d Cir. 1981). *cert. denied,* 455 U. S. 938.

The House committee report on the Insider Trading Sanctions Act of 1984 (see p. 1008 supra) seems to endorse the *respondeat superior* concept, which it says is not affected by the new treble damage action. Insider Trading Sanctions Act of 1983, H. R. Rep. No. 98-355, 98th Cong., 1st Sess. (1984) 10.

[50] 2 Code 793, Comment (3)(b).

[51] Kerch v. General Council of the Assemblies of God, 535 F. Supp. 494, 496-98 (N. D. Cal. 1982).

[52] See p. 1018 supra.

[53] G. A. Thompson & Co. v. Partridge, 636 F. 2d 945 (5th Cir. 1981). Contrast Drobbin v. Nicolet Instrument Corp., 631 F. Supp. 860, 885-86 (S. D. N. Y. 1986) (court applied a *negligence* standard by way of defense, stating that that standard was particularly appropriate with respect to violation of the reporting and disclosure requirements of the 1934 Act rather than its antifraud provisions).

[54] Durham v. Kelly, 810 F. 2d 1500 (9th Cir. 1987), and cases cited; cf. Metge

b. Agents, Participants, and Aiders and Abettors

Brokers or other agents of the seller — persons who are not sellers in the mystical sense of passing "title" — are normally held accountable under §17(a) of the 1933 Act, which literally applies to "any person" who engages in fraudulent or misleading practices "in the sale of any securities." By contrast, §12 specifies that "Any person who sells * * * shall be liable to the person purchasing * * * from him." Even so it is now quite clear that a broker for the seller is a "person who sells."[55] So, just as logically, is a broker who represents both sides.[56] And, since the term "offer" is defined to include the "solicitation of an offer to buy a security," it has been held that even a broker who represents the buyer alone "sells" to his customer within the meaning of §12(2) so as to be accountable for any false statements made in soliciting the customer's buy order.[57] In principle this applies equally to render liable under §12(1) a broker who solicits a buy order in violation of §5. At the same time, when the broker represents the buyer alone and executes a purely *unsolicited* order, it is difficult to see how he could be considered one who "sells" even within the meaning of the Securities Act.[58]

There is nothing basically incongruous about forcing a broker for either seller or buyer to assume ownership of the securities for

v. Baehler, 762 F. 2d 621, 631 (8th Cir. 1985), *cert. denied* sub nom. Metge v. Bankers Trust Co., 106 S. Ct. 798 and 832.

[55]Cady v. Murphy, 113 F. 2d 988 (1st Cir. 1940), *cert. denied,* 311 U. S. 705; Schillner v. H. Vaughan Clarke & Co., 134 F. 2d 875, 879 (2d Cir. 1943); First Trust & Savings Bank of Zanesville, Ohio v. Fidelity-Philadelphia Trust Co., 214 F. 2d 320, 324 (3d Cir. 1954), *cert. denied,* 348 U. S. 856; White Lighting Co. v. Wolfson, 68 Cal. 2d 336, 355, 356 and n. 13, 438 P. 2d 345, 357 and n. 13 (1968); Lawler v. Gilliam, 569 F. 2d 1283, 1287-88 (4th Cir. 1978); cf. Brown v. Cole, 155 Tex. 624, 629, 291 S. W. 2d 704, 708 (1956) (state act). But cf. Xaphes v. Merrill Lynch, Pierce, Fenner & Smith, Inc., 597 F. Supp. 213 (D. Me. 1984) (court refused to follow Cady v. Murphy under Maine's equivalent of §12(2) because of the Maine provision's legislative history).

[56]Cady v. Murphy, 113 F. 2d 988 (1st Cir. 1940), *cert. denied,* 311 U. S. 705; DeMarco v. Edens, 390 F. 2d 836, 844-45 (2d Cir. 1968) (dictum).

[57]Murphy v. Cady, 30 F. Supp. 466, 469 (D. Me. 1939), *aff'd on other grounds* sub nom. Cady v. Murphy, 113 F. 2d 988 (1st Cir. 1940), *cert. denied,* 311 U. S. 705; Boehm v. Granger, 181 Misc. 680, 42 N. Y. S. 2d 246 (Sup. Ct. 1943), *aff'd per curiam,* 268 App. Div. 855, 50 N. Y. S. 2d 845 (1st Dept. 1944); Smith v. Smith, 424 S. W. 2d 244 (Tex. Civ. App. 1968) (state act); Katz v. Amos Treat & Co., 411 F. 2d 1046, 1052-53 (2d Cir. 1969); see also SEC v. Chinese Consolidated Benevolent Assn., 120 F. 2d 738, 740 (2d Cir. 1941), *cert. denied,* 314 U. S. 618.

[58]Katz v. Amos Treat & Co., 411 F. 2d 1046, 1053 (2d Cir. 1969). This is apart from the fact that, so far as §12(1) is concerned, an unsolicited brokerage order would normally be exempted from §5 by §4(4).

the first time. When rescission is based on a contract theory — mistake, or breach of contract — only the party to the contract is liable. But, when it is predicated on fraud, privity is not essential. "To avoid unjust enrichment, general equitable principles indicate the preferability of the purchaser pursuing first the seller, rather than his partner in the fraud. However, as between the innocent purchaser and the wrongdoer who, though not a privy to the fraudulent contract, nonetheless induced the victim to make the purchase, equity requires the wrongdoer to restore the victim to the status quo."[59] Besides, it would be a strange construction that permitted the buyer to recover damages if he had resold the security, but not rescission; he could easily avoid such a rule in any event by reselling just before suit, and (conversely) the broker upon whom the security is forced by rescission can resell it if there is a market, take his loss, and (selling cost aside) be no worse off than if he had paid damages.[60]

If a broker may be liable under §12, it is hard to distinguish the case of an officer or director or employee or other non-broker agent of the seller who actively participates in the sale.[61]

There are, to be sure, a number of obstacles to the application of §12: When Congress provided in §11 for the liability of various persons connected with an issuer filing a registration statement, it set up an elaborate scheme of defenses in lieu of the scienter element in common law deceit. It also inserted a contribution provision in §11, as well as in the sections of the 1934 Act that contemplate multiple defendants.

On the other hand, there would still be a distinction under §12 between the liability of the seller proper and the liability of other persons, in that the seller proper would have the burden under the statute of proving his innocence but the plaintiff obviously would have the burden of proving that the other persons had participated in an unlawful sale,[62] a burden that (at least under §12(2) as distinguished from §12(1)) would almost inevitably involve proof by the plaintiff of some sort of scienter on their part. In other words, there would still be a marked contrast between §§11 and 12 in this regard: officers and directors of a corporate seller would in no event

[59] Gordon v. Burr, 506 F. 2d 1080, 1085 (2d Cir. 1974).

[60] This assumes a rescission measure rather than a deceit or warranty measure of damages. See p. 875 supra.

[61] In re Caesars Palace Securities Litigation, 360 F. Supp. 366, 383 (S. D. N. Y. 1973).

[62] Id. at 380 (determination of sufficiency of the participation must await discovery).

be liable automatically under §12(2) subject only to the privilege of somehow purging themselves.[63]

The Second Circuit *en banc* drew a similar contrast between §11 and Rule 10b-5 in holding that an outside (non-management) director has no 10b-5 "duty to convey" — that is, "to insure that all material, adverse information is conveyed to prospective purchasers" of the corporation's stock. His 10b-5 liability "can thus only be secondary, such as that of an aider and abettor, a conspirator, or a substantial participant in fraud perpetrated by others." Without such participation the plaintiff must prove scienter in the sense of "actual knowledge * * * [or] a willful, deliberate, or reckless disregard for the truth that is the equivalent of knowledge."[64] Although the Second Circuit had earlier read Rule 10b-5 as requiring scienter even with respect to one alleged to be a *primary* violator, it is quite clear from the opinion that the court would have required no less of the plaintiff under §12(2).[65]

Indeed, even though recklessness may suffice to constitute scienter as applied to the principal defendant, some of the 10b-5 decisions speak in terms of "knowledge" on the part of the person liable secondarily.[66] This is consistent with the common law of torts,

[63]As for §12(1), the court stated in Katz v. Amos Treat & Co., 411 F. 2d 1046, 1053 (2d Cir. 1969), that that section was not "intended to embrace a corporate officer or director merely because he has knowledge of a sale of unregistered stock and plays * * * a minor role in facilitating it." See also Katz v. David W. Katz & Co., CCH Fed. Sec. L. Rep. ¶99,669 (S. D. N. Y. 1984), and cases cited.

[64]Lanza v. Drexel & Co., 479 F. 2d 1277, 1289, 1305 (2d Cir. *en banc* 1973) (the offering was private, so that §11 did not apply); Klein v. Computer Devices, Inc., 602 F. Supp. 837, 840 (S. D. N. Y. 1985), citing the text; Mayer v. Oil Field Systems Corp., 803 F. 2d 749, 756 (2d Cir. 1986), citing the text (§12(2) and Rule 10b-5); but cf. In re AM Int'l, Inc. Securities Litigation, 606 F. Supp. 600, 605 (S. D. N. Y. 1985) (audit committee members, though not officers, were *held,* on the facts pleaded, to be "much closer to the position occupied by an insider director, than they are to a typical outside director").

[65]See esp. Lanza v. Drexel & Co., 479 F. 2d 1277, 1298 (2d Cir. *en banc* 1973); see also Aid Auto Stores, Inc. v. Cannon, 525 F. 2d 468, 470-71 (2d Cir. *per curiam* 1975) (both §12(2) and Rule 10b-5 require "knowledge" of the principal defendant's breach of trust).

But cf. Sanders v. John Nuveen & Co., 619 F. 2d 1222 (7th Cir. 1980), supra p. 895 n. 30, which equated an underwriter's duty under §12(2) in the sale of commercial paper exempted under §3(a)(3) to its duty under §11. The Seventh Circuit's reading is the harder to understand in view of the opinion's reference to the underwriter's failure to verify the audited statements or to review the auditor's work papers — conduct not required to make out even the double-negative defense in §11(b)(3)(C). See p. 900 supra.

[66]See Zabriskie v. Lewis, 507 F. 2d 546, 554 (10th Cir. 1974); Woodward v. Metro Bank of Dallas, 522 F. 2d 84, 94-100 (5th Cir. 1975); Rochez Bros., Inc. v. Rhoades, 527 F. 2d 880, 886-87 (3d Cir. 1975); Hirsch v. du Pont, 553 F. 2d 750, 759 (2d Cir. 1977); Edwards & Hanly v. Wells Fargo Securities Clearance

which makes a person liable for harm resulting to a third person from the tortious conduct of another only (insofar as is here relevant) if he "knows that the other's conduct constitutes a breach of duty and gives substantial assistance or encouragement to the other so to conduct himself."[67]

A number of tests have been suggested for what constitutes sufficient participation to come within §12:

In a 1953 case the Commission argued successfully as *amicus curiae,* on the analogy of the brokers' liability cases, that any person who lent *substantial assistance* to a wrongful sale should be liable under §12(2) — for example, a defendant who was the driver of a sightseeing tour around the citrus groves in which investment contracts were being sold and who allegedly made fraudulent representations to induce persons to buy.[68]

In a 1964 case the court thought that liability under §12(1) "must lie somewhere between the narrow view, which holds only the party to the sale, and the too-liberal view, which would hold all who remotely participated in the events leading up to the transaction." On analogy from the law of negligence, the court thought the test should be whether the injuries to the plaintiff flowed "directly and proximately from the actions of [the] particular defendant." But "The hunter who seduces the prey and leads it to the trap he has set is no less guilty than the hunter whose hand springs the snare." On this approach the court held the defendant (Roger) who had made the initial contact with the plaintiffs and convinced them to invest, as well as the defendant (vice-president of the defendant corporation) who had assisted Roger and "represented the symbol of authority which Roger said he lacked," and the president, who had signed the agreement.[69]

Corp., 602 F. 2d 478, 485 (2d Cir. 1979), *cert. denied,* 444 U. S. 1045 ("something closer to an actual intent to aid in the fraud"); Barker v. Henderson, Franklin, Starnes & Holt, 797 F. 2d 490, 496 (7th Cir. 1986), citing the text.

But there is authority, at least in SEC injunctive actions, that "liability predicated on aiding and abetting may be founded on less than actual knowledge and participation in the activity proscribed by" Rule 10b-5. SEC v. First Securities Co. of Chicago, 463 F. 2d 981, 987 (7th Cir. 1972), *cert. denied* sub nom. McKy v. Hochfelder, 409 U. S. 880; SEC v. Spectrum, Ltd., 489 F. 2d 535, 541 (2d Cir. 1973).

[67] Restatement (Second) of Torts §876(b).

[68] SEC brief as *amicus curiae,* Blackwell v. Bentsen, 203 F. 2d 690 (5th Cir. 1953), *cert. dismissed,* 347 U. S. 925.

[69] Lennerth v. Mendenhall, 234 F. Supp. 59, 65 (N. D. Ohio 1964). To the same effect, see Junker v. Crory, 650 F. 2d 1349, 1360 (5th Cir. 1981), and cases cited; SEC v. Seaboard Corp. (Admiralty Fund v. Hugh Johnson & Co., Inc.), 677 F. 2d 1289, 1294 (9th Cir. 1983); McFarland v. Memorex Corp., 581 F. Supp. 878 (N. D. Cal. 1984); Davis v. Avco Financial Services, Inc., 739 F.

In 1977, however, the Eighth Circuit rejected the proximate cause test as failing to focus on implementing statutory policy. Toward that end, one factor to be considered, the court thought, was whether the defendant was in a unique position to ask relevant questions, to require material information, or to disclose his findings.[70]

At the other extreme, a number of cases, some expressly influenced by the Supreme Court's recent approach to implied actions, reject *any* secondary liability under §12 except as provided in §15.[71]

Everything thus far said about holding participants under §12(2) should apply *a fortiori* to Rule 10b-5, because it does not in so many words refer to seller's liability to buyer as does §12. And there are in fact more cases under Rule 10b-5. But the opinions speak in

---

2d 1057, 1064-68 (6th Cir. 1984), *rehearing, and rehearing en banc, denied,* CCH Fed. Sec. L. Rep. ¶91,668 (6th Cir. 1984), *cert. denied,* 470 U. S. 1005, 472 U. S. 1012; Foster v. Jesup & Lamont Securities Co., Inc., 759 F. 2d 838 (11th Cir. 1985) (defendant's acting as "best efforts" underwriter, and plaintiff's reliance on that fact in buying from issuer's controlling person rather than defendant, did not make defendant a "seller"); Anderson v. Aurotek, 774 F. 2d 927 (9th Cir. 1985); Adalman v. Baker, Watts & Co., 807 F. 2d 359 (4th Cir. 1986).

In SEC v. Rogers, 790 F. 2d 1450, 1456 (9th Cir. 1986), the court held, for both §12 and SEC actions, that the defendant's conduct had to be "both necessary to, and a substantial factor in, the unlawful transaction"; that the first standard required that the participation be a "but for" cause; and that the second required that it be more than *de minimis.*

But cf. Dahl v. Pinter, 787 F. 2d 985 (5th Cir. 1986), *cert. granted* sub. nom. Pinter v. Dahl, 107 S. Ct. 1885: A buyer of unregistered securities in oil and gas ventures who promoted the investment to family and friends was not a seller under §12(1) even though his conduct was a substantial factor in causing the other purchases, since his solicitations were motivated only by his desire to enrich his friends and family and he received no commission by way of discount or otherwise. "Absent express direction by Congress, we decline to impose liability for mere gregariousness." Id. at 991.

In general, see Note, Seller Liability Under Section 12(2) of the Securities Act of 1933: A Proximate Cause-Substantial Factor Approach Limited by a Duty of Inquiry, 36 Vand. L. Rev. 361 (1983).

[70] Wasson v. SEC, 558 F. 2d 879, 885-86 (8th Cir. 1977); see also Jefferies & Co. v. United Mo. Bank of Kansas City, N. A., CCH Fed. Sec. L. Rep. ¶99,257 at 96,144 (W. D. Mo. 1983).

[71] In re Equity Funding Corp. of America Securities Litigation, 416 F. Supp. 161, 181 (C. D. Cal. 1976); Benoay v. Decker, 517 F. Supp. 490, 494 (E. D. Mich. 1981); Beck v. Cantor Fitzgerald & Co., Inc., 621 F. Supp. 1547, 1560-61 (N. D. Ill. 1985); Wagman v. FSC Securities Corp., CCH Fed. Sec. L. Rep. ¶92,445 (N. D. Ill. 1985). In any event, insofar as the plaintiff must prove scienter in order to hold an aider and abettor under §12(2), that section offers him no advantage over Rule 10b-5. Klein v. Computer Devices, Inc., 602 F. Supp. 837, 841 (S. D. N. Y. 1985); Hackett v. Village Court Associates, 602 F. Supp. 856, 858-59 (E. D. Wis. 1985).

For an exhaustive study with respect to §12(2), see O'Hara, Erosion of the Privity Requirement in Section 12(2) of the Securities Act of 1933: The Expanded Meaning of Seller, 31 U. C. L. A. L. Rev. 921 (1984).

terms of "aiding and abetting" — a concept that has its roots in the law of torts as well as the criminal law[72] — rather than "participation," perhaps because §12(2) at least (as distinguished from §12(1)) is not based on a *violation* of anything but merely imposes civil liability for false statements. It is on aider and abettor concepts, for example, that a non-broker-dealer can violate §15(c)(1) of the 1934 Act, which applies only to brokers and dealers.[73]

Some of the 10b-5 cases — including the very first — speak also

[72] Restatement (Second) of Torts §876(b), supra p. 1018-19. See, e. g., Brennan v. Midwestern United Life Ins. Co., 417 F. 2d 147, 151-54 (7th Cir. 1969), *cert. denied,* 397 U. S. 989; Rolf v. Blyth, Eastman Dillon & Co., Inc., 570 F. 2d 38, 44-48 (2d Cir. 1978); Monsen v. Consolidated Dressed Beef Co., Inc., 479 F. 2d 793 (3d Cir. 1978), *cert. denied* sub nom. First Pa. Bank, N. A. v. Monsen, 439 U. S. 930 (also §12(1) and (2)); In re Seagate Technology Securities Litigation, CCH Fed. Sec. L. Rep. ¶92,435 at 92,658 (N. D. Cal. 1985) (though the substantial factor test "defines the outer limit" for §12(2) liability, motions to dismiss aiding and abetting claims *denied*); Foltz v. U. S. News & World Report, 627 F. Supp. 1143, 1155-56 (D. D. C. 1986); see also Errion v. Connell, 236 F. 2d 447 (9th Cir. 1956).

But cf. In re National Mortgage Equity Corp. Mortgage Pool Certificates Securities Litigation, 636 F. Supp. 1138, 1169 (C. D. Cal. 1986); Landy v. FDIC, 486 F. 2d 139, 162-64 (3d Cir. 1973), *cert. denied,* 416 U. S. 960; In re Activision Securities Litigation, 621 F. Supp. 415, 522 (N. D. Cal. 1985), and cases cited: "The 'substantial participation' test thus reflects the outer limits of §12 liability. This court refuses plaintiffs' invitation to extend its boundaries further by recognizing aiding and abetting liability."

Moreover, aider and abettor liability will not be extended to §11 because of the specificity of those primarily liable. In re Equity Funding Corp. of America Securities Litigation, 416 F. Supp. 161, 181 (C. D. Cal. 1976); Hagert v. Glickman, Lurie, Eiger & Co., 520 F. Supp. 1028, 1034 (D. Minn. 1981); In re Flight Transportation Corp. Securities Litigation, 593 F. Supp. 612 (D. Minn. 1984), disapproving In re Caesars Palace Securities Litigation, 360 F. Supp. 366 (S. D. N. Y. 1973); Ahern v. Gaussoin, 611 F. Supp. 1465 (D. Ore. 1985); In re Seagate Technology Securities Litigation, CCH Fed. Sec. L. Rep. ¶92,435 at 92,657 (N. D. Cal. 1985); Bresson v. Thomson McKinnon Securities, Inc., 641 F. Supp. 338, 342 (S. D. N. Y. 1986).

So, too, one underwriter (even presumably a managing underwriter) is not *as such* an aider and abettor so as to be liable to persons who bought from other participants in the distribution. In re Gap Stores Securities Litigation, 79 F. R. D. 283, 307 (N. D. Cal. 1978); Akerman v. Oryx Communications, Inc., 810 F. 2d 336, 344 (2d Cir. 1987).

The House committee report on the Insider Trading Sanctions Act of 1984 (see p. 1008 supra) endorsed the judicial application of the aider and abettor concept. Insider Trading Sanctions Act of 1983, H. R. Rep. No. 98-355, 98th Cong., 1st Sess. (1983) 10.

In general, see Gilmore and McBride, Liability of Financial Institutions for Aiding and Abetting Violations of Securities Laws, 42 Wash. & Lee L. Rev. 811 (1985).

[73] The Commission has found officers and salesmen guilty of violating §15(c) in disciplinary proceedings. E. g., Nees v. SEC, 414 F. 2d 211, 219 (9th Cir. 1969); Luckhurst & Co., Inc., 40 SEC 539, 540 (1961). And it has also used the aider and abettor statute, Cr. Code §2, 18 U. S. C. §2, as a basis for injunction. E. g., SEC v. Barraco, 438 F. 2d 97 (10th Cir. 1971).

in terms of conspiracy.[74] And, although the line between primary and secondary actors is sometimes vague, an accounting firm, for example, might be held liable as a principal violator.[75]

All this is encapsulated in the Code (essentially as a restatement of existing law) as follows:

> An agent or other person who knowingly causes or gives substantial assistance to conduct by another person (herein a "principal") giving rise to liability under this Code (* * * except for section 1714 [successor to §16(b)]) with knowledge that the conduct is unlawful or a breach of duty, or involves a fraudulent or manipulative act, a misrepresentation, or nondisclosure of a material fact by an insider (as defined in section 1603(b) [successor to Rule 10b-5]), is liable as a principal.[76] A person may cause or give substantial assistance to conduct by inaction or silence when he has a duty to act or speak.

The second sentence, which was added in the course of the discus-

[74]In the *Kardon* case Judge Kirkpatrick used conspiracy language to sustain the complaint as against the company with which the defendants had negotiated a sale of assets. Kardon v. National Gypsum Co., 69 F. Supp. 512, 514-15 (E. D. Pa. 1946), *on the merits,* 73 F. Supp. 798 (E. D. Pa. 1947), *on requests for additional findings,* 83 F. Supp. 613 (E. D. Pa. 1947), supra p. 729. See also, e. g., Texas Continental Life Ins. Co. v. Dunne, 307 F. 2d 242, 249 (6th Cir. 1962); Dasho v. Susquehanna Corp., 380 F. 2d 262, 267 n. 2 (7th Cir. 1967), *cert. denied* sub nom. Bard v. Dasho, 389 U. S. 977; Shell v. Hensley, 430 F. 2d 819, 827 n. 13 (5th Cir. 1970); Ferguson v. OmniMedia, Inc., 469 F. 2d 194, 197 (1st Cir. 1972); First Interstate Bank of Nev., N. A. v. National Republic Bank of Chicago, CCH Fed. Sec. L. Rep. ¶91,994 at 90,933 (N. D. Ill. 1985); Ruder, Multiple Defendants in Securities Law Fraud Cases: Aiding and Abetting, Conspiracy, *In Pari Delicto,* Indemnification, and Contribution, 120 U. Pa. L. Rev. 597, 620-44 (1972).

[75]Chemical Bank v. Arthur Andersen & Co., 552 F. Supp. 439, 454-55 (S. D. N. Y. 1982), and cases cited, *rev'd on other grounds,* 726 F. 2d 930 (2d Cir. 1984), *cert. denied,* 469 U. S. 884. Cf. Klein v. Computer Devices, Inc., 591 F. Supp. 270, 278 (S. D. N. Y. 1984), *reargument on other grounds,* 602 F. Supp. 837 (S. D. N. Y. 1985) (participation can include "active participation in the transaction, or aiding and abetting, or conspiring with the seller"); Kaliski v. Hunt Int'l Resources Corp., 609 F. Supp. 649 (N. D. Ill. 1985) (the acts constituting the aiding and abetting must occur before the completion of the allegedly fraudulent transaction, although one *can* be held *primarily* liable for damages incurred as a direct result of "lulling activities"); Sheftelman v. N. L. Industries, Inc., CCH Fed. Sec. L. Rep. ¶92,040 at 91,190 (D. N. J. 1985) (the need "to prove a securities *violation* * * * in no way indicates that the primary *violator* need be named as a defendant").

[76]§1724(b)(1); see William R. Carter, Sec. Ex. Act Rel. 17,597, 22 SEC Dock. 292, 315-16 (1981), infra p. 1057; Woods v. Barnett Bank of Fort Lauderdale, 765 F. 2d 1004 (11th Cir. 1985), and cases cited at 1009 n. 8, *rehearing en banc denied,* 772 F. 2d 918 (11th Cir. 1985).

sions with the SEC, reflects the case law, which is by no means uniform.[77] But the reference to a "duty to act or speak" is consistent with the *Dirks* approach in the analogous situation of fixing a tippee's obligation to speak under Rule 10b-5.[78]

Liability in these cases is several, not joint.[79] When the broker is the innocent party as between himself and the selling principal, presumably he has a right to be indemnified by the principal under common law agency concepts. Such a right over would seem to lie under §12 or Rule 10b-5 itself when the broker represented only the buyer, so that the broker was in effect a principal vis-à-vis the seller.[80]

Subject to the exceptions involving controlling persons, agents, and participants — the last of which may sometimes permit *Z* to sue *X* as well as *Y* even though *X* sold to *Y*, who sold to *Z*, if *Z* can prove that *X* participated to the required degree in *Y*'s violation of §5 or *Y*'s fraud — it seems quite clear that §12 contemplates only

[77] See, e. g., SEC v. Coffey, 493 F. 2d 1304, 1317 (6th Cir. 1974) (dictum), and cases cited; Kerbs v. Fall River Industries, Inc., 502 F. 2d 731, 740 (10th Cir. 1974); Hochfelder v. Midwest Stock Exchange, 503 F. 2d 364, 374-75 (7th Cir. 1974), *cert. denied*, 419 U. S. 875; Woodward v. Metro Bank of Dallas, 522 F. 2d 84, 94-100 (5th Cir. 1975), and cases cited; IIT v. Cornfeld, 619 F. 2d 909, 925-27 (2d Cir. 1980); Brennan v. Midwestern United Life Ins. Co., 417 F. 2d 147, 154-55 (7th Cir. 1969), *cert. denied*, 397 U. S. 989; Metge v. Baehler, 762 F. 2d 621, 624-25 (8th Cir. 1985), *cert. denied* sub nom. Metge v. Bankers Trust Co., 106 S. Ct. 798 and 832 (on a balancing of the "knowledge" and "substantial assistance" factors, "in the absence of a duty to act or disclose, an aider-abettor case predicated on inaction of the secondary party must meet a high standard of intent"); Rudolph v. Arthur Andersen & Co., 800 F. 2d 1040, 1045 (11th Cir. 1986) (when the alleged aiding and abetting is mere silence on the part of an auditor — failure to disclose fraud — "the requirement of 'knowing' assistance does not require a conscious intent to aid the fraud if the aider and abettor was under a duty to disclose"); Kersh v. General Council of the Assemblies of God, 804 F. 2d 546, 552 (9th Cir. 1986); cf. Walck v. American Stock Exchange, Inc., 687 F. 2d 778, 791 (3d Cir. 1982), *cert. denied*, 461 U. S. 942 (only if defendant "*consciously* intended to assist in the perpetration of a wrongful act"). *Contra:* Wessel v. Buhler, 437 F. 2d 279, 283 (10th Cir. 1971).

[78] Dirks v. SEC, 463 U. S. 646, 653-64 (1983).

In general, see Note, The Private Action Against a Securities Fraud Aider and Abettor: Silent and Inactive Conduct, 29 Vand. L. Rev. 1233 (1976). On lawyers as aiders and abettors, see SEC v. National Student Marketing Corp., 457 F. Supp. 682 (D. D. C. 1978), infra p. 1051; William R. Carter, Sec. Ex. Act Rel. 17,597, 22 SEC Dock. 292 (1981), infra p. 1057. For a suggestion that the implication of secondary liability is no longer viable since the recent Supreme Court decisions on implied liabilities, see Fischel, Secondary Liability Under Section 10(b) of the Securities Act of 1934 [*sic*], 69 Calif. L. Rev. 80 (1981). But see Hokama v. E. F. Hutton & Co., 566 F. Supp. 636, 640-42 (C. D. Cal. 1983).

[79] Stadia Oil & Uranium Co. v. Wheelis, 251 F. 2d 269, 276 (10th Cir. 1957).

[80] Cf. American Bank & Trust Co. v. Barad Shaff Securities Corp., 335 F. Supp. 1276, 1279-80 (S. D. N. Y. 1972) (bank that bought stock for a customer who subsequently defaulted can recover from seller under §12(1)).

an action by a buyer against *his immediate seller.*[81] That is to say, in the case of the typical firm-commitment underwriting, the ultimate investor can recover only from the dealer who sold to him.[82] But the dealer in turn can recover over against the underwriter, and the latter (with some caveat by reason of the "preliminary negotiations clause of §2(3)) against the issuer, and each defendant can bring in his predecessor in the chain of distribution as a third-party defendant under the Federal Rules of Civil Procedure. Moreover, in the case of "best-efforts" distributions in which the distributors act as the issuer's agents, so that title passes from the issuer directly to the ultimate investor, the investor can proceed under §12 against the issuer, the underwriters, the broker-dealer, and the salesman with whom he dealt; for they are all "sellers."[83]

3. NONWAIVER PROVISIONS (HEREIN OF ARBITRATION)

In England before the Companies Act of 1900 the courts honored stipulations that bound the purchasers to waive the statutory liabilities as long as the stipulations were not too "tricky."[84] Since

[81] Surowitz v. Hilton Hotels Corp., 342 F. 2d 596, 603 (7th Cir. 1965), *rev'd on other grounds,* 383 U. S. 363 (1966); Wolf v. Frank, 477 F. 2d 467, 478 (5th Cir. 1973), *cert. denied,* 414 U. S. 975; Collins v. Signetics Corp., 605 F. 2d 110, 113-14 (3d Cir. 1979); Klein v. Computer Devices, Inc., 602 F. Supp. 837, 840 (S. D. N. Y. 1965), supra Supp. p. 906 n. 73; Fine v. Rubin, 623 F. Supp. 171, CCH Fed. Sec. L. Rep. ¶92,342 (N. D. Cal. 1985).

[82] Ackerman v. Clinical Data, Inc., — F. Supp. —, CCH Fed. Sec. L. Rep. ¶92,803 (D. Mass. 1986), and cases cited.

[83] DeMarco v. Edens, CCH Fed. Sec. L. Rep. ¶91,856 at 95,934 (S. D. N. Y. 1966), *aff'd on other grounds,* 390 F. 2d 836 (2d Cir. 1968). On the other side of the coin, the plaintiff, of course, must be a buyer. Ratner v. Sioux National Gas Corp., 770 F. 2d 512, 517 (5th Cir. 1985). But the term "purchaser" in §12(2) includes an investment adviser (or broker) buying for a customer's account, and such a purchaser "owns" the security for purposes of §12 if he had enough control or authority to effectuate a tender. Monetary Management Group of St. Louis, Inc. v. Kidder, Peabody & Co., Inc., 604 F. Supp. 764 (E. D. Mo. 1985), supra p. 891 n. 15.

[84] Greenwood v. Leather Shod Wheel Co., [1900] 1 Ch. 421 (C. A.); Cackett v. Keswick, [1902] 2 Ch. 456 (C. A.). Under the blue sky laws, the courts worry about "virtual nullification." Foreman v. Holsman, 10 Ill. 2d 551, 553-54, 141 N. E. 2d 31, 32 (1957); Irving v. Bankers' Mortgage Co., 169 Miss. 890, 151 So. 740 (1934); 6 Corbin, Contracts (1951) 982-83; more generally, see id. §§1515-16; but cf. DePolo v. Greig, 338 Mich. 703, 707, 62 N. W. 2d 441, 442 (1954) (extenuating circumstances leading to estoppel as well as waiver). In any event, a waiver will be disregarded if it was obtained by fraud. Lolkus v. Vander Wilt, 258 Iowa 1074, 141 N. W. 2d 600 (1966).

the turn of the century, however, this ready means of evasion has been unavailable in England, and here again Congress profited from the English experience.[85]

All six SEC statutes specify that any condition, stipulation, or provision binding any person to waive compliance with any provision of the Act or any rule of the Commission "shall be void."[86] Except in the case of the 1933 and 1934 Acts, this extends also to any *order* of the Commission. The provision in the 1934 Act refers, in addition, to "any rule of an exchange required" by that Act. Presumably this covers those disciplinary rules that all exchanges are required by §6(b) to adopt as a condition of registration, as well as any exchange rules altered or supplemented by the Commission pursuant to §19(c).[87]

[85]Companies Act 1985, 1985 Acts c. 6, §§57, 86(7).

[86]Sec. Act §14; Sec. Ex. Act §29(a); Holding Co. Act §26(a); Trust Ind. Act §327; Inv. Co. Act §47(a); Inv. Adv. Act §215(a); see also Unif. Sec. Act §410(g). See Stonehill v. Security National Bank, 68 F. R. D. 24, 33 (S. D. N. Y. 1975) (provision in loan guarantee allowing bank to recover on the guarantee even though the loan violated Regulation U); Annot., Construction and Application of §14 of Securities Act of 1933 and §29(a) of Securities Exchange Act of 1934, Voiding Waiver of Compliance with Statutory Provisions or Rules or Regulations, 26 A. L. R. Fed. 495 (1976).

[87]Brown v. Gilligan, Will & Co., 287 F. Supp. 766, 773 n. 13 (S. D. N. Y. 1968); but cf. Rospigliosi v. Clogher, 46 So. 2d 170 (Fla. 1950), *cert. denied*, 340 U. S. 853, where the court enforced a member firm's contract made in violation of an exchange rule prohibiting a registered employee from having an interest in a customer's account, because it had not been shown that this was a rule "required by the act."

The Florida court's result seems open to some question entirely apart from the nonwaiver provision of the Exchange Act. A customer is usually held to the established customs and usages of the market when he sends an order to a broker established in that market, even if the customer is ignorant of those usages. Bibb v. Allen, 149 U. S. 481, 489-90 (1893); Hawkins v. Merrill Lynch, Pierce, Fenner & Beane, 85 F. Supp. 104, 121 (W. D. Ark. 1949); Samuels v. Oliver, 130 Ill. 73, 22 N. E. 499 (1889); White v. Merrill Lynch, Pierce, Fenner & Smith, Inc., 90 N. J. Super. 565, 218 A. 2d 655 (1966); Lynch v. Maw, 3 Utah 2d 271, 282 P. 2d 841 (1955); see C. Meyer, The Law of Stockbrokers and Stock Exchanges and of Commodity Brokers and Commodity Exchanges (1931) 157-63; Annot., Regulations, Rules, Custom, or Usage of Stock or Produce Exchange or of Stock or Produce Broker as Affecting Customers, 79 A. L. R. 592 (1932). But cf. Gordon v. Diffenderfer, 317 Pa. 425, 430, 177 Atl. 21, 23 (1935); Mercury Investment Co. v. A. G. Edwards & Sons, 295 F. Supp. 1160, 1163 (S. D. Tex. 1969).

In practice, although the *Rospigliosi* opinion is silent on the point, the rules and customs of the exchange are usually made a part of the broker's contract with the customer. Clews v. Jamieson, 182 U. S. 461, 481-82 (1901); American Cotton Mills v. Monier, 61 F. 2d 852, 854 (4th Cir. 1932). If a customer is thus held to the usages of the exchange when they work to his disadvantage, should he not also benefit from usage and rules that are either expressly or impliedly a part of his contract? There is no indication in the *Rospigliosi* opinion that this argument was considered by the court. It was held merely that the record did

In view of these provisions, as well as the repeated holdings apart from the SEC statutes that a "hedge clause" or legend disclaiming liability has little if any legal effect as protection against civil liability for either intentional or negligent misstatements in the sale of securities,[88] the Commission's General Counsel in a published opinion questioned "whether the result, if not the purpose, of such a legend is to create in the mind of the investor a belief that he has given up legal rights and is foreclosed from a remedy which he might otherwise have either at common law or under the SEC statutes." Consequently, he ruled, "the anti-fraud provisions of the SEC statutes are violated by the employment of any legend, hedge clause or other provision which is likely to lead an investor to believe that he has in any way waived any right of action he may have."[89] The opinion

---

not establish that the plaintiff employee had come into court with unclean hands. The case generally was perhaps colored by the fact that it arose in the context of a suit for divorce of an alleged common law marriage between the plaintiff and his customer, although the court did not disturb the denial of a divorce on the ground that there had been no marriage.

In any event, it does not follow, of course, that *every* violation of an exchange rule should make a member's contract unenforceable against his customer, since this is not true even of a *contract* that is illegal. See c. 10F supra.

[88] Equitable Life Ins. Co. of Iowa v. Halsey, Stuart & Co., 312 U. S. 410, 419 (1941); Wolfe v. A. E. Kusterer & Co., 269 Mich. 424, 431, 257 N. W. 729, 731 (1934); People v. Federated Radio Corp., 244 N. Y. 33, 41, 154 N. E. 655, 658 (1926). In Wilko v. Swan, 346 U. S. 427, 433-34 (1953), there was agreement as to the invalidity under §14 of the provision in a margin agreement purporting to relieve the broker-dealer of liability for any "representation or advice by you or your employees or agents regarding the purchase or sale of any property." See also the opinion below, 201 F. 2d 439, 442-43 (2d Cir. 1953). But see Kennedy v. Josephthal & Co., Inc., 814 F. 2d 798 (1st Cir. 1987), where the inclusion of a clear and unambiguous warning in the confidential offering memorandum precluded proof of 10b-5 reliance by sophisticated investors.

The Restatement (Second) of Agency permits innocent principals to contract themselves out of liability for deceit, though not for rescission, because of an agent's unauthorized fraud. §§259, 260. But as to fraud see id., §166, Comment e, Illus.: "The *P* company employs *A* to sell its shares, instructing *A* not to make any representations except those contained in the prospectus. The prospectus states nothing as to the assets of the company, the number of shareholders, or the company affiliations. *A* knowingly makes untruthful statements concerning the assets of the company upon which *T* relies, and then contracts with *T* by a written contract in which it is stated that *A* is not authorized to make statements except those in the prospectus. It may be found that, from the known habit of stock salesmen and the necessity of making statements concerning the assets of the company, the *P* company intended that *A* should make such statements; if so, an action for deceit will lie against the principal." And the reporter's notes to §260 refer specifically to "the cases involving exculpatory clauses in prospectuses and contracts involving the purchase of shares of stock." 3 id. 417.

[89] See Meason v. Gilbert, 236 Ga. 862, 863, 226 S. E. 2d 49, 50 (1976) (state act). In *Meason* — which was decided on the basis of an earlier Georgia statute that contained no antiwaiver provision, see Gilbert v. Meason, 137 Ga. App. 1,

concluded that the type of legend in common use by brokers, dealers, and investment advisers — which states, in effect, that the information is obtained from specified sources and is believed to be reliable but that its accuracy is not guaranteed — is not objectionable if the representations as to the source of the information and the belief in its reliability are true.[90] That is to say, the facts may make such a hedge clause misleading in suggesting the employment of objective, careful procedures totally at variance with the deception engaged in by the firm issuing the market letter.[91]

There is authority that an acceleration clause in a purchase money note is not necessarily void,[92] but that a contractual provision for something in the nature of liquidated damages is.[93] And it should not be overlooked that the statutory provisions void waivers by *agreement* of some kind, so that they do not automatically preclude waiver (or estoppel or ratification) by *conduct*[94] or settlements of *existing* controversies.[95] At the same time, their very presence should help the person asserting a violation as against arguments directed by his adversary to ratification or estoppel as well as waiver by conduct.[96]

2-4, 222 S. E. 2d 835, 837 (1975) — the court held that, if in fact there had been non-prospectus representations, the use of an integration clause might itself be a prohibited "scheme or artifice to defraud"; but it regarded the particular clause not as a waiver but as "a recital of fact * * * merely having evidentiary value on the question" of the existence of such representations. *Meason* was followed in Doody v. E. F. Hutton & Co., Inc., 587 F. Supp. 829 (D. Minn. 1984), where the court held also that an indemnity clause contained in a subscription agreement that provided for the recovery of attorneys' fees and costs by the issuer and its broker if the investors committed a breach of their warranties not to sue for alleged oral misrepresentations was not enforceable.

[90] Op. Gen. Counsel, Sec. Act Rel. 3411 (1951); see also the present writer's letter as Chief Counsel, Div. of Trading & Ex., SEC, reprinted in 13 Inv. Dealers' Digest 30 (Mar. 17, 1947).

[91] Heft, Kahn & Infante, Inc., 41 SEC 379, 389 (1963); Linder, Bilotti & Co., Inc., 42 SEC 407, 408 (1964).

[92] Titan Group, Inc. v. Faggen, 513 F. 2d 234, 239 (2d Cir. 1975), *cert. denied,* 423 U. S. 840.

[93] Special Transportation Services, Inc. v. Balto, 325 F. Supp. 1185 (D. Minn. 1971).

[94] See p. 1034 infra.

[95] Goodman v. Epstein, 582 F. 2d 388, 402-04 (7th Cir. 1978) (a release is valid only with respect to ripened claims of which the releasing party had knowledge or that he could have discovered on reasonable inquiry); but cf. Royal Air Properties, Inc. v. Smith, 333 F. 2d 568, 571 (9th Cir. 1964), infra p. 1028 n. 96. Of course, the enforcement of post-controversy arbitration agreements (see p. 1029 n. 104 infra) argues *a fortiori* for the inapplicability of the nonwaiver provisions to settlement agreements.

[96] "Since under this section the corporation cannot be estopped by an express waiver, an implied waiver must likewise be void." Jefferson Lake Sulphur Co. v. Walet, 104 F. Supp. 20, 23-24 (E. D. La. 1952), *aff'd* sub nom. Walet v.

The most litigated questions in this area are the effect of the nonwaiver provisions on arbitration. These questions have led to the Supreme Court in no fewer than four cases:

(1) In the first case, *Wilko* v. *Swan,* the Court had to decide whether the nonwaiver provision in §14 of the 1933 Act invalidated a provision in a customer's margin agreement that any controversy between him and the securities firm should be determined by arbitration under the New York Arbitration Law. The United States Arbitration Act provides that the court shall stay the trial of any action "upon being satisfied that the issue involved * * * is referable to arbitration" under a written arbitration agreement.[97] The customer sued the firm under §12(2). There was thus presented a neat conflict between two socially desirable policies — arbitration with its advantages of speed and economy and protection of the rights of investors against persons with superior bargaining power. The District Court resolved this conflict in favor of the Securities Act, the Second Circuit reversed with one Judge dissenting, and the Supreme Court again reversed by a vote of seven to two.[98]

The Court concluded that the right to select the judicial forum was the kind of "provision" that could not be waived under §14, because "it is clear that the Securities Act was drafted with an eye to the disadvantages under which buyers labor."[99] The case did not involve a determination of "the quality of a commodity or the

---

Jefferson Lake Sulphur Co., 202 F. 2d 433, 435 (5th Cir. 1953), *cert. denied,* 346 U. S. 820; see also Kaiser-Frazer Corp. v. Otis & Co., 195 F. 2d 838, 843-44 n. 8 (2d Cir. 1952), *cert. denied,* 344 U. S. 856; Can-Am Petroleum Co. v. Beck, 331 F. 2d 371 (10th Cir. 1964); Rogen v. Ilikon Corp., 361 F. 2d 260, 268 (1st Cir. 1966) (court used §29(a) to void a contractual acknowledgement of nonreliance); Meyers v. C & M Petroleum Producers, Inc., 476 F. 2d 427, 429 (5th Cir. 1973), *cert. denied,* 414 U. S. 829; Fox v. Kane-Miller Corp., 398 F. Supp. 609, 624 (D. Md. 1975), *aff'd on other grounds,* 542 F. 2d 915 (4th Cir. 1976); Hayden v. McDonald, 742 F. 2d 423, 431-35 (8th Cir. 1984) (Minnesota law), citing the text; cf. Todaro v. E. F. Hutton & Co., Inc., CCH Blue Sky L. Rep. ¶71,957 at 70,412-13 (E. D. Va. 1982) (antiwaiver provision in Virginia version of Uniform Securities Act applies to waiver by conduct).

In Royal Air Properties, Inc. v. Smith, 333 F. 2d 568, 571 (9th Cir. 1964), the court, without mentioning §29(a), emphasized that waiver, as "the voluntary or intentional relinquishment of a known right," required full knowledge of a right rather than merely enough facts to put the plaintiff on inquiry. "To hold one to diligence in discovering his rights is reasonable in the case of laches and estoppel, where another has acted in the interim to his detriment," but not in the case of waiver, which is "unilaterally accomplished." Id. at 571; see also Burgess v. Premier Corp., 727 F. 2d 826, 831 (9th Cir. 1984).

[97] §3, 9 U. S. C. §3. Arbitration is required even in a state court when there is a "contract evidencing a transaction involving commerce." 9 U. S. C. §2.

[98] Wilko v. Swan, 107 F. Supp. 75 (S. D. N. Y. 1952) *rev'd,* 201 F. 2d 439 (2d Cir. 1953), *rev'd,* 346 U. S. 427 (1953).

[99] 346 U. S. at 435.

amount of money due under a contract," the Court said, but required "subjective findings on the purpose and knowledge of an alleged violator of the Act."[100]

(2) *Wilko* was decided in 1953. The Court did not address securities arbitration again for twenty-one years, during which attitudes toward arbitration as an alternative method of dispute resolution had grown more receptive. The Court then distinguished *Wilko* in *Scherk* v. *Alberto-Culver Co.*, a case of a sale of a business (later challenged under Rule 10b-5) pursuant to a contract in which the parties had bargained for arbitration under the rules of the International Chamber of Commerce in Paris.[101] But in 1985 the Court described that case *obiter* in 10b-5 terms without referring to its international flavor.[102] And, on the approach of noninterference between two "more or less equally sophisticated institutions,"[103] the Code includes a "de-internationalized" and flexible *Scherk* along with several other exceptions to *Wilko* whose substance has been developed by the lower courts:

(1) a good faith settlement of, or agreement to arbitrate, an existing dispute;[104]

[100] Id. at 435-36.

[101] 417 U. S. 506 (1974); see also S. A. Mineracão da Trinidade-Samitri v. Utah Int'l, Inc., 745 F. 2d 190 (2d Cir. 1984); cf. Mitsubishi Motors Corp. v. Soler Chrysler-Plymouth, Inc., 473 U. S. 614 (1985) (Court applied arbitration agreement to antitrust claim arising from an international transaction). In AVC Nederland B. V. v. Atrium Investment Partnership, 740 F. 2d 148, 155-60 (2d Cir. 1984), the court applied the *Scherk* approach to a forum-selection and choice-of-law clause specifying Dutch law and a Dutch forum in a contract between a Dutch company and a Dutch-owned Georgia corporation.

[102] Dean Witter Reynolds, Inc. v. Byrd, 470 U. S. 213, 215 n. 1 (1985).

[103] 2 Code 804, Comment (4).

[104] See Moran v. Paine, Webber, Jackson & Curtis, 422 Pa. 66, 220 A. 2d 624 (1966); Moran v. Paine, Webber, Jackson & Curtis, 389 F. 2d 242 (3d Cir. 1968); Murtagh v. University Computing Co., 490 F. 2d 810, 816 (5th Cir. 1974), *cert. denied,* 419 U. S. 835.

But there is no "existing" dispute unless the investor is aware of a dispute when the agreement is made. It is not enough "that the events giving rise to the claim have occurred prior to the" agreement. Malena v. Merrill Lynch, Pierce, Fenner & Smith, Inc., CCH Fed. Sec. L. Rep. ¶91,492 (E. D. N. Y. 1984).

Moreover, although "once the facts underlying a securities claim are in fact arbitrated the decision is binding," in the case of federal securities disputes "any doubt as to whether a particular item falls within the ambit of matters actually and necessarily submitted to arbitration must be resolved in favor of allowing access to the federal courts." Williams v. E. F. Hutton & Co., Inc., 753 F. 2d 117, 119-20 (D. C. Cir. 1985).

As the Court observed in *Wilko,* judicial power to vacate an award is limited by the Arbitration Act. 9 U. S. C. §10. Although "manifest disregard" of the law as distinct from error in its interpretation is theoretically subject to judicial review, how is a court to be made aware that the arbitrators *ignored* the applicable law instead of *misapplying* it? For expedition, the very purpose of arbitra-

(2) action taken pursuant to a rule of the Municipal Board under section 1103(a)(8)[105] or by any other self-regulatory organization to settle disputes between its members or participants;[106] or

(3) an advance agreement

(A) by a member of or participant in a self-regulatory organization to arbitrate any dispute;[107]

---

tion, dictates that awards may be made without a statement of reasons or a complete record. See generally Wilko v. Swan, 346 U. S. 427, 436-37 (1954); but cf. Sobel v. Hertz, Warner & Co., 469 F. 2d 1211 (2d Cir. 1972), *rev'g* 338 F. Supp. 287 (S. D. N. Y. 1971), where Judge Pollack, in remanding to the arbitrators for a statement of reasons, sought to differentiate controversies based on statutory duties as under §12(2) or Rule 10b-5 from ordinary commercial problems.

[105] This section authorizes the Board to provide for the binding arbitration of disputes relating to transactions in municipal securities so far as municipal brokers or dealers or their associates are concerned.

[106] This provision reflects §28(b)(1) and (2) of the 1934 Act, as amended in 1975 to add Clause (2) with respect to municipals. On the binding effect of arbitration agreements between members, see In re Revenue Properties Litigation Cases, 451 F. 2d 310 (1st Cir. 1971); Coenen v. R. W. Pressprich & Co., Inc., 453 F. 2d 1209 (2d Cir. 1972), *cert. denied,* 406 U. S. 949; Tullis v. Kohlmeyer & Co., 551 F. 2d 632 (5th Cir. 1977); N. Donald & Co. v. American United Energy Corp., 746 F. 2d 666 (10th Cir. 1984); Swink & Co., Inc. v Hereth, 784 F. 2d 866 (8th Cir. 1986); but cf. Allegaert v. Perot, 548 F. 2d 432 (2d Cir. 1977), *cert. denied,* 432 U. S. 910, which qualifies this proposition as not applying if the dispute involves a "wholesale fraud of institutional dimension." 548 F. 2d at 437. On the advantages of arbitration between members, see Legg, Mason & Co., Inc. v. Mackall & Coe, Inc., 351 F. Supp. 1367 (D. D. C. 1972). In Halliburton & Associates, Inc. v. Henderson, Few & Co., 774 F. 2d 441 (11th Cir. 1985), the court held that arbitration of a 1933 Act claim with respect to municipal securities was enforceable between municipal securities dealers even though the 1933 Act contains nothing comparable to §28(b).

[107] On the binding effect of a member-*customer* agreement on the *member,* see Axelrod & Co. v. Kordich, Victor & Neufeld, 451 F. 2d 838 (2d Cir. 1971); Goldberg v. Donaldson, Lufkin & Jenrette Securities Corp., 650 F. Supp. 222 (N. D. Ga. 1986) (dispute involving *former* member's *personal investment account*). Such an advance agreement is usually reflected in the rules of the self-regulatory organizations. Whether a plaintiff who became an exchange member *after* the eruption of a controversy is bound by an agreement to arbitrate depends on the circumstances. *Yes:* Coenen v. Pressprich & Co., Inc., 453 F. 2d 1209 (2d Cir. 1972), *cert. denied,* 406 U. S. 949. *No:* Laupheimer v. McDonnell & Co., Inc., 500 F. 2d 21 (2d Cir. 1974); De Lancie v. Birr, Wilson & Co., 648 F. 2d 1255 (9th Cir. 1981).

The Commission has expressed concern about the use of arbitration clauses in broker-dealer-customer agreements that purport to bind the *customer* to arbitrate all future disputes. If their meaning, effect, and enforceability are not specified, the Commission cautioned, this practice may be "inconsistent with just and equitable principles of trade" and also raise serious questions under the antifraud provisions. Sec. Ex. Act Rel. 15,984, 17 SEC Dock. 1167 (1979). But failure to comply with the release does not preclude arbitration of state law claims. In re Quick & Reilly, Inc., 103 A. D. 2d 958, 479 N. Y. S. 2d 576 (3d

(B) by any person to arbitrate a dispute arising under a rule of a self-regulatory organization (other than the Municipal Board), unless a violation of the rule is (i) a violation of this Code, or (ii) actionable under section 1721(a);[108] or

(C) between any persons if a court determines, on consideration of their financial and legal sophistication and the relationship between them, that the purposes of this Code do not require the application of section 1725(a).

On the strength of the arbitration cases, there is precedent for invalidating also a *choice-of-law* clause in a customer agreement.[109]

Dept. 1984).

In Sec. Ex. Act Rel. 20,397, 29 SEC Dock. 232 (1983), the Commission adopted Rule 15c2-2 to prohibit broker-dealers from using predispute arbitration clauses in customer agreements that purport to bind public customers to arbitration of claims arising under the SEC statutes. The rule also requires broker-dealers to disclose to existing public customers that they are not precluded from judicial recourse by such clauses. Failure to comply with the rule does not itself preclude arbitration. Steinberg v. Illinois Co., Inc., 685 F. Supp. 615 (N. D. Ill. 1986).

For the benefit of investors who do want to arbitrate, the Commission reaffirmed its support for arbitration as an important means for resolution of certain disputes between broker-dealers and their customers. For example, it recognized that the Uniform Code of Arbitration drafted by the Securities Industry Conference on Arbitration and adopted by the self-regulatory organizations [see Sec. Ex. Act Rel. 12,528, 9 SEC Dock. 833 (1976); Sec. Ex. Act Rel. 12,974, 10 SEC Dock. 955 (1976)] provided an efficient and economical procedure. But it noted further that its approval of the adoption of the Code by the self-regulatory organizations specifically took into account that public customers would be bound by arbitration agreements only after a dispute had arisen. Id. at 233 n. 1. On the Code, see Katsoris, The Arbitration of a Public Securities Dispute, 53 Ford. L. Rev. 279 (1984). The Arbitration Code contains a simplified small claim procedure.

Section 28(b)(3), which was §28(b)(2) before the 1975 amendments inserted the present §28(b)(2) with respect to arbitration rules of the Municipal Board, is not clear when it saves "the binding effect * * * of any action described in paragraph (1) or (2) on any person who has agreed to be bound thereby." See 2 Code 804, Comment (3)(b). At any rate, although one or two cases have applied §28(b) to the 1933 Act on an *in pari materia* approach (Brown v. Gilligan, Will & Co., 287 F. Supp. 766 (S. D. N. Y. 1968); Axelrod & Co. v. Kordich, Victor & Neufeld, 451 F. 2d 838, 843 (2d Cir. 1971)), most cases under the 1934 Act achieve parity between the two statutes by simply ignoring §28(b). E. g., Greater Continental Corp. v. Schechter, 422 F. 2d 1100, 1103-04 (2d Cir. 1970).

[108] This provision makes it plain that even nonmembers are bound by agreements to arbitrate rule disputes that are not actionable under the Code and do not involve illegal conduct under the Code.

[109] Dales v. Gruntal & Co., CCH Fed. Sec. L. Rep. ¶99,673 (C. D. Cal. 1984); cf. Hall v. Superior Court of Orange County, 150 Cal. App. 3d 411, 197 Cal. Rptr. 757 (1983) (blue sky nonwaiver provision). *Contra:* AVC Nederland B. V.

(3) The third Supreme Court case, *Dean Witter Reynolds, Inc.* v. *Byrd,* grappled with the complexities created when a complaint joins a state law claim that is arbitrable with a nonarbitrable federal claim arising out of the same transaction.[110] Before that decision in 1985, several circuits had developed an "intertwining" doctrine: "When arbitrable and nonarbitrable claims arise out of the same transaction, and are sufficiently intertwined factually and legally, the district court, under this view, may in its discretion deny arbitration as to the arbitrable claims and try all the claims together in federal court."[111] Those courts, acknowledging "the strong federal policy in favor of enforcing arbitration," offered

> two reasons why the district court nevertheless should decline to compel arbitration in this situation. First, they assert that such a result is necessary to preserve what they consider to be the court's exclusive jurisdiction over the federal securities claim; otherwise, they suggest, arbitration of an "intertwined" state claim might precede the federal proceeding and the fact-finding done by the arbitrator might thereby bind the federal court through collateral estoppel. The second reason they cite is efficiency; by declining to compel arbitration, the court avoids bifurcated proceedings and perhaps redundant efforts to litigate the same factual questions twice.[112]

But the Supreme Court decided unanimously that the Arbitration Act allowed no discretion in requiring "district courts to compel arbitration of pendent arbitrable claims when one of the parties files a motion to compel, even where the result would be the possibly inefficient maintenance of separate proceedings in different forums."

On the collateral estoppel point, the Court concluded "that neither a stay of proceedings, nor joined proceedings, is necessary to protect the federal interest in the federal-court proceeding, and that the formulation of collateral-estoppel rules affords adequate protection to the interest."[113] This was read by the Third Circuit as indicating "that, at least with respect to an important, nonarbitrable federal claim, a federal court should be hesitant to preclude the

v. Atrium Investment Partnership, 740 F. 2d 148, 155-60 (2d Cir. 1984) (court applied *Scherk* approach to both a choice-of-law clause and a forum-selection clause). The courts do not seem unreceptive to the latter. See Andrews v. Heinold Commodities, Inc., 771 F. 2d 184 (7th Cir. 1985); Abelson v. World Transportation, Inc., 631 F. Supp. 504 (S. D. Fla. 1986).

[110] 470 U. S. 213 (1985).

[111] Id. at 216-17.

[112] Id. at 217.

[113] Id. at 222.

litigation of the federal claim based on the collateral estoppel effects of a prior arbitration award" (although the particular award *was* given collateral estoppel effect).[114]

On the efficiency point, the Court observed that the overriding goal of the Arbitration Act was not "to promote the expeditious resolution of claims," but "to ensure judicial enforcement of privately made agreements to arbitrate."[115]

This case produced an anomalous fall-out so far as arbitration under the state blue sky laws is concerned. The state courts had previously followed *Wilko* under their own blue sky nonwaiver provisions.[116] But now, with an irreconcilable conflict between the federal mandate to arbitrate and a state provision that prevents arbitration, the state nonwaiver provision is preempted by the Federal Arbitration Act when "commerce" is involved.[117] Consequently the same questions that are nonarbitrable as a matter of federal law must be referred to arbitration when they arise under state law.

(4) In the most recent case the Court granted *certiorari* in order to resolve a sharp conflict between the Circuits on the question whether *Wilko,* which arose under §12(2) of the 1933 Act, extended to an *implied* action under Rule 10b-5. Since the decision in that

[114]Greenblatt v. Drexel Burnham Lambert, Inc., 763 F. 2d 1352, 1360-62 (11th Cir. 1985); see also Morgan, Olmstead, Kennedy & Gardner, Inc. v. U. S. Trust Co. of N. Y., 608 F. Supp. 1561 (S. D. N. Y. 1985) (arbitrable securities claims between exchange members were referred to arbitration "despite the presence of other parties in the larger dispute who are not subject to any arbitration agreement"); Hammerman v. Peacock, 654 F. Supp. 71 (D. D. C. 1987), and cases cited (arbitration decision can have *res judicata* or collateral estoppel effect even when underlying claim involves the SEC statutes). But cf. Sevinor v. Merrill Lynch, Pierce, Fenner & Smith, Inc., 807 F. 2d 16, 20 (1st Cir. 1986).

[115]470 U. S. at 219.

[116]Sandefer v. Reynolds Securities, Inc., 44 Colo. App. 343, 618 P. 2d 690 (1980); Shearson, Hammill & Co. v. Vouis, 247 So. 2d 733 (Fla. App. 1971); Kiehne v. Purdy, 309 N. W. 2d 60 (Minn. 1981); State *ex rel.* Geil v. Corcoran, 623 S. W. 2d 555 (Mo. App. 1981).

[117]Kroog v. Mait, 712 F. 2d 1148 (7th Cir. 1983), *cert. denied,* 465 U. S. 1007; see also Garmo v. Dean Witter Reynolds, Inc., 101 Wash. 2d 585, 681 P. 2d 253 (1984). In Southland Corp. v. Keating, 465 U. S. 1 (1984), the Supreme Court reached the same result under the identical nonwaiver provision of the California Franchise Investment Law, holding that the federal Arbitration Act created a substantive rule applicable in state as well as federal courts. The case of Oppenheimer & Co., Inc. v. Young, 456 So. 2d 1175 (Fla. 1984), where the court had distinguished *Southland* in the blue sky context, was vacated, 470 U. S. 1078 (1985), for further consideration in the light of the *Dean Witter Reynolds* case. See also Sager v. District Court, 698 P. 2d 250 (Colo. 1985), and Fairview Cemetery Assn. v. Eckberg, 385 N. W. 2d 812 (Minn. 1986), to the effect that *Sandefer* and *Kiehne* supra n. 116, were overruled by *Southland.*

case came down when this book was in final proof, it is considered in an appendix.[118]

4. In Pari Delicto, Estoppel, and Related Defenses

We have already touched on laches[119] and on waiver by conduct.[120] The blue sky cases on those defenses and their siblings — ratification, estoppel,[121] *in pari delicto,* and (in equity) unclean hands[122] — are too numerous to mention. Unfortunately they are also too variegated to permit generalization.[123] But they constitute a research resource beyond the blue sky area itself because of their precedential value with respect to the federal statutes.

In 1985 the Court was confronted with a 10b-5 case in which a tippee (who turned out to be a "dupee") complained that the defendant tippers had falsely stated that they were conveying inside information.[124] Reminding that "*pari*" means "equal," Justice Brennan stated that "a private action for damages in these circumstances may be barred on the grounds of the plaintiff's own culpability only where (1) as a direct result of his own actions, the plaintiff bears at least substantially equal responsibility for the violations he seeks to redress, and (2) preclusion of suit would not significantly interfere with the effective enforcement of the securities laws and protection of the investing public."[125] This holding was followed by the minor premise in the syllogism: "In the context of insider trading, we do not believe that a person [the tippee] whose liability

[118] McMahon v. Shearson/American Express, Inc., 107 S. Ct. 2332 (1987), infra App. D.

[119] See p. 1002 supra.

[120] See p. 1027 supra.

[121] It has been held that the defenses of estoppel and waiver by conduct are available to a §12(1) defendant. Straley v. Universal Uranium & Milling Corp., 289 F. 2d 370, 373-74 (9th Cir. 1961); Katz v. Amos Treat & Co., 411 F. 2d 1046, 1054-55 (2d Cir. 1969); Henderson v. Hayden, Stone, Inc., 461 F. 2d 1069, 1072 (5th Cir. 1972). *Query:* Is this consistent with strict liability?

[122] The unclean hands defense has been involved in relatively few SEC cases. Wolf v. Frank, 477 F. 2d 467, 474 (5th Cir. 1973), *cert. denied,* 414 U. S. 975; Lawler v. Gilliam, 569 F. 2d 1283, 1294 (4th Cir. 1978); Bertoglio v. Texas Int'l Co., 488 F. Supp. 630, 662 (D. Del. 1980), and cases cited; cf. Hall v. Johnston, 758 F. 2d 421, 422-23 (9th Cir. 1985) (plaintiff in action under Oregon Uniform Securities Act's equivalent of §12(1) *held* not subject to unclean hands defense based on his knowledge of nonregistration).

[123] See 3 Loss 1676-80; 6 id. 3818-19.

[124] Bateman Eichler, Hill Richards, Inc. v. Berner, 472 U. S. 299 (1985).

[125] Id. at 310-11.

is solely derivative [from the tipper] can be said to be as culpable as one whose breach of duty gave rise to that liability in the first place."[126]

Denying the doctrine in these circumstances "will best promote 'a high standard of business ethics * * * in every facet of the securities industry.' [Citation deleted.] Although a number of lower courts have reasoned that a broad rule of *caveat tippee* would better serve this goal, we believe the contrary position adopted by other courts represents the better view."[127]

On the question (left open in *Bateman*)[128] whether the defense should bar recovery against a brokerage firm whose only role was that of a controlling person, the mere fact that the plaintiffs might have traded on inside information was held not to bear on the defendant's failure to supervise or control its employees. But, if the defendant could show that the plaintiffs had participated in hiding the truth about the activities of the defendant's employees from the defendant, the plaintiffs might be barred.[129]

5. Indemnification, Contribution, and Insurance

The SEC statutes are silent on indemnification except for provisions in the Trust Indenture and Investment Company Acts.[130]

[126] Id. at 313.

[127] 472 U. S. at 315, quoting from SEC v. Capital Gains Research Bureau, Inc., 375 U. S. 180, 186-87 (1963).

[128] 472 U. S. at 314 n. 25.

[129] In re Olympia Brewing Co. Securities Litigation, CCH Fed. Sec. L. Rep. ¶92,461 (N. D. Ill. 1985).

In Dahl v. Pinter, 787 F. 2d 985 (5th Cir. 1986), *cert. granted* sub. nom. Printer v. Dahl, 107 S. Ct. 1885, a confusing opinion that produced a vigorous dissent from Judge Brown, the court distinguished *Bateman Eichler* as involving Rule 10b-5 rather than §12(1), the latter not requiring scienter, but held that the plaintiff was not estopped or subject to an *in pari delicto* or unclean hands defense by virtue of his having been aware that the securities were unregistered.

In Rothberg v. Rosenbloom, 808 F. 2d 252 (3d Cir. 1986), *cert. denied* sub. nom. Rosenbloom v. Rothberg, 107 S. Ct. 1895, a split court applied *Bateman Eichler* to a buyer's action on promissory notes given or guaranteed by the defendants, so that the case involved not *in pari delicto* but the "related" (id. at 254) defense of illegality by reason of the notes' having arisen out of a transaction allegedly in violation of Rule 10b-5.

[130] Section 315(d)(2) of the former statute permits the indenture to contain provisions protecting the trustee "from liability for any error of judgment made in good faith by a responsible officer * * * unless it shall be proved that such trustee was negligent in ascertaining the pertinent facts." Section 17(h) of the Investment Company Act nullifies all exculpatory clauses that purport to protect any director or officer against liability to the company or its security holders "by reason of willful misfeasance, bad faith, gross negligence or reckless disregard

Those civil liability provisions of the 1933 and 1934 Acts that contemplate more than one defendant do contain provisions on contribution. Section 11(f) of the 1933 Act provides:

> All or any one or more of the persons specified in subsection (a)[131] shall be jointly and severally liable, and every person who becomes liable to make any payment under this section may recover contribution as in cases of contract from any person who, if sued separately, would have been liable to make the same payment, unless the person who has become liable was, and the other was not, guilty of fraudulent misrepresentation.

In the 1934 Act §§9(e) (manipulation) and 18(b) (false filings) contain the same language except for the absence of the introductory reference to joint and several liability and the "unless" clause at the end. But, of course, the 1934 Act is silent, by hypothesis, with respect to contribution in the *implied* actions under Rule 10b-5 and other provisions.

Section 11(f) was taken almost bodily from the English Companies Act.[132] And its obvious purpose was to avoid the historic policy against contribution among joint tortfeasors, aside from the specific exception in the section. With that exception, the section presumably contemplates contribution *pro rata* as in contract rather than on a fault basis as in tort.[133]

---

of the duties involved in the conduct of his office." And §17(i) contains similar language with respect to investment advisers of registered investment companies or their principal underwriters.

The Commission has interpreted these provisions to prohibit indemnification for expenses and the amount of any judgment handed down against the specified categories of persons. In cases of settlement it has taken the position that indemnity may be offered only when the reasonable expenses of prosecution of a case to judgment would exceed the amount paid in settlement. 7 SEC Ann. Rep. 16 (1941), quoted in Inv. Co. Act Rel. 7221 (1972). See also Brown v. Bullock, 194 F. Supp. 207, 237-38 (S. D. N. Y. 1961), *aff'd en banc on other grounds,* 294 F. 2d 415 (2d Cir. 1961); Chabot v. Empire Trust Co., 301 F. 2d 458, 461 (2d Cir. 1962); SEC v. Continental Growth Fund, Inc., CCH Fed. Sec. L. Rep. ¶91,437 (S. D. N. Y. 1964); Steadman Security Corp. v. Steadman Associated Fund, CCH Fed. Sec. L. Rep. ¶99,009 (D. D. C. 1982). For the administrative view, see Inv. Co. Act Rel. 11,330, 20 SEC Dock. 1342 (1980); Inv. Co. Act Rel. 13,181, 27 SEC Dock. 916 (1983).

[131] Although this does not literally cover controlling persons liable under §15, they nevertheless fall within the scope of §11(f) because §15 specifies the same *prima facie* liability as §11. Laventhol, Krekstein, Horwath & Horwath v. Horwitch, 637 F. 2d 672 (9th Cir. 1980), *cert. denied* sub nom. Frank v. U. S. Trust Co., 452 U. S. 963.

[132] 19 & 20 Geo. 5, c. 23, §37(3) (1929).

[133] See Douglas and Bates, The Federal Securities Act of 1933, 43 Yale L. J. 171, 178-81 (1933). In Smith v. Mulvaney, CCH Fed. Sec. L. Rep. ¶92,084 (S. D. Cal. 1985), the court held that contribution under *Rule 10b-5* did not have to be *pro rata* but could be flexible — that the fact that the judgment against the issuer's majority shareholder (plaintiff in contribution) was greater than the

The issues that have proved much more serious in the administration of the 1933 Act relate to indemnification rather than contribution — to the question whether liability *inter se* may be governed by express contract. We have already noticed the Commission's use of its acceleration authority to enforce its anti-indemnification policy so far as §11 is concerned.[134] The Commission's codification of that policy in Regulation S-K[135] is carefully phrased to preserve the two exceptions that the Commission has traditionally followed:

(1) No objection is made to an agreement by a *controlling stockholder* in a secondary (or partially secondary) distribution to indemnify the issuer and its directors, officers, and experts. Since the offering is made solely for the benefit of the controlling stockholder, Congress could not have intended to foreclose his reimbursing the issuer (and indirectly the other stockholders) for any liability or expense the issuer might suffer by reason of §11, although it is arguable that the issuer's directors, officers, and experts should no more be relieved of their statutory duties in secondary than in primary distributions.

(2) It is common practice for the issuer and *underwriters* to enter into cross-indemnification agreements whereby (a) the underwriters agree to indemnify the issuer, its directors, and those officers signing the registration statement with respect to any information furnished by the underwriters expressly for the registration statement, and (b) the issuer agrees to indemnify the underwriters and their controlling persons as to everything else. The Commission grants acceleration in such cases as long as the "Johnson & Johnson formula"[136] is applied to any person who happens to be both (a) a director,

---

amount paid by the directors (defendants in contribution) in settlement failed, standing alone, to raise a triable issue. On contribution in general, see 3 Harper, James, and Gray, The Law of Torts (2d ed. 1986) §10.2; 2 Williston, Contracts (2d ed. 1959) §345.

[134] See pp. 128-29 supra. Indemnification provisions come to the Commission's attention also under the proxy rules when a company with a security registered under the Exchange Act (or a company subject to the Holding Company or Investment Company Act) seeks stockholder approval of an agreement or bylaw or charter amendment on indemnification.

[135] Item 512(i); see also Item 702. Although Item 512(i) preserves the "Johnson & Johnson formula," Item 510 extends the traditional policy beyond cases where acceleration is requested.

Of course, notwithstanding the uncertainty with respect to the enforceability of indemnification agreements, their setting forth the understanding of the parties is not without practical effect. For example, a contractual agreement that sets forth settlement *procedures* may provide the basis for an ultimate settlement. McLaughlin, Stapleton, and Harman, Indemnity and Contribution, in Practising Law Institute, Thirteenth Annual Institute on Securities Regulation (1982) 258-59.

[136] See p. 129 n. 21 supra.

officer, or controlling person of the issuer and (b) an underwriter or a partner or controlling person of an underwriter. In the case of secondary distributions, the formula would seem to apply in such interlocking situations when the *issuer* indemnifies the underwriters, but there should be no concern when the indemnification is provided by the selling stockholder. This special treatment of underwriters apparently has a historical explanation in the fears expressed during the early days of the Act that underwriters would be unwilling to assume the full risks of §11, with attendant danger to the country's economic recovery.[137]

There is a further anomaly in that the Commission has not raised similar objection to *insurance* against §11 liability, regardless of who bears the cost. This position was formalized in 1982 as Rule 461(c). Presumably the explanation lies in the insurance company's furnishing another pocket for plaintiffs.[138]

The Commission's view of §11 does not interfere, of course, with the issuer's reimbursing officers or directors who have been *successful* in defending §11 actions, with or without a prior agreement to do so, at least when they have won an adjudication on the merits.[139] The provisions for joint and several liability of all persons liable, and for contribution, militate in favor of such reimbursement; for a vigorous defense by any officers or directors who are sued will tend to reduce the chance that the issuer itself will be held liable. But (*pace* settlements) it is prudent not to place any reliance on indemnification against an adjudicated liability under §11. The *in*

[137] Professor Berle later wrote that the Reconstruction Finance Corporation was "erected into a huge capital banking institution" and that, "In effect, we broke the capital strike." Berle, Prologue to Federal Securities Law Symposium, 15 N. Y. L. F. 213, 214 (1969).

The Commission's failure to apply the formula to underwriters' indemnification does not assure that the particular indemnification will be honored. Cf. Globus v. Law Research Service, Inc. (*Globus I*), 418 F. 2d 1276 (2d Cir. 1969), *cert. denied*, 397 U. S. 913, infra p. 1039. On the other hand, a "technical" underwriter is in a different position from the investment banker, since his opportunity to participate in the preparation of the registration statement, or even to check its accuracy, may be virtually nil. See Cohen, in Symposium, The *BarChris* Case: Prospectus Liability, 24 Bus. Law. 523, 551-52 (1969).

[138] By way of recognizing the anti-indemnification provision in §17(h) of the Investment Company Act (supra p. 1035 n. 130), the rule's nonacceleration policy does extend to insurance of a director or officer of a registered investment company or a "business development company" (see p. 306 supra) against "willful misfeasance, bad faith, gross negligence or reckless disregard of the duties involved in the conduct of his or her office" if the cost is borne by any person other than the insured.

[139] Galdi v. Berg, 359 F. Supp. 698 (D. Del. 1973); Goldstein v. Alodex Corp., 409 F. Supp. 1201 (E. D. Pa. 1976); cf. Koch Industries, Inc. v. Vosko, 494 F. 2d 713, 725 (10th Cir. 1974); Collins v. Fitzwater, 277 Ore. 401, 560 P. 2d 1074 (1977) (state act).

terrorem purpose of individual liability is reinforced by the antiwaiver provision in §14.

What little case law there is under §11 (it must be remembered that there is relatively little case law under §11 altogether) supports the Commission's view.[140]

So does the leading case under Rule 10b-5, *Globus* v. *Law Research Service, Inc.* (*"Globus I"*) in the Second Circuit,[141] which did not involve §11 because the offering had been made under Regulation A. Indeed, it is interesting, in view of the Commission's tenderness to underwriters, that the court considered that "indemnification of the underwriter by the issuer is particularly suspect."[142] Emphasizing "at the outset that at this time we consider only the case where the underwriter has committed a sin graver than ordinary negligence," the court concluded "that to tolerate indemnity under these circumstances would encourage flouting the policy of the common law and the Securities Act."[143]

Thus the case is not a square holding under §11. Nevertheless, it seems quite likely from a paragraph of the opinion devoted to §11 that the court would have come out the same way if it *had* been a §11 case:

> Civil liability under section 11 and similar provisions was designed not so much to compensate the defrauded purchaser as to promote enforcement of the Act and to deter negligence by providing a penalty for those who fail in their duties. And Congress intended to impose a "high standard of trusteeship" on underwriters. Kroll, [Some Reflections on Indemnification Provisions and S. E. C. Liability Insurance in the Light of *BarChris* and *Globus,* 24 Bus. Law. 681, 687 (1969)]. Thus, what Professor Loss terms the "*in terrorem* effect" of civil liability, 3 Loss, supra, at 1831, might well be thwarted if underwriters were free to pass their liability on to the issuer. Underwriters who knew they could be indemnified simply by showing that the issuer was "more liable" than they (a process not too difficult when the issuer is inevitably closer to the facts) would have a tendency to be lax in their independent investigations.[144]

[140]In Laventhal, Krekstein, Horwath & Horwath v. Horwitch, 637 F. 2d 672, 676 (9th Cir. 1980), *cert. denied* sub. nom. Frank v. U. S. Trust Co., 452 U. S. 963, the court held, with little discussion except for citation of a 10b-5 case, that indemnification under §11 "would undermine the statutory purpose of assuring diligent performance of duty and deterring negligence." See Gould v. American-Hawaiian Steamship Co., 387 F. Supp. 163, 168 n. 11 (D. Del. 1974), *vacated and remanded on other grounds,* 535 F. 2d 761 (3d Cir. 1976).

[141]418 F. 2d 1276 (2d Cir. 1969), *cert. denied,* 397 U. S. 913.

[142]418 F. 2d at 1289.

[143]Id. at 1288.

[144]Ibid.

There are also *negligence* cases not arising under §11 in which indemnification has been denied.[145] The *Globus* court later approved *contribution.*[146] But there is a question whether these contribution cases survive recent Supreme Court decisions under the Equal Pay Act together with Title VII of the Civil Rights Act of

[145] Gould v. American-Hawaiian Steamship Co., 387 F. Supp. 163, 168-72 (D. Del. 1974), *remanded on other grounds,* 535 F. 2d 761 (3d Cir. 1976) (Rule 14a-9, the proxy fraud rule); Odette v. Shearson, Hammill & Co., Inc., 394 F. Supp. 946, 956-57 (S. D. N. Y. 1975) (§12(2)); see also Delta Holdings, Inc. v. National Distillers & Chemical Corp., — F. Supp. — , — , CCH Fed. Sec. L. Rep. ¶92,910 at 93,011 (S. D. N. Y. 1986).

[146] Globus Inc. v. Law Research Service, Inc. (*Globus II),* 318 F. Supp. 955 (S. D. N. Y. 1970), *aff'd per curiam,* 442 F. 2d 1346 (2d Cir. 1971), *cert. denied* sub nom. Law Research Service, Inc. v. Blair & Co., 404 U. S. 941; see also deHaas v. Empire Petroleum Co., 286 F. Supp. 809, 815-16 (D. Colo. 1968), *aff'd on this point,* 435 F. 2d 1223 (10th Cir. 1970); Gould v. American-Hawaiian Steamship Co., 387 F. Supp. 163, 168-72 (D. Del. 1974), *remanded on other grounds,* 535 F. 2d 761 (3d Cir. 1976). With respect to the holdings in both *Globus* cases, see also Heizer Corp. v. Ross, 601 F. 2d 330 (7th Cir. 1979); Stowell v. Ted S. Finkel Investment Services, Inc., 641 F. 2d 323 (5th Cir. 1981); Altman v. Josephthal & Co., Inc., CCH Fed. Sec. L. Rep. ¶99,421 (D. Mass. 1983); Seiler v. E. F. Hutton & Co., Inc., CCH Fed. Sec. L. Rep. ¶91,632 at 99,203 (D. N. J. 1984); Tri-State Bank of East Dubuque v. Dain Bosworth, Inc., CCH Fed. Sec. L. Rep. ¶92,751 (D. Neb. 1985); In re Nucorp Energy Securities Litigation, — F. Supp. — , CCH Fed. Sec. L. Rep. ¶93,224 (S. D. Cal 1987).

In any event, since contribution under Rule 10b-5 could lie only between knowing participants in the same fraud, an accounting firm charged under 10b-5 could not file a third-party complaint for contribution against other entities that were not alleged to be joint participants in the fraud claimed by the plaintiff shareholders. Kenneth Leventhal & Co. v. Joyner Wholesale Co., 736 F. 2d 29 (2d Cir. 1984); First Federal Savings & Loan Assn. of Pittsburgh v. Oppenheim, Appel, Dixon & Co., 634 F. Supp. 1341 (S. D. N. Y. 1986). But it has been held not to be "necessary that the alleged tort-feasors act in concert or in pursuance of a common design in order for them to be joint tort-feasors for purposes of contribution." Adalman v. Baker, Watts & Co., 599 F. Supp. 752, 755 (D. Md. 1984), *aff'd in part and rev'd in part on other grounds,* 807 F. 2d 359 (4th Cir. 1986).

In *First Federal,* supra, the court held also that, although contribution under the SEC laws and the effect of a release of an SEC claim were both governed by federal law (*Globus*), the absence of any federal statutory rule required a balancing of the state and federal interests affected, and so it adopted the New York rule as the federal rule.

On the complications created by partial settlements, see Laventhol, Krekstein, Horwath & Horwath v. Horwitch, 637 F. 2d 672 (9th Cir. 1980), *cert. denied* sub nom. Frank v. U. S. Trust Co., 452 U. S. 963; Adamski, Contribution and Settlement in Multiparty Actions Under Rule 10b-5, 66 Iowa L. Rev. 533 (1981).

For a comprehensive discussion of contribution and indemnification under Rule 10b-5 in historical terms, see McLean v. Alexander, 449 F. Supp. 1251, 1265-68 (D. Del. 1978), *rev'd on other grounds,* 599 F. 2d 1190 (3d Cir. 1979). See also Annot., Right to Contribution Among Defendants in Action Under §10(b) of Securities Exchange Act of 1934 or SEC Rule 10b-5, 62 A. L. R. Fed. 802 (1983). In general, see J. Bishop, The Law of Corporate Officers and Directors: Indemnification and Insurance (1981).

1964 in one case[147] and §4 of the Clayton Act in another.[148] Concluding that "a right to contribution may arise in either of two ways: first, through the affirmative creation of a right of action by Congress, either expressly or by clear implication; or, second, through the power of federal courts to fashion a federal common law of contribution,"[149] the Court refused to take the second route.

As Judge Friendly later said, the Supreme Court "left open the question whether federal courts could properly provide for contribution when an implied right of action was found to exist under the securities laws." For the statutes before the Supreme Court "expressly created the private damage actions and failed to provide for contribution, although §11(f) of the Securities Act of 1933 and §18(b) of the Securities Exchange Act demonstrated that Congress knew how to do this when it wished."[150] But one cannot ignore the *contra* argument that the contribution provisions in §§11(f) and 18(b) apply only for purposes of those sections, just as one does not apply the provisions on attorneys' fees in §11(e) of the 1933 Act and §§9(e) and 18(a) of the 1934 Act to actions under Rule 10b-5. So *query.*[151]

Under the Federal Rules of Civil Procedure anyone sued under §11 or one of the implied liabilities can bring in as third-party defendants those who may be liable to him by way of contribution or indemnification.[152] Under the broad provisions of §22(a) of the 1933 Act and §27 of the 1934 Act there will frequently (perhaps usually) be no problem of venue or personal service; indeed, even if it be assumed that the defendant's third-party complaint is based not on one of the statutory contribution provisions but on a contract of indemnification (or presumably a common law right of indemnification), such a complaint is ancillary to the principal cause of

[147] 29 U. S. C. §206(d); Tit. VII, §703, 42 U. S. C. §2000e-2; Northwest Airlines, Inc. v. Transport Workers Union, 451 U. S. 77 (1981).

[148] 15 U. S. C. §15; Texas Industries, Inc. v. Radcliff Materials, Inc., 451 U. S. 630 (1981).

[149] 451 U. S. at 638; see also id. at 90-91.

[150] Fogel v. Chestnutt, 668 F. 2d 100, 119 n. 17 (2d Cir. 1981); see also In re National Student Marketing Litigation, 517 F. Supp. 1345, 1348-49 (D. D. C. 1981); Seiler v. E. F. Hutton & Co., Inc., CCH Fed. Sec. L. Rep. ¶91,632 at 99,203 (D. N. J. 1984).

[151] In Noonan v. Granville-Smith, 532 F. Supp. 1007 (S. D. N. Y. 1982), *certificate of interlocutory appeal*, 535 F. Supp. 333 (S. D. N. Y. 1982), the court held that the Second Circuit's contribution holdings did survive.

When indemnification or contribution is foreclosed for any reason, and the person sought to be held is a lawyer, he might be liable for malpractice. Brennan v. Reed, Smith, Shaw & McClay, 304 Pa. Super. 399, 405-06, 450 A. 2d 740, 747-48 (1982).

[152] F. R. Civ. P. 14(a).

action created by §11 or implied under the 1934 Act, so that no independent basis of jurisdiction over the subject matter is required.[153] It has been held also that a §11 defendant's third-party complaint based on indemnification and breach of warranty and apparently contribution is not governed by the statute of limitations in the Securities Act.[154]

6. Attorneys' Fees and Security for Costs

If an officer's or director's right to look to the issuer for reimbursement of his litigation expenses is not altogether clear, what are his chances of being awarded his costs at the expense of the plaintiff in the principal action — or, better yet from his point of view, being secured against his costs in advance by the plaintiff's posting a surety bond?

In the absence of some statutory provision or rule of court, no advance security for costs may be required.[155] Under Rule 54(d) of the Federal Rules of Civil Procedure, costs are "allowed as of course to the prevailing party unless the court otherwise directs."[156]

---

[153] Miller v. Hano, 8 F. R. D. 67, 71 (E. D. Pa. 1947) (third-party complaint under §11(f) by underwriters against officers and directors); Lyons v. Marrud, Inc., 46 F. R. D. 451 (S. D. N. Y. 1968) (third-party complaint under §11(f) by underwriters against selling stockholders). The majority rule is the same with respect to venue. Lyons v. Marrud, Inc., CCH Fed. Sec. L. Rep. ¶92,307 at 97,455 (S. D. N. Y. 1968); Black & Co., Inc. v. Nova Tech, Inc., 333 F. Supp. 468, 473 (D. Ore. 1971).

[154] Metzger v. Breeze Corporations, Inc., 37 F. Supp. 693 (D. N. J. 1941); Lyons v. Marrud, Inc., CCH Fed. Sec. L. Rep. ¶92,307 at 97,456 (S. D. N. Y. 1968).

[155] McClure v. Borne Chemical Co., Inc., 292 F. 2d 824, 836-37 (3d Cir. 1961), *cert. denied,* 368 U. S. 939. There may, however, be a *contractual* condition of security for costs. See Chabot v. Empire Trust Co., 301 F. 2d 458 (2d Cir. 1962). And F. R. Civ. P. 65(c) requires security from an applicant for a temporary restraining order or preliminary injunction.

[156] The trial court has broad discretion with respect to the items of costs to be allowed. Fey v. Walston & Co., Inc., 493 F. 2d 1036, 1056 (7th Cir. 1974) (10b-5 churning case).

See also 28 U. S. C. §1912 (a Court of Appeals or the Supreme Court, when affirming a judgment, may give the prevailing party "just damages for his delay, and single or double costs"); F. R. App. P. 38 (to the same effect on a determination that an appeal is frivolous); Oscar Gruss & Son v. Lumbermens Mutual Casualty Co., 422 F. 2d 1278, 1285 (2d Cir. 1970); Zerman v. Jacobs, 751 F. 2d 82 (2d Cir. 1984); F. R. Civ. P. 37(a)(4), 37(b) (last par.) (failure to make or cooperate in discovery), considered in SEC v. Musella, CCH Fed. Sec. L. Rep. ¶91,647 (S. D. N. Y. 1984). Moreover, the plaintiff is entitled to the expenses

But costs normally do not include attorneys' fees when there is no specific statutory provision or rule.[157] To this "American rule" the courts have developed a number of exceptions:

(1) Under the "common fund" theory a plaintiff who has established a fund under the control of the court, classically in a stockholder's derivative or a class action, may recover his counsel fees from the fund.[158]

(2) This gradually developed into a broader "common benefit" theory. As Justice Harlan put it in *Mills* v. *Electric Auto-Lite Co.*:[159]

---

incurred in prosecuting a civil contempt. See cases cited, id. at 99,284.

The statutes in New York (Bus. Corp. Law §627) and a number of other states on security for costs in stockholders' derivative actions apply under the *Erie* doctrine to diversity cases in the federal courts. Cohen v. Beneficial Industrial Loan Corp., 337 U. S. 541 (1949). But those statutes, whether in the forum state or the state of incorporation, do not apply in federal question cases. McClure v. Borne Chemical Co., Inc., 292 F. 2d 824, 829-35 (3d Cir. 1961), *cert. denied,* 368 U. S. 939 (Rule 10b-5). Counts based on pendent jurisdiction are another matter unless amended out of the complaint. Lowey v. Vanderbilt, CCH Fed. Sec. L. Rep. ¶93,135 (S. D. N. Y. 1971). When a complaint is based on both federal and state law, "there should be no exaction of a joint undertaking covering all causes of action, but the requirement should be limited to those causes of action as to which the statute authorizes a bond." Fischman v. Raytheon Mfg. Co., 188 F. 2d 783, 789 (2d Cir. 1951); cf. Phelps v. Burnham, 327 F. 2d 812 (2d Cir. 1964); Lerman v. Tenney, 425 F. 2d 236 (2d Cir. 1970); Arceneaux v. Merrill Lynch, Pierce, Fenner & Smith, Inc., 595 F. Supp. 171, 174-75 (M. D. Fla. 1984), *aff'd on other grounds,* 767 F. 2d 1498 (11th Cir. 1985).

The inapplicability of state statutes on security to actions under the SEC statutes does not preclude application of the local court rules that exist (without limitation to stockholders' derivative actions) in some federal courts. But those rules are limited to "costs," which, as distinct from "expenses," usually involve a relatively small initial outlay. McClure v. Borne Chemical Co., supra, 292 F. 2d at 835; see, e. g., Leighton v. Paramount Pictures, Inc., 340 F. 2d 859, 861 (2d Cir. 1965), *cert. denied,* 381 U. S. 925 (court required $2000 bond of a "habitual *pro se* litigant whose claims were often conclusory and lacking in legal merit"); Competitive Associates, Inc. v. International Health Sciences, Inc., CCH Fed. Sec. L. Rep. ¶93,632 at 92,871-73 (S. D. N. Y. 1972) (court pretermitted question of propriety of costs under §11(e) by acting under local court rule).

[157] Alyeska Pipeline Service Co. v. Wilderness Society, 421 U. S. 240 (1975). This "American rule" is "unknown in the rest of the world." Ehrenzweig, Reimbursement of Counsel Fees and the Great Society, 54 Calif. L. Rev. 792, 793 (1966). And Professor Dawson concluded: "No adequate historical explanation for the American departure has ever been advanced, and in any event, the reasons commonly given — the spirit of individualism in frontier societies, the conception in earlier times of lawsuits as sporting contests, and the widespread hostility toward lawyers — are not persuasive now." Dawson, Lawyers and Involuntary Clients: Attorney Fees from Funds, 87 Harv. L. Rev. 1597, 1598 (1974).

[158] Trustees v. Greenough, 105 U. S. 527, 532 (1882).

[159] 396 U. S. 375, 391-95 (1970).

> While the general American rule is that attorneys' fees are not ordinarily recoverable as costs, both the courts and Congress have developed exceptions to this rule for situations in which overriding considerations indicate the need for such recovery. A primary judge-created exception has been to award expenses where a plaintiff has successfully maintained a suit, usually on behalf of a class, that benefits a group of others in the same manner as himself. * * *
>
> The fact that this suit has not yet produced, and may never produce, a monetary recovery from which the fees could be paid does not preclude an award based on this rationale. * * *
>
> Other cases have departed further from the traditional metes and bounds of the doctrine, to permit reimbursement in cases where the litigation has conferred a substantial benefit on the members of an ascertainable class, and where the court's jurisdiction over the subject matter of the suit makes possible an award that will operate to spread the costs proportionately among them. This development has been most pronounced in shareholders' derivative actions * * *.
>
> * * *
>
> * * * an increasing number of lower courts have acknowledged that a corporation may receive a "substantial benefit" from a derivative suit, justifying an award of counsel fees, regardless of whether the benefit is pecuniary in nature. * * *[160]

Five years after *Mills* the Supreme Court held in the *Alyeska*

[160] See also Sprague v. Ticonic National Bank, 307 U. S. 161 (1939); Hall v. Cole, 412 U. S. 1 (1973); Wolf v. Frank, 477 F. 2d 467 480 (5th Cir. 1973), *cert. denied,* 414 U. S. 975 (Rule 10b-5); Ramey v. Cincinnati Enquirer, Inc., 508 F. 2d 1188, 1194-96 (6th Cir. 1974), *cert. denied,* 422 U. S. 1048 (Rule 10b-5 and §14(a)); Kopet v. Esquire Realty Co., 523 F. 2d 1005 (2d Cir. 1975) (award in a §12(1) action apart from §11(e), infra pp. 1045-46); Smillie v. Park Chemical Co., 710 F. 2d 271, 275 (6th Cir. 1983).

But cf. Gerstle v. Gamble-Skogmo, Inc., 478 F. 2d 1281, 1308-10 (2d Cir. 1973) (court refused to extend *Mills* so as to charge counsel fees directly to defendant even when a fund *was* recovered); Isaacs Bros. v. Hibernia Bank, 481 F. 2d 1168, 1170 (9th Cir. 1973) (no substantial class benefit); Grace v. Ludwig, 484 F. 2d 1262, 1267-70 (2d Cir. 1973), *cert. denied,* 416 U. S. 905 (no fee for intervention in SEC proceeding under 1940 Act on behalf of minority stockholders); Wechsler v. Southeastern Properties, Inc., 506 F. 2d 631 (2d Cir. 1974) (private action based on a state proceeding); SEC v. Capital Counsellors, Inc., 512 F. 2d 654 (2d Cir. 1975) (unsuccessfully resisting a broker-dealer receivership); Bender v. Crown, 551 F. 2d 169 (7th Cir. 1977); Silberman v. Bogle, 683 F. 2d 62 (3d Cir. 1982).

See generally Dawson, Lawyers and Involuntary Clients in Public Interest Litigation, 88 Harv. L. Rev. 849, 867-70 (1975).

The result in *Mills* on remand was anticlimactic: The District Court found the exchange to be unfair and awarded damages that with prejudgment interest came to almost $2 million, but the Court of Appeals reversed. Mills v. Electric Auto-Lite Co., 552 F. 2d 1239 (7th Cir. 1977), *cert. denied,* 434 U. S. 922.

Pipeline case[161] that there was no inherent authority under federal law to award fees on any "private attorney general" theory — which the *Mills* case seemed to approach when it shifted from "common benefit" language to talk of "corporate therapeutics" that "furnish a benefit to *all* shareholders."[162] But the Court cited *Mills* with approval.[163]

(3) It "has long been established that even under the American common-law rule attorney's fees may be awarded against a party who has proceeded in bad faith."[164] But the courts are split on two important questions: whether the presence of a claim that is at least colorable precludes a finding of bad faith,[165] and whether pre-litigation conduct (acts forming the basis of the lawsuit as distinct from conduct during the litigation) may supply the necessary "bad faith."[166]

[161] Alyeska Pipeline Service Co. v. Wilderness Society, 421 U. S. 240, 262 (1975).

[162] 396 U. S. at 396 (italics are supplied).

[163] 421 U. S. at 258.

[164] Christiansburg Garment Co. v. Equal Employment Opportunity Commission, 434 U. S. 412, 419 (1978); see also Hall v. Cole, 412 U. S. 1, 5 (1973) (action "in bad faith, vexatiously, wantonly, or for oppressive reasons"); Alyeska Pipeline Service Co. v. Wilderness Society, 421 U. S. 240, 258-59 (1975); Kahan v. Rosenstiel, 424 F. 2d 161, 167 (3d Cir. 1970), *cert. denied* sub nom. Glen Alden Corp. v. Kahan, 398 U. S. 950 (10b-5 case involving "a willful and persistent 'defiance of the law' "); Goldman v. Belden, 580 F. Supp. 1373, 1381-82 (W. D. N. Y. 1984), *vacated on other grounds,* 754 F. 2d 1059 (2d Cir. 1985) (costs, including attorneys' fees, were assessed jointly and severally against plaintiff and his attorneys). But, although "awards of costs and attorney's fees * * * are entrusted to the sound discretion of the trial court," that court "must listen to a party's arguments and give reasons for its decision." Schwarz v. Folloder, 767 F. 2d 125, 127 (5th Cir. 1985).

Under 28 U. S. C. §1927 costs, including attorneys' fees, may be levied against an *attorney* to the extent that they result from his multiplying the proceedings "unreasonably and vexatiously." See also F. R. Civ. P. 11, last sentence. Both provisions are discussed in Suslick v. Rothschild Securities Corp., 741 F. 2d 1000 (7th Cir. 1984), and Rule 11 was applied against plaintiffs' counsel in Bush v. Rewald, 619 F. Supp. 585, 604-05 (D. Hawaii 1985). See also *Goldman,* supra.

[165] *Yes:* Browning Debenture Holders' Committee v. DASA Corp., 560 F. 2d 1078, 1088 (2d Cir. 1977); Suslick v. Rothschild Securities Corp., 741 F. 2d 1000, 1007 (7th Cir. 1984). *No:* Lipsig v. National Student Marketing Corp., 663 F. 2d 178, 182 (D. C. Cir. 1980).

[166] *Yes*: Adams v. Standard Knitting Mills, Inc., CCH Fed. Sec. L. Rep. ¶95,713 (E. D. Tenn. 1976); cf. Tse Zung Yao v. W. E. Hutton & Co., CCH Fed. Sec. L. Rep. ¶96,039 (S. D. N. Y. 1977) (but not in 10b-5 cases). *No:* Straub v. Vaisman & Co., Inc., 540 F. 2d 591, 599 (3d Cir. 1976) (award of fees on basis of underlying acts would amount to punitive damages); Huddleston v. Herman & McLean, 640 F. 2d 534, 559-60 (5th Cir. 1981), *aff'd in part and rev'd in part on other grounds* sub nom. Herman & MacLean v. Huddleston, 459 U. S. 375 (1983); Fowler v. Bearing Specialty Co., CCH Fed. Sec. L. Rep. ¶99,061 (N. D.

So far as the *express* liabilities are concerned, Congress did supply variant provisions on costs, including counsel fees:

In 1934 the fear of "strike suits"[167] led Congress to amend §11(e) of the Securities Act to provide both for security and for the award of counsel fees:

> In any suit under this or any other section of this title the court may, in its discretion, require an undertaking for the payment of the costs of such suit, including reasonable attorney's fees, and if judgment shall be rendered against a party litigant, upon the motion of the other party litigant, such costs may be assessed in favor of such party litigant (whether or not such undertaking has been required) if the court believes the suit or the defense to have been without merit, in an amount sufficient to reimburse him for the reasonable expenses incurred by him, in connection with such suit, such costs to be taxed in the manner usually provided for taxing of costs in the court in which the suit was heard.[168]

Abbreviated versions of the same provision appear in §9(e) of the Exchange Act, the section creating civil liability for manipulation, as well as §18 of that Act and the similar sections in the Holding Company and Trust Indenture Acts creating civil liabilities for false statements filed with the Commission, but not in the provisions on recovery of insiders' short-term trading profits or the voidability provisions like §29(b) of the Exchange Act. The language of §§9(e) and 18(a) of the Exchange Act (the latter of which is incorporated by reference into §16(a) of the Holding Company Act) is simply this:

> In any such suit the court may, in its discretion, require an undertaking for the payment of the costs of such suit, and assess reasonable costs, including reasonable attorneys' fees, against either party litigant.

The Senate committee stated in its report on the 1934 bill that "bad faith" was the intended test.[169] But the specific reference to

---

Cal. 1982); Woods v. Barnett Bank of Fort Lauderdale, 765 F. 2d 1004, 1014 (11th Cir. 1985), *rehearing en banc denied*, 772 F. 2d 918 (11th Cir. 1985).

[167] See Linchuck v. Cooper, 43 F. R. D. 382, 384 (S. D. N. Y. 1967); Rubin v. Long Island Lighting Co., 576 F. Supp. 608, 615 (E. D. N. Y. 1984).

[168] See Douglas and Bates, The Federal Securities Act of 1933, 43 Yale L. J. 171, 210, 215 (1933).

[169] S. Rep. No. 792, 73d Cong., 2d Sess. (1934) 17-18. But the cases attack the "bad faith" rubric with varying prose. Jackson v. Oppenheim, 533 F. 2d 826, 831 (2d Cir. 1976) (whether claim is "frivolous or brought in bad faith"); Driscoll v. Oppenheimer & Co., Inc., 500 F. Supp. 174 (N. D. Ill. 1980) ("a colorable basis" for claims precludes "bad faith"); Weil v. Investment/Indicators, Research & Management, Inc., 647 F. 2d 18, 22 (9th Cir. 1981) (whether claim "borders on the frivolous"); Junker v. Crory, 650 F. 2d 1349, 1364 n. 20

the "merit" of the action that Congress wrote into §11 of the Securities Act by amendment in 1934 simultaneously with the passage of the Exchange Act was omitted from the latter statute, only to reappear in strengthened form in §323(a) of the Trust Indenture Act. That section adds to the language of §18(a) of the Exchange Act the clause: "having due regard to the merits and good faith of the suit or defense."[170]

A number of observations on this kaleidoscope:

(1) On the one hand, the courts' creation of implied actions has not persuaded them to imply a right to counsel fees by analogy to the express provisions on fees.[171] On the other hand, the presence of §§9(e) and 18(a) has not prevented the award of fees under §16(b).[172] But there, of course, the analogy is to the production of a fund in a stockholder's derivative action.[173]

(2) The desire to escape the double danger of paying counsel fees and posting security was yet another reason for buyers with complaints to rush to Rule 10b-5 in the face of their express remedies under §§11 and 12(2).[174]

(3) *Query* whether §11(e) applies to actions under §17(a) on the assumption that such actions are possible.[175]

(5th Cir. 1981) (whether defense was "without merit"); Western Federal Corp. v. Erickson, 739 F. 2d 1439, 1444 (9th Cir. 1984) (since the defenses "did border on the frivolous," lower court acted within its discretion in awarding fees).

[170]Cf. Trust Ind. Act §315(e); Browning Debenture Holders' Committee v. DASA Corp., 560 F. 2d 1078, 1088 (2d Cir. 1977), *on remand*, 81 F. R. D. 407 (S. D. N. Y. 1978). Presumably all these provisions yield in the case of "a person who makes affidavit that he is unable to pay * * * costs or give security therefor." 28 U. S. C. §1915(a).

Under the South Carolina Uniform Securities Act, which refers simply to "reasonable attorneys' fees," the court in Bradley v. Hullander, 277 S. C. 327, 287 S. E. 2d 140 (1982), considered five criteria in determining the amount of the award: (1) the nature, extent, and difficulty of the required services; (2) the attorney's professional standing and reputation; (3) the success of his efforts; (4) whether the fee was fixed or contingent; and (5) the time devoted to the case.

There is also a provision in RICO, 18 U. S. C. §1964(c), supra p. 923, that gives the successful treble damage plaintiff an automatic right to "a reasonable attorney's fee." See James v. Meinke, CCH Fed. Sec. L. Rep. ¶91,933 (N. D. Tex. 1984).

[171]McClure v. Borne Chemical Co., Inc., 292 F. 2d 824, 836-37 (3d Cir. 1961), *cert. denied*, 368 U. S. 939; Van Alen v. Dominick & Dominick, 560 F. 2d 547, 553-54 (2d Cir. 1977).

[172]Mills v. Electric Auto-Lite Co., 396 U. S. 375, 390-91 (1970).

[173]See Smolowe v. Delendo Corp., 136 F. 2d 231, 241 (2d Cir. 1963), *cert. denied*, 320 U. S. 751.

[174]In 10b-5 and other implied liability cases the defendant (and, of course, the plaintiff if he wins) should not overlook the possibility of getting counsel fees under the blue sky law (the Uniform Securities Act is silent) or some other state statute. Compare Young v. Taylor, 466 F. 2d 1329, 1338 (10th Cir. 1972), with Hail v. Heyman-Christiansen, Inc., 536 F. 2d 908 (10th Cir. 1976).

[175]See pp. 977-80 supra. The court apparently *assumed* an affirmative answer

(4) Although §11(e) contains no standards with respect to requiring security and the 1934 Act provisions contain no standards at all, the courts have applied a basically "bad faith" standard throughout.[176]

(5) All the provisions, though even-handed so far as assessment of costs is concerned, favor defendants in that they cannot be required to post security regardless of how *mala fide* their defense may be.

(6) Perhaps because of the readiness with which the plaintiff's motives are attacked, at least in the case of stockholders' suits,[177] the judicial attitude toward requiring plaintiffs to post security for costs under these statutory provisions seems to be on the chary side.[178] On the analogy of the summary judgment procedure under Rule 56 of the Federal Rules of Civil Procedure, there must be a substantial showing.[179] The small amount of the plaintiff's holdings does not establish bad faith *per se.*[180] And the mere failure to present sufficient evidence to support the claims made does not itself warrant a determination of frivolousness.[181]

On the other side of the coin, plaintiffs have been ordered to post security on a variety of grounds: the "large amount of work necessary in the defense of the actions by the numerous defendants," when considered together with the filing of defendants' affidavits containing "such detailed facts as tend strongly to refute

---

in Klein v. Shields & Co., 470 F. 2d 1344, 1347-48 (2d Cir. 1972); see also Ruebe v. Pharmacodynamics, Inc., 348 F. Supp. 900, 916 (E. D. Pa. 1972).

[176] See p. 1046 n. 169 supra. In Nemeroff v. Abelson, 704 F. 2d 652 (2d Cir. 1983), the court concluded that the lower court had been warranted in finding that the plaintiff and his attorneys had *continued* the suit in bad faith after a certain date. In Zissu v. Bear, Stearns & Co., 805 F. 2d 75, 79-80 (2d Cir. 1986), a strike suit instituted for its nuisance and settlement value, the fees and costs totaled $555,000. In LeMaster v. Bull, 581 F. Supp. 1170, 1173 (E. D. Pa. 1984), the court held that the "punitive nature" of the fee provision in §11 indicated that fees should not be awarded for activities after the close of the action, such as the separate proceedings involved in execution on a money judgment, "unless the defendant's bad faith, meritless or frivolous actions have in some ways caused the added costs of execution."

[177] See McClure v. Borne Chemical Co., Inc., 292 F. 2d 824, 837 n. 13 (3d Cir. 1961), *cert. denied,* 368 U. S. 939.

[178] Ibid.; see also, e. g., Can-Am Petroleum Co. v. Beck, 331 F. 2d 371, 374 (10th Cir. 1964); Oil & Gas Income, Inc., v. Woods Exploration & Producing Co., Inc., 362 F. 2d 309 (5th Cir. 1966), *on later appeal* sub nom. Oil & Gas Income, Inc. v. Trotter, 395 F. 2d 753 (5th Cir. 1968); Klein v. Shields & Co., 470 F. 2d 1344, 1348 (2d Cir. 1972); Rucker v. Louisiana Co., Inc., 496 F. 2d 850, 853 (8th Cir. 1974); Nemeroff v. Abelson, 620 F. 2d 339 (2d Cir. 1980).

[179] Stella v. Kaiser, 83 F. Supp. 431 (S. D. N. Y. 1949).

[180] Ibid.

[181] Aid Auto Stores, Inc. v. Cannon, 525 F. 2d 468, 471 (2d Cir. *per curiam* 1975).

the allegations in the amended complaints as to the untrue statements and omissions in the Registration Statement";[182] the fact that the plaintiff's affidavits "do not dispel the notion that they knew of the alleged misleading statements and the like long before they presently assert";[183] naming three defendants as co-conspirators on the basis solely of hearsay and rumor;[184] and the small value of the plaintiff's shares ($800) in relation to the potential damages ($5 million), when considered together with the plaintiff's apparent attempt to reargue matters already decided in a prior litigation that had caused the defendant much expense.[185] There is also precedent for assessing substantial costs against a *defendant* whose defense was without merit and not made in good faith.[186]

[182] Montague v. Electronic Corp. of America, 76 F. Supp. 933, 936 (S. D. N. Y. 1948).

[183] Fischman v. Raytheon Mfg. Co., 9 F. R. D. 707, 711 (S. D. N. Y. 1949). But on appeal the court held that the bond requirement was premature: "Passing the question whether the judge's 'feeling' and 'notion' about the knowledge of the preferred stockholders sufficed to show a lack of 'merit,' we think that, as amendment of the complaint was permitted, consideration of whether a bond should be exacted must be postponed until the amended complaint has been filed." Id., 188 F. 2d 783, 788-89 (2d Cir. 1951).

[184] Miller v. Schweikart, 413 F. Supp. 1059 (S. D. N. Y. 1976).

[185] Dabney v. Alleghany Corp., 164 F. Supp. 28, 33 (S. D. N. Y. 1958).

[186] Stadia Oil & Uranium Co. v. Wheelis, 251 F. 2d 269, 277 (10th Cir. 1957).

CHAPTER 11

THE SEC LAWYER

In varying degrees the Commission and the securities Bar have rubbed each other on a number of fronts in recent years:

A. THE SEC LAWYER'S ROLE

The question whether a lawyer may have a duty not only to resign but also to "turn his client in" when he is aware of the client's intention to commit an illegal act became the subject of a *cause célèbre* (with inconclusive results) in the 1970s.

The case grew out of a merger of Interstate National Corporation ("Interstate") into National Student Marketing Corporation ("NSM").[1] Counsel for both companies were among the defendants. Judge Parker put the question thus:

> The principal question presented is whether the defendants violated or aided and abetted the violation of the anti-fraud provisions of the federal securities laws in two instances: (1) consummation of the NSMC merger; and (2) the immediately following sale of newly acquired NSMC stock by former Interstate principals, including certain of the defendants. These transactions are alleged to have occurred despite the prior receipt by the defendants of information which revealed that NSMC's interim financial statements, used in securing shareholder approval of the merger and available to the investing public generally, were grossly inaccurate and failed to show the true condition of the corporation. The information was included in a comfort letter prepared by NSMC's [accountants].[2]

The Commission contended that the contents of the comfort letter should have caused the attorneys to refuse to issue the required opinions and to demand resolicitation of the Interstate stock-

C. 11A [1]SEC v. National Student Marketing Corp., 457 F. Supp. 682 (D. D. C. 1978).
[2]Id. at 687.

holders. If the Interstate directors refused to resolicit, the Commission argued, "the attorneys should have withdrawn from the representation and informed the shareholders or the Commission."[3]

On the critical question of the lawyer's duty vis-à-vis a recalcitrant client, the opinion was anticlimactic:

> In view of the obvious materiality of the information, especially to attorneys learned in securities law, the attorneys' responsibilities to their corporate client required them to take steps to ensure that the information would be disclosed to the shareholders. However, it is unnecessary to determine the precise extent of their obligations here, since it is undisputed that they took no steps whatsoever to delay the closing pending disclosure to and resolicitation of the Interstate shareholders. But, at the very least, they were required to speak out at the closing concerning the obvious materiality of the information and the concomitant requirement that the merger not be closed until the adjustments were disclosed and approval of the merger was again obtained from the Interstate shareholders. Their silence was not only a breach of this duty to speak, but in addition lent the appearance of legitimacy to the closing * * *.[4]

Nevertheless, the Commission had simply failed to make out a case for injunctive relief. In view of the complaint's having "generated significant interest and an almost overwhelming amount of comment within the legal profession on the scope of a securities lawyer's obligation to his client and to the investing public,"[5] the very initiation of the action "has provided a necessary and worthwhile impetus for the profession's recognition and assessment of its responsibilities in this area."[6] And the court thought it "difficult to characterize the violations presented here as either 'willful, blatant, and often completely outrageous,' or as the 'garden variety fraud'

[3] Id. at 701.

[4] Id. at 713.

[5] Ibid. The court referred (id. at 714 n. 73) to the extensive bibliography in Hoffman, On Learning of a Corporate Client's Crime or Fraud — the Lawyer's Dilemma, 33 Bus. Law. 2389, 2404-05 n. 38 (1978). See also S. Goldberg (ed.), Expanding Responsibilities Under the Securities Laws (conference co-chaired by J. Flom and L. Loss 1973); Am. B. Foundation, Annotated Code of Professional Responsibility (1979) 321-26; for a critique of the Commission's view, see Lipman, The SEC's Reluctant Police Force: A New Role for Lawyers, 49 N. Y. U. L. Rev. 437 (1974); for a pungent criticism by a civil libertarian, see Freedman, A Civil Libertarian Looks at Securities Regulation, 35 Ohio St. L. J. 280, esp. at 285 (1974) (the SEC Bar is already a "wholly-owned subsidiary" of the Commission).

[6] 457 F. Supp. at 714.

urged by the Commission."[7] Altogether the court was "confident that [the lawyers] will take appropriate steps to ensure that their professional conduct in the future comports with the law."[8]

The pendency of this case produced a strong reaction from the Bar. Acting on the basis of a committee report that did not "believe that the policy of disclosure as embodied in the SEC laws warrants an exception to the basic confidentiality of the attorney-client relationship,"[9] the American Bar Association in 1975 adopted a Statement of Policy on the question of disclosure by lawyers in the SEC context:[10]

* * *

2. [The] vital confidentiality of consultation and advice would be destroyed or seriously impaired if it is accepted as a general principle that lawyers must inform the SEC or others regarding confidential information received by lawyers from their clients even though such action would not be permitted or required by the CPR * * *.[11]

3. In light of the foregoing considerations, it must be recognized that a lawyer cannot, consistently with his essential role as legal adviser, be regarded as a source of information concerning possible wrong-doing by clients. Accordingly, any principle of law which, except as permitted or required by the CPR, permits or obliges a lawyer to disclose to the SEC otherwise confidential information, should be established only by statute after full and careful consideration of the public interests involved, and should be resisted unless clearly mandated by law.

4. * * * In appropriate circumstances, a lawyer may be permitted or required by the Disciplinary Rules under the CPR to resign his engagement if his advice concerning disclosures is disregarded by the client and, if the conduct of a client clearly establishes his prospective commission of a crime or the past or prospective perpetration of a fraud in the course of the lawyer's representation, even to make the disclosures himself. However, the lawyer has neither the obligation nor the right to make disclosure when any rea-

[7] Id. at 716, quoting from SEC v. Manor Nursing Centers, Inc., 458 F. 2d 1082, 1101 (2d Cir. 1972).

[8] 457 F. Supp. at 717.

[9] Statement of Policy Adopted by the American Bar Association Regarding Responsibilities and Liabilities of Lawyers in Advising with Respect to the Compliance by Clients with Laws Administered by the Securities and Exchange Commission, 31 Bus. Law. 543, 547 (1975).

[10] Ibid.; see also The Code of Professional Responsibility and the Responsibility of Lawyers Engaged in Securities Law Practice — A Report by the Committee on Counsel Responsibility and Liability, 30 Bus. Law. 1289 (1975).

[11] The Code of Professional Responsibility was replaced in 1983 by the Model Rules of Professional Conduct.

sonable doubt exists concerning the client's failure to meet his obligation is not clearly established, except to the extent that the lawyer should consider appropriate action, as required or permitted by the CPR, in cases where the lawyer's opinion is expected to be relied on by third parties and the opinion is discovered to be not correct, whether because it is based on erroneous information or otherwise.

5. Efforts by the government to impose responsibility upon lawyers to assure the quality of their clients' compliance with the law or to compel lawyers to give advice resolving all doubts in favor of regulatory restrictions would evoke serious and far-reaching disruption in the role of the lawyer as counselor, which would be detrimental to the public, clients and the legal profession. In fulfillment of their responsibility to clients under the CPR, lawyers must be free to advise clients as to the full range of their legitimately available courses of action and the relative attendant risks involved. Furthermore, it is often desirable for the lawyer to point out those factors which may suggest a decision that is morally just as well as legally permissible. However, the decision as to the course to be taken should be made by the client. The client's actions should not be improperly narrowed through the insistence of an attorney who may, perhaps unconsciously, eliminate available choices from consideration because of his concern over possible personal risks if the position is taken which, though supportable, is subject to uncertainty or contrary to a known, but perhaps erroneous, position of the SEC or a questionable lower court decision. * * *

The CPR that was then in effect provided in relevant part:

CANON 4. A LAWYER SHOULD PRESERVE THE CONFIDENCES AND SECRETS OF A CLIENT

* * *

DISCIPLINARY RULES

DR 4-101 Preservation of Confidences and Secrets of a Client.

* * *

(C) A lawyer may reveal:

* * *

(3) The intention of his client to commit a crime and the information necessary to prevent the crime.

* * *

CANON 7. A LAWYER SHOULD REPRESENT A CLIENT ZEALOUSLY WITHIN THE BOUNDS OF THE LAW

* * *

DISCIPLINARY RULES

* * *

DR 7-102 Representing a Client Within the Bounds of the Law.

* * *

(B) A lawyer who receives information clearly establishing that:

(1) His client has, in the course of the representation, perpetrated a fraud upon a person or tribunal shall promptly call upon his client to rectify the same, and if his client refuses or is unable to do so, he shall reveal the fraud to the affected person or tribunal except when the information is protected as a privileged communication.

* * *[12]

Even apart from the limitation to "the course of the representation," the accent was pretty clearly on the "may" in DR1 101(C), on the past tense in the mandatory DR7-102(B)(1), and on the "except" clause. In any event, the successor Model Rules of Professional Conduct are even more emphatic. Although a lawyer "may not counsel or assist a client in conduct that is criminal or fraudulent,"[13] and "must withdraw" if his services "will be used by the client in materially furthering a course of criminal or fraudulent conduct,"[14] he may reveal information relating to representation of a client only (so far as is here relevant) with the client's consent or authorization or "to the extent the lawyer reasonably believes necessary * * * to prevent the client from committing a criminal act

[12] See the commentary in Am. B. Foundation, Annotated Code of Professional Responsibility (1979) 307.

[13] Comment to Rule 1.6, citing Rule 1.2(d).

[14] Comment to Rule 1.6, citing Rule 1.16(a)(1). The lawyer "may also withdraw or disaffirm any opinion, document, affirmation or the like." Comment to Rule 1.6.

that the lawyer believes is likely to result in imminent death or substantial bodily harm."[15] The word is "may," not "must." And even this limitation is reinforced by a scope note that the lawyer's exercise of discretion not to disclose "should not be subject to reexamination."

It must be remembered that the American Bar Association's ethical codifications are not in themselves law. Most states that have adopted the Model Rules or the predecessor Code have not in fact followed their provisions on confidentiality. Nevertheless, the organized Bar's view of the lawyer's duty is not without significance.

Questions of attorney-client relationship aside, we must still ask just what the SEC lawyer's duty is when, say, he drafts a registration statement or report.

The issuer's counsel has been aptly called the "quarterback" in preparing the nonfinancial portions of a 1933 Act registration statement,[16] though the underwriter's counsel may play a substantial role if the issuer's counsel is inexperienced. This does not give the lawyer the statutory status of an "expert" on virtually the whole registration statement.[17] Normally he is an "expert" only with respect to his required opinion that the stock being offered will be legally issued, fully paid and nonassessable, or any additional opinions he might give on such questions as title to property or the validity of a patent. Although counsel is not doing his job unless he asks searching questions of management — clients seldom come into a lawyer's office in any branch of the law with all the relevant facts neatly arranged on a silver platter — the truthfulness and completeness of a registration statement are in the last analysis management's responsibility.

Here again, however, the Commission has repeatedly cautioned that "the task of enforcing the securities laws rests in overwhelming measure on the bar's shoulders."[18] And, if a Commissioner's statement in an address to a Bar group that "a lawyer preparing a

[15] Rule 1.6(b)(1).

[16] R. Jennings and H. Marsh, Securities Regulation Cases and Materials (5th ed. 1982) 106. For a set of guidelines on the lawyer's role in the preparation of registration statements, see Assn. of the Bar of the City of N. Y., Report by Special Committee on Lawyers' Role in Securities Transactions, 32 Record A. B. C. N. Y. 345 (1977), 32 Bus. Law. 1879 (1977).

[17] Escott v. BarChris Construction Corp., 283 F. Supp. 643, 683 (S. D. N. Y. 1968); see pp. 900-01 supra.

[18] Emanuel Fields, 45 SEC 262, 266 n. 20 (1973), *aff'd without opinion* sub nom. Fields v. SEC, 495 F. 2d 1075 (D. C. Cir. 1974), quoted in William R. Carter, Sec. Ex. Act Rel. 17,597, 22 SEC Dock. 292, 297 n. 21 (1981), infra p. 1057; see also SEC v. Spectrum, Ltd., 489 F. 2d 535, 541-42 (2d Cir. 1973), infra p. 1063.

registration statement has an obligation to do more than simply act as the blind scrivener of the thoughts of his client" can be discounted as an able lawyer's rhetoric, it is not quite so easy to discount the further suggestion that "in securities matters (other than those where advocacy is clearly proper) the attorney will have to function in a manner more akin to that of the auditor than to that of the advocate."[19]

The suggestion has been heard that the SEC lawyer is counsel to "the situation." The phrase is not new. Louis Brandeis used it as a practicing lawyer in Boston. But an admirer has termed it "one of the most unfortunate phrases he ever casually uttered."[20] And surely some of his Beacon Hill adversaries must have asked, as some lawyers ask today, where they should address their bills to "the situation."[21]

B. DISCIPLINARY PROCEEDINGS

Three years after the *National Student Marketing* case the Commission returned to the question of the lawyer's obligation when a client won't listen — this time in the context of an administrative proceeding against several lawyers under Rule 2(e) of the Commission's Rules of Practice, which has to do with the disciplining of lawyers, accountants, and other experts.[1] The Commission's lengthy opinion is important for two reasons: its exposition of Rule 2(e), and its announcement of a new test for lawyers' conduct in the future.

The Commission in 1938 amended Rule 2 of its original Rules of Practice to disestablish its formal "SEC Bar," with specific admission requirements, but preserved the provision that authorized the Commission to "deny admission to, suspend, or disbar, any

[19] Sommer, The Emerging Responsibilities of the Securities Lawyer, CCH Fed. Sec. L. Rep. ¶79,631 at 83,689, 83,690 (1974).

[20] Frank, The Legal Ethics of Louis D. Brandeis, 17 Stan. L. Rev. 683, 702 (1965); see also id. at 698-703; A. Mason, Brandeis: A Free Man's Life (1956) 236.

[21] R. Jennings and H. Marsh, Securities Regulation Cases and Materials (5th ed. 1982) 1209.

For a comprehensive review, see Small, An Attorney's Responsibilities Under Federal and State Securities Laws: Private Counselor or Public Servant?, 61 Calif. L. Rev. 1189 (1973); for a philosophical analysis, see Rosenfeld, Between Rights and Consequences: A Philosophical Inquiry into the Foundations of Legal Ethics in the Changing World of Securities Regulation, 49 Geo. Wash. L. Rev. 462 (1981).

C. 11B [1] William R. Carter, Sec. Ex. Act Rel. 17,597, 22 SEC Dock. 292 (1981).

person who does not possess the requisite qualifications to represent others, or who is lacking in character, integrity, or proper professional conduct." Then:

> In September 1970, Rule 2(e) was again amended to provide for an automatic suspension from appearance or practice before the Commission by a person who (1) had been suspended or disbarred from practice or who has had his license to practice suspended or revoked by a state licensing authority, (2) had been convicted of a felony or of a misdemeanor involving moral turpitude, or (3) had been suspended or disbarred by a court of competent jurisdiction. In addition, a third category — subparagraph (1)(iii) of the Rule — was added to provide that the Commission may deny a professional the privilege of appearing or practicing before it for the willful violation, or the willful aiding and abetting of a violation, of the federal securities laws or the rules and regulations thereunder.[2]

Observing that the Second Circuit had referred to the rule as "an attempt by the Commission to protect the integrity of its own processes,"[3] the Commission concluded that both the promulgation of the rule and its application in the particular case were "clearly within our jurisdictional grant of authority."[4] More particularly:

(1) With respect to prosecutorial considerations:

> We are sensitive to the abuses that may occur when an administrative agency with prosecutorial responsibilities has the power to discipline attorneys representing regulated entities. * * * Although the potential for abuse does exist, "it is neither so great nor so unique to this agency that the Commission should decline to exercise its authority in this area."[5]
>
> * * * We are convinced that, at this time, our responsibilities do not permit us to
>
>> ignore or refuse to exercise an effective professional disciplinary tool under the appropriate circumstances. * * * [We believe] that Rule 2(e) should not be utilized as an enforcement tool against those who violate the federal securities laws and happen coincidentally also to be lawyers or accountants. But where such individuals engage in professional misconduct which impairs the integrity of the Commission's processes, the Com-

[2] Id. at 297. In Sec. Act Rel. 6662, 36 SEC Dock. 8056 (1986), the SEC invited comment on whether to amend Rule 2(e)(7), which provides that all 2(e) proceedings shall be nonpublic unless the Commission directs otherwise.

[3] 22 SEC Dock. at 294, quoting from Touche Ross & Co. v. SEC, 609 F. 2d 570, 582 (2d Cir. 1979).

[4] 22 SEC Dock. at 294.

[5] Id. at 295, citing Keating, Muething & Klekamp, Sec. Ex. Act Rel. 15,982 (1979), 17 SEC Dock. 1149, 1165 (Chairman Williams, concurring).

mission has an obligation to respond through the application of Rule 2(e).[6]

(2) By way of contrasting lawyers' and accountants' functions:

The duty of accountants to those who justifiably rely on those reports is well-recognized. But the traditional role of the lawyer as counselor is to advise his client, not the public, about the law. Rule 2(e) does not change the nature of that obligation. Nevertheless, if a lawyer violates ethical or professional standards, or becomes a conscious participant in violations of the securities laws, or performs his professional function without regard to the consequences, it will not do to say that because the lawyer's duty is to his client alone, this Commission must stand helplessly by while the lawyer carries his privilege of appearing and practicing before the Commission on to the next client.[7]

(3) How broadly to cast the net:

Not every violation of law * * * may be sufficient to justify invocation of the sanctions available under Rule 2(e). The violation must be of a character that threatens the integrity of the Commission's processes in the way that the activities of unqualified or unethical professionals do.[8]

(4) The Commission does not

distinguish between the professional advice of a lawyer given orally or in writing and similar advice which is embodied in drafting documents to be filed with the Commission. Liability in these circumstances should not turn on such artificial distinctions, particularly in light of the almost limitless range of forms which legal advice may take. Moreover, the opposite approach, which would permit a lawyer to avoid or reduce his liability simply by avoiding participation in the drafting process, may well have the undesirable effect of reducing the quality of the disclosure by the many to protect against the defalcations of the few.[9]

On its facts the case presented a picture of misleading filings, letters to stockholders, and press releases, with the respondents "in the uncomfortable position of attempting to provide disclosure advice to an aggressive client whose unreceptive management actively frustrated the giving of advice and ignored what advice managed to get through."[10] The Commission was not able to find the intent

[6] 22 SEC Dock. at 295-96. But see p. 1062 infra.
[7] Id. at 297.
[8] Id. at 314.
[9] Id. at 316.
[10] Id. at 309.

on the part of the lawyers that was essential to their being aiders and abettors. But it expressed the belief that the lawyers' conduct "raises serious questions about the obligations of securities lawyers"; and it stated that it was "hereby giving notice of its interpretation of 'unethical or improper professional conduct' " within Rule 2(e)(1)(ii):[11]

> When a lawyer with significant responsibilities in the effectuation of a company's compliance with the disclosure requirements of the federal securities laws becomes aware that his client is engaged in a substantial and continuing failure to satisfy those disclosure requirements, his continued participation violates professional standards unless he takes prompt steps to end the client's noncompliance.[12]

Further, the Commission reminded that it is the corporate client as an entity to which the corporation's lawyer owes allegiance.[13] Accordingly, in discharge of his obligation to "make all efforts within reason to persuade his client to avoid or terminate proposed illegal action," those efforts "could include, where appropriate, notification to the board of directors."[14]

Having said all this, the Commission concluded "that, in general, elemental notions of fairness dictate that the Commission should not establish new rules of conduct and impose them retroactively upon professionals who acted at the time without reason to believe that their conduct was unethical or improper."[15]

Query:

(1) Can the *Touche Ross* case,[16] which involved an accounting firm, be distinguished with respect to lawyers? Commissioner Karmel (as

[11] Id. at 320.
[12] Id. at 322.
[13] Id. at 321.
[14] Id. at 324. The Commisson also expatiated on the circumstances that would justify or impel resignation, although it anticipated that "cases where a lawyer has no choice but to resign would be rare and of an egregious nature." At the same time, it expressly disavowed dealing with the additional question of when a lawyer, aware of his client's intention to commit fraud or an illegal act, has a professional duty to disclose that fact either publicly or to an affected third party. Id. at 323 n. 78.

The SEC's General Counsel referred to Model Rule 1.13 as "not consistent" with *Carter's* holding, as he phrased it, "that, under the federal securities laws, lawyers engaged in a securities practice for a corporate client are required to present evidence of ongoing corporate violations of the securities laws to higher authorities in the corporation, including, if necessary, the board of directors." CCH Fed. Sec. L. Rep. ¶83,483 at 86,574 (1984).
[15] 22 SEC Dock. at 323.
[16] Touche, Ross & Co. v. SEC, 609 F. 2d 570, 582 (2d Cir. 1979). It was a

she then was) thought it might because of the Commission's express statutory authority to define accounting terms and require certification:[17]

> When Rule 2(e) is invoked to discipline attorneys for misconduct which does not directly obstruct the administrative process, in my opinion it is done so improperly as a matter of law and as a matter of policy. In the *Emanuel Fields* case[18] the Commission barred an attorney on the theory that the Commission can regulate the manner in which lawyers counsel clients and render opinions in securities transactions in order to protect investors. A primary rationale for so using Rule 2(e) has been that "the task of enforcing the securities laws rests in overwhelming measure on the bar's shoulders" and that given "its small staff, limited resources, and onerous tasks, the Commission is peculiarly dependent on the probity and diligence of the professionals who practice before it."[19] However, Congress did not authorize the Commission to conscript attorneys to enforce their clients' responsibilities under the federal securities laws. Furthermore, institutional limitations alone cannot justify the creation of a new remedy not contemplated by the Congress.
>
> I am firmly convinced that such conscription, or the promulgation and enforcement of regulatory standards of conduct for securities lawyers by the Commission, is very bad policy. It undermines the willingness and ability of the bar to exercise professional responsibility and sows the seeds for government abuse of power.
>
> A person's right to counsel is protected by various common law principles, the Administrative Procedure Act and the Sixth Amendment to the U. S. Constitution. When a prosecutorial agency like the Commission disciplines attorneys acting in a representative capacity, it necessarily impinges upon and interferes with a client's right to counsel. Because of the importance of the right to counsel to persons in their dealings with the government, it seems to me that government agencies, especially those with a prosecutorial function, should exercise caution in taking administrative action against attorneys. Such regulation necessarily gives an advocate pause, whether he is acting as an advisor or an adversary.[20]

---

stipulation of the final settlement of this action that the respondents would not seek judicial review of the court's injunction. Touche, Ross & Co., Acctg. Ser. Rel. 153A, 17 SEC Dock. 1107, 1115 (1979).

[17] Keating, Muething & Klekamp, Sec. Ex. Act Rel. 15,982, 17 SEC Dock. 1149, 1161-62 (1979) (dissenting opinion).

[18] Emanuel Fields, 45 SEC 262 (1973), *aff'd without opinion* sub nom. Fields v. SEC, 495 F. 2d 1085 (D. C. Cir. 1974).

[19] Id., 45 SEC at 6 n. 20.

[20] See also Daley and Karmel, Attorneys' Responsibilities at the Bar of the SEC, 24 Emory L. J. 747 (1975). For the opposite point of view, see, in addition to the majority opinion in *Keating*, supra n. 17, Sommer [then a Commissioner], Introduction [to Symposium: Enforcement of the Federal Securities Laws], 24

Again, when the Commission invited comment on whether its *Carter* interpretation should be expanded or modified, expressly stating that the invitation did not extend to the "previously considered * * * issue of its authority to adopt and administer Rule 2(e),"[21] an American Bar Association committee in its highly critical response expressed surprise "that the Commission thought that assertion could be dispositive of the issue presented by the Release."[22]

The fact is that for the first forty years or so there was only a handful of Rule 2(e) proceedings, involving egregious interference with the Commission's processes, whereas the volume later increased geometrically, with the Commission using the rule as a basis for regulating lawyers and accountants, even when there was no proceeding before the Commission, as long as the respondent's alleged conduct could be said somehow to have facilitated some violation of the federal securities laws.[23]

(2) *Should* the SEC as an enforcement agency with prosecutorial functions have authority to discipline lawyers *as lawyers?* Does the possibility of Rule 2(e) proceedings militate against vigorous advocacy on the part of counsel for persons who are under investigation or the subject of administrative proceedings? If the lawyer in such a case may himself become a subject of the investigation, isn't his self-interest brought into conflict with his client's? And what about the possibility of inconsistent requirements between the Commission on the one hand and the states or other agencies on the other hand? The Commission's staff, at least, has been heard to disclaim any attempt to criticize lawyers' actions as advocates as distinct from their actions as advisers. Will such a distinction stand up?[24]

(3) What about the Commission's proceeding against lawyers by

---

Emory L. J. 557, 564-66 (1975); Sonde, Professional Responsibility —A New Religion, or the Old Gospel?, 24 Emory L. J. 827 (1975).

[21] Sec. Act Rel. 6344, 23 SEC Dock. 826 (1981).

[22] SEC Standard of Conduct for Lawyers, 37 Bus. Law. 915, 917 (1982).

[23] Marsh, Rule 2(e) Proceedings, 35 Bus. Law. 987, 990-93 (1980). Since 1975, moreover, the Commission has used Rule 2(e) to discipline corporate officers who are lawyers or accountants. See Siedel, Rule 2(e) and Corporate Officers, 39 Bus. Law. 455 (1984). The other side of this coin is that the vast majority of the more than a hundred proceedings in the history of the rule have been either consent cases or based on injunctions, convictions, or disbarments. Indeed, many of the consent cases have been by way of settling injunctive actions. Greene, Lawyer Disciplinary Proceedings Before the Securities and Exchange Commission, 14 Sec. Reg. L. Rep. 168 (1982). But, of course, the pressure to consent in order to avoid the risk of a more harsh disposition is considerable.

[24] For an examination of these disparate roles that lawyers play, see Lorne, The Corporate and Securities Adviser, the Public Interest, and Professional Ethics, 76 Mich. L. Rev. 428 (1978).

way of injunctive relief? Fair enough if they have acted with scienter, even with its connotation of recklessness rather than knowledge of falsity with intent to defraud. But all that the Second Circuit required in a 1973 case was a showing of negligence in the preparation of legal opinions that permitted the distribution of unregistered securities in violation of the 1933 Act:

> In assessing liability as an aider and abettor * * * , the district judge formulated a requisite standard of culpability — actual knowledge of the improper scheme plus an intent to further that scheme — which we find to be a sharp and unjustified departure from the negligence standard which we have repeatedly held to be sufficient in the context of enforcement proceedings seeking equitable or prophylactic relief. * * *
>
> * * * The legal profession plays a unique and pivotal role in the effective implementation of the securities laws.[25]

Surely lawyers ought not to be held to *less* strict standards than others. Quite the contrary, they should be exemplars. Yet there is something disquieting about a court's telling a lawyer, under penalty of contempt: "Go thou and be nevermore negligent." If the lawyer, having had his fingers burned, is resolved to bend over backwards in advising future clients — as the Commission must surely hope — will he be able to do justice to his clients? Although the Commission need not allege more than negligence if it confines its complaint to §17(a)(2) and (3) of the 1933 Act,[26] presumably the Government would have to show more to get a conviction for criminal contempt. And we must rely here on the prosecutorial discretion of the Commission and the good sense of the courts.[27]

(4) Is there a solution that might achieve a consensus? The SEC and the American Bar Association's Standing Committee on Professional Discipline have tried to create a model disciplinary mechanism for lawyers who practice before federal and state agencies, so

[25] SEC v. Spectrum, Ltd., 489 F. 2d 535, 541-42 (2d Cir. 1973); see also SEC v. Management Dynamics, Inc., 515 F. 2d 801, 811 (2d Cir. 1975) (court referred to "the high degree of carelessness" in *Spectrum*); SEC v. Universal Major Industries Corp., 546 F. 2d 1044, 1047 (2d Cir. 1976), *cert. denied* sub nom. Homans v. SEC, 434 U. S. 834 (court referred to the lawyer's conduct in giving a private offering opinion as in fact "reckless"); but cf. SEC v. Haswell, 654 F. 2d 698 (10th Cir. 1981). For citations to a considerable number of injunctive proceedings against lawyers in 1966-72, see Mathews, SEC Civil Injunctive Actions, 5 Rev. Sec. Reg. 969, 970 n. 2 (1972).

[26] Aaron v. SEC, 446 U. S. 680 (1980), supra p. 783.

[27] See cases cited supra n. 25.

far without success.[28] The subject has generated so much emotion that those who worked on the Federal Securities Code — exhibiting either cowardice or statesmanship depending on the point of view — ultimately decided, after trying and abandoning various formulas, that "doing nothing seems the least imperfect course."[29] And this is one of six "separable issues" that the Commission, in announcing its approval of the Code, reserved the right to bring to the attention of Congress at any time.[30]

In 1982 the Commission's General Counsel, in a considered address, suggested among other propositions that, as a general matter, the Commission should institute 2(e) proceedings only if the alleged misconduct was a violation of established ethical rules at the state level and had a direct impact on the Commission's internal processes (for example, participation in the preparation of filed disclosure documents); that ordinarily invocation of Rule 2(e) with respect to lawyers who do not actually appear before the Commission and are not involved in the preparation of filed documents "could entangle the Commission in the regulation of lawyers' routine office practice"; that he would not recommend proceedings against lawyers appearing as advocates, because the threat of their institution could have a seriously chilling effect on zealous representation; and that the Commission should likewise be sensitive to the problems of parallel proceedings against client and attorney.[31]

[28] See 14 Sec. Reg. L. Rep. 1400, 1477-78 (1982). The Commission favored a federal statute that would give the federal courts jurisdiction to discipline lawyers for improper professional practices before federal agencies. But, because "the states, for a variety of reasons * * * , have not adequately disciplined lawyers who practice before federal agencies," the Commission was not willing to accept a statute that would merely give the appropriate state bar association exclusive jurisdiction, on complaint by a federal agency, to investigate and prosecute the complaint before a United States District Court, but without any requirement that the state authorities take any action. And the judges of the District Court for the District of Columbia unanimously rejected the Standing Committee's further proposal that their court promulgate standards of conduct for practitioners' direct appearance before an agency. See letter from Paul Gonson, Solicitor, SEC, to Michael Franck, Chairman, Standing Committee on Professional Discipline, ABA, CCH Fed. Sec. L. Rep. ¶83,241 (1982).

[29] 2 Code 832; see generally 2 id. at 832-33, Comment (10).

[30] Sec. Act Rel. 6242, 20 SEC Dock. 1483, 1484-85, 1512 (1980), reprinted in 2 Code (2d Supp.) 7, 15-16.

[31] Greene, Lawyer Disciplinary Proceedings Before the Securities and Exchange Commission, 14 Sec. Reg. L. Rep. 168, 169 (1982). More generally, see Brown and Mahony, Corporate Counsel, in Practising Law Institute, Fifteenth Annual Institute on Securities Regulation (1984) c. 4; Note, Liability of Attorneys for Legal Opinions Under the Federal Securities Laws, 27 B. C. L. Rev. 325 (1986) (Rule 2(e), SEC injunctive actions, and private actions).

C. MISCELLANEOUS ASPECTS OF THE SEC LAWYER'S WORK

Lawyer *qua* director aside,[1] there are two aspects of his work that are peculiar to the securities field:

(1) The first has to do with his preparation of written opinions — to the effect, for example, that an exemption from §5 is available for a proposed transaction. Here the Bar has the benefit of guidelines prepared by a committee of The Association of the Bar of the City of New York:[2]

GUIDELINE ONE

> Before rendering an opinion, a lawyer should ascertain the purpose for which the opinion is sought; whether the opinion is to be addressed to the client or another recipient; whether any persons other than the client or other addressee are intended to be entitled to rely on the opinion and, if so, their identity; and whether use by and reliance on the opinion should be expressly limited to a specific person or group of persons or to a particular purpose. * * *

GUIDELINE TWO

> A lawyer should not give an opinion (including one based on hypothetical facts or one that is legally correct as to the limited matters to which it is addressed), if he knows or suspects that the opinion is being sought to further an illegal securities transaction.

GUIDELINE THREE

> The lawyer should identify, consider and reach a conclusion concerning the legal questions posed by the requested opinion, performing such legal research as is reasonable to enable the lawyer to reach the opinion. In order to do so, he will in most instances have to identify and obtain factual information on which his legal analysis will depend. The lawyer generally obtains such factual information through inquiry of the client and, where appropriate, from others,

C. 11C [1]See Escott v. BarChris Construction Corp., 283 F. Supp. 643 (S. D. N. Y. 1968), supra p. 907; Feit v. Leasco Data Processing Equipment Corp., 332 F. Supp. 544 (E. D. N. Y. 1971), supra p. 912. On the lawyer's liability as aider and abettor, see SEC v. National Student Marketing Corp., 457 F. Supp. 682 (D. D. C. 1978), supra p. 1051; William R. Carter, Sec. Ex. Act Rel. 17,597, 22 SEC Dock. 292 (1981), supra p. 1057.

[2]Assn. of the Bar of the City of N. Y., Report by the Special Committee on Lawyers' Role in Securities Transactions, 32 Bus. Law. 1879 (1977). Copyright 1977 by the American Bar Association and reprinted with the permission of the Association and its Section of Corporation, Banking, and Business Law. The commentary is omitted.

and by reviewing materials provided to him for this purpose by the client or others. The lawyer should, therefore, satisfy himself that the client (and, if appropriate, others providing the lawyer with factual information or materials) is aware of the extent to which the lawyer is relying upon such information or materials in rendering the opinion and that there could be serious consequences if such information and materials are inaccurate or incomplete and, as a result, the legal opinion proves inapplicable or incorrect.

Guideline Four

A lawyer should not render an opinion based on factual information or material which he knows or suspects to be inaccurate in any material respect. Subject to the foregoing and except as stated in (a) and (b) below, a lawyer has no obligation independently to verify factual matters underlying his legal opinion, but in such opinion or otherwise he should make clear to the client and any other intended recipients of the opinion that he has not done so and, where appropriate, he should identify the factual information he has accepted or assumed without verification. A statement in the opinion as to reliance on officers' certificates and other documents will normally serve as adequate notice of the absence of independent verification by the lawyer of the factual matters to which such documents relate.

(a) A lawyer has no obligation to verify statements made, or other information provided, to him by a client or other intended recipient of an opinion unless he is aware of inconsistent information, or of experience or circumstances which reasonably alert him that such statements and information may be erroneous or incomplete in a material respect. Where he is aware of such inconsistencies, experience or circumstances, the doubts which they create should be resolved to the lawyer's satisfaction through further inquiry or other appropriate investigation before an opinion is given which is based on such statements or other information.

(b) When the lawyer's opinion requires his interpretation or checking of legal documents, such as contracts, certificates of incorporation, or the terms of securities, he should examine the relevant documents (or copies thereof) and should not rely on the client or others to summarize or paraphrase documents for this purpose unless otherwise warranted by accepted legal practice (such as reliance on real estate title abstracts) and disclosed in the opinion.

* * *

Guideline Seven

If in the lawyer's opinion the applicable law, or the application of that law to the particular facts, is sufficiently uncertain or unresolved so that there is a substantial possibility of differences of view among knowledgeable lawyers, the lawyer's own legal conclusion should be expressed in the context of that possibility. If the lawyer believes that the position reflected in his opinion is not in accordance with a position of responsible officials of the cognizant regulatory or administrative agency which is known to the lawyer, the lawyer should bring this to the attention of the client or other intended recipients of the opinion.

GUIDELINE EIGHT

If an opinion does not purport to address itself to an actual set of facts, it may be given on the basis of hypothetical facts if it states clearly the extent to which it is addressed only to hypothetical facts and that the opinion might be incorrect if the actual facts differ from the hypothetical facts. Opinions based on hypothetical facts, even though clearly identified as such, should not normally be given except when clearly limited, as to use and reliance, to the client or some other limited group with respect to whom the lawyer believes there will be no misunderstanding or misuse of the opinion.

These guidelines, together with other authority, inevitably leave room for the lawyer's exercise of discretion in particular cases.

The Commission cautioned in 1962 that, "if an attorney furnishes an opinion based solely upon hypothetical facts which he has made no effort to verify, and if he knows that his opinion will be relied upon as the basis for a substantial distribution of unregistered securities, a serious question arises as to the propriety of his professional conduct."[3] But presumably lawyers who give opinions on securities questions do not have to hire private detectives; for the same announcement referred to "the practice of responsible counsel not to furnish an opinion concerning the availability of an exemption from registration under the Securities Act for a contemplated distribution unless such counsel have themselves carefully examined all of the relevant circumstances and satisfied themselves, *to the extent possible,* that the contemplated transaction is, in fact, not a part of an unlawful distribution."[4]

The Eighth Circuit, in holding that it was not reckless for a lawyer to rely on a description of his corporate client's business by an officer who was a convicted felon, said: "To impose a standard

[3] Sec. Act Rel. 4445 (1962). Cf. Popham, Haik, Schnobrich, Kaufman & Doty, Ltd. v. Newcomb Securities Co., 751 F. 2d 1262 (D. C. Cir. 1985) (advice that client's investment offering was not a "security" could constitute malpractice, because the firm was apparently aware of the client's intention to market the offering in jurisdictions where the courts had held to the contrary and failed so to advise the client).

[4] Sec. Act Rel. 4445 (1962). Italics are supplied.

of independent factual inquiry in these circumstances would make it unreasonably difficult for clients to obtain expeditious legal advice, or for lawyers to maintain a busy practice."[5] And Judge Friendly covered both ends as well as the middle when he stated *obiter* that a lawyer had no privilege to assist in circulating a statement with regard to securities that he knew to be false simply because his client had furnished it to him;[6] that, at the other extreme, it would be unreasonable to hold a lawyer who was putting his client's description of a chemical process in understandable English to be guilty of fraud simply because of his failure to detect discrepancies between that description and the technical reports available to him in a physical sense but beyond his ability to understand; and that the case at Bar was in between.[7]

(2) In the last decade or so the Commission's relatively small enforcement arm has managed to extend its reach in a series of consent injunction cases by having the court appoint special counsel to supervise an investigation[8] and sometimes institute all necessary lawsuits on behalf of the corporate defendant,[9] or to administer a reimbursement fund and approve the corporate defendant's continued operations with authority in counsel's discretion to seek the Commission's approval of the institution of bankruptcy proceedings,[10] or to determine whether the defendant violated suitability standards and if so to order restitution to particular buyers.[11] Sometimes it is the corporate defendant that selects special counsel satisfactory to the Commission.[12]

Although the vast majority of these judgments have been entered by consent,[13] there are several reported cases that bless the proce-

[5] Stokes v. Lokken, 644 F. 2d 779, 783 n. 3 (8th Cir. 1981).

[6] See Kilmartin v. Wainwright, 580 F. Supp. 604, 608 (D. Mass. 1984) (counsel's "preparation of documents they knew to be misleading qualifies as 'substantial assistance' " so as to make them liable as aiders and abettors).

[7] SEC v. Frank, 388 F. 2d 486, 489 (2d Cir. 1968).

[8] SEC v. Clinton Oil Co., Litig. Rel. 5798, 1 SEC Dock. No. 8, p. 23 (D. Kan. 1973).

[9] SEC v. Charter Diversified Services, Litig. Rel. 6507, 5 SEC Dock. 147 (S. D. Cal. 1974).

[10] SEC v. Holiday Magic, Inc., CCH Fed. Sec. L. Rep. ¶94,526 (1974 N. D. Cal.).

[11] SEC v. American Agronomics Corp., Litig. Rels. 5372, 5539, 5568 (N. D. Ohio 1972).

[12] SEC v. Canadian Javelin, Ltd., CCH Fed. Sec. L. Rep. ¶94,720 (S. D. N. Y. 1974).

[13] For a criticism of this practice whereby "the agency quickly builds up numerous uncontested precedents justifying a novel theory or procedure," see Karmel, address to Securities Law Committee of Young Lawyers Division of ABA, Sec. Reg. L. Rep. No. 489, p. H-1 (1979).

dure.[14] But it is not clear what status special counsel has or whom he represents — the court, the Commission, or the defendant whom he sometimes investigates and sometimes champions in actions against third persons.[15] Since he is a hybrid between privately retained counsel and government investigator, nice questions have arisen with respect to attorney-client privilege and counsel's work product.[16]

D. LAWYER *VERSUS* ACCOUNTANT: CONTINGENT LIABILITIES

This last aspect of the securities lawyer's role pitted the legal and accounting professions against each other for some five years until a *modus vivendi* was reached in 1976.

Accountants have always disclosed contingent liabilities (which for some reason they now prefer to call "loss contingencies") in

[14] United States v. Handler, CCH Fed. Sec. L. Rep. ¶96,519 at 94,023-24 (C. D. Cal. 1978) (although the unlimited nature of the special counsel procedure set forth in a prior consent injunction might have created due process problems, counsel's self-initiated safeguards cured any defect); Handler v. SEC, 610 F. 2d 656 (9th Cir. 1979) (there was no unlawful delegation of governmental power to a private person in the consent appointment of special counsel whose report led to the conviction in United States v. Handler, supra); International Controls Corp. v. Hogan & Hartson, summarized in CCH Fed. Sec. L. Rep. ¶97,183 (S. D. N. Y. 1979) (special counsel monitoring a consent judgment was permitted to employ his own law firm to litigate claims held by the monitored company); cf. also cases cited supra p. 1006 n. 6; but cf. Brick v. Dominion Mortgage & Realty Trust, 442 F. Supp. 283, 307-08 (W. D. N. Y. 1977).

[15] See Gruenbaum and Oppenheimer, Special Investigative Counsel: Conflicts and Roles, 33 Rutgers L. Rev. 865 (1981).

[16] See SEC v. Canadian Javelin, Ltd., 451 F. Supp. 594 (D. D. C. 1978), *remanded on other grounds*, CCH Fed. Sec. L. Rep. ¶96,742 (D. C. Cir. 1978) (no attorney-client relationship between defendant and compliance counsel); Osterneck v. E. T. Barwick Industries, Inc., 82 F. R. D. 81 (N. D. Ga. 1979) (same, and also no work product privilege, with respect to special counsel to Special Review Committee); In re Subpoena Duces Tecum to Fulbright & Jaworski, 738 F. 2d 1367 (D. C. Cir. 1984) (special counsel's voluntary disclosure of documents to SEC in an attempt to ward off a formal investigation waived both attorney-client and attorney work product privileges, so that the documents were subject to discovery in later private action against the company and its directors); but cf. Diversified Industries, Inc. v. Meredith, 572 F. 2d 596 (8th Cir. *en banc* 1978) (special counsel retained by corporation itself to investigate and report on charges of corporate bribery of purchasing agents of other companies); In re LTV Securities Litigation, 89 F. R. D. 595, 619 (N. D. Tex. 1981) ("it is likely that corporations will be less willing to engage in the sort of self-investigation [by an Audit Committee that retained special counsel pursuant to a consent injunction] if the results of such an investigation can be discovered in parallel civil litigation"). For a general review, see In re International Systems & Controls Corp. Securities Litigation, 91 F. R. D. 552 (S. D. Tex. 1981).

notes to the financial statements. But contingent liabilities traditionally were confined to those arising out of lawsuits already filed or clearly threatened.[1] Controversy arose in the early 1970s when the accounting fraternity, out of concern presumably for their own liability, began to demand that their clients instruct counsel (thus avoiding the question of attorney-client privilege that would arise if counsel were quizzed directly) to inform the auditors with respect to potential lawsuits. Since this would be inviting lawsuits to be filed, the Bar balked. This impasse raised the spectre that the auditors might qualify their opinions not merely as to certainty but as to scope, thus indicating that an essential audit step had not been completed; and opinions qualified as to scope are not acceptable to the Commission.[2]

A compromise was approved by the ABA and the AICPA in January 1976. The statement issued by the two organizations is fairly lengthy.[3] Among other things, it states:[4]

> (5) *Loss Contingencies.* When properly requested by the client, it is appropriate for the lawyer to furnish to the auditor information concerning the following matters if the lawyer has been engaged by the client to represent or advise the client professionally with respect thereto and he has devoted substantive attention to them in the form of legal representation or consultation:
>
> (a) *overtly threatened or pending litigation,* whether or not specified by the client;
>
> (b) *a contractually assumed obligation* which the client has specifically identified and upon which the client his specifically requested, in the inquiry letter or a supplement thereto, comment to the auditor;
>
> (c) *an unasserted possible claim or assessment* which the client has specifically identified and upon which the client has specifically requested, in the inquiry letter or a supplement thereto, comment to the auditor.

C. 11D [1] The Commission has always required the financial statements in a 1933 Act registration statement to disclose a contingent liability under §12(1) arising out of any violation of §5 disclosed in the registration statement.

[2] See Sommer, Two Problems for Lawyers (address to Dallas B. Assn., Nov. 4, 1975).

[3] ABA Statement of Policy Regarding Lawyers' Responses to Auditors' Requests for Information, 31 Bus. Law. 1709 (1976). Several weeks later the AICPA approved Statement on Auditing Standards No. 12, which coordinates with the Statement of Policy.

[4] Id. at 1712, 1714.

* * *

(6) *Lawyer's Professional Responsibility.* * * * The lawyer also may be required under the Code of Professional Responsibility [now the Model Rules of Professional Conduct] to resign his engagement if his advice concerning disclosures is disregarded by the client. The auditor may properly assume that whenever, in the course of performing legal services for the client with respect to a matter recognized to involve an unasserted possible claim or assessment which may call for financial statement disclosure, the lawyer has formed a professional conclusion that the client must disclose or consider disclosure concerning such possible claim or assessment, the lawyer, as a matter of professional responsibility to the client, will so advise the client and will consult with the client concerning the question of such disclosure and the applicable requirement* of FAS 5.[5]

Be all this as it may, neither of the two priesthoods can absolve from legal liability when it exists. Both continue to face a conundrum that is inherent in a system of compulsory disclosure: You are counsel for a company whose annual report is due in a month. You have just stumbled on facts indicating that for a considerable period ending some years ago the company used a process on which another company held the dominant patent. An action for patent infringement would probably succeed and come close to bankrupting the company. But apparently you are the only person who knows of this contingent liability. The statute of limitations expires in two months. It is a crime under §32(a) of the 1934 Act (1) willfully to fail to file a required report (or to file it late) in violation of §13(a) or (2) "willfully and knowingly" to make or cause any

*Under FAS [Financial Accounting Standards Board] 5, when there has been no manifestation by a potential claimant of an awareness of a possible claim or assessment, disclosure of an unasserted possible claim is required only if the enterprise concludes that (i) it is probable that a claim will be asserted, (ii) there is a reasonable possibility, if the claim is in fact asserted, that the outcome will be unfavorable, and (iii) the liability resulting from such unfavorable outcome would be material to its financial condition.

[5]See also Introductory Analysis and Guides to Statement of Policy Regarding Lawyers' Responses to Auditors' Requests for Information — Prepared by the Committee on Audit Inquiry Responses, 31 Bus. Law. 1737 (1976); ABA Statement of Policy Regarding Lawyers' Responses to Auditors' Request for Information: Second Report of the Committee on Audit Inquiry Responses Regarding Initial Implementation, 32 Bus. Law. 177 (1976); Deer, Practical Problems and Procedures in Preparing Responses to Auditors' Inquiry Letters, in Practising Law Institute, Eighth Annual Institute on Securities Regulation (1977) c. 3.

statement in a required report that is "false or misleading with respect to any *material* fact."[6]

This is not a case of the lady or the tiger. It is a case of two equally ferocious beasts. Which door do you open?

[6] Italics are supplied. This, of course, is apart from the risk of potentially crushing civil liability under Rule 10b-5.

APPENDIX A

SEC STATUTES IN THE UNITED STATES CODE

Securities Act of 1933

§1	15 U. S. C. §77a
§2	§77b
* * *	
§26	§77z
Sch. A	§77aa
Sch. B	§77aa

Securities Exchange Act of 1934

§1	15 U. S. C. §78a
§2	§78b
* * *	
§11	§78k
§11A	§78k-1
§12	§78l
* * *	
§15	§78o
§15A	§78o-3[1]
§15B	§78o-4
§16	§78p
§17	§78q
§17A	§78q-1
§18	§78r
* * *	
§26	§78z
§27	§78aa
* * *	
§30	§78dd
§30A	§78dd-1
§31	§78ee
* * *	
§34	§78hh

Public Utility Holding Company Act of 1935

§1	15 U. S. C. §79a
§2	§79b
* * *	
§26	§79z
§27	§79z-1
* * *	

[1] 15 U. S. C. §§78o-1 and 78o-2, which are not properly part of the 1934 Act, were mechanically incidental to the 1936 amendments.

§32	§79z-6
§33 (short title)	§79

Trust Indenture Act of 1939

§301	15 U. S. C. §77aaa
§302	§77bbb

* * *

§26	§77zzz
§27	§77aaaa
§28	§77bbbb

Investment Company Act of 1940

§1	15 U. S. C. §80a-1
§2	§80a-2

* * *

§28	§80a-28
§29	—[2]
§30	§80a-29
§31	§80a-30

* * *

§65	§80a-64

Investment Advisers Act of 1940

§201	15 U. S. C. §80b-1
§202	§80b-2

* * *

§206A	§80b-6a

* * *

§221	§80b-21
§222	§80b-18a

Securities Investor Protection Act of 1970

§1	15 U. S. C. §78aaa
§2	§78bbb

* * *

§6	§78fff
§7	§78fff-1
§8	§78fff-2
§9	§78fff-3
§10	§78fff-4
§11	§78ggg

* * *

§16	§78lll

[2] Since §29 amended §§44 and 67 of the then Bankruptcy Act, it does not appear in 15 U. S. C.

APPENDIX B

SEC, SIPC, AND FEDERAL RESERVE RULES IN THE CODE OF FEDERAL REGULATIONS

The SEC rules under the 1933 and 1935 Acts simply begin with 100 and 1, respectively, and run consecutively. Those under the 1934, 1939, and 1940 Acts are keyed into the sections under which they are adopted (except for a few preliminary rules designated 0-1, 0-2, etc.). Thus Rule 10b-5 under the 1934 Act is the fifth rule adopted under §10(b) of that statute. In the case of the 1939 Act, whose first section is 301, the first two digits of the section numbers are ignored in numbering the rules.

All the rules of the SEC are officially reported in 17 Code Fed. Regs., c. II. The Commission's rule numbers (as well as SIPC's under the Securities Investor Protection Act of 1970) correlate with the U. S. C. numbers as follows:

Set of Rules	*Part Number of C. F. R.*	*Typical SEC Rule Number*	*Typical Section Number of 12 C. F. R.*
Organization; Conduct and Ethics; Information and Requests	200	—	§200.1
Rules of Practice	201	6(e)	§201.6(e)
Informal and Other Procedures	202	—	§202.1
Investigations	203	—	§203.1
Reg. S-X	210	1-01	§210.1-01

Set of Rules	*Part Number of C. F. R.*	*Typical SEC Rule Number*	*Typical Section Number of 12 C. F. R.*
Reg. S-K	229	Item 101	§229.101
Sec. Act	230	140	§230.140
Sec. Ex. Act	240	10b-5	§240.10b-5
Holding Co. Act	250	50	§250.50
Trust Ind. Act	260	10b-1	§260.10b-1
Inv. Co. Act	270	8b-1	§270.8b-1
Inv. Adv. Act	275	203-1	§275.203-1
Sec. Inv. Prot. Act (SIPC rules)	300	100	§300.100

The margin rules adopted by the Board of Governors of the Federal Reserve System under §§7 and 8 of the Securities Exchange Act of 1934 appear in 12 Code Fed. Regs.:

Reg.	*Part Number of 12 C. F. R.*
G	207
T	220
U	221
X	224

APPENDIX C

"ONE SHARE ONE VOTE"[1]

The December 1986 hearings were followed by a series of meetings of the staffs of the two New York exchanges and the NASD, together with the SEC's staff. At that time, the American Stock Exchange permitted the listing of common stock with *less than full* voting rights if specified requirements were met, and the NASD had no voting right restrictions at all.

When these staff discussions failed to reach agreement on a uniform rule, the Commission gave notice of a formal proceeding under §19(c), with further hearings to begin in July 1987, on the question whether to adopt Rule 19c-4, which would add to the rules of most of the exchanges as well as the NASD a prohibition against the listing on an exchange or the inclusion in NASDAQ of the equity securities of an issuer that issued securities or took other corporate action "that would have the effect of nullifying, restricting, or disparately reducing the per share voting rights of holders"

[1] See p. 432 supra. Professor Fischel of the University of Chicago in a 1986 study found the available empirical evidence to be "consistent with the view that the creation of dual class common stock is desirable for certain types of firms and inconsistent with the view that dual class common stock systematically harms investors." D. Fischel, Organized Exchanges and the Regulation of Dual Class Common Stock (1986) 2. And an SEC staff study of 63 companies that had adopted dual-class common stock from 1976 to 1986 concluded that the stock price results did not support the hypothesis that dual-class recapitalizations negatively affected shareholder wealth. Moreover, the evidence tended "to support the contention that dual class common stock is a viable form of corporate structure which allows growing firms, and firms owned by family entrepreneurs, to raise additional equity capital to finance rewarding investment projects without increasing debt or diluting voting control." SEC, Office of the Chief Economist, The Effects of Dual-Class Recapitalizations on the Wealth of Shareholders (June 1, 1987) 33-34. But the report was careful to add that the evidence did not "provide a blanket approval of dual-class recapitalization." Id. at 34. And a few weeks later a supplemental report that included 1986-87 data with respect to an additional 34 companies found "significant and negative abnormal stock returns at the announcement of the dual-class recapitalization." SEC, Office of the Chief Economist, Update — The Effects of Dual Class Recapitalizations on Shareholder Wealth: Including Evidence from 1986 and 1987 (July 15, 1987) 8.

of one or more classes of outstanding registered common stock of the issuer.[2]

In recognition of the fact that 46 NYSE-listed companies had issued disparate voting stock or amended their charters to limit the voting power of large shareholders, the proposed rule would carry a "grandfather" date of May 15, 1987.

[2] Sec. Ex. Act Rel. 24,623, 38 SEC Dock. 917 (1987).

APPENDIX D

ARBITRABILITY OF 10b-5 ACTIONS[1]

Although virtually all the Courts of Appeals had followed *Wilko,*[2] five Justices, in *Shearson/American Express, Inc.* v. *McMahon,*[3] refused to apply it to a claim under Rule 10b-5 (or presumably the Exchange Act and the other SEC statutes generally). The rationale is mixed:

First, Justice O'Connor stated for the majority,

> By its terms, §29(a) only prohibits waiver of the substantive obligations imposed by the Exchange Act. Because §27 does not impose any statutory duties, its waiver does not constitute a waiver of "compliance with any provision" of the Exchange Act under §29(a).[4]

The majority also referred to the Commission's "expansive power" since the 1975 amendment of §19 of the Exchange Act "to ensure the adequacy of the arbitration procedures employed by the SROs."[5] Indeed, the holding is expressly limited to cases where "the prescribed procedures are subject to the Commission's §19 authority."[6]

The basic determinant, however, quite clearly was the greater receptivity of the Court (shared latterly by the Commission as *amicus curiae*) to arbitration as an alternative method of dispute resolution since *Wilko.* The majority found it "difficult to reconcile *Wilko*'s mistrust of the arbitral process with this Court's subsequent decisions involving the Arbitration Act."[7]

Is there, then, life in *Wilko* after *Shearson*? "While *stare decisis* concerns may counsel against upsetting *Wilko*'s contrary conclusion under the Securities Act," Justice O'Connor wrote, "we refuse to extend *Wilko*'s reasoning to the Exchange Act in light of these in-

[1] See p. 1034 supra.
[2] The cases are collected in Shearson/American Express, Inc. v. McMahon, 107 S. Ct. 2333, 2349 nn. 6, 8 (1987) (Blackmun, J., dissenting).
[3] 107 S. Ct. 2333 (1987).
[4] Id. at 2338.
[5] Id. at 2341.
[6] Ibid.
[7] Id. at 2346, citing cases.

tervening regulatory developments," that is to say, the 1975 legislation.[8] Consequently the majority had somehow to distinguish *Wilko.* This they sought to do by reading *Wilko* to hold "that the plaintiff's waiver of the 'right to select the judicial forum' * * * was unenforceable only because arbitration was judged inadequate to enforce the statutory rights created by §12(2)[9] — a reading said to be supported by *Scherk* v. *Alberto-Culver Co.*[10]

Justice Blackmun's dissent, supported by Justices Brennan, Marshall, and Stevens, was sharp: The Court "approves the abandonment of the judiciary's role in the resolution of claims under the Exchange Act * * * at a time when the [securities] industry's abuses towards investors are more apparent than ever."[11] Moreover, "the arbitral process *at best* places the investor on an equal footing with the securities industry personnel against whom the charges are brought," and "there remains the danger that, *at worst,* compelling an investor to arbitrate claims puts him in a forum controlled by the securities industry."[12] As for the SEC's oversight of the self-regulatory organizations' arbitration procedures, the dissenters thought that the majority, following the Commission's recent about-face, were overly sanguine.

Surely reasonable persons can differ with respect to the relative weight to be given the clashing social policies of arbitration and investor protection. The majority did not attempt to distinguish *Wilko,* as several lower courts had done, by reference to the difference between express and implied rights of action; on that point they followed *sub silentio* the SEC's suggestion that the difference was meaningless for purposes of arbitrability.[13] And, although it would have been neater to overrule *Wilko* than to distinguish, that is easier for an academic to suggest than for a Justice to do.[14]

[8] Id. at 2341. *Scherk* and the other exceptions to *Wilko* developed by the lower courts cannot be consigned to history as long as *Wilko* is not expressly overruled by the Supreme Court.

[9] Id. at 2338.

[10] 417 U. S. 506 (1974), supra p. 1029.

[11] 107 S. Ct. at 2346.

[12] Id. at 2355.

[13] It *is* difficult to understand why, if arbitration was "inadequate to enforce the statutory rights created by §12(2)," as the majority stated, it was not just as inadequate with respect to Rule 10b-5. The majority seemed satisfied that the Commission's new supervisory authority made the difference.

[14] The Court was unanimous in holding that the treble damage claim under RICO was arbitrable.

Arbitration cannot be compelled, of course, unless there is an agreement to arbitrate. Accordingly, arbitration of a 10b-5 claim will be denied if the arbitration agreement excluded federal securities law claims. Hammerman v. Peacock, CCH Fed. Sec. L. Rep. ¶92,239 (D. D. C. 1985), *clarified,* 623 F. Supp. 719 (D. D. C. 1985).

TABLE OF CASES

This table includes the few SEC "no action" letters that are cited in the book.

Panzirer v. Wolf (663 F. 2d 365), 962, 963, 964
Pappas v. Moss (393 F. 2d 865), 803
Park & Tilford v. Schulte (160 F. 2d 984), 581
Parklane Hosiery Co. v. Shore (439 U. S. 322), 73
Parrent v. Midwest Rug Mills (455 F. 2d 123), 999
Parsons v. Hornblower & Weeks-Hemphill Noyes (571 F. 2d 203), 832
Parsons v. Hornblower & Weeks-Hemphill Noyes (447 F. Supp. 482), 832
Parvin v. Davis Oil Co. (524 F. 2d 112), 201
Pasley v. Freeman (3 D. & E. 51), 874
Passman v. Oliphant (46 A. D. 2d 878), 643
Passman v. Oliphant (77 Misc. 2d 431), 643
Patterson v. Hewitt (195 U. S. 309), 1002
Patterson v. New York (432 U. S. 197), 275
Paul v. Berkman (620 F. Supp. 638), 721
Paul v. Virginia (8 Wall. 168), 204, 206
Paul F. Newton & Co. v. Texas Commerce Bank (630 F. 2d 1111), 1014
Paul K. Peers, Inc. (42 SEC 539), 839
Paul S. Mullin & Associates v. Bassett (632 F. Supp. 632), 940
Paulson Inv. Co. v. Norbay Sec. (603 F. Supp. 615), 882
Pavlidis v. New England Patriots (737 F. 2d 1227), 479, 483
Pavlidis v. New England Patriots (CCH Fed. Sec. L. Rep. ¶99,431), 479
Pay Less Drug Stores v. Jewel Cos. (579 F. Supp. 1396), 556, 580
Payne, SEC v. (35 F. Supp. 873), 189
Pearlstein v. Scudder & German (429 F. 2d 1136), 662
Peat, Marwick, Mitchell & Co. (Acctg. Sec. Rel. 173), 159
Peat, Marwick, Mitchell & Co. (Acctg. Sec. Rel. 173A), 159
Peat, Marwick, Mitchell & Co. v. Wachovia Bank & Trust Co. (452 U. S. 954), 942, 998
Peek v. Derry (L. R. 37 Ch. Div. 541), 875
Peek v. Gurney (L. R. 6 H. L. 377), 875
Pegasus Fund v. Laraneta (617 F. 2d 1335), 781
Peil v. Speiser (806 F. 2d 1154), 961, 962
Pellegrino v. Nesbit (203 F. 2d 463), 548
Peltz, United States v. (433 F. 2d 48), 757, 799
Penn-Allen Broadcasting Co. v. Taylor (389 Pa. 490), 880
Penn Central Sec. Litig., In re (494 F. 2d 528), 921
Penn Central Sec. Litig., In re (347 F. Supp. 1327), 921
Penn Central Sec. Litig., In re (357 F. Supp. 869), 921
Pennaluna & Co. v. SEC (410 F. 2d 861), 276
Pennebaker v. Kimble (126 Ore. 317), 889
Pennicard v. Coe (124 Ore. 423), 879
Pennsylvania Co. for Ins. on Lives & Granting Annuities v. Deckert (123 F. 2d 979), 992
Penturelli v. Spector Cohen Gadon & Rosen (779 F. 2d 160), 176, 177, 201
Penturelli v. Spector Cohen Gadon & Rosen (640 F. Supp. 867), 993
People v. ________. *See* other

TABLE OF SEC RELEASES

Releases that are set out substantially in full, together with the pages at which they appear, are printed in italics.

Securities Act Releases

Securities Exchange Act Releases

INDEX